D1799561
KINNOS
WITH AN INTERLINEAR TRANSLATION

THE SCHOTTENSTEIN EDITION

קינות ותפלות לתשעה באב

KINNOS

THE COMPLETE TISHAH B'AV SERVICE
WITH AN INTERLINEAR TRANSLATION

The ArtScroll Series®

Rabbi Nosson Scherman / Rabbi Meir Zlotowitz
General Editors

A PROJECT OF THE

Mesorah Heritage Foundation

Published by

Me'sorah Publications, ltd

THE SCHOTTENSTEIN EDITION

KINNOS

THE COMPLETE TISHAH B'AV SERVICE WITH AN INTERLINEAR TRANSLATION

NUSACH ASHKENAZ / נוסח אשכנז

Edited by

Rabbi Menachem Davis

Contributing Editors:

Rabbi Avrohom Chaim Feuer

Rabbi Avie Gold

Rabbi Nosson Scherman

Rabbi Meir Zlotowitz

Designed by

Rabbi Sheah Brander

FIRST EDITION
First Impression . . . June 2010

Published and Distributed by
MESORAH PUBLICATIONS, Ltd.
4401 Second Avenue
Brooklyn, New York 11232

Distributed in Europe by
LEHMANNS
Unit E, Viking Business Park
Rolling Mill Road
Jarrow, Tyne & Wear NE32 3DP
England

Distributed in Australia & New Zealand by
GOLDS WORLD OF JUDAICA
3-13 William Street
Balaclava, Melbourne 3183
Victoria Australia

Distributed in Israel by
SIFRIATI / A. GITLER — BOOKS
6 Hayarkon Street
Bnei Brak 51127

Distributed in South Africa by
KOLLEL BOOKSHOP
Ivy Common 105 William Road
Norwood 2192, Johannesburg, South Africa

THE ARTSCROLL SERIES® / SCHOTTENSTEIN EDITION
THE ARTSCROLL INTERLINEAR KINNOS / TISHAH B'AV SERVICE
Nusach Ashkenaz

Hard cover — ISBN 10: 1-4226-0987-1 / ISBN 13: 978-1-4226-0987-3
Paperback — ISBN 10: 1-4226-0988-X / ISBN 13: 978-1-4226-0988-0

Typography by CompuScribe at ArtScroll Studios, Ltd., Brooklyn, NY
Bound by **Sefercraft, Inc.,** Brooklyn, NY

This volume is dedicated in honor of
our revered friend and spiritual guide

The Gaon and Mekubal,
Harav Yoshiyahu Yosef Pinto שליט״א

He is a worthy scion of the illustrious Pinto and Abuhatzeira families, which have provided our people with generations of awesomely great scholars of Torah and Kabbalah.

Harav Pinto carries the superhuman burden of twenty yeshivos on four continents. Hashem alone knows how many legions of Torah-true families – and what a magnificent future! – are being fashioned and nurtured thanks to his courage and unselfish devotion to our people.

It is fitting that this Schottenstein Edition of Interlinear Kinnos is dedicated to this great gaon. The Temple was destroyed because of Sinas Chinam, hatred without cause. With his uncompromising love of all Jews, Harav Pinto is preparing the way for the Redemption, the coming of Messiah, and the building of the Beis HaMikdash, may it be speedily in our time.

Jay and Jeanie Schottenstein
Joseph Aaron and Lindsay Brooke,
Jacob Meir and Jonah Philip
Jonathan Richard, and Jeffrey Adam

TABLE OF CONTENTS

Kinnos listed in alpabetical order

◆ The Interlinear Translation — How to Read it

There is a difficulty inherent in any interlinear translation of Hebrew to English: the fact that English and Hebrew are read in opposite directions. ArtScroll has developed a patented system of notations that helps the reader navigate the two languages simultaneously, without confusion.

These notations consist of the following:

1) single arrow notations ‹ between English phrases direct the reader's eye toward the next English phrase, reading right to left, for example:

« and her cities, ‹ O Zion ‹ Lament,

2) Double arrow notations « indicate a logical break between phrases, equivalent to a period, semicolon, dash and many commas.

3) Bold double arrow notations **«** indicate the completion of a sentence at the end of a verse.

With these double arrows, the reader need not search for commas, semicolons, and periods. This was done to make the translation as user-friendly as possible; it allows the reader to continue following the Hebrew moving to the left, without the distraction of looking for English punctuation marks on the *right* side of the English words.

The arrows also identify the specific Hebrew word or words that are translated by the English phrase. This is especially useful where two or more Hebrew words are translated as a unit.

For quotations, one further convention was used: Wherever text would normally be set off by quotation marks, the quotation has been set in italics.

◈ Publisher's Preface

The publication of ArtScroll's COMPLETE TISHAH B'AV SERVICE in 1991 brought about an amazing enhancement in the community's understanding of, and participation in, the *Kinnos* of Tishah B'Av. The liturgical lamentations of the day are a complex web of allusions to Tanach, Talmud, Midrash, and history, and they are rendered in language that combines spiritual feeling with complex poetry. For most people, the ArtScroll *Kinnos* brought an unprecedented level of comprehension.

Now, with the publication of this new entry in the SCHOTTENSTEIN EDITION INTERLINEAR SERIES, the day of mourning and hope will be even more meaningful. Dedicated by JAY AND JEANIE SCHOTTENSTEIN AND THEIR CHILDREN, this series brings a new level of understanding to Torah and *tefillah*, enabling people to understand their learning and prayers word for word and phrase by phrase.

The Interlinear Series was born in 2001 with the publication of *Tehillim / Psalms*. The response was so electrifying that it was imperative that it be followed up with many more such works, including Siddur, Machzor, Chumash, and others. Our original hope was that these interlinear works would initiate the same sort of awakening as the original ArtScroll Siddur achieved since its publication in 1984. That hope has been realized many times over.

The Schottenstein family has dedicated this volume in honor of HARAV YOSHIYAHU YOSEF PINTO, who works without respite to spread Torah over four continents.

The prophet promises that those who mourn for Jerusalem will merit to rejoice with her, as well. This volume will help us mourn, and we pray that it will help lead us to the rejoicing.

◈ Contents This *Kinnos*/Tishah B'Av Siddur is as complete as possible. It includes translations of all the prayers and Torah readings, and translations and commentaries on *Eichah* and the *Kinnos*. The services for the full day are self-contained so that the reader will be spared the annoying chore of turning back and forth or consulting multiple volumes. The Overview provides a perspective on Tishah B'Av.

Although the *Kinnos* are standard and identical in both Nusach Ashkenaz and Nusach Sefard, there are minor variations among the texts. The authors and editors of this work consulted many different editions of the *Kinnos* in order to arrive at the text that seemed to be correct. We emphasize, however, that the variations are relatively few.

⊱§ Translation The interlinear translation strives to maintain the literary flavor of the original ArtScroll translation that sought to balance the lofty beauty of the heavily nuanced text with a readily understood English rendering. Obviously, the word-by-word nature of this work constrains the fluidity of the language, but yet it does flow. Where a choice had to be made, we generally preferred fidelity to the text over inaccurate simplicity, but occasionally, we had to stray from the literal translation in order to capture the essence of a phrase in an accessible English idiom. Especially in the *Kinnos* we had to go beyond a strictly literal translation, and sometimes rely on the commentary to clarify the meaning of the text.

⊱§ Commentary Because ordinary Torah study is forbidden on Tishah B'Av, this volume contains no commentary on the regular prayer order or the Torah readings. There is commentary, however, on *Eichah* and the *Kinnos*, for their saddening content makes it permissible to study as well as recite them. In addition, each *Kinnah* / Lamentation is provided with an introduction giving its background and historical context.

⊱§ Laws and Instructions Clear instructions are provided throughout. More complex or lengthy halachos are discussed at the end of the volume in the *Laws* section, which the reader will find to be a very helpful guide. This section includes general halachos that are relevant to the regular prayer service. Throughout the volume, we refer to these laws by paragraph (§) number.

⊱§ Layout and Typography Though this *Kinnos*/Tishah B'Av Siddur's interlinear system sets it apart dramatically from others, it fundamentally maintains the pattern of the ArtScroll Siddur and Machzorim, which have been greatly praised for their ease of use and clarity of layout. With its clear instructions, copious subtitles, and precise page headings, this volume was designed to make the Tishah B'Av service easy for everyone to follow: paragraphs begin with bold-type words to facilitate the individual *tefillos;* portions said aloud by the *chazzan* are indicated by either the symbol ⁘ or the word *chazzan*.

An asterisk (*) after a word indicates that that word or phrase is treated in the commentary. Numbered footnotes give the Scriptural sources of countless verses that have been melded into the prayers, as well as variant readings. A footnote beginning "Cf." indicates that the Scriptural source is paraphrased.

⁂ Hebrew Grammar As a general rule in the Hebrew language, the accent is on the last syllable. Where the accent is on an earlier syllable, it is indicated with a *messeg*, a vertical line below the accented letter: שִֽׁירוּ. In the case of the *Shema* and the "Song at the Sea," which are given with the cantillation [*trop*], the accent follows the trop. A שְׁוָא נָע [*sh'va na*] is indicated by a hyphen mark above the letter: בָּרְכוּ; except for a *sh'va* on the first letter of a word, which is always a *sh'va na*. In identifying a *sh'va na*, we have followed the rules of the Vilna Gaon and Rabbi Yaakov Emden.

⁂ Acknowledgments

RABBI MENACHEM DAVIS has edited the entire project since its inception. He brings uncommon skills to this very difficult task and accomplishes it brilliantly. He has a rare sensitivity to the subtleties and nuances of Hebrew and English, and the ability to convert even complex syntactical constructions into the interlinear format.

This work is based on the original ArtScroll Tishah B'Av Service by RABBI AVROHOM CHAIM FEUER and RABBI AVIE GOLD. RABBI HERSH GOLDWURM זצ"ל compiled the Laws and reviewed most of the instructions. His contribution to ArtScroll was immense and his loss is still felt.

We are grateful to MRS. SERENA VEGH ע"ה AND HER CHILDREN who dedicated the original Tishah B'Av Siddur in memory of their husband and father REB AVROHOM ALTER VEGH ז"ל.

We are grateful to MR. PINCHAS (FRED) HERZKA ז"ל who, with untiring efforts over many years, succeeded in assembling the *Kinnos* for *Churban Europa* and having them accepted by large numbers of *kehillos*.

The design of the interlinear page remains a challenge even for our cherished friend and colleague REB SHEAH BRANDER, the acknowledged genius in this demanding field — and he has again produced a masterpiece. Reb Sheah was ably assisted in every facet of the production and layout by MRS. SURY ENGLARD and by SHLOIME BRANDER.

In this volume, we have utilized the services of ZEV TEICH, a brilliant technological consultant who designed systems to maximize the efficient functioning of the entire process.

REB ELI KROEN designed the cover with his customary good taste and imagination.

AVROHOM YITZCHOK DEUTSCH proofread the Hebrew text, assisted by RABBI ELIYAHU COHEN, to assure the greatest degree of accuracy. YAAKOV LERCHER expended much fruitful effort to assure that the text of the *Kinnos* is correct.

MOSHE DEUTSCH prepared the book for printing.

MRS. FRIMY EISNER reviewed everything for language, consistency, and accuracy. MRS. FAYGIE WEINBAUM and MRS. MINDY STERN proofread with their customary diligence. MRS. EDNA DAVIS made many valuable comments and suggestions.

AVROHOM BIDERMAN and MENDY HERZBERG always contribute expertise and efficiency in shepherding the production from beginning to end, whatever the need.

We are grateful to them all.

MRS. LEA BRAFMAN is our comptroller, but she is more. Her competence and dedication go far beyond a mere job title.

SHMUEL BLITZ directs our Jerusalem office with extraordinary efficiency, and his prowess helps in all our work, even when he is not directly involved.

With Hashem's help, ArtScroll / Mesorah has over 1,200 titles in print, and the SCHOTTENSTEIN INTERLINEAR SERIES is one of our crown jewels.

We are grateful for the *z'chus* of serving His people by bringing them closer to His Torah. We close with the prayer that this Tishah B'Av will be the last that is observed as a day of mourning. May the next one be a day of celebration for the final Redemption and the Third *Bais HaMikdash*.

Rabbi Meir Zlotowitz — Rabbi Nosson Scherman

Tammuz 5770 / June 2010
Brooklyn, N.Y.

⇸§ Editor's Preface

There are a mere six weeks between Tishah B'Av, when we recite *Kinnos,* lamentations over the destruction of the Holy Temples, and the week before Rosh Hashanah when we begin *Selichos,* prayers for forgiveness recited before and during the *Yamim Noraim,* the Days of Awe. That proximity brings into focus a startling contrast between the two sets of prayers. While the content, structure, and language of the *Kinnos* and *Selichos* are notably similar — written by many of the same authors — nevertheless, *Kinnos* seems to be lacking an essential feature that is found in *Selichos*: the recitation of the Thirteen Attributes of Mercy. While these are the keystone prayers of *Selichos,* their glaring absence in *Kinnos* demands an explanation.

The answer, I believe, lies in our focusing either on the past or on the future. *Kinnos* and Tishah B'Av concentrate on the past; on the awareness and appreciation of our loss — what we once had, what we once were, and what has become of it all; and how our failings were the cause of those tragedies. The goal of all our recitations on Tishah B'Av is to arrive at the feeling of מֵתוֹ מוּטָל לְפָנָיו, *the corpse of his dead dear one is lying on the ground before him.* The burial has not yet hidden the corpse from sight. We see it and are touched by it; it overwhelms us with grief; we cannot be comforted, we cannot be consoled. Consolation is for some time in the future when the wounds are no longer as fresh and as raw.

Selichos and the Days of Awe are primarily future oriented. We pray for a Good New Year, for forgiveness and atonement, so that the sins and failings of the past do not hold us back and drag us down. The promise of the Thirteen Attributes of Mercy is encouraging, replete with potential. With sincere repentance we can hope to be granted another year.

But why are the two — *Kinnos* and *Selichos* — so close together? An observation by R' Shimshon Pinkus zt"l may provide the answer. He points to the contrast between Noah and Mordechai. The Midrash places the onus for the flood on Noah; it is called Noah's flood. Why? It was not he who was wicked and evil. But as the Midrash quoted by *Rashi* (*Genesis* 7:7) states, Noah was a person of insufficient faith. He did not truly believe that the flood would come. Even though he spent 120 years building the ark in the face of ridicule and scorn, he did not believe that God would actually destroy the world. And therefore he did not pray to prevent what might not come. However, when Mordechai saw the decree *"to destroy, to murder, and to exterminate all the Jews"* he did not rationalize about Persia being a civilized nation, or that *"relief and deliverance will come to the Jews from another place."* Mordechai *did* believe that the evil decree *would* be carried out unless he and all the Jews mobilized in prayer, believing fully that their life depended on their actions. And so Mordechai *"cried a loud and bitter cry"* and saw to it that *"sackcloth and ashes were spread out for the masses."*

Through *Kinnos* and Tishah B'Av we see that the threat of annihilation is real; it has happened in the past and in the future, if we are complacent and cavalier about the threats the Jewish People face, can חַס וְשָׁלוֹם happen. We must cry on Tishah B'Av until we can no longer have tears to cry, so that when we say *Selichos* we will do so with the recognition that the weapons of mass destruction are pointed at us and there is no one on whom we can count to save us other than *Our Father Who is in Heaven.*

❧ ❧ ❧

Studying every nuance of every word of the *Kinnos,* trying to make clear and real the tragedies of the last 3,000 years, has been a sobering experience for me this last year. When I began to work on *Kinnos,* I asked R' Meir Zlotowitz if the ArtScroll *Kinnos* would not be obsolete when Mashiach arrives this year. He answered that it would then be an heirloom! But I have come to the realization that right now we are in need of more and better *Kinnos* tools right now, to hasten the Redemption. And there is hardly a better tool for this than the INTERLINEAR SERIES, sponsored by the Schottenstein family.

I wish to acknowledge the support and encouragement of many of the scholars who are part of the ArtScroll family. First and foremost, RABBI MEIR ZLOTOWITZ, the source of the vision and energy behind the unique ArtScroll dynamic. May he succeed in envisioning and incubating many more projects — to enlighten and to inspire. RABBI SHEAH BRANDER is one of the wonders of the publishing world. The interlinear format is one of the most challenging of layouts, even if there were unlimited time within which to produce it. In addition, the diversity of poetic styles of the *Kinnos* presents a truly daunting task. R' Sheah magically creates his masterpieces. But R' Sheah is much more than the supreme artisan of the printed word; he is also an editor par excellence and a *talmid chacham* of deep insight. His sage advice has improved the Interlinear Series in myriad ways. And perhaps more important, Reb Sheah is a friend.

Other scholars contributed to the interlinear project in those subtle ways that inspire and spur one's efforts to unanticipated heights. They include: RABBI NOSSON SCHERMAN, who is renowned for his eloquence and depth in expressing so many concepts of the ArtScroll oeuvre, and who is always available for consultation and for discovering the ideal way to express an elusive concept; RABBI MENACHEM SILBER, whose encyclopedic knowledge was readily proferred, and who provided access to critical volumes from his personal library; RABBI MOSHE ROSENBLUM, a consummate scholar of Hebrew, *Mikra,* and *piyut*; and RABBI AVROHOM SHERESHEVSKY, an expert in Hebrew grammar and *Mikra.*

In this volume my wife Edna once again served as an editor extraordinaire, assisting with numerous translations. All this, in addition to her inspiration and enthusiasm that continually encourage me to greater achievement. May Hashem grant that we be *zocheh* to enjoy further growth in Torah and *yiras Shamayim,* together with our children and all of *Klal Yisrael.*

Menachem Davis

Tammuz 5770 / June 2010
Brooklyn, N.Y.

❧ *An Overview* *Kinnos:* A Trail of Tears — From Tragedy to Triumph!

I. Tears: The Essence of the Soul

אָמַר ר׳ יוֹחָנָן: אוֹתוֹ הַיּוֹם [שֶׁחָזְרוּ הַמְּרַגְּלִים] עֶרֶב תִּשְׁעָה בְּאָב הָיָה. אָמַר הקב״ה, אַתֶּם בְּכִיתֶם בְּכִיָּה שֶׁל חִנָּם, וַאֲנִי קוֹבֵעַ לָכֶם בְּכִיָּה לְדוֹרוֹת.

Rabbi Yochanan said that this day [when the spies returned and delivered their derogatory report about Eretz Yisrael] was Tishah B'Av eve. The Holy One, Blessed is He, said, "You wept in vain. I will establish this date for you as a time of real weeping for all generations" (Taanis 29a).

Tears are uniquely suited to Tishah B'Av. Special dates in the Jewish calendar have their own tangible means to convey their essence. Rosh Hashanah has its *shofar,* Pesach has its *matzoh,* and so on. The mitzvah of Tishah B'Av is tears.

On the afternoon before Tishah B'Av, the *Chasam Sofer* would already be sobbing bitterly in anticipation of this day of misfortune. He collected every tear in a cup, and, when he ate his final meal before the fast, he would dip his bread into his tears and into ashes, as a sign of intense mourning. Thus would he fulfill the verse כִּי אֵפֶר כַּלֶּחֶם אָכָלְתִּי וְשִׁקֻּוַי בִּבְכִי מָסָכְתִּי, *For I have eaten ashes like bread, and mixed my drink with tears* (*Psalms* 102:10).

What is the significance of tears? Real tears, meaningful tears that are shed out of deep and sincere feelings, are the most genuine expression of the essence of the human personality. *Rav Hirsch* describes tears as "the sweat of the soul." When man is honestly moved or agitated, he sheds tears.

Maharal (*Netzach Yisrael* Ch. 8) explains that when the Jews were redeemed from Egypt, God was actually submitting them to a new process of creation, whereby a new national entity called "Israel" was being fashioned — a nation whose collective soul would be inextricably bound up with the teachings of the Torah and with the land of the Torah, *Eretz Yisrael*. When the Jewish people accepted the negative reports of the spies, however, they dramatically transformed their essential nature and ripped the Land of Israel out of the core of their being. They didn't merely accept the spies' report intellectually; rather, they shed real tears. Thereby they expressed the depths of their soul's antipathy for *Eretz Yisrael* — and thereby they severed their soul-bond with the Holy Land.

In order to forge a new soul-bond with the holy soil, the same tears that once dissolved our link to the Land of Israel must now be shed in love and yearning for our homeland. Once our souls are merged with the Land, the return of our bodies will follow.

II: My Soul Weeps in Secret

> בְּמִסְתָּרִים תִּבְכֶּה נַפְשִׁי מִפְּנֵי גֵוָה.
>
> *My soul shall weep in secrecy for your pride (Jeremiah 13:17).*
>
> *This teaches that God has a concealed place called* מִסְתָּרִים*, secrecy, where He weeps over the pride of Israel that was stripped from them and given to the nations of the world .... Some say that God weeps over the Divine glory which has been concealed from this world ....*
>
> *But how can we say God weeps; are we not told that* עֹז וְחֶדְוָה בִּמְקֹמוֹ*, strength and rejoicing are in His Presence? (I Chronicles 16:27).*
>
> *No, this is not a contradiction! On the inside [in secret], God weeps; on the outside, He appears to rejoice (Chagigah 5b).*

Perceiving the Real Loss

MAHARAL (NETZACH YISRAEL CHAPTER 9) reveals the location of God's secret hideaway — it is within the soul of every Jew. For the soul is really an aspect of God concealed within man, and that fundamental soul of man cries incessantly over the Destruction of the Temple. The average person is not in touch with his inner soul, with his real self, so he is oblivious to its weeping. The average person is aware only of his external facade, the outer world of the body, where everything appears to be fine and growing better — with abundant "strength and rejoicing."

The chassidic master, Reb Bunim of P'shis'cha, illustrated this concept with a parable of a king who amassed tremendous treasures and hid them in a secret storage room, deep inside his palace. One day the palace caught fire and burned down to the ground. The entire nation and the royal court cried over the loss of the beautiful palace, but the king cried more bitterly than any of them, for he alone knew the true extent of the loss. Only he knew of the enormous hidden treasure that went up in smoke.

Similarly, a person who is out of touch with his inner soul hardly appreciates the spiritual loss suffered with the Temple's destruction.

Rav Elya Lopian זצ"ל illustrated this with the following incident (see *Lev Eliahu I, Shevivei Or* 155):

Rav Moshe Isserles, the Rama, wrote in *Toras HaOlah* that when King Nebuchadnezzar came to destroy the First Temple, the Greek philosopher Plato accompanied him. After the Destruction, Plato met the prophet Jeremiah near the Temple Mount, weeping and wailing bitterly over the Temple ruins. Plato asked him two questions: 1) "Behold, you are the preeminent sage in Israel, is it befitting a man of your intellectual stature to cry over a building, which is really no more than a pile of sticks and stones?" 2) "This building is already in ruins; what good will your tears do now? Why cry over the past?"

Jeremiah responded, "Plato, as a world-renowned philosopher, you surely have many perplexing questions."

The Greek recited his long list of complicated problems. Humbly and quietly, Jeremiah solved them all in a few brief sentences. Plato was dumbfounded. "I can't believe that any mortal man can be so wise!"

Jeremiah pointed sadly to the Temple ruins and said, "All of this profound wisdom I derived from those 'sticks and stones,' and that is why I am crying. As for your second question, 'Why do I cry over the past,' this I cannot tell you because you will not be able to understand the answer."

Rav Elya Lopian related that Rav Simcha Zissel of Kelm explained Jeremiah's answer. Our tears are not for the past; rather, we cry for the future, because even though all the gateways to heaven were sealed at the time of the *Churban* [Destruction], the gateway of tears always remains open (*Berachos* 32b). Every tear we shed is collected in heaven and contributes to the reconstruction of the next Temple. This concept, which is so simple for any Jew to understand, is beyond the comprehension of a "rational," world-renowned Plato.

❦ ❦ ❦

JEREMIAH BEGAN OUR TRAIL of tears twenty-five centuries ago. Since then, tragically, the trail has been enlarged into an expanding stream, a mighty river, a surging torrent — and the tears continue to flow even in our days.

Transcending Sadness

Jeremiah poured all of his tears into *Eichah,* the Book of *Lamentations,* wherein he painfully predicted the travails of his tormented people. In his commentary to the *Rambam, Yad Hamelech* asks: The rule is that our Holy Scriptures, the Tanach, must be written by a proven prophet while he is under the influence and inspiration of רוּחַ הַקֹּדֶשׁ, the Divine spirit. The Talmud (*Shabbos* 30b) clearly teaches, however, that this holy spirit cannot envelop a person while he is in a state of sorrow, because it settles only on a person whose spirit enjoys the ecstasy of performing a mitzvah. If so, how could Jeremiah write the Book of *Lamentations* while he was shrouded in mourning?

Yad Hamelech explains that the spirit of prophecy rests upon men of greatness, who demonstrate nobility of character and generosity of spirit. Ordinarily, people who wallow in self-pity and are consumed by their personal woes lead narrow, self-centered lives, and are remote from the qualities of a prophet. Conversely, people who exult in performing God's commandments display a purity of character. But there is another proof of sterling character, one that is valid even in the vale of tears.

Jeremiah was not sad about himself or his plight; his personal situation concerned him not at all. Rather, his tears were over the miserable plight of his fellow Jews, and over the pain of God's Presence, which had been forced into exile. Consequently, Jeremiah's sorrow proved the greatness of his selfless personality, thus making him fit for prophetic inspiration.

III: A Tear Is Never Wasted

Rabbi Eliezer said: Since the day the Temple was destroyed, the heavenly gates of prayer have been shut, as it is written, "Though I cry out and I plead, He shuts out my prayer" (Lam. 3:8); nevertheless, the gates of tears have not been sealed, as it is written, "Hear my prayer, HASHEM, *listen to my outcry, be not mute to my tears" (Psalms 39:13) (Berachos 32b).*

Power of Tears

THE QUESTION HAS been asked: If the gates of tears are never locked, why did God make them in the first place? The Gerrer Rebbe explained that although sincere tears always gain admission above, the gates are needed to shut out false tears, which are abominable to God. We might add that although these gates are never locked, they are closed and can be opened only as far as the flow of tears will push them! Indeed, *Yaaros Devash* (II:11) observes that the numerical value of בֶּכִי, *weeping,* equals that of לֵב, *heart,* because tears are meaningful only if they are sincere expressions of the heart. Such tears are truly priceless.

Rav Aryeh Levin of Jerusalem was a man of rare compassion and sensitivity. Once, a distraught, recently widowed woman came to his home and cried uncontrollably. All his efforts to offer solace were to no avail, until the widow said, "Rabbi, I will accept your words of consolation on one condition. Please tell me, what happened to all of my tears? I prayed and prayed for my late husband, I recited chapter after chapter of *Tehillim,* and shed thousands upon thousands of tears. My very soul flowed into those tears. Were they all wasted?"

Gently, Rav Aryeh replied, "After a hundred and twenty years, when you will leave this world and ascend to the heavenly tribunal, you will see how meaningful and precious your tears were. You will discover that God himself gathered them in and counted every single teardrop and treasured it like a priceless gem. And you will discover that, whenever some harsh and evil decree was looming over the Jewish people, one of your tears came and washed the evil away, making it null and void. Even one sincere tear is a source of salvation!"

Hearing, this the woman burst into a fresh flow of tears — not tears of sorrow and grief, but tears of courage and hope.

Sometime later she came back to Reb Aryeh and said, "Rabbi, you remember what you told me? Please tell me again."

For the Nation's Sake

THE JEW WHO sheds tears for his personal concerns does so as the external, physical person. Deep inside the secret recesses of his soul, however, the Godly portion within him cries over one thing only — the loss of the Divine Presence, for that is the source of all other tragedies and the underlying reason for Jewish suffering.

Our personal suffering is a direct offshoot of the collective, national suffering of the Jewish people in exile. The Midrash (*Eichah Rabbasi* 1:25, see also *Sanhedrin* 104b) tells of a widow in Rabban Gamliel's neighborhood who would weep bitterly over her plight. When Rabban Gamliel heard her cries in the night, he would arise and cry over the destruction of the Temple and the Jewish exile. HaRav Mordechai Gifter explains that Rabban Gamliel knew that her personal woes were an outgrowth of Israel's general misfortune. When Israel is delivered collectively, all personal problems will be resolved as well.

For many years, Rabbi Yoel Sirkis, known as the *Bach,* could not arrange for the publication of *Bais Chadash,* his commentary on the *Tur Shulchan Aruch.* Whenever it was about to go to print, an unforeseen circumstance would arise and delay the printing. After many years of frustration, the *Bach* was heartbroken. One midnight, as he grieved over his personal misfortune, he stopped and berated himself, "How selfish of me to weep over my personal problems when there is a far greater tragedy in the world, the calamity of Israel in Exile!" So he took off his shoes like a mourner and recited *Tikkun Chatzos,* the midnight prayer for the Redemption of Israel.

Eventually, fatigue overcame the *Bach* and he fell asleep. A heavenly voice addressed him in a dream. "Know that for many years they have been displeased with you in heaven, because you became so engrossed in writing *Bais Chadash* that you neglected the recitation of *Tikkun Chatzos.* As great as Torah study is, one must never lose sight of the plight of the Jewish people. Tonight, for the first time in years, you cried over the collective misery of God and Israel — so you have regained favor in heaven."

Heart of Our Nation

TODAY'S JERUSALEM IS A magnificent urban complex replete with every type of religious institution necessary for Torah living. With its hundreds upon hundreds of synagogues, yeshivos, kollelim, mikvaos, charity funds, etc., the rebuilt Jerusalem of our times appears to adequately serve the spiritual needs of her devout citizens. Much impressed by appearances, the casual uninformed observer might well have reason to ask, "Why do we continue to plead so desperately for Jerusalem to be rebuilt? True, we have no Temple and we cannot sacrifice *korbanos,* but we can hardly say that the holy city still lays in ruins!"

This question can be answered with an analogy to the patient who receives a heart transplant. The patient is up and around and appears to be healthy, but he is filled with anxiety lest his new heart be rejected or malfunction. He is extremely vulnerable to infection, and distressingly susceptible to unexpected side effects. As advanced as technology may be, the new heart is not his own.

Similarly, the heart of mankind in general and the Jews in particular is the *Beis HaMikdash,* the Holy Temple. In that location, Adam was created and there God breathed life into his nostrils. God continued to pump vitality into mankind through the Temple until it was destroyed. Now, we are still maintained, but it is not the same. We are weak and fragile, susceptible to spiritual and moral contamination and disease. We are easily worn out. The whole system can collapse at any time.

The Temple and the Holy City are the heart of our nation; when they were destroyed we suffered a national cardiac arrest. If we are crippled as a nation, how can any individual be fully healthy? Only when Jerusalem is rebuilt will Israel be healed: As King David said, The Builder of Jerusalem is Hashem, He will gather in the outcasts of Israel: He is the Healer of the brokenhearted and the One Who binds up their sorrows (*Psalms* 147:2, 3).

IV: Jeremiah the Prophet: Fighting Fire With Tears

Jeremiah cursed the ninth day of Av, Tishah B'Av, the day of his birth (Midrash Iyov).

Every time Jeremiah admonished the Jewish people, they mocked, scorned, and humiliated him (Mishlei Rabbasi 1).

Unbridled Brazenness

JEREMIAH WAS PROBABLY the most unpopular prophet in history. For forty years he fearlessly hammered away at the people of Israel and warned them of God's impending retribution. Everything he said, he said publicly, in the marketplace, for all to hear. The people despised him for his prophecies. He was not just unpopular — he was scorned, hated, threatened, and persecuted. But he was never intimidated or silenced, because he spoke the word of God — and the word of God must be heard.

The one who detested Jeremiah most was King Yehoyakim. The height of King Yehoyakim's brazen defiance is described in Chapter 36 of the Book of *Jeremiah*.

In the fourth year of his reign, eighteen years before the *Churban,* God commanded Jeremiah to prepare a scroll upon which he would record God's prediction of the evil that would befall the land during the future *Churban.* Our Rabbis teach that Jeremiah, who was then in prison because of his intrepid prophecies, recorded the basic text of the Book of *Lamentations* (Chapters 1, 2, and 4). Because he was incarcerated, Jeremiah sent his devoted disciple Baruch ben Neriyah to the king's palace to read this prophetic warning to him. This took place on the eighth day of Kislev while the king was in his winter palace, which was warmed by a roaring fire. One of the king's officers began to read:

"Alas — she [Jerusalem] sits in solitude!" (*Lam.* 1:1).

"Who cares," responded Yehoyakim, "as long as I remain king!"

"She weeps bitterly in the night" (ibid. 1:2).

"Who cares," he shrugged, "as long as I remain king!"

"Judah has gone into exile because of suffering" (ibid. 1:3).

"Who cares! I am still king!"

"The roads of Zion are in mourning!" (ibid. 1:4).

"Who cares! I am still king!"

"Her adversaries have become her ruling monarch" (ibid. 1:5).

"That I will never accept! I must remain king!" (*Moed Katan* 26a).

Enraged, Yehoyakim seized a sharp razor, and cut out every Name of God from the scroll, and then threw God's Names and the holy scroll into the roaring fire — where it burnt until everything turned to ashes.

After the king committed this sacrilege, neither he nor any of his retinue felt any remorse or fear whatsoever. Ordinarily, when a sacred Torah Scroll goes up in flames and God's Name is obliterated, it is considered a calamity of the highest order, and one must tear his clothing in mourning and fast and repent. Not so Yehoyakim and his court; they rejoiced over the conflagration of the Torah.

For this, Yehoyakim was doomed to die a terrible death, with his remains treated like an animal's carcass, unburied and left to rot in the street. And his subjects, who tolerated his wickedness, were doomed to destruction by sword and fire.

Jeremiah's Mission

GOD TOLD JEREMIAH to take up the prophet's pen once again to rewrite the Book of *Lamentations* to which was now added Chapter Three, the longest and most tragic chapter of all. It begins: I am the man who has seen affliction by the rod of His anger (*Lam.* 3:1).

This was Jeremiah's sorrowful destiny. He saw the destruction looming closer and closer, yet he could do nothing to prevent it, because the people and their leaders refused to listen. He tried with all his might to get the people to cry, because he knew that nothing would extinguish the flame of God's fury like sincere tears of penitence; but their hearts were hardened and not a tear would they shed.

After the destruction of the Temple, Jeremiah resolved to follow the multitude of Jews who were led into captivity. When he found a blood-drenched trail, he knew he was in the right direction. All too soon, he came across dead bodies, severed limbs, and the pitiful corpses of tiny sucklings and babes. When he finally caught up with the captives, he hugged and kissed them, clung to them in warm embrace, and accompanied them all the way to the shores of the Euphrates River, in Babylonia, where he bid them farewell saying, "I must return to comfort the remnants of Israel who remain on the holy soil."

When the captives realized that the prophet was leaving them, they burst into tears. "Our dear father Jeremiah, how can you leave us?" they wept. With deep compassion, Jeremiah responded, "I hereby bring heaven and earth to testify that I tell you the absolute truth; if only you had cried sincerely but once while you were still in Zion, you never would have been exiled." With that, Jeremiah turned toward the Holy Land, shedding bitter tears (*Pesikta Rabbasi* 26).

A Cry for All Seasons

THE TEARS OF *KINNOS* are a never-ending stream. When I began to translate and elucidate the *Kinnos* on the day after Succos, I called my rebbe, HaRav Mordechai Gifter, and asked, "How can I get into the mood of writing about *Kinnos* just a day after Simchas Torah, while the happy tunes of joy still resonate in my ears and Tishah B'Av is still so far off in the future? Who can think of *Kinnos* now?"

He replied, "You are mistaken. *Kinnos* are not only for Tishah B'Av, they are for the entire year, except that throughout the year we recite *Kinnos* in a whisper, while on Tishah B'Av we shout them out loud! Whoever neglects *Kinnos* all year long and attempts to start reciting them on

Tishah B'Av will not succeed in saying them even then, because he will recite the verses without any feeling and he will become bored. We must cry and mourn over the *Churban* all year long, in every season, and then our *Kinnos* will reach their climax of pain on Tishah B'Av!"

This concept of regular mourning over the *Churban* is codified in the very first chapter of *Shulchan Aruch* (*Orach Chaim* 1:3): It is proper for every God-fearing person to feel pain and anguish over the destruction of the Holy Temple.

The *Sfas Emes* was once asked: "And what should someone do if he feels no anguish over the *Churban* of the Temple?" The Rebbi replied, "Then he should be consumed with pain and anguish over his own personal *Churban*. If a Jew doesn't feel real pain over the *Churban*, it shows that his soul is in a wretched, abysmal state!"

True, *kinnos* are for all year round — but when does one begin to develop a feeling for them? On Tishah B'Av. If one truly comprehends and feels the *Kinnos* he recites on this day, he will be inspired to refer back to them throughout the year. For this reason the halachah places special emphasis on understanding the meaning of every word in the *Kinnos*:

> *... the entire congregation should understand them — including the women and children — because women are obligated to hear the Kinnos like the men — and undoubtedly we must make certain that the young boys understand (Tur Shulchan Aruch, Orach Chaim §559).*

V: Tishah B'Av: The Birthday of Mashiach

> כֵּיוָן שֶׁחָרַב בֵּית הַמִּקְדָּשׁ נוֹלַד הַמָּשִׁיחַ.
> *From the moment the Temple was destroyed Mashiach was born (Midrash Abba Gorion).*
>
> *What is the name of the Messiah? Rav Yehudah said in the name of Rav Iva, "His name is Menachem, as it is written:* עַל אֵלֶּה אֲנִי בוֹכִיָּה עֵינִי עֵינִי יֹרְדָה מַּיִם כִּי רָחַק מִמֶּנִּי מְנַחֵם מֵשִׁיב נַפְשִׁי*, Over these things I weep; my eyes run with water because a comforter [Menachem] to revive my spirit is far from me (Lam. 1:16). ... On the day the Temple was destroyed the Messianic Savior of Israel was born. What is his name? Menachem [comforter]" (Midrash Eichah Rabbasi 1:57).*

No Contradiction

ON TISHAH B'AV we recite over forty *kinnos* expressing our pain and misery over the destruction of our Temple and the exile of the Jewish people. Scores of major Jewish themes are interwoven into the rich and complex tapestry of the *kinnos,* yet one fundamental concept is missing. There is no mention of Mashiach! This deletion is particularly puzzling since, according to many Rabbinic sources, Mashiach's birthday is on this very day of Tishah B'Av!

Perhaps the solution to this enigma may be found in the Redeemer's identity. He is מָשִׁיחַ בֶּן דָּוִד, Messiah the son of David, an extension and an amplification of the life and accomplishments of King David, "The Sweet Singer of Israel" (see Overview to ArtScroll *Tehillim*). The Psalmist was uniquely able to sing God's praises under even the most adverse circumstances. Indeed, the more David suffered, the more he praised God. The more intense the pain, the more intense the passion, because David extracted the precious nugget of goodness from within every grief.

For David and for the Messiah, his scion, there are no bleak, mournful *kinnos* / lamentations; there are only exultant *mizmorim* / songs. Indeed, this is precisely how *Mashiach* will redeem Israel from her travails, by teaching Jews how to discern the positive, productive forces that are encased within every negative experience. In all of the Scriptures, no one was as afflicted as David. No one was so misunderstood, no one had so many enemies. Job's suffering was unbearable, but it lasted for a relatively short while. But David's entire life was an endless succession of misfortune.

This is the wondrous secret of *Tehillim.* David cries out in pain, yet songs of joy pour forth from his lips. His words are those of melancholy and despair, yet a spirit of happiness saturates every syllable.

David could cry out, "Every night my bed I drench, with my tears I soak my couch" — and still he could exult, "Hashem has heard my plea, Hashem will accept my prayer" (*Psalms* 6:7,10). There was no contradiction, because David understood that his affliction and his acceptance were one (*Tzidkas HaTzaddik* 129).

To Cope With Heartbreak

ONE OF DAVID'S GREATEST MISFORTUNES was the rebellion of Absalom, his son. Thus, the Sages of the Talmud expound on the verse: מִזְמוֹר לְדָוִד בְּבָרְחוֹ מִפְּנֵי אַבְשָׁלוֹם בְּנוֹ. ה׳ מָה רַבּוּ צָרָי רַבִּים קָמִים עָלָי. *A song of David, as he fled from Absalom his son. Hashem, how many are my tormentors! The great rise up against me!* (*Psalms* 3:1, 2). In view of the tragic circumstances under which this psalm was composed — a revolution led by the son over whom he had doted! — the title "A song of David," seems to be incongruous. It should have been called a *kinnah* / lament! Said Rabbi Shimon ben Avishalom, this may be likened to a person in debt. Before he pays, he is worried and sad, but after he pays, he rejoices. So too with David. Since God had warned him, "I will raise up evil against you from out of your own house" (*II Samuel* 12:11), he was saddened. Perhaps a merciless slave or an illegitimate child would rise up in vengeance, without any mercy. Now that he saw that he was menaced by his own son, who, despite his treachery, indeed hesitated to follow Ahitophel's counsel that he pursue and slaughter his father, David sang in gratitude to God (*Berachos* 7b).

Similarly we read in *Psalms* how the Psalmist took a different view of the destruction of the Temple. Even in this catastrophe, he found cause to sing.

> מִזְמוֹר לְאָסָף אֱלֹהִים בָּאוּ גוֹיִם בְּנַחֲלָתֶךָ טִמְּאוּ אֶת הֵיכַל קָדְשֶׁךָ שָׂמוּ אֶת יְרוּשָׁלַם לְעִיִּים.
> *A song of Assaf, O God! The nations have entered into Your estate, they defiled the Sanctuary of Your holiness, they turned Jerusalem into a heap of rubble (Psalms 79:1).*

Since this woeful composition describes the Temple's destruction, the Midrash asks here too: מִזְמוֹר? קִינָה מִיבָּעֵי לֵהּ, *A song? This should be titled a kinnah!*

The Midrash answers with a parable. A king once erected a beautiful bridal canopy for his son's nuptials. The son, however, was so stubborn and rude that he infuriated his father. The king stormed into the wedding hall and vented his rage on the gorgeous canopy, ripping it to shreds.

So too did the stubbornness of Israel exceedingly anger God. However, He was merciful, and directed His anger at the stones and beams of the Holy Temple rather than at the Jews themselves. Although the people of Israel were severely punished, only the Temple was destroyed; the nation survived (*Rashi, Kiddushin* 31b).

Clearly, David/Messiah is able to transform every *kinnah* into a *mizmor,* song. Thus, it is impossible to include the concept of the hopeful, optimistic Mashiach in the despairing, despondent *kinnos* of Tishah B'Av. Where there is Mashiach, there can be no *kinnos*!

Measure for measure, God ordained Tishah B'Av to be a day of total grief. God thundered at the unfaithful generation of the Wilderness, "You utterly betrayed me by accepting the evil reports of the spies. You drowned yourselves in tears of desperation and self-pity as if there were absolutely no possibility for salvation. Therefore, on this very day, you and your descendants shall always be entirely immersed in sorrow and despair. You will be so blinded by tears that you will see no glimmer of hope arising from the messianic future!"

Thus, Jeremiah, the prophet who was born on Tishah B'Av, said, "Cursed be the day on which I was born, let not the day on which my mother gave birth to me have any blessing" (*Jeremiah* 20:14). But this very tragedy shall lead us to our ultimate triumph. Because the very fact that for thousands of years Jews the world over have forgotten the woes of the present and plunged themselves into an ocean of tears over a Holy Temple that they and their parents never saw, and lamented over a Holy Land upon which their feet never trod — this is Israel's supreme merit. The very fact that we return to our lament every Tishah B'Av, year after year, shows that we remember what was and lament what was lost, that we do have hope and that our faith is strong. Thus, as the *Kinnos* end, Jeremiah's accursed birthday is transformed into Mashiach's blessed birthday. Once again the *kinnah* is exchanged for a *mizmor.*

Therefore, the halachah reminds us that in certain ways Tishah B'Av is actually considered a מוֹעֵד, *holiday,* and we are enjoined from reciting the *Tachanun* supplication to demonstrate that our spirits have not been entirely crushed by this day of mourning (see *Shulchan Aruch, Orach Chaim* 559:4, 5). Indeed, we even conclude every *kinnah* on an upbeat note of נֶחָמָה, *consolation,* to demonstrate that in the merit of these bitter, heartrending lamentations we do have confidence in the redemption that lies ahead!

VI: Rabbi Elazar HaKalir: A Balm for Burning Eyes

Master Paytan

PIYUT, LITURGICAL POETRY, has been a hallowed and time-honored component of our prayer service for many centuries. Rabbi Elazar HaKalir is universally accepted as "the Father of the *Paytanim*" [liturgical poets], having achieved an unsurpassed degree of excellence in language and style, combined with a superior level of Torah scholarship.

Magen Avraham (*Orach Chaim* 68:1) quotes *Shibbolei Haleket* who writes, "I heard from my father who heard from his teachers that when the Kalir composed the *piyut* 'And the fiery angels face the celestial Throne,' a heavenly fire encircled him. This is what my father heard from his teachers. Indeed, Rabbi Shimon HaGadol, who was a miracle-worker, would recite that *piyut* every day."

Who Was He?

THE GREATEST MYSTERY surrounding the Kalir is his identity. Who was this awesome person? When and where did he live?

There are many versions of who he was and in which century he lived, but this is not the place to discuss the various opinions. However, *Arizal* gives us a remarkable teaching which provides an insight into the Kalir's role in the *Kinnos.* According to *Arizal,* he had the soul of Rabbi Elazar, the son of Rabbi Shimon bar Yochai, author of the Holy *Zohar.*

What is the meaning of the name *Kalir*? There are various opinions. I would humbly suggest the word *Kalir* is derived from קִילוֹרִין [*killorin,*] which means "a balm for the eyes" (see *Shabbos* 108b and *Yalkut Shimoni, Tehillim* §675). Incessant weeping and bitter tears had burned and reddened the eyes of the Jewish people. Rabbi Elazar the Kalir composed his beautiful, soul-stirring poems in order to soothe and cool the feverish eyes and hearts of his suffering brethren.

The World Survives

GENERATIONS UPON GENERATIONS of Jews have found an expression of their innermost spiritual pain and yearning in these *Kinnos* composed by those who expanded upon the dirges of Jeremiah. Surely the Holy One, Blessed is He, collects and cherishes our tears. Surely the treasury of tears has already been filled to overflowing by countless years of Jewish suffering. Surely the time has come to call a halt to the flow of tears and to replace our weeping with laughter.

May the tears we shed this Tishah B'Av be the last, and may we see the fulfillment of the Talmudic blessing: כָּל הַמִּתְאַבֵּל עַל יְרוּשָׁלַיִם זוֹכֶה וְרוֹאֶה בְּשִׂמְחָתָהּ, *Whoever mourns over Jerusalem is deserving to witness her joy!* (*Taanis* 30b).

Rabbi Avrohom Chaim Feuer
Miami Beach, Florida
17 Tammuz 5751

☙ *Prologue*

The All-Encompassing *Aleph-Beis*: From *Aleph* to *Tav*, and Back Again

(based on *The Wisdom in the Hebrew Alphabet*, by Rabbi Michael L. Munk)

In Jewish thought, the *Aleph-Beis* is unlike any other alphabet; it is not merely a haphazard collection of consonants whose order was determined by convention, but that could have been — or still could be — changed without loss of content. The individual letters, their names, graphic forms, *gematrios* [numerical equivalents], and respective positions in the *Aleph-Beis* are Divinely ordained. [See Overview of ArtScroll's *The Wisdom in the Hebrew Alphabet* for a discussion of the Divine forces represented by the letters and their various combinations.] A corollary of this principle is the halachic requirement that every letter in a Torah scroll, *mezuzah,* and *tefillin* must be written perfectly. No part of a letter may be omitted or distorted, nor may its individual integrity be compromised by contact with any other letter. Every word must be spelled correctly; a missing, extra, transposed, or blemished letter can invalidate the entire scroll.

In Scripture, as in our prayers and *kinnos,* we often find verses or phrases progressing through the Hebrew alphabet from *aleph* to *tav;* conversely, there are passages that reverse the order, beginning with *tav* and going back to *aleph.* What is the significance of these letter progressions?

Aleph to Tav: Completion

IN THE POPULAR IDIOM, something that is expressed or analyzed in its entirety is said to be covered מֵאָלֶף וְעַד תָּיו, *from aleph to tav.* Since the very order of the letters represents profound halachic and philosophic concepts, this expression is far more encompassing than the idiomatic "from A to Z" or from "*alpha* to *omega.*"

The use of an alphabetical sequence to praise God, or to describe a person or concept, denotes totality and perfection. For example, the passage of אֵשֶׁת חַיִל, *An Accomplished Woman* (*Proverbs* 31:10-31), describes in twenty-two alphabetically arranged verses the entire range of the woman's virtues in following the ways of Torah, the very Torah that was translated into human expression by means of these same twenty-two letters.

Complete Blessing and Tempered Curse

THE DEFINITE ARTICLE *the* is expressed in Hebrew by prefixing the letter ה to a word. Often, for extra emphasis, the word אֶת (or אֵת) is employed in addition to the prefix. Because it is spelled with the first and last letters of the *Aleph-Beis*, אֶת alludes to completion and perfection. Thus the Torah uses this emphatic article in describing the beginning of Creation: בְּרֵאשִׁית בָּרָא אֱלֹהִים אֵת הַשָּׁמַיִם וְאֵת הָאָרֶץ, *In the beginning of God's creating the heavens and the earth* (*Genesis* 1:1). This usage indicates that the universe was created in complete perfection, "from *aleph* to *tav*."

The detailed blessings promised those who observe the entire Torah begin with the א of אִם [*If you follow My decrees* ...] (*Leviticus* 26:3) and end with the ת of קוֹמְמִיּוּת, (*upright,* ibid. v. 13). This indicates that the commandments are as perfect as the universe in which they are to be fulfilled (*Maharal, Netzach*), and that the blessings bestowed as a reward for *mitzvah* observance are complete and all-encompassing.

Consolation Amid Tragedy

IN A LESS HAPPY USE, alphabetic acrostics are employed to symbolize totality of destruction and transgression. In the period before the destruction of the First Temple when Israel no longer deserved blessings, the prophet Jeremiah composed the Book of *Eichah* [*Lamentations*], which contains a series of lamentations. Its verses begin, respectively, with the twenty-two letters of the *Aleph-Beis,* in order to indicate that God's *full* fury was unleashed against the people of Israel, because "they transgressed the Torah, which was given them with the twenty-two letters" (*Sanhedrin* 104a).

But there is consolation even amid tragedy. Although the Temple has not been rebuilt, the Torah, symbolizing the completion and perfection of the full *Aleph-Beis,* remains the legacy of Israel. The month of tragedy, is called מְנַחֵם אָב, or *consolation of the Aleph-Beis* (*Kotzker*).

The Universal Cycle of Return: From Tav to Aleph

THE ENTIRE *ALEPH-BEIS* is a single unit in which all the letters are interrelated. Just as every part of the universe was created by God and is totally dependent on His mercy at all times, so too the *aleph* — symbol of God's uniqueness and primacy — is the root and leader of all the sacred letters. The letters can be compared to a flame; though tongues and sparks of fire spring out in many directions, they all originate from and are part of the same flame, because all forces emanate from the One God and are connected by an underlying unity.

Accordingly, Kabbalistic literature teaches that the *Aleph-Beis* — representing all Divine forces — does not culminate with the *tav,* but turns around to reunite again with the *aleph,* which symbolizes the יְחִידוֹ שֶׁל עוֹלָם, *the Unique One of the universe,* Who is אֵין סוֹף, *Infinite.* Having attained the level of *aleph* to *tav* by making his way to completion, one has not completed his task. The achievement has elevated him, given him new insights. From the vantage point of his *tav,* one looks back at his previous insights — and begins anew — because he now sees the *aleph,* the very beginning, with new eyes. He begins again, because the ladder climaxing in the *tav* has given him a new perspective on the *aleph,* which in turn leads him to ever higher levels of perfection as he ascends from letter to letter, from teaching to teaching, from aspiration to aspiration.

The Spiritual Cycle in the Universe

THE FORCE THAT DRAWS the holy letters back to the *aleph* reflects the spiritual cycle of the universe. At the beginning of Creation, nothing stood in opposition to the will of God. Heaven and earth, from the mightiest galaxies to the tiniest microbe, reflected only His will. They existed as testimony to the revelation of His Oneness. But this sublime era ceased with the creation of man. Only man has free will. Only he can accept powers other than the Divine; only he can disobey God's will. Adam and Eve did so when they let the serpent entice them into eating from the forbidden fruit in the Garden of Eden. Ever since, sin has been part of man's nature, with the result that God's Oneness is concealed [הֶסְתֵּר יִחוּדוֹ]. But man's aberration is not permanent; eventually the cycle will return to its starting point, when — in Messianic times — Hashem will be acknowledged by all mankind as the exclusive and absolute Ruler (*R' Moshe Chaim Luzatto*).

Every individual human being is challenged in his own life to make a spiritual cycle that will return him to his lofty origin. Thus, the cycle of striving for the *tav* and then of reinvigorating one's personal *aleph* is the mission of mankind as a whole and of every individual Jew.

The Continuous Cycle of Generations

KING SOLOMON DERIVES FROM the cycles in the universe an allegoric illustration of man's fate, which can change from darkness to light. In the words *the sun rises and the sun sets* (*Koheles* 1:5), Solomon expresses the idea of continuity. Before the "sun" of a righteous man sets, Providence causes the sun of another righteous man to rise. Before the sun of Moses set, God caused the sun of Joshua to rise. Before Sarah's sun set, Rebeccah's rose. On the day R' Akiva died, R' Yehudah HaNassi was born. And so, on and on, generations perish and new generations are born.

Jewish history is filled with the recurring phenomenon that periods of darkness and oppression are followed by periods of light and relief. In the midst of the Egyptian exile and slavery, Pharaoh learned from his astrologers of the imminent birth of Israel's redeemer. The king tried to prevent Moses' emergence by ordering the murder of all newborn males, but in that tragic hour of Israel's history, Moses was born (*Rashi*, *Exodus* 1:16). Divine Providence decreed that Israel's first redeemer — the very person the Egyptian ruler wanted to annihilate — was saved by Pharaoh's own daughter and raised in the royal palace. Indeed, light emerged from darkness!

Divine Providence has assured Israel that the greater the affliction, the closer and surer the redemption (*Sotah* 11a). Thus on the darkest day of the year, Tishah B'Av [the Ninth of Av], when the Jew mourns the destruction of both Holy Temples, he is consoled by the knowledge that the Messiah will be born on this very day, and Tishah B'Av will eventually become a joyous festival (*Midrash Abba Gurion*).

Imrei Emes finds an allusion to this thought in the fact that Tishah B'Av always falls on the same day of the week as the first day of the preceding Pesach. This indicates that the day inaugurating the redemption (from Egypt) also marks its end (the destruction of the Temple). However, in the life-cycle of Israel, as well as in the letter-cycle of the *Aleph-Beis*, "the beginning is anchored in the end and the end in its beginning." Thus our Sages assure us that Tishah B'Av contains in itself the spark of the final redemption, although we cannot see it in the present darkness.

This change from pain to joy is anticipated in *Eichah* (1:15), which calls the Ninth of Av a מוֹעֵד, *festival*. Hence, even during the exile, on that day Jews do not recite *Tachanun*, the weekday plea for salvation (*Orach Chaim* 559:4).

Even the stones that were retrieved from the debris of *Eretz Yisrael's* destruction and transported to Babylonia to erect new houses of worship and study will complete the cycle of Divine Providence. The synagogues and study halls of Babylonia — and, by extension, of Israel's every sojourn during the long exile — will, in the future, be established in *Eretz Yisrael (Megillah* 29a). *Maharsha* explains that the Third Temple will be as large as the entire city of Jerusalem because it will have to accommodate all the Jews returning from the Diaspora. For this purpose their synagogues and study halls will accompany them on their return to the land. These edifices will become merged with the Temple so that their combined area will cover the whole city. Thus we may conclude that spiritual intentions are never lost; they transcend all destruction and become the foundation of future redemptions.

The Celestial Order of the Holy Letters and Man's Aspiration for It

IN THE TIMELESS REALM before Creation, the letters existed in a sequence opposite that of the *Aleph-Beis*. They began with *tav* and proceeded in the backward order of ת,ש,ר,ק and so on, concluding with *aleph*. Those letters represented the pure Divine Spirit of the Almighty and were engraved with flaming fire in the כֶּתֶר, *Crown* of God (*Sefer Yetzirah*).

When the Almighty intended to create the world through the Divine letters, He did so in the order of ... ת,ש,ר,ק. Accordingly, the Midrash (*Yalkut* 1:1) relates: When the letters descended from the Crown of the Almighty and appeared before Him in order, each one to plead that the world should be created with it, the procession began with *tav* and continued until the plea of the *beis* was accepted.

א״ב for Mercy; תשר״ק for Judgment

THE ONLY DIVINE NAME FOUND in the first chapter of *Genesis* is אֱלֹהִים, *God [of Judgment*]. This teaches us that God intended the universe to be ruled by the scales of justice. Then He tempered Justice with Mercy, and this new process was indicated by the Torah in *Genesis* 2:4, where it begins to refer to God as ה' אֱלֹהִים, combining His Name of Mercy [י-ה-ו-ה] with His Name of Judgment [אֱלֹהִים].

The Midrash compares this to a king who wanted a warm drink, but had only very expensive and delicate stemware. The king thought, "If I pour in the hot water first, the thin glass will expand and crack. But if I pour in the cold water first, the thin glass will contract and snap." So he mixed the hot water with the cold and filled his glass with the warm water.

Similarly, God said, "If I create the world on the basis of Divine Mercy alone (represented by the Name *Hashem),* its sins will abound; on the basis of Divine Judgment alone *[Elohim],* it cannot endure. Therefore, I will create it on the basis of both Judgment and Mercy, and may it then stand!" Hence, the combined expression: *Hashem, Elohim.*

Thus, in telling of the Creation of the universe as a whole, *Elohim* is used and heaven is mentioned first, for, indeed, only the celestial beings can endure governance by Justice alone. But when man entered the scene, "earth" is mentioned first and the added use of *Hashem* signifies that His justice must be tempered with mercy (*Kli Yakar*).

The association of Mercy with Judgment at the creation of mankind did not effect the *essence* of the celestial letters. What changed was the *order* of the letters. By reversing their order — to begin with an *aleph* instead of *tav* — God mercifully indicated that the scheme of Creation was not intended to include only the celestial beings but was planned especially for the sake of man (*Maharal*).

The *Aleph-Beis* is a ladder and a link. It binds us to the spiritual origin of creation and life. It enables us to aspire to heights and to infuse all areas of existence with the celestial summit. It illuminates us with renewed aspiration for new life and redemption. It teaches us to pull ourselves from the *alpeh* of potential life to the *tav* of achievement — and then to begin again to attain ever-new levels of accomplishment until our aspirations for the Messianic times will be fulfilled.

◆§ The Names of God

The Four-Letter Name of HASHEM [י־ה־ו־ה] indicates that God is timeless and infinite, since the letters of this Name are those of the words הָיָה הֹוֶה וְיִהְיֶה, *He was, He is, and He will be.* This Name appears in some editions with vowel points [יְ־הֹ־וָ־ה] and in others, such as the present edition, without vowels. In either case, this Name is *never* pronounced as it is spelled.

During prayer, or when a blessing is recited, or when Torah verses are read, the Four-Letter Name should be pronounced as if it were spelled אֲדֹנָי, *Adōnoy,* the Name that identifies God as the Master of All. At other times, it should be pronounced הַשֵּׁם, *Hashem,* literally, "the Name."

According to the *Shulchan Aruch,* one should have both meanings — the Master of All and the Timeless, Infinite One — in mind when reciting the Four-Letter Name during prayer (*Orach Chaim* Ch. 5). According to the *Vilna Gaon,* however, one need have in mind only the meaning of the Name as it is pronounced — the Master of All (ibid.).

When the Name is spelled אֲדֹנָי in the prayer or verse, all agree that one should have in mind that God is the Master of All.

The Name אֱלֹהִים, *Elōhim, God,* refers to Him as the One Who is all-powerful and Who is in direct overlordship of the universe (ibid.). This is also used as a generic name for the angels, a court, rulers, and even idols. However, when the term אֱלֹהִים is used for the God of Israel, it means the One Omniscient God, Who is uniquely identified with His Chosen People.

In this work, the Four-Letter Name of God is translated "HASHEM," the pronunciation traditionally used for the Name to avoid pronouncing it unnecessarily. This pronunciation should be used when studying the meanings of the prayers. However, if one prays in English, he should say "God" or "Lord" or he should pronounce the Name in the proper Hebrew way — *Adōnoy* — in accord with the ruling of most halachic authorities.

◆§ Pronouncing the Names of God

The following table gives the pronunciations of the Name when it appears with a prefix. In all these cases, the accent is on the last syllable (*noy*). The phrase "מֹשֶׁה" מוֹצִיא "וְכָלֵב" מַכְנִיס is used as a mnemonic. The prefixes מ, ש, and ה do not absorb or assimilate the vowel from the first letter of God's Name, while the prefixes ו, כ, ל, and ב do absorb the vowel that follows.

בַּי־ה־ו־ה	—	*Ba-dōnoy*
דַי־ה־ו־ה	—	*Da-dōnoy*
הַי־ה־ו־ה	—	*Ha-adōnoy*
וַי־ה־ו־ה	—	*Va-dōnoy*
כַּי־ה־ו־ה	—	*Ka-dōnoy*
לַי־ה־ו־ה	—	*La-dōnoy*
מֵי־ה־ו־ה	—	*May-adōnoy*
שֶׁי־ה־ו־ה	—	*She-adōnoy*

Sometimes the Name appears with the vowelization יֱ־הֹ־וִ־ה. This version of the Name is pronounced as if it were spelled אֱלֹהִים, *Elōhim,* the Name that refers to God as the One Who is all-powerful. When it appears with a prefix לֵי־הֹ־וִ־ה, it is pronounced *Lay-lōhim.* We have translated this Name as *HASHEM / ELOHIM* to indicate that it refers to the aspects inherent in each of those Names.

◈ Erev Tishah B'Av

The laws regarding Tishah B'Av and Erev Tishah B'Av appear in a separate section at the end of this volume. Some of the main points are:

- Although the fast does not begin until sundown, the mourning of Tishah B'Av is manifested in many laws and customs that are observed during the afternoon before the fast. The last meal before the fast — the *se'udah hamafsekes* — is governed by many restrictions that limit the types of foods that may be eaten and the beverages that may be drunk (see Laws §5-16). Therefore, it is customary to eat a full meal before *Minchah* to prepare oneself for the fast, and to eat the *se'udah hamafsekes* after *Minchah*. That final meal customarily consists of bread, some of which is dipped in ashes, and a hard-boiled egg. One sits on the ground while eating this meal. Regarding food after the *se'udah hamafsekes*, see *Laws* §17-20.

- It is also customary to restrict one's learning on the afternoon before the fast to sad subject matter, i.e., laws pertaining to Tishah B'Av and mourning, and matters relevant to the destruction of the Holy Temple. See *Laws* §2. Regarding learning on Tishah B'Av or its eve when they fall on a Sabbath, see *Laws* §29. Concerning the *se'udah hamafsekes* in such a case, see *Laws* §23-24.

- Just before sunset, one must remove his leather shoes for the duration of Tishah B'Av, and commence the fast. If *Maariv* is recited before sundown, the shoes must be removed before *Barchu*. If Tishah B'Av or its eve fall on the Sabbath, the congregants remove their shoes after *Barchu*, but the *chazzan* recites the formula בָּרוּךְ הַמַּבְדִּיל בֵּין קוֹדֶשׁ לְחוֹל, and removes his shoes before *Barchu*. For a short summary of activities that are prohibited because of the fast-day aspect of Tishah B'Av, see *Laws* §31-41.

- The *Paroches* (Curtain) is removed from the Ark before *Maariv* and not replaced until *Minchah* (see p. 541).

FOR LAWS PERTAINING TO THE EVE OF TISHAH B'AV, SEE PAGE 1.

MAARIV / מעריב

ON SATURDAY NIGHT THE *CHAZZAN* RECITES THE FOLLOWING BEFORE *MAARIV*:

בָּרוּךְ הַמַּבְדִּיל בֵּין קֹדֶשׁ לְחוֹל.

‹ Blessed ‹ is He Who distinguishes ‹ between ‹ sacred ‹ and secular. «

HE THEN REMOVES HIS SHOES.

CONGREGATION, THEN *CHAZZAN*:

וְהוּא רַחוּם יְכַפֵּר עָוֹן וְלֹא יַשְׁחִית, וְהִרְבָּה

‹ He, ‹ the Merciful One, ‹ is forgiving ‹ of iniquity ‹ and does not destroy; « frequently

לְהָשִׁיב אַפּוֹ, וְלֹא יָעִיר כָּל חֲמָתוֹ.[1] ❖ יהוה

‹ He withdraws ‹ His anger, « not ‹ arousing ‹ all ‹ His wrath. « HASHEM,

הוֹשִׁיעָה, הַמֶּלֶךְ יַעֲנֵנוּ בְיוֹם קָרְאֵנוּ.[2]

save! « May the King ‹ answer us ‹ on the day ‹ we call. «

THE *CHAZZAN* SUMMONS THE CONGREGATION TO JOIN IN THE FORTHCOMING PRAYERS, BOWING AT בָּרְכוּ, *BLESS,* AND STRAIGHTENING UP AT 'ה, *HASHEM.*

בָּרְכוּ אֶת יהוה הַמְּבֹרָךְ.

Bless ‹ HASHEM, ‹ the blessed One. «

THE CONGREGATION, FOLLOWED BY *CHAZZAN,* RESPONDS, BOWING AT בָּרוּךְ, *BLESS,* AND STRAIGHTENING UP AT 'ה, *HASHEM.*

בָּרוּךְ יהוה הַמְּבֹרָךְ לְעוֹלָם וָעֶד.

Blessed is ‹ HASHEM, ‹ the blessed One, ‹ for ever ‹ and ever. «

ON SATURDAY NIGHT, THE CONGREGANTS REMOVE THEIR SHOES AT THIS POINT.

(1) *Psalms* 78:38. (2) 20:10.

Laws of Maariv (see also *Laws* §95-109 for the laws of *Shema*)

The ideal time for *Maariv* is after dark. However, if one recited *Maariv* earlier he must repeat the three chapters of *Shema* after dark.

As a general rule, no אָמֵן, *Amen,* or other prayer response may be recited between *Borchu* and *Shemoneh Esrei,* but there are exceptions. The main exception is "between chapters" [בֵּין הַפְּרָקִים] of the *Shema Blessings* — i.e., after each of the blessings, and between the three chapters of *Shema.* At those points, every אָמֵן (but not בָּרוּךְ הוּא וּבָרוּךְ שְׁמוֹ) may be said in response to any blessing. Some responses, however, are so important that they are permitted at any point in the *Shema* blessings. They are: (a) In *Kaddish,* אָמֵן יְהֵא שְׁמֵהּ רַבָּא . . . עָלְמַיָּא and the אָמֵן after דַּאֲמִירָן בְּעָלְמָא; and (b) the response to בָּרְכוּ.

No interruptions whatever are permitted during the two verses of שְׁמַע and בָּרוּךְ שֵׁם.

BLESSINGS OF THE SHEMA / ברכות קריאת שמע

בָּרוּךְ אַתָּה יהוה אֱלֹהֵינוּ מֶלֶךְ הָעוֹלָם, אֲשֶׁר

‹ Who « of the universe, ‹ King ‹ our God, ‹ HASHEM, ‹ are You, ‹ Blessed

בִּדְבָרוֹ מַעֲרִיב עֲרָבִים, בְּחָכְמָה פּוֹתֵחַ שְׁעָרִים,

« gates, ‹ opens ‹ with wisdom « evenings, ‹ brings on ‹ by His word

וּבִתְבוּנָה מְשַׁנֶּה עִתִּים, וּמַחֲלִיף אֶת הַזְּמַנִּים,

« the seasons, ‹ changes « periods, ‹ alters ‹ with understanding

וּמְסַדֵּר אֶת הַכּוֹכָבִים בְּמִשְׁמְרוֹתֵיהֶם בָּרָקִיעַ

« in the heavens ‹ in their constellations « the stars ‹ and orders

כִּרְצוֹנוֹ. בּוֹרֵא יוֹם וָלָיְלָה, גּוֹלֵל אוֹר מִפְּנֵי חֹשֶׁךְ

‹ darkness ‹ before ‹ light ‹ rolling away « and night, ‹ day ‹ He creates « as He wills.

וְחֹשֶׁךְ מִפְּנֵי אוֹר. וּמַעֲבִיר יוֹם וּמֵבִיא לָיְלָה,

« night, ‹ and brings ‹ day ‹ He removes « light. ‹ before ‹ and darkness

וּמַבְדִּיל בֵּין יוֹם וּבֵין לָיְלָה, יהוה צְבָאוֹת שְׁמוֹ.

« is His Name. ‹ Master of Legions, ‹ — HASHEM, « night ‹ and between ‹ day ‹ between ‹ and separates

❖ אֵל חַי וְקַיָּם, תָּמִיד יִמְלוֹךְ עָלֵינוּ, לְעוֹלָם וָעֶד.

« and ever. ‹ for ever ‹ over us, ‹ may He reign ‹ continually « and enduring, ‹ the living ‹ God

בָּרוּךְ אַתָּה יהוה, הַמַּעֲרִיב עֲרָבִים. (אָמֵן – Cong.)

« (Amen.) « evenings. ‹ Who brings on ‹ HASHEM, ‹ are You, ‹ Blessed

אַהֲבַת עוֹלָם בֵּית יִשְׂרָאֵל עַמְּךָ אָהָבְתָּ. תּוֹרָה

‹ Torah « have You loved. ‹ Your people ‹ Israel, ‹ the Family of « that is eternal, ‹ [With] a love

וּמִצְוֹת, חֻקִּים וּמִשְׁפָּטִים, אוֹתָנוּ לִמַּדְתָּ. עַל כֵּן

‹ Therefore, « have You taught us. « and ordinances ‹ decrees ‹ and commandments,

יהוה אֱלֹהֵינוּ, בְּשָׁכְבֵנוּ וּבְקוּמֵנוּ נָשִׂיחַ בְּחֻקֶּיךָ,

« Your decrees ‹ we will discuss « and upon our arising, ‹ upon our retiring « our God, ‹ HASHEM,

וְנִשְׂמַח בְּדִבְרֵי תוֹרָתֶךָ וּבְמִצְוֹתֶיךָ לְעוֹלָם וָעֶד.

« and ever. ‹ for ever ‹ and with Your commandments « of Your Torah ‹ with the words ‹ and we will rejoice

❖ כִּי הֵם חַיֵּינוּ, וְאֹרֶךְ יָמֵינוּ, וּבָהֶם נֶהְגֶּה יוֹמָם

For 〈 they 〈 are our life 〈 and the length 《 of our days 《 and about them 〈 we will meditate 〈 day

וָלָיְלָה. וְאַהֲבָתְךָ, אַל תָּסִיר מִמֶּנּוּ לְעוֹלָמִים. בָּרוּךְ

and night. 《 Your love 〈 do not 〈 remove 〈 from us 〈 forever. 《 Blessed 〈

אַתָּה יהוה, אוֹהֵב עַמּוֹ יִשְׂרָאֵל. (Cong. – אָמֵן)

are You, 〈 HASHEM, 〈 Who loves 〈 His people 〈 Israel. 《 (Amen.) 《

THE SHEMA / שמע

IMMEDIATELY BEFORE ITS RECITATION CONCENTRATE ON FULFILLING THE POSITIVE COMMANDMENT OF RECITING THE *SHEMA* TWICE DAILY. IT IS IMPORTANT TO ENUNCIATE EACH WORD CLEARLY AND NOT TO RUN WORDS TOGETHER. FOR THIS REASON, VERTICAL LINES HAVE BEEN PLACED BETWEEN TWO WORDS THAT ARE NOT SEPARATED BY A COMMA OR A DASH AND ARE APT TO BE SLURRED INTO ONE. SEE *LAWS* §95-109.

WHEN PRAYING WITHOUT A *MINYAN*, BEGIN WITH THE FOLLOWING THREE-WORD FORMULA:

אֵל מֶלֶךְ נֶאֱמָן.

God, 〈 King 〈 Who is trustworthy. 《

RECITE THE FIRST VERSE ALOUD, WITH THE RIGHT HAND COVERING THE EYES, AND CONCENTRATE INTENSELY UPON ACCEPTING GOD'S ABSOLUTE SOVEREIGNTY.

שְׁמַע | יִשְׂרָאֵל,* יהוה | אֱלֹהֵינוּ, יהוה | אֶחָד:[1]

Hear, 〈 O Israel:* 《 HASHEM 〈 is our God, 《 HASHEM is 〈 the One [and Only]. 《

IN AN UNDERTONE:

בָּרוּךְ שֵׁם כְּבוֹד מַלְכוּתוֹ לְעוֹלָם וָעֶד.[2]

Blessed 〈 is the Name 〈 of His glorious 〈 kingdom 〈 for ever 〈 and ever. 《

(1) *Deuteronomy* 6:4. (2) See *Pesachim* 56a.

שְׁמַע / The Shema

The recitation of the three paragraphs of Shema is required by the Torah, and one must have in mind that he is about to fulfill this commandment. Although one should try to concentrate on the meaning of all three paragraphs, one must concentrate at least on the meaning of the first verse (שְׁמַע) and the second verse (בָּרוּךְ שֵׁם) because the recitation of Shema represents fulfillment of the paramount commandment of acceptance of God's absolute sovereignty (קַבָּלַת עוֹל מַלְכוּת שָׁמַיִם). By declaring that God is One, Unique, and Indivisible, we subordinate every facet of our personalities and possessions — and our very lives — to His will.

שְׁמַע יִשְׂרָאֵל — *Hear, O Israel.* Although the commentators find many layers of profound meaning in this seminal verse, one should bear in mind at least the following points during its recitation:

□ At this point in history, HASHEM is only אֱלֹהֵינוּ, *our God,* for He is not acknowledged universally. Ultimately, however, all will recognize Him as ה׳ אֶחָד, *HASHEM, the One and Only* (*Rashi; Aruch HaShulchan* 61:4).

□ ה׳ — *HASHEM.* God is the Eternal One, Who was, is, and always will be [הָיָה הֹוֶה

WHILE RECITING THE FIRST PARAGRAPH (*DEUTERONOMY* 6:5-9), CONCENTRATE ON ACCEPTING THE COMMANDMENT TO LOVE GOD.

וְאָהַבְתָּ אֵת | יְהוָה | אֱלֹהֶיךָ, בְּכָל־לְבָבְךָ, וּבְכָל־

‹ with all « your heart, ‹ with all « your God, ‹ HASHEM, ‹ You shall love

נַפְשְׁךָ, וּבְכָל־מְאֹדֶךָ: וְהָיוּ הַדְּבָרִים הָאֵלֶּה, אֲשֶׁר |

‹ that ‹ — these matters « They should be « your resources. ‹ and with all ‹ your soul,

אָנֹכִי מְצַוְּךָ הַיּוֹם, עַל־לְבָבֶךָ: וְשִׁנַּנְתָּם לְבָנֶיךָ,

« to your children ‹ Teach them thoroughly « your heart. ‹ upon « today— ‹ command you ‹ I

וְדִבַּרְתָּ בָּם בְּשִׁבְתְּךָ בְּבֵיתֶךָ, וּבְלֶכְתְּךָ בַדֶּרֶךְ,

« on the way, ‹ while you walk « in your home, ‹ while you sit ‹ of them ‹ and speak

וּבְשָׁכְבְּךָ וּבְקוּמֶךָ: וּקְשַׁרְתָּם לְאוֹת | עַל־יָדֶךָ,

« your arm ‹ upon ‹ as a sign ‹ Bind them « and when you arise. ‹ when you lie down,

וְהָיוּ לְטֹטָפֹת בֵּין | עֵינֶיךָ: וּכְתַבְתָּם | עַל־מְזֻזוֹת

‹ the doorposts ‹ on ‹ And write them « your eyes. ‹ between ‹ *tefillin* ‹ and they shall be

בֵּיתֶךָ וּבִשְׁעָרֶיךָ:

« and upon your gates. ‹ of your house

WHILE RECITING THE SECOND PARAGRAPH (*DEUTERONOMY* 11:13-21), CONCENTRATE ON ACCEPTING ALL THE COMMANDMENTS AND ON THE CONCEPT OF REWARD AND PUNISHMENT.

וְהָיָה, אִם־שָׁמֹעַ תִּשְׁמְעוּ אֶל־מִצְוֹתַי אֲשֶׁר |

‹ that « My commandments ‹ to ‹ you continually hearken ‹ that if ‹ And it will come to pass

אָנֹכִי מְצַוֶּה | אֶתְכֶם הַיּוֹם, לְאַהֲבָה אֶת־יְהוָה |

‹ HASHEM, ‹ to love « today, ‹ you ‹ command ‹ I

[וַיִהְיֶה], and He is אָדוֹן, *Master*, of all.

□ אֱלֹהֵינוּ — *Our God*. He is All-Powerful (*Orach Chaim* 5).

אֶחָד — *The One [and Only]*. The word has two connotations: (a) There is no God other than HASHEM (*Rashbam*); and, (b) though we perceive God in many roles — kind, angry, merciful, wise, judgmental, and so on — these different attributes are not contradictory, even though human intelligence does not comprehend their harmony.

In saying the word אֶחָד, *the One and Only*, draw out the second syllable (חָ) a bit and emphasize the final consonant (ד). While drawing out the ח — a letter with the numerical value of eight — bear in mind that God is Master of the earth and the seven heavens. While clearly enunciating the final ד — which has the numerical value of four — bear in mind that God is Master in all four directions, meaning everywhere.

אֱלֹהֵיכֶם וּלְעָבְדוֹ, בְּכָל־לְבַבְכֶם וּבְכָל־נַפְשְׁכֶם:

« your soul ‹ and with all ‹ your heart ‹ with all « and to serve Him, ‹ your God,

וְנָתַתִּי מְטַר־אַרְצְכֶם בְּעִתּוֹ, יוֹרֶה וּמַלְקוֹשׁ,

« and late rain, ‹ the early rain « in its proper time, ‹ for your land ‹ rain ‹ — then I will provide

וְאָסַפְתָּ דְגָנֶךָ וְתִירֹשְׁךָ וְיִצְהָרֶךָ: וְנָתַתִּי | עֵשֶׂב |

‹ grass ‹ I will provide « and your oil. ‹ your wine, ‹ your grain, ‹ that you may gather in

בְּשָׂדְךָ לִבְהֶמְתֶּךָ, וְאָכַלְתָּ וְשָׂבָעְתָּ: הִשָּׁמְרוּ לָכֶם פֶּן־

‹ lest « for yourselves ‹ Beware « and be satisfied. ‹ and you will eat « for your cattle ‹ in your field

יִפְתֶּה לְבַבְכֶם, וְסַרְתֶּם וַעֲבַדְתֶּם | אֱלֹהִים | אֲחֵרִים

‹ of others ‹ gods ‹ and serve ‹ and you turn astray « be your heart ‹ seduced

וְהִשְׁתַּחֲוִיתֶם לָהֶם: וְחָרָה | אַף־יהוה בָּכֶם, וְעָצַר |

‹ He will restrain « against you. ‹ of HASHEM ‹ the wrath ‹ Then shall blaze « to them. ‹ and bow

אֶת־הַשָּׁמַיִם וְלֹא־יִהְיֶה מָטָר, וְהָאֲדָמָה לֹא תִתֵּן

‹ yield ‹ will not ‹ and the ground « rain ‹ so there will not be ‹ the heaven

אֶת־יְבוּלָהּ, וַאֲבַדְתֶּם | מְהֵרָה מֵעַל הָאָרֶץ הַטֹּבָה |

‹ the good land ‹ from upon « swiftly ‹ And you will be banished « its produce.

אֲשֶׁר | יהוה נֹתֵן לָכֶם: וְשַׂמְתֶּם | אֶת־דְּבָרַי | אֵלֶּה

‹ these words of Mine ‹ Place « you. ‹ gives ‹ HASHEM ‹ which

עַל־לְבַבְכֶם וְעַל־נַפְשְׁכֶם, וּקְשַׁרְתֶּם | אֹתָם לְאוֹת |

‹ for a sign ‹ them ‹ bind « your soul; ‹ and upon ‹ your heart ‹ upon

עַל־יֶדְכֶם, וְהָיוּ לְטוֹטָפֹת בֵּין | עֵינֵיכֶם: וְלִמַּדְתֶּם |

‹ Teach « your eyes. ‹ between ‹ *tefillin* ‹ and they shall be « your arm ‹ upon

אֹתָם | אֶת־בְּנֵיכֶם לְדַבֵּר בָּם, בְּשִׁבְתְּךָ בְּבֵיתֶךָ,

« in your home, ‹ while you sit « them, ‹ to discuss « to your children, ‹ them

וּבְלֶכְתְּךָ בַדֶּרֶךְ, וּבְשָׁכְבְּךָ וּבְקוּמֶךָ: וּכְתַבְתָּם | עַל־

‹ on ‹ And write them « and when you arise. ‹ when you lie down « on the way, ‹ while you walk

מְזוּזוֹת בֵּיתֶךָ וּבִשְׁעָרֶיךָ: לְמַעַן | יִרְבּוּ | יְמֵיכֶם

‹ your days ‹ to prolong ‹ In order « and upon your gates. ‹ of your house ‹ the doorposts

וִימֵי בְנֵיכֶם עַל הָאֲדָמָה | אֲשֶׁר נִשְׁבַּע | יְהוָה

‹ HASHEM swore ‹ that ‹ the land ‹ upon « of your children ‹ and the days

לַאֲבֹתֵיכֶם לָתֵת לָהֶם, כִּימֵי הַשָּׁמַיִם | עַל־הָאָרֶץ:

« the earth. ‹ on ‹ of the heaven ‹ like the days « them, ‹ to give « to your ancestors

***NUMBERS* 15:37-41**

וַיֹּאמֶר | יְהוָה | אֶל־מֹשֶׁה לֵּאמֹר: דַּבֵּר | אֶל־בְּנֵי |

‹ the Children ‹ to ‹ Speak « saying: ‹ Moses, ‹ to ‹ HASHEM Said

יִשְׂרָאֵל וְאָמַרְתָּ אֲלֵהֶם, וְעָשׂוּ לָהֶם צִיצִת עַל־כַּנְפֵי

‹ the corners ‹ on ‹ *tzitzis* ‹ for themselves ‹ that they are to make « to them ‹ and say ‹ of Israel

בִגְדֵיהֶם לְדֹרֹתָם, וְנָתְנוּ | עַל־צִיצִת הַכָּנָף פְּתִיל

‹ a thread ‹ of the corner ‹ the *tzitzis* ‹ upon ‹ And they are to place « throughout their generations. ‹ of their garments,

תְּכֵלֶת: וְהָיָה לָכֶם לְצִיצִת, וּרְאִיתֶם | אֹתוֹ וּזְכַרְתֶּם |

‹ and remember « it ‹ that you may see « *tzitzis,* ‹ for you ‹ And it shall constitute « of *techeiles.*

אֶת־כָּל־מִצְוֹת | יְהוָה וַעֲשִׂיתֶם | אֹתָם, וְלֹא־תָתוּרוּ |

‹ explore ‹ and do not « them; ‹ and perform « of HASHEM ‹ the commandments ‹ all

אַחֲרֵי לְבַבְכֶם וְאַחֲרֵי | עֵינֵיכֶם אֲשֶׁר־אַתֶּם זֹנִים |

‹ stray ‹ you ‹ which ‹ your eyes ‹ and after ‹ your heart ‹ after

אַחֲרֵיהֶם: לְמַעַן תִּזְכְּרוּ וַעֲשִׂיתֶם | אֶת־כָּל־מִצְוֹתָי,

« My commandments, ‹ all ‹ and perform ‹ you may remember ‹ So that « after them.

וִהְיִיתֶם קְדֹשִׁים לֵאלֹהֵיכֶם:

« to your God. ‹ holy ‹ and be

CONCENTRATE ON THE COMMANDMENT TO REMEMBER THE EXODUS FROM EGYPT.

אֲנִי יְהוָה | אֱלֹהֵיכֶם אֲשֶׁר הוֹצֵאתִי | אֶתְכֶם |

‹ you ‹ has removed ‹ Who ‹ your God, ‹ HASHEM, ‹ I am

מֵאֶֽרֶץ מִצְרַֽיִם לִהְיוֹת לָכֶם לֵאלֹהִים, אֲנִי |

‹ I am « a God; ‹ to you ‹ to be ‹ of Egypt ‹ from the land

יְהוָֹה | אֱלֹהֵיכֶם: אֱמֶת —

« – It is true . . . « your God. ‹ HASHEM

ALTHOUGH THE WORD אֱמֶת BELONGS TO THE NEXT PARAGRAPH, IT IS APPENDED TO THE CONCLUSION OF THE PREVIOUS ONE.

יהוה אֱלֹהֵיכֶם אֱמֶת, — *CHAZZAN* REPEATS

« **is true,** ‹ **your God,** ‹ **HASHEM,**

וֶאֱמוּנָה כָּל זֹאת, וְקַיָּם עָלֵֽינוּ, כִּי הוּא יהוה

‹ is HASHEM ‹ He ‹ that « for us ‹ and it is firmly established ‹ this, ‹ is all ‹ and faithful

אֱלֹהֵֽינוּ וְאֵין זוּלָתוֹ, וַאֲנַֽחְנוּ יִשְׂרָאֵל עַמּוֹ. הַפּוֹדֵֽנוּ

‹ He is the One Who redeems us « His people. ‹ Israel, ‹ and we are « but Him, ‹ and there is none « our God,

מִיַּד מְלָכִים, מַלְכֵּֽנוּ הַגּוֹאֲלֵֽנוּ מִכַּף כָּל הֶעָרִיצִים.

« the cruel tyrants. ‹ of all ‹ from the hand ‹ Who delivers us ‹ our King « of kings, ‹ from the power

הָאֵל הַנִּפְרָע לָֽנוּ מִצָּרֵֽינוּ, וְהַמְשַׁלֵּם גְּמוּל לְכָל

‹ upon all ‹ just retribution ‹ and Who repays « from our foes ‹ for us ‹ Who exacts vengeance ‹ He is the God

אֹיְבֵי נַפְשֵֽׁנוּ. הָעֹשֶׂה גְדֹלוֹת עַד אֵין חֵֽקֶר, וְנִפְלָאוֹת

‹ and wonders « comprehension, ‹ that are beyond ‹ great deeds ‹ Who performs « of our soul; ‹ the enemies

עַד אֵין מִסְפָּר.[1] הַשָּׂם נַפְשֵֽׁנוּ בַּחַיִּים, וְלֹא נָתַן

‹ allow ‹ and did not « in life ‹ our soul ‹ Who set « number. ‹ that are beyond

לַמּוֹט רַגְלֵֽנוּ.[2] הַמַּדְרִיכֵֽנוּ עַל בָּמוֹת אוֹיְבֵֽינוּ, וַיָּֽרֶם

‹ and raised « of our enemies ‹ the heights ‹ upon ‹ Who led us « our foot. ‹ to falter

קַרְנֵֽנוּ עַל כָּל שׂוֹנְאֵֽינוּ. הָעֽוֹשֶׂה לָּֽנוּ נִסִּים וּנְקָמָה

‹ and vengeance ‹ miracles ‹ for us ‹ Who wrought « who hate us; ‹ all ‹ above ‹ our pride

בְּפַרְעֹה, אוֹתוֹת וּמוֹפְתִים בְּאַדְמַת בְּנֵי חָם. הַמַּכֶּה

‹ Who struck « of Ham; ‹ of the offspring ‹ in the land ‹ and wonders ‹ signs « upon Pharaoh;

(1) *Job* 9:10. (2) *Psalms* 66:9.

בְּעֶבְרָתוֹ כָּל בְּכוֹרֵי מִצְרָיִם, וַיּוֹצֵא אֶת עַמּוֹ

‹ His people ‹ and removed « of Egypt ‹ the firstborn ‹ all ‹ in His anger

יִשְׂרָאֵל מִתּוֹכָם לְחֵרוּת עוֹלָם. הַמַּעֲבִיר בָּנָיו

‹ His children ‹ Who brought « everlasting; ‹ to freedom ‹ from their midst ‹ Israel

בֵּין גִּזְרֵי יַם סוּף, אֶת רוֹדְפֵיהֶם וְאֶת שׂוֹנְאֵיהֶם

‹ and those who hated them ‹ [while] those who pursued them « of Reeds ‹ of the Sea ‹ the split parts ‹ through

בִּתְהוֹמוֹת טִבַּע. וְרָאוּ בָנָיו גְּבוּרָתוֹ, שִׁבְּחוּ וְהוֹדוּ

‹ and gave thanks ‹ they praised « His power, ‹ When His children perceived « He sank. ‹ into the depths

לִשְׁמוֹ. ❖ וּמַלְכוּתוֹ בְּרָצוֹן קִבְּלוּ עֲלֵיהֶם. מֹשֶׁה

‹ Moses « upon themselves; ‹ they accepted ‹ willingly And His Kingship « to His Name.

וּבְנֵי יִשְׂרָאֵל לְךָ עָנוּ שִׁירָה בְּשִׂמְחָה רַבָּה, וְאָמְרוּ

‹ and said ‹ with great gladness « in song, ‹ exclaimed ‹ to You ‹ of Israel ‹ and the Children

כֻלָּם:

«unanimously:

מִי כָמֹכָה בָּאֵלִם יהוה, מִי כָּמֹכָה נֶאְדָּר בַּקֹּדֶשׁ,

« in holiness, ‹ mighty ‹ is like You, ‹ Who « HASHEM! *‹ among the heavenly powers, ‹ is like You ‹ Who*

נוֹרָא תְהִלֹּת, עֹשֵׂה פֶלֶא.[1] ❖ מַלְכוּתְךָ רָאוּ בָנֶיךָ

« did Your children behold, Your Majesty *« wonders! ‹ doing ‹ [beyond] praise, ‹ awesome*

בּוֹקֵעַ יָם לִפְנֵי מֹשֶׁה, זֶה אֵלִי[2] עָנוּ וְאָמְרוּ:

« then they said: « they exclaimed; ‹ *is my God!"* ‹ *"This* « Moses, ‹ before ‹ the Sea ‹ as You split

יהוה יִמְלֹךְ לְעֹלָם וָעֶד.[3]

« and ever! ‹ for ever ‹ shall reign ‹ HASHEM

❖ וְנֶאֱמַר: כִּי פָדָה יהוה אֶת יַעֲקֹב, וּגְאָלוֹ מִיַּד

‹ from the hand ‹ and delivered him « Jacob ‹ *HASHEM has redeemed ‹ For* ‹ And it is further said:

---

(1) *Exodus* 15:11. (2) 15:2. (3) 15:18.

חָזָק מִמֶּנּוּ.[1] בָּרוּךְ אַתָּה יהוה, גָּאַל יִשְׂרָאֵל.
« Israel. ‹ Who redeemed ‹ HASHEM, ‹ are You, ‹ Blessed « *than he.* ‹ *of one mightier*

(אָמֵן. — Cong.)
« (Amen.)

הַשְׁכִּיבֵנוּ יהוה אֱלֹהֵינוּ לְשָׁלוֹם, וְהַעֲמִידֵנוּ
‹ and raise us up, « in peace, ‹ our God, ‹ HASHEM, ‹ Lay us down to sleep,

מַלְכֵּנוּ לְחַיִּים. וּפְרוֹשׂ עָלֵינוּ סֻכַּת שְׁלוֹמֶךָ, וְתַקְּנֵנוּ
‹ Set us aright « of Your peace. ‹ the shelter ‹ over us ‹ Spread « to life. ‹ our King,

בְּעֵצָה טוֹבָה מִלְּפָנֶיךָ, וְהוֹשִׁיעֵנוּ לְמַעַן שְׁמֶךָ. וְהָגֵן
‹ Shield « of Your Name. ‹ for the sake ‹ and save us « from before You, ‹ that is good ‹ with counsel

בַּעֲדֵנוּ, וְהָסֵר מֵעָלֵינוּ אוֹיֵב, דֶּבֶר, וְחֶרֶב, וְרָעָב,
‹ famine, ‹ sword, ‹ plague, ‹ foe, ‹ from us ‹ remove « us;

וְיָגוֹן, וְהָסֵר שָׂטָן מִלְּפָנֵינוּ וּמֵאַחֲרֵינוּ, וּבְצֵל כְּנָפֶיךָ
‹ of Your wings ‹ and in the shadow « and from behind us, ‹ from before us ‹ spiritual impediment ‹ and remove « and woe;

תַּסְתִּירֵנוּ,[2] כִּי אֵל שׁוֹמְרֵנוּ וּמַצִּילֵנוּ אָתָּה, כִּי אֵל
‹ God, ‹ for « are You; ‹ and rescues us ‹ Who protects ‹ God ‹ For « shelter us.

מֶלֶךְ חַנּוּן וְרַחוּם אָתָּה.[3] ❖ וּשְׁמוֹר צֵאתֵנוּ וּבוֹאֵנוּ,
‹ and our coming ‹ our going ‹ Safeguard « are You. ‹ and Compassionate, ‹ Gracious ‹ King,

לְחַיִּים וּלְשָׁלוֹם מֵעַתָּה וְעַד עוֹלָם.[4] בָּרוּךְ
‹ Blessed « eternity. ‹ and for all ‹ from now ‹ and for peace ‹ for life

אַתָּה יהוה, שׁוֹמֵר עַמּוֹ יִשְׂרָאֵל לָעַד. (אָמֵן. — Cong.)
« (Amen.) « forever. ‹ Israel ‹ His people ‹ Who safeguards « HASHEM, ‹ are You,

SOME CONGREGATIONS OMIT THE FOLLOWING PRAYERS AND CONTINUE WITH HALF-*KADDISH* (P. 13).

בָּרוּךְ יהוה לְעוֹלָם, אָמֵן וְאָמֵן.[5] בָּרוּךְ יהוה
‹ is HASHEM ‹ Blessed « and Amen. ‹ Amen « forever, ‹ is HASHEM ‹ Blessed

(1) *Jeremiah* 31:10. (2) Cf. *Psalms* 17:8. (3) Cf. *Nehemiah* 9:31. (4) Cf. *Psalms* 121:8. (5) 89:53.

מִצִּיּוֹן, שֹׁכֵן יְרוּשָׁלָיִם, הַלְלוּיָהּ.[1] בָּרוּךְ יהוה

from Zion, He Who dwells in Jerusalem, Halleluyah! Blessed is HASHEM,

אֱלֹהִים אֱלֹהֵי יִשְׂרָאֵל, עֹשֵׂה נִפְלָאוֹת לְבַדּוֹ.

God, the God of Israel, Who does wondrous things by Himself.

וּבָרוּךְ שֵׁם כְּבוֹדוֹ לְעוֹלָם, וְיִמָּלֵא כְבוֹדוֹ אֶת כָּל

Blessed is the Name of His glory forever; and fill may His glory all

הָאָרֶץ, אָמֵן וְאָמֵן.[2] יְהִי כְבוֹד יהוה לְעוֹלָם,

the earth. Amen and Amen. May the glory of HASHEM endure forever;

יִשְׂמַח יהוה בְּמַעֲשָׂיו.[3] יְהִי שֵׁם יהוה מְבֹרָךְ,

let HASHEM rejoice in His works. Let the Name of HASHEM be blessed,

מֵעַתָּה וְעַד עוֹלָם.[4] כִּי לֹא יִטֹּשׁ יהוה אֶת עַמּוֹ

from this time until eternity. For HASHEM will not forsake His people

בַּעֲבוּר שְׁמוֹ הַגָּדוֹל, כִּי הוֹאִיל יהוה לַעֲשׂוֹת

for the sake of His Name, that is great, for HASHEM has vowed to make

אֶתְכֶם לוֹ לְעָם.[5] וַיַּרְא כָּל הָעָם וַיִּפְּלוּ עַל פְּנֵיהֶם,

you for Him a people. See did all the people and they fell on their faces

וַיֹּאמְרוּ, יהוה הוּא הָאֱלֹהִים, יהוה הוּא הָאֱלֹהִים.[6]

and they said, *HASHEM — He is the God! HASHEM — He is the God!*

וְהָיָה יהוה לְמֶלֶךְ עַל כָּל הָאָרֶץ, בַּיּוֹם הַהוּא

Then will HASHEM be King over all the world — on that day

יִהְיֶה יהוה אֶחָד וּשְׁמוֹ אֶחָד.[7] יְהִי חַסְדְּךָ יהוה

shall HASHEM be One and His Name be One. May Your kindness, HASHEM,

עָלֵינוּ, כַּאֲשֶׁר יִחַלְנוּ לָךְ.[8] הוֹשִׁיעֵנוּ יהוה אֱלֹהֵינוּ,

be upon us, just as we awaited You. Save us, HASHEM, our God,

---

(1) *Psalms* 135:21. (2) 72:18-19. (3) 104:31. (4) 113:2. (5) *I Samuel* 12:22.
(6) *I Kings* 18:39. (7) *Zechariah* 14:9. (8) *Psalms* 33:22.

וְקַבְּצֵנוּ מִן הַגּוֹיִם, לְהוֹדוֹת לְשֵׁם קָדְשֶׁךָ לְהִשְׁתַּבֵּחַ

‹ and to glory ‹ of Your Holiness ‹ the Name ‹ to thank « among the nations, ‹ from ‹ and gather us

בִּתְהִלָּתֶךָ.[1] כָּל גּוֹיִם אֲשֶׁר עָשִׂיתָ יָבוֹאוּ וְיִשְׁתַּחֲווּ

‹ and bow down ‹ will come ‹ You have made ‹ that ‹ the nations ‹ All « in Your praise!

לְפָנֶיךָ אֲדֹנָי, וִיכַבְּדוּ לִשְׁמֶךָ. כִּי גָדוֹל אַתָּה וְעֹשֵׂה

‹ and You work ‹ are You ‹ great ‹ For « to Your Name. ‹ and they will give glory « O Lord, ‹ before You,

נִפְלָאוֹת, אַתָּה אֱלֹהִים לְבַדֶּךָ.[2] וַאֲנַחְנוּ עַמְּךָ וְצֹאן

‹ and the sheep ‹ Your people « As for us, « alone. ‹ O God ‹ You « wonders,

מַרְעִיתֶךָ, נוֹדֶה לְּךָ לְעוֹלָם, לְדוֹר וָדֹר נְסַפֵּר

‹ we shall relate ‹ after generation ‹ for generation « forever; ‹ You ‹ we shall thank « of Your pasture,

תְּהִלָּתֶךָ.[3] בָּרוּךְ יהוה בַּיּוֹם. בָּרוּךְ יהוה בַּלָּיְלָה.

« by night; ‹ is HASHEM ‹ blessed « by day; ‹ is HASHEM ‹ Blessed « Your praise.

בָּרוּךְ יהוה בְּשָׁכְבֵנוּ. בָּרוּךְ יהוה בְּקוּמֵנוּ. כִּי בְיָדְךָ

‹ in Your hand ‹ For « when we arise. ‹ is HASHEM ‹ blessed « when we retire; ‹ is HASHEM ‹ blessed

נַפְשׁוֹת הַחַיִּים וְהַמֵּתִים. אֲשֶׁר בְּיָדוֹ נֶפֶשׁ כָּל חָי,

« the living ‹ of all ‹ is the soul ‹ in His hand ‹ That « and of the dead. ‹ of the living ‹ are the souls

וְרוּחַ כָּל בְּשַׂר אִישׁ.[4] בְּיָדְךָ אַפְקִיד רוּחִי, פָּדִיתָה

‹ You redeemed « my spirit; ‹ I shall entrust ‹ In Your hand « mankind. ‹ of all ‹ and the spirit

אוֹתִי, יהוה אֵל אֱמֶת.[5] אֱלֹהֵינוּ שֶׁבַּשָּׁמַיִם, יַחֵד שִׁמְךָ,

« to Your Name; ‹ bring unity « Who is in heaven, ‹ Our God, « of truth. ‹ God ‹ O HASHEM, ‹ me,

וְקַיֵּם מַלְכוּתְךָ תָּמִיד, וּמְלוֹךְ עָלֵינוּ לְעוֹלָם וָעֶד.

« and ever. ‹ for ever ‹ over us ‹ and reign « forever ‹ Your kingdom ‹ establish

(1) *Psalms* 106:47. (2) 86:9-10. (3) 79:13. (4) *Job* 12:10. (5) *Psalms* 31:6.

יִרְאוּ עֵינֵינוּ וְיִשְׂמַח לִבֵּנוּ וְתָגֵל נַפְשֵׁנוּ בִּישׁוּעָתְךָ

‹ in Your salvation « may our soul ‹ and exult « may our heart, ‹ rejoice « may our eyes, ‹ See

בֶּאֱמֶת, בֶּאֱמֹר לְצִיּוֹן מָלַךְ אֱלֹהָיִךְ.[1] יהוה מֶלֶךְ,[2]

« reigns, ‹ HASHEM « *has Your God.* ‹ *Reigned* « to Zion, ‹ when it is told « in truth,

יהוה מָלָךְ,[3] יהוה יִמְלֹךְ לְעֹלָם וָעֶד.[4] ❖ כִּי

‹ For « and ever. ‹ for ever ‹ shall reign ‹ HASHEM « has reigned, ‹ HASHEM

הַמַּלְכוּת שֶׁלְּךָ הִיא, וּלְעוֹלְמֵי עַד תִּמְלוֹךְ בְּכָבוֹד,

« in glory, ‹ You will reign ‹ and ever ‹ and for ever « is Yours ‹ the kingdom

כִּי אֵין לָנוּ מֶלֶךְ אֶלָּא אָתָּה. בָּרוּךְ אַתָּה יהוה,

« HASHEM, ‹ are You, ‹ Blessed « You. ‹ except for ‹ King ‹ we have no ‹ for

הַמֶּלֶךְ בִּכְבוֹדוֹ תָּמִיד יִמְלוֹךְ עָלֵינוּ לְעוֹלָם וָעֶד,

‹ and ever, ‹ for ever ‹ over us ‹ will He reign ‹ always ‹ Who in His glory ‹ the King

וְעַל כָּל מַעֲשָׂיו. (Cong. — אָמֵן.)

« (Amen.) « His creation. ‹ all ‹ and over

THE *CHAZZAN* RECITES חֲצִי קַדִּישׁ, HALF-*KADDISH*:

יִתְגַּדַּל וְיִתְקַדַּשׁ שְׁמֵהּ רַבָּא. (Cong. — אָמֵן.) בְּעָלְמָא דִּי

‹ that ‹ — in the world ‹ (Amen.) « that is great! — ‹ may His Name ‹ and be sanctified ‹ Grow exalted

בְּרָא כִרְעוּתֵהּ. וְיַמְלִיךְ מַלְכוּתֵהּ, בְּחַיֵּיכוֹן וּבְיוֹמֵיכוֹן וּבְחַיֵּי

‹ and in the lifetimes ‹ and in your days, ‹ in your lifetimes « to His kingship, ‹ and may He give reign « according to His will, ‹ He created

דְכָל בֵּית יִשְׂרָאֵל, בַּעֲגָלָא וּבִזְמַן קָרִיב. וְאִמְרוּ: אָמֵן.

« Amen. ‹ Now respond: « that comes soon. ‹ and at a time ‹ swiftly « of Israel, ‹ Family ‹ of the entire

CONGREGATION RESPONDS:

אָמֵן. יְהֵא שְׁמֵהּ רַבָּא מְבָרַךְ לְעָלַם וּלְעָלְמֵי עָלְמַיָּא.

« and for all eternity. ‹ forever ‹ be blessed ‹ that is great ‹ His Name ‹ May « Amen.

CHAZZAN CONTINUES:

יְהֵא שְׁמֵהּ רַבָּא מְבָרַךְ לְעָלַם וּלְעָלְמֵי עָלְמַיָּא. יִתְבָּרַךְ

‹ Blessed, « and for all eternity. ‹ forever ‹ be blessed ‹ that is great ‹ His Name ‹ May

(1) *Isaiah* 52:7. (2) *Psalms* 10:16. (3) 93:1 et al. (4) *Exodus* 15:18.

וְיִשְׁתַּבַּח וְיִתְפָּאַר וְיִתְרוֹמַם וְיִתְנַשֵּׂא וְיִתְהַדָּר וְיִתְעַלֶּה

‹ elevated, ‹ honored, ‹ upraised, ‹ exalted, ‹ glorified, ‹ praised,

וְיִתְהַלָּל שְׁמֵהּ דְּקֻדְשָׁא בְּרִיךְ הוּא (.Cong — בְּרִיךְ הוּא.)

« is He) ‹ (Blessed « is He ‹ Blessed ‹ of the Holy One, ‹ be the Name ‹ and lauded

— לְעֵלָּא מִן כָּל בִּרְכָתָא וְשִׁירָתָא תֻּשְׁבְּחָתָא וְנֶחֱמָתָא

‹ and consolation ‹ praise « and song, ‹ blessing ‹ any ‹ beyond

דַּאֲמִירָן בְּעָלְמָא. וְאִמְרוּ: אָמֵן. (.Cong — אָמֵן.)

« (Amen.) « Amen. ‹ Now respond: « in the world. ‹ that are uttered

SHEMONEH ESREI / שמונה עשרה — עמידה

TAKE THREE STEPS BACKWARD, THEN THREE STEPS FORWARD. REMAIN STANDING WITH FEET TOGETHER WHILE RECITING *SHEMONEH ESREI*. RECITE IT WITH QUIET DEVOTION AND WITHOUT INTERRUPTION, VERBAL OR OTHERWISE. ALTHOUGH ITS RECITATION SHOULD NOT BE AUDIBLE TO OTHERS, ONE MUST PRAY LOUDLY ENOUGH TO HEAR HIMSELF.

אֲדֹנָי שְׂפָתַי תִּפְתָּח, וּפִי יַגִּיד תְּהִלָּתֶךָ.[1]

« Your praise. ‹ may declare ‹ that my mouth « open, ‹ my lips ‹ O Lord,

PATRIARCHS / אבות

BEND THE KNEES AT בָּרוּךְ, *BLESSED*; BOW AT אַתָּה, *YOU*; STRAIGHTEN UP AT ה׳, *HASHEM*.

בָּרוּךְ אַתָּה יהוה אֱלֹהֵינוּ וֵאלֹהֵי אֲבוֹתֵינוּ, אֱלֹהֵי

‹ God « of our forefathers, ‹ and the God ‹ our God ‹ HASHEM, ‹ are You, ‹ Blessed

אַבְרָהָם, אֱלֹהֵי יִצְחָק, וֵאלֹהֵי יַעֲקֹב, הָאֵל הַגָּדוֹל

‹ [Who is] great, ‹ God « of Jacob; ‹ and God « of Isaac, ‹ God « of Abraham,

הַגִּבּוֹר וְהַנּוֹרָא, אֵל עֶלְיוֹן, גּוֹמֵל חֲסָדִים טוֹבִים,

‹ [that are] beneficent ‹ kindnesses ‹ Who bestows « the Most High, ‹ God ‹ and awesome; ‹ mighty,

וְקוֹנֵה הַכֹּל, וְזוֹכֵר חַסְדֵי אָבוֹת, וּמֵבִיא גוֹאֵל לִבְנֵי

‹ to the children ‹ a Redeemer ‹ and brings « of the Patriarchs, ‹ the kindnesses ‹ Who recalls « everything, ‹ and creates

בְנֵיהֶם, לְמַעַן שְׁמוֹ בְּאַהֲבָה. מֶלֶךְ עוֹזֵר וּמוֹשִׁיעַ וּמָגֵן.

« and Shield. ‹ Savior, ‹ Helper, ‹ O King, « with love. ‹ of His Name, ‹ for the sake « of their children,

(1) *Psalms* 51:17.

BEND THE KNEES AT בָּרוּךְ, *BLESSED*; BOW AT אַתָּה, *YOU*; STRAIGHTEN UP AT 'ה, *HASHEM.*

בָּרוּךְ אַתָּה יהוה, מָגֵן אַבְרָהָם.

« of Abraham. ‹ Shield « HASHEM, ‹ are You, ‹ Blessed

GOD'S MIGHT / גבורות

אַתָּה גִּבּוֹר לְעוֹלָם אֲדֹנָי, מְחַיֵּה מֵתִים אַתָּה, רַב לְהוֹשִׁיעַ. מְכַלְכֵּל חַיִּים בְּחֶסֶד, מְחַיֵּה מֵתִים בְּרַחֲמִים רַבִּים, סוֹמֵךְ נוֹפְלִים, וְרוֹפֵא חוֹלִים, וּמַתִּיר אֲסוּרִים, וּמְקַיֵּם אֱמוּנָתוֹ לִישֵׁנֵי עָפָר. מִי כָמוֹךָ בַּעַל גְּבוּרוֹת, וּמִי דּוֹמֶה לָּךְ, מֶלֶךְ מֵמִית וּמְחַיֶּה, וּמַצְמִיחַ יְשׁוּעָה. וְנֶאֱמָן אַתָּה לְהַחֲיוֹת מֵתִים. בָּרוּךְ אַתָּה יהוה, מְחַיֵּה הַמֵּתִים.

« are You; ‹ of the dead ‹ the Revivifier « O Lord, ‹ eternally, ‹ mighty ‹ You are ‹ the dead ‹ Who revivifies « with kindness, ‹ the living ‹ Who sustains « able to save, ‹ abundantly « the sick, ‹ Who heals « the fallen, ‹ Who supports « abundant, ‹ with mercy ‹ Who « in the dust. ‹ to those asleep ‹ His faith ‹ and Who maintains « the confined, ‹ Who releases ‹ Who causes death ‹ O King « to You, ‹ is comparable ‹ and who « of mighty deeds, ‹ O Master ‹ is like You, ‹ to revivify ‹ are You ‹ And faithful « salvation! ‹ and makes sprout ‹ and restores life « the dead. ‹ Who revivifies « HASHEM, ‹ are You, ‹ Blessed « the dead.

HOLINESS OF GOD'S NAME / קדושת השם

אַתָּה קָדוֹשׁ וְשִׁמְךָ קָדוֹשׁ, וּקְדוֹשִׁים בְּכָל יוֹם יְהַלְלוּךָ סֶּלָה. בָּרוּךְ אַתָּה יהוה, הָאֵל הַקָּדוֹשׁ.

‹ day ‹ every ‹ and holy ones « is holy, ‹ and Your Name ‹ are holy ‹ You «Who is Holy. ‹ the God «HASHEM, ‹ are You, ‹ Blessed « forever. ‹ praise You

INSIGHT / בינה

אַתָּה חוֹנֵן לְאָדָם דַּעַת, וּמְלַמֵּד לֶאֱנוֹשׁ בִּינָה.

« insight. ‹ to a [frail] mortal ‹ and teach « with wisdom ‹ man ‹ graciously endow ‹ You

AFTER THE SABBATH ADD [IF FORGOTTEN, DO NOT REPEAT *SHEMONEH ESREI*:

אַתָּה חוֹנַנְתָּנוּ לְמַדַּע תּוֹרָתֶךָ, וַתְּלַמְּדֵנוּ לַעֲשׂוֹת

‹ to perform ‹ and You have taught us « Your Torah ‹ [with the intelligence needed] to study ‹ have graciously endowed us ‹ You

חֻקֵּי רְצוֹנֶךָ, וַתַּבְדֵּל יהוה אֱלֹהֵינוּ בֵּין קֹדֶשׁ

‹ the sacred ‹ between « our God, ‹ HASHEM, « You have distinguished, « of Your will. ‹ the decrees

לְחוֹל, בֵּין אוֹר לְחוֹשֶׁךְ, בֵּין יִשְׂרָאֵל לָעַמִּים, בֵּין

‹between « and the peoples, ‹ Israel ‹between « and darkness, ‹ light ‹between « and the secular,

יוֹם הַשְּׁבִיעִי לְשֵׁשֶׁת יְמֵי הַמַּעֲשֶׂה. אָבִינוּ מַלְכֵּנוּ, הָחֵל

‹begin ‹ our King, ‹Our Father, « of work. ‹ days ‹ and the six ‹ the Seventh Day

עָלֵינוּ הַיָּמִים הַבָּאִים לִקְרָאתֵנוּ לְשָׁלוֹם, חֲשׂוּכִים מִכָּל

‹ of all ‹ devoid « for peace, ‹ that are approaching us ‹ the days ‹ for us

חֵטְא, וּמְנֻקִּים מִכָּל עָוֹן, וּמְדֻבָּקִים בְּיִרְאָתֶךָ. וְ. . .

‹ And ... « to fearing You. ‹ and devoted ‹ iniquity, ‹ of all ‹ cleansed « sin,

חָנֵּנוּ מֵאִתְּךָ דֵּעָה בִּינָה וְהַשְׂכֵּל. בָּרוּךְ אַתָּה

‹ are You, ‹ Blessed « and discernment. ‹ insight, ‹ [with] wisdom, ‹ from Yourself ‹ Endow us graciously

יהוה, חוֹנֵן הַדָּעַת.

« of wisdom. ‹ gracious Giver « HASHEM,

REPENTANCE / תשובה

הֲשִׁיבֵנוּ אָבִינוּ לְתוֹרָתֶךָ, וְקָרְבֵנוּ מַלְכֵּנוּ

‹ our King, ‹ and bring us near, « to Your Torah, ‹ our Father, ‹ Bring us back,

לַעֲבוֹדָתֶךָ, וְהַחֲזִירֵנוּ בִּתְשׁוּבָה שְׁלֵמָה לְפָנֶיךָ.

« before You. ‹ in complete repentance ‹ and influence us to return « to Your service,

בָּרוּךְ אַתָּה יהוה, הָרוֹצֶה בִּתְשׁוּבָה.

« repentance. ‹ Who desires « HASHEM, ‹ are You, ‹ Blessed

FORGIVENESS / סליחה

STRIKE THE LEFT SIDE OF THE CHEST WITH THE RIGHT FIST WHILE RECITING THE WORDS חָטָאנוּ, *SINNED,* AND פָּשָׁעְנוּ, *WILLFULLY SINNED.*

סְלַח לָנוּ אָבִינוּ כִּי חָטָאנוּ, מְחַל לָנוּ מַלְכֵּנוּ

‹ our King, ‹ us, ‹ pardon « we have sinned; ‹ for ‹ our Father, ‹ us, ‹ Forgive

כִּי פָשָׁעְנוּ, כִּי מוֹחֵל וְסוֹלֵחַ אָתָּה. בָּרוּךְ

‹ for ‹ we have willfully sinned; « for ‹ a Pardoner ‹ and Forgiver ‹ are You. « Blessed

אַתָּה יהוה, חַנּוּן הַמַּרְבֶּה לִסְלוֹחַ.

‹ are You, « HASHEM, ‹ the gracious One ‹ Who abundantly « forgives.

REDEMPTION / גאולה

רְאֵה בְעָנְיֵנוּ, וְרִיבָה רִיבֵנוּ, וּגְאָלֵנוּ[1] מְהֵרָה

‹ Behold ‹ our affliction, « champion ‹ our cause, « and redeem us ‹ speedily

לְמַעַן שְׁמֶךָ, כִּי גוֹאֵל חָזָק אָתָּה. בָּרוּךְ אַתָּה

‹ for the sake of ‹ Your Name, « for ‹ a Redeemer ‹ Who is powerful ‹ are You. « Blessed ‹ are You,

יהוה, גוֹאֵל יִשְׂרָאֵל.

« HASHEM, ‹ Redeemer ‹ of Israel. «

HEALTH AND HEALING / רפואה

רְפָאֵנוּ יהוה וְנֵרָפֵא, הוֹשִׁיעֵנוּ וְנִוָּשֵׁעָה, כִּי

‹ Heal us, ‹ HASHEM « — then we will be healed; « save us « — then we will be saved, « for ‹

תְהִלָּתֵנוּ אָתָּה,[2] וְהַעֲלֵה רְפוּאָה שְׁלֵמָה לְכָל

‹ the One we praise ‹ is You. « Bring ‹ healing ‹ that is complete ‹ for all ‹

מַכּוֹתֵינוּ, °°כִּי אֵל מֶלֶךְ רוֹפֵא נֶאֱמָן וְרַחֲמָן

« our ailments, ‹ for ‹ O God, ‹ [and] King, ‹ a Healer ‹ Who is faithful ‹ and compassionate ‹

°°AT THIS POINT ONE MAY INSERT A PRAYER FOR ONE WHO IS ILL:

יְהִי רָצוֹן מִלְּפָנֶיךָ, יהוה אֱלֹהַי וֵאלֹהֵי אֲבוֹתַי, שֶׁתִּשְׁלַח מְהֵרָה

‹ May it be ‹ the will ‹ before You, « HASHEM, ‹ my God, ‹ and the God ‹ of my forefathers, « that You send ‹ quickly ‹

רְפוּאָה שְׁלֵמָה מִן הַשָּׁמַיִם, רְפוּאַת הַנֶּפֶשׁ וּרְפוּאַת הַגּוּף

‹ a healing ‹ which is complete, « from ‹ heaven, « a healing ‹ of the spirit ‹ and a healing ‹ of the body «

FOR A MALE / FOR A FEMALE

לַחוֹלֶה / לַחוֹלָה (SICK ONE'S NAME) בֶּן / בַּת (MOTHER'S NAME) בְּתוֹךְ שְׁאָר

‹ to the sick one ‹ son of / daughter of ‹ among ‹ the other ‹

חוֹלֵי יִשְׂרָאֵל.

sick ones ‹ of Israel. «

CONTINUE ... כִּי אֵל (ABOVE)

(1) Cf. *Psalms* 119:153-154. (2) *Jeremiah* 17:14.

אָתָּה. בָּרוּךְ אַתָּה יהוה, רוֹפֵא חוֹלֵי עַמּוֹ יִשְׂרָאֵל.

« Israel. ‹ of His people ‹ the sick ‹ Who heals « HASHEM, ‹ are You, ‹ Blessed « are You.

YEAR OF PROSPERITY / ברכת השנים

בָּרֵךְ עָלֵינוּ יהוה אֱלֹהֵינוּ אֶת הַשָּׁנָה הַזֹּאת וְאֶת

‹ and « this year « our God — ‹ — O HASHEM, ‹ on our behalf ‹ Bless

כָּל מִינֵי תְבוּאָתָהּ לְטוֹבָה, וְתֵן בְּרָכָה עַל פְּנֵי

‹ the face ‹ on ‹ a blessing ‹ and give « for goodness; ‹ of its crops ‹ of the kinds ‹ all

הָאֲדָמָה, וְשַׂבְּעֵנוּ מִטּוּבֶךָ, וּבָרֵךְ שְׁנָתֵנוּ כַּשָּׁנִים

‹ like the years ‹ our year ‹ and bless « from Your bounty, ‹ and satisfy us « of the earth,

הַטּוֹבוֹת. בָּרוּךְ אַתָּה יהוה, מְבָרֵךְ הַשָּׁנִים.

« the years. ‹ Who blesses « HASHEM, ‹ are You, ‹ Blessed « that were good.

INGATHERING OF EXILES / קיבוץ גליות

תְּקַע בְּשׁוֹפָר גָּדוֹל לְחֵרוּתֵנוּ, וְשָׂא נֵס לְקַבֵּץ

‹ to gather ‹ a banner ‹ raise « for our freedom, ‹ the great *shofar* ‹ Sound

גָּלֻיּוֹתֵינוּ, וְקַבְּצֵנוּ יַחַד מֵאַרְבַּע כַּנְפוֹת הָאָרֶץ.[1]

« of the earth. ‹ corners ‹ from the four ‹ together ‹ and gather us « our exiles,

בָּרוּךְ אַתָּה יהוה, מְקַבֵּץ נִדְחֵי עַמּוֹ יִשְׂרָאֵל.

« Israel. ‹ of His people ‹ the dispersed ‹ Who gathers in « HASHEM, ‹ are You, ‹ Blessed

RESTORATION OF JUSTICE / דין

הָשִׁיבָה שׁוֹפְטֵינוּ כְּבָרִאשׁוֹנָה, וְיוֹעֲצֵינוּ

‹ and our counselors ‹ as [they were] in earliest times, ‹ our judges ‹ Restore

כְּבַתְּחִלָּה,[2] וְהָסֵר מִמֶּנּוּ יָגוֹן וַאֲנָחָה, וּמְלוֹךְ עָלֵינוּ

‹ over us ‹ and reign « and groan; ‹ sorrow ‹ from us ‹ remove « as at the beginning;

אַתָּה יהוה לְבַדְּךָ בְּחֶסֶד וּבְרַחֲמִים, וְצַדְּקֵנוּ

‹ and justify us « and compassion, ‹ with kindness « alone — ‹ HASHEM, ‹ — You,

(1) *Isaiah* 11:12. (2) Cf. 1:26.

בַּמִּשְׁפָּט. בָּרוּךְ אַתָּה יהוה, מֶלֶךְ אוֹהֵב צְדָקָה

‹ righteousness ‹ Who loves ‹ the King « HASHEM, ‹ are You, ‹ Blessed « through judgment.

וּמִשְׁפָּט.

« and judgment.

AGAINST HERETICS / ברכת המינים

וְלַמַּלְשִׁינִים אַל תְּהִי תִקְוָה, וְכָל הָרִשְׁעָה

‹ wickedness ‹ and may all « hope; ‹ let there not be ‹ And for slanderers

כְּרֶגַע תֹּאבֵד, וְכָל אוֹיְבֶיךָ מְהֵרָה יִכָּרֵתוּ, וְהַזֵּדִים

«The willful sinners « be cut down. ‹ speedily ‹ Your enemies ‹ and may all « perish; ‹ in an instant

מְהֵרָה תְעַקֵּר וּתְשַׁבֵּר וּתְמַגֵּר וְתַכְנִיעַ בִּמְהֵרָה

‹ speedily « and humble — ‹ cast down, ‹ smash, ‹ uproot, ‹ — may You speedily

בְיָמֵינוּ. בָּרוּךְ אַתָּה יהוה, שׁוֹבֵר אֹיְבִים

‹ enemies ‹ Who breaks « HASHEM, ‹ are You, ‹ Blessed « in our days.

וּמַכְנִיעַ זֵדִים.

« willful sinners. ‹ and humbles

THE RIGHTEOUS / צדיקים

עַל הַצַּדִּיקִים וְעַל הַחֲסִידִים, וְעַל זִקְנֵי עַמְּךָ בֵּית

‹ the Family ‹ of Your people ‹ the elders ‹ on « the devout, ‹ on ‹ the righteous, ‹ On

יִשְׂרָאֵל, וְעַל פְּלֵיטַת סוֹפְרֵיהֶם, וְעַל גֵּרֵי הַצֶּדֶק

‹ who are righteous ‹ the converts ‹ on « of their scholars, ‹ the remnant ‹ on « of Israel,

וְעָלֵינוּ, יֶהֱמוּ רַחֲמֶיךָ, יהוה אֱלֹהֵינוּ, וְתֵן שָׂכָר

‹ a reward ‹ and give « our God, ‹ HASHEM, « Your compassion, ‹ — may aroused be « and on ourselves

טוֹב לְכָל הַבּוֹטְחִים בְּשִׁמְךָ בֶּאֱמֶת, וְשִׂים חֶלְקֵנוּ

‹ our lot ‹ Put « in sincerity. ‹ in Your Name ‹ who believe ‹ to all ‹ which is good

עִמָּהֶם לְעוֹלָם, וְלֹא נֵבוֹשׁ כִּי בְךָ בָּטָחְנוּ. בָּרוּךְ

‹ Blessed « we trust. ‹ in You ‹ for ‹ feel ashamed, ‹ and we will not « forever, ‹ with them

אַתָּה יהוה, מִשְׁעָן וּמִבְטָח לַצַּדִּיקִים.

« of the righteous. ‹ and Assurance ‹ Mainstay « HASHEM, ‹ are You,

REBUILDING JERUSALEM / בנין ירושלים

וְלִירוּשָׁלַיִם עִירְךָ בְּרַחֲמִים תָּשׁוּב, וְתִשְׁכּוֹן

‹ and may You rest « may You return, ‹ in compassion ‹ Your City, ‹ And to Jerusalem,

בְּתוֹכָהּ כַּאֲשֶׁר דִּבַּרְתָּ, וּבְנֵה אוֹתָהּ בְּקָרוֹב בְּיָמֵינוּ

‹ in our days ‹ soon ‹ it ‹ May You rebuild « You have spoken. ‹ as ‹ within it,

בִּנְיַן עוֹלָם, וְכִסֵּא דָוִד מְהֵרָה לְתוֹכָהּ תָּכִין.

« may You establish. ‹ within it ‹ speedily, ‹ of David, ‹ and the throne « that is eternal, ‹ as a structure

בָּרוּךְ אַתָּה יהוה, בּוֹנֵה יְרוּשָׁלָיִם.

« of Jerusalem. ‹ Builder « HASHEM, ‹ are You, ‹ Blessed

DAVIDIC REIGN / מלכות בית דוד

אֶת צֶמַח דָּוִד עַבְדְּךָ מְהֵרָה תַצְמִיחַ, וְקַרְנוֹ

‹ and his pride « may You cause to flourish, ‹ speedily, « Your servant, ‹ of David ‹ offspring ‹ The

תָּרוּם בִּישׁוּעָתֶךָ, כִּי לִישׁוּעָתְךָ קִוִּינוּ כָּל הַיּוֹם.

« all day long. ‹ we hope ‹ for Your salvation ‹ because « through Your salvation, ‹ may You exalt

בָּרוּךְ אַתָּה יהוה, מַצְמִיחַ קֶרֶן יְשׁוּעָה.

« of salvation. ‹ the pride ‹ Who causes to flourish « HASHEM, ‹ are You, ‹ Blessed

ACCEPTANCE OF PRAYER / קבלת תפלה

שְׁמַע קוֹלֵנוּ יהוה אֱלֹהֵינוּ, חוּס וְרַחֵם

‹ and have compassion ‹ have pity « our God, ‹ HASHEM, ‹ our voice, ‹ Hear

עָלֵינוּ, וְקַבֵּל בְּרַחֲמִים וּבְרָצוֹן אֶת תְּפִלָּתֵנוּ, כִּי

‹ for « our prayer, ‹ and with favor ‹ with compassion ‹ and accept « on us,

אֵל שׁוֹמֵעַ תְּפִלּוֹת וְתַחֲנוּנִים אָתָּה. וּמִלְּפָנֶיךָ

« From before Yourself, « are You. ‹ and supplications ‹ prayers ‹ Who hears ‹ God

מַלְכֵּנוּ, רֵיקָם אַל תְּשִׁיבֵנוּ.°°

« turn us away, ‹ do not ‹ empty-handed ‹ our King,

°°AT THIS POINT ONE MAY INSERT THE FOLLOWING PERSONAL PRAYER FOR FORGIVENESS:

אָנָּא יהוה, חָטָאתִי עָוִיתִי וּפָשַׁעְתִּי לְפָנֶיךָ, מִיּוֹם הֱיוֹתִי

‹ I have existed ‹ from the day « before You, ‹ and willfully sinned « been iniquitous, ‹ I have sinned, ‹ HASHEM, ‹ Please,

עַל הָאֲדָמָה עַד הַיּוֹם הַזֶּה (וּבִפְרַט בַּחֵטְא . . .). אָנָּא יהוה,

‹ HASHEM, ‹ Please, « with the sin of . . .). ‹ (and especially « this very day ‹ until ‹ earth ‹ on

עֲשֵׂה לְמַעַן שִׁמְךָ הַגָּדוֹל, וּתְכַפֶּר לִי עַל חֲטָאַי וַעֲוֹנַי

‹ my iniquities, ‹ my inadvertent sins, ‹ for ‹ to me ‹ and grant atonement « which is great ‹ Your Name ‹ for the sake of ‹ act

וּפְשָׁעַי שֶׁחָטָאתִי וְשֶׁעָוִיתִי וְשֶׁפָּשַׁעְתִּי לְפָנֶיךָ, מִנְּעוּרַי עַד

‹ until ‹ from my youth « before You, ‹ and sinned willfully ‹ been iniquitous, ‹ [through which] I have sinned, « and my willful sins

הַיּוֹם הַזֶּה. וּתְמַלֵּא כָּל הַשֵּׁמוֹת שֶׁפָּגַמְתִּי בְּשִׁמְךָ הַגָּדוֹל.

« that is great. ‹ within Your Name ‹ that I have blemished ‹ the [Holy] Names ‹ all ‹ And make whole « this very day.

CONTINUE ... כִּי אַתָּה (P. 22)

°°AT THIS POINT ONE MAY INSERT THE FOLLOWING PERSONAL PRAYER FOR LIVELIHOOD:

אַתָּה הוּא יהוה הָאֱלֹהִים, הַזָּן וּמְפַרְנֵס וּמְכַלְכֵּל מִקַּרְנֵי

‹ from the horns « and supports, ‹ sustains, ‹ Who nourishes, ‹ the God ‹ HASHEM, ‹ Who ‹ It is You are

רְאֵמִים עַד בֵּיצֵי כִנִּים. הַטְרִיפֵנִי לֶחֶם חֻקִּי,[1] וְהַמְצֵא לִי

‹ for me ‹ provide « allotted to me; ‹ the bread ‹ Supply me with « of lice. ‹ the eggs ‹ to ‹ of *re'eimim*

וּלְכָל בְּנֵי בֵיתִי מְזוֹנוֹתַי קוֹדֶם שֶׁאֶצְטָרֵךְ לָהֶם, בְּנַחַת

‹ in contentment « for it; ‹ I have need ‹ before ‹ my food, « of my household, ‹ members ‹ and for all

וְלֹא בְצַעַר, בְּהֶתֵּר וְלֹא בְאִסּוּר, בְּכָבוֹד וְלֹא בְבִזָּיוֹן,

« in disgrace, ‹ but not ‹ in honor « in a forbidden manner, ‹ but not ‹ in a permissible manner « in pain, ‹ but not

לְחַיִּים וּלְשָׁלוֹם, מִשֶּׁפַע בְּרָכָה וְהַצְלָחָה, וּמִשֶּׁפַע בְּרֵכָה

‹ of the spring ‹ and from the flow « and success ‹ of blessing ‹ from the flow « and for peace; ‹ for life

עֶלְיוֹנָה, כְּדֵי שֶׁאוּכַל לַעֲשׂוֹת רְצוֹנֶךָ וְלַעֲסוֹק בְּתוֹרָתֶךָ

‹ in Your Torah ‹ and engage « Your will ‹ to do ‹ I be enabled ‹ so that « from On High,

(1) *Proverbs* 30:8.

וּלְקַיֵּם מִצְוֹתֶיךָ. וְאַל תַּצְרִיכֵנִי לִידֵי מַתְּנַת בָּשָׂר וָדָם.

« and blood; ‹ of flesh ‹ of the gifts of the hands ‹ make me needful ‹ Do not « Your commandments. ‹ and fulfill

וִיקֻיַּם בִּי מִקְרָא שֶׁכָּתוּב: פּוֹתֵחַ אֶת יָדֶךָ, וּמַשְׂבִּיעַ לְכָל

‹ *every* ‹ *and satisfy* ‹ *Your hand,* ‹ *You open* « that states, ‹ the verse ‹ in me ‹ and may there be fulfilled

חַי רָצוֹן.[1] וְכָתוּב: הַשְׁלֵךְ עַל יהוה יְהָבְךָ וְהוּא יְכַלְכְּלֶךָ.[2]

« *will sustain you.* ‹ *and He* ‹ *Your burden* ‹ *HASHEM* ‹ *upon* ‹ *Cast* ‹ and that states, « *[with its] desire,* ‹ *living thing*

CONTINUE ... **כִּי אַתָּה** (BELOW)

כִּי אַתָּה שׁוֹמֵעַ תְּפִלַּת עַמְּךָ יִשְׂרָאֵל בְּרַחֲמִים.

« with compassion. ‹ Israel ‹ of Your people ‹ the prayer ‹ hear ‹ You ‹ For

בָּרוּךְ אַתָּה יהוה, שׁוֹמֵעַ תְּפִלָּה.

« prayer. ‹ Who hears « HASHEM, ‹ are You, ‹ Blessed

TEMPLE SERVICE / עבודה

רְצֵה יהוה אֱלֹהֵינוּ בְּעַמְּךָ יִשְׂרָאֵל וּבִתְפִלָּתָם,

« and toward their prayer ‹ Israel ‹ toward Your people « our God, ‹ HASHEM, « Be favorable,

וְהָשֵׁב אֶת הָעֲבוֹדָה לִדְבִיר בֵּיתֶךָ. וְאִשֵּׁי יִשְׂרָאֵל

‹ of Israel ‹ The fire-offerings « of Your Temple. ‹ to the Holy of Holies ‹ the service ‹ and restore

וּתְפִלָּתָם בְּאַהֲבָה תְקַבֵּל בְּרָצוֹן, וּתְהִי לְרָצוֹן

‹ to Your favor ‹ and may it be « favorably, ‹ accept ‹ with love ‹ and their prayer

תָּמִיד עֲבוֹדַת יִשְׂרָאֵל עַמֶּךָ.

« Your people. ‹ of Israel ‹ the service ‹ always

וְתֶחֱזֶינָה עֵינֵינוּ בְּשׁוּבְךָ לְצִיּוֹן בְּרַחֲמִים. בָּרוּךְ

‹ Blessed « in compassion. ‹ to Zion ‹ Your return ‹ may our eyes ‹ Witness

אַתָּה יהוה, הַמַּחֲזִיר שְׁכִינָתוֹ לְצִיּוֹן.

« to Zion. ‹ His Presence ‹ Who restores « HASHEM, ‹ are You,

(1) *Psalms* 145:16. (2) 55:23.

THANKSGIVING [MODIM] / הוֹדָאָה

BOW AT מוֹדִים, *WE THANK YOU*; STRAIGHTEN UP AT 'ה, *HASHEM*.

מוֹדִים אֲנַחְנוּ לָךְ שָׁאַתָּה הוּא יהוה אֱלֹהֵינוּ

‹ our God ‹ HASHEM, ‹ Who are ‹ for it is You « You, ‹ We thank

וֵאלֹהֵי אֲבוֹתֵינוּ לְעוֹלָם וָעֶד. צוּר חַיֵּינוּ, מָגֵן

‹ Shield « of our lives, ‹ Rock « and ever; ‹ for ever ‹ of our forefathers ‹ and the God

יִשְׁעֵנוּ אַתָּה הוּא לְדוֹר וָדוֹר. נוֹדֶה לְּךָ וּנְסַפֵּר

‹ and relate ‹ You ‹ We shall thank « to generation. ‹ from generation ‹ [is what] You are « of our salvation

תְּהִלָּתֶךָ[1] עַל חַיֵּינוּ הַמְּסוּרִים בְּיָדֶךָ, וְעַל נִשְׁמוֹתֵינוּ

‹ our souls ‹ and for « into Your hands, ‹ that are committed ‹ our lives ‹ for « Your praise,

הַפְּקוּדוֹת לָךְ, וְעַל נִסֶּיךָ שֶׁבְּכָל יוֹם עִמָּנוּ, וְעַל

‹ and for « are with us; ‹ day ‹ that every ‹ Your miracles ‹ and for « to You; ‹ that are entrusted

נִפְלְאוֹתֶיךָ וְטוֹבוֹתֶיךָ שֶׁבְּכָל עֵת, עֶרֶב וָבֹקֶר

‹ morning, ‹ — evening, « times ‹ that are at all ‹ and favors ‹ Your wonders

וְצָהֳרָיִם. הַטּוֹב כִּי לֹא כָלוּ רַחֲמֶיךָ, וְהַמְּרַחֵם

‹ and the Compassionate One, « are Your compassions, ‹ exhausted ‹ never ‹ for ‹ The Beneficent One, « and afternoon.

כִּי לֹא תַמּוּ חֲסָדֶיךָ,[2] מֵעוֹלָם קִוִּינוּ לָךְ.

« in You. ‹ have we put our hope ‹ — always « were Your kindnesses ‹ ended ‹ never ‹ for

וְעַל כֻּלָּם יִתְבָּרַךְ וְיִתְרוֹמַם שִׁמְךָ מַלְכֵּנוּ

« our King, ‹ may Your Name be, ‹ and exalted ‹ blessed ‹ all these, ‹ For

תָּמִיד לְעוֹלָם וָעֶד.

« and ever. ‹ for ever ‹ continually,

BEND THE KNEES AT בָּרוּךְ, *BLESSED*; BOW AT אַתָּה, *YOU*; STRAIGHTEN UP AT 'ה, *HASHEM*.

וְכֹל הַחַיִּים יוֹדְוּךָ סֶּלָה, וִיהַלְלוּ אֶת שִׁמְךָ

‹ Your Name ‹ — and praise « forever! ‹ will gratefully acknowledge You, ‹ alive ‹ Everything

(1) Cf. *Psalms* 79:13. (2) Cf. *Lamentations* 3:22.

בֶּאֱמֶת, הָאֵל יְשׁוּעָתֵנוּ וְעֶזְרָתֵנוּ סֶלָה. בָּרוּךְ אַתָּה

‹ are You, ‹ Blessed « forever! ‹ and of our help, ‹ of our salvation ‹ O God « sincerely,

יהוה, הַטּוֹב שִׁמְךָ וּלְךָ נָאֶה לְהוֹדוֹת.

« to give thanks. ‹ it is fitting ‹ and to You ‹ is Your Name, ‹ *The Beneficent One* « HASHEM,

PEACE / שלום

שָׁלוֹם רָב עַל יִשְׂרָאֵל עַמְּךָ תָּשִׂים לְעוֹלָם,

« forever, ‹ establish ‹ Your people ‹ Israel ‹ upon « abundant, « Peace,

כִּי אַתָּה הוּא מֶלֶךְ אָדוֹן לְכָל הַשָּׁלוֹם.

« peace. ‹ of all ‹ Master « King, ‹ Who are ‹ it is You ‹ for

וְטוֹב בְּעֵינֶיךָ לְבָרֵךְ אֶת עַמְּךָ יִשְׂרָאֵל בְּכָל

‹ at every « Israel ‹ Your people ‹ to bless ‹ in Your eyes ‹ May it be good

עֵת וּבְכָל שָׁעָה בִּשְׁלוֹמֶךָ. בָּרוּךְ אַתָּה יהוה,

« HASHEM, ‹ are You, ‹ Blessed « with Your peace. ‹ hour ‹ and at every ‹ time

הַמְּבָרֵךְ אֶת עַמּוֹ יִשְׂרָאֵל בַּשָּׁלוֹם.

« with peace. ‹ Israel ‹ His people ‹ Who blesses

יִהְיוּ לְרָצוֹן אִמְרֵי פִי וְהֶגְיוֹן לִבִּי לְפָנֶיךָ,

« before You, ‹ of my heart — ‹ and the thoughts ‹ of my mouth ‹ — the expressions ‹ find favor ‹ May they

יהוה צוּרִי וְגֹאֲלִי.[1]

« and my Redeemer. ‹ my Rock ‹ HASHEM,

אֱלֹהַי, נְצוֹר לְשׁוֹנִי מֵרָע, וּשְׂפָתַי מִדַּבֵּר מִרְמָה,[2]

« deceitfully. ‹ from speaking ‹ and my lips « from evil ‹ my tongue ‹ guard ‹ My God,

וְלִמְקַלְלַי נַפְשִׁי תִדּוֹם, וְנַפְשִׁי כֶּעָפָר לַכֹּל תִּהְיֶה.

« be. ‹ to everyone ‹ like dust ‹ and let my soul « be silent; ‹ let my soul ‹ To those who curse me,

פְּתַח לִבִּי בְּתוֹרָתֶךָ, וּבְמִצְוֹתֶיךָ תִּרְדּוֹף נַפְשִׁי. וְכָל

‹ As for all « shall my soul pursue. ‹ so that Your commandments « to Your Torah, ‹ my heart ‹ Open

---

(1) *Psalms* 19:15. (2) Cf. 34:14.

הַחוֹשְׁבִים עָלַי רָעָה, מְהֵרָה הָפֵר עֲצָתָם וְקַלְקֵל

who plot against me evil, speedily nullify their counsel and disrupt

מַחֲשַׁבְתָּם.[1] עֲשֵׂה לְמַעַן שְׁמֶךָ, עֲשֵׂה לְמַעַן

their scheme. Act for the sake of Your Name; act for the sake

יְמִינֶךָ, עֲשֵׂה לְמַעַן קְדֻשָּׁתֶךָ, עֲשֵׂה לְמַעַן תּוֹרָתֶךָ.

of Your right hand; act for the sake of Your sanctity; act for the sake of Your Torah.

לְמַעַן יֵחָלְצוּן יְדִידֶיךָ, הוֹשִׁיעָה יְמִינְךָ וַעֲנֵנִי.[2]

In order that Your beloved ones may be released — save with Your right hand, and answer me.

SOME RECITE THE VERSE PERTAINING TO THEIR NAMES AT THIS POINT. SEE PAGE 643.

יִהְיוּ לְרָצוֹן אִמְרֵי פִי וְהֶגְיוֹן לִבִּי לְפָנֶיךָ, יהוה

May they find favor — the expressions of my mouth and the thoughts of my heart — before You, HASHEM,

צוּרִי וְגֹאֲלִי.[3]

my Rock and my Redeemer.

BOW. TAKE THREE STEPS BACK. BOW LEFT AND SAY ... עֹשֶׂה, *"HE WHO MAKES . . ."*; BOW RIGHT AND SAY ... הוּא, *"MAY HE . . ."*; BOW FORWARD AND SAY ... וְעַל כָּל יִשְׂרָאֵל, *"AND UPON ALL ISRAEL . . ."*.

עֹשֶׂה שָׁלוֹם בִּמְרוֹמָיו,[4] הוּא יַעֲשֶׂה שָׁלוֹם

He Who makes peace in His heights, may He make peace

עָלֵינוּ, וְעַל כָּל יִשְׂרָאֵל.[5] וְאִמְרוּ: אָמֵן.

upon us, and upon all Israel. Now respond: Amen.

יְהִי רָצוֹן מִלְּפָנֶיךָ, יהוה אֱלֹהֵינוּ וֵאלֹהֵי אֲבוֹתֵינוּ, שֶׁיִּבָּנֶה

May it be the will, before You, HASHEM, our God and the God of our forefathers, that

בֵּית הַמִּקְדָּשׁ בִּמְהֵרָה בְיָמֵינוּ, וְתֵן חֶלְקֵנוּ בְּתוֹרָתֶךָ.[6] וְשָׁם

rebuilt shall the Holy Temple be, speedily in our days. Grant that our portion be in Your Torah, so that there

נַעֲבָדְךָ בְּיִרְאָה, כִּימֵי עוֹלָם וּכְשָׁנִים קַדְמוֹנִיּוֹת. וְעָרְבָה לַיהוה

we may serve You with reverence, as in days of old and as in years gone by. And pleasing to HASHEM

מִנְחַת יְהוּדָה וִירוּשָׁלָיִם, כִּימֵי עוֹלָם וּכְשָׁנִים קַדְמוֹנִיּוֹת.[7]

let be the offering of Judah and Jerusalem, as in days of old and in years gone by.

(1) See *Berachos* 17a. (2) *Psalms* 60:7, 108:7. (3) 19:15. (4) *Job* 25:2. (5) Cf. *Berachos* 16b. (6) *Ethics of the Fathers* 5:24. (7) *Malachi* 3:4.

***SHEMONEH ESREI* ENDS HERE.**
REMAIN STANDING IN PLACE FOR AT LEAST A FEW MOMENTS BEFORE TAKING THREE STEPS FORWARD.

FULL KADDISH / קדיש שלם

THE *CHAZZAN* RECITES קַדִּישׁ שָׁלֵם, FULL *KADDISH.*

יִתְגַּדַּל וְיִתְקַדַּשׁ שְׁמֵהּ רַבָּא. (Cong. — אָמֵן.) בְּעָלְמָא דִּי

Grow exalted ‹ and be sanctified ‹ may His Name ‹ that is great! — « (Amen.) ‹ in the world ‹ that ‹

בְרָא כִרְעוּתֵהּ. וְיַמְלִיךְ מַלְכוּתֵהּ, בְּחַיֵּיכוֹן וּבְיוֹמֵיכוֹן וּבְחַיֵּי

He created ‹ according to His will, « and may He give reign ‹ to His kingship, « in your lifetimes ‹ and in your days, ‹ and in the lifetimes ‹

דְכָל בֵּית יִשְׂרָאֵל, בַּעֲגָלָא וּבִזְמַן קָרִיב. וְאִמְרוּ: אָמֵן.

of the entire ‹ Family ‹ of Israel, « swiftly ‹ and at a time ‹ that comes soon. « Now respond: ‹ Amen. «

CONGREGATION RESPONDS:

אָמֵן. יְהֵא שְׁמֵהּ רַבָּא מְבָרַךְ לְעָלַם וּלְעָלְמֵי עָלְמַיָּא.

Amen. « May ‹ His Name ‹ that is great ‹ be blessed ‹ forever ‹ and for all eternity. «

CHAZZAN CONTINUES:

יְהֵא שְׁמֵהּ רַבָּא מְבָרַךְ לְעָלַם וּלְעָלְמֵי עָלְמַיָּא. יִתְבָּרַךְ

May ‹ His Name ‹ that is great ‹ be blessed ‹ forever ‹ and for all eternity. « Blessed, ‹

וְיִשְׁתַּבַּח וְיִתְפָּאַר וְיִתְרוֹמַם וְיִתְנַשֵּׂא וְיִתְהַדָּר וְיִתְעַלֶּה

praised, ‹ glorified, ‹ exalted, ‹ upraised, ‹ honored, ‹ elevated, ‹

וְיִתְהַלָּל שְׁמֵהּ דְּקֻדְשָׁא בְּרִיךְ הוּא (Cong. — בְּרִיךְ הוּא)

and lauded ‹ be the Name ‹ of the Holy One, ‹ Blessed ‹ is He « (Blessed ‹ is He) «

— לְעֵלָּא מִן כָּל בִּרְכָתָא וְשִׁירָתָא תֻּשְׁבְּחָתָא וְנֶחֱמָתָא

beyond ‹ any ‹ blessing ‹ and song, « praise ‹ and consolation ‹

דַּאֲמִירָן בְּעָלְמָא. וְאִמְרוּ: אָמֵן. (Cong. — אָמֵן.)

that are uttered ‹ in the world. « Now respond: ‹ Amen. « (Amen.) «

CONGREGATION:

קַבֵּל בְּרַחֲמִים וּבְרָצוֹן אֶת תְּפִלָּתֵנוּ.

Accept ‹ with mercy ‹ and with favor ‹ our prayers. «

CHAZZAN CONTINUES:

תִּתְקַבֵּל צְלוֹתְהוֹן וּבָעוּתְהוֹן דְּכָל (בֵּית) יִשְׂרָאֵל קֳדָם

May accepted be ‹ the prayers ‹ and supplications ‹ of the entire ‹ (Family of) ‹ Israel ‹ before ‹

אֲבוּהוֹן דִּי בִשְׁמַיָּא. וְאִמְרוּ: אָמֵן. (Cong. — אָמֵן.)

‹ (Amen.) « Amen. ‹ Now respond: « is in Heaven. ‹ Who ‹ their Father

CONGREGATION:

יְהִי שֵׁם יהוה מְבֹרָךְ, מֵעַתָּה וְעַד עוֹלָם.[1]

« eternity. ‹ until ‹ from this time « be blessed, ‹ of HASHEM ‹ the Name ‹ Let

***CHAZZAN* CONTINUES:**

יְהֵא שְׁלָמָא רַבָּא מִן שְׁמַיָּא, וְחַיִּים עָלֵינוּ וְעַל כָּל

‹ all ‹ and upon ‹ upon us « and life, « Heaven, ‹ from ‹ that is abundant ‹ peace ‹ May there be

יִשְׂרָאֵל. וְאִמְרוּ: אָמֵן. (Cong. — אָמֵן.)

‹ (Amen.) « Amen. ‹ Now respond: « Israel.

CONGREGATION:

עֶזְרִי מֵעִם יהוה, עֹשֵׂה שָׁמַיִם וָאָרֶץ.[2]

« and earth. ‹ of heaven ‹ Maker « HASHEM, ‹ is from ‹ (My help

CHAZZAN BOWS; TAKES THREE STEPS BACK. BOWS LEFT AND SAYS ... עֹשֶׂה שָׁלוֹם, *"HE WHO MAKES PEACE ..."*; BOWS RIGHT AND SAYS ... הוּא, *"MAY HE ..."*; BOWS FORWARD AND SAYS ... וְעַל כָּל יִשְׂרָאֵל, *"AND UPON ALL ISRAEL ..."*; REMAINS IN PLACE FOR A FEW MOMENTS, THEN TAKES THREE STEPS FORWARD.

עֹשֶׂה שָׁלוֹם בִּמְרוֹמָיו, הוּא יַעֲשֶׂה שָׁלוֹם עָלֵינוּ, וְעַל כָּל

‹ all ‹ and upon ‹ upon us, ‹ peace ‹ make ‹ may He « in His heights, ‹ peace ‹ He Who makes

יִשְׂרָאֵל. וְאִמְרוּ: אָמֵן. (Cong. — אָמֵן.)

‹ (Amen.) « Amen. ‹ Now respond: « Israel.

ON SATURDAY NIGHT A MULTIWICKED CANDLE OR TWO ORDINARY CANDLES WITH FLAMES TOUCHING EACH OTHER ARE HELD UP AND THE FOLLOWING BLESSING IS RECITED. AFTER THE BLESSING THE FINGERS ARE HELD UP TO THE FLAME TO SEE THE REFLECTED LIGHT.

בָּרוּךְ אַתָּה יהוה אֱלֹהֵינוּ מֶלֶךְ הָעוֹלָם, בּוֹרֵא

‹ Who creates « of the universe, ‹ King ‹ our God, ‹ HASHEM, ‹ are You, ‹ Blessed

מְאוֹרֵי הָאֵשׁ.

« of fire. ‹ the illuminations

THE *CHAZZAN* JOINS THE CONGREGATION SITTING ON THE FLOOR OR ON LOW SEATS JUST AS MOURNERS DURING THE *SHIVAH* WEEK. ONLY ENOUGH LIGHTS ARE KEPT LIT TO ALLOW THE CONGREGATION TO READ *EICHAH* AND *KINNOS*. MANY CONGREGATIONS USE CANDLES INSTEAD OF ELECTRIC LIGHTS. *EICHAH* AND KINNOS ARE READ IN A LOW VOICE.

(1) Cf. *Psalms* 113:2. (2) 121:2.

THE BOOK OF EICHAH / מגילת איכה

[א] א אֵיכָה* | יָשְׁבָה בָדָד* הָעִיר רַבָּתִי עָם

[1] 1 ‹ How is it that* ‹ she sits «in solitude* ‹ – the city ‹ that had so many «people?

הָיְתָה כְּאַלְמָנָה* רַבָּתִי בַגּוֹיִם שָׂרָתִי בַּמְּדִינוֹת

‹ She has become «like a widow.* ‹ The greatest ‹ among nations, ‹ the princess ‹ among states,

[This commentary to *Eichah* has been abridged from that volume in the ArtScroll Tanach Series, by Rabbi Meir Zlotowitz.]

CHAPTER ONE

1. אֵיכָה — *How is it that.* The prophet Jeremiah wrote סֵפֶר אֵיכָה, the *Book of Lamentations.* This is the Scroll which King Yehoyakim burned *on the fire* that was in the brazier [*Jeremiah* 36:23].

[The book laments the fall of the Jews and Jerusalem after the חוּרְבָּן, *Destruction,* of the First Temple. Originally the book consisted of 3 acrostic chapters [1,2, and 4] which Jeremiah rewrote after the burning. He later added Chapter 3 consisting of three additional acrostics, as well as Chapter 5 (*Rashi; Moed Katan* 26a).

According to *Tzemach David,* the Destruction took place during the reign of King Zedekiah in the year 3338 from Creation [422 B.C.E.]. Judah was then exiled from the Land by Nebuchadnezzar. (The ten tribes had been exiled 133 years earlier.)

For a period of 52 years after the Destruction, Eretz Yisrael lay desolate: the roads and villages were uninhabited; not even cattle or birds inhabited the Land (*Yoma* 54a).

The Exile lasted 70 years until 3408, when Darius, son of Queen Esther and King Ahasuerus, permitted the rebuilding of the Temple. The Destruction of the Second Temple took place in the days of Rabban Yochanan ben Zakkai in the year 3828 (*Tzemach David*).

אֵיכָה יָשְׁבָה בָדָד — *How is it that she sits in solitude.* Three people uttered prophecies using the word אֵיכָה, *Eichah:* Moses, Isaiah, and Jeremiah... Rav Levi said: It is comparable to a bride that had three best men at her wedding: The first beheld her in her happiness; the second beheld her in her infidelity, and the third beheld her in her disgrace. In this vein, Moses beheld the Jews in their glory and happiness, and exclaimed: אֵיכָה אֶשָּׂא לְבַדִּי טָרְחֲכֶם, *How can I carry by myself your contentiousness?* (*Deut.* 1:12) [they presented all the difficulties of a large, growing, and flourishing nation]. Isaiah beheld them in their infidelity and exclaimed: אֵיכָה הָיְתָה לְזוֹנָה, *How has the faithful city become a harlot* (*Isaiah* 1:21)? Jeremiah beheld them in their disgrace and said: אֵיכָה יָשְׁבָה בָדָד, *How is it that she sits in solitude!* (*Midrash*).

The Book of *Lamentations* is written in a series of alphabetical acrostics. The *Talmud* notes: Why was Israel smitten with an alphabetical dirge? — Because they transgressed the Torah from *alef* to *tav,* from the first to the last letter of the alphabet (*Sanhedrin* 104b).

יָשְׁבָה בָדָד — *She sits in solitude.* Bereft of her inhabitants (*Rashi*) [*she* — Jerusalem personified as a woman].

הָיְתָה כְּאַלְמָנָה — *She has become like a widow.* The *Talmud* stresses the prefix כְּ, *as:* Jerusalem's widowhood was not total, but temporary; she is like a woman whose husband went to a foreign country, but with the intention of returning to her (*Sanhedrin* 104b).

Another interpretation: She *is* a widow — she is bereft of the ten tribes, but not of the tribes of Judah and Benjamin... The Rabbis said: She was widowed of *all* the tribes [all the tribes — including Judah and Benjamin — were exiled, and Jerusalem

הָיְתָה לָמַס׃ ב בָּכוֹ תִבְכֶּה* בַּלַּיְלָה וְדִמְעָתָהּ

has become ‹ a tribute [payer]. » **2** She weeps intensely* ‹ in the night, » and her tear ‹

עַל לֶחֱיָהּ אֵין־לָהּ מְנַחֵם מִכָּל־אֹהֲבֶיהָ כָּל־רֵעֶיהָ

is on ‹ her cheek; » there is not ‹ for her ‹ any comforter ‹ from all ‹ those who love her. » All ‹ her friends ‹

בָּגְדוּ בָהּ הָיוּ לָהּ לְאֹיְבִים׃ ג גָּלְתָה יְהוּדָה* מֵעֹנִי

have betrayed ‹ her; » they have turned ‹ for her ‹ into enemies. » **3** Judah has gone into exile* ‹ because of oppression ‹

וּמֵרֹב עֲבֹדָה הִיא יָשְׁבָה בַגּוֹיִם לֹא מָצְאָה מָנוֹחַ

and excessive ‹ servitude. » She ‹ dwelt ‹ among the nations, ‹ [where] she did not find ‹ a respite; »

כָּל־רֹדְפֶיהָ הִשִּׂיגוּהָ בֵּין הַמְּצָרִים׃* ד דַּרְכֵי צִיּוֹן

all ‹ her pursuers ‹ caught up to her ‹ between ‹ the narrow confines.* » **4** The roads ‹ of Zion ‹

---

was bereft of them] but she was never deserted by God (*Midrash*).

2. בָּכוֹ תִבְכֶּה — *She weeps intensely* [lit., *weeping she weeps*]. Many interpretations are offered for the use of בָּכוֹ תִּבְכֶּה, the double form of the verb בכה, *weep:*

According to the *Talmud*: Why this "double weeping"? — Once for the First Temple; once for the Second (*Sanhedrin* 104b).

Other explanations of the "double weeping" are: On account of Judah, and of Zion and Jerusalem; on account of the exile of the ten tribes, and of Judah and Benjamin.

Another interpretation: בָּכוֹ וּתְבַכֶּה, she weeps and makes others weep with her (*Midrash*).

The word בַּלַּיְלָה, *in* the *night*, refers to the *specific* night of Tishah B'Av, which, from the time of the מְרַגְּלִים, spies, has been mournfully observed as a night of weeping and meditation (*Lechem Dimah*) . . .

As the *Talmud* (*Sanhedrin* 104b) relates: When the מְרַגְּלִים (the spies sent by Moses to investigate the land of Canaan) returned with discouraging news, the *people wept that night* (*Numbers* 14:1). That night was the ninth of Av, and God said to Israel: You have wept without cause; therefore I will appoint [this date as a time of] weeping for you in future generations.

3. גָּלְתָה יְהוּדָה — *Judah has gone into exile* — from its land (*Rashi*).

Judah is a general term encompassing both the male and female members of the tribe of Judah (*Ibn Ezra*). [The term *Judah* also includes the tribe of Benjamin who was exiled together with Judah.]

The *Midrash* compares the exile of other nations to that of Israel:

Heathen nations also go into exile, however, since they eat the bread and drink the wine [of their enemies], they do not experience real exile [they do not experience privation]. For Israel, however, which is forbidden to eat their bread or drink their wine, the exile is real.

בֵּין הַמְּצָרִים — *Between the narrow confines*, by cornering them (*Rashi*).

Some understand this literally, but the *Midrash* understands the phrase בֵּין הַמְּצָרִים as *within the days of distress*, all who pursued her overtook her during the period between the 17th of Tammuz when the first breach in Jerusalem's walls was made and the 9th of Av [exactly 3 weeks later, when the Temple was destroyed].

[This phrase בֵּין הַמְּצָרִים, *between the*

אֲבֵלוֹת מִבְּלִי בָּאֵי מוֹעֵד כָּל־שְׁעָרֶיהָ שׁוֹמֵמִין

are in mourning, ‹ for lack ‹ of those who come ‹ at the appointed festivals. « All ‹ her gates ‹ are desolate, «

כֹּהֲנֶיהָ נֶאֱנָחִים בְּתוּלֹתֶיהָ נוּגוֹת וְהִיא מַר־לָהּ׃

her Kohanim ‹ sigh; « her maidens ‹ are afflicted, « and as for her, ‹ it is bitter ‹ for her. «

5 ה הָיוּ צָרֶיהָ לְרֹאשׁ אֹיְבֶיהָ שָׁלוּ כִּי־יהוה הוֹגָהּ עַל־

5 Her adversaries have become ‹ the head, « her enemies ‹ are at ease, « for ‹ HASHEM ‹ has afflicted her ‹ due to ‹

רֹב פְּשָׁעֶיהָ* עוֹלָלֶיהָ הָלְכוּ שְׁבִי* לִפְנֵי צָר׃ 6 ו וַיֵּצֵא

the abundance of her transgressions.* « Her young children ‹ have gone ‹ into captivity* ‹ before ‹ the adversary. « 6 Gone ‹

°מִבַּת־ [°מן בת־ כ׳] צִיּוֹן כָּל־הֲדָרָהּ הָיוּ שָׂרֶיהָ

from the daughter ‹ of Zion ‹ is all ‹ her splendor. « Her leaders were ‹

כְּאַיָּלִים לֹא־מָצְאוּ מִרְעֶה וַיֵּלְכוּ בְלֹא־כֹחַ לִפְנֵי

like deer ‹ that did not ‹ find ‹ pasture, « and walked on ‹ without ‹ strength ‹ before ‹

---

days of distress, is used today in halachic literature as well as in common Hebrew usage to refer to the period between the 17th of Tammuz and the 9th of Av.]

5. כִּי־ה׳ הוֹגָהּ עַל־רֹב פְּשָׁעֶיהָ — *For HASHEM has afflicted her due to the abundance of her transgressions.* The *Midrash*, as interpreted by the commentaries, notes that God's punishment was in direct proportion to Israel's many transgressions. Even הָיוּ צָרֶיהָ לְרֹאשׁ, *her adversaries have become the head*, was part of the punishment.

[The word רֹב, *abundance*, can also mean *majority, most*. Since the phrase is רֹב פְּשָׁעֶיהָ, *her many sins*, instead of כָּל פְּשָׁעֶיהָ, *all of her sins*, it is, perhaps, possible to translate the verse: *for God has afflicted her due to the majority of her transgressions*. In the final analysis, God *was* compassionate, for had He exacted punishment at that time for *all* her transgressions, *no one* would have survived.]

Harav David Cohen points out that *Rambam* in *Hilchos Teshuvah* 2:2 discusses the evaluation of iniquities and merits and concludes: *This evaluation takes into account not the number but the magnitude [the qualitative rather than the quantitative aspects] of merits and iniquities. There may be a single merit that outweighs many iniquities... and there may be one iniquity that offsets many merits... God alone makes this evaluation; He alone knows how to set off merits against iniquities.*

עוֹלָלֶיהָ הָלְכוּ שְׁבִי — *Her young children have gone into captivity.* The *Midrash* stresses that the children are the most beloved to God. According to this view, the Sanhedrin went into exile, but the *Shechinah* [God's Presence] did not go into exile with them; the priestly watches were exiled, but the *Shechinah* did not go into exile with them. However, when the children were exiled, the *Shechinah* went into exile with them. Therefore, it is written: *Her young children have gone into captivity before the adversary.* This is

רוֹדֵף׃* ז זָכְרָה יְרוּשָׁלַ͏ִם* יְמֵי עָנְיָהּ* וּמְרוּדֶיהָ כֹּל

the pursuer. 7 Remember did Jerusalem, in the days of her oppression* and her sorrow, all

מַחֲמֻדֶיהָ אֲשֶׁר הָיוּ מִימֵי קֶדֶם בִּנְפֹל עַמָּהּ בְּיַד־

her treasures that had been [hers] from the days ancient. With the fall of her people into the hand

צָר וְאֵין עוֹזֵר לָהּ רָאוּהָ צָרִים שָׂחֲקוּ עַל־

of the adversary and there was no one to help her, her adversaries saw her and rejoiced at

מִשְׁבַּתֶּהָ׃ ח חֵטְא חָטְאָה יְרוּשָׁלַ͏ִם עַל־כֵּן לְנִידָה

her cessation of celebrations. 8 A sin she did sin, Jerusalem; for this, a wanderer

הָיָתָה כָּל־מְכַבְּדֶיהָ הִזִּילוּהָ כִּי־רָאוּ עֶרְוָתָהּ גַּם־

has she become. All who [once] respected her disdain her, for they have seen her nakedness. Also

הִיא נֶאֶנְחָה וַתָּשָׁב אָחוֹר׃ ט טֻמְאָתָהּ בְּשׁוּלֶיהָ

she herself sighs and turns backward. 9 Her impurity is on her hems,

לֹא זָכְרָה אַחֲרִיתָהּ וַתֵּרֶד פְּלָאִים אֵין מְנַחֵם לָהּ

she did not keep in mind the consequences. She has sunk astonishingly, there is no one to comfort her.

רְאֵה יהוה אֶת־עָנְיִי כִּי הִגְדִּיל אוֹיֵב׃ י יָדוֹ פָּרַשׂ צָר

See, HASHEM, my misery, for has the enemy self aggrandize! 10 His hand did the enemy spread out

---

immediately followed by, *Gone from the daughter of Zion is all her splendor* [the *Shechinah*].

6. לִפְנֵי רוֹדֵף — *Before the pursuer. Rashi* observes that wherever else in Scripture the word רוֹדֵף appears it is spelled חָסֵר, defectively [רֹדֵף — without the ו, *vav*]. In our verse, however, the full spelling is used to imply that the Jews were pursued vigorously and fully.

7. זָכְרָה יְרוּשָׁלַם — *Remember did Jerusalem.* While in exile (*Rashi*).

יְמֵי עָנְיָהּ — *In the days of her oppression,* the Destruction which was the cause of her oppression (*Rashi*).

8. [The author now attributes all of the suffering described in verses 1-7 to Divine retribution for Jerusalem's grievous sins.]

The *Midrash*, commenting on the use of the double verb, חֵטְא חָטְאָה, *a sin did she sin*, explains: They sinned doubly and were punished doubly, as it is written: כִּי לָקְחָה מִיַּד ה׳ כִּפְלַיִם בְּכָל־חַטֹּאתֶיהָ — *For she received from the hand of HASHEM double for all her sins* (*Isaiah* 40:2); and they were comforted doubly, as it is written: נַחֲמוּ נַחֲמוּ עַמִּי, *Comfort, comfort My people* (ibid. 40:1).

Meshech Chachmah interprets the double verb: *Jerusalem sinned repeatedly* and grew accustomed to the fact, viewing

עַל כָּל־מַחֲמַדֶּיהָ כִּי־רָאֲתָה גוֹיִם בָּאוּ מִקְדָּשָׁהּ אֲשֶׁר

‹ about whom « her sanctuary, ‹ who invaded ‹ nations ‹ she saw ‹ for « her treasures; ‹ all ‹ over

צִוִּיתָה לֹא־יָבֹאוּ בַקָּהָל לָךְ׃* יא כָּל־עַמָּהּ נֶאֱנָחִים

‹ sigh, ‹ her people ‹ All 11 « Your congregation.* ‹ that they should not enter ‹ You had commanded

מְבַקְּשִׁים לֶחֶם נָתְנוּ °מַחֲמַדֵּיהֶם [°מחמודיהם כ׳]

‹ their treasures ‹ They traded « for bread. ‹ searching

בְּאֹכֶל לְהָשִׁיב נָפֶשׁ רְאֵה יהוה* וְהַבִּיטָה כִּי הָיִיתִי

‹ [famine] made me ‹ that ‹ and behold ‹ HASHEM,* ‹ Look, « their souls. ‹ to revive ‹ for food

זוֹלֵלָה׃ יב לוֹא אֲלֵיכֶם כָּל־עֹבְרֵי דֶרֶךְ הַבִּיטוּ וּרְאוּ

‹ and see ‹ Behold « on the road! ‹ who pass by ‹ all « happen to you, ‹ May it not 12 « like a glutton!

אִם־יֵשׁ מַכְאוֹב כְּמַכְאֹבִי אֲשֶׁר עוֹלַל לִי אֲשֶׁר

‹ that « to me, ‹ happened ‹ which ‹ like my pain ‹ any pain ‹ there is ‹ if

הוֹגָה יהוה בְּיוֹם חֲרוֹן אַפּוֹ׃* יג מִמָּרוֹם שָׁלַח־אֵשׁ

‹ a fire ‹ He sent ‹ From On High 13 « of His wrath.* ‹ of the flaring ‹ on the day ‹ HASHEM has afflicted me

---

it naturally, and feeling no remorse...

[As the *Talmud* (*Moed Katan* 27b) remarks: *As soon as a person has committed a sinful act and has repeated it,* נַעֲשֵׂית לוֹ כְּהֶיתֵּר, *it has become to him as though it were something permissible* (see *Overview*).]

According to the *Talmud*, a sin consists of two parts: the sinful act itself and the thoughts and satisfaction surrounding it. Each part of the sin is evaluated separately and punished separately (*Kiddushin* 40a). Therefore, the verse uses a twin expression of sin. In the same way, the thought leading up to a good deed and the satisfaction one derives from having performed it are rewarded by God along with the good deed itself (*Hagaon Rav Moshe Feinstein*).

10. אֲשֶׁר צִוִּיתָה לֹא־יָבֹאוּ בַקָּהָל לָךְ — *About whom You had commanded that they should not enter Your congregation.* When the enemies entered the Temple, Ammonites and Moabites entered among them. While the others ran to plunder the silver and gold, the Ammonites and Moabites ran to plunder the Torah itself to expunge the verse (*Deut.* 23:4): לֹא־יָבֹא עַמּוֹנִי וּמוֹאָבִי בִּקְהַל ה׳, *An Ammonite or Moabite shall not enter the Congregation of HASHEM* (*Midrash*).

11. רְאֵה ה׳ — *Look, HASHEM.* An impassioned plea. From this point on, Jerusalem, itself, laments. The Community of Israel says to the nations of the world: May there not occur to you what has occurred to me.

12. בְּיוֹם חֲרוֹן אַפּוֹ — *On the day of the flaming of His wrath*, the Ninth of Av when so many tragedies befell Israel throughout its history (*Shaar Bas Rabim*).

The *Midrash* stresses *the day*, i.e., that particular day upon which God's fierce anger was kindled: Had Israel repented that very day they could have cooled [averted] His anger.

בְּעַצְמֹתַי* וַיִּרְדֶּנָּה פָּרַשׂ רֶשֶׁת לְרַגְלַי הֱשִׁיבַנִי

‹ turned me ‹ for my feet, ‹ a net ‹ He spread « and He crushed each one.* ‹ into my bones,

אָחוֹר נְתָנַנִי שֹׁמֵמָה כָּל־הַיּוֹם דָּוָה: יד נִשְׂקַד* עֹל

‹ was the yoke ‹ Amassed **14** « suffering. ‹ day long ‹ all « desolate; ‹ He made me « backward.

פְּשָׁעַי בְּיָדוֹ יִשְׂתָּרְגוּ* עָלוּ עַל־צַוָּארִי הִכְשִׁיל

‹ He sapped « my neck; ‹ upon ‹ and came up ‹ they were twisted together* « in His hand; ‹ of my transgressions

כֹּחִי נְתָנַנִי אֲדֹנָי בִּידֵי לֹא־אוּכַל קוּם: טו סִלָּה

‹ Trampled **15** « to withstand. ‹ [of those] I am not able ‹ into the hands ‹ The Lord has given me over « my strength.

כָל־אַבִּירַי | אֲדֹנָי בְּקִרְבִּי קָרָא עָלַי מוֹעֵד*

‹ a set time ‹ against me ‹ He proclaimed « in my midst; ‹ has the Lord ‹ my warriors ‹ all

לִשְׁבֹּר בַּחוּרָי גַּת דָּרַךְ אֲדֹנָי לִבְתוּלַת בַּת־יְהוּדָה:*

« of Judah.* ‹ daughter ‹ [upon] the maiden ‹ the Lord trod ‹ As in a winepress « my young men. ‹ to crush

טז עַל־אֵלֶּה | אֲנִי בוֹכִיָּה* עֵינִי | עֵינִי יֹרְדָה מַּיִם

« [tears like] water, ‹ sheds ‹ my eye ‹ my eye, « weep;* ‹ I ‹ these things ‹ Over **16**

כִּי־רָחַק מִמֶּנִּי מְנַחֵם מֵשִׁיב נַפְשִׁי הָיוּ בָנַי

‹ My children have become « my spirit. ‹ one who can revive ‹ is any comforter, ‹ from me ‹ far away ‹ because

---

13. מִמָּרוֹם שָׁלַח אֵשׁ בְּעַצְמֹתַי — *From On High He sent a fire into my bones.* The *Midrash* understands this literally: God Himself sent a fire to burn the Temple so the heathens could not boast that they themselves destroyed it.

14. נִשְׂקַד ... יִשְׂתָּרְגוּ — *Amassed . . . they were twisted together.* Instead of constantly doling out small, proportioned punishment for every one of Zion's sins whenever she transgressed, God collected all her transgressions, noting and remembering them. He then metaphorically twisted them together into a heavy garment which he thrust upon her neck in one heavy, cumulative load, effectively weighing her down, and sapping her strength until she was unable to withstand the enemy.

15. קָרָא עָלַי מוֹעֵד — *He proclaimed against me a set time,* the Ninth of Av (*Taanis* 29a). [See comm. to verse 2, s.v. בַּלַּיְלָה].

[Since Tishah B'Av is referred to as מוֹעֵד, *set time, festival,* the Sages state that halachically, as on a holiday, *Tachanun* is not said during *Minchah* services on *Erev Tishah B'Av* (*Shulchan Aruch, Orach Chaim* 552).

לִבְתוּלַת בַּת־יְהוּדָה — The *maiden daughter of Judah,* Jerusalem (*Rashi*).

16. עַל־אֵלֶּה אֲנִי בוֹכִיָּה — *Over these things I weep.* The verb בוֹכִיָּה implies a constant action: *I weep incessantly;* or *I have become*

שׁוֹמֵמִים כִּי גָבַר אוֹיֵב: יז פֵּרְשָׂה צִיּוֹן בְּיָדֶיהָ
forlorn, « for ‹ prevailed ‹ has the enemy. « 17 Spread out ‹ did Zion ‹ her hands [in prayer]; «

אֵין מְנַחֵם לָהּ צִוָּה יהוה לְיַעֲקֹב סְבִיבָיו צָרָיו
there was no one ‹ who could comfort ‹ her. « HASHEM commanded ‹ against Jacob ‹ that his enemies should surround him. «

הָיְתָה יְרוּשָׁלַםִ לְנִדָּה בֵּינֵיהֶם: יח צַדִּיק הוּא יהוה
Jerusalem has become ‹ like a pariah ‹ among them. « 18 Righteous ‹ is ‹ HASHEM, «

כִּי־פִיהוּ מָרִיתִי שִׁמְעוּ־נָא כָל־°הָעַמִּים [°עמים כ׳]
for ‹ His utterance ‹ I have disobeyed. « Hear, ‹ now, ‹ all ‹ [you] peoples ‹

וּרְאוּ מַכְאֹבִי בְּתוּלֹתַי וּבַחוּרַי הָלְכוּ בַשֶּׁבִי:
and behold ‹ my pain: « My maidens ‹ and my young men ‹ have gone ‹ into captivity. «

יט קָרָאתִי לַמְאַהֲבַי הֵמָּה רִמּוּנִי* כֹּהֲנַי וּזְקֵנַי בָּעִיר
19 I called ‹ for those who love me ‹ but they ‹ deceived me.* « My Kohanim ‹ and my elders ‹ in the city ‹

גָּוָעוּ כִּי־בִקְשׁוּ אֹכֶל לָמוֹ וְיָשִׁיבוּ אֶת־נַפְשָׁם:
perished; « for ‹ they sought ‹ food ‹ for themselves ‹ that would revive ‹ their souls. «

כ רְאֵה יהוה* כִּי־צַר־לִי מֵעַי חֳמַרְמָרוּ נֶהְפַּךְ לִבִּי
20 See, ‹ HASHEM,* ‹ that ‹ painful ‹ it is to me; « my insides ‹ churn! « Turned over ‹ is My heart ‹

---

known as a habitual weeper (*Lechem Dimh*). Various causes for her weeping are offered in the *Midrash*, which relates many harrowing incidents of barbarous atrocities which befell the Jews at the time of the Destruction (1:16). [The post-Holocaust generation understands only too well how the Jewish people can suffer at the hands of cruel and bestial people. Indeed, the atrocities of the Nazis are also foreshadowed in the lament of Jeremiah.]

18. Zion itself resumes the lament, and confesses publicly and without reservation that God is righteous and justified in what He has done.

19. קָרָאתִי לַמְאַהֲבַי הֵמָּה רִמּוּנִי — *I called for those who love me but they deceived me. Those who love me* — those who feigned friendship (*Rashi*) [the neighboring countries — Egypt, Moab, Ammon, with whom Judea had hoped to form an alliance].

The Rabbis interpret this verse as an allusion to the false prophets who made me love their idol worship. הֵמָּה רִמּוּנִי, *they deceived me*, by incessantly uttering false prophecies of reassurance decrying Jeremiah's calls for repentance, until they caused me to go into exile.

20. רְאֵה ה׳ — *See,* HASHEM. [This verse begins with a supplication to God to bear witness to the extent of Zion's affliction, and culminates with an appeal (verse 22)

בְּקִרְבִּי כִּי מָרוֹ מָרִיתִי מִחוּץ שִׁכְּלָה־חֶרֶב בַּבַּיִת

inside me, 〈 for 〈 I have utterly rebelled. 《 Outside 〈 cause bereavement 〈 did the sword, 《 indoors 〈

כַּמָּוֶת: כא שָׁמְעוּ כִּי נֶאֱנָחָה אָנִי* אֵין מְנַחֵם לִי

it was deathlike. 《 21 They heard 〈 that 〈 sighing 〈 I was,* 《 there was no one 〈 who could comfort 〈 me. 《

כָּל־אֹיְבַי שָׁמְעוּ רָעָתִי שָׂשׂוּ כִּי אַתָּה עָשִׂיתָ*

All 〈 my enemies 〈 heard 〈 of my plight 〈 and rejoiced, 《 for 〈 it was You 〈 Who caused this.* 《

הֵבֵאתָ יוֹם־קָרָאתָ וְיִהְיוּ כָמוֹנִי: כב תָּבֹא כָל־

[If only] you brought about 〈 the day 〈 You proclaimed, 《 so that they be [punished] 〈 like me! 《 22 Let there come 〈 all 〈

רָעָתָם לְפָנֶיךָ וְעוֹלֵל לָמוֹ כַּאֲשֶׁר עוֹלַלְתָּ לִי

their wickedness 〈 before You, 《 and do 〈 to them 〈 as 〈 You did 〈 to me 〈

עַל כָּל־פְּשָׁעָי כִּי־רַבּוֹת אַנְחֹתַי וְלִבִּי דַוָּי:

for 〈 all 〈 my transgressions. 《 For 〈 many 〈 are my sighs, 《 and my heart 〈 suffers. 《

[ב] א אֵיכָה יָעִיב בְּאַפּוֹ | אֲדֹנָי אֶת־בַּת־צִיּוֹן*

[2] 1 How is it that 〈 becloud 〈 in His anger 〈 the Lord does 〈 to 〈 the daughter 〈 of Zion? 《

הִשְׁלִיךְ מִשָּׁמַיִם אֶרֶץ תִּפְאֶרֶת יִשְׂרָאֵל* וְלֹא־זָכַר

He cast down 〈 from heaven 〈 to earth 〈 the glory 〈 of Israel.* 《 He did not remember 〈

---

for Divine retribution against the enemy.]

21. שָׁמְעוּ כִּי נֶאֱנָחָה אָנִי — *They heard that sighing I was. Those who love me* [referred to above in verses 2 and 19] heard me sigh and did not even comfort me; my real enemies, on the other hand, actually rejoiced upon hearing my plight, knowing You have caused it (*Ibn Ezra*).

כִּי אַתָּה עָשִׂיתָ — *For it was You Who caused this* [i.e., my misfortune emanated from Your will]. You are the cause of their hating us because You prohibited us from eating their food or marrying their children. Had we socialized and intermarried with them, would they not have compassion upon us and on their offspring? (*Midrash; Rashi*).

Lechem Dimah notes that here [unlike verse 12] Zion prays that the enemies be punished for rejoicing at her downfall. And lest anyone think that Zion might then rejoice at her enemies' downfall, the verse concludes: No, there is no room for rejoicing! *My groans are many, and my heart is sick.*

CHAPTER TWO

1. בַּת־צִיּוֹן — *The daughter of Zion.* A poetic form, used to denote Jerusalem; its populace.

הִשְׁלִיךְ מִשָּׁמַיִם אֶרֶץ תִּפְאֶרֶת יִשְׂרָאֵל — *He cast down from heaven to earth the glory of Israel.* After having raised up the Jews to the uppermost heavens, He cast them

הֲדֹם־רַגְלָיו* בְּיוֹם אַפּוֹ: ב בִּלַּע אֲדֹנָי° וְלֹא [°לא כ׳]

the stool ‹ for His feet* ‹ on the day ‹ of His wrath. « 2 The Lord destroyed ‹ and did not ‹

חָמַל אֵת כָּל־נְאוֹת יַעֲקֹב* הָרַס בְּעֶבְרָתוֹ מִבְצְרֵי

have pity ‹ on all ‹ the dwellings ‹ of Jacob;* « He razed ‹ in His anger ‹ the fortresses ‹

בַת־יְהוּדָה הִגִּיעַ לָאָרֶץ חִלֵּל מַמְלָכָה וְשָׂרֶיהָ:*

of the daughter ‹ of Judah; « He brought [them] down ‹ to the ground; « He defiled ‹ the kingdom ‹ and its officers.* «

ג גָּדַע* בָּחֳרִי־אַף כֹּל קֶרֶן יִשְׂרָאֵל הֵשִׁיב אָחוֹר

3 He cut down,* ‹ in burning ‹ anger, ‹ all ‹ the pride ‹ of Israel; « He drew ‹ back ‹

יְמִינוֹ מִפְּנֵי אוֹיֵב וַיִּבְעַר בְּיַעֲקֹב* כְּאֵשׁ לֶהָבָה

His right hand ‹ because of ‹ the enemy. « [His anger] burned ‹ through Jacob* ‹ like a fire ‹ that is flaming, «

אָכְלָה סָבִיב: ד דָּרַךְ קַשְׁתּוֹ כְּאוֹיֵב נִצָּב יְמִינוֹ

consuming ‹ on all sides. « 4 He bent ‹ His bow ‹ like an enemy; « poised ‹ was His right hand ‹

---

down to the nethermost depths — not gradually, but in one thrust (*Rashi*).

וְלֹא־זָכַר הֲדֹם־רַגְלָיו — *He did not remember the stool for His foot,* the בֵּית הַמִּקְדָּשׁ, *the Holy Temple* (*Midrash; Rashi*).

The *Midrash* notes, homiletically, that הֲדֹם, *footstool,* has the same spelling as הַדָּם, *the blood:* God in His anger preferred not to remember Abraham's blood of circumcision or the blood in which they wallowed in Egypt, and which they put on the doorposts there (II:1).

2. אֵת כָּל־נְאוֹת יַעֲקֹב — *All the dwellings of Jacob.* The *Midrash* homiletically translates נְאוֹת יַעֲקֹב, *the beauty of Jacob* — referring to the Torah Sages who were martyred during the Destruction.

חִלֵּל מַמְלָכָה וְשָׂרֶיהָ — *He defiled the kingdom and its officers.* This refers to Israel which is called מַמְלֶכֶת כֹּהֲנִים, *a kingdom of priests* (*Rashi*); also, to Zedekiah, king of Judah (*Midrash*).

3. גָּדַע — *He cut down,* i.e., the branches only, leaving the root intact so it could eventually grow back (*Lechem Dimah*).

The *Midrash* notes that when the enemy entered Jerusalem, they took the mighty men of Israel and bound their hands behind them. The Holy One, Blessed is He, saw their distress, so He, too — anthropomorphically — *withdrew His right hand behind Him* [i.e., symbolizing His endurance of the many indignities heaped upon His glory by the heathens, as if His hands, so to speak, were behind His back, powerless to avenge] (*Yefei Anaf*).

וַיִּבְעַר בְּיַעֲקֹב — *[His anger] burned through Jacob.* The *Midrash* comments: When punishment comes into the world, no one feels it as much as [the patriarch] Jacob; and when there is good in the world, no one rejoices as much as Jacob, i.e., Jacob feels it more keenly than the other patriarchs because he experienced the most tribulations in raising his family (*Torah Temimah*).

4. In this verse Hashem is depicted, not only in His passive role as One Who withdrew His support, but as One Who actively participated in Israel's destruction.

כְּצָר וַיַּהֲרֹג כֹּל מַחֲמַדֵּי־עָיִן* בְּאֹהֶל בַּת־צִיּוֹן

like a foe; He slew all who were of pleasant appearance.* In the tent of the daughter of Zion

שָׁפַךְ כָּאֵשׁ חֲמָתוֹ: ה הָיָה אֲדֹנָי | כְּאוֹיֵב* בִּלַּע

He poured out like fire His wrath. 5 The Lord became like an enemy.* He destroyed

יִשְׂרָאֵל בִּלַּע כָּל־אַרְמְנוֹתֶיהָ שִׁחֵת מִבְצָרָיו וַיֶּרֶב

Israel; He destroyed all [Jerusalem's] palaces, He destroyed [the nation's] fortresses. He multiplied

בְּבַת־יְהוּדָה תַּאֲנִיָּה וַאֲנִיָּה: ו וַיַּחְמֹס כַּגַּן* שֻׂכּוֹ*

within the daughter of Judah mourning and grief. 6 He cut down like a garden* His Tabernacle,*

שִׁחֵת מֹעֲדוֹ* שִׁכַּח יהוה | בְּצִיּוֹן מוֹעֵד וְשַׁבָּת*

He destroyed His meeting place.* HASHEM caused to be forgotten in Zion festivals and Sabbaths,

וַיִּנְאַץ בְּזַעַם־אַפּוֹ מֶלֶךְ וְכֹהֵן: ז זָנַח אֲדֹנָי | מִזְבְּחוֹ*

and He scorned in the wrath of His anger king and Kohen. 7 The Lord rejected His altar,*

וַיַּהֲרֹג כֹּל מַחֲמַדֵּי־עָיִן — *He slew all who were of pleasant appearance.*

Rav Tanchum ben Yirmiyah said this refers to the children who were as dear to their parents as the apple of their eye. The Rabbis said this refers to the members of the Sanhedrin who were as dear to Israel as the apple of their eye (*Midrash*).

5\. הָיָה ה׳ כְּאוֹיֵב... — *The Lord became like an enemy...* After all of the above, the Jews did not repent. Still, God restrained Himself. The verse *likens* His anger to that of an enemy, but He did not *become* an enemy. Also, בִּלַּע יִשְׂרָאֵל, *He destroyed Israel*, but not כָּל יִשְׂרָאֵל, *all of Israel;* בִּלַּע כָּל־אַרְמְנוֹתֶיהָ, *He destroyed all [Jerusalem's palaces];* and thus vented His anger by directing His actions עַל עֵצִים וַאֲבָנִים, *on wood and stone* [on inanimate objects, rather than on human lives], so as to avoid the total slaughter of the Jews themselves (*Palgei Mayim*).

6\. וַיַּחְמֹס כַּגַּן שֻׂכּוֹ — *He cut down like a garden His Tabernacle. His Tabernacle,* related to סֻכָּה, *sukkah* (*Ibn Ezra*), His dwelling place (*Rashi*) — the קֹדֶשׁ קָדָשִׁים, *Holy of Holies* (*Palgei Mayim*).

The *Midrash* notes that the word for Tabernacle, שֻׂכּוֹ [*sukko*], can be read שֻׁכּוֹ [*shukko*], *His appeasement*: when He cut down [Jerusalem] as one cuts down a garden, שֶׁכָּכָה חֲמָתוֹ שֶׁל הקב״ה, *God's wrath was appeased* [having vented His anger on wood and stone].

כַּגַּן — *Like a garden.* As one cuts vegetables in a garden. Jerusalem became like a garden which had been deprived of its water (*Midrash*) [and nothing looks as desolate as a garden stripped of its plants].

שִׁחֵת מֹעֲדוֹ — *He destroyed His meeting place,* the קֹדֶשׁ קָדָשִׁים, *the Holiest of the Holies,* where God *presents Himself* [נועד] to His children [*Exodus* 25:22] (*Rashi*).

שִׁכַּח ה׳ בְּצִיּוֹן מוֹעֵד וְשַׁבָּת — *HASHEM caused to be forgotten in Zion festivals and Sabbaths* [as a result of God's destruction of the Temple and sacrifices, it was as if the festivals and Sabbath were forgotten].

7\. זָנַח ה׳ מִזְבְּחוֹ — *The Lord rejected His altar.* The Holy One, Blessed is He, said

נִאֵר מִקְדָּשׁוֹ הִסְגִּיר בְּיַד־אוֹיֵב חוֹמֹת אַרְמְנוֹתֶיהָ

He repudiated ‹ His Sanctuary; « He handed over ‹ into the hand ‹ of the enemy ‹ the walls ‹ of her palaces. «

קוֹל נָתְנוּ בְּבֵית־יהוה כְּיוֹם מוֹעֵד:* ח חָשַׁב יהוה |

A tumult ‹ they raised ‹ in the House ‹ of HASHEM ‹ as on the day ‹ of a festival.* «

8 HASHEM resolved ‹

לְהַשְׁחִית* חוֹמַת בַּת־צִיּוֹן נָטָה קָו לֹא־הֵשִׁיב

to destroy* ‹ the wall ‹ of the daughter ‹ of Zion. « He stretched out ‹ the [surveyor's] line ‹ and did not ‹ hold back ‹

יָדוֹ מִבַּלֵּעַ וַיַּאֲבֶל־חֵל וְחוֹמָה יַחְדָּו אֻמְלָלוּ:

His hand ‹ from destroying. « He made to mourn ‹ rampart ‹ and wall; « together ‹ they crumble. «

ט טָבְעוּ בָאָרֶץ שְׁעָרֶיהָ* אִבַּד וְשִׁבַּר בְּרִיחֶיהָ

9 Sunk ‹ into the earth ‹ have her gates,* « He has demolished ‹ and shattered ‹ her bars. «

מַלְכָּהּ וְשָׂרֶיהָ בַגּוֹיִם אֵין תּוֹרָה* גַּם־נְבִיאֶיהָ

Her king ‹ and her officers ‹ are among the nations ‹ without ‹ Torah;* « even ‹ her prophets ‹

---

to Israel: Do you provoke Me because you rely on the sacrifices which you offer to Me? Here, have them! They are thrown in your face (*Midrash*).

כְּיוֹם מוֹעֵד — *As on the day of a festival.* The heathens clamored joyously at the destruction of the Temple, matching the fervor of Israel's joyous chants on its holiday (*Alshich; Rashi*).

8. חָשַׁב ה׳ לְהַשְׁחִית — *HASHEM resolved to destroy.* The *Midrash* explains that the resolve was not new — but an old one, as it is written: כִּי עַל־אַפִּי וְעַל־חֲמָתִי הָיְתָה לִּי הָעִיר הַזֹּאת לְמִן־הַיּוֹם אֲשֶׁר בָּנוּ אוֹתָהּ, *For this city [Jerusalem] has aroused My anger and My wrath in Me from the day that they built it* (*Jer.* 32:31) [and God, in a sense, restrained Himself until then].

9. טָבְעוּ בָאָרֶץ שְׁעָרֶיהָ — *Sunk into the earth have her gates.* According to the *Midrash* the gates sunk into the ground [i.e., miraculously, and were not destroyed by the enemy], because when Solomon brought the אֲרוֹן הַבְּרִית, *Ark of the Covenant,* into Jerusalem, the gates paid honor to the Ark by rising to allow the Ark to enter [*Shabbos* 30a]. *Rashi* adds that the gates were invulnerable to the enemy because they were the handiwork of King David [*Sotah* 9a].

Minchas Shai explains that the ט, *tes,* of טָבְעוּ, *sunk,* is small to allude to ט, *the Ninth,* of Av when the Temple was destroyed.

אֵין תּוֹרָה — *Without Torah;* with no one to provide religious instruction (*Rashi*). [All the most important people — king, princes, priests — in whose hands lay the religious administration of the country are either gone or not functioning.]

Most commentators and the *Midrash* attach this clause to the preceding and translate: *Her king and her officers are among the nations where there is no Torah.* Hence, the *Midrash* concludes: Should a person tell you there is חָכְמָה, *wisdom,* among the nations, believe it; but if he tells you there is Torah among the nations, do not believe it.

לֹא־מָצְאוּ חָזוֹן מֵיהוָה: י יֵשְׁבוּ לָאָרֶץ יִדְּמוּ* זִקְנֵי

did not ‹ find ‹ a vision ‹ from HASHEM. » 10 They sit ‹ on the ground, ‹ they are silent* » — the elders ‹

בַת־צִיּוֹן הֶעֱלוּ עָפָר עַל־רֹאשָׁם חָגְרוּ שַׂקִּים הוֹרִידוּ

of the daughter ‹ of Zion; » they have brought up ‹ ashes ‹ onto ‹ their heads, ‹ they donned ‹ sack-cloths. » Lowered ‹

לָאָרֶץ רֹאשָׁן בְּתוּלֹת יְרוּשָׁלָם: יא כָּלוּ בַדְּמָעוֹת

to the ground ‹ their heads, ‹ [have] the maidens ‹ of Jerusalem. » 11 Exhausted ‹ of tears ‹

עֵינַי חֳמַרְמְרוּ מֵעַי נִשְׁפַּךְ לָאָרֶץ כְּבֵדִי עַל־שֶׁבֶר

are my eyes, » churned ‹ are my insides, » spilled out ‹ onto the ground ‹ is my liver, » at ‹ the shattering ‹

בַּת־עַמִּי בֵּעָטֵף עוֹלֵל וְיוֹנֵק בִּרְחֹבוֹת קִרְיָה:

of the daughter ‹ of my people, » while they faint » — infants ‹ and nursing children [do] — » in the streets ‹ of the City. »

יב לְאִמֹּתָם יֹאמְרוּ* אַיֵּה דָּגָן וָיָיִן* בְּהִתְעַטְּפָם כֶּחָלָל

12 To their mothers ‹ they say:* » *Where is there* ‹ *grain* ‹ *and wine?** » as they lose consciousness ‹ like a dying man ‹

בִּרְחֹבוֹת עִיר בְּהִשְׁתַּפֵּךְ נַפְשָׁם אֶל־חֵיק אִמֹּתָם:

in the streets ‹ of the town, » as ebb away ‹ does their soul ‹ in ‹ the bosom ‹ of their mothers. »

---

10. In this verse, the prophet depicts the elders — who no longer have a worldly occupation to keep them occupied, and who have suffered and endured so much — mourning for Zion. They have no words, no prayers, only silent resignation. Note also the poetic contrast between the זְקֵנִים, *elders*, and בְּתוּלוֹת, *maidens*, as depicting the extremes of the population spectrum (*Kol Yaakov; Lechem Dimah*).

יֵשְׁבוּ לָאָרֶץ יִדְּמוּ — *They sit on the ground, they are silent.* [The Biblical classic form of mourning includes strewing dust on the head, wearing sackcloth, and bowing the head.]

This verse is cited as a basis for the halachic custom of sitting on the ground on Tishah B'Av. The 12th-century *Sefer HaEshkol* says: After the final meal, we go to the synagogue without shoes and sit on the ground, as it is written: *They sit on the ground, they are silent.*

11. [In a personal interjection of special grief, the prophet laments the tragic sight of children languishing from hunger in the streets.]

12. לְאִמֹּתָם יֹאמְרוּ — *To their mothers they* [the swooning children mentioned in the last verse] *say.*

אַיֵּה דָּגָן וָיָיִן — *Where is there grain and wine?*

It is obvious that fine grain (bread) and good wine were not available during the siege, and the verse could not be suggesting that the children seriously expected to receive these foods during the famine; the children would have been satisfied with any morsels of food to still their hunger pangs. Rather, as they swooned from hunger, they beseeched their mothers, remembering their past comforts, and saying, *"What happened to the fine food which*

יג מָה־°אֲעִידֵךְ [°אעודך כ׳] מָה אֲדַמֶּה־לָּךְ* הַבַּת

‹ O daughter « to you,* ‹ can I compare ‹ What « can I bear witness for you? ‹ About what 13

יְרוּשָׁלַםִ מָה אַשְׁוֶה־לָּךְ וַאֲנַחֲמֵךְ* בְּתוּלַת בַּת־צִיּוֹן

« of Zion? ‹ daughter ‹ O maiden ‹ and [thereby] comfort you,* ‹ to you ‹ can I equate ‹ What « of Jerusalem?

כִּי־גָדוֹל כַּיָּם שִׁבְרֵךְ מִי יִרְפָּא־לָךְ׃ יד נְבִיאַיִךְ*

‹ Your prophets* 14 « you? ‹ can heal ‹ who « is your ruin; ‹ as the sea ‹ vast ‹ For

חָזוּ לָךְ שָׁוְא וְתָפֵל וְלֹא־גִלּוּ עַל־עֲוֺנֵךְ לְהָשִׁיב

‹ to bring you back ‹ your iniquity, ‹ about ‹ and they did not expose [to you] « and foolish things, ‹ useless ‹ for you ‹ envisioned

°שְׁבוּתֵךְ [°שביתך כ׳] וַיֶּחֱזוּ לָךְ מַשְׂאוֹת שָׁוְא

‹ of uselessness ‹ visions ‹ to you ‹ they prophesied « from your waywardness;

וּמַדּוּחִים׃ טו סָפְקוּ עָלַיִךְ כַּפַּיִם* כָּל־עֹבְרֵי דָּרֶךְ

« on the way; ‹ those who pass ‹— [did] all « their hands [in dismay]* ‹ because of you ‹ They slapped 15 « and deception.

שָׁרְקוּ וַיָּנִעוּ רֹאשָׁם* עַל־בַּת יְרוּשָׁלָםִ הֲזֹאת

‹ *Is this* « of Jerusalem, [saying:] ‹ the daughter ‹ at ‹ their head* ‹ and they shook ‹ they whistled

---

you used to feed us?" (*Lechem Dimah*).

13. מָה־אֲעִידֵךְ מָה אֲדַמֶּה־לָּךְ — *About what can I bear witness for you? What can I compare to you?* What instance can I cite of any other nation that suffered a calamity equal to yours? (*Zohar; Alshich*).

The *Midrash*, interpreting the verb אֲעִידֵךְ, *witness*, by its other meaning, *warn*, translates: [God said:] How many prophets did I send to warn you [of the consequences of your evil ways]? I.e., what more could I have done for you? (*Torah Temimah*).

מָה אַשְׁוֶה־לָּךְ וַאֲנַחֲמֵךְ — *What can I equate to you and thereby comfort you?* Whose suffering and circumstances can be likened to yours, so that you can be comforted by the comparison? (*Lechem Dimah*).

Human nature is such that in times of trouble one finds comfort in hearing of others who experienced similar tribulations (*Rashi*) (II:12).

14. נְבִיאַיִךְ — *Your prophets*, i.e., those prophets — whom you believed to have the most spiritual and moral insight — prophesied falsely, and whitewashed your iniquities, soothing you into self-righteousness by indulging in deceptive oracles (*Rav Arama*).

Alshich concludes: Not only did your prophets not reprimand you for your transgressions, they actually led you astray from God with their vain and deceptive prophecies. Indeed, who can heal such a nation? And if you expect to derive comfort from passersby who will see your suffering and commiserate with you, you are sadly mistaken ... [see *Alshich* next verse].

15. סָפְקוּ עָלַיִךְ כַּפַּיִם ... שָׁרְקוּ וַיָּנִעוּ רֹאשָׁם — *They slapped because of you their hands . . . they whistled and they shook their head* — upon witnessing your disaster (*Kiflayim L'Sushiyah*).

... In mock and derision, not over your

הָעִיר* שֶׁיֹּאמְרוּ כְּלִילַת יֹפִי מָשׂוֹשׂ לְכָל־הָאָרֶץ:

« the Earth? ‹ for all ‹ a joy « of beauty, ‹ is the perfection ‹ that they say ‹ the city

טז פָּצוּ* עָלַיִךְ פִּיהֶם כָּל־אֹיְבַיִךְ שָׁרְקוּ וַיַּחַרְקוּ־שֵׁן

«their teeth. ‹ and they gnashed ‹ they whistled « your enemies; ‹ — [did] all « their mouths ‹ because of you ‹ They opened wide* 16

אָמְרוּ בִּלָּעְנוּ אַךְ זֶה הַיּוֹם שֶׁקִּוִּינֻהוּ מָצָאנוּ רָאִינוּ:*

« we have seen [it]! ‹ we have found [it], « that we hoped for; ‹ is the day ‹ this ‹ Indeed, « We have destroyed [her]! « They said,*

יז עָשָׂה יהוה אֲשֶׁר זָמָם* בִּצַּע אֶמְרָתוֹ אֲשֶׁר

‹ which ‹ His decree ‹ He carried out « He planned; ‹ what ‹ HASHEM has done 17

צִוָּה מִימֵי־קֶדֶם* הָרַס וְלֹא חָמָל וַיְשַׂמַּח עָלַיִךְ

‹ because of you ‹ He brought rejoicing « show pity. ‹ and did not ‹ He devastated « ancient;* ‹ from days ‹ He ordained

---

loss, Jerusalem, but for themselves, as the Sages proclaimed: Had the heathens known how much they would lose by destroying the Temple, they would not have done it. The Divine blessing that had rested upon the entire world left with the Destruction (*Alshich*).

[*Rashi* implies that this verse refers to a sincere manifestation of grief which one naturally expresses upon seeing such a precipitous decline in someone who was once great. Perhaps, in this light, we can differentiate between this verse and the next. In this verse the prophet laments the fact that Zion's state is so lamentable that *all* neutral *passersby* will be sincerely moved to commiserate at the great loss. The next verse, however, speaks of the confirmed אוֹיֵב, *enemy*, who jeers and gnashes his teeth, openly displaying *joy* at her present condition.]

הֲזֹאת הָעִיר... — *Is this the city...?* [This is what the passersby are moved to say, remembering her past glory, and seeing her in her present state of destruction.]

16. פָּצוּ — *They opened wide.* [*Lamentations* is written in the form of an alphabetical acrostic, but in this chapter, and also in chapters 3 and 4, the verse beginning with פ precedes that of ע. The name of the letter פ means mouth; the name of the letter ע means eye.] Rashi notes: Why did he place the פ before the ע? Because they [the Spies — (*Sanhedrin* 104b; see also comm. to 1:2)] spoke with their mouths what they had not seen with their eyes [thus putting one before the other].

According to *Lechem Dimah, Rashi* is referring [not to the Spies as in *Sanhedrin,* 104b, but] to the enemies who cast diatribes at Israel long before the actual Destruction took place. Hence, the sequence of the verses: First, פָּצוּ, *All your enemies jeered at you,* then, עָשָׂה ה׳ ... הָרַס, *HASHEM has done ... He devasted.*

מָצָאנוּ רָאִינוּ — *We have found it, we have seen it.* The *Arizal* explains that the enemy had hoped for the day when they could burn the Temple themselves. They were disappointed because *"we found it, we saw it,"* they found that God had already sent down the fire that burned the Temple [see commentary 1:13].

17. עָשָׂה ה׳ אֲשֶׁר זָמָם — *HASHEM has done what He planned.*

Although most human plans are never executed, God's resolve was carried through in its entirety (*Lechem Dimah*).

אֲשֶׁר צִוָּה מִימֵי־קֶדֶם — *Which He ordained from days ancient.* According to *Rashi*

אוֹיֵב* הֵרִים קֶרֶן צָרָיִךְ׃ יח צָעַק לִבָּם אֶל־אֲדֹנָי

to the enemy;* « He raised up ‹ the pride ‹ of your foes. « 18 Cry out ‹ did their heart ‹ to ‹ the Lord. «

חוֹמַת בַּת־צִיּוֹן הוֹרִידִי כַנַּחַל דִּמְעָה יוֹמָם וָלַיְלָה

O wall ‹ of the daughter ‹ of Zion: « Shed ‹ like a river ‹ tears, ‹ day ‹ and night; «

אַל־תִּתְּנִי פוּגַת לָךְ אַל־תִּדֹּם בַּת־עֵינֵךְ׃* יט קוּמִי |

do not ‹ give ‹ respite ‹ to yourself, « let not ‹ be still ‹ the pupil ‹ of your eyes.* « 19 Arise, ‹

רֹנִּי °בַלַּיְלָה [°בליל כ׳]* לְרֹאשׁ אַשְׁמֻרוֹת* שִׁפְכִי

cry out ‹ at night* ‹ at the beginning ‹ of the watches!* « Pour out ‹

כַמַּיִם לִבֵּךְ נֹכַח פְּנֵי אֲדֹנָי* שְׂאִי אֵלָיו כַּפַּיִךְ׃

like water ‹ your heart ‹ before ‹ the Presence ‹ of the Lord;* « lift up ‹ to Him ‹ your hands [in prayer] «

עַל־נֶפֶשׁ עוֹלָלַיִךְ* הָעֲטוּפִים בְּרָעָב בְּרֹאשׁ כָּל־

for ‹ the life ‹ of your young children,* « who faint ‹ from hunger ‹ at the head ‹ of every ‹

---

this refers to the warnings in the Torah of the dire results of disobedience (e.g., *Leviticus* 26:27).

וַיְשַׂמַּח עָלַיִךְ אוֹיֵב — *He brought rejoicing because of you to the enemy.* God Himself rejoices with Israel when good befalls them; but when anything bad befalls them, He lets others do the rejoicing (*Midrash*).

18. אַל־תִּתְּנִי פוּגַת לָךְ אַל־תִּדֹּם בַּת־עֵינֵךְ — *Do not give respite to yourself, let not be still the pupil of your eye.*

"The greatest sin of all is that we, in our time, stopped mourning properly for Jerusalem. I am convinced that, in punishment for this, our exile has lasted so long, we have never been able to find rest, and we are always being persecuted. Historically, whenever we found some security in any of the lands of our exile, we forgot Jerusalem and did not place it at the foremost place in our minds" (*Rav Yaakov Emden*).

19. [This verse is a continuation of the last, in which the prophet exhorts the sufferers to pray unrestrainedly to God.]

בַלַּיְלָה — *At night.* [See commentary on 1:2.]

Midrash Lekach Tov comments that *night* refers to the night of Tishah B'Av which should be observed annually as an eve of weeping and lamentation.

The כְּתִיב, *written form,* of the *night* is לֵיל, and refers to the earlier part of the evening, which is the רֹאשׁ אַשְׁמֻרוֹת, *beginning of the first two watches,* and is the most effective time (*Lechem Dimah*).

לְרֹאשׁ אַשְׁמֻרוֹת — *At the beginning of the watches,* the night being divided into three equal *watches* (*Rashi*).

שִׁפְכִי כַמַּיִם לִבֵּךְ נֹכַח פְּנֵי ה׳ — *Pour out like water your heart before the Presence of the Lord.* And confess your guilt (*Ibn Yachya*).

Wherever *Hashem's* name appears as אדני, it refers to the *Shechinah.* Therefore, first *pour out* your heart like water at the 'departure' of the *Shechinah,* and then pray for the *life of your infants,* i.e., for your own needs (*Lechem Dimah*).

עַל־נֶפֶשׁ עוֹלָלַיִךְ — *For the life* [lit., *soul*] *of your young children.* Most commentators understand *children* literally, referring to

חוּצוֹת׃ כ רְאֵה יהוה וְהַבִּיטָה לְמִי עוֹלַלְתָּ כֹּה אִם־

street. » **20** Look, ‹ HASHEM, ‹ and behold, » to whom ‹ You have done ‹ so. » How can it be ‹

תֹּאכַלְנָה נָשִׁים פִּרְיָם* עֹלְלֵי טִפֻּחִים* אִם־יֵהָרֵג

[that] women eat ‹ their own offspring,* ‹ the young children ‹ that they care for?* » How can it be ‹ [that] there be slain ‹

בְּמִקְדַּשׁ אֲדֹנָי כֹּהֵן וְנָבִיא׃ כא שָׁכְבוּ לָאָרֶץ חוּצוֹת

in the Sanctuary ‹ of the Lord ‹ a Kohen ‹ and a prophet? » **21** They lie ‹ on the ground ‹ in the streets »

נַעַר וְזָקֵן בְּתוּלֹתַי וּבַחוּרַי נָפְלוּ בֶחָרֶב הָרַגְתָּ

— the youth ‹ and the old man [do]; » my maidens ‹ and my young men ‹ have fallen ‹ by the sword. » You slew [them] ‹

בְּיוֹם אַפֶּךָ טָבַחְתָּ לֹא חָמָלְתָּ׃* כב תִּקְרָא כְיוֹם

on the day ‹ of Your wrath; » You slaughtered [them] ‹ and You did not show pity.* » **22** You summoned, ‹ as if on a day ‹

---

the starving children in verses 11 and 12. *Midrash Lekach Tov* seems to understand it as the fainting children [citizens] of personified Jerusalem — who had been exiled בְּרֹאשׁ כָּל־חוּצוֹת, in foreign heathen countries [בְּחוּץ לָאָרֶץ] throughout the world.

Lechem Dimah interprets the verse: *Pour out like water your heart in the Presence of the Lord*, and if that is ineffective because your merits are insufficient, then *lift up to Him your hands as if* you were praying for *the life of your young children who faint* etc.

20. [In this verse, the thoughts of the prophet revert to Hashem.]

אִם־תֹּאכַלְנָה נָשִׁים פִּרְיָם — *How can it be [that] women eat their own offspring?* An incredulous question: Has it ever happened to any other nation that their afflictions should result in the ghastly extreme of mothers eating their offspring, עֹלְלֵי טִפֻּחִים, *the young children that they care for*, whom they previously fondled and cared for like all compassionate mothers? Is such a thing right? (*Alshich; Palgei Mayim*).

Wouldn't it have been sufficient to let them die from starvation without having their mothers eat them? (*Ibn Yachya*).

[Apparently, not only mothers were reduced to such a state of cruelty:] Rav Yochanan said: Fathers, too, ate the flesh of their sons and daughters at the Destruction of both the First and Second Temples. Jeremiah lamented this horror by crying, *"Therefore shall fathers eat the sons in your midst, and the sons shall eat their fathers"* [Ezek. 5:10] (*Pesikta Rabbasi*).

עֹלְלֵי טִפֻּחִים — *The young children that they care for*, objects of their caressing (*Ibn Ezra*).

The *Talmud* relates the incident of a child, Doeg ben Yosef, whose father died and he was left in his mother's care. Everyday she would lovingly measure him בְּטְפָחֶהָ, *with her handbreadth*, and give his [extra] weight in gold to the Temple. When the enemy prevailed, however, she slaughtered him and ate him. It was to her that Jeremiah referred when he lamented to God: *How can it be [that] women eat their own offspring*, עֹלְלֵי טִפֻּחִים, *the young children they measured by handbreadths?* [A play on *tipuchim — that they care for; caressed* — read as *tefuchim — measured by handbreadths* — as a sign of love, as in this story] (*Yoma* 38b; *Midrash; Rashi*).

21. הָרַגְתָּ בְּיוֹם אַפֶּךָ טָבַחְתָּ לֹא חָמָלְתָּ — *You slew [them] on the day of Your wrath; You*

מוֹעֵד* מְגוּרַי מִסָּבִיב וְלֹא הָיָה בְּיוֹם אַף־יְהֹוָה

of a festival,* ‹ those who live near me ‹ all around. « And there was not ‹ on the day ‹ of the wrath ‹ of HASHEM ‹

פָּלִיט וְשָׂרִיד אֲשֶׁר־טִפַּחְתִּי וְרִבִּיתִי אֹיְבִי כִלָּם׃

anyone who escaped ‹ or who survived. « Those whom ‹ I took care of ‹ and I raised, ‹ my enemy ‹ has annihilated them. «

[ג] א אֲנִי הַגֶּבֶר* רָאָה עֳנִי בְּשֵׁבֶט עֶבְרָתוֹ׃ ב אוֹתִי

[3] 1 I ‹ am the man* ‹ who has seen ‹ affliction ‹ by the rod ‹ of His anger. « 2 Me ‹

נָהַג וַיֹּלַךְ חֹשֶׁךְ וְלֹא־אוֹר׃ ג אַךְ בִּי* יָשֻׁב יַהֲפֹךְ

has He driven ‹ and led ‹ into darkness ‹ without ‹ light. « 3 Only ‹ against me* ‹ did He repeatedly ‹ turn ‹

יָדוֹ* כָּל־הַיּוֹם׃ ד בִּלָּה בְשָׂרִי וְעוֹרִי* שִׁבַּר עַצְמוֹתָי׃

His hand* ‹ all ‹ day long. « 4 He has worn away ‹ my flesh ‹ and my skin;* « He broke ‹ my bones. «

---

slaughtered them and did not show pity.

Had the Destruction come on a day other than *the day of Your wrath,* i.e., Tishah B'Av, it would have been tempered with mercy and restraint. Having come on the day You specifically set aside for display of Your anger, it was untempered and complete (*Lechem Dimah*).

22. כְּיוֹם מוֹעֵד — *As if on a day of a festival.* The enemy's swarming over Jerusalem and the Temple was reminiscent of the throngs of Jewish pilgrims who would swarm into Jerusalem on the festivals (*Ibn Shuib*).

CHAPTER THREE

1. אֲנִי הַגֶּבֶר — *I am the man.* Jeremiah, in a personal statement, laments that he saw more affliction than all the other prophets who foretold the Destruction of the Temple. For it was destroyed not in their days, but in his (*Rashi*). (It had been noted that the numerical value of אֲנִי הַגֶּבֶר, *I am the man* [=271], equals יִרְמְיָהוּ, *Jeremiah* [*Tzfunos Yisrael*]).

[Chapter 3 is composed of a triple acrostic. It is written in the form of three-verse units, each verse beginning with the same letter.]

2. [In the verses 2-16 the sufferer proceeds to describe his suffering figuratively in a series of more or less isolated pictures. The translation, which already incorporates much of the exegesis of the Sages, makes the verses, for the most part, readily understandable. The commentary, in this chapter, has therefore been intended mainly to remove surface difficulties.]

3. אַךְ בִּי — *Only against me,* I alone am the constant recipient of His punishment (*Rashi*).

Sifsei Chachamim personifies the phrase as referring specifically to Jeremiah: *On no prophet but me* [see comm. 3:1].

All nations sin but toward no other nation is God so zealous in exacting retribution as toward Israel (*Rav Yosef Kara*).

יָשֻׁב יַהֲפֹךְ יָדוֹ — *Did He repeatedly turn His hand.* In punishment, anthropomorphically, as if — so to speak — He wants the punishment to be constant; when one hand tires, He uses the other (*Toras Chesed*).

Alshich translates: He removed His compassionate hand [i.e., His protection] from me.

4. [The verse speaks of man's total physical suffering:]

בִּלָּה בְשָׂרִי וְעוֹרִי — *He has worn away my flesh and my skin.* The flesh and skin — which are sensitive to pain — He wore

ה בָּנָה עָלַי וַיַּקַּף רֹאשׁ וּתְלָאָה: ו בְּמַחֲשַׁכִּים

5 He built [a siege tower] ‹ against me ‹ and encircled [me] ‹ with bitterness ‹ and hardship. « 6 In utter darkness ‹

הוֹשִׁיבַנִי כְּמֵתֵי עוֹלָם: ז גָּדַר בַּעֲדִי* וְלֹא אֵצֵא

He has placed me ‹ like those who are dead ‹ eternally. « 7 He has built a wall ‹ opposite me* ‹ so I cannot go out; «

הִכְבִּיד נְחָשְׁתִּי: ח גַּם כִּי אֶזְעַק וַאֲשַׁוֵּעַ* שָׂתַם

He has made weighty ‹ my copper [chains]. « 8 Even ‹ when ‹ I cry out ‹ and plead,* « He has shut out ‹

תְּפִלָּתִי:* ט גָּדַר דְּרָכַי בְּגָזִית נְתִיבֹתַי עִוָּה: י דֹּב

my prayer.* « 9 He has walled up ‹ my roads ‹ with hewn stones; « my paths ‹ He has made crooked. « 10 A bear ‹

אֹרֵב הוּא לִי* °אֲרִי [°אריה כ׳] בְּמִסְתָּרִים: יא דְּרָכַי

lying in ambush ‹ He is ‹ to me,* « a lion ‹ in hidden places. « 11 My paths ‹

---

away. The bones — which have no tactile sensation — He crushed (*Ibn Ezra*).

7. גָּדַר בַּעֲדִי — *He has built a wall opposite* [lit., *hedged*] *me.* The prophet alludes to our long exile. God has, in effect, walled us in, so that the dark exile imprisons us. The verses continue that he weighed us down with oppression and closed the door to our prayers (*Lechem Dimah*).

8. גַּם כִּי אֶזְעַק וַאֲשַׁוֵּעַ — *Even when I cry out and plead.* Rav Eliezer said: From the day the Temple was destroyed, the gates of prayer have been shut, as it is written: *Though I would cry out and plead, He shut out my prayer* (*Berachos* 32b).

This refers to insincere private prayer; public prayer or sincere private prayer is always accepted (*Torah Temimah*).

שָׂתַם תְּפִלָּתִי — *He has shut out my prayer* by closing the "windows" of Heaven (*Rashi*); and by placing an "iron barrier" between Him and Israel (*Mikdash Lekach Tov*).

The *Midrash* notes that prayers said with a congregation are more acceptable than those said alone or after the congregation has finished. [This is suggested by the fact that the word תְּפִלָּתִי, my *prayer*, is in the singular; this indicating that, had a quorum prayed, their supplication would have been heard (*Torah Temimah*).] If ten righteous men pray and a wicked person joins them, would Hashem say, "I refuse to hear their prayers because of this single wicked person"? But if a person comes after the congregation is finished, and stands alone in prayer, his every deed and thought is scrutinized.

10. דֹּב אֹרֵב הוּא לִי — *A bear lying in ambush He is to me.* [The verse does not make it clear who is referred to: God; or His delegate — the enemy.]

According to *Rashi*, the subject is the Holy One, Blessed is He, Who has become like a lurking bear.

The *Midrash* however, interprets *bear* as referring to Nebuchadnezzar or, prophetically, to Vespasian. *Lion* refers to Nebuzaradan [the general who made the final attack during the First Destruction], or to Trajan [the conquering general during the Second Destruction].

According to many commentators (*Alshich; Ibn Yachya; Kol Yehudah*), the verse refers to the enemy who lay in hiding ready to pounce upon Israel without warning.

סוֹרֵר וַיְפַשְּׁחֵנִי שָׂמַנִי שֹׁמֵם: יב דָּרַךְ קַשְׁתּוֹ

He has strewn with thorns / and split me open; / He made me / desolate. / **12** He bent / his bow

וַיַּצִּיבֵנִי* כַּמַּטָּרָא לַחֵץ: יג הֵבִיא בְּכִלְיוֹתָי בְּנֵי

and set me up* / as a target / for the arrow. / **13** He shot / into my kidneys / the arrows

אַשְׁפָּתוֹ: יד הָיִיתִי שְּׂחֹק לְכָל־עַמִּי* נְגִינָתָם כָּל־

of His quiver. / **14** I have become / a laughingstock / to all / the peoples;* / [the theme of] their songs / all

הַיּוֹם:* טו הִשְׂבִּיעַנִי בַמְּרוֹרִים הִרְוַנִי לַעֲנָה: טז וַיַּגְרֵס

day long.* / **15** He sated me / with bitter [herbs], / filled me up / with wormwood. / **16** He shattered

בֶּחָצָץ שִׁנָּי הִכְפִּישַׁנִי בָּאֵפֶר:* יז וַתִּזְנַח מִשָּׁלוֹם

with gravel / my teeth, / He forced me down / into ashes.* / **17** Rejected / from achieving peace

נַפְשִׁי נָשִׁיתִי טוֹבָה: יח וָאֹמַר אָבַד נִצְחִי וְתוֹחַלְתִּי

was my soul, / I have forgotten / goodness. / **18** And I said: / *Gone* / *is my world* / *and my expectation*

מֵיהוה: יט זְכָר־עָנְיִי וּמְרוּדִי לַעֲנָה וָרֹאשׁ:

from HASHEM. / **19** Remember / my affliction / and my sorrow, / the wormwood / and bitter gall.

---

12. דָּרַךְ קַשְׁתּוֹ וַיַּצִּיבֵנִי — *He bent his bow and set me up. Lechem Dimah* notes that the order is reversed. Usually one first sets up his target and then takes aim. The verse implies the enemy kept him in constant terror by keeping his bow bent and aimed at him.

[Being *walled in so he could not get out* and *walled up with hewn stones,* as described in verses 7-9, he was certainly an easy target!]

14. הָיִיתִי שְׂחֹק לְכָל־עַמִּי — *I have become a laughingstock to all my people* [i.e., an object of derision]. עַמִּי, *my people,* is explained as: The people in whose midst I dwell (*Lechem Dimah*).

The *Targum* translates: פְּרִיצֵי, *the impudent (scorners) of my nation.*

The *Midrash* explains this as referring to "the nations of the world who sit in theaters and circuses. After they eat and drink and become intoxicated, they sit and discuss me, scoffing at me."

According to *Palgei Mayim,* Jeremiah is lamenting how, whenever he prophesied oracles of reproof and impending disaster, the Jews would laugh and taunt him. Because of their inattentiveness to his prophecies, disaster fell.

נְגִינָתָם כָּל־הַיּוֹם — *Their songs all day long* [I became the theme of their satirical songs].

15. The *Midrash,* linking בַמְּרוֹרִים with מָרוֹר, *the bitter herbs,* eaten at the Passover *Seder,* notes that the night of the week on which the first day of Passover occurs is always the same as the night on which Tishah B'Av falls.

16. הִכְפִּישַׁנִי בָּאֵפֶר — *He forced me down into ashes,* He covered me with ashes (*Rashi*).

כ זָכֹ֤ור תִּזְכּ֔וֹר °וְתָשׁ֥וֹחַ [°ותשיח כ׳] עָלַ֖י נַפְשִֽׁי׃

« is my soul. ‹ upon me ‹ and bent over « [My soul] remembers [this] well, 20

כא זֹ֛את אָשִׁ֥יב אֶל־לִבִּ֖י* עַל־כֵּ֥ן אוֹחִֽיל׃ כב חַֽסְדֵ֤י

‹ The kindness 22 « I have hope: ‹ [and] therefore ‹ my heart, ‹ to ‹ I take ‹ This 21

יהוה֙ כִּ֣י לֹא־תָ֔מְנוּ* כִּ֥י לֹא־כָל֖וּ רַחֲמָֽיו׃ כג חֲדָשִׁים֙

‹ they are new 23 « is His mercy; ‹ exhausted ‹ not ‹ that « it has not ended; ‹ — it is certain that « of HASHEM

לַבְּקָרִ֔ים* רַבָּ֖ה אֱמוּנָתֶֽךָ׃* כד חֶלְקִ֤י יהוה֙ אָמְרָ֣ה

‹ says « is *HASHEM,* ‹ *My portion* 24 « is Your faithfulness.* ‹ great « every morning;*

The *Talmud* relates that on the eve of Tishah B'Av, after Rav would complete his regular meal, he would dip a morsel of bread into ashes and say, "This is the essence of the Erev Tishah B'Av meal, in fulfillment of the verse: ... *He forced me down into ashes*" (*Yerushalmi Taanis* 4:6).

20. The *Midrash* translates: זָכוֹר תִּזְכּוֹר, *You will surely remember* [O God,] the nations of the world and will punish them for oppressing me, but while waiting for the vengeance, תָשׁוֹחַ עָלַי נַפְשִׁי, *my soul is despondent* [I haven't the patience to wait any longer]. A proverb declares: While the fat one grows lean, the lean one expires.

21. זֹאת אָשִׁיב אֶל־לִבִּי — [Yet,] *this I bear in mind.* After my heart told me that it *lost its expectation from* HASHEM [verse 18], I bore this in mind and thus restored my faith (*Rashi*).

[Verses 19-21 represent the transition from the despair (which culminates in verse 18) and the doctrine of hope which is achieved by recalling God's mercy in verses 22-38.]

In the time to come when the era of redemption arrives, God will say to Israel, "My sons, I wonder how you waited for Me all these years." And they will answer, "Lord of the universe, had it not been for Your Torah which You gave us, the heathen peoples would long ago have caused us to perish."

Therefore, it is stated: זֹאת אָשִׁיב אֶל־לִבִּי, *This I take to my heart,* and זֹאת, *this,* indicates nothing else than the Torah, as it is said וְזֹאת הַתּוֹרָה, *And this is the Torah* [*Deut.* 4:44] (*Midrash*).

22. [This verse begins the expression of faith and hope alluded to in the previous verse and continues through verse 38.]

חַסְדֵי ה׳ כִּי לֹא־תָמְנוּ — *The kindness of* HASHEM *— it is certain that it has not ended* [it is inexhaustible]. *Rashi,* whose translation we followed, gives an alternate translation: חַסְדֵי ה׳, *it is due to* HASHEM*'s kindness,* כִּי לֹא־תָמְנוּ, *that we were not annihilated for our transgressions,* כִּי לֹא־כָלוּ רַחֲמָיו — *because His mercies are not exhausted* [see *Numbers* 17-28].

23. חֲדָשִׁים לַבְּקָרִים — *They are new every morning* [Your kindnesses are renewed from day to day (*Rashi*)]. *Alshich* interprets the subject of this verse as the soul of man: *God renews man's life every morning, and I have faith that He will continue to do so in the future and redeem us.*

The *Talmud* interprets esoterically that each day God creates a band of new angels who utter a song before Him and then pass away (*Chagigah* 14a).

רַבָּה אֱמוּנָתֶךָ — *Great is your faithfulness,* great is Your promise; and it is great to believe in Your fulfilling and guarding whatever You promised (*Rashi*).

One earns great merit by believing in You (*Lechem Dimah*).

נַפְשִׁי עַל־כֵּן אוֹחִיל לוֹ: כה טוֹב יהוה לְקֹוָו* לְנֶפֶשׁ

my soul, therefore, *I place hope in Him.* 25 Good is HASHEM to those who trust in Him,* to the soul

תִּדְרְשֶׁנּוּ: כו טוֹב וְיָחִיל וְדוּמָם לִתְשׁוּעַת יהוה:

that seeks Him. 26 It is good that one should hope and patiently await the salvation of HASHEM.

כז טוֹב לַגֶּבֶר כִּי־יִשָּׂא עֹל בִּנְעוּרָיו: כח יֵשֵׁב בָּדָד

27 It is good for a man that he bear a yoke in his youth. 28 One should sit in solitude

וְיִדֹּם כִּי נָטַל עָלָיו: כט יִתֵּן בֶּעָפָר פִּיהוּ אוּלַי

and await patiently, for [God] has placed [the burden] upon him. 29 Let him put into the dust his mouth; perhaps

יֵשׁ תִּקְוָה:* ל יִתֵּן לְמַכֵּהוּ לֶחִי יִשְׂבַּע בְּחֶרְפָּה:

there is yet hope.* 30 Let him offer to the one who hits him a cheek, let him be sated with disgrace.

לא כִּי לֹא יִזְנַח לְעוֹלָם* אֲדֹנָי: לב כִּי אִם־הוֹגָה

31 For not reject forever* [will] the Lord; 32 but rather, He afflicts

וְרִחַם כְּרֹב °חֲסָדָיו [°חסדו ק']: לג כִּי לֹא עִנָּה

and then has mercy according to the abundance of His kindness. 33 For He does not torment

25. טוֹב ה׳ לְקֹוָו — *Good is HASHEM to those who trust in Him.* The *Midrash* cites an apparent contradiction between this verse and the verse in *Psalms* 145:9 stating that Hashem is good to all, not only to those who trust in Him. The *Midrash* explains with a parable: When one waters his orchard, he waters all of it. When one hoes, however, he hoes only the better plants. [So, too, in normal times, God provides for everyone equally, but in a time of punishment and destruction, only those who hope in Him are worthy of individual intervention (*Torah Temimah*).]

26-27. Since we are certain that God will not eternally neglect us, the prudent thing to do is to accept God's afflictions submissively, in quiet resignation, and silently anticipate God's ultimate salvation. As for the suffering he inflicts upon us in the interim ... *It is better to bear the yoke in one's youth* — while one is young and has the vigor to withstand the tribulations — rather than when old and lacking the stamina (*Alshich*).

29. אוּלַי יֵשׁ תִּקְוָה — *There is yet hope*, that God will forgive him (*Alshich*).

When Rabbi [the compiler of the *Mishnah*] reached these verses [29-31], he wept (*Midrash*), because even after all the indignities which were heaped upon Israel, the prophet still said אוּלַי, *perhaps*, as if hope was still doubtful (*Torah Temimah*).

31. [In the last several verses, the prophet exhorted man to completely debase himself in resignation before God. Now, he justifies his advice by extolling the compassion of God.]

כִּי לֹא יִזְנַח לְעוֹלָם ה׳ — *For not reject forever will the Lord*, [His anger is of limited duration], and it is therefore good to be submissive [silent] (*Rashi*).

מִלִּבּוֹ* וַיַּגֶּה בְּנֵי־אִישׁ: לד לְדַכֵּא תַּחַת רַגְלָיו כֹּל

‹ all ‹ His feet ‹ under ‹ crushing 34 « of men, ‹ the children ‹ nor afflict [for no cause] « capriciously,*

אֲסִירֵי אָרֶץ:* לה לְהַטּוֹת מִשְׁפַּט־גָּבֶר* נֶגֶד פְּנֵי

‹ the presence ‹ before ‹ for a man* ‹ justice ‹ [nor allow] to pervert 35 « of the earth; ‹ the prisoners

עֶלְיוֹן: לו לְעַוֵּת אָדָם בְּרִיבוֹ אֲדֹנָי לֹא רָאָה:

« countenance. ‹ does not ‹ — the Lord « in his grievance ‹ a man ‹ wronging 36 « of the Most High,

לז מִי זֶה אָמַר וַתֶּהִי אֲדֹנָי לֹא צִוָּה: לח מִפִּי עֶלְיוֹן

‹ of the Most High ‹ From the mouth 38 « ordain it. ‹ did not ‹ [if] the Lord « and it took place, ‹ that decreed [something] ‹ is it ‹ Who 37

לֹא תֵצֵא הָרָעוֹת וְהַטּוֹב:* לט מַה־יִּתְאוֹנֵן אָדָם

‹ — [should] a person « should he complain ‹ Of what 39 « and that are good?* ‹ [decrees] that are bad ‹ emanate ‹ do there not

חַי גֶּבֶר עַל־°חֲטָאָיו* [°חטאו כ׳]: מ נַחְפְּשָׂה

‹ Let us search 40 « his sins!* ‹ [and complain] about ‹ [Let him be] a strong man « who is alive?

God waits for man to repent (*Alshich*).

33. כִּי לֹא עִנָּה מִלִּבּוֹ — *For He does not torment capriciously*, He has no desire to punish capriciously; everything is in retribution for one's sins (*Rashi; Alshich*).

34. כֹּל אֲסִירֵי אָרֶץ — *All the prisoners of the earth*. This phrase is a poetic description referring to all mankind. Are we not all *prisoners* on God's *earth* with no way to escape His providence? (*Alshich*).

35. לְהַטּוֹת מִשְׁפַּט־גָּבֶר — *[Nor allow] to pervert justice for a man*. According to *Rashi*, this verse, too, continues the theme begun in verse 33, enumerating what Hashem does not capriciously do or allow.

37-40. *Rashi* groups together three verses and explains: One should never ascribe his suffering to chance, because from whom else but from God does good and evil emanate? Therefore, why should a man complain? Let everyone put the blame on his own sins! — and [verse 40] search his ways and repent.

הָרָעוֹת וְהַטּוֹב — *That are bad and that are good*. *Palgei Mayim*, in contrast to *Rashi*, takes this phrase as a statement and explains that although everything *does* emanate from God, the choice of man's actions — bad or good — is not Divine, but human ...

Thus, the *Rambam* [in his *Hilchos Teshuvah* and *Eight Chapters*] writes that man is mistaken in ascribing to God his evil ways — as if they were Divinely forced upon him. When justice is meted out to him, why should someone complain that he was coerced? גֶּבֶר עַל־חֲטָאָו, he is a *strong man* over his sins! Let him conquer his evil ways! Where there is knowledge of God there is free choice.

מַה־יִּתְאוֹנֵן אָדָם חַי גֶּבֶר עַל־חֲטָאָו — *Of what should he complain — [should] a person who is alive? ... a strong man about his sins!* Let him be thankful that he is alive! Rav Levi said: The Holy One, Blessed is He, declared: Your existence is in My hand,

דְּרָכֵינוּ וְנַחְקֹרָה* וְנָשׁוּבָה עַד־יהוה:* מא נִשָּׂא לְבָבֵנוּ

‹our hearts [in prayer] ‹Let us lift **41** «HASHEM.* ‹unto ‹and let us return ‹and let us investigate [them]* ‹our ways

אֶל־כַּפָּיִם* אֶל־אֵל בַּשָּׁמָיִם: מב נַחְנוּ פָשַׁעְנוּ* וּמָרִינוּ

«and rebelled; ‹have transgressed* ‹We **42** «in heaven. ‹God ‹to ‹our hands* ‹together with

---

and, being alive, you complain! Rav Huna said: Let him stand up like a brave man, acknowledge his sins, and not complain. Rav Berachiah explained the verse: Why does man complain against Him Who lives eternally? If a man wishes to complain, let it be about his own sins! (*Midrash*).

This כְּתִיב, *written form,* is חֶטְאוֹ, *his sin* [in the singular], while the קְרִי, *reading,* is חֲטָאָיו, *his sins. Shaar Bas Rabim* points out that someone should be particularly concerned about his *first* sin. He dare not overlook it, or take it lightly, because עֲבֵרָה גּוֹרֶרֶת עֲבֵרָה, *one sin leads to another sin* (*Pirkei Avos* 4:2), and his entire future might very well depend upon how he reacted to that first sin.

Similarly, *Rav Yonasan Eyebescheutz* points out that one should not overlook even a single transgression — however minor it appears — rather, *man should complain about every single sin.*

40. נַחְפְּשָׂה דְרָכֵינוּ וְנַחְקֹרָה — *Let us search our ways and let us investigate [them].* This is the climax of the previous verses. Since man has only his own sins to blame for any misfortunes emanating from God, he should not grumble and recriminate. Instead, let us search our conduct to find the cause of our suffering, and then repent (*Kiflayim LeSushiyah*).

As the *Talmud* advises: If a man sees that pain and suffering visit him, let him examine his conduct, as it says: *Let us examine our ways and return to HASHEM* (*Berachos* 5a).

This verse is reminiscent of *Zephaniah* 1:12: *I will search Jerusalem with candles.* One should search his ways so that his repentance will reach *up to HASHEM* — to His Throne of Glory (*Midrash Lekach Tov*).

Rav Galanti elaborates that this soul-searching must be accomplished in a manner similar to meticulous searching with the light of a candle — in every nook and crevice — as required when searching for *chametz* before Passover. The simile here refers to the soul which is likened to light [נֵר ה׳ נִשְׁמַת אָדָם, *the light of God is the soul of man*]. When one is guided by his soul and conducts the search properly throughout every nook and cranny of his being — even in areas where he least suspects it — he will inevitably discover some *chametz,* the symbol of sin and improper behavior. When he removes the *chametz,* his repentance will surely reach *'up to HASHEM's* Throne of Glory.'

וְנָשׁוּבָה עַד־ה׳ — *And let us return unto HASHEM.* The *Midrash* and commentators explain the use of the more forceful עַד, *unto,* rather than the more direct אֶל, *to,* by quoting the Talmudic dictum [*Yoma* 86b]: גְּדוֹלָה תְּשׁוּבָה שֶׁמַּגַּעַת עַד כִּסֵּא הַכָּבוֹד, *Great is repentance for it reaches* [עַד] *unto the Throne of Glory.* Thus, the verse alludes to a concept often stressed by our Sages: A repenter rises above the status of a sinner who falls short of the ideal. Repentance raises one to the level of the most righteous.

41. נִשָּׂא לְבָבֵנוּ אֶל־כַּפָּיִם — *Let us lift our hearts [in prayer] together with our hands.* The translation follows the first of *Rashi's* two interpretations: When we lift our hands [in prayer] to God, let us lift our hearts along with him [i.e., in utmost sincerity] broken-heartedly — before God.

Prayer is efficacious only when the external lifting of the hands is accompanied by the internal lifting of the heart (*Alshich*).

As the *Talmud* explains: A man's prayer is answered only if he takes his heart in his hands [i.e., is sincere] (*Taanis* 8a).

42. נַחְנוּ פָשַׁעְנוּ — *We have trangressed ... You have not forgiven.* In trangressing,

אַתָּה לֹא סָלָחְתָּ: מג סַכֹּתָה בָאַף וַתִּרְדְּפֵנוּ הָרַגְתָּ

‹You have slain « and pursued us; ‹ with anger ‹ You have covered [Yourself] **43** « forgiven. ‹ have not ‹ You

לֹא חָמָלְתָּ: מד סַכֹּתָה בֶעָנָן לָךְ מֵעֲבוֹר תְּפִלָּה:*

« of any prayer.* ‹ to prevent the passage « Yourself, ‹ in a cloud ‹ You have covered **44** « shown pity. ‹ and You have not

מה סְחִי וּמָאוֹס תְּשִׂימֵנוּ בְּקֶרֶב הָעַמִּים: מו פָּצוּ

‹Open wide **46** « of the nations. ‹ in the midst ‹ do You make us ‹ and repugnance ‹ Filth **45**

עָלֵינוּ פִּיהֶם* כָּל־אֹיְבֵינוּ: מז פַּחַד וָפַחַת הָיָה לָנוּ

« ours, ‹ were ‹ and pitfalls ‹ Panic **47** « our enemies. ‹ [did] all « their mouths, ‹ against us

הַשֵּׁאת וְהַשָּׁבֶר: מח פַּלְגֵי־מַיִם תֵּרַד עֵינִי* עַל־

‹ over ‹ do my eyes* ‹ shed ‹ of water ‹ Streams **48** « and destruction. ‹ desolation

שֶׁבֶר בַּת־עַמִּי: מט עֵינִי נִגְּרָה וְלֹא תִדְמֶה מֵאֵין

‹ [it is] without ‹ still; ‹ and is not ‹ flows ‹ My eye **49** « of my people. ‹ of the daughter ‹ the shattering

הֲפֻגוֹת: נ עַד־יַשְׁקִיף וְיֵרֶא יהוה מִשָּׁמָיִם:

« from heaven. « — HASHEM — « and takes notice ‹ He gazes down ‹ until **50** « respite;

---

we have been true to *our* nature and Evil Inclination; but *You* have not conformed to *Your* Merciful ways, You did not forgive (*Midrash; Rashi; Alshich*).

Ibn Ezra views this verse as a separate lament: *We have transgressed*, and did not repent. Therefore, *You have not forgiven.*

44. סַכֹּתָה בֶעָנָן . . . מֵעֲבוֹר תְּפִלָּה — *You have covered in a cloud . . . to prevent the passage of any prayer.*

Cloud is used here allegorically, as if the cloud formed a barrier between our prayers and Hashem (*Ibn Ezra*).

The *Talmud* relates that Rava would not proclaim a fast on a cloudy day because "God wrapped Himself *in a cloud so that prayer cannot pass*" (*Berachos* 32b).

46. [Verses 46-48 which begin with פ precede, rather than follow, verses 49-51 which begin with the earlier Hebrew letter ע. (See comm. to 2:16).]

פָּצוּ עָלֵינוּ פִּיהֶם — *Open wide against us their mouths.* Instead of completely ignoring us — as one would normally ignore *filth and repugnance* — our enemies taunted and jeered at us, giving us no peace; not even allowing us to wallow, undisturbed, in our misery (*Ibn Yachya*).

Ibn Ezra relates שֵׁאת to שׁוֹאָה, *sudden catastrophe.*

48. פַּלְגֵי־מַיִם תֵּרַד עֵינִי — *Streams of water shed do my eyes. Eye* is singular. If only one eye produces such streams of water, how much more so both eyes! (*Alshich*).

51. This is a personal lament of Jeremiah who was of an aristocratic, priestly family. He anguished that his weeping eye figuratively contorted his face and aggrieved his spirit more than any inhabitant of the

נא עֵינִי עוֹלְלָה לְנַפְשִׁי מִכֹּל בְּנוֹת עִירִי: נב צוֹד

51 My eye [by its tears] › has sullied › me › more than all › the daughters › of my city. » 52 Snare ›

צָדוּנִי כַּצִּפּוֹר אֹיְבַי חִנָּם: נג צָמְתוּ בַבּוֹר חַיָּי

they did ensnare me › like a bird, » [so did] my enemies › without cause. » 53 They closed off › in the pit › my life, »

וַיַּדּוּ־אֶבֶן בִּי: נד צָפוּ־מַיִם עַל־רֹאשִׁי* אָמַרְתִּי

and they threw › stones › at me. » 54 Flood › did the water › over › my head;* » I said [to myself], ›

נִגְזָרְתִּי: נה קָרָאתִי שִׁמְךָ יהוה* מִבּוֹר תַּחְתִּיּוֹת:

I am cut off! » 55 I called › on Your Name, › HASHEM,* › from the pit's › lowest depths. »

נו קוֹלִי שָׁמָעְתָּ אַל־תַּעְלֵם אָזְנְךָ לְרַוְחָתִי לְשַׁוְעָתִי:

56 My voice › You have heard; » do not › shut › Your ear › to [my prayer for] my relief, » to my cry. »

נז קָרַבְתָּ בְּיוֹם אֶקְרָאֶךָּ אָמַרְתָּ אַל־תִּירָא:* נח רַבְתָּ

57 You drew near › on the day › I called You; » You said, › *Do not* › *fear!** » 58 You fought, ›

---

city. His family was particularly affected, and suffered more than others because, as priests, they had been selected for holiness and the service of God (*Rashi*).

54. צָפוּ־מַיִם עַל־רֹאשִׁי אָמַרְתִּי נִגְזָרְתִּי — *Flood did the water over my head; I said [to myself], "I am cut off!"* When a man is in water up to his hips, there is still hope, but when water — here allegorically referring to the heathen nations — flows *over* one's head, one gives up all hope. Rather, קָרָאתִי שִׁמְךָ ה׳, *I called on Your Name,* HASHEM (*Rashi*).

55-56. שִׁמְךָ ה׳ — *Your Name,* HASHEM. When one is in great anguish, drained of strength, he merely calls out the name of a passerby with such anguish that the hearer immediately discerns the gravity of the situation and responds. Here, too, he simply called God's Name hoping that קוֹלִי שָׁמָעְתָּ, *You heard my voice,* and therefore אַל־תַּעְלֵם אָזְנְךָ לְרַוְחָתִי לְשַׁוְעָתִי, *do not shut Your ear to [my prayer for] my relief, to my cry* (*Kiflayim LeSushiyah*).

As Jonah called upon You from inside the fish and from the depths of the sea, so does Israel call upon You from its exile among the nations — likened to the depths of a pit — to hear their prayers and deliver them (*Midrash Lekach Tov*).

57. אַל־תִּירָא — *Do not fear!* [The utterance, *Do not fear!*, is a constant refrain throughout Scripture, and was said not only on segregated occasions but to virtually every one of the fathers of our people; it is a Divine promise that Israel need not fear. To mention several: *Do not fear, Avram, I am a shield for you* (*Genesis* 15:1); *Do not fear* (Isaac,) *for I am with you* (ibid. 26:24); *Do not fear,* (Jacob,) *of descending to Egypt* (ibid. 46:3); *Fear him not,* (Moses)... (*Numbers* 21:34); *Fear not,* (Children of Israel,) *and do not lose resolve* (*Deuteronomy* 1:21); *Fear not,* (Joshua,) *and do not lose resolve* (*Joshua* 8:1); to Gideon (*Judges* 6:23); to Elijah (*II Kings* 1:15); to Hezekiah (*II Kings* 19:6); to Isaiah (*Isaiah* 7:4); to Jeremiah (*Jeremiah* 1:8); to Daniel (*Daniel* 10:12).]

אֲדֹנָי רִיבֵי נַפְשִׁי גָּאַלְתָּ חַיָּי׃ נט רָאִיתָה יהוה

O Lord, | the battles | of my soul; | You redeemed | my life. | 59 You have seen, | HASHEM,

עַוָּתָתִי שָׁפְטָה מִשְׁפָּטִי׃ ס רָאִיתָה כָּל־נִקְמָתָם כָּל־

the injustices [I suffer]; | judge | my cause. | 60 You have seen | all | their vengeance, | all

מַחְשְׁבֹתָם לִי׃ סא שָׁמַעְתָּ חֶרְפָּתָם יהוה* כָּל־

their schemes | against me. | 61 You have heard | their verbal abuse, | HASHEM,* | all

מַחְשְׁבֹתָם עָלָי׃ סב שִׂפְתֵי קָמַי וְהֶגְיוֹנָם עָלַי כָּל־

their schemes | regarding me. | 62 The lips | of my antagonists | and their thoughts | are against me | all

הַיּוֹם׃* סג שִׁבְתָּם וְקִימָתָם הַבִּיטָה אֲנִי מַנְגִּינָתָם׃

day long.* | 63 Their sitting down | and their rising up, | You scrutinize; | I | am [the theme] of their songs.

סד תָּשִׁיב לָהֶם גְּמוּל יהוה כְּמַעֲשֵׂה יְדֵיהֶם׃*

64 Pay back | to them | what they deserve, | HASHEM, | in accordance with the deeds | of their hands.*

סה תִּתֵּן לָהֶם מְגִנַּת־לֵב תַּאֲלָתְךָ לָהֶם׃ סו תִּרְדֹּף

65 Give | them | a grief-filled | heart; | may Your curse | be upon them! | 66 Pursue them

בְּאַף וְתַשְׁמִידֵם מִתַּחַת שְׁמֵי יהוה׃*

in anger | and destroy them | from beneath | the heavens | of HASHEM.*

61-63. שָׁמַעְתָּ חֶרְפָּתָם ה׳ — *You have heard their verbal abuse,* HASHEM. *Alshich* translates the verse as referring to their blasphemies against Hashem: *You have heard how they reviled You,* HASHEM, *and how they designed against me.*

Most commentators, however, see *Israel* as being the object of their insults, and explain verses 61-63 as referring to designs of the enemy — in thought, word, and action.

כָּל־הַיּוֹם — *All day long.* Even though my enemies already accomplished many of their evil plans, their mind is not at ease. They continue to plan and talk about me incessantly *all day long,* as if their power of speech was given them just to deride me (*Lechem Dimah*).

64-66. [In the verses that follow, Hashem is asked to mete out retribution to Israel's enemies, in kind, for all their evil.]

כְּמַעֲשֵׂה יְדֵיהֶם — *In accordance with the deeds of their hands.* For having acted in consonance with, and as emissaries of, God's will in bringing about punishment to Israel — for that they are absolved. However, כְּמַעֲשֵׂה יְדֵיהֶם, for what they added *of their own hands,* of their viciousness and overzealousness beyond the bounds expected of them — for that Hashem is asked to punish them (*Lechem Dimah*).

וְתַשְׁמִידֵם מִתַּחַת שְׁמֵי ה׳ — *And destroy them from beneath the heavens of* HASHEM — Do not punish them with exile, as You punished us. Destroy them from the face

[ד] א אֵיכָה֙ יוּעַ֣ם זָהָ֔ב* יִשְׁנֶ֖א הַכֶּ֣תֶם הַטּ֑וֹב

[4] 1 How is it that dimmed is the gold?* Altered is the gold that is the finest?

תִּשְׁתַּפֵּ֙כְנָה֙ אַבְנֵי־קֹ֔דֶשׁ בְּרֹ֖אשׁ כָּל־חוּצֽוֹת׃ ב בְּנֵ֤י

Poured out are the stones of sanctity at the head of all the streets? 2 The children

צִיּוֹן֙ הַיְקָרִ֔ים* הַמְסֻלָּאִ֖ים בַּפָּ֑ז אֵיכָ֤ה נֶחְשְׁבוּ֙

of Zion who were precious,* who were valued like fine gold — how is it that they are considered

לְנִבְלֵי־חֶ֔רֶשׂ מַעֲשֵׂ֖ה יְדֵ֥י יוֹצֵֽר׃ ג גַּם־°תַּנִּים֙ [°תנין כ׳]

like [fragile] jugs of earthenware, the work of the hands of a potter? 3 Even *tanim*

חָ֣לְצוּ שַׁ֔ד* הֵינִ֖יקוּ גּוּרֵיהֶ֑ן בַּת־עַמִּ֣י לְאַכְזָ֔ר

draw out the breast* and suckle their young; [but] the daughter of my people has become cruel,

°כַּיְעֵנִ֖ים [°כי ענים כ׳] בַּמִּדְבָּֽר׃ ד דָּבַ֨ק לְשׁ֥וֹן יוֹנֵ֛ק

like ostriches in the desert. 4 Adhere does the tongue of the suckling

---

of the earth (*Rav Galanti*).

The obliteration should be so complete that they should have no descendants, and that no one will be able to say, 'This tree, or camel, or lamb belongs to him' [i.e., there will be no trace of identity left] (*Midrash*).

[Thus, with the plea that God utterly wipe out the enemy, the chapter closes.]

CHAPTER FOUR

1. אֵיכָה יוּעַם זָהָב — *How is it that dimmed is the gold?* The *gold* figuratively refers to the people of Jerusalem. It has become covered over, dull only in its external appearance and brilliance, but not in substance (*Midrash; Rashi; Ibn Yachya*).

Rashi comments that this elegy was originally pronounced over יֹאשִׁיָּהוּ, King Josiah, as mentioned in *II Chronicles* 35:25. (See commentary to *Kinnah* 11, p. 182.) Jeremiah also incorporated within it the references to Zion.

2. בְּנֵי צִיּוֹן הַיְקָרִים — *The children of Zion who were precious.* [The verse laments how Zion's precious inhabitants, once greatly esteemed, are now treated like common clay.]

Midrash Lekach Tov, commenting on the precious character of the people of Jerusalem, notes that when residents of Jerusalem sat down to eat they would hang a cloth over their door as a signal to the poor that they might come to share their meal [see also *Bava Basra* 93b].

3. גַּם־תַּנִּים חָלְצוּ שַׁד — *Even tanim will offer the breast.* [The word תַּנִּים, *tanim,* refers to a wild animal but its exact identity is unknown. The word usually means *reptile* or *fish* and in modern Hebrew, תַּן means *jackal.* Since the specific guidance of Talmudic sources is lacking, we have left the word untranslated.]

Although *tanim* are vicious, they display warmth and kindness to their young by nursing them. Jeremiah laments how, as a result of the ravages and stress of famine, the usually compassionate Jewish mothers became cruel and placed their own lives before their children's. They consumed whatever food was available, and allowed their children to go hungry, ignoring their cries for food (*Rashi*).

אֶל־חִכּוֹ בַּצָּמָא* עוֹלָלִים שָׁאֲלוּ לֶחֶם פֹּרֵשׂ אֵין

to its palate from thirst;* young children beg for bread, there is no one to extend [it]

לָהֶם: ה הָאֹכְלִים לְמַעֲדַנִּים נָשַׁמּוּ בַּחוּצוֹת הָאֱמֻנִים

to them. 5 Those who are used to eating delicacies lie desolate in the streets; those who were brought up

עֲלֵי תוֹלָע חִבְּקוּ אַשְׁפַּתּוֹת: ו וַיִּגְדַּל עֲוֹן בַּת־עַמִּי*

in scarlet clothing embrace [what they find] in garbage heaps. 6 Greater is the iniquity of the daughter of my people

מֵחַטַּאת סְדֹם* הַהֲפוּכָה כְמוֹ־רָגַע* וְלֹא־חָלוּ בָהּ

than the sin of Sodom,* which was overturned as if in an instant,* and there did not act against her

יָדָיִם: ז זַכּוּ נְזִירֶיהָ מִשֶּׁלֶג צַחוּ מֵחָלָב אָדְמוּ עֶצֶם

[human] hands. 7 [Then] purer were her princes than snow, whiter than milk; ruddier was their appearance

---

According to many commentators, *tanim* figuratively refers to the vicious enemy who חָלְצוּ שַׁד, *bared the breast,* forced Jewish women to nurse their enemy's children with the tragic result that the nursing mothers had no milk left for their own children. The Jewish daughters, unable to respond to the needs of their children who cried *like ostriches in the desert*, seemed to be אַכְזָר, *cruel* (*Alshich, Palgei Mayim*).

At very least, the Jews could expect that the enemy's children who were nursed by Jewish women should display some compassion for the women who reared them. This, too, was not forthcoming. They were as cruel as ostriches in the desert (*Lechem Dimah*).

4. לְשׁוֹן יוֹנֵק ... בַּצָּמָא — *The tongue of the suckling ... from thirst.* Since, in the previous verse, *the daughter of my people has become cruel*, the sucklings who depend on their mothers for milk are described as dying of thirst, whereas the עוֹלָלִים, *young children*, beg for bread (*Kiflayim LeSushiyah*).

The *Midrash* relates how the enemy also destroyed the conduits which carried water through the land. Even when a father took his thirsty child to the conduit, he found no water.

5. In this verse Jeremiah further laments the fall of the people from their previous heights to the nethermost depths to which they have fallen. People, who were brought up eating *only* the finest delicacies and dressed only in the most luxurious clothing, lay faint from hunger in the streets, and scrounged through garbage heaps for the most meager scraps of food (*Lechem Dimah*).

6. וַיִּגְדַּל עֲוֹן ... מֵחַטַּאת סְדֹם — *Greater is the iniquity ... than the sin of Sodom.* The punishment of Zion, greater than that of Sodom [see next comm.], proves that their iniquity was greater than Sodom's (*Rashi*).

הַהֲפוּכָה כְמוֹ־רָגַע — *Which was overturned as if in an instant*, Sodom was destroyed instantly — without the suffering of a prolonged siege. Hence its sin is considered not as grave as Jerusalem's, which was punished with famine, sieges, war — and an exile which still endures! (*Rashi; Lechem Dimah*).

7-8. [The dramatic "then and now" comparisons demonstrate the ravages of famine and war upon the nobility. Formerly they

מִפְּנִינִים סַפִּיר גִּזְרָתָם: ח חָשַׁךְ מִשְּׁחוֹר תָּאֳרָם

than rubies; [like] sapphire was their body; 8 [now] darker than blackness is their appearance,

לֹא נִכְּרוּ בַּחוּצוֹת* צָפַד עוֹרָם עַל־עַצְמָם יָבֵשׁ

they were not recognized in the streets;* shriveled is their skin upon their bones; it is dry,

הָיָה כָעֵץ: ט טוֹבִים הָיוּ חַלְלֵי־חֶרֶב* מֵחַלְלֵי רָעָב

it became like wood. 9 Better off were those killed by the sword* than those killed by famine,

שֶׁהֵם יָזֻבוּ מְדֻקָּרִים מִתְּנוּבֹת שָׂדָי: י יְדֵי נָשִׁים

for the former [died from the blood] flowing from their stab wounds [rather than from lack] of the produce of my fields. 10 The hands of women

רַחֲמָנִיּוֹת בִּשְּׁלוּ יַלְדֵיהֶן* הָיוּ לְבָרוֹת לָמוֹ בְּשֶׁבֶר

who were compassionate have cooked their own children;* they became food for them with the devastation

בַּת־עַמִּי: יא כִּלָּה יהוה אֶת־חֲמָתוֹ* שָׁפַךְ חֲרוֹן

of the daughter of my people. 11 HASHEM has expended all of His fury,* He has poured out the flaring

אַפּוֹ וַיַּצֶּת־אֵשׁ בְּצִיּוֹן וַתֹּאכַל יְסוֹדֹתֶיהָ:

of His wrath; He kindled a fire in Zion and it consumed its foundations.

---

were princelike figures of grace and nobility, while now they are *blacker than soot.*]

8. לֹא נִכְּרוּ בַּחוּצוֹת — *They were not recognized in the streets.* The *Midrash* relates of Rav Zadok that the ravages of the Destruction bore so hard upon him that his body never returned to normal although he lived for many years after the Destruction.

9. טוֹבִים הָיוּ חַלְלֵי־חֶרֶב — *Better off were those killed by the sword* or: *The good* [people] *were the victims of the sword* because they died a swift death, one preferable to the slow agony of famine (*Alshich*).

10. [The extent of the depravity is described. (See also 2:20.)]

יְדֵי נָשִׁים רַחֲמָנִיּוֹת בִּשְּׁלוּ יַלְדֵיהֶן — *The hands of women who were compassionate have cooked their own children.*

The impending Destruction and the ravages and famine of war caused compassionate mothers to become so depraved that *with their own hands they cooked their children* and they consumed them without even leaving flesh for other members of the family (*Alshich*).

Rav Almosnino comments that they cooked their own *dead* children, but did not murder them.

The *Shelah* comments that this phrase also contains moralistic criticism of overly compassionate and over-indulgent mothers who, for example, let their children sleep late rather than go to synagogue or to school. With this "misplaced compassion" they "cook" and destroy their children's souls.

11. כִּלָּה ה׳ אֶת חֲמָתוֹ — *HASHEM has expended all of His fury.* The fury, pent up

יב לֹא הֶאֱמִינוּ מַלְכֵי־אֶרֶץ* °כֹּל [°וכל כ׳] יֹשְׁבֵי תֵבֵל

12 They did not believe it « — the kings ‹ of the earth ‹ and all ‹ the inhabitants ‹ of the world — «

כִּי יָבֹא צַר וְאוֹיֵב בְּשַׁעֲרֵי יְרוּשָׁלָ͏ִם: יג מֵחַטֹּאת

that ‹ there would [ever] enter ‹ an adversary ‹ and an enemy ‹ into the gates ‹ of Jerusalem. « 13 It was for the sins ‹

נְבִיאֶיהָ* עֲוֺנֹת כֹּהֲנֶיהָ הַשֹּׁפְכִים בְּקִרְבָּהּ דַּם

of her prophets, ‹ the iniquities ‹ of her Kohanim, « who had shed ‹ in her midst ‹ the blood ‹

צַדִּיקִים: יד נָעוּ עִוְרִים בַּחוּצוֹת* נְגֹאֲלוּ בַּדָּם

of the righteous. « 14 Wander ‹ did the blind men ‹ through the streets, « defiled ‹ with blood, «

בְּלֹא יוּכְלוּ יִגְּעוּ בִּלְבֻשֵׁיהֶם: טו סוּרוּ טָמֵא קָרְאוּ

so that [people] were not ‹ able ‹ to touch ‹ their garments. « 15 Go away, ‹ unclean one! « they shouted ‹

לָמוֹ סוּרוּ סוּרוּ אַל־תִּגָּעוּ כִּי נָצוּ גַּם־נָעוּ אָמְרוּ

at them; « Go away, ‹ go away, ‹ do not ‹ touch! « For ‹ they were loathsome, ‹ even ‹ with [their own] filth. « [People] said ‹

---

within Him for many years [see comm. to 2:8], was expended when He exacted vengeance upon them.

12. לֹא הֶאֱמִינוּ מַלְכֵי־אֶרֶץ — *They did not believe it — the kings of the earth.* The miraculous defeat of Sennacherib [*II Chronicles* 32] created the impression that Jerusalem was impregnable (*Midrash Lekach Tov*).

They didn't realize that because its sanctity had been defiled, it had become vulnerable (*Alshich*).

13. מֵחַטֹּאת נְבִיאֶיהָ — *It was for the sins of her prophets,* i.e., she became vulnerable to such calamity because of the sins of her false prophets (*Rashi*).

[These prophets gave her false security by indulging in deceptive oracles, and did not exhort her to repent. Compare *Jeremiah* 8:10-12: *From prophet to priest, all deal in falsehood. They relieved the [impending] disaster of the daughter of My people by making light [of it], saying, "Peace! peace!" But there is no peace... Therefore they will fall among the fallen.* This caused the blood of the righteous to be shed in their midst.]

A different approach is taken by *Rav Alkabetz* in interpreting verses 12-13: The priests and prophets of Israel were renowned throughout the world for their holiness and sincerity. Therefore: *The kings of the earth could not believe that Jerusalem would be made vulnerable as a result of any sins,* and if it were to become subject to conquest, it could be *on the fault of her priests and prophets.*

14-15. נָעוּ עִוְרִים בַּחוּצוֹת — *Wander did the blind men through the streets.* This translation follows *Rashi* who explains: When the blind wandered through the streets, their feet slipped in the blood of the murdered Jews who lay throughout the city.

Ibn Ezra interprets עִוְרִים as an adverb and translates: they wandered through the streets *blindly.*

בַגּוֹיִם לֹא יוֹסִפוּ לָגוּר:* טז פְּנֵי יהוה חִלְּקָם

among the nations: ‹ They will not any longer ‹ live [among us].* « 16 The [angry] countenance ‹ of HASHEM ‹ has scattered them; «

לֹא יוֹסִיף לְהַבִּיטָם פְּנֵי כֹהֲנִים לֹא נָשָׂאוּ*

He does not any longer ‹ look [favorably] upon them; « [because] the presence ‹ of the Kohanim ‹ they did not respect,* «

°וּזְקֵנִים [°זקנים כ׳] לֹא חָנָנוּ: יז °עוֹדֵינוּ [°עודינה כ׳]

to the elders ‹ they were not gracious. « 17 Still, we are ‹

תִּכְלֶינָה עֵינֵינוּ אֶל־עֶזְרָתֵנוּ הָבֶל* בְּצִפִּיָּתֵנוּ

longingly looking ‹ with our eyes ‹ for ‹ our help ‹ that is useless;* « in our expectations ‹

צִפִּינוּ אֶל־גּוֹי לֹא יוֹשִׁעַ: יח צָדוּ צְעָדֵינוּ מִלֶּכֶת

we looked ‹ to ‹ a nation ‹ that would not ‹ save [us]. « 18 They stalk ‹ our steps ‹ [preventing us] from walking ‹

בִּרְחֹבֹתֵינוּ* קָרַב קִצֵּנוּ מָלְאוּ יָמֵינוּ כִּי־בָא קִצֵּנוּ:

in our streets.* « Near ‹ is our end; « completed ‹ are our days, « for ‹ come ‹ has our end. «

יט קַלִּים הָיוּ רֹדְפֵינוּ מִנִּשְׁרֵי שָׁמַיִם עַל־הֶהָרִים

19 Swifter ‹ were ‹ our pursuers ‹ than eagles ‹ of the sky. « Over ‹ the mountains ‹

אָמְרוּ בַּגּוֹיִם לֹא יוֹסִפוּ לָגוּר — *[People] said among the nations: "They will not any longer live [among us]."* The nations predicted that the Jews will never again return to their land to dwell as before (*Ibn Ezra; Akeidas Yitzchak*) because [next verse] God is the One Who exiled them (*Alshich*).

Other commentators translate: For the nations resolved — after seeing Israel's defilement — that they will not allow her to dwell [peacefully] in their lands, and they will compel her to wander about (*Lechem Dimah*).

[In this chapter, too, the verse beginning with פ precedes the verse beginning with ע. See comm. to 2:16.]

16. פְּנֵי כֹהֲנִים לֹא נָשָׂאוּ — *The presence of the Kohanim they did not respect.* The end of the verse gives the reason that God dispersed the Jews and avoided looking after them: Because they showed no regard for the priests and elders, God showed no regard, as it were, for them (*Alshich*).

17. עוֹדֵינוּ תִּכְלֶינָה עֵינֵינוּ אֶל־עֶזְרָתֵנוּ הָבֶל — *Still, we are longingly looking with our eyes for our help that is useless.* [The verse reproduces the state of mind that prevailed in the last days of the siege, when nearly everyone sustained the hope that outside help would arrive. From *Jeremiah* 37:5-11 we know that the advance of the Egyptian army caused the Babylonians to retreat from Jerusalem, but as Jeremiah predicted, the relief was only temporary. The Egyptians never came to save them, and the Babylonians returned as Jeremiah predicted.]

18. These verses describe the miserable state of the Jews who remained in Judea under Chaldean rule (*Ibn Shuib*).

צָדוּ צְעָדֵינוּ מִלֶּכֶת בִּרְחֹבֹתֵינוּ — *They stalk our steps [preventing us] from walking*

דְּלָקֻנוּ בַּמִּדְבָּר אָרְבוּ לָנוּ׃ כ רוּחַ אַפֵּינוּ מְשִׁיחַ

they chased us; « in the desert ‹ they lay in ambush ‹ for us. » 20 The breath ‹ of our nostrils, ‹ the anointed one ‹

יהוה* נִלְכַּד בִּשְׁחִיתוֹתָם אֲשֶׁר אָמַרְנוּ בְּצִלּוֹ

of HASHEM,* ‹ was caught ‹ in their traps, » the one of whom ‹ we said: » *Under his shadow* ‹

נִחְיֶה בַגּוֹיִם׃ כא שִׂישִׂי וְשִׂמְחִי בַּת־אֱדוֹם

we will live ‹ *among the nations.* » 21 Rejoice ‹ and exult, ‹ O daughter ‹ of Edom, »

יוֹשֶׁבֶת° [יושבתי° כ׳] בְּאֶרֶץ עוּץ* גַּם־עָלַיִךְ

who dwells ‹ in the land ‹ of Uz;* » [but] also ‹ to you ‹

תַּעֲבָר־כּוֹס* תִּשְׁכְּרִי וְתִתְעָרִי׃* כב תַּם־עֲוֹנֵךְ

will pass ‹ the [bitter] cup,* » you will become drunk [from it] ‹ and you will vomit [it] out.* » 22 Fully expiated ‹ is your iniquity, ‹

in our streets: they ambushed us (*Rashi*), so that when a Jew went to market they would pounce upon him screaming, "There goes a Jew!" (*Lekach Tov*).

20. רוּחַ אַפֵּינוּ מְשִׁיחַ ה׳ — *The breath of our nostrils, the anointed one of HASHEM.* [The expression רוּחַ אַפֵּינוּ, *the breath of our nostrils*, occurs only here, and poetically expresses the very essence of national hope and identity — its very survival and "breath of life" — which focused on the monarch, God's anointed.]

21. שִׂישִׂי וְשִׂמְחִי בַּת־אֱדוֹם — *Rejoice and exult, O daughter of Edom.* These words are spoken sarcastically, as if to say: Rejoice while you can, because you will not escape punishment for your sins (*Midrash Lekach Tov*).

Ibn Ezra explains that Edom is referred to here because of its implacable hatred for Israel. They rejoiced at Jerusalem's downfall, as it is written (*Psalms* 137:7): *Remember, HASHEM, for the offspring of Edom, the day of Jerusalem, for those who say, "Destroy! Destroy! to its very foundation!"* [See also *Obadiah* 1:10-14 for a description of the malice which Edom demonstrated on the day of Jerusalem's disaster.]

According to *Rashi* and the *Midrash*, this verse refers not to contemporary Edom but prophetically to the Romans [whom the Sages identify with Biblical Edom] who Jeremiah foresaw would destroy the Second Temple.

יוֹשֶׁבֶת בְּאֶרֶץ עוּץ — *Who dwells in the land of Uz.* [The Arameans' land bordering upon Edom (see *Jeremiah* 25:20) and named after its early Edomite settler, Uz, son of Seir (*Gen.* 36:28).]

גַּם־עָלַיִךְ תַּעֲבָר־כּוֹס — *[But] also to you will pass the [bitter] cup*, the cup of punishment (*Rashi*).

תִּשְׁכְּרִי וְתִתְעָרִי — *You will become drunk [from it] and you will vomit [it] out* [you will drink so much from the cup of punishment and wrath that you will get intoxicated from its abundance, and, like a drunken man, will vomit].

Rav Yonasan Eyebescheutz notes that the curse of vomiting is that as a result of vomiting she will have room to drink more from the cup of punishment.

[It is perhaps possible to relate תִּתְעָרִי to the Edomite outcry against Jerusalem (*Psalms* 137:7: עָרוּ עָרוּ, *"Destroy! Destroy!"*). Just as you Edomites called excessively for Jerusalem's destruction, so

בַּת־צִיּוֹן* לֹא יוֹסִיף לְהַגְלוֹתֵךְ* פָּקַד עֲוֹנֵךְ בַּת־

O daughter of Zion;* He will not again exile you.* [But] He will recall your iniquity, O daughter

אֱדוֹם גִּלָּה עַל־חַטֹּאתָיִךְ׃

of Edom; He will reveal about your sins.

[ה] א זְכֹר יהוה מֶה־הָיָה לָנוּ* °הַבִּיטָה [°הביט כ׳]

[5] 1 Remember, HASHEM, what has come upon us;* look

וּרְאֵה אֶת־חֶרְפָּתֵנוּ׃* ב נַחֲלָתֵנוּ נֶהֶפְכָה לְזָרִים

and see our disgrace.* 2 Our inheritance has been turned over to strangers,

---

will you drink excessively from the cup of destruction and be destroyed.]

22. תַּם־עֲוֹנֵךְ בַּת־צִיּוֹן — *Fully expiated is your iniquity, O daughter of Zion,* you have been punished for all your sins (*Rashi*).

You have been punished in one blow for the accumulation of all your iniquity (*Alshich*).

The *Midrash* notes that [the miseries and calamities related in] the Book of *Lamentations* were better for Israel than the forty years during which Jeremiah exhorted and prophesied. Because of the Destruction of the Temple, all Israel's sins were expiated that very day.

לֹא יוֹסִיף לְהַגְלוֹתֵךְ — *He will not again exile you,* beyond the Edomite [Roman, current] exile (*Rashi*).

[*Rashi* thus understands the subject *He* as referring to God.]

Ibn Ezra suggests that the subject is *your iniquity* [your iniquity will never again cause you to be exiled].

[The verse closes this chapter with the prophetic consolation that the worst of God's wrath upon the Jews has passed, and that now it is time for Edom's Day of Judgment.]

CHAPTER FIVE

[Chapter Five is composed of 22 verses like Chapters 1, 2, and 4; it differs from the previous four chapters in that it is not alphabetically arranged.]

1. זְכֹר ה׳ מֶה־הָיָה לָנוּ — *Remember, HASHEM, what has come upon us.* Remember the sufferings we endured before the Destruction, as well as our present disgraceful condition (*Ibn Ezra*).

Israel spoke before the Holy One, Blessed is He: We are subject to forgetfulness, but You are not. Since there is no forgetfulness before You, please remember... (*Midrash*).

Alshich interprets this as alluding not to former *suffering,* but to former *glory* (see below).

הַבִּיטָה וּרְאֵה אֶת־חֶרְפָּתֵנוּ — *Look and see our disgrace. Remember,* God, those who died at the hands of our enemies, and *look and see* the disgrace which we survivors suffer (*Lechem Dimah*).

Alshich explains that the suffering of a poor man who has never seen wealth cannot be compared with the greater suffering of a wealthy man who has been reduced to pauperdom — who is now publicly disgraced at having to beg for his very sustenance. Thus the exiles, who were thrust from the heights of glory to the lowest conditions of servility, commiserated over their fate and lamented: זְכֹר ה׳ מֶה־הָיָה לָנוּ, *Remember, HASHEM, what we have been* — during our time of royalty. And as You remember our former grandeur, הַבִּיטָה, *look,* at our present condition in exile, וּרְאֵה אֶת־חֶרְפָּתֵנוּ, *and see our disgrace* now, compared with our former glory.

בָּתֵּינוּ לְנָכְרִים: ג יְתוֹמִים הָיִינוּ °וְאֵין [°אין כ׳] אָב*

our houses ‹ to foreigners. « 3 Orphans ‹ have we become, ‹ without ‹ a father;* «

אִמֹּתֵינוּ כְּאַלְמָנוֹת: ד מֵימֵינוּ בְּכֶסֶף שָׁתִינוּ* עֵצֵינוּ

our mothers ‹ are like widows. « 4 Our water ‹ for money ‹ we must drink,* « our wood ‹

בִּמְחִיר יָבֹאוּ: ה עַל צַוָּארֵנוּ נִרְדָּפְנוּ יָגַעְנוּ

for a price ‹ comes [to us]. « 5 [With the yoke] upon ‹ our necks ‹ we are pursued; « we became exausted, ‹

°וְלֹא [°לא כ׳] הוּנַּח־לָנוּ:* ו מִצְרַיִם נָתַנּוּ יָד אַשּׁוּר

but there was no ‹ rest ‹ for us.* « 6 To the Egyptians ‹ we extended ‹ a hand, « and to Assyria, ‹

לִשְׂבֹּעַ לָחֶם: ז אֲבֹתֵינוּ חָטְאוּ °וְאֵינָם [°אינם כ׳]

to be sated ‹ with bread. « 7 Our fathers ‹ have sinned ‹ and are no more, «

°וַאֲנַחְנוּ [°אנחנו כ׳] עֲוֹנֹתֵיהֶם סָבָלְנוּ:* ח עֲבָדִים

but we, ‹ their iniquities ‹ have borne.* « 8 Slaves ‹

---

3. יְתוֹמִים הָיִינוּ וְאֵין אָב — *Orphans have we become, without a father. Without a father* refers to our relationship with God who is called *our Father* — God has, in a sense, removed Himself from us, leaving us *without a father* (*Alshich*).

Lechem Dimah [who also interprets *father* as God] notes that the כְּתִיב, written text, has אֵין אָב, *there is no father,* without the connecting prefix ו, *and.* It is therefore intended to be understood as a separate clause: The ravages of war made us *become orphans* from our natural father; in addition to that calamity, אֵין אָב, *there is no father,* because God has hidden Himself, so to speak, from us. But this verse is not to be understood as suggesting that God is no longer the Father of Israel, ח״ו, but that *He is not there,* in the sense that He maintains a distance instead of being available and paternal to His children.

4. מֵימֵינוּ בְּכֶסֶף שָׁתִינוּ — *Our water for money we must drink.* Because, due to the enemy, they were afraid to fetch it from the river. Instead, they were forced to purchase it at a high price from the enemy (*Rashi*) who had taken possession of their wells (*Alshich*).

Even the wells and trees which had been common property were sold at exorbitant prices due to the siege (*Ibn Ezra*).

5. וְלֹא הוּנַּח־לָנוּ — *But there was no rest for us.* They acquired everything we had by imposing taxes and levies (*Rashi*).

The *Midrash* translates וְלֹא הוּנַּח־לָנוּ, *and we were given no rest.*

6. מִצְרַיִם נָתַנּוּ יָד — *To the Egyptians we extended a hand.* The *Midrash* relates that the Jews had traded their oil with Egypt for foodstuff which they then sent to Assyria in the hope that, if the enemy were to advance, Egypt and Assyria would come to their assistance. Ultimately the pact was fruitless; when the attack came, her "allies" ignored her [see also 4:17]. The futility of this ill-fated arrangement is now lamented by the prophet (*Torah Temimah*).

7. אֲבֹתֵינוּ חָטְאוּ וְאֵינָם וַאֲנַחְנוּ עֲוֹנֹתֵיהֶם סָבָלְנוּ — *Our fathers have sinned and are no more, but we, their iniquities have borne.* Several interpretations are given for this

מָשְׁלוּ בָנוּ פֹּרֵק אֵין מִיָּדָם: ט בְּנַפְשֵׁנוּ נָבִיא

ruled / over us, / a redeemer / there was not / from their hands. / **9** Risking our lives / we must bring

לַחְמֵנוּ מִפְּנֵי חֶרֶב הַמִּדְבָּר: י עוֹרֵנוּ כְּתַנּוּר נִכְמָרוּ

our bread, / because of / the sword / of the wilderness. / **10** Our skin / like in an oven / became heated,

מִפְּנֵי זַלְעֲפוֹת רָעָב: יא נָשִׁים בְּצִיּוֹן עִנּוּ בְּתֻלֹת

because of / the fever / of famine. / **11** Women / in Zion / they did ravage; / maidens

בְּעָרֵי יְהוּדָה:* יב שָׂרִים בְּיָדָם נִתְלוּ פְּנֵי זְקֵנִים

in the towns / of Judah.* / **12** Leaders / by them / were hanged, / the face / of the elders

---

important verse. A comprehensive selection follows:

Ibn Ezra comments that our misfortune is the result of our sins which intermingled with the sins of our ancestors for which they were not punished according to the doctrine of פֹּקֵד עֲוֹן אָבֹת עַל־בָּנִים ... [לְשֹׂנְאָי], *Who visits the sin of fathers upon children ... [for My enemies]* (*Exodus* 20:5). [*Ramban*, quoting the *Talmud* (*Sanhedrin* 27b), explains that God punishes children for the sins of the fathers only if the children persist in committing those sins.]

The *Arizal* offers an interpretation to harmonize the apparent contradiction between the verses *punishing the* עָוֹן, *sin, of fathers upon children* (*Exodus* 20:5), and אִישׁ בְּחֶטְאוֹ יוּמָתוּ, *a man for his own sin shall be put to death* (*Deuteronomy* 24:16). He points out — in addition to the Talmudic explanation above that the verse in *Exodus* applies only when the children persist in their fathers' ways — that there is also a distinction between עָוֹן, *iniquity*, and חֵטְא, *sin*. *Iniquity* [referring to the verse in *Exodus*] applies to מֵזִיד, *willful* transgressions, for which, according to the Torah, children share the guilt. The verse in *Deuteronomy*, however, refers to חֵטְא, *unintentional* trangressions, for which children are not punished. Thus, the *Arizal* explains our verse [as does *Ibn Yachya, Lechem Dimah*]: *Our fathers* חָטְאוּ, *sinned unintentionally*, וְאֵינָם, *and they are not* — we are not being held accountable for them; וַאֲנַחְנוּ עֲוֹנֹתֵיהֶם סָבָלְנוּ, *but for* עֲוֹנֹתֵיהֶם, *their intentional trangressions* — for those we *do* suffer.

[It must be stressed that the Jews were *not* suggesting that their suffering was *wholly* the result of their fathers' sins. They admitted complicity, too, as evidenced by the outcry in verse 16: אוֹי־נָא לָנוּ כִּי חָטָאנוּ, *woe now to us, for we have sinned*. Rather, as suggested by *Ibn Ezra* (above), they acknowledged their share of the iniquity. Added together with the sins of their ancestors, the cumulative guilt was the cause of their present predicament.]

Lechem Dimah explains that it would be more appropriate for the fathers to receive their own punishment. But since אֵינָם, *they are no more*, it is only just their children — who according to halachah are enjoined to say after a father's death, אֲנִי כַּפָּרַת מִשְׁכָּבוֹ, *"I am the atonement for his repose"* — who should accept responsibility. As the *Alshich* notes, no atonement is necessary for חֲטָאִים, *the unintentional sins* of parents, because death atones for them. For עֲוֹנוֹת, *intentional trangressions*, however, death does not suffice; suffering is a required part of the atonement. Children, therefore, should accept the obligation to atone for the sins of their parents.

11. נָשִׁים בְּצִיּוֹן עִנּוּ בְּתֻלֹת בְּעָרֵי יְהוּדָה — *Women in Zion they did ravage; maidens in the towns of Judah.* As if the sufferings of famine were not punishment enough,

לֹא נֶהְדָּרוּ: יג בַּחוּרִים טְחוֹן נָשָׂאוּ וּנְעָרִים בָּעֵץ

‹ carrying wood ‹ and youths « they bear, ‹ the millstone ‹ Young men 13 « shown any respect. ‹ was not

כָּשָׁלוּ:* יד זְקֵנִים מִשַּׁעַר שָׁבָתוּ בַּחוּרִים מִנְּגִינָתָם:*

« from their music.* ‹ young men « have ceased, ‹ from the gates ‹ The elders 14 « stumble.*

טו שָׁבַת מְשׂוֹשׂ לִבֵּנוּ נֶהְפַּךְ לְאֵבֶל מְחוֹלֵנוּ: טז נָפְלָה

« It fell 16 « is our dancing. ‹ into mourning ‹ changed « of our hearts; ‹ is the joy ‹ Ceased 15

עֲטֶרֶת רֹאשֵׁנוּ אוֹי־נָא לָנוּ כִּי חָטָאנוּ:* יז עַל־זֶה

‹ this ‹ For 17 « we have sinned.* ‹ for ‹ to us, ‹ now ‹ woe « of our head [did]; ‹ — the crown

---

the slaves [verse 8] ravaged our wives (*Ibn Ezra*).

The greater the sanctity of the place, the more heinous their sins. In Judah, the enemy limited himself to ravaging בְּתֻלֹת, *unmarried maidens;* in the higher sanctity of Zion, the environs of Jerusalem and the Temple, he was brazen and defiant enough toward God to show his contempt and ravage נָשִׁים, *married women* (*Kiflayim LeSushiyah*).

Lechem Dimah explains that when the Babylonian soldiers marched on Zion, they first passed through the towns of Judah. Not yet being sure of their own strength, they limited their ravages to unmarried maidens. But by the time they reached Jerusalem, the tide of war was going with them and they were fully confident of victory. Then they stopped at nothing, even ravaging married women.

The *Targum* translates: Married women in Zion were ravaged by Arameans [Edomites; *Ibn Yachya* and *Lechem Dimah* version of *Targum* reads *Romans*]; *maidens in the towns of Judah* by Chaldeans (Babylonians).

13. וּנְעָרִים בָּעֵץ כָּשָׁלוּ — *And youths carrying wood stumble.* Rav Yehoshua ben Levi said: Three hundred children were found hung by the enemy on one branch (*Midrash*).

According to *Alshich*: The children grew so weak that they would stumble over a branch lying on the road.

14. זְקֵנִים מִשַּׁעַר שָׁבָתוּ בַּחוּרִים מִנְּגִינָתָם — *The elders from the gates have ceased, young men from their music.* [It had been the custom for elders to station themselves at the gates (see *Ruth* 4:1; *Esther* 2:21). Now the gates lie desolate (see above 1:4).]

Elders here refer to the wise men, as the *Talmud* states: כִּי אֵין זָקֵן אֶלָּא מִי שֶׁקָּנָה חָכְמָה, for זָקֵן, *elder,* means only one who has acquired wisdom [*Kiddushin* 32b]. They have departed from the *gates of Halachah.* Similarly, *young men* refers to the young students who would study Mishnah by heart, and put the words to a melody as an aid to memorization. They, too, sang no longer (*Lechem Dimah*).

In verses 11-14, we have a description of how the enemy attacked every segment of the population in every social strata: married women and maidens; officers and elders; young men and children (*Rav Almosnino*).

16. אוֹי־נָא לָנוּ כִּי חָטָאנוּ — *Woe now to us, for we have sinned.* Now that the Temple is destroyed, how will we atone for our sins? Previously, a sinner would offer a sacrifice to atone for his sins. Now there is no longer a Temple. Woe to us! (*Lechem Dimah*).

[This is an obvious confession, a recognition that everything that has befallen them is the result — and just reward — for their sinful ways (see comm. to verse 7).]

הָיָה דָוֶה לִבֵּנוּ* עַל־אֵלֶּה חָשְׁכוּ עֵינֵינוּ:* יח עַל

‹ for **18** « were our eyes: ‹ darkened ‹ these things ‹ for « our heart faint,* ‹ was

הַר־צִיּוֹן שֶׁשָּׁמֵם* שׁוּעָלִים הִלְּכוּ־בוֹ: יט אַתָּה יהוה

‹ HASHEM, ‹ Yet You, **19** « upon it. ‹ prowled ‹ foxes « which became desolate,* ‹ Zion ‹ Mount

לְעוֹלָם תֵּשֵׁב* כִּסְאֲךָ לְדוֹר וָדוֹר: כ לָמָּה לָנֶצַח

‹ eternally ‹ Why **20** « to generation. ‹ is from generation ‹ Your throne « are enthroned,* ‹ forever

תִּשְׁכָּחֵנוּ תַּעַזְבֵנוּ לְאֹרֶךְ יָמִים: כא הֲשִׁיבֵנוּ יהוה |

‹ HASHEM, ‹ Bring us back, **21** « of days? ‹ for the length ‹ forsake us « do You forget us,

אֵלֶיךָ °וְנָשׁוּבָה* [°ונשוב כ׳] חַדֵּשׁ יָמֵינוּ כְּקֶדֶם:*

« as of old. ‹ our days ‹ renew « and we shall return;* ‹ to You,

---

17-18. עַל־זֶה הָיָה דָוֶה לִבֵּנוּ — *For this our heart was faint* [or *sick*], etc. For what is described in the next verse (the desolation of Mount Zion with foxes prowling it) (*Rashi*).

Alshich interprets the first half of this verse as referring to remorse over her sins which were the cause of Destruction; the second half of the verse to the desolation of Mount Zion.

The *Midrash* comments: Just as a woman who separates from her husband for a few days because of impurity is called דָוָה, *sick* [*Leviticus* 15:33], how much more should *we* be called דָוֶה, *sick*, for being separated from the "house of our life," the Temple, for these many years!

עַל־אֵלֶּה חָשְׁכוּ עֵינֵינוּ — *For these things darkened were our eyes* from excessive weeping *(Ibn Ezra)*.

For none of our other catastrophes and suffering did our hearts grow so faint or did we weep so much, as for *"Mount Zion which became desolate, foxes prowled upon it" (Rav Yosef Kara; Palgei Mayim)*.

עַל הַר־צִיּוֹן שֶׁשָּׁמֵם ... — *For Mount Zion which became desolate, foxes prowled upon it.* Its desolation is so utter, that foxes, which usually dwell in ruins, prowl freely and undisturbed over it (*Alshich; Ibn Ezra*).

[In this context *Mount Zion* is used poetically in place of Mount Moriah — the actual site of the Temple.]

19-20. אַתָּה ה׳ לְעוֹלָם תֵּשֵׁב — *Yet You, HASHEM, forever are enthroned.* Although the manifestation of Your Kingship on earth is in ruins, nevertheless, Your dominion will never cease. You are enthroned forever. So if Your incorporeality is undiminished, and our sins only affect material manifestations of Your holiness, *why do You ignore us eternally? (Alshich)*.

[It follows that since Hashem's Kingship *is ageless*, His throne itself will ultimately be restored.] Is there enthronement without a throne; a king without a consort? [Jerusalem is the throne: Israel the consort (*Torah Temimah*)] (*Midrash*).

21. הֲשִׁיבֵנוּ ה׳ אֵלֶיךָ וְנָשׁוּבָה — *Bring us back, HASHEM, to You, and we shall return* [or *repent*]. Israel addresses God: All we ask is for some Divine assistance. If You initiate the action, and draw us near to You, then we will repent our sins and return to You wholeheartedly (*Lechem Dimah*).

The *Midrash* relates that there is a constant dispute, so to speak, between Hashem and Israel. God insists: שׁוּבוּ אֵלַי

כב כִּי אִם־מָאֹס מְאַסְתָּנוּ* קָצַפְתָּ עָלֵינוּ עַד־מְאֹד:

22 For ‹ even if ‹ You had utterly rejected us,* « You have already raged ‹ against us ‹ to ‹ an extreme. «

THE FOLLOWING VERSE IS RECITED ALOUD BY THE CONGREGATION, THEN BY THE READER:

הֲשִׁיבֵנוּ יהוה | אֵלֶיךָ וְנָשׁוּבָה

Bring us back, ‹ HASHEM, ‹ to You, ‹ and we shall return; «

חַדֵּשׁ יָמֵינוּ כְּקֶדֶם:

renew ‹ our days ‹ as of old. «

וְאָשׁוּבָה אֲלֵיכֶם, [First] *return to Me and* [then] *I will return to you* (*Malachi* 3:7); and Israel answers: הֲשִׁיבֵנוּ ה׳ אֵלֶיךָ וְנָשׁוּבָה, [First] *bring us back,* HASHEM, *to You and* [then] *we shall return.* Neither side gives in and thus the dispute, as to who will take the initiative, continues . . .

. . .The *Maggid of Kozhnitz* explains homiletically that this is why we face the Master of the universe and say: לָמָּה לָנֶצַח תִּשְׁכָּחֵנוּ, נִצָּחוֹן, *why for the sake of victory, do You forget us,* Your children? Whom are you defeating: Your foolish stubborn children? Concede, O Merciful God, this one time! הֲשִׁיבֵנוּ ה׳ אֵלֶיךָ וְנָשׁוּבָה, *Bring us back,* HASHEM, *to You, and we shall return!*

Ibn Ezra translates הֲשִׁיבֵנוּ, *bring us back,* in the physical sense: *Bring us back* to the city of the Dwelling Place of Your Name, [Jerusalem,] and we will resume serving You as before.

חַדֵּשׁ יָמֵינוּ כְּקֶדֶם — *Renew our days as of old.* As it is written (*Malachi* 3:4): *Then shall the offering of Judah and Jerusalem be pleasant to* HASHEM, כִּימֵי עוֹלָם, *as in the days of old,* וּכְשָׁנִים קַדְמוֹנִיּוֹת, *and as in ancient years* (*Midrash*) — Renew our days as You did when You took us out of Egypt (*Ibn Shuib*).

22. כִּי אִם־מָאֹס מְאַסְתָּנוּ — *For even if You had utterly rejected us* [lit., *reject, You rejected us*], *You have already raged against us to an extreme.* Although we sinned, You did not have to increase rage against us as much as You did (*Rashi*).

The use of the double verb מָאֹס מְאַסְתָּנוּ, *Reject, You rejected us,* is interpreted as referring prophetically to both Temples (*Alshich*).

Pesikta d'Rav Kahana translates: *If it is "rejection," then You completely rejected us; but You are very 'wroth' against us.* That is, if God has *rejected* Israel, then there is no hope. If, however, He is no more than *wrathful,* then there is hope, for He Who is angered is likely to become reconciled.

Rav Levi Yitzchak of Berditchev explains these verses as follows:

Someone may divorce his wife for one of two reasons: for having found in her עֶרְוַת דָּבָר, an immorality; or because she no longer finds favor in his eyes. If he divorces her for the former reason, he may never remarry her; if for the latter, he may remarry her. This is how these verses הֲשִׁיבֵנוּ, *Bring us back,* are to be understood. You did not divorce us because of עֶרְוַת דָּבָר, that our behavior was so improper that You cannot ever take us back. Rather, You divorced us, כִּי אִם־מָאֹס מְאַסְתָּנוּ, because *You had utterly rejected us*; i.e. we no longer found favor in Your eyes. As such You may bring us back to You.

הֲשִׁיבֵנוּ ה׳ — *Bring us back . . .* HASHEM. It is customary to repeat verse 21 rather than end with the words of rebuke in verse 22. We act similarly at the conclusion of *Isaiah, Malachi,* and *Ecclesiastes* [and thus end these books on a comforting note] (*Rashi*).

KINNAH 1 / קינה א

זְכֹר יהוה* מֶה הָיָה לָנוּ,[1] אוֹי,

Remember, HASHEM,* what has happened to us, O woe!

הַבִּיטָה וּרְאֵה אֶת חֶרְפָּתֵנוּ,[2] אוֹי, מֶה הָיָה לָנוּ.

Look and see our disgrace, O woe! What has happened to us!

נַחֲלָתֵנוּ נֶהֶפְכָה לְזָרִים,[3] אוֹי,

Our inheritance, [Israel] has been turned over to strangers, O woe!

בָּתֵּינוּ לְנָכְרִים,[4] אוֹי, מֶה הָיָה לָנוּ.

Our homes [turned over] to foreigners, O woe! What has happened to us!

יְתוֹמִים הָיִינוּ וְאֵין אָב,[5] אוֹי,

Orphans we have become, without a father, O woe!

אִמּוֹתֵינוּ מְקוֹנְנוֹת בְּחֹדֶשׁ אָב, אוֹי, מֶה הָיָה לָנוּ.

Our mothers lament in the month of Av, O woe! What has happened to us!

(1) *Eichah* 5:1. (2) Ibid. (3) 5:2.(4) Ibid. (5) 5:3.

זְכֹר ה׳ — *Remember, HASHEM.* Many of the *kinnos* are arranged according to the verses of one or more chapters of *Eichah* (the Book of *Lamentations*). This first *kinnah* is based on the fifth chapter. Each stanza contains two lines. The first stich is the opening phrase of the corresponding verse in *Eichah*, followed by the word אוֹי, *O woe!* The second stich rhymes with the first and is either the *paytan's* extension of the verse's lament, or his explanation of why the tragedy described in the first stich occurred. The phrase, 'אוֹי מֶה הָיָה לָנוּ, *O woe! What has happened to us!*' is inserted at the end of the stanza. This format allows us to focus carefully on each tragedy and to respond with a personal sigh of grief, 'אוֹי, *O woe . . .*' The last four verses of *Eichah* appear at the end of the *kinnah* in their entirety, without the added phrases.

In some early editions of *Kinnos* this *kinnah* does not appear. Instead, there is an instruction that reads, "The *chazzan* repeats [the chapter beginning] זְכֹר ה׳, *Remember,* HASHEM, and inserts אוֹי, *O woe!*, in the middle of each verse, and אוֹי מֶה הָיָה לָנוּ, *O woe! What has befallen us!*, at the end. From the verse אַתָּה ה׳, *Yet You,* HASHEM, he omits the insertions . . . but recites the verses as they appear in *Eichah* . . . ."

Whether this *kinnah* is recited in the words of *Eichah* or in the words of the *paytan*, the repetition of the last chapter of Jeremiah's lament emphasizes that the Destruction of the Temples did not bring an end to Jewish suffering and tragedy; on the contrary, it marked the beginning of what seems like an interminable series of exiles and massacres. Nevertheless, if we return to HASHEM, He will return us to Him and to His Land.

מֵימֵינוּ בְּכֶסֶף שָׁתִינוּ,[1] אוֹי,

Our own water ‹ only after paying money ‹ do we drink, « O woe!

כִּי נִסּוּךְ הַמַּיִם בָּזִינוּ,* אוֹי, מֶה הָיָה לָנוּ.

Because ‹ the [Succos] libation ‹ of water ‹ we scorned,* « O woe! « What ‹ has happened ‹ to us! «

עַל צַוָּארֵנוּ נִרְדָּפְנוּ,[2] אוֹי,

[With a yoke] upon ‹ our necks ‹ we are pursued, « O woe!

כִּי שִׂנְאַת חִנָּם רָדַפְנוּ,[3] אוֹי, מֶה הָיָה לָנוּ.

Because ‹ hatred ‹ without justification ‹ we pursued, « O woe! « What ‹ has happened ‹ to us! «

מִצְרַיִם נָתַנּוּ יָד,[4] אוֹי,

To the Egyptians ‹ we extended ‹ a hand, « O woe!

וְאַשּׁוּר צָדוּנוּ כְּצַיָּד, אוֹי, מֶה הָיָה לָנוּ.

While Assyria ‹ hunted us ‹ like a hunter, « O woe! « What ‹ has happened ‹ to us! «

אֲבוֹתֵינוּ חָטְאוּ וְאֵינָם,[5] אוֹי,

Our fathers ‹ sinned ‹ and are no more, « O woe!

וַאֲנַחְנוּ סוֹבְּלִים אֶת עֲוֹנָם,[6] אוֹי, מֶה הָיָה לָנוּ.

But we ‹ bear the burden ‹ of their iniquities, « O woe! « What ‹ has happened ‹ to us! «

עֲבָדִים מָשְׁלוּ בָנוּ,[7] אוֹי,

Slaves ‹ ruled ‹ over us, « O woe!

כִּי שִׁלּוּחַ עֲבָדִים בִּטַּלְנוּ,[8] אוֹי, מֶה הָיָה לָנוּ.

Because ‹ the liberation ‹ of the [Hebrew] slaves ‹ we discontinued, « O woe! « What ‹ has happened ‹ to us! «

(1) *Eichah* 5:4. (2) 5:5. (3) See *Yoma* 9b. (4) *Eichah* 5:6. (5) 5:7.
(6) Cf. Ibid. (7) 5:8. (8) See *Exodus* 21:2 and *Jeremiah* 34:8ff.

כִּי נִסּוּךְ הַמַּיִם בָּזִינוּ — *Because the [Succos] libation of water we scorned.* It is axiomatic that God rewards and punishes מִדָּה כְּנֶגֶד מִדָּה, *measure for measure.* Therefore, when retribution is visited upon the nation, there must be a cause-and-effect relationship between the deed in whose wake that retribution comes and the specific form it takes. In thirteen of the next fifteen stanzas, the *paytan* traces these relationships.

בְּנַפְשֵׁנוּ נָבִיא לַחְמֵנוּ,[1] אוֹי,

« our bread, ‹ do we bring ‹ Risking our lives — « O woe!

כִּי קָפַצְנוּ מֵעֲנִי יָדֵינוּ,[2] אוֹי, מֶה הָיָה לָנוּ.

« our hands, « — from [giving to] the poor — ‹ we have closed ‹ Because — « to us! ‹ has happened ‹ What « O woe!

עוֹרֵנוּ כְּתַנּוּר נִכְמָרוּ,[3] אוֹי,

« was shriveled, ‹ like [from] an oven ‹ Our skin — « O woe!

כִּי כְבוֹדָם בְּקָלוֹן הֵמִירוּ,[4] אוֹי, מֶה הָיָה לָנוּ.

« they have exchanged, ‹ for disgrace ‹ their dignity [God and the Torah] ‹ Because — « to us! ‹ has happened ‹ What « O woe!

נָשִׁים בְּצִיּוֹן עִנּוּ,[5] אוֹי,

« they ravaged, ‹ in Zion ‹ Women — « O woe!

כִּי אִישׁ אֶת אֵשֶׁת רֵעֵהוּ טִמְּאוּ וְזָנוּ,[6]

« [through] adultery, ‹ he defiled ‹ of his neighbor ‹ the wife ‹ [every] man ‹ Because

אוֹי, מֶה הָיָה לָנוּ.

« to us! ‹ has happened ‹ What « O woe!

שָׂרִים בְּיָדָם נִתְלוּ,[7] אוֹי,

« were hanged, ‹ by their hands ‹ Leaders — « O woe!

כִּי גְזֵלַת הֶעָנִי[8] חָמְסוּ וְגָזָלוּ, אוֹי, מֶה הָיָה לָנוּ.

« and they stole, ‹ [what] they plundered ‹ from the poor, ‹ of what they robbed ‹ Because — « to us! ‹ has happened ‹ What « O woe!

בַּחוּרִים טְחוֹן* נָשָׂאוּ,[9] אוֹי,

« do they bear, ‹ the millstone* ‹ Young men, — « O woe!

כִּי בְּבֵית זוֹנָה* נִמְצָאוּ,[10] אוֹי, מֶה הָיָה לָנוּ.

« they were found, ‹ of a harlot* ‹ in the house ‹ Because — « to us! ‹ has happened ‹ What « O woe!

(1) *Eichah* 5:9. (2) Cf. *Deuteronomy* 15:7. (3) *Eichah* 5:10. (4) Cf. *Hosea* 4:7; cf. *Jeremiah* 2:11. (5) *Eichah* 5:11. (6) Cf. *Ezekiel* 18:11. (7) *Eichah* 5:12. (8) Cf. *Isaiah* 3:14. (9) *Eichah* 5:13. (10) Cf. *Jeremiah* 5:7.

טְחוֹן . . . בְּבֵית זוֹנָה — *The millstone . . . in the house of a harlot.* The Sages understand the root טחן, literally, *grind,* as a euphemism for adultery (*Sotah* 10a;

זְקֵנִים מִשַּׁעַר שָׁבָתוּ,[1] אוֹי,

The elders / from the gates / have ceased, / O woe!

כִּי מִשְׁפַּט יָתוֹם וְאַלְמָנָה עִוְּתוּ,[2] אוֹי, מֶה הָיָה לָנוּ.

Because / the judgment / of the orphan / and the widow / they corrupted, / O woe! / What / has happened / to us!

שָׁבַת מְשׂוֹשׂ לִבֵּנוּ,[3] אוֹי,

Ceased / is the joy / of our hearts, / O woe!

כִּי נִבְטְלוּ עוֹלֵי רְגָלֵינוּ, אוֹי, מֶה הָיָה לָנוּ.

Because / discontinued / were the pilgrimages / of our festivals, / O woe! / What / has happened / to us!

נָפְלָה עֲטֶרֶת רֹאשֵׁנוּ,[4] אוֹי,

It fell / — [did] the crown / of our head, / O woe!

כִּי נִשְׂרַף בֵּית מִקְדָּשֵׁנוּ,[5] אוֹי, מֶה הָיָה לָנוּ.

Because / was burnt / the Temple / of our holiness, / O woe! / What / has happened / to us!

עַל זֶה הָיָה דָוֶה לִבֵּנוּ,[6] אוֹי,

For / this / was / our heart faint, / O woe!

כִּי נִבְטַל כְּבוֹד בֵּית מַאֲוָיֵינוּ,[7] אוֹי, מֶה הָיָה לָנוּ.

Because / was cancelled / the glory / of the House / of our Aspirations, / O woe! / What / has happened / to us!

עַל הַר צִיּוֹן שֶׁשָּׁמֵם,[8] אוֹי,

For / Mount / Zion / which became desolate, / O woe!

כִּי הַר הַבַּיִת מְשׁוֹמֵם,[9] אוֹי, מֶה הָיָה לָנוּ.

Because / the Mount / of the Temple / is in ruins, / O woe! / What / has happened / to us!

---

(1) *Eichah* 5:14. (2) Cf. *Deuteronomy* 27:19. (3) *Eichah* 5:15. (4) 5:16. (5) Cf. *Isaiah* 64:10. (6) *Eichah* 5:17. (7) Cf. *Mussaf,* Sabbath Rosh Chodesh. (8) *Eichah* 5:18. (9) Alternate text: כִּי נִתַּן עָלָיו שִׁקּוּץ מְשׁוֹמֵם, *For there was placed upon it an abominable idol that is mute.* Cf. *Daniel* 9:27 and Mishnah *Taanis* 4:6.

Eichah Rabbah 5:13). Hence, the burden of carrying a heavy millstone is apt punishment for frequenting the harlot's house.

אַתָּה יהוה לְעוֹלָם תֵּשֵׁב כִּסְאֲךָ לְדוֹר וָדוֹר.

Yet You, HASHEM, forever are enthroned, Your throne is from generation to generation.

לָמָּה לָנֶצַח תִּשְׁכָּחֵנוּ תַּעַזְבֵנוּ לְאֹרֶךְ יָמִים.

Why eternally do You forget us, forsake us for the length of days?

הֲשִׁיבֵנוּ יהוה אֵלֶיךָ וְנָשׁוּבָה חַדֵּשׁ יָמֵינוּ כְּקֶדֶם.

Bring us back, HASHEM, to You, and we shall return; renew our days as of old.

כִּי אִם מָאֹס מְאַסְתָּנוּ קָצַפְתָּ עָלֵינוּ עַד מְאֹד.

For even if You had utterly rejected us, You have already raged against us to an extreme.

הֲשִׁיבֵנוּ יהוה אֵלֶיךָ וְנָשׁוּבָה חַדֵּשׁ יָמֵינוּ כְּקֶדֶם.[1]

Bring us back, HASHEM, to You, and we shall return; renew our days as of old.

(1) *Eichah* 5:19-22.

ON SATURDAY NIGHT:

KINNAH 2 / קִינָה ב

אֵיךְ מִפִּי בֵּן וּבַת, הֲגוּת קִינוֹת רַבַּת,

« in profusion, ‹ lamentations ‹ are voiced ‹ and daughter ‹ of son ‹ [that] from the mouth ‹ O how is it

תְּמוּר שִׁירִים וְחֶדְוַת,

« and jubilation? ‹ songs ‹ instead of

וִיהִי נֹעַם[1] נִשְׁבַּת,* בְּמוֹצָאֵי שַׁבָּת.

« of the Sabbath. ‹ at the departure ‹ is omitted* ‹ the pleasantness" ‹ The [prayer,] "May

אוֹי, כִּי נִגְזְרָה גְזֵרָה, בָּחֳרִי אַף[2] וְגַם עֶבְרָה,[3]

« with wrath; ‹ as well as ‹ anger ‹ with flaring ‹ the decree ‹ there was issued ‹ For « O woe!

וְאַפּוֹ בָּנוּ חָרָה, וּבָעֲרָה חֲמָתוֹ כְּלַבַּת,[2]

« like a flame! ‹ and burn did His fury ‹ flared ‹ against us ‹ His anger

וִיהִי נֹעַם נִשְׁבַּת, בְּמוֹצָאֵי שַׁבָּת.

« of the Sabbath. ‹ at the departure ‹ is omitted ‹ the pleasantness" ‹ The [prayer,] "May

אוֹי, כִּי בָתֵּינוּ שֻׁנּוּ,[4] וּבְתוּלוֹתֵינוּ עֻנּוּ,[5]

« they ravished; ‹ and our maidens « they turned over, ‹ our homes [to strangers] ‹ For « O woe!

וּפָנֵינוּ נִשְׁתַּנּוּ, וְגַם הוּשְׁחֲרוּ[6] כְּמַחֲבַת,

« like a frying pan. ‹ blackened ‹ and also ‹ are distorted ‹ our faces

וִיהִי נֹעַם נִשְׁבַּת, בְּמוֹצָאֵי שַׁבָּת.

« of the Sabbath. ‹ at the departure ‹ is omitted ‹ the pleasantness" ‹ The [prayer,] "May

(1) *Psalms* 90:17 - 91:16. (2) Cf. *Eichah* 2:3.
(3) Cf. *Isaiah* 13:9. (4) Cf. *Eichah* 5:2. (5) Cf. 5:11. (6) Cf. 4:8.

וִיהִי נֹעַם נִשְׁבַּת — *The [prayer] "May the Pleasantness" is omitted.* Although this prayer (*Psalms* 90:17-91:16) is usually recited at the departure of the Sabbath, it is omitted when Tishah B'Av follows immediately after the Sabbath. This is because the prayer was composed by Moses in honor of the completion of the מִשְׁכָּן [*Mishkan*], *Tabernacle*, in the Wilderness (*Midrash Tehillim*). Since the

אוֹי, כִּי שַׁדְּדוּנוּ צָרִים, וְגַם הִפִּילוּ בָנוּ פְּגָרִים,

« corpses, ‹ among us ‹ cast down ‹ and also « have enemies, ‹ plundered us ‹ For « O woe!

בְּנֵי צִיּוֹן הַיְּקָרִים,[1] הָיוּ נְצוּרִים כְּבָבַת,

« like the pupil [of the eye]. ‹ protected ‹ who had been « who were precious, ‹ of Zion, ‹ the children

וִיהִי נֹעַם נִשְׁבַּת, בְּמוֹצָאֵי שַׁבָּת.

« of the Sabbath. ‹ at the departure ‹ is omitted ‹ the pleasantness" ‹ The [prayer,] "May

אוֹי, כִּי נָפְלָה עֲטֶרֶת,[2] וְגָבְרָה כָּתֵף סוֹרֶרֶת,[3]

« that rebelled [against God]; ‹ has the shoulder ‹ and prevailed « has the crown[like Temple], ‹ fallen ‹ For « O woe!

וְחָדַל הוֹד וְתִפְאֶרֶת, צִמְצוּם שֶׁכֵּן חִבַּת,[4]

« with love. ‹ [His] Presence ‹ [where He] had concentrated « and splendor, ‹ have majesty ‹ ceased [from the Temple]

וִיהִי נֹעַם נִשְׁבַּת, בְּמוֹצָאֵי שַׁבָּת.

« of the Sabbath. ‹ at the departure ‹ is omitted ‹ the pleasantness" ‹ The [prayer,] "May

אוֹי, כִּי נֻטְּלָה מְנוֹרָה, וּקְטֹרֶת לְבוֹנָה הַטְּהוֹרָה,

« that is pure; ‹ of the frankincense ‹ and the incense « was the Menorah, ‹ taken away ‹ For « O woe!

וְנִבְזֶה גָּזִית[5] מְיֻקָּרָה, אֻכְּלָה אֶרֶץ זָבַת,

« of flowing [milk and honey]. ‹ the land ‹ as has been consumed « that had been cherished; ‹ is the hewn-stone [Sanhedrin chamber] ‹ disdained

וִיהִי נֹעַם נִשְׁבַּת, בְּמוֹצָאֵי שַׁבָּת.

« of the Sabbath. ‹ at the departure ‹ is omitted ‹ the pleasantness" ‹ The [prayer,] "May

(1) Cf. *Eichah* 4:2. (2) Cf. 5:16. (3) Cf. *Zechariah* 7:11; *Nehemiah* 9:29. (4) Cf. *Vayikra Rabbah* 29:4. (5) Cf. *Middos* 5:4.

Mishkan served the same function as the *Beis HaMikdash*, it would be unseemly to recite this prayer on the anniversary of the Destruction (*Matteh Moshe* 729, cited in *Taamei HaMinhagim*). Additionally, as stated in *Taanis* (29a), the Temple was destroyed on the day after the Sabbath (*R' Asher b'R' Yosef*).

KINNAH 3 / קינה ג

בְּלֵיל זֶה* יִבְכָּיוּן וְיֵילִילוּ בָנַי,

« shall my children, ‹ and wail, ‹ weep ‹ On this night

בְּלֵיל זֶה חָרַב בֵּית קָדְשִׁי וְנִשְׂרְפוּ אַרְמוֹנַי,[1]

« were my palaces; ‹ and burnt down ‹ my Holy Temple ‹ was destroyed ‹ [for] on this night

וְכָל בֵּית יִשְׂרָאֵל יֶהְגּוּ בִּיגוֹנַי,

« about my agony, ‹ shall voice [laments] ‹ of Israel ‹ House ‹ the entire

וְיִבְכּוּ אֶת הַשְּׂרֵפָה אֲשֶׁר שָׂרַף יהוה.[2]

« HASHEM has burned. ‹ that ‹ the burning ‹ over ‹ and they shall weep

בְּלֵיל זֶה תְּיַלֵּל מַר עֲנִיָּה נֶחְדֶּלֶת,

« [whose glory] has ceased; ‹ the impoverished one [Israel], ‹ bitterly ‹ shall wail ‹ On this night,

וּמִבֵּית אָבִיהָ בְּחַיִּים מֻבְדֶּלֶת,

« was estranged; ‹ even while He is alive ‹ of her Father ‹ and who from the Temple

וְיָצְאָה מִבֵּיתוֹ וְנִסְגַּר הַדֶּלֶת,

« was the door [to redemption]; ‹ and closed ‹ from his house ‹ she went forth

וְהָלְכָה בַּשְּׁבִיָּה בְּכָל פֶּה נֶאֱכֶלֶת,

« she was devoured, ‹ mouth ‹ where by every ‹ into captivity ‹ she went

(1) Cf. *II Chronicles* 36:19; see *II Kings* 25:9. (2) *Leviticus* 10:6.

בְּלֵיל זֶה — *On this night.* When the Spies returned after forty days of reconnoitering the Land of Canaan, they produced a terribly slanderous report about the Land. Rather than have faith in God's promise to bring them to a land of flowing milk and honey where they would live under Divine protection, the nation chose to believe the Spies' discouraging word, and they wept that night (*Numbers* 13:25 - 14:1). God was infuriated at Israel's treachery and declared, "Since you shed tears on this night for no reason, I shall give you many reasons to cry on this night!" (*Taanis* 29a).

Thus, the date of Tishah B'Av became a day of repeated tragedies throughout Jewish history. The Mishnah enumerates five of these dire events: (a) Because the nation believed the Spies' malicious report, the guilty ones were sentenced to die in the wilderness, before the nation would enter the Land; (b-c) the First and Second Temples were destroyed; (d) Bar Kochba's revolt was crushed and his stronghold at Beitar was captured by the Romans [so

בְּיוֹם שֻׁלְּחָה בָּאֵשׁ בּוֹעֶרֶת וְאוֹכֶלֶת,

« and consuming — ‹ that is flaming ‹ with a fire ‹ she was ignited ‹ on the very day

וְאֵשׁ עִם גַּחֶלֶת יָצְאָה מֵאֵת יהוה.[1]

« HASHEM. ‹ from ‹ went forth ‹ the coal ‹ and ‹ where the fire

בְּלֵיל זֶה יִבְכָּיוּן וְיֵילִילוּ בָנַי . . .

« shall my children . . . ‹ and wail, ‹ weep ‹ On this night,

בְּלֵיל זֶה הַגַּלְגַּל סִבֵּב הַחוֹבָה,*

« an inauspicious date;* ‹ turned to ‹ the cycle [of the calendar] ‹ On this night,

רִאשׁוֹן גַּם שֵׁנִי בֵּיתִי נֶחֱרָבָה,[2]

« were destroyed; ‹ of My Temples ‹ the Second ‹ as well as ‹ the First

וְעוֹד לֹא רֻחָמָה[3] **בַּת הַשּׁוֹבֵבָה,***[4]

« who is rebellious;* ‹ is the daughter ‹ worthy of mercy ‹ not ‹ and still

(1) Cf. *Numbers* 16:35. (2) Mishnah *Taanis* 4:6. (3) *Hosea* 1:7. (4) *Jeremiah* 31:21, 49:4.

many Jews were slain at that time that the non-Jews fertilized their vineyards for seven years with the blood of the Jews killed at Beitar (*Gittin* 57a)]; and (e) the Roman governor Turnus Rufus had the city of Jerusalem razed and plowed under (*Taanis* 26b).

The *paytan* places this lament into the mouth of either Jerusalem (which *Eichah* describes as a widow) or the nation as a whole lamenting to her children (the exiles) about the bitter tragedies which have befallen her. Alternatively, the narrator of the *kinnah* is addressing his own children to explain the reasons for the sadness of the day.

הַגַּלְגַּל סִבֵּב הַחוֹבָה — *The cycle [of the calendar] turned to an inauspicious date.* The Mishnah states that both the First and Second Temples were destroyed on the Ninth of Av (*Taanis* 26b). The Talmud adduces verses that verify this date for the First Temple, then seeks proof that the second Destruction also occurred on Tishah B'Av. The following *baraisa* is cited: מְגַלְגְּלִין זְכוּת לְיוֹם זַכַּאי וְחוֹבָה לְיוֹם חַיָּיב, *They [the Heavenly Court] make a good event occur on an auspicious date, and a bad event on an inauspicious date* (ibid. 29a; *Arachin* 11b).

וְעוֹד לֹא רֻחָמָה בַּת הַשּׁוֹבֵבָה — *And still not worthy of mercy is the daughter who is rebellious.* God appeared to the prophet Hosea in a vision and ordered him to concretize Israel's wayward lust for idolatry in a most dramatic manner: *Go take unto yourself a wife of harlotry and [beget] children of harlotry, for the land is straying completely from following HASHEM* (*Hosea* 1:2). The prophet did so and three children were born to him. God told him what to name each baby — names that describe His displeasure with the nation. The second child, a daughter, was to be called לֹא רֻחָמָה, *Lo-Ruchamah* [lit., *unworthy of mercy* or *unpitied*] (ibid. 1:6). When the nation will be exiled, learn its lesson, and return to God's service, her name will be

הֻשְׁקְתָה מֵי רוֹשׁ[1] וְאֶת בִּטְנָהּ צָבָה,[2]*
« was swollen; ‹ and her belly ‹ of bitter gall ‹ water ‹ she was given to drink

וְשֻׁלְּחָה מִבֵּיתוֹ[3] וְגַם נָשְׁתָה טוֹבָה,[4]
« what good is; ‹ forgotten ‹ and has even ‹ from His House ‹ she was banished

גְּדוֹלָה הַשִּׂנְאָה מֵאֵת אֲשֶׁר אֲהֵבָהּ,[5]*
« [He formerly] loved her; ‹ to which ‹ than the extent ‹ is [God's] hatred [now] ‹ greater

וּכְאַלְמְנוּת חַיּוּת[6] כְּאִשָּׁה נֶעֱזָבָה,[7]
« who has been abandoned. ‹ like a wife « of the living, ‹ [she] is like a widow

וַתֹּאמֶר צִיּוֹן עֲזָבַנִי יהוה.[8]
« has HASHEM. ‹ forsaken me « And Zion said:

בְּלֵיל זֶה יִבְכָּיוּן וְיֵילִילוּ בָּנַי . . .
« shall my children . . . ‹ and wail, ‹ weep ‹ On this night,

בְּלֵיל זֶה קָדַרְתִּי וְחָשְׁכוּ הַמְּאוֹרוֹת,[9]
« were the luminaries, ‹ and turned dark ‹ I was blackened ‹ On this night,

לְחֻרְבַּן בֵּית קָדְשִׁי וּבִטּוּל מִשְׁמָרוֹת,[10]
« of the [priestly] watches. ‹ and the cancellation ‹ of my Holy Temple ‹ because of the destruction

בְּלֵיל זֶה סַבּוּנִי אֲפָפוּנִי צָרוֹת,
‹ have troubles, ‹ and surrounded me ‹ encircled me ‹ On this night,

---

(1) Cf. 9:14. (2) Cf. *Numbers* 5:21. (3) Cf. *Deuteronomy* 24:1.
(4) Cf. *Eichah* 3:17. (5) Cf. *II Samuel* 13:15. (6) Cf. 20:3. (7) Cf. *Isaiah* 54:6.
(8) 49:14. (9) Cf. *Joel* 2:20, 4:15. (10) See introduction to *Kinnah* 10.

---

changed to רֻחָמָה, *Ruchamah, An Object of Mercy* (ibid. 2:3).

הֻשְׁקְתָה מֵי רוֹשׁ וְאֶת בִּטְנָהּ צָבָה — *She was given to drink water of bitter gall and her belly was swollen.* Although *Rashi* (*Jeremiah* 9:14) renders מֵי רֹאשׁ as *snake venom* and *Radak* translates *bitter grass,* from the context of the *kinnah* it is obvious that the *paytan* alludes to the ordeal and degradation of the סוֹטָה, the *wayward wife,* as described in Scripture (*Numbers* 5:11-31).

גְּדוֹלָה הַשִּׂנְאָה . . . אֲהֵבָהּ — *Greater is [God's] hatred [now] ... [He formerly] loved her.* As proof, the two Temples together lasted fewer than one thousand years while the exile has lasted [almost two] thousand years (*R' Asher b'R' Yosef; Matteh Levi*).

וְגַם קָרָא מוֹעֵד[1] בְּדִין חָמֵשׁ גְּזֵרוֹת,
« decrees. ‹ through the five ‹ for punishment ‹ [this date] as a set time ‹ He proclaimed ‹ and additionally,

בְּכִי חִנָּם בָּכוּ[2] וְנִקְבַּע לַדּוֹרוֹת,
« [a weeping] for all generations; ‹ so it was designated ‹ did they weep, ‹ without cause ‹ A weeping

יַעַן כִּי הָיְתָה סִבָּה מֵעִם יהוה.[3]
« HASHEM. ‹ from ‹ such a plan ‹ there was ‹ it is that ‹ for this reason

בְּלֵיל זֶה יִבְכָּיוּן וְיֵילִילוּ בָנַי . . .
« shall my children . . . ‹ and wail, ‹ weep ‹ On this night,

בְּלֵיל זֶה אֵרְעוּ בוֹ חָמֵשׁ מְאֹרָעוֹת,[4]
« tragedies: ‹ five ‹ thereon ‹ there occurred ‹ On this night,

גָּזַר עַל אָבוֹת בִּפְרֹעַ פְּרָעוֹת,[5]
« wantonly, ‹ when they rebelled ‹ [our] ancestors ‹ against ‹ He decreed

וְדָבְקוּ בוֹ צָרוֹת רַבּוֹת וְרָעוֹת,[6]
« and terrible, ‹ that were many ‹ were troubles ‹ to [this day] ‹ and attached

יוֹם מוּכָן הָיָה בִּפְגֹעַ פְּגָעוֹת,
« by misfortunes. ‹ to be struck ‹ it was ‹ designated ‹ a day

וְהֶעֱמִיד הָאוֹיֵב* וְהֵרִים קוֹל זְוָעוֹת,
« that was terrifying: ‹ a cry ‹ and he raised « the enemy,* ‹ [God] set [against us]

קוּם כִּי זֶה הַיּוֹם אֲשֶׁר אָמַר יהוה.[7]
« *HASHEM has said [we should destroy His Temple]!* ‹ *of which* ‹ *is the day* ‹ *this* ‹ *For* ‹ *Arise!*

בְּלֵיל זֶה יִבְכָּיוּן וְיֵילִילוּ בָנַי . . .
« shall my children . . . ‹ and wail, ‹ weep ‹ On this night,

---

(1) Cf. *Eichah* 1:15. (2) Cf. *Sanhedrin* 104b; *Bamidbar Rabbah* 16:20. (3) *I Kings* 12:15.
(4) Mishnah *Taanis* 4:6. (5) *Judges* 5:2; see commentators there for other interpretations of this phrase.
(6) Some editions read מְצֵרוֹת וְגַם רָעוֹת, *tormenting and also terrible.* (7) Cf. *Judges* 4:14.

וְהֶעֱמִיד הָאוֹיֵב — *[God] set [against us] the enemy.* Some commentaries understand 'the enemy' as the subject of the verb and render: *Set up did the enemy [an idol in the Temple].* This interpretation is difficult because the Mishnah (*Taanis* 4:6) lists that event as one of the five tragedies of the Seventeenth of Tammuz, while this stanza of the *kinnah* recounts the tragic events of Tishah B'Av.

KINNAH 4 / קינה ד

שׁוֹמְרוֹן קוֹל תִּתֵּן[1] מְצָאוּנִי עֲוֹנַי,[2]

Shomron ‹ a voice [of lament] ‹ raise, ‹ Befallen me ‹ have [the punishments] for my sins! «

לְאֶרֶץ אַחֶרֶת יָצְאוּנִי בָנַי,[3]

To another land ‹ go away from me ‹ did my children! «

וְאָהֳלִיבָה תִּזְעַק נִשְׂרְפוּ אַרְמוֹנַי,[4]

Then Oholivah ‹ screams, « Burnt down ‹ were my palaces! «

וַתֹּאמֶר צִיּוֹן עֲזָבַנִי יהוה.[5]

And Zion says, « Abandoned me ‹ has HASHEM! «

לֹא לָךְ אָהֳלִיבָה חֲשׁוֹב עָנְיֵךְ כְּעָנְיִי,

[Oholah:] It is not ‹ [right] for you, « Oholivah, « to consider ‹ your suffering ‹ as [equal to] my suffering! «

הֲתַמְשִׁילִי חָלְיֵךְ לְשִׁבְרִי וּלְחָלְיִי,

Can you compare ‹ your sickness ‹ to my injury ‹ and to my sickness? «

אֲנִי אָהֳלָה סוּרָה בָּגַדְתִּי בְּקָשְׁיִי,

I, ‹ Oholah, ‹ [am now] displaced, « I have rebelled ‹ in my stubbornness, «

וְקָם עָלַי כַּחֲשִׁי וְעָנָה בִי מֶרְיִי,[6]

but risen ‹ against me ‹ has my deceitfulness, « and testified ‹ against me ‹ has my defiance, «

---

(1) Cf. *Eichah* 2:7. (2) Cf. *II Kings* 7:9; *Deuteronomy* 4:30. (3) Cf. *Jeremiah* 10:20.
(4) Cf. *II Chronicles* 36:19. (5) *Isaiah* 49:14. (6) Cf. *Job* 16:8.

שׁוֹמְרוֹן — *Shomron.* This *kinnah* is based on chapter 23 of *Ezekiel,* where God bids the prophet to expose the sins of the Jewish people. Then unfolds the shocking parable of two faithless wives who seek fulfillment of their unnatural lusts through numerous lovers. Ezekiel tells of two sisters, אָהֳלָה, *Oholah,* and אָהֳלִיבָה, *Oholivah,* who are both married to the same man. Oholah is identified as Shomron [Samaria, capital of the Northern Kingdom, also called the Kingdom of Israel, which comprised ten of the tribes] and Oholivah as Jerusalem [capital of the Southern Kingdom, also called the Kingdom of Judah, which comprised Judah and Benjamin]. Both are 'wed' to one 'husband', God, but both brazenly betray Him.

The names, אָהֳלָה, *Oholah,* and אָהֳלִיבָה, *Oholivah,* are both derived from אֹהֶל, a *tent* or *dwelling place.* However, אָהֳלָה is a contraction of הָאֹהֶל שֶׁלָּהּ, *her tent,* because God had no part in the tabernacles

וּלְמִקְצַת הַיָּמִים[1] שִׁלַּמְתִּי נִשְׁיִי,[2]
«my debts [for my sins].‹ I paid ‹ of a short time ‹ and at the end

וְתִגְלַת פִּלְאֶסֶר[3] אָכַל אֶת פִּרְיִי,
« my [womb's] fruits, ‹ devoured ‹ [The Assyrian king] Tiglath-pileser

חֶמְדָּתִי פָּשַׁט וְהִצִּיל אֶת עֶדְיִי,[4]*
« my jewelry,* ‹ and confiscated ‹ he stripped away ‹ my precious possessions

וְלַחֲלַח וְחָבוֹר[5] נָשָׂא אֶת שִׁבְיִי,
« my captives. ‹ [his successor Shalmaneser] carried away ‹ and to Habor ‹ then to Halah

דֹּמִּי אָהֳלִיבָה וְאַל תִּבְכִּי כְּבִכְיִי,
« as I weep! ‹ weep ‹ and do not ‹ Oholivah ‹ [Therefore,] be silent

שְׁנוֹתַיִךְ אָרְכוּ וְלֹא אָרְכוּ שָׁנָי.*
« were my years!* ‹ but not prolonged ‹ were prolonged, ‹ Your years [in the Land]

וְאָהֳלִיבָה תִּזְעַק נִשְׂרְפוּ אַרְמוֹנַי,
« were my palaces! ‹ Burnt down « screams, ‹ Then Oholivah

(1) *Daniel* 1:18 (2) Cf. *II Kings* 4:7. (3) *II Kings* 15:29. (4) Cf. *Exodus* 33:6. (5) See *II Kings* 17:3-6.

of Shomron. They were *her own tents* which she had dedicated to the golden calves Jeroboam ben Nevat had erected (see *I Kings* 12:28). On the other hand, אָהֳלִיבָה is a contraction of הָאֹהֶל שֶׁלִּי בָּהּ, *My Tent is within her* — the Tent of God, the *Beis HaMikdash*. These names place Judah, in which God's Temple stood, in sharp contrast to Shomron.

The wicked city of Shomron, with the abominations of its citizens, epitomizes all of the evil of the Ten Tribes. That segment of Israel became so corrupted that to this day those tribes are lost in exile and the possibility of their ultimate return remains the subject of considerable Talmudic debate (see *Sanhedrin* 110b and *Ramban, Sefer HaGeulah, shaar* I).

In this *kinnah*, the author compares the tragedies which befell both Judah and Samaria by means of a debate raging between the two. Each capital claims — and vehemently defends its claim — that it suffered more at the hand of the marauding enemy.

The composer of the *kinnah*, R' Shlomo ibn Gabirol (11th-century Spain), used the letters of his name שְׁלֹמֹה to begin the respective stanzas.

חֶמְדָּתִי . . . עֶדְיִי — *My precious possessions . . . my jewelry.* Some commentators understand these expressions as allusions to the two Temples. We have rejected that interpretation because Oholah is the speaker, but the Temples had stood in Oholivah's state.

שְׁנוֹתַיִךְ אָרְכוּ וְלֹא אָרְכוּ שָׁנָי — *Your years [in the Land] were prolonged, but not prolonged were my years!* Oholah, the North-

וַתֹּאמֶר צִיּוֹן עֲזָבַנִי יהוה.

«has HASHEM! ‹ Abandoned me « And Zion says,

מְשִׁיבָה אָהֳלִיבָה אֲנִי כֵּן נֶעֱקַשְׁתִּי,

« acted crookedly, ‹ similarly ‹ I « Oholivah: ‹ Responds

וּבְאַלּוּף נְעוּרַי[1] כְּאָהֳלָה בָּגַדְתִּי,

« I rebelled! ‹ like Oholah, ‹ of my youth, ‹ and against [God,] the Mentor

דֹּמִּי אָהֳלָה כִּי יְגוֹנִי זָכַרְתִּי,

« do I remember; ‹ my agony ‹ for ‹ Oholah, ‹ Be silent,

נָדַדְתְּ אַתְּ אַחַת וְרַבּוֹת נָדַדְתִּי,

« was I exiled. ‹ while many times « but once, ‹ were you ‹ exiled

הִנֵּה בְּיַד הַכַּשְׂדִּים פַּעֲמַיִם נִלְכַּדְתִּי,

« was I taken; ‹ twice ‹ of the Chaldeans ‹ by the hand ‹ Indeed,

וּשְׁבִיָּה עֲנִיָּה לְבָבֶל יָרַדְתִּי,

« did I descend; ‹ to Babylon ‹ afflicted, ‹ as a captive,

וְנִשְׂרַף הַהֵיכָל אֲשֶׁר בּוֹ נִכְבַּדְתִּי,

« I was honored. ‹ through it ‹ that ‹ was the Temple ‹ and burnt down

וּלְשִׁבְעִים שָׁנָה בְּבָבֶל נִפְקַדְתִּי,

« I was recalled [by God]; ‹ in Babylon ‹ years ‹ After seventy

וְשַׁבְתִּי לְצִיּוֹן עוֹד וְהֵיכָל יָסַדְתִּי,

« I established. ‹ and the [Second] Temple ‹ once again ‹ to Zion ‹ I returned

גַּם זֹאת הַפַּעַם מְעַט לֹא עָמַדְתִּי,

‹ I had not lasted ‹ even a brief time ‹ time ‹ this ‹ Also

עַד לְקָחַנִי אֱדוֹם וְכִמְעַט אָבַדְתִּי,

« was I annihilated. ‹ and nearly ‹ Edom seized me ‹ before

וְעַל כָּל הָאֲרָצוֹת נָפְצוּ הֲמוֹנַי,

« my multitudes. ‹ were dispersed ‹ the lands ‹ all ‹ Throughout

(1) Cf. *Jeremiah* 3:4.

וְאָהֳלִיבָה תִּזְעַק נִשְׂרְפוּ אַרְמוֹנַי,

« were my palaces! ‹ Burnt down « screams, ‹ Then Oholivah

וַתֹּאמֶר צִיּוֹן עֲזָבַנִי יהוה.

« has HASHEM! ‹ Abandoned me « And Zion says,

הַחוֹמֵל עַל דַּל חֲמוֹל עַל דַּלּוּתָם,*

« their poverty.* ‹ on ‹ take pity « the pauper, ‹ on ‹ O You Who takes pity

וּרְאֵה שִׁמְמוֹתָם[1] וְאֹרֶךְ גָּלוּתָם,

« of their exile. ‹ and the length ‹ their desolation ‹ See

אַל תִּקְצוֹף עַד מְאֹד[1] וּרְאֵה שִׁפְלוּתָם,

« their degradation. ‹ rather see « an extreme, ‹ to ‹ be angered ‹ Do not

וְאַל לָעַד תִּזְכּוֹר עֲוֹנָם[2] וְסִכְלוּתָם,

« and their foolishness. ‹ their sins ‹ remember ‹ forever ‹ Do not

רְפָא נָא אֶת שִׁבְרָם[3] וְנַחֵם אֲבֵלוּתָם,

« in their bereavement; ‹ and console [them] ‹ their wounds ‹ please, ‹ Heal,

כִּי אַתָּה סִבְרָם וְאַתָּה אֱיָלוּתָם,

« their Strength. ‹ and You are ‹ their Hope ‹ You are ‹ for

חַדֵּשׁ יָמֵינוּ כִּימֵי קַדְמוֹנַי,[4]

« of my youth; ‹ as the days ‹ our days ‹ Renew

כִּנְאֻמֶךָ בּוֹנֵה יְרוּשָׁלַיִם יהוה.[5]

« is HASHEM. ‹ of Jerusalem ‹ The Builder « as You have said:

(1) Cf. *Daniel* 9:18. (2) Cf. *Isaiah* 64:8. (3) Cf. *Psalms* 60:4. (4) Cf. *Eichah* 5:21. (5) *Psalms* 147:2.

ern Kingdom of Samaria, was exiled more than one hundred thirty years before Oholivah, the Southern Kingdom of Judah.

דַּלּוּתָם — *Their poverty.* Until this point, the *kinnah* has been a one-on-one debate between Oholah and Oholivah. Thus, the statements are all in first- or second-person singular. The last stanza, however, is the *paytan's* supplication for the restitution of both, and consequently is couched in third-person plural. The *paytan* prays for the reunification of the two Kingdoms with Jerusalem as the focal point as it was in *the days of the nation's youth.*

KINNAH 5 / קינה ה

עַד אָנָה בְּכִיָּה בְּצִיּוֹן וּמִסְפֵּד בִּירוּשָׁלָיִם,
Until ‹ when ‹ must there be weeping ‹ in Zion ‹ and lamenting ‹ in Jerusalem? «

תְּרַחֵם צִיּוֹן[1] וְתִבְנֶה חוֹמוֹת יְרוּשָׁלָיִם.[2]
Show mercy ‹ to Zion ‹ and rebuild ‹ the walls ‹ of Jerusalem! «

אָז בַּחֲטָאֵינוּ חָרַב מִקְדָּשׁ,
At that time, ‹ through our sins, ‹ destroyed ‹ was the Temple, «

וּבַעֲוֹנוֹתֵינוּ נִשְׂרַף הֵיכָל.
and through our iniquities ‹ burnt down ‹ was the Sanctuary. «

בָּאָרֶץ חֻבְּרָה לָהּ[3] קָשְׁרָה מִסְפֵּד,*
On earth ‹ those united ‹ with it ‹ joined ‹ in lament,* ‹

וּצְבָא הַשָּׁמַיִם נָשְׂאוּ קִינָה.
while the legions ‹ of heaven ‹ raised ‹ an elegy. «

עַד אָנָה בְּכִיָּה בְּצִיּוֹן וּמִסְפֵּד בִּירוּשָׁלָיִם,
Until ‹ when ‹ must there be weeping ‹ in Zion ‹ and lamenting ‹ in Jerusalem? «

תְּרַחֵם צִיּוֹן וְתִבְנֶה חוֹמוֹת יְרוּשָׁלָיִם.
Show mercy ‹ to Zion ‹ and rebuild ‹ the walls ‹ of Jerusalem! «

(1) *Psalms* 102:14. (2) Cf. 51:20. (3) Cf. 122:3.

עַד אָנָה — *Until when?* The theme of this *kinnah* is derived from the *Midrash* which teaches that at the time of the Temple's destruction the celestial star formations called מַזָּלוֹת [*mazalos*], *constellations*, joined in Israel's mourning (*Yalkut Shimoni* II:1008). The Rabbis teach that the term מַזָּל is cognate with נוֹזֵל, *flow*, because God causes His blessings to flow to earth, with the *mazalos* acting as conduits and transformers that bring His infinite beneficence down to the finite world. The varying positions of the *mazolos* with relation to both time and earth will affect this heavenly flow in such manner that it can be said that mankind is under the influence or control of the *mazalos*. Nevertheless, the Talmud (*Shabbos* 156a) teaches that אֵין מַזָּל לְיִשְׂרָאֵל, *Mazal does not control Israel. Rashi* explains that since *mazal* is nothing more than a tool in God's hands, a Jew can overcome his *mazal* by appealing to God through prayer or righteous deeds and He will rearrange the *mazalos* to be favorable to the petitioner. This *kinnah* describes how, on Tishah B'Av, God aligned all of the *mazalos* against Israel, so that they were all positioned in a way that would cause a negative, harmful flow upon Israel. The *paytan* records how each of the *mazalos* cried because it had a hand in this terrible tragedy.

בָּאָרֶץ חֻבְּרָה לָהּ קָשְׁרָה מִסְפֵּד — *On earth those united with it joined in lament.* Just

גַּם בָּכוּ בְּמֶרֶר שִׁבְטֵי יַעֲקֹב,

« of Jacob, ‹ did the tribes ‹ bitterly ‹ cry ‹ Also

וְאַף מַזָּלוֹת יִזְּלוּ דִמְעָה.

« tears. ‹ shed ‹ the constellations ‹ and even

דִּגְלֵי יְשֻׁרוּן חָפוּ רֹאשָׁם,[1]

« their heads; ‹ hid [in shame] ‹ of Yeshurun [Israel] ‹ The bannered tribes

וְכִימָה וּכְסִיל[2] קָדְרוּ פְּנֵיהֶם.

« their countenance. ‹ blackened ‹ and Orion ‹ the Pleiades

עַד אָנָה בְּכִיָּה בְּצִיּוֹן וּמִסְפֵּד בִּירוּשָׁלָיִם,

« in Jerusalem? ‹ and lamenting ‹ in Zion ‹ must there be weeping ‹ when ‹ Until

תְּרַחֵם צִיּוֹן וְתִבְנֶה חוֹמוֹת יְרוּשָׁלָיִם.

« of Jerusalem! ‹ the walls ‹ and rebuild ‹ to Zion ‹ Show mercy

הֶעְתִּירוּ אָבוֹת וְלֹא שָׁמַע אֵל,[3]

« did God; ‹ listen ‹ but not ‹ did the Patriarchs ‹ Entreat

צָעֲקוּ בָנִים וְלֹא עָנָה אָב.[4]

« did the Father. ‹ respond ‹ but not « did the children, ‹ scream

וְקוֹל הַתּוֹר*[5] נִשְׁמַע בַּמָּרוֹם,

« on high, ‹ was heard ‹ of the turtledove* ‹ And the voice

(1) Cf. *Jeremiah* 14:3. (2) See *Ibn Ezra* to *Amos* 5:8 for the identifications and locations of these star clusters; see also *Ibn Ezra* to *Job* 9:9.
(3) See *Eichah Rabbah, Pesichta* 24. (4) Cf. *Exodus* 22:22. (5) *Song of Songs* 2:12.

as *the angels, the multitudes of above, together with Your people Israel, assembled below,* join to crown God with praises (as stated in the *Kedushah* of *Mussaf* according to the Nusach Sefard rite), so after the Destruction, did Israel on earth and the legions of angels in heaven unite in lamenting the destruction of the *Beis HaMikdash* (See *Eichah Rabbah, Pesichta* 24).

Some editions read בָּעִיר שֶׁחֻבְּרָה לָהּ, *in the city joined to it* [to Jerusalem], and refer to celestial Jerusalem which, as the Talmud (*Taanis* 5a) teaches, is joined to the terrestrial Jerusalem. Accordingly, the *paytan* tells us that the Heavenly City united with the angels in mourning the destruction of its earthly counterpart. (See also *Rashi* to *Psalms* 122:3.)

וְקוֹל הַתּוֹר — *And the voice of the turtledove.* This is variously explained as an allusion to Moses (*Shir HaShirim Rabbah* 2:12), Israel (see *Psalms* 74:19 with *Rashi*),

וְרוֹעֶה נֶאֱמָן לֹא הִטָּה אֹזֶן.

« an ear. ‹ attend ‹ did not ‹ Who is Faithful [God] ‹ yet the Shepherd

עַד אָנָה בְּכִיָּה בְצִיּוֹן וּמִסְפֵּד בִּירוּשָׁלָיִם,

« in Jerusalem? ‹ and lamenting ‹ in Zion ‹ must there be weeping ‹ when ‹ Until

תְּרַחֵם צִיּוֹן וְתִבְנֶה חוֹמוֹת יְרוּשָׁלָיִם.

« of Jerusalem! ‹ the walls ‹ and rebuild ‹ to Zion ‹ Show mercy

זֶרַע קֹדֶשׁ[1] לָבְשׁוּ שַׂקִּים,

« sackcloth, ‹ wore ‹ of holiness ‹ The offspring

וּצְבָא הַשָּׁמַיִם גַּם הֵם שַׂק הוּשַׂם כְּסוּתָם.[2]

« for their garments. ‹ was assigned ‹ sack-cloth « for them — ‹ — also « of heaven ‹ and the legions

חָשַׁךְ הַשֶּׁמֶשׁ וְיָרֵחַ[3] קָדַר,

« was blackened, ‹ and the moon ‹ was the sun ‹ Darkened

וְכוֹכָבִים וּמַזָּלוֹת אָסְפוּ נָגְהָם.[4]

« their shine. ‹ held back ‹ and the constellations ‹ the stars

עַד אָנָה בְּכִיָּה בְצִיּוֹן וּמִסְפֵּד בִּירוּשָׁלָיִם,

« in Jerusalem? ‹ and lamenting ‹ in Zion ‹ must there be weeping ‹ when ‹ Until

תְּרַחֵם צִיּוֹן וְתִבְנֶה חוֹמוֹת יְרוּשָׁלָיִם.

« of Jerusalem! ‹ the walls ‹ and rebuild ‹ to Zion ‹ Show mercy

טָלֶה רִאשׁוֹן* בָּכָה בְּמַר נֶפֶשׁ,

« of soul, ‹ with bitterness ‹ bleated ‹ the first [constellation],* ‹ The **Ram,**

עַל כִּי כְבָשָׂיו לַטֶּבַח הוּבָלוּ.[5]

« were led. ‹ to the slaughter ‹ his lambs ‹ that ‹ for the reason

(1) Cf. *Isaiah* 6:13. (2) 50:3. (3) Cf. 13:10. (4) Cf. *Joel* 2:10. (5) Cf. *Isaiah* 53:7.

or the Torah (some editions even read וְקוֹל הַתּוֹרָה צוֹעֵק בְּמָרָה, *the voice of the Torah cries out bitterly*).

טָלֶה רִאשׁוֹן — *The Ram, the first [constellation].* Each of the *mazalos,* whose plaints the *paytan* now enumerates, corresponds to another month of the Hebrew calendar (*Sefer Yetzirah* 5:2). The Ram which corresponds to the first month, Nissan, is called רִאשׁוֹן, *the first.*

יְלָלָה הִשְׁמִיעַ **שׁוֹר** בַּמְּרוֹמִים,

‹ on high, ‹ by the **Bull** ‹ was made heard ‹ Wailing

כִּי עַל צַוָּארֵנוּ* נִרְדָּפְנוּ[1] כֻּלָּנוּ.

« — all of us. ‹ we were pursued ‹ our necks* ‹ [with the yoke] upon ‹ because

עַד אָנָה בְּכִיָּה בְצִיּוֹן וּמִסְפֵּד בִּירוּשָׁלָיִם,

« in Jerusalem? ‹ and lamenting ‹ in Zion ‹ must there be weeping ‹ when ‹ Until

תְּרַחֵם צִיּוֹן וְתִבְנֶה חוֹמוֹת יְרוּשָׁלָיִם.

« of Jerusalem! ‹ the walls ‹ and rebuild ‹ to Zion ‹ Show mercy

כּוֹכַב **תְּאוֹמִים** נִרְאָה חָלוּק,

« separated, ‹ appeared ‹ of the **Twins** ‹ The constellation

כִּי דַּם אַחִים נִשְׁפַּךְ כַּמַּיִם.

« like water. ‹ was spilled ‹ of brothers ‹ the blood ‹ because

לָאָרֶץ בִּקֵּשׁ לִנְפּוֹל **סַרְטָן**,

‹ did the **Crab** ‹ to fall ‹ — desire « To the earth

כִּי נִתְעַלַּפְנוּ מִפְּנֵי צָמָא.[2]

« thirst. ‹ from ‹ we fainted ‹ because

(1) Cf. *Eichah* 5:5. (2) Cf. *Amos* 8:13.

The *paytan* reversed the order of the tenth and eleventh constellations. Perhaps he did this to juxtapose the verses of the Rainbow and the Bucket, both of which speak of water. The chart below enumerates the twelve constellations.

עַל צַוָּארֵנוּ — *[With the yoke] upon our necks,* with the yoke of heavy labor

HEBREW NAME	ASTRONOMICAL NAME	MONTH
טָלֶה / RAM OR LAMB	ARIES (THE RAM)	NISSAN
שׁוֹר / BULL	TAURUS (THE BULL)	IYAR
תְּאוֹמִים / TWINS	GEMINI (THE TWINS)	SIVAN
סַרְטָן / CRAB	CANCER (THE CRAB)	TAMMUZ
אַרְיֵה / LION	LEO (THE LION)	AV
בְּתוּלָה / MAIDEN	VIRGO (THE VIRGIN)	ELUL
מֹאזְנַיִם / SCALES	LIBRA (THE SCALES)	TISHREI
עַקְרָב / SCORPION	SCORPIO (THE SCORPION)	CHESHVAN
קֶשֶׁת / RAINBOW	SAGITTARIUS (THE ARCHER)	KISLEV
גְּדִי / GOAT OR KID	CAPRICORN (THE GOAT)	TEVES
דְּלִי / BUCKET	AQUARIUS (THE WATER BEARER)	SHEVAT
דָּגִים / FISH	PISCES (THE FISH)	ADAR

עַד אָנָה בְּכִיָּה בְּצִיּוֹן וּמִסְפֵּד בִּירוּשָׁלָיִם,

« in Jerusalem? ‹ and lamenting ‹ in Zion ‹ must there be weeping ‹ when ‹ Until

תְּרַחֵם צִיּוֹן וְתִבְנֶה חוֹמוֹת יְרוּשָׁלָיִם.

« of Jerusalem! ‹ the walls ‹ and rebuild ‹ to Zion ‹ Show mercy

מָרוֹם נִבְעַת מִקּוֹל אַרְיֵה,

« of the **Lion**, ‹ by the voice ‹ were terrified ‹ The heavens

כִּי שַׁאֲגָתֵנוּ לֹא עָלְתָה לַמָּרוֹם.[1]

« on high. ‹ ascend ‹ did not ‹ our roaring ‹ because

נֶהֶרְגוּ בְתוּלוֹת וְגַם בַּחוּרִים,[2]

« young men, ‹ and also ‹ were maidens ‹ Slain

כִּי עַל כֵּן **בְּתוּלָה** קָדְרָה פָנֶיהָ.

« its face. ‹ blackened ‹ the **Maiden** ‹ of that ‹ because

עַד אָנָה בְּכִיָּה בְּצִיּוֹן וּמִסְפֵּד בִּירוּשָׁלָיִם,

« in Jerusalem? ‹ and lamenting ‹ in Zion ‹ must there be weeping ‹ when ‹ Until

תְּרַחֵם צִיּוֹן וְתִבְנֶה חוֹמוֹת יְרוּשָׁלָיִם.

« of Jerusalem! ‹ the walls ‹ and rebuild ‹ to Zion ‹ Show mercy

סִבֵּב **מֹאזְנַיִם** וּבִקֵּשׁ תְּחִנָּה,[3]

« with supplication, ‹ and beseeched ‹ did the **Scales** ‹ Tilt [in our favor]

כִּי נִבְחַר לָמוֹ מָוֶת מֵחַיִּים.[4]

« over life. ‹ had death become ‹ for them [Israel], ‹ preferable ‹ because,

עַקְרָב לָבַשׁ פַּחַד וּרְעָדָה,

« and trepidation, ‹ fear ‹ wore ‹ The **Scorpion**

(1) Some editions read כִּי שַׁאֲגָתֵנוּ עָלְתָה לַמָּרוֹם, *when our roaring ascended on high.*
(2) Cf. *Eichah* 2:21. (3) Cf. *Daniel* 9:3. (4) Cf. *Jeremiah* 8:3; some editions read לָנוּ, *for us,* instead of לָמוֹ, *for them;* some read כִּי נִכְרַע לָנוּ כַּף מָוֶת מֵחַיִּים, *because outweigh for us did the death side of the scale over that of life.*

(*Rashi* to *Eichah* 5:5). According to the Midrash, this refers to a decree issued by the wicked Adrianus: Every Jew must shave himself bald; any Jew found with a single hair on his head or neck would be beheaded (*Eichah Rabbah* 5:5).

Others note that in another context the word צַוָּאר, *neck,* alludes to the *Beis HaMikdash* (*Megillah* 16b). Thus, the verse means that we were pursued

כִּי בְּחֶרֶב וּבְרָעָב שְׁפָטָֽנוּ צוּרֵֽנוּ.

« did our Creator. ‹ judge us « and hunger, ‹ to receive sword ‹ because

עַד אָֽנָה בְּכִיָּה בְּצִיּוֹן וּמִסְפֵּד בִּירוּשָׁלָֽיִם,

« in Jerusalem? ‹ and lamenting ‹ in Zion ‹ must there be weeping ‹ when ‹ Until

תְּרַחֵם צִיּוֹן וְתִבְנֶה חוֹמוֹת יְרוּשָׁלָֽיִם.

« of Jerusalem! ‹ the walls ‹ and rebuild ‹ to Zion ‹ Show mercy

פַּלְגֵי מַֽיִם[1] הוֹרִידוּ דִמְעָה כַּנַּֽחַל,[2]

« like a river, ‹ tears ‹ they shed ‹ of water, ‹ [Like] streams

כִּי אוֹת **בַּקֶּשֶׁת** לֹא נִתַּן לָֽנוּ.*

« upon us.* ‹ bestowed ‹ was not ‹ of the **Rainbow** ‹ the sign ‹ because

צָֽפוּ מַֽיִם עַל רֹאשֵֽׁנוּ,[3]

« our heads, ‹ over ‹ did the water ‹ Flood [of suffering]

וּבִדְלִי מָלֵא חִכֵּֽנוּ יָבֵשׁ.

« was parched. ‹ our palate « was full, ‹ and although the **Bucket**

עַד אָֽנָה בְּכִיָּה בְּצִיּוֹן וּמִסְפֵּד בִּירוּשָׁלָֽיִם,

« in Jerusalem? ‹ and lamenting ‹ in Zion ‹ must there be weeping ‹ when ‹ Until

תְּרַחֵם צִיּוֹן וְתִבְנֶה חוֹמוֹת יְרוּשָׁלָֽיִם.

« of Jerusalem! ‹ the walls ‹ and rebuild ‹ to Zion ‹ Show mercy

קֵרַֽבְנוּ קָרְבָּן וְלֹא נִתְקַבֵּל,

« accepted, ‹ but it was not ‹ an offering, ‹ We brought

וּגְדִי פָּסַק שְׂעִיר חַטֹּאתֵֽנוּ.

« sin-offering. ‹ our he-goat ‹ ceased being ‹ and the **Goat**

(1) Cf. *Eichah* 3:48; *Psalms* 119:136. (2) Cf. *Eichah* 2:18. (3) Cf. 3:54.

because we acted treacherously to the Temple.

כִּי אוֹת בַּקֶּשֶׁת לֹא נִתַּן לָנוּ — *Because the sign of the Rainbow was not bestowed upon us.* As indicated by the chart, the constellation קֶשֶׁת may be rendered either *Rainbow* or *Archer's Bow;* the *paytan* uses the former. The sign of the rainbow was given to Noah as an omen that (a) the people have lapsed into sinfulness, and (b) even though the world deserves another Flood, it will not come because

רַחֲמָנִיּוֹת בִּשְּׁלוּ יַלְדֵיהֶן,[1]

« their own children, ‹ cooked ‹ Compassionate women

וּמַזַּל **דָּגִים** הֶעְלִים עֵינָיו.

« its eyes. ‹ averted ‹ of **Fish** ‹ and the constellation

עַד אָנָה בְּכִיָּה בְּצִיּוֹן וּמִסְפֵּד בִּירוּשָׁלָיִם,

« in Jerusalem? ‹ and lamenting ‹ in Zion ‹ must there be weeping ‹ when ‹ Until

תְּרַחֵם צִיּוֹן וְתִבְנֶה חוֹמוֹת יְרוּשָׁלָיִם.

« of Jerusalem! ‹ the walls ‹ and rebuild ‹ to Zion ‹ Show mercy

שָׁכַחְנוּ שַׁבָּת[2] בְּלִבּוֹת שׁוֹבָבִים,[3]

« that are wayward, « with hearts ‹ [to observe] the Sabbath, ‹ We have forgotten

שַׁדַּי שִׁכַּח כָּל צִדְקוֹתֵינוּ.

« our righteousness. ‹ all ‹ has caused to be forgotten ‹ so the Almighty

תְּקַנֵּא לְצִיּוֹן קִנְאָה גְדוֹלָה,[4]

‹ that is great, ‹ with vengeance ‹ Zion ‹ Avenge

וְתָאִיר לְרַבָּתִי עָם[5] מְאוֹר נָגְהֶךָ.

« that shines. ‹ with Your light ‹ people ‹ [the City] of so many ‹ illuminate

תְּרַחֵם צִיּוֹן כַּאֲשֶׁר אָמַרְתָּ, וּתְכוֹנְנֶהָ כַּאֲשֶׁר דִּבַּרְתָּ,

« You have spoken. ‹ as ‹ and establish her « You have said, ‹ as ‹ to Zion ‹ Show mercy

תְּמַהֵר יְשׁוּעָה וְתָחִישׁ גְּאֻלָּה, וְתָשׁוּב לִירוּשָׁלַיִם

‹ to Jerusalem ‹ and return ‹ redemption ‹ and accelerate ‹ salvation ‹ Hasten

בְּרַחֲמִים רַבִּים.

« that is abundant. ‹ with mercy

(1) Cf. 4:10. (2) See *Shabbos* 119b. (3) Cf. *Isaiah* 57:17. (4) Cf. *Zechariah* 1:14, 8:2. (5) *Eichah* 1:1.

of God's promise to Noah (see *Genesis* 9:12-16). We lament because the rainbow was not sent to stop the flood of our tragedies.

כַּכָּתוּב עַל יַד נְבִיאֶךָ, לָכֵן כֹּה אָמַר יהוה,

As it is written by the hand of Your prophet: Therefore, thus said HASHEM,

שַׁבְתִּי לִירוּשָׁלַיִם בְּרַחֲמִים, בֵּיתִי יִבָּנֶה בָּהּ,

I shall return to Jerusalem with mercy, My House shall be rebuilt within it,

נְאֻם יהוה צְבָאוֹת, וְקָו יִנָּטֶה עַל יְרוּשָׁלָיִם.[1]

the word of HASHEM, Master of Legions, and a [surveyor's] string shall be stretched over Jerusalem.

וְנֶאֱמַר, עוֹד קְרָא לֵאמֹר, כֹּה אָמַר יהוה צְבָאוֹת,

And it is said: Once again call out, saying, Thus said HASHEM, Master of Legions,

עוֹד תְּפוּצֶנָה עָרַי מִטּוֹב, וְנִחַם יהוה עוֹד

'Once again overflow shall My cities with abundance, and HASHEM will comfort once again

אֶת צִיּוֹן, וּבָחַר עוֹד בִּירוּשָׁלָיִם.[2] וְנֶאֱמַר, כִּי

Zion and He will choose once again Jerusalem.' And it is said: For

נִחַם יהוה צִיּוֹן, נִחַם כָּל חָרְבוֹתֶיהָ, וַיָּשֶׂם מִדְבָּרָהּ

HASHEM will comfort Zion, He will comfort all her ruins, He will make her wilderness

כְּעֵדֶן, וְעַרְבָתָהּ כְּגַן יהוה, שָׂשׂוֹן וְשִׂמְחָה יִמָּצֵא

like Eden, and her wasteland like a garden of HASHEM; joy and gladness will be found

בָּהּ, תּוֹדָה וְקוֹל זִמְרָה.[3]

in her, thanksgiving and the sound of music.

AT THIS POINT, SOME CONGREGATIONS HAVE INTRODUCED THE CUSTOM OF RECITING A KINNAH LAMENTING THE TRAGEDY OF THE SIX MILLION JEWS MURDERED DURING THE HOLOCAUST. TWO KINNOS OF THIS GENRE APPEAR ON PAGES 510-519.

---

(1) *Zechariah* 1:16. (2) 1:17. (3) *Isaiah* 51:3. See *Radak* and *Metzudos David* on the use of the past tense, as if it had already happened.

וִיהִי נֹעַם, USUALLY RECITED ON SATURDAY NIGHT, IS NOT RECITED ON TISHAH B'AV; **וְאַתָּה קָדוֹשׁ** IS RECITED EVEN ON WEEKNIGHTS.

THE PRIMARY PART OF **וְאַתָּה קָדוֹשׁ** IS THE *KEDUSHAH* RECITED BY THE ANGELS. THESE VERSES ARE PRESENTED IN BOLD TYPE AND IT IS PREFERABLE THAT THE CONGREGATION RECITE THEM ALOUD AND IN UNISON. HOWEVER, THE INTERPRETIVE TRANSLATION IN ARAMAIC (WHICH FOLLOWS THE VERSES IN BOLD TYPE) SHOULD BE RECITED SOFTLY.

וְאַתָּה קָדוֹשׁ יוֹשֵׁב תְּהִלּוֹת יִשְׂרָאֵל.[1] וְקָרָא זֶה

Yet You are / the Holy One, / enthroned / upon the praises / of Israel. / And one [angel] will call

אֶל זֶה וְאָמַר: **קָדוֹשׁ, קָדוֹשׁ, קָדוֹשׁ יהוה**

to / another / and say: / ***Holy,*** / ***holy,*** / ***holy*** / ***is HASHEM,***

צְבָאוֹת, מְלֹא כָל הָאָרֶץ כְּבוֹדוֹ.[2] וּמְקַבְּלִין דֵּין

Master of Legions, / ***filled*** / ***is the whole*** / ***world*** / ***[with] His glory.*** / And they receive [permission] / one

מִן דֵּין וְאָמְרִין: קַדִּישׁ בִּשְׁמֵי מְרוֹמָא עִלָּאָה בֵּית

from / the other / and say: / *Holy* / *in the lofty heavens* / *on high,* / *the abode*

שְׁכִינְתֵּהּ, קַדִּישׁ עַל אַרְעָא עוֹבַד גְּבוּרְתֵּהּ, קַדִּישׁ

of His Presence; / *holy* / *on* / *earth,* / *the product* / *of His might;* / *holy*

לְעָלַם וּלְעָלְמֵי עָלְמַיָּא, יהוה צְבָאוֹת מַלְיָא כָל

forever / *and to all eternity* / *is HASHEM,* / *Master of Legions;* / *filled* / *is the whole*

אַרְעָא זִיו יְקָרֵהּ.[3] ❖ וַתִּשָּׂאֵנִי רוּחַ, וָאֶשְׁמַע אַחֲרַי

world / *with the radiance* / *of His glory.* / A wind lifted me, / and I heard / behind me

קוֹל רַעַשׁ גָּדוֹל: **בָּרוּךְ כְּבוֹד יהוה מִמְּקוֹמוֹ.**[4]

the sound / of a great noise: / ***Blessed*** / ***is the glory*** / ***of HASHEM*** / ***from His place.***

וּנְטָלַתְנִי רוּחָא, וְשִׁמְעֵת בַּתְרַי קָל זִיעַ סַגִּיא

A wind lifted me, / and I heard / behind me / the sound / of the great noise

דִּמְשַׁבְּחִין וְאָמְרִין: בְּרִיךְ יְקָרָא דַיהוה מֵאֲתַר בֵּית

of those who were praising / and saying: / *Blessed* / *is the honor* / *of HASHEM* / *from the place* / *of the abode*

(1) Cf. *Psalms* 22:40. (2) *Isaiah* 6:30. (3) *Targum Yonasan*. (4) *Ezekiel* 3:12.

שְׁכִינְתֵּהּ.[1] **יהוה יִמְלֹךְ לְעֹלָם וָעֶד.**[2] יהוה מַלְכוּתֵהּ

‹ – His kingdom «HASHEM « **and ever.** ‹ **for ever** ‹ **shall reign** ‹ **HASHEM** « *of His Presence.*

קָאֵם לְעָלַם וּלְעָלְמֵי עָלְמַיָּא.[3] יהוה אֱלֹהֵי אַבְרָהָם

‹ of Abraham, ‹ God ‹ HASHEM, « and to all eternity. ‹ forever ‹ stands

יִצְחָק וְיִשְׂרָאֵל אֲבֹתֵינוּ, שָׁמְרָה זֹּאת לְעוֹלָם,

‹ forever ‹ this ‹ may You preserve ‹ our forefathers, ‹ and Israel, ‹ Isaac,

לְיֵצֶר מַחְשְׁבוֹת לְבַב עַמֶּךָ, וְהָכֵן לְבָבָם אֵלֶיךָ.[4]

« to You. ‹ their heart ‹ and may You direct « of Your people, ‹ of the heart ‹ of the thoughts ‹ as the product

וְהוּא רַחוּם, יְכַפֵּר עָוֹן וְלֹא יַשְׁחִית, וְהִרְבָּה

‹ frequently « destroy; ‹ and does not ‹ of iniquity ‹ is forgiving ‹ the Merciful One, ‹ And He,

לְהָשִׁיב אַפּוֹ, וְלֹא יָעִיר כָּל חֲמָתוֹ.[5] כִּי אַתָּה אֲדֹנָי

‹ O Lord, ‹ You, ‹ For « of His wrath. ‹ all ‹ arousing ‹ not « His anger, ‹ He withdraws

טוֹב וְסַלָּח, וְרַב חֶסֶד לְכָל קֹרְאֶיךָ.[6] צִדְקָתְךָ

‹ Your righteousness « who call upon You. ‹ to all ‹ kind ‹ and abundantly « and forgiving, ‹ are good

צֶדֶק לְעוֹלָם, וְתוֹרָתְךָ אֱמֶת.[7] תִּתֵּן אֱמֶת לְיַעֲקֹב,

« to Jacob, ‹ truth ‹ Grant « is truth. ‹ and Your Torah « ever-lasting, ‹ is a right-eousness

חֶסֶד לְאַבְרָהָם, אֲשֶׁר נִשְׁבַּעְתָּ לַאֲבֹתֵינוּ מִימֵי קֶדֶם.[8]

« of old. ‹ from days ‹ to our forefathers ‹ you swore ‹ as « to Abraham, ‹ kind-ness

בָּרוּךְ אֲדֹנָי יוֹם יוֹם יַעֲמָס לָנוּ, הָאֵל יְשׁוּעָתֵנוּ סֶלָה.[9]

« Selah. « of our salvation, ‹ the God ‹ us up [with blessings], ‹ He loads ‹ by day ‹ day « is the Lord; ‹ Blessed

יהוה צְבָאוֹת עִמָּנוּ, מִשְׂגָּב לָנוּ אֱלֹהֵי יַעֲקֹב סֶלָה.[10]

« Selah. « of Jacob, ‹ is the God ‹ for us ‹ a stronghold « is with us, ‹ Master of Legions, ‹ HASHEM,

---

(1) *Targum Yonasan.* (2) *Exodus* 15:18. (3) *Targum Onkelos.* (4) *I Chronicles* 29:18.
(5) *Psalms* 78:38. (6) 86:5. (7) 119:142. (8) *Micah* 7:20. (9) *Psalms* 68:20. (10) 46:8.

יהוה צְבָאוֹת, אַשְׁרֵי אָדָם בֹּטֵחַ בָּךְ.[1] יהוה הוֹשִׁיעָה,

HASHEM, › Master of Legions, › praiseworthy › is the man › who trusts › in You. » HASHEM, › save! »

הַמֶּלֶךְ יַעֲנֵנוּ בְיוֹם קָרְאֵנוּ.[2] בָּרוּךְ הוּא אֱלֹהֵינוּ

May the King › answer us › on the day › we call. » Blessed › is He, › our God, ›

שֶׁבְּרָאָנוּ לִכְבוֹדוֹ, וְהִבְדִּילָנוּ מִן הַתּוֹעִים, וְנָתַן לָנוּ

Who created us › for His glory, » and separated us › from › those who stray, » and gave › us ›

תּוֹרַת אֱמֶת, וְחַיֵּי עוֹלָם נָטַע בְּתוֹכֵנוּ. הוּא

the Torah › of truth, » and life › eternal › implanted › within us. » May He ›

יִפְתַּח לִבֵּנוּ בְּתוֹרָתוֹ, וְיָשֵׂם בְּלִבֵּנוּ אַהֲבָתוֹ וְיִרְאָתוֹ

open › our heart › to His Torah » and imbue › our heart › with love of Him › and awe of Him ›

וְלַעֲשׂוֹת רְצוֹנוֹ וּלְעָבְדוֹ בְּלֵבָב שָׁלֵם, לְמַעַן לֹא נִיגַע

and [the will] to do › His will › and to serve Him › with a heart › that is whole, » so that › we do not › toil ›

לָרִיק, וְלֹא נֵלֵד לַבֶּהָלָה.[3] יְהִי רָצוֹן מִלְּפָנֶיךָ, יהוה

in vain › nor › produce › for futility. » May it be › the will › before You, › HASHEM, »

אֱלֹהֵינוּ וֵאלֹהֵי אֲבוֹתֵינוּ, שֶׁנִּשְׁמֹר חֻקֶּיךָ בָּעוֹלָם הַזֶּה,

our God › and the God › of our forefathers, » that we observe › Your decrees › in This World, ›

וְנִזְכֶּה וְנִחְיֶה וְנִרְאֶה וְנִירַשׁ טוֹבָה וּבְרָכָה לִשְׁנֵי

and that we merit › that we live › and we see › and we inherit › goodness › and blessing › in the years ›

יְמוֹת הַמָּשִׁיחַ וּלְחַיֵּי הָעוֹלָם הַבָּא. לְמַעַן יְזַמֶּרְךָ

of Messianic times › and for the life › of the World › to Come. » So that › sing to You ›

כָבוֹד וְלֹא יִדֹּם, יהוה אֱלֹהַי לְעוֹלָם אוֹדֶךָּ.[4] בָּרוּךְ

[might] my soul, › and not › be silenced; » HASHEM, › my God, › forever › will I thank You. » Blessed ›

הַגֶּבֶר אֲשֶׁר יִבְטַח בַּיהוה, וְהָיָה יהוה מִבְטַחוֹ.[5]

is the man › who › trusts › in HASHEM, » then will › HASHEM be › his security. »

---

(1) *Psalms* 84:13. (2) 20:10. (3) Cf. *Isaiah* 65:23. (4) *Psalms* 30:13. (5) *Jeremiah* 17:7.

בִּטְחוּ בַיהוה עֲדֵי עַד, כִּי בְּיָהּ יהוה צוּר עוֹלָמִים.[1]

« of the worlds. ‹ is the strength ‹ HASHEM, ‹ in God, ‹ for « forever, ‹ in HASHEM ‹ Trust

❖ וְיִבְטְחוּ בְךָ יוֹדְעֵי שְׁמֶךָ, כִּי לֹא עָזַבְתָּ דֹּרְשֶׁיךָ,

‹ those who seek You, ‹ You have not forsaken ‹ for « Your Name, ‹ those who know « in You, ‹ And they will trust

יהוה.[2] יהוה חָפֵץ לְמַעַן צִדְקוֹ, יַגְדִּיל תּוֹרָה וְיַאְדִּיר.[3]

« and glorious. ‹ to make the Torah great ‹ of [Israel's] righteousness, ‹ for the sake ‹ desired, ‹ HASHEM « HASHEM.

THE *CHAZZAN* RECITES קַדִּישׁ שָׁלֵם בְּלֹא תִּתְקַבֵּל.

יִתְגַּדַּל וְיִתְקַדַּשׁ שְׁמֵהּ רַבָּא. (Cong. — אָמֵן.) בְּעָלְמָא דִּי

‹ that ‹ in the world ‹ (Amen.) « that is great! — ‹ may His Name ‹ and be sanctified ‹ Grow exalted

בְרָא כִרְעוּתֵהּ. וְיַמְלִיךְ מַלְכוּתֵהּ, בְּחַיֵּיכוֹן וּבְיוֹמֵיכוֹן וּבְחַיֵּי

‹ and in the lifetimes ‹ and in your days, ‹ in your lifetimes « to His kingship, ‹ and may He give reign « according to His will, ‹ He created

דְכָל בֵּית יִשְׂרָאֵל, בַּעֲגָלָא וּבִזְמַן קָרִיב. וְאִמְרוּ: אָמֵן.

« Amen. ‹ Now respond: « that comes soon. ‹ and at a time ‹ swiftly « of Israel, ‹ Family ‹ of the entire

CONGREGATION RESPONDS:

אָמֵן. יְהֵא שְׁמֵהּ רַבָּא מְבָרַךְ לְעָלַם וּלְעָלְמֵי עָלְמַיָּא.

« and for all eternity. ‹ forever ‹ be blessed ‹ that is great ‹ His Name ‹ May « Amen.

CHAZZAN CONTINUES:

יְהֵא שְׁמֵהּ רַבָּא מְבָרַךְ לְעָלַם וּלְעָלְמֵי עָלְמַיָּא. יִתְבָּרַךְ

‹ Blessed, « and for all eternity. ‹ forever ‹ be blessed ‹ that is great ‹ His Name ‹ May

וְיִשְׁתַּבַּח וְיִתְפָּאַר וְיִתְרוֹמַם וְיִתְנַשֵּׂא וְיִתְהַדָּר וְיִתְעַלֶּה

‹ elevated, ‹ honored, ‹ upraised, ‹ exalted, ‹ glorified, ‹ praised,

וְיִתְהַלָּל שְׁמֵהּ דְּקֻדְשָׁא בְּרִיךְ הוּא (Cong. — בְּרִיךְ הוּא) —

« is He) ‹ (Blessed « is He ‹ Blessed ‹ of the Holy One, ‹ be the Name ‹ and lauded

לְעֵלָּא מִן כָּל בִּרְכָתָא וְשִׁירָתָא תֻּשְׁבְּחָתָא וְנֶחֱמָתָא

‹ and consolation ‹ praise « and song, ‹ blessing ‹ any ‹ beyond

דַּאֲמִירָן בְּעָלְמָא. וְאִמְרוּ: אָמֵן. (Cong. — אָמֵן.)

« (Amen.) « Amen. ‹ Now respond: « in the world. ‹ that are uttered

(1) *Isaiah* 26:4. (2) *Psalms* 9:11. (3) *Isaiah* 42:21.

CONGREGATION:

יְהִי שֵׁם יהוה מְבֹרָךְ, מֵעַתָּה וְעַד עוֹלָם.[1]

« eternity. ‹ until ‹ from this time « be blessed, ‹ of HASHEM ‹ the Name ‹ Let

CHAZZAN CONTINUES:

יְהֵא שְׁלָמָא רַבָּא מִן שְׁמַיָּא, וְחַיִּים עָלֵינוּ וְעַל כָּל

‹ all ‹ and upon ‹ upon us « and life, « Heaven, ‹ from ‹ that is abundant ‹ peace ‹ May there be

יִשְׂרָאֵל. וְאִמְרוּ: אָמֵן. (Cong. — אָמֵן.)

« (Amen.) « Amen. ‹ Now respond: « Israel.

CONGREGATION:

עֶזְרִי מֵעִם יהוה, עֹשֵׂה שָׁמַיִם וָאָרֶץ.[2]

« and earth. ‹ of heaven ‹ Maker « HASHEM, ‹ is from ‹ (My help

CHAZZAN BOWS; TAKES THREE STEPS BACK. BOWS LEFT AND SAYS ... עֹשֶׂה שָׁלוֹם, *"HE WHO MAKES PEACE ..."*; BOWS RIGHT AND SAYS ... הוּא, *"MAY HE ..."*; BOWS FORWARD AND SAYS ... וְעַל כָּל יִשְׂרָאֵל, *"AND UPON ALL ISRAEL ..."*; REMAINS IN PLACE FOR A FEW MOMENTS, THEN TAKES THREE STEPS FORWARD.

עֹשֶׂה שָׁלוֹם בִּמְרוֹמָיו, הוּא יַעֲשֶׂה שָׁלוֹם עָלֵינוּ, וְעַל כָּל

‹ all ‹ and upon ‹ upon us, ‹ peace ‹ make ‹ may He « in His heights, ‹ peace ‹ He Who makes

יִשְׂרָאֵל. וְאִמְרוּ: אָמֵן. (Cong. — אָמֵן.)

« (Amen.) « Amen. ‹ Now respond: « Israel.

STAND WHILE RECITING עָלֵינוּ, *"IT IS OUR DUTY ..."*

עָלֵינוּ לְשַׁבֵּחַ לַאֲדוֹן הַכֹּל, לָתֵת גְּדֻלָּה לְיוֹצֵר

‹ to the Molder ‹ greatness ‹ to ascribe « of all, ‹ the Master ‹ to praise ‹ It is our duty

בְּרֵאשִׁית, שֶׁלֹּא עָשָׂנוּ כְּגוֹיֵי הָאֲרָצוֹת, וְלֹא

‹ and has not « of the lands, ‹ like the nations ‹ for He has not made us « of primeval creation,

שָׂמָנוּ כְּמִשְׁפְּחוֹת הָאֲדָמָה. שֶׁלֹּא שָׂם חֶלְקֵנוּ

‹ our portion ‹ assigned ‹ for He has not « of the earth; ‹ like the families ‹ established us

כָּהֶם, וְגוֹרָלֵנוּ כְּכָל הֲמוֹנָם. (שֶׁהֵם מִשְׁתַּחֲוִים

‹ bow ‹ (For they « their multitudes. ‹ like all ‹ nor our lot ‹ like theirs

לְהֶבֶל וָרִיק, וּמִתְפַּלְּלִים אֶל אֵל לֹא יוֹשִׁיעַ.[3])

« save.) ‹ who does not ‹ a god ‹ to ‹ and pray ‹ and emptiness ‹ to vanity

(1) *Psalms* 113:2. (2) 121:2. (3) *Isaiah* 45:20.

BOW WHILE RECITING וַאֲנַחְנוּ כּוֹרְעִים וּמִשְׁתַּחֲוִים, "BUT WE BEND OUR KNEES, BOW."

וַאֲנַחְנוּ כּוֹרְעִים וּמִשְׁתַּחֲוִים וּמוֹדִים, לִפְנֵי מֶלֶךְ

But we | bend our knees, | bow, | and acknowledge our thanks | before | the King

מַלְכֵי הַמְּלָכִים הַקָּדוֹשׁ בָּרוּךְ הוּא. שֶׁהוּא נוֹטֶה

over kings | of kings, | the Holy One, | Blessed is | He. | He | stretches out

שָׁמַיִם וְיֹסֵד אָרֶץ,[1] וּמוֹשַׁב יְקָרוֹ בַּשָּׁמַיִם מִמַּעַל,

heaven | and establishes | earth's foundation, | the seat | of His homage | is in the heavens | above,

וּשְׁכִינַת עֻזּוֹ בְּגָבְהֵי מְרוֹמִים. הוּא אֱלֹהֵינוּ, אֵין עוֹד.

and the Presence | of His power | is in the loftiest | heights. | He is | our God | and there is none | other.

אֱמֶת מַלְכֵּנוּ, אֶפֶס זוּלָתוֹ, כַּכָּתוּב בְּתוֹרָתוֹ: וְיָדַעְתָּ

True | is our King, | there is nothing | beside Him, | as it is written | in His Torah: | *You are to know*

הַיּוֹם וַהֲשֵׁבֹתָ אֶל לְבָבֶךָ, כִּי יהוה הוּא הָאֱלֹהִים

this day | *and take* | *to* | *your heart,* | *that* | *HASHEM* | *He is* | *the God*

בַּשָּׁמַיִם מִמַּעַל וְעַל הָאָרֶץ מִתָּחַת, אֵין עוֹד.[2]

— in heaven | *above* | *and on* | *the earth* | *below —* | *there is none* | *other.*

עַל כֵּן נְקַוֶּה לְּךָ, יהוה אֱלֹהֵינוּ, לִרְאוֹת מְהֵרָה

Therefore | we put our hope | in You, | HASHEM, | our God, | that we may see | very soon

בְּתִפְאֶרֶת עֻזֶּךָ, לְהַעֲבִיר גִּלּוּלִים מִן הָאָרֶץ,

the splendor | of Your might, | to remove | detestable idolatry | from | the earth,

וְהָאֱלִילִים כָּרוֹת יִכָּרֵתוּן, לְתַקֵּן עוֹלָם בְּמַלְכוּת

and false gods | will be utterly cut off, | to perfect | the universe | through the sovereignty

שַׁדַּי. וְכָל בְּנֵי בָשָׂר יִקְרְאוּ בִשְׁמֶךָ, לְהַפְנוֹת אֵלֶיךָ

of the Almighty. | Then all | humanity | will call | upon Your Name, | to turn | toward You

כָּל רִשְׁעֵי אָרֶץ. יַכִּירוּ וְיֵדְעוּ כָּל יוֹשְׁבֵי תֵבֵל, כִּי

all | the wicked | of the earth. | May they recognize | and know | — all | the inhabitants | of the world — | that

(1) *Isaiah* 51:13. (2) *Deuteronomy* 4:39.

לְךָ תִּכְרַע כָּל בֶּרֶךְ, תִּשָּׁבַע כָּל לָשׁוֹן.[1] לְפָנֶיךָ

‹ Before You, « tongue. ‹ every ‹ should swear « knee, ‹ every ‹ should bend ‹ to You

יהוה אֱלֹהֵינוּ יִכְרְעוּ וְיִפֹּלוּ, וְלִכְבוֹד שִׁמְךָ יְקָר

‹ homage ‹ of Your Name ‹ and to the glory « and cast themselves down, ‹ they will bend their knees ‹ our God, ‹ HASHEM,

יִתֵּנוּ. וִיקַבְּלוּ כֻלָּם אֶת עוֹל מַלְכוּתֶךָ, וְתִמְלֹךְ

‹ that You may reign « of Your kingship, ‹ the yoke ‹ will all ‹ and accept « they will offer,

עֲלֵיהֶם מְהֵרָה לְעוֹלָם וָעֶד. כִּי הַמַּלְכוּת שֶׁלְּךָ הִיא

« is Yours, ‹ the kingdom ‹ For « and ever. ‹ for ever ‹ very soon ‹ over them

וּלְעוֹלְמֵי עַד תִּמְלוֹךְ בְּכָבוֹד, כַּכָּתוּב בְּתוֹרָתֶךָ:

« in Your Torah: ‹ as it is written « in glory, ‹ You will reign ‹ and ever ‹ and for ever

יהוה יִמְלֹךְ לְעֹלָם וָעֶד.[2] וְנֶאֱמַר: וְהָיָה יהוה

‹ *HASHEM* ‹ *Then will* « And it is said: « *and ever.* ‹ *for ever* ‹ *shall reign* ‹ *HASHEM*

לְמֶלֶךְ עַל כָּל הָאָרֶץ, בַּיּוֹם הַהוּא יִהְיֶה יהוה

‹ *HASHEM* ‹ *shall* ‹ *— on that day* « *the world* ‹ *all* ‹ *over* ‹ *be King*

אֶחָד וּשְׁמוֹ אֶחָד.[3]

« *be One.* ‹ *and His Name* ‹ *be One*

SOME CONGREGATIONS RECITE THE FOLLOWING AFTER עָלֵינוּ, *ALEINU.*

אַל תִּירָא מִפַּחַד פִּתְאֹם, וּמִשֹּׁאַת רְשָׁעִים כִּי

‹ when ‹ of the wicked ‹ nor the holocaust « [that comes] suddenly, ‹ terror ‹ Do not fear

תָבֹא.[4] עֻצוּ עֵצָה וְתֻפָר, דַּבְּרוּ דָבָר וְלֹא יָקוּם, כִּי

‹ for « stand, ‹ and it shall not ‹ your speech ‹ speak « and it will be annulled; ‹ a conspiracy ‹ Plan « it comes.

עִמָּנוּ אֵל.[5] וְעַד זִקְנָה אֲנִי הוּא, וְעַד שֵׂיבָה אֲנִי

‹ I ‹ [your] elder years, ‹ and even till « I remain unchanged; ‹ [your] old age, ‹ Even till « is God. ‹ with us

אֶסְבֹּל, אֲנִי עָשִׂיתִי וַאֲנִי אֶשָּׂא, וַאֲנִי אֶסְבֹּל וַאֲמַלֵּט.[6]

« and rescue [you]. ‹ shall carry [you] ‹ I « shall bear [you]; ‹ and I ‹ created [you] ‹ I « shall carry [you].

---

(1) Cf. *Isaiah* 45:23. (2) *Exodus* 15:18. (3) *Zechariah* 14:9. (4) *Proverbs* 3:25. (5) *Isaiah* 8:10. (6) 46:4.

IN THE PRESENCE OF A *MINYAN*, MOURNERS RECITE קַדִּישׁ יָתוֹם, THE MOURNER'S *KADDISH* (SEE LAWS §132-134). [A TRANSLITERATION OF THIS *KADDISH* APPEARS ON PAGE 647.]

יִתְגַּדַּל וְיִתְקַדַּשׁ שְׁמֵהּ רַבָּא. (Cong.—אָמֵן.) בְּעָלְמָא דִּי

‹ that ‹ in the world ‹ (Amen.) « that is great! — ‹ may His Name ‹ and be sanctified ‹ Grow exalted

בְּרָא כִרְעוּתֵהּ. וְיַמְלִיךְ מַלְכוּתֵהּ, בְּחַיֵּיכוֹן וּבְיוֹמֵיכוֹן וּבְחַיֵּי

‹ and in the lifetimes ‹ and in your days, ‹ in your lifetimes « to His kingship, ‹ and may He give reign « according to His will, ‹ He created

דְכָל בֵּית יִשְׂרָאֵל, בַּעֲגָלָא וּבִזְמַן קָרִיב. וְאִמְרוּ: אָמֵן.

« Amen. ‹ Now respond: « that comes soon. ‹ and at a time ‹ swiftly « of Israel, ‹ Family ‹ of the entire

CONGREGATION RESPONDS:

אָמֵן. יְהֵא שְׁמֵהּ רַבָּא מְבָרַךְ לְעָלַם וּלְעָלְמֵי עָלְמַיָּא.

« and for all eternity. ‹ forever ‹ be blessed ‹ that is great ‹ His Name ‹ May « Amen.

MOURNER CONTINUES:

יְהֵא שְׁמֵהּ רַבָּא מְבָרַךְ לְעָלַם וּלְעָלְמֵי עָלְמַיָּא. יִתְבָּרַךְ

‹ Blessed, « and for all eternity. ‹ forever ‹ be blessed ‹ that is great ‹ His Name ‹ May

וְיִשְׁתַּבַּח וְיִתְפָּאַר וְיִתְרוֹמַם וְיִתְנַשֵּׂא וְיִתְהַדָּר וְיִתְעַלֶּה

‹ elevated, ‹ honored, ‹ upraised, ‹ exalted, ‹ glorified, ‹ praised,

וְיִתְהַלָּל שְׁמֵהּ דְּקֻדְשָׁא בְּרִיךְ הוּא (Cong.—בְּרִיךְ הוּא) —

« is He) ‹ (Blessed « is He ‹ Blessed ‹ of the Holy One, ‹ be the Name ‹ and lauded

לְעֵלָּא מִן כָּל בִּרְכָתָא וְשִׁירָתָא תֻּשְׁבְּחָתָא וְנֶחֱמָתָא

‹ and consolation ‹ praise « and song, ‹ blessing ‹ any ‹ beyond

דַּאֲמִירָן בְּעָלְמָא. וְאִמְרוּ: אָמֵן. (Cong.—אָמֵן.)

« (Amen.) « Amen. ‹ Now respond: « in the world. ‹ that are uttered

יְהֵא שְׁלָמָא רַבָּא מִן שְׁמַיָּא, וְחַיִּים עָלֵינוּ וְעַל כָּל

‹ all ‹ and upon ‹ upon us « and life, « Heaven, ‹ from ‹ that is abundant ‹ peace ‹ May there be

יִשְׂרָאֵל. וְאִמְרוּ: אָמֵן. (Cong.—אָמֵן.)

« (Amen.) « Amen. ‹ Now respond: « Israel.

BOW; TAKE THREE STEPS BACK; BOWS LEFT AND SAY ... עֹשֶׂה שָׁלוֹם, *"HE WHO MAKES PEACE ..."*; BOW RIGHT AND SAY ... הוּא, *"MAY HE ..."*; BOW FORWARD AND SAY ... וְעַל כָּל יִשְׂרָאֵל, *"AND UPON ALL ISRAEL ..."*; REMAIN IN PLACE FOR A FEW MOMENTS, THEN TAKE THREE STEPS FORWARD.

עֹשֶׂה שָׁלוֹם בִּמְרוֹמָיו, הוּא יַעֲשֶׂה שָׁלוֹם עָלֵינוּ, וְעַל כָּל

‹ all ‹ and upon ‹ upon us, ‹ peace ‹ make ‹ may He « in His heights, ‹ peace ‹ He Who makes

יִשְׂרָאֵל. וְאִמְרוּ: אָמֵן. (Cong.—אָמֵן.)

« (Amen.) « Amen. ‹ Now respond: « Israel.

UPON ARISING / השכמת הבוקר

A JEW SHOULD WAKE UP WITH GRATITUDE TO GOD FOR HAVING RESTORED HIS FACULTIES AND WITH A LIONLIKE RESOLVE TO SERVE HIS CREATOR. BEFORE GETTING OFF THE BED OR COMMENCING ANY OTHER CONVERSATION OR ACTIVITY, HE DECLARES HIS GRATITUDE:

מוֹדֶה אֲנִי לְפָנֶיךָ, מֶלֶךְ חַי וְקַיָּם, שֶׁהֶחֱזַרְתָּ

‹ for You have returned « and eternal, ‹ living ‹ King, « before You, ‹ I give thanks

בִּי נִשְׁמָתִי בְּחֶמְלָה — רַבָּה אֱמוּנָתֶךָ.

« is Your faithfulness! ‹— abundant « with compassion ‹ my soul ‹ within me

WASH THE FINGERS, BUT NOT THE PALMS, ACCORDING TO THE RITUAL PROCEDURE: PICK UP THE VESSEL OF WATER WITH THE RIGHT HAND, PASS IT TO THE LEFT, AND POUR WATER OVER THE RIGHT. THEN WITH THE RIGHT HAND POUR OVER THE LEFT. FOLLOW THIS PROCEDURE UNTIL WATER HAS BEEN POURED OVER EACH HAND THREE TIMES. (WHILE THE FINGERS ARE STILL DAMP, THEY MAY BE USED TO REMOVE MUCUS FROM THE EYES.) THEN, RECITE:

רֵאשִׁית חָכְמָה יִרְאַת יהוה, שֵׂכֶל טוֹב לְכָל

‹ to all ‹ good understanding [is given] « of HASHEM, ‹ is the fear ‹ of wisdom ‹ The beginning

עֹשֵׂיהֶם, תְּהִלָּתוֹ עֹמֶדֶת לָעַד.[1] בָּרוּךְ שֵׁם כְּבוֹד

‹ of His glorious ‹ is the Name ‹ Blessed « forever. ‹ endures ‹ His praise « their practitioners;

מַלְכוּתוֹ לְעוֹלָם וָעֶד.

« and ever. ‹ for ever ‹ kingdom

ציצית, טלית, ותפילין

TZITZIS, TALLIS, AND TEFILLIN

THE *TALLIS KATTAN (TZITZIS)* IS WORN, BUT THE BLESSING IS OMITTED. THE *TALLIS* AND *TEFILLIN* ARE NOT WORN AT *SHACHARIS*, BUT ARE WORN AT *MINCHAH*.

SOME CONGREGATIONS OMIT CERTAIN PASSAGES OF THE PRAYERS PRECEDING אֵיזֶהוּ מְקוֹמָן (P. 128). CUSTOMS REGARDING WHETHER AND WHICH PASSAGES ARE OMITTED VARY GREATLY; THEREFORE WE HAVE NOT OMITTED ANY PASSAGES. EACH CONGREGATION SHOULD FOLLOW ITS ESTABLISHED CUSTOM.

MORNING BLESSINGS / ברכות השחר

RECITE THE FOLLOWING COLLECTION OF VERSES UPON ENTERING THE SYNAGOGUE:

מַה טֹּבוּ אֹהָלֶיךָ יַעֲקֹב, מִשְׁכְּנֹתֶיךָ יִשְׂרָאֵל.[2]

« O Israel. ‹ your dwelling places, « O Jacob, ‹ are your tents, ‹ goodly ‹ How

(1) *Psalms* 111:10. (2) *Numbers* 24:5.

וַאֲנִי בְּרֹב חַסְדְּךָ אָבוֹא בֵיתֶךָ, אֶשְׁתַּחֲוֶה אֶל

‹ toward ‹ I will prostrate myself « Your house; ‹ will I enter ‹ of Your kindness ‹ through the abundance ‹ As for me,

הֵיכַל קָדְשְׁךָ בְּיִרְאָתֶךָ.[1] יהוה אָהַבְתִּי מְעוֹן

‹ the shelter ‹ I love ‹ HASHEM, « in awe of You. ‹ of Your Holiness ‹ the Sanctuary

בֵּיתֶךָ, וּמְקוֹם מִשְׁכַּן כְּבוֹדֶךָ.[2] וַאֲנִי אֶשְׁתַּחֲוֶה

‹ shall prostrate myself ‹ I « of Your glory. ‹ of the residence ‹ and the place ‹ of Your House,

וְאֶכְרָעָה, אֶבְרְכָה לִפְנֵי יהוה עֹשִׂי.[3] וַאֲנִי, תְפִלָּתִי

‹ may my prayer « As for me, « my Maker. ‹ HASHEM ‹ before ‹ I shall kneel « and bow,

לְךָ יהוה עֵת רָצוֹן, אֱלֹהִים בְּרָב חַסְדֶּךָ, עֲנֵנִי

‹ answer me ‹ of Your kindness, ‹ in the abundance ‹ O God, « that is favorable; ‹ be at a time ‹ HASHEM, ‹ to You,

בֶּאֱמֶת יִשְׁעֶךָ.[4]

« of Your salvation. ‹ with the truth

אֲדוֹן עוֹלָם אֲשֶׁר מָלַךְ בְּטֶרֶם כָּל יְצִיר נִבְרָא.

« was created. ‹ form ‹ any ‹ before ‹ reigned ‹ Who ‹ of the universe ‹ Master

לְעֵת נַעֲשָׂה בְחֶפְצוֹ כֹּל, אֲזַי מֶלֶךְ שְׁמוֹ נִקְרָא.

« was proclaimed. ‹ His Name ‹ as "King" ‹ then « all things, ‹ when His will created ‹ At the time

וְאַחֲרֵי כִּכְלוֹת הַכֹּל, לְבַדּוֹ יִמְלוֹךְ נוֹרָא.

« the Awesome one. « will reign, ‹ He alone « of all, ‹ the end ‹ After

וְהוּא הָיָה וְהוּא הֹוֶה, וְהוּא יִהְיֶה בְּתִפְאָרָה.

« in splendor. ‹ Who shall remain ‹ and He ‹ Who is ‹ and He ‹ Who was ‹ It is He

וְהוּא אֶחָד וְאֵין שֵׁנִי לְהַמְשִׁיל לוֹ לְהַחְבִּירָה.

« or to be His equal. ‹ to Him ‹ to compare ‹ second ‹ and there is no ‹ is One ‹ He

בְּלִי רֵאשִׁית בְּלִי תַכְלִית, וְלוֹ הָעֹז וְהַמִּשְׂרָה.

« and the dominion. ‹ is the power ‹ — His « conclusion, ‹ without « beginning, ‹ Without

(1) *Psalms* 5:8. (2) 26:8. (3) Cf. 95:6. (4) 69:14.

וְהוּא אֵלִי וְחַי גֹּאֲלִי, וְצוּר חֶבְלִי בְּעֵת צָרָה.

He is ‹ my God, « my living ‹ Redeemer, « a Rock [to save] ‹ [from] my pain ‹ in a time ‹ of distress. «

וְהוּא נִסִּי וּמָנוֹס לִי, מְנָת כּוֹסִי בְּיוֹם אֶקְרָא.

He is ‹ my banner, « a refuge ‹ for me, « the portion ‹ of my cup ‹ on the day ‹ I call. «

בְּיָדוֹ אַפְקִיד רוּחִי בְּעֵת אִישַׁן וְאָעִירָה.

Into His hand ‹ I shall entrust ‹ my spirit ‹ when ‹ I go to sleep ‹ — and I shall awaken! «

וְעִם רוּחִי גְּוִיָּתִי, יהוה לִי וְלֹא אִירָא.

With ‹ my spirit ‹ my body shall remain; « HASHEM ‹ is with me, « I shall not fear. «

יִגְדַּל אֱלֹהִים חַי וְיִשְׁתַּבַּח, נִמְצָא וְאֵין עֵת אֶל

Exalted be ‹ God ‹ Who lives, ‹ and may He be praised. « He exists, ‹ and there is no ‹ time limitation ‹ for ‹

מְצִיאוּתוֹ. אֶחָד וְאֵין יָחִיד כְּיִחוּדוֹ, נֶעְלָם וְגַם אֵין

His existence. « He is One, « and there is no ‹ unity ‹ like His Oneness. « [He is] inscrutable ‹ and indeed ‹ there is no ‹

סוֹף לְאַחְדּוּתוֹ. אֵין לוֹ דְּמוּת הַגּוּף וְאֵינוֹ

limit ‹ to His Oneness. « He has no ‹ semblance ‹ of a body, « nor is He ‹

גוּף, לֹא נַעֲרוֹךְ אֵלָיו קְדֻשָּׁתוֹ. קַדְמוֹן לְכָל דָּבָר

corporeal, « nor ‹ can we compare ‹ to Him ‹ [in] His Holiness. « He preceded ‹ every ‹ entity ‹

אֲשֶׁר נִבְרָא, רִאשׁוֹן וְאֵין רֵאשִׁית לְרֵאשִׁיתוֹ.

that ‹ was created « — the First, ‹ and nothing ‹ precedes ‹ His precedence. «

הִנּוֹ אֲדוֹן עוֹלָם לְכָל נוֹצָר, יוֹרֶה גְדֻלָּתוֹ וּמַלְכוּתוֹ.

He is ‹ Master ‹ of the universe, « To every ‹ creature ‹ He teaches ‹ His greatness ‹ and His sovereignty. «

שֶׁפַע נְבוּאָתוֹ נְתָנוֹ, אֶל אַנְשֵׁי סְגֻלָּתוֹ וְתִפְאַרְתּוֹ.

The abundance ‹ of His prophecy ‹ did He grant ‹ to ‹ the people ‹ of His choosing ‹ and of His splendor. «

לֹא קָם בְּיִשְׂרָאֵל כְּמֹשֶׁה עוֹד, נָבִיא[1] וּמַבִּיט

There did not ‹ rise ‹ in Israel ‹ [anyone] like Moses ‹ ever again « — a prophet ‹ who gazes at ‹

(1) Cf. *Deuteronomy* 34:10.

אֶת תְּמוּנָתוֹ.[1] תּוֹרַת אֱמֶת נָתַן לְעַמּוֹ אֵל, עַל

〈 by 〈 — did God, 〈 to His people 〈 He gave 〈 of truth 〈 A Torah 《 His image.

יַד נְבִיאוֹ נֶאֱמַן בֵּיתוֹ.[2] לֹא יַחֲלִיף הָאֵל וְלֹא

〈 nor 〈 will God amend 〈 Never 《 of His household. 〈 the most trusted 〈 of His prophet, 〈 means

יָמִיר דָּתוֹ, לְעוֹלָמִים לְזוּלָתוֹ. צוֹפֶה וְיוֹדֵעַ סְתָרֵינוּ,

《 our secrets, 〈 and knows 〈 He scrutinizes 《 for any other one. 〈 for all eternity, 《 His law, 〈 will He exchange

מַבִּיט לְסוֹף דָּבָר בְּקַדְמָתוֹ. גּוֹמֵל לְאִישׁ חֶסֶד

〈 with kindness 〈 man 〈 He recompenses 《 at its inception. 〈 of a matter 〈 the outcome 〈 He perceives

כְּמִפְעָלוֹ, נוֹתֵן לְרָשָׁע רָע כְּרִשְׁעָתוֹ. יִשְׁלַח לְקֵץ

〈 at the End 〈 He will send 《 according to his wickedness. 〈 evil 〈 to the wicked one 〈 He assigns 《 according to his deed;

הַיָּמִין מְשִׁיחֵנוּ, לִפְדּוֹת מְחַכֵּי קֵץ יְשׁוּעָתוֹ. מֵתִים

〈 The dead 《 salvation. 〈 His final 〈 those longing for 〈 to redeem 《 our Messiah, 〈 of Days

יְחַיֶּה אֵל בְּרֹב חַסְדּוֹ, בָּרוּךְ עֲדֵי עַד שֵׁם תְּהִלָּתוֹ.

《 of His praise. 〈 is the Name 〈 and ever 〈 for ever 〈 blessed 《 of His kindness, 〈 in the abundance 〈 will God revive

MORNING BLESSINGS / ברכות השחר

ALTHOUGH MANY HOLD THAT THE BLESSING עַל נְטִילַת יָדָיִם SHOULD BE RECITED IMMEDIATELY AFTER THE RITUAL WASHING OF THE HANDS UPON ARISING, OTHERS CUSTOMARILY RECITE IT AT THIS POINT. SIMILARLY, SOME RECITE אֲשֶׁר יָצַר IMMEDIATELY AFTER RELIEVING THEMSELVES IN THE MORNING, WHILE OTHERS RECITE IT HERE.

בָּרוּךְ אַתָּה יהוה אֱלֹהֵינוּ מֶלֶךְ הָעוֹלָם, אֲשֶׁר

〈 Who 《 of the universe, 〈 King 〈 our God, 〈 HASHEM, 〈 are You, 〈 Blessed

קִדְּשָׁנוּ בְּמִצְוֹתָיו, וְצִוָּנוּ עַל נְטִילַת יָדָיִם.

《 the hands. 〈 washing 〈 regarding 〈 and has commanded us 〈 with His commandments 〈 has sanctified us

בָּרוּךְ אַתָּה יהוה אֱלֹהֵינוּ מֶלֶךְ הָעוֹלָם, אֲשֶׁר

〈 Who 《 of the universe, 〈 King 〈 our God, 〈 HASHEM, 〈 are You, 〈 Blessed

יָצַר אֶת הָאָדָם בְּחָכְמָה, וּבָרָא בוֹ נְקָבִים נְקָבִים,

〈 all manner of openings 〈 within him 〈 and created 《 with wisdom, 〈 man 〈 fashioned

(1) Cf. *Numbers* 12:8. (2) Cf. 12:7.

חֲלוּלִים חֲלוּלִים. גָּלוּי וְיָדוּעַ לִפְנֵי כִסֵּא כְבוֹדֶךָ,

« of Your glory, ‹ the throne ‹ before ‹ and known ‹ It is obvious « and all manner of cavities.

שֶׁאִם יִפָּתֵחַ אֶחָד מֵהֶם, אוֹ יִסָּתֵם אֶחָד

‹ [even] one ‹ would be blocked ‹ or « of them ‹ [even] one ‹ there would be ruptured ‹ that if

מֵהֶם, אִי אֶפְשַׁר לְהִתְקַיֵּם וְלַעֲמוֹד לְפָנֶיךָ. בָּרוּךְ

‹ Blessed « before You. ‹ and to stand ‹ to survive ‹ be possible ‹ it would not « of them,

אַתָּה יהוה, רוֹפֵא כָל בָּשָׂר וּמַפְלִיא לַעֲשׂוֹת.

« in His acts. ‹ and is wondrous ‹ flesh, ‹ all ‹ Who heals « HASHEM, ‹ are You,

AT THIS POINT, SOME RECITE אֱלֹהַי נְשָׁמָה (P. 103).

BLESSINGS OF THE TORAH / ברכות התורה

IT IS FORBIDDEN TO STUDY OR RECITE TORAH PASSAGES BEFORE RECITING THE FOLLOWING BLESSINGS. HOWEVER, THESE BLESSINGS NEED NOT BE REPEATED IF ONE STUDIES AT VARIOUS TIMES OF THE DAY. ALTHOUGH MANY SIDDURIM BEGIN A NEW PARAGRAPH AT וְהַעֲרֶב נָא, ACCORDING TO THE VAST MAJORITY OF COMMENTATORS THE FIRST BLESSING DOES NOT END UNTIL לְעַמּוֹ יִשְׂרָאֵל.

בָּרוּךְ אַתָּה יהוה אֱלֹהֵינוּ מֶלֶךְ הָעוֹלָם, אֲשֶׁר

‹ Who « of the universe, ‹ King ‹ our God, ‹ HASHEM, ‹ are You, ‹ Blessed

קִדְּשָׁנוּ בְּמִצְוֹתָיו, וְצִוָּנוּ לַעֲסוֹק בְּדִבְרֵי תוֹרָה.

« of Torah. ‹ in the words ‹ to engross ourselves ‹ and commanded us ‹ with His commandments ‹ has sanctified us

וְהַעֲרֶב נָא יהוה אֱלֹהֵינוּ אֶת דִּבְרֵי תוֹרָתְךָ בְּפִינוּ

‹ in our mouth ‹ of Your Torah, ‹ the words « our God, ‹ HASHEM, « please, ‹ Sweeten,

וּבְפִי עַמְּךָ בֵּית יִשְׂרָאֵל. וְנִהְיֶה אֲנַחְנוּ וְצֶאֱצָאֵינוּ

‹ and our offspring ‹ — we « that we may be « of Israel, ‹ the house ‹ of Your people ‹ and in the mouth

וְצֶאֱצָאֵי עַמְּךָ בֵּית יִשְׂרָאֵל, כֻּלָּנוּ יוֹדְעֵי שְׁמֶךָ

‹ of Your Name ‹ knowers « all of us — ‹ of Israel, ‹ the House ‹ of Your people, ‹ and the offspring

וְלוֹמְדֵי תוֹרָתֶךָ לִשְׁמָהּ. בָּרוּךְ אַתָּה יהוה, הַמְּלַמֵּד

‹ Who teaches « HASHEM, ‹ are You, ‹ Blessed « for its own sake. ‹ of Your Torah ‹ and students

תּוֹרָה לְעַמּוֹ יִשְׂרָאֵל.

« Israel. ‹ to His people ‹ Torah

בָּרוּךְ אַתָּה יהוה אֱלֹהֵינוּ מֶלֶךְ הָעוֹלָם, אֲשֶׁר בָּחַר בָּנוּ מִכָּל הָעַמִּים וְנָתַן לָנוּ אֶת תּוֹרָתוֹ. בָּרוּךְ אַתָּה יהוה, נוֹתֵן הַתּוֹרָה.

Blessed are You, HASHEM, our God, King of the universe, Who selected us from all the peoples and gave us His Torah. Blessed are You, HASHEM, Giver of the Torah.

יְבָרֶכְךָ יהוה וְיִשְׁמְרֶךָ. יָאֵר יהוה פָּנָיו אֵלֶיךָ וִיחֻנֶּךָּ. יִשָּׂא יהוה פָּנָיו אֵלֶיךָ, וְיָשֵׂם לְךָ שָׁלוֹם.[1]

May HASHEM bless you and safeguard you. May HASHEM illuminate His countenance for you and be gracious to you. May HASHEM turn His countenance to you and establish for you peace.

אֵלּוּ דְבָרִים שֶׁאֵין לָהֶם שִׁעוּר: הַפֵּאָה וְהַבִּכּוּרִים וְהָרֵאָיוֹן וּגְמִילוּת חֲסָדִים וְתַלְמוּד תּוֹרָה.[2]

These are the precepts that have no prescribed measure: the corner of a field [which must be left for the poor], the first-fruit offering, the pilgrimage, the bestowal of kindness and study of Torah.

אֵלּוּ דְבָרִים שֶׁאָדָם אוֹכֵל פֵּרוֹתֵיהֶם בָּעוֹלָם הַזֶּה וְהַקֶּרֶן קַיֶּמֶת לוֹ לָעוֹלָם הַבָּא. וְאֵלּוּ הֵן: כִּבּוּד אָב וָאֵם, וּגְמִילוּת חֲסָדִים, וְהַשְׁכָּמַת בֵּית הַמִּדְרָשׁ שַׁחֲרִית וְעַרְבִית, וְהַכְנָסַת אוֹרְחִים, וּבִקּוּר חוֹלִים, וְהַכְנָסַת כַּלָּה, וּלְוָיַת הַמֵּת,

These are the precepts of which a person enjoys their fruits in This World but whose principal remains intact for him in the World to Come. These are they: honoring [one's] father and mother, the bestowal of kindness, early attendance at the house of study morning and evening, hospitality to guests, visiting the sick, providing for a bride, escorting the dead,

(1) *Numbers* 6:24-26. (2) Mishnah *Pe'ah* 1:1.

וְעִיּוּן תְּפִלָּה, וַהֲבָאַת שָׁלוֹם בֵּין אָדָם

‹ man ‹ between ‹ peace ‹ bringing « in prayer, ‹ absorption

לַחֲבֵרוֹ — וְתַלְמוּד תּוֹרָה כְּנֶגֶד כֻּלָּם.[1]

« to them all. ‹ is equivalent ‹ of Torah ‹ — and the study « and his fellow

אֱלֹהַי, נְשָׁמָה שֶׁנָּתַתָּ בִּי טְהוֹרָה הִיא. אַתָּה

‹ You « is pure. ‹ within me ‹ that You placed ‹ the soul « My God,

בְרָאתָהּ אַתָּה יְצַרְתָּהּ, אַתָּה נְפַחְתָּהּ בִּי, וְאַתָּה

‹ You « into me, ‹ breathed it ‹ You ‹ fashioned it, ‹ You ‹ created it,

מְשַׁמְּרָהּ בְּקִרְבִּי, וְאַתָּה עָתִיד לִטְּלָהּ מִמֶּנִּי,

‹ from me ‹ take it ‹ will eventually ‹ and You ‹ within me, ‹ safeguard it

וּלְהַחֲזִירָהּ בִּי לֶעָתִיד לָבֹא. כָּל זְמַן שֶׁהַנְּשָׁמָה

‹ that the soul ‹ the time ‹ All « to Come. ‹ in the Time ‹ to me ‹ and restore it

בְקִרְבִּי, מוֹדֶה אֲנִי לְפָנֶיךָ, יהוה אֱלֹהַי וֵאלֹהֵי

‹ and the God ‹ my God ‹ HASHEM, ‹ before You, ‹ I give thanks « is within me,

אֲבוֹתַי, רִבּוֹן כָּל הַמַּעֲשִׂים, אֲדוֹן כָּל הַנְּשָׁמוֹת.

« souls. ‹ of all ‹ Lord « works, ‹ of all ‹ Master « of my forefathers,

בָּרוּךְ אַתָּה יהוה, הַמַּחֲזִיר נְשָׁמוֹת לִפְגָרִים מֵתִים.

« that are dead. ‹ to the bodies ‹ souls ‹ Who restores « HASHEM, ‹ are You, ‹ Blessed

THE CHAZZAN RECITES THE FOLLOWING BLESSINGS ALOUD, AND THE CONGREGATION RESPONDS אָמֵן TO EACH BLESSING. NEVERTHELESS, EACH PERSON MUST RECITE THESE BLESSINGS FOR HIMSELF. SOME PEOPLE RECITE THE BLESSINGS ALOUD FOR ONE ANOTHER SO THAT EACH ONE CAN HAVE THE MERIT OF RESPONDING אָמֵן MANY TIMES.

בָּרוּךְ אַתָּה יהוה אֱלֹהֵינוּ מֶלֶךְ הָעוֹלָם, אֲשֶׁר

‹ Who « of the universe, ‹ King ‹ our God, ‹ HASHEM, ‹ are You, ‹ Blessed

נָתַן לַשֶּׂכְוִי בִינָה[2] לְהַבְחִין בֵּין יוֹם וּבֵין לָיְלָה.

« and night. ‹ day ‹ between ‹ to distinguish ‹ understanding ‹ the heart ‹ gave

בָּרוּךְ אַתָּה יהוה אֱלֹהֵינוּ מֶלֶךְ הָעוֹלָם,

« of the universe, ‹ King ‹ our God, ‹ HASHEM, ‹ are You, ‹ Blessed

שֶׁלֹּא עָשַׂנִי גּוֹי.

« a gentile. ‹ make me ‹ Who did not

---

(1) Tractate *Shabbos* 127a. (2) Cf. *Job* 38:36.

בָּרוּךְ אַתָּה יהוה אֱלֹהֵינוּ מֶלֶךְ הָעוֹלָם,

« of the universe, ‹ King ‹ our God, ‹ HASHEM, ‹ are You, ‹ Blessed

שֶׁלֹּא עָשַׂנִי עָבֶד.

« a slave. ‹ make me ‹ Who did not

בָּרוּךְ אַתָּה יהוה אֱלֹהֵינוּ מֶלֶךְ הָעוֹלָם,

« of the universe, ‹ King ‹ our God, ‹ HASHEM, ‹ are You, ‹ Blessed

MEN SAY:

שֶׁלֹּא עָשַׂנִי אִשָּׁה.

« a woman. ‹ make me ‹ Who did not

WOMEN SAY:

שֶׁעָשַׂנִי כִּרְצוֹנוֹ.

« according to His will. ‹ Who made me

בָּרוּךְ אַתָּה יהוה אֱלֹהֵינוּ מֶלֶךְ הָעוֹלָם,

« of the universe, ‹ King ‹ our God, ‹ HASHEM, ‹ are You, ‹ Blessed

פּוֹקֵחַ עִוְרִים.[1]

« to the blind. ‹ Who gives sight

בָּרוּךְ אַתָּה יהוה אֱלֹהֵינוּ מֶלֶךְ הָעוֹלָם,

« of the universe, ‹ King ‹ our God, ‹ HASHEM, ‹ are You, ‹ Blessed

מַלְבִּישׁ עֲרֻמִּים.

« the naked. ‹ Who clothes

בָּרוּךְ אַתָּה יהוה אֱלֹהֵינוּ מֶלֶךְ הָעוֹלָם,

« of the universe, ‹ King ‹ our God, ‹ HASHEM, ‹ are You, ‹ Blessed

מַתִּיר אֲסוּרִים.[2]

« the bound. ‹ Who releases

בָּרוּךְ אַתָּה יהוה אֱלֹהֵינוּ מֶלֶךְ הָעוֹלָם,

« of the universe, ‹ King ‹ our God, ‹ HASHEM, ‹ are You, ‹ Blessed

זוֹקֵף כְּפוּפִים.[3]

« those who are bent. ‹ Who straightens

בָּרוּךְ אַתָּה יהוה אֱלֹהֵינוּ מֶלֶךְ הָעוֹלָם,

« of the universe, ‹ King ‹ our God, ‹ HASHEM, ‹ are You, ‹ Blessed

רוֹקַע הָאָרֶץ עַל הַמָּיִם.[4]

« the waters. ‹ upon ‹ the earth ‹ Who spreads out

(1) *Psalms* 146:8. (2) 146:7. (3) 146:8. (4) Cf. 136:6.

SOME POSTPONE THE RECITAL OF THIS BLESSING UNTIL THEY DON LEATHER SHOES AFTER THE FAST HAS ENDED.

בָּרוּךְ אַתָּה יהוה אֱלֹהֵינוּ מֶלֶךְ הָעוֹלָם,

« of the universe, ‹ King ‹ our God, ‹ HASHEM, ‹ are You, ‹ Blessed

שֶׁעָשָׂה לִי כָּל צָרְכִּי.

« my needs. ‹ with all ‹ me ‹ Who has provided

בָּרוּךְ אַתָּה יהוה אֱלֹהֵינוּ מֶלֶךְ הָעוֹלָם,

« of the universe, ‹ King ‹ our God, ‹ HASHEM, ‹ are You, ‹ Blessed

הַמֵּכִין מִצְעֲדֵי גָבֶר.[1]

« of man. ‹ the footsteps ‹ Who establishes

SOME POSTPONE THE RECITAL OF THIS BLESSING UNTIL THEY DON *TEFILLIN* AT *MINCHAH*.

בָּרוּךְ אַתָּה יהוה אֱלֹהֵינוּ מֶלֶךְ הָעוֹלָם,

« of the universe, ‹ King ‹ our God, ‹ HASHEM, ‹ are You, ‹ Blessed

אוֹזֵר יִשְׂרָאֵל בִּגְבוּרָה.

« with strength. ‹ Israel ‹ Who girds

בָּרוּךְ אַתָּה יהוה אֱלֹהֵינוּ מֶלֶךְ הָעוֹלָם,

« of the universe, ‹ King ‹ our God, ‹ HASHEM, ‹ are You, ‹ Blessed

עוֹטֵר יִשְׂרָאֵל בְּתִפְאָרָה.

« with splendor. ‹ Israel ‹ Who crowns

בָּרוּךְ אַתָּה יהוה אֱלֹהֵינוּ מֶלֶךְ הָעוֹלָם,

« of the universe, ‹ King ‹ our God, ‹ HASHEM, ‹ are You, ‹ Blessed

הַנּוֹתֵן לַיָּעֵף כֹּחַ.[2]

« strength. ‹ to the weary ‹ Who gives

ALTHOUGH MANY *SIDDURIM* BEGIN A NEW PARAGRAPH AT וִיהִי רָצוֹן, THE FOLLOWING IS ONE LONG BLESSING THAT ENDS AT לְעַמּוֹ יִשְׂרָאֵל.

בָּרוּךְ אַתָּה יהוה אֱלֹהֵינוּ מֶלֶךְ הָעוֹלָם, הַמַּעֲבִיר

‹ Who removes « of the universe, ‹ King ‹ our God, ‹ HASHEM, ‹ are You, ‹ Blessed

שֵׁנָה מֵעֵינָי וּתְנוּמָה מֵעַפְעַפָּי. וִיהִי רָצוֹן מִלְּפָנֶיךָ,

« before You, ‹ the will ‹ And may it be « from my eyelids. ‹ and slumber ‹ from my eyes ‹ sleep

(1) Cf. *Psalms* 37:23. (2) Cf. *Isaiah* 40:29.

יהוה אֱלֹהֵינוּ וֵאלֹהֵי אֲבוֹתֵינוּ, שֶׁתַּרְגִּילֵנוּ בְּתוֹרָתֶךָ
HASHEM, 〈 our God 〈 and the God 〈 of our forefathers, 《 that You accustom us 〈 to [study] Your Torah 〈

וְדַבְּקֵנוּ בְּמִצְוֹתֶיךָ, וְאַל תְּבִיאֵנוּ לֹא לִידֵי חֵטְא,
and attach us 〈 to Your commandments; 《 and do not 〈 bring us 〈 neither 〈 into the influence 〈 of inadvertent sin, 〈

וְלֹא לִידֵי עֲבֵרָה וְעָוֹן, וְלֹא לִידֵי נִסָּיוֹן, וְלֹא
nor 〈 into the influence 〈 of transgression 〈 and sin, 〈 nor 〈 into the influence 〈 of temptation, 〈 nor 〈

לִידֵי בִזָּיוֹן, וְאַל תַּשְׁלֶט בָּנוּ יֵצֶר הָרָע.
into the influence 〈 of scorn. 《 And do not 〈 allow to dominate 〈 over us 〈 the Inclination 〈 for Evil. 《

וְהַרְחִיקֵנוּ מֵאָדָם רָע וּמֵחָבֵר רָע. וְדַבְּקֵנוּ
Distance us 〈 from a person 〈 who is evil 〈 and from a companion 〈 who is evil, 《 and attach us 〈

בְּיֵצֶר הַטּוֹב וּבְמַעֲשִׂים טוֹבִים, וְכוֹף אֶת יִצְרֵנוּ
to the Inclination 〈 for Good 〈 and to deeds 〈 that are good. 《 And compel 〈 our [Evil] Inclination 〈

לְהִשְׁתַּעְבֶּד לָךְ. וּתְנֵנוּ הַיּוֹם וּבְכָל יוֹם לְחֵן
to be subservient 〈 to You. 《 Allow us to elicit 〈 today 〈 and every 〈 day 〈 grace, 〈

וּלְחֶסֶד וּלְרַחֲמִים בְּעֵינֶיךָ וּבְעֵינֵי כָל רוֹאֵינוּ,
kindness, 〈 and mercy 〈 in Your eyes 〈 and in the eyes 〈 of all 〈 who see us, 《

וְתִגְמְלֵנוּ חֲסָדִים טוֹבִים. בָּרוּךְ אַתָּה יהוה, גּוֹמֵל
and bestow upon us 〈 kindnesses 〈 that are beneficent. 《 Blessed 〈 are You, 〈 HASHEM, 《 Who bestows 〈

חֲסָדִים טוֹבִים לְעַמּוֹ יִשְׂרָאֵל.
kindnesses 〈 that are beneficent 〈 to His people 〈 Israel. 《

יְהִי רָצוֹן מִלְּפָנֶיךָ, יהוה אֱלֹהַי וֵאלֹהֵי אֲבוֹתַי,
May it be 〈 the will 〈 before You, 《 HASHEM, 〈 my God 〈 and the God 〈 of my forefathers, 《

שֶׁתַּצִּילֵנִי הַיּוֹם וּבְכָל יוֹם מֵעַזֵּי פָנִים וּמֵעַזּוּת
that You rescue me 〈 today 〈 and every 〈 day 〈 from those who are brazen-faced 〈 and from brazen- 〈

פָּנִים, מֵאָדָם רָע, וּמֵחָבֵר רָע, וּמִשָּׁכֵן רָע, וּמִפֶּגַע

faced-ness, « from a person ‹ who is evil, ‹ from a companion ‹ who is evil, ‹ from a neighbor ‹ who is evil, ‹ from a mishap ‹

רָע, וּמִשָּׂטָן הַמַּשְׁחִית, מִדִּין קָשֶׁה וּמִבַּעַל דִּין

that is evil, ‹ and from a spiritual impediment ‹ which is destructive, « from legal proceedings ‹ that are harsh, ‹ and from an opponent ‹

קָשֶׁה, בֵּין שֶׁהוּא בֶן בְּרִית, וּבֵין שֶׁאֵינוֹ בֶּן בְּרִית.

who is harsh, « whether ‹ he is ‹ a member ‹ of the covenant ‹ or whether ‹ he is not ‹ a member ‹ of the covenant. «

THE AKEIDAH / עקדה

אֱלֹהֵינוּ וֵאלֹהֵי אֲבוֹתֵינוּ, זָכְרֵנוּ בְּזִכָּרוֹן טוֹב לְפָנֶיךָ,

Our God ‹ and the God ‹ of our forefathers, « remember us ‹ with a memory ‹ that is favorable ‹ before You, «

וּפָקְדֵנוּ בִּפְקֻדַּת יְשׁוּעָה וְרַחֲמִים מִשְּׁמֵי שְׁמֵי קֶדֶם.

and recall us ‹ with a recollection ‹ of salvation ‹ and mercy ‹ from the loftiest ‹ heavens ‹ of primeval. «

וּזְכָר לָנוּ יהוה אֱלֹהֵינוּ אַהֲבַת הַקַּדְמוֹנִים אַבְרָהָם

Remember ‹ on our behalf « – O HASHEM, ‹ our God – « the love ‹ of the Patriarchs, ‹ Abraham, ‹

יִצְחָק וְיִשְׂרָאֵל עֲבָדֶיךָ, אֶת הַבְּרִית וְאֶת הַחֶסֶד

Isaac, ‹ and Israel, ‹ Your servants, « the covenant, ‹ the kindness ‹

וְאֶת הַשְּׁבוּעָה שֶׁנִּשְׁבַּעְתָּ לְאַבְרָהָם אָבִינוּ בְּהַר הַמּוֹרִיָּה,

and the oath ‹ that You swore ‹ to Abraham ‹ our father ‹ at Mount ‹ Moriah, «

וְאֶת הָעֲקֵדָה שֶׁעָקַד אֶת יִצְחָק בְּנוֹ עַל גַּבֵּי הַמִּזְבֵּחַ,

and the *Akeidah,* ‹ when he bound ‹ Isaac ‹ his son ‹ on ‹ top ‹ of the altar, «

כַּכָּתוּב בְּתוֹרָתֶךָ:

as it is written ‹ in Your Torah: «

Genesis 22:1-19 / בראשית כב:א-יט

וַיְהִי אַחַר הַדְּבָרִים הָאֵלֶּה, וְהָאֱלֹהִים נִסָּה

And it happened ‹ after ‹ these things ‹ that God ‹ tested ‹

אֶת אַבְרָהָם, וַיֹּאמֶר אֵלָיו, אַבְרָהָם. וַיֹּאמֶר, הִנֵּנִי.

Abraham. « He said ‹ to him, ‹ *Abraham,* « and he replied, ‹ *Here I am.* «

וַיֹּאמֶר קַח נָא אֶת בִּנְךָ, אֶת יְחִידְךָ, אֲשֶׁר אָהַבְתָּ,

« *you love* ‹ *whom* ‹ *your only one,* ‹ *your son,* ‹ *please,* ‹ *Take,* ‹ And He said,

אֶת יִצְחָק, וְלֶךְ לְךָ אֶל אֶרֶץ הַמֹּרִיָּה, וְהַעֲלֵהוּ

‹ *bring him up* « *of Moriah;* ‹ *the Land* ‹ *to* ‹ *yourself* ‹ *and get* « *— Isaac —*

שָׁם לְעֹלָה עַל אַחַד הֶהָרִים אֲשֶׁר אֹמַר אֵלֶיךָ.

« *to you.* ‹ *I shall indicate* ‹ *which* ‹ *of the mountains* ‹ *one* ‹ *upon* « *as an offering,* ‹ *there*

וַיַּשְׁכֵּם אַבְרָהָם בַּבֹּקֶר, וַיַּחֲבֹשׁ אֶת חֲמֹרוֹ, וַיִּקַּח

‹ he took « his donkey; ‹ and he saddled « in the morning, ‹ Abraham rose early

אֶת שְׁנֵי נְעָרָיו אִתּוֹ, וְאֵת יִצְחָק בְּנוֹ, וַיְבַקַּע עֲצֵי

‹ wood ‹ He split « his son. ‹ and Isaac, « with him, ‹ young men ‹ his two

עֹלָה, וַיָּקָם וַיֵּלֶךְ אֶל הַמָּקוֹם אֲשֶׁר אָמַר לוֹ

‹ to him ‹ indicated ‹ which ‹ the place ‹ toward ‹ and went ‹ and rose « for the offering,

הָאֱלֹהִים. בַּיּוֹם הַשְּׁלִישִׁי, וַיִּשָּׂא אַבְרָהָם אֶת עֵינָיו,

« his eyes, ‹ Abraham raised ‹ On the third day « did God.

וַיַּרְא אֶת הַמָּקוֹם מֵרָחֹק. וַיֹּאמֶר אַבְרָהָם אֶל

‹ to ‹ Abraham said « from afar. ‹ the place ‹ and perceived

נְעָרָיו, שְׁבוּ לָכֶם פֹּה עִם הַחֲמוֹר, וַאֲנִי וְהַנַּעַר

‹ *and the lad* ‹ *[while] I* « *the donkey,* ‹ *with* ‹ *here* ‹ *[by] yourselves* ‹ *Stay* « his young men,

נֵלְכָה עַד כֹּה, וְנִשְׁתַּחֲוֶה וְנָשׁוּבָה אֲלֵיכֶם.

« *to you.* ‹ *and we will return* ‹ *we will prostrate ourselves* « *there;* ‹ *until* ‹ *will go*

וַיִּקַּח אַבְרָהָם אֶת עֲצֵי הָעֹלָה, וַיָּשֶׂם עַל יִצְחָק

‹ Isaac, ‹ on ‹ and placed it « for the offering, ‹ the wood ‹ Abraham took

בְּנוֹ, וַיִּקַּח בְּיָדוֹ אֶת הָאֵשׁ וְאֶת הַמַּאֲכֶלֶת, וַיֵּלְכוּ

‹ and they went, « and the knife, ‹ the fire ‹ in his hand ‹ He took « his son.

שְׁנֵיהֶם יַחְדָּו. וַיֹּאמֶר יִצְחָק אֶל אַבְרָהָם אָבִיו,

« his father, ‹ Abraham ‹ to ‹ [Then] Isaac spoke « together. ‹ the two of them

וַיֹּאמֶר, אָבִי. וַיֹּאמֶר, הִנֶּנִּי בְנִי. וַיֹּאמֶר, הִנֵּה הָאֵשׁ

‹ *the fire* ‹ *Here are* ‹ And he said, « *my son.* ‹ *Here I am,* ‹ And he said, « *My father!* ‹ and he said:

וְהָעֵצִים, וְאַיֵּה הַשֶּׂה לְעֹלָה. וַיֹּאמֶר אַבְרָהָם,

« Abraham said: « *for the offering?* ‹ *is the lamb* ‹ *but where* ‹ *and the wood,*

אֱלֹהִים יִרְאֶה לּוֹ הַשֶּׂה לְעֹלָה, בְּנִי, וַיֵּלְכוּ

‹ And they went, « *my son.* ‹ *for the offering,* ‹ *the lamb* ‹ *for Himself* ‹ *will seek out* ‹ *God*

שְׁנֵיהֶם יַחְדָּו. וַיָּבֹאוּ אֶל הַמָּקוֹם אֲשֶׁר אָמַר לוֹ

‹ indicated to him ‹ which ‹ the place ‹ at ‹ They arrived « together. ‹ the two of them

הָאֱלֹהִים, וַיִּבֶן שָׁם אַבְרָהָם אֶת הַמִּזְבֵּחַ, וַיַּעֲרֹךְ

‹ and arranged ‹ the altar ‹ did Abraham ‹ there ‹ and build « God had,

אֶת הָעֵצִים, וַיַּעֲקֹד אֶת יִצְחָק בְּנוֹ, וַיָּשֶׂם אֹתוֹ

‹ him ‹ and he placed ‹ his son, ‹ Isaac, ‹ he bound « the wood;

עַל הַמִּזְבֵּחַ מִמַּעַל לָעֵצִים. וַיִּשְׁלַח אַבְרָהָם

‹ Abraham stretched out « the wood. ‹ atop ‹ the altar ‹ on

אֶת יָדוֹ, וַיִּקַּח אֶת הַמַּאֲכֶלֶת לִשְׁחֹט אֶת בְּנוֹ.

« his son. ‹ to slaughter ‹ the knife ‹ and took ‹ his hand

וַיִּקְרָא אֵלָיו מַלְאַךְ יהוה מִן הַשָּׁמַיִם, וַיֹּאמֶר,

‹ and he said, « heaven, ‹ from ‹ of HASHEM ‹ an angel ‹ to him ‹ And there called

אַבְרָהָם, אַבְרָהָם. וַיֹּאמֶר, הִנֵּנִי. וַיֹּאמֶר, אַל

‹ *Do not* « And he said, « *Here I am.* ‹ And he said, « *Abraham!* ‹ *Abraham!*

תִּשְׁלַח יָדְךָ אֶל הַנַּעַר, וְאַל תַּעַשׂ לוֹ מְאוּמָה, כִּי

‹ *for* « *anything,* ‹ *to him* ‹ *do* ‹ *nor* ‹ *the lad* ‹ *against* ‹ *your hand* ‹ *stretch out*

עַתָּה יָדַעְתִּי כִּי יְרֵא אֱלֹהִים אַתָּה, וְלֹא חָשַׂכְתָּ

‹ withheld ‹ since you have not « are you, ‹ of God ‹ a fearer ‹ that ‹ I know ‹ now

אֶת בִּנְךָ אֶת יְחִידְךָ מִמֶּנִּי. וַיִּשָּׂא אַבְרָהָם אֶת עֵינָיו

‹ his eyes ‹ Abraham raised « from Me. ‹ your only one, ‹ your son,

וַיַּרְא, וְהִנֵּה אַיִל, אַחַר, נֶאֱחַז בַּסְּבַךְ בְּקַרְנָיו,

« by its horns. ‹ in the thicket ‹ caught ‹ — afterward « a ram! ‹ — behold « and saw

וַיֵּלֶךְ אַבְרָהָם וַיִּקַּח אֶת הָאַיִל, וַיַּעֲלֵהוּ לְעֹלָה

‹ as an offering ‹ and brought it ‹ the ram ‹ and he took ‹ Abraham went

תַּחַת בְּנוֹ. וַיִּקְרָא אַבְרָהָם שֵׁם הַמָּקוֹם הַהוּא יהוה

‹ HASHEM ‹ of that site ‹ the name ‹ Abraham called « of his son. ‹ instead

יִרְאֶה, אֲשֶׁר יֵאָמֵר הַיּוֹם, בְּהַר יהוה יֵרָאֶה. וַיִּקְרָא

‹ And there called « is seen. ‹ HASHEM ‹ On the mountain « this day: ‹ it is said ‹ as « Yireh,

מַלְאַךְ יהוה אֶל אַבְרָהָם שֵׁנִית מִן הַשָּׁמָיִם. וַיֹּאמֶר,

‹ and he said, « heaven ‹ from ‹ a second time ‹ Abraham ‹ to ‹ of HASHEM ‹ an angel

בִּי נִשְׁבַּעְתִּי נְאֻם יהוה, כִּי יַעַן אֲשֶׁר עָשִׂיתָ

‹ you have done ‹ since ‹ that « of HASHEM — ‹ — the word « I swear ‹ By Myself

אֶת הַדָּבָר הַזֶּה, וְלֹא חָשַׂכְתָּ אֶת בִּנְךָ אֶת יְחִידֶךָ.

« your only one, ‹ your son, ‹ withheld ‹ and have not ‹ this thing

כִּי בָרֵךְ אֲבָרֶכְךָ, וְהַרְבָּה אַרְבֶּה אֶת זַרְעֲךָ כְּכוֹכְבֵי

‹ like the stars ‹ your offspring ‹ and greatly shall I increase ‹ I shall surely bless you ‹ that

הַשָּׁמַיִם, וְכַחוֹל אֲשֶׁר עַל שְׂפַת הַיָּם, וְיִרַשׁ זַרְעֲךָ

‹ will your offspring ‹ and inherit « of the sea; ‹ the shore ‹ is on ‹ which ‹ and like the sand ‹ of the heavens

אֵת שַׁעַר אֹיְבָיו. וְהִתְבָּרְכוּ בְזַרְעֲךָ כֹּל גּוֹיֵי הָאָרֶץ,

« of the earth, ‹ the nations ‹ will all ‹ by your offspring ‹ and bless themselves « of their enemies; ‹ the gates

עֵקֶב אֲשֶׁר שָׁמַעְתָּ בְּקֹלִי. וַיָּשָׁב אַבְרָהָם אֶל נְעָרָיו,

« his young men, ‹ to ‹ Abraham returned « *to My voice.* ‹ *you have listened* ‹ *because*

וַיָּקֻמוּ וַיֵּלְכוּ יַחְדָּו אֶל בְּאֵר שָׁבַע, וַיֵּשֶׁב אַבְרָהָם

‹ and Abraham stayed « Beer-Sheba, ‹ to ‹ together ‹ and went ‹ and they rose

בִּבְאֵר שָׁבַע.

« at Beer-Sheba.

רִבּוֹנוֹ שֶׁל עוֹלָם, יְהִי רָצוֹן מִלְּפָנֶיךָ, יהוה אֱלֹהֵינוּ

‹ our God, ‹ HASHEM, « before You ‹ the will ‹ May it be « the universe! ‹ of ‹ Master

וֵאלֹהֵי אֲבוֹתֵינוּ, שֶׁתִּזְכָּר לָנוּ בְּרִית אֲבוֹתֵינוּ. כְּמוֹ שֶׁכָּבַשׁ

‹ suppress ‹ Just as « of our forefathers. ‹ the covenant ‹ for our sake ‹ that You remember « of our forefathers, ‹ and the God

אַבְרָהָם אָבִינוּ אֶת רַחֲמָיו מִבֶּן יְחִידוֹ, וְרָצָה לִשְׁחוֹט

‹ to slaughter ‹ and was willing « his only one, ‹ regarding his son, ‹ his mercy ‹ our forefather ‹ did Abraham

אוֹתוֹ כְּדֵי לַעֲשׂוֹת רְצוֹנֶךָ, כֵּן יִכְבְּשׁוּ רַחֲמֶיךָ אֶת כַּעַסְךָ

‹ Your anger ‹ may Your mercy ‹ suppress ‹ so « Your will, ‹ to do ‹ in order ‹ him

מֵעָלֵינוּ, וְיִגֹּלּוּ רַחֲמֶיךָ עַל מִדּוֹתֶיךָ, וְתִכָּנֵס אִתָּנוּ לִפְנִים

‹ beyond ‹ with us ‹ May You step « Your (strict) attributes. ‹ may Your mercy ‹ and overwhelm « from upon us,

מִשּׁוּרַת דִּינֶךָ, וְתִתְנַהֵג עִמָּנוּ, יהוה אֱלֹהֵינוּ, בְּמִדַּת הַחֶסֶד

‹ of kindness ‹ with the attribute « our God — ‹ — O HASHEM, « with us ‹ and conduct Yourself « of Your law, ‹ the line

וּבְמִדַּת הָרַחֲמִים. וּבְטוּבְךָ הַגָּדוֹל, יָשׁוּב חֲרוֹן אַפְּךָ מֵעַמְּךָ

‹ from Your people, « wrath ‹ may Your burning ‹ turn away « that is great, ‹ In Your goodness « of mercy. ‹ and with the attribute

וּמֵעִירְךָ וּמֵאַרְצְךָ וּמִנַּחֲלָתֶךָ. וְקַיֶּם לָנוּ, יהוה אֱלֹהֵינוּ,

‹ our God, ‹ HASHEM, ‹ for us, ‹ Fulfill « and from Your heritage. ‹ from Your land, ‹ from Your city,

אֶת הַדָּבָר שֶׁהִבְטַחְתָּנוּ עַל יְדֵי מֹשֶׁה עַבְדֶּךָ, כָּאָמוּר:

« as it is said: « Your servant, ‹ of Moses, ‹ the hand ‹ by ‹ that You pledged to us ‹ the declaration

וְזָכַרְתִּי אֶת בְּרִיתִי יַעֲקוֹב, וְאַף אֶת בְּרִיתִי יִצְחָק, וְאַף

‹ *and also* « *with Isaac,* ‹ *My covenant* ‹ *also* « *with Jacob;* ‹ *My covenant* ‹ *I shall remember*

אֶת בְּרִיתִי אַבְרָהָם אֶזְכֹּר, וְהָאָרֶץ אֶזְכֹּר.[1]

« shall I remember. ‹ and the land « shall I remember; ‹ with Abraham ‹ My covenant

לְעוֹלָם יְהֵא אָדָם יְרֵא שָׁמַיִם בְּסֵתֶר וּבַגָּלוּי,

« and in public, ‹ [both] in private ‹ of Heaven, ‹ be fearing ‹ a person ‹ should ‹ Always

וּמוֹדֶה עַל הָאֱמֶת, וְדוֹבֵר אֱמֶת בִּלְבָבוֹ, וְיַשְׁכֵּם

‹ and one should arise early « within his heart, ‹ the truth ‹ speaking « the truth, ‹ acknowledging

וְיֹאמַר:

« and proclaim:

רִבּוֹן כָּל הָעוֹלָמִים, לֹא עַל צִדְקוֹתֵינוּ אֲנַחְנוּ

‹ that we ‹ our righteousness ‹ because of ‹ It is not « worlds! ‹ of all ‹ Master

מַפִּילִים תַּחֲנוּנֵינוּ לְפָנֶיךָ, כִּי עַל רַחֲמֶיךָ הָרַבִּים.

« that is abundant. ‹ Your mercy ‹ because of ‹ but « before You, ‹ our supplications ‹ cast

מָה אֲנַחְנוּ, מֶה חַיֵּינוּ, מֶה חַסְדֵּנוּ, מַה צִּדְקוֹתֵינוּ,

« is our righteousness? ‹ What « is our kindness? ‹ What « is our life? ‹ What « are we? ‹ What

מַה יְּשׁוּעָתֵנוּ, מַה כֹּחֵנוּ, מַה גְּבוּרָתֵנוּ. מַה נֹּאמַר

‹ can we say ‹ What « is our might? ‹ What « is our strength? ‹ What « is our salvation? ‹ What

לְפָנֶיךָ, יהוה אֱלֹהֵינוּ וֵאלֹהֵי אֲבוֹתֵינוּ, הֲלֹא כָּל

‹ all ‹ Are not « of our forefathers? ‹ and the God ‹ our God, ‹ HASHEM, « before You,

הַגִּבּוֹרִים כְּאַיִן לְפָנֶיךָ, וְאַנְשֵׁי הַשֵּׁם כְּלֹא הָיוּ,

« existed, ‹ as if they had never ‹ of renown ‹ and people « before You, ‹ like nothing ‹ the mighty

וַחֲכָמִים כִּבְלִי מַדָּע, וּנְבוֹנִים כִּבְלִי הַשְׂכֵּל. כִּי

‹ For « of intelligence? ‹ as if devoid ‹ and the perceptive « of wisdom ‹ as if devoid ‹ the wise

(1) *Leviticus* 26:42.

רֹב מַעֲשֵׂיהֶם תֹּהוּ, וִימֵי חַיֵּיהֶם הֶבֶל לְפָנֶיךָ,

« before You. ‹ are worthless ‹ of their lives ‹ and the days ‹ is useless ‹ of their deeds ‹ the multitude

וּמוֹתַר הָאָדָם מִן הַבְּהֵמָה אָיִן, כִּי הַכֹּל הָבֶל.[1]

« is vain. ‹ all ‹ for « is non-existent, ‹ beast ‹ over ‹ of man ‹ The preeminence

אֲבָל אֲנַחְנוּ עַמְּךָ, בְּנֵי בְרִיתֶךָ, בְּנֵי אַבְרָהָם

‹ of Abraham, ‹ children « of Your covenant, ‹ members « Your people, ‹ we are ‹ But

אֹהַבְךָ שֶׁנִּשְׁבַּעְתָּ לּוֹ בְּהַר הַמּוֹרִיָּה, זֶרַע יִצְחָק

‹ of Isaac, ‹ the offspring « Moriah; ‹ at Mount ‹ to him ‹ that You swore « Your beloved,

יְחִידוֹ שֶׁנֶּעֱקַד עַל גַּב הַמִּזְבֵּחַ, עֲדַת יַעֲקֹב בִּנְךָ

‹ Your son, ‹ of Jacob, ‹ the community « of the altar; ‹ top ‹ on ‹ who was bound ‹ his only son,

בְּכוֹרֶךָ, שֶׁמֵּאַהֲבָתְךָ שֶׁאָהַבְתָּ אוֹתוֹ וּמִשִּׂמְחָתְךָ

‹ and the joy ‹ him ‹ with which You loved ‹ who — because of Your love « Your firstborn,

שֶׁשָּׂמַחְתָּ בּוֹ, קָרָאתָ אֶת שְׁמוֹ יִשְׂרָאֵל וִישֻׁרוּן.

« and Jeshurun. ‹ Israel ‹ his name ‹ — You called « in him ‹ with which You delighted

לְפִיכָךְ אֲנַחְנוּ חַיָּבִים לְהוֹדוֹת לְךָ, וּלְשַׁבֵּחֲךָ,

‹ to praise You, ‹ You, ‹ to thank ‹ are obliged ‹ we ‹ Therefore,

וּלְפָאֶרְךָ, וּלְבָרֵךְ וּלְקַדֵּשׁ וְלָתֵת שֶׁבַח וְהוֹדָיָה

‹ and thanks ‹ praise ‹ and to offer ‹ to sanctify, ‹ to bless, « to glorify You,

לִשְׁמֶךָ. אַשְׁרֵינוּ, מַה טּוֹב חֶלְקֵנוּ, וּמַה נָּעִים גּוֹרָלֵנוּ,

‹ our lot, ‹ pleasant ‹ how ‹ is our portion, ‹ good ‹ how « We are fortunate, « to Your Name.

וּמַה יָּפָה יְרֻשָּׁתֵנוּ. אַשְׁרֵינוּ, שֶׁאֲנַחְנוּ מַשְׁכִּימִים

‹ come early ‹ for we « We are fortunate, « our heritage! ‹ beautiful ‹ and how

וּמַעֲרִיבִים, עֶרֶב וָבֹקֶר וְאוֹמְרִים פַּעֲמַיִם בְּכָל יוֹם:

« day: ‹ each ‹ twice ‹ and proclaim « and morning, ‹ evening « and stay late,

(1) *Ecclesiastes* 3:19.

שְׁמַע ׀ יִשְׂרָאֵל, יְהוָה ׀ אֱלֹהֵינוּ, יְהוָה ׀ אֶחָד:[1]

« the One [and Only]. ‹ HASHEM is « is our God, ‹ HASHEM « O Israel: ‹ Hear,

IN AN UNDERTONE:

בָּרוּךְ שֵׁם כְּבוֹד מַלְכוּתוֹ לְעוֹלָם וָעֶד.[2]

« and ever. ‹ for ever ‹ kingdom ‹ of His glorious ‹ is the Name ‹ Blessed

SOME CONGREGATIONS COMPLETE THE FIRST CHAPTER OF THE *SHEMA* (FOLLOWING PARAGRAPH) AT THIS POINT, ALTHOUGH MOST OMIT IT. HOWEVER IF YOU FEAR THAT YOU WILL NOT RECITE THE FULL *SHEMA* LATER IN *SHACHARIS* BEFORE THE PRESCRIBED TIME HAS ELAPSED, RECITE ALL THREE CHAPTERS OF *SHEMA* (P. 167-170) HERE.

Deuteronomy 6:5-9 / דברים ו:ה-ט

וְאָהַבְתָּ אֵת ׀ יְהוָה ׀ אֱלֹהֶיךָ, בְּכָל־לְבָבְךָ, וּבְכָל־

‹ with all ‹ your heart, ‹ with all « your God, ‹ HASHEM, ‹ You shall love

נַפְשְׁךָ, וּבְכָל־מְאֹדֶךָ: וְהָיוּ הַדְּבָרִים הָאֵלֶּה, אֲשֶׁר ׀ אָנֹכִי

‹ I ‹ that ‹ — these matters « They should be « your resources. ‹ and with all ‹ your soul,

מְצַוְּךָ הַיּוֹם, עַל־לְבָבֶךָ: וְשִׁנַּנְתָּם לְבָנֶיךָ, וְדִבַּרְתָּ בָּם

« of them ‹ and speak « to your children ‹ Teach them thoroughly « your heart. ‹ upon « today— ‹ command you

בְּשִׁבְתְּךָ בְּבֵיתֶךָ, וּבְלֶכְתְּךָ בַדֶּרֶךְ, וּבְשָׁכְבְּךָ וּבְקוּמֶךָ:

« and when you arise. ‹ when you lie down, « on the way, ‹ while you walk ‹ in your home, ‹ while you sit

וּקְשַׁרְתָּם לְאוֹת ׀ עַל־יָדֶךָ, וְהָיוּ לְטֹטָפֹת בֵּין ׀ עֵינֶיךָ:

« your eyes. ‹ between ‹ *tefillin* ‹ and they shall be « your arm ‹ upon ‹ as a sign ‹ Bind them

וּכְתַבְתָּם ׀ עַל־מְזֻזוֹת בֵּיתֶךָ וּבִשְׁעָרֶיךָ:

« and upon your gates. ‹ your house ‹ the door-posts of ‹ on ‹ And write them

אַתָּה הוּא עַד שֶׁלֹּא נִבְרָא הָעוֹלָם, אַתָּה

‹ You are « the world was created. « before ‹ the One Who [existed] ‹ You are

הוּא מִשֶּׁנִּבְרָא הָעוֹלָם, אַתָּה הוּא בָּעוֹלָם הַזֶּה,

‹ in This World, ‹ the One Who [exists] ‹ You are « after the world was created. ‹ the One Who [exists]

וְאַתָּה הוּא לָעוֹלָם הַבָּא. קַדֵּשׁ אֶת שִׁמְךָ

‹ Your Name ‹ Sanctify « to Come. ‹ in the World ‹ the One Who [will exist] ‹ and You are

(1) *Deuteronomy* 6:4. (2) See *Pesachim* 56a.

עַל מַקְדִּישֵׁי שְׁמֶךָ, וְקַדֵּשׁ אֶת שִׁמְךָ בְּעוֹלָמֶךָ.

through ‹ those who sanctify ‹ Your Name, « and sanctify ‹ Your Name ‹ in Your universe. «

וּבִישׁוּעָתְךָ תָּרִים וְתַגְבִּיהַּ קַרְנֵנוּ. בָּרוּךְ אַתָּה

Through Your salvation ‹ may You exalt ‹ and raise ‹ our pride. « Blessed ‹ are You, ‹

יהוה, מְקַדֵּשׁ אֶת שִׁמְךָ בָּרַבִּים. (Cong. – אָמֵן.)

HASHEM, « Who sanctifies ‹ Your Name ‹ among the multitudes. « (Amen.) «

אַתָּה הוּא יהוה אֱלֹהֵינוּ,[1] בַּשָּׁמַיִם וּבָאָרֶץ

You are ‹ the One Who is ‹ HASHEM, ‹ our God, ‹ in heaven ‹ and on earth ‹

וּבִשְׁמֵי הַשָּׁמַיִם הָעֶלְיוֹנִים. אֱמֶת, אַתָּה הוּא רִאשׁוֹן

and in the loftiest heavens ‹ on high. « It is true, ‹ that You are ‹ the One Who is ‹ the First ‹

וְאַתָּה הוּא אַחֲרוֹן, וּמִבַּלְעָדֶיךָ אֵין אֱלֹהִים.[2]

and You are ‹ the One Who is ‹ the Last, « and other than You ‹ there is no ‹ God. «

קַבֵּץ קֹוֶיךָ מֵאַרְבַּע כַּנְפוֹת הָאָרֶץ.[3] יַכִּירוּ וְיֵדְעוּ

Gather in ‹ those who yearn for You, ‹ from the four ‹ corners ‹ of the earth. « May they recognize ‹ and know «

כָּל בָּאֵי עוֹלָם כִּי אַתָּה הוּא הָאֱלֹהִים לְבַדְּךָ

— all ‹ who come ‹ [into] the world — « that ‹ You are ‹ the One Who is ‹ God ‹ alone ‹

לְכֹל מַמְלְכוֹת הָאָרֶץ. אַתָּה עָשִׂיתָ אֶת הַשָּׁמַיִם

over all ‹ the kingdoms ‹ of the earth. « You ‹ made ‹ the heavens, ‹

וְאֶת הָאָרֶץ,[4] אֶת הַיָּם, וְאֶת כָּל אֲשֶׁר בָּם.[5] וּמִי

and the earth, ‹ the sea, ‹ and all ‹ that is ‹ in them. « Who is there ‹

בְּכָל מַעֲשֵׂה יָדֶיךָ בָּעֶלְיוֹנִים אוֹ בַתַּחְתּוֹנִים שֶׁיֹּאמַר

among all ‹ the work ‹ of Your hands « — those above ‹ or ‹ those below — « who can say ‹

לְךָ, מַה תַּעֲשֶׂה. אָבִינוּ שֶׁבַּשָּׁמַיִם, עֲשֵׂה עִמָּנוּ

to You, ‹ *What* ‹ *are You doing?* « Our Father ‹ Who is in Heaven, « perform ‹ for us ‹

(1) *Jeremiah* 14:22. (2) Cf. *Isaiah* 44:6. (3) Cf. 11:12. (4) *II Kings* 19:15. (5) Cf. *Nehemiah* 9:6.

חֶסֶד בַּעֲבוּר שִׁמְךָ הַגָּדוֹל שֶׁנִּקְרָא עָלֵינוּ,[1] וְקַיֵּם

‹ Fulfill « upon us. ‹ that has been proclaimed ‹ of Your great Name, ‹ for the sake ‹ kindness

לָנוּ יהוה אֱלֹהֵינוּ מַה שֶּׁכָּתוּב: בָּעֵת הַהִיא אָבִיא

‹ *I will bring* ‹ *At that time* « which is written: ‹ that « our God, ‹ HASHEM, « for us,

אֶתְכֶם, וּבָעֵת קַבְּצִי אֶתְכֶם, כִּי אֶתֵּן אֶתְכֶם לְשֵׁם

‹ *for renown* ‹ *you* ‹ *I will designate* ‹ *for* « *you,* ‹ *I will gather* ‹ *and at [that] time* « *you [in]*

וְלִתְהִלָּה בְּכֹל עַמֵּי הָאָרֶץ, בְּשׁוּבִי אֶת שְׁבוּתֵיכֶם

‹ *your captivity,* ‹ *when I bring back* « *of the earth,* ‹ *the peoples* ‹ *among all* ‹ *and praise*

לְעֵינֵיכֶם, אָמַר יהוה.[2]

« *HASHEM.* ‹ *said* « *before your own eyes,*

SOME CONGREGATIONS OMIT CERTAIN PASSAGES OF THE PRAYERS PRECEDING אֵיזֶהוּ מְקוֹמָן (P. 128). CUSTOMS REGARDING WHETHER AND WHICH PASSAGES ARE OMITTED VARY GREATLY; THEREFORE WE HAVE NOT OMITTED ANY PASSAGES. EACH CONGREGATION SHOULD FOLLOW ITS ESTABLISHED CUSTOM.

OFFERINGS / קרבנות

THE LAVER / הכיור

וַיְדַבֵּר יהוה אֶל מֹשֶׁה לֵּאמֹר. וְעָשִׂיתָ כִּיּוֹר

‹ a laver ‹ You shall make « saying: ‹ Moses, ‹ to ‹ HASHEM spoke

נְחֹשֶׁת, וְכַנּוֹ נְחֹשֶׁת, לְרָחְצָה, וְנָתַתָּ אֹתוֹ בֵּין אֹהֶל

‹ the Tent ‹ between ‹ it ‹ and you shall place « for washing; ‹ of copper, ‹ and its base ‹ of copper,

מוֹעֵד וּבֵין הַמִּזְבֵּחַ, וְנָתַתָּ שָׁמָּה מָיִם. וְרָחֲצוּ אַהֲרֹן

‹ – Aaron « They shall wash « water. ‹ there ‹ and you shall put « and the Altar, ‹ of Appointment

וּבָנָיו מִמֶּנּוּ, אֶת יְדֵיהֶם וְאֶת רַגְלֵיהֶם. בְּבֹאָם אֶל

‹ into ‹ When they enter « and their feet. ‹ their hands ‹ from [the laver] « and his sons —

אֹהֶל מוֹעֵד יִרְחֲצוּ מַיִם וְלֹא יָמֻתוּ, אוֹ בְגִשְׁתָּם

‹ when they approach ‹ or « perish, ‹ so that they not ‹ with water ‹ they shall wash ‹ of Appointment ‹ the Tent

---

(1) *Jeremiah* 14:9. (2) *Zephaniah* 3:20.

אֶל הַמִּזְבֵּחַ לְשָׁרֵת לְהַקְטִיר אִשֶּׁה לַיהוה. וְרָחֲצוּ

‹ They shall wash « to HASHEM. ‹ a fire-offering ‹ to burn « to serve, ‹ the Altar ‹ to

יְדֵיהֶם וְרַגְלֵיהֶם וְלֹא יָמֻתוּ, וְהָיְתָה לָהֶם חָק

‹ a decree ‹ for them ‹ and this shall be « perish; ‹ so that they not ‹ and their feet ‹ their hands

עוֹלָם, לוֹ וּלְזַרְעוֹ לְדֹרֹתָם.[1]

« throughout their generations. ‹ and for his offspring ‹ for him « that is eternal

THE TAKING OF ASHES / תרומת הדשן

וַיְדַבֵּר יהוה אֶל מֹשֶׁה לֵּאמֹר. צַו אֶת אַהֲרֹן

‹ Aaron ‹ Command « saying: ‹ Moses ‹ to ‹ HASHEM spoke

וְאֶת בָּנָיו לֵאמֹר, זֹאת תּוֹרַת הָעֹלָה, הִוא הָעֹלָה

‹ the elevation-offering ‹ — it is « of the elevation-offering ‹ is the teaching ‹ This « saying: ‹ and his sons,

עַל מוֹקְדָה עַל הַמִּזְבֵּחַ כָּל הַלַּיְלָה עַד הַבֹּקֶר,

« morning, ‹ until ‹ night ‹ all ‹ the Altar ‹ on ‹ the pyre ‹ [that stays] on

וְאֵשׁ הַמִּזְבֵּחַ תּוּקַד בּוֹ. וְלָבַשׁ הַכֹּהֵן מִדּוֹ בַד,

« of linen, ‹ his garment ‹ shall the *Kohen* ‹ Don « on it. ‹ shall be kept burning ‹ of the Altar ‹ and the fire

וּמִכְנְסֵי בַד יִלְבַּשׁ עַל בְּשָׂרוֹ, וְהֵרִים אֶת הַדֶּשֶׁן

‹ the ashes ‹ He is to lift up « his flesh. ‹ upon ‹ shall he don ‹ of linen ‹ and breeches

אֲשֶׁר תֹּאכַל הָאֵשׁ אֶת הָעֹלָה עַל הַמִּזְבֵּחַ,

« the Altar, ‹ upon ‹ of the elevation-offering ‹ the fire consumed ‹ that

וְשָׂמוֹ אֵצֶל הַמִּזְבֵּחַ. וּפָשַׁט אֶת בְּגָדָיו, וְלָבַשׁ

‹ and don ‹ his garments ‹ Then he shall remove « the Altar. ‹ next to ‹ and he shall place it

בְּגָדִים אֲחֵרִים, וְהוֹצִיא אֶת הַדֶּשֶׁן אֶל מִחוּץ

‹ the outside ‹ to ‹ the ashes ‹ then he shall remove « other garments;

(1) *Exodus* 30:17-21.

לַמַּחֲנֶה, אֶל מָקוֹם טָהוֹר. וְהָאֵשׁ עַל הַמִּזְבֵּחַ

of the camp, to a place which is pure. The fire on the Altar

תּוּקַד בּוֹ, לֹא תִכְבֶּה, וּבִעֵר עָלֶיהָ הַכֹּהֵן עֵצִים

shall be kept burning on it; it may not be extinguished, and burn on it shall the *Kohen* wood

בַּבֹּקֶר בַּבֹּקֶר, וְעָרַךְ עָלֶיהָ הָעֹלָה, וְהִקְטִיר עָלֶיהָ

each and every morning. He is to prepare upon it the elevation-offering and burn upon it

חֶלְבֵי הַשְּׁלָמִים. אֵשׁ תָּמִיד תּוּקַד עַל הַמִּזְבֵּחַ,

the fats of the peace-offering. A fire that is permanent shall be kept burning on the Altar;

לֹא תִכְבֶּה.[1]

it may not be extinguished.

THE TAMID OFFERING / קרבן התמיד

SOME AUTHORITIES HOLD THAT THE FOLLOWING (UNTIL קְטֹרֶת) SHOULD BE RECITED STANDING.

יְהִי רָצוֹן מִלְּפָנֶיךָ, יהוה אֱלֹהֵינוּ וֵאלֹהֵי אֲבוֹתֵינוּ,

May it be the will before You HASHEM, our God, and the God of our forefathers,

שֶׁתְּרַחֵם עָלֵינוּ וְתִמְחָל לָנוּ עַל כָּל חַטֹּאתֵינוּ, וּתְכַפֵּר

that You have mercy on us and pardon us for all our unintentional sins, atone

לָנוּ אֶת כָּל עֲוֹנוֹתֵינוּ, וְתִסְלַח לְכָל פְּשָׁעֵינוּ, וְתִבְנֶה

for us all our iniquities, and forgive all our willful sins; and that You rebuild

בֵּית הַמִּקְדָּשׁ בִּמְהֵרָה בְיָמֵינוּ, וְנַקְרִיב לְפָנֶיךָ קָרְבַּן

the Holy Temple speedily, in our days, so that we may offer before You the offering

הַתָּמִיד שֶׁיְּכַפֵּר בַּעֲדֵנוּ, כְּמוֹ שֶׁכָּתַבְתָּ עָלֵינוּ בְּתוֹרָתֶךָ עַל

that is continual, that it may atone for us, as You have written for us in Your Torah, by

יְדֵי מֹשֶׁה עַבְדֶּךָ, מִפִּי כְבוֹדֶךָ, כָּאָמוּר:

the hand of Moses, Your servant, from Your glorious mouth, as it is said:

וַיְדַבֵּר יהוה אֶל מֹשֶׁה לֵּאמֹר. צַו אֶת בְּנֵי יִשְׂרָאֵל

HASHEM spoke to Moses, saying: Command the Children of Israel

(1) *Leviticus* 6:1-6.

וְאָמַרְתָּ אֲלֵהֶם, אֶת קָרְבָּנִי לַחְמִי לְאִשַּׁי, רֵיחַ נִיחֹחִי,

« that is satisfying, ‹ My aroma « for My fires, ‹ My food ‹ My offering, « them: ‹ and tell

תִּשְׁמְרוּ לְהַקְרִיב לִי בְּמוֹעֲדוֹ. וְאָמַרְתָּ לָהֶם, זֶה

‹ This is « them: ‹ And you are to tell « in its appointed time. ‹ Me ‹ to offer ‹ you are to be scrupulous

הָאִשֶּׁה אֲשֶׁר תַּקְרִיבוּ לַיהוה, כְּבָשִׂים בְּנֵי שָׁנָה

‹ first year, ‹ in their ‹ male lambs, « to HASHEM: ‹ you are to offer ‹ that ‹ the fire-offering

תְּמִימִם, שְׁנַיִם לַיּוֹם, עֹלָה תָמִיד. אֶת הַכֶּבֶשׂ אֶחָד

‹ The one lamb « that is continual. ‹ an elevation-offering ‹ daily, ‹ two ‹ unblemished,

תַּעֲשֶׂה בַבֹּקֶר, וְאֵת הַכֶּבֶשׂ הַשֵּׁנִי תַּעֲשֶׂה בֵּין הָעַרְבָּיִם.

« in the afternoon; ‹ you shall do ‹ that is second ‹ and the lamb « in the morning, ‹ you shall do

וַעֲשִׂירִית הָאֵיפָה סֹלֶת לְמִנְחָה, בְּלוּלָה בְּשֶׁמֶן

‹ with oil ‹ mixed « for a meal-offering, ‹ of fine flour ‹ of an *ephah* ‹ with a tenth

כָּתִית רְבִיעִת הַהִין. עֹלַת תָּמִיד, הָעֲשֻׂיָה בְּהַר

‹ at Mount ‹ that was done « that is continual, ‹ It is the elevation-offering « of a *hin*. ‹ a quarter ‹ from crushed [olives]

סִינַי, לְרֵיחַ נִיחֹחַ, אִשֶּׁה לַיהוה. וְנִסְכּוֹ רְבִיעִת הַהִין

‹ of a *hin* ‹ is a quarter ‹ And its libation « to HASHEM. ‹ a fire-offering « that is satisfying, ‹ for an aroma « Sinai,

לַכֶּבֶשׂ הָאֶחָד, בַּקֹּדֶשׁ הַסֵּךְ נֶסֶךְ שֵׁכָר לַיהוה.

« to HASHEM. ‹ of fermented wine ‹ a libation ‹ pour ‹ on the Holy [Altar] « for each lamb,

וְאֵת הַכֶּבֶשׂ הַשֵּׁנִי תַּעֲשֶׂה בֵּין הָעַרְבָּיִם, כְּמִנְחַת

‹ like the meal-offering « in the afternoon; ‹ you are to do ‹ that is second ‹ And the lamb

הַבֹּקֶר וּכְנִסְכּוֹ תַּעֲשֶׂה, אִשֵּׁה רֵיחַ נִיחֹחַ לַיהוה.[1]

« to HASHEM. ‹ that is satisfying ‹ for an aroma ‹ a fire-offering « shall you do, ‹ and like its libation ‹ of the morning

(1) *Numbers* 28:1-8.

וְשָׁחַט אֹתוֹ עַל יֶרֶךְ הַמִּזְבֵּחַ צָפֹנָה לִפְנֵי יהוה,

«HASHEM, ‹ before « on the north, ‹ of the Altar ‹ the side ‹ on ‹ it ‹ He is to slaughter

וְזָרְקוּ בְּנֵי אַהֲרֹן הַכֹּהֲנִים אֶת דָּמוֹ עַל הַמִּזְבֵּחַ

‹ the Altar, ‹ upon ‹ its blood « the *Kohanim* — ‹ of Aaron ‹ — the sons « and they shall throw

סָבִיב.[1]

« all around.

יְהִי רָצוֹן מִלְּפָנֶיךָ, יהוה אֱלֹהֵינוּ וֵאלֹהֵי אֲבוֹתֵינוּ,

« of our forefathers, ‹ and the God ‹ our God ‹ HASHEM, « before You, ‹ the will ‹ May it be

שֶׁתְּהֵא אֲמִירָה זוּ חֲשׁוּבָה וּמְקֻבֶּלֶת וּמְרֻצָּה לְפָנֶיךָ כְּאִלּוּ

‹ as if « before You ‹ and favorable ‹ and acceptable, ‹ worthy « — this recital — « that it be

הִקְרַבְנוּ קָרְבַּן הַתָּמִיד בְּמוֹעֲדוֹ וּבִמְקוֹמוֹ וּכְהִלְכָתוֹ.

« and according to its requirement. ‹ in its place, ‹ in its set time, ‹ the continual-offering ‹ we had offered

INCENSE / קטרת

אַתָּה הוּא יהוה אֱלֹהֵינוּ שֶׁהִקְטִירוּ אֲבוֹתֵינוּ לְפָנֶיךָ

‹ before You ‹ that our forefathers burned « our God, ‹ HASHEM, « the One, ‹ You are

אֶת קְטֹרֶת הַסַּמִּים בִּזְמַן שֶׁבֵּית הַמִּקְדָּשׁ קַיָּם, כַּאֲשֶׁר

‹ as « stood, ‹ when the Holy Temple ‹ in the time ‹ spices ‹ the incense

צִוִּיתָ אוֹתָם עַל יְדֵי מֹשֶׁה נְבִיאֶךָ, כַּכָּתוּב בְּתוֹרָתֶךָ:

« in Your Torah: ‹ as is written ‹ Your prophet, ‹ of Moses ‹ the hand ‹ by ‹ them ‹ You commanded

וַיֹּאמֶר יהוה אֶל מֹשֶׁה, קַח לְךָ סַמִּים, נָטָף

‹– stacte, « spices ‹ [for] yourself ‹ Take « Moses: ‹ to ‹ HASHEM Said

וּשְׁחֵלֶת וְחֶלְבְּנָה, סַמִּים וּלְבֹנָה זַכָּה, בַּד בְּבַד

‹ of equal weight « that is pure; ‹ and frankincense ‹ spices « and galbanum — ‹ onycha,

יִהְיֶה. וְעָשִׂיתָ אֹתָהּ קְטֹרֶת, רֹקַח, מַעֲשֵׂה רוֹקֵחַ,

« of a perfumer, ‹ the handiwork ‹ a spice-compound, ‹ into incense, ‹ it ‹ You shall make « shall they be.

(1) *Leviticus* 1:11.

מְמֻלָּח, טָהוֹר, קֹדֶשׁ. וְשָׁחַקְתָּ מִמֶּנָּה הָדֵק, וְנָתַתָּה

‹ and you shall place « finely ‹ some of it ‹ You shall grind « and holy. ‹ pure ‹ thoroughly mixed,

מִמֶּנָּה לִפְנֵי הָעֵדֻת בְּאֹהֶל מוֹעֵד אֲשֶׁר אִוָּעֵד לְךָ

‹ you ‹ I shall designate a time to meet ‹ where « of Appointment, ‹ in the Tent ‹ the Testimony ‹ before ‹ some of it

שָׁמָּה, קֹדֶשׁ קָדָשִׁים תִּהְיֶה לָכֶם.[1] וְנֶאֱמַר: וְהִקְטִיר

‹ Burn « It is also written: « for you. ‹ it shall be ‹ of holies ‹ holy « there;

עָלָיו אַהֲרֹן קְטֹרֶת סַמִּים, בַּבֹּקֶר בַּבֹּקֶר בְּהֵיטִיבוֹ

‹ when he prepares ‹ each and every morning « spices, ‹ the incense ‹ shall Aaron ‹ upon it

אֶת הַנֵּרֹת יַקְטִירֶנָּה. וּבְהַעֲלֹת אַהֲרֹן אֶת הַנֵּרֹת

‹ the lamps ‹ And when Aaron ignites « he is to burn it. ‹ the lamps

בֵּין הָעַרְבַּיִם יַקְטִירֶנָּה, קְטֹרֶת תָּמִיד לִפְנֵי

‹ before ‹ that is continual ‹ an incense « he is to burn it, ‹ in the afternoon,

יהוה לְדֹרֹתֵיכֶם.[2]

« throughout your generations. ‹ HASHEM,

Talmud, *Kereisos* 6a; *Yerushalmi Yoma* 4:5 / כריתות ו., ירושלמי יומא ד:ה

תָּנוּ רַבָּנָן, פִּטּוּם הַקְּטֹרֶת כֵּיצַד. שְׁלֹשׁ מֵאוֹת

‹ hundred ‹ Three « how is it done? « of the incense mixture, ‹ The formulation « did the Rabbis: ‹ Taught

וְשִׁשִּׁים וּשְׁמוֹנָה מָנִים הָיוּ בָהּ. שְׁלֹשׁ מֵאוֹת וְשִׁשִּׁים

‹ sixty- ‹ hundred ‹ three « in it: ‹ were ‹ *maneh* ‹ eight ‹ sixty-

וַחֲמִשָּׁה כְּמִנְיַן יְמוֹת הַחַמָּה — מָנֶה לְכָל יוֹם,

« day, ‹ for each ‹ — a *maneh* « of the solar [year] ‹ of days ‹ corresponding to the number ‹ five

פְּרַס בְּשַׁחֲרִית וּפְרַס בֵּין הָעַרְבָּיִם; וּשְׁלֹשָׁה מָנִים

‹ *maneh* ‹ and three « in the afternoon; ‹ and half ‹ in the morning ‹ half

יְתֵרִים, שֶׁמֵּהֶם מַכְנִיס כֹּהֵן גָּדוֹל מְלֹא חָפְנָיו

‹ his hands ‹ the amount that fills « the *Kohen Gadol,* « would bring, ‹ from which « extra,

(1) *Exodus* 30:34-26 (2) 30:7-8.

בְּיוֹם הַכִּפֻּרִים. וּמַחֲזִירָם לְמַכְתֶּשֶׁת בְּעֶרֶב

[into the Holiest of the Holies] on Yom Kippur. He would return them to the mortar on the day before

יוֹם הַכִּפֻּרִים, וְשׁוֹחֲקָן יָפֶה יָפֶה כְּדֵי שֶׁתְּהֵא דַקָּה

Yom Kippur, and grind them very thoroughly so that it would be the finest

מִן הַדַּקָּה. וְאַחַד עָשָׂר סַמָּנִים הָיוּ בָהּ, וְאֵלּוּ הֵן:

of the fine. Eleven kinds of spices were in it, and these are they:

(א) הַצֳּרִי, (ב) וְהַצִּפֹּרֶן, (ג) הַחֶלְבְּנָה, (ד) וְהַלְּבוֹנָה, מִשְׁקַל

stacte, onycha, galbanum, and frankincense, weighing

שִׁבְעִים שִׁבְעִים מָנֶה; (ה) מוֹר, (ו) וּקְצִיעָה, (ז) שִׁבֹּלֶת נֵרְדְּ,

each seventy *maneh;* myrrh, cassia, spikenard,

(ח) וְכַרְכֹּם, מִשְׁקַל שִׁשָּׁה עָשָׂר שִׁשָּׁה עָשָׂר מָנֶה;

saffron, weighing each sixteen *maneh;*

(ט) הַקֹּשְׁטְ שְׁנֵים עָשָׂר, (י) וְקִלּוּפָה שְׁלֹשָׁה, (יא) וְקִנָּמוֹן

costus, twelve [*maneh;*] aromatic bark, three; and cinnamon,

תִּשְׁעָה. בֹּרִית כַּרְשִׁינָה תִּשְׁעָה קַבִּין, יֵין קַפְרִיסִין

nine. [Additionally,] lye of Carshina nine *kav;* wine of Cyprus

סְאִין תְּלָתָא וְקַבִּין תְּלָתָא, וְאִם אֵין לוֹ יֵין קַפְרִיסִין,

three *se'ah* and three *kav* — if he has no wine of Cyprus,

מֵבִיא חֲמַר חִוַּרְיָן עַתִּיק, מֶלַח סְדוֹמִית רֹבַע הַקָּב;

he brings wine that is white that is old — salt of Sodom, a quarter of a *kav;*

מַעֲלֶה עָשָׁן כָּל שֶׁהוּא. רַבִּי נָתָן הַבַּבְלִי אוֹמֵר:

and *maaleh ashan* a minute amount. Rabbi Nassan the Babylonian says:

אַף כִּפַּת הַיַּרְדֵּן כָּל שֶׁהוּא. וְאִם נָתַן בָּהּ דְּבַשׁ,

Also amber of the Jordan a minute amount. If he placed in it fruit-honey,

פְּסָלָהּ. וְאִם חִסַּר אַחַת מִכָּל סַמָּנֶיהָ, חַיָּב מִיתָה.

« to the death penalty. ‹ he is liable ‹ its spices, ‹ of all ‹ any one ‹ he left out ‹ And if « he invalidated it.

רַבָּן שִׁמְעוֹן בֶּן גַּמְלִיאֵל אוֹמֵר: הַצֳּרִי אֵינוֹ

‹ is nothing ‹ Stacte « says: ‹ Gamliel ‹ ben ‹ Shimon ‹ Rabban

אֶלָּא שְׂרָף הַנּוֹטֵף מֵעֲצֵי הַקְּטָף. בֹּרִית כַּרְשִׁינָה

‹ of Carshina, ‹ Lye « of balsam. ‹ from trees ‹ that drips ‹ the sap ‹ but

לָמָּה הִיא בָאָה, כְּדֵי לְיַפּוֹת בָּהּ אֶת הַצִּפֹּרֶן, כְּדֵי

‹ in order « the onycha, ‹ with it ‹ to refine ‹ In order « brought? ‹ is it ‹ why

שֶׁתְּהֵא נָאָה. יֵין קַפְרִיסִין לָמָּה הוּא בָא, כְּדֵי

‹ In order « brought? ‹ is it ‹ why ‹ of Cyprus, ‹ Wine « pleasing. ‹ that it should be

לִשְׁרוֹת בּוֹ אֶת הַצִּפֹּרֶן, כְּדֵי שֶׁתְּהֵא עַזָּה. וַהֲלֹא

‹ But is not « pungent. ‹ that it should be ‹ in order ‹ the onycha ‹ in it ‹ to soak

מֵי רַגְלַיִם יָפִין לָהּ, אֶלָּא שֶׁאֵין מַכְנִיסִין מֵי רַגְלַיִם

‹ urine ‹ bring ‹ they do not ‹ Nevertheless « for that? ‹ more suitable ‹ urine

בַּמִּקְדָּשׁ מִפְּנֵי הַכָּבוֹד.

« respect. ‹ out of ‹ into the Temple

תַּנְיָא, רַבִּי נָתָן אוֹמֵר: כְּשֶׁהוּא שׁוֹחֵק, אוֹמֵר

« [the one in charge] would say, ‹ would grind [the incense], ‹ As he « says: ‹ Nassan ‹ Rabbi « It is taught:

הָדֵק הֵיטֵב, הֵיטֵב הָדֵק, מִפְּנֵי שֶׁהַקּוֹל יָפֶה

‹ is beneficial ‹ the sound ‹ because « *grind,* ‹ *thoroughly* ‹ *thoroughly,* ‹ *Grind*

לַבְּשָׂמִים. פִּטְּמָהּ לַחֲצָאִין, כְּשֵׁרָה; לִשְׁלִישׁ

‹ but as to a third « it was fit for use, ‹ in half-quantities, ‹ If one mixed it « for the spices.

וְלִרְבִיעַ, לֹא שָׁמַעְנוּ. אָמַר רַבִּי יְהוּדָה: זֶה הַכְּלָל

« the general rule: ‹ This is « Yehudah: ‹ Rabbi ‹ Said « — we have not heard [the law]. « or a quarter

— אִם כְּמִדָּתָהּ, כְּשֵׁרָה לַחֲצָאִין; וְאִם חִסַּר אַחַת

‹ If ‹ in its proper proportion, « it is fit for use ‹ [even] in half the full amount. « But if ‹ he left out ‹ any one ‹

מִכָּל סַמָּנֶיהָ, חַיָּב מִיתָה.

‹ of all ‹ its spices, ‹ he is liable ‹ to the death penalty. «

תַּנְיָא, בַּר קַפָּרָא אוֹמֵר: אַחַת לְשִׁשִּׁים אוֹ

It is taught: « Bar ‹ Kappara ‹ says: « Once ‹ every sixty ‹ or ‹

לְשִׁבְעִים שָׁנָה הָיְתָה בָאָה שֶׁל שִׁירַיִם לַחֲצָאִין.

seventy ‹ years, ‹ it would ‹ reach « — the accumulated leftovers — « half the yearly quantity. «

וְעוֹד תָּנֵי בַּר קַפָּרָא: אִלּוּ הָיָה נוֹתֵן בָּהּ קוֹרְטוֹב

Furthermore ‹ taught ‹ Bar ‹ Kappara: « If ‹ one had ‹ put ‹ into it ‹ a *kortov* ‹

שֶׁל דְּבַשׁ, אֵין אָדָם יָכוֹל לַעֲמֹד מִפְּנֵי רֵיחָהּ.

of ‹ fruit-honey, « no ‹ person ‹ could have ‹ withstood ‹ its scent. «

וְלָמָּה אֵין מְעָרְבִין בָּהּ דְּבַשׁ, מִפְּנֵי שֶׁהַתּוֹרָה

Why ‹ did they not ‹ mix ‹ into it ‹ fruit-honey? « Because ‹ the Torah ‹

אָמְרָה: כִּי כָל שְׂאֹר וְכָל דְּבַשׁ לֹא תַקְטִירוּ

said: « *For* ‹ *any* ‹ *leaven* ‹ *or any* ‹ *fruit-honey,* ‹ *you are not to burn* ‹

מִמֶּנּוּ אִשֶּׁה לַיהוה.[1]

from them ‹ *a fire-offering* ‹ *to* HASHEM. «

RECITE THREE TIMES:

יהוה צְבָאוֹת עִמָּנוּ, מִשְׂגָּב לָנוּ אֱלֹהֵי יַעֲקֹב,

HASHEM, ‹ Master of Legions, ‹ is with us, « a stronghold ‹ for us ‹ is the God ‹ of Jacob, «

סֶלָה.[2]

Selah! «

RECITE THREE TIMES:

יהוה צְבָאוֹת, אַשְׁרֵי אָדָם בֹּטֵחַ בָּךְ.[3]

HASHEM, ‹ Master of Legions, ‹ praiseworthy ‹ is the man ‹ who trusts ‹ in You. «

(1) *Leviticus* 2:11. (2) *Psalms* 46:8. (3) 84:13.

RECITE THREE TIMES:

יהוה הוֹשִׁיעָה, הַמֶּלֶךְ יַעֲנֵנוּ בְיוֹם קָרְאֵנוּ.[1]

« we call! ‹ on the day ‹ answer us ‹ May the King « save! ‹ HASHEM,

אַתָּה סֵתֶר לִי, מִצַּר תִּצְּרֵנִי, רָנֵּי פַלֵּט, תְּסוֹבְבֵנִי, סֶלָה.[2] וְעָרְבָה לַיהוה מִנְחַת יְהוּדָה וִירוּשָׁלָיִם, כִּימֵי עוֹלָם וּכְשָׁנִים קַדְמֹנִיּוֹת.[3]

« You envelop me, ‹ of rescue, ‹ with glad song « You preserve me; ‹ from distress « for me; ‹ a shelter ‹ You are

« and Jerusalem, ‹ of Judah ‹ let be the offering ‹ to HASHEM ‹ And pleasing « Selah!

« gone by. ‹ and in years ‹ of old ‹ as in days

Talmud *Yoma* 33a / יומא לג.

אַבַּיֵּי הֲוָה מְסַדֵּר סֵדֶר הַמַּעֲרָכָה מִשְּׁמָא דִגְמָרָא וְאַלִּבָּא דְאַבָּא שָׁאוּל: מַעֲרָכָה גְדוֹלָה קוֹדֶמֶת לְמַעֲרָכָה שְׁנִיָּה שֶׁל קְטֹרֶת; וּמַעֲרָכָה שְׁנִיָּה שֶׁל קְטֹרֶת קוֹדֶמֶת לְסִדּוּר שְׁנֵי גִזְרֵי עֵצִים; וְסִדּוּר שְׁנֵי גִזְרֵי עֵצִים קוֹדֵם לְדִשּׁוּן מִזְבֵּחַ הַפְּנִימִי; וְדִשּׁוּן מִזְבֵּחַ הַפְּנִימִי קוֹדֵם לַהֲטָבַת חָמֵשׁ נֵרוֹת; וַהֲטָבַת חָמֵשׁ נֵרוֹת קוֹדֶמֶת לְדַם הַתָּמִיד; וְדַם

« the tradition, ‹ based on ‹ of the Altar service, ‹ the order ‹ list ‹ would ‹ Abaye

‹ precedes ‹ The [arrangement of the] large pyre « with Abba Shaul: ‹ and in accordance

‹ of ‹ the secondary pyre « the incense-offering; ‹ of ‹ that of the secondary pyre

‹ of two ‹ the placement « of wood; ‹ logs ‹ of two ‹ the placement ‹ precedes ‹ the incense-offering

‹ the removal of ashes « that is inside; ‹ from the Altar ‹ the removal of ashes ‹ precedes ‹ of wood ‹ logs

‹ the cleaning « lamps [of the Menorah]; ‹ of the five ‹ the cleaning ‹ precedes ‹ that is inside ‹ from the Altar

‹ the blood « of the continual-offering; ‹ the [throwing of the] blood ‹ precedes ‹ lamps ‹ of the five

(1) *Psalms* 20:10. (2) 32:7. (3) *Malachi* 3:4.

הַתָּמִיד קוֹדֵם לַהֲטָבַת שְׁתֵּי נֵרוֹת; וַהֲטָבַת

‹of the continual-offering ‹precedes ‹the cleaning ‹of the [other] two «lamps; ‹the cleaning

שְׁתֵּי נֵרוֹת קוֹדֶמֶת לִקְטֹרֶת; וּקְטֹרֶת קוֹדֶמֶת

‹of the two ‹lamps ‹precedes «the incense; ‹the incense ‹precedes

לְאֵבָרִים; וְאֵבָרִים לְמִנְחָה; וּמִנְחָה לַחֲבִתִּין;

«the [burning of the] limbs [of the *tamid*]; ‹the [burning of the] limbs «[precedes] the meal-offering; ‹the meal-offering «[precedes] the pan-cakes;

וַחֲבִתִּין לִנְסָכִין; וּנְסָכִין לְמוּסָפִין; וּמוּסָפִין

‹the pan-cakes «[precede] the wine-libations; ‹the wine-libations «[precede] the *mussaf*-offering; ‹the *mussaf*-offering

לְבָזִיכִין; וּבָזִיכִין קוֹדְמִין לְתָמִיד שֶׁל בֵּין הָעַרְבָּיִם,

«[precedes] the bowls [of frankincense]; ‹the bowls ‹precede ‹the continual-offering ‹of «the afternoon,

שֶׁנֶּאֱמַר: וְעָרַךְ עָלֶיהָ הָעֹלָה, וְהִקְטִיר עָלֶיהָ חֶלְבֵי

«for it is said: ‹*And he is to arrange* ‹*upon it* ‹*the elevation-offering* ‹*and burn* ‹*upon it* ‹*the fats*

הַשְּׁלָמִים.[1] עָלֶיהָ הַשְׁלֵם כָּל הַקָּרְבָּנוֹת כֻּלָּם.

«*of the peace-offerings;* ‹"*upon it*" ‹you are to complete ‹all ‹the [day's] offerings «in their entirety.

אָנָּא בְּכֹחַ גְּדֻלַּת יְמִינְךָ תַּתִּיר צְרוּרָה. אב״ג ית״ץ

«We beg You! ‹With the strength ‹of the greatness ‹of Your right hand, ‹untie «the bundled [sins].

קַבֵּל רִנַּת עַמְּךָ שַׂגְּבֵנוּ טַהֲרֵנוּ נוֹרָא. קר״ע שט״ן

‹Accept ‹the prayer «of Your people; ‹strengthen us, ‹purify us, «O Awesome One.

נָא גִבּוֹר דּוֹרְשֵׁי יִחוּדְךָ כְּבָבַת שָׁמְרֵם. נג״ד יכ״ש

‹Please, «O Strong One ‹— those who foster «Your Oneness, ‹like the pupil of an eye «guard them.

בָּרְכֵם טַהֲרֵם רַחֲמֵם צִדְקָתְךָ תָּמִיד גָּמְלֵם. בט״ר צת״ג

‹Bless them, ‹purify them, «show them pity; ‹may Your righteousness ‹always «recompense them.

---

(1) *Leviticus* 6:5.

חֲסִין קָדוֹשׁ בְּרוֹב טוּבְךָ נַהֵל עֲדָתֶךָ. חק״ב טנ״ע

« Your congregation. ‹ guide ‹ of Your goodness ‹ with the abundance « Holy One, ‹ Powerful One,

יָחִיד גֵּאֶה לְעַמְּךָ פְּנֵה זוֹכְרֵי קְדֻשָּׁתֶךָ. יג״ל פז״ק

« Your holiness. ‹ those who proclaim « turn, ‹ to Your people ‹ Exalted One, ‹ Unique One,

שַׁוְעָתֵנוּ קַבֵּל וּשְׁמַע צַעֲקָתֵנוּ יוֹדֵעַ תַּעֲלֻמוֹת. שק״ו צי״ת

« of mysteries. ‹ O Knower « our cry, ‹ and hear « accept, ‹ Our entreaty

בָּרוּךְ שֵׁם כְּבוֹד מַלְכוּתוֹ לְעוֹלָם וָעֶד.

« and ever. ‹ for ever ‹ kingdom ‹ of His glorious ‹ is the Name ‹ Blessed

רִבּוֹן הָעוֹלָמִים, אַתָּה צִוִּיתָנוּ לְהַקְרִיב קָרְבַּן הַתָּמִיד

‹ the continual-offering ‹ to bring ‹ commanded us ‹ You « of the worlds, ‹ Master

בְּמוֹעֲדוֹ, וְלִהְיוֹת כֹּהֲנִים בַּעֲבוֹדָתָם, וּלְוִיִּם בְּדוּכָנָם, וְיִשְׂרָאֵל

‹ and Israelites « on their platform, ‹ Levites « at their assigned service, ‹ *Kohanim* ‹ and that there be « at its set time,

בְּמַעֲמָדָם. וְעַתָּה בַּעֲוֹנוֹתֵינוּ חָרַב בֵּית הַמִּקְדָּשׁ וּבָטַל

‹ and discontinued ‹ was the Holy Temple, ‹ destroyed « through our sins, ‹ But now, « at their station.

הַתָּמִיד, וְאֵין לָנוּ לֹא כֹהֵן בַּעֲבוֹדָתוֹ, וְלֹא לֵוִי בְּדוּכָנוֹ,

« on his platform, ‹ a Levite ‹ nor « at his service, ‹ a *Kohen* « and we have neither « was the continual-offering;

וְלֹא יִשְׂרָאֵל בְּמַעֲמָדוֹ. וְאַתָּה אָמַרְתָּ: וּנְשַׁלְּמָה פָרִים

‹ *for the bulls* ‹ *Let us compensate* « said: ‹ But You « at his station. ‹ Israelite ‹ nor

שְׂפָתֵינוּ.[1] לָכֵן יְהִי רָצוֹן מִלְּפָנֶיךָ, יהוה אֱלֹהֵינוּ וֵאלֹהֵי

‹ and the God ‹ our God ‹ HASHEM, « before You, ‹ the will ‹ may it be ‹ Therefore, « *with our lips.*

אֲבוֹתֵינוּ, שֶׁיְּהֵא שִׂיחַ שִׂפְתוֹתֵינוּ חָשׁוּב וּמְקֻבָּל וּמְרֻצֶּה

‹ and favorable ‹ acceptable, ‹ worthy, « of our lips — ‹ — the prayer « that it be « of our forefathers,

לְפָנֶיךָ, כְּאִלּוּ הִקְרַבְנוּ קָרְבַּן הַתָּמִיד בְּמוֹעֲדוֹ, וְעָמַדְנוּ עַל

‹ at ‹ and we had stood « at its set time ‹ the continual-offering ‹ we had brought ‹ as if « before You,

מַעֲמָדוֹ.

« its station.

(1) *Hosea* 14:3.

Mishnah, Zevachim Chapter 5 / משנה זבחים פרק ה

[א] **אֵיזֶהוּ** מְקוֹמָן שֶׁל זְבָחִים. קָדְשֵׁי קָדָשִׁים

[1] What is the location of the offerings? The holiest of the holy offerings,

שְׁחִיטָתָן בַּצָּפוֹן. פַּר וְשָׂעִיר שֶׁל יוֹם הַכִּפּוּרִים

their slaughter is in the north. The bull and the he-goat of Yom Kippur

שְׁחִיטָתָן בַּצָּפוֹן, וְקִבּוּל דָּמָן בִּכְלִי שָׁרֵת בַּצָּפוֹן.

— their slaughter is in the north and the reception of their blood in a vessel of service is in the north.

וְדָמָן טָעוּן הַזָּיָה עַל בֵּין הַבַּדִּים, וְעַל הַפָּרֹכֶת,

Their blood requires sprinkling upon the area between the poles [of the Holy Ark], and toward the Curtain [of the Holy of Holies]

וְעַל מִזְבַּח הַזָּהָב. מַתָּנָה אַחַת מֵהֶן מְעַכֶּבֶת. שְׁיָרֵי

and upon the Altar of gold. [The omission of even] one application [of blood] of these prevents [atonement]. The leftover

הַדָּם הָיָה שׁוֹפֵךְ עַל יְסוֹד מַעֲרָבִי שֶׁל מִזְבַּח

blood he would pour onto the western base of the Altar

הַחִיצוֹן; אִם לֹא נָתַן, לֹא עִכֵּב.

outside; but if he did not apply [the leftover blood to the base], he has not prevented [atonement].

[ב] **פָּרִים** הַנִּשְׂרָפִים וּשְׂעִירִים הַנִּשְׂרָפִים שְׁחִיטָתָן

[2] The bulls that are completely burned and he-goats that are completely burned — their slaughter

בַּצָּפוֹן, וְקִבּוּל דָּמָן בִּכְלִי שָׁרֵת בַּצָּפוֹן. וְדָמָן טָעוּן

is in the north, and the reception of their blood in a vessel of service is in the north. Their blood requires

הַזָּיָה עַל הַפָּרֹכֶת וְעַל מִזְבַּח הַזָּהָב. מַתָּנָה אַחַת מֵהֶן

sprinkling toward the Curtain and upon the Altar of Gold. [The omission of even] one application [of blood] of them

מְעַכֶּבֶת. שְׁיָרֵי הַדָּם הָיָה שׁוֹפֵךְ עַל יְסוֹד מַעֲרָבִי

prevents [atonement]. The leftover blood he would pour onto the western base

שֶׁל מִזְבֵּחַ הַחִיצוֹן; אִם לֹא נָתַן, לֹא עִכֵּב. אֵלּוּ

of 〈 the Altar 〈 outside; « but if he did not apply [the leftover blood to the base], « he has not prevented [atonement]. « Both these 〈

וְאֵלּוּ נִשְׂרָפִין בְּבֵית הַדֶּשֶׁן.

and those [the Yom Kippur offerings] 〈 are burned 〈 in the place 〈 where the Altar ashes [are deposited]. «

[ג] **חַטֹּאת** הַצִּבּוּר וְהַיָּחִיד — אֵלּוּ הֵן חַטֹּאת

[3] Sin-offerings 〈 of the community 〈 and of the individual « — these 〈 are 〈 the sin-offerings 〈

הַצִּבּוּר, שְׂעִירֵי רָאשֵׁי חֳדָשִׁים וְשֶׁל מוֹעֲדוֹת —

of the community: « the he-goats 〈 of Rosh Chodesh 〈 and of 〈 the Festivals «

שְׁחִיטָתָן בַּצָּפוֹן, וְקִבּוּל דָּמָן בִּכְלִי שָׁרֵת בַּצָּפוֹן.

— their slaughter 〈 is in the north 〈 and the reception 〈 of their blood 〈 in a vessel 〈 of service 〈 is in the north. «

וְדָמָן טָעוּן אַרְבַּע מַתָּנוֹת עַל אַרְבַּע קְרָנוֹת. כֵּיצַד,

Their blood 〈 requires 〈 four 〈 applications, 〈 [one] on 〈 [each of] the four 〈 corners [of the Altar]. « How is it done? «

עָלָה בַכֶּבֶשׁ, וּפָנָה לַסּוֹבֵב וּבָא לוֹ לְקֶרֶן דְּרוֹמִית

[The *Kohen*] ascended 〈 the [Altar] ramp, 〈 turned 〈 to the surrounding ledge 〈 and arrived 〈 at the corner 〈 which is south- 〈

מִזְרָחִית, מִזְרָחִית צְפוֹנִית, צְפוֹנִית מַעֲרָבִית,

east, 〈 [then at] the east- 〈 north [corner], 〈 the north- 〈 west [corner], 〈

מַעֲרָבִית דְּרוֹמִית. שִׁירֵי הַדָּם הָיָה שׁוֹפֵךְ עַל

and the west- 〈 south [corner]. « The leftover 〈 blood 〈 he would 〈 pour 〈 onto 〈

יְסוֹד דְּרוֹמִי. וְנֶאֱכָלִין לִפְנִים מִן הַקְּלָעִים, לְזִכְרֵי

the southern base. « They are eaten 〈 inside 〈 of 〈 the [Courtyard] curtains, « by males 〈

כְהֻנָּה, בְּכָל מַאֲכָל, לְיוֹם וָלַיְלָה, עַד חֲצוֹת.

of the priesthood, « in any manner 〈 of preparation, « on the day [of offering] 〈 and on the following night 〈 until 〈 midnight. «

[ד] **הָעוֹלָה** קֹדֶשׁ קָדָשִׁים. שְׁחִיטָתָהּ בַּצָּפוֹן,

[4] The elevation-offering ‹ is among the holiest ‹ of the holy offerings. « Its slaughter ‹ is in the north ‹

וְקִבּוּל דָּמָהּ בִּכְלִי שָׁרֵת בַּצָּפוֹן. וְדָמָהּ טָעוּן שְׁתֵּי

and the reception ‹ of its blood ‹ in a vessel ‹ of service ‹ is in the north. « Its blood ‹ requires ‹ two ‹

מַתָּנוֹת שֶׁהֵן אַרְבַּע; וּטְעוּנָה הַפְשֵׁט וְנִתּוּחַ,

applications ‹ that are equivalent to four. « It requires ‹ flaying ‹ and dismemberment, «

וְכָלִיל לָאִשִּׁים.

and it is entirely consumed ‹ by the fire. «

[ה] **זִבְחֵי** שַׁלְמֵי צִבּוּר וַאֲשָׁמוֹת, אֵלּוּ הֵן אֲשָׁמוֹת:

[5] Sacrifices ‹ of peace-offerings ‹ of the community ‹ and guilt-offerings « these —‹ are ‹ the guilt-offerings: «

אֲשַׁם גְּזֵלוֹת, אֲשַׁם מְעִילוֹת, אֲשַׁם שִׁפְחָה

the guilt-offering ‹ for thefts, « the guilt-offering ‹ for misuse of sacred objects, « the guilt-offering ‹ [for violating] a maidservant ‹

חֲרוּפָה, אֲשַׁם נָזִיר, אֲשַׁם מְצוֹרָע, אָשָׁם תָּלוּי.

who was betrothed, « the guilt-offering ‹ of a nazirite, « the guilt-offering ‹ of a *metzora,* « and the guilt-offering ‹ in case of doubt «

שְׁחִיטָתָן בַּצָּפוֹן, וְקִבּוּל דָּמָן בִּכְלִי שָׁרֵת בַּצָּפוֹן,

— their slaughter ‹ is in the north ‹ and the reception ‹ of their blood ‹ in a vessel ‹ of service ‹ is in the north. «

וְדָמָן טָעוּן שְׁתֵּי מַתָּנוֹת שֶׁהֵן אַרְבַּע. וְנֶאֱכָלִין

Their blood ‹ requires ‹ two ‹ applications ‹ that are equivalent to four. « They are eaten ‹

לִפְנִים מִן הַקְּלָעִים לְזִכְרֵי כְהֻנָּה, בְּכָל מַאֲכָל,

inside ‹ of ‹ the [Courtyard] curtains, « by males ‹ of the priesthood, « in any manner ‹ of preparation, «

לְיוֹם וָלַיְלָה, עַד חֲצוֹת.

on the day [of offering] ‹ and on the [following] night ‹ until ‹ midnight. «

[ו] **הַתּוֹדָה** וְאֵיל נָזִיר קָדָשִׁים קַלִּים. שְׁחִיטָתָן

[6] The thanksgiving-offering ‹ and the ram ‹ of a Nazirite ‹ are offerings of holiness ‹ of a lesser degree. « Their slaughter ‹

בְּכָל מָקוֹם בָּעֲזָרָה, וְדָמָן טָעוּן שְׁתֵּי מַתָּנוֹת

is in any ‹ place ‹ in the Courtyard, « and their blood ‹ requires ‹ two ‹ applications ‹

שֶׁהֵן אַרְבַּע. וְנֶאֱכָלִין בְּכָל הָעִיר, לְכָל אָדָם,

that are equivalent to four. « They are eaten ‹ through-out ‹ the City [of Jerusalem] « by any ‹ person, «

בְּכָל מַאֲכָל, לְיוֹם וָלַיְלָה, עַד חֲצוֹת. הַמּוּרָם

in any manner ‹ of preparation, « on the day [of offering] ‹ and on the [following] night ‹ until ‹ midnight. « The [priestly] portion separated ‹

מֵהֶם כַּיּוֹצֵא בָהֶם, אֶלָּא שֶׁהַמּוּרָם נֶאֱכָל לַכֹּהֲנִים,

from them ‹ is to be treated ‹ like them, « except that ‹ the separated portion ‹ may be eaten ‹ [only] by the *Kohanim,* ‹

לִנְשֵׁיהֶם וְלִבְנֵיהֶם וּלְעַבְדֵיהֶם.

by their wives, ‹ by their children, ‹ and by their slaves. «

[ז] **שְׁלָמִים** קָדָשִׁים קַלִּים. שְׁחִיטָתָן בְּכָל מָקוֹם

[7] The peace-offerings ‹ are offerings of holiness ‹ of a lesser degree. « Their slaughter ‹ is in any ‹ place ‹

בָּעֲזָרָה, וְדָמָן טָעוּן שְׁתֵּי מַתָּנוֹת שֶׁהֵן אַרְבַּע.

in the Courtyard, « and their blood ‹ requires ‹ two ‹ applications ‹ that are equivalent to four. «

וְנֶאֱכָלִין בְּכָל הָעִיר, לְכָל אָדָם, בְּכָל מַאֲכָל,

They are eaten ‹ through-out ‹ the City [of Jerusalem] « by any ‹ person, « in any manner ‹ of preparation, «

לִשְׁנֵי יָמִים וְלַיְלָה אֶחָד. הַמּוּרָם מֵהֶם כַּיּוֹצֵא

for two ‹ days ‹ and the [intervening] night. « The [priestly] portion separated ‹ from them ‹ is to be treated ‹

בָהֶם, אֶלָּא שֶׁהַמּוּרָם נֶאֱכָל לַכֹּהֲנִים, לִנְשֵׁיהֶם

like them, « except that ‹ the separated portion ‹ may be eaten ‹ [only] by the *Kohanim,* ‹ by their wives, ‹

וְלִבְנֵיהֶם וּלְעַבְדֵיהֶם.

by their children, ‹ and by their slaves. «

[ח] **הַבְּכוֹר** וְהַמַּעֲשֵׂר וְהַפֶּסַח קָדָשִׁים קַלִּים.

[8] The firstborn, the tithe of animals, and the *pesach*-offering are offerings of holiness of a lesser degree:

שְׁחִיטָתָן בְּכָל מָקוֹם בָּעֲזָרָה, וְדָמָן טָעוּן

Their slaughter is in any place in the Courtyard, and their blood requires

מַתָּנָה אֶחָת, וּבִלְבָד שֶׁיִּתֵּן כְּנֶגֶד הַיְסוֹד. שׁוֹנָה

a single application, provided he applies it above the base. They differ

בַּאֲכִילָתָן: הַבְּכוֹר נֶאֱכָל לַכֹּהֲנִים, וְהַמַּעֲשֵׂר לְכָל

in their consumption: The firstborn is eaten by *Kohanim*, and the tithe by any

אָדָם. וְנֶאֱכָלִין בְּכָל הָעִיר, בְּכָל מַאֲכָל, לִשְׁנֵי

person. They are eaten throughout the City [of Jerusalem] in any manner of preparation, for two

יָמִים וְלַיְלָה אֶחָד. הַפֶּסַח אֵינוֹ נֶאֱכָל אֶלָּא

days and the [intervening] night. The *pesach*-offering is not eaten except

בַלַּיְלָה, וְאֵינוֹ נֶאֱכָל אֶלָּא עַד חֲצוֹת, וְאֵינוֹ נֶאֱכָל

at night, and is not eaten except until midnight, and is not eaten

אֶלָּא לִמְנוּיָו, וְאֵינוֹ נֶאֱכָל אֶלָּא צָלִי.

except by those registered for it; and is not eaten [in any manner of preparation] except roasted.

——*Baraisa DeR' Yishmael* Introduction to *Sifra* / ברייתא דר' ישמעאל – ספרא, פתיחה——

רַבִּי יִשְׁמָעֵאל אוֹמֵר: בִּשְׁלשׁ עֶשְׂרֵה מִדּוֹת

Rabbi Yishmael says: Through thirteen rules

הַתּוֹרָה נִדְרֶשֶׁת בָּהֶן. (א) מִקַּל וָחֹמֶר;

the Torah is elucidated thereby: (1) through a conclusion inferred from a lenient law to a strict one;

(ב) וּמִגְּזֵרָה שָׁוָה; (ג) מִבִּנְיַן אָב מִכָּתוּב אֶחָד,

(2) through tradition that similar words in different contexts are meant to create a connection between the two topics; (3) through [establishing] a general principle from one passage

וּמִבִּנְיַן אָב מִשְּׁנֵי כְתוּבִים; (ד) מִכְּלָל וּפְרָט;

and through establishing a general principle from two passages; (4) through a generalization [limited by] a specification;

(ה) וּמִפְּרָט וּכְלָל; (ו) כְּלָל וּפְרָט וּכְלָל, אִי אַתָּה דָן

(5) through a specification [broadened by] a generalization; (6) through a generalization [followed by] a specification [followed by another] generalization — you may not infer [anything]

אֶלָּא כְּעֵין הַפְּרָט; (ז) מִכְּלָל שֶׁהוּא צָרִיךְ לִפְרָט,

except that which is similar to the specification; (7) through a generalization that requires a specification [to clarify its meaning];

וּמִפְּרָט שֶׁהוּא צָרִיךְ לִכְלָל; (ח) כָּל דָּבָר שֶׁהָיָה בִּכְלָל

or a specification that requires a generalization [to clarify its meaning]; (8) any item that was included in a generalization,

וְיָצָא מִן הַכְּלָל לְלַמֵּד, לֹא לְלַמֵּד עַל עַצְמוֹ יָצָא,

but was then singled out from the generalization in order to teach something — it is not to teach only about itself that it was singled out,

אֶלָּא לְלַמֵּד עַל הַכְּלָל כֻּלּוֹ יָצָא; (ט) כָּל דָּבָר שֶׁהָיָה

but to apply its teaching to the generalization in its entirety that it was singled out; (9) any item that was included

בִּכְלָל וְיָצָא לִטְעוֹן טוֹעַן אֶחָד שֶׁהוּא כְעִנְיָנוֹ,

in a generalization, but was then singled out to discuss a provision of one kind that is similar to the general category,

יָצָא לְהָקֵל וְלֹא לְהַחֲמִיר; (י) כָּל דָּבָר שֶׁהָיָה בִּכְלָל

was singled out to be more lenient and not to be more stringent; (10) any item that was included in a general statement,

וְיָצָא לִטְעוֹן טֹעַן אַחֵר שֶׁלֹּא כְעִנְיָנוֹ, יָצָא לְהָקֵל

but was then singled out to discuss a provision of a different kind, that is not similar to the general category, was singled out to be both more lenient

וּלְהַחֲמִיר; (יא) כָּל דָּבָר שֶׁהָיָה בִּכְלָל וְיָצָא לִדּוֹן

and more stringent; (11) any item that was included in a generalization, but was then singled out to be treated

בַּדָּבָר הֶחָדָשׁ, אִי אַתָּה יָכוֹל לְהַחֲזִירוֹ לִכְלָלוֹ, עַד

as a new case, you are not permitted to return it to its general statement unless

שֶׁיַּחֲזִירֶנּוּ הַכָּתוּב לִכְלָלוֹ בְּפֵרוּשׁ; (יב) דָּבָר הַלָּמֵד

it is returned by Scripture to its generalization explicitly; (12) a matter elucidated

מֵעִנְיָנוֹ, וְדָבָר הַלָּמֵד מִסּוֹפוֹ; (יג) וְכֵן שְׁנֵי כְתוּבִים

from its context, or a matter elucidated from the passage following it; (13) similarly, two passages

הַמַּכְחִישִׁים זֶה אֶת זֶה, עַד שֶׁיָּבוֹא הַכָּתוּב הַשְּׁלִישִׁי

that contradict one another « [cannot be resolved] until there comes ‹ a third passage ‹

וְיַכְרִיעַ בֵּינֵיהֶם.

and reconciles « between them. «

יְהִי רָצוֹן מִלְּפָנֶיךָ, יהוה אֱלֹהֵינוּ וֵאלֹהֵי

May it be ‹ the will ‹ before You, « HASHEM, ‹ our God ‹ and the God ‹

אֲבוֹתֵינוּ, שֶׁיִּבָּנֶה בֵּית הַמִּקְדָּשׁ בִּמְהֵרָה בְיָמֵינוּ,

of our forefathers, « that rebuilt ‹ shall the Holy Temple be, ‹ speedily ‹ in our days. «

וְתֵן חֶלְקֵנוּ בְּתוֹרָתֶךָ.[1] וְשָׁם נַעֲבָדְךָ בְּיִרְאָה כִּימֵי

Grant that ‹ our portion ‹ be in Your Torah, « and there ‹ may we serve You ‹ with reverence « as in days ‹

עוֹלָם וּכְשָׁנִים קַדְמוֹנִיּוֹת.[2]

of old ‹ and as in years ‹ gone by. «

THE RABBI'S KADDISH / קדיש דרבנן

IN THE PRESENCE OF A *MINYAN*, MOURNERS RECITE קַדִּישׁ דְּרַבָּנָן, THE RABBIS' *KADDISH* (SEE *LAWS* §135-136). [A TRANSLITERATION OF THIS *KADDISH* APPEARS ON PAGE 646.]

יִתְגַּדַּל וְיִתְקַדַּשׁ שְׁמֵהּ רַבָּא. (Cong. — אָמֵן.) בְּעָלְמָא דִּי

Grow exalted ‹ and be sanctified ‹ may His Name ‹ that is great! — « (Amen.) ‹ in the world ‹ that ‹

בְרָא כִרְעוּתֵהּ. וְיַמְלִיךְ מַלְכוּתֵהּ, בְּחַיֵּיכוֹן וּבְיוֹמֵיכוֹן וּבְחַיֵּי

He created « according to His will, « and may He give reign ‹ to His kingship, « in your lifetimes ‹ and in your days, ‹ and in the lifetimes ‹

דְכָל בֵּית יִשְׂרָאֵל, בַּעֲגָלָא וּבִזְמַן קָרִיב. וְאִמְרוּ: אָמֵן.

of the entire ‹ Family ‹ of Israel, « swiftly ‹ and at a time ‹ that comes soon. « Now respond: ‹ Amen. «

CONGREGATION RESPONDS:

אָמֵן. יְהֵא שְׁמֵהּ רַבָּא מְבָרַךְ לְעָלַם וּלְעָלְמֵי עָלְמַיָּא.

Amen. « May ‹ His Name ‹ that is great ‹ be blessed ‹ forever ‹ and for all eternity. «

MOURNER CONTINUES:

יְהֵא שְׁמֵהּ רַבָּא מְבָרַךְ לְעָלַם וּלְעָלְמֵי עָלְמַיָּא. יִתְבָּרַךְ

May ‹ His Name ‹ that is great ‹ be blessed ‹ forever ‹ and for all eternity. « Blessed, ‹

(1) *Ethics of the Fathers* 5:24. (2) *Malachi* 3:4.

וְיִשְׁתַּבַּח וְיִתְפָּאַר וְיִתְרוֹמַם וְיִתְנַשֵּׂא וְיִתְהַדָּר וְיִתְעַלֶּה

‹ elevated, ‹ honored, ‹ upraised, ‹ exalted, ‹ glorified, ‹ praised,

וְיִתְהַלָּל שְׁמֵהּ דְּקֻדְשָׁא בְּרִיךְ הוּא (Cong. — בְּרִיךְ הוּא) —

« is He) ‹ (Blessed « is He ‹ Blessed ‹ of the Holy One, ‹ be the Name ‹ and lauded

לְעֵלָּא מִן כָּל בִּרְכָתָא וְשִׁירָתָא תֻּשְׁבְּחָתָא וְנֶחֱמָתָא

‹ and consolation ‹ praise « and song, ‹ blessing ‹ any ‹ beyond

דַּאֲמִירָן בְּעָלְמָא. וְאִמְרוּ: אָמֵן. (Cong. — אָמֵן.)

« (Amen.) « Amen. ‹ Now respond: « in the world. ‹ that are uttered

עַל יִשְׂרָאֵל וְעַל רַבָּנָן, וְעַל תַּלְמִידֵיהוֹן וְעַל כָּל

‹ all ‹ and upon ‹ their disciples ‹ upon ‹ the teachers, ‹ upon ‹ Israel, ‹ Upon

תַּלְמִידֵי תַלְמִידֵיהוֹן, וְעַל כָּל מָאן דְּעָסְקִין בְּאוֹרַיְתָא,

‹ in the study of Torah, ‹ who engage ‹ those ‹ all ‹ and upon ‹ of their disciples ‹ of the disciples

דִּי בְאַתְרָא[1] הָדֵין וְדִי בְכָל אֲתַר וַאֲתַר. יְהֵא לְהוֹן

‹ for them ‹ may there be « other place; ‹ in any ‹ or who are ‹ in this place ‹ who are

וּלְכוֹן שְׁלָמָא רַבָּא, חִנָּא וְחִסְדָּא וְרַחֲמִין, וְחַיִּין אֲרִיכִין,

‹ that is long, ‹ life « and mercy, ‹ kindness, ‹ grace, ‹ that is abundant, ‹ peace ‹ and for you

וּמְזוֹנֵי רְוִיחֵי, וּפֻרְקָנָא מִן קֳדָם אֲבוּהוֹן דִּי בִשְׁמַיָּא

‹ in Heaven ‹ Who is ‹ their Father ‹ before ‹ from « and salvation ‹ that is ample, ‹ nourishment

(וְאַרְעָא). וְאִמְרוּ: אָמֵן. (Cong. — אָמֵן.)

« (Amen.) « Amen. ‹ Now respond: « (and on earth).

יְהֵא שְׁלָמָא רַבָּא מִן שְׁמַיָּא, וְחַיִּים עָלֵינוּ וְעַל כָּל

‹ all ‹ and upon ‹ upon us « and life, « Heaven, ‹ from ‹ that is abundant ‹ peace ‹ May there be

יִשְׂרָאֵל. וְאִמְרוּ: אָמֵן. (Cong. — אָמֵן.)

« (Amen.) « Amen. ‹ Now respond: « Israel.

BOW; TAKE THREE STEPS BACK. BOW LEFT AND SAY ... עֹשֶׂה שָׁלוֹם, *"HE WHO MAKES PEACE ..."*; BOW RIGHT AND SAY ... הוּא, *"MAY HE ..."*; BOW FORWARD AND SAY ... וְעַל כָּל יִשְׂרָאֵל, *"AND UPON ALL ISRAEL ..."*; REMAIN IN PLACE FOR A FEW MOMENTS, THEN TAKE THREE STEPS FORWARD.

עֹשֶׂה שָׁלוֹם בִּמְרוֹמָיו, הוּא יַעֲשֶׂה שָׁלוֹם עָלֵינוּ, וְעַל כָּל

‹ all ‹ and upon ‹ upon us ‹ peace ‹ make ‹ may He « in His heights, ‹ peace ‹ He Who makes

יִשְׂרָאֵל. וְאִמְרוּ: אָמֵן. (Cong. — אָמֵן.)

« (Amen.) « Amen. ‹ Now respond: « Israel.

(1) In *Eretz Yisrael* add קַדִּישָׁא, *holy.*

INTRODUCTORY PSALM TO PESUKEI D'ZIMRAH

Psalm 30 / תהלים ל

מִזְמוֹר שִׁיר חֲנֻכַּת הַבַּיִת לְדָוִד. אֲרוֹמִמְךָ

A psalm, ‹ a song ‹ for the inauguration ‹ of the Temple, ‹ by David. « I will exalt You, ‹

יהוה כִּי דִלִּיתָנִי, וְלֹא שִׂמַּחְתָּ אֹיְבַי לִי. יהוה

HASHEM, ‹ for ‹ You have drawn me up, ‹ and not ‹ let my foes rejoice ‹ over me. « HASHEM, ‹

אֱלֹהָי, שִׁוַּעְתִּי אֵלֶיךָ וַתִּרְפָּאֵנִי. יהוה הֶעֱלִיתָ מִן

my God, ‹ I cried out ‹ to You ‹ and You healed me. « HASHEM, ‹ You have raised up ‹ from ‹

שְׁאוֹל נַפְשִׁי, חִיִּיתַנִי מִיָּרְדִי בוֹר. זַמְּרוּ לַיהוה

the lower world ‹ my soul; « You have preserved me ‹ from my descent ‹ to the grave. « Sing ‹ to HASHEM, ‹

חֲסִידָיו, וְהוֹדוּ לְזֵכֶר קָדְשׁוֹ. כִּי רֶגַע בְּאַפּוֹ, חַיִּים

His devout ones, ‹ and give thanks ‹ to His Holy Name. « For ‹ but a moment ‹ His anger endures; « life ‹

בִּרְצוֹנוֹ, בָּעֶרֶב יָלִין בֶּכִי וְלַבֹּקֶר רִנָּה. וַאֲנִי

results from His favor. « In the evening ‹ one lies down ‹ weeping, ‹ but with dawn « — a cry of joy! « I ‹

אָמַרְתִּי בְשַׁלְוִי, בַּל אֶמּוֹט לְעוֹלָם. יהוה בִּרְצוֹנְךָ

had said ‹ in my serenity, « *I would not falter,* ‹ *ever.* « But, HASHEM, ‹ [it is only] through Your favor ‹

הֶעֱמַדְתָּה לְהַרְרִי עֹז, הִסְתַּרְתָּ פָנֶיךָ הָיִיתִי נִבְהָל.

that You supported ‹ my greatness ‹ to be mighty; « when You concealed ‹ Your face, ‹ I was ‹ confounded. «

אֵלֶיךָ יהוה אֶקְרָא, וְאֶל אֲדֹנָי אֶתְחַנָּן. מַה בֶּצַע

To You, ‹ HASHEM, ‹ I would call ‹ and to ‹ the Lord ‹ I would appeal. « What ‹ gain is there ‹

בְּדָמִי, בְּרִדְתִּי אֶל שָׁחַת, הֲיוֹדְךָ עָפָר, הֲיַגִּיד

in my death, ‹ in my descent ‹ to ‹ the Pit? « Will the dust acknowledge You? « Will it declare ‹

אֲמִתֶּךָ. שְׁמַע יהוה וְחָנֵּנִי, יהוה הֱיֵה עֹזֵר לִי.

Your truth? « Hear, ‹ O HASHEM, ‹ and favor me; « HASHEM, ‹ be ‹ my Helper! «

הָפַכְתָּ מִסְפְּדִי לְמָחוֹל לִי, פִּתַּחְתָּ שַׂקִּי, וַתְּאַזְּרֵנִי

‹ and You girded me ‹ my sack-cloth ‹ You undid « for me, ‹ into dancing ‹ my lament ‹ You have transformed

שִׂמְחָה. לְמַעַן יְזַמֶּרְךָ כָבוֹד וְלֹא יִדֹּם, יהוה אֱלֹהַי

‹ my God, ‹ HASHEM « be silenced, ‹ and not ‹ [might] my soul ‹ sing to you ‹ So that « with gladness.

לְעוֹלָם אוֹדֶךָּ.

« will I thank You. ‹ forever

MOURNER'S KADDISH / קדיש יתום

IN THE PRESENCE OF A *MINYAN,* MOURNERS RECITE קַדִּישׁ יָתוֹם, THE MOURNER'S *KADDISH* (SEE *LAWS* §132-134). [A TRANSLITERATION OF THIS *KADDISH* APPEARS ON PAGE 647.]

יִתְגַּדַּל וְיִתְקַדַּשׁ שְׁמֵהּ רַבָּא. (Cong. — אָמֵן.) בְּעָלְמָא דִּי

‹ that ‹ in the world ‹ (Amen.) « that is great! — ‹ may His Name ‹ and be sanctified ‹ Grow exalted

בְּרָא כִרְעוּתֵהּ. וְיַמְלִיךְ מַלְכוּתֵהּ, בְּחַיֵּיכוֹן וּבְיוֹמֵיכוֹן וּבְחַיֵּי

‹ and in the lifetimes ‹ and in your days, ‹ in your lifetimes « to His kingship, ‹ and may He give reign « according to His will, « He created

דְכָל בֵּית יִשְׂרָאֵל, בַּעֲגָלָא וּבִזְמַן קָרִיב. וְאִמְרוּ: אָמֵן.

« Amen. ‹ Now respond: « that comes soon. ‹ and at a time ‹ swiftly « of Israel, ‹ Family ‹ of the entire

CONGREGATION RESPONDS:

אָמֵן. יְהֵא שְׁמֵהּ רַבָּא מְבָרַךְ לְעָלַם וּלְעָלְמֵי עָלְמַיָּא.

« and for all eternity. ‹ forever ‹ be blessed ‹ that is great ‹ His Name ‹ May « Amen.

MOURNER CONTINUES:

יְהֵא שְׁמֵהּ רַבָּא מְבָרַךְ לְעָלַם וּלְעָלְמֵי עָלְמַיָּא. יִתְבָּרַךְ

‹ Blessed, « and for all eternity. ‹ forever ‹ be blessed ‹ that is great ‹ His Name ‹ May

וְיִשְׁתַּבַּח וְיִתְפָּאַר וְיִתְרוֹמַם וְיִתְנַשֵּׂא וְיִתְהַדָּר וְיִתְעַלֶּה

‹ elevated, ‹ honored, ‹ upraised, ‹ exalted, ‹ glorified, ‹ praised,

וְיִתְהַלָּל שְׁמֵהּ דְּקֻדְשָׁא בְּרִיךְ הוּא (Cong. — בְּרִיךְ הוּא) —

« is He) ‹ (Blessed « is He ‹ Blessed ‹ of the Holy One, ‹ be the Name ‹ and lauded

לְעֵלָּא מִן כָּל בִּרְכָתָא וְשִׁירָתָא תֻּשְׁבְּחָתָא וְנֶחֱמָתָא

‹ and consolation ‹ praise « and song, ‹ blessing ‹ any ‹ beyond

דַּאֲמִירָן בְּעָלְמָא. וְאִמְרוּ: אָמֵן. (Cong. — אָמֵן.)

that are uttered 〈 in the world. 《 Now respond: 〈 Amen. 《 (Amen.) 《

יְהֵא שְׁלָמָא רַבָּא מִן שְׁמַיָּא, וְחַיִּים עָלֵינוּ וְעַל כָּל

May there be 〈 peace 〈 that is abundant 〈 from 〈 Heaven, 《 and life, 《 upon us 〈 and upon 〈 all 〈

יִשְׂרָאֵל. וְאִמְרוּ: אָמֵן. (Cong. — אָמֵן.)

Israel. 《 Now respond: 〈 Amen. 《 (Amen.) 〈

BOW; TAKE THREE STEPS BACK. BOW LEFT AND SAY ... עֹשֶׂה שָׁלוֹם, *"HE WHO MAKES PEACE ..."*; BOW RIGHT AND SAY ... הוּא, *"MAY HE ..."*; BOW FORWARD AND SAY ... וְעַל כָּל יִשְׂרָאֵל, *"AND UPON ALL ISRAEL ..."*; REMAIN IN PLACE FOR A FEW MOMENTS, THEN TAKE THREE STEPS FORWARD.

עֹשֶׂה שָׁלוֹם בִּמְרוֹמָיו, הוּא יַעֲשֶׂה שָׁלוֹם עָלֵינוּ, וְעַל כָּל

He Who makes 〈 peace 〈 in His heights, 《 may He 〈 make 〈 peace 〈 upon us, 〈 and upon 〈 all 〈

יִשְׂרָאֵל. וְאִמְרוּ: אָמֵן. (Cong. — אָמֵן.)

Israel. 《 Now respond: 〈 Amen. 《 (Amen.) 〈

Permitted Responses During *Pesukei D'Zimrah*

From this point until after *Shemoneh Esrei* conversation is forbidden. During *Pesukei D'Zimrah* [from בָּרוּךְ שֶׁאָמַר until יִשְׁתַּבַּח, p. 160] certain congregational and individual responses [e.g., בָּרוּךְ הוּא וּבָרוּךְ שְׁמוֹ] are omitted. The following responses, however, should be made: אָמֵן, *Amen,* after any blessing; *Kaddish; Borchu; Kedushah;* and the Rabbis' *Modim.* Additionally, one should join the congregation in reciting the first verse of the *Shema,* and may recite the אֲשֶׁר יָצַר blessing if he had to relieve himself during *Pesukei D'Zimrah.*

If one is in the middle of *Pesukei D'Zimrah* and the congregation has already reached the Torah reading, it is preferable that he not be called to the Torah. However, if (a) one is the only *Kohen* or Levite present, or (b) the *gabbai* inadvertently called him to the Torah, then he may recite the blessings and even read the portion softly along with the Torah reader.

If after beginning *Pesukei D'Zimrah* one realizes that he has forgotten to recite the morning Blessings of the Torah (p. 101), he should pause to recite them and their accompanying verses. Likewise, if he fears that he will not reach the *Shema* before the prescribed time (see *Laws* §109), he should recite all three paragraphs of *Shema.*

In all cases of permitted responses it is preferable to respond between psalms, whenever possible. Thus, for example, if one realizes that the congregation is approaching *Kedushah,* he should not begin a new psalm, but should wait for the congregation to recite *Kedushah,* then continue his prayers.

The responses permitted above do not apply during the final blessings of בָּרוּךְ שֶׁאָמַר [בָּרוּךְ אַתָּה ה' מֶלֶךְ מְהֻלָּל בַּתִּשְׁבָּחוֹת] and יִשְׁתַּבַּח [from the words בָּרוּךְ אַתָּה ה', *Blessed are You,* HASHEM, until the blessing's conclusion] where no interruptions are permitted.

PESUKEI D'ZIMRAH / פסוקי דזמרה

(SOME RECITE THIS SHORT KABBALISTIC DECLARATION OF INTENT BEFORE BEGINNING *PESUKEI D'ZIMRAH*:)

הֲרֵינִי מְזַמֵּן אֶת פִּי לְהוֹדוֹת וּלְהַלֵּל וּלְשַׁבֵּחַ אֶת בּוֹרְאִי.

« my Creator. ‹ and to praise ‹ to laud, ‹ to thank, ‹ my mouth ‹ prepare ‹ I now

לְשֵׁם יִחוּד קֻדְשָׁא בְּרִיךְ הוּא וּשְׁכִינְתֵּיהּ עַל יְדֵי הַהוּא

‹ Him ‹ through ‹ and His Presence, « is He, ‹ Blessed « of the Holy One, ‹ of the unification ‹ For the sake

טָמִיר וְנֶעְלָם, בְּשֵׁם כָּל יִשְׂרָאֵל.

« Israel. ‹ of all ‹— [I pray] in the name « and Who is inscrutable ‹ Who is hidden

PESUKEI D'ZIMRAH BEGINS WITH THE RECITAL OF בָּרוּךְ שֶׁאָמַר, *BLESSED IS HE WHO SPOKE ...*, WHICH IS RECITED WHILE STANDING. THE *TZITZIS* ARE NOT HELD DURING ITS RECITATION, AND ARE NOT KISSED AT ITS CONCLUSION.

בָּרוּךְ שֶׁאָמַר וְהָיָה הָעוֹלָם, בָּרוּךְ הוּא. בָּרוּךְ

‹ Blessed « is He. ‹ — blessed ‹ and the world came into being ‹ He Who spoke, ‹ Blessed is

עֹשֶׂה בְרֵאשִׁית, בָּרוּךְ אוֹמֵר וְעֹשֶׂה, בָּרוּךְ גּוֹזֵר

‹ is He Who decrees ‹ blessed « and Who does; ‹ is He Who speaks ‹ blessed « Creation; ‹ is He Who maintains

וּמְקַיֵּם, בָּרוּךְ מְרַחֵם עַל הָאָרֶץ, בָּרוּךְ מְרַחֵם עַל

‹ on ‹ is He Who has mercy ‹ blessed « the earth; ‹ on ‹ is He Who has mercy ‹ blessed « and Who Fulfills;

הַבְּרִיּוֹת, בָּרוּךְ מְשַׁלֵּם שָׂכָר טוֹב לִירֵאָיו, בָּרוּךְ

‹ blessed « to those who fear Him; ‹ that is good ‹ a reward ‹ is He Who gives ‹ blessed « the creatures;

חַי לָעַד וְקַיָּם לָנֶצַח, בָּרוּךְ פּוֹדֶה וּמַצִּיל,

« and Who rescues ‹ is He Who redeems ‹ blessed « to eternity; ‹ and Who endures ‹ forever ‹ is He Who lives

בָּרוּךְ שְׁמוֹ. בָּרוּךְ אַתָּה יהוה אֱלֹהֵינוּ מֶלֶךְ הָעוֹלָם,

« of the universe, ‹ King ‹ our God, ‹ HASHEM, ‹ are You, ‹ Blessed « is His Name! ‹— blessed

הָאֵל הָאָב הָרַחֲמָן הַמְּהֻלָּל בְּפֶה עַמּוֹ, מְשֻׁבָּח

‹ praised « of His people, ‹ by the mouth ‹ Who is lauded « Who is merciful, ‹ the Father ‹ the God,

וּמְפֹאָר בִּלְשׁוֹן חֲסִידָיו וַעֲבָדָיו. וּבְשִׁירֵי דָוִד עַבְדֶּךָ

and glorified / by the tongue / of His devout ones / and His servants. / And through the psalms / of David / Your servant

נְהַלֶּלְךָ יהוה אֱלֹהֵינוּ, בִּשְׁבָחוֹת וּבִזְמִרוֹת. נְגַדֶּלְךָ

we shall laud You, / HASHEM, / our God, / with praises / and songs, / we shall exalt You,

וּנְשַׁבֵּחֲךָ וּנְפָאֶרְךָ וְנַזְכִּיר שִׁמְךָ וְנַמְלִיכְךָ, מַלְכֵּנוּ

praise You, / glorify You, / mention / Your Name, / and proclaim Your reign, / our King,

אֱלֹהֵינוּ. ❖ יָחִיד, חֵי הָעוֹלָמִים, מֶלֶךְ מְשֻׁבָּח וּמְפֹאָר

our God. / O Unique One, / Life-giver / of the worlds, / King, / [that] praised / and glorified

עֲדֵי עַד שְׁמוֹ הַגָּדוֹל. בָּרוּךְ אַתָּה יהוה, מֶלֶךְ

eternally / is His Name, / that is great. / Blessed / are You, / HASHEM, / the King

מְהֻלָּל בַּתִּשְׁבָּחוֹת. (.אָמֵן – Cong.)

Who is lauded / with praises. / (Amen.)

I Chronicles 16:8-36 / דברי הימים א טז:ח-לו

הוֹדוּ לַיהוה קִרְאוּ בִשְׁמוֹ, הוֹדִיעוּ בָעַמִּים

Give thanks / to HASHEM, / declare / His Name, / make known / among the peoples

עֲלִילֹתָיו. שִׁירוּ לוֹ, זַמְּרוּ לוֹ, שִׂיחוּ בְּכָל

His actions. / Sing / to Him, / make music / to Him, / speak / of all

נִפְלְאֹתָיו. הִתְהַלְלוּ בְּשֵׁם קָדְשׁוֹ, יִשְׂמַח לֵב

His wonders. / Glory / in the Name, / of His Holiness, / glad will be / the heart

מְבַקְשֵׁי יהוה. דִּרְשׁוּ יהוה וְעֻזּוֹ, בַּקְּשׁוּ פָנָיו

of those who seek / HASHEM. / Search out / HASHEM / and His might, / seek / His Presence

תָּמִיד. זִכְרוּ נִפְלְאֹתָיו אֲשֶׁר עָשָׂה, מֹפְתָיו

always. / Remember / His wonders / that / He performed, / His marvels

וּמִשְׁפְּטֵי פִיהוּ. זֶרַע יִשְׂרָאֵל עַבְדּוֹ, בְּנֵי יַעֲקֹב

and the judgments / of His mouth. / O seed / of Israel, / His servant, / O children / of Jacob,

בְּחִירָיו. הוּא יהוה אֱלֹהֵינוּ, בְּכָל הָאָרֶץ

‹ the earth ‹ over all « our God, ‹ HASHEM, ‹ He is « His chosen ones.

מִשְׁפָּטָיו. זִכְרוּ לְעוֹלָם בְּרִיתוֹ, דָּבָר צִוָּה לְאֶלֶף

‹ for a thousand ‹ He commanded ‹ — the Word « His covenant ‹ forever ‹ Remember « are His judgments.

דּוֹר. אֲשֶׁר כָּרַת אֶת אַבְרָהָם, וּשְׁבוּעָתוֹ לְיִצְחָק.

« to Isaac. ‹ and His oath « with Abraham ‹ He made ‹ — that « generations

וַיַּעֲמִידֶהָ לְיַעֲקֹב לְחֹק, לְיִשְׂרָאֵל בְּרִית עוֹלָם.

« everlasting, ‹ as a covenant ‹ for Israel « as a statute, ‹ for Jacob ‹ Then He established it

לֵאמֹר, לְךָ אֶתֵּן אֶרֶץ כְּנָעַן, חֶבֶל נַחֲלַתְכֶם.

« *of your inheritance.* ‹ *the lot* ‹ *of Canaan,* ‹ *the Land* ‹ *I shall give* ‹ *To you* ‹ saying,

בִּהְיוֹתְכֶם מְתֵי מִסְפָּר, כִּמְעַט וְגָרִים בָּהּ. וַיִּתְהַלְּכוּ

‹ and they wandered « there; ‹ dwelling ‹ hardly « in number, ‹ but few ‹ When you were

מִגּוֹי אֶל גּוֹי, וּמִמַּמְלָכָה אֶל עַם אַחֵר. לֹא הִנִּיחַ

‹ — He did not allow « another people. ‹ to ‹ from one kingdom ‹ nation, ‹ to ‹ from nation

לְאִישׁ לְעָשְׁקָם, וַיּוֹכַח עֲלֵיהֶם מְלָכִים. אַל תִּגְּעוּ

‹ *Dare not touch* « kings: ‹ for their sake ‹ and He rebuked « to rob them, ‹ any man

בִּמְשִׁיחָי, וּבִנְבִיאַי אַל תָּרֵעוּ. שִׁירוּ לַיהוה כָּל

‹ every-one ‹ to HASHEM, ‹ Sing « *harm.* ‹ *do no* ‹ *and to My prophets* ‹ *My anointed ones,*

הָאָרֶץ, בַּשְּׂרוּ מִיּוֹם אֶל יוֹם יְשׁוּעָתוֹ. סַפְּרוּ בַגּוֹיִם

‹ among the nations ‹ Relate « His salvation. ‹ day ‹ to ‹ from day ‹ announce « on earth,

אֶת כְּבוֹדוֹ, בְּכָל הָעַמִּים נִפְלְאוֹתָיו. כִּי גָדוֹל

‹ great ‹ That « His wonders: ‹ peoples ‹ among all « His glory,

יהוה וּמְהֻלָּל מְאֹד, וְנוֹרָא הוּא עַל כָּל אֱלֹהִים.

« powers. ‹ all ‹ above ‹ is He ‹ and awesome « exceedingly, ‹ and lauded ‹ is HASHEM

❖ כִּי כָּל אֱלֹהֵי הָעַמִּים אֱלִילִים, (PAUSE) וַיהוה שָׁמַיִם

‹ heaven ‹ — but HASHEM « are worthless ‹ of the peoples ‹ the gods ‹ all ‹ For

עָשָׂה. הוֹד וְהָדָר לְפָנָיו, עֹז וְחֶדְוָה בִּמְקֹמוֹ.

« are in His place. ‹ and delight ‹ might « are before Him, ‹ and majesty ‹ Glory « did make!

הָבוּ לַיהוה מִשְׁפְּחוֹת עַמִּים, הָבוּ לַיהוה כָּבוֹד

‹ honor ‹ unto HASHEM ‹ render « of the peoples, ‹ O families ‹ unto HASHEM, ‹ Render

וָעֹז. הָבוּ לַיהוה כְּבוֹד שְׁמוֹ, שְׂאוּ מִנְחָה וּבֹאוּ

‹ and come ‹ an offering ‹ raise up « [worthy of] His Name, ‹ honor ‹ to HASHEM ‹ Render « and might.

לְפָנָיו, הִשְׁתַּחֲווּ לַיהוה בְּהַדְרַת קֹדֶשׁ. חִילוּ

‹ Tremble « of His holy place. ‹ in the beauty ‹ before HASHEM ‹ bow down « before Him;

מִלְּפָנָיו כָּל הָאָרֶץ, אַף תִּכּוֹן תֵּבֵל בַּל תִּמּוֹט.

« topple. ‹ so that it cannot ‹ is the world ‹ firmly established ‹ indeed, « on earth, ‹ every-one ‹ before Him,

יִשְׂמְחוּ הַשָּׁמַיִם וְתָגֵל הָאָרֶץ, וְיֹאמְרוּ בַגּוֹיִם,

‹ among the nations, ‹ and they will say ‹ the earth ‹ and rejoice will ‹ the heavens ‹ Glad will be

יהוה מָלָךְ. יִרְעַם הַיָּם וּמְלוֹאוֹ, יַעֲלֹץ הַשָּׂדֶה

‹ the field ‹ exult will « and its fullness; ‹ the sea ‹ Roar will « *has reigned!* ‹ *HASHEM*

וְכָל אֲשֶׁר בּוֹ. אָז יְרַנְּנוּ עֲצֵי הַיָּעַר, מִלִּפְנֵי

‹ before « of the forest ‹ the trees ‹ sing joyously will ‹ Then « in it. ‹ that is ‹ and everything

יהוה, כִּי בָא לִשְׁפּוֹט אֶת הָאָרֶץ. הוֹדוּ לַיהוה

‹ to HASHEM, ‹ Give thanks « the earth. ‹ to judge ‹ He will have arrived ‹ for ‹ HASHEM,

כִּי טוֹב, כִּי לְעוֹלָם חַסְדּוֹ. וְאִמְרוּ הוֹשִׁיעֵנוּ אֱלֹהֵי

‹ *O God* ‹ *Save us,* ‹ And say, « is His kindness! ‹ forever enduring ‹ for « He is good, ‹ for

יִשְׁעֵנוּ, וְקַבְּצֵנוּ וְהַצִּילֵנוּ מִן הַגּוֹיִם, לְהוֹדוֹת לְשֵׁם

‹ *the Name* ‹ *to thank* « *among the nations,* ‹ *from* ‹ *and rescue us* ‹ *and gather us* « *of our salvation,*

קָדְשֶׁךָ, לְהִשְׁתַּבֵּחַ בִּתְהִלָּתֶךָ. בָּרוּךְ יהוה אֱלֹהֵי

‹ the God ‹ is HASHEM, ‹ Blessed « *in Your praise!* ‹ *and to glory* ‹ *of Your Holiness,*

יִשְׂרָאֵל מִן הָעוֹלָם וְעַד הָעֹלָם, וַיֹּאמְרוּ כָל הָעָם,

‹ the people — ‹ — all ‹ and let them say ‹ the World [to Come] ‹ to ‹ [This] World ‹ from ‹ of Israel,

אָמֵן, וְהַלֵּל לַיהוה. ❖ רוֹמְמוּ יהוה אֱלֹהֵינוּ וְהִשְׁתַּחֲווּ

‹ and bow down ‹ our God, ‹ HASHEM, ‹ Exalt « *to HASHEM!* ‹ *and praise* ‹ *Amen*

לַהֲדֹם רַגְלָיו, קָדוֹשׁ הוּא.[1] רוֹמְמוּ יהוה אֱלֹהֵינוּ

‹ our God, ‹ HASHEM, ‹ Exalt « is He! ‹ holy « at His footstool;

וְהִשְׁתַּחֲווּ לְהַר קָדְשׁוֹ, כִּי קָדוֹשׁ יהוה אֱלֹהֵינוּ.[2]

« our God. ‹ is HASHEM, ‹ holy ‹ for « of His Holiness; ‹ at the Mount ‹ and bow down

וְהוּא רַחוּם יְכַפֵּר עָוֹן וְלֹא יַשְׁחִית, וְהִרְבָּה

‹ frequently, « destroy; ‹ and does not ‹ of iniquity ‹ is forgiving ‹ the Merciful One, ‹ Nevertheless He,

לְהָשִׁיב אַפּוֹ, וְלֹא יָעִיר כָּל חֲמָתוֹ.[3] אַתָּה יהוה,

‹ HASHEM, ‹ You, « His entire wrath. ‹ arousing ‹ not « His anger, ‹ He withdraws

לֹא תִכְלָא רַחֲמֶיךָ מִמֶּנִּי, חַסְדְּךָ וַאֲמִתְּךָ תָּמִיד

‹ always ‹ and Your truth ‹ may Your kindness « from me; ‹ Your mercy ‹ withhold ‹ do not

יִצְּרוּנִי.[4] זְכֹר רַחֲמֶיךָ יהוה, וַחֲסָדֶיךָ, כִּי מֵעוֹלָם

‹ eternal ‹ for ‹ and Your kindnesses, ‹ HASHEM, ‹ Your mercies, ‹ Remember « protect me.

הֵמָּה.[5] תְּנוּ עֹז לֵאלֹהִים, עַל יִשְׂרָאֵל גַּאֲוָתוֹ,

« is His grandeur ‹ Israel ‹ upon « to God; ‹ [invincible] might ‹ Acknowledge « are they.

וְעֻזּוֹ בַּשְּׁחָקִים. נוֹרָא אֱלֹהִים מִמִּקְדָּשֶׁיךָ, אֵל

‹ God « from Your Sanctuaries; ‹ O God, ‹ You are awesome, « is in the skies. ‹ — as His might

יִשְׂרָאֵל הוּא נֹתֵן עֹז וְתַעֲצֻמוֹת לָעָם, בָּרוּךְ

‹ blessed « to the people; ‹ and power ‹ might ‹ Who grants ‹ — it is He « of Israel

(1) *Psalms* 99:5. (2) 99:9. (3) 78:38. (4) 40:12. (5) 25:6.

אֱלֹהִים.[1] אֵל נְקָמוֹת יהוה, אֵל נְקָמוֹת הוֹפִיעַ.

« appear! ‹ of vengeance, ‹ O God « HASHEM; ‹ of vengeance, ‹ O God « is God.

הִנָּשֵׂא שֹׁפֵט הָאָרֶץ, הָשֵׁב גְּמוּל עַל גֵּאִים.[2]

«the haughty. ‹ to ‹ retribution ‹ render « of the earth, ‹ O Judge ‹ Arise,

לַיהוה הַיְשׁוּעָה, עַל עַמְּךָ בִרְכָתֶךָ סֶּלָה.[3]

« Selah. « is Your blessing, ‹ Your people ‹ upon « is Salvation, ‹ To HASHEM

❖ יהוה צְבָאוֹת עִמָּנוּ, מִשְׂגָּב לָנוּ אֱלֹהֵי יַעֲקֹב

«of Jacob, ‹ is the God ‹ for us ‹ a stronghold « is with us, ‹ Master of Legions, ‹ HASHEM,

סֶלָה.[4] יהוה צְבָאוֹת, אַשְׁרֵי אָדָם בֹּטֵחַ בָּךְ.[5]

« in You. ‹ who trusts ‹ is the man ‹ praiseworthy ‹ Master of Legions, ‹ HASHEM, « Selah.

יהוה הוֹשִׁיעָה, הַמֶּלֶךְ יַעֲנֵנוּ בְיוֹם קָרְאֵנוּ.[6]

« we call. ‹ on the day ‹ answer us ‹ May the King « save! ‹ HASHEM,

הוֹשִׁיעָה אֶת עַמֶּךָ, וּבָרֵךְ אֶת נַחֲלָתֶךָ, וּרְעֵם

‹tend them « Your inheritance; ‹ and bless ‹ Your nation, ‹ Save

וְנַשְּׂאֵם עַד הָעוֹלָם.[7] נַפְשֵׁנוּ חִכְּתָה לַיהוה, עֶזְרֵנוּ

‹ our help « for HASHEM; ‹ longed ‹ Our soul « forever. ‹ and raise them up

וּמָגִנֵּנוּ הוּא. כִּי בוֹ יִשְׂמַח לִבֵּנוּ, כִּי בְשֵׁם קָדְשׁוֹ

‹ of His Holiness ‹ in the Name ‹ for « our hearts; ‹ will be gladdened ‹ in Him ‹ For « is He. ‹ and our shield

בָטָחְנוּ. יְהִי חַסְדְּךָ יהוה עָלֵינוּ, כַּאֲשֶׁר יִחַלְנוּ

‹ we awaited ‹ just as « be upon us, ‹ HASHEM, ‹ Your kindness, ‹ May « we trusted.

לָךְ.[8] הַרְאֵנוּ יהוה חַסְדֶּךָ, וְיֶשְׁעֲךָ תִּתֶּן לָנוּ.[9]

« us. ‹ grant ‹ and Your salvation « Your kindness, ‹ HASHEM, ‹ Show us, « You.

קוּמָה עֶזְרָתָה לָנוּ, וּפְדֵנוּ לְמַעַן חַסְדֶּךָ.[10] אָנֹכִי

‹ I am « of Your kindness! ‹ for the sake ‹ And redeem us « us! ‹ Assist ‹ Arise!

---

(1) *Psalms* 68:35-36. (2) 94:1-2. (3) 3:9. (4) 46:8. (5) 84:13.
(6) 20:10. (7) 28:9. (8) 33:20-22. (9) 85:8. (10) 44:27.

יהוה אֱלֹהֶיךָ הַמַּעַלְךָ מֵאֶרֶץ מִצְרָיִם, הַרְחֶב

‹ Open wide « of Egypt. ‹ from the land ‹ Who raised you ‹ your God, ‹ HASHEM,

פִּיךָ וַאֲמַלְאֵהוּ.[1] אַשְׁרֵי הָעָם שֶׁכָּכָה לּוֹ, אַשְׁרֵי

‹ praiseworthy « is their lot; ‹ that such ‹ is the people ‹ Praiseworthy « and I will fill it. ‹ your mouth

הָעָם שֶׁיהוה אֱלֹהָיו.[2] ❖ וַאֲנִי בְּחַסְדְּךָ בָטַחְתִּי, יָגֵל

‹ exult will « I trust; ‹ in Your kindness ‹ But as for me, « is their God. ‹ that HASHEM ‹ is the people

לִבִּי בִּישׁוּעָתֶךָ, אָשִׁירָה לַיהוה, כִּי גָמַל עָלָי.[3]

« with me. ‹ He has dealt kindly ‹ for « to HASHEM, ‹ I will sing « in Your salvation. ‹ my heart

מִזְמוֹר לְתוֹדָה, *A PSALM OF THANKGIVING,* IS RECITED WHILE STANDING.

Psalm 100 / תהלים ק

מִזְמוֹר לְתוֹדָה, הָרִיעוּ לַיהוה כָּל הָאָרֶץ.

« the earth. ‹ all ‹ to HASHEM, ‹ call out « of thanksgiving, ‹ A psalm

עִבְדוּ אֶת יהוה בְּשִׂמְחָה, בֹּאוּ לְפָנָיו בִּרְנָנָה.

« with joyous song. ‹ before Him ‹ come « with gladness, ‹ HASHEM ‹ Serve

דְּעוּ כִּי יהוה הוּא אֱלֹהִים, הוּא עָשָׂנוּ, וְלוֹ

‹ and His ‹ made us ‹ He « is God; ‹ He ‹ HASHEM, ‹ that ‹ Know

אֲנַחְנוּ, עַמּוֹ וְצֹאן מַרְעִיתוֹ. בֹּאוּ שְׁעָרָיו בְּתוֹדָה,

« with thanksgiving, ‹ His gates ‹ Enter « of His pasture. ‹ and the sheep ‹ His people « are we,

חֲצֵרֹתָיו בִּתְהִלָּה, הוֹדוּ לוֹ, בָּרְכוּ שְׁמוֹ. ❖ כִּי טוֹב

‹ good ‹ For « His Name. ‹ bless ‹ to Him, ‹ give thanks « with praise; ‹ His courtyards

יהוה, לְעוֹלָם חַסְדּוֹ, וְעַד דֹּר וָדֹר אֱמוּנָתוֹ.

« is His faithfulness. ‹ to generation ‹ generation ‹ and from « His kindness, ‹ forever endures « is HASHEM,

THE FOLLOWING PRAYER SHOULD BE RECITED WITH SPECIAL INTENSITY.

יְהִי כְבוֹד יהוה לְעוֹלָם, יִשְׂמַח יהוה בְּמַעֲשָׂיו.[4]

« in His works. ‹ let HASHEM rejoice « endure forever, ‹ of HASHEM ‹ the glory ‹ May

(1) *Psalms* 81:11. (2) 144:15. (3) 13:6. (4) 104:31.

יְהִי שֵׁם יהוה מְבֹרָךְ, מֵעַתָּה וְעַד עוֹלָם. מִמִּזְרַח

Let Name ‹ the HASHEM ‹ of ‹ be blessed « this time from ‹ until ‹ eternity. « the rising From ‹

שֶׁמֶשׁ עַד מְבוֹאוֹ, מְהֻלָּל שֵׁם יהוה. רָם עַל

of the sun ‹ to ‹ its setting, « praised ‹ is the Name ‹ of HASHEM. « High ‹ above ‹

כָּל גּוֹיִם יהוה, עַל הַשָּׁמַיִם כְּבוֹדוֹ.[1] יהוה שִׁמְךָ

all ‹ nations ‹ is HASHEM, « above ‹ the heavens ‹ is His glory. « HASHEM, ‹ Your Name is ‹

לְעוֹלָם, יהוה זִכְרְךָ לְדֹר וָדֹר.[2] יהוה בַּשָּׁמַיִם

forever, « HASHEM, ‹ Your memorial is ‹ from generation ‹ to generation. « HASHEM ‹ in heaven ‹

הֵכִין כִּסְאוֹ, וּמַלְכוּתוֹ בַּכֹּל מָשָׁלָה.[3] יִשְׂמְחוּ

has established ‹ His throne « and His kingdom ‹ over all ‹ does reign. « Glad will be ‹

הַשָּׁמַיִם וְתָגֵל הָאָרֶץ, וְיֹאמְרוּ בַגּוֹיִם יהוה מָלָךְ.[4]

the heavens ‹ and rejoice will ‹ the earth, « and they will proclaim ‹ among the nations, ‹ HASHEM ‹ *has reigned!* «

יהוה מֶלֶךְ,[5] יהוה מָלָךְ,[6] יהוה יִמְלֹךְ לְעֹלָם וָעֶד.[7]

HASHEM ‹ reigns, « HASHEM ‹ has reigned, « HASHEM ‹ shall reign ‹ for ever ‹ and ever. «

יהוה מֶלֶךְ עוֹלָם וָעֶד, אָבְדוּ גוֹיִם מֵאַרְצוֹ.[8] יהוה

HASHEM ‹ is King ‹ for ever ‹ and ever, « [then] the nations will have vanished ‹ from His earth. « HASHEM ‹

הֵפִיר עֲצַת גּוֹיִם, הֵנִיא מַחְשְׁבוֹת עַמִּים.[9] רַבּוֹת

annuls ‹ the counsel ‹ of nations; « He thwarts ‹ the designs ‹ of peoples. « Many ‹

מַחֲשָׁבוֹת בְּלֶב אִישׁ, וַעֲצַת יהוה הִיא תָקוּם.[10] עֲצַת

are the designs ‹ that are in the heart ‹ of man, « but the counsel ‹ of HASHEM « – only it ‹ will prevail. « The counsel ‹

יהוה לְעוֹלָם תַּעֲמֹד, מַחְשְׁבוֹת לִבּוֹ לְדֹר וָדֹר.[11]

of HASHEM ‹ forever ‹ will endure, « the designs ‹ of His heart ‹ from generation ‹ to generation. «

---

(1) *Psalms* 113:2-4. (2) 135:13. (3) 103:19. (4) *I Chronicles* 16:31. (5) *Psalms* 10:16. (6) 93:1 et al. (7) *Exodus* 15:18. (8) *Psalms* 10:16. (9) 33:10. (10) *Proverbs* 19:21. (11) *Psalms* 33:11.

כִּי הוּא אָמַר וַיֶּהִי, הוּא צִוָּה וַיַּעֲמֹד.[1] כִּי בָחַר יהוה

‹ HASHEM has chosen ‹ For « and it endured. ‹ commanded ‹ He « and it came to be; ‹ spoke ‹ He ‹ For

בְּצִיּוֹן, אִוָּהּ לְמוֹשָׁב לוֹ.[2] כִּי יַעֲקֹב בָּחַר לוֹ יָהּ,

« by God, ‹ for His own ‹ was selected ‹ Jacob ‹ For « for Him. ‹ for a habitation ‹ He has desired it « Zion;

יִשְׂרָאֵל לִסְגֻלָּתוֹ.[3] כִּי לֹא יִטֹּשׁ יהוה עַמּוֹ, וְנַחֲלָתוֹ

‹ and His heritage « His people, ‹ will HASHEM ‹ forsake not ‹ Because « as His treasure. ‹ Israel

לֹא יַעֲזֹב.[4] ❖ וְהוּא רַחוּם יְכַפֵּר עָוֹן וְלֹא

‹ and does not ‹ of iniquity ‹ is forgiving ‹ the Merciful One, ‹ Nevertheless, He, « He will not abandon.

יַשְׁחִית, וְהִרְבָּה לְהָשִׁיב אַפּוֹ, וְלֹא יָעִיר כָּל

‹ all ‹ arousing ‹ not « His anger, ‹ He withdraws ‹ frequently « destroy;

חֲמָתוֹ.[5] יהוה הוֹשִׁיעָה, הַמֶּלֶךְ יַעֲנֵנוּ בְיוֹם קָרְאֵנוּ.[6]

« we call. ‹ on the day ‹ answer us ‹ May the King « save! ‹ HASHEM, « of His wrath.

אַשְׁרֵי יוֹשְׁבֵי בֵיתֶךָ, עוֹד יְהַלְלוּךָ סֶּלָה.[7] אַשְׁרֵי

‹ Praiseworthy « Selah. ‹ they will praise You, ‹ continually « in Your house, ‹ are those who dwell ‹ Praiseworthy

הָעָם שֶׁכָּכָה לּוֹ, אַשְׁרֵי הָעָם שֶׁיהוה אֱלֹהָיו.[8]

« is their God. ‹ that HASHEM ‹ is the people ‹ praiseworthy « is their lot; ‹ that such ‹ is the people

Psalm 145 / תהלים קמה

תְּהִלָּה לְדָוִד, אֲרוֹמִמְךָ אֱלוֹהַי הַמֶּלֶךְ, וַאֲבָרְכָה

‹ and I will bless « the King, ‹ my God ‹ I will exalt You, « by David: ‹ A psalm of praise

שִׁמְךָ לְעוֹלָם וָעֶד. **בְּ**כָל יוֹם אֲבָרְכֶךָּ, וַאֲהַלְלָה

‹ and I will laud « I will bless You, ‹ day ‹ Every « and ever. ‹ for ever ‹ Your Name

שִׁמְךָ לְעוֹלָם וָעֶד. **גָּ**דוֹל יהוה וּמְהֻלָּל מְאֹד,

« exceedingly, ‹ and lauded ‹ is HASHEM ‹ Great « and ever. ‹ forever ‹ Your Name

(1) *Psalms* 33:9. (2) 132:13. (3) 135:4 (4) 94:14. (5) 78:38. (6) 20:10. (7) 84:5. (8) 144:15.

וְלִגְדֻלָּתוֹ אֵין חֵקֶר. דּוֹר לְדוֹר יְשַׁבַּח מַעֲשֶׂיךָ,

and His greatness ‹ is beyond investigation. « Generation ‹ to generation ‹ will praise ‹ Your actions, «

וּגְבוּרֹתֶיךָ יַגִּידוּ. הֲדַר כְּבוֹד הוֹדֶךָ, וְדִבְרֵי

and Your mighty deeds ‹ they will recount. « The splendrous ‹ glory ‹ of Your majesty, « and Your deeds ‹

נִפְלְאֹתֶיךָ אָשִׂיחָה. וֶעֱזוּז נוֹרְאוֹתֶיךָ יֹאמֵרוּ,

that are wondrous ‹ I shall discuss. « And of the might ‹ of Your awesome deeds ‹ they will speak, «

וּגְדוּלָּתְךָ אֲסַפְּרֶנָּה. זֵכֶר רַב טוּבְךָ יַבִּיעוּ, וְצִדְקָתְךָ

and Your greatness ‹ I shall relate. « A recollection ‹ of Your abundant goodness ‹ they will utter, « and of Your righteousness ‹

יְרַנֵּנוּ. חַנּוּן וְרַחוּם יהוה, אֶרֶךְ אַפַּיִם וּגְדָל חָסֶד.

they will sing joyfully. « Gracious ‹ and merciful ‹ is HASHEM, « slow ‹ to anger, ‹ and great ‹ in [bestowing] kindness. «

טוֹב יהוה לַכֹּל, וְרַחֲמָיו עַל כָּל מַעֲשָׂיו. יוֹדוּךָ יהוה

HASHEM is good ‹ to all; « His mercies ‹ are on ‹ all ‹ His creations. « They will thank You, ‹ HASHEM «

כָּל מַעֲשֶׂיךָ, וַחֲסִידֶיךָ יְבָרְכוּכָה. כְּבוֹד מַלְכוּתְךָ

— all ‹ Your creations, « and Your devout ones ‹ will bless You. « Of the glory ‹ of Your kingdom ‹

יֹאמֵרוּ, וּגְבוּרָתְךָ יְדַבֵּרוּ. לְהוֹדִיעַ לִבְנֵי הָאָדָם

they will speak, « and of Your power ‹ they will declare. « To inform ‹ mankind ‹

גְּבוּרֹתָיו, וּכְבוֹד הֲדַר מַלְכוּתוֹ. מַלְכוּתְךָ מַלְכוּת

of His mighty deeds, « and of the glorious ‹ splendor ‹ of His kingdom. « Your kingdom ‹ is a kingdom ‹

כָּל עֹלָמִים, וּמֶמְשַׁלְתְּךָ בְּכָל דּוֹר וָדֹר. סוֹמֵךְ יהוה

[spanning] all ‹ eternities, « and Your dominion ‹ is throughout ‹ generation ‹ after generation. « HASHEM supports ‹

לְכָל הַנֹּפְלִים, וְזוֹקֵף לְכָל הַכְּפוּפִים. עֵינֵי כֹל אֵלֶיךָ

all ‹ those who are fallen, « and straightens ‹ all ‹ those who are bent. « The eyes ‹ of all ‹ to You ‹

יְשַׂבֵּרוּ, וְאַתָּה נוֹתֵן לָהֶם אֶת אָכְלָם בְּעִתּוֹ.

do look with hope, « and You ‹ give ‹ them ‹ their food ‹ in its proper time. «

CONCENTRATE INTENTLY WHILE RECITING THE VERSE פּוֹתֵחַ, *"YOU OPEN . . ."*

פּוֹתֵחַ אֶת יָדֶךָ, וּמַשְׂבִּיעַ לְכָל חַי רָצוֹן. צַדִּיק

‹ Righteous « [with its] desire. ‹ living thing ‹ every ‹ and satisfy « Your hand, ‹ You open

יהוה בְּכָל דְּרָכָיו, וְחָסִיד בְּכָל מַעֲשָׂיו. קָרוֹב

‹ Close « His deeds. ‹ in all ‹ and magnanimous « His ways, ‹ in all ‹ is HASHEM

יהוה לְכָל קֹרְאָיו, לְכֹל אֲשֶׁר יִקְרָאֻהוּ בֶאֱמֶת.

« sincerely. ‹ call upon Him ‹ who ‹ to all « who call upon Him, ‹ to all ‹ is HASHEM

רְצוֹן יְרֵאָיו יַעֲשֶׂה, וְאֶת שַׁוְעָתָם יִשְׁמַע וְיוֹשִׁיעֵם.

« and He will save them. ‹ He will hear, ‹ and their cry « He will do; ‹ of those who fear Him ‹ The will

שׁוֹמֵר יהוה אֶת כָּל אֹהֲבָיו, וְאֵת כָּל הָרְשָׁעִים

‹ the wicked ‹ but all « who love Him; ‹ all ‹ HASHEM protects

יַשְׁמִיד. ❖ תְּהִלַּת יהוה יְדַבֶּר פִּי, וִיבָרֵךְ כָּל בָּשָׂר

‹ flesh ‹ may all ‹ and bless « may my mouth declare, ‹ of HASHEM ‹ The praise « He will destroy.

שֵׁם קָדְשׁוֹ לְעוֹלָם וָעֶד. וַאֲנַחְנוּ נְבָרֵךְ יָהּ מֵעַתָּה

‹ from this time ‹ God ‹ will bless ‹ But we « and ever. ‹ for ever ‹ of His Holiness ‹ the Name

וְעַד עוֹלָם, הַלְלוּיָהּ.[1]

« Halleluyah! « eternity. ‹ until

——— Psalm 146 / תהלים קמו ———

הַלְלוּיָהּ, הַלְלִי נַפְשִׁי אֶת יהוה. אֲהַלְלָה יהוה

‹ HASHEM ‹ I will praise « HASHEM! ‹ O my Soul ‹ Praise « Halleluyah!

בְּחַיָּי, אֲזַמְּרָה לֵאלֹהַי בְּעוֹדִי. אַל תִּבְטְחוּ בִנְדִיבִים,

« on nobles, ‹ Do not rely « while I exist. ‹ to my God ‹ I will make music « while I live,

בְּבֶן אָדָם שֶׁאֵין לוֹ תְשׁוּעָה. תֵּצֵא רוּחוֹ, יָשֻׁב

‹ he returns ‹ does his spirit ‹ When depart « salvation. ‹ for he holds no ‹ [nor] on a human being,

(1) *Psalms* 115:18.

לְאַדְמָתוֹ, בַּיּוֹם הַהוּא אָבְדוּ עֶשְׁתֹּנֹתָיו. אַשְׁרֵי

‹ Praiseworthy is he « do all his plans. ‹ perish ‹ on that day « to his earth,

שֶׁאֵל יַעֲקֹב בְּעֶזְרוֹ, שִׂבְרוֹ עַל יהוה אֱלֹהָיו. עֹשֶׂה

‹ [He is] the Maker « his God. ‹ HASHEM, ‹ is in ‹ whose hope « is his help, ‹ of Jacob ‹ whom the God

שָׁמַיִם וָאָרֶץ, אֶת הַיָּם וְאֶת כָּל אֲשֶׁר בָּם, הַשֹּׁמֵר

‹ He safeguards « is in them; ‹ that ‹ and all ‹ the sea ‹ and earth, ‹ of heaven

אֱמֶת לְעוֹלָם. עֹשֶׂה מִשְׁפָּט לַעֲשׁוּקִים, נֹתֵן לֶחֶם

‹ bread ‹ He gives « for the exploited, ‹ justice ‹ He does « forever. ‹ truth

לָרְעֵבִים, יהוה מַתִּיר אֲסוּרִים. יהוה פֹּקֵחַ עִוְרִים,

« to the blind; ‹ gives sight ‹ HASHEM « the bound; ‹ releases ‹ HASHEM « to the hungry.

יהוה זֹקֵף כְּפוּפִים, יהוה אֹהֵב צַדִּיקִים. יהוה

‹ HASHEM « the righteous. ‹ loves ‹ HASHEM « the bent; ‹ straightens ‹ HASHEM

שֹׁמֵר אֶת גֵּרִים, יָתוֹם וְאַלְמָנָה יְעוֹדֵד, וְדֶרֶךְ

‹ but the way « He encourages; ‹ and widow ‹ orphan « strangers, ‹ protects

רְשָׁעִים יְעַוֵּת. ❖ יִמְלֹךְ יהוה לְעוֹלָם, אֱלֹהַיִךְ

‹ your God, « forever; ‹ HASHEM shall reign « He contorts. ‹ of the wicked

צִיּוֹן, לְדֹר וָדֹר; הַלְלוּיָהּ.

« Halleluyah! « to generation, ‹ from generation ‹ O Zion,

Psalm 147 / תהלים קמז

הַלְלוּיָהּ; כִּי טוֹב זַמְּרָה אֱלֹהֵינוּ, כִּי נָעִים

‹ pleasant ‹ for « to our God, ‹ to make music ‹ it is good ‹ For « Halleluyah!

נָאוָה תְהִלָּה. בּוֹנֵה יְרוּשָׁלַיִם יהוה, נִדְחֵי יִשְׂרָאֵל

‹ of Israel ‹ the outcasts « is HASHEM; ‹ of Jerusalem ‹ The Builder « is praise. ‹ and befitting

יְכַנֵּס. הָרוֹפֵא לִשְׁבוּרֵי לֵב, וּמְחַבֵּשׁ לְעַצְּבוֹתָם.

« their sorrows. ‹ and the One Who bandages « of the brokenhearted ‹ He is the Healer « He will gather in.

מוֹנֶה מִסְפָּר לַכּוֹכָבִים, לְכֻלָּם שֵׁמוֹת יִקְרָא. גָּדוֹל

‹ Great « He assigns. ‹ names ‹ to all of them « of the stars, ‹ the number ‹ He counts

אֲדוֹנֵינוּ וְרַב כֹּחַ, לִתְבוּנָתוֹ אֵין מִסְפָּר. מְעוֹדֵד

‹ Encourage « calculation. ‹ is beyond ‹ His understanding « in strength; ‹ and abundant ‹ is our Lord

עֲנָוִים יהוה, מַשְׁפִּיל רְשָׁעִים עֲדֵי אָרֶץ. עֱנוּ

‹ Call out « the ground. ‹ to ‹ the wicked ‹ He lowers « does HASHEM; ‹ the humble

לַיהוה בְּתוֹדָה, זַמְּרוּ לֵאלֹהֵינוּ בְכִנּוֹר. הַמְכַסֶּה

‹ It is He Who covers « with the harp. ‹ to our God ‹ sing « with thanks, ‹ to HASHEM

שָׁמַיִם בְּעָבִים, הַמֵּכִין לָאָרֶץ מָטָר, הַמַּצְמִיחַ

‹ Who makes sprout « rain, « for the earth ‹ Who prepares « with clouds, ‹ the heavens

הָרִים חָצִיר. נוֹתֵן לִבְהֵמָה לַחְמָהּ, לִבְנֵי עֹרֵב

‹ ravens ‹ to young « its food, ‹ to an animal ‹ He gives « grass. ‹ [on] the mountains

אֲשֶׁר יִקְרָאוּ. לֹא בִגְבוּרַת הַסּוּס יֶחְפָּץ, לֹא

‹ and not « does He desire, ‹ of the horse ‹ the strength ‹ Not « cry out. ‹ that

בְשׁוֹקֵי הָאִישׁ יִרְצֶה. רוֹצֶה יהוה אֶת יְרֵאָיו,

« those who fear Him, ‹ HASHEM desires « does He favor. ‹ of man ‹ the thighs

אֶת הַמְיַחֲלִים לְחַסְדּוֹ. שַׁבְּחִי יְרוּשָׁלַיִם אֶת יהוה;

« HASHEM, ‹ O Jerusalem ‹ Praise « for His kindness. ‹ those who yearn

הַלְלִי אֱלֹהַיִךְ צִיּוֹן. כִּי חִזַּק בְּרִיחֵי שְׁעָרָיִךְ, בֵּרַךְ

‹ and [He has] blessed « of your gates, ‹ the bars ‹ He has strengthened ‹ For « O Zion. ‹ your God, ‹ laud

בָּנַיִךְ בְּקִרְבֵּךְ. הַשָּׂם גְּבוּלֵךְ שָׁלוֹם, חֵלֶב חִטִּים

‹ wheat ‹ [and with] the choicest « peaceful, ‹ your borders ‹ [It is He] Who makes « in your midst. ‹ your children

יַשְׂבִּיעֵךְ. הַשֹּׁלֵחַ אִמְרָתוֹ אָרֶץ, עַד מְהֵרָה יָרוּץ

‹ runs ‹ swiftly « earthward; ‹ His utterance ‹ [It is He] Who dispatches « He satiates you.

דְּבָרוֹ. הַנֹּתֵן שֶׁלֶג כַּצָּמֶר, כְּפוֹר כָּאֵפֶר יְפַזֵּר.

« He scatters. ‹ like ashes ‹ frost « like fleece, ‹ snow ‹ [It is He] Who gives «His word.

מַשְׁלִיךְ קַרְחוֹ כְפִתִּים, לִפְנֵי קָרָתוֹ מִי יַעֲמֹד.

« can stand? ‹ who ‹ His cold ‹ — before « like crumbs ‹ His ice ‹ He hurls

יִשְׁלַח דְּבָרוֹ וְיַמְסֵם, יַשֵּׁב רוּחוֹ יִזְּלוּ מָיִם. ❖ מַגִּיד

‹ He relates « the waters flow. ‹ His wind, ‹ He blows « and it melts them; ‹ His command ‹ He issues

דְּבָרָיו לְיַעֲקֹב, חֻקָּיו וּמִשְׁפָּטָיו לְיִשְׂרָאֵל. לֹא עָשָׂה

‹ He did not do « to Israel. ‹ and judgments ‹ His statutes « to Jacob, ‹ His Words

כֵן לְכָל גּוֹי, וּמִשְׁפָּטִים בַּל יְדָעוּם; הַלְלוּיָהּ.

« Halleluyah! « — they know them not, « such judgments « nation; ‹ for any other ‹ so

Psalm 148 / תהלים קמח

הַלְלוּיָהּ; הַלְלוּ אֶת יהוה מִן הַשָּׁמַיִם, הַלְלוּהוּ

‹ praise Him « the heavens; ‹ from ‹ HASHEM ‹ Praise « Halleluyah!

בַּמְּרוֹמִים. הַלְלוּהוּ כָל מַלְאָכָיו, הַלְלוּהוּ כָּל

‹ all ‹ praise Him, « His angels; ‹ all ‹ Praise Him, « in the heights:

צְבָאָיו. הַלְלוּהוּ שֶׁמֶשׁ וְיָרֵחַ, הַלְלוּהוּ כָּל כּוֹכְבֵי

‹ stars ‹ all ‹ praise Him, « and moon; ‹ sun ‹ Praise Him, « His legions.

אוֹר. הַלְלוּהוּ שְׁמֵי הַשָּׁמָיִם, וְהַמַּיִם אֲשֶׁר מֵעַל

‹ above ‹ that are ‹ and the waters « the loftiest heavens ‹ Praise Him, « that are bright.

הַשָּׁמָיִם. יְהַלְלוּ אֶת שֵׁם יהוה, כִּי הוּא צִוָּה

‹ commanded ‹ He ‹ for « of HASHEM, ‹ the Name ‹ Let them praise « the heavens.

וְנִבְרָאוּ. וַיַּעֲמִידֵם לָעַד לְעוֹלָם, חָק נָתַן וְלֹא

‹ that will not ‹ He issued ‹ a decree « and ever, ‹ for ever ‹ And He established them « and they were created.

יַעֲבוֹר. הַלְלוּ אֶת יהוה מִן הָאָרֶץ, תַּנִּינִים וְכָל

‹ and all ‹ sea giants « the earth: ‹ from ‹ HASHEM ‹ Praise « be broken.

תְּהֹמוֹת. אֵשׁ וּבָרָד, שֶׁלֶג וְקִיטוֹר, רוּחַ סְעָרָה

‹ of the storm ‹ the wind « and vapor, ‹ snow ‹ and hail, ‹ Fire « [watery] depths.

עֹשָׂה דְבָרוֹ. הֶהָרִים וְכָל גְּבָעוֹת, עֵץ פְּרִי וְכָל

‹ and all ‹ yielding fruit ‹ trees « hills; ‹ and all ‹ the mountains « His word; ‹ fulfilling

אֲרָזִים. הַחַיָּה וְכָל בְּהֵמָה, רֶמֶשׂ וְצִפּוֹר כָּנָף.

« with wings; ‹ and birds ‹ crawling things ‹ cattle, ‹ and all ‹ beasts « cedars;

מַלְכֵי אֶרֶץ וְכָל לְאֻמִּים, שָׂרִים וְכָל שֹׁפְטֵי אָרֶץ.

« on earth; ‹ judges ‹ and all ‹ princes « regimes, ‹ and all ‹ of the earth ‹ kings

בַּחוּרִים וְגַם בְּתוּלוֹת, זְקֵנִים עִם נְעָרִים. ❖ יְהַלְלוּ

‹ Let them praise « youths. ‹ together with ‹ old men ‹ maidens, ‹ and also ‹ young men

אֶת שֵׁם יהוה, כִּי נִשְׂגָּב שְׁמוֹ לְבַדּוֹ; הוֹדוֹ עַל אֶרֶץ

‹ earth ‹ is above ‹ His glory ‹ alone; ‹ is His Name ‹ exalted ‹ for ‹ of HASHEM, ‹ the Name

וְשָׁמָיִם. וַיָּרֶם קֶרֶן לְעַמּוֹ, תְּהִלָּה לְכָל חֲסִידָיו,

« His devout ones, ‹ for all ‹ [causing] praise « of His nation, ‹ the pride ‹ He has exalted « and heaven.

לִבְנֵי יִשְׂרָאֵל עַם קְרֹבוֹ; הַלְלוּיָהּ.

« Halleluyah! « with whom He is intimate, ‹ the people ‹ of Israel, ‹ for the Children

Psalm 149 / תהלים קמט

הַלְלוּיָהּ; שִׁירוּ לַיהוה שִׁיר חָדָשׁ, תְּהִלָּתוֹ

‹ His praise « that is new; ‹ a song ‹ to HASHEM ‹ Sing « Halleluyah!

בִּקְהַל חֲסִידִים. יִשְׂמַח יִשְׂרָאֵל בְּעֹשָׂיו, בְּנֵי צִיּוֹן

‹ of Zion ‹ let the Children « in its Maker; ‹ Let Israel rejoice « of the devout. ‹ is in the congregation

יָגִילוּ בְמַלְכָּם. יְהַלְלוּ שְׁמוֹ בְמָחוֹל, בְּתֹף וְכִנּוֹר

‹ and harp ‹ with drums « with dancing; ‹ His Name ‹ Let them praise « in their King. ‹ rejoice

יְזַמְּרוּ לוֹ. כִּי רוֹצֶה יהוה בְּעַמּוֹ, יְפָאֵר עֲנָוִים

‹ the humble ‹ He adorns « His people; ‹ HASHEM desires ‹ For « to Him. ‹ let them make music

בִּישׁוּעָה. יַעְלְזוּ חֲסִידִים בְּכָבוֹד, יְרַנְּנוּ עַל

with salvation. « Exult ‹ let the devout ‹ in glory, « let them sing joyously ‹ upon ‹

מִשְׁכְּבוֹתָם. רוֹמְמוֹת אֵל בִּגְרוֹנָם, וְחֶרֶב פִּיפִיּוֹת

their beds. « The lofty praises ‹ of God ‹ are in their throats, « and a sword, « double edged, «

בְּיָדָם. לַעֲשׂוֹת נְקָמָה בַּגּוֹיִם, תּוֹכֵחוֹת בַּלְאֻמִּים.

is in their hand « — to execute ‹ vengeance ‹ among the nations, « rebukes ‹ among the regimes; «

❖ לֶאְסֹר מַלְכֵיהֶם בְּזִקִּים, וְנִכְבְּדֵיהֶם בְּכַבְלֵי

to bind ‹ their kings ‹ with chains, « and their nobles ‹ with shackles ‹

בַרְזֶל. לַעֲשׂוֹת בָּהֶם מִשְׁפָּט כָּתוּב, הָדָר הוּא

of iron; « to execute ‹ upon them ‹ the judgment ‹ that was written. « [That judgment day,] a splendor ‹ it will be ‹

לְכָל חֲסִידָיו; הַלְלוּיָהּ.

for all ‹ His devout ones, ‹ Halleluyah! «

Psalm 150 / תהלים קנ

הַלְלוּיָהּ; הַלְלוּ אֵל בְּקָדְשׁוֹ, הַלְלוּהוּ בִּרְקִיעַ עֻזּוֹ.

Halleluyah! « Praise ‹ God ‹ in His Sanctuary; « praise Him ‹ in the firmament ‹ of His power. «

הַלְלוּהוּ בִגְבוּרֹתָיו, הַלְלוּהוּ כְּרֹב גֻּדְלוֹ. הַלְלוּהוּ

Praise Him ‹ for His mighty acts; « praise Him ‹ as befits the abundance ‹ of His greatness. « Praise Him ‹

בְּתֵקַע שׁוֹפָר, הַלְלוּהוּ בְּנֵבֶל וְכִנּוֹר. הַלְלוּהוּ בְּתֹף

with the blast ‹ of the *shofar;* « praise Him ‹ with lyre ‹ and harp. « Praise Him ‹ with drum ‹

וּמָחוֹל, הַלְלוּהוּ בְּמִנִּים וְעוּגָב. הַלְלוּהוּ בְצִלְצְלֵי

and dance; « praise Him ‹ with organ ‹ and flute. ‹ Praise Him ‹ with cymbals ‹

שָׁמַע, הַלְלוּהוּ בְּצִלְצְלֵי תְרוּעָה. ❖ כֹּל הַנְּשָׁמָה

clanging; ‹ Praise Him ‹ with trumpets ‹ resounding. « Let all ‹ souls ‹

תְּהַלֵּל יָהּ, הַלְלוּיָהּ. כֹּל הַנְּשָׁמָה תְּהַלֵּל יָהּ; הַלְלוּיָהּ.

praise ‹ God, « Halleluyah! « Let all ‹ souls ‹ praise ‹ God, « Halleluyah! «

בָּרוּךְ יהוה לְעוֹלָם, אָמֵן וְאָמֵן.[1] בָּרוּךְ

‹ Blessed « and Amen. ‹ Amen « forever, ‹ is HASHEM ‹ Blessed

יהוה מִצִּיּוֹן, שֹׁכֵן יְרוּשָׁלָיִם, הַלְלוּיָהּ.[2] בָּרוּךְ

‹ Blessed « Halleluyah! « in Jerusalem, ‹ He Who dwells « from Zion, ‹ is HASHEM

יהוה אֱלֹהִים אֱלֹהֵי יִשְׂרָאֵל, עֹשֵׂה נִפְלָאוֹת

‹ wondrous things ‹ Who does « of Israel, ‹ the God ‹ God, ‹ is HASHEM,

לְבַדּוֹ. ❖ וּבָרוּךְ שֵׁם כְּבוֹדוֹ לְעוֹלָם, וְיִמָּלֵא כְבוֹדוֹ

‹ may His glory ‹ and fill « forever; ‹ of His glory ‹ is the Name ‹ Blessed « by Himself.

אֶת כָּל הָאָרֶץ, אָמֵן וְאָמֵן.[3]

« and Amen. ‹ Amen « the earth. ‹ all

ONE MUST STAND FROM וַיְבָרֶךְ דָּוִיד UNTIL AFTER THE PHRASE אַתָּה הוּא ה' הָאֱלֹהִים; HOWEVER, THERE IS A GENERALLY ACCEPTED CUSTOM TO REMAIN STANDING UNTIL AFTER COMPLETING בָּרְכוּ (P. 162).

I Chronicles 9:10-13 / דברי הימים א כט:י-יג

וַיְבָרֶךְ דָּוִיד אֶת יהוה לְעֵינֵי כָּל הַקָּהָל,

« the congregation. ‹ of all ‹ in the sight ‹ HASHEM ‹ And David blessed

וַיֹּאמֶר דָּוִיד: בָּרוּךְ אַתָּה יהוה אֱלֹהֵי יִשְׂרָאֵל אָבִינוּ,

« our forefather, ‹ of Israel ‹ the God ‹ HASHEM, ‹ are You, ‹ Blessed « David said:

מֵעוֹלָם וְעַד עוֹלָם. לְךָ יהוה הַגְּדֻלָּה וְהַגְּבוּרָה

‹ the strength, ‹ is the greatness, ‹ HASHEM, ‹ Yours, « the World [to Come]. ‹ to ‹ from [This] World

וְהַתִּפְאֶרֶת וְהַנֵּצַח וְהַהוֹד, כִּי כֹל בַּשָּׁמַיִם וּבָאָרֶץ;

« and on earth [is Yours] ‹ in heaven ‹ everything ‹ for « and the majesty; ‹ the triumph, ‹ the glory,

לְךָ יהוה הַמַּמְלָכָה וְהַמִּתְנַשֵּׂא לְכֹל לְרֹאשׁ.

« leader. ‹ over every ‹ and the sovereignty ‹ is the kingdom, ‹ HASHEM, ‹ Yours,

IT IS CUSTOMARY TO SET ASIDE SOMETHING FOR CHARITY AT THIS POINT.

וְהָעֹשֶׁר וְהַכָּבוֹד מִלְּפָנֶיךָ, וְאַתָּה מוֹשֵׁל בַּכֹּל,

« over everything; ‹ rule ‹ and You « [come] from before You ‹ and honor ‹ Wealth

(1) *Psalms* 89:53. (2) 135:21. (3) 72:18-19.

וּבְיָדְךָ כֹּחַ וּגְבוּרָה, וּבְיָדְךָ לְגַדֵּל וּלְחַזֵּק לַכֹּל.

«anyone. ‹ or to strengthen ‹ to make great ‹ and it is in Your hand « and strength ‹ is power ‹ in Your hand

וְעַתָּה אֱלֹהֵינוּ מוֹדִים אֲנַחְנוּ לָךְ, וּמְהַלְּלִים

‹ and we praise « You ‹ we thank « our God, ‹ So now,

לְשֵׁם תִּפְאַרְתֶּךָ.

« of Your splendor. ‹ the Name

Nehemiah 9:6-11 / נחמיה ט:ו-יא

אַתָּה הוּא יהוה לְבַדֶּךָ, אַתָּה עָשִׂיתָ אֶת הַשָּׁמַיִם

« the heavens, ‹ have made ‹ You « alone. ‹ HASHEM, ‹ Who are, ‹ It is You

שְׁמֵי הַשָּׁמַיִם וְכָל צְבָאָם, הָאָרֶץ וְכָל אֲשֶׁר

‹ that is ‹ and everything ‹ the earth « their legions, ‹ and all ‹ the loftiest heavens

עָלֶיהָ, הַיַּמִּים וְכָל אֲשֶׁר בָּהֶם, וְאַתָּה מְחַיֶּה

‹ give life ‹ and You « in them; ‹ that is ‹ and everything ‹ the seas « upon it,

אֶת כֻּלָּם, וּצְבָא הַשָּׁמַיִם לְךָ מִשְׁתַּחֲוִים. ❖ אַתָּה

‹ It is You « do bow. ‹ to You ‹ of heaven ‹ and the legions ‹ to all of them;

הוּא יהוה הָאֱלֹהִים אֲשֶׁר בָּחַרְתָּ בְּאַבְרָם,

« Abram, ‹ selected ‹ [You] Who « the God, ‹ HASHEM ‹ Who are

וְהוֹצֵאתוֹ מֵאוּר כַּשְׂדִּים, וְשַׂמְתָּ שְׁמוֹ אַבְרָהָם.

« Abraham. ‹ his name ‹ and designated « of Ur Kasdim ‹ brought him out

וּמָצָאתָ אֶת לְבָבוֹ נֶאֱמָן לְפָנֶיךָ —

« before You ‹ faithful ‹ his heart ‹ You found

— וְכָרוֹת עִמּוֹ הַבְּרִית לָתֵת אֶת אֶרֶץ הַכְּנַעֲנִי

‹ of the Canaanite, ‹ the land ‹ to give ‹ the covenant ‹ with him ‹ — and You established

הַחִתִּי הָאֱמֹרִי וְהַפְּרִזִּי וְהַיְבוּסִי וְהַגִּרְגָּשִׁי, לָתֵת

‹ — to give [it] « and the Girgashite ‹ the Jebusite, ‹ the Perizzite, ‹ the Amorite, ‹ the Hittite,

לְזַרְעוֹ, וַתָּקֶם אֶת דְּבָרֶיךָ, כִּי צַדִּיק אָתָּה. וַתֵּרֶא

‹ You observed « are You. ‹ righteous ‹ for ‹ Your word, ‹ and You upheld « to his offspring;

אֶת עֳנִי אֲבֹתֵינוּ בְּמִצְרָיִם, וְאֶת זַעֲקָתָם שָׁמַעְתָּ
the suffering ‹ of our forefathers ‹ in Egypt, « and their outcry ‹ You heard ‹

עַל יַם סוּף. וַתִּתֵּן אֹתֹת וּמֹפְתִים בְּפַרְעֹה וּבְכָל
at ‹ the Sea ‹ of Reeds. « You imposed ‹ signs ‹ and wonders ‹ upon Pharaoh ‹ and upon all ‹

עֲבָדָיו וּבְכָל עַם אַרְצוֹ, כִּי יָדַעְתָּ כִּי הֵזִידוּ
his servants, ‹ and upon all ‹ the people ‹ of his land, « for ‹ You knew ‹ that ‹ they sinned flagrantly ‹

עֲלֵיהֶם, וַתַּעַשׂ לְךָ שֵׁם כְּהַיּוֹם הַזֶּה. ❖ וְהַיָּם בָּקַעְתָּ
against them; « and You made ‹ for Yourself ‹ a name ‹ as [clear as] this [very] day. « The Sea ‹ You split ‹

לִפְנֵיהֶם, וַיַּעַבְרוּ בְתוֹךְ הַיָּם בַּיַּבָּשָׁה, וְאֶת רֹדְפֵיהֶם
before them, « and they crossed ‹ in the midst ‹ of the Sea ‹ on dry land; « but their pursuers ‹

הִשְׁלַכְתָּ בִמְצוֹלֹת, כְּמוֹ אֶבֶן בְּמַיִם עַזִּים.
You hurled ‹ into the depths, ‹ like ‹ a stone ‹ into waters ‹ that are turbulent. «

THE SONG AT THE SEA / שירת הים

Exodus 14:30-15:19 / שמות יד:ל-טו:יט

וַיּוֹשַׁע יהוה בַּיּוֹם הַהוּא אֶת־יִשְׂרָאֵל מִיַּד
HASHEM saved ‹ on that day, ‹ Israel ‹ from the hand ‹

מִצְרָיִם, וַיַּרְא יִשְׂרָאֵל אֶת־מִצְרַיִם מֵת עַל־שְׂפַת
of Egypt, « and Israel saw ‹ the Egyptians ‹ dead ‹ on ‹ the shore ‹

הַיָּם: ❖ וַיַּרְא יִשְׂרָאֵל אֶת־הַיָּד הַגְּדֹלָה אֲשֶׁר
of the sea. « And Israel saw ‹ the hand, ‹ that is great, ‹ that ‹

עָשָׂה יהוה בְּמִצְרַיִם, וַיִּירְאוּ הָעָם אֶת־יהוה,
HASHEM inflicted ‹ upon Egypt, « and fear ‹ did the people ‹ HASHEM, ‹

וַיַּאֲמִינוּ בַּיהוה וּבְמֹשֶׁה עַבְדּוֹ:
and they had faith ‹ in HASHEM ‹ and in Moses, ‹ His servant. «

אָז יָשִׁיר־ מֹשֶׁה וּבְנֵי יִשְׂרָאֵל אֶת־הַשִּׁירָה הַזֹּאת

Then ‹ choose to sing ‹ did Moses ‹ and the Children ‹ of Israel ‹ this song ‹

לַיהוָה, וַיֹּאמְרוּ לֵאמֹר, אָשִׁירָה לַיהוָה כִּי־גָאֹה

to HASHEM, « and they said, ‹ saying [the following]: « I shall sing ‹ to HASHEM ‹ for ‹ He is exalted ‹

גָּאָה, סוּס וְרֹכְבוֹ רָמָה בַיָּם: עָזִּי וְזִמְרָת יָהּ

[above] the arrogant, « the horse ‹ with its rider ‹ He hurled ‹ into the sea. « My might ‹ and my praise ‹ is God, «

וַיְהִי־לִי לִישׁוּעָה, זֶה אֵלִי וְאַנְוֵהוּ, אֱלֹהֵי אָבִי

and He was ‹ for me ‹ a salvation. « This ‹ is my God, ‹ and I will build Him a Sanctuary; « the God ‹ of my father, ‹

וַאֲרֹמְמֶנְהוּ: יְהוָה אִישׁ מִלְחָמָה, יְהוָה שְׁמוֹ:

and I will exalt Him. « HASHEM ‹ is Master ‹ of war, ‹ HASHEM ‹ is his Name. «

מַרְכְּבֹת פַּרְעֹה וְחֵילוֹ יָרָה בַיָּם, וּמִבְחַר שָׁלִשָׁיו

The chariots ‹ of Pharaoh ‹ and his army ‹ He hurled ‹ into the sea; « and the pick ‹ of his officers ‹

טֻבְּעוּ בְיַם־סוּף: תְּהֹמֹת יְכַסְיֻמוּ, יָרְדוּ בִמְצוֹלֹת

were mired ‹ in the Sea ‹ of Reeds. « Deep waters ‹ covered them; « they descended ‹ in the depths ‹

כְּמוֹ־אָבֶן: יְמִינְךָ יְהוָה נֶאְדָּרִי בַּכֹּחַ, יְמִינְךָ יְהוָה

like ‹ stone. « Your right hand, ‹ HASHEM, ‹ is adorned ‹ with strength; « Your right hand, ‹ HASHEM, ‹

תִּרְעַץ אוֹיֵב: וּבְרֹב גְּאוֹנְךָ תַּהֲרֹס קָמֶיךָ, תְּשַׁלַּח

smashes ‹ the enemy. « In Your abundant ‹ grandeur ‹ You shatter ‹ Your opponents; « You dispatch ‹

חֲרֹנְךָ יֹאכְלֵמוֹ כַּקַּשׁ: וּבְרוּחַ אַפֶּיךָ נֶעֶרְמוּ מַיִם,

Your wrath, ‹ it consumes them ‹ like straw. « At a blast ‹ from Your nostrils, « heaped up ‹ were the waters; «

נִצְּבוּ כְמוֹ־נֵד נֹזְלִים, קָפְאוּ תְהֹמֹת בְּלֶב־יָם:

stand up straight ‹ as ‹ a wall ‹ did the running water, « congealed ‹ were the deep waters ‹ in the heart ‹ of the sea. «

אָמַר אוֹיֵב, אֶרְדֹּף אַשִּׂיג אֲחַלֵּק שָׁלָל, תִּמְלָאֵמוֹ

The enemy declared: « I will pursue, ‹ I will overtake, ‹ I will divide ‹ plunder; « satisfied with them ‹

נַפְשִׁי, אָרִיק חַרְבִּי, תּוֹרִישֵׁמוֹ יָדִי: נָשַׁפְתָּ בְרוּחֲךָ

« will my desires be; ‹ I will unsheathe « my sword, ‹ impoverish them « will my hand. ‹ You blew « with Your wind;

כִּסָּמוֹ יָם, צָלְלוּ כַּעוֹפֶרֶת בְּמַיִם, אַדִּירִים: מִי־

‹ enshroud them « did the sea; ‹ sink ‹ like lead ‹ in the waters « did the mighty ones. ‹ Who

כָמֹכָה בָּאֵלִם יהוה, מִי כָּמֹכָה נֶאְדָּר בַּקֹּדֶשׁ,

‹ is like You ‹ among the heavenly powers, « HASHEM! ‹ Who ‹ is like You, ‹ mighty « in holiness,

נוֹרָא תְהִלֹּת עֹשֵׂה פֶלֶא: נָטִיתָ יְמִינְךָ, תִּבְלָעֵמוֹ

‹ awesome « [beyond] praise, ‹ doing « wonders! ‹ You stretched out « Your right hand; ‹ swallow them

אָרֶץ: נָחִיתָ בְחַסְדְּךָ עַם־זוּ גָּאָלְתָּ, נֵהַלְתָּ בְעָזְּךָ

« did the earth. ‹ You guided ‹ in Your kindness ‹ this people « that You redeemed; ‹ You led [them] ‹ with Your might

אֶל־נְוֵה קָדְשֶׁךָ: שָׁמְעוּ עַמִּים יִרְגָּזוּן, חִיל אָחַז

‹ to ‹ the abode « of Your holiness. ‹ Hear « did peoples; « they were agitated; ‹ terror ‹ gripped

יֹשְׁבֵי פְּלָשֶׁת: אָז נִבְהֲלוּ אַלּוּפֵי אֱדוֹם, אֵילֵי

‹ the dwellers « of Philistia. ‹ Then ‹ were confounded ‹ the chieftains « of Edom, ‹ the powers

מוֹאָב יֹאחֲזֵמוֹ רָעַד, נָמֹגוּ כֹּל יֹשְׁבֵי כְנָעַן: תִּפֹּל

« of Moab ‹ – grip them « did trembling; ‹ dissolved ‹ were all ‹ the dwellers « of Canaan. ‹ Fall

עֲלֵיהֶם אֵימָתָה וָפַחַד, בִּגְדֹל זְרוֹעֲךָ יִדְּמוּ כָּאָבֶן,

‹ upon them ‹ may fear « and terror, ‹ at the greatness ‹ of Your arm ‹ may they be still « as stone;

עַד־יַעֲבֹר עַמְּךָ יהוה, עַד־יַעֲבֹר עַם־זוּ קָנִיתָ:

‹ until ‹ pass through ‹ do Your people, « HASHEM, ‹ until ‹ pass through ‹ do this people « that You have acquired.

תְּבִאֵמוֹ וְתִטָּעֵמוֹ בְּהַר נַחֲלָתְךָ, מָכוֹן לְשִׁבְתְּךָ

‹ You shall bring them ‹ and implant them ‹ on the mount « of Your heritage, ‹ the foundation ‹ of Your dwelling-place,

פָּעַלְתָּ יהוה, מִקְּדָשׁ אֲדֹנָי כּוֹנְנוּ יָדֶיךָ: יהוה |

‹ which You have made, « HASHEM: ‹ the Sanctuary, ‹ my Lord, « that Your hands established. ‹ HASHEM

יִמְלֹךְ לְעֹלָם וָעֶד: יהוה | יִמְלֹךְ לְעֹלָם וָעֶד: (יהוה
shall reign ‹ for ever ‹ and ever. « HASHEM ‹ shall reign ‹ for ever ‹ and ever. « HASHEM «

מַלְכוּתֵהּ קָאֵם לְעָלַם וּלְעָלְמֵי עָלְמַיָּא.) כִּי בָא
— His kingdom ‹ stands ‹ forever ‹ and to all eternity. « When ‹ come ‹

סוּס פַּרְעֹה בְּרִכְבּוֹ וּבְפָרָשָׁיו בַּיָּם וַיָּשֶׁב יהוה
did the cavalry ‹ of Pharaoh ‹ with his chariots ‹ and horsemen ‹ into the sea, « and turn back ‹ did HASHEM ‹

עֲלֵהֶם אֶת־מֵי הַיָּם וּבְנֵי יִשְׂרָאֵל הָלְכוּ בַיַּבָּשָׁה
upon them ‹ the waters ‹ of the sea, « the Children ‹ of Israel ‹ walked ‹ on the dry bed ‹

בְּתוֹךְ הַיָּם: ❖ כִּי לַיהוה הַמְּלוּכָה, וּמֹשֵׁל בַּגּוֹיִם.[1]
amid ‹ the sea. « For ‹ to HASHEM belongs ‹ the kingship « and He rules ‹ the nations. «

וְעָלוּ מוֹשִׁעִים בְּהַר צִיּוֹן, לִשְׁפֹּט אֶת הַר עֵשָׂו,
Ascend ‹ will the saviors ‹ up Mount ‹ Zion ‹ to judge ‹ the mountain ‹ of Esau, «

וְהָיְתָה לַיהוה הַמְּלוּכָה.[2] וְהָיָה יהוה לְמֶלֶךְ
and to HASHEM will be ‹ the kingship. « Then will ‹ HASHEM ‹ be King ‹

עַל כָּל הָאָרֶץ, בַּיּוֹם הַהוּא יִהְיֶה יהוה אֶחָד
over ‹ all ‹ the world « — on that day ‹ shall ‹ HASHEM ‹ be One ‹

וּשְׁמוֹ אֶחָד.[3] (וּבְתוֹרָתְךָ כָּתוּב לֵאמֹר: שְׁמַע
and His Name ‹ be One. « (And in Your Torah ‹ it is written, ‹ saying: « Hear ‹

יִשְׂרָאֵל, יהוה אֱלֹהֵינוּ, יהוה אֶחָד.[4])
O Israel: « HASHEM ‹ is our God, ‹ HASHEM is ‹ the One [and Only].) «

STAND WHILE RECITING ... יִשְׁתַּבַּח. THE FIFTEEN EXPRESSIONS OF PRAISE — ... שִׁיר וּשְׁבָחָה — בְּרָכוֹת וְהוֹדָאוֹת — SHOULD BE RECITED WITHOUT PAUSE, PREFERABLY IN ONE BREATH.

יִשְׁתַּבַּח שִׁמְךָ לָעַד, מַלְכֵּנוּ הָאֵל הַמֶּלֶךְ הַגָּדוֹל
Praised ‹ may Your Name be ‹ forever, « our King, « the God, ‹ the King ‹ Who is great ‹

וְהַקָּדוֹשׁ, בַּשָּׁמַיִם וּבָאָרֶץ. כִּי לְךָ נָאֶה, יהוה
and Who is holy, « in heaven ‹ and on earth. « Because ‹ for you ‹ are fitting, « HASHEM, ‹

(1) *Psalms* 22:29. (2) *Obadiah* 1:21. (3) *Zechariah* 14:9. (4) *Deuteronomy* 6:4.

אֱלֹהֵינוּ וֵאלֹהֵי אֲבוֹתֵינוּ, שִׁיר וּשְׁבָחָה, הַלֵּל

〈 lauding 〈 and praise, 〈 song 《 of our forefathers, 〈 and the God 〈 our God

וְזִמְרָה, עֹז וּמֶמְשָׁלָה, נֶצַח גְּדֻלָּה וּגְבוּרָה, תְּהִלָּה

〈 praise 〈 and strength, 〈 greatness, 〈 triumph, 〈 and dominion, 〈 power 〈 and hymns,

וְתִפְאֶרֶת, קְדֻשָּׁה וּמַלְכוּת, בְּרָכוֹת וְהוֹדָאוֹת מֵעַתָּה

〈 from this time 〈 and thanksgivings 〈 blessings 〈 and sovereignty, 〈 holiness 〈 and glory,

וְעַד עוֹלָם. ❖ בָּרוּךְ אַתָּה יהוה, אֵל מֶלֶךְ גָּדוֹל

〈 [Who is] exalted 〈 King 〈 God, 《 HASHEM, 〈 are You, 〈 Blessed 《 eternity. 〈 until

בַּתִּשְׁבָּחוֹת, אֵל הַהוֹדָאוֹת, אֲדוֹן הַנִּפְלָאוֹת, הַבּוֹחֵר

〈 Who chooses 《 of wonders, 〈 Master 《 of thanksgivings, 〈 God 《 through praises,

בְּשִׁירֵי זִמְרָה, מֶלֶךְ אֵל חֵי הָעוֹלָמִים. (Cong. – אָמֵן.)

《 (Amen.) 《 of the worlds. 〈 Life-giver 〈 God, 〈 — King, 《 that are melodious, 〈 songs [of praise]

THE *CHAZZAN* RECITES חֲצִי קַדִּישׁ HALF-*KADDISH*:

יִתְגַּדַּל וְיִתְקַדַּשׁ שְׁמֵהּ רַבָּא. (Cong. – אָמֵן.) בְּעָלְמָא דִּי

〈 that 〈 — in the world 〈 (Amen.) 《 that is great! — 〈 may His Name 〈 and be sanctified 〈 Grow exalted

בְּרָא כִרְעוּתֵהּ. וְיַמְלִיךְ מַלְכוּתֵהּ, בְּחַיֵּיכוֹן וּבְיוֹמֵיכוֹן וּבְחַיֵּי

〈 and in the lifetimes 〈 and in your days, 〈 in your lifetimes 《 to His kingship, 〈 and may He give reign 《 according to His will, 〈 He created

דְכָל בֵּית יִשְׂרָאֵל, בַּעֲגָלָא וּבִזְמַן קָרִיב. וְאִמְרוּ: אָמֵן.

《 Amen. 〈 Now respond: 《 that comes soon. 〈 and at a time 〈 swiftly 《 of Israel, 〈 Family 〈 of the entire

CONGREGATION RESPONDS:

אָמֵן. יְהֵא שְׁמֵהּ רַבָּא מְבָרַךְ לְעָלַם וּלְעָלְמֵי עָלְמַיָּא.

《 and for all eternity. 〈 forever 〈 be blessed 〈 that is great 〈 His Name 〈 May 《 Amen.

CHAZZAN CONTINUES:

יְהֵא שְׁמֵהּ רַבָּא מְבָרַךְ לְעָלַם וּלְעָלְמֵי עָלְמַיָּא. יִתְבָּרַךְ

〈 Blessed, 《 and for all eternity. 〈 forever 〈 be blessed 〈 that is great 〈 His Name 〈 May

וְיִשְׁתַּבַּח וְיִתְפָּאַר וְיִתְרוֹמַם וְיִתְנַשֵּׂא וְיִתְהַדַּר וְיִתְעַלֶּה

〈 elevated, 〈 honored, 〈 upraised, 〈 exalted, 〈 glorified, 〈 praised,

וְיִתְהַלָּל שְׁמֵהּ דְּקֻדְשָׁא בְּרִיךְ הוּא (Cong. — בְּרִיךְ הוּא.) —

« is He) ‹ (Blessed « is He ‹ Blessed ‹ of the Holy One, ‹ be the Name ‹ and lauded

לְעֵֽלָּא מִן כָּל בִּרְכָתָא וְשִׁירָתָא תֻּשְׁבְּחָתָא וְנֶחֱמָתָא

‹ and consolation ‹ praise « and song, ‹ blessing ‹ any ‹ beyond

דַּאֲמִירָן בְּעָלְמָא. וְאִמְרוּ: אָמֵן. (Cong. — אָמֵן.)

« (Amen.) « Amen. ‹ Now respond: « in the world. ‹ that are uttered

THE *CHAZZAN* SUMMONS THE CONGREGATION TO JOIN IN THE FORTHCOMING PRAYERS, BOWING AT בָּרְכוּ, AND STRAIGHTENING UP AT 'ה.

בָּרְכוּ אֶת יהוה הַמְּבֹרָךְ.

« the blessed One. ‹ HASHEM, ‹ Bless

THE CONGREGATION, FOLLOWED BY *CHAZZAN*, RESPONDS, BOWING AT בָּרוּךְ, AND STRAIGHTENING UP AT 'ה.

בָּרוּךְ יהוה הַמְּבֹרָךְ לְעוֹלָם וָעֶד.

« and ever. ‹ for ever ‹ the blessed One, ‹ HASHEM, ‹ Blessed is

BLESSINGS OF THE SHEMA / ברכות קריאת שמע

IT IS PREFERABLE THAT ONE SIT WHILE RECITING THE FOLLOWING SERIES OF PRAYERS — PARTICULARLY THE *KEDUSHAH* VERSES, קָדוֹשׁ קָדוֹשׁ קָדוֹשׁ AND בָּרוּךְ כְּבוֹד — UNTIL *SHEMONEH ESREI*.

בָּרוּךְ אַתָּה יהוה אֱלֹהֵינוּ מֶלֶךְ הָעוֹלָם, יוֹצֵר

‹ Who forms « of the universe, ‹ King ‹ our God, ‹ HASHEM, ‹ are You, ‹ Blessed

אוֹר וּבוֹרֵא חֹשֶׁךְ, עֹשֶׂה שָׁלוֹם וּבוֹרֵא אֶת הַכֹּל.[1]

« all. ‹ and creates ‹ peace ‹ Who makes « darkness, ‹ and creates ‹ light

(1) Cf. *Isaiah* 45:7.

Interruptions During the Blessings of the *Shema*

As a general rule, no אָמֵן or other prayer response may be recited between בָּרְכוּ and *Shemoneh Esrei*, but there are exceptions. The main exception is "between chapters" [בֵּין הַפְּרָקִים] of the *Shema* Blessings — i.e., after יוֹצֵר הַמְּאוֹרוֹת and הַבּוֹחֵר ... בְּאַהֲבָה, and between the three chapters of *Shema*. At those points, אָמֵן (but not בָּרוּךְ הוּא וּבָרוּךְ שְׁמוֹ) may be responded to any blessing. Some responses, however, are so important that they are permitted at any point in the *Shema* blessings. They are: (a) In *Kaddish*, אָמֵן יְהֵא שְׁמֵהּ רַבָּא ... עָלְמַיָּא and the אָמֵן after דַּאֲמִירָן בְּעָלְמָא; (b) the response to בָּרְכוּ (even of one called to the Torah); and (c) during the *chazzan's* repetition of *Shemoneh Esrei:* 1) in *Kedushah,* the verses קָדוֹשׁ קָדוֹשׁ קָדוֹשׁ ... כְּבוֹדוֹ and בָּרוּךְ כְּבוֹד ה' מִמְּקוֹמוֹ; 2) the אָמֵן after הָאֵל הַקָּדוֹשׁ; 3) the three words מוֹדִים אֲנַחְנוּ לָךְ.

During the recital of the two verses שְׁמַע and בָּרוּךְ שֵׁם, absolutely no interruptions are permitted.

הַמֵּאִיר לָאָרֶץ וְלַדָּרִים עָלֶיהָ בְּרַחֲמִים, וּבְטוּבוֹ

‹ and in His goodness « with compassion, ‹ upon it, ‹ and those who dwell ‹ the earth ‹ He Who illuminates

מְחַדֵּשׁ בְּכָל יוֹם תָּמִיד מַעֲשֵׂה בְרֵאשִׁית. מָה

‹ How « of Creation ‹ the work «perpetually— ‹ day, ‹ —every « He renews

רַבּוּ מַעֲשֶׂיךָ יהוה, כֻּלָּם בְּחָכְמָה עָשִׂיתָ, מָלְאָה

‹ full «You made; ‹ with wisdom ‹ all of them « HASHEM; ‹ are Your works, ‹ abundant

הָאָרֶץ קִנְיָנֶךָ.[1] הַמֶּלֶךְ הַמְּרוֹמָם לְבַדּוֹ מֵאָז, הַמְּשֻׁבָּח

‹ Who is praised, ‹ from before Creation, ‹ in solitude ‹ Who was exalted ‹ [You are] the King « with Your possessions. ‹ is the earth

וְהַמְּפֹאָר וְהַמִּתְנַשֵּׂא מִימוֹת עוֹלָם. אֱלֹהֵי עוֹלָם,

«of eternity, ‹ God « of old. ‹ since days ‹ and upraised ‹ glorified,

בְּרַחֲמֶיךָ הָרַבִּים רַחֵם עָלֵינוּ, אֲדוֹן עֻזֵּנוּ, צוּר

‹ our rocklike ‹ of our power, ‹ O Master « on us; ‹ have compassion ‹ that is abundant ‹ with Your compassion

מִשְׂגַּבֵּנוּ, מָגֵן יִשְׁעֵנוּ, מִשְׂגָּב בַּעֲדֵנוּ. אֵל בָּרוּךְ גְּדוֹל

‹Who is great ‹ The blessed God, « for us. ‹ Who is a stronghold ‹ of our salvation, ‹ O Shield ‹ stronghold,

דֵּעָה, הֵכִין וּפָעַל זָהֳרֵי חַמָּה, טוֹב יָצַר כָּבוֹד

‹provides honor ‹ that which He fashioned ‹ the Beneficent One, « of the sun; ‹ the rays ‹ and produced ‹ prepared « in knowledge,

לִשְׁמוֹ, מְאוֹרוֹת נָתַן סְבִיבוֹת עֻזּוֹ, פִּנּוֹת צְבָאָיו

« of His legions, ‹ The leaders « His power. ‹ all around ‹ did He place ‹ Luminaries « for His Name.

קְדוֹשִׁים רוֹמְמֵי שַׁדַּי, תָּמִיד מְסַפְּרִים כְּבוֹד אֵל

‹of God ‹ the honor ‹ relate ‹ constantly «the Almighty, ‹ who exalt ‹ holy ones

וּקְדֻשָּׁתוֹ. תִּתְבָּרַךְ יהוה אֱלֹהֵינוּ עַל שֶׁבַח מַעֲשֵׂה

‹ work ‹ the praiseworthy ‹ for ‹ our God, ‹ HASHEM, ‹ May You be blessed, « and His sanctity.

יָדֶיךָ, וְעַל מְאוֹרֵי אוֹר שֶׁעָשִׂיתָ, יְפָאֲרוּךָ, סֶּלָה.

« forever. ‹ may [people] glorify You « that You have made, ‹ of light ‹ the luminaries ‹ and for « of Your hands,

(1) *Psalms* 104:24.

תִּתְבָּרַךְ צוּרֵנוּ מַלְכֵּנוּ וְגֹאֲלֵנוּ, בּוֹרֵא קְדוֹשִׁים.

« of holy ones; ‹ Creator « and our Redeemer, ‹ our King ‹ our Rock, ‹ May You be blessed,

יִשְׁתַּבַּח שִׁמְךָ לָעַד מַלְכֵּנוּ, יוֹצֵר מְשָׁרְתִים, וַאֲשֶׁר

‹ and Whose « of ministering angels; ‹ O Fashioner « our King, ‹ forever, ‹ may Your Name be praised

מְשָׁרְתָיו כֻּלָּם עוֹמְדִים בְּרוּם עוֹלָם, וּמַשְׁמִיעִים

‹ and proclaim ‹ of the universe ‹ at the summit ‹ stand ‹ all ‹ ministering angels

בְּיִרְאָה יַחַד בְּקוֹל דִּבְרֵי אֱלֹהִים חַיִּים וּמֶלֶךְ

‹ and King ‹ of the living God ‹ the words « loudly, ‹ together, « with awe,

עוֹלָם.[1] כֻּלָּם אֲהוּבִים, כֻּלָּם בְּרוּרִים, כֻּלָּם גִּבּוֹרִים,

« mighty; ‹ they are all « flawless; ‹ they are all « beloved; ‹ They are all « of the universe.

וְכֻלָּם עֹשִׂים בְּאֵימָה וּבְיִרְאָה רְצוֹן קוֹנָם. ❖ וְכֻלָּם

‹ And they all « of their Maker. ‹ the will ‹ and reverence ‹ with trepidation ‹ do ‹ and they all

פּוֹתְחִים אֶת פִּיהֶם בִּקְדֻשָּׁה וּבְטָהֳרָה, בְּשִׁירָה

‹ with song « and in purity, ‹ in holiness ‹ their mouth ‹ open

וּבְזִמְרָה, וּמְבָרְכִים וּמְשַׁבְּחִים וּמְפָאֲרִים וּמַעֲרִיצִים

‹ revere, ‹ glorify, ‹ praise, ‹ and bless, « and with hymn,

וּמַקְדִּישִׁים וּמַמְלִיכִים —

« and declare the kingship — ‹ sanctify

אֶת שֵׁם הָאֵל הַמֶּלֶךְ הַגָּדוֹל הַגִּבּוֹר וְהַנּוֹרָא

« and Who is awesome; ‹ mighty ‹ Who is great, ‹ the King ‹ of God, ‹ of the Name

קָדוֹשׁ הוּא.[2] ❖ וְכֻלָּם מְקַבְּלִים עֲלֵיהֶם עֹל מַלְכוּת

‹ of the sovereignty ‹ the yoke ‹ upon themselves ‹ accept ‹ Then they all « is He. ‹ holy

שָׁמַיִם זֶה מִזֶּה, וְנוֹתְנִים רְשׁוּת זֶה לָזֶה, לְהַקְדִּישׁ

‹ to sanctify « to another, ‹ one ‹ permission ‹ and grant « from the other, ‹ one « of heaven,

(1) Cf. *Jeremiah* 10:10. (2) Cf. *Deuteronomy* 10:17; *Psalms* 99:3.

לְיוֹצְרָם, בְּנַחַת רוּחַ בְּשָׂפָה בְרוּרָה וּבִנְעִימָה.

« and with sweet melody. « that is clear, ‹ with articulation « of spirit, ‹ with calmness « the One Who formed them,

קְדֻשָּׁה כֻּלָּם כְּאֶחָד עוֹנִים וְאוֹמְרִים בְּיִרְאָה:

« with reverence: ‹ and say ‹ proclaim, ‹ as one ‹ all of them ‹ Sanctification

CONGREGATION RECITES ALOUD IN UNISON:

קָדוֹשׁ קָדוֹשׁ קָדוֹשׁ יהוה צְבָאוֹת,

« Master of Legions; ‹ is HASHEM, ‹ holy ‹ holy, ‹ Holy,

מְלֹא כָל הָאָרֶץ כְּבוֹדוֹ.[1]

« with His glory. ‹ world ‹ is the whole ‹ filled

❖ **וְהָאוֹפַנִּים** וְחַיּוֹת הַקֹּדֶשׁ בְּרַעַשׁ גָּדוֹל מִתְנַשְּׂאִים

‹ raise themselves ‹ with great noise, « and the holy *Chayos*, ‹ Then the *Ofanim*

לְעֻמַּת שְׂרָפִים. לְעֻמָּתָם מְשַׁבְּחִים וְאוֹמְרִים:

« and proclaim: ‹ they offer praise ‹ facing them « the *Seraphim*; ‹ toward

CONGREGATION RECITES ALOUD IN UNISON:

בָּרוּךְ כְּבוֹד יהוה מִמְּקוֹמוֹ.[2]

« from His place. ‹ of HASHEM ‹ is the glory ‹ Blessed

לְאֵל בָּרוּךְ נְעִימוֹת יִתֵּנוּ. לְמֶלֶךְ אֵל חַי וְקַיָּם,

‹ and enduring, ‹ living ‹ the God, ‹ to the King, « do they offer; ‹ sweet melodies ‹ Who is blessed ‹ To the God

זְמִרוֹת יֹאמֵרוּ וְתִשְׁבָּחוֹת יַשְׁמִיעוּ. כִּי הוּא לְבַדּוֹ

‹ alone ‹ He ‹ For « do they proclaim. ‹ and praises ‹ do they sing ‹ hymns

פּוֹעֵל גְּבוּרוֹת, עֹשֶׂה חֲדָשׁוֹת, בַּעַל מִלְחָמוֹת,

« of wars, ‹ is Master « new things, ‹ makes « mighty deeds, ‹ performs

זוֹרֵעַ צְדָקוֹת, מַצְמִיחַ יְשׁוּעוֹת, בּוֹרֵא רְפוּאוֹת,

« cures, ‹ creates « of salvations, ‹ brings about the sprouting « kindnesses, ‹ sows

נוֹרָא תְהִלּוֹת, אֲדוֹן הַנִּפְלָאוֹת. הַמְחַדֵּשׁ בְּטוּבוֹ

‹ in His goodness ‹ Who renews ‹ of wonders, ‹ is the Master « beyond praise, ‹ is awesome

(1) *Isaiah* 6:3. (2) *Ezekiel* 3:12.

בְּכָל יוֹם תָּמִיד מַעֲשֵׂה בְרֵאשִׁית. כָּאָמוּר: לְעֹשֵׂה

‹ *[Give thanks] to Him Who makes* « As it is said: « of Creation. ‹ the work ‹ perpetually, ‹ day, ‹ every

אוֹרִים גְּדֹלִים, כִּי לְעוֹלָם חַסְדּוֹ.[1] אוֹר חָדָשׁ עַל

‹ on ‹ A new light « *is His kindness.* ‹ *enduring forever* ‹ *for* « *the great luminaries,*

צִיּוֹן תָּאִיר, וְנִזְכֶּה כֻלָּנוּ מְהֵרָה לְאוֹרוֹ. בָּרוּךְ אַתָּה

‹ are You, ‹ Blessed « [to benefit from] its light. ‹ speedily, ‹ all of us, ‹ and may we merit, « may You shine, ‹ Zion

יהוה, יוֹצֵר הַמְּאוֹרוֹת. (–Cong. אָמֵן.)

« Amen. « the luminaries. ‹ Who fashions « HASHEM,

אַהֲבָה רַבָּה אֲהַבְתָּנוּ יהוה אֱלֹהֵינוּ, חֶמְלָה

‹ with a compassion « our God; ‹ HASHEM, ‹ have You loved us, ‹ With an abundant love

גְדוֹלָה וִיתֵרָה חָמַלְתָּ עָלֵינוּ. אָבִינוּ מַלְכֵּנוּ,

« our King, ‹ Our Father, « to us. ‹ have You shown compassion ‹ and exceeding ‹ that is great

בַּעֲבוּר אֲבוֹתֵינוּ שֶׁבָּטְחוּ בְךָ, וַתְּלַמְּדֵם חֻקֵּי חַיִּים,

« of life, ‹ the decrees ‹ and to whom You taught ‹ in You ‹ who trusted ‹ of our forefathers ‹ for the sake

כֵּן תְּחָנֵּנוּ וּתְלַמְּדֵנוּ. אָבִינוּ הָאָב הָרַחֲמָן הַמְרַחֵם,

‹ Who acts mercifully, ‹ the merciful Father ‹ Our Father, « and teach us. ‹ may You be gracious to us ‹ so

רַחֵם עָלֵינוּ, וְתֵן בְּלִבֵּנוּ לְהָבִין וּלְהַשְׂכִּיל, לִשְׁמוֹעַ

‹ to listen, ‹ and comprehend, ‹ to understand ‹ in our hearts ‹ and instill « upon us, ‹ have mercy

לִלְמוֹד וּלְלַמֵּד, לִשְׁמֹר וְלַעֲשׂוֹת וּלְקַיֵּם אֶת כָּל

‹ all ‹ and fulfill ‹ perform, ‹ observe, ‹ teach, ‹ learn,

דִּבְרֵי תַלְמוּד תּוֹרָתֶךָ בְּאַהֲבָה. וְהָאֵר עֵינֵינוּ

‹ our eyes ‹ Enlighten « with love. ‹ of Your Torah ‹ of the teaching ‹ the words

בְּתוֹרָתֶךָ, וְדַבֵּק לִבֵּנוּ בְּמִצְוֹתֶיךָ, וְיַחֵד לְבָבֵנוּ

‹ our hearts ‹ and unify « to Your commandments, ‹ our hearts ‹ attach « in your Torah,

(1) *Psalms* 136:7.

לְאַהֲבָה וּלְיִרְאָה אֶת שְׁמֶךָ,[1] וְלֹא נֵבוֹשׁ לְעוֹלָם

to love, and to fear Your Name, so that we not be ashamed for ever

וָעֶד. כִּי בְשֵׁם קָדְשְׁךָ הַגָּדוֹל וְהַנּוֹרָא בָּטָחְנוּ, נָגִילָה

and ever; for in the Name of Your holiness that is great and awesome do we trust — may we exult

THE *TZITZIS* ARE NOT GATHERED AND ARE NOT KISSED DURING THE *SHEMA*.

וְנִשְׂמְחָה בִּישׁוּעָתֶךָ. וַהֲבִיאֵנוּ לְשָׁלוֹם מֵאַרְבַּע

and rejoice in Your salvation. Bring us in peace from the four

כַּנְפוֹת הָאָרֶץ, וְתוֹלִיכֵנוּ קוֹמְמִיּוּת לְאַרְצֵנוּ. כִּי אֵל

corners of the earth and lead us with upright pride to our land. For the God

פּוֹעֵל יְשׁוּעוֹת אָתָּה, וּבָנוּ בָחַרְתָּ מִכָּל עַם וְלָשׁוֹן.

Who performs salvations are You, and us You have chosen from among all peoples and tongues.

❖ וְקֵרַבְתָּנוּ לְשִׁמְךָ הַגָּדוֹל סֶלָה בֶּאֱמֶת, לְהוֹדוֹת

And You have brought us close to Your Name that is great forever in truth, to offer thanks

לְךָ וּלְיַחֶדְךָ בְּאַהֲבָה. בָּרוּךְ אַתָּה יהוה, הַבּוֹחֵר

to You, and proclaim Your Oneness with love. Blessed are You, HASHEM, Who chooses

בְּעַמּוֹ יִשְׂרָאֵל בְּאַהֲבָה. (—Cong. אָמֵן.)

His people Israel with love. Amen

THE SHEMA / שמע

IMMEDIATELY BEFORE ITS RECITATION CONCENTRATE ON FULFILLING THE POSITIVE COMMANDMENT OF RECITING THE *SHEMA* TWICE DAILY.

IT IS IMPORTANT TO ENUNCIATE EACH WORD CLEARLY AND NOT TO RUN WORDS TOGETHER. FOR THIS REASON, VERTICAL LINES HAVE BEEN PLACED BETWEEN TWO WORDS THAT ARE NOT SEPARATED BY A COMMA OR A DASH AND ARE APT TO BE SLURRED INTO ONE. SEE *LAWS* §95-109.

WHEN PRAYING WITHOUT A *MINYAN*, BEGIN WITH THE FOLLOWING THREE-WORD FORMULA:

אֵל מֶלֶךְ נֶאֱמָן.

God, King Who is trustworthy.

RECITE THE FIRST VERSE ALOUD, WITH THE RIGHT HAND COVERING THE EYES, AND CONCENTRATE INTENSELY UPON ACCEPTING GOD'S ABSOLUTE SOVEREIGNTY.

שְׁמַע | יִשְׂרָאֵל, יהוה | אֱלֹהֵינוּ, יהוה | אֶחָד:[2]

Hear, O Israel:* HASHEM is our God, HASHEM is the One [and Only].

(1) Cf. *Psalms* 86:11. (2) *Deuteronomy* 6:4.

IN AN UNDERTONE:

בָּרוּךְ שֵׁם כְּבוֹד מַלְכוּתוֹ לְעוֹלָם וָעֶד.[1]

« and ever. ‹ for ever ‹ kingdom ‹ of His glorious ‹ is the Name ‹ Blessed

WHILE RECITING THE FIRST PARAGRAPH (*DEUTERONOMY* 6:5-9), CONCENTRATE ON ACCEPTING THE COMMANDMENT TO LOVE GOD.

וְאָהַבְתָּ אֵת | יהוה | אֱלֹהֶיךָ, בְּכָל־לְבָבְךָ, וּבְכָל־

‹ with all « your heart, ‹ with all « your God, ‹ HASHEM, ‹ You shall love

נַפְשְׁךָ, וּבְכָל־מְאֹדֶךָ: וְהָיוּ הַדְּבָרִים הָאֵלֶּה, אֲשֶׁר |

‹ that ‹ — these matters « They should be « your resources. ‹ and with all ‹ your soul,

אָנֹכִי מְצַוְּךָ הַיּוֹם, עַל־לְבָבֶךָ: וְשִׁנַּנְתָּם לְבָנֶיךָ,

« to your children ‹ Teach them thoroughly « your heart. ‹ upon « today— ‹ command you ‹ I

וְדִבַּרְתָּ בָּם בְּשִׁבְתְּךָ בְּבֵיתֶךָ, וּבְלֶכְתְּךָ בַדֶּרֶךְ,

« on the way, ‹ while you walk « in your home, ‹ while you sit ‹ of them ‹ and speak

וּבְשָׁכְבְּךָ וּבְקוּמֶךָ: וּקְשַׁרְתָּם לְאוֹת | עַל־יָדֶךָ,

« your arm ‹ upon ‹ as a sign ‹ Bind them « and when you arise. ‹ when you lie down,

וְהָיוּ לְטֹטָפֹת בֵּין | עֵינֶיךָ: וּכְתַבְתָּם | עַל־מְזֻזוֹת

‹ the doorposts ‹ on ‹ And write them « your eyes. ‹ between ‹ *tefillin* ‹ and they shall be

בֵּיתֶךָ וּבִשְׁעָרֶיךָ:

«and upon your gates.‹ of your house

WHILE RECITING THE SECOND PARAGRAPH (*DEUTERONOMY* 11:13-21), CONCENTRATE ON ACCEPTING ALL THE COMMANDMENTS AND ON THE CONCEPT OF REWARD AND PUNISHMENT.

וְהָיָה, אִם־שָׁמֹעַ תִּשְׁמְעוּ אֶל־מִצְוֹתַי אֲשֶׁר |

‹ that « My commandments ‹ to ‹ you continually hearken ‹ that if ‹ And it will be

אָנֹכִי מְצַוֶּה | אֶתְכֶם הַיּוֹם, לְאַהֲבָה אֶת־יהוה |

‹ HASHEM, ‹ to love « today, ‹ you ‹ command ‹ I

אֱלֹהֵיכֶם וּלְעָבְדוֹ, בְּכָל־לְבַבְכֶם וּבְכָל־נַפְשְׁכֶם:

« your soul ‹ and with all ‹ your heart ‹ with all « and to serve Him, ‹ your God,

(1) See *Pesachim* 56a.

וְנָתַתִּי מְטַר־אַרְצְכֶם בְּעִתּוֹ, יוֹרֶה וּמַלְקוֹשׁ,

« and late rain, ‹ the early rain « in its proper time, ‹ for your land ‹ rain ‹ — then I will provide

וְאָסַפְתָּ דְגָנֶךָ וְתִירֹשְׁךָ וְיִצְהָרֶךָ: וְנָתַתִּי | עֵשֶׂב |

‹ grass ‹ I will provide « and your oil. ‹ your wine, ‹ your grain, ‹ that you may gather in

בְּשָׂדְךָ לִבְהֶמְתֶּךָ, וְאָכַלְתָּ וְשָׂבָעְתָּ: הִשָּׁמְרוּ לָכֶם פֶּן־

‹ lest « for yourselves ‹ Beware « and be satisfied. ‹ and you will eat « for your cattle ‹ in your field

יִפְתֶּה לְבַבְכֶם, וְסַרְתֶּם וַעֲבַדְתֶּם | אֱלֹהִים | אֲחֵרִים

‹ of others ‹ gods ‹ and serve ‹ and you turn astray « be your heart ‹ seduced

וְהִשְׁתַּחֲוִיתֶם לָהֶם: וְחָרָה | אַף־יְהוָה בָּכֶם, וְעָצַר |

‹ He will restrain « against you. ‹ of HASHEM ‹ the wrath ‹ Then shall blaze « to them. ‹ and bow

אֶת־הַשָּׁמַיִם וְלֹא־יִהְיֶה מָטָר, וְהָאֲדָמָה לֹא תִתֵּן

‹ yield ‹ will not ‹ and the ground « rain ‹ so there will not be ‹ the heaven

אֶת־יְבוּלָהּ, וַאֲבַדְתֶּם | מְהֵרָה מֵעַל הָאָרֶץ הַטֹּבָה |

‹ the good land ‹ from upon « swiftly ‹ And you will be banished « its produce.

אֲשֶׁר | יְהוָה נֹתֵן לָכֶם: וְשַׂמְתֶּם | אֶת־דְּבָרַי | אֵלֶּה

‹ these words of Mine ‹ Place « you. ‹ gives ‹ HASHEM ‹ which

עַל־לְבַבְכֶם וְעַל־נַפְשְׁכֶם, וּקְשַׁרְתֶּם | אֹתָם לְאוֹת |

‹ for a sign ‹ them ‹ bind « your soul; ‹ and upon ‹ your heart ‹ upon

עַל־יֶדְכֶם, וְהָיוּ לְטוֹטָפֹת בֵּין | עֵינֵיכֶם: וְלִמַּדְתֶּם |

‹ Teach « your eyes. ‹ between ‹ *tefillin* ‹ and they shall be « your arm ‹ upon

אֹתָם | אֶת־בְּנֵיכֶם לְדַבֵּר בָּם, בְּשִׁבְתְּךָ בְּבֵיתֶךָ,

« in your home, ‹ while you sit « them, ‹ to discuss « to your children, ‹ them

וּבְלֶכְתְּךָ בַדֶּרֶךְ, וּבְשָׁכְבְּךָ וּבְקוּמֶךָ: וּכְתַבְתָּם | עַל־

‹ on ‹ And write them « and when you arise. ‹ when you lie down « on the way, ‹ while you walk

מְזוּזוֹת בֵּיתֶךָ וּבִשְׁעָרֶיךָ: לְמַעַן | יִרְבּוּ | יְמֵיכֶם

‹ your days ‹ to prolong ‹ In order « and upon your gates. ‹ of your house ‹ the doorposts

וִימֵי בְנֵיכֶם עַל הָאֲדָמָה | אֲשֶׁר נִשְׁבַּע | יְהֹוָה

‹ HASHEM swore ‹ that ‹ the land ‹ upon « of your children ‹ and the days

לַאֲבֹתֵיכֶם לָתֵת לָהֶם, כִּימֵי הַשָּׁמַיִם | עַל־הָאָרֶץ:

« the earth. ‹ on ‹ of the heaven ‹ like the days « them, ‹ to give « to your ancestors

THE *TZITZIS* ARE NOT KISSED DURING THE LAST PARAGRAPH OF *SHEMA* (*NUMBERS* 15:37-41)

וַיֹּאמֶר | יְהֹוָה | אֶל־מֹשֶׁה לֵּאמֹר: דַּבֵּר | אֶל־בְּנֵי |

‹ the Children ‹ to ‹ Speak « saying: ‹ Moses, ‹ to ‹ HASHEM said

יִשְׂרָאֵל וְאָמַרְתָּ אֲלֵהֶם, וְעָשׂוּ לָהֶם צִיצִת

‹ *tzitzis* ‹ for themselves ‹ that they are to make « to them ‹ and say ‹ of Israel

עַל־כַּנְפֵי בִגְדֵיהֶם לְדֹרֹתָם, וְנָתְנוּ | עַל־צִיצִת

‹ the *tzitzis* ‹ upon ‹ And they are to place « throughout their generations. ‹ of their garments, ‹ the corners ‹ on

הַכָּנָף פְּתִיל תְּכֵלֶת: וְהָיָה לָכֶם לְצִיצִת, וּרְאִיתֶם |

‹ that you may see « *tzitzis,* ‹ for you ‹ And it shall constitute « of *techeiles.* ‹ a thread ‹ of the corner

אֹתוֹ וּזְכַרְתֶּם | אֶת־כָּל־מִצְוֹת | יְהֹוָה וַעֲשִׂיתֶם |

‹ and perform « of HASHEM ‹ the commandments ‹ all ‹ and remember « it

אֹתָם, וְלֹא־תָתֻרוּ | אַחֲרֵי לְבַבְכֶם וְאַחֲרֵי | עֵינֵיכֶם

‹ your eyes ‹ and after ‹ your heart ‹ after ‹ explore ‹ and do not « them;

אֲשֶׁר־אַתֶּם זֹנִים | אַחֲרֵיהֶם: לְמַעַן תִּזְכְּרוּ וַעֲשִׂיתֶם |

‹ and perform ‹ you may remember ‹ So that « after them. ‹ stray ‹ you ‹ which

אֶת־כָּל־מִצְוֹתָי, וִהְיִיתֶם קְדֹשִׁים לֵאלֹהֵיכֶם:

« to your God. ‹ holy ‹ and be « My commandments, ‹ all

CONCENTRATE ON FULFILLING THE COMMANDMENT TO REMEMBER THE EXODUS FROM EGYPT.

אֲנִי יְהֹוָה | אֱלֹהֵיכֶם אֲשֶׁר הוֹצֵאתִי | אֶתְכֶם |

‹ you ‹ has removed ‹ Who ‹ your God, ‹ HASHEM, ‹ I am

מֵאֶרֶץ מִצְרַיִם לִהְיוֹת לָכֶם לֵאלֹהִים, אֲנִי |

‹ I am « a God; ‹ to you ‹ to be ‹ of Egypt ‹ from the land

יְהֹוָה | אֱלֹהֵיכֶם: אֱמֶת —

« – It is true . . . « your God. ‹ HASHEM

ALTHOUGH THE WORD אֱמֶת BELONGS TO THE NEXT PARAGRAPH, IT IS APPENDED TO THE CONCLUSION OF THE PREVIOUS ONE.

***CHAZZAN* REPEATS:**

יהוה אֱלֹהֵיכֶם אֱמֶת,

« is true, ‹ your God, ‹ HASHEM,

וְיַצִּיב וְנָכוֹן וְקַיָּם וְיָשָׁר וְנֶאֱמָן וְאָהוּב וְחָבִיב

‹ cherished, ‹ beloved, ‹ faithful, ‹ fair, ‹ and enduring, ‹ established ‹ and certain,

וְנֶחְמָד וְנָעִים וְנוֹרָא וְאַדִּיר וּמְתֻקָּן וּמְקֻבָּל וְטוֹב

‹ good, ‹ accepted, ‹ correct, ‹ powerful, ‹ awesome, ‹ pleasant, ‹ desirable,

וְיָפֶה הַדָּבָר הַזֶּה עָלֵינוּ לְעוֹלָם וָעֶד. אֱמֶת

« True – « and ever. ‹ forever ‹ to us ‹ is this affirmation ‹ and beautiful

אֱלֹהֵי עוֹלָם מַלְכֵּנוּ צוּר יַעֲקֹב, מָגֵן יִשְׁעֵנוּ,

« of our salvation. ‹ is the Shield ‹ of Jacob ‹ the Rock « is our King; ‹ of the universe ‹ the God

לְדֹר וָדֹר הוּא קַיָּם, וּשְׁמוֹ קַיָּם, וְכִסְאוֹ נָכוֹן,

« is well established; ‹ and His Throne ‹ endures ‹ and His Name ‹ endures ‹ He ‹ after generation ‹ Generation

וּמַלְכוּתוֹ וֶאֱמוּנָתוֹ לָעַד קַיֶּמֶת. וּדְבָרָיו חָיִים

‹ are living ‹ His words « endure. ‹ forever ‹ and faithfulness ‹ His sovereignty

וְקַיָּמִים, נֶאֱמָנִים וְנֶחֱמָדִים לָעַד וּלְעוֹלְמֵי עוֹלָמִים.

« and to all eternity; ‹ forever ‹ and desirable ‹ faithful ‹ and enduring,

עַל אֲבוֹתֵינוּ וְעָלֵינוּ, עַל בָּנֵינוּ וְעַל דּוֹרוֹתֵינוּ, וְעַל

‹ and for « our generations, ‹ and for ‹ our children ‹ for « and for us, ‹ our forefathers ‹ for

כָּל דּוֹרוֹת זֶרַע יִשְׂרָאֵל עֲבָדֶיךָ.

« [who are] Your servants. ‹ of Israel, ‹ of the offspring ‹ the generations ‹ all

עַל הָרִאשׁוֹנִים וְעַל הָאַחֲרוֹנִים, דָּבָר טוֹב וְקַיָּם

‹ and enduring ‹ is good ‹ the matter ‹ the later generations, ‹ and for ‹ the earlier generations ‹ For

לְעוֹלָם וָעֶד, אֱמֶת וֶאֱמוּנָה חֹק וְלֹא יַעֲבֹר. אֱמֶת

‹ It is true « be breached: ‹ that cannot ‹ a decree ‹ and faithful, ‹ it is true « and ever; ‹ for ever

שָׁאַתָּה הוּא יהוה אֱלֹהֵינוּ וֵאלֹהֵי אֲבוֹתֵינוּ,

« of our forefathers, ‹ and the God ‹ our God ‹ HASHEM, ‹ that You are

❖ מַלְכֵּנוּ מֶלֶךְ אֲבוֹתֵינוּ, גֹּאֲלֵנוּ גֹּאֵל אֲבוֹתֵינוּ,

« of our forefathers, ‹ the Redeemer ‹ our Redeemer, « of our forefathers, ‹ and the King ‹ our King

יוֹצְרֵנוּ צוּר יְשׁוּעָתֵנוּ, פּוֹדֵנוּ וּמַצִּילֵנוּ מֵעוֹלָם

‹ — this has always ‹ *and our Rescuer* ‹ *our Liberator* « of our salvation; ‹ the Rock ‹ our Molder,

שְׁמֶךָ, אֵין אֱלֹהִים זוּלָתֶךָ.

« but You. ‹ God ‹ There is no « been Your Name.

עֶזְרַת אֲבוֹתֵינוּ אַתָּה הוּא מֵעוֹלָם, מָגֵן וּמוֹשִׁיעַ

‹ and Savior ‹ Shield « always, ‹ You have been ‹ of our forefathers ‹ The help

לִבְנֵיהֶם אַחֲרֵיהֶם בְּכָל דּוֹר וָדוֹר. בְּרוּם עוֹלָם

‹ of the universe ‹ At the zenith « generation. ‹ in every ‹ after them ‹ for their children

מוֹשָׁבֶךָ, וּמִשְׁפָּטֶיךָ וְצִדְקָתְךָ עַד אַפְסֵי אָרֶץ.

« of the earth. ‹ the ends ‹ extend to ‹ and Your righteousness ‹ and Your justice ‹ is Your dwelling,

אַשְׁרֵי אִישׁ שֶׁיִּשְׁמַע לְמִצְוֹתֶיךָ, וְתוֹרָתְךָ וּדְבָרְךָ

‹ and Your word ‹ and Your teaching ‹ Your commandments, ‹ who obeys ‹ is the person ‹ Praiseworthy

יָשִׂים עַל לִבּוֹ. אֱמֶת אַתָּה הוּא אָדוֹן לְעַמֶּךָ

‹ for Your people ‹ the Master ‹ that You are ‹ It is true « his heart. ‹ upon ‹ places

וּמֶלֶךְ גִּבּוֹר לָרִיב רִיבָם. אֱמֶת אַתָּה הוּא רִאשׁוֹן

‹ the First ‹ that You are ‹ It is true « their cause. ‹ to champion ‹ and a mighty King

וְאַתָּה הוּא אַחֲרוֹן, וּמִבַּלְעָדֶיךָ אֵין לָנוּ מֶלֶךְ[1]

‹ king, ‹ we have no ‹ and other than You « the Last, ‹ and that You are

גּוֹאֵל וּמוֹשִׁיעַ. מִמִּצְרַיִם גְּאַלְתָּנוּ יהוה אֱלֹהֵינוּ,

« our God, ‹ HASHEM, ‹ You redeemed us, ‹ From Egypt « or savior. ‹ redeemer,

(1) Cf. *Isaiah* 44:6.

וּמִבֵּית עֲבָדִים פְּדִיתָנוּ. כָּל בְּכוֹרֵיהֶם הָרָגְתָּ,

« You slew, ‹ their firstborn ‹ All « You liberated us. ‹ of slavery ‹ and from the house

וּבְכוֹרְךָ גָּאָלְתָּ, וְיַם סוּף בָּקַעְתָּ, וְזֵדִים טִבַּעְתָּ,

« You drowned; ‹ the willful sinners « You split; ‹ of Reeds ‹ the Sea « you redeemed; ‹ but Your firstborn

וִידִידִים הֶעֱבַרְתָּ, וַיְכַסּוּ מַיִם צָרֵיהֶם, אֶחָד מֵהֶם

‹ of them ‹ even one « their foes; ‹ and the water covered « You brought across; ‹ the dear ones

לֹא נוֹתָר.[1] עַל זֹאת שִׁבְּחוּ אֲהוּבִים וְרוֹמְמוּ אֵל,

« God; ‹ and exalted ‹ the beloved ones praised ‹ this, ‹ For « left. ‹ was not

וְנָתְנוּ יְדִידִים זְמִרוֹת שִׁירוֹת וְתִשְׁבָּחוֹת, בְּרָכוֹת

‹ blessings, ‹ praises, ‹ songs, ‹ hymns, ‹ the dear ones offered

וְהוֹדָאוֹת, לְמֶלֶךְ אֵל חַי וְקַיָּם, רָם וְנִשָּׂא, גָּדוֹל

‹ great ‹ and uplifted, ‹ exalted ‹ and enduring, ‹ Who is living ‹ the God ‹ to the King, ‹ and thanksgivings

וְנוֹרָא, מַשְׁפִּיל גֵּאִים, וּמַגְבִּיהַּ שְׁפָלִים, מוֹצִיא

‹ frees « the lowly, ‹ and lifts ‹ the haughty ‹ Who humbles « and awesome,

אֲסִירִים, וּפוֹדֶה עֲנָוִים, וְעוֹזֵר דַּלִּים, וְעוֹנֶה לְעַמּוֹ

‹ to His people ‹ and Who responds « the poor, ‹ and helps ‹ the humble, ‹ liberates ‹ the captive,

בְּעֵת שַׁוְּעָם אֵלָיו.

« to Him. ‹ they cry out ‹ when

RISE FOR *SHEMONEH ESREI*. SOME TAKE THREE STEPS BACKWARD AT THIS POINT; OTHERS DO SO BEFORE צוּר יִשְׂרָאֵל.

❖ תְּהִלּוֹת לְאֵל עֶלְיוֹן, בָּרוּךְ הוּא וּמְבֹרָךְ. מֹשֶׁה

‹ Moses « Who is blessed — ‹ One ‹ — the blessed « the Most High « to God ‹ Praises

וּבְנֵי יִשְׂרָאֵל לְךָ עָנוּ שִׁירָה בְּשִׂמְחָה רַבָּה

« with great joy, ‹ a song ‹ proclaimed ‹ to You ‹ of Israel ‹ and the Children

וְאָמְרוּ כֻלָּם:

« unanimously: « and said:

(1) *Psalms* 106:11.

מִי כָמֹכָה בָּאֵלִם יהוה, מִי כָּמֹכָה נֶאְדָּר

‹ mighty ‹ is like You, ‹ Who « HASHEM! ‹ among the heavenly powers, ‹ is like You ‹ Who

בַּקֹּדֶשׁ, נוֹרָא תְהִלֹּת עֹשֵׂה פֶלֶא.[1]

«wonders! ‹ doing «[beyond] praise, ‹ awesome « in holiness,

❖ שִׁירָה חֲדָשָׁה שִׁבְּחוּ גְאוּלִים לְשִׁמְךָ עַל

‹ at ‹ Your Name ‹ the redeemed ones praised ‹ [With] a new song

שְׂפַת הַיָּם, יַחַד כֻּלָּם הוֹדוּ וְהִמְלִיכוּ וְאָמְרוּ:

« and said: ‹ acknowledged Your sovereignty, ‹ gave thanks, ‹ all of them ‹ together « of the Sea, ‹ the shore

יהוה יִמְלֹךְ לְעֹלָם וָעֶד.[2]

« and ever! ‹ for ever ‹ shall reign ‹ HASHEM

IT IS FORBIDDEN TO INTERRUPT OR PAUSE BETWEEN גָּאַל יִשְׂרָאֵל AND *SHEMONEH ESREI*, EVEN FOR קַדִּישׁ, קְדוּשָּׁה, בָּרְכוּ, OR אָמֵן.

❖ **צוּר יִשְׂרָאֵל,** קוּמָה בְּעֶזְרַת יִשְׂרָאֵל, וּפְדֵה

«and liberate, ‹ of Israel ‹ to the aid ‹ arise ‹ of Israel, ‹ Rock

כִנְאֻמֶךָ יְהוּדָה וְיִשְׂרָאֵל. גֹּאֲלֵנוּ יהוה צְבָאוֹת שְׁמוֹ,

« is His Name, ‹ *Master of Legions* ‹ HASHEM, ‹ Our redeemer, « and Israel. ‹ Judah « as You pledged,

קְדוֹשׁ יִשְׂרָאֵל.[3] בָּרוּךְ אַתָּה יהוה, גָּאַל יִשְׂרָאֵל.

« Israel. ‹ Who redeemed «HASHEM, ‹ are You, ‹ Blessed « of Israel. ‹ the Holy One

SHEMONEH ESREI / שמונה עשרה — עמידה

TAKE THREE STEPS BACKWARD, THEN THREE STEPS FORWARD. REMAIN STANDING WITH FEET TOGETHER WHILE RECITING *SHEMONEH ESREI*. RECITE IT WITH QUIET DEVOTION AND WITHOUT INTERRUPTION, VERBAL OR OTHERWISE. ALTHOUGH ITS RECITATION SHOULD NOT BE AUDIBLE TO OTHERS, ONE MUST PRAY LOUDLY ENOUGH TO HEAR HIMSELF.

אֲדֹנָי שְׂפָתַי תִּפְתָּח, וּפִי יַגִּיד תְּהִלָּתֶךָ.[4]

« Your praise. ‹ may declare ‹ that my mouth « open, ‹ my lips ‹ O Lord,

PATRIARCHS / אבות

BEND THE KNEES AT בָּרוּךְ; BOW AT אַתָּה; STRAIGHTEN UP AT ה׳.

בָּרוּךְ אַתָּה יהוה אֱלֹהֵינוּ וֵאלֹהֵי אֲבוֹתֵינוּ, אֱלֹהֵי

‹ God « of our forefathers, ‹ and the God ‹ our God ‹ HASHEM, ‹ are You, ‹ Blessed

(1) *Exodus* 15:11. (2) 15:18. (3) *Isaiah* 47:4. (4) *Psalms* 51:17.

אַבְרָהָם, אֱלֹהֵי יִצְחָק, וֵאלֹהֵי יַעֲקֹב, הָאֵל הַגָּדוֹל

‹ [Who is] great, ‹ God « of Jacob; ‹ and God « of Isaac, ‹ God « of Abraham,

הַגִּבּוֹר וְהַנּוֹרָא, אֵל עֶלְיוֹן, גּוֹמֵל חֲסָדִים טוֹבִים,

‹ [that are] beneficent ‹ kindnesses ‹ Who bestows « the Most High, ‹ God ‹ and awesome; ‹ mighty,

וְקוֹנֵה הַכֹּל, וְזוֹכֵר חַסְדֵי אָבוֹת, וּמֵבִיא גוֹאֵל לִבְנֵי

‹ to the children ‹ a Redeemer ‹ and brings « of the Patriarchs, ‹ the kindnesses ‹ Who recalls « everything, ‹ and creates

בְנֵיהֶם, לְמַעַן שְׁמוֹ בְּאַהֲבָה. מֶלֶךְ עוֹזֵר וּמוֹשִׁיעַ וּמָגֵן.

« and Shield. ‹ Savior, ‹ Helper, ‹ O King, « with love. ‹ of His Name, ‹ for the sake « of their children,

BEND THE KNEES AT בָּרוּךְ; BOW AT אַתָּה; STRAIGHTEN UP AT 'ה.

בָּרוּךְ אַתָּה יהוה, מָגֵן אַבְרָהָם.

« of Abraham. ‹ Shield « HASHEM, ‹ are You, ‹ Blessed

GOD'S MIGHT / גבורות

אַתָּה גִּבּוֹר לְעוֹלָם אֲדֹנָי, מְחַיֵּה מֵתִים אַתָּה,

« are You; ‹ of the dead ‹ the Revivifier « O Lord, ‹ eternally, ‹ mighty ‹ You are

רַב לְהוֹשִׁיעַ. מְכַלְכֵּל חַיִּים בְּחֶסֶד, מְחַיֵּה מֵתִים

‹ the dead ‹ Who revivifies « with kindness, ‹ the living ‹ Who sustains « able to save, ‹ abundantly

בְּרַחֲמִים רַבִּים, סוֹמֵךְ נוֹפְלִים, וְרוֹפֵא חוֹלִים,

« the sick, ‹ Who heals « the fallen, ‹ Who supports « abundant, ‹ with mercy

וּמַתִּיר אֲסוּרִים, וּמְקַיֵּם אֱמוּנָתוֹ לִישֵׁנֵי עָפָר. מִי

‹ Who « in the dust. ‹ to those asleep ‹ His faith ‹ and Who maintains « the confined, ‹ Who releases

כָמוֹךָ בַּעַל גְּבוּרוֹת, וּמִי דּוֹמֶה לָּךְ, מֶלֶךְ מֵמִית

‹ Who causes death ‹ O King « to You, ‹ is comparable ‹ and who « of mighty deeds, ‹ O Master ‹ is like You,

וּמְחַיֶּה, וּמַצְמִיחַ יְשׁוּעָה. וְנֶאֱמָן אַתָּה לְהַחֲיוֹת

‹ to revivify ‹ are You ‹ And faithful « salvation! ‹ and makes sprout ‹ and restores life

מֵתִים. בָּרוּךְ אַתָּה יהוה, מְחַיֵּה הַמֵּתִים.

« the dead. ‹ Who revivifies « HASHEM, ‹ are You, ‹ Blessed « the dead.

DURING THE *CHAZZAN'S* REPETITION, *KEDUSHAH* (P. 176) IS RECITED AT THIS POINT.

KEDUSHAH / קדושה

WHEN RECITING *KEDUSHAH*, ONE MUST STAND WITH HIS FEET TOGETHER AND AVOID ANY INTERRUPTIONS. ONE SHOULD RISE ON HIS TOES WHEN SAYING THE WORDS ,קָדוֹשׁ, קָדוֹשׁ, קָדוֹשׁ; בָּרוּךְ (OF בָּרוּךְ כְּבוֹד); AND יִמְלֹךְ.

נְקַדֵּשׁ אֶת שִׁמְךָ בָּעוֹלָם, כְּשֵׁם שֶׁמַּקְדִּישִׁים אוֹתוֹ בִּשְׁמֵי

‹ in heaven ‹ it ‹ they sanctify ‹ just as « in this world ‹ Your Name ‹ We shall sanctify

מָרוֹם, כַּכָּתוּב עַל יַד נְבִיאֶךָ, וְקָרָא זֶה אֶל זֶה וְאָמַר:

« *and say:* ‹ *another* ‹ *to* ‹ *And one [angel] will call* « Your prophet, ‹ by ‹ as it is written « above,

קָדוֹשׁ קָדוֹשׁ קָדוֹשׁ יהוה צְבָאוֹת, מְלֹא כָל הָאָרֶץ כְּבוֹדוֹ.[1]

« *with His glory.* ‹ *world* ‹ *is the whole* ‹ *filled* « *Master of Legions,* ‹ *is* HASHEM, ‹ *holy* ‹ *holy,* ‹ *Holy,*

CHAZZAN:

לְעֻמָּתָם בָּרוּךְ יֹאמֵרוּ:

« they proclaim: ‹ *Blessed* ‹ Facing them,

ALL:

בָּרוּךְ כְּבוֹד יהוה, מִמְּקוֹמוֹ.[2]

« *from His place.* ‹ *of* HASHEM ‹ *is the glory* ‹ *Blessed*

CHAZZAN:

וּבְדִבְרֵי קָדְשְׁךָ כָּתוּב לֵאמֹר:

« saying: ‹ it is written ‹ that are holy ‹ And in Your Writings

ALL:

יִמְלֹךְ יהוה לְעוֹלָם, אֱלֹהַיִךְ צִיּוֹן לְדֹר וָדֹר, הַלְּלוּיָהּ.[3]

« *Halleluyah!* « *to generation,* ‹ *from generation* ‹ *O Zion,* ‹ *your God,* « *forever;* ‹ HASHEM *shall reign*

***CHAZZAN* ONLY CONCLUDES:**

לְדוֹר וָדוֹר נַגִּיד גָּדְלֶךָ וּלְנֵצַח נְצָחִים קְדֻשָּׁתְךָ נַקְדִּישׁ,

« we shall sanctify. ‹ Your holiness ‹ and for all eternity « Your greatness ‹ we shall relate ‹ to generation ‹ From generation

וְשִׁבְחֲךָ אֱלֹהֵינוּ מִפִּינוּ לֹא יָמוּשׁ לְעוֹלָם וָעֶד, כִּי אֵל

‹ O God, ‹ for, « and ever, ‹ for ever ‹ leave ‹ shall not ‹ from our mouth « our God, ‹ Your praise,

מֶלֶךְ גָּדוֹל וְקָדוֹשׁ אָתָּה. בָּרוּךְ אַתָּה יהוה, הָאֵל הַקָּדוֹשׁ.

« Who is holy. ‹ the God « HASHEM, ‹ are You, ‹ Blessed « are You. ‹ and holy ‹ great ‹ a King,

***CHAZZAN* CONTINUES אַתָּה חוֹנֵן ... (P. 177).**

(1) *Isaiah* 6:3. (2) *Ezekiel* 3:12. (3) *Psalms* 146:10.

HOLINESS OF GOD'S NAME / קדושת השם

אַתָּה קָדוֹשׁ וְשִׁמְךָ קָדוֹשׁ, וּקְדוֹשִׁים בְּכָל יוֹם

‹ day ‹ every ‹ and holy ones « is holy, ‹ and Your Name ‹ are holy ‹ You

יְהַלְּלְוּךָ סֶּלָה. בָּרוּךְ אַתָּה יהוה, הָאֵל הַקָּדוֹשׁ.

« Who is Holy. ‹ the God « HASHEM, ‹ are You, ‹ Blessed « forever. ‹ praise You

INSIGHT / בינה

אַתָּה חוֹנֵן לְאָדָם דַּעַת, וּמְלַמֵּד לֶאֱנוֹשׁ בִּינָה.

« insight. ‹ to a [frail] mortal ‹ and teach « with wisdom ‹ man ‹ graciously endow ‹ You

חָנֵּנוּ מֵאִתְּךָ דֵּעָה בִּינָה וְהַשְׂכֵּל. בָּרוּךְ אַתָּה

‹ are You, ‹ Blessed « and discernment. ‹ insight, ‹ [with] wisdom, ‹ from Yourself ‹ Endow us graciously

יהוה, חוֹנֵן הַדָּעַת.

« of wisdom. ‹ gracious Giver « HASHEM,

REPENTANCE / תשובה

הֲשִׁיבֵנוּ אָבִינוּ לְתוֹרָתֶךָ, וְקָרְבֵנוּ מַלְכֵּנוּ

‹ our King, ‹ and bring us near, « to Your Torah, ‹ our Father, ‹ Bring us back,

לַעֲבוֹדָתֶךָ, וְהַחֲזִירֵנוּ בִּתְשׁוּבָה שְׁלֵמָה לְפָנֶיךָ.

« before You. ‹ in complete repentance ‹ and influence us to return « to Your service,

בָּרוּךְ אַתָּה יהוה, הָרוֹצֶה בִּתְשׁוּבָה.

« repentance. ‹ Who desires « HASHEM, ‹ are You, ‹ Blessed

FORGIVENESS / סליחה

STRIKE THE LEFT SIDE OF THE CHEST WITH THE RIGHT FIST WHILE RECITING THE WORDS חָטָאנוּ, *SINNED,* AND פָּשָׁעְנוּ, *WILLFULLY SINNED.*

סְלַח לָנוּ אָבִינוּ כִּי חָטָאנוּ, מְחַל לָנוּ מַלְכֵּנוּ

‹ our King, ‹ us, ‹ pardon « we have sinned; ‹ for ‹ our Father, ‹ us, ‹ Forgive

כִּי פָשָׁעְנוּ, כִּי מוֹחֵל וְסוֹלֵחַ אָתָּה. בָּרוּךְ

‹ Blessed « are You. ‹ and Forgiver ‹ a Pardoner ‹ for « we have willfully sinned; ‹ for

אַתָּה יהוה, חַנּוּן הַמַּרְבֶּה לִסְלוֹחַ.

« forgives. ‹ Who abundantly ‹ the gracious One « HASHEM, ‹ are You,

REDEMPTION / גאולה

רְאֵה בְעָנְיֵנוּ, וְרִיבָה רִיבֵנוּ, וּגְאָלֵנוּ[1] מְהֵרָה

‹ speedily ‹ and redeem us « our cause, ‹ champion « our affliction, ‹ Behold

לְמַעַן שְׁמֶךָ, כִּי גוֹאֵל חָזָק אָתָּה. בָּרוּךְ אַתָּה

‹ are You, ‹ Blessed « are You. ‹ Who is powerful ‹ a Redeemer ‹ for « Your Name, ‹ for the sake of

יהוה, גּוֹאֵל יִשְׂרָאֵל.

« of Israel. ‹ Redeemer « HASHEM,

DURING HIS REPETITION, THE *CHAZZAN* RECITES עֲנֵנוּ AT THIS POINT. SEE *LAWS* §61-63. [IF HE FORGOT TO RECITE IT AT THIS POINT, HE MAY INSERT IT IN שְׁמַע קוֹלֵנוּ (P. 182), BUT WITHOUT THE CONCLUDING BLESSING.]

עֲנֵנוּ יהוה עֲנֵנוּ, בְּיוֹם צוֹם תַּעֲנִיתֵנוּ, כִּי בְצָרָה

‹ in distress ‹ for « of our public gathering for fasting ‹ on this day « answer us, ‹ HASHEM, ‹ Answer us,

גְדוֹלָה אֲנָחְנוּ. אַל תֵּפֶן אֶל רִשְׁעֵנוּ, וְאַל תַּסְתֵּר

‹ hide ‹ do not « our wickedness, ‹ to ‹ pay attention ‹ Do not « are we. ‹ that is great

פָּנֶיךָ מִמֶּנּוּ, וְאַל תִּתְעַלַּם מִתְּחִנָּתֵנוּ. הֱיֵה נָא קָרוֹב

‹ near ‹ Please be « our supplication. ‹ ignore ‹ and do not «from us, ‹ Your Face

לְשַׁוְעָתֵנוּ, יְהִי נָא חַסְדְּךָ לְנַחֲמֵנוּ, טֶרֶם נִקְרָא

‹ we call ‹ – before « comfort us ‹ Your kindness ‹ please let « to our outcry;

אֵלֶיךָ עֲנֵנוּ, כַּדָּבָר שֶׁנֶּאֱמַר: וְהָיָה טֶרֶם יִקְרָאוּ

‹ *they call,* ‹ *[that] before* ‹ *And it will be* « is said: ‹ as it « answer us, « to You

וַאֲנִי אֶעֱנֶה, עוֹד הֵם מְדַבְּרִים וַאֲנִי אֶשְׁמָע.[1] כִּי

‹ For « *will hear.* ‹ *I* ‹ *[yet] speak,* ‹ *they* ‹ *[that] while* « *will answer;* ‹ *I*

אַתָּה יהוה הָעוֹנֶה בְּעֵת צָרָה, פּוֹדֶה וּמַצִּיל בְּכָל

‹ in every ‹ and rescues ‹ Who redeems « of distress, ‹ in time ‹ are the One Who responds ‹ HASHEM, ‹ You,

עֵת צָרָה וְצוּקָה. בָּרוּךְ אַתָּה יהוה, הָעוֹנֶה בְּעֵת צָרָה.

« of distress. ‹ in time ‹ Who responds « HASHEM, ‹ are You, ‹ Blessed « and woe. ‹ of distress ‹ time

(1) Cf. *Psalms* 119:153-154. (2) *Isaiah* 65:24.

HEALTH AND HEALING / רפואה

רְפָאֵנוּ יהוה וְנֵרָפֵא, הוֹשִׁיעֵנוּ וְנִוָּשֵׁעָה, כִּי

Heal us, HASHEM — then we will be healed; save us — then we will be saved, for

תְהִלָּתֵנוּ אָתָּה,[1] וְהַעֲלֵה רְפוּאָה שְׁלֵמָה לְכָל

the One we praise is You. Bring healing that is complete for all

מַכּוֹתֵינוּ, °°כִּי אֵל מֶלֶךְ רוֹפֵא נֶאֱמָן וְרַחֲמָן

our ailments, for O God, [and] King, a Healer Who is faithful and compassionate

אָתָּה. בָּרוּךְ אַתָּה יהוה, רוֹפֵא חוֹלֵי עַמּוֹ יִשְׂרָאֵל.

are You. Blessed are You, HASHEM, Who heals the sick of His people Israel.

YEAR OF PROSPERITY / ברכת השנים

בָּרֵךְ עָלֵינוּ יהוה אֱלֹהֵינוּ אֶת הַשָּׁנָה הַזֹּאת וְאֶת

Bless on our behalf — O HASHEM, our God — this year and

כָּל מִינֵי תְבוּאָתָהּ לְטוֹבָה, וְתֵן בְּרָכָה עַל פְּנֵי

all the kinds of its crops for goodness; and give a blessing on the face

הָאֲדָמָה, וְשַׂבְּעֵנוּ מִטּוּבֶךָ, וּבָרֵךְ שְׁנָתֵנוּ כַּשָּׁנִים

of the earth, and satisfy us from Your bounty, and bless our year like the years

°°AT THIS POINT ONE MAY INSERT A PRAYER FOR ONE WHO IS ILL:

יְהִי רָצוֹן מִלְּפָנֶיךָ, יהוה אֱלֹהַי וֵאלֹהֵי אֲבוֹתַי, שֶׁתִּשְׁלַח מְהֵרָה

May it be the will before You, HASHEM, my God, and the God of my forefathers, that You send quickly

רְפוּאָה שְׁלֵמָה מִן הַשָּׁמַיִם, רְפוּאַת הַנֶּפֶשׁ וּרְפוּאַת הַגּוּף

a healing which is complete, from heaven, a healing of the spirit and a healing of the body

FOR A MALE / FOR A FEMALE

לַחוֹלֶה / לַחוֹלָה (SICK ONE'S NAME) בֶּן / בַּת (MOTHER'S NAME) בְּתוֹךְ שְׁאָר

to the sick one son of / daughter of among the other

חוֹלֵי יִשְׂרָאֵל.

sick ones of Israel.

CONTINUE ... כִּי אֵל (ABOVE)

(1) Cf. *Jeremiah* 17:14.

הַטּוֹבוֹת. בָּרוּךְ אַתָּה יהוה, מְבָרֵךְ הַשָּׁנִים.

« the years. ‹ Who blesses « HASHEM, ‹ are You, ‹ Blessed « that were good.

INGATHERING OF EXILES / קיבוץ גליות

תְּקַע בְּשׁוֹפָר גָּדוֹל לְחֵרוּתֵנוּ, וְשָׂא נֵס לְקַבֵּץ גָּלֻיּוֹתֵינוּ, וְקַבְּצֵנוּ יַחַד מֵאַרְבַּע כַּנְפוֹת הָאָרֶץ.[1] בָּרוּךְ אַתָּה יהוה, מְקַבֵּץ נִדְחֵי עַמּוֹ יִשְׂרָאֵל.

‹ to gather ‹ a banner ‹ raise « for our freedom, ‹ the great *shofar* ‹ Sound

« of the earth. ‹ corners ‹ from the four ‹ together ‹ and gather us « our exiles,

« Israel. ‹ of His people ‹ the dispersed ‹ Who gathers in « HASHEM, ‹ are You, ‹ Blessed

RESTORATION OF JUSTICE / דין

הָשִׁיבָה שׁוֹפְטֵינוּ כְּבָרִאשׁוֹנָה, וְיוֹעֲצֵינוּ כְּבַתְּחִלָּה,[2] וְהָסֵר מִמֶּנּוּ יָגוֹן וַאֲנָחָה, וּמְלוֹךְ עָלֵינוּ אַתָּה יהוה לְבַדְּךָ בְּחֶסֶד וּבְרַחֲמִים, וְצַדְּקֵנוּ בַּמִּשְׁפָּט. בָּרוּךְ אַתָּה יהוה, מֶלֶךְ אוֹהֵב צְדָקָה וּמִשְׁפָּט.

‹ and our counselors ‹ as [they were] in earliest times, ‹ our judges ‹ Restore

‹ over us ‹ and reign « and groan; ‹ sorrow ‹ from us ‹ remove « as at the beginning;

‹ and justify us « and compassion, ‹ with kindness « alone — ‹ HASHEM, ‹ — You,

‹ righteousness ‹ Who loves ‹ the King « HASHEM, ‹ are You, ‹ Blessed « through judgment.

« and judgment.

AGAINST HERETICS / ברכת המינים

וְלַמַּלְשִׁינִים אַל תְּהִי תִקְוָה, וְכָל הָרִשְׁעָה כְּרֶגַע תֹּאבֵד, וְכָל אוֹיְבֶיךָ מְהֵרָה יִכָּרֵתוּ, וְהַזֵּדִים

‹ wickedness ‹ and may all « hope; ‹ let there not be ‹ And for slanderers

« The willful sinners « be cut down. ‹ speedily ‹ Your enemies ‹ and may all « perish; ‹ in an instant

(1) *Isaiah* 11:12. (2) Cf. 1:26.

מְהֵרָה תְעַקֵּר וּתְשַׁבֵּר וּתְמַגֵּר וְתַכְנִיעַ בִּמְהֵרָה

‹ speedily « and humble — ‹ cast down, ‹ smash, ‹ uproot, ‹ — may You speedily

בְּיָמֵינוּ. בָּרוּךְ אַתָּה יהוה, שׁוֹבֵר אֹיְבִים

‹ enemies ‹ Who breaks « HASHEM, ‹ are You, ‹ Blessed « in our days.

וּמַכְנִיעַ זֵדִים.

« willful sinners. ‹ and humbles

THE RIGHTEOUS / צדיקים

עַל הַצַּדִּיקִים וְעַל הַחֲסִידִים, וְעַל זִקְנֵי עַמְּךָ בֵּית

‹ the Family ‹ of Your people ‹ the elders ‹ on « the devout, ‹ on ‹ the righteous, ‹ On

יִשְׂרָאֵל, וְעַל פְּלֵיטַת סוֹפְרֵיהֶם, וְעַל גֵּרֵי הַצֶּדֶק

‹ who are righteous ‹ the converts ‹ on « of their scholars, ‹ the remnant ‹ on « of Israel,

וְעָלֵינוּ, יֶהֱמוּ רַחֲמֶיךָ, יהוה אֱלֹהֵינוּ, וְתֵן שָׂכָר

‹ a reward ‹ and give « our God, ‹ HASHEM, « Your compassion, ‹ — may aroused be « and on ourselves

טוֹב לְכָל הַבּוֹטְחִים בְּשִׁמְךָ בֶּאֱמֶת, וְשִׂים חֶלְקֵנוּ

‹ our lot ‹ Put « in sincerity. ‹ in Your Name ‹ who believe ‹ to all ‹ which is good

עִמָּהֶם לְעוֹלָם, וְלֹא נֵבוֹשׁ כִּי בְךָ בָּטָחְנוּ. בָּרוּךְ

‹ Blessed « we trust. ‹ in You ‹ for ‹ feel ashamed, ‹ and we will not « forever, ‹ with them

אַתָּה יהוה, מִשְׁעָן וּמִבְטָח לַצַּדִּיקִים.

« of the righteous. ‹ and Assurance ‹ Mainstay « HASHEM, ‹ are You,

REBUILDING JERUSALEM / בנין ירושלים

וְלִירוּשָׁלַיִם עִירְךָ בְּרַחֲמִים תָּשׁוּב, וְתִשְׁכּוֹן

‹ and may You rest « may You return, ‹ in compassion ‹ Your City, ‹ And to Jerusalem,

בְּתוֹכָהּ כַּאֲשֶׁר דִּבַּרְתָּ, וּבְנֵה אוֹתָהּ בְּקָרוֹב בְּיָמֵינוּ

‹ in our days ‹ soon ‹ it ‹ May You rebuild « You have spoken. ‹ as ‹ within it,

בִּנְיַן עוֹלָם, וְכִסֵּא דָוִד מְהֵרָה לְתוֹכָהּ תָּכִין.

« may You establish. ‹ within it ‹ speedily, ‹ of David, ‹ and the throne « that is eternal, ‹ as a structure

בָּרוּךְ אַתָּה יהוה, בּוֹנֵה יְרוּשָׁלָיִם.

« of Jerusalem. ‹ Builder « HASHEM, ‹ are You, ‹ Blessed

DAVIDIC REIGN / מלכות בית דוד

אֶת צֶמַח דָּוִד עַבְדְּךָ מְהֵרָה תַצְמִיחַ, וְקַרְנוֹ

‹ and his pride « may You cause to flourish, ‹ speedily, « Your servant, ‹ of David ‹ offspring ‹ The

תָּרוּם בִּישׁוּעָתֶךָ, כִּי לִישׁוּעָתְךָ קִוִּינוּ כָּל הַיּוֹם.

« all day long. ‹ we hope ‹ for Your salvation ‹ because « through Your salvation, ‹ may You exalt

בָּרוּךְ אַתָּה יהוה, מַצְמִיחַ קֶרֶן יְשׁוּעָה.

« of salvation. ‹ the pride ‹ Who causes to flourish « HASHEM, ‹ are You, ‹ Blessed

ACCEPTANCE OF PRAYER / קבלת תפלה

שְׁמַע קוֹלֵנוּ יהוה אֱלֹהֵינוּ, חוּס וְרַחֵם

‹ and have compassion ‹ have pity « our God, ‹ HASHEM, ‹ our voice, ‹ Hear

עָלֵינוּ, וְקַבֵּל בְּרַחֲמִים וּבְרָצוֹן אֶת תְּפִלָּתֵנוּ, כִּי

‹ for « our prayer, ‹ and with favor ‹ with compassion ‹ and accept « on us,

אֵל שׁוֹמֵעַ תְּפִלּוֹת וְתַחֲנוּנִים אָתָּה. וּמִלְּפָנֶיךָ

« From before Yourself, « are You. ‹ and supplications ‹ prayers ‹ Who hears ‹ God

מַלְכֵּנוּ, רֵיקָם אַל תְּשִׁיבֵנוּ.°°

« turn us away, ‹ do not ‹ empty-handed ‹ our King,

°°AT THIS POINT IN THE SILENT *SHEMONEH ESREI* ONE MAY INSERT THE FOLLOWING PERSONAL PRAYER FOR FORGIVENESS:

אָנָּא יהוה, חָטָאתִי עָוִיתִי וּפָשַׁעְתִּי לְפָנֶיךָ, מִיּוֹם הֱיוֹתִי

‹ I have existed ‹ from the day « before You, ‹ and willfully sinned « been iniquitous, ‹ I have sinned, ‹ HASHEM, ‹ Please,

עַל הָאֲדָמָה עַד הַיּוֹם הַזֶּה (וּבִפְרַט בַּחֵטְא . . .). אָנָּא יהוה,

‹ HASHEM, ‹ Please, « with the sin of . . .). ‹ (and especially « this very day ‹ until ‹ earth ‹ on

עֲשֵׂה לְמַעַן שִׁמְךָ הַגָּדוֹל, וּתְכַפֶּר לִי עַל חֲטָאַי וַעֲוֹנַי

‹ my iniquities ‹ my inadvertent sins, ‹ for ‹ to me ‹ and grant atonement « which is great ‹ Your Name ‹ for the sake of ‹ act

וּפְשָׁעַי שֶׁחָטָאתִי וְשֶׁעָוִיתִי וְשֶׁפָּשַׁעְתִּי לְפָנֶיךָ, מִנְּעוּרַי עַד

‹ until ‹ from my youth « before You, ‹ and sinned willfully ‹ been iniquitous, ‹ [through which] I have sinned, « and my willful sins

הַיּוֹם הַזֶּה. וּתְמַלֵּא כָּל הַשֵּׁמוֹת שֶׁפָּגַמְתִּי בְּשִׁמְךָ הַגָּדוֹל.

« that is great. ‹ within Your Name ‹ that I have blemished ‹ the [Holy] Names ‹ all ‹ And make whole « this very day.

CONTINUE ... **כִּי אַתָּה** (P. 184)

°°AT THIS POINT DURING THE SILENT *SHEMONEH ESREI* ONE MAY INSERT THE FOLLOWING PERSONAL PRAYER FOR LIVELIHOOD:

אַתָּה הוּא יהוה הָאֱלֹהִים, הַזָּן וּמְפַרְנֵס וּמְכַלְכֵּל מִקַּרְנֵי

‹ from the horns « and supports, ‹ sustains, ‹ Who nourishes, ‹ the God ‹ HASHEM, ‹ Who are ‹ It is You

רְאֵמִים עַד בֵּיצֵי כִנִּים. הַטְרִיפֵנִי לֶחֶם חֻקִּי,[1] וְהַמְצֵא לִי

‹ for me ‹ provide « allotted to me; ‹ the bread ‹ Supply me with « of lice. ‹ the eggs ‹ to ‹ of *re'eimim*

וּלְכָל בְּנֵי בֵיתִי מְזוֹנוֹתַי קוֹדֶם שֶׁאֶצְטָרֵךְ לָהֶם, בְּנַחַת

‹ in contentment « for it; ‹ I have need ‹ before ‹ my food, « of my household, ‹ members ‹ and for all

וְלֹא בְצַעַר, בְּהֶתֵּר וְלֹא בְאִסּוּר, בְּכָבוֹד וְלֹא בְבִזָּיוֹן,

« in disgrace, ‹ but not ‹ in honor « in a forbidden manner, ‹ but not ‹ in a permissible manner « in pain, ‹ but not

לְחַיִּים וּלְשָׁלוֹם, מִשֶּׁפַע בְּרָכָה וְהַצְלָחָה, וּמִשֶּׁפַע בְּרֵכָה

‹ of the spring ‹ and from the flow « and success ‹ of blessing ‹ from the flow « and for peace; ‹ for life

עֶלְיוֹנָה, כְּדֵי שֶׁאוּכַל לַעֲשׂוֹת רְצוֹנֶךָ וְלַעֲסוֹק בְּתוֹרָתֶךָ

‹ in Your Torah ‹ and engage « Your will ‹ to do ‹ I be enabled ‹ so that « from On High,

וּלְקַיֵּם מִצְוֹתֶיךָ. וְאַל תַּצְרִיכֵנִי לִידֵי מַתְּנַת בָּשָׂר וָדָם.

« and blood; ‹ of flesh ‹ of the gifts of the hands ‹ make me needful ‹ Do not « Your commandments. ‹ and fulfill

וִיקֻיַּם בִּי מִקְרָא שֶׁכָּתוּב: פּוֹתֵחַ אֶת יָדֶךָ, וּמַשְׂבִּיעַ לְכָל

‹ *every* ‹ *and satisfy* ‹ *Your hand,* ‹ *You open* « that states, ‹ the verse ‹ in me ‹ and may there be fulfilled

חַי רָצוֹן.[2] וְכָתוּב: הַשְׁלֵךְ עַל יהוה יְהָבְךָ וְהוּא יְכַלְכְּלֶךָ.[3]

« *will sustain you.* ‹ *and He* ‹ *Your burden* ‹ *HASHEM* ‹ *upon* ‹ *Cast* ‹ and that states, « *[with its] desire,* ‹ *living thing*

CONTINUE ... **כִּי אַתָּה** (P. 184)

(1) *Proverbs* 30:8. (2) *Psalms* 145:16. (3) 55:23.

כִּי אַתָּה שׁוֹמֵעַ תְּפִלַּת עַמְּךָ יִשְׂרָאֵל בְּרַחֲמִים.

For ‹ You ‹ hear ‹ the prayer ‹ of Your people ‹ Israel ‹ with compassion. «

בָּרוּךְ אַתָּה יהוה, שׁוֹמֵעַ תְּפִלָּה.

Blessed ‹ are You, ‹ HASHEM, « Who hears ‹ prayer. «

TEMPLE SERVICE / עבודה

רְצֵה יהוה אֱלֹהֵינוּ בְּעַמְּךָ יִשְׂרָאֵל וּבִתְפִלָּתָם,

Be favorable, « HASHEM, ‹ our God, « toward Your people ‹ Israel ‹ and toward their prayer «

וְהָשֵׁב אֶת הָעֲבוֹדָה לִדְבִיר בֵּיתֶךָ. וְאִשֵּׁי יִשְׂרָאֵל

and restore ‹ the service ‹ to the Holy of Holies ‹ of Your Temple. « The fire-offerings ‹ of Israel ‹

וּתְפִלָּתָם בְּאַהֲבָה תְקַבֵּל בְּרָצוֹן, וּתְהִי לְרָצוֹן

and their prayer ‹ with love ‹ accept ‹ favorably, « and may it be ‹ to Your favor ‹

תָּמִיד עֲבוֹדַת יִשְׂרָאֵל עַמֶּךָ.

always ‹ the service ‹ of Israel ‹ Your people. «

וְתֶחֱזֶינָה עֵינֵינוּ בְּשׁוּבְךָ לְצִיּוֹן בְּרַחֲמִים. בָּרוּךְ

Witness ‹ may our eyes ‹ Your return ‹ to Zion ‹ in compassion. « Blessed ‹

אַתָּה יהוה, הַמַּחֲזִיר שְׁכִינָתוֹ לְצִיּוֹן.

are You, ‹ HASHEM, « Who restores ‹ His Presence ‹ to Zion. «

THANKSGIVING [MODIM] / הודאה

BOW AT מוֹדִים, *WE THANK YOU*; STRAIGHTEN UP AT ה׳, *HASHEM.*
IN HIS REPETITION THE *CHAZZAN* RECITES THE ENTIRE מוֹדִים ALOUD,
WHILE THE CONGREGATION RECITES מוֹדִים דְּרַבָּנָן (P. 185) SOFTLY.

מוֹדִים אֲנַחְנוּ לָךְ שָׁאַתָּה הוּא יהוה אֱלֹהֵינוּ

We thank ‹ You, « for it is You ‹ Who are ‹ HASHEM, ‹ our God ‹

וֵאלֹהֵי אֲבוֹתֵינוּ לְעוֹלָם וָעֶד. צוּר חַיֵּינוּ, מָגֵן

and the God ‹ of our forefathers ‹ for ever ‹ and ever; « Rock ‹ of our lives, « Shield ‹

יִשְׁעֵנוּ אַתָּה הוּא לְדוֹר וָדוֹר. נוֹדֶה לְּךָ וּנְסַפֵּר

of our salvation « [is what] You are ‹ from generation ‹ to generation. « We shall thank ‹ You ‹ and relate ‹

תְּהִלָּתֶךָ[1] עַל חַיֵּינוּ הַמְּסוּרִים בְּיָדֶךָ, וְעַל נִשְׁמוֹתֵינוּ

‹ our souls ‹ and for «into Your hands ‹ that are committed ‹our lives‹ for « Your praise,

הַפְּקוּדוֹת לָךְ, וְעַל נִסֶּיךָ שֶׁבְּכָל יוֹם עִמָּנוּ, וְעַל

‹ and for « are with us; ‹ day ‹ that every ‹ Your miracles ‹ and for « to You; ‹ that are entrusted

נִפְלְאוֹתֶיךָ וְטוֹבוֹתֶיךָ שֶׁבְּכָל עֵת, עֶרֶב וָבֹקֶר

‹morning, ‹ — evening,« times ‹ that are at all ‹ and favors ‹ Your wonders

וְצָהֳרָיִם. הַטּוֹב כִּי לֹא כָלוּ רַחֲמֶיךָ, וְהַמְּרַחֵם

‹ and the Compassionate One, « are Your compassions, ‹exhausted ‹ never ‹ for ‹ The Beneficent One, « and afternoon.

כִּי לֹא תַמּוּ חֲסָדֶיךָ,[2] מֵעוֹלָם קִוִּינוּ לָךְ.

« in You. ‹have we put our hope ‹ — always « were Your kindnesses ‹ ended ‹ never ‹ for

MODIM OF THE RABBIS / מודים דרבנן

מוֹדִים אֲנַחְנוּ לָךְ, שָׁאַתָּה הוּא יהוה אֱלֹהֵינוּ וֵאלֹהֵי

‹ and the God ‹ our God ‹ HASHEM, ‹ Who are ‹ for it is You « You, ‹ We thank

אֲבוֹתֵינוּ, אֱלֹהֵי כָל בָּשָׂר, יוֹצְרֵנוּ, יוֹצֵר בְּרֵאשִׁית. בְּרָכוֹת

‹ Blessings « of the universe. ‹ the Molder ‹ our Molder, « flesh, ‹ of all ‹ the God « of our forefathers,

וְהוֹדָאוֹת לְשִׁמְךָ הַגָּדוֹל וְהַקָּדוֹשׁ, עַל שֶׁהֶחֱיִיתָנוּ וְקִיַּמְתָּנוּ.

« and You have sustained us. ‹ You have given us life ‹ for « and that is holy, ‹ that is great ‹ [are due] to Your Name ‹ and thanks

כֵּן תְּחַיֵּנוּ וּתְקַיְּמֵנוּ, וְתֶאֱסוֹף גָּלֻיּוֹתֵינוּ לְחַצְרוֹת קָדְשֶׁךָ,

« of Your Sanctuary, ‹ to the Courtyards ‹ our exiles ‹ and gather « and sustain us, ‹ may You continue to give us life ‹ So

לִשְׁמוֹר חֻקֶּיךָ וְלַעֲשׂוֹת רְצוֹנֶךָ, וּלְעָבְדְּךָ בְּלֵבָב שָׁלֵם,

« wholeheartedly. ‹ and to serve You « Your will, ‹ to do « Your decrees, ‹ to observe

עַל שֶׁאֲנַחְנוּ מוֹדִים לָךְ. בָּרוּךְ אֵל הַהוֹדָאוֹת.

« of thanksgivings. ‹ is the God ‹ Blessed «You. ‹ to thank ‹ [inspiring] us ‹[We thank You] for

(1) Cf. *Psalms* 79:13. (2) Cf. *Lamentations* 3:22.

וְעַל כֻּלָּם יִתְבָּרַךְ וְיִתְרוֹמַם שִׁמְךָ מַלְכֵּנוּ

« our King, ‹ may Your Name be, ‹ and exalted ‹ blessed ‹ all these, ‹ For

תָּמִיד לְעוֹלָם וָעֶד.

« and ever. ‹ for ever ‹ continually,

BEND THE KNEES AT בָּרוּךְ, *BLESSED*; BOW AT אַתָּה, *YOU*; STRAIGHTEN UP AT ה׳, *HASHEM*.

וְכֹל הַחַיִּים יוֹדְוּךָ סֶּלָה, וִיהַלְּלוּ אֶת שִׁמְךָ

‹ Your Name ‹ — and praise « forever! ‹ will gratefully acknowledge You, ‹ alive ‹ Everything

בֶּאֱמֶת, הָאֵל יְשׁוּעָתֵנוּ וְעֶזְרָתֵנוּ סֶלָה. בָּרוּךְ אַתָּה

‹ are You, ‹ Blessed « forever! ‹ and of our help, ‹ of our salvation ‹ O God « sincerely,

יהוה, הַטּוֹב שִׁמְךָ וּלְךָ נָאֶה לְהוֹדוֹת.

« to give thanks. ‹ it is fitting ‹ and to You ‹ is Your Name, ‹ *The Beneficent One* « HASHEM,

---

THE *CHAZZAN* DOES NOT RECITE THE PRIESTLY BLESSING AT *SHACHARIS.*

PEACE / שלום

שִׂים שָׁלוֹם, טוֹבָה, וּבְרָכָה, חֵן, וָחֶסֶד וְרַחֲמִים,

‹ and compassion ‹ kindness, ‹ graciousness, ‹ blessing, ‹ goodness, ‹ peace, ‹ Establish

עָלֵינוּ וְעַל כָּל יִשְׂרָאֵל עַמֶּךָ. בָּרְכֵנוּ אָבִינוּ,

‹ our Father, ‹ Bless us, « Your people. ‹ of Israel ‹ all ‹ and upon ‹ upon us

כֻּלָּנוּ כְּאֶחָד בְּאוֹר פָּנֶיךָ, כִּי בְאוֹר פָּנֶיךָ נָתַתָּ

‹ You gave ‹ of Your countenance ‹ with the light ‹ for « of Your countenance, ‹ with the light « as one, « all of us

לָּנוּ, יהוה אֱלֹהֵינוּ, תּוֹרַת חַיִּים וְאַהֲבַת חֶסֶד,

‹ of kindness, ‹ and a love ‹ of life ‹ the Torah « our God, ‹ HASHEM, ‹ us,

וּצְדָקָה, וּבְרָכָה, וְרַחֲמִים, וְחַיִּים, וְשָׁלוֹם. וְטוֹב

‹ And may it be good « and peace. ‹ life, ‹ compassion, ‹ blessing, ‹ righteousness,

בְּעֵינֶיךָ לְבָרֵךְ אֶת עַמְּךָ יִשְׂרָאֵל בְּכָל עֵת וּבְכָל

‹ and at every ‹ time ‹ at every « Israel, ‹ Your people ‹ to bless ‹ in Your eyes

שָׁעָה בִּשְׁלוֹמֶךָ. בָּרוּךְ אַתָּה יהוה, הַמְּבָרֵךְ אֶת עַמּוֹ

hour, with Your peace. Blessed are You, HASHEM, Who blesses His people

יִשְׂרָאֵל בַּשָּׁלוֹם.

Israel with peace.

ALTHOUGH THE *CHAZZAN'S* REPETITION ENDS HERE, HE SHOULD ADD THE NEXT VERSE IN AN UNDERTONE. INDIVIDUALS CONTINUE:

יִהְיוּ לְרָצוֹן אִמְרֵי פִי וְהֶגְיוֹן לִבִּי לְפָנֶיךָ,

May they find favor — the expressions of my mouth and the thoughts of my heart — before You,

יהוה צוּרִי וְגֹאֲלִי.[1]

HASHEM, my Rock and my Redeemer.

אֱלֹהַי, נְצוֹר לְשׁוֹנִי מֵרָע, וּשְׂפָתַי מִדַּבֵּר מִרְמָה,[2]

My God, guard my tongue from evil and my lips from speaking deceitfully.

וְלִמְקַלְלַי נַפְשִׁי תִדּוֹם, וְנַפְשִׁי כֶּעָפָר לַכֹּל תִּהְיֶה.

To those who curse me, let my soul be silent; and let my soul be like dust to everyone.

פְּתַח לִבִּי בְּתוֹרָתֶךָ, וּבְמִצְוֹתֶיךָ תִּרְדּוֹף נַפְשִׁי. וְכָל

Open my heart to Your Torah, so that Your commandments shall my soul pursue. As for all

הַחוֹשְׁבִים עָלַי רָעָה, מְהֵרָה הָפֵר עֲצָתָם וְקַלְקֵל

who plot against me evil, speedily nullify their counsel and disrupt

מַחֲשַׁבְתָּם.[3] עֲשֵׂה לְמַעַן שְׁמֶךָ, עֲשֵׂה לְמַעַן

their scheme. Act for the sake of Your Name; act for the sake

יְמִינֶךָ, עֲשֵׂה לְמַעַן קְדֻשָּׁתֶךָ, עֲשֵׂה לְמַעַן תּוֹרָתֶךָ.

of Your right hand; act for the sake of Your sanctity; act for the sake Your Torah.

לְמַעַן יֵחָלְצוּן יְדִידֶיךָ, הוֹשִׁיעָה יְמִינְךָ וַעֲנֵנִי.[4]

In order that Your beloved ones may be released — save with Your right hand, and answer me.

(1) *Psalms* 19:15. (2) Cf. 34:14. (3) See *Berachos* 17a. (4) *Psalms* 60:7, 108:7.

SOME RECITE THE VERSE PERTAINING TO THEIR NAMES AT THIS POINT. SEE PAGE 643.

יִהְיוּ לְרָצוֹן אִמְרֵי פִי וְהֶגְיוֹן לִבִּי לְפָנֶיךָ, יהוה צוּרִי וְגֹאֲלִי.[1]

May they ‹ find favor ‹ — the expressions ‹ of my mouth ‹ and the thoughts ‹ of my heart — ‹ before You, « HASHEM, ‹ my Rock ‹ and my Redeemer. «

BOW. TAKE THREE STEPS BACK. BOW LEFT AND SAY ... עֹשֶׂה, *"HE WHO MAKES ..."*; BOW RIGHT AND SAY ... הוּא, *"MAY HE ..."*; BOW FORWARD AND SAY ... וְעַל כָּל יִשְׂרָאֵל, *"AND UPON ALL ISRAEL ..."*.

עֹשֶׂה שָׁלוֹם בִּמְרוֹמָיו,[2] הוּא יַעֲשֶׂה שָׁלוֹם עָלֵינוּ, וְעַל כָּל יִשְׂרָאֵל.[3] וְאִמְרוּ: אָמֵן.

He Who makes ‹ peace ‹ in His heights, « may He ‹ make ‹ peace ‹ upon us, « and upon ‹ all ‹ Israel. « Now respond: ‹ Amen. «

יְהִי רָצוֹן מִלְּפָנֶיךָ, יהוה אֱלֹהֵינוּ וֵאלֹהֵי אֲבוֹתֵינוּ, שֶׁיִּבָּנֶה בֵּית הַמִּקְדָּשׁ בִּמְהֵרָה בְיָמֵינוּ, וְתֵן חֶלְקֵנוּ בְּתוֹרָתֶךָ.[4] וְשָׁם נַעֲבָדְךָ בְּיִרְאָה, כִּימֵי עוֹלָם וּכְשָׁנִים קַדְמוֹנִיּוֹת. וְעָרְבָה לַיהוה מִנְחַת יְהוּדָה וִירוּשָׁלָיִם, כִּימֵי עוֹלָם וּכְשָׁנִים קַדְמוֹנִיּוֹת.[5]

May it be ‹ the will, ‹ before You, « HASHEM, ‹ our God ‹ and the God ‹ of our forefathers, « that ‹ shall the Holy Temple be rebuilt, ‹ speedily ‹ in our days. « Grant that ‹ our portion ‹ be in Your Torah, « so that there ‹ we may serve You ‹ with reverence, « as in days ‹ of old ‹ and as in years ‹ gone by. « And pleasing ‹ to HASHEM ‹ let be the offering ‹ of Judah ‹ and Jerusalem, « as in days ‹ of old ‹ and in years ‹ gone by. «

THE INDIVIDUAL'S RECITATION OF *SHEMONEH ESREI* ENDS HERE.

THE INDIVIDUAL REMAINS STANDING IN PLACE UNTIL THE *CHAZZAN* RECITES KEDUSHAH — OR AT LEAST UNTIL THE *CHAZZAN* BEGINS HIS REPETITION — THEN HE TAKES THREE STEPS FORWARD. THE *CHAZZAN* HIMSELF, OR ONE WHO IS PRAYING ALONE, SHOULD REMAIN IN PLACE FOR A FEW MOMENTS BEFORE TAKING THREE STEPS FORWARD.

THE *CHAZZAN* RECITES HALF-*KADDISH*:

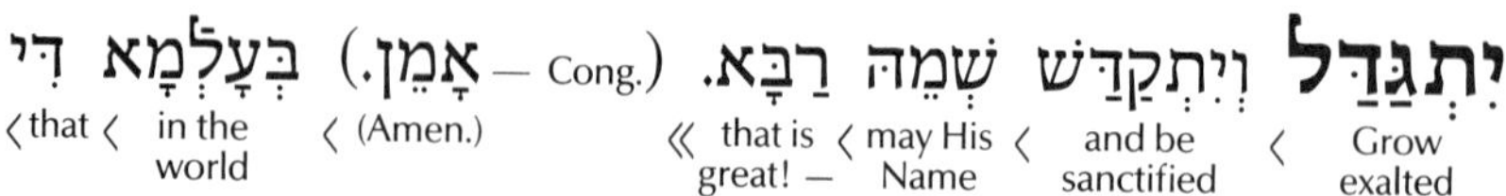

יִתְגַּדַּל וְיִתְקַדַּשׁ שְׁמֵהּ רַבָּא. (Cong. — אָמֵן.) בְּעָלְמָא דִּי

Grow exalted ‹ and be sanctified ‹ may His Name ‹ that is great! — « (Amen.) ‹ in the world ‹ that ‹

(1) *Psalms* 19:15. (2) *Job* 25:2. (3) Cf. *Berachos* 16b. (4) *Ethics of the Fathers* 5:24. (5) *Malachi* 3:4.

בְּרָא כִרְעוּתֵהּ. וְיַמְלִיךְ מַלְכוּתֵהּ, בְּחַיֵּיכוֹן וּבְיוֹמֵיכוֹן וּבְחַיֵּי

He created according to His will, and may He give reign to His kingship, in your lifetimes and in your days, and in the lifetimes

דְכָל בֵּית יִשְׂרָאֵל, בַּעֲגָלָא וּבִזְמַן קָרִיב. וְאִמְרוּ: אָמֵן.

of the entire Family of Israel, swiftly and at a time that comes soon. Now respond: Amen.

CONGREGATION RESPONDS:

אָמֵן. יְהֵא שְׁמֵהּ רַבָּא מְבָרַךְ לְעָלַם וּלְעָלְמֵי עָלְמַיָּא.

Amen. May His Name that is great be blessed forever and for all eternity.

MOURNER CONTINUES:

יְהֵא שְׁמֵהּ רַבָּא מְבָרַךְ לְעָלַם וּלְעָלְמֵי עָלְמַיָּא. יִתְבָּרַךְ

May His Name that is great be blessed forever and for all eternity. Blessed,

וְיִשְׁתַּבַּח וְיִתְפָּאַר וְיִתְרוֹמַם וְיִתְנַשֵּׂא וְיִתְהַדָּר וְיִתְעַלֶּה

praised, glorified, exalted, upraised, honored, elevated,

וְיִתְהַלָּל שְׁמֵהּ דְּקֻדְשָׁא בְּרִיךְ הוּא (Cong. — בְּרִיךְ הוּא) —

and lauded be the Name of the Holy One, Blessed is He (Blessed is He)

לְעֵלָּא מִן כָּל בִּרְכָתָא וְשִׁירָתָא תֻּשְׁבְּחָתָא וְנֶחֱמָתָא

beyond any blessing and song, praise and consolation

דַּאֲמִירָן בְּעָלְמָא. וְאִמְרוּ: אָמֵן. (Cong. — אָמֵן.)

that are uttered in the world. Now respond: Amen. (Amen.)

הוצאת ספר תורה

REMOVAL OF THE TORAH FROM THE ARK

FROM THE MOMENT THE ARK IS OPENED UNTIL THE TORAH IS RETURNED TO IT, ONE MUST CONDUCT HIMSELF WITH THE UTMOST RESPECT AND AVOID UNNECESSARY CONVERSATION. IT IS COMMENDABLE TO KISS THE TORAH AS IT IS CARRIED TO THE *BIMAH* (READING TABLE) AND BACK TO THE ARK.

ALL RISE AND REMAIN STANDING UNTIL THE TORAH IS PLACED ON THE *BIMAH*.
THE ARK IS OPENED; BEFORE THE TORAH IS REMOVED THE CONGREGATION RECITES:

וַיְהִי בִּנְסֹעַ הָאָרֹן, וַיֹּאמֶר מֹשֶׁה, קוּמָה יהוה

It would be that when the Ark would travel, Moses would say: *Arise, HASHEM,*

וְיָפֻצוּ אֹיְבֶיךָ, וְיָנֻסוּ מְשַׂנְאֶיךָ מִפָּנֶיךָ.[1] כִּי מִצִּיּוֹן

and let Your foes be scattered, Let flee those who hate You from before You. For from Zion

(1) *Numbers* 10:35.

תֵּצֵא תוֹרָה, וּדְבַר יהוה מִירוּשָׁלָיִם.[1] בָּרוּךְ שֶׁנָּתַן

will come forth ‹ the Torah, « and the word ‹ of HASHEM ‹ from Jerusalem. « Blessed ‹ is He Who gave ‹

תּוֹרָה לְעַמּוֹ יִשְׂרָאֵל בִּקְדֻשָּׁתוֹ.

the Torah ‹ to His people ‹ Israel ‹ in His holiness. «

Zohar, Vayakhel 206a / זוהר ויקהל רו:א

בְּרִיךְ שְׁמֵהּ דְּמָרֵא עָלְמָא, בְּרִיךְ כִּתְרָךְ וְאַתְרָךְ.

Blessed ‹ is the Name ‹ of the Master ‹ of the universe; « blessed ‹ is Your crown ‹ and Your place. «

יְהֵא רְעוּתָךְ עִם עַמָּךְ יִשְׂרָאֵל לְעָלַם, וּפֻרְקַן

May Your favor be ‹ with ‹ Your people ‹ Israel ‹ forever, « and the salvation ‹

יְמִינָךְ אַחֲזֵי לְעַמָּךְ בְּבֵית מַקְדְּשָׁךְ, וּלְאַמְטוּיֵי

of Your right hand ‹ may You display ‹ to Your people ‹ in Your holy Temple, « to extend ‹

לָנָא מִטּוּב נְהוֹרָךְ, וּלְקַבֵּל צְלוֹתָנָא בְּרַחֲמִין.

to us ‹ of the goodness ‹ of Your light, « and to accept ‹ our prayers ‹ with mercy. «

יְהֵא רַעֲוָא קֳדָמָךְ, דְּתוֹרִיךְ לָן חַיִּין בְּטִיבוּתָא,

May it be ‹ the will ‹ before You ‹ that You extend ‹ for us ‹ life ‹ with goodness, «

וְלֶהֱוֵי אֲנָא פְּקִידָא בְּגוֹ צַדִּיקַיָּא, לְמִרְחַם עָלַי

and it should be that ‹ I ‹ am counted ‹ among ‹ the righteous; « that You have mercy ‹ on me «

וּלְמִנְטַר יָתִי וְיַת כָּל דִּי לִי וְדִי לְעַמָּךְ יִשְׂרָאֵל.

and protect ‹ me, « and all ‹ that ‹ is mine « and [all] that ‹ belongs to Your people ‹ Israel. «

אַנְתְּ הוּא זָן לְכֹלָּא, וּמְפַרְנֵס לְכֹלָּא, אַנְתְּ הוּא

It is You ‹ Who ‹ nourishes ‹ all ‹ and sustains ‹ all; « it is You ‹ Who ‹

שַׁלִּיט עַל כֹּלָּא. אַנְתְּ הוּא דְּשַׁלִּיט עַל מַלְכַיָּא,

rules ‹ over ‹ everything. « It is You ‹ Who ‹ rules ‹ over ‹ kings, ‹

וּמַלְכוּתָא דִּילָךְ הִיא. אֲנָא עַבְדָּא דְקֻדְשָׁא בְּרִיךְ

and kingship ‹ is Yours. « I am ‹ a servant ‹ of the Holy One, ‹ Blessed ‹

(1) *Isaiah* 2:3.

הוּא, דְּסָגִידְנָא קַמֵּהּ וּמִקַּמָּא דִּיקַר אוֹרַיְתֵהּ

‹ of His Torah ‹ the glory ‹ and before ‹ before Him ‹ and prostrate myself « is He,

בְּכָל עִדָּן וְעִדָּן. לָא עַל אֱנָשׁ רָחִיצְנָא, וְלָא עַל

‹ on ‹ nor « do I put trust, ‹ any man ‹ in ‹ Not « times. ‹ at all

בַּר אֱלָהִין סָמִיכְנָא, אֶלָּא בֶּאֱלָהָא דִשְׁמַיָּא, דְּהוּא

‹ Who is ‹ of heaven, ‹ on the God ‹ — only « do I rely ‹ any angel

אֱלָהָא קְשׁוֹט, וְאוֹרַיְתֵהּ קְשׁוֹט, וּנְבִיאוֹהִי קְשׁוֹט,

« are true, ‹ Whose prophets « is truth, ‹ Whose Torah « of truth, ‹ the God

וּמַסְגֵּא לְמֶעְבַּד טַבְוָן וּקְשׁוֹט. בֵּהּ אֲנָא רָחִיץ,

« trust, ‹ I ‹ In Him « and truth. ‹ with kindness ‹ acts ‹ and Who abundantly

וְלִשְׁמֵהּ קַדִּישָׁא יַקִּירָא אֲנָא אֵמַר תֻּשְׁבְּחָן. יְהֵא

‹ May it be « praises. ‹ declare ‹ I ‹ and glorious — ‹ — holy ‹ and to His Name,

רַעֲוָא קֳדָמָךְ, דְּתִפְתַּח לִבָּאִי בְּאוֹרַיְתָא, וְתַשְׁלִים

‹ and that You fulfill « to the Torah, ‹ my heart ‹ that You open ‹ before You ‹ the will

מִשְׁאֲלִין דְּלִבָּאִי, וְלִבָּא דְכָל עַמָּךְ יִשְׂרָאֵל, לְטַב

‹ for good, ‹ Israel ‹ Your people ‹ of all ‹ and the heart ‹ of my heart ‹ the wishes

וּלְחַיִּין וְלִשְׁלָם. (אָמֵן.)

« (Amen.) « and for peace. ‹ for life,

THE TORAH SCROLL IS REMOVED FROM THE ARK AND PRESENTED TO THE *CHAZZAN,* WHO ACCEPTS IT IN HIS RIGHT ARM. HE TURNS TO THE ARK, BOWS WHILE RAISING THE TORAH, AND RECITES:

גַּדְּלוּ לַיהוה אִתִּי, וּנְרוֹמְמָה שְׁמוֹ יַחְדָּו.[1]

« in unison. ‹ His Name ‹ and let us exalt « with me, ‹ of HASHEM ‹ Declare the greatness

THE *CHAZZAN* TURNS TO HIS RIGHT AND CARRIES THE TORAH TO THE *BIMAH,* AS THE CONGREGATION RESPONDS:

לְךָ יהוה הַגְּדֻלָּה וְהַגְּבוּרָה וְהַתִּפְאֶרֶת וְהַנֵּצַח

‹ the triumph, ‹ the glory, ‹ the strength, ‹ is the greatness, ‹ HASHEM, ‹ Yours,

(1) *Psalms* 34:4.

וְהַהוֹד, כִּי כֹל בַּשָּׁמַיִם וּבָאָרֶץ, לְךָ יהוה הַמַּמְלָכָה

‹ and the majesty; ‹ for ‹ everything ‹ in heaven « and on earth [is Yours] ‹ Yours, ‹ HASHEM, ‹ is the kingdom,

וְהַמִּתְנַשֵּׂא לְכֹל לְרֹאשׁ.[1] רוֹמְמוּ יהוה אֱלֹהֵינוּ

‹ and the sovereignty ‹ over every leader. « Exalt ‹ HASHEM, ‹ our God,

וְהִשְׁתַּחֲווּ לַהֲדֹם רַגְלָיו, קָדוֹשׁ הוּא. רוֹמְמוּ יהוה

‹ and bow down at His footstool; « holy ‹ is He! « Exalt ‹ HASHEM,

אֱלֹהֵינוּ וְהִשְׁתַּחֲווּ לְהַר קָדְשׁוֹ, כִּי קָדוֹשׁ יהוה

‹ our God, ‹ and bow down ‹ at the Mount ‹ of His holiness; « for ‹ holy ‹ is HASHEM,

אֱלֹהֵינוּ.[2]

« our God.

AS THE *CHAZZAN* CARRIES THE TORAH, THE CONGREGATION RECITES:

אַב הָרַחֲמִים, הוּא יְרַחֵם עַם עֲמוּסִים, וְיִזְכֹּר

‹ Father of compassion! « May He ‹ have mercy ‹ on the nation « that is borne [by Him], ‹ and may He remember

בְּרִית אֵיתָנִים, וְיַצִּיל נַפְשׁוֹתֵינוּ מִן הַשָּׁעוֹת

‹ the covenant ‹ of the [spiritually] mighty ones. « May He rescue ‹ our souls ‹ from ‹ the times

הָרָעוֹת, וְיִגְעַר בְּיֵצֶר הָרַע מִן הַנְּשׂוּאִים, וְיָחֹן

« that are bad, ‹ and denounce ‹ the Evil Inclination ‹ from ‹ [harming] those carried by Him, « graciously grant

אוֹתָנוּ לִפְלֵיטַת עוֹלָמִים, וִימַלֵּא מִשְׁאֲלוֹתֵינוּ

‹ us ‹ eternal deliverance, « and fulfill ‹ our requests

בְּמִדָּה טוֹבָה יְשׁוּעָה וְרַחֲמִים.

‹ in good measure, ‹ with salvation ‹ and mercy. «

THE TORAH IS PLACED ON THE *BIMAH* AND PREPARED FOR READING.
THE GABBAI USES THE FOLLOWING FORMULA TO CALL A *KOHEN* TO THE TORAH:

וְתִגָּלֶה וְתֵרָאֶה מַלְכוּתוֹ עָלֵינוּ בִּזְמַן קָרוֹב, וְיָחֹן

‹ And be revealed ‹ and become visible ‹ may His Kingship ‹ over us ‹ at a time ‹ that comes soon, « and May He be gracious

פְּלֵיטָתֵנוּ וּפְלֵיטַת עַמּוֹ בֵּית יִשְׂרָאֵל לְחֵן וּלְחֶסֶד

‹ to our remnant ‹ and the remnant ‹ of His people, ‹ the Family « of Israel, ‹ for graciousness, ‹ for kindness,

(1) *I Chronicles* 29:11. (2) *Psalms* 99:5,9.

וּלְרַחֲמִים וּלְרָצוֹן. וְנֹאמַר אָמֵן. הַכֹּל הָבוּ גֹדֶל לֵאלֹהֵינוּ וּתְנוּ

for mercy, and for favor. And let us respond: Amen. Everyone ascribe greatness to our God and give

כָּבוֹד לַתּוֹרָה. °כֹּהֵן קְרָב, יַעֲמֹד (NAME) בֶּן (FATHER'S NAME) הַכֹּהֵן.

honor to the Torah. *Kohen,* approach! Arise, (NAME) son of (FATHER'S NAME) the *Kohen!*

°IF NO *KOHEN* IS PRESENT, THE *GABBAI* SAYS:

אֵין כַּאן כֹּהֵן יַעֲמֹד (NAME) בֶּן (FATHER'S NAME) יִשְׂרָאֵל (לֵוִי)

No *Kohen* is present. Arise (NAME) son of (FATHER'S NAME) the Israelite (Levite),

בִּמְקוֹם כֹּהֵן.

in place of a *Kohen!*

בָּרוּךְ שֶׁנָּתַן תּוֹרָה לְעַמּוֹ יִשְׂרָאֵל בִּקְדֻשָּׁתוֹ. (תּוֹרַת יהוה

Blessed is He Who gave Torah to His people Israel in His holiness. (The Torah of HASHEM

תְּמִימָה מְשִׁיבַת נָפֶשׁ, עֵדוּת יהוה נֶאֱמָנָה מַחְכִּימַת

is perfect, restoring the soul; the testimony of HASHEM is trustworthy, making wise

פֶּתִי. פִּקּוּדֵי יהוה יְשָׁרִים מְשַׂמְּחֵי לֵב, מִצְוַת יהוה

the simple one. The orders of HASHEM are upright, gladdening the heart; the command of HASHEM

בָּרָה מְאִירַת עֵינָיִם.[1] יהוה עֹז לְעַמּוֹ יִתֵּן, יהוה יְבָרֵךְ

is clear, enlightening the eyes. HASHEM, strength to His nation will give; HASHEM will bless

אֶת עַמּוֹ בַשָּׁלוֹם.[2] הָאֵל תָּמִים דַּרְכּוֹ, אִמְרַת יהוה צְרוּפָה,

His people with peace. The God! Perfect is His way; the utterance of HASHEM is flawless;

מָגֵן הוּא לְכֹל הַחֹסִים בּוֹ.[3])

a shield He is for all who take refuge in Him).

CONGREGATION, THEN GABBAI:

וְאַתֶּם הַדְּבֵקִים בַּיהוה אֱלֹהֵיכֶם, חַיִּים כֻּלְּכֶם הַיּוֹם.[4]

And you who cling to HASHEM, your God, you are alive — all of you — today.

THE LAWS OF THE TORAH READING ARE FOUND ON PAGE 640.

---

(1) *Psalms* 19:8-9. (2) 29:11. (3) *II Samuel* 22:31; cf. *Psalms* 18:31. (4) *Deuteronomy* 4:4.

BLESSINGS FOR THE TORAH / ברכות התורה

THE READER SHOWS THE *OLEH* (PERSON CALLED TO THE TORAH) THE PLACE IN THE TORAH. THE *OLEH* TOUCHES THE TORAH WITH ITS BELT OR MANTLE OF THE TORAH, AND KISSES IT. HE THEN BEGINS THE BLESSING, BOWING AT בָּרְכוּ, AND STRAIGHTENING UP AT 'ה.

בָּרְכוּ אֶת יהוה הַמְּבֹרָךְ.

《 the blessed One. 〈 HASHEM, 〈 Bless

CONGREGATION, FOLLOWED BY *OLEH*, RESPONDS, BOWING AT בָּרוּךְ, AND STRAIGHTENING UP AT 'ה.

בָּרוּךְ יהוה הַמְּבֹרָךְ לְעוֹלָם וָעֶד.

《 and ever. 〈 for ever 〈 the blessed One, 〈 is HASHEM, 〈 Blessed

OLEH CONTINUES:

בָּרוּךְ אַתָּה יהוה אֱלֹהֵינוּ מֶלֶךְ הָעוֹלָם, אֲשֶׁר

〈 Who 《 of the universe, 〈 King 〈 our God, 〈 HASHEM, 〈 are You, 〈 Blessed

בָּחַר בָּנוּ מִכָּל הָעַמִּים, וְנָתַן לָנוּ אֶת תּוֹרָתוֹ.

《 His Torah. 〈 us 〈 and gave 〈 the peoples 〈 from all 〈 us 〈 selected

בָּרוּךְ אַתָּה יהוה, נוֹתֵן הַתּוֹרָה. (Cong. – אָמֵן.)

《 of the Torah. 〈 Giver 《 HASHEM, 〈 are You, 〈 Blessed 《 (Amen.)

AFTER HIS TORAH PORTION HAS BEEN READ, THE *OLEH* RECITES:

בָּרוּךְ אַתָּה יהוה אֱלֹהֵינוּ מֶלֶךְ הָעוֹלָם, אֲשֶׁר

〈 Who 《 of the universe, 〈 King 〈 our God, 〈 HASHEM, 〈 are You, 〈 Blessed

נָתַן לָנוּ תּוֹרַת אֱמֶת, וְחַיֵּי עוֹלָם נָטַע בְּתוֹכֵנוּ.

《 within us. 〈 He implanted 〈 of eternity 〈 and the life 《 of truth 〈 the Torah 〈 us 〈 gave

בָּרוּךְ אַתָּה יהוה, נוֹתֵן הַתּוֹרָה. (Cong. – אָמֵן.)

《 of the Torah. 〈 Giver 《 HASHEM, 〈 are You, 〈 Blessed 《 (Amen.)

THE *MI SHEBEIRACH* PRAYER FOR A SICK PERSON APPEARS ON PAGE 198.

TORAH READING / קריאת התורה

Deuteronomy 4:25-40 / דברים ד:כה־מ

כהן – כִּי־תוֹלִיד בָּנִים וּבְנֵי בָנִים וְנוֹשַׁנְתֶּם בָּאָרֶץ

KOHEN 〈 When you give birth 〈 to children 〈 and children 〈 of children 〈 and you will have been long 《 in the Land,

Torah Reading

The Torah reading of Tishah B'Av encapsules Jewish history: the spiritual sloth that leads to idolatry and exile, the encouragement that it is in our power to arouse God's mercy — and that it is surely in His power to bring about the final redemption. In his warning that exile may be impending, Moses says that the main source of tragedy is that *you will*

וְהִשְׁחַתֶּם וַעֲשִׂיתֶם פֶּסֶל תְּמוּנַת כֹּל וַעֲשִׂיתֶם

‹ and you will do « of anything, ‹ an image ‹ a statue, ‹ and make ‹ you will grow corrupt

הָרַע בְּעֵינֵי יהוה־אֱלֹהֶיךָ לְהַכְעִיסוֹ: הַעִידֹתִי בָכֶם

‹ against you ‹ I call to testify « to anger Him. ‹ your God, ‹ of HASHEM, ‹ in the eyes ‹ that which is evil

הַיּוֹם אֶת־הַשָּׁמַיִם וְאֶת־הָאָרֶץ כִּי־אָבֹד תֹּאבֵדוּן מַהֵר

‹ quickly ‹ you will certainly perish ‹ that ‹ and earth ‹ heaven ‹ this day

מֵעַל הָאָרֶץ אֲשֶׁר אַתֶּם עֹבְרִים אֶת־הַיַּרְדֵּן שָׁמָּה

‹ thereto ‹ the Jordan ‹ are crossing ‹ you ‹ that ‹ the Land ‹ from upon

לְרִשְׁתָּהּ לֹא־תַאֲרִיכֻן יָמִים עָלֶיהָ כִּי הִשָּׁמֵד תִּשָּׁמֵדוּן:

« you will be utterly destroyed. ‹ for « upon it, ‹ of days ‹ you shall not have length « to possess;

וְהֵפִיץ יהוה אֶתְכֶם בָּעַמִּים וְנִשְׁאַרְתֶּם מְתֵי מִסְפָּר

‹ in number ‹ few ‹ and you will be left « among the peoples, ‹ you ‹ HASHEM will scatter

בַּגּוֹיִם אֲשֶׁר יְנַהֵג יהוה אֶתְכֶם שָׁמָּה: וַעֲבַדְתֶּם־שָׁם

‹ there ‹ You will serve « thereto. ‹ you ‹ HASHEM will lead ‹ where ‹ among the nations

אֱלֹהִים מַעֲשֵׂה יְדֵי אָדָם עֵץ וָאֶבֶן אֲשֶׁר לֹא־יִרְאוּן

‹ see, ‹ do not ‹ which ‹ and stone, ‹ of wood « of man, ‹ of the hands ‹ the work « gods,

וְלֹא יִשְׁמְעוּן וְלֹא יֹאכְלוּן וְלֹא יְרִיחֻן: וּבִקַּשְׁתֶּם

‹ You will seek « smell. ‹ and do not ‹ eat, ‹ and do not ‹ hear, ‹ and do not

מִשָּׁם אֶת־יהוה אֱלֹהֶיךָ וּמָצָאתָ כִּי תִדְרְשֶׁנּוּ בְּכָל־

‹ with all ‹ you search for Him ‹ if « and you will find [Him], ‹ your God, ‹ HASHEM, ‹ from there

לְבָבְךָ וּבְכָל־נַפְשֶׁךָ:

« your soul. ‹ and with all ‹ your heart

---

have been long in the land. For all its imperfections, the generation that experienced the Exodus and the miracles of the Wilderness and the conquest of the Land would not be quick to sin so grievously. But as the years and generations go by, people tend to grow stale, to take their advantages for granted, to forget the sense of freshness and spiritual striving that brought them to their high plateau

לוי — בַּצַּר לְךָ וּמְצָאוּךָ כֹּל הַדְּבָרִים הָאֵלֶּה בְּאַחֲרִית

LEVITE When in distress you are, and befallen you have all these things, at the end

הַיָּמִים וְשַׁבְתָּ עַד־יהוה אֱלֹהֶיךָ וְשָׁמַעְתָּ בְּקֹלוֹ: כִּי

of days, you will return unto HASHEM, your God, and you shall listen to His voice. For

אֵל רַחוּם יהוה אֱלֹהֶיךָ לֹא יַרְפְּךָ וְלֹא יַשְׁחִיתֶךָ

a God Who is merciful is HASHEM, your God, He will not let go of you and He will not destroy you,

וְלֹא יִשְׁכַּח אֶת־בְּרִית אֲבֹתֶיךָ אֲשֶׁר נִשְׁבַּע לָהֶם: כִּי

and He will not forget the covenant of your forefathers that He swore to them. For

שְׁאַל־נָא לְיָמִים רִאשֹׁנִים אֲשֶׁר־הָיוּ לְפָנֶיךָ לְמִן־הַיּוֹם

ask now regarding the days of yore that were before you, from the day

אֲשֶׁר בָּרָא אֱלֹהִים | אָדָם עַל־הָאָרֶץ וּלְמִקְצֵה הַשָּׁמַיִם

when God created man upon the earth, and from [the one] end of heaven

וְעַד־קְצֵה הַשָּׁמָיִם הֲנִהְיָה כַּדָּבָר הַגָּדוֹל הַזֶּה אוֹ

to [the other] end of heaven: Has there been anything like this great thing or

הֲנִשְׁמַע כָּמֹהוּ: הֲשָׁמַע עָם קוֹל אֱלֹהִים מְדַבֵּר מִתּוֹךְ־

has there been heard anything like it? Has a people heard the voice of God speaking from the midst

הָאֵשׁ כַּאֲשֶׁר־שָׁמַעְתָּ אַתָּה וַיֶּחִי: אוֹ | הֲנִסָּה אֱלֹהִים

of the fire as you have heard, and survived? Or has any god performed miracles

לָבוֹא לָקַחַת לוֹ גוֹי מִקֶּרֶב גּוֹי בְּמַסֹּת בְּאֹתֹת

to come to take for himself a nation from amidst a nation, with trials, with signs,

---

of success. Once that happens and they begin to look for new stimuli, they will begin to explore the lifestyle of their neighbors and experiment with it. In ancient times, this meant idolatry. Today, it can mean any of the numerous isms and beliefs that have led Jews astray once they have grown weary of their eternal tradition and sought more fashionable ways of life and belief.

But the Torah assures us that even after the exile takes place, there is always hope. From its place of distress, Israel will seek God and find Him, and the nation will repent and return to God. The Torah exhorts us to remember that God redeemed

וּבְמוֹפְתִים וּבְמִלְחָמָה וּבְיָד חֲזָקָה וּבִזְרוֹעַ נְטוּיָה

and with wonders, / and with war, / and with a hand / that is strong, / and with an arm / that is outstretched,

וּבְמוֹרָאִים גְּדֹלִים כְּכֹל אֲשֶׁר־עָשָׂה לָכֶם יְהוָה

and with awesome [deeds] / that are great, / compared to everything / that / He did / for you / — HASHEM,

אֱלֹהֵיכֶם בְּמִצְרַיִם לְעֵינֶיךָ׃ אַתָּה הָרְאֵתָ לָדַעַת

your God [did] — / in Egypt / before your eyes? / You / have been shown / [in order] to know

כִּי יְהוָה הוּא הָאֱלֹהִים אֵין עוֹד מִלְבַדּוֹ׃

that / HASHEM / —He is / the God! / There is none / other / besides Him!

ישראל (מפטיר) — מִן־הַשָּׁמַיִם הִשְׁמִיעֲךָ אֶת־קֹלוֹ לְיַסְּרֶךָּ

YISRAEL (MAFTIR) — From / heaven / He caused you to hear / His voice / in order to discipline you,

וְעַל־הָאָרֶץ הֶרְאֲךָ אֶת־אִשּׁוֹ הַגְּדוֹלָה וּדְבָרָיו שָׁמַעְתָּ

and on / earth / He showed you / His fire / that is great, / and His words / you heard

מִתּוֹךְ הָאֵשׁ׃ וְתַחַת כִּי אָהַב אֶת־אֲבֹתֶיךָ וַיִּבְחַר

from the midst / of the fire. / And it is because / He loved / your forefathers, / and He chose

בְּזַרְעוֹ אַחֲרָיו וַיּוֹצִאֲךָ בְּפָנָיו בְּכֹחוֹ הַגָּדֹל מִמִּצְרָיִם׃

his offspring / after him, / [that] He took you out / before Himself / with His strength / that is great / from Egypt;

לְהוֹרִישׁ גּוֹיִם גְּדֹלִים וַעֲצֻמִים מִמְּךָ מִפָּנֶיךָ לַהֲבִיאֲךָ

to drive out / nations / that are greater / and mightier / than you are / from before you, / to bring you,

לָתֶת־לְךָ אֶת־אַרְצָם נַחֲלָה כַּיּוֹם הַזֶּה׃ וְיָדַעְתָּ הַיּוֹם

to give / you / their land / as an inheritance, / as it is this day. / You are to know / this day

---

us in an unprecedented display of mercy and love. His love for us stems from the covenant with the Patriarchs, a phenomenon that is eternal and can never be diminished by sin or exile. Therefore we must always be aware that redemption *will* come again, and that it is in our hands to hasten it through repentance.

Thus, the Torah reading is a ray of hope amid the gloom and tragedy of Tishah B'Av. The Destruction of the Temple and the resultant exile are still with us, and this is the day that does not let us forget that. But exile is not more a part of our history than is redemption. The difference is that exile, long though

וַהֲשֵׁבֹתָ֮ אֶל־לְבָבֶךָ֒ כִּ֚י יהוה֙ ה֣וּא הָֽאֱלֹהִ֔ים בַּשָּׁמַ֣יִם

‹— in heaven « the God ‹ He is ‹ HASHEM ‹ that « your heart, ‹ to ‹ and take

מִמַּ֔עַל וְעַל־הָאָ֖רֶץ מִתָּ֑חַת אֵ֖ין ע֑וֹד׃ וְשָֽׁמַרְתָּ֞

‹ You shall observe « other. ‹ there is none « below — ‹ the earth ‹ and on ‹ above

אֶת־חֻקָּ֣יו וְאֶת־מִצְוֺתָ֗יו אֲשֶׁ֨ר אָנֹכִ֤י מְצַוְּךָ֙ הַיּ֔וֹם

« this day, ‹ command you ‹ I ‹ that ‹ and His commandments ‹ His decrees

אֲשֶׁר֙ יִיטַ֣ב לְךָ֔ וּלְבָנֶ֖יךָ אַחֲרֶ֑יךָ וּלְמַ֙עַן֙ תַּאֲרִ֣יךְ

‹ you will prolong ‹ and so that « after you, ‹ and to your children ‹ to you ‹ He will do good ‹ so that

יָמִים֙ עַל־הָ֣אֲדָמָ֔ה אֲשֶׁ֨ר יהוה אֱלֹהֶ֛יךָ נֹתֵ֥ן לְךָ֖

‹ to you, ‹ gives ‹ your God, ‹ HASHEM, ‹ that ‹ the Land ‹ upon ‹ your days

כָּל־הַיָּמִֽים׃

« the days. ‹ for all

PRAYER FOR A SICK MAN / מי שברך לחולה (זכר)

מִי שֶׁבֵּרַךְ אֲבוֹתֵינוּ אַבְרָהָם יִצְחָק וְיַעֲקֹב, מֹשֶׁה אַהֲרֹן

‹ Aaron, ‹ Moses, ‹ and Jacob, ‹ Isaac, ‹ Abraham, ‹ our forefathers ‹ Who blessed ‹ The One

דָּוִד וּשְׁלֹמֹה, הוּא יְבָרֵךְ וִירַפֵּא אֶת הַחוֹלֶה (PATIENT'S NAME) בֶּן

‹ son of ‹ the sick person ‹ and heal ‹ bless ‹ — may He « and Solomon ‹ David,

(MOTHER'S NAME) °°בַּעֲבוּר שֶׁ(SUPPLICANT'S NAME) יִתֵּן לִצְדָקָה בַּעֲבוּרוֹ.

« on his behalf. ‹ to charity ‹ will contribute ‹ because

MANY CONGREGATIONS SUBSTITUTE:

°°בַּעֲבוּר שֶׁכָּל הַקָּהָל מִתְפַּלְּלִים בַּעֲבוּרוֹ.

« for him. ‹ prays ‹ congregation ‹ the entire ‹ because

בִּשְׂכַר זֶה, הַקָּדוֹשׁ בָּרוּךְ הוּא יִמָּלֵא רַחֲמִים עָלָיו, לְהַחֲלִימוֹ

‹ to restore his health, ‹ for him ‹ with compassion ‹— may He be filled « is He ‹ Blessed ‹ the Holy One, ‹ for this, ‹ In reward

וּלְרַפְּאתוֹ וּלְהַחֲזִיקוֹ וּלְהַחֲיוֹתוֹ, וְיִשְׁלַח לוֹ מְהֵרָה רְפוּאָה

‹ a recovery ‹ speedily ‹ him ‹ And may He send « and to revivify him. ‹ to strengthen him, ‹ to heal him,

---

it may be, is a temporary condition; the coming of Messiah is the permanent and natural state of Jewry, may it happen speedily in our days.

שְׁלֵמָה מִן הַשָּׁמַיִם, לִרְמַ״ח אֵבָרָיו, וּשְׁסָ״ה גִּידָיו, בְּתוֹךְ

‹ among «sinews, ‹ and 365 ‹ organs ‹ for his 248 « heaven ‹ from ‹ that is complete

שְׁאָר חוֹלֵי יִשְׂרָאֵל, רְפוּאַת הַנֶּפֶשׁ, וּרְפוּאַת הַגּוּף,

«of the body, ‹ and a recovery ‹ of the spirit ‹ a recovery « of Israel, ‹ sick people ‹ the other

הַשְׁתָּא בַּעֲגָלָא וּבִזְמַן קָרִיב. וְנֹאמַר: אָמֵן. (Cong. – אָמֵן.)

«(Amen.) « Amen. ‹ Now let us respond: «that comes soon. ‹ and at a time ‹ swiftly, ‹ now,

PRAYER FOR A SICK WOMAN / מי שברך לחולה (נקבה)

מִי שֶׁבֵּרַךְ אֲבוֹתֵינוּ אַבְרָהָם יִצְחָק וְיַעֲקֹב, מֹשֶׁה אַהֲרֹן

‹ Aaron, ‹ Moses, ‹ and Jacob, ‹ Isaac, ‹ Abraham, ‹ our forefathers ‹ Who blessed ‹ The One

דָּוִד וּשְׁלֹמֹה, הוּא יְבָרֵךְ וִירַפֵּא אֶת הַחוֹלָה (PATIENT'S NAME) בַּת

‹daughter of ‹ the sick person ‹ and heal ‹ bless ‹ — may He « and Solomon ‹ David,

(MOTHER'S NAME) °°בַּעֲבוּר שֶׁ(SUPPLICANT'S NAME) יִתֵּן לִצְדָקָה בַּעֲבוּרָהּ.

« on her behalf. ‹ to charity ‹ will contribute ‹ because

MANY CONGREGATIONS SUBSTITUTE:

°°בַּעֲבוּר שֶׁכָּל הַקָּהָל מִתְפַּלְּלִים בַּעֲבוּרָהּ.

« for her. ‹ prays ‹ congregation ‹ the entire ‹ because

בִּשְׂכַר זֶה, הַקָּדוֹשׁ בָּרוּךְ הוּא יִמָּלֵא רַחֲמִים עָלֶיהָ, לְהַחֲלִימָהּ

‹ to restore her health, ‹ for her ‹ with compassion ‹— may He be filled « is He ‹ Blessed ‹ the Holy One, ‹ for this, ‹ In reward

וּלְרַפְּאתָהּ וּלְהַחֲזִיקָהּ וּלְהַחֲיוֹתָהּ, וְיִשְׁלַח לָהּ מְהֵרָה

‹speedily ‹ her ‹ And may He send « and to revivify her. ‹ to strengthen her, ‹ to heal her,

רְפוּאָה שְׁלֵמָה מִן הַשָּׁמַיִם, לְכָל אֵבָרֶיהָ, וּלְכָל גִּידֶיהָ,

«sinews, ‹ and all her ‹ organs ‹ for all her « heaven ‹ from ‹ that is complete ‹ a recovery

בְּתוֹךְ שְׁאָר חוֹלֵי יִשְׂרָאֵל, רְפוּאַת הַנֶּפֶשׁ, וּרְפוּאַת הַגּוּף,

«of the body, ‹ and a recovery ‹ of the spirit ‹ a recovery « of Israel, ‹ sick people ‹ the other ‹ among

הַשְׁתָּא בַּעֲגָלָא וּבִזְמַן קָרִיב. וְנֹאמַר: אָמֵן. (Cong. – אָמֵן.)

«(Amen.) « Amen. ‹ Now let us respond: «that comes soon. ‹ and at a time ‹ swiftly, ‹ now,

WHEN THE TORAH READING HAS BEEN COMPLETED, THE READER RECITES HALF-*KADDISH*:

יִתְגַּדַּל וְיִתְקַדַּשׁ שְׁמֵהּ רַבָּא. (Cong. — אָמֵן.) בְּעָלְמָא דִּי

〈 that 〈 in the world 〈 (Amen.) 《 that is great! — 〈 may His Name 〈 and be sanctified 〈 Grow exalted

בְּרָא כִרְעוּתֵהּ. וְיַמְלִיךְ מַלְכוּתֵהּ, בְּחַיֵּיכוֹן וּבְיוֹמֵיכוֹן וּבְחַיֵּי

〈 and in the lifetimes 〈 and in your days, 〈 in your lifetimes 《 to His kingship, 〈 and may He give reign 《 according to His will, 《 He created

דְכָל בֵּית יִשְׂרָאֵל, בַּעֲגָלָא וּבִזְמַן קָרִיב. וְאִמְרוּ: אָמֵן.

《 Amen. 〈 Now respond: 《 that comes soon. 〈 and at a time 〈 swiftly 《 of Israel, 〈 Family 〈 of the entire

CONGREGATION RESPONDS:

אָמֵן. יְהֵא שְׁמֵהּ רַבָּא מְבָרַךְ לְעָלַם וּלְעָלְמֵי עָלְמַיָּא.

《 and for all eternity. 〈 forever 〈 be blessed 〈 that is great 〈 His Name 〈 May 《 Amen.

MOURNER CONTINUES:

יְהֵא שְׁמֵהּ רַבָּא מְבָרַךְ לְעָלַם וּלְעָלְמֵי עָלְמַיָּא. יִתְבָּרַךְ

〈 Blessed, 《 and for all eternity. 〈 forever 〈 be blessed 〈 that is great 〈 His Name 〈 May

וְיִשְׁתַּבַּח וְיִתְפָּאַר וְיִתְרוֹמַם וְיִתְנַשֵּׂא וְיִתְהַדָּר וְיִתְעַלֶּה

〈 elevated, 〈 honored, 〈 upraised, 〈 exalted, 〈 glorified, 〈 praised,

וְיִתְהַלָּל שְׁמֵהּ דְּקֻדְשָׁא בְּרִיךְ הוּא (Cong. — בְּרִיךְ הוּא) —

《 is He) 〈 (Blessed 《 is He 〈 Blessed 〈 of the Holy One, 〈 be the Name 〈 and lauded

לְעֵלָּא מִן כָּל בִּרְכָתָא וְשִׁירָתָא תֻּשְׁבְּחָתָא וְנֶחֱמָתָא

〈 and consolation 〈 praise 《 and song, 〈 blessing 〈 any 〈 beyond

דַּאֲמִירָן בְּעָלְמָא. וְאִמְרוּ: אָמֵן. (Cong. — אָמֵן.)

《 (Amen.) 《 Amen. 〈 Now respond: 《 in the world. 〈 that are uttered

HAGBAHAH AND GELILAH / הגבהה וגלילה

ALL STAND. THE TORAH IS RAISED FOR ALL TO SEE.
EACH PERSON LOOKS AT THE TORAH AND RECITES ALOUD:

וְזֹאת הַתּוֹרָה אֲשֶׁר שָׂם מֹשֶׁה לִפְנֵי בְּנֵי

〈 the Children 〈 before 〈 Moses placed 〈 that 〈 is the Torah 〈 This

יִשְׂרָאֵל,[1] עַל פִּי יהוה בְּיַד מֹשֶׁה.[2]

《 of Moses. 〈 through the hand 《 of HASHEM, 〈 the word 〈 according to 《 of Israel,

(1) *Deuteronomy* 4:44. (2) *Numbers* 9:23.

SOME ADD:

עֵץ חַיִּים הִיא לַמַּחֲזִיקִים בָּהּ, וְתֹמְכֶיהָ מְאֻשָּׁר.[1] דְּרָכֶיהָ

‹ Its ways « are praiseworthy. ‹ and its supporters « it, ‹ for those who grasp ‹ is it ‹ of life ‹ A tree

דַּרְכֵי נֹעַם, וְכָל נְתִיבוֹתֶיהָ שָׁלוֹם.[2] אֹרֶךְ יָמִים בִּימִינָהּ,

« are at its right; ‹ of days ‹ Length « are peace. ‹ its paths ‹ and all « of pleasantness, ‹ are ways

בִּשְׂמֹאלָהּ עֹשֶׁר וְכָבוֹד.[3] יהוה חָפֵץ לְמַעַן צִדְקוֹ, יַגְדִּיל

‹ that He make great « of [Israel's] righteousness, ‹ for the sake « desired, ‹ HASHEM « and honor. ‹ are wealth ‹ at its left

תּוֹרָה וְיַאְדִּיר.[4]

« and [make it] glorious. ‹ the Torah

BLESSING BEFORE THE HAFTARAH / ברכה לפני ההפטרה

AFTER THE TORAH SCROLL HAS BEEN TIED AND COVERED, THE *OLEH* FOR *MAFTIR* RECITES THE *HAFTARAH* BLESSING:

בָּרוּךְ אַתָּה יהוה אֱלֹהֵינוּ מֶלֶךְ הָעוֹלָם, אֲשֶׁר

‹ Who « of the universe, ‹ King ‹ our God, « HASHEM, ‹ are You, ‹ Blessed

בָּחַר בִּנְבִיאִים טוֹבִים, וְרָצָה בְדִבְרֵיהֶם הַנֶּאֱמָרִים

‹ that were uttered ‹ with their words ‹ and was pleased ‹ good prophets ‹ has chosen

בֶּאֱמֶת, בָּרוּךְ אַתָּה יהוה, הַבּוֹחֵר בַּתּוֹרָה וּבְמֹשֶׁה

‹ and Moses, ‹ the Torah ‹ Who chooses ‹ HASHEM, ‹ are You, ‹ Blessed « with truth.

עַבְדּוֹ, וּבְיִשְׂרָאֵל עַמּוֹ, וּבִנְבִיאֵי הָאֱמֶת וָצֶדֶק.

« and righteousness. ‹ of truth ‹ and the prophets ‹ His people, ‹ and Israel, ‹ His servant,

(Cong. — אָמֵן.)

« (Amen.)

(1) *Proverbs* 3:18. (2) 3:17. (3) 3:16. (4) *Isaiah* 42:21.

◆§ The Haftarah

Unlike the Torah reading, which is primarily hopeful, the *Haftarah* is an almost unrelieved dirge. Indeed, it is read with the sad cantillation of *Eichah* until the last two verses, which, with their brief depiction of what is worthwhile and praiseworthy in human beings, points the way toward ultimate salvation. Jeremiah, the prophet of the Destruction and the author of *Eichah*, directed this harsh prophecy at his wayward brethren, in the vain hope that it would stir them to repent.

The *Haftarah* begins with a picture of the terror that the people felt. Their towns and farms were desolate and they fled to the cities, but there, too, they found no refuge. Foolishly and vainly they asked,

HAFTARAH / הפטרה

Jeremiah 8:13-9:23 / ירמיה ח:יג-ט:כג

אָסֹף אֲסִיפֵם נְאֻם־יְהֹוָה אֵין עֲנָבִים בַּגֶּפֶן וְאֵין

‹ and no ‹ on the vine ‹ grapes ‹ There will be no « of HASHEM. ‹ the word « I shall utterly destroy them —

תְּאֵנִים בַּתְּאֵנָה וְהֶעָלֶה נָבֵל וָאֶתֵּן לָהֶם יַעַבְרוּם:

« will be taken away from them. ‹ to them ‹ and what I have given « will wither, ‹ the leaf « on the fig tree, ‹ figs

עַל־מָה אֲנַחְנוּ יֹשְׁבִים הֵאָסְפוּ וְנָבוֹא אֶל־עָרֵי

‹ the cities ‹ to ‹ and let us come ‹ Gather together « remain [here]? ‹ do we ‹ what ‹ For [reason]

הַמִּבְצָר וְנִדְּמָה־שָּׁם כִּי יְהֹוָה אֱלֹהֵינוּ הֲדִמָּנוּ

« has silenced us ‹ our God, ‹ HASHEM, ‹ for « there; ‹ and we will be silent « with fortifications,

וַיַּשְׁקֵנוּ מֵי־רֹאשׁ כִּי חָטָאנוּ לַיהֹוָה: קַוֵּה לְשָׁלוֹם

‹ for peace, ‹ We may hope « to HASHEM. ‹ we have sinned ‹ for « of bitter gall, ‹ water ‹ and He has given us to drink

וְאֵין טוֹב לְעֵת מַרְפֵּה וְהִנֵּה בְעָתָה: מִדָּן נִשְׁמַע

‹ was heard ‹ From Dan « terror. ‹ but there is ‹ of healing, ‹ [we hope] for a time « goodness; ‹ but there is no

נַחְרַת סוּסָיו מִקּוֹל מִצְהֲלוֹת אַבִּירָיו רָעֲשָׁה

‹ quaked ‹ of his mighty men ‹ of the footsteps ‹ at the sound « of his steeds, ‹ the snorting

כָּל־הָאָרֶץ וַיָּבוֹאוּ וַיֹּאכְלוּ אֶרֶץ וּמְלוֹאָהּ עִיר

‹ the city « and its fullness, ‹ the land ‹ and they will devour ‹ they are coming « the land; ‹ all

וְיֹשְׁבֵי בָהּ: כִּי הִנְנִי מְשַׁלֵּחַ בָּכֶם נְחָשִׁים צִפְעֹנִים

« that are venomous, ‹ serpents ‹ among you ‹ sending forth ‹ indeed, I am ‹ For « in it. ‹ and the inhabitants

---

Is HASHEM not in Zion, is its king not within it? — as if the God Whom they had spurned and the king who had been shorn of his power would help them.

Then Jeremiah speaks of his personal despair at the degradation of his people. He is blackened. There is no balm to soothe his hurt. He wishes his eyes had enough tears for him to express his heartbreak. On the other hand, when he views their grievous sins, he wishes there were an inn in an isolated desert where he could escape from them. They are immoral and traitorous to God. Their

אֲשֶׁר אֵין־לָהֶם לָחַשׁ וְנִשְּׁכוּ אֶתְכֶם נְאֻם־יהוה:

« of HASHEM. ‹ — the word « you ‹ and they shall bite « [susceptibility to] snake-charms, ‹ have ‹ do not ‹ which

מַבְלִיגִיתִי עֲלֵי יָגוֹן עָלַי לִבִּי דַוָּי: הִנֵּה־קוֹל

‹ the voice ‹ Indeed, « is sick. ‹ my heart ‹ but within me « the sorrow, ‹ against ‹ I seek fortitude

שַׁוְעַת בַּת־עַמִּי מֵאֶרֶץ מַרְחַקִּים הַיהוה אֵין בְּצִיּוֹן

« *in Zion,* ‹ *is not* ‹ *Is it so that* HASHEM « far away: ‹ from a land ‹ of my people ‹ of the daughter ‹ of the cry

אִם־מַלְכָּהּ אֵין בָּהּ מַדּוּעַ הִכְעִסוּנִי בִּפְסִלֵיהֶם

« *with their graven idols,* ‹ *have they angered Me* ‹ [HASHEM replies:] *Why* « *within it?* ‹ *is not* ‹ *its King* ‹ *could it be that*

בְּהַבְלֵי נֵכָר: עָבַר קָצִיר כָּלָה קָיִץ וַאֲנַחְנוּ לוֹא

‹ have not ‹ but we « is the summer, ‹ finished « has the harvest season, ‹ passed « *of foreigners?* ‹ *with the worthless beliefs*

נוֹשָׁעְנוּ: עַל־שֶׁבֶר בַּת־עַמִּי הָשְׁבָּרְתִּי קָדַרְתִּי

« I am blackened, « I have been shattered; ‹ of my people ‹ of the daughter ‹ the calamity ‹ Over « been saved.

שַׁמָּה הֶחֱזִקָתְנִי: הַצֳרִי אֵין בְּגִלְעָד אִם־רֹפֵא אֵין

‹ is not ‹ Could it be that a doctor « in Gilead? ‹ Is it so that there is no balm « has gripped me. ‹ astonishment

שָׁם כִּי מַדּוּעַ לֹא עָלְתָה אֲרֻכַת בַּת־עַמִּי: מִי־

‹ If only someone « of my people? ‹ of the daughter ‹ the cure ‹ arisen ‹ has there not ‹ why ‹ For then « there?

יִתֵּן רֹאשִׁי מַיִם וְעֵינִי מְקוֹר דִּמְעָה וְאֶבְכֶּה יוֹמָם

‹ day ‹ then I would cry « of tears, ‹ into a spring ‹ and my eye ‹ into water ‹ my head ‹ would make

וָלַיְלָה אֵת חַלְלֵי בַת־עַמִּי: מִי־יִתְּנֵנִי בַמִּדְבָּר

‹ in the desert ‹ would grant that I were ‹ If only someone « of my people. ‹ of the daughter ‹ the slain ‹ for ‹ and night

---

tongues are like bows shooting arrows of falsehood and slander. Consequently, God must smelt them and test them, in the hope that through punishment and suffering they will repent. So the punishment comes, and it is harsh indeed, but the behavior of the nation leaves God no alternative.

Why did it happen? the prophet asks. Because they forsook the Torah, upon

מְלוֹן אֹרְחִים וְאֶעֶזְבָה אֶת־עַמִּי וְאֵלְכָה מֵאִתָּם כִּי

‹ for « away from them; ‹ and go ‹ my people ‹ then I would forsake « for travelers, ‹ [in] an inn

כֻּלָּם מְנָאֲפִים עֲצֶרֶת בֹּגְדִים: וַיַּדְרְכוּ אֶת־לְשׁוֹנָם

« their tongue, ‹ They draw « of traitors. ‹ an assembly ‹ adulterers, ‹ they are all

קַשְׁתָּם שֶׁקֶר וְלֹא לֶאֱמוּנָה גָּבְרוּ בָאָרֶץ כִּי

‹ for « in the land, ‹ that they have taken power ‹ through truthful justice ‹ and it is not « of falsehood, ‹ their bow

מֵרָעָה אֶל־רָעָה | יָצָאוּ וְאֹתִי לֹא־יָדָעוּ נְאֻם־יְהוָה:

« of HASHEM. ‹ — the word « they did not know ‹ and Me « they progress, ‹ evil ‹ to ‹ from evil

אִישׁ מֵרֵעֵהוּ הִשָּׁמֵרוּ וְעַל־כָּל־אָח אַל־תִּבְטָחוּ כִּי

‹ for « place your trust; ‹ do not ‹ brother ‹ any ‹ and in « beware, ‹ from his neighbor ‹ Every man

כָּל־אָח עָקוֹב יַעְקֹב וְכָל־רֵעַ רָכִיל יַהֲלֹךְ: וְאִישׁ

‹ Every man « goes about. ‹ spreading slander ‹ neighbor ‹ and every « acts with guile, ‹ brother ‹ every

בְּרֵעֵהוּ יְהָתֵלּוּ וֶאֱמֶת לֹא יְדַבֵּרוּ לִמְּדוּ לְשׁוֹנָם

‹ their tongue ‹ they train « they do not speak; ‹ and the truth « deceives his neighbor,

דַּבֵּר־שֶׁקֶר הַעֲוֵה נִלְאוּ: שִׁבְתְּךָ בְּתוֹךְ מִרְמָה

« deceit; ‹ is amid ‹ Your dwelling « they toil. ‹ at being iniquitous « falsehood, ‹ to speak

בְּמִרְמָה מֵאֲנוּ דַעַת־אוֹתִי נְאֻם־יְהוָה: לָכֵן כֹּה אָמַר

‹ says ‹ thus ‹ Therefore, « of HASHEM. ‹ — the word « Me ‹ to know ‹ they refuse ‹ because of [their] deceit

יְהוָה צְבָאוֹת הִנְנִי צוֹרְפָם וּבְחַנְתִּים כִּי־אֵיךְ אֶעֱשֶׂה

‹ *can I do [otherwise]* ‹ *how* ‹ *for* « *and I shall test them;* ‹ *purify them* ‹ *Indeed, I shall* « Master of Legions: ‹ HASHEM,

מִפְּנֵי בַּת־עַמִּי: חֵץ שָׁחוּט לְשׁוֹנָם מִרְמָה דִבֵּר

« *speaking;* ‹ *with deceit* ‹ *is their tongue,* ‹ *that kills* ‹ *Like an arrow* « *of My people?* ‹ *of the daughter* ‹ *because of the [evil]*

---

which the Sages comment that God declares, *I wish they had forsaken Me, but not forsaken My Torah, because its spiritual glow would have turned them back to the good.* This has remained a lesson for all time: The Torah is Israel's

בְּפִיו שָׁלוֹם אֶת־רֵעֵהוּ יְדַבֵּר וּבְקִרְבּוֹ יָשִׂים אָרְבּוֹ׃

with his mouth, ‹ about peace ‹ with ‹ his neighbor ‹ he speaks, « while inside of him ‹ he lays ‹ his ambush. «

הַעַל־אֵלֶּה לֹא־אֶפְקָד־בָּם נְאֻם־יְהֹוָה אִם בְּגוֹי אֲשֶׁר־

For ‹ these ‹ shall I not punish ‹ them? « — the word ‹ of HASHEM — « Shall it be that ‹ against a nation ‹ that is ‹

כָּזֶה לֹא תִתְנַקֵּם נַפְשִׁי׃ עַל־הֶהָרִים אֶשָּׂא בְכִי

like this ‹ not ‹ take vengeance ‹ shall My soul? « Regarding ‹ the mountains ‹ I shall take up ‹ a weeping ‹

וָנֶהִי וְעַל־נְאוֹת מִדְבָּר קִינָה כִּי נִצְּתוּ מִבְּלִי־אִישׁ

and a wailing, « and regarding ‹ the pastures ‹ of the wilderness ‹ a lamentation, « for ‹ they are desolate ‹ without ‹ a man ‹

עֹבֵר וְלֹא שָׁמְעוּ קוֹל מִקְנֶה מֵעוֹף הַשָּׁמַיִם וְעַד־

passing by ‹ and they do not hear ‹ the sound ‹ of flocks; « from the birds ‹ of heaven ‹ to ‹

בְּהֵמָה נָדְדוּ הָלָכוּ׃ וְנָתַתִּי אֶת־יְרוּשָׁלַםִ לְגַלִּים מְעוֹן

the animals, ‹ they have wandered off ‹ and gone away. « I shall transform ‹ Jerusalem ‹ into mounds of rubble, ‹ a lair ‹

תַּנִּים וְאֶת־עָרֵי יְהוּדָה אֶתֵּן שְׁמָמָה מִבְּלִי יוֹשֵׁב׃

of jackals; « and the cities ‹ of Judah ‹ I shall transform ‹ into desolation, ‹ without ‹ inhabitants. «

מִי־הָאִישׁ הֶחָכָם וְיָבֵן אֶת־זֹאת וַאֲשֶׁר דִּבֶּר פִּי־יְהֹוָה

Who ‹ is the man ‹ who is wise ‹ who will understand ‹ this, « the one whom ‹ there spoke ‹ the mouth ‹ of HASHEM ‹

אֵלָיו וְיַגִּדָהּ עַל־מָה אָבְדָה הָאָרֶץ נִצְּתָה כַמִּדְבָּר

to him ‹ and let him explain it: « For what reason ‹ did the land perish, « becoming parched ‹ like a desert, ‹

מִבְּלִי עֹבֵר׃ וַיֹּאמֶר יְהֹוָה עַל־עָזְבָם אֶת־תּוֹרָתִי

without ‹ passers-by? « And HASHEM said: « It is because of ‹ their forsaking ‹ My Torah ‹

---

ultimate hope of restoration to its former position of glory.

The *Haftarah* concludes with another timeless guide to the road map of life. Let people never seek their glory in transient and inconsequential matters such as ordinary wisdom, strength, and wealth. Only knowledge of God is worthwhile, and if that is someone's priority, then even his wisdom, strength, and wealth are praiseworthy, because they have become his tools in the service of God.

אֲשֶׁר נָתַתִּי לִפְנֵיהֶם וְלֹא־שָׁמְעוּ בְקוֹלִי וְלֹא־הָלְכוּ

‹ follow ‹ and they did not « My voice ‹ and they did not heed « before them, ‹ I placed ‹ that

בָהּ: וַיֵּלְכוּ אַחֲרֵי שְׁרִרוּת לִבָּם וְאַחֲרֵי הַבְּעָלִים

‹ the Baal-idols, ‹ and after « of their heart, ‹ the visions ‹ after ‹ And they went « [My Torah].

אֲשֶׁר לִמְּדוּם אֲבוֹתָם: לָכֵן כֹּה־אָמַר יהוה צְבָאוֹת

‹ Master of Legions, ‹ HASHEM, ‹ said ‹ thus ‹ Therefore, « their fathers taught them! ‹ which

אֱלֹהֵי יִשְׂרָאֵל הִנְנִי מַאֲכִילָם אֶת־הָעָם הַזֶּה לַעֲנָה

« wormwood, « — this people — « feeding them ‹ Indeed, I am « of Israel: ‹ the God

וְהִשְׁקִיתִים מֵי־רֹאשׁ: וַהֲפִצוֹתִים בַּגּוֹיִם אֲשֶׁר

‹ whom ‹ among nations ‹ I shall scatter them « of bitter gall. ‹ water ‹ and I am giving them to drink

לֹא יָדְעוּ הֵמָּה וַאֲבוֹתָם וְשִׁלַּחְתִּי אַחֲרֵיהֶם

‹ after them ‹ I shall send « [nor] their fathers; ‹ [neither] they « they have not known,

אֶת־הַחֶרֶב עַד כַּלּוֹתִי אוֹתָם: כֹּה אָמַר יהוה

‹ HASHEM, ‹ said ‹ thus « them! ‹ I destroy ‹ until ‹ the sword

צְבָאוֹת הִתְבּוֹנְנוּ וְקִרְאוּ לַמְקוֹנְנוֹת וּתְבוֹאֶינָה

« that they should come, ‹ the women lamenters ‹ and summon ‹ Perceive [the situation], « Master of Legions:

וְאֶל־הַחֲכָמוֹת שִׁלְחוּ וְתָבוֹאנָה: וּתְמַהֵרְנָה וְתִשֶּׂנָה

‹ and raise up ‹ Let them hurry « that they should come. ‹ send ‹ the wise women ‹ and for

עָלֵינוּ נֶהִי וְתֵרַדְנָה עֵינֵינוּ דִּמְעָה וְעַפְעַפֵּינוּ יִזְּלוּ־

‹ will flow ‹ and our eyelids « with tears, ‹ will our eyes ‹ and gush « a wailing, ‹ for us

מָיִם: כִּי קוֹל נְהִי נִשְׁמַע מִצִּיּוֹן אֵיךְ שֻׁדָּדְנוּ בֹּשְׁנוּ

‹ We are ashamed « have we been plundered! ‹ How « from Zion: ‹ is heard ‹ of wailing ‹ the sound ‹ For « with water.

מְאֹד כִּי־עָזַבְנוּ אָרֶץ כִּי הִשְׁלִיכוּ מִשְׁכְּנוֹתֵינוּ:

« have our dwellings! ‹ cast us out ‹ for « the land, ‹ we have left ‹ for ‹ greatly,

כִּֽי־שְׁמַ֤עְנָה נָשִׁים֙ דְּבַר־יהוה וְתִקַּ֥ח אָזְנְכֶ֖ם דְּבַר־

‹ the word ‹ let your ears ‹ and absorb « of HASHEM, ‹ to the word ‹ women, ‹ listen, ‹ For

פִּ֑יו וְלַמֵּ֤דְנָה בְנֽוֹתֵיכֶם֙ נֶ֔הִי וְאִשָּׁ֥ה רְעוּתָ֖הּ קִינָֽה׃

« [teach] a lamentation. ‹ to her friend ‹ and each woman « wailing, ‹ to your daughters ‹ and teach « of His mouth,

כִּי־עָ֤לָה מָ֙וֶת֙ בְּחַלּוֹנֵ֔ינוּ בָּ֖א בְּאַרְמְנוֹתֵ֑ינוּ לְהַכְרִ֤ית

‹ to eliminate « into our palaces, ‹ it has come « through our windows, ‹ death ‹ there has ascended ‹ For

עוֹלָל֙ מִח֔וּץ בַּחוּרִ֖ים מֵרְחֹבֽוֹת׃ דַּבֵּ֗ר כֹּ֚ה נְאֻם־

‹ is the word ‹ Thus « Speak: « from the streets. ‹ the young men « from the yards, ‹ infants

יהוה וְֽנָפְלָה֙ נִבְלַ֣ת הָֽאָדָ֔ם כְּדֹ֖מֶן עַל־פְּנֵ֣י הַשָּׂדֶ֑ה

« *of the field,* ‹ *the surface* ‹ *upon* ‹ *like dung* ‹ *of humans* ‹ *the corpses* ‹ *There will fall* « *of* HASHEM:

וּכְעָמִ֛יר מֵאַחֲרֵ֥י הַקֹּצֵ֖ר וְאֵ֥ין מְאַסֵּֽף׃ כֹּ֣ה ׀ אָמַ֣ר

‹ said ‹ Thus « *to gather it in.* ‹ *with no one* ‹ *the harvester* ‹ *[falling] behind* ‹ *and like a sheaf*

יהוה אַל־יִתְהַלֵּ֤ל חָכָם֙ בְּחָכְמָת֔וֹ וְאַל־יִתְהַלֵּ֥ל

« *glorify himself* ‹ *and let [him] not* « *with his wisdom,* « *— the wise man —* ‹ *glorify himself* « *Let [him] not* « HASHEM:

הַגִּבּ֖וֹר בִּגְבֽוּרָת֑וֹ אַל־יִתְהַלֵּ֥ל עָשִׁ֖יר בְּעָשְׁרֽוֹ׃ כִּ֣י

‹ *But* « *with his wealth.* ‹ *glorify himself* « *—the wealthy man —* « *let [him] not* « *with his strength,* « *— the strong man —*

אִם־בְּזֹ֞את יִתְהַלֵּ֣ל הַמִּתְהַלֵּ֗ל הַשְׂכֵּל֮ וְיָדֹ֣עַ אוֹתִי֒

« *Me.* ‹ *and knowing* ‹ *contem-plating* « *— the one who glorifies himself:* « *should [he] glorify himself* ‹ *with this* ‹ *rather,*

כִּ֚י אֲנִ֣י יהוה עֹ֥שֶׂה חֶ֛סֶד מִשְׁפָּ֥ט וּצְדָקָ֖ה בָּאָ֑רֶץ

« *in the land,* ‹ *and righteousness* ‹ *justice,* ‹ *kindness,* ‹ *Who does* ‹ *HASHEM* ‹ *I am* ‹ *For*

כִּֽי־בְאֵ֥לֶּה חָפַ֖צְתִּי נְאֻם־יהוה׃

« of HASHEM. ‹ — the word « *do I desire* ‹ *in these* ‹ *for*

BLESSINGS AFTER THE HAFTARAH / ברכות לאחר ההפטרה

AFTER THE *HAFTARAH* IS READ, THE *OLEH* FOR *MAFTIR* RECITES THE FOLLOWING BLESSINGS:

בָּרוּךְ אַתָּה יהוה אֱלֹהֵינוּ מֶלֶךְ הָעוֹלָם, צוּר
‹Rock «of the universe, ‹ King ‹ our God, «HASHEM, ‹ are You, ‹ Blessed

כָּל הָעוֹלָמִים, צַדִּיק בְּכָל הַדּוֹרוֹת, הָאֵל הַנֶּאֱמָן
« Who is trustworthy, ‹the God « generations, ‹ in all ‹ Righteous ‹ eternities, ‹ of all

הָאוֹמֵר וְעֹשֶׂה, הַמְדַבֵּר וּמְקַיֵּם, שֶׁכָּל דְּבָרָיו אֱמֶת
‹ are true ‹ of His words ‹ Who all « and fulfills, ‹ Who speaks « and does, ‹ Who says

וָצֶדֶק. נֶאֱמָן אַתָּה הוּא יהוה אֱלֹהֵינוּ, וְנֶאֱמָנִים
‹ and trustworthy ‹ our God, ‹HASHEM, ‹ are You, ‹ Trustworthy « and righteous.

דְּבָרֶיךָ, וְדָבָר אֶחָד מִדְּבָרֶיךָ אָחוֹר לֹא יָשׁוּב רֵיקָם,
« unfulfilled, ‹ returns ‹ never ‹ back « of Your words ‹ [even] one word « are Your words;

כִּי אֵל מֶלֶךְ נֶאֱמָן (וְרַחֲמָן) אָתָּה. בָּרוּךְ אַתָּה
‹ are You, ‹ Blessed « are You. ‹ (and compassionate) ‹ trustworthy ‹ King, ‹ a God, ‹ for

יהוה, הָאֵל הַנֶּאֱמָן בְּכָל דְּבָרָיו. (Cong. — אָמֵן.)
«His words. ‹ in all ‹ Who is trustworthy ‹ the God « HASHEM, « (Amen.)

רַחֵם עַל צִיּוֹן כִּי הִיא בֵּית חַיֵּינוּ, וְלַעֲלוּבַת
‹ and to [Israel,] who is humiliated « [that is the focus of] our life; ‹ is the place ‹ it ‹ for ‹ Zion, ‹ on ‹ Have mercy

נֶפֶשׁ תּוֹשִׁיעַ בִּמְהֵרָה בְיָמֵינוּ. בָּרוּךְ אַתָּה יהוה,
«HASHEM, ‹ are You, ‹ Blessed « in our days. ‹ speedily, ‹ bring salvation ‹ to her very soul,

מְשַׂמֵּחַ צִיּוֹן בְּבָנֶיהָ. (Cong. — אָמֵן.)
« through her children. ‹ Zion ‹ Who gladdens « (Amen.)

שַׂמְּחֵנוּ יהוה אֱלֹהֵינוּ בְּאֵלִיָּהוּ הַנָּבִיא עַבְדֶּךָ,
« Your servant, ‹ the prophet, ‹ with Elijah ‹ our God, ‹ HASHEM, ‹ Gladden us,

וּבְמַלְכוּת בֵּית דָּוִד מְשִׁיחֶךָ, בִּמְהֵרָה יָבֹא

‹ may he come, ‹ speedily « Your anointed one; ‹ of David, ‹ of the House ‹ and with the kingdom

וְיָגֵל לִבֵּנוּ, עַל כִּסְאוֹ לֹא יֵשֶׁב זָר וְלֹא יִנְחֲלוּ

‹ and do not [allow to] inherit « any stranger, ‹ sit ‹ may there never ‹ his throne ‹ On « and then our hearts will exult.

עוֹד אֲחֵרִים אֶת כְּבוֹדוֹ, כִּי בְשֵׁם קָדְשְׁךָ נִשְׁבַּעְתָּ

‹ You swore ‹ of your Holiness ‹ by the Name ‹ for « his honor, ‹ others ‹ any longer

לוֹ, שֶׁלֹּא יִכְבֶּה נֵרוֹ לְעוֹלָם וָעֶד. בָּרוּךְ אַתָּה

‹ are You, ‹ Blessed « and ever. ‹ forever ‹ would his lamp be ‹ extinguished ‹ that not « to him

יהוה, מָגֵן דָּוִד. (אָמֵן. — Cong.)

« (Amen.) « of David. ‹ Shield « HASHEM,

RETURNING THE TORAH / הכנסת ספר תורה

CHAZZAN TAKES THE TORAH IN HIS RIGHT ARM AND RECITES:

יְהַלְלוּ אֶת שֵׁם יהוה, כִּי נִשְׂגָּב שְׁמוֹ לְבַדּוֹ —

« alone; ‹ is His Name ‹ exalted ‹ for ‹ of HASHEM, ‹ the Name ‹ Let them praise

CONGREGATION RESPONDS:

— הוֹדוֹ עַל אֶרֶץ וְשָׁמָיִם. וַיָּרֶם קֶרֶן לְעַמּוֹ, תְּהִלָּה

‹ [causing] praise « of His people, ‹ the pride ‹ He has exalted « and heaven. ‹ earth ‹ is above ‹ His glory

לְכָל חֲסִידָיו, לִבְנֵי יִשְׂרָאֵל עַם קְרֹבוֹ, הַלְלוּיָהּ.[1]

« Halleluyah! « with whom He is intimate. ‹ the people ‹ of Israel, ‹ for the Children « His devout ones, ‹ for all

AS THE TORAH IS CARRIED TO THE ARK THE CONGREGATION RECITES PSALM 24, לְדָוִד מִזְמוֹר.

לְדָוִד מִזְמוֹר; לַיהוה הָאָרֶץ וּמְלוֹאָהּ, תֵּבֵל

‹ the inhabited land « and its fullness, ‹ is the earth ‹ HASHEM's « a psalm. ‹ By David,

וְיֹשְׁבֵי בָהּ. כִּי הוּא עַל יַמִּים יְסָדָהּ, וְעַל נְהָרוֹת

‹ rivers ‹ and upon ‹ founded it, ‹ seas ‹ upon ‹ He ‹ For « in it. ‹ and those who dwell

(1) *Psalms* 148:13-14.

יְכוֹנְנֶהָ. מִי יַעֲלֶה בְהַר יהוה, וּמִי יָקוּם בִּמְקוֹם

‹ in the place ‹ may stand ‹ and who ‹ of HASHEM, ‹ the mountain ‹ may ascend ‹ Who « established it.

קָדְשׁוֹ. נְקִי כַפַּיִם וּבַר לֵבָב, אֲשֶׁר לֹא נָשָׂא

‹ sworn ‹ has not ‹ who « heart; ‹ and pure ‹ hands ‹ One with clean « of His sanctity?

לַשָּׁוְא נַפְשִׁי וְלֹא נִשְׁבַּע לְמִרְמָה. יִשָּׂא בְרָכָה

‹ a blessing ‹ He will receive « deceitfully. ‹ sworn ‹ and has not « by My soul, ‹ in vain

מֵאֵת יהוה, וּצְדָקָה מֵאֱלֹהֵי יִשְׁעוֹ. זֶה דּוֹר

‹ the generation ‹ This is « of his salvation. ‹ from the God ‹ and just kindness « HASHEM ‹ from

דֹּרְשָׁיו, מְבַקְשֵׁי פָנֶיךָ, יַעֲקֹב, סֶלָה. שְׂאוּ שְׁעָרִים

‹ O gates ‹ Raise up, « Selah. « [the nation of] Jacob, ‹ Your Presence — ‹ those who strive for « of those who seek Him,

רָאשֵׁיכֶם, וְהִנָּשְׂאוּ פִּתְחֵי עוֹלָם, וְיָבוֹא מֶלֶךְ

‹ — the king « so that He may enter ‹ [you] everlasting entrances, ‹ and be uplifted, « your heads,

הַכָּבוֹד. מִי זֶה מֶלֶךְ הַכָּבוֹד, יהוה עִזּוּז וְגִבּוֹר,

« and the strong; ‹ the mighty ‹ HASHEM, « of Glory? ‹ King ‹ is this ‹ Who « of Glory.

יהוה גִּבּוֹר מִלְחָמָה. שְׂאוּ שְׁעָרִים רָאשֵׁיכֶם, וּשְׂאוּ

‹ and raise up, « your heads, ‹ O gates, ‹ Raise up, « in battle. ‹ the strong ‹ HASHEM,

פִּתְחֵי עוֹלָם, וְיָבֹא מֶלֶךְ הַכָּבוֹד. מִי הוּא זֶה מֶלֶךְ

‹ King ‹ this ‹ is He, ‹ Who « of Glory. ‹ — the king « so that He may enter ‹ [you] everlasting entrances,

הַכָּבוֹד, יהוה צְבָאוֹת הוּא מֶלֶךְ הַכָּבוֹד, סֶלָה.

« Selah! « of Glory, ‹ the King ‹ He is ‹ Master of Legions, ‹ HASHEM, « of Glory?

AS THE TORAH IS PLACED INTO THE ARK, THE CONGREGATION RECITES THE FOLLOWING VERSES:

וּבְנֻחֹה יֹאמַר, שׁוּבָה יהוה רִבְבוֹת אַלְפֵי יִשְׂרָאֵל.[1]

« *of Israel.* ‹ *thousands* ‹ *to the myriad* ‹ *HASHEM,* ‹ *Return,* « he would say: ‹ And when it rested

(1) *Numbers* 10:36.

קוּמָה יהוה לִמְנוּחָתֶךָ, אַתָּה וַאֲרוֹן עֻזֶּךָ. כֹּהֲנֶיךָ

Arise 〈 HASHEM, 〈 to Your resting place, 《 You 〈 and the Ark 〈 of Your strength. 《 Let Your *Kohanim* 〈

יִלְבְּשׁוּ צֶדֶק, וַחֲסִידֶיךָ יְרַנֵּנוּ. בַּעֲבוּר דָּוִד עַבְדֶּךָ

be clothed 〈 in righteousness, 《 and Your devout ones 〈 will sing joyously. 《 For the sake 〈 of David, 〈 Your servant, 《

אַל תָּשֵׁב פְּנֵי מְשִׁיחֶךָ.[1] כִּי לֶקַח טוֹב נָתַתִּי לָכֶם,

turn not away 〈 the face 〈 of Your anointed. 《 For 〈 a good teaching 〈 have I given 〈 you; 《

תּוֹרָתִי אַל תַּעֲזֹבוּ.[2] ❖ עֵץ חַיִּים הִיא לַמַּחֲזִיקִים

My Torah 〈 do not 〈 forsake. 《 A tree 〈 of life 〈 it is 〈 for those who grasp 〈

בָּהּ, וְתֹמְכֶיהָ מְאֻשָּׁר.[3] דְּרָכֶיהָ דַרְכֵי נֹעַם, וְכָל

it, 《 and its supporters 〈 are praiseworthy. 《 Its ways 〈 are ways 〈 of pleasantness, 《 and all 〈

נְתִיבוֹתֶיהָ שָׁלוֹם.[4] הֲשִׁיבֵנוּ יהוה אֵלֶיךָ וְנָשׁוּבָה,

its paths 〈 are peace. 《 Bring us back, 〈 HASHEM, 〈 to You, 〈 and we shall return, 《

חַדֵּשׁ יָמֵינוּ כְּקֶדֶם.[5]

renew 〈 our days 〈 as of old. 《

(1) *Psalms* 132:8-10. (2) *Proverbs* 4:2. (3) 3:18. (4) 3:17. (5) *Lamentations* 5:21.

KINNAH 6 / קינה ו

שָׁבַת*[1] סוּרוּ[2] מֶנִּי שִׁמְּעוּנִי עוֹבְרַי,[3]

« When ceased [did our joy],* ‹ Go away « *from me!* ‹ proclaimed to me ‹ those who expelled me. «

סְחִי וּמָאוֹס הֱשִׂימוּנִי[4] בְּעֶדְרֵי חֲבֵרַי,[5]

Filth ‹ and repugnance ‹ did they make of us ‹ amidst the flocks ‹ of my fellow [nations]. «

סַכּוֹתָה[6] מִשְׁכַּן מִסְּכוֹת דְּבִירַי,

You have covered ‹ Your [heavenly] Tabernacle, « so as not to listen ‹ to my entreaties. «

סַכּוֹתָ[7] וְהֻבְלְגוּ גִּבּוֹרַי,

You have covered [Yourself]; « thus overpowered ‹ were my warriors. «

סָפְקוּ כַף[8] וּמָעֲדוּ אֵבָרַי,[9] כִּסְלָה כָּל אַבִּירַי.[10]

[My enemies] clapped ‹ their hands [in derision] ‹ and tremble ‹ did my limbs ‹ when they trampled ‹ all ‹ my warriors. «

נָפְלָה[11] עוֹדֵינוּ[12] בְּצוּל דְּכוּיָה,

[Jerusalem] has fallen, ‹ it remains ‹ in [Babylon's] depths ‹ destroyed. «

(1) *Eichah* 5:15. (2) 4:15. (3) Some editions read עוֹכְרַי, *those who besmirched me.* (4). Cf. *Eichah* 3:45. (5) Cf. *Song of Songs* 1:7. (6) *Eichah* 3:44. (7) Cf. 3:43. (8) 2:15. (9) Cf. *II Samuel* 22:37; *Psalms* 18:37. (10) Cf. *Eichah* 1:15. (11) 5:16. (12) Cf. 4:17.

שָׁבַת — *When ceased [did our joy].* R' Elazar HaKalir, one of the earliest and most prolific *paytanim* (composers of liturgical poems), was a master at weaving seemingly diverse elements into a well-constructed, albeit difficult to understand, whole. In this first *kinnah* of the morning service, he has linked the verses of the respective chapters of *Eichah* into an intricate chain according to the following formula:

(a) each stanza contains six lines that correspond to the six alphabets of *Eichah* (Chapters one, two, and four contain 22 verses each, and are arranged according to an *aleph-beis* acrostic; Chapter Three comprises three verses beginning with א, three with ב, and so on);

(b) the first line of each sextet begins with the opening word or phrase of the corresponding verse in Chapter Five of *Eichah* (these do not follow an *aleph-beis* format), and is followed by the opening word or phrase of the corresponding verse in Chapter Four;

(c) the next three lines correspond to the respective triad of verses in Chapter Three, each set in the reverse order of its appearance in *Eichah;*

(d) the fifth line of each stanza corresponds to the verses in Chapter Two; and

(e) the final line is taken in its entirety from Chapter One, and determines the stanza's rhyme syllable. [All the words

עֵינִי[1] חִכְּתָה לַחֲזוֹן בֶּן בֶּרֶכְיָה,*
« of Berechiah,* ‹ of [Zechariah] the son ‹ for the prophetic vision ‹ longs ‹ My eye

עַד[2] פִּלְאֵי גִלְגָּל* חֲבוּיָה,[3]
« [that vision] remains hidden. ‹ [like those] of Gilgal,* ‹ miracles ‹ but until [we see]

עֵינִי[4] מְעוֹלֶלֶת בִּיוָנִית נְכוּיָה,*
« we are mired.* ‹ because in thick mud « sullied me, ‹ My eye [with tears]

עָשָׂה[5] וְנִחַם וַיִּקְרָא לִבְכִיָּה,[6]
‹ to cry, ‹ then summoned [Israel] « then regretted it, ‹ [God] caused [the Destruction],

וְנָם עַל אֵלֶּה אֲנִי בוֹכִיָּה.[7]
« *weep.* ‹ *I* ‹ *these things* ‹ *Over* ‹ saying,

(1) *Eichah* 3:51. (2) 3:50. (3) Some editions read חֲכוּיָה, *awaited.*
(4) *Eichah* 3:49. (5) 2:17. (6) Cf. *Isaiah* 22:12. (7) *Eichah* 1:16.

and phrases taken from *Eichah* appear in bold type in the Hebrew text.]

The concluding stanza deviates from the established pattern. Its first five lines contain an acrostic of the author's name אֶלְעָזָר, *Elazar,* and it closes with the refrain of the following *kinnah,* thus serving as a connective between the two.

Interestingly, the *kinnah* includes only eight stanzas taken from the last eight verses (or, in Chapter Three, the last eight triads) of the chapter of *Eichah.* Many commentators therefore regard this *kinnah* as the conclusion of a 14-stanza *kerovah* (*piyut* recited at various points during the *chazzan's* repetition of the *Shemoneh Esrei*) written by R' Elazar HaKalir, and recited by some congregations. That *kerovah* is based on the first 14 verses of *Eichah's* chapters.

לַחֲזוֹן בֶּן בֶּרֶכְיָה — *For the prophetic vision of [Zechariah] the son of Berechiah.* Zechariah's prophecies are full of hope and optimism. The Talmud points especially to his proclamation: *Thus says* HASHEM, *Master of Legions, "Old men and old women will once again sit in the streets of Jerusalem, each with his staff in his hand because of advanced age. And the streets of the city will be filled with boys and girls playing in its streets"* (*Zechariah* 8:4-5; see *Makkos* 24b).

פִּלְאֵי גִלְגָּל — *Miracles [like those] of Gilgal.* While the Israelites were encamped at Gilgal, they won many battles in miraculous fashion. For example, at Gibeon, God caused the sun to remain in the skies long after it should have set. Thus, Joshua and his forces were able to annihilate the enemy before they had a chance to retreat under cover of night. Additionally, God caused a heavy hailstorm to rain upon the five armies allied against Israel so that *more had died by the hailstones than had been put to the sword by the Children of Israel* (*Joshua* 10:11).

בִּיוָנִית נְכוּיָה — *Because in thick mud we are mired.* The word בִּיוָנִית is derived

עַל[1] פְּנֵי[2] פְרָת נֻפְּצוּ חֲסִידֶיהָ,*

On the surface of the Euphrates were shattered her pious ones;*

פַּלְגֵי[3] סוּף זָכְרָה כְּעָרוּ יְסוֹדֶיהָ,[4]

[yet] the split streams of the Sea of Reeds she remembered even while being destroyed was her foundation.

פַּחַד[5] חֵטְא שִׁילֹה* תָּכַף סוֹדֶיהָ,

The fearful threat of the sins of Shiloh* was swiftly fulfilled by those conspiring against her.

פָּצוּ[6] חֲזִירֵי יַעַר[7] אַיֵּה חֲסִידֶיהָ,

Open wide [their mouth] did the boars of the forest, [asking,] *Where are her pious ones?*

פָּצוּ[8] מַעֲשֶׂה עֶרְיָה לְנַדֶּיהָ, פֵּרְשָׂה צִיּוֹן בְּיָדֶיהָ.[9]

They declared that acts of adultery caused her to wander. Spread out did Zion her hands [to heaven].

עַל הַר צִיּוֹן[10] צָדוּ[11] שְׁאוֹנֵי מְדָנַי,

On Mt. Zion an ambush was laid by the hordes of my enemy.

(1) *Eichah* 5:17. (2) 4:16. (3) 3:48. (4) Cf. *Psalms* 137:7. (5) *Eichah* 3:47. (6) 3:46. (7) Cf. *Psalms* 80:14. (8) *Eichah* 2:16. (9) 1:17. (10) 5:18. (11) 4:18.

from יָוֵן, *thick mud* (as in *Psalms* 40:3 and 69:3). Thus, the phrase means that we are mired in a quagmire of troubles.

Alternatively, the word is derived from יָוָן, *Greece*, and is an allusion to חָכְמַת יְוָנִית, *Greek wisdom*, a form of sign-language code instrumental (to a degree) in sowing the seeds that led to the Destruction of the Second Temple (see *Menachos* 64b; see also *Bava Kamma* 83a).

עַל פְּנֵי פְרָת נֻפְּצוּ חֲסִידֶיהָ — *On the surface of the Euphrates were shattered her pious ones.* The Midrash teaches that when Nebuchadnezzar saw the renowned Levite singers who once sang in the Temple, he demanded that they serenade him as he feasted merrily over his victory, *"Sing for us from the songs of Zion!"* (*Psalms* 137:3). Without any hesitation, the Levites hung their precious musical instruments on the trees and deliberately mutilated their fingers, making it impossible for them to play the stringed instruments. Thus they did flatly refuse to play for Nebuchadnezzar but declared, *"How can we sing the song of HASHEM?* (ibid. 137:4). We cannot make any more music with these crippled hands!" (*Pesikta Rabasi* 31).

פַּחַד חֵטְא שִׁילֹה — *The fearful threat of the sins of Shiloh.* Jeremiah had warned the nation that just as the Tabernacle at Shiloh had come to destruction because of the sins of the sons of Eli, the *Kohen Gadol*, so would the *Beis HaMikdash* be destroyed because of the people's sinfulness (see *Jeremiah* 7:12 and 26:6). And now that his message had been ignored, his terrifying prophecy came true.

צָפוּ עַל רָאשִׁי[1] צִיּוֹן זְדוֹנַי,

[The enemy] flooded 〈 over 〈 the heads 〈 of Zion 〈 like treacherous waters. «

צָמְתוּ[2] בְּנֹב לַעֲמוֹד[3]* זְדוֹנַי,

They gathered 〈 at Nob 〈 to stand [against me]* 〈 my evil enemies [did]. «

צוֹד[4] נָצַרְתָּ לְעוֹרֵר מְדָנַי,

To ensnare, 〈 You preserved [memory of that sin] 〈 in order to incite 〈 my foes. «

צָעַק[5] עַמִּי בִּימֵי בֶן דִּינַי,* צַדִּיק הוּא יהוה.[6]

Cry out 〈 did my nation 〈 in the days 〈 of the son 〈 of Dinai,* « *Righteous* 〈 *is* 〈 *HASHEM!* «

אַתָּה[7] קַלִּים[8] הִכְבַּדְתָּ וּמֵעֶדְיִי עֶרְמוּנִי,

You 〈 to the lowly [nation] 〈 granted respect, « and of my glorious jewelry 〈 they denuded me. «

קֵרַבְתָּ[9] בֹּא אֵלַי וַיַּחֲרִימוּנִי,

You expedited 〈 their coming 〈 against me 〈 and they destroyed me. «

---

(1) Cf. *Eichah* 3:54. (2) 3:53. (3) See *Isaiah* 10:32. (4) *Eichah* 3:52; some editions read צוּר, but that is erroneous since the corresponding verse in *Eichah* reads צוֹד (*Beis Levi*). (5) *Eichah* 2:18. (6) 1:18. (7) 5:19. (8) 4:19. (9) Cf. 3:57.

בְּנֹב לַעֲמוֹד — *At Nob to stand [against me].* King Saul, in his mistaken belief that the *Kohanim* of the Tabernacle at Nob were conspiring with David against him, had 85 *Kohanim* slain, along with their wives, children, neighbors, and cattle (*I Samuel* 22:12-19). The Talmud reports that on the day of that slaughter, God ordained that retribution for that act will take place (in a later year) on the ninth of Av (*Sanhedrin* 95a).

בֶן דִּינַי — *The son of Dinai.* This as a reference to King Josiah who was so concerned about judging (דין) correctly that at age eighteen he returned all the judgments that he had made from the time he became king at age eight, since they might have been in error (*Shabbos* 56b). Further, Josiah understood and accepted Hashem's judgment against him, (as mentioned in *Kinnah* 11, from *Eichah Rabbah* 1:53). Josiah's final words were *Righteous is HASHEM* (*Arugas HaBosem*).

Alternately, the reference is to Eliezer ben Dinai, an infamous murderer (*Sotah* 47a; *Kesubos* 27a). Josephus (*Antiquities* XX, 8:5) describes how he was captured and brought to Rome for trial. *Shir HaShirim Rabbah* (2:7) refers to a man named Dinai — who led an unsuccessful revolt against Roman domination and brought swift retribution and heavy bloodshed — which may have been Eliezer or a different person (*R' Asher b' R' Yosef*).

קָרָאתִי[1] לְיוֹשְׁבֵי גִבְעוֹן עוֹד הֵם זֵרְמוּנִי,
‹ I called ‹ to the natives ‹ of Gibeon [for help], « but likewise, ‹ they ‹ swept me away. «

קוֹלִי לְהַשְׁמִיעַ[2] בַּעֲרָב* הִגְרִימוּנִי,
‹ My voice ‹ was raised [for relief] « in Arabia,* « but they caused my death. «

קוּמִי[3] עֲבוֹרִי בְּהָתֵל הֶעֱרִימוּנִי,
Arise! « Travel through [safely]! « mockingly ‹ were they treacherous to me. «

קָרָאתִי לַמְאַהֲבַי* הֵמָּה רִמּוּנִי.[4]
‹ I called ‹ for those who love me,* ‹ but they « deceived me.

לָמָּה[5] רוּחַ אַפֵּינוּ[6] לַטֶּבַח שָׁמָרוּ,[7]
‹ Why was it ‹ that the breath ‹ of our nostrils, [King Josiah,] ‹ to slaughter « they eagerly awaited?

רָאִיתָ[8] כִּי כְתַנּוּר עוֹרָם[9] כָּמָרוּ,[10]
‹ You have seen ‹ that ‹ like in an oven ‹ their skin « they heated.

רָאִיתָ[11] כִּי עָמָל וָכַעַס[12] בְּאִוּוּיְךָ גָּמָרוּ,
‹ You have seen ‹ that ‹ annoying ‹ and angering [acts] ‹ in the place of Your desire [Temple] « they consummated.

רַבְתָּ[13] בְּיַד יְחֶזְקֵאל לִנְקוֹם כְּמוֹ מָרוּ,
‹ You rebuked [Israel] ‹ at the hand « of Ezekiel, ‹ [warning] of retribution ‹ matching « their rebelliousness.

(1) *Eichah* 3:55. (2) Cf. 3:56. (3) 2:19. (4) 1:19. (5) 5:20. (6) 4:20. (7) See prefatory comments to *Kinnah* 11. (8) Cf. *Eichah* 3:60. (9) Some editions read עוֹרִי, *my skin*; some read עוֹרֵנוּ, *our skin*. (10) Cf. *Eichah* 5:10. (11) Cf. 3:59. (12) Cf. *Psalms* 10:14. (13) *Eichah* 3:58.

בַּעֲרָב — *In Arabia.* When the captive Israelites were led through the Ishmaelite lands of Arabia, the local populace met them and appeared interested in helping them. The Arabs pretended friendship and sympathy, and offered food and drink. However, the bread they offered had been oversalted in order to cause the Jews great and painful thirst. Then the Ishmaelites proferred leather canteens filled, not with water, but with air. When the captives raised the containers to their mouths, the hot, stagnant air entered their bodies and they died (*Tanchuma, Yisro* 5).

לַמְאַהֲבַי — *For those who love me.* The prophet compares alliance with foreign nations (rather than a return to God and reliance on His salvation) to an illicit affair with a pseudolover.

רְאֵה[1] וְנַכְחִידֵם מִגּוֹי[2] אָמָרוּ,

See, *Let us obliterate them from nationhood,* [our enemies] said!

רְאֵה יהוה כִּי צַר לִי מֵעַי חֳמַרְמָרוּ.[3]

See, HASHEM, that it is painful to me; my insides churn!

הֲשִׁיבֵנוּ[4] שִׂישִׂי[5] שִׁמַּע לְגוֹי צְאָנִי,

Bring us back [to You]; as *Rejoice [now for you too will be punished]* You declared to the nation which exiled us.

שִׁבְתָּם[6] רְמוֹס חֲצֵרַי[7] לְהַדְכִּיאֵנִי,

Their dwelling places trample, just as in my courtyards they strove to crush me.

שִׂפְתֵי[8] מְשׁוֹרְרֵי דְּבִיר דָּמְמוּ לְהַדְאִיבֵנִי,

The lips of the singers in the Temple they silenced, to cause me grief.

שָׁמַעְתָּ[9] זְמוֹרוֹת אַף[10] הֵכִין לְטַאטְאֵנִי,

You heard how they expelled flatulence in anger as they prepared to sweep me away.

שָׁכְבוּ[11] וְנָדוּ חָצָץ[12] לְהַבְרִיאֵנִי,[13]*

When [my nation] camped on their way to exile, mixed with pebbles was [the bread] they were given to eat.*

שָׁמְעוּ כִּי נֶאֱנָחָה אָנִי.[14]

They heard that sighing I was.

כִּי[15] תָם[16] חֲקַקְתָּ בְּכֵס אוֹפַנֶּיךָ,

Because of [the image of] the perfect one [Jacob] that You engraved upon the throne of Your Chariot,

(1) *Eichah* 2:20. (2) *Psalms* 83:5. (3) *Eichah* 1:20. (4) 5:21. (5) 4:21. (6) 3:63. (7) *Isaiah* 1:12. (8) *Eichah* 3:62. (9) 3:61. (10) Cf. *Ezekiel* 8:17; see the commentaries there. (11) *Eichah* 2:21. (12) Cf. 3:16. (13) Cf. *II Samuel* 3:35. (14) *Eichah* 1:21. (15) 5:22. (16) 4:22; see *Rashi* to *Ezekiel* 1:5.

חָצָץ לְהַבְרִיאֵנִי — *Mixed with pebbles was [the bread] they were given to eat.* God had told the prophet (*Ezekiel* 12:3) to prepare easily portable cooking utensils for use during the trip into exile. The purpose of the command was that others might follow his example and thus be prepared to cope with the rigors of the journey. But the people jeered at him and did not obey. Therefore, the exiles had to knead their dough in pits dug into the ground and their bread became mixed with grit (*Rashi* to *Eichah* 3:16).

תָּשִׁיב לָהֶם גְּמוּל[1] כְּאָז חֲזוּת פָּנֶיךָ,[2]

« Your face [at the Splitting of the Sea]; ‹ when [Israel] beheld ‹ as [You did] then ‹ what they deserve ‹ to them ‹ pay back

תִּרְדּוֹף[3] לְצַלְמוֹן יוֹעֲצֵי[4] עַל צְפוּנֶיךָ,[5]

« Your sheltered ones; ‹ against [Israel,] ‹ — all those who plot « into the darkest shadows ‹ pursue them

תִּתֵּן[6] לְהַבְהֵב נוֹתְצֵי פְנִינֶיךָ,

« Your precious gems [the Temples]. ‹ those who smashed ‹ to [eternal] burning ‹ consign

תִּקְרָא[7] לְשַׁכְּרָם כּוֹס כָּמוּס בְּפִנֶּיךָ,[8]

« in Your corners. ‹ hidden ‹ the cup [of retribution] ‹ to drink to intoxication ‹ Summon them

תָּבֹא כָל רָעָתָם לְפָנֶיךָ.[9]

« before You. ‹ their wickedness ‹ all ‹ Let there come

תָּבֹא אֶל צָר אֲשֶׁר כִּלָּנוּ,

« to destroy us completely. ‹ who [sought] ‹ the tormentor ‹ upon ‹ May [retribution] come

לִמְבוֹא חֲמָת[10] בְּחֵמָה נִהֲלָנוּ,

« he led us; ‹ in fury ‹ to Hamath ‹ To the approach

עַד לַחֲלַח וְחָבוֹר הִגְלָנוּ,[11]

« he exiled us. ‹ and Habor ‹ Halah ‹ unto

זָקֵן וּבָחוּר וּבְתוּלָה כִּבְלָנוּ,[12]

« — he shackled us [all]. « and maiden ‹ youth, ‹ Old man,

רָם הַבֵּט נָא עַמְּךָ כֻלָּנוּ,[13]

« are we all. ‹ that Your nation ‹ now, ‹ see, « O Supreme One,

זְכוֹר יהוה מֶה הָיָה לָנוּ.[14]

« upon us! ‹ has come ‹ what ‹ HASHEM, ‹ Remember,

---

(1) *Eichah* 3:64. (2) Cf. *Psalms* 17:15. (3) 3:66. (4) Some editions read יוֹעֲצֵי רַע, *those who plot evil.* (5) Cf. *Psalms* 83:4. (6) *Eichah* 3:65. (7) 2:22. (8) Some editions read בְּפָנֶיךָ, *before You.* (9) 1:22. (10) Cf. *Amos* 6:14. (11) *II Kings* 17:6. (12) Cf. *Jeremiah* 51:22. (13) *Isaiah* 64:8. (14) *Eichah* 5:1.

KINNAH 7 / קינה ז

אֵיכָה אַצְתָּ בְאַפֶּךָ,* לְאַבֵּד בְּיַד אֲדוֹמִים אֱמוּנֶיךָ,

« of the Edomites, ‹ at the hand ‹ to eradicate ‹ in Your anger* ‹ did You rush ‹ How

וְלֹא זָכַרְתָּ בְּרִית בֵּין הַבְּתָרִים[1]

‹ the Parts ‹ Between ‹ the Covenant ‹ and You did not recall

אֲשֶׁר בֵּרַרְתָּ לִבְחוּנֶיךָ,

« the ones You tested? ‹ You selected ‹ by which

וּבְכֵן בִּטֵּינוּ, זְכוֹר יהוה מֶה הָיָה לָנוּ.[2]

« *upon us!* ‹ *has come* ‹ *what* ‹ *HASHEM,* ‹ *Remember,* « we have declaimed, ‹ Therefore

אֵיכָה גָּעַרְתָּ בְּגַעֲרָתֶךָ, לְגַלּוֹת בְּיַד גֵּאִים גְּאוּלֶיךָ,

« those You had [once] redeemed, ‹ of the haughty ones ‹ at the hand ‹ to exile ‹ with Your rebuke, ‹ did You reproach ‹ How

וְלֹא זָכַרְתָּ דְּלִיגַת דִּלּוּג דֶּרֶךְ* אֲשֶׁר דִּלַּגְתָּ לִדְגָלֶיךָ,

« for Your flag-bearing tribes? ‹ You had shortened ‹ that ‹ road* ‹ of the shortened ‹ the skipping over ‹ and You did not recall

וּבְכֵן דִּבַּרְנוּ, זְכוֹר יהוה מֶה הָיָה לָנוּ.

« *upon us!* ‹ *has come* ‹ *what* ‹ *HASHEM,* ‹ *Remember,* « we have spoken, ‹ Therefore

(1) *Genesis* Ch. 15 (2) *Eichah* 5:1.

אֵיכָה אַצְתָּ בְאַפֶּךָ — *How did You rush in Your anger.* This *kinnah,* by R' Elazar HaKalir — who signed his name, אֶלְעָזָר, in the acrostic of the final stanza — follows a complex alphabetical form. Each of the first eleven stanzas is constructed in the following manner:

אֵיכָה א. . .תָּ בְּא. . .ךָ, לְא. . . בְּיַד א. . .ים א. . .ךָ,
וְלֹא זָכַרְתָּ ב. . . ב. . . ב. . ., אֲשֶׁר ב. . .תָּ לב. . .ךָ,
וּבְכֵן ב. . .נוּ זְכוֹר ה׳ מֶה הָיָה לָנוּ.
אֵיכָה ג. . .תָּ בְּג. . .ךָ, לְג. . . בְּיַד ג. . .ים ג. . .ךָ,
וְלֹא זָכַרְתָּ ד. . . ד. . . ד. . ., אֲשֶׁר ד. . .תָּ לד. . .ךָ,
וּבְכֵן ד. . .נוּ זְכוֹר ה׳ מֶה הָיָה לָנוּ.

The alphabet is repeated five times for odd-numbered letters (א,ג,ה . . .) and six times for even-numbered letters (ב,ד,ו . . .). This repetition alludes to the Five Books of the Torah and the Six Orders of the Mishnah. Even the merit of Torah study was ineffective in protecting Israel when its actions became degenerate (*Kol BeRamah*).

דְּלִיגַת דִּלּוּג דֶּרֶךְ — *The skipping over of the shortened road.* When the Israelites left Sinai, they traveled three days and arrived at Kadosh Barnea — an eleven-day journey under usual circumstances! (See *Rashi* to *Deut.* 1:2.) Alternatively, this

אֵיכָה הֲגִתָ בְּהֶגְיוֹנֶךָ, לַהֲדוֹף בְּיַד הוֹלְלִים הֲמוֹנֶיךָ,

How ‹ did You conceive ‹ in Your thoughts ‹ to push ‹ into the hand ‹ of the unruly revelers ‹ Your multitudes, «

וְלֹא זָכַרְתָּ וְעוּד וֶתֶק וֶסֶת* אֲשֶׁר וְעַדְתָּ לְוְעוּדֶיךָ,

and You did not recall ‹ the Assembly Hall, ‹ the strong-hold ‹ of the [yearly] cycle,* ‹ that ‹ You had designated ‹ for those You meet with? «

וּבְכֵן וְקוֹנַנּוּ, זְכוֹר יהוה מֶה הָיָה לָנוּ.

There-fore, ‹ we have lamented, « *Remem-ber,* ‹ *HASHEM,* ‹ *what* ‹ *has come* ‹ *upon us!* «

אֵיכָה זָנַחְתָּ בְּזַעְמֶךָ לְזַלְזֵל בְּיַד זָרִים זְבוּלֶךָ,

How ‹ did You abandon ‹ in Your rage ‹ to allow derision « — at the hand ‹ of strangers — « of Your Temples, «

וְלֹא זָכַרְתָּ חִתּוּן חֻקֵּי חוֹרֵב אֲשֶׁר חָקַקְתָּ לַחֲמוּלֶיךָ,

and You did not recall ‹ the betrothal of [Israel] ‹ to the Laws ‹ of Horeb [Sinai] ‹ that ‹ You had carved ‹ for those You show compassion to? «

וּבְכֵן חִוִּינוּ, זְכוֹר יהוה מֶה הָיָה לָנוּ.

There-fore ‹ we have conveyed, « *Remem-ber,* ‹ *HASHEM,* ‹ *what* ‹ *has come* ‹ *upon us!* «

אֵיכָה טָרַחְתָּ בְּטָרְחֶךָ,*

How ‹ did You trouble Yourself ‹ in Your exertion* ‹

לִטְרוֹף בְּיַד טוֹרְפִים[1] טְלָאֶיךָ,

to have torn asunder, ‹ by the hand ‹ of the predators, ‹ Your sheep, «

וְלֹא זָכַרְתָּ יְקַר יְדִידוּת יֹשֶׁר אֲשֶׁר יִחַדְתָּ לְיוֹדְעֶיךָ,

and You did not recall ‹ the [merit of the] honored, ‹ beloved ‹ upright [Torah] ‹ that ‹ You designated ‹ for those who know You? «

(1) Some editions read טְמֵאִים, *the unclean.*

---

refers to the 400-year period of slavery prophesied in the Covenant Between the Parts (*Genesis* 15:13) that was condensed to 210 years, from Jacob's arrival in Egypt until the Exodus (see *Targum* to *Song of Songs* 2:8).

וְעוּד וֶתֶק וֶסֶת — *The Assembly Hall, the stronghold of the [yearly] cycle.* This alludes to the *Beis HaMikdash,* the spiritual stronghold at which all of Israel would assemble during three seasons (*Pesach, Shavuos, Succos*) each year.

אֵיכָה טָרַחְתָּ בְּטָרְחֶךָ — *How did You trouble Yourself in Your exertion.* For 18 years a heavenly voice resounded through the halls of Nebuchadnezzar's palace. It

וּבְכֵן יְלָלְנוּ, זְכוֹר יהוה מֶה הָיָה לָנוּ.

Therefore ‹ we have wailed, « Remember, ‹ *HASHEM,* ‹ what ‹ has come ‹ upon us! «

אֵיכָה כּוֹנַנְתָּ בְּכַעְסֶךָ, לְכַלּוֹת בְּיַד כְּפִירִים[1] כַּרְמֶךָ,

How ‹ did You focus ‹ in Your anger, ‹ to devastate ‹ at the hand ‹ of the lion [-like enemy] ‹ Your vineyard [Israel], «

וְלֹא זָכַרְתָּ לֹא לִזְנוֹחַ לְעוֹלָם[2]

and You did not recall ‹ [Your promise] not ‹ to reject [them] ‹ forever ‹

אֲשֶׁר לִמַּדְתָּ לִלְקוּחֶיךָ,

that ‹ You taught ‹ Your acquired people? «

וּבְכֵן לָהַגְנוּ, זְכוֹר יהוה מֶה הָיָה לָנוּ.

Therefore ‹ we have spoken, « Remember, ‹ *HASHEM,* ‹ what ‹ has come ‹ upon us! «

אֵיכָה מִלַּלְתָּ בְּמוֹאֲסֶךָ,

How ‹ did You speak ‹ in Your disdain, ‹

לִמְחוֹת בְּיַד מוֹנִים מְנַשְּׂאֶיךָ,

of eradicating ‹ at the hand ‹ of oppressors ‹ those who had exalted You, «

וְלֹא זָכַרְתָּ נְשִׂיאַת נוֹצַת נֶשֶׁר[3]

and You did not recall ‹ the bearing [of Israel] ‹ on the feathers ‹ of an eagle ‹

אֲשֶׁר נָשָׂאתָ לִנְשׂוּאֶיךָ,

when ‹ You carried ‹ those whom You had exalted? «

וּבְכֵן נָהִינוּ, זְכוֹר יהוה מֶה הָיָה לָנוּ.

Therefore ‹ we have moaned, « Remember, ‹ *HASHEM,* ‹ what ‹ has come ‹ upon us! «

אֵיכָה שַׂחְתָּ בְּסַעֲרָךְ, לְסַגֵּר בְּיַד סְעֵפִים סַהֲדֶיךָ,

How ‹ did You speak out ‹ in Your stormy rage ‹ to deliver ‹ into the hand ‹ of plotters of evil ‹ those who testify to You, «

(1) Some editions read כּוֹשְׁלִים, *sinners.* (2) Cf. *Eichah* 3:31. (3) Cf. *Exodus* 19:4.

cried, "O perpetrator of evil! Go destroy your Master's Temple, for His children do not listen to Him" (*Midrash Eichah,* intro. 23).

וְלֹא זָכַרְתָּ עֹז עֲדִי עֲדָיִים*[1] אֲשֶׁר עִטַּרְתָּ לַעֲבָדֶיךָ,

and You did not recall ‹ the ‹ mighty [Torah's] twin crowns* ‹ with which ‹ You crowned ‹ Your servants? «

וּבְכֵן עָנִינוּ, זְכוֹר יהוה מֶה הָיָה לָנוּ.

Therefore ‹ we have responded, « Remember, ‹ *HASHEM,* ‹ *what* ‹ *has come* ‹ *upon us!* «

אֵיכָה פַּצְתָּ בְּפַחְדֶּךָ, לְפַגֵּר בְּיַד פָּרִיצִים פְּלִיאֶיךָ,

How ‹ did You utter ‹ in Your fearsomeness, ‹ to make corpses « by the hand ‹ of lawbreakers — « of the people You did wonders for, «

וְלֹא זָכַרְתָּ צַהֲלַת צְבִי צַדִּיק[2]

and You did not recall ‹ the joyous song ‹ of the desirable ‹ righteous one ‹

אֲשֶׁר צָפַנְתָּ לִצְבָאֶיךָ,[3]

that ‹ You have concealed ‹ for Your legions [Israel]? «

וּבְכֵן צָעַקְנוּ, זְכוֹר יהוה מֶה הָיָה לָנוּ.

There-fore ‹ we have shouted, « *Remember,* ‹ *HASHEM,* ‹ *what* ‹ *has come* ‹ *upon us!* «

אֵיכָה קָרָאתָ בִּקְרִיאָתֶךָ,

How ‹ did You proclaim ‹ in Your proclamation, ‹

לַקְנוֹת[4] בְּיַד קָמִים קְרוּאֶיךָ,

to give over ‹ to the hand ‹ of those who oppose You ‹ those You had once summoned, «

וְלֹא זָכַרְתָּ רֶגֶשׁ רֶכֶב רִבּוֹתַיִם*[5]

and You did not recall ‹ the assembly ‹ of [Your] entourage ‹ of [two and] twenty thousand,* ‹

---

(1) Cf. *Ezekiel* 16:7. (2) Cf. *Isaiah* 24:16; some editions read, צַהֲלַת צְבִי צֶדֶק, *the joyous song of the desirable* [*Land* (cf. *Ezekiel* 20:15) *of*] *righteousness* (cf. *Isaiah* 1:21).
(3) Cf. *Psalms* 31:20. (4) Some editions read לְקַנּוֹת, *to effect a transfer.* (5) Cf. *Psalms* 68:18.

עֲדִי עֲדָיִים — *[Torah's] twin crowns.* When Israel was asked to accept the Torah, the nation cried out, נַעֲשֶׂה וְנִשְׁמָע, *We will do and we will hear* (*Exodus* 24:7), placing נַעֲשֶׂה, *we will do,* before נִשְׁמָע, *we will hear.* Thus they undertook to fulfill all of God's commandments, even before they knew what was expected of them. This devotion was rewarded when 600,000 ministering angels approached Israel and placed two crowns upon each Jew's head — one for נַעֲשֶׂה, and one for נִשְׁמָע (*Shabbos* 88a).

רֶגֶשׁ רֶכֶב רִבּוֹתַיִם — *The assembly of [Your] entourage of [two and] twenty thousand.* The translation and interpolation are

אֲשֶׁר רָצִיתָ לְרֵעֶיךָ,

« to Your friends? ‹ You chose ‹ at which [to appear]

וּבְכֵן רָגַנְנוּ, זְכוֹר יהוה מֶה הָיָה לָנוּ.

« *upon us!* ‹ *has come* ‹ *what* ‹ *HASHEM,* ‹ *Remember,* « we have complained regretfully, ‹ Therefore

אֵיכָה שָׁאַפְתָּ בְּשַׁאֲפֶךָ,

‹ in Your desire, ‹ did You strive ‹ How

לְשַׁלּוֹת בְּיַד שׁוֹדְדִים שְׁלֵמֶיךָ,

« Your perfect ones, ‹ of pillagers ‹ at the hand ‹ to disperse

וְלֹא זָכַרְתָּ תֹּקֶף תַּלְתַּלֵּי תֹּאַר

‹ beauty ‹ of the Temple Mount's ‹ the strength ‹ and You did not recall

אֲשֶׁר תִּכַּנְתָּ לִתְמִימֶיךָ,

« for Your wholesome ones? ‹ You prepared ‹ which

וּבְכֵן תָּאַנְנוּ, זְכוֹר יהוה מֶה הָיָה לָנוּ.

« *upon us!* ‹ *has come* ‹ *what* ‹ *HASHEM,* ‹ *Remember,* « we have mourned, ‹ Therefore

תָּאַנְנוּ לִשְׁפּוֹךְ [דְּמָעוֹת] כַּמַּיִם,

‹ like water, « [tears] ‹ pouring out ‹ We have mourned;

עַל מֶה בְּיוֹם זֶה נִשְׁבֵּינוּ פַּעֲמַיִם,

« twice. ‹ we were taken captive ‹ on this day ‹ the fact that ‹ because of

זָכְרִי בִּהְיוֹתִי בְּשַׁלְוָה יוֹשֶׁבֶת בִּירוּשָׁלַיִם,

« in Jerusalem. ‹ dwelling ‹ in serenity ‹ how I was ‹ I recall

רָגַנְתִּי וְעַתָּה אַאֲדֶה עַד חוּג שָׁמַיִם.

« of heaven. ‹ the sphere ‹ up to ‹ [with my laments] I shall soar ‹ but now, ‹ I have complained regretfully,

---

based on a midrashic account of God's descent upon Mount Sinai. The psalmist states: *The chariot of God is twenty thousand, thousands of angels, my Lord is among them, at Sinai in holiness* (*Psalms* 68:18). R' Avudimi of Haifa explained that 22,000 ["20,000" plus 2,000, the minimum that can be called "thousands"] ministering angels accompanied God when He descended upon Mount Sinai to give the Torah to Israel (see *Rashi* to *Psalms* 68:18).

KINNAH 8 / קינה ח

אַאֲדֶה* עַד חוּג שָׁמַיִם, אַאֲלֶה אִתִּי שָׁמַיִם,

« would the heavens! ‹ join with me ‹ I would lament [until] « of heaven; ‹ the sphere ‹ up to ‹ Would that I could soar*

אָאוֹר יוֹם מַחֲרִיבִי פַּעֲמַיִם,

« twice. ‹ on which I was destroyed ‹ the day ‹ I would curse

אֶתְאוֹנֵן מִי יִתֵּן רֹאשִׁי מַיִם.[1]

« were [a stream of] water. ‹ that my head ‹ can grant ‹ Who « I would lament,

אַבְחִין בִּבְכִי לֵיל מִדְבָּר,[2]

« in the wilderness; ‹ of that night ‹ the crying ‹ I would review

אֶבְחֲנָה לֵיל מִלֵּיל* וּמִדְבָּר מִמִּדְבָּר,*

« from the wilderness [of the nations].* ‹ and [that] wilderness « from the night [of destruction],* ‹ [that] night ‹ I would differentiate

אֲבַכֶּה אִתִּי עוֹלַת מִדְבָּר,[3]

« from the wilderness, ‹ all who ascended ‹ with me ‹ I would inspire to cry

אֶשְׁאַג מִי יִתְּנֵנִי בַמִּדְבָּר.[4]

« *in the Wilderness [of Sinai].* ‹ *can grant that I were [once again]* ‹ *Who* « as I would roar,

(1) *Jeremiah* 8:23, see *Targum*. (2) Some editions read יְלֵל מִדְבָּר, *the wailing of the wilderness*. (3) Cf. *Song of Songs* 3:6. (4) *Jeremiah* 9:1.

אַאֲדֶה — *Would that I could soar.* The translation of this rare word is based on הִנֵּה כַנֶּשֶׁר יִדְאֶה, *Indeed! It shall fly as an eagle* (*Jeremiah* 48:40). Alternatively the word is related to אֵיד, which *Targum* (*Job* 21:30) renders תְּבִירָא, *destruction*, and *Ibn Ezra* explains as a *dark cloud.*

אֶבְחֲנָה לֵיל מִלֵּיל — *I would differentiate [that] night from the night [of destruction].* On that first tragic night of Tishah B'Av in the wilderness, the nation heard the Spies' slanderous reports regarding the Land of Canaan, and they wept. But that was a בְּכִיָּה שֶׁל חִנָּם, *an uncalled-for* (or, *needless*) *weeping.* The tragic events that occurred on later Tishah B'Avs, however, were the source of true weeping. Thus we distinguish between tonight's weeping and that first night's weeping.

וּמִדְבָּר מִמִּדְבָּר — *And [that] wilderness from the wilderness [of the nations]*, between the Wilderness of Sinai where we ate the heavenly manna, drank from the Well of Miriam, and were protected by the Clouds of Glory, and the wilderness of exile where we were starving, thirsty, and at the mercy of the elements and both four-legged and two-legged predators.

אֶגָּדַע וְאֶנָּשֵׁל כְּנֹקֶף זַיִת,

[My limbs] are amputated, ‹ [my fruit] has been stripped ‹ like a beaten ‹ olive tree. «

אֲגָרֶה אִתִּי כָּל בְּנֵי בַיִת,

I would provoke ‹ [to cry] with me ‹ all ‹ the members ‹ of the household; «

אֶגְרוֹם שֶׁיֹּאמַר בַּעַל הַבַּיִת,

I would cause ‹ that He would say « — the Master ‹ of the Household — «

אֲרַשֶּׁה מִי יִתְּנֵנִי שָׁמִיר וָשַׁיִת.[1]

I wish to express, ‹ *if only* ‹ *I could allow Myself* ‹ *[to burn Israel's enemies as if] thorns* ‹ *and thistles!* «

אֲדַוֶּה בְּכָל לֵב לְהַמְצִיאֵהוּ,

I would suffer pain ‹ within all ‹ my heart ‹ in order that He be close [to me]. «

אֲדַעָה מִלִּין בָּם לְאַמְּצֵהוּ.

Would that I knew ‹ the words ‹ with which ‹ to strengthen [my ties] to Him. «

אֶדְאַג אַיֵּה רוֹעֶה וְלֹא אֶמְצָאֵהוּ,

I would worry, ‹ *Where is* ‹ *the Shepherd?* « — but not ‹ be able to find Him. «

אֲקוֹנֵן מִי יִתֵּן יָדַעְתִּי וְאֶמְצָאֵהוּ.[2]

I would lament, ‹ *Who* ‹ *can grant* ‹ *that I discover [where],* « *so that I might find him.* «

אֶהָפְכָה וְאֶתְהַפְּכָה כְּאוֹפָן בְּמִלַּי,

I would turn around ‹ and turn around again ‹ like a spinning wheel ‹ with my words, «

אֶהְגֶּה פָּנִים בְּפָנִים לְתַנּוֹת עֲמָלַי,

I would speak [with Him] ‹ face ‹ to face ‹ to bemoan ‹ my woes. «

אָהֲהוּ חֶרֶס וָסַהַר מִלְּהַגִּיהַּ לְמוּלַי,

Howl together ‹ would the sun ‹ and the moon, « refusing to shine ‹ toward me. «

(1) Cf. *Isaiah* 27:4. (2) *Job* 23:3.

אֶצְרַח מִי יִתֵּן אֵפוֹא וְיִכָּתְבוּן מִלָּי.[1]

I would shriek, ‹ Who ‹ can grant ‹ now ‹ that recorded would be ‹ my words [of lamentation].

אוֹרַח מִשְׁפְּטֵי גוֹנְבֵי עֱלִי,*

The ways ‹ that were righteous ‹ of the smugglers [of first fruits] ‹ hidden in the pestle,*

אוֹדִיעַ בְּבִצְעִי וּמַעֲלִי,

I would reveal ‹ [the decree was] for my graft ‹ and my treachery.

אוּמְלְלוּ מַזָּלוֹת בְּקָרְעִי מְעִילִי,

Distraught were even ‹ the constellations ‹ when I ripped ‹ my garments [at the Temple's destruction],

אֶפְעֶה מִי יִתֵּן שׁוֹמֵעַ לִי.[2]

I would cry out, ‹ Who ‹ can grant ‹ that He listen ‹ to me!

אָזְדָה כְּהוּפְרָה הָאֲבִיּוֹנָה,*[3]

[The Divine Presence] departed ‹ when dissipated ‹ was the desire [for the Temple];*

אֶזְכְּרָה כִּי הָיִיתִי מְחֻתָּנָה,

I would remember ‹ that ‹ I was once ‹ wed [to God through the Torah];

(1) *Job* 19:23. (2) Cf. 31:35. (3) Cf. *Ecclesiates* 12:5.

גּוֹנְבֵי עֱלִי — *Of the smugglers [of first fruits] hidden in the pestle.* Once, the foreign overlords of *Eretz Yisrael* forbade the bringing of *bikkurim* (first-fruit offerings) to Jerusalem and stationed sentries on the roads to prevent the Jews from doing so. Pious men of that generation arose and placed baskets of *bikkurim*, covered with dried figs, into large wooden vessels shaped like pestles, which were used for pressing dried figs into cakes, and carried them on their shoulders to Jerusalem. When the sentries inquired about the contents, the Jews would say that they were taking the dried figs to a mortar where they would press them with their pestle. Therefore, they were given the appellation *pestle-smugglers* because they would *smuggle past the hearts*, deceiving the sentries with the pretext of the pestle (*Taanis* 28a).

הָאֲבִיּוֹנָה — *Was the desire [for the Temple].* The translation follows *Rashi* and *Ibn Ezra* (*Ecclesiastes* 12:5) who render "lust for conjugal pleasures." Some regard this as a compound word from אָב, *father* or *patriarch*, and יוֹנָה, *dove*, thus, Abraham, Isaac, and Jacob, the Patriarchs of Israel, the nation compared to a dove (see e.g., *Song of Songs* 2:14). The verse then alludes to the Talmudic teaching, תַּמּוּ זְכוּת אָבוֹת, *the merits of the Patriarchs*

אַזִּיל פְּלָגִים כִּבְרֵכָה הָעֶלְיוֹנָה,[1]

I would shed tears ‹ that stream forth ‹ as from the Pool ‹ that was Highest; «

אֶעֱגוֹר מִי יִתֶּן לִּי אֵבֶר כַּיּוֹנָה.[2]

I would yearningly exclaim, « *Who* ‹ *can grant* ‹ *that I had* ‹ *wings* ‹ *like a dove.* «

אָח נִפְשַׁע מִקִּרְיַת עֹז[3] אֶל צוֹר,

Brother [Israel] ‹ separated by sinfulness ‹ from [Jerusalem,] the city ‹ that is mighty ‹ and exiled to ‹ Tyre; «

אָחוּ בְּלִי מָיִם[4] בְּאַף לַעֲצוֹר,

like a meadow ‹ without ‹ water, « for in God's wrath ‹ was [rain] withheld. «

אָחַז קָמוֹת לִקְצוֹר וְעוֹלֵלוֹת לִבְצוֹר,

[The enemy] grasped ‹ the standing grain [adults] ‹ to be reaped ‹ and the unripe grapes [children] ‹ to be harvested; «

אָשִׂיחָה מִי יוֹבִילֵנִי עִיר מָצוֹר.[5]

I would speak, ‹ *Who [can grant]* ‹ *that I be brought* ‹ *to the city* ‹ *that is fortified!* «

אֶטַּע אָהֳלֵי אַפַּדְנִי[6] בְּצַלְמָוֶת,

I would pitch ‹ the tents ‹ of my palace ‹ in the shadow of death [in exile]; «

אָטוּסָה וְאֶשְׁכּוֹנָה[7] עַד חֲצַר מָוֶת,*

I would fly off ‹ and I would find rest ‹ even in ‹ the Courtyard ‹ of Death,* «

אֶטַּפֵּל אֶת הַמְחַכִּים לַמָּוֶת,*

[where] I would associate ‹ with ‹ those who wait ‹ for death.* «

(1) Cf. *II Kings* 18:17; *Isaiah* 7:3. (2) *Psalms* 55:7. (3) *Proverbs* 18:19; see *Nazir* 23a. (4) *Job* 8:11. (5) *Psalms* 60:11. (6) Cf. *Daniel* 11:45. (7) Cf. *Psalms* 55:7.

have ended (*Shabbos* 55a), and means that since we no longer had the merits of the אָבוֹת to protect us, the Temple was destroyed (*Matteh Levi*).

חֲצַר מָוֶת ... הַמְחַכִּים לַמָּוֶת — *The Courtyard of Death . . . those who wait for death.* חֲצַרְמָוֶת, *Hazar-maveth,* was a seventh-generation descendant of Noah. According to the Midrash, he was the progenitor of a tribe of impoverished people who ate animal fodder, dressed in papyrus reed garments, and eagerly anticipated death

אֲנָהֶה מִי גֶבֶר יִחְיֶה וְלֹא יִרְאֶה מָּוֶת.[1]

I would wail, ‹ Who ‹ is the man ‹ who lives ‹ and will not ‹ see ‹ death? [So let me die!]

אֱיָלוּתִי לְעֶזְרָתִי[2] תַּרְתִּי חֲזוֹת,

For my Strength, [God,] ‹ coming to my assistance, ‹ I sought ‹ to witness.

אֲיֻמָּתִי בְּכָל שָׁנָה אוֹמֶרֶת הִיא הַשָּׁנָה הַזֹּאת,

My awe-inspiring nation ‹ every ‹ year ‹ proclaims, ‹ This is it; ‹ this is the year [of redemption]!

אֲיַדַּע לַכֹּל כִּי מוּדַעַת זֹאת,[3]

I shall make known [its coming] ‹ to everyone, ‹ for ‹ universally known ‹ shall this be,

אִם לֹא כִּי יַד יהוה עָשְׂתָה זֹאת.[4]

for if ‹ not ‹ that ‹ the hand ‹ of God ‹ had wrought ‹ all this, [it could not have happened]!

אֶכּוֹף לְךָ רֹאשׁ יהוה חֵילִי,

I shall bow ‹ to You [in penitence], ‹ my head, ‹ HASHEM, ‹ my source of strength;

אֶכְרַע לְךָ בֶּרֶךְ לְחַתֵּל מַחֲלִי,

I shall bend ‹ to You ‹ my knee [in supplication], ‹ to bandage ‹ my [exile-] wounds.

אֲכַתִּירְךָ בְּשִׁיר מִשִּׁירֵי מְחוֹלִי,*

I shall crown You ‹ with song, ‹ from the melodies ‹ of my dancing.*

אֲכַוֵּן מִי יִתֶּנְךָ כְּאָח לִי.[5]

I will concentrate [in my prayer], ‹ Who ‹ can grant that You be ‹ as a brother ‹ to me!

(1) *Psalms* 89:49. (2) 22:20. (3) *Isaiah* 12:5. (4) *Job* 12:9. (5) *Song of Songs* 8:1.

(*Bereishis Rabbah* 37:8). The *paytan* compares the plight of exiled Israel to the lives of those unfortunates.

מְחוֹלִי — *Of my dancing.* The word may be related to מָחוֹל, *a circle dance.* Accordingly the stich is based on the verse, *You have transformed my lament into dancing for me* . . . (*Psalms* 30:12), and means that when redemption comes You will have changed מַחֲלִי, *my exile-wounds,* into מְחוֹלִי, *my dancing.* Alternatively, the מַחֲלַת, *machalas,* is a musical

אַל תִּשְׁכַּח צַעֲקַת אֲרִיאֵל,[1]

« of Ariel [the Beis HaMikdash], ‹ the scream ‹ forget ‹ Do not

אֵלָיו לֶאֱגוֹר יְהוּדָה וְיִשְׂרָאֵל,

« and Israel. ‹ Judah ‹ to assemble ‹ to him

אַלְפֵי שִׁנְאָן[2] אֲשֶׁר מָסַר אֵל,

« God designated [to guard Jerusalem], ‹ whom ‹ of protective angels ‹ the thousands

לֵאמֹר מִי יִתֵּן מִצִּיּוֹן יְשׁוּעַת יִשְׂרָאֵל.[3]

« *of Israel!* ‹ *the salvation* ‹ *that out of Zion [shall emerge]* ‹ *can grant* ‹ *Who* « saying,

יִשְׂרָאֵל מֵעֵת בִּדְרָכַי לֹא הָלָכוּ,

« *they ceased to follow;* ‹ *along My pathways* ‹ *from the moment* ‹ [God responds:] *Israel*

עֲזָבוּנִי וַעֲזַבְתִּים וּפָנַי מֵהֶם נֶהְפָּכוּ,

« *was turned away!* ‹ *from them* ‹ *and My countenance* ‹ *so I abandoned them* ‹ *they abandoned Me,*

רָגַנְתִּי וְהֵלַלְתִּי* וּמֵעַי וְלִבִּי נִשְׁפָּכוּ,

« were spilled out [in grief]; ‹ and my heart ‹ and my innards ‹ and I groaned,* ‹ I grumbled

אֵיכָה תִּפְאַרְתִּי מֵרַאֲשׁוֹתַי הִשְׁלִיכוּ.

« they have cast down? ‹ from my head ‹ my splendor ‹ How is it that

(1) See commentary to *Kinnah* 37. (2) *Psalms* 68:18. (3) 53:7.

instrument used by the Levite orchestra in the Temple (see *Psalms* 53:1 and 88:1). The word מַחֲלַת [and מְחוֹלִי] can also be cognate with מַחֲלָה, *sickness*, and refer to Israel's heartache over the Destruction of the two Temples (*Rashi* to *Psalms* ibid.).

רָגַנְתִּי וְהֵלַלְתִּי — *I grumbled and I groaned.* The speaker here may be God continuing His lament from the previous two lines: *Israel abandoned Me . . . and My splendor from My head they have cast down [Divine crowns from the prayers of the righteous* (see *Chagigah* 13b with *Tosafos*)]. Alternatively, the lament may refer to Israel's words: From the time God abandoned me . . . the enemy nations have thrown my splendor [the *Beis HaMikdash*] from my head [Jerusalem].

KINNAH 9 / קינה ט

אֵיכָה תִּפְאַרְתִּי מֵרַאֲשׁוֹתַי הִשְׁלִיכוּ,*

《they have cast down,* 〈 from My head 〈 My splendor 〈 How is it that

וּכְנֶגֶד כִּסֵּא הַכָּבוֹד* צֶלֶם הִמְלִיכוּ,

《 they enthroned, 〈 an idol 〈 of Glory* 〈 to [My Heavenly] Throne 〈 and parallel

בְּחַלְּלָם* תְּנַאי אֲשֶׁר חוֹזַי נִמְלָכוּ,

〈had advised,〈 My prophets 〈 that 〈 the condition 〈 when they [Israel] violated*

אֵיכָה תִּפְאַרְתִּי מֵרַאֲשׁוֹתַי הִשְׁלִיכוּ — *How is it that My splendor from My head they have cast down. Parashas Bechukosai* (*Leviticus*, Chapters 26-27) begins with the idyllic blessings that await the Jewish people if they prove themselves worthy of God's esteem. The portion proceeds to the תּוֹכָחָה, *Admonition*, a terrifying prediction of the curses and plagues which will inevitably befall the Jewish people if they betray their solemn covenant with God. This composition [by R' Elazar HaKalir] vividly depicts how Israel did indeed turn away from God and progressively forfeited, one by one, the blessings which God had in store for them and how ultimately their evil ways forced God to fulfill the harsh prophecies of the admonition.

Appropriately, the acrostic of this *kinnah* is arranged according to the אַתְ בַּשׁ order of the alphabet. In this arrangement, the first letter of the *aleph-beis* is paired with the last, the second letter is exchanged for the second to last, and so on. This pattern alludes to Israel who foolishly exchanged the first and best, God, for the last and worst, the idols.

The first word of each quatrain is taken from the respective verse of the second chapter of *Eichah*, thus forming an *aleph-beis* acrostic. The second word begins with the complementary letter in the אַתְ בַּשׁ formation. The last stich of each stanza is the opening of the corresponding verse in *Leviticus* 26:3-24 and appears in bold type.

Throughout this *kinnah*, the *paytan* shifts back and forth between first, second, and third person. This indicates a continuously changing narrator. In some stanzas, God (as it were) mourns His splendor, the *Beis HaMikdash*, that "they" [a reference to either the wicked king Manasseh (see *II Kings* 21:4-7) during the First Temple era; or the pagan conquerors of the Second Temple] turned into a sanctuary for idolatry. In other stanzas, Israel ruefully laments its forsaking מֵרַאֲשׁוֹתַי תִּפְאַרְתִּי, *my splendor from my head*, the Torah's laws (see commentary to בְּחַלְּלָם, below). And in some stanzas the gentile nations taunt Israel in its degradation.

Alternatively, the entire *kinnah* represents the words of one speaker, so distraught in his mourning that he variously refers to himself introspectively in the first person, admonishes himself as an outsider using the second person, and hangs his guilt on a third party, but realizes that he means himself.

וּכְנֶגֶד כִּסֵּא הַכָּבוֹד — *Parallel to [My Heavenly] Throne of Glory.* The Midrash teaches that the celestial Throne of Glory rests directly above the *Beis HaMikdash* on earth (*Mechilta* cited by *Rashi* to *Exodus* 15:17; *Targum* to *Jeremiah* 17:12).

בְּחַלְּלָם — *When they [Israel] violated.* This reference to Israel in the third person indicates that God is the speaker. However, some editions read בְּחַלְּלִי, *when I violated*, implying that Israel is the speaker. (See commentary above.)

וְנָם אִם בְּחֻקֹּתַי תֵּלֵכוּ.[1]

« you go. ‹ by My decrees ‹ If « and He declared,

לָמָּה[2] תָרִיבוּ אֵלַי כֻּלְּכֶם,[3]

« — all of you? « with Me ‹ do you quarrel ‹ Why

חָזְקוּ עָלַי דִּבְרֵיכֶם,[4]

« have your words been. ‹ against Me ‹ Harsh

מִיֶּדְכֶם הָיְתָה זֹּאת לָכֶם.[5]

« to you. ‹ has this happened ‹ From your own hand

בִּלַּע שׁוֹפְטַי בְּמוֹעֲצוֹת עִוְּתָם,

« they perverted; ‹ because of the advice ‹ my judges ‹ He swallowed up

וּפָנִים הִסְתִּיר מֵהֶם כְּשָׁר עַוָּתָתָם,

« their injustices. ‹ when He saw ‹ from them ‹ He concealed ‹ and His countenance

וַיּוֹמַר לְאָבָק מִטְרָם[6] לְהַבְעִיתָם,

« to frighten them, ‹ their rain ‹ into dust ‹ He transformed

חֵלֶף וְנָתַתִּי גִשְׁמֵיכֶם בְּעִתָּם.[7]

« *in their proper time.* ‹ *your rains* ‹ *I will provide* « instead of [the blessing]:

סְחִי וּמָאוֹס שָׂמַנִי,[8] כִּלָּה בְאַפּוֹ וַיִּשְׂטְמֵנִי,[9]

« and He despised me. ‹ with His wrath ‹ He destroyed [me] « did He make me; ‹ and repugnant [to the nations] ‹ Filth

נִחוּמָיו מְהֵרָה יְשַׁעַשְׁעוּנִי.[10]

« cheer me. ‹ swiftly ‹ May His comforting

גָּדַע רוּם קַרְנָם[11] וְעָלוּמָם הִקְצִיר,[12]

« He cut short; ‹ and their youth ‹ of their pride ‹ the pinnacle ‹ He cut down

וּבְאִבְחַת חֶרֶב שַׁעֲרֵיהֶם הֵצִיר,[13]

« he laid siege. ‹ to their gates ‹ of the sword ‹ with the butchery

---

(1) *Leviticus* 26:3. (2) Some early editions omit this stanza. (3) *Jeremiah* 2:29. (4) *Malachi* 3:13. (5) Cf. 1:9. (6) Cf. *Deuteronomy* 28:24. (7) *Leviticus* 26:4. (8) Cf. *Eichah* 3:45. (9) Cf. *Job* 16:9. (10) Cf. *Psalms* 94:19. (11) Cf. *Eichah* 2:3. (12) Cf. *Psalms* 89:46. (13) Cf. *Ezekiel* 21:20.

מְזֵי רָעָב עָשׂ בְּקָצִיר,

« during the [abundant] harvest; ‹ He caused them ‹ of famine ‹ The bloating

תְּמוּר וְהִשִּׂיג לָכֶם דַּיִשׁ אֶת בָּצִיר.[1]

« *until the grape harvest.* « *— the season of threshing —* « *for you* ‹ *And it shall reach* « instead of [the blessing]:

דָּרַךְ קַשְׁתּוֹ וְכִלָּה בְּחֶרֶץ,

« with intensity, ‹ and destroyed ‹ His bow ‹ He bent

וְכַבַּרְזֶל עִפֵּל שְׁמֵי אֶרֶץ,[2]

« fortified [to withhold rain]. ‹ the heavens, ‹ He strengthened ‹ and as with iron

פְּרָצַנִי שְׁלֹשׁ עֶשְׂרֵה פֶּרֶץ,*

« breaches,* ‹ with thirteen ‹ He breached me

תַּחַת וְנָתַתִּי שָׁלוֹם בָּאָרֶץ.[3]

« *in the Land.* ‹ *peace* ‹ *And I will provide* « instead of [the blessing],

הָיָה צוּרְכֶם וּמָעֻזְּכֶם וּמִשְׂגַּבְּכֶם,

« and your Stronghold, ‹ your Fortification, ‹ your Rock, ‹ He had been

הָפַךְ לְאַכְזָר וְנִלְחַם בָּכֶם,

« against you. ‹ and wages war ‹ to be ruthless ‹ but He has transformed

הַנּוֹצַרְכֶם רִחֲקְכֶם, חוֹשַׁקְכֶם תִּעֲבְכֶם,

« despises you. ‹ He Who desired you « has set you afar; ‹ He Who guarded you

וְאַיֵּה הַבְטָחַת וּרְדַפְתֶּם אֶת אוֹיְבֵיכֶם.[4]

« *your enemies?* ‹ *And you will pursue* « the promise: ‹ And where is

(1) *Leviticus* 26:5. (2) Cf. 26:19. (3) 26:6. (4) 26:7.

שָׁלֹשׁ עֶשְׂרֵה פֶּרֶץ — *With thirteen breaches.* A latticework fence, ten handbreadths high, stood within the walls surrounding the Temple Mount. This fence, called the סוֹרֵג, *soreig*, served as a boundary, past which neither a Jew contaminated by contact with a corpse nor a gentile was permitted to enter. When the Greeks conquered the Land during the Second Temple era, they angrily broke through the *soreig* in thirteen places to register their indignation at being denied entrance. In subsequent years, the Hasmonean kings repaired these breaches (see *Middos* 2:3 with *Tos. Yom Tov; Shekalim* 6:8).

וַיַּחֲמוֹס פִּנַּת צֶדֶק מְלֵאָה,
« had been filled, ‹ that with righteousness ‹ the cornerstone [of the world], ‹ He cut down [Jerusalem,]

כִּי בְּמַשְׂכִּיּוֹתֶהָ מָצָא כָּל טֻמְאָה,
« of abomination. ‹ every manner ‹ He found ‹ beneath her [stone] floors ‹ because

וּמְכַבְּדֶיהָ הִזִּילוּהָ כְּדָוָה מְטֻמָּאָה,[1]
« in defilement, ‹ like a woman who suffers ‹ denigrated her ‹ Those who had respected her

בְּשִׁנּוּי **וְרָדְפוּ מִכֶּם חֲמִשָּׁה מֵאָה.**[2]
« *[against] a hundred.* ‹ *five* ‹ *of you* ‹ *There will pursue* « replacing [the blessing]:

זָנַח עֶלְיוֹן קִרְיַת מוֹעֲדֵיכֶם,
« of your festival [assemblies], ‹ the metropolis ‹ has the Exalted One ‹ Rejected

וְהֶאֱבִיל שַׁעֲרֵי חֵיל עֲמִידַת רַגְלֵיכֶם,
« your feet. ‹ where stood ‹ of the rampart ‹ to the gates ‹ and brought mourning

מִי בִקֵּשׁ זֹאת[3] פָּץ וְהִגְלְכֶם,
« as He exiled you, ‹ He declared, ‹ *this [trampling of My courtyards]?* ‹ *requested* ‹ *Who*

וְגָמַר אֹמֶר **וּפָנִיתִי אֲלֵיכֶם.**[4]
« *to you!* ‹ *And I will turn My attention* « His assurance, ‹ and He terminated

חָשַׁב שְׂנוֹא אוֹם לֻקַּט כַּשּׁוֹשָׁן[5]
« like a rose [from the thorns], ‹ that had been selected ‹ the nation ‹ to despise ‹ He planned

וּמֵחֵלֶב עוֹלָלֶיהָ אוֹתָהּ דִּשָּׁן,*
« were fertilized.* ‹ [the enemy's orchards] ‹ of her [slaughtered] infants ‹ and with the fat [of the flesh]

(1) Cf. *Eichah* 1:8. (2) *Leviticus* 26:8. (3) *Isaiah* 1:12. (4) *Leviticus* 26:9. (5) Cf. *Song of Songs* 2:2.

וּמֵחֵלֶב עוֹלָלֶיהָ אוֹתָהּ דִּשָּׁן — *And with the fat [of the flesh] of her [slaughtered] infants [the enemy's orchards] were fertilized.* The heathen farmers fertilized their vineyards for seven years with the blood of the slaughtered Jews (*Gittin* 57a).

קִיטוֹר חֻפָּתָהּ הוּעֲלָה כַּכִּבְשָׁן,[1]

« as from a furnace, ‹ went up « her wedding canopy, «The smoke from [the Temple,]

וְשָׁאֲלוּ אַיֵּה דָגָן תְּמוּר וַאֲכַלְתֶּם יָשָׁן נוֹשָׁן.[2]

« well-preserved foods. ‹ your old, ‹ And you shall prefer to eat « in place of [the promise]: « the grain? ‹ Where is « and the [starving] people asked,

טָבְעוּ נִכְסוּ רוֹבְדֵי דוּכָנִי,*

« of my [Temple] platform.* ‹ were [those who stood] on the tiers ‹ and slaughtered ‹ Drowned

בְּגֵיא חֲמַת כְּנִקְטַל מְכַהֲנַי,*

« my Kohanim.* ‹ [when] were murdered ‹ of Hamath, ‹ In the valley

הֲרֵי כַּמָּה שָׁנִים גֻּלָּה יְסוֹד מְכוֹנִי,

« of my [Temple's] foundation, ‹ the footing ‹ was revealed ‹ years since ‹ it is many ‹ Indeed,

וְסָע מִתּוֹכִי אֹמֶר וְנָתַתִּי מִשְׁכָּנִי.[3]

« My sanctuary [in your midst]. ‹ I shall place « is He Who said: ‹ from my midst ‹ and gone away

יָשְׁבוּ מְבַכִּים מִנַּאַק מְתֵיכֶם,*[4]

« of those dying among you.* ‹ because of the cries ‹ weeping ‹ They sat down

בְּאַרְבַּע מִיתוֹת הִפִּיל מְתֵיכֶם,

« your people: ‹ He struck down ‹ forms of death ‹ With four

(1) Cf. *Genesis* 19:28. (2) *Leviticus* 26:10. (3) 26:11. (4) Cf. *Job* 24:12.

דוּכָנִי — *My [Temple] platform.* The *Kohanim* would ascend a platform to bless the nation with the Priestly Blessing, and the Levite orchestra would ascend to accompany the daily Altar service.

כְּנִקְטַל מְכַהֲנַי — *When . . . were murdered my Kohanim.* This refers to the tragic events following immediately after the Destruction of the First Temple. Nebuzaradan, the chief executioner for the Babylonian king, captured Seraiah the *Kohen Gadol* and his deputy Zefaniah, along with seventy other officials, and transported them to Babylonia. There he delivered them into the hands of King Nebuchadnezzar, who executed them at Rivlah in the land of Hamath (see *II Kings* 25:18-21).

מִנַּאַק מְתֵיכֶם — *Because of the cries of those dying among you* [lit., *the cry of your dead*]. Since the dead cannot cry, the phrase must refer to the cry of those in the throes of death. Alternatively, it

חֶרֶב וְרָעָב וְחַיָּה וְדֶבֶר* שִׁחֶתְכֶם,[1]

« He destroyed you. ‹ and the plague* ‹ wild beast, ‹ starvation, ‹ [with] the sword,

כְּסָר צִלָּם פָּץ[2] **וְהִתְהַלַּכְתִּי בְּתוֹכְכֶם.**[3]

« *in your midst.* ‹ *And I will walk* « Who had pledged, ‹ their protective shadow [God], ‹ And as was removed

כָּלוּ לְשׁוֹד כְּרֶגַע אָהֳלֵיכֶם,

« were all your tents, ‹ in but one moment ‹ by pillage ‹ Totally destroyed

וּבָכֶם נִשְׁבָּעוּ* מְהוֹלְלֵיכֶם,[4]

« would those who ridicule you. ‹ as a curse* ‹ and use you

לְחֵיקְכֶם נִשְׁפְּכוּ נַפְשׁוֹת עוֹלְלֵיכֶם,[5]

« of your infants, ‹ the souls ‹ ebbs away ‹ Into your bosom

בְּמָאָסְכֶם שִׂיחַ אֲנִי יהוה אֱלֹהֵיכֶם.[6]

« *your God.* ‹ *HASHEM,* ‹ *I am* « the utterance, ‹ because you despised

לְאִמּוֹתָם כִּלְכּוּל אַנֵּה שִׁוְּעוּ,

« they cried out, « — *where is it?* « *The food* « To their mothers,

וְצוּר לְמַלְאָכָיו שָׂח מֶנִּי שְׁעוּ,[7]

« *do not intercede!* ‹ *With Me* « declared, ‹ to His angels ‹ But the Rock [God]

אֶרֶץ הַכַּרְמֶל[8] **הֲבֵאתִים וְשֶׁעֱשָׁעוּ,**

« where they found all delights, ‹ I brought them ‹ that is fruitful ‹ To a land

וְשָׂנְאוּ מוֹכִיחַ וְאִם לֹא תִשְׁמָעוּ.[9]

« *you will not listen ....* ‹ *But if* « the One Who rebukes, ‹ but they scorned

---

(1) Cf. *Ezekiel* 14:21. (2) Cf. *Numbers* 14:9. (3) *Leviticus* 26:12. (4) Cf. *Psalms* 102:9. (5) Cf. *Eichah* 2:12. (6) *Leviticus* 26:13. (7) Cf. *Isaiah* 22:4; see *Rashi* there. (8) Cf. *Jeremiah* 2:7. (9) *Leviticus* 26:14.

---

means the screams of the relatives of the dead.

וְדֶבֶר — *And the plague.* This indicates that הִפִּיל, *He struck down,* refers to God, as germ warfare was unknown at that time.

וּבָכֶם נִשְׁבָּעוּ — *And use you as a curse.* If one of the enemy took an oath and wished to reinforce it, he would say, "If I am not telling the truth, may I be cursed in the worst possible way, in the manner

מָה אֲעִידֵךְ* יְשִׁישַׁיִךְ עִם גּוּרַיִךְ[1] בּוֹסָסוּ,

About what more ‹ can I testify against you,* ‹ [when both] your elders ‹ and ‹ your young cubs ‹ have been trampled? «

אוֹמְרִים עַל סוּס נָנוּס* עַל כֵּן נָסוּ,[2]

They [rejected rebuke] saying, « *On* ‹ *horses* ‹ *we will flee!** « And so ‹ they fled [not to return]! «

נִלְאֵיתִי נְשׂוֹא[3] עֲוֹנוֹתֵיכֶם כְּהוּעֲמָסוּ,

I am weary ‹ from carrying ‹ your sins, ‹ for they are loaded up [upon Me]. «

וַאֲיַסֶּרְכֶם כְּנַמְתִּי אִם בְּחֻקֹּתַי תִּמְאָסוּ.[4]

Therefore, I have disciplined you ‹ as I declared, « *And if* ‹ *My decrees* ‹ *you consider loathsome ....* «

נְבִיאַיִךְ תָּעוּ* תַּרְמִית שָׁוְא חֲזוֹת,[5]

Your [false] prophets ‹ misled you* ‹ with deceit ‹ and useless ‹ visions. «

וָאֶדְרוֹשׁ לִסְלוֹחַ וּפַצְתִּי אֵי לְזֹאת,[6]

I sought ‹ to forgive you, « [but without repentance] I cried out, « *How shall I [pardon]* ‹ *for this?* «

(1) Cf. *II Chronicles* 36:16-17. (2) Cf. *Isaiah* 30:16. (3) 1:14. (4) Cf. *Leviticus* 26:15. (5) Cf. *Eichah* 2:14; *Micah* 3:5-7; *Ezekiel* 13:8-10. (6) *Jeremiah* 5:7.

---

which the conquered Jews suffer!" (*Rashi* to *Psalms* 12:9).

מָה אֲעִידֵךְ — *About what more can I testify against you . . .?* The word אֲעִידֵךְ is derived from the root עוד, which can mean either *warn, admonish,* or *testify.* The translation here follows *Midrash Eichah* (2:13). According to others, the phrase means, *Whom can I bring to testify to you* that their suffering equals yours? (*Zohar; Targum; Rashi*), for צָרַת רַבִּים חֲצִי נֶחָמָה, *general suffering is half of assuagement;* grieving and troubles are easier to bear when one knows that there are others in the same dire circumstances (*Ibn Kaspi*).

עַל סוּס נָנוּס — *On horses we will flee!* When warned by the prophets that the only way to avert impending disaster is a combination of repentance and quiet confidence in God's salvation, the nation proudly refused to pay heed. Instead they replied, "We will flee on horseback!" They meant, "We will ally ourselves with Egypt, who will supply us with mighty steeds. Thus shall we escape the threat of annihilation. Then, when the enemy leaves our land, we will return home safe and sound!" For this, God caused them to flee, but did not allow them to return (*Isaiah* 30:15-16 with *Rashi*).

תָּעוּ — *Misled you.* Since this *kinnah* follows an אַתְּ בַּשׁ pattern (see above), a word beginning with ט (the letter corresponding to נ in אַתְּ בַּשׁ) is expected here. Perhaps the proper reading here is טָעוּ, *caused to err* or *erred,* which is homophonous with תָּעוּ and similar in meaning. Moreover, the only appearance of the root טעה in Scripture (*Ezekiel* 13:10) speaks of the "prophets" whose vain visions lulled

פִּתִּיתִים וּכְנֶגְדִּי הֵשִׁיבוּ עַזּוּת,

« with ‹ they ‹ but « I tried to induce
brazenness. responded to me them [to repent],

וְאָנַפְתִּי וְשַׁחְתִּי אַף אֲנִי אֶעֱשֶׂה זֹּאת.[1]

« *this ....* ‹ *will do* ‹ *I* ‹ *Then* « and I ‹ I was
also declared, infuriated

סָפְּקוּ חָרְקוּ שָׁרְקוּ מוֹנַי,[2]

« — so did my « and they ‹ they gnashed ‹ They
tormentors, whistled [their teeth], clapped,

מִבִּפְנִים וּמִבַּחוּץ לְהַצְמִית אֱמוּנַי,[3]

« my faithful ‹ to cut down ‹ and from ‹ [as they prepared]
ones, without from within

כִּי בְּנֵי זֵדִים חִלְּלוּ צְפוּנַי,

« my hidden ‹ des- ‹ of the im- ‹ the ‹ be-
treasures. ecrated moral ones sons cause

לְרָעָה וְלֹא לְטוֹבָה נָם וְנָתַתִּי פָּנַי.[4]

« *My* ‹ *I will* « He ‹ for good, ‹ and ‹ To inflict
attention .... *turn* said, not harm

פָּצוּ זֵדִים לִפְנֵי מִי תְּחַלֶּה,

« *do you* ‹ *Whom* ‹ *Before* « did the im- ‹ Taunt
pray? moral ones,

עַם כֶּבֶד עָוֹן[5] **פָּקַד וַיִּלְאֶה,**

« *and is* ‹ *He has* « *by* ‹ *weighed* ‹ *[You*
wearied [by *called you* *iniquity;* *down* *are] a*
your sins]. *to account* *people*

לֹא תְחַכּוּ עוֹד לְמוֹפֵת וָפֶלֶא,

« *and a* ‹ *for a sign* ‹ *any* ‹ *wait* ‹ *Therefore,*
wonder. *longer* *do not*

אָנַף וְנָסַע וְנָם וְאִם עַד אֵלֶּה.[6]

« *these [pun-* ‹ *despite* ‹ *And* « and ‹ and He has ‹ He is
ishments] .... *if* He said, departed, angered

(1) *Leviticus* 26:16. (2) Cf. *Eichah* 2:15. (3) Cf. 1:20; *Deuteronomy* 32:25.
(4) *Leviticus* 26:17. (5) *Isaiah* 1:4. (6) *Leviticus* 26:18.

the nation into a false sense of security. Indeed, the wording of the *kinnah* seems to be based on that passage (ibid. 13:9-10). Nevertheless, we have retained the word תָּעוּ because in similar passages (e.g., *Micah* 3:5-7) the root תעה is used in Scripture, and because that is how it appears in virtually all editions.

עָשָׂה וַיָּרֶם קָדְקֹד בְּנֵי שָׁאוֹן,[1]
« that are tumultuous, ‹ of the ones ‹ the heads ‹ and raised ‹ He acted

וְדָמִי שִׁכְּרַנִי בְּגֵיא צִמָּאוֹן,
« that is waterless [in exile]; ‹ in the valley ‹ He made me drunk ‹ and on my own blood

וּבְכָל שָׁנָה וְשָׁנָה הוֹסִיף יָגוֹן עַל אוֹן,
« to [my] mourning, ‹ anguish ‹ He added ‹ after year ‹ year ‹ and every

מֵעֵת כָּעַס וְנָם **וְשָׁבַרְתִּי אֶת גְּאוֹן.**[2]
« *the pride [of your might].* ‹ *And I will break* « and He said, ‹ He was angered ‹ since the moment

צָעַק הוֹי הוֹי וְאַשְׁפָּתוֹ הֵרִיק,
« He emptied [against me]. ‹ though His quiver ‹ *Woe!* ‹ *Woe!* « [God] cried out,

מִפֹּה וּמִפֹּה הֵבִיא עָלַי מַעֲרִיק,
« pursuers. ‹ against me ‹ He brought ‹ and from there ‹ From here

וּבְלַעֲגֵי מָעוֹג שִׁנֵּי צָר הֶחֱרִיק,[3]
« He caused to gnash [at me]. ‹ of the oppressor ‹ the teeth « to obtain a loaf of bread, ‹ And with mocking slander

וְכִלָּה כֹּחִי בִּנְאֻם **וְתַם לָרִיק.**[4]
« *in vain will [your strength be].* ‹ *And spent* « with the statement, ‹ my strength ‹ He drained

קוּמִי דָּפְקִי שַׁוְּעִי אַל דֳּמִי,[5]
« *be silent!* ‹ *Do not* « cry out, « and pound [on heaven's gates], ‹ Arise

וּתְנִי כְּאוֹב מֵאֶרֶץ[6] קוֹלֵךְ וָדֹמִּי,
« then remain silent. ‹ your voice, « [rising] from the earth — ‹ — as [the sound of] « Give out [in prayer]

(1) *Jeremiah* 48:45. (2) *Leviticus* 26:19. (3) Cf. *Psalms* 35:16.
(4) *Leviticus* 26:20. (5) Cf. *Psalms* 83:2. (6) Cf. *Isaiah* 29:4.

מֵי רוֹשׁ הִשְׁקַנִי וְהִדְמִי,

« thus silencing me. ‹ He made me drink ‹ of bitter gall ‹ Water

וְחָשַׁךְ הִלּוּכִי בִּנְאֻם וְאִם תֵּלְכוּ עִמִּי.[1]

« *with Me [with indifference].* ‹ *you will walk* ‹ *But if* « when He declared, ‹ my walking ‹ He darkened

רְאֵה גּוֹרָל אִוִּיתָ הוּשַּׂם לְרוֹעִים לְעִיַּת,[2]

« into [rubble] heaps, ‹ through a clamoring ‹ has been made ‹ You had once desired ‹ the portion ‹ Behold,

וְלִקְאַת מִדְבָּר הָיִיתִי דְמוּיַת,[3]

« to resemble. ‹ I have come ‹ of the wilderness ‹ and to a bird

גּוֹלָה כְּנוּיַת וְסוּרָה גְנוּיַת,[4]

« I am humiliated, ‹ and as *Displaced* ‹ I am nicknamed, ‹ As *Exile*

בְּשָׁמְעִי וְהִשְׁלַחְתִּי בָכֶם אֶת חַיַּת.[5]

« *the wildlife.* ‹ *against you* ‹ *And I will incite* « when I hear [the curse],

שָׁכְבוּ בְּעִלּוּף כְּתוֹא מִכְמָר וְאֵין דּוֹלֶה,[6]

« to pull it out. ‹ with no one ‹ in a hunter's net ‹ like a wild ox ‹ in a faint ‹ They lie

הַמְּלֵאִים גַּעַר וְאֵין מַרְפֵּא עוֹלֶה,

« has emerged. ‹ healing ‹ but no « of [God's] rebuke, ‹ [They are] full

הֲרֵי כַּמֶּה שָׁנִים הֲמָמַנִי לְהִתְכַּלֶּה,

« seeking [my] destruction. ‹ that [the enemy] has crushed me. ‹ years ‹ it is many ‹ Indeed,

אֲנוּשִׁים בְּוִכּוּחַ וְאִם בְּאֵלֶּה.[7]

« *by these [punishments] ....* ‹ *And if* « by the admonition, ‹ We are extremely pained

---

(1) *Leviticus* 26:21. (2) Cf. *Psalms* 79:1. (3) 102:7. (4) Cf. *Isaiah* 49:21. (5) *Leviticus* 26:22. (6) Cf. *Isaiah* 51:20. (7) *Leviticus* 26:23.

תִּקְרָא אֵיד עוֹלַלְתָּ עַל אַדְמוֹנִי,

« the red one [Edom], ‹ for « — as You did [against me] — « a day of doom ‹ Designate

לְסַחֲפוֹ וּלְשַׁסְּפוֹ שִׁבְעָתַיִם כְּאוֹנִי,

« than my pain. ‹ seven times more ‹ and to hew him down ‹ to sweep him away

תָּהוֹם צָרַי בְּצֵאת קוֹל מֵאַרְמוֹנִי,

« from my palace, ‹ does the cry ‹ when go forth ‹ my enemies ‹ Confound

כְּנֶהֱמַמְתִּי בְּרִיב וְהָלַכְתִּי אַף אֲנִי.[1]

« *I [with indifference]....* ‹ *— even* « *Because I will walk* ‹ by the [enemy] attack, ‹ as I was stunned

אַף אֲנִי לָכוּד* בְּיוֹקֶשׁ שִׁכָּרוֹן,

« of drunkenness. ‹ in the snare ‹ have been trapped* ‹ I ‹ Also

עָרְבָה שִׂמְחָה וְהִשְׁבִּית חָרוֹן,

« was [His] anger. ‹ [yet with the destruction,] ended ‹ has been the joy, ‹ Darkened

לָאָרֶץ אֵשֵׁב וְאֶהְגֶּה בְּגָרוֹן,

« with my throat, ‹ and I will express ‹ I will sit ‹ Down on the earth

אֵיכָה יָשְׁבָה חֲבַצֶּלֶת הַשָּׁרוֹן.[2]

« *of Sharon!* ‹ *— the Rose* « *that it [Israel] sits* ‹ *how is it*

(1) *Leviticus* 26:24. (2) *Song of Songs* 2:1.

אַף אֲנִי לָכוּד — *Also I have been trapped.* Many a *kinnah* of the series attributed to R' Elazar HaKalir ends with a stanza that links it with the following *kinnah*, the closing word or stich of one is identical with the opening word or stich of the next. Such a linking stanza is evident between *Kinnos* 7-8, 8-9, 11-12 and 19-20, and such is the nature of this stanza. However, many early editions do not contain this stanza, which leads to the contention that it is not the work of R' Elazar, but was inserted by some later *paytan* in order to connect this and the following *kinnah*. Indeed, *Maharil* argues that *Kinnah* 15 was originally juxtaposed with this *kinnah* and he would recite that *kinnah* at this point (see commentary there for his reasoning). If so, this stanza could not have been part of the original *kinnah*, as it would be entirely out of place.

KINNAH 10 / קינה י

אֵיכָה יָשְׁבָה חֲבַצֶּלֶת הַשָּׁרוֹן,[1]*

« of Sharon!* ‹ — the Rose « that it sits [alone] ‹ How is it

וְדָמַם רוֹן מִפִּי נוֹשְׂאֵי אָרוֹן,*

« the Ark;* ‹ of those who carried ‹ from the mouths ‹ is the joy ‹ and silenced

וְנָעוּ מִמִּשְׁמְרוֹתָם כֹּהֲנִים בְּנֵי אַהֲרֹן,

« of Aaron, ‹ the sons ‹ were the *Kohanim,* ‹ from their watches ‹ and removed

(1) *Song of Songs* 2:1.

אֵיכָה יָשְׁבָה חֲבַצֶּלֶת הַשָּׁרוֹן — *How is it that it sits [alone] — the Rose of Sharon.* The Talmud (*Taanis* 26a-27a) teaches that the early prophets, David and Samuel, established 24 מִשְׁמְרוֹת כְּהוּנָה, *priestly watches,* to scrupulously perform the Temple services. Each *mishmar* (watch) served for one week, on a rotation basis. The names of the watches in the First Temple are enumerated in *I Chronicles,* Chapter 24. This *kinnah* describes the watches of the Second Temple, which were then known under different names. According to many commentators, these new names were the names of each *mishmar's* home city. This is the approach followed in the translation and commentary. Some commentators explain the new names as pejoratives and expound on the particular offense by which each *mishmar* earned its nickname. The commentary includes only those pejorative interpretations found in the Talmud.

In composing this *kinnah,* R' Elazar HaKalir used the opening word or phrase of the respective verses in the first chapter of *Eichah* to begin each stanza. Thus, the stanzas contain an alphabetical acrostic. The name of the corresponding *mishmar* appears in the last line. The relevant words appear in bold type.

חֲבַצֶּלֶת הַשָּׁרוֹן — *The Rose of Sharon.* The *Beis HaMikdash* was affectionately called חֲבַצֶּלֶת, *Rose.* The Midrash teaches that חֲבַצֶּלֶת is a contraction of the words חֲבוּיָה בְּצֵל, *sheltered in the shade,* in good times God loved Israel and their Temple so much that He hovered over them and provided them with the most intense protection under the shade of His Divine Presence, the *Shechinah* (*Shir HaShirim Rabbah* 2).

וְדָמַם רוֹן מִפִּי נוֹשְׂאֵי אָרוֹן — *And silenced is the joy from the mouths of those who carried the Ark.* According to *Rambam* (*Sefer HaMitzvos, asei* 34 and *shoresh* 3), the *Kohanim* were the bearers of the Ark throughout the generations. Only during the early years in the Wilderness, when there were very few *Kohanim,* did the *Leviim* carry the Ark. *Ramban* (ibid.) disagrees and states that the *Leviim* were charged with carrying the Ark whenever this would become necessary throughout the generations. Most commentators to *kinnos* follow *Ramban's* view. Thus, רוֹן refers to the *joyous song* the Levite bearers of the Ark sang on the platform in the Temple courtyard. Indeed, the Talmud relates that the Levite choir was interrupted in mid-verse when the enemy conquered the *Beis HaMikdash* (*Taanis* 29a). However, the translation of רוֹן as *joy* [see *Psalms* 30:6 where רִנָּה, synonymous with רוֹן, is used as the opposite of בְּכִי, *weeping*], rather than *joyous song,* allows the *kinnah* to be understood even

כְּנִמְסַר הַבַּיִת בִּמְסָרְבֵי מָרוֹן.*

when given over 〈 was the Temple 〈 to the rebels 〈 of **Maron.*** 《

בָּכֹה תִבְכֶּה מְחֻמֶּשֶׁת סְפָרִים,*

Intensely does she weep 《 — the [nation] of the Five 〈 Books —* 《

כְּנֶהֱרַג כֹּהֵן וְנָבִיא בְּיוֹם הַכִּפּוּרִים,

when slain 〈 was the priest 〈 and prophet [Zechariah] 〈 on the Day 〈 of Atonement, 《

וְעַל דָּמוֹ נִשְׁחֲטוּ פְּרָחִים כִּצְפִירִים,

and in vengeance 〈 for his blood 〈 were butchered 〈 blossoming children 〈 like goats, 《

וְנָדוּ כְּצִפֳּרִים, כֹּהֲנֵי צִפּוֹרִים.*

and wandered 〈 like birds 〈 did the *Kohanim* 〈 of **Sepphoris.*** 《

גָּלְתָה מֵאַרְצָהּ כַּלָּה מְקֻשָּׁטָה,

Exiled 〈 from her land 〈 was the bride 〈 who was bejeweled

בַּעֲוֹן מַעַשְׂרוֹת וּשְׁמִטָּה,

because of the iniquity 〈 of the tithes 〈 and the Sabbatical year. 《

---

according to *Rambam's* view that the *Kohanim* bore the Ark.

בִּמְסָרְבֵי מָרוֹן — *To the rebels of Maron.* The town of Maron was situated on a mountain and could only be reached by a narrow road (see *Rosh Hashanah* 18a and *Eruvin* 22b). It was the home of the first *mishmar*, יְהוֹיָרִיב, *Jehoiarib*. The Talmud states that it was during this *mishmar's* tour of duty that Jerusalem was captured (*Taanis* 29a), and expounds on the name Jehoiarib: **יָ־הּ הֵרִיב** עִם בָּנָיו עַל שֶׁמָּרוּ וְסָרְבוּ בוֹ, *God contended with His children because they were rebellious and defiant against Him* (*Yerushalmi Taanis* 4:5).

מְחֻמֶּשֶׁת סְפָרִים — *The [nation] of the Five Books.* This refers either to Israel, the Torah nation (as indicated by the interpolation), or to the Torah itself which metaphorically wept bitterly when Zechariah was assassinated (see *Kinnah* 34).

כֹּהֲנֵי צִיפּוֹרִים — *The Kohanim of Sepphoris.* The city of קִטְרוֹן, *Kitron* (see *Judges* 1:30), was also called צִיפּוֹרֵי or צִיפּוֹרִים, *Sepphoris,* because it sat on a mountaintop like a high-soaring צִיפּוֹר, *bird* (*Megillah* 6a). It was the hometown of the second watch, יְדַעְיָה, *Jedaiah*, whose name the Talmud explains as **יָדַע יָ־הּ**, *God knew*, what evil was in the depths of their hearts and so He exiled them לְצִיפּוֹרִין, *to Sepphoris*, or, in a variant reading, כְּצִיפּוֹרִים, *like birds* (*Yerushalmi Taanis* 4:5). The *paytan* merges both readings.

וּבְאַרְבַּעַת שְׁפָטִים* הֻשְׁפָּטָה,

« was her sentence, ‹ types of affliction* ‹ To suffer four

וּמֵעֶדְיָהּ הֻפְשָׁטָה, מִשְׁמֶרֶת **מִפְשָׁטָה.**

« of **Mifshatah.** ‹ — the watch « she was stripped ‹ and of her ornaments [the priestly garb]

דַּרְכֵי הֵיכָל שָׁמְמוּ כְּנִפְרַץ כָּתְלוֹ,

« was its wall; ‹ when breached ‹ were desolate ‹ to the Sanctuary ‹ The roads

וְהַמְּעִיל כְּנִקְרַע פְּתִילוֹ,

« were its threads [of *techeiles*]. ‹ when ripped ‹ as was the [*Kohen Gadol's*] tunic

הוּרַד וְהֻשְׁפַּל מִתִּלּוֹ,

« from its Mount, ‹ and lowered ‹ [The Temple] was pulled down

וְנָע מִשְּׁתִילוֹ, כֹּהֵן **עַיָּתָה לוֹ.***

« **Lo.*** ‹ [from] **Aysah-** ‹ was the *Kohen* ‹ from the place of his origin ‹ and uprooted

הָיוּ אוֹיְבִים מַלְעִיבִים בְּלוֹחֲמֵי לֶחֶם,[1]

« in the battle [for Torah observance], ‹ those who fought ‹ ridiculing ‹ The enemy were

כְּבִטְּלוּ הֲלֹא פָרוֹס לָרָעֵב לַחְמֶם,[2]

« *your bread?* ‹ *with the hungry* ‹ *divide* ‹ *Should you not* « when they violated [the verse],

וְהֻרְעֲבוּ וְהֻצְמְאוּ מִמַּיִם וּמִלֶּחֶם,

« and for bread, ‹ for water ‹ and thirsted ‹ So they hungered

(1) Cf. *Proverbs* 9:5; *Chagigah* 14a. (2) *Isaiah* 58:7.

וּבְאַרְבַּעַת שְׁפָטִים — *To suffer four types of affliction:* sword, starvation, wild beast, and plague (see *Ezekiel* 14:21; see also *Kinnah* 9).

עַיָּתָה לוֹ — *Aysah-Lo.* This was the city of the fourth watch, שְׂעוֹרִים, *Seorim*. Perhaps it is identical with עַיַּת, *Aiath,* the first city taken by Sennacherib when he moved against Jerusalem (*Isaiah* 10:28 with *Rashi*). The *Vilna Gaon* identifies

כְּבֻטְּלוּ שְׁתֵּי הַלֶּחֶם, מִבֵּית לֶחֶם.*

when discontinued ‹ was the two- ‹ loaf offering, ‹ from **Bethlehem.*** «

וַיֵּצֵא הֲדַר אוֹם בַּכֶּסֶף נֶחְפֶּת,[1]

Gone ‹ is the splendor ‹ from the nation ‹ that with silver ‹ was coated, «

וּתְמוּרוֹ אֵפֶר עַל רֹאשָׁהּ חִפֵּת,

in its place ‹ ashes ‹ over ‹ her head ‹ did cover. «

וְנֵרוֹת נִכְבּוּ וּמְנוֹרָה נִכְפָּת,

The candles ‹ have been extinguished ‹ and the Menorah ‹ has been turned over, «

כְּפָשְׁעוּ בְּלֶחֶם וּפַת, נִלְכְּדָה יוֹדְפַת.*[2]

when they sinned, ‹ [withholding from the poor,] bread « [— even] a slice — « captured ‹ was **Yodpath.*** «

זָכְרָה זְמַן אֲשֶׁר נַעֲשֶׂה וְנִשְׁמָע[3] **הֵשִׁיבוּ,**

Remember ‹ the moment ‹ when ‹ *We will do* ‹ *and we will obey!* ‹ they replied. «

וְעַתָּה עֲנוֹת אָמֵן לֹא אָבוּ,

But now ‹ even to respond ‹ *Amen* ‹ [acknowledging their sin] they do not choose. «

לַעֲנָה וָרוֹשׁ[4] **שָׂבְעוּ וְרָווּ,**

With wormwood ‹ and bitter gall ‹ they were sated ‹ and quenched; «

וְהֻקְצוּ וְהָלְעֲבוּ, כֹּהֲנֵי עֵילְבוּ.

shunned ‹ and shamed ‹ were the *Kohanim* ‹ of **Aylevu.** «

---

(1) Cf. *Psalms* 68:14 with *Rashi*. (2) Some editions read יוּרְפַּת, *Yurfath*. (3) *Exodus* 24:7. (4) Cf. *Eichah* 3:15.

---

that place with Gilgal.

מִבֵּית לֶחֶם — *From Bethlehem.* The fifth watch, מַלְכִּיָּה, *Malciah*, was headquartered in Bethlehem. Additionally, בֵּית לֶחֶם, literally, *House of Bread*, alludes to the *Beis HaMikdash*. For as the Midrash teaches, as long as the Show Bread was placed on the שֻׁלְחָן, *Table*, each Sabbath, and the Two Loaves were brought every Shavuos in the Temple, the nation's flour and bread would be blessed. But since these were stopped, blessing no longer lies in the bread. Nonetheless, in the future they will be restored (*Yalkut Shimoni* II:565).

יוֹדְפַת — *Yodpath.* A Galilean fortress, mentioned in *Arachin* (32a) as a city that was walled from the time Joshua entered the land.

חֵטְא חָטְאָה וְאָמְרָה לֶאֱלִיל זֶה אֵל,

« *God!* ‹ *This is* « of the idol, ‹ when she said ‹ she did sin ‹ A sin

וְהִלְעִיגָה וְתִעְתְּעָה בְּחוֹזֵי אֵל,

« of God; ‹ at the prophets ‹ and scoffed ‹ She ridiculed

עֲבוּר כֵּן הֶקְנְאָה בְּמַרְגִּיזֵי אֵל,

« God, ‹ through those who anger ‹ He took revenge ‹ of that ‹ because

וַיֵּצֵא מִמְּעוֹן אֵל, **כְּפַר עֻזִּיאֵל.**

« **Uziel.** ‹ [must the *Kohanim* of] **Kfar** ‹ of God ‹ from the abode ‹ and depart

טֻמְאָתָהּ הֶחֱנִיפָה תֵּבֵל, וְנַעֲלָה רַב הַחוֹבֵל,

« has the Captain. ‹ and ascend [to His abode] « the [inhabited] world, ‹ has corrupted ‹ Her contamination

וְעָנָן אֲבַק רַגְלָיו כְּאָבֵל,

« like a mourner, ‹ on His feet ‹ are as dust ‹ The clouds

וְאֵין מִתְכַּרְבֵּל, בְּכֹהֲנֵי **אַרְבֵּל.**

« of **Arbel.** ‹ among the *Kohanim* ‹ who clads himself in the [priestly garments] ‹ and there is no one

יָדוֹ פֵּרַשׂ **צָר** בְּבֵית זְבוּל,

« of [Divine] habitation, ‹ against the house ‹ did the enemy, ‹ spread out ‹ His hand

כִּי כְלָיָה חִיַּבְתִּי כְּדוֹר הַמַּבּוּל,

« of the Flood. ‹ like the generation ‹ did I deserve ‹ destruction ‹ for

כִּסְאוֹ הֵשִׁית לְחִבּוּל וְנִבּוּל,

« and degradation, ‹ to mutilation ‹ He subjected ‹ [Instead, God's] throne

וַיֵּצֵא בְּכֶבֶל כָּבוּל, כֹּהֵן **כָּבוּל.**[1]*

« of **Cabul.*** ‹ did the *Kohanim* ‹ chained, ‹ by leg irons ‹ as go out,

(1) See *Joshua* 19:27 and *I Kings* 9:13.

כָּבוּל — *Cabul.* In return for supplying many of the materials for the *Beis HaMikdash* and Solomon's Palace, King Hiram of Tyre was presented with

כָּל עַמָּהּ קוֹנְנוּ קִינָה,

« a lamentation, ‹ chanted ‹ of her nation ‹ All

כִּי הִכְעִיסוּ לְאֵל קַנָּא,

« Who is jealous; ‹ the God ‹ they angered ‹because

בְּגוֹי נָבָל אוֹתָם קִנָּא,

« He took revenge, ‹ against them « that is vile, ‹ through a nation

וְנָדְדָה מִקִּנָּהּ, מִשְׁמֶרֶת **אֶלְקָנָה.**

« of **Elkanah.** ‹ did the watch ‹ from its nest ‹ and wander

לֹא לַמָּרוֹם עַיִן צָפַת,

« gaze; ‹ did [their] eye ‹ heavenward ‹ Not

וְכֶסֶף עַל חֶרֶשׂ חִפַּת,

« was plated, ‹ earthen-ware ‹ that over ‹ [Their piety was like] silver

וּבְחִזּוּק מוּסָר הֻרְפַּת,[1]

« [their hands] were weakened, ‹ of their suffering ‹ and through the intensity

וְנֶהֱרַס וְנִלְפַּת, כֹּהֵן **צְפַת.**

« of **Safed.** ‹ were the *Kohanim* ‹ and captured ‹ so that canceled

מִמָּרוֹם הִשְׁמִיעַ נִלְאֵתִי טְעוֹן,[2]

« *of bearing [your sins].* ‹ *I am weary* « He sounded [the cry], ‹ From on high

וְהִכַּנִי בְּעִוָּרוֹן וּבְשִׁגָּעוֹן,

« and madness. ‹ with blindness ‹ Then He afflicted me

(1) Cf. *Proverbs* 4:13. (2) Cf. *Isaiah* 1:14.

twenty cities in the land of Cabul, but he was not satisfied (*I Kings* 9:10-13). The Talmud explains that the inhabitants of this area of the Galilee were so wealthy that they would attire themselves in silver and gold. If so, why was Hiram displeased? Because such wealthy people would not serve him properly (*Shabbos* 54a). According to the Talmud, Cabul was destroyed because there was strife among its citizens (*Yerushalmi Taanis* 4:5).

וּפָקַד עָלַי עֲוֹן נוֹב וְגִבְעוֹן,[1]

« and the Gibeonites, ‹ of [the massacre] of Nob ‹ the iniquity ‹ against me ‹ He remembered

וְנָעָה מִמָּעוֹן, מִשְׁמֶרֶת בֵּית כֹּהֵן מָעוֹן.

« of *Kohanim* from **Beis Ma'on.** ‹ did the watch ‹ from the Temple ‹ and depart

נִשְׂקַד עוֹל עֲוֹן וְנִכְאָב,

« and it causes me pain. ‹ of my iniquities ‹ has the yoke ‹ Amassed

כְּהוּשַׁבְתִּי אֲנוּנָה מִבְּלִי אָב,

« [my] Father, ‹ without ‹ like a mourning daughter, ‹ When I was forced to sit

וְנִמְנַעְתִּי מִלְּצַפְצֵף בְּמִנִּים וְעֻגָב,

« and flute, ‹ the organ ‹ from playing ‹ and I was prevented

וְנָשְׂאָה עָלַי קִינָה, מִשְׁמֶרֶת יֶשֶׁבְאָב.*

« of **Jeshebeab.*** ‹ did the watch ‹ a lament ‹ for me ‹ raise

סִלָּה אַבִּירַי מוֹרֵי הוֹרָיָה,

« of [God's] Law, ‹ the teachers « my warriors, ‹ He has trampled

וְלֹא נִזְכַּר לִי עֲקֵדַת מוֹרִיָּה,

« on [Mount] Moriah; ‹ was the [merit] of the binding [of Isaac] ‹ on my behalf ‹ recalled ‹ and not

וּמֵרֹב מֶרֶד וּמְרִיָּה,

« and defiance, ‹ of my rebellion ‹ and because of the enormity

(1) See *I Samuel* 22:19.

יֶשֶׁבְאָב — *Jeshebeab.* Although the *paytan* does not refer to any of the other watches by their Scriptural names as recorded in *I Chronicles* (24:7-18), in this case he makes an exception. According to those who interpret the names used by the *paytan* as geographical locations (see the opening comment to this *kinnah*), it is not unreasonable to assume that this *mishmar* lived in a town that bore its name. Following the opinion that these names are allusions to the sins of the *Kohanim* (see ibid.), *Beis Levi* surmises that this *mishmar* was righteous in all its deeds. Thus, it was not given a pejorative nickname. This view is borne out by the Talmud's statement (*Succah* 56b) that Bilgah, the *mishmar* following Jeshebeab,

הוּצָּגָה עֵרוֹם וְעֶרְיָה,[1] מִשְׁמֶרֶת **מַעַדְיָה.**[2]
« was the watch of **Maadiah.** ‹ and bare ‹ naked ‹ put on display,

עַל גַּבִּי חָרְשׁוּ חוֹרְשִׁים וְהֶאֱרִיכוּ מַעֲנִית,[3]
« the furrow, ‹ they lengthened « the plowers, ‹ plowed ‹ my back ‹ On

וְהֵרִיקוּ עָלַי חֶרֶב וַחֲנִית,[4]
« and spear; ‹ sword ‹ against me ‹ they unsheathed

וְהִרְבֵּיתִי צוֹמוֹת וְתַעֲנִית,
« and afflictions; ‹ fasts ‹ so I have increased

וּמִצּוּרַת תָּבְנִית,[5] יָצְאָה **יְוָנִית.**
« did the [watch of] **Yevanis.** ‹ depart ‹ [of the Temple] design ‹ and from the form

פֵּרְשָׂה וְאֵין יָד שׁוֹלֵחַ,
« sent [to help]. ‹ hand ‹ but there was no ‹ She spread [her hands in prayer],

כִּי לֹא הֶאֱמִינָה בְּהַשְׁכֵּם וְשָׁלוֹחַ,[6]
« were sent [to admonish her]. ‹ in [God's prophets] who from early on ‹ she did not believe ‹ Because

וְהֻשְׁבְּתָה בְּרִית מֶלַח,[7]
« of Salt, ‹ was the [Temple service] Covenant ‹ Discontinued

וְאֵין שֶׁמֶן מְמֻלָּח, בְּרֹאשׁ **מַמְלָח.**
«[of the *Kohen Gadol*] from **Mamlah.** ‹ on the head « thoroughly mixed, « was there [anointment] oil, ‹ and no more

צַדִּיק הוּא יהוה כִּי פִיהוּ מָרַת,[8]
« was disobeyed. ‹ His utterance ‹ for ‹ HASHEM ‹ is ‹ Righteous

(1) Cf. *Hosea* 2:5; Cf. *Ezekiel* 16:7. (2) Some editions read מַעַרְיָה, *Maariah.* (3) Cf. *Psalms* 129:3. (4) Cf. *Ezekiel* 28:7. (5) 43:11. (6) Cf. *Jeremiah* 25:4; 29:19. (7) Cf. *Leviticus* 2:13. (8) Cf. *Eichah* 1:18.

would arrive late (or not at all) when it was their week to serve in the Temple. At those times, the *Kohanim* of Jeshebeab would dutifully remain at their posts. For this, Bilgah's watch was punished (see ibid.) and Jeshebeab was rewarded.

וְעָרוּ עָרוּ עַד הַיְסוֹד בָּהּ[1] הוּעֲרַת,

Destroy! 《 *Destroy* 〈 *until* 〈 *the very foundation* 〈 *of it* 〈 *was bared.* 《

וּתְמוּר עָזִּי וְזִמְרָת,[2] קִינִים עָלֶיהָ נֶחֱרַת,

Instead of [singing], 《 *[God is] my might* 〈 *and my praise,* 《 laments 〈 for her 〈 were engraved, 《

וּבְקַצְוֵי אֶרֶץ נִזְרַת **נִצְרַת.**

and to the ends 〈 of the earth 〈 was scattered 〈 [the watch] of **Nitzrath.** 《

קָרָאתִי לְצוּרִי וְקוֹלִי לֹא עָרַב,

I called out 〈 to my Rock, 〈 but my voice 〈 was not 〈 pleasing. 《

וְקוֹנַנְתִּי בְּיַעַר בַּעֲרָב,

I lamented 〈 in the forest 〈 of Arabia, 《

וְכָבָה נֵר הַדּוֹלֵק בְּמַעֲרָב,

for extinguished 〈 was the Lamp 〈 which burnt [continuously] 〈 on the west [of the Menorah], 《

וְרֵיחוֹ לֹא עָרַב, **מֵאֲכָלָהּ עָרַב.**

and [the incense's] fragrance 〈 was not 〈 pleasing 〈 [that was brought by the watch] from **Achalah** 〈 **Arav.** 《

רְאֵה כִּי הֻסְעַרְתִּי כָּאֳנִיָּה, בְּתַאֲנִיָּה וַאֲנִיָּה,[3]

Behold, 〈 that 〈 I am storm tossed 〈 like a [floundering] ship, 《 through mourning 〈 and grief; 《

וּקְהָלִי כַּצֹּאן לַטֶּבַח[4] מְנוּיָה,

my congregation 〈 resembles a flock 〈 that for slaughter 〈 is prepared, 《

וְגָעָה מֵחֲנוּיָה, **מִגְדַּל נוּנִיָּה.**

and exiled 〈 from Chanuyah [in Jerusalem] 〈 was [the watch from] **Migdal** 〈 **Nuniyah.** 《

(1) Cf. *Psalms* 137:7. (2) *Exodus* 15:2. (3) *Eichah* 2:5. (4) Cf. *Jeremiah* 12:3.

שָׁמְעוּ כִּי יָצָאתִי בַּשִּׁבְיָה,

« in captivity, ‹ I went out ‹ that ‹ [When] they heard

וְנִשְׂרְפָה דַּת מָרוֹם שְׁבוּיָה,[1]*

« was captured,* ‹ that from On High ‹ was the Law ‹ and that burnt

וְהוּשַׁתִּי לְשַׁמָּה וְעַרְבּוּבְיָה,

« amid chaos, ‹ into a wasteland ‹ I was made

וּמֵהֶסְתֵּר חֲבוּיָה, נָדְדָה בֵּית חוֹבִיָּה.

« **Hoviah.** ‹ [the watch from] **Bais** ‹ went into exile « where [God's Presence] was hidden, ‹ and from the concealing [Temple]

שָׁמְעוּ כִּי נִזְהֲמְתִּי בְּצַחֲנָה, וְסָתַם מִמֶּנִּי תְּחִנָּה,

« for supplication, ‹ from me ‹ and that [God] blocked [the path] « by the stench [of my sins], ‹ I was befouled ‹ that ‹ They heard

וְלֹא נָתַן לִי רַחֲמִים וַחֲנִינָה,

« or favor. ‹ mercy ‹ upon me ‹ bestow ‹ and did not

וּמִקִּרְיַת חָנָה,[2] נָעָה כְּפַר יוֹחֲנָה.

« **Yohanah.** ‹ [the watch from] **Kfar** ‹ wandered « where [David] encamped, ‹ So from the City

תָּבֹא רָעַת שָׁמוּנִי הַדָּמִין,

‹ limb from limb, ‹ who tore me ‹ evil upon those ‹ May there come

(1) Cf. *Psalms* 68:19. (2) Cf. *Isaiah* 29:1.

דַּת מָרוֹם שְׁבוּיָה — *The Law that from On High was captured.* During the 40-day period that Moses was atop Mount Sinai, he ascended to heaven to receive the Torah to bring it down to Israel. When the ministering angels complained to God that a mortal did not belong among them, He replied, "He has ascended to take the Torah."

The angels argued, "This precious treasure, which was hidden away for the equivalent of 974 generations before the world was created, should not be given to mortal man."

God then summoned Moses to counter the arguments of the angels. Moses reasoned with them, "Angels do not need the Torah. You have no parents to honor, no possibility of conforming to the requirements of *kashrus*, and no Egyptian bondage to remember."

The holy angels admitted the truth of Moses' words and consented to allow the Torah out of the heavenly domain, for

וְשָׁתוּ שְׁעָרַי שׁוֹמֵמִין,[1]
« desolate; ‹ my gates ‹ and who made

וְהֵשִׁיב אָחוֹר יָמִין,[2]
« His right hand, ‹ back ‹ [God] drew

וּבַעֲוֹן פְּסִילִים נָעָה גִּנְּתוֹן צַלְמִין.
« **Ginthon-Tzalmin.** ‹ wandered [the watch from] « of idols, ‹ and because of the iniquity

תָּבֹא תַמְרִיחַ, וְחָשְׁכִּי תַּזְרִיחַ,
« shine [Your] light, ‹ and [upon] my darkness ‹ and spread [healing] ointment ‹ O come

וְכַדֶּשֶׁא עַצְמוֹתֵינוּ תַּפְרִיחַ,[3]
« make to flourish. ‹ our [dry] bones « and like the grass,

וְרֵיחַ נִיחוֹחֵינוּ כְּקֶדֶם תָּרִיחַ,
« You shall smell; ‹ as of old « that are pleasing, ‹ And our [offering] aromas

וּמִשֻּׁלְחָנְךָ תַּאֲרִיחַ, שׁוּלֵי חֲמַת אָרִיחַ.
« **Ariach.** ‹ [watch from] **Hamath-** ‹ to the final ‹ offer hospitality ‹ and from your Altar-table

(וַיְקוֹנֵן יִרְמְיָהוּ עַל יֹאשִׁיָּהוּ.)*
« Josiah.)* ‹ over ‹ did Jeremiah ‹ (And lament

(1) Cf. *Eichah* 1:4. (2) Cf. 2:3. (3) Cf. *Isaiah* 66:14.

they realized that its precepts apply only to man and to his world (*Shabbos* 88b).

Since the angels sought to keep the Torah captive in the heavens until Moses captured it for mankind by his convincing arguments, the *paytan* describes the Torah as "captured from on High."

וַיְקוֹנֵן . . . יֹאשִׁיָּהוּ — *And lament did Jeremiah over Josiah.* Although this verse is printed at the end of this *kinnah* in many editions, the consensus of the commentators considers it a mistake. It is really the opening verse of the next *kinnah,* and that is how it appears in most early editions.

KINNAH 11 / קינה יא

וַיְקוֹנֵן יִרְמְיָהוּ עַל יֹאשִׁיָּהוּ.*[1]

« Josiah.* ‹ over ‹ did Jeremiah ‹ And lament

(1) *II Chronicles* 35:25.

וַיְקוֹנֵן יִרְמְיָהוּ עַל יֹאשִׁיָּהוּ — *And lament did Jeremiah over Josiah.* This *kinnah* is the most important and authentic lament we recite on Tishah B'Av (except for the Book of *Eichah*) because its recitation was ordained by the prophet Jeremiah [Yirmeyahu] himself following the tragic death of King Josiah [Yoshiyahu]: . . .*And all of Judah and Jerusalem mourned over Yoshiyahu. And Yirmeyahu lamented over Yoshiyahu; and all of the male singers and the female singers have mentioned Yoshiyahu in their laments to this day and made them a statute in Israel, and behold, they are written in the Book of Lamentations* (*II Chronicles* 35:24, 25).

Why was the death of Yoshiyahu considered a tragedy of such proportion that it must be remembered by *all* of Israel for *all* time? Because *never* in all of Jewish history was there a leader as great as this king who sparked a massive nationwide wave of *teshuvah*, repentance, which had such a positive effect on Israel that the First Temple was almost saved from doom and preserved for future generations — as Scripture states: *And like him there was no king before him who returned to* HASHEM *with all his heart and all his soul and with all his resources in accordance with all the Torah teachings of Moses, and after him no one arose like him* (*II Kings* 23:25).

Yoshiyahu's grandfather, the notorious King Menasheh, had fanatically dedicated the early years of his reign to a campaign of utterly stripping the Jewish people of every vestige of true faith in God. With single-minded devotion, Menasheh planted idols in every corner of his kingdom, even in the Holy of Holies itself! Although Menasheh repented in his later years, it was beyond his ability to rip out the bitter root of idolatry he had planted so deeply within the heart of the Jewish people.

Amon, Menasheh's son, was an idolater who corrupted Judah for two years until he was assassinated by his palace guards. His son *Yoshiyahu was eight years old when he began his reign and he reigned thirty-one years in Jerusalem* (*II Kings* 22:1).

So thoroughly had Yoshiyahu's predecessors eradicated the Torah's influence from the Jewish people that it appears that the king of the Jewish people *never saw a Sefer Torah* for the first 18 years of his reign. In the eighteenth year, the *Kohen Gadol*, Hilkiah [Chilkiyahu, father of the prophet Yirmeyahu], began to make long-overdue repairs to the Temple structure. In the course of this work, he discovered a Torah Scroll which had been hidden for generations — since the time of the wicked King Ahaz, father of Hezekiah [Chizkiyahu] and grandfather of Menasheh (*Metzudas David*). Chilkiyahu was shocked when he opened the Scroll to the תּוֹכָחָה, *Admonition*, recorded in *Deuteronomy* (Chs. 27 and 28): HASHEM *will carry off [to captivity] both you and the king whom you shall raise over yourself, to a nation which neither you nor your fathers have known* (*Deut.* 28:36); and, אָרוּר אֲשֶׁר לֹא־יָקִים אֶת דִּבְרֵי הַתּוֹרָה־הַזֹּאת לַעֲשׂוֹת אוֹתָם, *Cursed be he who does not uphold all the words of this Torah, to perform them* (*Deut.* 27:26). When King Yoshiyahu heard this, he was so shaken that he ripped his clothing (*II Kings* 22:11; *II Chron.* 34:19) in anguish over all the years he had neglected the Torah out of sheer ignorance. Then he cried out, עָלֵינוּ לְהָקִים, *It is incumbent upon us to uphold [the Torah]!* (*Yerushalmi Sotah* 5:4; *Midrash HaGadol, Devarim* 27:26).

אֵיכָה אֱלִי* קוֹנְנוּ מֵאֵלָיו,

« for one of the mightiest [kings], ‹ they lamented ‹ as a lament* ‹ *Eichah*

Yoshiyahu swiftly convened a massive assembly of all the leaders and elders of Judah and Jerusalem and read to them from this new-found treasure, the Torah Scroll. Together, they entered a solemn covenant to keep all the teachings of the Torah with all their heart and soul. Yoshiyahu appointed agents to search out and destroy every vestige of idolatry in the land. They were successful in eradicating every *apparent* heathen image and the vast majority of people did join in Yoshiyahu's penitence, but a stubborn minority persisted in the pagan beliefs that had taken such firm root over the generations. They invented an ingenious method for concealing their idols. They split their doors in two and they split their idols in two, down the middle. They attached one half of the idol to each half door in such a way that when the doors were closed the two idol halves came together to be whole, but when the doors were opened the idol was split in half and each piece was concealed behind the open door. When Yoshiyahu's detectives came to search for idols they opened the doors and found nothing (*Eichah Rabbah* 1:53). This *kinnah* laments that these surreptitious idolaters undermined all of Yoshiyahu's efforts to purify Israel.

In the last year of Yoshiyahu's reign, Pharaoh Necho, the king of Egypt, which is southwest of Israel, decided to wage war against Assyria, which lies northeast of Israel. He asked Yoshiyahu for permission to march his troops through his land as this was the fastest and shortest route to Assyria. However, Yoshiyahu refused because God promised that when the Jewish people do His will, . . . *a sword will not pass through your land* (*Leviticus* 26:6). This means that the blessing of peace will be so pervasive that (a) foreign armies will not even attempt to use *Eretz Yisrael* en route to battle with a different country (*Sifra* and *Rashi* ibid.), and (b) the Jews will be so strong and meritorious that no army would be able to force its way through (see *Taanis* 22a,b).

Yirmeyahu the prophet sent word to Yoshiyahu to allow Pharaoh to pass through. He warned Yoshiyahu that his generation was not as righteous as he imagined and that there were still significant groups of secret idolaters. Tragically, Yoshiyahu, in his righteous zeal, refused to face reality and continued to entertain illusions of total perfection for the Jewish people (*Eichah Rabbah* 1:53). The king then sought the advice of the prophetess Huldah who he felt would see things in a more sympathetic light. And, despite the fact that Huldah's prophetic response was as harsh as Yirmeyahu's, Yoshiyahu ignored both prophets. He went to do battle with Pharaoh Necho to prevent him from crossing his land.

This *kinnah* describes King Yoshiyahu's tragic and untimely death, when, with his last breath, he remorsefully repented his sin against God's words that he had heard from the prophets. But it was too late. Not only was Yoshiyahu personally doomed, but the entire kingdom of Judah was now set on a course of irrevocable, ultimate destruction. Hence, the enormous tragedy of Yoshiyahu's death, because with him died the very last hope and opportunity to save the Temple and the Jewish people.

אֵיכָה אֱלִי — *"Eichah" as a lament.* Specifically, this refers to the fourth chapter of the Book of *Eichah*, which also begins with the word אֵיכָה. That elegy was originally pronounced over Yoshiyahu's death and is the *kinnah* referred to in the verse from *II Chronicles* that introduces this *kinnah* (*Rashi* to *Eichah* 4:1). For this reason the *paytan* begins each line of this *kinnah* with the first word of the corresponding verse in *Eichah* 4.

בֶּן שְׁמוֹנֶה שָׁנָה הֵחֵל לִדְרוֹשׁ מֵאֱלֹהָיו,*[1]

« for His God.* ‹ to search ‹ began ‹ years ‹ of eight ‹ who at the age

בְּנֵי חָם* בְּעָבְרָם חָנוּ עָלָיו,

« against him, ‹ encamped ‹ when they passed through ‹ of Ham* ‹ Yet the sons

וְלֹא הֻזְכַּר לוֹ שִׂגּוּי מִפְעָלָיו.

« of his [meritorious] deeds. ‹ of the grandeur ‹ for him ‹ was recalled ‹ nothing

גַּם בְּכָל מַלְכֵי יִשְׂרָאֵל אֲשֶׁר קָמוּ לִגְדּוֹר,

« to close the breach [of idolatry], ‹ rose up ‹ who ‹ of Israel ‹ the kings ‹ among all ‹ Even

לֹא קָם כָּמוֹהוּ מִימוֹת אֲבִיגְדּוֹר,*[2]

« of Avigdor [Moses].* ‹ since the days ‹ like him ‹ rose up ‹ no one

דָּבַק בּוֹ חֵטְא לֵיצָנֵי הַדּוֹר,

« of that generation — ‹ of the scorners ‹ did the sin ‹ to him ‹ Adhere

אֲשֶׁר קָמוּ אַחַר הַדֶּלֶת לְסִדּוֹר.[3]

« to arrange [idols]. ‹ the door ‹ behind ‹ arose, [intending] ‹ those who

הָאוֹכְלִים זֶרַע שִׁיחוֹר,

« of the Nile, ‹ the produce ‹ Those who ate

(1) Cf. *II Chronicles* 34:3. (2) Cf. *II Kings* 23:25. (3) Cf. *Isaiah* 57:8.

בֶּן שְׁמוֹנֶה שָׁנָה הֵחֵל לִדְרוֹשׁ מֵאֱלֹהָיו — *Who at the age of eight years began to search for His God.* Actually, it was Yoshiyahu's reign that began when he was eight years old. And it was in the eighth year of his reign (when he was 16 years old) that Yoshiyahu felt the first stirrings of *teshuvah* in his heart and *began to search for the God of David, his ancestor (II Chronicles* 34:3, see *Malbim*). Nevertheless, since a newly crowned king is considered like a newborn baby (see *Yoma* 22b), the *paytan* refers to Yoshiyahu in the eighth year of his reign as an eight-year-old.

בְּנֵי חָם — *The sons of Ham.* This refers to Pharaoh Necho (see above) of Egypt. מִצְרַיִם, *Mitzrayim*, the progenitor of Egypt, was a son of חָם, *Ham*, the son of Noah (see *Genesis* 10:6).

אֲבִיגְדּוֹר — *Avigdor [Moses].* The Talmud (*Megillah* 13a) and Midrash (*Vayikra Rabbah* 1:3) record ten names by which Moses was known: Moshe, Toviah, Yered, Avi Gedor (or Avigdor), Chaver, Avi Socho, Yekusiel, Avi Zanoach, Shemayah, and Nesanel (see *I Chronicles* 4:18, 24:6).

כְּתְמוֹ הַטּוֹב פְּחָמוּ מִשְּׁחוֹר,

[Josiah's countenance —] like gold ‹ that is the finest — « [were able] to darken blacker than charcoal. «

וַיִּגְדַּל עָוֹן וְהֵשִׁיב יָמִין אָחוֹר,[1]

[As] grew greater ‹ did iniquity, « He drew ‹ His right hand ‹ back; «

וְעוֹד לֹא שָׁלַח יָדוֹ מִן הַחוֹר.[2]

and as yet ‹ He has not extended ‹ His hand ‹ through ‹ the opening. «

זַכּוּ אֲמָרָיו כְּנָם דַּת לְהָקִים,

Pure ‹ were his words ‹ when he spoke ‹ of the Law ‹ to uphold; «

בִּצַּע אֶמְרָתוֹ[3] בְּאָרוּר אֲשֶׁר לֹא יָקִים,[4]

and he ripped ‹ his hem ‹ when he heard, *Cursed* ‹ *is one who* ‹ *will not* ‹ *uphold [the Torah].* «

חָשַׁךְ תָּאֳרוֹ כְּנֶאֱצוּ רְחוֹקִים,

But darkened ‹ were his features ‹ when defiant [of God] ‹ were the estranged [Jews]; «

בְּבֶצַע מוֹאֲסֵי דַּת וְחֻקִּים.

through the corruption ‹ of those who despised ‹ the Law ‹ and the statutes. «

טוֹבִים רָעִים[5] נִקְרָאוּ בְּשָׁלְחוֹ מַלְאָךְ,

Good ‹ were the bad ones ‹ called ‹ when [Pharaoh Necho] sent ‹ a messenger [saying], «

מַה לִּי וָלָךְ הַיּוֹם לְתַלְאָךְ,[6]

What is there ‹ *between me* ‹ *and you* ‹ *today* ‹ *to weary you [in battle]?* «

יְדֵי עַם הָאָרֶץ דָּמִים בְּמַלְאָךְ,

The hands ‹ *of the people* ‹ *of the land* ‹ *with blood* ‹ *you will be filling;* «

תֵּעָנֵשׁ בְּבִצְעִי אֶת פְּנֵי פִּלְאָךְ.

and you will be punished ‹ *[for preventing me] from* ‹ *fulfilling* ‹ *the desire* ‹ *of your miracle worker [God].* «

(1) Cf. *Eichah* 2:3. (2) Cf. *Song of Songs* 5:4. (3) *Eichah* 2:17. (4) *Deuteronomy* 27:26.
(5) Some editions read טוֹבִים רֵעִים נִקְרְאוּ, *They were called good friends.* (6) Cf. *II Chronicles* 35:21.

כִּלָּה הֲמוֹנֵי לֶכֶת אֲרַם נַהֲרַיִם,
[But] he [Josiah] stopped ‹ his [Pharaoh's] hordes ‹ from marching ‹ to Mesopotamia, «

לְמַעַן לֹא תַעֲבוֹר חֶרֶב[1] כָּל שֶׁהוּא בְּאֶפְרָיִם,
so that ‹ there should not ‹ pass ‹ a sword ‹ of any ‹ sort ‹ through Ephraim. «

וְלֹא שָׁמַע לַחוֹזֶה לָשׁוּב אֲחוֹרַיִם,
He failed ‹ to heed ‹ the seer [Jeremiah] ‹ [who said] to turn ‹ back, «

כִּי גְּזֵרָה נִגְזְרָה לְסַכְסֵךְ מִצְרַיִם בְּמִצְרָיִם.[2]*
for ‹ a decree ‹ was [Divinely] decreed ‹ to incite strife ‹ of Egyptian ‹ against Egyptian.* «

מֵחַטֹּאת סְתִירַת מְזוּזוֹת,
This resulted from the sin ‹ of concealing ‹ [idols behind] the doorposts, «

חֲזוֹן עֲנְּתוֹתִי[3] הֵחֵלּוּ לְבַזּוֹת,
when the prophecies ‹ [of Jeremiah,] from Anathoth ‹ they began ‹ to scorn. «

נָעוּ עֲנָמִים לְחוּמוֹ לְהַבְזוֹת.
Move onward ‹ did the Anamite [Egyptians] ‹ [Josiah's] flesh ‹ to desecrate; «

וְלֹא הֵסֵב פָּנָיו[4] וְסָפְדוּ עַל זֹאת.*
yet he did not turn ‹ his face [to retreat], « and they eulogized him with, « *For* ‹ *this ....* * «

סוּרוּ הֵעִידוּ עַד לֹא שְׁאִיָּה,
Turn back! ‹ they warned ‹ while ‹ there is not yet ‹ destruction, «

(1) Cf. *Leviticus* 26:6. (2) Cf. *Isaiah* 19:2. (3) See *Jeremiah* 1:1. (4) Cf. *II Chronicles* 35:22.

מִצְרַיִם בְּמִצְרָיִם — *Egyptian against Egyptian.* According to the prophecy of Isaiah (19:2), Egypt would be destroyed through internal strife as *I will cause Egyptian to contend against Egyptian; each man to wage battle against his brother and against his friend; city against city and kingdom against kingdom.*

עַל זֹאת — *"For this ...."* Yirmeyahu bemoaned the death of Yoshiyahu with the words: ... עַל זֹאת, *For this, don sackloth, lament and mourn, for of* H*ASHEM's burning wrath has not receded from us* (*Jeremiah* 4:8; see *Rashi*).

וַיְמָאֵנוּ סוּר וּמָט יְסוֹד* נְשִׁיָּה,

but he refused ‹ to turn back, ‹ and collapse ‹ did [righteous Josiah,] the foundation* ‹ of the world. «

פְּנֵי קְרָב כְּקָרֵב וְלֹא עָלְתָה לוֹ רְטִיָּה,[1]

To the frontline ‹ of the battle ‹ when he approached, « there was not ‹ available ‹ to him ‹ healing [salvation], «

וַיּוֹרוּ הַמּוֹרִים לַמֶּלֶךְ יֹאשִׁיָּה.[2]

for they shot, « did the archers, « at King ‹ Josiah. «

עוֹדֶנּוּ עוֹצֵם עֵינָיו בְּגֵוָיו נוֹחֲצִים,

While he was still ‹ closing ‹ his eyes, « into his body ‹ they continued swiftly; «

חֵץ אַחַר חֵץ מוֹרִים וְלוֹחֲצִים,

arrow ‹ after ‹ arrow ‹ they were shooting ‹ and pressing. «

צָדוּהוּ וְשָׂמוּהוּ כַּמַּטָּרָה לַחִצִּים,

They trapped him, ‹ and made him ‹ a target ‹ for [their] arrows, «

וַיִּזְרְקוּ בוֹ שְׁלֹשׁ מֵאוֹת חִצִּים.[3]

and shot ‹ into him ‹ three ‹ hundred ‹ arrows. «

קַלִּים[4] הִטּוּ אַחֲרָיו אֹזֶן מוֹצָא פִּיהוּ,

The swift-footed [Jeremiah] ‹ inclined ‹ behind him, ‹ to hear ‹ [the words] that would come out ‹ of his mouth; «

וְעַד מִצּוּי נֶפֶשׁ מַעֲשָׂיו הֱפִיהוּ,

and until ‹ the forcing out ‹ of his soul, ‹ his deeds ‹ adorned him. «

רוּחַ שְׂפָתָיו הִפְצָה מִפִּיהוּ,

The breath ‹ of his lips ‹ burst forth ‹ from his mouth, «

(1) Some editions read שְׁעִיָּה which can mean either *salvation* or *prayer*.
(2) Cf. *II Chronicles* 35:23; some editions read הַיּוֹרִים (as in the Scriptural verse), rather than הַמּוֹרִים, but the meaning is the same. (3) *Eichah Rabbah* 1:53; cf. *Sanhedrin* 48b. (4) Cf. *Isaiah* 18:2.

יְסוֹד — *[Righteous Josiah,] the foundation.* The interpolation is based on the verse: וְצַדִּיק יְסוֹד עוֹלָם, *a righteous person is the foundation of the world* (*Proverbs*

צַדִּיק הוּא יהוה* כִּי מָרִיתִי פִּיהוּ.[1]
Righteous ‹ is ‹ HASHEM* ‹ for ‹ I have disobeyed ‹ His utterance. «

שִׂישִׂי נוֹף* כִּי קִנֵּא זַעַם,
Rejoice [for now], ‹ O Nof,* « because ‹ [God] shall avenge ‹ with fury, «

לְשַׁלֵּם שְׁאוֹנָם בַּעֲוֹן בִּצְעָם,[2]
repaying ‹ [your] hordes ‹ for the sin ‹ of their corruption. «

תַּם כֶּתֶם הַטּוֹב עַם זוּ* בְּפִשְׁעָם,
Died ‹ has the golden one [Joshiah] ‹ that was the finest, « due to this people* ‹ in their guilt, «

וַיְקוֹנֵן עָלָיו כָּל אֵיכָה יוּעַם.[3]
and lament ‹ for him [did Jeremiah] ‹ all of: « How is it ‹ that dimmed [is the gold] .... «

תָּם בְּמִקְרֶה אֶחָד* כּוֹס מְגִדּוֹ לִשְׁתּוֹת,
[The righteous Josiah] died ‹ in the same way [as the wicked Ahab],* « when the cup ‹ of bitterness at Megiddo ‹ he drank; «

בְּמוֹעֵד שְׁנַת הַשְּׁמִטָּה[4] **כְּגַע הַקָּהֵל לֶאֱתוֹת,**
it was the Festival [of Succos] ‹ in a year ‹ [following the] Sabbatical year ‹ when arrived the time ‹ for the national assembly ‹ to approach. «

---

(1) Cf. *Eichah* 1:18; *Eichah Rabbah* 1:53. (2) Alternatively: *Because God's fury has avenged, repaying [Israel's] multitudes for the sin of their corruption.* (3) *Eichah* Ch. 4. (4) *Deuteronomy* 31:10; see *Sotah* 41a.

10:25; see *Chagigah* 12b).

צַדִּיק הוּא ה׳... — *"Righteous is HASHEM ...."* With three hundred well-aimedarrows, the Egyptians pierced Yoshiyahu's body like a sieve. As the king breathed his last, Yirmeyahu swiftly ran over to his side to catch the dying words of this great *tzaddik*. Yoshiyahu completely accepted the punishment that God had meted out to him and realized that he deserved it. *"Righteous is HASHEM for I have disobeyed His utterance* — and I disobeyed the utterances of His representative, the prophet Yirmeyahu!" (*Midrash Eichah* 1:53).

נוֹף — *Nof*, an Egyptian city mentioned in *Isaiah* (19:13), *Jeremiah* (2:16 et al.), and *Ezekiel* (30:13,16) and usually identified with Memphis.

עַם זוּ — *Due to this people.* In the Song of the Sea, Israel is called עַם זוּ גָּאָלְתָּ, *this people that You redeemed* (*Exodus* 15:13), and עַם זוּ קָנִיתָ, *this people that You have acquired* (ibid. 15:16). Moreover, Isaiah (43:21) calls Israel, עַם זוּ יָצַרְתִּי לִי, *this people I fashioned for Myself*. Based on these passages, the *paytanim* often refer to Israel as עַם זוּ, *this people*.

בְּמִקְרֶה אֶחָד — *In the same way [as the wicked Ahab]*, who also succumbed to an enemy archer's arrow on the battlefield (see *I King* 22:34-35).

תָּלָה בְּעֶשְׂרִים וּשְׁתַּיִם* מֵהֲרוֹס שָׁתוֹת,

« of the Temple, ‹ the utter destruction ‹ for twenty-two [years]* ‹ [God] suspended

כִּי סִפְּדוּ לוֹ אֵיכָה בְּעֶשְׂרִים וּשְׁתַּיִם אוֹתִיּוֹת.

« letters [of the *aleph-beis*]. ‹ [composed according to] the twenty-two « with *Eichah,* ‹ [Josiah] ‹ they eulogized ‹ because

אוֹתוֹת קִינוֹת* לְבָטָה מְחוֹלִי,

« my dance, ‹ degenerated ‹ of lament* ‹ Into signs

עֵת כִּי שָׁכַחְתִּי מְחוֹלְלִי,[1]

« the One Who fashioned me; ‹ I forgot ‹ that ‹ at the time

זַמּוֹתִי כִּי לָעַד יַאֲהִילִי,

« He would shelter me [with the Temple], ‹ eternally ‹ that ‹ I expected

רָשַׁעְתִּי וְנָסַעְתִּי וְנֶטַשׁ אָהֳלִי.

« was my Tent. ‹ for abandoned [by God] « and was [exiled, always] traveling, ‹ but I was wicked

(1) Cf. *Deuteronomy* 32:18.

בְּעֶשְׂרִים וּשְׁתַּיִם — *For twenty-two [years].* The calculation of these years is as follows: After the death of Yoshiyahu, his son Jehoahaz [Yehoachaz] reigned for three months, Jehoiakim [Yehoyakim] for 11 years, Jehoiachin [Yehoyachin] for three months and ten days, and the last king of Judah, Zedekiah [Zidkiyahu], for 11 years, for a total of 22 years, six months, and ten days (*Beis Levi*).

אוֹתוֹת קִינוֹת — *Into signs of lament.* The singular noun אוֹת can mean either *letter of the alphabet* or *sign.* Usually the plural אוֹתוֹת is used for *signs* and the plural אוֹתִיּוֹת for *letters.* But sometimes they are interchanged. Thus, some render this phrase *alphabetically arranged lamentations.*

KINNAH 12 / קינה יב

אָהֳלִי* אֲשֶׁר תָּאַבְתָּ עַד לֹא בְרֵאשִׁית*

« Creation —* ‹ there was not yet ‹ — while ‹ You desired ‹ that ‹ My Tent,*

עִם כִּסֵּא כָבוֹד לְצָרְפוֹ,*

« to link,* ‹ of Glory, ‹ [Your] Throne ‹ with

לָמָּה לָנֶצַח[1] שֻׁדַּד בְּיַד שׁוֹדְדִים,

« of plunderers? ‹ by the hand ‹ is it plundered ‹ forever ‹ why

וְנִהְיֵיתָ כְּרוֹעֶה בְּעֹטְיָה[2] וְרָעַשְׁתָּ וְרָגַנְתָּ,

« and you grumbled, ‹ as You stormed ‹ veiled in mourning [for his lost flocks], ‹ like a shepherd ‹ [And why] have You become

וְעַתָּה מַה לִּי פֹה.[3]

« *here?* ‹ *should I [remain]* ‹ *why* ‹ *And now,*

אָהֳלִי אֲשֶׁר קוֹמַמְתָּ לְאֵיתָנֵי אֶרֶץ,[4]

« of the Land, ‹ for the powerful [Patriarchs] ‹ You erected ‹ that ‹ My Tent

(1) *Eichah* 5:20. (2) Cf. *Song of Songs* 1:7. (3) *Isaiah* 52:5.
(4) Some editions read לְאֵיתָנֵי עוֹלָם, *the powerful of the world,* or, *the powerful of yore.*

אָהֳלִי — *My Tent.* Each stanza begins אָהֳלִי, *My Tent,* which variously alludes to either the *Mishkan* (Tabernacle) that accompanied Israel through the Wilderness for 40 years, or to one or the other of the two Temples. According to *Ibn Ezra* (*Eichah* 2:4), the *Beis HaMikdash* is referred to as a tent, because just as when fire touches a tent, it begins to burn instantly, so did the *Beis HaMikdash* catch fire in an instant.

The *kinnah* is a series of triplets, each of which follows the same pattern: (a) The first line begins אָהֳלִי אֲשֶׁר, *My Tent that,* followed by a letter of the reverse alphabetical arrangement known as תַּשְׁרַק; and ends with the syllable פוֹ or פּוֹ; (b) the second line begins לָמָּה לָנֶצַח, *why forever . . .,* followed by the next letter of תַּשְׁרַק; and ends with the syllable ־ים; (c) the third line begins וְנִהְיֵיתָ כְּ־, *[And why] have You become . . .,* followed by a תַּשְׁרַק letter; (d) the second part of the line is a Scriptural passage that ends with the word פֹה or פֹּה.

The final stanza contains an acrostic of the author's name אֶלְעָזָר, *Elazar.*

עַד לֹא בְרֵאשִׁית — *While there was not yet Creation.* The Talmud states that the *Beis HaMikdash* is one of seven things (or concepts) created before the world. The other six are: תּוֹרָה, *Torah;* תְּשׁוּבָה, *repentance;* גַּן עֵדֶן, *the Garden of Eden;* גֵּיהִנֹּם, *Hell;* כִּסֵּא הַכָּבוֹד, *[God's] Throne of Glory;* and שְׁמוֹ שֶׁל מָשִׁיחַ, *the name of the Messiah* (*Pesachim* 54a; *Nedarim* 39b).

עִם כִּסֵּא כָבוֹד לְצָרְפוֹ — *With [Your] Throne of Glory to link.* According to the

בְּחֶרְדַּת מִי אֵיפֹא,[1]*

« *and where [is he who will destroy the Temple]?* ‹ *Who [is he]* « with [Isaac's] trembling [and asking],

לָמָּה לָנֶצַח צָמַת בְּיַד צָרִים,

« of adversaries? ‹ by the hand ‹ is it destroyed ‹ forever ‹ Why

וְנִהְיֵיתָ כְּצִפּוֹר בּוֹדֵד עַל גָּג[2] מַר צוֹרֵחַ,

« screeching, ‹ bitterly « a rooftop, ‹ upon ‹ alone ‹ like a bird ‹ [And why] have You become

מַה לִּידִידִי פֹּה.[3]

« *here?* ‹ *is My beloved doing* ‹ *What*

אָהֳלִי אֲשֶׁר פִּצְתָּ לְמַעֲנוֹ לְצִיר,

« to the emissary [Moses], ‹ regarding it ‹ You expressed ‹ that ‹ My Tent

וְאַתָּה עֲמוֹד עִמָּדִי פֹּה,[4]

« *here [for instruction about the Tabernacle],* ‹ *with Me* ‹ *stand* ‹ *But as for you,*

לָמָּה לָנֶצַח עֻרְעַר בְּיַד עֲרֵלִים,[5]

« of the uncircumcised? ‹ by the hand ‹ is it razed ‹ forever ‹ why

וְנִהְיֵיתָ כְּשׂוֹנֵא וְצָר,[6]

« and an adversary? ‹ like an enemy ‹ [And why] have You become

וְאַיֵּה אִוּוּי מוֹשָׁב פֹּה.[7]

« to be here [in Zion]? ‹ for Your habitation ‹ [Your] desire ‹ Where is

---

(1) Cf. *Genesis* 27:33. (2) *Psalms* 102:8. (3) Cf. *Jeremiah* 11:15. (4) Cf. *Deuteronomy* 5:28. (5) Some editions read עוֹבְדֵי כּוֹכָבִים, *star worshipers;* some read נָכְרִים, *strangers;* and some read אוֹיְבִים, *enemies.* Obviously, the hand of the censor has been at work here, and the whims of the various censors had to be adhered to by the printing shops. (6) Cf. *Eichah* 2:5. (7) Cf. *Psalms* 132:13.

Midrash, the *Throne of Glory* in heaven is directly above the *Beis HaMikdash* on earth (*Mechilta* cited by *Rashi* to *Exodus* 15:17; *Targum* to *Jeremiah* 17:12).

בְּחֶרְדַּת מִי אֵיפֹא — *With [Isaac's] trembling [and asking], "Who [is he] and where [is he who will destroy the Temple]?"* According to the *paytan,* Isaac did not tremble because Jacob had pre-empted Esau's blessing. Rather, Isaac saw in a

אָהֳלִי אֲשֶׁר נָחִיתָ בְּעַנְנֵי הוֹד,

« of splendor, ‹ with clouds ‹ You guided ‹ that ‹ My Tent

לְזֹאת אֲשֶׁר יֶשְׁנוֹ פֹּה וְאֵינֶנּוּ פֹּה,[1]

« here, ‹ [and for those who] are not ‹ here ‹ are ‹ who ‹ for those

לָמָּה לָנֶצַח מוּאָס בְּיַד מוֹרְדִים,

« of rebels? ‹ by the hand ‹ is it made contemptible ‹ forever ‹ why

וְנִהְיֵיתָ כְּגִבּוֹר לֹא יוּכַל לְהוֹשִׁיעַ,[2]

‹ to save, [with the enemy mocking,] ‹ able ‹ not ‹ like a warrior ‹ [And why] have You become

מַה לְּךָ פֹה וּמִי לְךָ פֹּה.[3]

« *here?* ‹ *have You* ‹ *and whom* ‹ *here* ‹ *What have You*

אָהֳלִי אֲשֶׁר כּוֹנַנְתָּ מוּל מָכוֹן לְשִׁבְתְּךָ*[4]

‹ of Your [celestial] dwelling place* ‹ the foundation ‹ oppo- site ‹ You positioned carefully ‹ that ‹ My Tent

לְחוֹפֵף לְחֻפּוֹ,

« like a canopy, ‹ that hovers over it

לָמָּה לָנֶצַח יוּעָה בְּיַד יְהִירִים,

« of the arrogant? ‹ by the hand ‹ is it swept aside ‹ forever ‹ why

וְנִהְיֵיתָ כְּטָס בְּחָלָל וְאֵין עוֹד נָבִיא,

‹ a prophet, ‹ any longer ‹ for there is not « in an empty void, ‹ like [a bird] flying ‹ [And why] have You become

וְנָמְתָּ הַאֵין פֹּה.[5]

« *here [a prophet]?* ‹ *Is there not* « as You have said,

(1) Cf. *Deuteronomy* 29:14. (2) *Jeremiah* 14:9. (3) *Isaiah* 22:16. (4) Cf. *Exodus* 15:17. (5) *I Kings* 22:7.

prophetic vision that descendants of the one standing before him would someday destroy the *Beis HaMikdash*.

כּוֹנַנְתָּ מוּל מָכוֹן לְשִׁבְתְּךָ — *You positioned carefully opposite the foundation of Your [celestial] dwelling place.* The Midrash teaches that the celestial *Beis HaMikdash* is aligned with the terrestrial *Beis HaMikdash* (*Tanchuma, Mishpatim* 18, cited by *Rashi* to *Exodus* 28:17).

אָהֳלִי אֲשֶׁר חָנִיתָ מֵאָז בְּתָאָיו מִפֹּה וּמִפֹּה,[1]

« and on that side, ‹ on this side ‹ in its chambers ‹ since time long past ‹ You encamped ‹ where ‹ My Tent

לָמָּה לָנֶצַח זֻנַּח בְּיַד זָרִים,

« of strangers? ‹ in the hand ‹ [and left] forsaken ‹ is it ‹ forever ‹ why

וְנִהְיֵיתָ כְּוָתִיק יוֹצֵא חוּצָה,

« outside, ‹ who escaped [from his house] ‹ like a veteran ‹ [And why] have You become

וְלֹא עֲבֹר פֹּה.

« here? ‹ to return ‹ not

אָהֳלִי אֲשֶׁר הֲכִנוֹתָ

‹ You established ‹ where ‹ My Tent

לְהַשְׁלִיךְ בּוֹ לְפָנֶיךָ גּוֹרָל* פֹּה,[2]

« here, ‹ of lots* ‹ in Your Presence ‹ in it ‹ the casting

לָמָּה לָנֶצַח דּוּחָה בְּיַד דָּמִים,[3]

« of the Edomites? ‹ into the hand ‹ is it pushed away ‹ forever ‹ why

וְנִהְיֵיתָ כְּגֵר בָּאָרֶץ, וְנַמְתָּ

‹ and announced ‹ in the land, ‹ like a foreigner ‹ [And why] have You become

כִּי לֹא נָסוֹב עַד בּוֹאוֹ פֹּה.[4]

« here [to terrestrial Jerusalem]? ‹ [Israel] returns ‹ until ‹ You would not return [to Your celestial Temple] ‹ that

אָהֳלִי אֲשֶׁר בַּעֲוֹן בִּצְעִי, חָשְׁכוּ כּוֹכְבֵי נִשְׁפּוֹ,[5]

« of its twilight, ‹ the stars ‹ had darkened ‹ of my illicit gain, ‹ because of the sin ‹ that, ‹ My Tent

---

(1) Cf. *Ezekiel* 40:21. (2) Cf. *Joshua* 18:6. (3) Some editions read either דּוּמִים (see *Rashi* to *Isaiah* 21:11) or דּוֹמִים (a contraction of אֲדוֹמִים), both of which mean *Edomites;* some editions read אֲחֵרִים, *others*. Once again, the censors have left their stamp on this *kinnah*. (4) *I Samuel* 16:11. (5) Cf. *Job* 3:8.

גּוֹרָל — *Lots.* Four times each day the *Kohanim* would assemble in the *Beis HaMikdash.* At those times lots would be drawn to determine who would perform the various aspects of the Altar service. The method by which the selections were

לָמָּה לָנֶצַח אֻפַּל בְּיַד אֻמּוֹת,
« of the nations? ‹ at the hand ‹ is it blackened ‹ forever ‹ why

וְנִהְיֵיתָ כְּאוֹרֵחַ בַּמָּלוֹן,
« at an inn [begging], ‹ like a transient ‹ [And why] have You become

וְעוֹד מִי לְךָ פֹה.[1]
« *here [for me to rest]?* ‹ *do you have* ‹ *where* ‹ *In addition,*

אָחוֹר וָקֶדֶם[2] מִפֹּה וּמִפֹּה,*
« and from there,* ‹ from here « and before [the Temple's destruction], ‹ After

לְכָל דּוֹר וָדוֹר נוֹדַע קִצְפּוֹ וְחֶפּוֹ,
« and His protective shelter. ‹ are [God's] anger ‹ made known ‹ after generation ‹ gener- ation ‹ in every

עַל מֶה מִכָּל אוֹם שָׁת עָלַי כַּפּוֹ,
« His [punishing] hand? ‹ upon me ‹ has He laid ‹ nations, ‹ of all ‹ what ‹ For reason,

זֹאת בַּעֲלִיל כִּי פִּיד חָקוּק בְּכַפּוֹ,
« on His palm; ‹ is engraved ‹ my destruction ‹ since ‹ is evident, ‹ This

רְפוּאָתִי בְטוּחָה כִּי רֶגַע בְּאַפּוֹ,[3]
« endures His anger. ‹ for but a moment ‹ since « is certain, ‹ [yet,] my healing

וְעַד עַתָּה אֵיכָה יָעִיב בְּאַפּוֹ.[4]
« in His anger? ‹ He has beclouded [me] ‹ how is it that ‹ now ‹ Still, until

(1) *Genesis* 19:12. (2) Cf. *Psalms* 139:5. (3) 30:6. (4) *Eichah* 2:1.

made and the particular tasks assigned at each lottery are discussed in Chapter Two of Tractate *Yoma*.

אָחוֹר וָקֶדֶם מִפֹּה וּמִפֹּה — *After and before . . . from here and from there.* The translation of the first part of this phrase in a temporal sense follows *Matteh Levi* who understands it as an allusion to the generations following and preceding the Destruction. Alternatively, the phrase is spatial in meaning and is translated, *West and east, from here and from there* (see *Targum* to *Isaiah* 9:11 and *Job* 23:8).

KINNAH 13 / קינה יג

אֵי כֹּה* אֹמֶר כּוֹרֶת לְאָב בְּפֶצַח,

Where is [the merit of the word] *so,** of the proclamation promised to [our] father [Abraham] in an utterance

בִּבְרִית בֵּין הַבְּתָרִים כֹּה יִהְיֶה[1] לָנֶצַח,

at the Covenant Between the Parts, *So numerous shall [your offspring] be for eternity?*

וְהֵן עַתָּה בֻּלְּעוּ עֲצָמַי בְּרֶצַח,

Indeed now, swallowed up have my bones been murderously.

לָמָה אֱלֹהִים זְנַחְתָּ לָנֶצַח.[2]

Why, O God, have you abandoned us for [what seems] an eternity?

אֵי כֹּה גָּשׁ כְּשֶׂה לְעוֹלָה לִרְצוֹתֶךָ,

Where is [the merit of the word] *so,* [when Abraham] approached [with his son] as with a sheep for a burnt-offering to appease You?

נֵלְכָה עַד כֹּה[3] פִּתּוּ בְּעֵדוֹתֶיךָ,

[Saying] *We will go until there,* they persuaded [the others to wait], [so as to fulfill] Your commandments.

וְהֵן עַתָּה דָּקְרוּ כְּפֶלַח רֵעִיָּתֶךָ,

But indeed now, they have skewered like a piece of fruit Your beloved ones.

יֶעְשַׁן אַפְּךָ בְּצֹאן מַרְעִיתֶךָ.[2]

[Why] does it smolder — Your wrath — against the sheep of Your pasture?

---

(1) *Genesis* 15:5. (2) *Psalms* 74:1. (3) *Genesis* 22:5.

אֵי כֹּה ... — *Where is [the merit of the word] "so." The* Midrash teaches that the *mitzvah* of *Bircas Kohanim* (the Priestly Blessing), which is introduced with the word כֹּה, *"so" shall you bless the Children of Israel*, was given in the merit of the three Patriarchs, about each of whom Scripture uses the word כֹּה, *so*. Regarding Abraham it is written, כֹּה, *so shall your offspring be* (*Genesis* 15:5); about Isaac it is said, *I and the lad* [i.e., Isaac] *will go* כֹּה, *so far* [yonder] (ibid. 22:5); and of Jacob the Torah states, כֹּה, *so shall you say to the House of Jacob*

אֵי כֹּה הַבְטָחַת עֲקֻדִּים נְקֻדִּים[1] בְּמַשּׁוּאוֹת,

Where is ‹ [the merit of the word] *so,* « in the promise [to Jacob] ‹ [of an abundance] of ringed ‹ and speckled [sheep] ‹ in the vision at night? «

אִם כֹּה יֹאמַר[2] כֹּה יוּחַשׁ אוֹת,

If [with sheep marked] ‹ **so** [is your wage], « [Laban] would say, « thus ‹ was swiftly fulfilled ‹ the sign. «

וְהֵן עַתָּה וּכִּחַתְּ עִיר מְלֵאָה תְּשׁוּאוֹת,[3]

But indeed ‹ now ‹ You admonished ‹ the City, [Jerusalem,] ‹ once filled ‹ with multitudes. «

הָרִימָה פְעָמֶיךָ לְמַשֻּׁאוֹת.[4]

Lift up ‹ Your footsteps [to punish the enemy] ‹ who wreaked the ruin [of the City]. «

אֵי כֹּה זָם וְהָרַג מִצְרִי בְּגַן נָעוּל[5] בַּקֹּדֶשׁ,

Where is ‹ [the merit of the word] *so,* « when with full intent ‹ [Moses] killed ‹ an Egyptian ‹ in midst [of the Israelites, who are like] a garden ‹ locked in ‹ with holiness? «

וַיִּפֶן כֹּה וָכֹה[6] חֻתַּם בַּעֲדַת קֹדֶשׁ,

He turned ‹ like **so** ‹ and like **so**, « and [the Egyptian's death] was kept sealed ‹ within the congregation [of Israel] ‹ that is holy. «

וְהֵן עַתָּה חֶלְקָם אֻכַּל חֹדֶשׁ,[7]

But indeed ‹ now, « their portion ‹ was devoured ‹ in the [tragic] month, «

כָּל הֵרַע אוֹיֵב בַּקֹּדֶשׁ.[4]

when everything ‹ was harmed ‹ by the enemy ‹ in the Sanctuary. «

---

(1) *Genesis* 31:11-13. (2) 31:8. (3) Cf. *Isaiah* 22:2. (4) *Psalms* 74:3. (5) Cf. *Song of Songs* 4:12; see *Shemos Rabbah* 1:29. (6) *Exodus* 2:12. (7) Cf. *Hosea* 5:7, see *Rashi* there.

(*Exodus* 19:3; *Bereishis Rabbah* 43:8).

When God utilizes the term כֹּה, He demonstrates an intense degree of הַשְׁגָּחָה פְּרָטִית, *Divine Providence*, and reveals manifest love for His Chosen People. This *kinnah* laments that all the merits of the Patriarchs, the *Kohanim*, and various other personages and events that Scripture describes with the word כֹּה, *so*, could not prevent the Temple's destruction when Israel turned away from God's service, and God concealed His Presence from the nation.

The events recalled are: בְּרִית בֵּין הַבְּתָרִים, *the Covenant Between the Parts* (*Genesis* Ch. 15); עֲקֵדַת יִצְחָק, *the offering of Isaac* (ibid., Ch. 22); the dream in which Jacob was promised prosperity despite Laban's dishonesty in paying Jacob's wages (ibid. 31:1-16); Moses' killing an Egyptian task-

אֵי כֹּה טוֹב* כְּשֻׁלַּח גְּאוֹל עֲבָדֶיךָ,

Where is [the merit of the word] *so,* with Tov[iah, Moses],* when he was sent to redeem Your servants?

כֹּה תֹאמַר[1] **לְשַׁלַּח עָם לְעָבְדֶךָ,**

So [You said], shall you say, sent out must this nation be to serve You.

וְהֵן עַתָּה יָשְׁבוּ בוֹגְדִים בְּבֵית וְעוּדֶיךָ,

But indeed now, occupy do traitors Your House of Meeting:

שָׁאֲגוּ צֹרְרֶיךָ בְּקֶרֶב מוֹעֲדֶיךָ.[2]

Roared have your oppressors amidst Your meeting place.

אֵי כֹּה כְּרִיתוּת חֲדָשׁוֹת בְּרִיתוֹת,*

Where is [the merit of the word] *so,* when were established new covenants,*

(1) *Exodus* 3:14. (2) *Psalms* 74:4.

master who had been beating a Jew (*Exodus* 2:11-12); Moses' encounter with God at the Burning Bush, where he was charged with redeeming the Israelite slaves from Egypt (ibid. 3:1-4:17); the Covenant of Circumcision and the *pesach*-offering (ibid. 12:43-50); the Giving of the Torah at Mount Sinai (ibid. Chs. 19-20); the Priestly Blessing (*Numbers* 6:22-27); Balaam's attempted curses that were transformed into blessings (ibid. Chs. 22-24); the selection of the Tribe of Levi to minister in the Sanctuary (ibid. 8:5-22); the conquest of Jericho (*Joshua* Ch. 6); and the more than four hundred prophecies recorded in Scripture that begin with the words כֹּה אָמַר ה׳, *so said* HASHEM.

The first line of each stanza begins אֵי כֹּה, *Where is [the merit of the word] "so,"* followed by the respective letter of the *aleph-beis.* The third line begins וְהֵן עַתָּה, *But indeed now . . .,* followed by the next letter of the alphabet. The last stich of each stanza is taken from the first ten verses of Psalm 74. The author of the *kinnah,* R' Elazar HaKalir (whose name, atypically, does not appear), draws upon the verses of this psalm to express Israel's bewilderment and confusion over the drastic change in their relationship with God, a change that brought about their ruination.

טוֹב — *Tov[iah, Moses].* Expounding on the verse that describes the birth of Moses, *And she [Yocheved] saw that he [her newborn son] was* טוֹב, *good* (*Exodus* 2:2), the Talmud explains that she named him טוֹבִיָּה, which means *God is good* (*Sotah* 12a). Pharaoh's daughter named him מֹשֶׁה, *Moses,* three months later when she drew him out of the waters of the Nile (*Exodus* 2:10).

[Although popularly pronounced as if it were spelled טוּבְיָה, *Tuvyah,* lit., *goodness of God,* the proper vowelization of this name is טוֹבִיָּה (see for example, *Zechariah* 6:10 and *Ezra* 2:60).]

כְּרִיתוּת חֲדָשׁוֹת בְּרִיתוֹת — *When were established new covenants.* When the Israelites were to be set free from Egyptian slavery, they had no merits by which to be redeemed. So God gave them the *mitzvah* of the *pesach*-offering, but forbade the uncircumcised from partaking of it

בְּכֹה אָמַר כַּחֲצוֹת לַיְלָה בְּמוֹפְתֵי אוֹתוֹת,[1]

« signs! ‹ [I shall go out] with miraculous ‹ of the night ‹ At about the middle « says [HASHEM]: ‹ with the word **So**

וְהֵן עַתָּה לְהֵקוּ בְּנַעֲלֵיהֶם לֶאֱתוֹת,

« to come [into the Temple]. ‹ wearing their shoes ‹ they have gathered ‹ now, ‹ But indeed

שָׂמוּ אוֹתוֹתָם אוֹתוֹת.*[2]

« *to be signs [for them]!** ‹ *their [Israel's] signs* ‹ *They [mistakenly] made*

אֵי כֹּה מִשְׁמַע וּמֹשֶׁה עָלָה,

« ascended [Mount Sinai]? ‹ when Moses ‹ which was heard « [the merit of the word] **so**, ‹ Where is

כֹּה תֹאמַר[3] לִנְוַת בַּיִת מְעֻלָּה,

« who are distinguished [women]. ‹ in the home ‹ unto the dwellers ‹ *shall you say* ‹ [God said,] **So**

וְהֵן עַתָּה נֶאֱצוּהָ בְּנֵי עַוְלָה,

« of iniquity [do], ‹ — the sons ‹ they blaspheme Him ‹ now, ‹ But indeed

יִוָּדַע כְּמֵבִיא לְמַעְלָה.[4]

« *on [God] above.* ‹ *as bringing [an attack]* ‹ and *it had been regarded*

(1) *Exodus* 11:4. (2) *Psalms* 74:4. (3) *Exodus* 19:3. (4) *Psalms* 74:5; some editions read, וְהֵן עַד עַתָּה לֹא שָׁבוּ בְּנֵי גוֹלָה, *Behold how, until now, the exiles have not returned*, but this fits neither the alphabetic nor the repetitive aspects of the *kinnah*. It may be the result of a censor's whim.

(*Exodus* 12:44,48). Since most of them had not been circumcised in Egypt, they had to submit to the covenant of *milah* before they could offer the *pesach*. Then the blood of the *milah* and the blood of the offerings mingled. And it was in the merit of these two blood-related *mitzvos* that the nation was redeemed (*Shemos Rabbah* 19:5). The *paytan* refers to these *mitzvos* as "new covenants," since one, the *pesach*, was indeed new, and the other, *milah*, had fallen into disuse and was then renewed.

שָׂמוּ אוֹתוֹתָם אוֹתוֹת — *They [mistakenly] made their [Israel's] signs to be signs [for them].* These words refer to the destruction of the First *Beis HaMikdash* at the hands of Nebuchadnezzar. He received heavenly signs which were meant to encourage his assault on Jerusalem and he was wise enough to pay heed to those messages. Thus *they* [the attackers] *made their* [Heaven-sent] *signs to be* [meaningful] *signs*.

Nebuchadnezzar had not been sure whether to attack Israel or Ammon, so he had consulted seers, who foretold victory over Israel. He then shot arrows into the air, aimed in all directions. He observed that all of the arrows flew toward the south, in the direction of the Holy Land (Babylon is in the north). Thus assured,

(1) *Numbers* 6:23. (2) Cf. *Song of Songs* 3:7. (3) *Psalms* 74:5.

he confidently marched to Jerusalem (*Midrash Shocher Tov* 74:4).

Some interpret the passage as an allusion to the Destruction of the Second *Beis HaMikdash.* The Talmud describes how Titus entered the Temple, unsheathed his sword, and stabbed the holy פָּרוֹכֶת, *Partition Curtain,* for he imagined that he could thereby cut God away from Israel. Blood began to flow from the curtain. Titus interpreted this as an אוֹת, *sign,* that he had slain God Himself (*Gittin* 56b). The blood was actually a Divine sign to Israel that God was "suffering" over their tragic plight. Thus, *they* [the Romans] made אוֹתוֹתָם, *their signs* [the ones intended for encouraging Israel], for אוֹתוֹת, *signs* [for themselves and in their own favor] (*Sforno*).

שִׁשִּׁים אוֹתִיּוֹת הַקְּדוּמוֹת — *The sixty-letter premier [benediction].* בִּרְכַּת כֹּהֲנִים, *the Priestly Blessing,* contains exactly sixty letters. These are alluded to in the verse, *Behold the couch of the King of Peace, sixty of Israel's mightiest warriors surround it* (*Song of Songs* 3:7). Since all the blessings promised in the Torah are contingent upon Israel's fulfillment of the *mitzvos* (see, e.g., *Leviticus* 22:3-13 and *Deuteronomy* 28:1-14), while the Priestly Blessing is given with no conditions attached, it is called "the premier benediction" (*Beis Levi*).

בִּסְבָךְ עֵץ קַרְדֻּמּוֹת — *As against the thicket of the trees [the gates of the Temple] are the axes [wielded].* The Talmud (*Sanhedrin* 96b) relates that when the Babylonian multitudes laid siege to Jerusalem, King Nebuchadnezzar sent to his general Nebuzaradan 300 mules laden with axes made of specially hardened iron which could smash through barriers of iron. At first the Babylonians were entirely unsuccessful and they wasted this entire stock of unique weapons on an assault on just one of Jerusalem's many gates, all to no avail; the axes shattered while the gate held firm. Nebuzaradan was completely demoralized and he wished to lift the siege and retreat, for he feared that he would meet the disastrous fate of Sennacherib whose vast army perished to a man when he besieged the Holy City. But a בַּת קוֹל, *heavenly voice,* resounded and said to Nebuzaradan, "Don't be hasty. The moment has just arrived for the Temple to be destroyed and the Sanctuary to be consumed in fire." Nebuzaradan had but one axe left in his arsenal. He threw it at the gate and it didn't even strike it with

אֵי כֹּה פָּץ לָקוֹב עָם וּבֵרַךְ עַם קְדוֹשֶׁיךָ,

Where is ‹ [the merit of the word] *so,* ‹‹ when [Balaam] opened his mouth ‹ to curse ‹ the nation, ‹‹ but instead blessed ‹ Your nation ‹ that is holy? ‹‹

בְּשׁוּב **וְכֹה** תְדַבֵּר[1] הוּמַר לִקְדוֹשֶׁיךָ,

With [Your command,] *Return* ‹ *[to Balak,] and* **so** ‹ *shall you say,* ‹‹ [the curses] were transformed ‹ [into blessings] for Your holy ones. ‹‹

וְהֵן עַתָּה צָרוּ עַל עִיר קָדְשֶׁךָ,

But indeed, ‹ now, ‹ they have laid siege ‹ to ‹ Your City ‹ that is holy; ‹‹

שִׁלְּחוּ בָאֵשׁ מִקְדָּשֶׁךָ.[2]

they have sent ‹ up in flames ‹ Your Sanctuary. ‹‹

אֵי כֹּה קִיחַת לְוִיִּם שְׁלֵמֶיךָ,

Where is ‹ [the merit of the word] *so,* ‹‹ with the taking [into Your service] ‹ of the Levites, ‹‹ Your perfect [attendants], ‹‹

כֹּה תַעֲשֶׂה לָהֶם לְטַהֲרָם[3] לְבֵית עוֹלָמֶיךָ,

[with the words], **So** ‹ *shall you do* ‹ *to them* ‹ *to purify them* ‹ for your Eternal Temple? ‹‹

וְהֵן עַתָּה רָעֲשׁוּ וְהִרְעִישׁוּ שָׁמֶיךָ,

But indeed, ‹ now, ‹ they have shaken [the Temple on earth], ‹‹ causing to tremble ‹ [the Temple in] Your heaven; ‹‹

לָאָרֶץ חִלְּלוּ מִשְׁכַּן שְׁמֶךָ.[2]

to the ground ‹ they have desecrated ‹ the Abode ‹ of Your Name. ‹‹

אֵי כֹּה שִׁבְעַת שׁוֹפְרוֹת עֶרֶץ,

Where is ‹ [the merit of the word] *so,* ‹‹ [when at Jericho] the seven ‹ ram's horns ‹ were powerfully [blown]? ‹‹

(1) *Numbers* 23:5. (2) *Psalms* 74:7. (3) Cf. *Numbers* 8:7.

its metal head, but with its dull wooden handle, yet it smashed the iron gate wide open! This fulfilled King David's prophetic lamentation, *It is regarded as an attack on [God] above, its axes are in the wooden thicket* (*Psalms* 74:5), i.e., this wondrous assault on the gates of the earthly Temple below was tantamount to an attack on the celestial Temple Above (*Rashi* ibid.).

כֹּה תַעֲשֶׂה שֵׁשֶׁת יָמִים[1] לְהַפִּיל חוֹמָה לָאָרֶץ,

[You said,] **So** 〈 shall you do 〈 for six 〈 days, 〈 to topple 〈 the wall 〈 to the earth. «

וְהֵן עַתָּה שְׁעָרִים טָבְעוּ בָאָרֶץ,[2]

But indeed, 〈 now, 〈 the gates [of the Temple] 〈 have sunk 〈 into the earth; «

שָׂרְפוּ כָל מוֹעֲדֵי אֵל בָּאָרֶץ.[3]

[and] they have burned 〈 all 〈 of the meeting places 〈 of God 〈 on earth. «

אֵי **כֹּה** תְּשׁוּעוֹת אֲסָמֵי אוֹצָר,

Where is 〈 [the merit of the word] *so,* « assuring salvation 〈 from the abundance 〈 of the storehouse [the Temple], «

בְּ**כֹה** אָמַר אֲשֶׁר לַחוֹזִים נָצָר,[4]

[with the words], **So** 〈 *says [HASHEM],* « that 〈 for His prophets 〈 He preserved. «

וְהֵן עַתָּה תְּפֻחוּ פִרְחַי בֶּחָצֵר,

But indeed, 〈 now, 〈 bloated [from starvation], 〈 My young *kohanim* 〈 lie in [the Temple] courtyard. «

עַד מָתַי אֱלֹהִים יְחָרֶף צָר.[5]

Until 〈 when, 〈 O God, « revile 〈 will the tormentor? «

---

(1) *Joshua* 6:3. (2) Cf. *Eichah* 2:9. (3) *Psalms* 74:8.
(4) Some editions read אֲשֶׁר לַדּוֹרוֹת נָצָר, *for the generations designated.* (5) *Psalms* 74:10.

KINNAH 14 / קינה יד

אֵיכָה* אֶת אֲשֶׁר כְּבָר עָשׂוּהוּ,[1]
« they had done it, ‹ already ‹ which ‹ that for ‹ How is it*

תָּבַע מֶנִּי לִגְבּוֹת נְשִׁיֵּהוּ,
« of His debt. ‹ the repayment ‹ from me ‹ [God] demanded

אֲשֶׁר עַד לֹא שְׁחָקִים נִמְתָּחוּ,
‹ been stretched out, ‹ had the heavens ‹ not yet ‹ while ‹ For

בְּשֶׁלִּי רָמַז הֱיוֹת אֶרֶץ תֹּהוּ.[2]
«*is astonishingly [empty].* ‹ *the earth,* [the Temple,] ‹ it would be that « He hinted, « because of me,

בִּלַּע בְּאוֹת עַרְבִית וְשַׁחֲרִית,[3]
« and [of rebuilding as] morning; ‹ [of Destruction as] evening ‹ an omen ‹ He revealed

(1) *Ecclesiastes* 2:12. (2) *Genesis* 1:2. (3) Cf. 1:5.

אֵיכָה — *How is it.* From the very beginning of Creation, God foresaw that the *Beis HaMikdash* would be built, destroyed, and rebuilt. Thus, the Torah states: בְּרֵאשִׁית בָּרָא אֱלֹהִים, *In the beginning God created* (*Genesis* 1:1), an allusion to building . . .; then, וְהָאָרֶץ הָיְתָה תֹהוּ וָבֹהוּ, *the earth was astonishingly empty* (1:2), a hint of destruction . . .; finally, וַיֹּאמֶר אֱלֹהִים יְהִי אוֹר, *God said, "Let there be light"* (1:3), indicating a rebuilding (*Midrash Bereishis Rabbah* 2:5). This *kinnah* describes how all the Patriarchs and forebears of the Jewish people were privy to foreknowledge regarding the first two phases, but were not permitted to learn the secret of the third phase — the time of the End — when the Temple will be rebuilt.

R' Moshe Chaim Luzzatto explains in *Daas Tevunos* that God created the forces of evil in this world — and allows them to temporarily overpower the good — to provide the good with an opportunity to summon forth all of its latent inner strength and to ultimately obliterate evil. The triumph of the dark forces over those of light is always temporary, because the light is destined to burst out with hitherto untapped brilliance to ultimately wash away the stain of darkness. The Midrash (ibid.) concludes that the prophet Isaiah also had this idea in mind when he proclaimed: *Arise and shine, for your light has arrived, and the glory of* HASHEM *has dawned upon you. For, behold, darkness shall shroud the earth and deep gloom the nations, but* HASHEM *will dawn over you and His glory will be visible over you. And the nations shall walk by your shining light and kings by the brightness of your rising!* (*Isaiah* 60:1-3).

In the intricate tapestry of this *kinnah*, R' Elazar HaKalir wove together a triple *aleph-beis* and his signature (for the most part doubled). Each group of three stanzas is arranged in the following format: The first words of stanzas one and two are taken from the respective verses in Chapter Two of *Eichah;* the next word and the first word of line three begin with the same letter as that

גֵּאֶה מַגִּיד מֵרֵאשִׁית אַחֲרִית,[1]

« the final outcome. ‹ at the very beginning, ‹ announced ‹ thus the Glorious One

בָּנוּי וְחָרֵב וּבָנוּי בְּאַחֲרִית,

« in the end, ‹ and then rebuilt ‹ and destroyed ‹ It would be built

וּמֵחוֹבִי קַלְקָלָתוֹ הֶחֱרִית.

« was engraved. ‹ that its ruination ‹ yet it was because of my guilt

הֶחֱרִית אִישׁוֹן חֹשֶׁךְ מְיֻדָּע,

« so that it would be known, ‹ and the dark [of the Temple's Destruction] ‹ the blackness ‹ God engraved [in the Torah]

וְקַדְמוֹנִים חֲזָוּהוּ מְגֻדָּע,

« cut down. ‹ had visions of it ‹ and the ancient [Patriarchs and prophets]

אָז לְרָאשֵׁי דוֹרוֹת נִתּוּצוֹ נוֹדַע,

« was known. ‹ its shattering ‹ of the generations ‹ to the leaders ‹ Long ago

עַד לֹא עֲשׂוּי קַרְנוֹתָיו גָּדַע.[2]

« was already cut down. ‹ [the Temple's] pride ‹ completed, ‹ not yet ‹ While

גָּדַע גֹּבַהּ קוֹמַת יְצִיר צָר,*

« He had fashioned;* ‹ the being « stature of [Adam,] ‹ the towering ‹ He cut down

זֶה סֵפֶר[3] לְפָנָיו הוּבְצָר,

«was revealed; ‹ before him ‹ book [of the descendants of Adam] ‹ this very

---

(1) *Isaiah* 46:10. (2) *Eichah* 2:3. (3) *Genesis* 5:1.

---

word; the third stanzas of the respective group contain a double acrostic of the author's name, אֶלְעָזָר בֵּירַבִּי קַלִּיר, *Elazar son of R' Kalir;* the last word of the second stanza is repeated as the first word of the third, and the last word of the third is repeated as the first word of the following stanza.

גָּדַע גֹּבַהּ קוֹמַת יְצִיר צָר — *He cut down the towering stature of [Adam,] the being He had fashioned.* Before Adam sinned by eating the forbidden fruit, he stood from the earth to heaven (see *Chagigah* 12a). His spiritual capacity was virtually limitless. There was no facet of creation, from the most mundane to the most sublime,

גָּלְמִי רָאוּ עֵינֶיךָ[1] הִפְצַר,

[when] my unshaped [future] form › was seen by › Your eyes, » [Adam] prayed for their wellbeing, »

כְּהֶעֱבִיר לְפָנָיו כָּל נֶעֱצָר.*

as You passed › before him › all [the unborn souls] › stored [in heaven].* »

דָּרַךְ דֹּחַף מִבֵּית הָאוֹצָר,

Just as he stepped in, » he was pushed out › of the house › of treasure [Eden]. »

וְהֶרְאָהוּ כִּי הַמַּצָּע קָצָר,*[2]

Thus God demonstrated to him › that › the sleeping pad › is too short.* »

דָּוֶה לִבּוֹ כְּבָט בְּבִיאַת צָר,

Suffer › did [Adam's] heart › upon foreseeing › the entry › of the enemy [into the Temple]; »

וַיְקוֹנֵן עָלָיו אֵיכָה בְּאַיֶּכָּה*[3] בְּעֵת צָר.

and he lamented › over [the Temple's destruction] » — [saying,] *Eichah!* » [but caused by Adam's sin when God's called], *Ayechah? Where are you?* —* » in the time › of distress? »

(1) *Psalms* 139:16. (2) Cf. *Isaiah* 28:20. (3) *Genesis* 3:9.

that Adam did not encompass. Nothing was hidden from him. More — no one ever comprehended better than he how each of his actions could determine the course of creation. However, after Adam sinned, God laid His hand upon him and diminished his stature until he was able to hide *among the trees of the Garden* (*Genesis* 3:8; *Bereishis Rabbah* 19:9).

כְּהֶעֱבִיר לְפָנָיו כָּל נֶעֱצָר — *As You passed before him all [the unborn souls] stored [in heaven].* Adam foresaw the fate of all future generations, as Scripture relates: זֶה סֵפֶר תּוֹלְדֹת אָדָם, *This is the account* [lit., *book*] *of the descendants of Adam* (*Genesis* 5:1). The Talmud (*Avodah Zarah* 5a) explains that this verse implies that God showed Adam every generation with its expositors, sages, and leaders.

כִּי הַמַּצָּע קָצָר — *That the sleeping pad is too short;* when man arrogantly defies God there is no room for both of them to dwell together, and man must be dismissed. Interestingly, this verse also alludes to the Destruction of the *Beis HaMikdash*. The Talmud (*Sanhedrin* 103b; *Yoma* 9b) relates that when the sinful King Menasheh placed an idol in the Sanctuary, God said, "The couch is too short to support a man and his two wives"; the *Beis HaMikdash*, in which God made His Presence rest, could not tolerate the rival, idolatrous worship. And so it was to be destroyed.

אֵיכָה בְּאַיֶּכָּה — *"Eichah!" but caused by Adam's sin . . . "Where are you?"* When Adam and Eve tried to hide their nakedness after eating the forbidden fruit, God

צוּר הֶרְאָה לוֹ מַה שֶּׁהָיָה,

« was already done: ‹ that the [Temple Destruction] ‹ him, [the enemy,] ‹ showed ‹ The Rock

נֻתַּץ קִיר נָטוּי וְגָדֵר הַדְּחוּיָה,[1]

« already toppled. ‹ and a fence ‹ that already was leaning ‹ was a wall ‹ smashed

לְדוֹרוֹת לִמֵּד נְהוֹת נְהִי נִהְיָה,[2]

‹ that came to be ‹ a lamentation ‹ to lament ‹ God taught « But for the generations,

עַל שֶׁבֶר אֲשֶׁר הָיָה.

« it actually happened. ‹ when ‹ the Destruction ‹ over

הָיָה הַנּוֹעָר מִמִּזְרָח,[3]

« to come from the East, ‹ [Abraham,] the one inspired ‹ It was when

בֵּין בְּתָרִים[4] אוֹרוֹ כְּזָרַח,

« shone forth, ‹ his light [of prophecy] ‹ the Parts ‹ who at [the Covenant] Between

וְהֶרְאָהוּ אַרְבַּע מַלְכֻיּוֹת בְּרֶדֶם וְצָרַח,

‹ and he screamed, « while [Abraham] slept, ‹ Kingdoms ‹ [the subjugation by] the Four ‹ that [God] showed him

כִּי טָבַע שַׁעַר הַמִּזְרָח.[5]

« at the East. ‹ did the [Temple] Gate ‹ sink [into the earth] ‹ for

וַיַּחְמוֹס וַיְנַצֵּל זֵרָהּ,

« of her crown. ‹ and stripped her ‹ He cut down [the Temple]

(1) Cf. *Psalms* 62:4. (2) Cf. *Micah* 2:4. (3) Cf. *Isaiah* 41:2.
(4) See *Genesis* 15. (5) Cf. *Eichah* 2:9.

approached to admonish them with the word, "אַיֶּכָּה, *Where are you?"* The *paytan* plays on the similarity between that word and אֵיכָה, *How is it*. Both words are spelled with the same letters and differ only in vowelization. Thus, they are taken as an allusion that the ultimate cause of the Destruction was Adam's initial sin. The commentators disagree regarding the speaker of the word אֵיכָה in this comparison. Either it was said by God after the actual Destruction, or it was spoken by Adam when he was shown the vision of the Destruction.

וַיַּרְא הַשְׁלָכַת נִזְרָהּ,*

« of her crown;* ‹ the throwing-away ‹ [Abraham] saw

וְאֵימָה נוֹפֶלֶת עָלָיו כִּבְזוּרָה,[1]

« when [he saw his children] scattered. ‹ upon him ‹ was falling ‹ and a fear

וְצִדֵּק מִדַּת הַדִּין כְּאָז רָאָה.

« [given all that] he foresaw. ‹ even then « of Strict Justice, ‹ of the [Divine] Attribute ‹ Yet, he affirmed the righteousness

רָאָה עֵרוֹם וְעֶרְיָה[2] וְנֶאֱנַח,

« and he sighed, ‹ and bare ‹ [his exiled children] naked ‹ He foresaw

וְלַעֲקוּדוֹ סוֹד זֶה פִּעֲנַח,

« he revealed; ‹ this secret [of the exile] ‹ and to his bound [son Isaac]

עָשְׁשָׁה מִכַּעַס עֵינוֹ[3] וְלֹא נָח

‹ and he could not rest « was his eye, ‹ because of anger ‹ dimmed

מֵרְאוֹת גִּזְעוֹ טוֹב זָנַח.[4]

« forsaking. ‹ the Benevolent One « his offspring, ‹ because he saw

זָנַח זֹהַר תָּם בַּמַּחֲזֶה,

« in the vision [that Israel would ascend and not descend], ‹ did the wholesome one [Jacob] ‹ the glorious promise ‹ Forsake

(1) Cf. *Genesis* 15:12. (2) Cf. *Ezekiel* 16:7. (3) Cf. *Psalms* 6:8. (4) Cf. *Hosea* 8:3.

נִזְרָהּ . . . זֵרָהּ — *Her crown . . . her crown.* Some commentators understand this as an allusion to the three crowns spoken of in *Avos* (4:17). They are the crowns of Torah scholarship, priesthood, and kingship. When the *Beis HaMikdash* was destroyed, Israel had to forfeit these three crowns. This interpretation is difficult because only two crowns are mentioned in the *kinnah.*

Perhaps the *paytan* means to teach that although the crown of priesthood was lost with the Destruction, and the crown of kingship was lost with the Exile, the crown of Torah can never be removed from the Jewish people, despite their centuries-long homeless wandering through the Diaspora.

Alternatively, this refers to the three "crowned" vessels in the Sanctuary: הָאָרוֹן, *the Ark,* in which the Tablets of the Ten Commandments rested (see *Exodus* 25:11); הַשֻּׁלְחָן, *the Table,* for the *Panim* Loaves (ibid. 25:24); and הַמִּזְבֵּחַ,

כִּי לֹא הֶאֱמִין* בִּנְאֻם זֶה,

《this pronouncement; 〈 he did not believe 〈 for

זָן עֵינוֹ בַּמָּקוֹם הַזֶּה,

《 [from God's sanctity revealed] in this place, 〈 his eyes 〈 yet when he nourished

וְשָׁר שִׁמּוּמוֹ וַיְקוֹנֵן אֵין זֶה.[1]

《 *will this be!* 〈 *Gone* 《 and lamented, 〈 its devastation 〈 he foresaw

חָשַׁב חֲשׁוּשׁ בְּעוֹלִים וְיוֹרְדִים,

《 who then descend [the celestial ladder], 〈 would be among the ascenders 〈 and was worried [that he too] 〈 He pondered

וַיָּבֶן כִּי בוֹ יִהְוּ רוֹדִים,

《 oppressively rule. 〈 [the nations] would 〈 over him 《 that [for his lack of faith], 〈 then he under-stood

חֲנִיכָיו עַל מֶה בְּדִינוֹ חֲרֵדִים,

《 are they terrorized, 〈 of His judgment 〈 what grounds 〈 on 《 His disciples [Israel],

וּמֵהֶם תָּבַע זְבוּל מוֹרְדִים.

《 by [the heathen] rebels? 〈 [the Destruction of] the Temple 〈 He demands 〈 and from them

(1) *Genesis* 28:17.

the Golden *Altar*, upon which the Incense was offered (ibid. 30:3). The Talmud correlates: (a) the Altar's crown with the crown of priesthood that Aaron merited and took for his descendants; (b) the Table's crown with the crown of kingship (as in the expression, שֻׁלְחָן שֶׁל מְלָכִים, *a royal table*) that David merited and took for his offspring; and (c) the Ark's crown with the crown of Torah scholarship, but that crown is still available and whoever desires to wear it can attain it [through diligent study] (*Yoma* 72b).

כִּי לֹא הֶאֱמִין — *For he did not believe.* The Midrash relates that when God showed our father Jacob, in the vision of the ladder, that all the major empires ascend and then descend the ladder, He invited Jacob to ascend also. However, Jacob expressed his fear that just as each of the empires ascended for a while, but then descended, the same would happen to Israel. God assured Jacob that if he would ascend the ladder, Israel would never descend. Despite the Divine assurance, Jacob was still afraid and didn't ascend. The Midrash continues that Jacob's failure to trust the Divine assurance was a sin and because of it, Israel would be subjugated by each of the empires in this world for a time (*Vayikra Rabbah* 29:2; *Tanchuma Vayetze* 2:2; *Pesikta D'Rav Kahana* 23:2).

מוֹרְדִים זְבוּל וּמַצְפּוּנָיו נִבְעוּ,[1]
« were revealed, ‹ and its hidden [treasures] ‹ the Temple ‹ [To heathen] rebels

וּמַסְמְרוֹת נְעָלֵימוֹ* בְּקַרְקָעִיתוֹ קָבְעוּ,
« they stuck.* ‹ into its floor ‹ studding their shoes ‹ and the nails

זִיו שְׁעָרָיו מִנִּי מַה נִּתְבָּעוּ,
« were they demanded? ‹ why ‹— from me « gates ‹ Its shining

וְהִנָּם טְמוּנִים בָּאָרֶץ כִּי טָבָעוּ.[2]
« they have sunk. ‹ for ‹ in the earth ‹ hidden ‹ Indeed they are

טָבְעוּ טוֹרְדִים לֵידַע זְמָן,
« the time [for the final redemption], ‹ to discover ‹ did [Jacob's] weary [sons] ‹ Demand

כִּי לְגַלּוֹת קֵץ אָב זִמֵּן,[3]
« ready. ‹ was their father ‹ the End [of Days] ‹ to reveal ‹ for

טוֹב מִשֶּׁגִּלָּה לוֹ קֵץ מְזֻמָּן,
« that was appointed, ‹ the End ‹ to him [Jacob] ‹ after revealing ‹ But the Benevolent One

הֵשַׁע וְהִבְלִיג[4] וְקֵץ כָּמָן.
« He hid. ‹ so that the End [of Days] « and held it back, ‹ turned it away [from him]

יָשְׁבוּ וְשָׁאֲלוּ לְאָב לֵידַע,
‹ to make known ‹ their father ‹ and beseeched ‹ They sat

זְמַן קֵץ הַפְּלָאוֹת מָתַי יִתְוַדַּע,[5]
« would it be disclosed. ‹ — when « so wondrous ‹ of the End ‹ the time

(1) Cf. *Obadiah* 1:6. (2) Cf. *Eichah* 2:9. (3) See *Rashi* to *Genesis* 49:1.
(4) Cf. *Psalms* 39:14. (5) Cf. *Daniel* 12:6.

וּמַסְמְרוֹת נְעָלֵימוֹ — *And the nails studding their shoes.* In the place so holy that the *Kohanim* were prohibited from wearing shoes while performing the Temple Service, these brazen heathens came tramping in with their nail-studded shoes.

יִקְוּ לְיוֹם יְשׁוּעָה וְלֹא נוֹדַע,

« but it will not be known, ‹ of salvation, ‹ for the day ‹ They waited hopefully

עַד כִּי בְעִתּוֹ יוּחַשׁ[1] וְיִתְוַדַּע.

« and be known. ‹ it will come quickly ‹ at its designated time ‹ when ‹ until

יִתְוַדַּע רָז לִבָּם נִסְתַּכְּלוּ,

‹ looked [heavenward], ‹ their hearts ‹ the secret [of the End] ‹ To discover

וְנִכְסָה מֵהֶם וְלֹא יוּכָלוּ,

« and they were unable [to uncover it]. ‹ from them ‹ but it was concealed

רֵעֶיךָ מִקִּנְאַת בֵּיתְךָ נֶאֱכָלוּ,[2]

« are consumed, ‹ for [the Destruction of] Your House ‹ from the desire for vengeance ‹ Your beloved ones [Israel]

וּבְיָגוֹן חַיֵּימוֹ כָּלוּ.[3]

« are spent. ‹ their lives ‹ and in sorrow

כָּלוּ כִּסְלֵי צִיר כְּשֻׁלָּח,

« when he was sent to [Pharaoh]; ‹ of the emissary [Moses] ‹ were the hopes ‹ Spent

וְנָם שְׁלַח נָא בְּיַד תִּשְׁלָח,[4]

« *[of whomever] You will send;* ‹ *through the hand* ‹ *please,* ‹ he said, *Send,*

כִּי מַה בֶּצַע לִי לְהִשְׁתַּלָּח,

« to be sent [since the Jews will be exiled again], ‹ for me ‹ gain will there be ‹ what ‹ for

וְאַחֲרַי גִּלְעָדִי יְשֻׁלָּח.

« will be sent [to herald the final redemption]? ‹ [Elijah] the Gileadite ‹ and after me

לְאִמּוֹתָם לִבְּבוּ עוֹלְלֵי סוּף,

« at the [Sea of] Reeds, ‹ did the infants ‹ ask with heartfelt sincerity ‹ Of their mothers

---

(6) Cf. *Isaiah* 60:22. (2) Cf. *Psalms* 69:10. (3) Cf. 31:11. (4) *Exodus* 4:13.

אֵיזֶה יוֹם הַכָּסוּף,

« that is yearned for? ‹ the day ‹ Which is

לִבָּם הֵכִין לְשׁוֹרֵר מִסּוּף,[1]

« from the [Sea of] Reeds, ‹ to sing ‹ He prepared ‹ Their hearts

יהוה יִמְלוֹךְ בִּזְרְוֹעַ חָשׂוּף.[2]

« *that is uncovered!* ‹ *through [the power of] His arm* ‹ *shall reign* ‹ *HASHEM*

חָשׂוּף זְרוֹעוֹ בְּיַד רָמָה,

« upraised, ‹ with His hand ‹ is His arm ‹ Uncovered

וְנִגְלָה בִּימִין רוֹמֵמָה,[3]

« upraised. ‹ through [His] right hand ‹ and [His strength] is revealed

בָּנִים כְּשָׁרוּ חֵמָה זְרוּמָה,

« streaming [quickly in Babylon], ‹ [His] wrath ‹ when they saw ‹ The sons [of Israel]

קָצְרָה נַפְשָׁם בְּגֵיא אֱדוֹם לָדַעַת עַל מָה.

« what [reason the exile is so long]. ‹ for ‹ to know « of Edom, ‹ in the [exile of the] valley ‹ was their spirit ‹ impatient

מַה מָּצֵאתָ עַוְלָתָה בִּי,

‹ *in Me* ‹ *that is iniquitous* ‹ *did you find* ‹ [God responded,] *What*

כִּי בָגוֹד בָּגַדְתָּ בִּי,[4]

« *against Me?* ‹ *have you rebelled* ‹ *rebelliously* ‹ *that*

מִמִּדְבָּר הֱמַרְתָּ בִּי,[5]

« *against Me,* ‹ *you have rebelled* ‹ *Since the Wilderness*

וְעַד עַתָּה לֹא הֶאֱמַנְתָּ בִּי.

« *in Me!* ‹ *you still do not believe* ‹ *now* ‹ *and even unto*

1) See *Sotah* 30b. (2) Cf. *Isaiah* 52:10. (3) Cf. *Psalms* 118:16. (4) Cf. *Jeremiah* 5:11. (5) Cf. 2:11.

נְבִיאֶיךָ נִטְעֵי אֲבִיגְדוֹר,[1]
‹ of Avigdor [Moses], ‹ the plantings ‹ Your prophets,

נִשְׁתַּבְּרוּ פְּרָצוֹת לִגְדּוֹר,
« they had [to seek] to repair. ‹ by the many breaches ‹ were broken

נִגְלֵיתִי בְּיוֹם נָקָם[2] לְסַדּוֹר,
« [I told them] to arrange, ‹ of retribution ‹ [and prophecy regarding] a day ‹ I revealed Myself [to them]

וְלֹא קִדְּשׁוּ פָּרִיצֵי הַדּוֹר.
« of the generation. ‹ were the wanton sinners ‹ sanctified [through repentance] ‹ but not

הַדּוֹר יָזְמוּ דַּעַת סוֹד וְדָפְקוּ,
« and pushed [to hasten it], ‹ the secret [time of Messiah's advent] ‹ to know ‹ endeavored ‹ [The Sages of the] generation

הִשְׁבַּעְתִּי אֶתְכֶם*[3] שָׁמְעוּ וּפָקְקוּ,
« and they sealed [their mouths]. ‹ they heard [from God], ‹ *on you* ‹ but then *I imposed an oath*

יַחַד כְּשָׁמְעָם כֵּן נִתְמַקְמָקוּ,
‹ their [hearts] melted « this, ‹ when they heard ‹ Together

וְעַל כַּפַּיִם סָפָקוּ.
« they slapped [in dismay]. ‹ and their hands

סָפְקוּ שָׁשׂוּ בָּאֵי הָאָרֶץ,
« the Land [with Joshua], ‹ did those who entered ‹ and rejoice ‹ But clapped [their hands]

(1) See commentary to *Kinnah* 11. (2) Cf. *Isaiah* 63:4. (3) *Song of Songs* 2:7; 3:5; 5:8; 8:4.

הִשְׁבַּעְתִּי אֶתְכֶם — *But then I imposed an oath on you.* This phrase appears four times in *Song of Songs* (2:7, 3:5, 5:8, 8:4). According to the Midrash, God made Israel take four oaths: That it would not rebel against the sovereign governments; that it would not seek to hasten the End; that it would not reveal the Torah's mysteries to other nations; and that it would not attempt to ascend from the Diaspora by force (*Shir Rabbah* 2:7). When these oaths were demanded of them, the people's hearts melted in anguish.

כִּנְפָּלוּ בְּיָדָם מַלְכֵי אֶרֶץ,
« of the land; ‹ did the kings ‹ into their hands ‹ when fall

סִבְּרוּ כִּי יִשְׁעָם יִרֶץ,
« would show them favor, ‹ their Savior ‹ that ‹ they hoped

וְעַל יָדָם יִתְכּוֹנֵן מְשׂוֹשׂ כָּל הָאָרֶץ.[1]
« the earth. ‹ of all ‹ [Jerusalem,] the joy ‹ would be established ‹ their hand, ‹ and, that through

פָּצוּ פִּיהֶם חַג לַיהוה בְּשִׁילֹה,[2]
« *in Shiloh!* ‹ *for* HASHEM ‹ *A festival* ‹ their mouths [to announce], ‹ They opened

דִּמּוּ כִּי לָעַד יִהְיֶה שָׁם מוֹשְׁלוֹ,
« His reign; ‹ there ‹ would continue ‹ forever ‹ that ‹ They imagined

פָּעֲלוּ שֶׁקֶר וְהִשִּׁילוֹ, עַד כִּי יָבֹא שִׁילֹה.*[3]
« Shiloh [the Messiah].* ‹ arrives ‹ when ‹ — until « so He shed them prematurely ‹ deceitfully, ‹ but they acted

שִׁילֹה רִצָּה כַּחַלָּה מֵעִסָּה,*
« from the dough,* ‹ as if it were *challah* ‹ [God] found favor, ‹ In Shiloh

וְנִמְאַס כַּאֲשֶׁר בּוֹ נַעֲשָׂה,[4]
« were committed [abominations]. ‹ there ‹ when ‹ but it became abhorrent

רְאוּ מַה עֲבֵרָה עוֹשָׂה,
« accomplishes, ‹ sin ‹ what ‹ Observe

לְכֹל אֲשֶׁר חָפֵץ עָשָׂה.[5]
« He does. ‹ He pleases ‹ with [the One Who] whatever

(1) *Psalms* 48:3. (2) Cf. *Judges* 21:19. (3) *Genesis* 49:10. (4) See *I Samuel* 2:11 ff. (5) Cf. *Psalms* 115:3.

שִׁילֹה — *Shiloh [the Messiah.]* The Talmud states four opinions regarding the Messiah's given name: מְנַחֵם, *Menachem;* שִׁילֹה, *Shiloh;* יִנּוֹן, *Yinon;* and חֲנִינָה, *Chaninah* (*Sanhedrin* 98b). It is noteworthy that the initial letters of these four names spell מָשִׁיחַ, *Messiah.*

שִׁילֹה רִצָּה כַּחַלָּה מֵעִסָּה — *In Shiloh [God] found favor, as if it were challah from the dough.* Shiloh was the site of the first permanent Tabernacle. The *paytan* compares this to *challah,* the first portion of dough separated from each batch and presented to a *Kohen.*

עָשָׂה עִמִּי אוֹת[1] בִּצְבְיוֹן,

« when He was pleased; ‹ a sign [of hope] ‹ for me ‹ He displayed

וּלְעִתּוֹ חָשׁ עָלַי קִשְׁיוֹן,

« [our] stubborn defiance. ‹ for ‹ He hastened [retribution] ‹ but at its time,

עֻלַּפְתִּי כְּחוֹרֶב בְּצָיוֹן,[2]

« in a parched land, ‹ as if from scorching heat ‹ I fell faint,

עַד אֲשֶׁר יוֹפִיעַ אֱלֹהִים מִצִּיּוֹן.[3]

« from Zion. ‹ God appears ‹ when ‹ [not revived] until

צָעַק צִיּוֹן אֵיךְ נָתַן, לָשׂוּם עָלַי גּוֹי אֵיתָן,[4]

« *that is powerful;* ‹ *a nation* ‹ *over me* ‹ *there to be placed* ‹ *How did [God] allow* « did Zion, ‹ Cry out,

צָהַל וְרָקַע עַל הַמִּפְתָּן, וּבַחֲמָתוֹ חִתִּיתוֹ נָתָן.[5]

« *instilled?* ‹ *terror of it* « *and with its fury,* « *the [Temple's] threshold,* ‹ *on* ‹ *trampled* ‹ *that cheerfully*

נָתַן בַּעֲתוּתוֹ עֵת הוֹבִילַנִי רוֹקְמִי,

« did the One Who knit me together; ‹ when bring me [into Canaan] ‹ at the time ‹ His awe [upon the nations] ‹ He set

תַּרְתִּי לָעַד בָּהּ לְקוֹמְמִי,

« I would be established. ‹ within it ‹ that for eternity ‹ I imagined

בֹּשְׁתִּי וְגַם נִכְלַמְתִּי[6] בֵּל בַּהֲקִימִי,

« was erected [inside the Temple]; ‹ [when the idol] Bel ‹ humiliated ‹ and also ‹ But I was shamed

וּבָחֳרִי אַף נָם לִי קוּמִי.

« *Get up [and leave this Land]!* « me, ‹ He told ‹ anger ‹ and with a burning

קוּמִי קָשַׁבְתִּי בְּהַזְנָחָה,

« in [His] abandonment, ‹ is what I heard ‹ *Get up!*

---

(1) Cf. *Psalms* 86:17. (2) *Isaiah* 25:5. (3) Cf. *Psalms* 50:2.
(4) Cf. *Jeremiah* 5:15. (5) Cf. *Ezekiel* 32:26. (6) *Jeremiah* 31:18.

קוּמִי וּלְכִי כִּי לֹא זֹאת הַמְּנוּחָה,[1]
« the resting place! ‹ this is not ‹ For « and go out! ‹ Get up,

קַצְתִּי בְחַיַּי[2] מֵאֲנָחָה,
« because of [my incessant] groaning, ‹ with my life, ‹ I have become disgusted

וְהִגַּשְׁתִּי וְלֹא עָרְבָה מִנְחָה.[3]
« was my offering. ‹ pleasing [to Him] ‹ I brought [offerings to God], but not

רְאֵה רֹעַ נַפְשִׁי זְנוּחָה,
‹ that has been rejected ‹ of my spirit ‹ the wretched state ‹ Behold

מִשָּׁלוֹם וּמִשַּׁלְוָה וּמֵהֲנָחָה,
« and from composure, ‹ from serenity, ‹ from peace,

רְטוּשָׁה בְּהָרֵי נֶשֶׁף[4] זְנוּחָה, גַּם שָׁם לֹא נָחָה.
« to find rest. ‹ not able ‹ there ‹ and also « forsaken, ‹ of darkness ‹ and in [Exile's] mountains ‹ torn apart

נָחָה יָדוֹ בָּם וּבָהּ נִכְווּ,
« they were burnt, ‹ and by it ‹ [heavily] upon them ‹ His hand ‹ [God] laid

אֲנוּשִׁים* עַל רֹאשָׁם כְּרָכְבוּ,[5]
« rode. ‹ over their heads ‹ as lowly people*

יָגְעוּ עַל נַהֲרוֹת בָּבֶל[6] כְּנִתְעַכְּבוּ,*
« when they were detained;* ‹ of Babylon ‹ the rivers ‹ along ‹ They were worn down

וְכִעוֹלְלוּ עוֹלְלוּ חוּצָה שָׁכְבוּ.[7]
« lying [asleep]. ‹ out in the open « was done to them, ‹ for what they had done

(1) Cf. *Micah* 2:10. (2) *Genesis* 27:46. (3) Cf. *Malachi* 3:3-4.
(4) Cf. *Jeremiah* 13:16. (5) Cf. *Psalms* 66:12. (6) 137:1. (7) Cf. *Eichah* 2:21.

אֲנוּשִׁים — *Lowly people.* The translation follows *Rashi* (*Jeremiah* 17:9) who renders אָנֻשׁ as *sickly*. According to *Targum* (ibid.) the word means *powerful*. Some editions of *Kinnos* read אֱנוֹשִׁים, *frail mortals.*

יָגְעוּ עַל נַהֲרוֹת בָּבֶל כְּנִתְעַכְּבוּ — *They were worn down along the rivers of Babylon when they were detained.* When the Jewish captives arrived at the Euphrates River, Nebuchadnezzar and his retinue were sailing lei-

שָׁכְבוּ שׁוֹבִים גְּוִיָּם מַדְקִירִים,[1]

« stabbing, ‹ the [Jewish captives'] bodies « did the captors, ‹ Slept [peacefully]

מִתְעוֹלְלִים בָּמוֹ כְּמוֹ בְקָרִים,

« they were cattle. ‹ as if ‹ with them ‹ making sport

שֶׁהֵם יָזֻבוּ מִדְּקָרִים,[2]

« from their stab wounds, ‹ have [their blood] flowing ‹ For they,

וּמֵי פְּרָת קְרָבֵימוֹ דוֹקְרִים.*

« their innards.* ‹ ulcerate ‹ of the Euphrates ‹ while the waters

תִּקְרָא תֹּקֶף טֶבַח וּמֶסֶךְ לְמַבְקִירִים,

« for those who considered [our blood] ownerless, ‹ and the cup [of poison] ‹ [day of] slaughter ‹ a powerful ‹ Proclaim

קִיר עֶרְוָה מְקַרְקְרִים,

« they breached, ‹ that was bared ‹ those who the [Temple] wall

וְכָל עַם וְלָשׁוֹן בָּם סוֹקְרִים,

« watched them; ‹ and tongues ‹ nations ‹ while all

וַעֲלֵיהֶם מְקוֹנְנִים בְּנֵי צִיּוֹן הַיְקָרִים.[3]

« *who were precious.* ‹ *of Zion* ‹ *The children* ‹ [the nations just] lamented: ‹ and over them

(1) Some editions read גְּוִיָּם מַבְקִירִים, *having left their bodies to the elements.*
(2) *Eichah* 4:9. (3) 4:2.

surely on the river while being entertained by musicians. The nobles of Israel trudged by the riverbank, naked and chained together with heavy iron shackles. Nebuchadnezzar noticed them and asked of his attendants, "Why are these captives allowed to walk with noble, upright bearing? Is there no burden we can place on them to bend them over?" The cruel overseers filled huge casks with sand and placed them on the captives' backs until they doubled over from the weight. At that moment all the Jews burst out in tears and their anguished cries arose to the highest heavens (*Midrash Tehillim* 137).

Many editions read גָּעוּ, *they cried,* in place of יָגְעוּ, *they were worn down.* Both versions allude to the same Midrash. However, the format of the *kinnah* indicates that this verse should begin with the letter י.

וּמֵי פְּרָת קְרָבֵימוֹ דוֹקְרִים — *While the waters of the Euphrates ulcerate their innards.* Why did the Jews weep so bitterly by the

הַיְקָרִים קוֹל בְּרָמָה הִשְׁמִיעוּ לִבְכֹּה,[1]

« weeping: ‹ be heard ‹ on high ‹ let a voice ‹ The precious [Patriarchs]

לָמָּה זֶה וְעַל מַה זֶּה הִקְרָנוּ כֹּה,

« *so?* ‹ *happen to us* ‹ *did this* ‹ *what* ‹ *And for* ‹ *is this?* ‹ *Why*

יַחַד זֶה אוֹמֵר בְּכֹה וְזֶה אוֹמֵר בְּכֹה,

« *That is the reason.* ‹ said, ‹ and the other « *This is the reason,* ‹ said, ‹ this one ‹ In unison,

רָגְנוּ לְהָמִיר לְשׁוֹן אֵיכָה

« *How?* ‹ the lamenting expression, ‹ that they wanted to transform ‹ but all complained

בִּלְשׁוֹן אֵי כֹּה.[2]

« *"So [says* HASHEM*"].* « *Where is [the Divine promise of],* ‹ into the expression of promise,

(1) Cf. *Jeremiah* 31:14. (2) See commentary to *Kinnah* 13.

river of Babylon? R' Yochanan taught that the Jews were entirely unaccustomed to the harsh, sharp nature of the waters of the Euphrates River, so it had a lethal effect on them. Far more Jews died as a result of drinking these foreign waters than fell to the sword of Nebuchadnezzar! (*Midrash Tehillim* 137).

KINNAH 15 / קינה טו

אֵיכָה אַשְׁפָּתוֹ* פָּתוּחַ כְּקֶבֶר,[1]

« like a grave [waiting for death], ‹ is open ‹ His quiver* ‹ How is it that

וּלְרוֹדַי בְּאַף הוֹסִיף אֵבֶר, אֲנִי הַגֶּבֶר.

« the man [who has seen affliction by the rod of His anger]. ‹ I am « a wing. ‹ He has added ‹ with fury ‹ and to those who rule over me

אֵיכָה אֶשָּׂא עֲוֹן הָג, וְחֻסַּם פִּי מִפֶּלֶל לַהֲג,

« crying out. ‹ from prayer ‹ was my mouth ‹ Thus, sealed « [God] said? « *[their] sin,* ‹ *can I bear* ‹ *How*

אוֹתִי נָהַג.

« has He driven [into unrelieved darkness]. ‹ Me

אֵיכָה אָץ זַעְמוֹ לִשְׁפּוֹךְ,

« to pour out, ‹ His wrath « He has rushed, ‹ How is it that

הֲכִיל נִלְאֵיתִי וְנָם שְׁפוֹךְ,[2] אַךְ בִּי יָשׁוּב יַהֲפוֹךְ.

« turn [His hand]. ‹ did He repeatedly ‹ against me ‹ But only « *Pour forth!* « And so He said, « *I have tired!* ‹ [saying,] *Of holding back*

זָכוֹר אֲפִיפָתִי בְּשָׁרָב,

« with withering heat in the parched Wilderness, ‹ for which He surrounded me during my wandering ‹ He remembers [my sin with the Golden Calf]

וְנָם כִּי יִנָּטוּ צִלְלֵי עָרֶב,[3]

« *of [Exiles's] evening,* ‹ *the shadows* ‹ *shall lengthen* ‹ *When* « He said,

וְהֵבֵאתִי עֲלֵיכֶם חָרֶב.

« *a sword [as final punishment for that sin]!* ‹ *against you* ‹ *I will bring*

---

(1) Cf. *Jeremiah* 5:16. (2) Cf. 6:11. (3) 6:4.

אֵיכָה אַשְׁפָּתוֹ — *How is it that His quiver.* The longest and most intricate of our Tishah B'Av recitations, this *kinnah* was composed by R' Elazar HaKalir, based on two Scriptural sources. As explained in the Overview, the longest and the most sorrowful section of Jeremiah's *Eichah* is the third chapter which he composed after King Yehoyakim brazenly burnt the original version of *Eichah*.

בָּכֹה תִבְכֶּה בְּעֵת כֹּל חָסַרְתִּי,

« did I lose, ‹ that everything ‹ At the time « and weeps, ‹ She [Zion] weeps

וּכְעָזְבִי אֹרַח יִסְּרָנִי,[1] בִּלָּה בְשָׂרִי וְעוֹרִי.

« He punished me; ‹ the [righteous] path ‹ and when I abandoned « and my skin. ‹ my flesh ‹ He has worn away

בִּלַּע בַּיִת לָרוּם מֻזְקָף,

« had been erected, ‹ that to lofty heights ‹ the Temple ‹ He destroyed

וְכַבַּרְזֶל סֻבְּכֵי נִקַּף,[2] בָּנָה עָלַי וַיַּקַּף.

« been pruned [my major branches — the righteous]. ‹ have my branches ‹ and as with iron « and encircled me [with troubles]. ‹ around me ‹ He built siege walls

בְּנֵי בִטְנִי לֶאֱכוֹל[3] הִקְשִׁיבַנִי,

« so he [Moses] informed me. « I would be forced to eat, ‹ of my womb ‹ [It was foretold that] the children

מִפְּנֵי צָר אָחוֹר הֱשִׁיבַנִי,[4] בְּמַחֲשַׁכִּים הוֹשִׁיבַנִי.

« He forced us, ‹ to retreat ‹ the oppressor ‹ [And this occurred when] from before « He placed me. ‹ [and] in darkness [like the eternally dead]

נַחֲלוֹתֵינוּ בְּנֶטְשׁוּ בְּיַד לוֹחֵם,

« of the [enemy] soldier, ‹ into the hand ‹ when it was abandoned ‹ Our heritage [the Temple]

נָם לֹא אָחוּס וְלֹא אֲרַחֵם,[5]

« nor show compassion [for you], ‹ I will not have pity « He said,

בְּשִׁבְרִי לָכֶם מַטֵּה לֶחֶם.

« of bread! ‹ the staff ‹ for you ‹ When I break

(1) Cf. *Proverbs* 15:10. (2) Cf. *Isaiah* 10:34. (4) Cf. *Deuteronomy* 28:53.
(5) Cf. *Psalms* 44:11. (5) *Jeremiah* 13:14.

That chapter vividly foretells the impending *Churban* in alphabetic sequence, using three verses for every letter of the Hebrew alphabet. Essential segments of all those verses are cited in this *kinnah*. The second major component of this lament is the *Tochachah / Admonition* recorded in *Leviticus* (Ch. 26), in which Moses graphically predicted the Destruction of the First Temple, which came to pass in Jeremiah's day some 900 years later. *Ramban* in his commentary

גָּלְתָה גְּהוּצָה לַעֲטוֹת עֲדִי,

« with [spiritual] crowns [at Sinai]. ‹ [in order] to adorn herself ‹ who cleansed herself [of sin] ‹ Exiled is she

מֵחֻפָּה לִגְלוֹת בְּהִתְעַתְּדִי, גָּדַר בַּעֲדִי.

« *opposite me [to keep me in exile].* ‹ *[She cries,] He has built a wall* « she was destined [because of the Golden Calf]. ‹ to be exiled ‹ From the bridal canopy

גָּדַע גְּאוֹן נָדִיב וָשׁוֹעַ,[1]

« and the magnanimous, ‹ of the generous ‹ the pride ‹ He cut down

וְהֵשִׁיב יָמִין אָחוֹר[2] **מִלְּהוֹשִׁיעַ,**

‹ not to save, ‹ back, ‹ His right hand ‹ and He drew

גַּם כִּי אֶזְעַק וַאֲשַׁוֵּעַ.

« and plead. ‹ I would cry out ‹ when ‹ even

גַּם גָּבַר עָלַי פּוֹרְכִי,

« did those who enslaved me with crushing labor, ‹ me ‹ over-power ‹ Even [when]

וּבְנַאֲקִי סָתַם חֲרַכִּי, גָּדַר דְּרָכַי.

« my roads. ‹ He walled up « the lattice spaces [of heaven to my pleas]; ‹ He sealed ‹ and when I screamed [in prayer],

יְתוֹמִים גְּרוּשִׁים מֵאֲחֻזּוֹת,

« from ancestral estates, ‹ banished ‹ [We were] like orphans

וְלֹא שָׁב אַפּוֹ בְּכָל זֹאת,[3]

« this [suffering], ‹ despite all ‹ has His anger ‹ sub-sided ‹ yet, not

וְאָמַר אִם בְּזֹאת.

« *in spite of this [you do not listen to Me ... I will punish you seven times for your sins]!* ‹ *If* « rather He said,

(1) *Isaiah* 32:5. (2) Cf. *Eichah* 2:3. (3) Cf. *Isaiah* 5:25.

on the Torah (ibid.) demonstrates how each and every one of Moses' warnings came true when Israel's sins finally forced God to unleash His anger against them. Thus, after every three verses from the Book of *Eichah*, the *kinnah* cites the corresponding verse from the *Tochachah*.

דַּרְכֵי דִיץ סָךְ לְהַאֲבִילִי, וּלְגָלוּת שֵׁשַׁךְ הוֹבִילִי,

The roads ‹ once jubilant [with pilgrims] ‹ He has fenced [with thorns], ‹ to cause me to mourn. « And into the exile ‹ of Babylon ‹ He led me [on these very same roads]. «

דֹּב אֹרֵב הוּא לִי.

[Like] a bear ‹ lying in ambush ‹ He is ‹ to me. «

דָּרַךְ דּוֹחֵק עַל בָּמוֹתַי לְהִשְׂתָּרֵר,

Trample ‹ did the attacker ‹ on ‹ my high places ‹ to display his sovereignty. «

שְׁעוּ מֶנִּי בִּבְכִי אֲמָרֵר,[1] דְּרָכַי סוֹרֵר.

[Please] turn ‹ from me, ‹ so that through weeping ‹ I may express [my] bitterness. « My paths ‹ He has strewn with thorns. «

דָּבַק דּוֹלְקִי וְצָדַנִי בְּרִשְׁתּוֹ,

Caught up to me ‹ has my pursuer ‹ and he has snared me ‹ in his net, «

עָלַי לִלְטוֹשׁ מַחֲרַשְׁתּוֹ,[2] דָּרַךְ קַשְׁתּוֹ.

[as a weapon] against me ‹ he has honed ‹ his plow blade; « he bent ‹ his bow [and set me as a target for his arrow]. «

מֵימֵינוּ דָּלַח[3] וְנָם אֲשִׁימְכֶם,

Our waters ‹ He churned and muddied ‹ and said, « *I will devastate you!* «

גֵּיא גָלוּת אֲטִילְכֶם לְהַכְלִימְכֶם,

[Into] the valley ‹ of exile ‹ I will cast you ‹ to humiliate you. «

וְהָלַכְתִּי עִמָּכֶם.

I will walk ‹ with you [with the fury of indifference]. «

(1) Cf. *Isaiah* 22:4. (2) *I Samuel* 13:20. (3) *Ezekiel* 32:2.

In the complex format of this *kinnah,* each letter of the *aleph-beis* appears ten times in the following manner: The respective letter is represented by four three-line stanzas. The first word in Stanza One of each four-stanza group is the first word of the corresponding verse in Chapter One of *Eichah;* the next word begins with the same letter of the alphabet. Stanza Two follows the same format but the first word is from Chapter Two of *Eichah.* And in Stanza Three the first word is from Chapter Four. The third stich of each of these three stanzas is the opening phrase from the respective verses of Chapter Three (which has three verses

הָיוּ הָהּ לְיוֹם בִּכְיוֹתַי,

There were [cries of] ‹ Ho ‹ on the day ‹ of my weeping, «

וְצָרֶבֶת אֵשׁ כְּוִיּוֹתַי, הֵבִיא בְּכִלְיוֹתָי.

[and the hot tears] scarred [my face] ‹ with a fiery burn. « He shot [his arrows] ‹ into my kidneys. «

הָיָה הוֹלֵךְ לְפָנַי מַזְעִימִי, וְכֶעָסִיס דָּמִי הִטְעִימִי,[1]

He would ‹ walk [with arrogance] ‹ ahead of me « — the one who enraged me, « and as if it were sweet nectar, « my own blood ‹ he forced me to taste. «

הָיִיתִי שְׂחוֹק לְכָל עַמִּי.

I have become ‹ a laughing-stock ‹ to all ‹ the peoples. «

הָאוֹכְלִים הֶקְדֵּשׁ פֶּסַח בְּלֵיל שִׁמּוּרִים,

Those who would eat ‹ the sacred flesh ‹ of the *pesach*-offering ‹ on the night ‹ that is guarded, «

הֶאֱכִילָם בְּכָפָן רָאשֵׁי חֲמוֹרִים,[2]

He fed them ‹ during famine ‹ the heads ‹ of donkeys. «

הִשְׂבִּיעַנִי בַּמְּרוֹרִים.

He sated me ‹ with bitter [herbs]. «

עַל צַוָּארֵנוּ הִשְׂרִיג וְחִלֵּל שְׁכֶם,[3]

Upon ‹ our necks [as a yoke] ‹ He twisted together ropes [of our sins] ‹ and crippled ‹ our shoulder [where the Temple rested], «

וְנָם אֶפְקוֹד עַל עֲוֹנוֹתֵיכֶם,

for He said, ‹ *I shall visit [upon you] retribution* ‹ *for* ‹ *your iniquities!* «

וַאֲכַלְתֶּם בְּשַׂר בְּנֵיכֶם.

And you will eat ‹ *the flesh* ‹ *of your sons.* «

---

(1) Cf. *Isaiah* 49:26. (2) Cf. *II Kings* 6:25. (3) Cf. *Deuteronomy* 33:12 and *Rashi*.

---

for each letter). Thus, the group's *aleph-beis* letter appears three times in each of these stanzas: the first two words of line one and the first word of line three, for a total of nine times. The fourth stanza of each group begins with the first word of the respective verse in Chapter Five of *Eichah*. This is followed by a word beginning with the group's code letter (its tenth appearance). The final stich of this stanza is the opening phrase of the corresponding verse from *Leviticus* 26:25-46. [Some

וַיֵּצֵא וְקָדְקֹד סִפַּח[1] וְרִצֵּץ,
And He went forth; « heads « He afflicted with leprosy « [so that the enemy] would smash [them], «

וְחִזֵּק מוֹסְרֵי בִּי וָאֶתְלוֹצָץ,[2]
and He tightened « my bonds « about me, « because I scorned [the admonitions of His prophets], «

וַיַּגְרֵס בֶּחָצָץ.
He shattered « with gravel my teeth. «

וַיַּחְמֹס וַיְנַצֵּל מֶעֶדְיִי[3] לְהַכְפִּישִׁי,
He pillaged [the Holy Temple] « and stripped me « of my [spiritual] adornments, « covering me with dust, «

וּמִגָּבְהָהּ לִתְהוֹם הִרְפִּישִׁי, וַתִּזְנַח מִשָּׁלוֹם נַפְשִׁי.
[He lowered me] from the loftiest heights « to the depths « to cover me in mire and muck. « Rejected « from achieving peace « was my soul. «

וַיִּגְדַּל וְכָבֵד נַאַק רִצְחִי,
Grew stronger « and more intense « did the cry « of my murdered one, «

וּבְקָדְקֳדִי עָלָה צְוָחִי, וָאֹמַר אָבַד נִצְחִי.
until in my skull « rever-berated « my scream. « And I said, « *Gone* « *is my world!* «

מִצְרַיִם וְכוּשׁ שָׁח אֲשִׁיבְכֶם,[4]
Back to Egypt « *and Kush,* « said God, « *I shall return you;* «

וְאֶשְׁפָּטְכֶם כִּזְמוֹתֵיכֶם,
and I shall judge you « *in accordance with your scheming;* «

וְהִשְׁמַדְתִּי אֶת בָּמוֹתֵיכֶם.
And I will demolish « *your lofty buildings.* «

(1) Cf. *Isaiah* 3:17 and *Metzudos David.* (2) Cf. *Isaiah* 28:22.
(3) Cf. *Exodus* 33:6. (4) Cf. *Deuteronomy* 28:68.

commentators assume that this *kinnah* is a companion to *Kinnah* 9, in which the stanzas end with the first phrases of the verses from *Leviticus* 26:3-24.]

זָכְרָה זֹאת כִּי נִבְאַשׁ נִרְדִּי,

« did my nard [spice]. ‹ become putrid ‹ when ‹ this [sin with the Golden Calf] ‹ He [God] remembered

וּלְכַלָּה פָּץ מִכָּבוֹד רְדִי, **זְכָר** עָנְיִי וּמְרוּדִי.

« and my sorrow. ‹ my affliction ‹ Remember « *descend!* ‹ *From [your place of] honor* « He ordered, ‹ Therefore to the bride

זָנַח זְבוּל וְלֵב הִקְשִׁיחַ,

« he stiffened, ‹ and His heart ‹ His Temple ‹ He abandoned

וּבְהִתְעַבְּרוֹ עִם מָשִׁיחַ,[1] **זָכוֹר** תִּזְכּוֹר וְתָשִׂיחַ.[2]

« and is bent over. ‹ [My soul] remembers [this] well, « the anointed one [King Josiah]. ‹ with ‹ [because] of His anger

זְכוּת זְקֵנַי וּפָעֳלָם אָבִיא,

« I shall bring [to God's attention], ‹ and their achievement ‹ of my ancestors ‹ The merit

כִּי בְּכֵן פָּרַץ נְתִיבִי, **זֹאת** אָשִׁיב אֶל לִבִּי.

« my heart [and therefore I have hope]. ‹ to ‹ I take ‹ This « my path. ‹ for [God] to breach ‹ it would be just ‹ because otherwise

אֲבוֹתֵינוּ זָעֲקוּ וְכָלוּ מִדִּבָּה,

« because of the [spies'] slander; ‹ and were annihilated ‹ cried ‹ Our forefathers

וְשָׂח עַל רָעָתֵנוּ כִּי רַבָּה,[3]

« it is great, ‹ for ‹ our wickedness ‹ because of « and He proclaimed,

וְנָתַתִּי אֶת עָרֵיכֶם חָרְבָּה.

« *into ruin.* ‹ *your cities* ‹ *I will turn*

חֵטְא חָז כִּי בֶּעָוֹן נִכְתָּמְנוּ,[4]

« we were stained; ‹ by iniquity ‹ for « He saw, ‹ Sin [within us]

---

(1) See commentary to *Kinnah* 11. (2) *Eichah* 3:20; as evidenced by the rhyme scheme, the paytan used the כְּתִיב, Masoretic spelling, in place of the קְרִי, Masoretic pronunciation (וְתָשִׂיחַ instead of וְתָשׁוּחַ or וְתָשֹׁחַ); nevertheless, most editions read וְתָשׁוּחַ.
(3) *I Samuel* 12:17. (4) Cf. *Jeremiah* 2:22.

תְּמוּר כִּי בְּצִחְיוֹן נִזְהָמְנוּ,

« we filthied ourselves. ‹ in the Wilderness, ‹ for, exchanging [God for the Golden Calf]

חַסְדֵי יהוה כִּי לֹא תָמְנוּ.

« it has not ended. ‹ — it is certain that « of HASHEM ‹ [Yet,] the kindness

חָשַׁב חוֹרְשִׁי לְקַרְקֵר (קִיר)[1] יְקָרִים,

« of the precious ones, ‹ [the wall] ‹ to tear down ‹ did the one who plowed over me ‹ Plan

וּמַר יִבְכָּיוּן[2] מַכָּתִי סוֹקְרִים,

« perceive, ‹ who my wounds ‹ weep [did the angels] ‹ and bitterly

חֲדָשִׁים לַבְּקָרִים.

« every morning. ‹ they, [the angels,] are new

חָשַׁךְ חֲזוֹן מַגִּישֵׁי אִשִּׁי,

« my fire [offerings], ‹ [of the *Kohanim*] who bring ‹ the prophetic vision ‹ He made dark

קִיר כְּעִוֵּר לְגַשְּׁשִׁי,[3] חֶלְקִי יהוה אָמְרָה נַפְשִׁי.

« my soul. ‹ says « *is* HASHEM, ‹ [Nevertheless,] *My portion* « I must grope. ‹ like the blind, ‹ for the wall

עֲבָדִים חִסְּמוּנִי מִלִּגְדּוֹר פֶּרֶץ,

« the breach, ‹ from repairing ‹ prevented us ‹ [The Babylonian soldier-] slaves

וְתוֹכָחוֹת קָשׁוֹת פָּץ בְּחֶרֶץ,

« with determination, ‹ He had spoken ‹ that were harsh ‹ because admonitions

וַהֲשִׁמּוֹתִי אֲנִי אֶת הָאָרֶץ.

« the land. « — I will — « And I will make desolate

---

(1) Many editions omit the word in parentheses; if included, it refers to the walls of the *Beis HaMikdash*. (2) *Isaiah* 33:7. (3) Cf. 59:10.

טֻמְאָתָהּ טָפְלָה וְנָטָה קָו,[1]

« the measuring line [for retribution]. ‹ so [God] stretched out « she [Zion] attached [to the Temple], ‹ Her [idolatrous] defilement

וְלֹא נָסוֹג אָחוֹר מִקּוָֹיו,

« from those who trust in Him; ‹ back ‹ Yet He did not turn

טוֹב יהוה לְקוָֹיו.

« to those who trust in Him. ‹ is HASHEM ‹ [for] good

טָבְעוּ טִירוֹתַי וּפִי צַר דָּמָם,[2]

« was silenced, ‹ because of suffering, ‹ and my mouth, « did my palaces, ‹ Sink into the earth

וְכָל עוֹבֵר עָלַי שָׁרַק וְשָׁמָם,[3]

« and were amazed [at such punishment]. ‹ whistled ‹ by me ‹ passed ‹ and whoever

טוֹב וְיָחִיל וְדוּמָם.

« *and patiently await [the salvation of* HASHEM*].* ‹ *that one should hope* ‹ *[Still, I declare,] It is good*

טוֹבִים טַפִּים נִכְלוּ בְּהוֹסִיפִי לִמְעוֹל,

« to betray [God], ‹ when I continued ‹ were exterminated ‹ infants ‹ The finest

וּכְמַעֲלָלַי חָרָה בִּי לִפְעוֹל,

« into action. ‹ against me, ‹ [God's anger] flared ‹ and in proportion to my misdeeds,

טוֹב לַגֶּבֶר כִּי יִשָּׂא עוֹל.

« a yoke [in his youth]. ‹ he bear ‹ that ‹ for a man ‹ It is good

בְּנַפְשֵׁנוּ נָבִיא טֶרֶף נִכְרֶה,[4]

« do we prepare a meal, « our food, ‹ do we purchase ‹ With [danger to] our lives

כִּי כְּמוֹ בָּרַחַת וּבַמִּזְרֶה,[5]

« or a winnowing shovel, ‹ with a pitchfork ‹ as if ‹ for

---

(1) *Eichah* 2:8. (2) Alternatively: *the mouth of the tormentor was silent.* (3) Cf. *Jeremiah* 18:16, 19:8. (4) Some editions read טֶרֶף נִבְרֶה, *our food is supplied.* (5) *Isaiah* 30:24.

נָם וְאֶתְכֶם אֱזָרֶה.

« *I will scatter [among the nations].* ‹ *And you* ‹ [thus fulfilling] the spoken [curse,]

יָדוֹ יָרָה בִּי אוּר כִּסְדוֹם,

« as [He did] against Sodom, ‹ fire ‹ at me ‹ threw ‹ His hand

וְעַל כָּל אֵלֶּה הוֹנָאַתְנִי בַּת אֱדוֹם,

« of Edom. ‹ the [Roman] daughter ‹ He caused to torment me « that, ‹ to all ‹ and in addition

יֵשֵׁב בָּדָד וְיִדֹּם.

« and await patiently [for God has placed the burden upon him]. ‹ in solitude ‹ One should sit

יֵשְׁבוּ יְגוֹנִים בְּנֵי עֱלֵי חוּפֵּיהוּ,

« His sheltering canopy, ‹ over [the destruction of] ‹ do my children ‹ in anguish ‹ Sit

כִּי כָבֵד עָלַי אַכְפֵּהוּ,[1] יִתֵּן בֶּעָפָר פִּיהוּ.

« weighs His [God's] authority. ‹ upon me ‹ heavy ‹ because

« his mouth, [perhaps there is yet hope]. ‹ into the dust ‹ [Therefore] let him put

יְדֵי יוֹסְרַי שָׁתוּ בִּי מְחִי,

« blows, ‹ upon me ‹ have inflicted ‹ of those who punish me ‹ The hands

וְקָשַׁבְתִּי מִפִּי צַר שְׁחִי, יִתֵּן לְמַכֵּהוּ לֶחִי.

« *Bend low,* ‹ of the tormentor, ‹ from the mouth ‹ and I have heard

« *a cheek.* « *to the one who hits him,* ‹ *let him offer*

עוֹרֵנוּ יוּעַם כְּחֶרֶשׂ בַּקֶּרֶץ,

« because of repeated killings, ‹ like earthenware ‹ has become dark ‹ Our skin

וּגְוִיּוֹתֵינוּ שַׂמְנוּ כָּאָרֶץ,[2]

« like the ground. ‹ we made ‹ and [submissively,] our bodies

אָז תִּרְצֶה הָאָרֶץ.

« will the land. ‹ appease God ‹ Then

(1) Cf. *Job* 33:7; some editions read אַפֵּהוּ, *His [God's] anger.*
(2) Cf. *Isaiah* 51:23; some editions read בָּאָרֶץ, *(we placed our bodies) on the ground.*

כָּל כְּבוֹד תָּאֳרֵנוּ הֻכְלָם,

« has been humiliated, ‹ of our features ‹ the splendor ‹ [Although] all

וְצוּר אוֹרְחוֹתָיו חֶסֶד[1] כֻּלָּם, כִּי לֹא יִזְנַח לְעוֹלָם.

« forever [will the Lord]. ‹ reject ‹ not ‹ For « — all of them; « reflect total kindness ‹ — His paths « [we have faith that] of the Rock

כָּלוּ[2] כִמְעַט כִּי בִי נִלְחָם,

« He Himself waged war, ‹ against us ‹ for « almost, ‹ [We] were annihilated

וְעַל הָרָעָה הוּא נִחָם,[3] כִּי אִם הוֹגָה וְרִחָם.

« He [later] has mercy. « He afflicts [at first], ‹ even if ‹ For « reconsidered. ‹ He ‹ the evil [with which He afflicted us] ‹ but then over

כִּלָּה כַעְסוֹ וְהִצִּית לְהָבוֹ,

« his flame, ‹ when He kindled ‹ His anger ‹ He expended

וּבְתַכְלִית שְׁשָּׁה מְאוֹרֵי אוֹר* כִּבּוֹ,

« had cooled off,* ‹ of fire ‹ of the luminaries ‹ of six [annual cycles] ‹ which at the end

כִּי לֹא עִנָּה מִלִּבּוֹ.

« capriciously. ‹ He does not torment ‹ for

נָשִׁים בִּפְרוּעוֹת יוֹשְׁבוֹת שַׁמָּה,

« devastated, ‹ sat ‹ with their hair uncovered ‹ Women

בְּכָל שָׁנָה וְשָׁנָה מַזְכִּירוֹת אַשְׁמָה,

« the sins [that brought about the Destruction]. ‹ they recall ‹ after year [on Tishah B'Av] ‹ year ‹ and every

כָּל יְמֵי הָשַּׁמָּה.

« of its desolation. ‹ the days ‹ All

(1) Cf. *Psalms* 25:10. (2) Some editions read כָּלִינוּ, which includes the interpolated "*we*" of the translation; however, since this stich corresponds to *Eichah* 2:11, it should begin כָּלוּ. (3) Cf. *Joel* 2:13.

שִׁשָּׁה מְאוֹרֵי אוֹר — *Six [annual cycles] of the luminaries.* When the nation's sinfulness reached the maximum that God would overlook, He commanded the angel Gabriel to throw two coals from the celestial fires upon the city of Jerusalem (see *Ezekiel* 10:2). For six years, Gabriel allowed the coals to cool in his hands before

לֹא אֲלֵיכֶם לוֹחֲצֵי גִילָיו,

« those who emulate [God's ways]! ‹ who tyrannize ‹ upon you ‹ [God did] not [bring suffering]

וְעַל בָּנָיו הֶעֱבִיר גַּלָּיו,[1] לְדַכֵּא תַּחַת רַגְלָיו.

« His feet. ‹ under ‹ crushing [them] « His [destructive] waves, ‹ did God cause to roll ‹ His own sons ‹ Rather, upon

לְאִמּוֹתָם עֵת כָּמְהוּ מִשֶּׁבֶר,

« for food. ‹ they were craving ‹ when ‹ [Children cried out] to their mothers

יַעַן כִּי גָרוֹן פָּתְחוּ כְּקֶבֶר,[2] לְהַטּוֹת מִשְׁפַּט גָּבֶר.

« for a man. ‹ justice ‹ to pervert « like a grave, ‹ had been opened ‹ their [parents'] throats ‹ [The children were punished] for the reason that

לֹא לִמְחוֹת[3] פָּץ לְעַם קְרוֹבוֹ,

« with whom He was intimate. ‹ to the people ‹ did He speak ‹ to eradicate ‹ Not

וְאֵיךְ מִתַּעַר הוֹצִיא חַרְבּוֹ,[4] לְעַוֵּת אָדָם בְּרִיבוֹ.

« in his grievance? ‹ a man ‹ wronging «His sword, ‹ did He draw ‹ from its sheath ‹ How then

שָׂרִים לְכוּדִים הוֹצִיא מִשְּׁעָרִים,

« from the gateways [of Jerusalem], ‹ [the enemy] took out ‹ as captives ‹ The noblemen

תֵּת כַּתְּאֵנִים הַשּׁוֹעָרִים,[5]

« that are rotten, ‹ like figs ‹ and treated them

לְעוֹלֵל אֶת הַנִּשְׁאָרִים.[6]

« even the few scattered survivors. ‹ harvesting

(1) Cf. *Psalms* 42:8. (2) Cf. 5:10. (3) Cf. *II Kings* 14:27. (4) Cf. *Ezekiel* 21:8. (5) *Jeremiah* 29:17. (6) Cf. 6:9.

he actually threw them. He was certain that Israel's repentance would soon be forthcoming. When he realized that the people were steadfast in their evil ways, he decided to cast the fire upon them in a way that would wipe them out without a trace remaining. But God intervened, "Gabriel, Gabriel, take your time; take your time, for among them there are some who treat one another righteously."

But then an accusing angel appeared before the Throne of Glory and said, "Master of the universe, will this wicked

מִמָּרוֹם מְגִלָּה כָּתַב וָנֶהִי,

« [containing the terms] *moaning,* ‹ He wrote ‹ a scroll ‹ From Above

קִינִים וָהֶגֶה וָהִי,[1] **מִי זֶה אָמַר וַתֶּהִי.**

« and woe. «*murmuring,* ‹ *lamenting,* « and it took place? ‹ that decreed [something] ‹ is it ‹ [For] Who

מָה אֲעִידֵךְ מְאוּמָה מִלְּהֶרָצֶה,[2]

« would bring consolation? ‹ that in the slightest way ‹ can I adduce for you ‹ What example [of another nation's suffering]

נְתוּנָה בְּיַד מֵרִיב וּמִתְנַצֶּה,[3] **מִפִּי עֶלְיוֹן לֹא תֵצֵא.**

« and a foe? ‹ of an antagonist ‹ into the hand ‹ [Has another nation] been delivered « From the mouth ‹ of the Most High ‹ do there not ‹ emanate decrees that are bad [and that are good]?

מֵחַטֹּאת מַדִּיחַי שָׁוְא[4] **אֲקוֹנֵן,**

« I shall lament. ‹ after worthlessness ‹ of those who led you astray ‹ Over the sins

מְנַחֲמִי כְּמִיַּיִן מִתְרוֹנֵן,[5] **מַה יִּתְאוֹנֵן.**

« arousing Himself. ‹ He is as one from wine ‹ Yet my Comforter [is only beginning], « should he complain? ‹ Of what

בַּחוּרִים מוֹטְטוּ כָּשַׁל בִּי לְהָרֵב,

« within me increasingly, ‹ they stumbled « stagger, ‹ Youths

וּשְׁכִינָה הוּעֲלָה מִקֶּרֶב,

« from our midst. ‹ ascended [and departed] ‹ while the Divine Presence

וְכָשְׁלוּ אִישׁ בְּאָחִיו כְּמִפְּנֵי חָרֶב.

« a sword. ‹ as if from before ‹ over his brother ‹ one man ‹ And they will stumble

---

(1) Cf. *Ezekiel* 2:9. (2) See commentary to *Kinnah* 9.
(3) Cf. *Isaiah* 58:4. (4) Cf. *Eichah* 2:14. (5) Cf. *Psalms* 78:65.

---

man be permitted to say haughtily, 'I have destroyed God's Home, and burned His Sanctuary?' "

Immediately, God replied, "If so, let fire descend from above and burn it!" (*Midrash Eichah* 1:41).

נִשְׂקַד נֵטֶל עוֹל פּוֹרְכֵינוּ,

《 of those who crush us, 〈 of the yoke 〈 is the load 〈 Amassed

וַיִּתְעֵב שַׁי עוֹרְכֵינוּ, נַחְפְּשָׂה דְרָכֵינוּ.

《 our ways [and return unto HASHEM]. 〈 [Therefore,] let us search 《 that we ordered [before Him]. 〈 offerings and prayers 〈 for He has rejected

נְבִיאַיִךְ נִאֲצוּ לִקְרוֹץ עַפְעַפַּיִם,[1]

《 eyelids; 〈 with winking 〈 caused abomination 〈 Your [false] prophets

וְאִכְזְרוּ עָלֵינוּ אֶרֶךְ אַפַּיִם,

《 the One Who [is otherwise] slow to anger. 〈 against us 〈 they caused to be harsh

נִשָּׂא לְבָבֵנוּ אֶל כַּפָּיִם.

《 our hands [to God in heaven]! 〈 together with 〈 our hearts [in prayer] 〈 Let us lift

נָעוּ וְנָדוּ רֹאשׁ[2] בְּמַהֲמוֹרֵינוּ,

《 at the deep pits [of our woes]; 〈 their heads [in disbelief] 〈 and wagged 〈 [Everyone] shook

רְשָׁעִים מַפִּילִים בְּמִכְמוֹרֵינוּ,[3]

《 into our nets [were amazed at our tragedy]. 〈 who made us fall 〈 even the wicked

נַחְנוּ פָשַׁעְנוּ וּמָרֵינוּ.

《 and rebelled [but God has not yet forgiven]. 〈 have transgressed 〈 [All because] we

זְקֵנִים וְנִינָם לָרֹב סְגוּיִם,

《 and greatly increased, 〈 [although] their number was large 〈 and their offspring 〈 Grandparents

אֲכָלוּם וֶהֱשִׁיתוּם מָשָׁל בַּגּוֹיִם,[4]

《 among the nations. 〈 into a byword [for misfortune] 〈 and made them 〈 [the conquerors] devoured them

כְּנָם וַאֲבַדְתֶּם בַּגּוֹיִם.

《 *among the nations.* 〈 *You will become lost* 《 As He had said,

(1) Cf. *Proverbs* 10:10. (2) Cf. *Jeremiah* 18:16. (3) Cf. *Psalms* 141:10. (4) 44:15.

סִלָּה שָׂמֵי קְטוֹרָה בְּאַף,[1]*

« for [God] to smell,* ‹ incense [on the Golden Altar] ‹ were [the *Kohanim*] who placed ‹ Trampled

וָאֶפְעַר פִּי וָאֶשְׁאַף,[2] **סַכּוֹתָה בָאַף.**

« and I gasped [in bewilderment], ‹ my mouth ‹ while I opened wide « in anger. ‹ [for] You have covered Yourself

סִפְּקוּ שׂוֹטְנַי כַּף וָאֶשְׁתּוֹנָן,

« and caused me sharp pain, ‹ [their] hands [with glee over my sorrows] ‹ did my antagonists ‹ Clap

וָאֶזְעַק חָמָס[3] **וָאֶתְאוֹנָן, סַכּוֹתָה בֶעָנָן.**

« and I lamented in mourning, « over the injustice [against me], ‹ and I would cry out « in a cloud [to prevent the passage of any prayer]. ‹ [because] You have covered [Yourself]

סוּרוּ טָמֵא סָחוּ מַאֲשִׁימֵינוּ,

« our destroyers, ‹ spoke « *unclean one,* « *Go Away,*

בְּהִנָּתֵן כַּבַּרְזֶל שָׁמֵינוּ, סְחִי וּמָאוּס תְּשִׂימֵנוּ.

« were our skies [allowing no rainfall]. ‹ as hard as iron ‹ when rendered « do You make us [in the midst of the nations]. ‹ and repugnant ‹ [Thus,] as filth

שָׁבַת מְשׂוֹשׂ שִׂמְחַת מְשׁוֹרְרִים,

« of the singers, ‹ jubilation ‹ has the rejoicing ‹ Ceased

וְרוֹדְפַי קַלּוּ מִנְּשָׁרִים,

‹ than eagles ‹ were swifter ‹ for my pursuers

לְאַבֵּד הַנִּשְׁאָרִים.

« the survivors. ‹ to destroy

עַל אֵלֶּה עֲשָׁקוּנוּ בְּחֵרוּפֵיהֶם,

« with their curses, ‹ they oppressed us ‹ these [sins] ‹ Because of

(1) Cf. *Deuteronomy* 33:10. (2) Cf. *Psalms* 119:131. (3) Cf. *Habakkuk* 1:2; see also *Job* 19:7.

שָׂמֵי קְטוֹרָה בְּאַף — *Were [the Kohanim] who placed incense [on the Golden Altar] for [God] to smell.* The *paytan* plays on the dual meaning of the word אַף. The Torah verse that this stich paraphrases reads, יָשִׂימוּ קְטוֹרָה בְּאַפֶּךָ, *They shall place incense*

וְהִגְדִּילוּ שְׁאוֹן גִּדּוּפֵיהֶם, פָּצוּ עָלַי פִּיהֶם.

and they intensified ‹ the din ‹ of their blasphemies, « [when] they opened wide ‹ against us ‹ their mouths. «

פָּצוּ פָּעֲרוּ פֶּה מִבְּאֵר שַׁחַת,

They opened ‹ and spread wide ‹ their mouth ‹ wider than the Well ‹ of Destruction, «

וְאִטְּרוּ עָלַי[1] בְּתוֹכַחַת, פַּחַד וָפַחַת.

they closed off [any escape] ‹ from before me ‹ through [God's] rebuke; « panic ‹ and pitfalls [were ours]. «

פְּנֵי פְאֵר חֻפַּת מְעוֹנִי

The appearance ‹ of the majesty ‹ of my canopied ‹ Temple ‹

הִקְמִיל וְהֵקִים מְעַנִּי, פַּלְגֵי מַיִם תֵּרַד עֵינִי.

He cut down; « He established [in its stead] ‹ my oppressor. « [Therefore,] streams ‹ of water ‹ does my eye shed. «

נָפְלָה עֲטֶרֶת עֹז מַשְׁעֵנָם,

Fallen ‹ is their crown ‹ of strength, « their [pillar of] support; «

וְצָר[2] בְּשִׁבְעָה דִינִים דָּנָם,[3]

for [God,] like a foe, « with seven ‹ harsh punishments ‹ afflicted them. «

וְהִתְוַדּוּ אֶת עֲוֹנָם.

Then they will confess ‹ their sin. «

פֵּרְשָׂה פוֹצְצָה אוֹי כִּי סֻגָּרָה,

[Zion] spread [her arms], ‹ she exclaimed, « *Woe!* « for ‹ she was turned over [into captivity]! «

תְּמוּר עֹז מָתְנֶיהָ בְּשַׂק חָגְרָה,

Instead of ‹ powerfully ‹ [girding] her loins, « with sackcloth ‹ she now girds herself. «

עֵינִי נִגְּרָה.

My eye ‹ will flow [with tears without respite]. «

---

(1) Cf. *Psalms* 69:15. (2) See *Eichah* 2:4. (3) See *Leviticus* 26:18, 24, 28.

---

before You. The literal meaning of בְּאַפֶּךָ is *in Your nose*, hence *before You.* The word אַף can also mean *anger* or *fury*, for flaring nostrils are a sign of anger (see *Rashi*

עָשָׂה עֶבְרָתוֹ וַיֶּחֱרָה,

« but He continues to seethe, « what His anger [demanded], ‹ [God] carried out

וְעָרַף אֶת מְדוֹן מְגָרָה,[1] עַד יַשְׁקִיף וְיֵרֶא.

« were the instigators. ‹ that of the strife [alienating God from Israel] ‹ those [evil-doers] ‹ and He beheaded

« and takes notice [of our shame]. ‹ He gazes down ‹ [Yet, how long must we wait] until

עוֹדֶנּוּ עָף כָּבוֹד וְעָלָה,

« ascending [heavenward], ‹ does the [Divine] Glory ‹ to soar ‹ Continue

וְעֶשֶׂר מַסָּעוֹת[2] הוּעֲלָה, עֵינִי עוֹלְלָה.

« [away from the Temple] it ascended. ‹ stages ‹ in ten

« has sullied [me by its tears]. ‹ [Over this] my eye

עַל זֶה פָּסַק נוֹי נָעֳמָם,

« of their pleasant [Temple], ‹ to the beauty ‹ there came an end ‹ this ‹ Because of

וְשָׂח לֹא אֶעֶזְבֵם בְּכַף זוֹעֲמָם,

« *of [the enemies] who make them furious,* ‹ *into the hands* ‹ *I shall never abandon them* «*yet [God] stated,*

אַף אֲנִי אֵלֵךְ עִמָּם.[3]

« *with them [into exile].* ‹ *will go* ‹ *I* ‹ *for indeed*

צַדִּיק צָר צְעָדַי לִסְפּוֹר,[4]

« and took account of them, ‹ my footsteps ‹ would guard ‹ The Righteous One

וּכְעִקַּלְתִּי יֹשֶׁר וָאֶכְפּוֹר, צוֹד צָדוּנִי כַּצִּפּוֹר.

« and denied [God's sovereignty], ‹ what was straight ‹ but since I made crooked

« like a bird. ‹ and they ensnared me ‹ [the enemy] hunted me

(1) Cf. *Proverbs* 15:18. (2) See *Rosh Hashanah* 31a. (3) See *Megillah* 29a. (4) Cf. *Job* 31:4.

to *Exodus* 15:8). Thus, *Malbim* expounds regarding the Scriptural verse: Both anger and incense enter through the nose, one to torment the soul, the other to restore it.

צָעַק צוּרִי וְסִכֵּךְ מֵעֲבוֹר,

« [to prevent my prayers] from passing through; ‹ and covered over [the heavens] ‹ did my Rock ‹ Shout [a command]

וּבְחַלְּלִי עָרַךְ לִשְׁבּוֹר, צָמְּתוּ בַּבּוֹר.

« in the pit. ‹ [And me] they locked « to break [the Temple]. ‹ He prepared His weapons « and when I profaned [God's sanctity],

צָדוּ צְעָדַי וְסָע דּוֹרְשִׁי,

« had the One Who had sought my welfare; ‹ but departed « my footsteps, ‹ [The enemy] sought to ambush

וְכַעֲלוֹתָם עָלַי לְדוֹרְשִׁי,[1] צָפוּ מַיִם עַל רֹאשִׁי.

« my head. ‹ over ‹ did the water ‹ then flood « and sought my harm, ‹ me ‹ and when [the enemy] came against

עַל הַר צִיּוֹן צָבְאוּ לְהַכְרִיתִי,

« to annihilate me, ‹ [the enemy legions] mustered ‹ Zion ‹ Mount ‹ On

וְצוּר שָׂח אֶחְמוֹל עַל שְׁאֵרִיתִי,

‹ *My [people's] remnant* ‹ *on* ‹ *I will take pity* « said, ‹ but the Rock

וְזָכַרְתִּי אֶת בְּרִיתִי.

« *My covenant [with them].* ‹ *and I will remember*

קָרָאתִי קָשׁוֹב חֶרְפַּת מוֹנַי,

« *of my oppressors!* ‹ *to the abuse* « *Listen carefully [O God],* « I called out,

עַל הַלֶּחִי מַכִּים בָּנַי, קָרָאתִי שִׁמְךָ יהוה.

« *HASHEM.* ‹ *on Your Name,* ‹ *I called* « *my sons!* ‹ *they smack* ‹ *the cheek* ‹ *On*

קוּמִי קִרְאִי כִּי לֹא יִכָּלֵם,

« He will not put you to shame! ‹ for « Call out [O Israel to your God], ‹ Rise up!

(1) Some editions read כַּיָּם לְגָרְשִׁי, *like the [rolling] sea to drive me away.*

עַל יֶתֶר לְמַקְנִיאַי יְשַׁלֵּם,[1]

« He will surely repay. ‹ of those who torment me ‹ the haughtiness ‹ For

קוֹלִי שָׁמַעְתָּ אַל תַּעְלֵם.

« shut [Your ear to my prayer]. ‹ do not « You have heard; ‹ My voice

קַלִּים קְדָחוּנִי וְעִלַּמְתָּ מַרְאֶךָ,

« to what You saw, ‹ but You were oblivious ‹ burnt me, ‹ [The Babylonians,] an inferior nation,

הָשֵׁב בַּגּוֹיִם מוֹרָאֶךָ,[2] קָרַבְתָּ בְּיוֹם אֶקְרָאֶךָ.

« I called You. ‹ on the day ‹ You drew near « the fear of You. ‹ among the nations ‹ re-establish

אַתָּה יהוה קֵץ אַל תְּכַזֵּב,[3]

« prove false, ‹ do not ‹ the set time [of the Redemption] ‹ HASHEM, ‹ O You,

עַד מָתַי כְּחֹרֶשׁ אֵעָזֵב,[4] וְהָאָרֶץ תֵּעָזֵב.

« *will be abandoned.* ‹ [As You stated,] *The land* « shall I be abandoned? ‹ like a [desolate] forest ‹ when ‹ until

רְאֵה רֹגֶז מַכַּת אֱנוֹשִׁי,

« that is mortal, ‹ by my wound ‹ the turmoil caused ‹ Behold

וָאוֹמַר בְּהִנָּטְשִׁי בַּנֶּשִׁי, רַבְתָּ אֲדֹנָי רִיבֵי נַפְשִׁי.

« *of my soul.* ‹ *the battles* ‹ *O Lord,* ‹ *You fought,* « in oblivion, ‹ [even though] I seem to be forsaken ‹ yet I shall [still] say

רְאֵה רֹב בְּעָתוּתִי, הֲשִׁמּוֹתָ כָּל עֲדָתִי,

« community, ‹ my entire ‹ because You have devastated « terror, ‹ my extraordinary ‹ Behold

רָאִיתָה יהוה עַוָּתָתִי.

« the injustices [I suffer]. ‹ HASHEM, ‹ You have seen,

(1) Cf. *Psalms* 31:24. Some editions read וְיִתְעַנְּגוּ לְרֹב שָׁלוֹם, *and may they delight in abundant peace,* cf. *Psalms* 37:11.
(2) Cf. 9:21. (3) Cf. *Habakkuk* 2:3. (4) Cf. *Isaiah* 17:9.

רוּחַ רָפְתָה[1] בִּי מֵאֵימָתָם,
« because of fear of them, ‹ within me ‹ grew weak ‹ My spirit

לְבַלְּעֵי הֶעֱלוּ חֲמָתָם, רָאִיתָה כָּל נִקְמָתָם.
« their wrath. ‹ they arouse ‹ for in order to swallow me « their vengeance. ‹ all ‹ You have seen

לָמָּה בְּרָחוֹק תַּעֲמוֹד[2] בְּדַבְּרָם עַזּוֹת,[3]
« brazenness? ‹ when they speak ‹ do You stand ‹ at a distance ‹ Why

נַמְתָּ הַנְּשַׁמָּה אוֹשִׁיב פְּרָזוֹת,[4]
« and [it will be secure] without walls? « I shall restore, ‹ the desolate [city of Jerusalem] ‹ Have You not said,

וְאַף גַּם זֹאת.
« this [that they have done, I shall not annul My covenant with them]. ‹ despite all ‹ But yet

שָׁמְעוּ שֶׁנּוּקַשְׁתִּי בִּדְחִיפָתָם,
« from their attacks, ‹ that I was battered ‹ They [the enemy] heard

וּכְיֶלֶק עָלָה עֵיפָתָם, שָׁמַעְתָּ חֶרְפָּתָם.
« their darkness. ‹ rose up against me ‹ so like a swarm of locusts « their verbal abuse [regarding me]? ‹ You have heard

שָׁכְבוּ שׁוֹחֲחִים בָּנַי מִיגוֹנָם,
« from their agony, ‹ were my sons ‹ bent over ‹ Lying

וְשׁוֹבֵיהֶם גָּאָה מְאֹד גְּאוֹנָם,
« did their haughtiness, ‹ exceedingly ‹ — swell « while their captors

שִׂפְתֵי קָמַי וְהֶגְיוֹנָם.
« and their thoughts [are against me]. ‹ of my antagonists ‹ the lips

שִׂישִׂי שׁוֹסָתִי כִּי בִי יַד מֻטָּה,
« fallen, ‹ has the [punishing] hand of [God] ‹ against me ‹ for ‹ O you who plundered me, ‹ Rejoice,

(1) Cf. *Judges* 8:3. (2) Cf. *Psalms* 10:1. (3) Cf. *Proverbs* 18:23. (4) Cf. *Zechariah* 2:8.

מֻשְׁפֶּלֶת עַד[1] **שְׁאוֹל מָטָּה,**

« below. ‹ the grave ‹ unto ‹ and I have been dragged down

שִׁבְתָּם וְקִימָתָם הַבִּיטָה.

« You [should] scrutinize. ‹ and their rising up [to take action] ‹ Their sitting down [to plot against me]

הֲשִׁיבֵנוּ שָׁלֵם שִׁלּוּם שָׁנִים,[2]

« for the years [we suffered in exile]. ‹ and repay us ‹ to [Jeru-] salem ‹ Return us

וְתֹאמַר אֶפְדֵּם מִשְּׁאוֹנִים,

« *from the roaring masses!* ‹ *I shall redeem them* « And say,

וְזָכַרְתִּי לָהֶם בְּרִית רִאשׁוֹנִים.

« *of the original ancestors.* ‹ *the covenant* ‹ *for them* ‹ *And I will remember*

תָּבֹא תָּשׁוּר מְעַנַּי לָמוּל,

« in order to cut me down, ‹ those who afflict me ‹ and observe ‹ Come

הֵם שָׁגְבוּ חַיִל וְאִוּוּיֶךָ אָמוּל,

« they would destroy. ‹ in order that Your desirous [Temple] ‹ military feats ‹ performed mighty ‹ they

תָּשִׁיב לָהֶם גְּמוּל.

« what they deserve. ‹ to them ‹ Pay back

תִּקְרָא תְּגַלֶּה יוֹם כָּמוּס בְּלֵב,

« in [Your] heart. ‹ concealed ‹ the date [of redemption] ‹ and reveal ‹ Proclaim

וּמְחַפְּשֵׂי עוֹלוֹת[3] **לִפְעוֹל מִלֵּב,**[4]

« from their hearts, ‹ to work [evil] ‹ for pretexts ‹ But as for those who search

תִּתֵּן לָהֶם מְגִנַּת לֵב.

« heart. ‹ a grief-filled ‹ them ‹ give

---

(1) Cf. *Isaiah* 57:9. (2) Cf. *Psalms* 90:15. (3) Cf. 64:7. (4) Cf. 58:3. Some editions read וְהֵטִיבָה לָנוּ לְהָסִיר מִמֶּנּוּ מְגִינַּת לֵב, *be good to us, to remove from us a grief-filled heart.*

תַּם תַּכְלִית תָּקְפָּם לְלָכְדֵם,
« and conquer them, ‹ of their power ‹ the essence ‹ Let be ended

יִפְּלוּ בְּלִי לְהַעֲמִידֵם.[1]
« to allow them to rise, ‹ never ‹ let them fall,

תִּרְדּוֹף בְּאַף וְתַשְׁמִידֵם.
« and destroy them. ‹ in anger ‹ pursue them

כִּי תָמִיד דּוֹקְרִים וְשׂוֹחֲקִים,
« and ridicule us, ‹ stab ‹ continuously ‹ Because [our enemies]

וּמִתּוֹרָתְךָ אָנוּ לֹא רוֹחֲקִים,
« distanced, ‹ are never ‹ we ‹ yet from Your Torah

הֲשִׁיבֵנוּ וְהוֹרֵנוּ אֵלֶּה הַחֻקִּים.[2]
« *are the decrees* [that God gave . . . at Mount Sinai, through the hand of Moses]. ‹ *these* ‹ and teach us [how to observe] ‹ O bring us back

---

(1) Some editions read תַּצִּילֵנִי מִמּוֹקְשֵׁי בְּנֵי אָדָם, *save me from the snares of humankind,* / שׂוֹטְנִים לְהַפִּיל בְּלִי לְהַעֲמִידָם, *accusers to humble that they never be permitted to arise;* some editions read תְּשַׁלַּח חִישׁ עֶזְרְךָ, *dispatch swiftly Your assistance,* / וְרַחֵם עַל בָּנֶיךָ, *and have mercy on Your sons,* / הַמְצַפִּים לִישׁוּעָתֶךָ, *who long for Your salvation.*
(2) *Leviticus* 26:46.

KINNAH 16 / קינה טז

זָכוֹר* אֲשֶׁר עָשָׂה צַר בִּפְנִים,[1]*

‹Remember* ‹ what ‹ the oppressor [Titus] did ‹‹ inside [the Temple];*

(1) Cf. *Zechariah* 14:10; some editions read בִּפְנַיִם, *within.*

זכור — *Remember.* The Roman general Titus — whose words and actions represent the unique arrogance and ruthlessness of the entire Roman nation, the seed of the proud and bloodthirsty Esau — destroyed the Second Temple. The Talmud (*Gittin* 56b) relates that he began his assault on Jerusalem with an insolent declaration of war — not merely against the Jews — but against the Almighty, God of Israel, Himself! Titus shouted out the verse from Scripture: אֵי, אֱלֹהֵימוֹ צוּר חָסָיוּ בוֹ, *Where is their God, the Rock in Whom they have trusted? (Deuteronomy* 32:37).

Avos d'Rabbi Nosson (1:6) states that King David had Titus in mind when he supplicated before God: אַל תְּבוֹאֵנִי רֶגֶל גַּאֲוָה, *Let not the foot of the arrogant overtake me (Psalms* 36:12), because Titus' insufferable arrogance against God was unsurpassed. When he entered the Temple sanctuary he pounded on the altar and taunted: "O Wolf! O Wolf! You are a monarch and I am a monarch! Come, let us do battle with one another!"

Nor was Titus alone in this defiance. He was merely continuing the attitude of his father Vespasian, who had begun the siege against Jerusalem and had continued it until he was elected Emperor of Rome. Then he appointed his son Titus to complete the destruction of the city. Therefore many Midrashim which describe the destruction refer to one or the other of these wicked men, or to both.

God allowed the brutal Roman legions to vanquish their Jewish victims. Jerusalem was reduced to rubble; the Temple was destroyed. The human toll was staggering: "The number of captives was 97,000. The number of those who perished (from starvation or pestilence) or were slaughtered by the sword was one million and one hundred thousand" (Josephus, *Wars of the Jews* VI, 9:3). Even after Jerusalem fell, the Romans relentlessly hunted down every Jew they could find. Thus, they supplied victims for cruel torture for the amusement of Titus and his cohorts in sensational celebrations throughout the Roman Empire.

To emphasize how important this victory over the Jews was, a special coin was minted and issued to commemorate this event. On one side appears the head of Vespasian garlanded by a victory wreath; the reverse side depicts a Roman legionnaire leaning on his spear, while a forlorn figure representing the Jews weeps piteously under a palm tree. The inscription reads, *Judea Capta* — Judah is a captive! Moreover, Titus had a huge monument erected to mark this great triumph, an arch upon which are engraved scenes of the sacred vessels being plundered from the *Beis HaMikdash.* This Arch of Titus, which has endured for almost 2000 years, is one of the most dramatic structures of the Imperial Capital, and is a constant reminder to us that we have not yet fully repented the sins that vouchsafed to Titus the power to destroy our *Beis HaMikdash.*

This *kinnah,* by R' Elazar HaKalir, depicts Titus' wicked acts when he entered and destroyed the Temple. The first and third line of each quatrain begin with the opening words of the corresponding verses in Chapter Five of *Eichah* and appear in bold type. The second words of those lines form an *aleph-beis* acrostic.

זָכוֹר אֲשֶׁר עָשָׂה צַר בִּפְנִים — *Remember what the oppressor [Titus] did inside [the Temple].* The Talmud *(Gittin* 56b) relates that when Titus entered the Holy

שָׁלַף חַרְבּוֹ וּבָא לִפְנַי וְלִפְנִים,

he unsheathed ‹ his sword ‹ and entered ‹ within ‹ the innermost [chamber, the Holiest of the Holies]. «

נַחֲלָתֵנוּ בְּעֵת כְּטִמֵּא לֶחֶם הַפָּנִים,

[Throughout] our heritage ‹ he struck terror ‹ when he desecrated ‹ the bread ‹ of surfaces, «

וְגִדֵּר פָּרֹכֶת בַּעֲלַת שְׁתֵּי פָנִים.[1]*

and he stabbed ‹ the Partition Curtain ‹ having ‹ two ‹ sides.* «

יְתוֹמִים גֹּעֵל בְּמָגֵן מְאָדָּם,[2]*

The orphaned [nation] ‹ he defiled ‹ with a shield ‹ red with blood;* «

וַיְמַדֵּד קָו[3] כְּמַרְאֵה אֲדַמְדָּם,

and he measured them [for death] ‹ along a line ‹ whose appearance ‹ was blood-red. «

מֵימֵינוּ דָּלַח וְהִשְׁכִּיר חִצָּיו מִדָּם,[4]

Our waters ‹ he muddied, ‹ and he inebriated ‹ his arrows ‹ with blood, «

כְּיָצָא מִן הַבַּיִת וְחַרְבּוֹ מְלֵאָה דָם.

as he emerged ‹ from ‹ the Temple ‹ with his sword ‹ full ‹ of blood. «

(1) Some editions read בְּבַעֲלַת שְׁתֵּי פָנִים, *with a double-edged [blade].*
(2) Cf. *Nahum* 2:4. (3) Cf. *II Samuel* 8:2. (4) Cf. *Deuteronomy* 32:42.

Temple he cursed and blasphemed the God of Israel. He dragged a prostitute into the Holy of Holies and unrolled a holy Torah scroll and committed unspeakably lewd acts upon it. He then unsheathed his sword (already bloodied with the blood of countless Jewish victims) and slashed the פָּרוֹכֶת, *Partition Curtain* (that separated the Sanctuary from the Holiest of the Holies), to shreds. A miracle occurred and blood began to flow from the curtain. Thus Titus imagined that he had actually pierced and slain God Himself!

פָּרֹכֶת בַּעֲלַת שְׁתֵּי פָנִים — *The Partition Curtain having two sides.* The *Paroches* was woven in an intricate manner with various designs depicted on each of its sides. Two views are stated in the Talmud: (a) "A lion on one side, and a lion on the other": the same picture was visible from either side (or, as some explain, the front view of the lion on the front of the curtain, and the back view of the same lion on the reverse); or, (b) "a lion on one side, and an eagle on the other": totally different scenes on each side (*Yerushalmi Shekalim* 8:2).

יְתוֹמִים גֹּעֵל בְּמָגֵן מְאָדָּם — *The orphaned [nation] he defiled with a shield red with blood.* Josephus (*Wars of the Jews* VI, 5:1) described the misery and destruction brought about by Titus:

"There was a shout of the Roman le-

עַל הֲגוּתוֹ הַוּוֹת גָּבֶר,

[We mourn] over ‹ the plans ‹ for treachery ‹ of the man [Titus], «

וְנָטָה אֶל אֵל יָדוֹ לְמוּלוֹ לְגַבֵּר,[1]

who stretched out ‹ against ‹ God ‹ his hand, « against Him ‹ attempting to overpower. «

מִצְרַיִם וְכָל לְאוֹם אִם בָּם גָּבַר,

[He bragged,] Egypt ‹ and every other ‹ nation, ‹ even if ‹ [eventually,] them ‹ He conquered, «

אֲנִי בְּתוֹךְ אִוּוּיו אָרוּץ אֵלָיו בְּצַוָּאר.[2]*

*I « — even within ‹ His own beloved [Temple] — « I shall rush ‹ toward Him ‹ with [haughty] neck.** «

אֲבוֹתֵינוּ זָרָה כְּהִכְנִיסוּ[3] **בַּחוּרָיו אֻכְּלָה אֵשׁ,**[4]

In our ancestors [times], ‹ an alien [fire] ‹ when they brought it [into the Tabernacle], « His young men, [Aaron's sons,] ‹ were consumed ‹ by fire, «

וְזֶה זוֹנָה צוֹעָה הִכְנִיס[5] **וְלֹא נִכְוָה בָּאֵשׁ,***

while this [Titus], « a harlot ‹ who was wanton ‹ brought inside [the Holiest of the Holies], « yet he was not burnt ‹ by the fire.* «

עֲבָדִים חִתּוּ בְּתוֹכוֹ לַבַּת אֵשׁ,

[The Babylonians,] a slave-nation ‹ stoked ‹ within it ‹ the flames ‹ of fire; «

(1) Cf. *Job* 15:25. (2) 15:26. (3) *Psalms* 78:63. (4) See *Leviticus* 10:1-2. (5) Cf. *Jeremiah* 2:20.

gions as they marched together, and a sad clamor of the people, now surrounded by fire and sword .... Many who were worn away by starvation so that their mouths were almost closed, when they saw the Holy House on fire they exerted their last strength and broke out in groans and outcry. The mountains around the city returned the echo and increased the noise .... The Temple Mount was seething with fire in every part, and the blood was even more than the fire . . . for the ground was not visible because of the dead bodies that covered it; the soldiers went over heaps of those bodies in pursuit of those fleeing from them."

בְּצַוָּאר — *With [haughty] neck.* The translation is based upon *Rashi's* interpretation of this phrase in *Job* 15:26 (see also *Psalms* 75:6). Alternatively, it is an allusion to the Temple and Altar, both of which are compared to the straight neck of stately stature (see commentaries to *Song of Songs* 4:4 and 7:5).

בַּחוּרָיו אֻכְּלָה אֵשׁ . . . וְלֹא נִכְוָה בָּאֵשׁ — *His young men, [Aaron's sons,] were consumed by fire . . . yet he was not burnt by*

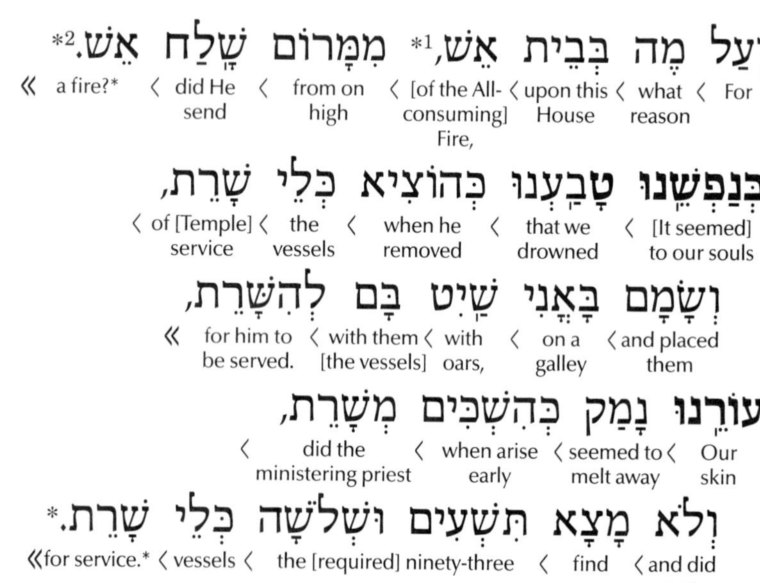

וְעַל מֶה בְּבֵית אֵשׁ,*¹ מִמָּרוֹם שָׁלַח אֵשׁ.*²
For reason 〈 what 〈 upon this House 〈 [of the All-consuming] Fire, 〈 from on high 〈 did He send 〈 a fire?* «
בְּנַפְשֵׁנוּ טָבַעְנוּ כְּהוֹצִיא כְּלֵי שָׁרֵת,
[It seemed] to our souls 〈 that we drowned 〈 when he removed 〈 the vessels 〈 of [Temple] service 〈
וְשָׂמָם בָּאֳנִי שַׁיִט בָּם לְהִשָּׁרֵת,
and placed them 〈 on a galley 〈 with oars, 〈 with them [the vessels] 〈 for him to be served. «
עוֹרֵנוּ נָמַק כְּהִשְׁכִּים מְשָׁרֵת,
Our skin 〈 seemed to melt away 〈 when arise early 〈 did the ministering priest 〈
וְלֹא מָצָא תִּשְׁעִים וּשְׁלֹשָׁה כְּלֵי שָׁרֵת.*
and did not 〈 find 〈 the [required] ninety-three 〈 vessels 〈 for service.* «

(1) *Cf. Deuteronomy* 4:24. (2) *Eichah* 1:13.

---

the fire. These two eldest sons of Aaron were pious and holy but they erred in their service on the very day of the Tabernacle's inauguration, Rosh Chodesh Nissan 2449. Bolts of fire burst forth from the Holiest of the Holies, entered their nostrils and consumed their innards, yet their outer flesh and garments remained perfectly intact. The fact that they were punished so severely for their error, while Titus, who intentionally committed every form of atrocity and sacrilege, was left unscathed, demonstrates that they entered the House of God when it was at the height of its sanctity, and God's Presence permeated its environs with unsurpassed intimacy and intensity. Therefore, the slightest deviation caused a serious flaw in the awesome level of sanctity maintained at that moment. Titus, however, entered the Temple only after God's Presence had departed in anger over the sins of Israel. Therefore, his victory was truly a hollow one, because he destroyed an empty shell, a meaningless facade. Although Titus' intentions were entirely evil, God left him unharmed. This demonstrated that Titus was unwittingly a tool of the Divine will to destroy the Temple from which the sins of Israel had chased the protective *Shechinah.*

בְּבֵית אֵשׁ — *Upon the House [of the All-consuming] Fire.* Alternatively, the *Beis HaMikdash* is the House of the Altar and Menorah fires, both of which had miraculous elements: The Altar fire was never extinguished, even though it stood in the open air (see *Avos* 5:7); the נֵר מַעֲרָבִי, *western lamp,* of the Menorah would still be burning, long after the other lamps (with the same amount of oil and same size wicks) had gone out (see *Shabbos* 22b).

וְעַל מֶה... מִמָּרוֹם שָׁלַח אֵשׁ — *For what reason . . . from On High did He send a fire?* The translation treats the entire line as a rhetorical question. Alternatively, it comprises a question and answer: *How could this happen to the House of Fire? — He sent a fire from on high!*

תִּשְׁעִים וּשְׁלֹשָׁה כְּלֵי שָׁרֵת — *The [required] ninety-three vessels for service.* Each morning, the *Kohanim* of the day's watch would remove exactly ninety-three vessels needed for the Temple service (*Tamid*

נָשִׁים כְּשָׁרוּ כִּי בָא עָרִיץ,

« did the ruthless one, ‹ enter ‹ that ‹ [were terrified] when they saw ‹ The women

בְּקַרְקַע הַבַּיִת נְעָלָיו הֶחֱרִיץ,[1]

« scratched grooves. ‹ his [spiked] shoes ‹ of the Temple ‹ and that in the floor

שָׂרִים* לְפָתוּ כְּבוֹא פָרִיץ,

« the wanton one, ‹ when entered ‹ were terror-struck ‹ Princes*

בְּבֵית קֹדֶשׁ הַקֳּדָשִׁים צַחֲנָתוֹ הִשְׁרִיץ.

« he spawned. ‹ his foul stench ‹ of the Holies ‹ Holiest ‹ In the Temple's

בַּחוּרִים מִבַּחוּץ צָגוּ מְחֻזָּקִים,

« resolute, ‹ stood ‹ outside ‹ The young men

וְתָרוּ כִּי יוּזַק בְּשִׁשִּׁים רִבּוֹא מַזִּיקִים,*

« of demons [there].* ‹ myriads ‹ by the sixty ‹ [Titus] would be harmed ‹ that ‹ they thought

זְקֵנִים נִבְעֲתוּ כְּהִרְשׁוּהוּ מִשְּׁחָקִים[2]

‹ from heaven ‹ when permission was given ‹ panicked ‹ Elders

עֲשׂוֹת רְצוֹנוֹ וְהוּא אָסוּר בָּאזִקִּים.[3]

« in chains. ‹ [appeared to be] bound ‹ while [God] « his will, ‹ for [Titus] to do

(1) See *Kinnah* 13. (2) Some editions read מְחֻזָּקִים, *from the powerful [heavens].* (3) *Jeremiah* 40:1.

3:4). On the morning of the day on which the *Beis HaMikdash* was to fall, the *Kohanim* could not find all ninety-three vessels — something that had never happened before.

שָׂרִים — *Princes.* This refers either to the nobility of Jerusalem, or to the heavenly angels who are called שָׂרִים. When the sinful were admonished that Jerusalem would be destroyed unless they would mend their ways, they replied, "We know the Divine Names that are the lifeblood of the various angels appointed over the elements. Should we be attacked, we will call upon the angels to surround us with walls of water, or fire, or iron." But God confounded them by exchanging each angel's role with another's. Thus, when the people called upon the angels that formerly protected them, the answer was always the same, "That is no longer within my realm." These angels now cringed because they were unable to help Israel (*Yalkut Shimoni II*:1023).

וְתָרוּ כִּי יוּזַק בְּשִׁשִּׁים רִבּוֹא מַזִּיקִים — *They thought that [Titus] would be harmed by the sixty myriads of demons [there].* When the Roman enemies came to destroy

שָׁבַת סוֹטֵן וַיָּבֹא אַדְמוֹן,

When withdrew ‹ the Satanic one [Babylon], ‹ there arrived ‹ the Red One [Rome]; «

וַיְסַבֵּב חוֹמָה וַיְעַוֵּת הָמוֹן,

he surrounded ‹ the wall ‹ and made desolate ‹ the populace. «

נָפְלָה עֶבְרָה עַל נִינֵי פִּצֵּל לַח וְלוּז וְעַרְמוֹן,[1]

Fall ‹ did the wrath [of God] ‹ upon ‹ the descendants ‹ of [Jacob] who had peeled ‹ fresh [rods] ‹ of hazel ‹ and of chestnut, «

עַד כִּי נֻטַּשׁ מִדּוּק אַרְמוֹן.

until [the point] ‹ when ‹ abandoned ‹ by heaven ‹ was the palace. «

עַל פֶּתַח הַר הַבַּיִת הֵחֵל לָבֹא,

Upon ‹ the entrance ‹ of the Mount ‹ of the Temple ‹ [Titus] began ‹ to advance, «

בְּיַד אַרְבָּעָה רָאשֵׁי טַפְסְרָיו לְהַחֲרִיבוֹ,

through the hand ‹ of his four ‹ chief ‹ commanders ‹ to destroy it. «

עַל צַד מַעֲרָבִי לְזֵכֶר הִשְׁרִיד בּוֹ,*

On ‹ the side ‹ to the West, « as a memorial, « he left a remnant ‹ of it,* «

(1) See *Genesis* 30:37.

Jerusalem, six hundred thousand demons waited at the gateway of the Temple to attack and harm them. However, the demons realized that God Himself witnessed the atrocities the Romans perpetrated, yet remained silent, as it is written: *He withdrew His right hand in the presence of the enemy.* Therefore the demons said, "If God does not interfere, we too will not interfere!" (*Devarim Rabbah* 1:17).

עַל צַד מַעֲרָבִי לְזֵכֶר הִשְׁרִיד בּוֹ — *On the side to the West, as a memorial, he left a remnant of it.* The Midrash states: When Vespasian besieged Jerusalem, he assigned four different generals to raze the four sections of the city. The western sector fell to the lot of a general named Pangar. In heaven it was decreed that the Western Wall of the Temple Mount should not be destroyed and, indeed, while the other three generals destroyed their sectors, Pangar allowed the Western Wall to stand intact. Vespasian summoned him and demanded an explanation, to which Pangar responded, "I swear that my intention is only to glorify your reputation, O royal master! Had I obliterated every last vestige of this metropolis of Jerusalem, later generations would have no idea of the scope of your victory, for they might think that Jerusalem was no more than a tiny town. But now that I have left over this massive Western Wall as a memorial, it will be known for all

וְצָג אַחַר כָּתְלֵנוּ וְלֹא רָב רִיבוֹ.

« for its cause. ‹ fight ‹ but did not « our wall, ‹ behind ‹ and [God] stood

אַתָּה קָצַפְתָּ וְהִרְשֵׁיתָ לְפַנּוֹת,

« to empty [the Temple], ‹ that You allowed them ‹ were so enraged ‹ You, [God,]

יְלָדִים אֲשֶׁר אֵין בָּהֶם כָּל מְאוּם מִשָּׁם לְהַפְנוֹת,[1]

« [You allowed] to remove. ‹ from there [Jerusalem] « blemish, ‹ any ‹ in them ‹ there was not ‹ that ‹ and the children

לָמָּה רָגְשׁוּ גוֹיִם[2] **וְלֹא שָׁעַתָּ אֶל הַמִּנְחָה פְּנוֹת,**[3]

« to turn toward it? ‹ my offering, ‹ to ‹ while You did not pay attention ‹ do [You allow] the nations to gather [against me] ‹ Why

וְשִׁלְּחוּם בְּאֶרֶץ עוּץ בְּשָׁלֹשׁ סְפִינוֹת.*

« ships.* ‹ in three ‹ of Uz ‹ to the land ‹ They sent them [the children]

הֲשִׁיבֵנוּ שִׁוְּעוּ כְּבָאוּ בְּנִבְכֵי יָם,[4]

« of the sea, ‹ into the depths ‹ as they sank ‹ they cried out ‹ *Bring us back!* [to eternal life]

(1) *Daniel* 1:4. (2) *Psalms* 2:1. (3) Cf. *Malachi* 2:13. (4) Cf. *Job* 38:16.

time that your majesty conquered a major city of colossal proportions!"

The Emperor said to him, "You have defended yourself very well; nevertheless, since you failed to follow my command, you must climb to the top of a tower and throw yourself off. If you survive, I will let you live; but if you die, then indeed you will have received the death penalty you deserve!" Pangar threw himself from the top of a tower and was killed, for Rabban Yochanan ben Zakkai had uttered a curse against him, saying, "Your own heart knows what your real intentions are! You claim to have preserved the Western Wall for the glory of Vespasian, but in your heart you know full well that you desire a memorial to commemorate the utter defeat and destruction of the Jewish people!" (*Midrash Eichah* 1:32).

וְשִׁלְּחוּם בְּאֶרֶץ עוּץ בְּשָׁלֹשׁ סְפִינוֹת — *They sent them [the children] to the land of Uz in three ships.* This is based on the narrative related in the Talmud *(Gittin* 57b) and the Midrash *(Midrash Eichah)* and presented here in composite form: Vespasian (or Titus) filled three galleys with four hundred of the finest youths of Jerusalem, boys and girls, and sent them off to Rome for immoral purposes. The children realized this and preferred taking their own lives to living in sin, yet they were uncertain whether suicide is permissible under such circumstances. They feared they might forfeit their share in the World to Come. God inspired them with a holy spirit to expound a verse from Scripture which gave them guidance and comfort: *My Lord promised, "I will bring back from Bashan* (those threatened by בּוּשָׁה, *immoral disgrace), I will bring back from the depths of the sea"* (God will revivify

וְשִׁתְּפוּ עַצְמָם יַחַד לִנְפּוֹל בַּיָּם,

as they joined 〈 themselves [in a pact] 〈 together 〈 to fall 〈 into the sea. 《

שִׁיר וְתִשְׁבָּחוֹת שׁוֹרְרוּ כְּעַל יָם,

Song 〈 and praises 〈 they sang 〈 as [Israel did] at 〈 the Sea [of Reeds], 《

כִּי עָלֶיךָ הוֹרַגְנוּ[1] בִּמְצוּלוֹת יָם.

Because 〈 *for Your sake* 〈 *we are killed* 〈 *in the depths* 〈 *of the Sea!* 《

כִּי תְהוֹמוֹת בָּאוּ עַד נַפְשָׁם,

Even as 〈 the depths 〈 reached 〈 until 〈 their souls, 《

כָּל זֹאת בָּאַתְנוּ וְלֹא שְׁכַחֲנוּךָ חִלּוּ לְמַמָּשָׁן,[2]

All 〈 *this* 〈 *has befallen us,* 〈 *yet we have not forgotten You!* 《 they prayed 〈 to their Real One, 《

תִּקְוָתָם נָתְנוּ לְמֵשִׁיב מִבָּשָׁן,[3]

Their hope 〈 they placed 〈 in the One [Who promised] to bring [them] back 〈 from Bashan, 《

וּבַת קוֹל נִשְׁמְעָה עוּרָה לָמָּה תִישָׁן.[4]

and an echo 〈 of a voice [from heaven] 〈 was heard, 《 *Awaken!* 《 *Why* 〈 *do You seem to sleep?* 《

(1) *Psalms* 44:23. (2) Cf. 44:21. (3) Cf. 68:23. (4) 44:24.

and reward those who drown themselves in the sea in order to preserve their purity and to sanctify God's Name) (*Psalms* 68:23). Upon hearing this, all the maidens leaped into the sea without any hesitation. The youths immediately followed their inspiring example.

As they performed this ultimate act of *Kiddush Hashem*, Sanctification of God's Holy Name, those on the first ship cried out, *"Have we forgotten the Name of our God and extended our hands to a strange god?"* (ibid. 44:21). Those on the second ship cried out, *"Is it not so that God can examine this? For He knows the secrets of the heart!"* (44:22). Those on the third ship cried out, *"Because for Your sake we are killed all the time, we are considered as sheep for slaughter"* (44:23).

Concerning these young and innocent martyrs Jeremiah laments, *"Over these people I weep; my eyes run with water .... My children have been destroyed, because the enemy has prevailed"* (*Lamentations* 1:16). And about them does the remainder of this *kinnah* speak.

KINNAH 17 / קינה יז

אֵם* תֹּאכַלְנָה נָשִׁים פִּרְיָם עוֹלְלֵי טִפּוּחִים,[1]

How [could it be that]* women ate their offspring, the young children that they cared for?

אַלְלַי לִי.[2]

— Woe unto me!

(1) *Eichah* 2:20. (2) *Job* 10:15.

אֵם — *How [could it be that].* This *kinnah* describes in horrible detail how the scope of the Destruction was not merely confined to material objects. Rather, this event ripped out the very moral fiber of the people and utterly distorted their essential personality traits. The Talmud teaches that the Jewish nation is identified by three basic qualities: they are רַחֲמָנִים, בַּיְשָׁנִים, וְגוֹמְלֵי חֲסָדִים, *compassionate, modest, and performers of kindness* (*Yevamos* 79a). The intense suffering of the Destruction crazed the Jewish People and stripped them of the most elementary, normal human feelings and emotions, to the point where mothers relished the opportunity to cook the flesh of their own babes in order to still their hunger, and children were not revolted to consume the remains of their dead parents.

Concurrently, the heathen conquerors, already barbaric, were roused to an unprecedented level of cruelty and depravity and perpetrated every form of unspeakable atrocity against their Jewish victims.

In the closing stanza of this *kinnah*, the author, R' Elazar HaKalir, reveals the true reason for this atmosphere of utter inhumanity. It all stemmed from the astonishing crime which the Jewish nation committed as a whole. Two hundred and fifty years before the destruction of the Temple, in the reign of King Joash, the prophet and priest Zechariah ben Jehoiada admonished the nation, in the person of the king, in the Temple courtyard on Yom Kippur. So perverted were the people that instead of heeding the rebuke of their spiritual leader, they allowed the cold-blooded stoning and murder of their holiest leader, on the holiest day of the year, in the holiest location on earth. It was this crime which totally corrupted the Jewish people and distorted their nature, and for this God exacted terrible vengeance at the time of the Temple's Destruction.

Each line of the *kinnah* begins with אֵם . . . ת, *How*, followed by the third-person feminine prefix. The second letter of the second word of each line forms the *aleph-beis*. The letters א מ ת spell the word אֱמֶת, *truth* or *it is true*. Perhaps this is an allusion to that which the *paytan* writes in the closing stanza, namely, that God was in full accord with the punishments described in the first twenty-two verses of the *kinnah*. Similarly, we find that when the Sages wished to eradicate the overpowering *yetzer hara* of idolatry from Israel, a note fell from heaven on which was written אֱמֶת, *it is true*. This proved that God agreed to their plan, for אֱמֶת is the signet of God (*Yoma* 69b; *Sanhedrin* 63a).

The significance of the letters א מ ת is that they come at the beginning, middle, and end of the *aleph-beis*. Thus they allude to the fact that God is the First, the Last, and has no equal or partner (*Yerushalmi Sanhedrin* 1:1). Accordingly, with this scheme, as with the alphabetical arrangement, the *paytan* intimates that the sins of the generation ran the gamut from א to ת.

אִם תְּבַשֵּׁלְנָה נָשִׁים רַחֲמָנִיּוֹת יְלָדִים[1]

How [could it be that] ‹ boil ‹ would women ‹ who were compassionate ‹ [their own] children

הַמְּדוּדִים טְפָחִים טְפָחִים,* אַלְלַי לִי.

whom they had measured ‹ handbreadth ‹ by handbreadth?* « Woe — ‹ unto me! «

אִם תְּגֻזְּנָה פְּאַת רֹאשָׁם

How [could it be that] ‹ torn out ‹ were the hair tresses ‹ from their heads ‹

וְתִקְשַׁרְנָה לְסוּסִים פּוֹרְחִים,* אַלְלַי לִי.

by being tied ‹ to horses ‹ swiftly galloping?* « Woe — ‹ unto me! «

אִם תִּדְבַּק לְשׁוֹן יוֹנֵק לְחֵיךְ:[2]

How [could it be that] ‹ adhere ‹ would the tongue ‹ of the nursing baby ‹ to its palate ‹

בְּצִמָּאוֹן צְחִיחִים, אַלְלַי לִי.

through thirst ‹ that is desiccating? « Woe — ‹ unto me! «

אִם תְּהוֹמֶינָה זוֹ לְעֻמַּת זוֹ

How [could it be that] ‹ cry in turmoil ‹ would one [mother] ‹ facing ‹ another, «

בּוֹאִי וּנְבַשֵּׁל אֶת בָּנֵינוּ צוֹרְחִים, אַלְלַי לִי.

Come, ‹ *let us boil* ‹ *our children* ‹ *who are shrieking [from hunger]!* « Woe — ‹ unto me! «

אִם תִּוָּעַדְנָה זוֹ לְזוֹ תְּנִי בְנֵךְ

How [could it be that] ‹ [after eating one of their babies,] the two met ‹ and one [said] ‹ to the other, « *Give* ‹ *your son!* «

(1) Cf. *Eichah* 4:10. (2) Cf. 4:4; *Psalms* 137:6.

טְפָחִים טְפָחִים — *Handbreadth by handbreadth.* The Talmud relates that when Doeg ben Yosef died, his widow was left with a young son. Each year, she would measure his growth by handbreadths and donate an equivalent amount of gold coins to the Temple treasury in honor of her son. But when the siege intensified against Jerusalem, she was caught in the throes of starvation until she slaughtered and ate her precious son (*Yoma* 38b).

וְתִקְשַׁרְנָה לְסוּסִים פּוֹרְחִים — *By being tied to horses swiftly galloping.* The Midrash recounts how, after the Destruction,

וְהוּא חָבוּי מְנֻתָּח נְתָחִים,[1] אַלְלַי לִי.

But he | was hidden away | already cut | to pieces? — Woe | unto me!

אִם תְּזֻמֶּינָה בְּשַׂר אָבוֹת לַבָּנִים*

How [could it be that] | prepared | was the flesh | of the fathers | for [their] sons [to eat]*

בִּמְעָרוֹת וְשִׁיחִים, אַלְלַי לִי.

in caves | and ditches? — Woe | unto me!

אִם תְּחֻיַּבְנָה בָּנוֹת

How [could it be that] | condemned to die | were daughters

אֶל חֵיק אִמּוֹתָם נִתְפָּחִים,[2] אַלְלַי לִי.

in | the bosom | of their mothers, | swollen [from starvation]? — Woe | unto me!

אִם תָּטֹסְנָה רוּחוֹת עוֹלְלִים

How [could it be that] | soar [heavenward] | did the spirits | of young children

בִּרְחוֹבוֹת קִרְיָה תְּפוּחִים,[3] אַלְלַי לִי.

[who were lying] in the streets | of the city, | their bodies swollen? — Woe | unto me!

אִם תְּיַקֶּרְנָה בְּשִׁכּוּל רֶחֶם וְצִמּוּק שָׁדַיִם[4]

How [could it be that] | weighed down [were women] | by miscarriage | of womb | and shriveling | of breast,

(1) See *II Kings* 6:28-29. (2) Cf. *Eichah* 2:12. (3) Cf. 2:11. (4) Cf. *Hosea* 9:14.

Miriam bas Baisos, wife of the *Kohen Gadol* Yehoshua ben Gamla, was tied by her hair to the tails of Arabian steeds and was dragged from Jerusalem to Lud (*Midrash Eichah* 1:47).

בְּשַׂר אָבוֹת לַבָּנִים — The *flesh of the fathers . . . for [their] sons [to eat].* When the siege was at its peak and the hunger most intense, one man of a group went out to find a corpse they could scavenge. When he chanced upon his own father's body, he buried it in a shallow grave and made a sign to enable him to recognize the spot. Then he returned empty-handed to his comrades. They sent out a second man to seek food. He returned with a corpse which they proceeded to eat. Later the first scout asked, "I was unable to find anything to eat. Where did you find this body?" The second described how he had exhumed it from a freshly dug grave which was marked in such and such a

וְאֵם עַל בָּנִים שָׁחִים, אַלְלַי לִי.
‹ and that mother ‹ over ‹ [dying] sons ‹ is bent over? ‹ — Woe ‹ unto me!

אִם תִּכָּשַׁלְנָה שְׁמוֹנֶה מֵאוֹת מָגִנִּים
‹ How [could it be that] ‹ trapped ‹ were eight ‹ hundred [young *Kohanim*] ‹ [who bore] shields,

בַּעֲרַב אֱלוֹחִים, אַלְלַי לִי.
‹ in Arabia ‹ where they fell to foul decay? ‹ — Woe ‹ unto me!

אִם תְּלֻהַטְנָה רוּחָם בְּמִינֵי מְלוּחִים
‹ How [could it be that] ‹ set on fire ‹ was their breath ‹ with a variety ‹ of salty foods

וְנוֹדוֹת נְפוּחִים,* אַלְלַי לִי.
‹ and [they died trying to drink from] wineskins ‹ inflated with [hot, stale] air?* ‹ — Woe ‹ unto me!

אִם תִּמָּעַטְנָה מֵאֶלֶף מֵאָה וּמִמֵּאָה עֲשָׂרָה
‹ How [could it be that] ‹ they were decimated ‹ from one thousand ‹ to one hundred, ‹ and from one hundred ‹ to ten,

עַד אֶחָד[1] לְמַפָּחִים, אַלְלַי לִי.
‹ until ‹ but one [remained] ‹ as a source of terrible sorrow? ‹ — Woe ‹ unto me!

אִם תָּנֹסְנָה לְמָסַךְ הֵיכָל
‹ How [could it be that] ‹ flee ‹ to the sheltering ‹ Sanctuary

שְׁמוֹנִים אֶלֶף כֹּהֲנִים פִּרְחִים, אַלְלַי לִי.
‹ did eighty ‹ thousand ‹ priest ‹ youths? ‹ — Woe ‹ unto me!

(1) Cf. *Amos* 5:3.

manner. And the first screamed, "Woe is me! For I have eaten my father's flesh!" (*Midrash Eichah* 1:45).

וְנוֹדוֹת נְפוּחִים — *Wineskins inflated with [hot, stale] air.* Various Midrashim describe how, when the captives were led through the lands of Arabia, the Ishmaelites met them on the way and appeared to be friendly and sympathetic. They offered bread and other foods, all of which

אִם תִּשָּׂרַפְנָה שָׁם כָּל אוֹתָם הַנְּפָשׁוֹת

How [could it be that] ‹ burned ‹ there ‹ were all ‹ those ‹ souls ‹

כְּקוֹצִים כְּסוּחִים, אַלְלַי לִי.

like thorn ‹ cuttings? « — Woe ‹ unto me! «

אִם תֵּעָרַפְנָה עַל דַּם נָקִי

How [could it be that] ‹ beheaded ‹ over ‹ the blood ‹ of an innocent [Zechariah], ‹

שְׁמוֹנִים אֶלֶף כֹּהֲנִים מְשׁוּחִים,[1] אַלְלַי לִי.

were eighty ‹ thousand ‹ *Kohanim* ‹ who were anointed? « — Woe ‹ unto me! «

אִם תְּפַחְנָה נְפָשׁוֹת מְדֻקָּרִים

How [could it be that] ‹ swollen ‹ were the souls [of the starving defenders] ‹ who were stabbed ‹

מֵרֵיחַ תְּנוּבוֹת שִׂיחִים,[2] אַלְלַי לִי.

by the aroma ‹ of the produce ‹ of the trees? « — Woe ‹ unto me! «

אִם תִּצָּבַרְנָה עַל אֶבֶן אַחַת

How [could it be that] ‹ heaped ‹ on ‹ one stone, «

תִּשְׁעָה קַבִּין מוֹחֵי יְלָדִים מֻנָּחִים, אַלְלַי לִי.

nine ‹ *kabs* ‹ of brains ‹ of children ‹ were placed? « — Woe ‹ unto me! «

אִם תּוּקַּעְנָה שְׁלֹשׁ מֵאוֹת יוֹנְקִים

How [could it be that] ‹ hung [to die] ‹ were three ‹ hundred ‹ nursing babies; «

---

(1) See *Kinnah* 34. (2) Cf. *Eichah* 4:9.

---

had been oversalted. Soon the Jews asked for something to drink. The Ishmaelites offered them leather canteens that they had filled with air and left hanging in the sun. Thinking they were full of refreshing liquid, the unfortunate captives — whose hands were tied behind their back — bit off the plugs with their teeth. The hot, stagnant air in the bags filled their lungs and killed them (*Tanchuma Yisro* 5; *Midrash Eichah; Yerushalmi Taanis* 4:5).

עַל שׂוֹכָה אַחַת מְתוּחִים, אַלְלַי לִי.
〈 on 〈 a single branch 〈 they were stretched out? 《 — Woe 〈 unto me! 《

אִם תֵּרָאֶינָה רַכּוֹת וַעֲנֻגּוֹת[1] כְּבוּלוֹת
〈 How [could it be that] 〈 were seen 〈 delicate, 〈 and pampered women 〈 bound in chains, 〈

עַל יַד רַב טַבָּחִים, אַלְלַי לִי.
〈 by 〈 the hand 〈 of the chief 〈 butcher? 《 — Woe 〈 unto me! 《

אִם תִּשְׁכַּבְנָה בֵּין שְׁפַתַּיִם*[2]
〈 How [could it be that] 〈 violated 〈 among 〈 the open roadsides* 〈

בְּנוֹת נְדִיבִים מְשֻׁבָּחִים, אַלְלַי לִי.
〈 were the daughters 〈 of nobles 〈 who were distinguished? 《 — Woe 〈 unto me! 《

אִם תִּתְעַלַּפְנָה הַבְּתוּלוֹת וְהַבַּחוּרִים
〈 How [could it be that] 〈 faint 〈 did the young maidens 〈 and the young men 〈

בְּצִמָּאוֹן צְחִיחִים, אַלְלַי לִי.
〈 from thirst 〈 that was desiccating? 《 — Woe 〈 unto me! 《

וְרוּחַ הַקֹּדֶשׁ לְמוּלָם מַרְעִים,
〈 But the Holy Spirit 〈 back to them 〈 thundered: 《

הוֹי עַל כָּל שְׁכֵנַי הָרָעִים,
〈 *Woe* 〈 *unto* 〈 *all* 〈 *My neighbors* 〈 *who are wicked!* 《

(1) Cf. *Deuteronomy* 28:56. (2) Cf. *Psalms* 68:14, *Genesis* 49:14.

בֵּין שְׁפַתָּיִם — *Among the open roadsides* [lit., *between the borders*]. The translation and interpretation follow *Rashi* (*Genesis* 49:14 and *Psalms* 68:14). The captive women were not permitted to sleep in the cities they passed on their way to Babylon, but had to sleep out in the open, exposed to the elements. Some interpret that these women were publicly violated when they were made to lie on the roadsides.

Various other interpretations of this phrase are possible: The noble daughters were forced to work as kitchen slaves and had to sleep among the racks of pots (see *Ibn Ezra* to *Psalms* 68:14); they were

מַה שֶׁהִקְרָאָם מוֹדִיעִים,

« they publicize, ‹ which befell them, ‹ Those [tragedies]

וְאֵת אֲשֶׁר עָשׂוּ לֹא מוֹדִיעִים,

« they do not publicize. ‹ they perpetrated, ‹ which ‹ but that [evil]

אִם תֹּאכַלְנָה נָשִׁים פִּרְיָם מַשְׁמִיעִים,

« they proclaim, « their offspring?" ‹ women ate ‹ "How [could it be that]

וְאִם יֵהָרֵג בְּמִקְדַּשׁ יהוה כֹּהֵן וְנָבִיא

« and a prophet?" ‹ a Kohen ‹ of HASHEM ‹ in the Sanctuary ‹ there be slain ‹ but "How [could it be that]

לֹא מַשְׁמִיעִים.

« they do not proclaim!

---

forced to till the soil and sleep between the furrows (see *Rashbam* to *Genesis* 49:14); they were forced to carry heavy double burdens and collapsed under their weight (see *Sforno* ibid.). None of these views are mutually exclusive, for all of these atrocities may have been perpetrated against the captives.

KINNAH 18 / קינה יח

וְאַתָּה אָמַרְתָּ* הֵיטֵב אֵיטִיב עִמָּךְ,[1]
And You have said,* "I will surely do good with you!"

וְנִפְלֵינוּ אֲנִי וְעַמָּךְ,[2]
[And You agreed to Moses' request,] "Let us be made distinct — I and Your people."

וְלָמָּה בְּנֵי בְלִיַּעַל חִלְּלוּ שְׁמָךְ,
So, why, when people who are wicked desecrated Your Name,

וְלֹא שָׁפַכְתָּ עֲלֵיהֶם זַעְמָךְ.
You did not pour out upon them Your fury?

אַתָּה גִּדַּלְתָּ וְרוֹמַמְתָּ בָּנִים[3] לְהָנֵק,
You have raised and elevated children, nurturing [from the Land of milk and honey],

כַּאֲשֶׁר יִשָּׂא הָאוֹמֵן אֶת הַיּוֹנֵק,[4]
as a nurse carries a nursing baby.

וְלָמָּה דוֹדָנִים דָּצוּ לְזַנֵּק,
So, why [did You allow] their cousins [Ishmael] to joyously leap forth [against us];

וְאַרְיֵה גּוּרוֹתָיו לְחַנֵּק.[5]
as the leonine [Nebuchadnezzar] [Israel's] young cubs strangled?

אַתָּה הֵינַקְתָּ דְּבַשׁ מִסֶּלַע,[6]
You suckled [Israel] with honey from a rock,

(1) *Genesis* 32:13. (2) Cf. *Exodus* 33:16. (3) Cf. *Isaiah* 1:2. (4) *Numbers* 11:12. (5) Cf. *Nahum* 2:13. (6) Cf. *Deuteronomy* 32:13.

וְאַתָּה אָמַרְתָּ — *And You have said.* The stark contrast between God's extremely close relationship with the Jewish people in early times and His aloofness at the time of the Destruction is highlighted in this *kinnah*, by R' Elazar HaKalir. Each odd-numbered line begins with the word אַתָּה, *You,* and describes some aspect of the closeness that permeated the relationship in the past. Each even-numbered line begins וְלָמָּה, *So, why* have You, O God, permitted such drastic change? The second words of the respective lines form an alphabetical acrostic. The final stanza acknowledges that God is righteous in all His deeds, and we must accept responsibility for the bitter tragedies that are the consequences of our misguided action.

It is not clear why the first stanza begins with a connective ו, *and,* while the

וַתּוֹצִיא נוֹזְלִים מִסֶּלַע,[1]

« from the rock. ‹ flowing waters ‹ and You brought forth

וְלָמָּה שׁוֹפְטֵיהֶם נִשְׁמְטוּ בִידֵי סֶלַע,[2]

« [their hearts] of stone, ‹ through ‹ go astray ‹ did their judges ‹ So, why

וְעוֹלְלֵיהֶם נֻפְּצוּ אֶל הַסֶּלַע.[3]

« the rock? ‹ against ‹ to be smashed ‹ and [cause] their infants

אַתָּה זָנַחְתָּ וַתִּמְאַס[4] כָּל גּוֹי,

« nation, ‹ every ‹ and rejected ‹ abandoned ‹ You

לָקַחַת גּוֹי מִקֶּרֶב גּוֹי,[5]

« another nation. ‹ from amidst ‹ one nation ‹ in order to take

וְלָמָּה חָשׁ וְעָלָה עַל אַרְצִי גּוֹי,

‹ a [heathen] nation ‹ my land ‹ against ‹ there should arise ‹ did [You allow] that speedily ‹ So, why

וְאָמְרוּ לְכוּ וְנַכְחִידֵם מִגּוֹי.[6]

« *from nationhood.* ‹ *let us obliterate them* ‹ *Come* « that said,

אַתָּה טֵאטֵאתָ שִׁשִּׁים וּשְׁמוֹנִים,*

« and the eighty [concubinelike peoples]* ‹ the sixty [queenlike peoples] ‹ swept away ‹ You

לְהָבִיא גּוֹי שׁוֹמֵר אֱמוּנִים,

« the faith. ‹ which guards ‹ the one nation ‹ in order to bring forth

(1) Cf. *Psalms* 78:16. (2) Cf. 141:6. (3) Cf. 137:9. (4) Cf. 89:39. (5) Cf. *Deuteronomy* 4:34. (6) *Psalms* 83:5.

remaining stanzas do not. If anything, the opposite would be expected. Indeed, many old editions omit the opening ו.

שִׁשִּׁים וּשְׁמוֹנִים — *The sixty [queenlike peoples] and the eighty [concubinelike peoples].* This is based on the verse: שִׁשִּׁים הֵמָּה מְלָכוֹת וּשְׁמֹנִים פִּילַגְשִׁים, *There are sixty queens and eighty concubines* (*Song of Songs* 6:8). *Rashi* (ibid.), based on the Midrash, explains that *sixty queens* refers to the offspring of Abraham who were noble people, when compared to the rest of the world. The family heads directly descended from him were: the sixteen of Keturah; Isaac and his two children; Ishmael and his twelve family heads; the twelve sons of Jacob; and the sixteen family heads of Esau; a total of sixty. The vast majority of these nations were rejected by God in favor of Israel. *Eighty concubines* refers to Noah and his descendants until Abraham. The family heads descending from those leaving the Ark to rebuild and repopulate the earth

וְלָמָּה יָזְמוּ מוֹאָבִים וְעַמּוֹנִים,
So, why ‹ did [You allow] to conspire ‹ the Moabites ‹ and the Ammonites ‹

לְעַם זוּ[1] בַּכְּרוּבִים מוֹנִים.*
against this nation, ‹ because of the Cherubim ‹ to denounce them [as idolaters]?* «

אַתָּה כּוֹנַנְתָּ לְשֶׁבֶת הוֹדֶךָ,[2]
You ‹ aligned [Your Temple on earth] ‹ with the [celestial] throne ‹ of Your majesty, «

הַר זֶה קָנְתָה יְמִינְךָ וְיָדֶךָ,[3]
this mountain ‹ acquired by ‹ Your right hand ‹ with Your [other] hand. «

וְלָמָּה לְאָחוֹר הֵשַׁבְתָּ יְמִין יָדֶךָ,[4]
Why, then, ‹ backward ‹ did You withdraw ‹ Your [strongest] right ‹ hand ‹

וַתְּנַבֵּל כִּסֵּא כְבוֹדֶךָ.[5]
thereby dishonoring ‹ Your Throne ‹ of Glory? «

אַתָּה מָרוֹם לְעוֹלָם יהוה[6] וְרִאשׁוֹן,
You ‹ remain exalted ‹ forever, ‹ HASHEM! « and You are the very first. «

כּוֹנַנְתָּ מָרוֹם מֵרִאשׁוֹן,[7]
You established ‹ the exalted [Throne] ‹ from the first, [before Creation]. «

וְלָמָּה נִאֵץ רָשָׁע[8] בְּפֶה וְלָשׁוֹן,
So, why ‹ did [You allow] the wicked one to blaspheme You ‹ with his mouth ‹ and tongue, «

---

(1) See commentary to *Kinnah* 11. (2) See commentary to *Kinnah* 5. (3) Cf. *Psalms* 78:54. (4) Cf. *Eichah* 2:3. (5) Cf. *Jeremiah* 14:21. (6) Cf. *Psalms* 92:9. (7) Cf. *Jeremiah* 17:12. (8) Cf. *Psalms* 10:13.

---

add up to eighty. And just as queens are superior to concubines, so are Abraham and his descendants more esteemed than all others.

בַּכְּרוּבִים מוֹנִים — *Because of the Cherubim to denounce them [as idolaters].* The Midrash relates that when the Babylonian hordes entered into the Holy Temple, the troops of Ammon and Moab joined them. However, whereas all the marauders greedily looted silver, gold, and precious treasures, the Ammonites and Moabites turned their attention exclusively toward destroying the Torah which states: *An Ammonite or Moabite shall not enter into the congregation of* HASHEM *(Deuteronomy* 23:4). Furthermore, they burst into the Holiest of the Holies and seized the two golden

עַד כִּי נָגַע צָר בְּאִישׁוֹן.

« the pupil of Your eye? ‹ did the enemy ‹ touch ‹ then that ‹ until

אַתָּה שַׂשְׂתָּ לְטוֹב עֲלֵימוֹ,

« upon them, ‹ to bestow goodness ‹ rejoiced ‹ You

בְּשִׂיחַ תְּבִאֵמוֹ וְתִטָּעֵמוֹ,[1]

« *and You shall implant them [on the mount of Your heritage].* ‹ *You shall bring them,* « with the statement,

וְלָמָּה עָרִיץ* חֵרֵף וְאָמַר אֵי אֱלֹהֵימוֹ,[2]

‹ *their God* ‹ *Where is* « and declare, ‹ to blaspheme ‹ [did You allow] the tyrant [Titus]* ‹ So, why

אֲשֶׁר יֹאכַל חֵלֶב זְבָחֵימוֹ.

« *of their offerings?* ‹ *the fats* ‹ *would eat* ‹ *Who*

אַתָּה פוֹרַרְתָּ בְעָזְּךָ יָם,[3]*

« the sea,* ‹ with Your might ‹ shattered ‹ You

וַתָּסֶךְ בִּדְלָתַיִם יָם,[4]

« the seawaters. ‹ with double doors ‹ then You held back

וְלָמָּה צָלַלְתִּי עַד נִבְכֵי יָם,[5]

« of the sea, ‹ the hidden depths ‹ unto ‹ am I now sinking [in tragedy] ‹ So, why

(1) *Exodus* 15:17. (2) *Deuteronomy* 32:37. (3) *Psalms* 74:13. (4) Cf. *Job* 38:8. (5) 38:16.

Cherubs which were atop the Ark-cover. They placed them on display in an open cage and paraded them all around Jerusalem. They mocked the Jews with derision and scorn, saying, "Didn't you all think that the Jews were special because they spurned idolatry? Look what we found in their holiest inner sanctum! Graven images! They are no better than the rest of us!"(*Midrash Eichah* intro. 9; 1:4).

עָרִיץ — *The tyrant Titus.* According to the Talmud (*Gittin* 56b), the wicked Titus shouted, *"Where is their God?"* as he desecrated the inner sanctum of the Temple (see commentary to *kinnah* 16).

Beis Levi says that afterward, Titus and his soldiers offered animal sacrifices to their pagan gods in the ruins of our Holy Temple. All the while they mocked the God of Israel, saying, "Since He allows us to worship other gods in His Temple, He must venerate our gods too. Why, then, does He not come to partake of the choicest of our sacrifices?"

אַתָּה פוֹרַרְתָּ בְעָזְּךָ יָם — *You shattered with Your might the sea.* You split the Sea of Reeds so Israel could cross on dry land. When the Egyptians entered, You returned the waters to their natural condition to drown them, yet You kept Israel safe from the raging, flooding waters, by holding them back as if with a dike of double doors.

וַיִּגְדַּל שִׁבְרִי כַּיָּם.[1]

and grown as vast ‹ has my ruination ‹ as the sea? «

וְאַתָּה קָדוֹשׁ יוֹשֵׁב תְּהִלּוֹת קְדוֹשִׁים,[2]

You are ‹ the Holy One, ‹ enthroned ‹ upon the praises ‹ of the holy ones, «

בְּקֶרֶב יְשִׁישִׁים הַמְּקֻדָּשִׁים,

[You dwell] in the midst ‹ of the elders [the Sanhedrin] ‹ who are sanctified. «

וְלָמָּה רָגְשׁוּ גוֹיִם עַם קְדֵשִׁים,[3]

So, why ‹ gather together ‹ do the nations, « peoples ‹ of licentiousness, «

וְהֵשִׁימוּ בֵּית קֹדֶשׁ הַקֳּדָשִׁים.

and they made desolate ‹ the chamber ‹ of the Holiest ‹ of the Holies? «

וְאַתָּה שְׁמַע אֱלֹהֵינוּ כִּי הָיִינוּ חֶרְפָּה,

And You, ‹ hear ‹ O our God, ‹ that ‹ we have become ‹ [an object of] derision, «

וְסֻכָּתְךָ בָּאֵשׁ נִשְׂרָפָה,

while Your Tabernacle ‹ in fire ‹ was burnt. «

וְלָמָּה תְבַלַּע נַחֲלַת[4] חֻפָּה,

So, why ‹ do You swallow up ‹ the heritage ‹ You once sheltered? «

תַּצְמִיחַ תְּרוּפָה וְעָלֵינוּ חוֹפְפָה.

Make to sprout ‹ a healing balm ‹ and over us ‹ hover protectively! «

וְאַתָּה צַדִּיק עַל כָּל הַבָּא,[5]

And You ‹ are righteous ‹ in ‹ all ‹ that comes; «

לְךָ אֲדֹנָי הַצְּדָקָה וְנַצְדִּיקְךָ בְּחִבָּה,

Yours, ‹ O Lord, ‹ is righteousness, « and we shall proclaim Your righteousness ‹ with love. «

(1) Cf. *Eichah* 2:13. (2) Cf. *Psalms* 22:4; some editions omit the prefix ו from this and the next two verses that begin וְאַתָּה. (3) Cf. 2:1. (4) Cf. *II Samuel* 20:19. (5) *Nehemiah* 9:33.

וְלָמָּה נָהֶינוּ וְלָנוּ הַדִּבָּה,

« are the [evil] words? ‹ when ours « do we moan, ‹ So, why

כִּי כָל זֹאת בָּאַתְנוּ בְּחוֹבָה.

« as a result of [our] guilt! ‹ has befallen us ‹ this ‹ all ‹ For

KINNAH 19 / קינה יט

לְךָ אֲדֹנָי הַצְּדָקָה*
‹ is righteousness,* ‹ O Lord, ‹ Yours,

בְּאוֹתוֹת אֲשֶׁר הִפְלֵאתָ מֵאָז וְעַד עָתָּה,
« now; ‹ until ‹ from then ‹ You have wondrously displayed ‹ that ‹ because of the signs

וְלָנוּ בֹּשֶׁת הַפָּנִים
‹ is shamefacedness, ‹ and ours

בִּבְחִינָה אֲשֶׁר נִצְרַפְנוּ[1] וְאוֹתָנוּ תִּעַבְתָּ.
« You despised. ‹ [but we failed] and us « You sought to purify us, ‹ with which ‹ because of the tests

לְךָ אֲדֹנָי הַצְּדָקָה
‹ is righteousness, ‹ O Lord, ‹ Yours,

בְּגוֹי מִקֶּרֶב גּוֹי לָקַחַת בְּמַסּוֹת,[2]
« with miracles; ‹ You have taken ‹ another nation, ‹ from amidst ‹ because [our] nation

וְלָנוּ בֹּשֶׁת הַפָּנִים
‹ is shamefacedness, ‹ and ours

בְּדֹפִי אֲשֶׁר נִמְצָא בָנוּ כְּמַעֲשֵׂיהֶם עָשׂוֹת.
« we emulated. ‹ as [Egypt's abominable] deeds ‹ within us ‹ found ‹ that is ‹ because of the fault

לְךָ אֲדֹנָי הַצְּדָקָה
‹ is righteousness, ‹ O Lord, ‹ Yours,

בְּהָלְכוּ אֱלֹהִים לִפְדּוֹת לוֹ לְעָם,[3]
« as a people; ‹ unto Himself ‹ to redeem [us] ‹ because God went

(1) Cf. *Jeremiah* 9:6. (2) *Deuteronomy* 4:34. (3) *II Samuel* 7:23.

לְךָ ה׳ הַצְּדָקָה — *Yours, O Lord, is righteousness.* R' Elazar HaKalir based this *kinnah* on the Midrash (*Tanchuma, Re'eh* 16) which expounds on the verse continuing the theme expressed in the preceding *kinnah's* conclusion — *Yours, O Lord, is righteousness* (*Daniel* 9:7). R' Elazar HaKalir illustrates a number of applications of this verse. Each odd-numbered line begins with the opening phrase of the Scriptural verse לְךָ ה׳ הַצְּדָקָה, *Yours, O Lord, is righteousness,* and each even-numbered line begins with the phrase וְלָנוּ בֹּשֶׁת הַפָּנִים, *and ours is shamefacedness.* The next word of each line begins with the respective letter of the *aleph-beis* after the prefix בְּ, *because of* or *in regard to.*

וְלָנוּ בֹּשֶׁת הַפָּנִים
‹ is shamefacedness, ‹ and ours

בְּוַיַּמְרוּ עַל יָם בְּיַם סוּף[1] גּוֹי בֵּאלֹהָיו בְּפִשְׁעָם.
« sinning! ‹ against its God ‹ the nation « of Reeds; ‹ at the Sea ‹ the sea ‹ by ‹ because [our forefathers] rebelled

לְךָ אֲדֹנָי הַצְּדָקָה
‹ is righteousness, ‹ O Lord, ‹ Yours,

בְּזֵכֶר וְאַתֶּם עֵדַי וַאֲנִי אֱלֹהִים,[2]
« *God!* ‹ *and I am* ‹ *My witnesses,* ‹ the proclamation, *You are* ‹ when we recall

וְלָנוּ בֹּשֶׁת הַפָּנִים
‹ is shamefacedness, ‹ and ours

בְּחָרְפֵנוּ יהוה בְּסִין קוּם עֲשֵׂה לָנוּ אֱלֹהִים.[3]
« *gods!* ‹ *for us* ‹ *and make* ‹ [by demanding of Aaron], *Rise up* ‹ in [the Wilderness of] Sin ‹ HASHEM ‹ because we blasphemed

לְךָ אֲדֹנָי הַצְּדָקָה
‹ is righteousness, ‹ O Lord, ‹ Yours,

בְּטַעַם שֶׁהִטְעַמְתָּנוּ כְּצַפִּיחִית בִּדְבָשׁ,[4]
« [fried] in honey; ‹ — like a cake « [of the manna] You gave us to taste ‹ because of the taste

וְלָנוּ בֹּשֶׁת הַפָּנִים
‹ is shamefacedness, ‹ and ours

בְּיוֹם הִקְרַבְנוּ לְפָנָיו סֹלֶת וְשֶׁמֶן וּדְבָשׁ.*[5]
« and honey.* ‹ with oil ‹ of fine flour ‹ before it ‹ we brought an offering ‹ because on the day [we made the Golden Calf],

(1) *Psalms* 106:7. (2) Cf. *Isaiah* 43:12. (3) *Exodus* 32:1. (4) 16:31. (5) Cf. *Ezekiel* 16:19.

הִקְרַבְנוּ לְפָנָיו סֹלֶת וְשֶׁמֶן וּדְבָשׁ — *We brought an offering before it of fine flour with oil and honey.* Regarding Israel's sinfulness with idolatry, the prophet Ezekiel admonishes that their betrayal is all the more shocking because God's own special gifts to Israel were used as offerings to idols. *My bread which I gave you — fine flour, oil, and honey did I feed you — you placed it before them . . .* (*Ezekiel* 16:19). *Rashi* cites a Midrash that this refers to the manna that was placed in worship before the Golden Calf. *Rashi* there cites the verses from *Nehemiah* (9:18-19) that

לְךָ אֲדֹנָי הַצְּדָקָה

‹ is righteousness, ‹ O Lord, ‹ Yours,

בְּכַלְכּוּל מָן וּבְאֵר וְעַמּוּד עָנָן,

« of cloud; ‹ and the pillar ‹ the well, ‹ with the manna, ‹ because You sustained us

וְלָנוּ בֹּשֶׁת הַפָּנִים

‹ is shamefacedness, ‹ and ours

בְּלֶחֶם הַקְּלוֹקֵל[1]* אֲבוֹתֵינוּ בְּאָהֳלֵיהֶם בְּרָגְנָן.[2]

« they slandered. ‹ when in their tents ‹ that our forefathers [called the manna] ‹ *that is insubstantial,** ‹ because of, *the bread*

לְךָ אֲדֹנָי הַצְּדָקָה

‹ is righteousness, ‹ O Lord, ‹ Yours,

בַּמִּדְבָּר לֹא חָסַרְנוּ דָּבָר,[3]

« a thing; ‹ we did not lack ‹ because in the Wilderness

וְלָנוּ בֹּשֶׁת הַפָּנִים

‹ is shamefacedness, ‹ and ours

בְּנֶאָצוֹת לָבָן וַחֲצֵרוֹת וְדִי זָהָב[4]* כִּמְדֻבָּר.

« as related [by Moses]. ‹ zahab* ‹ and Di- ‹ Hazeroth, ‹ at Laban, ‹ because of the blasphemies

לְךָ אֲדֹנָי הַצְּדָקָה

‹ is righteousness, ‹ O Lord, ‹ Yours,

בְּסִיחוֹן וְעוֹג[5] וְכָל מַמְלְכוֹת כְּנָעַן,[6]

« of Canaan; ‹ the kingdoms ‹ and all ‹ and Og ‹ because of [the war with] Sihon

(1) *Numbers* 21:5. (2) Cf. *Deuteronomy* 1:27. (3) Cf. 2:7.
(4) 1:1. (5) See *Numbers* 21:21-35. (6) See *Joshua* Ch. 12.

state: *Although they had made themselves a molten calf . . . You, in Your great compassion, did not forsake them in the Wilderness . . . .*

בְּלֶחֶם הַקְּלוֹקֵל — *Because of the bread that is insubstantial.* The word קְלוֹקֵל means either *destructive* (see *Metzudos* to *Jeremiah* 4:24) or *extremely light* (see *Ibn Ezra* to *Numbers* 21:5). *Rashi* (*Numbers* 21:5 and *Avodah Zarah* 5b) explains that since the manna is perfect food, it is digested in its entirety, producing no waste material. After a period of eating nothing but manna, the people no longer had the need to defecate. Instead of showing thankfulness for this miraculous food, they complained, "This bread will destroy us. It enters our bodies but does

וְלָנוּ בֹּשֶׁת הַפָּנִים

〈 is shamefacedness, 〈 and ours

בְּעָכָן אֲשֶׁר מָעַל בְּחֵרֶם בְּלִי מְצֹא מַעַן.[1]

« an excuse [for his crime]. 〈 finding 〈 without 〈 from the consecrated property [of Jericho] 〈 took for himself 〈 who 〈 because of Achan

לְךָ אֲדֹנָי הַצְּדָקָה

〈 is righteousness, 〈 O Lord, 〈 Yours,

בְּפֹעַל אֲשֶׁר פָּעַלְתָּ בְּאַרְבָּעָה עָשָׂר מוֹשִׁיעִים,*

« saviors [the Judges];* 〈 through the fourteen 〈 You accomplished 〈 that 〈 because of the actions

וְלָנוּ בֹּשֶׁת הַפָּנִים

〈 is shamefacedness, 〈 and ours

בְּצֶלֶם מִיכָה כִּי בוֹ אֲנַחְנוּ פוֹשְׁעִים.[2]

« transgressors. 〈 we are 〈 through it 〈 for « of Micah, 〈 because of the idol

לְךָ אֲדֹנָי הַצְּדָקָה

〈 is righteousness, 〈 O Lord, 〈 Yours,

(1) See *Joshua* 7:10-26. (2) See *Judges* Chs. 17-18.

not leave. Eventually we will be bloated and become sick and die." The Talmud (*Avodah Zarah* 5a-b) cites this as an example of כְּפוּי טוֹבָה, *ingratitude.*

לָבָן וַחֲצֵרוֹת וְדִי זָהָב — *Laban, Hazeroth, and Di-zahab.* Moses began his reprimand to the nation before his death with a seemingly innocent recollection of their itinerary through the Wilderness. Close inspection reveals a deeper meaning to Moses' words. Firstly, not all the places enumerated by Moses appear elsewhere in the Torah. This raises the question of why they were omitted from the list of encampments given in *Numbers* (Ch. 33). Secondly, at each of the places mentioned by Moses that does appear earlier, the nation struck a rebellious pose. Three of the names on Moses' litany are לָבָן, *Laban,* חֲצֵרוֹת, *Hazeroth,* and דִי זָהָב, *Di-zahab* (*Deuteronomy* 1:1). *Rashi* cites a Midrash that לָבָן is not a place but means *white* and refers to the manna which the Torah describes as white (*Exodus* 16:31). Thus, Laban alludes to the Israelites' ingratitude when they grumbled about the manna.

חֲצֵרוֹת is mentioned elsewhere and was the site of both Korah's uprising and Miriam's *tzaraas* punishment when she spoke slanderously about her brother Moses (see *Numbers* 12:14-16).

דִי זָהָב, literally, *sufficient gold,* is also not a place. Rather, it alludes to the Golden Calf made by the nation because God had endowed them with abundant gold (see also *Hosea* 2:10).

בְּאַרְבָּעָה עָשָׂר מוֹשִׁיעִים — *Through the fourteen saviors [the Judges].* These are the fourteen leaders of Israel from the death of Moses until the era of the prophets which began with Samuel. They were called

בְּקִימַת שִׁילֹה וְנוֹב וְגִבְעוֹן* וּבֵית עוֹלָמִים,

« Eternal [in Jerusalem]; ‹ and the Temple ‹ and Gibeon,* ‹ and Nob, ‹ at Shiloh, ‹ because You erected [Sanctuaries]

וְלָנוּ בֹּשֶׁת הַפָּנִים

‹ is shamefacedness, ‹ and ours

בְּרֶשַׁע שֶׁנִּמְצָא בָנוּ שֶׁחָרְבוּ וּבָם אָנוּ נִכְלָמִים.

« are shamed. ‹ we ‹ and in their loss ‹ that caused each one's destruction, ‹ in us ‹ that was found ‹ because of the evil

לְךָ אֲדֹנָי הַצְּדָקָה

‹ is righteousness, ‹ O Lord, ‹ Yours,

בִּשְׁנֵי חֻרְבָּנוֹת שֶׁחָרְבוּ בְּבִצְעֵנוּ וַאֲנַחְנוּ קַיָּמִים,

« endure; ‹ we ourselves « were due to our corruption, ‹ that were destroyed ‹ Destructions [of the Temples] ‹ because [although] the two

וְלָנוּ בֹּשֶׁת הַפָּנִים

‹ is shamefacedness, ‹ and ours

בְּשׁוּבֵנוּ אֵלֶיךָ בְּכָל לֵב שֶׁתָּשׁוּב אֵלֵינוּ בְּרַחֲמִים.

« with compassion. ‹ to us ‹ so that You would return « heart, ‹ with full ‹ to You ‹ because we [should have] repented

לְךָ אֲדֹנָי הַצְּדָקָה

‹ is righteousness, ‹ O Lord, ‹ Yours,

בְּתֵשַׁע מֵאוֹת שָׁנָה*

‹ years* ‹ hundred ‹ because of the nine

שֶׁהָיְתָה שִׂנְאָה כְּבוּשָׁה מִלְּהִשָּׁמַע,

« and not proclaimed; ‹ was suppressed ‹ the hatred [over our sins] ‹ when it was that

---

שׁוֹפְטִים, *Judges,* and their tenures are the subject of the Scriptural Book of that name.

שִׁילֹה וְנוֹב וְגִבְעוֹן — *Shiloh, and Nob, and Gibeon.* These were the successive sites of the Tabernacle before the בֵּית עוֹלָמִים, *Temple Eternal,* was erected by King Solomon.

בְּתֵשַׁע מֵאוֹת שָׁנָה — *Because of the nine hundred years.* When Israel left Egypt, some of the nation carried out idols with them. For close to nine hundred years, God remained silent. But when idolatry became rampant in the days of Ezekiel, God revived the memory of that treachery and admonished the nation for it (*Vayikra Rabbah* 7:1; cited by *Rashi* to *Ezekiel* 20:5).

וְלָנוּ בֹּשֶׁת הַפָּנִים

‹ is shamefacedness, ‹ and ours

כְּתָבַע אִישׁ חֲמוּדוֹת,

‹ greatly beloved [to rebuild the Temple though we were not worthy,] ‹ did [Daniel] the man ‹ because implore

הַטֵּה אֱלֹהַי אָזְנְךָ וּשְׁמַע.[1]

« *and listen!* ‹ *Your ear,* ‹ *my God,* ‹ [and prayed,] *Incline,*

(1) *Daniel* 9:18.

KINNAH 20 / קינה כ

הַטֵּה אֱלֹהַי אָזְנְךָ,*[1]

‹ Incline, ‹ my God, ‹ Your ear*

לְתִפְלֶצֶת מְנַאֶצֶת מִי לִי בַשָּׁמָיִם,*[2]

‹ to the frightening ones ‹ who blaspheme saying, « Whom ‹ do I have [to fear] ‹ in heaven?* «

וּשְׁמַע שַׁאֲגַת צוֹרְרֶיךָ הָאֹמְרִים עָרוּ עָרוּ

‹ And listen ‹ to the roaring ‹ of Your enemies ‹ who say, « Destroy! ‹ Destroy! ‹

עַד הַיְסוֹד[3] שַׁעַר הַשָּׁמָיִם.*[4]

‹ to ‹ the very foundation ‹ of [the Temple,] ‹ the gate ‹ of heaven.* «

הַטֵּה אֱלֹהַי אָזְנְךָ,

‹ Incline, ‹ my God, ‹ Your ear

לְרִגְשַׁת הַדּוֹבֶרֶת עַל צַדִּיק עָתָק,*[5]

‹ to the gathering ‹ of those who speak ‹ against ‹ the Righteous One ‹ falsehood;* «

(1) *Daniel* 9:18. (2) *Psalms* 73:25. (3) 137:7. (4) *Genesis* 28:17. (5) Cf. *Psalms* 31:19.

הַטֵּה אֱלֹהַי אָזְנְךָ — *Incline, my God, Your ear.* As in the preceding *kinnah,* R' Elazar HaKalir based this composition on a verse from the Book of *Daniel, Incline, my God, Your ear, and listen* (9:18). The contention of this lament is that the gentile marauders, who are supposedly God's agents to punish Israel and to destroy the Temple, are not merely enemies of the Jewish people; rather, they are the enemies of God Himself. This is vividly and unquestionably evident by the way in which they curse, blaspheme, and taunt God. Therefore Israel argues with God, "How can You, O God, allow these heathens to continue unchecked? They claim that since the Temple site remains desolate it proves that God was destroyed together with His Abode! You, O God, must stop them because they are far greater enemies of heaven than we are, despite our sins. Therefore we beseech You, O God, to return, rebuild the Temple and demonstrate how mistaken they are!"

In each stanza the first line begins הַטֵּה אֱלֹהַי אָזְנְךָ לְ..., *Incline, my God, Your ear, to . . .,* and the second line begins וּשְׁמַע, *and listen.* These phrases are followed by a word beginning with the respective letter of the reverse-alphabetical formulation known as תַּשְׁרַק.

מִי לִי בַשָּׁמָיִם — *"Whom do I have [to fear] in heaven?"* According to the translation, these words were spoken by the Roman soldier in direct defiance of God, as if to say, "I need fear no one in heaven." Alternatively, these are Israel's words: The heathens ask *whom I have in heaven* to protect me. They claim that even God has forsaken me.

שַׁעַר הַשָּׁמָיִם — *The gate of heaven.* When Jacob awoke from his prophetic vision of the angels ascending and descending a ladder stretching from earth to heaven, he declared, *"How awesome is this place! This is none other than the House of God and this is the gate of heaven!"* (*Genesis* 28:17).

עָתָק — *Falsehood.* The translation follows

וּשְׁמַע קוֹל שָׁאוֹן מֵעִיר[1] בְּחֵמָה שְׁפוּכָה לְשַׁתֵּק.

《 silence it. 《 poured out, 〈 with wrath 《 [coming] from the [conqueror's] city; 〈 of tumult 〈 to the sound 〈 and listen

הַטֵּה אֱלֹהַי אָזְנְךָ,

〈 Your ear 〈 my God, 〈 Incline,

לְצִיר שֻׁלַּח וְנָם קוּמוּ וְנָקוּמָה עָלֶיהָ לַמִּלְחָמָה,[2]

《 *in war!* 〈 *against her [Jerusalem]* 〈 *And let us rise up* 《 *Arise!* 《 and who proclaimed, 〈 who was sent [to all the nations] 〈 to the emissary

וּשְׁמַע פַּלָּצוּת הוֹמִים

《 of those who scream, 〈 to the frightening sound 〈 And listen

בָּא הָעֵת אִתּוֹ בְּבֵיתוֹ לְהִלָּחֵמָה.

《 *to wage war!* 〈 *in His Home [theTemple]* 〈 *against Him [God],* 〈 *has the time* 〈 *Come*

הַטֵּה אֱלֹהַי אָזְנְךָ,

〈 Your ear 〈 my God, 〈 Incline,

לְעָצוּ עֵצָה וְחָשְׁבוּ מְזִמָּה בַּל יוּכָלוּ,

《 that they cannot carry out; 〈 an evil scheme 〈 and devised 〈 a conspiracy 〈 to those who planned

וּשְׁמַע שִׂיחַת נוֹעֲצוּ לֵב יַחְדָּו עָלֶיךָ[3] עֲלוֹת נִסְתַּכָּלוּ.

《 they were foolish. 《 to rise up; 〈 against You 〈 with a single mind 〈 of those who took counsel 〈 to the talk 〈 and listen

הַטֵּה אֱלֹהַי אָזְנְךָ,

〈 Your ear 〈 my God, 〈 Incline,

לְנִאֲצוּ וְשִׁלְּחוּ בָאֵשׁ מִקְדָּשׁ מוֹרָא,[4]

《 that is awe inspiring; 〈 the Temple 〈 in flame 〈 and sent up 〈 to those who blasphemed

וּשְׁמַע מְחָרְפֶיךָ מַדְמִימֵי תוֹדָה וְקוֹל זִמְרָה.[5]

《 of music. 〈 and the sound 〈 thanksgiving 〈 who silence 《 to those who revile You, 〈 and listen

---

(1) *Isaiah* 66:6. (2) *Obadiah* 1:1. (3) *Psalms* 83:6. (4) Cf. 74:7. (5) *Isaiah* 51:3.

Rashi's first interpretation of this word in *Psalms* 31:19. Alternatively, *Rashi* has *harsh*; thus, in this *kinnah*, *"those who speak harshly about the Righteous One."*

הַטֵּה אֱלֹהַי אָזְנְךָ, לְלֵצִים לָצוֹן חָמְדוּ לָהֶם,[1]

« for themselves, ‹ they covet ‹ who *mockery* ‹ to the scorners ‹ Your ear ‹ my God, ‹ Incline,

וּשְׁמַע כָּל חֶרְפָּתָם אֲשֶׁר חֵרְפוּךָ[2]

« they disgrace You, ‹ with which ‹ their disgrace ‹ to all ‹ and listen

וְהַפֵּל אֵימָתְךָ עֲלֵיהֶם.

« upon them. ‹ Your terror ‹ and make fall

הַטֵּה אֱלֹהַי אָזְנְךָ,

‹ Your ear ‹ my God, ‹ Incline,

לְיָהֲרוּ וְהוֹצִיאוּ כְרוּבִים בִּרְחוֹבוֹת מְחַזְּרִים,

« paraded them around; ‹ and through the streets ‹ the Cherubim [from the Holiest of Holies] ‹ took out ‹ to those who with hauteur

וּשְׁמַע טַרְחוֹת טִנּוּפָם* כְּהֶעֱלוּ עַל מִזְבַּחֲךָ חֲזִירִים.

« swine. ‹ Your Altar ‹ on ‹ when they offered up ‹ with their filth* ‹ how they burdened [You] ‹ and listen to

הַטֵּה אֱלֹהַי אָזְנְךָ,

‹ Your ear ‹ my God, ‹ Incline,

לְחִלְּלוּ וְטִנְּפוּ בֵּית קֹדֶשׁ הַקֳּדָשִׁים,

« of the Holies; ‹ of the Holiest ‹ the chamber ‹ and made filthy ‹ to those who desecrated

וּשְׁמַע זֵדִים מְזָרְקִים לְמוּלָךְ מִילוֹת קְדוֹשִׁים.*

« [cruelly severed] from the holy ones.* ‹ the circumcised organs ‹ toward You ‹ flung ‹ to how the wanton ones ‹ and listen

הַטֵּה אֱלֹהַי אָזְנְךָ,

‹ Your ear ‹ my God, ‹ Incline,

(1) Cf. *Proverbs* 1:22. (2) *Psalms* 79:12.

טִנּוּפָם — *With their filth.* Idolatrous offerings are considered nothing more than filth, as the prophet (*Isaiah* 28:8) declares: *For all the tables [i.e., altars] are full of vomit and excrement, without the Omnipresent* (see *Avos* 3:4). Moreover, the idols themselves are so considered, as it is written: צֵא תֹּאמַר לוֹ, *Go out and say unto him [the idol], "You are excrement!"* (ibid. 30:22; see *Radak* there, and *Maharshal* to *Shabbos* 82a).

מִילוֹת קְדוֹשִׁים — *The circumcised organs . . . from the holy ones.* The Amalekites would mutilate their Jewish victims, then throw their organs skyward while calling out blasphemously to God, "Here, this is what You have chosen! Take what is Yours!" (*Midrash Tanchuma, Ki Seitzei* 10).

לְלוֹעֲזִים מְעִיזִים מֵצַח לְכוּ וְנִלָּחֲמָה אִתּוֹ בְּבֵיתוֹ,

« *in His own House [the Temple];* ‹ *against Him [God],* ‹ *and wage war* ‹ [who declare], *Let us go forth* ‹ brow ‹ of brazen ‹ to the foreign speakers

וּשְׁמַע הַוּוֹת הוֹלְלִים מְהַלְּלִים כִּי אֵין הָאִישׁ בְּבֵיתוֹ.[1]

« *in His House!* ‹ *The Man is not* ‹ that « who scorn, ‹ of the scorners ‹ the treacherous thoughts ‹ and listen to

הַטֵּה אֱלֹהַי אָזְנְךָ, לְדוֹבֶרֶת אֲנִי וְאַפְסִי עוֹד,[2]

« *else!* ‹ *And except for me there is nothing* « *I am!* ‹ to those who boast, ‹ Your ear ‹ my God, ‹ Incline,

וּשְׁמַע גִּדּוּפֶיהָ וְחֵרוּפֶיהָ מִשְׁתַּחֶצֶת עַד כִּסְאֲךָ עוֹד.

« itself. ‹ Your Throne ‹ reaches up to ‹ whose arrogance ‹ and disgraceful curses ‹ to the [nation's] blasphemy ‹ And listen

הַטֵּה אֱלֹהַי אָזְנְךָ,

‹ Your ear ‹ my God, ‹ Incline,

לְבוֹזָה וּמַלְעֶגֶת[3] מַה תּוֹחִילִי וְאֵינוֹ נִבְנֶה,

« *be rebuilt!* ‹ *[Your Temple] will never* « *are you hoping?* ‹ *For what* « and ridiculing, ‹ to the disparaging

וּשְׁמַע בְּכִיַּת מַסְפִּידִים וְקוֹרְאִים[4] וּמְחַכִּים מָתַי יִבָּנֶה.

« *will it be rebuilt?* ‹ *When* « and longingly yearn, ‹ and cry out ‹ of those who mourn ‹ to the weeping ‹ And listen

הַטֵּה אֱלֹהַי אָזְנְךָ,

‹ Your ear ‹ my God, ‹ Incline,

לְאוֹמְרִים עָזַב וְשָׁכַח וְנָטַשׁ וְלָעַד שׁוֹמֵם,

« will it be desolate. ‹ and forever « and forsaken, ‹ and forgotten, ‹ that [the Temple] is abandoned, ‹ to those who claim

וּשְׁמַע אֶנְקָתֵנוּ, וְקַנֵּא קִנְאָתֵנוּ,

« on our need for zealousness; ‹ and zealously act ‹ to our anguished cry ‹ And listen

וְהָאֵר פָּנֶיךָ עַל מִקְדָּשְׁךָ הַשָּׁמֵם.[5]

« which is desolate. ‹ Your Sanctuary ‹ upon ‹ Your countenance ‹ and shine

---

(1) *Proverbs* 7:19. (2) *Isaiah* 47:8. (3) Cf. *Nehemiah* 2:19. (4) Some editions read וְקוֹרְעִים, *and rend [their garments],* in place of וְקוֹרְאִים, *and cry out.* (5) *Daniel* 9:17.

KINNAH 21 / קינה כא

אַרְזֵי הַלְּבָנוֹן* אַדִּירֵי הַתּוֹרָה,

《 of the Torah, 〈 mighty ones 〈 of Lebanon,* 〈 Cedars

בַּעֲלֵי תְרֵיסִין* בְּמִשְׁנָה וּבִגְמָרָא,

《and of Gemara, 〈 of Mishnah 〈 of the shields*〈 masters

אַרְזֵי הַלְּבָנוֹן — *Cedars of Lebanon.* This *kinnah,* whose author is unknown [although some ascribe it to יְחִיאֵל בֶּן מֵאִיר, whose name may appear in the acrostic], is a dramatic highlight of the Tishah B'Av service. It depicts the tragic execution of the עֲשָׂרָה הֲרוּגֵי מַלְכוּת, *Ten Martyrs.*

Numerous *piyutim, kinnos,* and *selichos* have been written about the Ten Martyrs, all of which seemingly place them as contemporaneous. It should be noted, however, that while all ten of these righteous men were murdered by the Romans during the Mishnaic period, their executions did not take place at the same time, nor could they have, since two of the ten did not even live in the same generation as the other eight. Namely, Rabban Shimon ben Gamliel and Rabbi Yishmael the *Kohen Gadol* lived before the Destruction of the Second Temple, and were murdered shortly thereafter, while the others were all killed after the Bar Kochba revolt, more than sixty years later. The liturgical accounts of the martyrdom were not meant as historical records, but as dramatic accounts of the story, in order to evoke feelings of loss and repentance on the part of the congregation.

The Talmud teaches, "The death of the righteous is a tragedy equal to the burning of the Temple of our God" (*Rosh Hashanah* 18a). Thus, it is appropriate to mourn the loss of these righteous sages on Tishah B'Av, the day our Temple was destroyed in fire.

In the *chazzan's* repetition of the *Amidah* during *Mussaf* on Yom Kippur, the Day of Atonement, we read another *piyut* describing the death of the Ten Martyrs titled אֵלֶּה אֶזְכְּרָה, *These do I recall.* It is included in the Yom Kippur service because the Talmud (*Moed Katan* 28a) states, "The death of the righteous atones for the sins of Israel," and it is on Yom Kippur that we seek to arouse the merit of the martyrs. The Yom Kippur version of this story is lengthier and explains that the death of the Ten Martyrs was an atonement for the sin of the ten sons of Jacob who were involved in the sale of Joseph into slavery (see *Genesis* Ch. 37). That heartless deed sowed the seeds of future dissension and senseless hatred in Israel. But it was not until the Second Temple was destroyed due to שִׂנְאַת חִנָּם, *baseless hatred,* that Israel reaped the bitter fruits of that deed (*Yoma* 9b). Then, after the Temple's destruction, God brought about the death of ten holy martyrs who sanctified His Name in atonement for the sin of the ten brothers. For it was the still-present influence of their act that continued to prevent their offspring from living in brotherhood and harmony.

This *kinnah* lists only eight of the Ten Martyrs. In the Yom Kippur liturgy and other sources the other two are given as Rabbi Chanina ben Chachinai, one of Rabbi Akiva's earlier disciples, and Rabbi Yehudah (or Elazar) ben Dama. Some versions add the name of Rabbi Yehudah HaNachtom in place of ben Dama.

אַרְזֵי הַלְּבָנוֹן — *Cedars of Lebanon.* The righteous are thus described by the psalmist: *A righteous man like a date palm will flourish,* כְּאֶרֶז בַּלְּבָנוֹן יִשְׂגֶּה, *like a cedar in Lebanon he will grow tall* (*Psalms* 92:13).

בַּעֲלֵי תְרֵיסִין — *Masters of the shields.* The Talmud uses this phrase when referring

גִּבּוֹרֵי כֹחַ* עֲמֵלֶיהָ בְּטָהֳרָה,

powerful in strength,* toiling over it in purity,

דָּמָם נִשְׁפַּךְ וְנָשְׁתָה גְבוּרָה,

their blood was spilt and removed [from us] was [their heroic] strength.

הִנָּם קְדוֹשֵׁי הֲרוּגֵי מַלְכוּת עֲשָׂרָה,

Indeed, they are the holy Martyrs executed by the [Roman] government — Ten,

וְעַל אֵלֶּה אֲנִי בוֹכִיָּה וְעֵינִי נִגָּרָה.[1]

and for these do I weep and my eye overflows.

זֹאת בְּזָכְרִי אֶזְעַק בְּמָרָה,

This when I remember I cry out in bitterness.

חֶמְדַּת יִשְׂרָאֵל כְּלֵי הַקֹּדֶשׁ נֵזֶר וַעֲטָרָה,

The most desirable in Israel, the vessels that are holy, the crown and the tiara,

טְהוֹרֵי לֵב קְדוֹשִׁים מֵתוּ בְּמִיתָה חֲמוּרָה,

pure of heart and consecrated, they died a death that was harsh.

יַדּוּ גוֹרָל* מִי רִאשׁוֹן לַחֶרֶב בְּרוּרָה,

They cast lots* [to determine] whom first to be killed by the sword would be chosen.

(1) Cf. *Eichah* 1:16; 3:49.

to the sages in the academy of Rabban Gamliel, *Nasi* of Israel and son of Rabban Shimon, the first of the Ten Martyrs. Among those described with this title was Rabbi Chutzpis the Interpreter, ninth of the Martyrs (*Berachos* 27b). They are called masters of the shields either because they metaphorically do battle with each other in debating the fine points of Torah law, or because of their role in enforcing the law as interpreted by the *Nasi* and his academy (*Aruch*).

גִּבּוֹרֵי כֹחַ — *Powerful in strength.* Perhaps this is an even greater accolade than earlier ones, for the psalmist depicts the angels with this term (see *Psalms* 103:20).

יַדּוּ גוֹרָל — *They cast lots.* Rabban Shimon ben Gamliel and Rabbi Yishmael the *Kohen Gadol* were seized by the Romans at the time of the Temple's destruction. When they were about to be killed, each begged the executioner, "Please kill me first, so that I will not be forced to witness the death of my beloved colleague!" The executioner was amazed by the pure love for each other and said, "In that case we will cast lots to decide who should die first!"

כִּנְפוֹל גּוֹרָל עַל רַבָּן שִׁמְעוֹן*

When fall the lot ‹ did ‹ on ‹ Rabban ‹ Shimon [ben Gamliel],* «

פָּשַׁט צַוָּארוֹ וּבָכָה כְּנִגְזְרָה גְזֵרָה,*

he bared ‹ his neck, « and wept, « as was decreed ‹ by the decree.* «

לְרַבָּן שִׁמְעוֹן[1] חָזַר הַהֶגְמוֹן לְהָרְגוֹ בְּנֶפֶשׁ נְצוּרָה,

To Rabban ‹ Shimon ‹ turned ‹ the official, to kill him ‹ with a soul ‹ wrapped [in evil]. «

מִזֶּרַע אַהֲרֹן* שָׁאַל בְּבַקָּשָׁה

[Rabbi Yishmael, the *Kohen Gadol*,] the descendant ‹ of ‹ Aaron* ‹ asked ‹ permission ‹

לִבְכּוֹת עַל בֶּן הַגְּבִירָה,

to cry ‹ over ‹ this son ‹ of royalty. «

(1) Some editions read רַבִּי יִשְׁמָעֵאל, *Rabbi Yishmael.*

רַבָּן שִׁמְעוֹן — *Rabban Shimon [ben Gamliel]*, the נָשִׂיא, *Prince*, of Israel, a great-grandson of Hillel and a direct descendant of the royal family of King David. He was the first of the Ten Martyrs to die. *Mishnah Berurah* (53:35) quotes *Sefer Chassidim* who relates that when Rabban Shimon ben Gamliel was about to die he asked Rabbi Yishmael, "My dear brother, why am I being subjected to die such an ignominious death [like a common criminal]?"

Rabbi Yishmael replied, "Perhaps when you preached in public before the masses you were filled with too much personal pleasure and you thereby benefited personally from words of Torah?" Rabban Shimon responded, "My brother, you have comforted and consoled me!"

וּבָכָה כְּנִגְזְרָה גְזֵרָה — *And wept, as was decreed by the decree.* The much more detailed version in the *piyut* אֵלֶּה אֶזְכְּרָה (see above) relates that the Roman ruler informed the martyrs that they would be executed as retribution for the sale of Joseph by his brothers. They asked for a three-day period during which they would determine whether their deaths had been decreed by the Heavenly Tribunal. Rabbi Yishmael the *Kohen Gadol* uttered God's secret Name by which miracles can be performed, and ascended to heaven. There he met the angel Gabriel who told him, "Accept it upon yourselves . . . for I have heard . . . that you have been destined for this."

The *kinnah* informs us that Rabban Shimon wept as he heard Rabbi Yishmael report that their deaths had been decreed in heaven.

מִזֶּרַע אַהֲרֹן — *The descendant of Aaron.* Although his name is not mentioned in this *kinnah*, other sources identify him as Rabbi Yishmael ben Elisha the *Kohen Gadol* (see *Kinnah* 23). According to those sources, the Roman governor who condemned Rabbi Yishmael to death had a daughter who was impressed with the Rabbi's appearance, for he was as handsome as Joseph in his prime. She begged her father to spare the Rabbi for her personal gratification. Her father replied, "If it is his face that impresses you, we can preserve it." In an incredible display of cruelty, the governor gave orders that Rabbi Yishmael be skinned alive and the

נָטַל רֹאשׁוֹ וּנְתָנוֹ עַל אַרְכֻּבּוֹתָיו מְנוֹרָה הַטְּהוֹרָה,*

« *that is pure!** ‹ [and lamented], *O lamp* ‹ his knees ‹ on ‹ and placed it ‹ [Rabban Shimon's severed] head ‹ He took

שָׂם עֵינָיו עַל עֵינָיו וּפִיו עַל פִּיו בְּאַהֲבָה גְמוּרָה,

« that was absolute. ‹ in love ‹ his mouth ‹ upon ‹ and his mouth ‹ his eyes, ‹ upon ‹ his eyes ‹ He placed

עָנָה וְאָמַר פֶּה הַמִּתְגַּבֵּר בַּתּוֹרָה,

« *in Torah,* ‹ *that strengthened itself* ‹ *O mouth* « and said, ‹ He cried out

פִּתְאוֹם נִקְנְסָה עָלָיו מִיתָה מְשֻׁנָּה וַחֲמוּרָה,

« *and harsh!* ‹ *terrible* ‹ *a death* ‹ *upon you* ‹ *was unfairly decreed* ‹ *suddenly*

צִוָּה לְהַפְשִׁיט אֶת רֹאשׁוֹ בְּתַעַר הַשְּׂכִירָה,

« sharp for hire. ‹ with a razor, ‹ [Rabbi Yishmael's] head ‹ from ‹ to strip the skin ‹ [The official] ordered

קִיֵּם בְּעוֹרוֹ אָמְרוּ לְנַפְשֵׁךְ שְׁחִי וְנַעֲבֹרָה.[1]

« *that we may pass over [you]!"* ‹ *"Bow down* « *to your soul,* ‹ *They [the enemy] said* « with his skin: ‹ He fulfilled [the prophecy]

רָשָׁע הַפּוֹשֵׁט עֵת הִגִּיעַ לִמְקוֹם תְּפִלִּין מִצְוַת בָּרָה,

« that is clear and bright, ‹ the mitzvah « of the *tefillin,* ‹ the place ‹ he reached ‹ at the moment « who flayed [him], ‹ The wicked one

(1) *Isaiah* 51:23.

skin on his face be mounted like a trophy and preserved in fragrant balsam. They flayed the flesh off his face until they reached the top of his head where *tefillin* were positioned. Until that point Rabbi Yishmael bore the excruciating physical pain in silence, but when they stripped him of this precious spiritual possession he let out a terrifying scream.

The Talmud relates that once every seventy years the Romans would reenact the following scene: A healthy man (representing Esau) would ride on the back of a cripple (symbolic of Jacob, who had a temporary limp after doing battle with the angel — see *Genesis* 32:24-32). "Esau" would be wearing the garments once worn by Adam and later the property of Esau and would hold aloft the preserved head of Rabbi Yishmael. All this, to prove Esau's continued supremacy over Jacob, Israel (*Avodah Zarah* 11b with *Rashi*).

מְנוֹרָה הַטְּהוֹרָה — *O lamp that is pure!* Torah scholars are beacons of light that guide people along the paths that lead to heaven. Or, in the words of King Solomon: נֵר מִצְוָה וְתוֹרָה אוֹר, *A mitzvah is a lamp and the Torah is light* (*Proverbs* 6:23).

צָעַק צְעָקָה* וְנִזְדַּעְזְעָה עוֹלָם וָאֶרֶץ הִתְפּוֹרְרָה.

He [Rabbi Yishmael] screamed ‹ a scream* ‹ that caused the quaking ‹ of the world ‹ and the earth ‹ crumbled. «

מֵאַחֲרָיו הֵבִיאוּ אֶת רַבִּי עֲקִיבָא*

After him ‹ they brought ‹ Rabbi ‹ Akiva* ‹

עוֹקֵר הָרִים וְטוֹחֲנָן זוֹ בְּזוֹ בִּסְבָרָה,

who would uproot ‹ mountains [of halachic problems] ‹ and grind them ‹ one ‹ against the other ‹ by thorough analysis. «

וְסָרְקוּ אֶת בְּשָׂרוֹ בְּמַסְרֵק שֶׁל בַּרְזֶל לְהִשְׁתַּבְּרָה,

They combed ‹ his flesh ‹ with a comb ‹ of ‹ iron ‹ in order to break him. «

יָצְתָה נִשְׁמָתוֹ בְּאֶחָד וּבַת קוֹל אָמְרָה,

Depart ‹ did his soul ‹ while [he was declaring *God is*] *One* ‹ and an echo ‹ of a voice [from heaven] ‹ proclaimed, «

אַשְׁרֶיךָ רַבִּי עֲקִיבָא גּוּפְךָ טָהוֹר בְּכָל מִינֵי טָהֳרָה.

Fortunate are you, ‹ *Rabbi* ‹ *Akiva;* « *your body* ‹ *is pure* ‹ *in every* ‹ *kind* ‹ *of purity!* «

צָעַק צְעָקָה — *Screamed a scream.* Our text discontinues the alphabetical acrostic after the first twenty letters and omits the letter ש and ת. However, some of the manuscript texts of *Kinnos* do have lines for the letters ש and ת.

רַבִּי עֲקִיבָא — *Rabbi Akiva.* Rabbi Akiva's death at the age of 120 took place about sixty years after the destruction of the Temple (circa 135 C.E.). After Bar Kochba's unsuccessful uprising against the Romans, they enacted extremely harsh decrees proscribing the practice of Judaism in general and prohibiting the study and teaching of Torah in particular. Rabbi Akiva believed that without Torah study the Jewish people suffer a demise worse than death, so he ignored the Roman decree and taught Torah at massive public gatherings. The Romans imprisoned him and finally executed him on Yom Kippur.

Rabbi Akiva was tortured to death in this barbaric manner:

It was the time of the morning *Shema* reading when R' Akiva was taken out to be murdered publicly. During his frightful ordeal he accepted God's sovereignty upon himself by reciting the *Shema* joyously, oblivious to the pain. Turnus Rufus, the Roman commander who ordered the barbarous execution, was flabbergasted. "Have you no feeling of pain that you can laugh in the face of such intense suffering!" he exclaimed. Even R' Akiva's own students wondered, "Our teacher, even to this extent?"

The dying sage explained, "All my life I was concerned over a phrase of the Torah. We are taught in the *Shema* to accept God's sovereignty and decrees upon ourselves, בְּכָל נַפְשְׁךָ, *with all your soul* (*Deuteronomy* 6:5); this implies that we must serve God even if it means forfeiting our life. I used to wonder if I would ever have the privilege of serving God to such a degree. Now that the chance has come to me, shall I not grasp it with joy?"

בֶּן בָּבָא רַבִּי יְהוּדָה* אַחֲרָיו,

« came after him. «Yehudah* — ‹— Rabbi « Bava ‹ Ben

הֱבִיאוּ בְּשִׁבְרוֹן לֵב וְאַזְהָרָה,

« and warning [him not to grant *Semichah*]; ‹ his heart, ‹ [after] breaking down ‹ They brought [him]

נֶהֱרַג בֶּן שִׁבְעִים שָׁנָה בִּידֵי אֲרוּרָה,

« of the cursed [nation]. ‹ at the hands ‹ years ‹ of seventy ‹ at the age ‹ he was killed

יוֹשֵׁב בְּתַעֲנִית הָיָה נָקִי וְחָסִיד בִּמְלַאכְתּוֹ לְמַהֲרָה.

« always swift. ‹ and in doing his work [of mitzvos], ‹ and pious, ‹ clean « was he; ‹ fasting ‹ Always

רַבִּי חֲנִינָא[1] בֶּן תְּרַדְיוֹן* אַחֲרָיו

«came after him, ‹ Teradyon* ‹ ben ‹ Chanina ‹ Rabbi

מַקְהִיל קְהִלּוֹת בְּצִיּוֹן שְׁעָרָה,

« gates. ‹ within Zion's ‹ crowds [to study Torah] ‹ [condemned for] assembling

(1) Some editions read חֲנַנְיָה or חֲנַנְיָא, *Chananiah.*

He recited the first verse of *Shema — Hear, O Israel,* HASHEM *is our God,* HASHEM *is One* — and as he drew out the word אֶחָד, *One,* his soul left him.

A heavenly voice was heard saying, "You are praiseworthy, Rabbi Akiva, for your soul left you as you proclaimed God's Oneness! . . . You are praiseworthy, Rabbi Akiva, for you are ready to enter the life of the World to Come" (*Berachos* 61b; *Yerushalmi Berachos* 9:5).

בֶּן בָּבָא רַבִּי יְהוּדָה — *Ben Bava — Rabbi Yehudah.* Moses ordained his disciple Joshua, thus investing him with the God-given authority to render halachic judgments and to impose certain fines. The chain of *Semichah* ordination remained unbroken, handed down from teacher to disciple, for almost fifteen centuries until the Romans issued a decree prohibiting Rabbis (under pain of death) from ordaining their students. Rabbi Yehudah ben Bava was determined to guarantee the perpetuation of the chain of *Semichah.* He secretly ordained five of his greatest disciples near a mountain pass in a secluded area between the cities of Usha and Shefaram. These illustrious students were: Rabbi Meir, Rabbi Yehudah bar Illai, Rabbi Shimon bar Yochai, Rabbi Yossi ben Chalafta, and Rabbi Elazar ben Shamua, the tenth martyr (other opinions add a sixth disciple, Rabbi Nechemiah; see *Sanhedrin* 13b-14a).

Unfortunately, the Romans heard about this convocation and sent troops to execute the master and his disciples. Seventy-year-old Rabbi Yehudah ben Bava commanded his students, "Run away, my sons, and I will stand firm before them like an immovable boulder." Rabbi Yehudah blocked the narrow mountain path with his body and the Romans could not budge him. Only after they pierced his body with three hundred iron spears and made him like a sieve did he fall dead.

רַבִּי חֲנִינָא בֶּן תְּרַדְיוֹן — *Rabbi Chanina ben Teradyon.* The Talmud (*Avodah Zarah* 18a) teaches that the pretext to execute Rabbi Chanina was that he violated the

יוֹשֵׁב וְדוֹרֵשׁ וְסֵפֶר תּוֹרָה עִמּוֹ,

While he sat ‹ and expounded ‹ with a Scroll ‹ of the Torah ‹ with him, «

וְהִקִּיפוּהוּ בַּחֲבִלֵי זְמוֹרָה,

they surrounded him ‹ with bundles ‹ of vines. «

אֶת הָאוּר הִצִּיתוּ בָהֶם וּכְרָכוּהוּ בְּסֵפֶר תּוֹרָה,

The fire ‹ they kindled ‹ in them, « and they wrapped him ‹ in the Scroll ‹ of the Torah. «

סְפוֹגִין שֶׁל צֶמֶר הִנִּיחוּ עַל לִבּוֹ שֶׁלֹּא יָמוּת מְהֵרָה.

Tufts ‹ of ‹ [water-soaked] wool ‹ they placed ‹ on ‹ his heart, ‹ so that he would not die ‹ quickly. «

חָסִיד רַבִּי יֶשֵׁבָב הַסּוֹפֵר* הֲרָגוּהוּ עַם עֲמוֹרָה,

The pious one, ‹ Rabbi ‹ Yeshevav ‹ the Scribe,* « kill him ‹ did the people [wicked as those] ‹ of [Sodom and] Gomorrah. «

זְרָקוּהוּ וְהִשְׁלִיכוּהוּ לַכְּלָבִים וְלֹא הֻקְבַּר בִּקְבוּרָה,

They cast him down ‹ and threw him ‹ to the dogs, « so he was not buried ‹ in a [proper] grave. «

יָצְתָה בַּת קוֹל עָלָיו

There went out ‹ an echo ‹ of a voice [from heaven] ‹ [that said] about him ‹

Roman edict against teaching the Torah publicly. The Romans wrapped him in the Torah Scroll that he always kept with him and set it afire. To prolong his agony, they packed his chest with water-soaked wool. To his horrified daughter and student, Rabbi Chanina said, "The parchment is consumed, but the letters fly up in the air." The Roman executioner was deeply moved by Rabbi Chanina's holiness and asked, "If I remove the wool from your heart, will I have a share in the World to Come?" Rabbi Chanina promised that he would, whereupon the Roman removed the wet wool and put more wood on the fire, so that the agony would end quickly. Then, the Roman threw himself into the fire and died. A heavenly voice proclaimed, "Rabbi Chanina and his executioner are about to enter the World to Come."

רַבִּי יֶשֵׁבָב הַסּוֹפֵר — *Rabbi Yeshevav the Scribe.* Rabbi Yeshevav was Rabbi Akiva's colleague. It was said of him that he was as great as Moses in every respect other than prophecy. The Romans murdered him while he was reciting the *Shema,* as he was reading the portion dealing with the *mitzvah* of the *tzitzis* fringes. He died on a high level of purity for he had been fasting all that day, but the Romans were determined to subject his remains to degradation. They refused to allow him to be buried; instead, they had wild dogs drag his pure and holy body through the streets.

שֶׁלֹּא הִנִּיחַ כְּלוּם מִתּוֹרַת מֹשֶׁה לְשָׁמְרָה.

« without observing it. ‹ of Moses ‹ from the Torah ‹ any detail ‹ that he did not leave

וְאַחֲרָיו רַבִּי חוּצְפִּית* בְּיוֹם עֶבְרָה,

« of wrath; ‹ on the day ‹ Chutzpis* ‹ [they killed] Rabbi ‹ And after him

עוֹף הַפּוֹרֵחַ נִשְׂרַף בַּהֶבֶל פִּיו כִּבַמְּדוּרָה.

« as if on the Altar pyre. ‹ of his mouth [teaching Torah] ‹ by the breath ‹ would be burnt ‹ flying [above him] ‹ a bird

צַדִּיק רַבִּי אֶלְעָזָר בֶּן שַׁמּוּעַ*

‹ Shamua* ‹ ben ‹ Elazar ‹ Rabbi ‹ The righteous

בָּאַחֲרוֹנָה נֶהֱרַג בְּמַדְקִירָה,

« by stabbing. ‹ he was killed « was the last;

יוֹם עֶרֶב שַׁבָּת הָיָה זְמַן קִדּוּשׁ וַיְקַדֵּשׁ וַיִּקְרָא,

« and he recited. ‹ so he began the *Kiddush* ‹ for sanctifying [the Sabbath] ‹ at the time ‹ of the Sabbath ‹ the eve ‹ It was on the day

חֶרֶב שָׁלְפוּ עָלָיו וְלֹא הִנִּיחוּהוּ בַּחַיִּים לְגָמְרָהּ,

« to finish it. ‹ alive ‹ leave him ‹ and did not ‹ against him, ‹ they drew ‹ A sword

---

רַבִּי חוּצְפִּית — *Rabbi Chutzpis.* In Talmudic times, a מְתוּרְגְּמָן, literally, *interpreter*, would repeat and explain the lecture of the *rosh yeshivah*. The Midrash compares Rabbi Chutzpis the Interpreter with R' Yonasan ben Uziel, also a famous interpreter. It is about R' Yonasan ben Uziel that the Talmud (*Succah* 28a) relates that a bird flying over him while he studied Torah was immediately burned.

Rabbi Chutzpis was one day short of his 130th birthday and his last wish was for one more day of life in order to recite the *Shema* for another evening and morning. But his wish was not granted.

The Romans devised a particularly sadistic barbarism for Rabbi Chutzpis. Since he was renowned for his rhetorical skill and his golden tongue, before they killed him they cut out his tongue and tossed it into the trash heap. This was a particularly disturbing torture, for Rabbi Chutzpis never used his tongue to speak anything other than words of Torah. The Talmud relates that when Elisha ben Avuyah, a well-known Sage of Mishnaic times, saw Rabbi Chutzpis' tongue being chewed up by a swine in the trash heap, he could not fathom that a just God would allow such "injustice," and he turned heretic. The Talmud, however, explains Rabbi Chutzpis' degradation as proof that שְׂכַר מִצְוָה בְּהַאי עַלְמָא לֵיכָּא, *reward for mitzvah observance is not forthcoming in this world*, but in the World to Come (*Kiddushin* 39b).

רַבִּי אֶלְעָזָר בֶּן שַׁמּוּעַ — *Rabbi Elazar ben Shamua.* One of the five great disciples ordained by Rabbi Yehudah ben Bava (see above), he was the last of the Ten Martyrs. He was killed at the age of 105.

יָצְתָה נִשְׁמָתוֹ בְּבָרָא אֱלֹהִים[1] יוֹצֵר וְצָר צוּרָה.

Depart ‹ did his soul ‹ with *God created,* « [acknowledging Him as] the Creator ‹ Who fashioned ‹ [every creature's] form. «

כָּהֵנָּה וְכָהֵנָּה הוֹסִיפוּ בְּנֵי עַוְלָה לְעַנּוֹת בִּגְעָרָה,

In this manner ‹ and again in this manner, « continue ‹ do the sons ‹ of iniquity ‹ to torture [us] ‹ with reproof. «

בִּסְקִילָה שְׂרֵפָה הֶרֶג וְחֶנֶק מִי יוּכַל לְשַׁעֲרָה,

With stoning, ‹ burning, ‹ beheading, ‹ and strangling — « who ‹ is able ‹ to even estimate [the enormity of the tragedy]? «

נוֹתֶרֶת מִמֶּנָּה יֹאכְלוּ אֲרָיוֹת שֶׂה פְזוּרָה,[2]

What remained ‹ of it ‹ the lions would consume « — the flock ‹ that is scattered. «

חֲזֵה הַתְּנוּפָה וְשׁוֹק* הַתְּרוּמָה[3]

The breast [of the offering] ‹ that was waved ‹ and the thigh* [of the offering] ‹ that was raised-up «

טָרְפוּ אַרְיֵה וְהַכְּפִירָה,

— tear apart ‹ did the lion ‹ and the lioness. «

יֵיטִיב יהוה וְלֹא יוֹסִיף עוֹד לְיַסְּרָה,[4]

May HASHEM show [His] benevolence [to us], ‹ and may He not continue ‹ any more ‹ to punish [us]. «

אַמֵּיץ בִּרְכַּיִם כּוֹשְׁלוֹת[5]

Strengthen ‹ the knees ‹ that are faltering, «

חֵלֶק יַעֲקֹב[6] וּמוֹשִׁיעַ בְּעֵת צָרָה,[7]

O You Who are the portion ‹ of Jacob, ‹ and his savior ‹ in times ‹ of trouble. «

לְצֶדֶק יִמְלֹךְ מֶלֶךְ,[8] יֹאמַר שָׁלְמוּ יְמֵי אֶבְלֵךְ,[9]

For righteousness ‹ shall He [God] reign ‹ as King. « He will say [to Israel], « *Ended will be* ‹ *the days* ‹ *of your mourning!* «

לְאוֹרוֹ נִסַּע וְנֵלֵךְ.

Then in His light ‹ we shall journey forth ‹ and walk! «

(1) *Genesis* 2:3. (2) Cf. *Jeremiah* 50:17. (3) Cf. *Leviticus* 7:34. (4) Cf. 26:18. (5) Cf. *Isaiah* 35:3. (6) *Jeremiah* 10:16. (7) Cf. 14:8. (8) *Isaiah* 32:1. (9) 60:20.

חֲזֵה . . . וְשׁוֹק — *The breast . . . and the thigh.* The flesh of these innocent victims was regarded as the choicest and finest of the priestly sacrificial gifts.

KINNAH 22 / קינה כב

הַחֲרִישׁוּ מִמֶּנִּי* וַאֲדַבֵּרָה, וְיַעֲבוֹר עָלַי מָה,[1]

Be silent ‹ and do not answer me* ‹ so that I may speak; « let happen ‹ to me ‹ what may. «

חָמָס אֶזְעַק וְשׁוֹד[2] **לְךָ שׁוֹכֵן שָׁמַיְמָה,**

About violence ‹ I shall scream « — and pillage — « to You, ‹ Who dwells ‹ in the Heavens. «

הֱצִיקַתְנִי רוּחִי וְלֹא אוּכַל אֲדַמָּה,

Press me ‹ does my spirit ‹ and I am not able ‹ to remain silent; «

כַּיּוֹלֵדָה אֶפְעֶה אֶשְׁאַף וְאֶשְׁמָה,[3]

like a woman in labor ‹ I shall cry out, ‹ I shall desire [revenge], ‹ and I shall seek to destroy. «

מִסְפֵּד מַר אֶעֱשֶׂה וַאֲקוֹנֵן בִּנְהִימָה,

A eulogy ‹ that is bitter ‹ I shall compose ‹ and I shall lament ‹ in a loud growl. «

דִּבְרֵי שַׁאֲגוֹתַי יִתְּכוּ כְּיַמָּה,[4]

The words ‹ of my roars ‹ shall roll out ‹ like [the waves of] the sea. «

סְפָדִי עַל עֲדָתִי אֲשֶׁר נִתְּנָה לְשַׁמָּה,

My eulogy ‹ is for ‹ my community ‹ which ‹ has been given over ‹ to destruction. «

אָרִיד בְּשִׂיחִי וְאָהִימָה,[5] **וְקוֹל נְהִי אָרִימָה.**

I shall lament ‹ as I speak ‹ and I shall moan aloud, « and the sound ‹ of lament ‹ I shall raise. «

(1) Cf. *Job* 13:13. (2) Cf. *Habakkuk* 1:2-3. (3) *Isaiah* 42:14. (4) Cf. *Job* 3:24. (5) *Psalms* 55:3.

הַחֲרִישׁוּ מִמֶּנִּי — *Be silent and do not answer me.* In vivid prose and sharp detail this *kinnah,* of unknown authorship, captures the anguish of a survivor of an unknown massacred community whose emotions are still storming and seething and whose tears are not yet dry. It describes the untenable tragedy of loving parents forced to slaughter their cherished children by their own hand, to save them from excruciating torture and mutilation at the hand of the enemy. All this was performed in a spirit of utmost piety and purity to sanctify the Name of God. Furthermore, it describes how the greatest Torah scholars were murdered and how their books and manuscripts were mercilessly consigned to the flames.

It concludes with a question and a challenge to God, "How long will You continue to witness this indifferently? . . . Will You not seek revenge for the blood spilled like gushing streams?"

The particular tragedy about which

אֵיךְ שָׁבַת מָשׂוֹשׂ וְעָרְבָה שִׂמְחָה,
How is it that ‹ cease ‹ has joy ‹ and darkened ‹ has gladness; ‹‹

כָּל פָּנִים פָּארוּר[1] וְכָל רֹאשׁ קָרְחָה,
every ‹ face ‹ is blackened ‹ and every ‹ head ‹ is bald, ‹

וְכָל זָקָן גְּדוּעָה[2] וְעַל כָּל לֵב אֲנָחָה,
every ‹ beard ‹ is cut ‹ and on ‹ every ‹ heart ‹ is a sigh, ‹‹

מֵאָז נִתְעוֹרֵר גּוֹי עַז דּוֹרֵשׁ שׁוּחָה,[3]
from when ‹ arouse itself ‹ did the nation ‹ that is powerful, ‹‹ to seek ‹ [to cast us into] the pit. ‹‹

סִלָּה אַבִּירַי[4] הוֹגֵי עֹז מִבְטֶחָה,
He trampled ‹ all my warriors, ‹‹ those who study ‹ our stronghold ‹ that is secure [the Torah]. ‹‹

בְּתוּלוֹתַי וּבַחוּרַי נָסַח בִּנְסִיחָה,
My maidens ‹ and my young men, ‹ he uprooted ‹ with devastation; ‹‹

בְּרֹאשׁ כָּל חוּצוֹת[5] נִבְלָתָן כַּסּוּחָה,[6]
at the head ‹ of every ‹ street ‹ their corpses ‹ are cut down. ‹‹

עוֹלָלַי וְטַפַּי נֶחְשָׁבוּ כְּצֹאן טִבְחָה,[7]
My infants ‹ and my babies ‹ were considered ‹ to be like sheep ‹ for the slaughter. ‹‹

אֵילִילָה עַל זֹאת[8] וְדִמְעָתִי עַל לֶחָה,[9]
I shall wail ‹ about ‹ this, ‹‹ and my tear ‹ is on ‹ [my] cheek. ‹‹

הֵאָסְפוּ אֵלַי דְּוּוּיֵי צֹאן נִדָּחָה.
Gather ‹ to me, ‹‹ O suffering ‹ sheep ‹ that are lost, ‹‹

לְהַרְבּוֹת הַבְּכִי וּלְהָרִים צְוָחָה,
to intensify ‹ [your] weeping ‹ and to make even louder ‹ [your] outcry. ‹‹

(1) Cf. *Joel* 2:6. (2) Cf. *Jeremiah* 48:37; some editions read גְּרוּעָה, *diminished,* which is the word used in Scriptures. (3) Some editions read כּוֹרֶה שׁוּחָה, *to dig a pit;* cf. *Jeremiah* 18:22. (4) Cf. *Eichah* 1:15. (5) 2:19. (6) Cf. *Isaiah* 5:25. (7) Cf. *Psalms* 44:23. (8) Cf. *Micah* 1:8. (9) Cf. *Eichah* 1:2.

this *kinnah* was written is unknown. It very aptly describes any one of many massacres and pogroms that have formed a large part of Jewish history.

הֵילִילוּ שָׁמַיִם וְזַעֲקִי אֲדָמָה.

« O Earth. ‹ and shout out, «O Heaven, ‹ Howl,

אָרִיד בְּשִׂיחִי וְאָהִימָה, וְקוֹל נְהִי אָרִימָה.

« I shall raise. ‹ of lament ‹ and the sound « and I shall moan aloud, ‹ as I speak ‹ I shall lament

אֶרְאֶלִּים* צְאוּ וְצַעֲקוּ[1] מָרָה,

« bitterly, ‹ and shout ‹ go out ‹ O *Erelim,**

סְפוֹד תַּמְרוּר[2] הֵאָגְדוּ בַּחֲבוּרָה,

« in groups, ‹ assemble ‹ most bitter ‹ for eulogy

קוֹל כַּחוֹלָה צָרָה כְּמַבְכִּירָה,[3]

« of one giving birth to a first child. ‹ with the pain ‹ like a woman in labor, ‹ cry

הִתְאוֹנְנוּ עַל עֲדַת שֶׂה פְּזוּרָה,

« that are scattered, ‹ of sheep ‹ the flock ‹ for ‹ Mourn

עָלֵימוֹ כִּי נִגְזְרָה גְזֵרָה, בָּחֳרִי אַף וָזַעַם וְעֶבְרָה,[4]

« and wrath. ‹ and fury ‹ anger, ‹ with flaring ‹ was the decree ‹ issued ‹ because ‹ [mourn] for them

וְנִתְוַעֲדוּ בִּפְרִישׁוּת וּבְטָהֳרָה,

‹ and purity ‹ in abstinence ‹ They gathered themselves

לְקַדֵּשׁ שֵׁם הַגָּדוֹל וְהַנּוֹרָא,

« and Awesome, ‹ that is Great ‹ the Name ‹ to sanctify

וְאִישׁ אֶת אָחִיו חִזְּקוּ בְּעֶזְרָה,[5]

« with support, ‹ would strengthen ‹ to his brother ‹ and each man

לְהִדָּבֵק בְּיִרְאָה טְהוֹרָה,

« that is pure, ‹ with reverence ‹ to [be able to] embrace [God]

(1) Cf. *Isaiah* 33:7. (2) Cf. *Jeremiah* 6:26. (3) Cf. 4:31. (4) Cf. *Psalms* 78:49. (5) Cf. *Isaiah* 41:6.

אֶרְאֶלִּים — *Erelim*. We lack the vocabulary to distinguish between the varieties of angels. *Rambam* (*Yesodei HaTorah* 2:7) enumerates ten levels: *Chayos, Ofanim, Erelim, Chashmalim, Seraphim, Malachim, Elohim, Bnei Elohim, Cheruvim*, and *Ishim*.

בְּלִי כְּרוֹעַ לַעֲבוֹדָה זָרָה, וְלֹא חָסוּ גֶּבֶר וּגְבִירָה,

« nor a woman — ‹ — neither a man « They did not show pity « strange gods. ‹ to worship ‹ to kneel ‹ and not

עַל בָּנִים צְפִירַת תִּפְאָרָה,

« of glory. ‹ were like a coronet ‹ the children [whose faces] ‹ for

אֲבָל אָזְרוּ גְבוּרָה יְתֵרָה,

‹ that was extraordinary ‹ with courage ‹ they girded themselves ‹ Instead,

לַהֲלוֹם רֹאשׁ וְלִקְרוֹץ שִׁדְרָה,

« spine. ‹ and sever ‹ head ‹ to smash

וְאֵלֵימוֹ דִּבְּרוּ בַּאֲמִירָה,

« in declaration, ‹ they spoke ‹ Then to them

לֹא זָכִינוּ לְגַדֶּלְכֶם לַתּוֹרָה,

« *for the Torah,* ‹ *to raise you* ‹ *We did not merit*

נַקְרִיבְכֶם כְּעוֹלָה וְהַקְטָרָה,

« *caused to go up in smoke [before God].* ‹ *like a burnt-offering* ‹ *[instead] we must offer you as a sacrifice*

וְנִזְכֶּה עִמָּכֶם לְאוֹרָה, הַצְּפוּנָה מֵעֵין כֹּל וַעֲלוּמָה.

« *and hidden.* ‹ *of all* ‹ *from the eyes* ‹ *that is concealed* ‹ *the light* ‹ *sharing with you* ‹ *May we merit*

אָרִיד בְּשִׂיחִי וְאָהִימָה, וְקוֹל נְהִי אָרִימָה.

« I shall raise. ‹ of lament ‹ and the sound « and I shall moan aloud, ‹ as I speak ‹ I shall lament

אָז הִסְכִּימוּ גְּדוֹלִים וּקְטַנִּים,

‹ and the children ‹ the adults ‹ agreed ‹ Then

לְקַבֵּל בְּאַהֲבָה דִּין שׁוֹכֵן מְעוֹנִים,

« in the heavens. ‹ of the One Who dwells ‹ the verdict ‹ in love ‹ to accept

וּזְקֵנִים דְּשֵׁנִים וְרַעֲנַנִּים,[1] הֵם הָיוּ תְּחִלָּה נִדּוֹנִים,

« judged [to be executed]. ‹ the first ‹ who were ‹ it was they « and fresh, ‹ [though still] vigorous ‹ The aged

(1) Cf. *Psalms* 92:15.

וְיָצְאוּ לִקְרָאתָם עַזֵּי פָנִים,

‹ Come out ‹ against them ‹ did the brazen-faced [enemy]

וְנֶהֶרְגוּ הֲמוֹנִים הֲמוֹנִים,

‹ and slaughtered ‹ were multitudes ‹ upon multitudes,«

וְנִתְעָרְבוּ פְּדָרִים עִם פַּרְשְׁדוֹנִים,

‹ intermingled in a [gruesome] mix ‹ were fats ‹ with « intestinal wastes.

וְהָאָבוֹת אֲשֶׁר הָיוּ רַחֲמָנִים,

‹ Then the fathers ‹ who ‹ were once «compassionate,

נֶהֶפְכוּ לְאַכְזָר כַּיְּעֵנִים,[1]

‹ turned ‹ cruel « as ostriches,

וְהִפִּיסוּ עַל אָבוֹת וְעַל בָּנִים,

‹ and they cast lots ‹ over ‹ parents ‹ and over «children,

וּמִי שֶׁגּוֹרָל עָלָה לוֹ רִאשׁוֹנִים,

‹ and whomever ‹ the lot ‹ brought him up « first,

הוּא נִשְׁחַט בַּחֲלָפוֹת וְסַכִּינִים,

‹ he ‹ was slaughtered ‹ with slaughtering blades « and knives.

וּבַחוּרִים עֲלֵי תוֹלָע אֱמוּנִים,[2]

‹ Youths ‹ who in ‹ fine scarlet clothing ‹ were brought up

הֵם לָחֲכוּ עָפָר כַּתַּנִּינִים,[3]

‹ they now ‹ licked ‹ the dust « like serpents;

וְהַכַּלּוֹת לְבוּשׁוֹת שָׁנִים,

‹ and brides ‹ dressed ‹ in scarlet

מְעֻלָּפוֹת בִּזְרוֹעוֹת חֲתָנִים,

‹ fainted ‹ in the arms «of their husbands,

(1) Cf. *Eichah* 4:3. (2) Cf. 4:5. (3) Cf. *Micah* 7:17.

מְנֻתָּחוֹת בְּחֶרֶב וְכִידוֹנִים,

« and spears. ‹ by sword ‹ were butchered

זִכְרוּ זֹאת קְהַל עֲדַת נְבוֹנִים,

« of the wise, ‹ congregation ‹ assembled ‹ this, ‹ Remember

וְאַל תֶּחֱשׁוּ מֵהַרְבּוֹת קִינִים,

« lamentations! ‹ from reciting many ‹ be silenced ‹ and dare not

וְהַסְפִּידוּ עַל חֲסִידִים וַהֲגוּנִים,

‹ and proper ones ‹ the pious ‹ over ‹ Eulogize

אֲשֶׁר צָלְלוּ בַּמַּיִם הַזֵּידוֹנִים,

« that were treacherous. ‹ in the waters ‹ sank ‹ who

לְזֶכֶר זֹאת נַפְשִׁי עֲגוּמָה.

« is grieved. ‹ my soul ‹ of this, ‹ At the memory

אָרִיד בְּשִׂיחִי וְאָהִימָה, וְקוֹל נְהִי אָרִימָה.

« I shall raise. ‹ of lament ‹ and the sound « and I shall moan aloud, ‹ as I speak ‹ I shall lament

תּוֹרָה תּוֹרָה חִגְרִי שַׂק וְהִתְפַּלְּשִׁי בָּאֲפָרִים,

« in ashes, ‹ and roll yourself ‹ in sackcloth ‹ gird yourself ‹ O Torah, ‹ Torah,

אֵבֶל יָחִיד עֲשִׂי לָךְ וּמִסְפַּד תַּמְרוּרִים,[1]

« most bitter, ‹ with a eulogy ‹ on yourself, ‹ accept ‹ as if for an only child ‹ mourning

עַל תּוֹפְשֵׂי מְשׁוֹטַיִךְ וּפוֹרְשֵׂי מַכְמוֹרִים,

« the nets, ‹ and who spread ‹ the oars ‹ those who wield ‹ over

מַלָּחַיִךְ וְחוֹבְלַיִךְ בְּמַיִם אַדִּירִים,[2]

« that are mighty. ‹ through the waters [of the sea of Talmud] ‹ and your pilots ‹ your sailors

עוֹרְכֵי מַעֲרָכֵךְ, מְיַשְּׁרֵי הֲדוּרִים,[3]

« the twisted paths; ‹ those who straighten ‹ [Torah themes] in orderly arrangements, ‹ Those who organize

(1) Cf. *Jeremiah* 6:26. (2) Cf. *Ezekiel* 27:27-29. (3) Cf. *Isaiah* 45:2.

מְפַעַנְחֵי צְפוּנֶיךָ וּמְגַלֵּי מִסְתּוֹרִים,

« its secrets. ‹ and who uncover ‹ Your hidden [wisdom] ‹ who elucidate

מִי יְקַצֶּה בִּגְבָעוֹת וּמִי יְסַתֵּת בֶּהָרִים,

« the mountains? ‹ will [now] quarry ‹ and who « the hills, ‹ will [now] cut through ‹ Who

וּמִי יְפָרֵק הֲוָיוֹת וּמִי יְתָרֵץ שְׁבָרִים,

« the [questions about] contradictions? ‹ will [now] answer ‹ and who « the issues, ‹ will [now] resolve ‹ Who

מִי יַפְלִיא נְזִירוּת וּמִי יַעֲרוֹךְ נְדָרִים,

« the [annulment of] oaths? ‹ will [now] arrange ‹ and who « the Nazirites [by their vows], ‹ will [now] separate ‹ Who

מִי יְשַׂדֵּד מַעֲמַקָּיִךְ וְחַתּוּ אִכָּרִים,

« have the farmers [Torah scholars] been? ‹ when smashed ‹ your depths [of your fields] ‹ will plow through ‹ Who

וּמִי יִלְחוֹם מִלְחֲמוֹתַיִךְ וְיָשׁוּב לַשְּׁעָרִים,

« to the gates [of the House of Study], ‹ and return [Israel] ‹ your [Torah] battles ‹ will wage ‹ And who

כְּלֵי מִלְחָמָה אָבְדוּ וְנָפְלוּ גִבּוֹרִים.[1]

« have the warriors? ‹ and fallen ‹ are lost, ‹ of war ‹ [now that] the weapons

אַשְׁרֵיהֶם מַשְׂכִּילִים כָּרָקִיעַ זוֹהֲרִים,[2]

« shine, ‹ who like the firmament ‹ wise [martyrs] ‹ Fortunate are those

בִּמְנוּחוֹת שָׁלוֹם נָחוּ יְשָׁרִים,

« these upright ones. ‹ rest « that are peaceful, ‹ in resting places

אוֹי וַאֲבוֹי שׁוֹד וָשֶׁבֶר לְנוֹתָרִים,

« for those left alive, ‹ and destruction ‹ plunder « Alas! « Woe!

לִמְדִיבַת נֶפֶשׁ[3] וַחֲבָלִים וְצִירִים,

« and pains [of childbirth]; ‹ like the pangs ‹ soul, ‹ for those of distressed

(1) Cf. *II Samuel* 1:27. (2) Cf. *Daniel* 12:3. (3) Cf. *Deuteronomy* 28:65.

לְכִלְיוֹן עֵינַיִם[1] צַלְמָוֶת וְלֹא סְדָרִים,

for those longing [for salvation] ‹ with [wearied] eyes, « [seeing only] the shadow of death › and the lack ‹ of order. «

עֶרֶב אֹמְרִים מִי יִתֵּן צְפָרִים,

In the evening ‹ *they say,* ‹ *Who* ‹ *can give [back]* ‹ *[this] morning!* «

וּבֹקֶר מְצַפִּים מִי יְגַלֶּה אוֹרִים,*

And in the morning ‹ *they only hope,* ‹ *Who* ‹ *will remove* ‹ *the daylight [and bring evening]?** «

מִמַּרְאֵה עֵינֵימוֹ אֲשֶׁר הֵמָּה שָׁרִים,[2]

because of what they see ‹ with their eyes « — that which ‹ they ‹ see. «

מִחוּץ שְׁכְּלָה חֶרֶב וְאֵימָה מֵחֲדָרִים,[3]*

On the outside ‹ cause bereavement ‹ will the sword ‹ while terror ‹ [reigns] within.* «

עַד מָתַי תַּבִּיט רוֹאֶה כָּל סְתָרִים,

Until ‹ when ‹ will You watch [indifferently], « You Who sees ‹ all ‹ hidden things? «

קַנֵּא לְתוֹרָתְךָ אֲשֶׁר שְׂרָפוּהָ זָרִים,

Be zealous ‹ over Your Torah, ‹ which ‹ burn it ‹ did strangers; «

קְלָאוּהָ פְּרָעוּהָ קְרָעוּהָ לִגְזָרִים,

they roasted it, ‹ they opened it up, ‹ and they tore it ‹ into shreds. «

כְּסִירִים סְבוּכִים[4] הִגְדִּילוּ הַמְּדוּרִים,

As with [bundles] of thorn brush ‹ all entangled, « they enlarged ‹ the bonfires [of sacred scrolls]. «

(1) Cf. *Deuteronomy* 28:65. (2) Cf. 28:67. (3) Cf. 32: 25. (4) *Nahum* 1:10.

מִי יְגַלֶּה אוֹרִים — *Who will remove the daylight [and bring evening]?* The root גלה has two diametrically opposite meanings. It can mean *to exile, to remove,* or *to uncover, to reveal.* The translation uses the first meaning. Alternatively, the phrase may be translated according to the second meaning, *O who will reveal the nighttime luminaries?*

מִחוּץ...מֵחֲדָרִים — *On the outside ... within* [lit., *from the chambers*]. The translation follows one of the interpretations given by *Rashi* (*Deuteronomy* 32:25). According to *Rashi's* other interpretations: *On the outside* refers to the battlefield outside the city, and *chambers* refers to the fugitives from the battlefield who succumbed to the terror throbbing in the chamber of

הַעַל אֵלֶּה תִתְאַפַּק[1] אֲדוֹן כָּל יְצוּרִים,

« created? ‹ of ‹ O « You shall ‹ these ‹ Can it be
everything Master restrain Yourself, [deeds] that over

תִּנְקוֹם דָּם הַנִּשְׁפָּךְ כַּמַּיִם הַמֻּגָּרִים,[2]

« flowing downhill, ‹ like water ‹ poured out ‹ the ‹ Avenge
blood

מִשּׁוֹד עֲנִיִּים מֵאֶנְקַת סְעוּרִים,[3]

« of the ‹ for the cry ‹ of the ‹ for the
storm-tossed. poor, plundering

עַם שָׁבֵי פֶשַׁע[4] לְעוּנִים וּמְרוּרִים רַחֲמָה,

« have mercy; « and bitterness, ‹ who are « transgression, ‹ who ‹ [Upon]
filled with repent the
wormwood people

אוֹתָם בַּל תַּחֲרִימָה, קַרְנָם הַגְבִּיהַּ וְהָרִימָה.[5]

« and exalt. ‹ elevate ‹ their « to be annihilated; ‹ do not ‹ them
pride allow

אָרִיד בְּשִׂיחִי וְאָהִימָה, וְקוֹל נְהִי אָרִימָה.

« I shall ‹ of ‹ and the « and I shall ‹ as I speak ‹ I shall
raise. lament sound moan aloud, lament

(1) *Isaiah* 64:11. (2) *Micah* 1:4. (3) Cf. *Psalms* 12:6. (4) *Isaiah* 59:20. (5) *Psalms* 75:11.

their hearts; or, *outside* alludes to overt idolatry (see, e.g., *Jeremiah* 11:13) and *chambers* to covert idolatry (see, e.g., *Ezekiel* 8:12).

KINNAH 23 / קינה כג

וְאֶת נָוִי חַטָּאתִי הִשְׁמִימָה,*
« caused its destruction,* ‹ my sin « my Temple, ‹ Regarding

וְדִמְעָתִי עַל לֶחְיִי[1] אַזְרִימָה.
« I shall cause to stream; ‹ my cheeks ‹ on ‹ so my tears

וּבְיוֹם זֶה נְהִי נִהְיָה[2] אָרִימָה,
« I shall raise it. « came to be, ‹ a lament ‹ and on this day [the 9th of Av]

וְאָהִימָה מִיָּמִים יָמִימָה.[3]
« to year. ‹ from year ‹ And I shall moan

אֱבֶל לֵב וְנִחוּם חָדַל חָדוֹל,
« has absolutely ceased, ‹ but consolation «does the heart, ‹ Mourn

וּמִכָּל כְּאֵב צִירִי נִבְדַּל בָּדוֹל,
« is absolutely set apart, ‹ [this] my pain ‹ [other] pain, ‹ and from all

עַל בֵּן וּבַת רַבִּי יִשְׁמָעֵאל כֹּהֵן גָּדוֹל,
« *Gadol;* ‹ the *Kohen* ‹ Yishmael ‹ of Rabbi ‹ and the daughter ‹ the son ‹ regarding

זִכְרָם יְקוֹד בִּלְבָבִי אָשִׂימָה.
« I shall set. ‹ in my heart ‹ as a fire ‹ their memory

וְאָהִימָה מִיָּמִים יָמִימָה.
« to year. ‹ from year ‹ And I shall moan

(1) *Cf. Lamentations* 1:2. (2) *Micah* 2:4. (3) *Exodus* 13:10.

וְאֶת נָוִי חַטָּאתִי הִשְׁמִימָה — *Regarding my Temple, my sin caused its destruction.* The story of the son and daughter of R' Yishmael ben Elisha, the *Kohen Gadol,* (see *kinnah* 21) is related in the Talmud (*Gittin* 58a). It is interesting to note that the Midrash contains a very similar, though more complicated, narrative about the son and daughter of Tzaddok HaKohen (*Midrash Eichah* 1:46). In each case, the young pair's moral purity set an example of chastity and righteousness that became an example for future generations. Neither youth nor maiden complained about the personal tragedy each underwent. Rather, it was the

עֵת נִשְׁבּוּ וְנָפְלוּ לִשְׁנֵי אֲדוֹנִים,

« masters, ‹ to two ‹ they fell « they were captured, ‹ At the time

וְהֵם שְׁכֵנִים זֶה לְעֻמַּת זֶה חוֹנִים,

« did they dwell; ‹ the other ‹ opposite ‹ — the one « neighbors ‹ who were

וַיְסַפְּרוּ זֶה לָזֶה עִנְיָנִים,

« their affairs. « to the other — ‹ — the one ‹ they recounted

זֶה אָמַר מִשְּׁבִיַּת צִיּוֹנִים,

‹ *of Zion* ‹ *From the captivity* « said, ‹ One

שָׁבִיתִי שִׁפְחָה לְבוּשַׁת שָׁנִים,

« *in scarlet-wool,* ‹ *dressed* ‹ *a maidservant* ‹ *I have captured*

כַּלְּבָנָה בְּזִיו וּקְלַסְתֵּר פָּנִים,

« *of [her] face,* ‹ *and in the features* ‹ *in luminance* ‹ *as the moon*

וּבְתֹאַר כִּקְצִיעָה וִימִימָה.*

« *and Jemimah!** ‹ *as Keziah* ‹ *and in form [as beautiful]*

וְאָהִימָה מִיָּמִים יָמִימָה.

« to year. ‹ from year ‹ And I shall moan

רֵעֵהוּ סִפֵּר לוֹ בִּכְפָלַיִם,

« with double [those praises], ‹ to him ‹ reported ‹ His neighbor

הֵן אֲנִי מִשְּׁבִי יְרוּשָׁלַיִם,

« *of Jerusalem [have come],* ‹ *from the captivity* ‹ *I* ‹ *Indeed [too]*

---

chillul Hashem, the desecration of God's Holy Name, that was the point of their plaints. And it was for this reason that Jeremiah prophetically wailed and lamented for this brother and sister so many centuries earlier.

וּבְתֹאַר כִּקְצִיעָה וִימִימָה — *And in form [as beautiful] as Keziah and Jemimah.* Job had three daughters: Jemimah, Keziah, and Keren-happuch. *And there were not found any women as beautiful as the daughters of Job anywhere in the land* (Job 42:15).

שָׁבִיתִי עֶבֶד יְפֵה עֵינַיִם,
« eyes, ‹ with beautiful ‹ a man-servant ‹ where I captured

כַּשֶּׁמֶשׁ בְּתָקְפּוֹ עֵת צָהֳרַיִם,
« of noon! ‹ at the time ‹ in its full splendor ‹ as the sun

בֹּא וּנְזַוְּגֵם וּנְחַלְּקָה בֵּינֹתַיִם,
‹ between us ‹ and divide ‹ let us pair them ‹ Come,

בְּוְלָדוֹת כְּמוֹ כּוֹכְבֵי שָׁמַיִם,
« of the heavens! ‹ the stars ‹ [who will be] like ‹ their children

לְשֵׁמַע זֹאת תְּצַלֶּנָה אָזְנַיִם,[1]
« all ears; ‹ will ring ‹ this ‹ On hearing

לְזֵכֶר זֹאת אֶת מַדַּי אַפְרִימָה.
« I shall rend! ‹ my robe ‹ this, ‹ to commemorate

וְאָהִימָה מִיָּמִים יָמִימָה.
« to year. ‹ from year ‹ And I shall moan

כְּהִסְכִּימוּ עַל זֹאת שְׁנֵיהֶם יַחַד,
« together, ‹ — the two of them « this [plan] ‹ to ‹ Once they agreed

לָעֶרֶב זִוְּגוּם בְּחֶדֶר אֶחָד,
« in one room. ‹ they paired them together ‹ that evening

וְהָאֲדוֹנִים מִבַּחוּץ לִבָּם כְּאֶחָד,
« as one, ‹ their hearts « were outside, ‹ The masters

וְהֵם בּוֹכִים בְּמַר נֶפֶשׁ וָפַחַד,
« and with fear, ‹ of soul ‹ with bitterness ‹ were weeping ‹ but [the couple]

עַד בֹּקֶר בִּכְיָתָם לֹא הִדְמִימָה.
« stilled. ‹ was not ‹ their weeping ‹ morning ‹ until

וְאָהִימָה מִיָּמִים יָמִימָה.
« to year. ‹ from year ‹ And I shall moan

(1) *Cf. Jeremiah* 19:3.

זֶה יִסְפּוֹד בְּחִיל וּבְקִיר לֵב יִמְסֶה,

« was melting, ‹ of [his] heart ‹ so that even the wall « trembling, ‹ mourned ‹ He

נִין אַהֲרֹן אֵיךְ לְשִׁפְחָה יְהִי נוֹשֵׂא,

« *wed?* ‹ *he will be* ‹ *that to a maid-servant* ‹ *how can it be* « *of Aaron,* ‹ *A descendant*

וְהִיא גַּם הִיא תְּיַלֵּל בְּתִגְרַת שׁוֹסֶה,

« of her captor, ‹ over the blows ‹ was wailing « she — ‹ — also « While she

בַּת יוֹכֶבֶד אֵיךְ לְעֶבֶד תִּנָּשֵׂא,

« *she will be wed?* ‹ *that to a slave* ‹ *how can it be* « *of Yocheved,* ‹ *A daughter*

אוֹי כִּי זֹאת גְּזַר אוֹמֵר וְעֹשֶׂה,

« and does [it]. ‹ of [God], the One Who says [something] ‹ the decree ‹ this is ‹ For ‹ Woe!

לְזֹאת יִבְכּוּ עָשׁ וּכְסִיל וְכִימָה.[1]

« and the Pleiades! ‹ Orion, ‹ [do the constellations] Ursa Minor, ‹ weep « For this [tragedy],

וְאֶהֱימָה מִיָּמִים יָמִימָה.

« to year. ‹ from year ‹ And I shall moan

אוֹר בֹּקֶר זֶה אֶת זֶה כְּהִכִּירוּ,

« when they recognized, ‹ another ‹ one ‹ of dawn, ‹ At the light

הוֹי אָחִי וְהוֹי אָחוֹת הִגְבִּירוּ.

« they intensified [their cries]. « *Sister!* ‹ *and Woe!* « *My brother!* ‹ *Woe!*

וְנִתְדַּבְּקוּ יַחַד וְנִתְחַבְּרוּ,

« and were united, ‹ together ‹ They embraced

עַד יָצְתָה נִשְׁמָתָם בִּנְשִׁימָה.

« in the same breath. ‹ did their souls ‹ leave them ‹ until

וְאֶהֱימָה מִיָּמִים יָמִימָה.

« to year. ‹ from year ‹ And I shall moan

(1) *Job* 9:9; see commentary to *Kinnah* 5.

לָזֹאת יְקוֹנֵן יִרְמְיָהוּ בְּשְׁאִיָּה,

« amidst the Destruction, ‹ Jeremiah ‹ lamented ‹ For this

גְּזֵרָה זֹאת תָּמִיד אֲנִי בוֹכִיָּה,

« *shall weep,* ‹ *I* ‹ *continually* ‹ *Over this [decree]*

וּבִלְבָבִי יֵקַד יְקוֹד[1] וּכְוִיָּה,

« *and a burn;* ‹ *a flame* ‹ *is kindled* ‹ *and in my heart*

עַל בֵּן וּבַת מִסְפֵּד רַב אַרְעִימָה.[2]

« *I will thunder forth.* ‹ *that is great* ‹ *a lament* ‹ *and daughter* ‹ *[this] son* ‹ *for*

אָרִיד בְּשִׂיחִי וְאָהִימָה,[3]

‹ *and I shall moan,* « *as I speak,* ‹ *I shall lament*

וְקוֹל נְהִי אָרִימָה.

« *I shall raise.* ‹ *of lament* ‹ *and the sound*

(1) *Isaiah* 10:16. (2) Some editions read אַעֲצִימָה, but the meaning is the same. (3) *Psalms* 55:3.

KINNAH 24 / קינה כד

עַל חֻרְבַּן בֵּית הַמִּקְדָּשׁ,
Over 〈 the Destruction 〈 of the Temple, 〈

כִּי הוּרַס וְכִי הוּדַשׁ,
that 〈 was torn down 〈 and that 〈 was trampled upon, 《

אֶסְפּוֹד בְּכָל שָׁנָה וְשָׁנָה מִסְפֵּד חָדָשׁ,
I shall lament 〈 every 〈 year 〈 after year 〈 with an elegy 〈 that is new, 《

עַל הַקֹּדֶשׁ וְעַל הַמִּקְדָּשׁ.
for 〈 the holy [vessels] 〈 and for 〈 the Sanctuary. 《

תִּסְתֵּר לְאַלֵּם תַּרְשִׁישִׁים* מֵרוֹן,
You hid Yourself 〈 in order to silence 〈 the celestial angels* 〈 from [their] songs, 《

כְּזִעְזַעְתָּ עוֹלָם מִפְּנֵי חָרוֹן,
When You made shudder 〈 the world 〈 because of 〈 Your flaring anger, 《

כִּלְהֲטָה הָאֵשׁ בֵּין שְׁנֵי בַּדֵּי אָרוֹן.
[and] when flare 〈 did the fire 〈 between 〈 the two 〈 poles 〈 of the Ark. 《

עַל חֻרְבַּן בֵּית הַמִּקְדָּשׁ — *Over the Destruction of the Temple.* This *kinnah,* by Rabbi Elazar HaKalir, focuses on yet another tragic aspect of the Temple's Destruction. Not only was the Temple edifice destroyed but its furnishings, adornments, and holy vessels were plundered too. Each one of these components was designed to reflect the celestial Temple in the heavens above where the ministering angels offer their fiery and awesome paeans of praise to the Almighty. Moreover, each corresponded to some particular natural phenomenon (such as rain or dew). Here we lament the fact that these very adornments and vessels were ignominiously vandalized by the vile hand of Nebuchadnezzar and then sent as gifts to adorn the pagan temples of the Babylonian Empire. Here we mourn this terrible degradation that befell both the terrestrial and celestial Temples. Here we grieve over the diminution of benefits derived from the phenomena of nature.

Beginning with the second stanza, the *kinnah* follows a reverse-alphabetical format.

לְאַלֵּם תַּרְשִׁישִׁים — *In order to silence the celestial angels.* On three occasions when the angels in their heavenly array were about to begin their daily songs of God's praises, He stopped them: during the Flood in Noah's time; when the Egyptians were drowning in the Sea of Reeds; and at the Destruction of the *Beis HaMikdash* (*Midrash Eichah,* intro. 24, as interpreted by *Yefei Anaf*). The *paytan* alludes to the Flood and the drowning with the words, *when You made shudder the world because of Your flaring anger,* and to the

שְׁנֵי מִקְדָּשִׁים אֲשֶׁר בְּמַעֲלָה וּבְמַטָּה,

« and below ‹ above ‹ that are ‹ Temples, ‹ When these two

זֶה עַל גַּב זֶה[1] הוּאֲפְלוּ בַּעֲלָטָה,

« in darkness, ‹ were both enshrouded « of the other — ‹ top ‹ on ‹— one

וְנַמְתָּ אַחֲרִישׁ וְאֶתְאַפַּק[2] וְאַבִּיטָה.

« *I will observe.* « *I will hold myself back,* « *I will be silent,* « You said,

רָאשֵׁי הַבַּדִּים כִּנְגְנָזוּ* מִבֵּין הַפָּרוֹכוֹת,*

« the Curtains,* ‹ from inside ‹ were hidden* ‹ of the poles [of the Ark] ‹ When the heads

וְאַרְבַּע גֶּחָלִים* בִּדְבִיר מְהַלְּכוֹת,

« went around, ‹ throughout the Sanctuary ‹ [flaming] coals* ‹ four

וְאַרְבָּעִים יְסוֹד עַד תְּהוֹם מְלַחֲכוֹת.

« were seared. ‹ the depths ‹ unto ‹ foundation pillars ‹ and the forty

קֹדֶשׁ הַקֳּדָשִׁים מִבֵּית קֹדֶשׁ כְּנִבְדַּד,

« was isolated, ‹ of holiness ‹ from being a habitation ‹ of the Holies ‹ When the Holiest

שַׁחְתָּ וְהֵילַלְתָּ אָהֳלִי שֻׁדַּד,[3]

« *is plundered!* ‹ *My Tent* « and You wailed, ‹ You proclaimed

(1) See *kinnah* 5. (2) *Isaiah* 42:14. (3) *Jeremiah* 10:20.

Destruction with, *when flare did the fire between the two poles of the Ark* (*Beis Levi*).

כִּנְגְנָזוּ — *When the . . . were hidden.* The Talmudic Sages discuss the fate of the Ark. Some maintain that it was taken by Nebuchadnezzar when he conquered the First Temple. Others hold, and this is the opinion of the *paytan*, that when King Josiah was informed by the prophets of the impending Destruction, he had the Ark removed from its place in the Holiest of the Holies and hidden in one of the underground passageways that Solomon had built beneath the *Beis HaMikdash* (*Yoma* 54b; *Shekalim* 6:2).

מִבֵּין הַפָּרוֹכוֹת — *From inside the Curtains.* Although the Torah speaks of only one *Paroches*-Curtain in the Tabernacle, there were two in the Second Temple (see *Yoma* 47a).

וְאַרְבַּע גֶּחָלִים — *Four [flaming] coals.* While the enemy was debating how to set fire to the *Beis HaMikdash*, the angels were debating with God (as it were) whether to permit the Destruction to take place. Finally, the Divine Attribute of Strict Justice came to the fore and said, "Master of the

וַנַּמְתָּ אַכֶּה כַּף עַל כַּף[1] וְאֶשְׁאַג הֵידָד.[2]

And you said, « I shall clap, « one palm ‹ on ‹ the [other] palm, « and I shall roar, « *"O woe!"* «

צְפִירַת תִּפְאַרְתְּךָ כְּנִתְּנָה בְּיַד צָר,

The crown ‹ of Your glory [the Temple] ‹ when it was delivered ‹ into the hand ‹ of the enemy «

וְכָל כְּלֵי חֶמְדָּה אִוּוּי בֵּית הָאוֹצָר,[3]

— with all ‹ the vessels ‹ so precious, « the most desirable ‹ of the house ‹ of treasure. «

וּלְךָ הַכֹּחַ וְהַגְּבוּרָה[4] וְנָמוּ עָצָר.

To You belongs ‹ the power ‹ and the strength, « [yet You allowed] them to exult, « *He has been restrained!* «

פְּנֵי הַכִּסֵּא אָז אֻפָּלוּ,

Then [the heavens,] facing ‹ the Throne ‹ were darkened, «

וְגָבְהֵי שָׁמַיִם לְקַדְרוּת הוּשְׁפָּלוּ,

and the heights ‹ of heaven ‹ into blackness ‹ were plunged, «

יָכִין וּבוֹעַז[5] לְהִשְׁתַּבֵּר כְּנָפָלוּ,

when [the Temple pillars] Yachin ‹ and Boaz ‹ were smashed ‹ as they fell. «

עֲשָׂרָה שֻׁלְחָנוֹת*[6] אָז שֻׁלָּלוּ,

Ten ‹ Tables* ‹ then ‹ were taken as booty; «

(1) Cf. *Ezekiel* 21:22. (2) See *Jeremiah* 48:33 with *Rashi*. (3) Cf. *Hosea* 13:15. (4) Cf. *I Chronicles* 29:11. (5) See *I Kings* 7:21. (6) See *II Chronicles* 4:8.

world, do You want this wicked man to be able to boast, 'I have destroyed God's Temple! I have burnt His Sanctuary!' No! It is better that a heavenly fire be sent down upon it . . . Then, if the Babylonians claim supremacy because of their victory, Jerusalem will be able to retort, 'You have slain an already dying lion! You have ground already milled flour! You have kindled an already burned city!'" (*Midrash Eichah* 1:41). Suddenly the conquerors looked up and saw four flaming coals descend from heaven upon the four corners of the Temple and set it afire (*Pesikta Rabbah* 27:6).

עֲשָׂרָה שֻׁלְחָנוֹת — *Ten Tables*. The Torah ordains that a Golden Table be placed in the Sanctuary, upon which the *Panim*-breads are arranged. When King Solomon built the *Beis HaMikdash*, he enhanced that Table by placing five more to its right and five to its left (see *Rashi* to *II Chronicles* 4:8). These should not be

וּלְעוֹרְכֵיהֶם נָמוּ אַיֵּה אֲדוֹן אֵלּוּ,

and to [the *Kohanim*] who once set them, 《 [the enemy] said, 《 *Where is* 〈 *the Master* 〈 *of these [tables]?* 《

לְאוֹצְרוֹת שִׁנְעָר לִקְדֵשִׁים כְּהוּנְחָלוּ.

To the treasure houses 〈 of Shinar [Babylon] 〈 for the use of harlots 〈 they were allotted. 《

שְׂרָפִים עוֹמְדִים[1] נָעוּ מִמַּעֲמָד,

The Seraphim 〈 who stood [above His Throne] 〈 had to move 〈 from their positions 〈

כְּנֶהֶרְסוּ מְכוֹנוֹת[2] מִתּוֹךְ מַחֲמָד,

when were demolished 〈 the bases [of the washstands] 〈 within 〈 the [Temple of God's] delight, 《

וְזֵדִים קָרְאוּ יְמֵי הַשְּׁמָד.

while the immoral ones 〈 proclaimed [that period as] 〈 *The Days* 〈 *of Destruction.* 《

נְחֹשֶׁת יָם[3] וַעֲשָׂרָה כִּיּוֹרוֹת,[4]

The copper 〈 sea [basin] 〈 and the ten 〈 washbasins 《

כְּנִמְסְרוּ לַבֵּל וְהִנָּם שְׁבוּרוֹת,*

when they were given over 〈 to the [worship of] Bel, 《 indeed they 〈 were broken* 《

וּשְׁנֵי הַמְּאוֹרוֹת מֵאָז קְדוֹרוֹת.[5]

— and the two 〈 luminaries, [the sun and the moon,] 〈 since then 〈 are darkened. 《

מַעֲשֵׂה הָאוֹפַנִּים אֲשֶׁר בַּמֶּרְכָּבָה,[6]

The construction 〈 of the wheels [of the copper bases] 〈 [paterned on the wheels] that were 〈 in the [Celestial] Chariot, 《

כְּהוּרְדוּ לָאָרֶץ זֹהַר הָרָקִיעַ כָּבָה,

when they were lowered 〈 to the ground, 《 the brilliance 〈 of the firmament 〈 was dimmed, 《

---

(1) See commentary to *Kinnah* 22, s.v. אֶרְאֶלִים, *Erelim.* (2) See *I Kings* 7:27ff. (3) See 7:23 ff. (4) See 7:38. (5) Cf. *Joel* 2:10. (6) Cf. *I Kings* 7:33.

---

confused with the thirteen tables of the Second Temple (see *Shekalim* 6:4), which served an entirely different purpose.

וְהִנָּם שְׁבוּרוֹת — *Indeed, they were broken.* When these sturdy copper vessels were brought to Babylon for idol-

חוֹלֵשׁ עַל גּוֹיִם*[1] לִפְנֵי כְרוּבִים בָּא.

«entered.‹ of the Cherubim ‹ into the presence ‹ the nations* ‹ of ‹ because [Nebuchadnezzar] who caused the weakening

לוֹיוֹת הַמּוּרָד[2] מֵעֵת הוּרָדוּ,

« they were taken down, ‹ from the moment « that were engraved [on the basin], ‹ The [cherub] couples

וְהַטְּלָלִים לִבְרָכָה לֹא יָרָדוּ,

«descended, ‹ no longer ‹ for blessing ‹ the dew

כְּלָבִים רָעִים עַל בָּמֳתֵי עָב דָּדוּ.[3]

« ascended. « cloud wreathed, « the heights, ‹ above ‹ that were wicked ‹ while the dogs [Nebuchadnezzar's hordes]

כָּל כְּלֵי כֶסֶף וּכְלֵי הַזָּהָב,

‹ of gold ‹ and the vessels ‹ of silver ‹ the vessels ‹ All

קֻצְּצוּ וְשֻׁסּוּ מִבֵּית הַלַּהַב,

« [going up in] flame; ‹ from the [Temple] ‹ and pillaged ‹ were chopped up

בְּצֵאת הֶהָדָר שָׁחֲחוּ עוֹזְרֵי רָהַב.[4]

« with strength. ‹ are [the angels] who assist ‹ bent down « the splendor, ‹ and when departed

יוֹם אֲשֶׁר נִקְרָא מְהוּמָה וּמְבוּכָה,[5]

« *and Confusion,* ‹ *Chaos* ‹ was called ‹ which ‹ On the day

לַהֲקַת מַלְאָכִים כְּאִשָּׁה מְצֵרָה נְבוֹכָה,

« were left bewildered, « in labor, ‹ like a woman « of angels, ‹ the assembly

(1) *Isaiah* 14:12.(2) See *I Kings* 7:29. (3) Cf. *Isaiah* 14:14. (4) Cf. *Eichah* 1:6; *Job* 9:13. (5) Cf. *Isaiah* 22:5.

atrous purposes, they suddenly broke apart of their own accord (*Arugas HaBosem*).

חוֹלֵשׁ עַל גּוֹיִם — *[Nebuchadnezzar] who caused the weakening of the nations.* Nebuchadnezzar would degrade the kings of the lands he had captured by making them his personal servants. Daily lots would be cast to determine which king would serve him each day. According to the Sages, he also used them for immoral purposes (*Rashi* to *Isaiah* 14:12).

דִּבּוּר פָּתַח וְעָנוּ אַחֲרָיו אֵיכָה.

« *Eichah.* « after Him, ‹ and [the angels] answered « began, ‹ until [God] speaking [the lamentations]

טָסוּ עַמּוֹנִים וּמוֹאָבִים, וְהוֹצִיאוּ הַכְּרוּבִים,

« the Cherubim, ‹ and took out ‹ and the Moabites ‹ did the Ammonites ‹ Swoop in

וּבִכְלִיבָה הָיוּ אוֹתָם מְסַבְּבִים,

« parade around, ‹ them ‹ they would ‹ and in a cage

הִנֵּה כְּכָל הַגּוֹיִם בֵּית יְהוּדָה חֲשׁוּבִים.[1]

«*to be considered.* ‹ *of Judah* ‹ *is the House* ‹ *the nations* ‹ *[idolatrous] like all* « saying, *Behold,*

חֵיל שַׂרְפֵי הַקֹּדֶשׁ[2] חֻלַּף מִגְּדֻלָּתוֹ,

« in their positions of authority, ‹ were replaced ‹ that are holy ‹ of Seraphim ‹ The legions

וְאֵל אַדִּיר שְׁמוֹ לֹא אָבָה תְהִלָּתוֹ,[3]

« to be praised, ‹ desire ‹ did not « His Name, ‹ Mighty is « and God,

לְגַלִּים הוּשַׂם בֵּית תְּפִלָּתוֹ.

« of Prayer. ‹ His House ‹ was turned ‹ when into heaps [of ruins]

זַמָּרֵי שַׁחַק הֶחֱשׁוּ מִנֹּעַם,

« from their pleasant [singing], ‹ were silenced ‹ of the heavens ‹ The [angelic] singers

וְנָם מַה לָּכֶם פֹּה אֵין הַיּוֹם טַעַם,

« *permission [to sing]!* ‹ *today* ‹ *There has not [been given]* « *here?* ‹ *are you doing* ‹ *What* « because He said,

מַה תְּקַלְּסוּן לַמֶּלֶךְ בִּשְׁעַת הַזַּעַם.

« *of the fury?* ‹ *at the time* ‹ *to the King* ‹ *can you offer praise* ‹ *How*

וְהַכֹּהֲנִים וְהַלְוִיִּם עַל מִשְׁמְרוֹתָם נִשְׁחָטִים,

« were slaughtered; ‹ their watches ‹ at ‹ and the Levites ‹ The *Kohanim*

---

(1) Cf. *Ezekiel* 25:8. (2) Some editions read שַׂרְפֵי מַעְלָה, *celestial* or *exalted Seraphim.*
(3) See commentary above.

וְעַל מַחְלְקוֹתָם שַׁעֲטַת אִסְטַרְדְּיוֹטִים,

« of the [Roman] commanders, ‹ despite the clamor ‹ their posts ‹ they were at

וְנָמוּ אַיֵּה מֶלֶךְ אָסוּר בָּרְהָטִים.[1]

« *to those who run to fulfill His commands?* ‹ *Who is bound* ‹ *the King* ‹ *Where is* ‹ who asked,

הַכֵּלִים וְהַמְשַׁמְּשִׁים בַּשְּׁבִי הוֹלְכִים,

« have gone; ‹ into captivity ‹ and those who minister [with them] ‹ The vessels

וְהַשָּׂרִים וְהַסְּגָנִים בַּכֶּבֶל מְשׁוּכִים,

« were dragged away, ‹ in shackles ‹ and the assistants ‹ the nobles

וּתְמוּר בַּדִּים שַׂק חָגְרוּ מַלְאָכִים.

« did the angels. ‹ gird themselves ‹ in sack-cloth, « of fine linen, ‹ and instead

דָּץ לָבִיא וּפָקַח עֵינָיו,

« his eyes, ‹ and opened up ‹ did the lion[-like Nebuchadnezzar] ‹ Rejoice

וְהִנֵּה מִיכָאֵל מְהַלֵּךְ לְפָנָיו,

« before him; ‹ going ‹ [the angel] Michael ‹ and there was

וְשָׂרִים* הוֹלְכִים כַּעֲבָדִים חָזוּ הֲמוֹנָיו.

« [Nebuchadnezzar's] hordes. ‹ witnessed « like slaves, ‹ going [into exile] ‹ and [the sight of Jewish] nobles*

גַּאֲוָה עָטָה וְכִבָּה הַמְּנוֹרָה,

« the Menorah, ‹ and extinguished ‹ wrapped himself ‹ [Nebuchadnezzar] in arrogance

וְנָטָה יָדוֹ אֶל אֵל[2] הַמּוֹרָא,

« so Awesome, ‹ God ‹ against ‹ his hand ‹ then he stretched out

(1) *Song of Songs* 7:6. (2) Cf. *Job* 15:25.

וְשָׂרִים — *And . . . [Jewish] nobles.* Alternatively, this alludes to the Midrash that tells how, when Nebuchadnezzar ordered crushing burdens placed on the captives' backs to break their noble stature, armies of angels descended to help the Jews bear their loads (*Midrash Tehillim* 137). Thus, the שָׂרִים are the *celestial princes.*

וַיַּחֲשִׁיךְ אוֹר עוֹטֶה אוֹרָה.[1]

« in light. ‹ [of God] Who is enveloped ‹ the light ‹ and darkened

בְּשַׁאֲגוֹ כַּאֲרִי בִּדְבִיר בֵּל,

« — [Nebuchadnezzar worshiper of] Bel [did] — « in the Holiest of the Holies ‹ like a lion ‹ When he roared

בָּרַח דּוֹדִי וּכְעַל מֵת מִתְאַבֵּל,

« He mourned; ‹ the dead ‹ and as for ‹ did my Beloved ‹ flee

פִּקְדוֹן הָרוּחוֹת בּוֹ בַּלַּיְלָה לֹא קִבֵּל.*

« He did not accept. ‹ on that night ‹ then ‹ souls* ‹ the deposited

אָמַר לַמַּשְׁחִיתִים חֲמָתִי הִתַּכְתִּי,[2]

« *I have poured out,* ‹ *My fury [over Jerusalem]* « to the destructive angels, ‹ [God] said

אֶת יְדִידוּת נַפְשִׁי בְּכַף אוֹיְבֶיהָ נָתַתִּי,

« *I have placed;* ‹ *of her enemies* ‹ *into the hand* ‹ *of My soul [Israel]* ‹ *the beloved*

עָזַבְתִּי אֶת בֵּיתִי וְאֶת נַחֲלָתִי נָטַשְׁתִּי.[3]

« *I have forsaken.* ‹ *and My inheritance [Israel]* ‹ *My Temple* ‹ *I have abandoned*

(1) Cf. *Psalms* 104:2. (2) Cf. *II Chronicles* 34:25. (3) Cf. *Jeremiah* 12:7.

פִּקְדוֹן הָרוּחוֹת בּוֹ בַּלַּיְלָה לֹא קִבֵּל — *The deposited souls then on that night He did not accept.* Every night, when a person retires, his soul ascends to the heavens where it is held in safekeeping until morning (see *Psalms* 31:6). Moreover, it is invigorated and returned to its body in a fresh and renewed state, as it is stated: *They are new every morning; great is Your faithfulness* (*Eichah* 3:23). The *paytan* teaches us that on the night of the Destruction, God accepted no souls, for no one was able to sleep. Or, perhaps, no one could fall asleep because God would not accept the souls.

KINNAH 25 / קינה כה

מִי יִתֵּן רֹאשִׁי מַיִם* וְעֵינִי מְקוֹר נוֹזְלַי,

« of my flowing [tears], ‹ a well-spring ‹ and my eye ‹ were water,* ‹ that my head ‹ can grant ‹ Who

וְאֶבְכֶּה כָּל יְמוֹתַי וְלֵילַי,[1]

« and my nights, ‹ my days ‹ all ‹ that I might weep

אֶת חַלְלֵי טַפַּי וְעוֹלָלַי, וִישִׁישֵׁי קְהָלַי,

« of my congregation. ‹ and of the old ones « and my infants, ‹ of my children ‹ the slaughtered ones ‹ for

וְאַתֶּם עֲנוּ אֲבוֹי אוֹי[2] וְאַלְלַי,

« and *Alas!* « *Oy!* « *Woe!* ‹ respond [to my cry], « And you,

וּבְכֵן בָּכֹה בֶּכֶה[3] רַב וְהֶרֶב,

« and profuse, ‹ that is intense ‹ a crying ‹ cry ‹ And thus

עַל בֵּית יִשְׂרָאֵל וְעַל עַם יהוה כִּי נָפְלוּ בֶּחָרֶב.[4]

« by the sword! ‹ they have fallen ‹ for « of HASHEM, ‹ the nation ‹ and over ‹ of Israel ‹ the House ‹ over

(1) Cf. *Jeremiah* 8:23. (2) Cf. *Proverbs* 23:29. (3) Cf. *Ezra* 10:1. (4) Cf. *II Samuel* 1:12.

מִי יִתֵּן רֹאשִׁי מַיִם — *Who can grant that my head were water.* Significantly, this is the first *kinnah* recited on the Ninth of Av that is clearly unrelated to the destruction of the two Temples. Indeed, this elegy mourns the calamity that befell the Jewish communities of the Rhineland — Worms, Speyer, and Mainz (Mayence) — in the year 1096, during the First Crusade, over one thousand years after the destruction of the Second Temple. The inclusion of this lament in the Tishah B'Av ritual serves to demonstrate that the source and cause of all Jewish tragedies in exile can and must be traced back to the Destruction of our Temple. The following incident illustrates this concept vividly.

When the Jewish people became aware of the awesome devastation that befell our nation at the hands of the murderous Nazis in World War II, many sought to establish a new day of national mourning to commemorate *Churban Europa.* The contemporary Torah leaders were consulted. Among the responses was that of the *Brisker Rav, R' Yitzchak Zev Soloveitchik,* who said that the reply to this question lies in the *kinnah* before us. Why didn't the great Rabbis and Sages of that generation — among them the greatest of the *Rishonim,* including *Rashi* — establish a *new* day of national mourning to commemorate that *new* tragedy? The author of this *kinnah* addresses this question and offers this insight:

Place, please, upon your hearts a eulogy that is bitter to compose, / because equal is their massacre in deserving mourning and rolling in dust / to the burning of the House of our God, the

וְדָמוֹעַ תִּדְמַע[1] עֵינִי וְאֵלְכָה לִי שְׂדֵה בוֹכִים,

Flow with copious tears ‹ shall my eye, « and I shall go ‹ myself ‹ to the field ‹ of weepers. «

וַאֲבַכֶּה עִמִּי מָרֵי לֵבָב הַנְּבוֹכִים,

I shall arouse to weep ‹ with me ‹ the bitter ‹ of heart, ‹ who are bewildered, «

עַל בְּתוּלוֹת הַיָּפוֹת וִילָדִים הָרַכִּים,

over ‹ the maidens ‹ who were beautiful ‹ and the children ‹ who were tender, «

בְּסִפְרֵיהֶם נִכְרָכִים וְלַטֶּבַח נִמְשָׁכִים,

in their scrolls ‹ were they wrapped ‹ and to the slaughter ‹ were they dragged. «

אָדְמוּ עֶצֶם[2] מִפְּנִינִים סַפִּירִים וְנוֹפְכִים,

Ruddier ‹ was their appearance ‹ than rubies, « [more beautiful] than sapphires ‹ and other gems, «

כְּמוֹ טִיט חוּצוֹת[3] נִדָּשִׁים וְנִשְׁלָכִים,

yet like ‹ the mud ‹ in the streets ‹ they were trampled ‹ and discarded. «

סוּרוּ טָמֵא קָרְאוּ לָמוֹ[4] מִלִּקְרַב.

Go away, ‹ unclean one! « they shouted ‹ at them, « lest they come close. «

עַל בֵּית יִשְׂרָאֵל וְעַל עַם יהוה כִּי נָפְלוּ בֶּחָרֶב.

Over ‹ the House ‹ of Israel ‹ and over ‹ the nation ‹ of HASHEM, « for ‹ they have fallen ‹ by the sword! «

(1) *Jeremiah* 13:17. (2) *Eichah* 4:7. (3) *II Samuel* 22:43. (4) *Eichah* 4:15.

Hall and the Sanctuary. / Since [one] may not add a set day [of mourning] over ruin and conflagration, / nor may one [mourn] earlier — but rather delay. / Instead of that, today [on Tishah B'Av], my mourning I will arouse / and I will eulogize and I will wail and I will weep with a soul that is bitter, / and my moans are heavy from morning until evening.

Thus, the essential purpose of this *kinnah* is to drive home this lesson: There are really no *new* tragedies befalling Israel. All of our woes stem from one tragic source: the Destruction of the Temple on Tishah B'Av. To establish a new day of mourning would detract from the significance of Tishah B'Av and obscure its lesson and message. (See *Rashi* to *II Chronicles* 35:25.)

This *kinnah* also answers other major questions. Why does the exile continue? Why does God visit fresh calamities upon His people? Where have we gone astray?

One of the main reasons for the continuation of our exile is because Jews are often quite content and comfortable in their adopted, alien homelands and have

וְתֵרַד עֵינַי דִּמְעָה[1] וְאֵילִילָה וְאָנוּדָה,

« and I will shake [my head], ‹ and I will lament ‹ tears ‹ shall my eyes ‹ Stream down

וְלִבְכִּי וְלַחֲגוֹר שַׂק אֶקְרָא לְהַסְפִּידָה,

‹ and to eulogize « I will call, « sackcloth, ‹ to put on ‹ and to cry,

מִפָּז יְקָרָה וְזָהָב חֲמוּדָה,

« more desirable, ‹ [than] gold « is precious, ‹ what more than fine gold

פְּנִימָה כְּבוּדָּה[2] כְּבוֹד כָּל כְּלֵי חֶמְדָּה,

« that are cherished, ‹ vessels ‹ of all ‹ the [most] honored « their glory, ‹ within [is concealed]

רְאִיתִיהָ קְרוּעָה שְׁכוּלָה וְגַלְמוּדָה,[3]

« and forlorn ‹ bereft of children, ‹ ripped, ‹ and now I see it

הַתּוֹרָה וְהַמִּקְרָא וְהַמִּשְׁנָה וְאַגָּדָה,

« and the Aggadah. ‹ the Mishnah, ‹ the Scripture, ‹ — [namely,] the Torah,

עֲנוּ וְקוֹנְנוּ זֹאת לְהַגִּידָה,

« as the pronouncement, ‹ and have this ‹ and lament ‹ Raise your voice

אֵי תוֹרָה תַּלְמִיד וְהַלּוֹמְדָהּ,

« *and the one who studied it?* ‹ *the student,* ‹ *the Torah,* ‹ *Where are*

(1) *Jeremiah* 13:17. (2) *Psalms* 45:14. (3) *Isaiah* 49:21.

all but lost their desire to return to the poverty and hardships of *Eretz Yisrael.* Slowly the Jew ceases to identify with his true home, the Holy Land, and begins to feel intense pride in his citizenship in his new country.

The destruction of the Jewish community of Worms in the German Rhineland was the work of the crusaders. How ironic! The crusaders were willing to leave everything behind — homes, families, occupations — in order to conquer the Holy Land they called Palestine, while the Jews themselves were filled with no such longing for their redemption and return to their homeland! In heaven, this irony did not go unnoticed, but aroused a terrible denunciation against the Jewish people, and especially against the Jews of Worms and her neighboring communities.

The classic work on Jewish history, *Seder HaDoros,* by *R' Yechiel Halperin,* records the following observation in his entry for the year 5380 (1620):

> The author of the commentary *Sefer Meiras Eynayim (SMA)* on the *Shulchan Aruch* explained why the Jewish community of Worms suffered far more persecution, pogroms, and evil decrees than other congregations.

הֲלֹא הַמָּקוֹם מֵאֵין יוֹשֵׁב חָרֵב.[1]

« is desolate! ‹ dwelling there ‹ with no one ‹ the place ‹ Indeed,

עַל בֵּית יִשְׂרָאֵל וְעַל עַם יהוה כִּי נָפְלוּ בֶּחָרֶב.

« by the sword! ‹ they have fallen ‹ for « of HASHEM, ‹ the nation ‹ and over ‹ of Israel ‹ the House ‹ Over

(1) Cf. *Jeremiah* 26:9.

That *kehillah* was founded by Jewish exiles who made their way to Germany following the Destruction of the First Temple. After seventy years of exile, many Jews returned from Babylon to *Eretz Yisrael* and Jerusalem, but none returned from Worms. The community in Jerusalem wrote to the *kehillah* in Worms and urged them to join their new settlement in Jerusalem ... but the complacent Jews of Worms dismissed this invitation out of hand. Instead, they responded, "You stay where you are in the great Jerusalem, and we will continue to stay where we are in our little Jerusalem!" This arrogant response was due to the prosperity and prestige the Jews of Worms enjoyed in the eyes of the local gentiles and their princes.

The success of Worms was its undoing! The prosperity of the Jew in exile is nothing more than a Divine test to see whether it will cause the Jew to forget his homeland and his heritage. Worms and the Rhineland failed and suffered bitterly. Before World War I a large portion of Germany's Jewish population failed because, as *Meshech Chochmah* (*Bechukosai*) observes, "They began to call Berlin, Jerusalem!"

◆§ The Calamity of the First Crusade

On November 27, 1095, in Clermont (southeastern France) Pope Urban II called upon faithful Christians to join in arms to liberate the city of Jerusalem and its holy sites from the hands of the Moslem infidels who occupied it. Those who answered the call affixed crosses to their garments, and the campaign became known as *le Croisade* (from *croix*, French for *cross*), or the Crusade. At first, the Crusade seemed to pose no threat to the Jews who resided in peace with their Christian neighbors, but soon enough it became clear that the crusaders did not wish to wait until they reached far-off Palestine to "avenge the blood of their savior." In truth, it was their envy of the prosperous Jewish communities that incited the vulgar rabble and the greedy nobility to punish "the murderers of their lord" wherever they passed. It was rumored that the French leader of the Crusades, Godfrey of Bouillon, had taken a solemn vow that he would avenge the blood of the crucifixion with the blood of the Jews and that he would not tolerate even one Jewish soul remaining alive.

Early in the year 1096, the French communities, threatened with extinction if they did not submit to baptism, called upon the great Jewish communities on the Rhine to ordain a day of public fasting and prayer. The Rhenish Jews complied and prayed fervently for the welfare of their French brethren. However, they themselves felt perfectly secure, enjoying as they did the special favor of the Emperor and the local nobility.

But all too soon, the frenzied mobs of crusaders poured into Germany, thirsty for Jewish blood, and hungry for Jewish riches.

In the early spring, in the weeks between Pesach and Shavuos, violence broke out and atrocities escalated. The three Jewish communities of Speyer, Worms, and Mainz felt the main brunt of the carnage, and their calamity is described in this *kinnah* (see commentary below).

וְעַפְעַפַּי יִזְּלוּ מַיִם[1] דֶּמַע לְהַגִּירָה,

« flowing, ‹ with tears « with water, ‹ will flow ‹ My eyelids

וַאֲקוֹנֵן מַר עֲלֵי הֲרוּגֵי אַשְׁפִּירָה,*

« of Speyer.* ‹ the martyrs ‹ over ‹ bitterly ‹ as I lament

בַּשֵּׁנִי בִּשְׁמוֹנָה בוֹ בְּיוֹם מַרְגּוֹעַ הָקְרָה,

« it happened. ‹ of tranquility [the Sabbath] ‹ on the day « in it, ‹ on the eighth day ‹ In the second [month, Iyar]

מֵרְגוֹעַ לִרְגוֹעַ נֶחְלְפוּ לְהַבְעֵירָה,

« into a conflagration. ‹ was it transformed ‹ to tumult ‹ From tranquility

נֶהֶרְגוּ בַּחוּרֵי חֶמֶד[2] וִישִׁישֵׁי הֲדָרָה,

« of splendor. ‹ with old men ‹ who were handsome, ‹ were young men ‹ Murdered

נֶאֶסְפוּ יַחַד נַפְשָׁם הִשְׁלִימוּ בְּמוֹרָא.

« in reverence, ‹ they surrendered ‹ and their souls « together, ‹ They assembled

עַל יִחוּד שֵׁם הַמְּיֻחָד יִחֲדוּ שֵׁם בִּגְבוּרָה,

« heroically. ‹ of [God's] Name ‹ they declared the unity ‹ that is the One and Only, ‹ of the Name ‹ the unification ‹ for

גִּבּוֹרֵי כֹחַ עוֹשֵׂי דְבָרוֹ[3] לִמְהֵרָה,

« swiftly. «His word ‹ who fulfill ‹ in strength ‹ Mighty

וְכֹהֲנַי וַעֲלָמַי נִגְוְעוּ כֻּלְּהֶם עֲשָׂרָה.

« were ten. ‹ — all of them « perished ‹ and my young men ‹ And my *Kohanim*

וּבְמַר יְגוֹנִי וְעָצְבִּי יֶלֶל אֲחַבֵּירָה,

« I shall compose, ‹ elegies « and my sadness, ‹ of my agony ‹ In the bitterness

(1) Cf. *Jeremiah* 9:17. (2) *Ezekiel* 23:12. (3) *Psalms* 103:20.

הֲרוּגֵי אַשְׁפִּירָה — *The martyrs of Speyer.* On the Sabbath, the eighth of Iyar [May 3, 1096], the crusaders surrounded the synagogue in Speyer. They were unable to breach its fortifications, and the assembled worshipers were able to repel their attack. Frustrated, the frenzied mob threw itself upon any Jew it could find outside the synagogue. Altogether they murdered ten men. In addition they attacked

קְהִלּוֹת הַקֹּדֶשׁ הֲרִיגָתָם הַיּוֹם בְּזָכְרָה,
« of the holy congregations « — their murder — « today ‹ in remembrance; «

קְהַל וַרְמַיְזָא* בְּחוּנָה וּבְחוּרָה,
the community ‹ of Worms,* « tested ‹ and chosen. «

גְּאוֹנֵי אֶרֶץ וּנְקִיֵּי טָהֳרָה,
Talmudic masters ‹ of the land, « unsullied in their ‹ purity. «

פַּעֲמַיִם קִדְּשׁוּ שֵׁם הַמְּיֻחָד בְּמוֹרָא.
Twice ‹ they sanctified ‹ the Name ‹ that is the One and Only ‹ in reverence. «

בְּעֶשְׂרִים וּשְׁלֹשָׁה בְּחֹדֶשׁ זִיו[1] לְטַהֲרָה,
On the twenty-third day ‹ of the month ‹ of Ziv [Iyar], ‹ in purity, «

וּבַחֹדֶשׁ הַשְּׁלִישִׁי בִּקְרִיאַת הַלֵּל לְשׁוֹרְרָה,
and in the third month [Sivan], ‹ while reciting ‹ the *Hallel* [on Rosh Chodesh] ‹ in song, «

הִשְׁלִימוּ נַפְשָׁם בְּאַהֲבָה קְשׁוּרָה,
they surrendered ‹ their soul, ‹ with love ‹ bound up. «

אָהִימָה עֲלֵיהֶם בִּבְכִי יְלֵל לְחַשְׁרָה,
I moan ‹ over them ‹ with a crying ‹ wail, ‹ saturated [with tears]; «

כְּלוּלֵי כֶּתֶר עַל רֹאשָׁם לַעֲטָרָה.
those perfected ‹ with a crown ‹ upon ‹ their heads ‹ as glorious adornment. «

(1) *I Kings* 6:1.

one woman who was given the choice of death or conversion. She gladly chose the former and died a martyr's death and proved to be an example for many other Jews who preferred to sanctify God's Name in death, rather than to abandon Him in life.

קְהַל וַרְמַיְזָא — *The community of Worms.* On the twenty-third of Iyar [Sunday, May 18, 1096], a large force of crusaders, led by Count Emicho, mercilessly attacked the Jews of Worms who had remained confidently in their homes. There they felt safe, relying on the promises of protection offered by their Christian neighbors. Many were slain by the crusaders and their small children were seized for forced baptism. Jewish homes were pillaged and destroyed. The greedy mob even stripped the clothing from their victims' corpses, leaving them naked. Eventually, some Jews who had found refuge in the bishop's palace managed to send clothes to cover their shame.

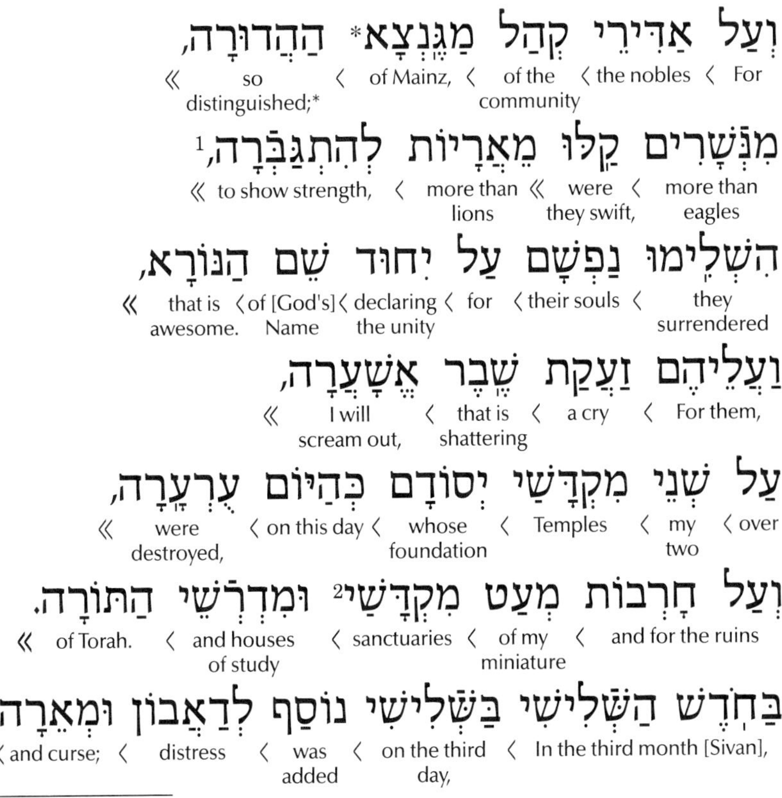

וְעַל אַדִּירֵי קְהַל מַגֶּנְצָא* הַהֲדוּרָה,

For ‹ the nobles ‹ of the community ‹ of Mainz, ‹ so distinguished;* «

מִנְּשָׁרִים קַלּוּ מֵאֲרָיוֹת לְהִתְגַּבְּרָה,[1]

more than eagles ‹ were they swift, « more than lions ‹ to show strength, «

הִשְׁלִימוּ נַפְשָׁם עַל יִחוּד שֵׁם הַנּוֹרָא,

they surrendered ‹ their souls ‹ for ‹ declaring the unity ‹ of [God's] Name ‹ that is awesome. «

וַעֲלֵיהֶם זַעֲקַת שֶׁבֶר אֶשָׁעֲרָה,

For them, ‹ a cry ‹ that is shattering ‹ I will scream out, «

עַל שְׁנֵי מִקְדָּשַׁי יְסוֹדָם כְּהַיּוֹם עֹרְעֲרָה,

over ‹ my two ‹ Temples ‹ whose foundation ‹ on this day ‹ were destroyed, «

וְעַל חָרְבוֹת מְעַט מִקְדָּשַׁי[2] וּמִדְרְשֵׁי הַתּוֹרָה.

and for the ruins ‹ of my miniature ‹ sanctuaries ‹ and houses of study ‹ of Torah. «

בַּחֹדֶשׁ הַשְּׁלִישִׁי בַּשְּׁלִישִׁי נוֹסַף לְדַאֲבוֹן וּמְאֵרָה,

In the third month [Sivan], ‹ on the third day, ‹ was added ‹ distress ‹ and curse; «

(1) Cf. *II Samuel* 1:23. (2) Cf. *Ezekiel* 11:16.

But for the Jews of Worms the suffering was not over. God had singled them out for double tragedy. On the following Sunday, Rosh Chodesh Sivan [May 25,] the crusaders and local rabble attacked the bishop's palace to kill the many Jews who had taken refuge there. After fierce combat the crusaders prevailed and slew every Jew they could find. When the attack came, the victims were in the midst of reciting *Hallel* (*Psalms* 113-118); with God's praises on their lips they sanctified His Name. A youth named Simchah Cohen planned to avenge his father and seven brothers who had been murdered by the crusaders. He pretended that he would accept baptism, and was taken to the church. At the moment he was to receive the sacrament, he whipped out a concealed knife and lashed out at those around him, stabbing the bishop's nephew in the act. Needless to say, the brave youth was torn to pieces by the infuriated bystanders.

All told, eight hundred Jews fell victim to the crusaders on those two Sundays in Worms.

קְהַל מַגֶּנְצָא — *The community of Mainz.* Terribly alarmed by the massacre at Speyer and Worms, the Jews of Mainz petitioned for the bishop's protection and paid him 400 pieces of silver for his promise. However, on the third of Sivan [May 27, 1096], when Count Emicho and his multitudes arrived at the gates of the city, the burghers were only too happy to welcome the crusaders and join in their attack on the Jews. The populace led the

הַחֹדֶשׁ אֲשֶׁר נֶהְפַּךְ לְיָגוֹן וְצָרָה,

« and distress, ‹ into sorrow ‹ was turned ‹ that ‹ in the month

בְּיוֹם מַתַּן דָּת שִׂבַּרְתִּי לְהִתְאַשְּׁרָה,

« to be strengthened [in the merit of the Torah], ‹ I had hoped ‹ of the Law [Shavuos] ‹ of the giving ‹ on the day

וּבְיוֹם נְתִינָתָהּ כְּמוֹ כֵן אָז חֲזָרָה,

« it was returned. ‹ then, ‹ way, ‹ in the same ‹ of its being given, ‹ but on the day

עָלְתָה לָהּ לַמָּרוֹם לִמְקוֹם מְדוֹרָהּ,

« of its dwelling, ‹ [back to] the place « to on high, ‹ itself ‹ It arose

עִם תִּיקָהּ וְנַרְתִּקָהּ וְהַדּוֹרְשָׁהּ וְחוֹקְרָהּ,

« and its examiner, ‹ its expounder « and its case, ‹ its cover ‹ together with

לוֹמְדֶיהָ וְשׁוֹנֶיהָ בְּאִישׁוֹן כְּמוֹ בְאוֹרָה,

« by the light [of day]. ‹ just as ‹ in the darkness [of night] ‹ and those who review it ‹ those who study it

שִׂימוּ נָא עַל לְבַבְכֶם[1] מִסְפֵּד מָר לְקַשְּׁרָה,

« to compose, ‹ that is bitter ‹ a eulogy ‹ your hearts ‹ upon ‹ please, ‹ Place,

כִּי שְׁקוּלָה הֲרִיגָתָם לְהִתְאַבֵּל וּלְהִתְעַפְּרָה,

‹ and rolling in dust ‹ in deserving mourning ‹ is their massacre ‹ equal ‹ because

כִּשְׂרֵפַת בֵּית אֱלֹהֵינוּ הָאוּלָם וְהַבִּירָה,

« and the Sanctuary. ‹ the Hall ‹ of our God, ‹ of the House ‹ to the burning

וְכִי אֵין לְהוֹסִיף מוֹעֵד שֶׁבֶר וְתַבְעֵרָה,

« and conflagration, ‹ over ruin ‹ a set day [of mourning] ‹ add ‹ [one] may not ‹ Since

(1) Cf. *Haggai* 2:18.

crusaders to all the Jewish hiding places. The Jews, led by R' Klonimos ben R' Meshullam, valiantly resisted, but were outnumbered and weakened by their penitential fasting. After a brief struggle, a general massacre ensued. The victims, more than one thousand pure Jewish souls, were ignominiously thrown into nine large ditches for mass burial.

Throughout the spring and early summer, the crusaders continued to maraud and sack once proud and venerable Jewish

וְאֵין לְהַקְדִּים זוּלָתִי לְאַחֲרָה,

‹ nor may one ‹ [mourn] earlier « — but rather ‹ delay. «

תַּחַת כֵּן הַיּוֹם לִוְיָתִי אֲעוֹרְרָה,

‹ Instead ‹ of ‹ today [on Tishah B'Av], that, ‹ my mourning ‹ I will arouse, «

וְאֶסְפְּדָה וְאֵילִילָה וְאֶבְכֶּה בְּנֶפֶשׁ מָרָה,

‹ and I will eulogize ‹ and I will wail ‹ and I will weep ‹ with a soul ‹ that is bitter, «

וְאַנְחָתִי כָּבְדָה מִבֹּקֶר וְעַד עָרֶב,

‹ and my moans ‹ are heavy ‹ from morning ‹ until ‹ evening, «

עַל בֵּית יִשְׂרָאֵל וְעַל עַם יהוה כִּי נָפְלוּ בֶּחָרֶב.

‹ over ‹ the House ‹ of Israel ‹ and over ‹ the nation « of HASHEM, ‹ for ‹ they have fallen « by the sword!

וְעַל אֵלֶּה אֲנִי בוֹכִיָּה[1] וְלִבִּי נוֹהֵם נְהִימוֹת,

‹ Over ‹ these things ‹ I ‹ weep ‹ and my heart ‹ moans « loud moans,

וְאֶקְרָא לַמְּקוֹנְנוֹת וְאֶל הַחֲכָמוֹת,[2]

‹ and I call ‹ for the women lamenters ‹ and for « the wise women.

אֱלִי וְאֶלְיָה כֻּלָּם הוֹמוֹת,

‹ *Eliy* ‹ or *Elya,* ‹ they all « cry out [words of lament].

הֲיֵשׁ מַכְאוֹב לְמַכְאוֹבִי[3] לְדַמּוֹת,

‹ Is there ‹ any pain ‹ that to my pain « compares?

מִחוּץ תְּשַׁכֶּל חֶרֶב וּמֵחֲדָרִים אֵמוֹת,[4]

‹ On the outside, ‹ cause bereavement « will the sword, ‹ while indoors « there will be terrors [of plague].

(1) *Eichah* 1:16. (2) Cf. *Jeremiah* 9:16. (3) Cf. *Eichah* 1:12. (4) Cf. *Deuteronomy* 32:25.

communities, many of which had stood for over a thousand years. They brought death and destruction to Cologne, Trier, Regensburg, Metz, and Prague. In all, it is estimated that over 5,000 Jews lost their lives during the First Crusade. But worse than that, the Crusades introduced the idea of organized, massive, widespread terror against the Jews on a vast, sweeping scale; an idea that would continue, and find its ultimate, horrible expression in the awesome Nazi Holocaust.

חֲלָלַי חַלְלֵי חֶרֶב מוּטָלִים עֲרֻמִּים וַעֲרֻמּוֹת,

My dead bodies, ‹ the corpses ‹ of the sword, « are strewn about, « naked men ‹ and naked women. «

נִבְלָתָם כְּסוּחָה[1] לְחַיַּת אֶרֶץ וְלַבְּהֵמוֹת,

Their bodies ‹ like carrion ‹ for the wild beasts ‹ of the land ‹ and for the animals «

יוֹנֵק עִם אִישׁ שֵׂיבָה[2] עֲלָמִים וַעֲלָמוֹת.

— a nursing infant ‹ with ‹ a man ‹ of old age, « young men ‹ and young maidens. «

מִתַעְתְּעִים בָּמוֹ מוֹנַי וּמַרְבִּים כְּלִמּוֹת,

Scoff ‹ at them ‹ do my tormentors ‹ and intensely ‹ humiliate them. «

אֵי אֱלֹהֵימוֹ אָמְרוּ צוּר חָסָיוּ בוֹ[3] עַד מוֹת,

Where is ‹ their God, « they taunt, « the Rock ‹ that they sought refuge ‹ in Him ‹ until ‹ death? «

יָבֹא וְיוֹשִׁיעַ וְיַחֲזִיר נְשָׁמוֹת,

Let Him come ‹ and save ‹ and restore ‹ souls! «

חֲסִין יָהּ מִי כָמוֹךָ[4] נוֹשֵׂא אֲלֻמּוֹת,[5]

O strong One, ‹ God, « who ‹ is like You, « Who patiently bears ‹ the bundles [of their iniquities]? «

תֶּחֱשֶׁה וְתִתְאַפַּק[6] וְלֹא תַחְגּוֹר חֵמוֹת,[7]

Will You remain silent ‹ and hold back, ‹ and not ‹ gird Yourself ‹ in burning wrath, «

בְּאָמוֹר אֵלַי מַלְעִיגַי אִם אֱלֹהִים הוּא יָרֶב,[8]

when say ‹ to me ‹ do those who mock me, « *If indeed ‹ a God ‹ He is, « let Him fight [on your behalf]!* «

עַל בֵּית יִשְׂרָאֵל וְעַל עַם יהוה כִּי נָפְלוּ בֶּחָרֶב.

over ‹ the House ‹ of Israel ‹ and over ‹ the nation ‹ of HASHEM, « for ‹ they have fallen ‹ by the sword! «

עֵינִי עֵינִי יוֹרְדָה מַּיִם[9] כִּי נֶהְפַּךְ לְאֵבֶל[10] מְשׁוֹרֵר,

My eye ‹ my eye ‹ sheds ‹ [tears like] water, « for ‹ turned ‹ to mourning ‹ has our singer, «

(1) *Isaiah* 5:25. (2) *Deuteronomy* 32:25. (3) Cf. 32:37. (4) Cf. *Psalms* 89:9. (5) Cf. 126:6. (6) Cf. *Isaiah* 42:14. (7) Cf. *Psalms* 76:11. (8) *Judges* 6:31. (9) *Eichah* 1:16. (10) 5:15.

וְעֻגָּבִי לְקוֹל בּוֹכִים[1] מִלְּהָפִיג וּלְקָרֵר,

« or calming. ‹ without respite « of weeping, ‹ to the sound ‹ and my flute

מִי יָנוּד לִי[2] וּמִי מַחֲזִיק לְהִתְעוֹרֵר,[3]

« to revive me? ‹ will hold [my hand] ‹ And who « for me? ‹ will shake [his head] ‹ Who

חֵמָה כִּי יָצְאָה וְסַעַר מִתְגּוֹרֵר,[4]

« gathered [to harm me]. ‹ while a storm [of anger] « went forth, ‹ against me ‹ [God's] wrath

אֲכָלַנִי הֱמָמַנִי[5] הַצַּר הַצּוֹרֵר,[6]

« the tormentor. ‹ did the enemy, ‹ and panic me ‹ Consume me

שִׁבַּר עַצְמוֹתַי[7] זוֹרֵר וּמְפָרֵר,

« and pulverized [them]. ‹ crushed « my bones, ‹ He shattered

סִלָּה כָּל אַבִּירַי[8] הַטַּבּוּר וְהַשָּׁרֵר,

« and umbilicus. ‹ [who were my center, the] navel « my warriors, ‹ all ‹ He trampled

רְטִיָּה וּמָזוֹר אֵין לְבָרֵר,

« [from which] to choose, ‹ there is none « or medicine, ‹ Bandage

מַכָּתִי אֲנוּשָׁה[9] בְּאֵין מַתְעִיל וּמְזוֹרֵר,

« or to apply medicinal powder. ‹ to bandage [it] ‹ with no one ‹ is acute, ‹ [because] my wound

עַל כֵּן אָמַרְתִּי שְׁעוּ מֶנִּי אֲמָרֵר,

‹ *I will make myself bitter* « *from me;* ‹ *Turn away* « I said, ‹ that reason ‹ For

בִּבְכִי[10] דִּמְעָתִי עַל לֶחֱיִי[11] לְצָרֵב,

« *to sear them,* ‹ *my cheeks* ‹ *will fall on* ‹ *my tears* « *with weeping;*

עַל בֵּית יִשְׂרָאֵל וְעַל עַם יהוה כִּי נָפְלוּ בֶּחָרֶב.

« *by the sword!* ‹ *they have fallen* ‹ *for* « *of* HASHEM, ‹ *the nation* ‹ *and over* ‹ *of Israel* ‹ *the House* ‹ *over*

(1) *Job* 30:31. (2) Cf. *Isaiah* 51:19. (3) Cf. 64:6. (4) *Jeremiah* 30:23. (5) Cf. 51:34. (6) *Numbers* 10:9. (7) *Eichah* 3:4. (8) 1:15. (9) *Jeremiah* 15:18. (10) *Isaiah* 22:4. (11) *Eichah* 1:2.

KINNAH 26 / קינה כו

אָז* בַּהֲלוֹךְ יִרְמְיָהוּ עַל* קִבְרֵי אָבוֹת,

‹ Then* ‹ when approach* ‹ did Jeremiah ‹ near ‹ the graves ‹ of the Patriarchs

וְנָם עֲצָמוֹת חֲבִיבוֹת, מָה אַתֶּם שׁוֹכְבוֹת,

« and said, ‹ *O bones* « *that are beloved,* ‹ *what* ‹ *are you doing* « *lying still?*

בְּנֵיכֶם גָּלוּ וּבָתֵּיהֶם חֲרֵבוֹת,

‹ *Your sons* ‹ *have gone into exile* ‹ *and their homes* « *are destroyed;*

וְאַיֵּה זְכוּת אָבוֹת בְּאֶרֶץ תַּלְאוּבוֹת.[1]*

‹ *where is* ‹ *the merit* ‹ *of their ancestors* ‹ *in a land* « *of drought?**

(1) *Hosea* 13:5.

אָז — *Then.* In this work, R' Elazar HaKalir retells the Midrashic account (*Midrash Eichah* intro. 24) of God's reaction to the Destruction. When He saw the ruins of the burnt Sanctuary, God cried to Jeremiah, "I feel like a father whose only son died on his wedding day! Go, summon Abraham, Isaac, Jacob, and Moses from their graves. They know how to weep (and perhaps they will arouse My mercy to return Israel to their land)." Jeremiah went to the Cave of Machpelah in Hebron to arouse the Patriarchs and to the banks of the Jordan River to awaken Moses. They all went to visit the ruins of the Temple. As they passed from gate to desolate gate, they wailed and cried and rent their garments in mourning. Yet, all their tears and pleas failed to arouse God's mercy, that He pledge to guarantee Israel's final redemption and return, for Israel had sinned terribly and God's fury was aroused.

God relented only after the Matriarchs led by Rachel joined in with their impassioned plea and God's response is recorded by the Prophet Jeremiah:

Thus says HASHEM, *"A voice is heard in Ramah, lamentation and bitter weeping, Rachel is weeping for her children, she refuses to be comforted over her children for they are not here." Thus says* HASHEM, *"Restrain your voice from weeping and hold back your eyes from tears, for your efforts will be rewarded," says* HASHEM, *"and they will return from the land of the enemy. And there is hope for your future," says* HASHEM, *"for your children shall be restored to their own borders!"* (*Jeremiah* 31:14-16).

אָז בַּהֲלוֹךְ יִרְמְיָהוּ עַל — *Then when approach did Jeremiah* [lit., *walked upon*]. Since Jeremiah was a *Kohen* (see *Jeremiah* 1:1), he was forbidden from contaminating himself to the dead. Therefore, he could not have entered the Cave of Machpelah (see *Rashi* to *Ezekiel* 37:2, where Ezekiel, also a *Kohen*, was led around a valley filled with bones to prophesy regarding those bones, but was not permitted to enter the valley). Thus, עַל, *upon*, has been translated according to its alternate meaning, *near* (see *Targum* and *Rashi* to *Numbers* 2:20) and the phrase הֲלוֹךְ עַל ... is rendered *did approach.*

בְּאֶרֶץ תַּלְאוּבוֹת — *In a land of drought*, an allusion to the Wilderness of Sinai where their ancestors accepted the Torah. As the prophet (*Jeremiah* 2:2) states: *So said* HASHEM, *"I shall remember for your sake the kindness of your younger days ... how you followed Me in the Wilderness in an unsown land."*

גָּעוּ כֻּלָּם בְּקִינִים עַל חֶסְרוֹן בָּנִים,

« of their children; ‹ the loss ‹ over ‹ in lamentations « — all of them — « They cried out

דּוֹבְבוּ בְּקוֹל תַּחֲנוּנִים פְּנֵי שׁוֹכֵן מְעוֹנִים,

« in the high heavens, ‹ Who dwells ‹ before [God] ‹ of supplication ‹ in a voice ‹ they spoke

וְאַיֵּה הַבְטָחַת וְזָכַרְתִּי לָהֶם בְּרִית רִאשׁוֹנִים.[1]

« of the original ancestors"? ‹ the covenant ‹ for them ‹ "And I will remember ‹ the assurance, ‹ Where is

הֵם הֵמִירוּ כְבוֹדוֹ בְּתֹהוּ,[2] וְלֹא פָחֲדוּ וְלֹא רָהוּ,[3]

« and they were not broken. ‹ and they were not afraid « for utter nothingness, ‹ My honor ‹ exchanged ‹ [God replied,] *They*

וָאַעְלִים עֵינַי מֵהֶם[4] וְלֹא שָׁבוּ וְלֹא נָהוּ,

« and they did not follow [after Me]; ‹ yet they did not repent « from them, ‹ My eyes ‹ Then I hid

וְאֵיךְ אֶתְאַפַּק עַל אֲמִירַת לֹא הוּא.[5]

« "He is not [the Lord]"? « the statement, ‹ over ‹ can I restrain [My anger] ‹ and how

זָעַק אַב הֲמוֹן[6] בַּעֲבוּרָם, וְחִנֵּן פְּנֵי אֵל רָם,

« the Most High, ‹ God, ‹ before ‹ and he pleaded « on their behalf, ‹ of the multitude ‹ did [Abraham] the father ‹ Then cry out

חִנָּם נֻסֵּיתִי עֶשֶׂר בְּחִינוֹת עֲבוּרָם,

« for their sake, ‹ tests ‹ with ten ‹ was I tried ‹ For nothing

וְהֵן חָזִיתִי שִׁבְרָם,

« their ruination! ‹ I must witness ‹ and now,

וְאַיֵּה הַבְטָחַת אַל תִּירָא אַבְרָם.[7]

« O Abram!"? ‹ fear, ‹ "Do not ‹ the assurance ‹ Where is

טָעוּ לְהוֹרוֹת[8] בַּעֲבוֹדוֹת זָרוֹת,

« of idols. ‹ worship ‹ by permitting ‹ [God responded,] *They erred*

---

(1) *Leviticus* 26:45. (2) Cf. *Jeremiah* 2:11. (3) Cf. *Isaiah* 44:8. (4) Cf. 1:15. (5) *Jeremiah* 5:12.
(6) Cf. *Genesis* 17:4. (7) 15:1. (8) Some editions read לְהַזְרוֹת, *to become estranged.*

יָעֲצוּ לַחְצוֹב בֹּארוֹת בֹּארוֹת נִשְׁבָּרוֹת,[1]

They devised plans ‹ to dig [for themselves] ‹ cisterns « — cisterns ‹ that are broken, «

וְאֵיךְ אֶתְאַפַּק עַל בִּטּוּל עֲשֶׂרֶת הַדִּבְּרוֹת.

and how can I restrain [My anger] ‹ over ‹ the violation ‹ of the Ten ‹ Commandments? «

כֹּה צָוַח יִצְחָק פְּנֵי שׁוֹכֵן שַׁחַק,

Similarly ‹ Isaac screamed ‹ before [God] ‹ Who dwells ‹ in heaven, «

לַשָּׁוְא בִּי טֶבַח הוּחַק, וְהֵן זַרְעִי נִשְׁחַק וְנִמְחַק,

Was it for nothing ‹ that of me ‹ being prepared for slaughter ‹ was inscribed [in the Torah]? « And now ‹ my seed ‹ is crushed ‹ and obliterated. «

וְאַיֵּה הַבְטָחַת וְאֶת בְּרִיתִי אָקִים אֶת יִצְחָק.[2]

Where is ‹ the assurance, « "And My covenant ‹ I shall fulfill ‹ with ‹ Isaac"? «

מָרוּ בְּיִרְמְיָה, וְטִמְּאוּ הַר הַמּוֹרִיָּה,

[God responded,] They rebelled ‹ against Jeremiah ‹ and they defiled ‹ Mount ‹ Moriah. «

נִלְאֵיתִי נְשׂוֹא[3] גְּעִיָּה עוֹלָה לִי מִנְּשִׁיָּה,

I am weary ‹ of bearing ‹ the cry ‹ that rises ‹ to Me ‹ from [the land of] oblivion; «

וְאֵיךְ אֶתְאַפַּק עַל הֲרִיגַת זְכַרְיָה.[4]

and how ‹ can I restrain [My anger] ‹ from avenging ‹ the murder ‹ of Zechariah? «

סָח יֶלֶד בְּתֶלֶף, דְּמָעוֹת כְּתַנִּין זוֹלֵף,

Then spoke [Jacob] ‹ who was born ‹ to learning, « with tears ‹ like a [slithering] serpent ‹ flowing [to the ground], «

עוֹלָלַי אֲשֶׁר טִפַּחְתִּי[5] בְּעֶלֶף,

My infants ‹ whom ‹ I took care of ‹ to exhaustion, «

וְאֵיךְ גָּזוּ מֶנִּי בְּחֵלֶף

how ‹ they have been cut off ‹ from me, ‹ by a butcher's knife! «

(1) Cf. *Jeremiah* 2:13. (2) *Genesis* 17:21. (3) *Isaiah* 1:14. (4) See *Kinnah* 34. (5) Cf. *Eichah* 2:22.

וְאֵיךְ הֻפְרַע מֶנִּי דָּמִים בְּדָמִים כַּמָּה אֶלֶף.

How ‹ *has there been exacted* ‹ *from me* ‹ *blood,* « *for [Zechariah's] blood,* « *so many* ‹ *thousands!* «

פָּץ רוֹעֶה נֶאֱמָן, כָּפוּשׁ בְּאֵפֶר וּמֶדְמָן,

Burst forth ‹ did the shepherd [Moses] ‹ who is faithful, « while sunk ‹ in ashes ‹ and covered in dung, «

צֹאן אֲשֶׁר בְּחֵיקִי הֶאֱמַן,[1] אֵיךְ גָּזוּ בְּלֹא זְמַן,

The lambs, ‹ *which* ‹ *at my bosom* ‹ *were nursed,* « *how* ‹ *were they sheared* ‹ *when it was not* ‹ *their time!* «

וְאַיֵּה הַבְטָחַת כִּי לֹא אַלְמָן.[2]

Where is ‹ *the assurance,* « *"For* ‹ *not* ‹ *a widower [shall Israel be]"?* «

קוֹל בְּכִי לֵאָה מְתוֹפֶפֶת עַל לְבָבֶיהָ,[3]

The sound ‹ of the weeping ‹ of Leah, « as she beats ‹ on ‹ her heart; «

רָחֵל אֲחוֹתָהּ מְבַכָּה עַל בָּנֶיהָ,[4]

Rachel, ‹ her sister, ‹ weeps ‹ for ‹ her children; «

וְזִלְפָּה מַכָּה פָּנֶיהָ, בִּלְהָה מְקוֹנֶנֶת בִּשְׁתֵּי יָדֶיהָ.

Zilpah ‹ slapping ‹ her own face [from grief]; « and Bilhah ‹ lamenting ‹ with her two ‹ hands [outstretched]. «

שׁוּבוּ תְמִימִים לִמְנוּחַתְכֶם,

[God responds,] Return, ‹ *O wholesome ones,* ‹ *to your place of rest,* «

מַלֵּא אֲמַלֵּא כָּל מִשְׁאֲלוֹתֵיכֶם,

I shall surely fulfill ‹ *all* ‹ *your requests.* «

שֻׁלַּחְתִּי בָּבֶלָה לְמַעַנְכֶם,[5]

I was sent ‹ *to Babylon,* ‹ *for your sake.* «

הִנְנִי מְשׁוֹבֵב גָּלוּת בְּנֵיכֶם.

Indeed, ‹ *I shall bring back* ‹ *from exile* ‹ *your children!* «

---

(1) Cf. *Numbers* 11:12. (2) *Jeremiah* 51:5. (3) Cf. *Nahum* 2:8.
(4) Cf. *Jeremiah* 31:14. (5) See *Minchas Shai* to *Isaiah* 43:14.

KINNAH 27 / קינה כז

אָז בִּמְלֹאת סֵפֶק יָפָה כְּתִרְצָה,*

Then, when filled was the measure [of sin] by [Israel] who is as beautiful as Tirtzah,*

הֵן אֶרְאֶלָּם[1] צָעֲקוּ חוּצָה,[2]

indeed, the *Erelim* cried out outside.

בֶּן חִלְקִיָּהוּ מֵאַרְמוֹן כְּיָצָא,

As [Jeremiah] the son of Hilkiyah departed, from the Temple

אִשָּׁה יְפַת תֹּאַר מְנֻוֶּלֶת מָצָא.

a woman of beautiful features who was filthy he met.

גּוֹזְרַנִי עָלַיִךְ בְּשֵׁם אֱלֹהִים וְאָדָם,

[He said:] I command you, in the Name of God and man,

אִם שֵׁד לַשֵּׁדִים אַתְּ אוֹ לִבְנֵי אָדָם,

[to reveal] whether a demon — of the realm of demons — you are or of the children of man.

(1) See commentary to *kinnah* 22. (2) *Isaiah* 33:7.

אָז בִּמְלֹאת סֵפֶק — *Then, when filled was the measure [of sin].* According to some versions, this *kinnah* by R' Elazar HaKalir appears *before* the preceding *kinnah*. The end of this *kinnah* relates how Jeremiah awakened the Patriarchs at the Cave of Machpelah and thus serves as an appropriate introduction to *Kinnah* 26 which narrates the pleas of the Patriarchs after they were aroused. According to our sequence, this *kinnah* comes later because its main theme is an event that occurred after the Destruction, as related in *Pesikta Rabbosi* (27): When Jeremiah returned to Jerusalem he met a woman sitting on a mountaintop, clothed in black, her hair disheveled. "Who will console me?" she cried out.

Jeremiah responded sternly, "If you are a real woman, speak to me, but if you are a spirit, depart!"

"I am your mother, Zion!" the woman responded.

Jeremiah said to her, "God, Himself, will console you! Mortal men built you and mortal men destroyed you. But in the future, God Himself will rebuild you as Scripture states: *The Builder of Jerusalem is Hashem*" (*Psalms* 147:2).

The *kinnah* follows an alphabetical format, and is a conversation between Jeremiah, Israel, God, and the Patriarchs.

יָפָה כְּתִרְצָה — *Beautiful as Tirtzah.* Israel is described with this phrase in *Song of Songs* (6:4). The translation follows *Ibn Ezra* there, who explains that Tirtzah refers to the province of that name mentioned elsewhere in Scripture (see, e.g., *I Kings* Chs. 14-16). *Rashi*, however, translates homiletically, and understands

דְּמוּת יָפְיֵךְ כִּבְשַׂר וָדָם,

« and blood, ‹ resembles flesh ‹ of your beauty ‹ The appearance

פַּחְדֵּךְ וְיִרְאָתֵךְ כְּמַלְאָכִים לְבַדָּם.

« uniquely! ‹ is like the angels ‹ and awe [that you induce] ‹ but the terror

הֵן לֹא שֵׁד אֲנִי וְלֹא גֹּלֶם פַּחַת,

« that is worthless. ‹ a lump [of clay] ‹ nor « am I, ‹ a demon ‹ not « Indeed, [she replied],

יְדוּעָה הָיִיתִי בְּשׁוּבָה וָנַחַת,[1]

« and rest. ‹ when there was tranquility ‹ was I ‹ Rather, renowned

הֵן לְאֶחָד אֲנִי וְלִשְׁלֹשָׁה וְשִׁשִּׁים וְאַחַת,

« and the one [Moses]; ‹ and the sixty [myriads] ‹ and to the three [Patriarchs], ‹ I belong, ‹ to the one [Abraham] ‹ Indeed,

וְלִשְׁנֵים עָשָׂר וּלְשִׁבְעִים וְאַחַת.

« one [Sanhedrin]! ‹ and the seventy- ‹ to the twelve [tribes]

זֶה הָאֶחָד אַבְרָהָם הָיָה,

« it was, ‹ Abraham « the one, ‹ This

וּבֵין הַשְּׁלֹשָׁה אָבוֹת שְׁלִישִׁיָּה,

« trio. ‹ the Patriarch « the three, ‹ and [I was] among

חֹק שְׁנֵים עָשָׂר הֵן הֵן שִׁבְטֵי יָהּ,

« of God, ‹ the tribes ‹ they are ‹ indeed ‹ of the twelve ‹ The rule

וְשִׁשִּׁים רִבּוֹא וְשִׁבְעִים וְאֶחָד סַנְהֶדְרֵי יָהּ.

« of God. ‹ are the Sanhedrin ‹ one ‹ And the seventy- « myriads. ‹ [numbering] sixty

טַעֲמִי הַקְשִׁיבִי וַעֲשִׂי תְּשׁוּבָה,

« repentence, ‹ and undergo ‹ listen ‹ [Jeremiah responded,] To my advice

(1) *Isaiah* 30:15.

כְּתִרְצָה as a contraction of כְּשֶׁאַתְּ רְצוּיָה, *when you find favor*; in other words, Israel is beautiful when it follows God's will and thereby finds favor in His eyes.

יַעַן הֱיוֹתֵךְ כָּל כַּךְ חֲשׁוּבָה,

« distinguished. ‹ to such an extent ‹ that you are ‹ for the reason

יָפֶה לָךְ בְּעֶלֶץ וְלִשְׂמוֹחַ בְּטוֹבָה,

« in goodness, ‹ and to rejoice ‹ to exult ‹ for you ‹ It is proper

וְלֹא לְקָרֵא עוֹד בַּת הַשּׁוֹבֵבָה.

« who is rebellious! ‹ the daughter ‹ any more ‹ to be called ‹ not

כִּי אֵיךְ אֶשְׂמַח וְקוֹלִי מָה אָרִים,

« can I raise? ‹ how ‹ and my voice [in song] « can I rejoice? ‹ how ‹ But

הֵן עוֹלָלַי נִתְּנוּ בְּיַד צָרִים,

« of my enemies! ‹ into the hands ‹ were delivered ‹ my infants ‹ Indeed,

לָקוּ נְבִיאַי וְדָמָם מֻגָּרִים,

« flowed. ‹ and their blood ‹ were My prophets ‹ Beaten

גָּלוּ מְלָכַי וְשָׂרַי וְכֹהֲנַי וַהֲרֵי הֵם בְּקוֹלָרִים.

« in prisoner's collars. ‹ they are now ‹ and indeed, ‹ and my priests ‹ my ministers ‹ were my kings, ‹ Exiled

מְלוֹן מִקְדָּשִׁי בַּעֲוֹנִי נָדָד,

« was forced to wander, ‹ because of my iniquity « that is holy, ‹ My Dwelling Place

דּוֹדִי מֵאָז נָדַד וַיִּדַּד,

« and fled. ‹ has wandered ‹ since then ‹ my Beloved

נֹעַם אָהֳלִי בְּעַל כָּרְחִי שֻׁדַּד,

« was plundered. ‹ my will ‹ against « of my Tent, ‹ The pleasantness

רַבָּתִי עָם אֵיכָה יָשְׁבָה בָדָד.[1]

« in solitude! ‹ it now sits ‹ how is it that « people, ‹ [The city] that had so many

---

(1) Cf. *Eichah* 1:1.

שָׂחָה הָאִשָּׁה לַנָּבִיא יִרְמְיָה,

« Jeremiah, ‹ to the prophet ‹ The woman spoke [further]

סַח לֵאלֹהֶיךָ בְּעַד מַכַּת סוֹעֲרָה עֲנִיָּה,

« *suffering [people of Israel],* ‹ *the storm-tossed,* ‹ *the blows upon* ‹ *concerning* ‹ *to your God* ‹ *Pray*

עַד יַעֲנֶה אֵל וְיֹאמַר דַּיָּהּ,

« *"Enough!"* « *and says,* ‹ *God responds* ‹ *until*

וְיַצִּילֵנִי מֵחֶרֶב וְשִׁבְיָה.

« *and captivity.* ‹ *from sword* ‹ *and saves me*

פִּלֵּל תְּחִנָּה לִפְנֵי קוֹנוֹ,

« his Creator, ‹ before ‹ in supplication ‹ [Jeremiah] prayed

מָלֵא רַחֲמִים רַחֵם כְּאָב עַל בְּנוֹ,

« *his son!* ‹ *on* ‹ *as a father* ‹ *have mercy [on us]* « *of mercy,* ‹ *[You Who are] full*

צָעַק מַה לְּאָב שֶׁהֶגְלָה בְּנוֹ,

« *His son?* ‹ *when He has exiled* ‹ *a Father feel* ‹ *How does* « [God] cried,

וְגַם אוֹי לַבֵּן שֶׁעַל שֻׁלְחַן אָב אֵינוֹ.

« *is not present!* ‹ *of his Father* ‹ *the table* ‹ *that at* ‹ *unto the son,* ‹ *woe* ‹ *And also*

קוּם לָךְ יִרְמְיָה לָמָּה תֶחֱשֶׁה,

« *should you be silent?* ‹ *Why* « *Jeremiah!* ‹ *yourself,* ‹ *Rouse*

לֵךְ קְרָא לְאָבוֹת וְאַהֲרֹן וּמֹשֶׁה,

« *and Moses!* ‹ *and Aaron* ‹ *the Patriarchs,* ‹ *call* ‹ *Go*

רוֹעִים יָבֹאוּ קִינָה לְהִנָּשֵׂא,

« *arouse,* ‹ *and lamentations* ‹ *come* ‹ *Let these shepherds*

כִּי זְאֵבֵי עֶרֶב טָרְפוּ אֶת הַשֶּׂה.

« *the lamb.* ‹ *have torn apart* ‹ *of the night* ‹ *the wolves* ‹ *because*

שׁוֹאֵג הָיָה יִרְמְיָהוּ הַנָּבִיא,

« the prophet; ‹ Jeremiah ‹ did ‹ Roar

עַל מַכְפֵּלָה נוֹהֵם כְּלָבִיא,
« like a lion, ‹ he roared ‹ the [Cave of] Machpelah ‹ at

תְּנוּ קוֹל בִּבְכִי אֲבוֹת הַצְּבִי,
« *of the desired [nation]!* ‹ *O Patriarchs* « *in weeping,* ‹ *[your] voice* ‹ *Give forth*

תָּעוּ בְנֵיכֶם וַהֲרֵי הֵם בַּשֶּׁבִי.
« *in captivity!* ‹ *they are* ‹ *and indeed,* « *have your children,* ‹ *Strayed*

וְאִם כְּאָדָם עָבְרוּ בְרִית,
« *the Covenant,* ‹ *they violated* ‹ *like mortals* ‹ [The Patriarchs replied,] *And if,*

אַיֵּה זְכוּת כְּרוּתֵי בְרִית.
« *the covenant?* ‹ *[of us,] with whom was established* ‹ *the merit* ‹ *where is*

מָה אֶעֱשֶׂה לָכֶם בָּנַי,
« *My children?* ‹ *for you,* ‹ *can I do* ‹ [God answered,] *What*

גְּזֵרָה הִיא מִלְּפָנַי.
« *from before Me!* ‹ *it is* ‹ *A decree*

שָׁמֵם מִקְדָּשׁ מִבְּלִי בָּאֵי מוֹעֵד,[1]
« *at the appointed festivals,* ‹ *of those who come* ‹ *for lack* ‹ *is the Temple* ‹ *Desolate*

עַל כִּי יְדִידִים נִתְּנוּ לְהִמָּעֵד,
to falter! ‹ *were wont* ‹ *[My] beloved ones* ‹ *that* ‹ *for the reason*

תְּשִׁיבֵם כְּמֵאָז* סוֹמֵךְ וְסוֹעֵד,
« *and Sustainer,* ‹ *O Supporter* « *as it was then,** ‹ *Return them*

תְּרַחֵם צִיּוֹן כִּי בָא מוֹעֵד.[2]
« — *the appointed time [of redemption]!* « *it has come* ‹ *for* « *have mercy on Zion,*

(1) *Eichah* 1:4. (2) Cf. *Psalms* 102:14.

תְּשִׁיבֵם כְּמֵאָז — *Return them as it was then.* It is unclear whether this last verse is spoken by Jeremiah, by the Patriarchs, or by the *paytan.*

KINNAH 28 / קינה כח

אֵיךְ תְּנַחֲמוּנִי* הֶבֶל,[1] וְכִנּוֹרִי נֶהְפַּךְ לְאֵבֶל,[2]

« to mourning? ‹ has turned ‹ when my harp « in vain, ‹ can you console me* ‹ How

בְּנַחֲלַת חֶבֶל,[3] כָּבֵד עָלַי עוֹל סֵבֶל, וְאֵיךְ אֶנָּחֵם.

« can I be consoled? ‹ So how « of suffering! ‹ is the yoke ‹ upon me ‹ heavy « measured portion [Israel], ‹ In the inherited

בְּזֶה יוֹם בְּכָל שָׁנָה, עִדַּן עָלַי שִׁנָּה,

« have changed [to mourning], ‹ for me ‹ the times « year, ‹ every ‹ day [9th of Av], ‹ On this

וְהִנְנִי עֲגוּמָה וַעֲגוּנָה, יוֹתֵר מֵאֶלֶף שָׁנָה,*

« years.* ‹ than a thousand ‹ for more ‹ and deserted ‹ anguished ‹ and indeed, I am

וְאֵיךְ אֶנָּחֵם.

« can I be consoled? ‹ So how

גָּבַר חָרוֹן, וְנִגְנַז אָרוֹן,[4]

« was the Holy Ark; ‹ and secreted ‹ did [God's] flaring anger ‹ Prevail

בְּמִשְׁנֶה שִׁבָּרוֹן,[5] בְּמִסָּרְבֵי מָרוֹן,[6] וְאֵיךְ אֶנָּחֵם.

« can I be consoled? ‹ So how « of Maron. ‹ because of the rebels ‹ disaster ‹ with double

(1) *Job* 21:34. (2) Cf. 30:31. (3) Cf. *Deuteronomy* 32:9. (4) See commentary to *Kinnah* 24. (5) Cf. *Jeremiah* 17:18. (6) See commentary to *Kinnah* 10.

אֵיךְ תְּנַחֲמוּנִי — *How can you console me?* This alphabetical composition by R' Elazar HaKalir highlights the futility of our attempts to find consolation for the tragedy of Israel's destruction. The calamity was so enormous that it is absolutely unforgettable. Its harsh effects are still felt today, even though many centuries have elapsed. Indeed, the opening words of this *kinnah* declare that any attempt at comfort is futile. The burden of witnessing the desolation of *Eretz Yisrael* and the suffering of the Jewish people is beyond endurance. The *kinnah* ends with a proclamation that even though there can be no consolation as long as the nation remains in exile, there is always hope for redemption and ultimate consolation.

It is not clear from the context whether the speaker of this *kinnah* is God, the nation, or the individual lamenter.

יוֹתֵר מֵאֶלֶף שָׁנָה — *For more than a thousand years.* This *kinnah* is usually ascribed to R' Elazar HaKalir, who lived, according to various opinions, somewhere between the second and seventh centuries C.E. In any case, he did not live a thousand years after the Destruction. Assumedly, this line originally read something like כַּמָּה מֵאוֹת שָׁנָה, *many hundreds of years,*

דִּירָתִי חֳרֵבָה, וְעֶדְרִי נִשְׁבָּה,

My dwelling ‹ is in ruins ‹ and my flock ‹ is captured, ‹

וְרַבַּת אָהֳלִיבָה,[1] בָּדָד יָשְׁבָה,[2] וְאֵיךְ אֶנָּחֵם.

and the [City that had] so many, ‹ Oholivah [Jerusalem], ‹ now in solitude ‹ sits! « So how ‹ can I be consoled? «

הוּעַל אַרְיֵה* מִסֻּבְּכוֹ,[3] עַל אֲרִיאֵל וְהִסְבִּיכוֹ,

Arise ‹ did the lion [Nebuchadnezzar]* ‹ from his lair, ‹ to go against ‹ God's lion-like Temple ‹ and entangled it; «

וְהֶגְלָה מִסֻּכּוֹ, מִנְחָתוֹ וְנִסְכּוֹ, וְאֵיךְ אֶנָּחֵם.

and banished ‹ from His Tabernacle, ‹ His meal-offering ‹ and His libation. « So how ‹ can I be consoled? «

וְהָרַג הֲמוֹנִים, מְשׁוּחֵי שְׁמָנִים,

And he killed ‹ multitudes ‹ of those anointed ‹ with oils [*Kohanim*]. «

בְּאִוּוּי נִמְנִים, פִּרְחֵי כֹהֲנִים, אֲלָפִים שְׁמוֹנִים,

In the desirable [Temple] ‹ they were counted « — the young ‹ *Kohanim* — « in thousands, ‹ eighty. «

וְאֵיךְ אֶנָּחֵם.

So how ‹ can I be consoled? «

(1) See *Kinnah* 4. (2) Cf. *Eichah* 1:1. (3) Cf. *Jeremiah* 4:7.

but was changed by a later copyist who updated the *kinnah*. Alternatively, if he was (as *Tosafos* and the *Rosh* record) a second-century Tanna, then he may have had in mind the original Tishah B'Av of the Spies' slanderous report about *Eretz Yisrael*. That event would have preceded him by some fourteen centuries, a period of "more than a thousand years."

אַרְיֵה — *The lion [Nebuchadnezzar].* Throughout the Talmud and Midrash, and based on the Book of *Daniel* (Ch. 8), Israel's long series of exiles and persecutions are always treated as four main periods of subjugation to foreign oppressors, either in *Eretz Yisrael* or in the Diaspora. These periods are known collectively as אַרְבַּע מַלְכֻיּוֹת, *the Four Kingdoms* (*Daniel* 8:22), and each is called by the name of the empire dominant in the world at that particular time. The first, called גָּלוּת בָּבֶל, *the Babylonian Exile*, began when Nebuchadnezzar king of Babylon conquered the Land of Israel and destroyed the First Temple. The second, called גָּלוּת מָדַי וּפָרַס, *the Median-Persian Exile* (ibid. 8:20), began when that empire captured the Babylonians and became the leading world power. Although the Medes permitted the Jewish return to *Eretz Yisrael* and the building of the Second Temple, the early years of that *Beis HaMikdash* were still considered a part of the exile, because Israel was not sovereign in its Land. During the entire third period, גָּלוּת יָוָן, *the*

זִנְּבָם כְּחִוִּי[1] וְהִדְבִּיא, בְּעֶזְרַת הַמַּלְבִּיא,[2]

« of the lionlike [Temple] ‹ in the Courtyard ‹ and cause [their blood] to flow ‹ like a snake ‹ He attacked them from behind

אַרְיוֹךְ* כְּמוֹ לָבִיא, עַל דַּם כֹּהֵן וְנָבִיא,[3]

« and prophet [Zechariah]. ‹ of the *Kohen* ‹ the blood ‹ because of « and the lion [Nebuchadnezzar] — ‹ — Arioch [Nebuzaradan]*

וְאֵיךְ אֶנָּחֵם.

« can I be consoled? ‹ So how

חָרַשׁ לְמַשּׁוּאוֹת, עִיר מְלֵאָה תְשׁוּאוֹת,[4]

«with tumultuous multitudes, ‹ [once] filled ‹ the city « to destruction; ‹ [Turnus Rufus] plowed [Jerusalem]

וּבָתֵּי סוֹפְרִים וּמִשְׁנִיּוֹת, יוֹתֵר מֵאַרְבַּע מֵאוֹת,

« hundred. ‹ four ‹ more than ‹ and Mishnah ‹ studying Scripture ‹ and schools

וְאֵיךְ אֶנָּחֵם.

« can I be consoled? ‹ So how

טָסָה מָדַי, לְאַבֵּד חֲמוּדַי,

« my cherished ones; ‹ to exterminate ‹ did Media ‹ Fly swiftly

וּמָשְׁלָה בְּמַחֲמַדַּי, בְּקָרְעִי מַדַּי, וְאֵיךְ אֶנָּחֵם.

« can I be consoled? ‹ So how « my robes [in grief]. ‹ when I tore ‹ over my precious [Temple], ‹ and ruled

(1) Some editions read בְּאִוּוּי, *in the desirable [Temple].* (2) Some editions read בַּעֲזָרַת, but the meaning is unchanged. (3) See *Kinnah* 34. (4) Cf. *Isaiah* 22:2.

Greek Exile (ibid. 8:21), paradoxically, Israel lived on its Land and the Temple stood. Nevertheless, it was a very turbulent era marked with civil strife, foreign domination, vicious antireligious campaigns, and the rejection of Torah values by a large number of Jews who adopted Greek culture with all its abominations. The downfall of the Greek Empire and the rise of Rome marked the beginning of גָּלוּת אֱדוֹם, *the Edomite* or *Roman Exile.* It is this millennia-long exile that we are still in today. The *kinnah* now speaks of these Four Kingdoms and their respective atrocities.

אַרְיוֹךְ — *Arioch [Nebuzaradan].* In *II Kings* (Ch. 25) and in *Jeremiah* (Chs. 39, 52, et al.), Nebuchadnezzar's general is called נְבוּזַרְאֲדָן רַב טַבָּחִים, *Nebuzaradan the chief executioner.* In *Daniel* (2:14), he is called אַרְיוֹךְ רַב טַבָּחַיָּא, *Arioch the chief executioner.* According to the Midrash,

יָעֲצָה לְחַנֵּק, בְּנֵי גוּר מְזַנֵּק,[1]
« that was prancing [Dan], ‹ of the lion cub ‹ the descendants ‹ to strangle ‹ [Haman] took counsel

בְּפֶה אֶחָד לְשַׁנֵּק, זָקֵן וְיָשִׁישׁ עוֹלֵל וְיוֹנֵק,
« and the nursing babies. ‹ the infants « and the aged, ‹ the old ‹ to tear apart ‹ with one bite

וְאֵיךְ אֶנָּחֵם.
« can I be consoled? ‹ So how

כָּבְדָה שְׁלִישִׁית, עַל קֹדֶשׁ רֵאשִׁית,[2]
« considered His first-fruit ‹ the holy [nation] ‹ against « was the third kingdom [Greece], ‹ Even more oppressive

בְּשֶׁצֶף חֲרִישִׁית, בָּתָה לְהָשִׁית, וְאֵיךְ אֶנָּחֵם.
« to make it. ‹ into a wasteland ‹ that was deafening, ‹ with a stream [of wrath] « can I be consoled? ‹ So how

לָחֲצָה לְחַלֵּק, בְּנֵי חָלָק וְחוֹלֵק,
« from [God Who] took [Jacob] as His portion; ‹ of the smooth-skinned [Jacob] ‹ the sons ‹ to separate ‹ She [Greece] pressured

שֶׁאֵין לָכֶם חֵלֶק, בְּשֵׁם אֵשׁ דּוֹלֵק,[3] וְאֵיךְ אֶנָּחֵם.
« *that is Consuming!* ‹ *of [God,] the Fire* ‹ *in the Name* ‹ *any portion* ‹ *for you* ‹ *[saying,] There is not* « can I be consoled? ‹ So how

מָרְדָה אֱדוֹם, עֲדוּשַׁת אָדוֹם,
« that were red, ‹ [named for] the lentils « did Edom, ‹ Rebel [against God]

וְאָצָה בְזָדוֹן, לְאַבֵּד כֵּס וַהֲדוֹם,[4] וְאֵיךְ אֶנָּחֵם.
« and His Footstool. ‹ [God's] Throne ‹ to obliterate ‹ defiantly ‹ and they hurried « can I be consoled? ‹ So how

נוֹעֲדוּ עִם אַדְמוֹן, מוֹאָב וְעַמּוֹן,
« and Ammon, ‹ were Moab ‹ Edom ‹ with ‹ Allied

(1) Cf. *Deuteronomy* 33:22. (2) Cf. *Jeremiah* 2:3. (3) Some editions read אֵל דּוֹלֵק, *the fiery God.* (4) Cf. *Isaiah* 66:1; see also *Ezekiel* 43:7.

his name was Nebuzaradan, but he was called Arioch (a diminutive of *Ari, lion*) because he roared at the Jewish captives, giving them no rest until they reached the banks of the Euphrates (*Midrash Eichah* 5:5).

לְהַשְׁבִּית אָמוֹן,* וּלְהַחֲרִיב אַרְמוֹן, וְאֵיךְ אֲנָּחֵם.

to eradicate ‹ the nurturing [Torah],* ‹ and to destroy ‹ the palatial [Temple]. « So how ‹ can I be consoled? «

סִלָּה כָל אַבִּירַי,[1] וְעֶדְרֵי חֲבֵרַי,[2]

He trampled ‹ all ‹ my warriors ‹ and the flocks ‹ of my friends [Israel]; «

וְהֻבְלָגוּ גִּבּוֹרַי, לְעֵין כָּל עוֹבְרַי, וְאֵיךְ אֲנָּחֵם.

overpowered ‹ were my warriors ‹ before the eyes ‹ of all ‹ who passed by me. « So how ‹ can I be consoled? «

עָיְפָה נַפְשִׁי לְהוֹרְגִים,[3] לְמִסְפַּר הַהֲרוּגִים,

Exhausted ‹ is my spirit ‹ by the killers, « by the number ‹ of those murdered, «

כְּאַיָּל עוֹרְגִים,[4] וְעָלֶיךָ נֶהֱרָגִים,[5] וְאֵיךְ אֲנָּחֵם.

who like a deer ‹ call longingly, ‹ and for Your sake ‹ are killed. « So how ‹ can I be consoled? «

פִּלְּצוּ בְּיוֹם קְרָב, בְּמִזְרָח וּבְמַעֲרָב,

They were horrified ‹ on the day ‹ of battle, « in the East ‹ and in the West, «

עַל דָּמָם מְעֹרָב, קָהָל וְעַם רָב,*[6] וְאֵיךְ אֲנָּחֵם.

over ‹ their blood ‹ being mixed ‹ with [the blood] of the congregation ‹ and the nation ‹ that is great.* « So how ‹ can I be consoled? «

צָרוֹת עַל צָרוֹת, זוֹ מִזּוֹ מְצִירוֹת,

Calamities ‹ upon ‹ calamities, ‹ each one, ‹ more than the previous one, ‹ causes tragedy, «

---

(1) *Eichah* 1:15. (2) *Song of Songs* 1:7. (3) *Jeremiah* 4:31.
(4) Cf. *Psalms* 42:2. (5) Cf. 44:23. (6) *Ezekiel* 26:7.

לְהַשְׁבִּית אָמוֹן — *To eradicate the nurturing [Torah].* The Talmud relates that when the enemies entered the Temple, Ammonites and Moabites entered among them. While the others ran to plunder the silver and gold, the Ammonites and Moabites ran to plunder the Torah itself to erase the verse (*Deuteronomy* 23:4), לֹא יָבֹא עַמּוֹנִי וּמוֹאָבִי בִּקְהַל ה׳, *An Ammonite or Moabite shall not enter the Assembly of* HASHEM (*Yevamos* 13b). The intention of Ammon and Moab in performing this brazen act was not merely to expunge the verse. There were many other Torah Scrolls in the land which still contained that verse; tearing it from the Temple Scroll would not have changed their forbidden status. Rather, their sole aim was to defy God and His Torah with impunity (*Lechem Dimah*).

קָהָל וְעַם רָב — *Congregation and the nation that is great.* Ironically, this phrase, used by the *paytan* to describe the masses

גְּדוֹלוֹת וּבְצוּרוֹת[1] אֲרֻכּוֹת וְלֹא קְצָרוֹת,
great ‹ and unstoppable, « long lasting ‹ and not ‹ brief. «

וְאֵיךְ אֶנָּחֵם.
So how ‹ can I be consoled? «

קָשְׁרוּ צִנָּתָם, וְחָגְרוּ חֲנִיתָם וְאָסְפוּ מַחֲנוֹתָם,
They tied on ‹ their shields ‹ and belted ‹ their spears; « they gathered ‹ their camps, «

וְהֶאֱרִיכוּ לְמַעֲנִיתָם,[2]* וְאֵיךְ אֶנָּחֵם.
they lengthened ‹ their furrow.* « So how ‹ can I be consoled? «

רַבּוֹת אַנְחוֹתַי וַעֲצוּמוֹת קִינוֹתַי,
Many ‹ are my sighs ‹ and powerful ‹ are my laments; «

רַבּוּ נַהֲמוֹתַי, וְאַתָּה יהוה עַד מָתַי,[3] וְאֵיךְ אֶנָּחֵם.
my moanings are many, « so [I ask] You, ‹ *HASHEM,* « *until* ‹ *when?* « So how ‹ can I be consoled? «

שָׁמַעְתָּ חֶרְפָּתָם, חֵרְפוּנִי בִּשְׂפָתָם,
You have heard ‹ their verbal abuse ‹ [as] they slandered me ‹ with their lips; «

שִׁבְתָּם וְקִימָתָם, אֲנִי מַנְגִּינָתָם,[4] וְאֵיךְ אֶנָּחֵם.
whether during their sitting ‹ or while they stand, « I am ‹ the theme of their [derisive] songs. « So how ‹ can I be consoled? «

תִּקְוַתְכֶם אֵיפוֹא, מַה לָּכֶם פֹּה,[5]
Your hope, « *where is it?* « *What* ‹ *are you doing* ‹ *here?* «

חָרָה אַפּוֹ, וְאֵין עוֹד לְרַפֹּא, וְאֵיךְ אֶנָּחֵם.
Flared ‹ *has His anger [against you]* ‹ *and there is nothing* ‹ *any longer* ‹ *to cure [you]!* « So how ‹ can I be consoled? «

---

(1) Cf. *Jeremiah* 33:3. (2) Cf. *Psalms* 129:3. (3) 6:4. (4) Cf. *Eichah* 3:61-63. (5) *Cf. I Kings* 19:9.

---

murdered by Nebuchadnezzar's hordes, is used by the prophet to describe those very hordes (see *Ezekiel* 26:7).

וְהֶאֱרִיכוּ לְמַעֲנִיתָם — *They lengthened their furrow.* The plowman never pauses while he is in the middle of a furrow, but waits until he reaches the end of the line. Thus, the longer the furrow, the longer the oxen must toil, without any respite. This alludes to Israel in exile, who suffered over a lengthy period, without relief (*Radak* to *Psalms* 129:3).

תְּשׁוּבוֹתֵיכֶם נִשְׁאֲרָה מָֽעַל,

« *lies!* ‹ *remain* ‹ *Your answers [of the future redemption]*

הוֹנוּנִי עוֹבְדֵי הַבָּֽעַל,

« of the Baal. ‹ do the worshipers ‹ continue to taunt me

עַד יַשְׁקוּף[1] מִמָּֽעַל, מוֹרִיד שְׁאוֹל וַיָּֽעַל,[2]*

« and raises us up [out of exile].* ‹ to the grave, ‹ [until] He lowers [our enemies] « from above; ‹ He gazes down ‹ [And this will continue] until

וְאָז אֶנָּחֵם.

« I will be consoled! ‹ And then

(1) Cf. *Eichah* 3:50. (2) *I Samuel* 2:6.

מוֹרִיד שְׁאוֹל וַיָּֽעַל — *[Until] He lowers [our enemies] to the grave, and raises us up [out of exile].* Alternatively, this is a descriptive phrase: *He Who lowers to the grave, then raises.* Accordingly this means: Just as God causes people to die and will eventually resurrect them, so has He caused us to sink to the depths of exile and will eventually redeem us.

KINNAH 29 / קינה כט

אֲמַרְתִּי* שְׁעוּ מִנִּי בִּבְכִי אֲמָרֵר,[1]

I said,* ‹ Turn away ‹ from me; ‹ with weeping ‹ I will make myself bitter. «

מַר נַפְשִׁי וְרוּחִי אֲקָרֵר,

The bitterness ‹ of my soul ‹ and my spirit ‹ I will soothe [by crying] «

עִם לִוְיָתָן* הָעֲתִידִים לְעוֹרֵר.[2]

with ‹ the lamentation of those* ‹ who are prepared ‹ to arouse [their grief]. «

בִּבְכִי יַעְזֵר*[3] עֲלֵי יְגוֹנֵךְ,

Through weeping, ‹ assist* ‹ in overcoming ‹ your agony, «

בַּת עַמִּי הִתְאַבְּכִי בְגִינֵךְ,

O daughter ‹ of my nation, ‹ roll in the dust ‹ over your sorrow! «

(1) Cf. *Isaiah* 22:4. (2) Cf. *Job* 3:8 [7]. (3) Cf. *Isaiah* 16:9; cf. *Jeremiah* 48:32.

אֲמַרְתִּי — *I said.* This *kinnah* is a bitter narrative that recounts the brave martyrdom and slaughter of innocent Jews at the hand of their enemy. It laments children being butchered cruelly for the sanctification of God's Name while their fathers are forced to witness this scene, reciting the *Shema* to proclaim that despite these unspeakable tragedies their faith was not shaken. The author cries out to God to avenge the blood of Israel and to speedily bring the redemption.

Each stanza comprises three lines. The third line is a Scriptural-verse fragment and determines the rhyme. The initial letters of the respective stanzas form the *aleph-beis*, followed by the composer's signature, קָלוֹנִימוֹס הַקָּטָן, *Klonimos the lesser.* Perhaps he is Klonimos Yehudah who composed *Kinnah* 25. If so, the events described here occurred during the First Crusade, in 1096. It is not surprising, therefore, that the medieval censors laid a heavy hand on this *kinnah*, as is obvious from the number and genre of the variant readings for some of the stanzas.

לִוְיָתָן — *The lamentation of those.* The translation follows *Ibn Ezra* (to *Job* 3:8 [7]) in his first explanation. Accordingly, the word is third-person feminine plural possessive, a contraction of לִוְיָה שֶׁלָּהֶן. Alternatively, the word is a proper noun and refers to the huge sea creature *Leviathan*, as if the sailors on an about-to-capsize ship were bemoaning their fate to become food for the Leviathan (*Ibn Ezra* ibid.). *Rashi* (ibid.) understands the word as *their conjugality*, i.e., as bereaved partners mourning over the spouse of their youth. In the *kinnah* this alludes to Israel lamenting its wayward infidelity in worshiping idols and in forsaking her first Husband, God, Who, in return, banished her from His House.

בִּבְכִי יַעְזֵר — *Through weeping, assist.* In the verses from which this phrase is borrowed (*Isaiah* 16:9 and *Jeremiah* 48:32), the word יַעְזֵר is a proper noun, the name of a Moabite city. Nevertheless, the translation

אַל תִּתְּנִי פוּגַת לָךְ, וְאַל תִּדּוֹם בַּת עֵינֵךְ.[1]

« of your eyes. ‹ the pupil ‹ be still ‹ let not « to yourself, ‹ respite ‹ give ‹ Do not

גְּעִי בִּבְכִיָּה מְעֻטֶּרֶת בַּעֲלִיזוּת,

‹ with joyfulness ‹ you who crowned « with weeping, ‹ Cry out

הָיִית מִקֶּדֶם וְהִנָּךְ לִבְזוּת,

« shamed. ‹ but you are now ‹ in the past ‹ had you been

אֵיכָה נִהְיְתָה הָרָעָה הַזֹּאת.[2]

« — this evil? « did it happen ‹ How

דֳּמִי אַל תִּתְּנִי[3] פְּלֵטָה הַנִּשְׁאָרָה,

« remnant, ‹ O you the escaped « give [Him], ‹ do not ‹ Silence

הָרִימִי קוֹל וְזַעֲקִי מָרָה,

« bitterly, ‹ and cry out ‹ [your] voice ‹ raise

כִּי שֶׁבֶר עַל שֶׁבֶר נִקְרָא.[4]

« occurred. ‹ catas- trophe ‹ upon ‹ catas- trophe ‹ be- cause

הֵן לְאֻמִּים עֵת נִקְבָּצוּ,

« they gathered together, ‹ — at the time « all the nations ‹ Indeed,

חַי עָלֶיךָ כְּרוֹת בְּרִית[5] כְּחָפֵצוּ,

« as was their desire. ‹ a covenant, ‹ they established ‹ against You ‹ O Life-giver,

עַל עַמְּךָ יַעֲרִימוּ סוֹד וְיִתְיָעֲצוּ.[6]

« and they take counsel. ‹ in secret ‹ they plot deviously ‹ Your people ‹ Against

וְנִכְּלוּ מְזִמּוֹת נְטוֹת אֲשׁוּרַי לְמְעוֹד,

« to cause me to falter; ‹ my steps [from righteousness] ‹ to turn ‹ in [evil] schemes, ‹ They conspired

(1) *Eichah* 2:18. (2) *Judges* 20:3. (3) Cf. *Isaiah* 62:7. (4) *Jeremiah* 4:20. (5) Cf. *Psalms* 83:6. (6) 83:4.

treats it as a derivative of the root עזר, *to help* or *assist*, because that interpretation seems more apt. Although the word's vowelization seems to contradict this view, it is not uncommon for *paytanim* to speak in wordplay and conundrum.

מִדְּאָגָה וּמִפַּחַד לִרְעוֹד,[1]

« to make me tremble. ‹ and from fear ‹ from anxiety

אָמְרוּ לְכוּ וְנַכְחִידֵם מִגּוֹי

« *from nationhood,* ‹ *let us obliterate them* ‹ *Come,* «*They said,*

וְלֹא יִזָּכֵר שֵׁם יִשְׂרָאֵל עוֹד.[2]

« *any longer!* ‹ *of Israel* ‹ *will be the name* ‹ *remembered* ‹ *so that not*

זֹאת הִשְׁמִיעוּ בְּנֵי מִקְרָאָיו,

« of those He summoned, ‹ the sons ‹ proclaimed ‹ Thus

לוֹ נְיַחֵל אִם יְקַטְּלֵנוּ[3] נַעֲרִיץ לְמוֹרָאָיו,

« *His awesomeness,* ‹ *we will revere* « *He to kill us,* ‹ *even were* ‹ *would we yearn,* ‹ *For Him*

הֵכִין יהוה זֶבַח הִקְדִּישׁ קְרוּאָיו.[4]

« *those He invited.* ‹ *He has consecrated* « *a sacrifice,* *HASHEM* ‹ *has* ‹ *for prepared*

חֲלָלַי אָז הִרְבּוּ וְהָרְגוּ טוֹבַי,

« my good ones; ‹ and slaughtered ‹ they increased ‹ then ‹ My slain ones

יִסְּרוּנִי קָשׁוֹת צָרַי וְאוֹיְבַי,

« and my enemies, ‹ did my tormentors ‹ severely ‹ torture me

הַמַּכּוֹת הָאֵלֶּה הֻכֵּיתִי בֵּית מְאַהֲבָי.[5]

« of my [ostensible] lovers. ‹ in the house ‹ inflicted upon me ‹ these are the wounds

טוֹב וּמֵטִיב הַבֵּט בְּצָרוֹתֵינוּ,

« our troubles, ‹ observe « and Who does good, ‹ [O God] Who is good

הִשְׁמִידוּ גִּבּוֹרַי בְּחֶתֶף מֵאַרְצֵנוּ,

‹ from our land, ‹ all at once ‹ my warriors ‹ for they destroyed

---

(1) Some editions read אַחֲרֵי הַהֶבֶל לְהַהְבִּיל וּמִפָּנָיו לִרְעוֹד, *to misguide me after the futile [idolatry], and to tremble before it.*

(2) *Psalms* 83:5. (3) Cf. *Job* 13:15. (4) *Zephaniah* 1:7. (5) Cf. *Zechariah* 13:6.

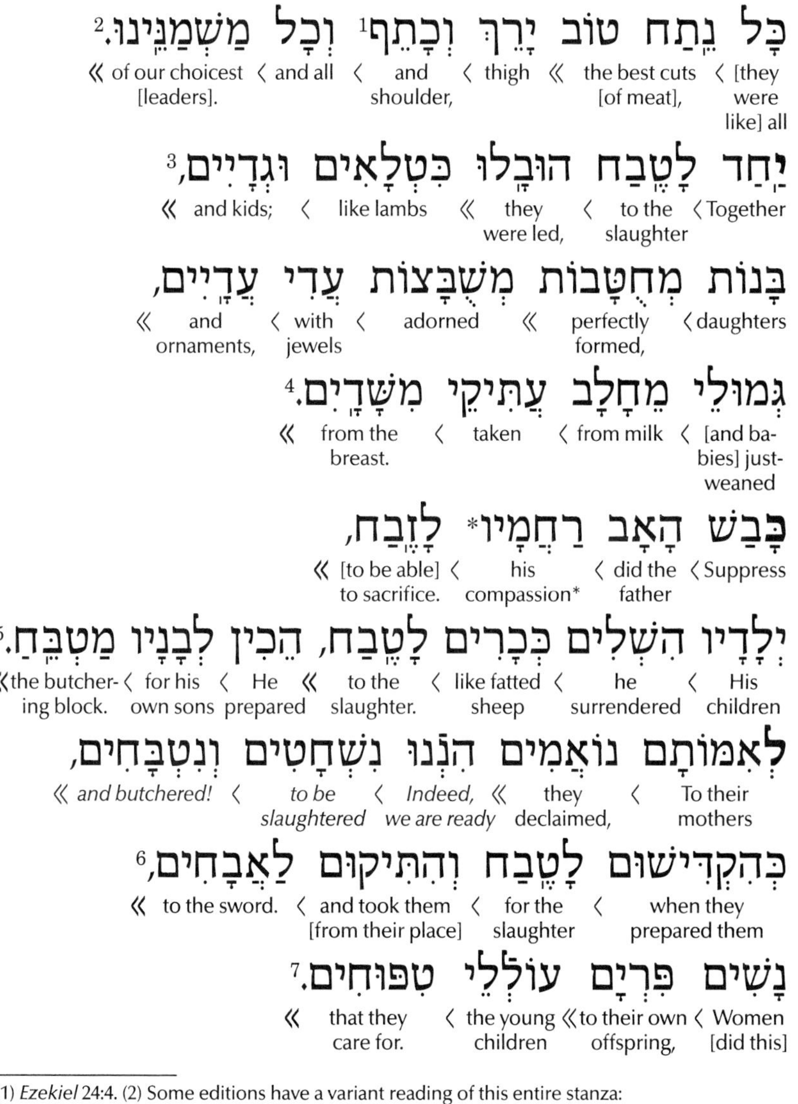

כָּל נֵתַח טוֹב יָרֵךְ וְכָתֵף[1] וְכָל מַשְׁמַנֵּינוּ.[2]

[they were like] all 〈 the best cuts [of meat], 《 thigh 〈 and shoulder, 〈 and all 〈 of our choicest [leaders]. 《

יַחַד לָטֶבַח הוּבָלוּ כִּטְלָאִים וּגְדָיִים,[3]

Together 〈 to the slaughter 〈 they were led, 《 like lambs 〈 and kids; 《

בָּנוֹת מְחֻטָּבוֹת מְשֻׁבָּצוֹת עֲדִי עֲדָיִים,

daughters 〈 perfectly formed, 《 adorned 〈 with jewels 〈 and ornaments, 《

גְּמוּלֵי מֵחָלָב עַתִּיקֵי מִשָּׁדָיִם.[4]

[and babies] just-weaned 〈 from milk 〈 taken 〈 from the breast. 《

כָּבַשׁ הָאָב רַחֲמָיו* לִזְבֹּחַ,

Suppress 〈 did the father 〈 his compassion* 〈 [to be able] to sacrifice. 《

יְלָדָיו הִשְׁלִים כְּכָרִים לָטֶבַח, הֵכִין לְבָנָיו מַטְבֵּחַ.[5]

His children 〈 he surrendered 〈 like fatted sheep 〈 to the slaughter. 《 He prepared 〈 for his own sons 〈 the butchering block. 《

לְאִמּוֹתָם נוֹאֲמִים הִנְנוּ נִשְׁחָטִים וְנִטְבָּחִים,

To their mothers 〈 they declaimed, 《 *Indeed, we are ready* 〈 *to be slaughtered* 〈 *and butchered!* 《

כְּהִקְדִּישׁוּם לָטֶבַח וְהִתִּיקוּם לַאֲבָחִים,[6]

when they prepared them 〈 for the slaughter 〈 and took them [from their place] 〈 to the sword. 《

נָשִׁים פִּרְיָם עוֹלְלֵי טִפּוּחִים.[7]

Women [did this] 〈 to their own offspring, 《 the young children 〈 that they care for. 《

(1) *Ezekiel* 24:4. (2) Some editions have a variant reading of this entire stanza: טֶנֶף צַחֲנָתָם מֵאַנְתִּי בָּם לְהִשְׁתַּתֵּף, *to the smelly filth of their idols I refused to become a partner,* / הִשְׁמִידוּ גִּבּוֹרֵי כֻּלָּם בְּחֶתֶף, *obliterated were all our warriors in one fell swoop,* / כָּל נֵתַח טוֹב יָרֵךְ וְכָתֵף, *[they were like] all the best cuts of meat, thigh and shoulder.* (3) Cf. *Isaiah* 53:7. (4) 28:9. (5) Cf. 14:21. (6) Cf. *Jeremiah* 12:3. (7) *Eichah* 2:20.

כָּבַשׁ הָאָב רַחֲמָיו — *Suppress did the father his compassion.* The next series of stanzas describes how parents made the supreme sacrifice in sanctification of God's Name by offering their children to the crusader's sword, rather than to his baptismal font. And all the while affirming their faith in the One True God by reciting the *Shema.*

מִי יִשְׁמַע וְלֹא יִדְמַע,

« shed tears? ‹ and not ‹ can hear [this] ‹ Who

הַבֵּן נִשְׁחָט וְהָאָב קוֹרֵא אֶת שְׁמַע,

« the *Shema!* ‹ recites ‹ and the father ‹ is slaughtered ‹ The son

מִי רָאָה כָּזֹאת וּמִי שָׁמַע.[1]

« has heard? ‹ and who « anything like this, ‹ has seen ‹ Who

נְוַת בַּיִת הַיָּפָה בְּתוּלַת בַּת יְהוּדָה,

« of Judah, ‹ daughter ‹ the maiden « and is beautiful, ‹ within [His] house ‹ The one who dwells

צַוָּארָהּ פָּשְׁטָה וּמַאֲכֶלֶת הִשְׁחִיזָה וְחִדְּדָה,

« and sharpened [the knife]; ‹ she honed « she stretched out [for the slaughter]; ‹ her neck

עַיִן רָאֲתָה וַתְּעִידָהּ.[2]

« and testified to this [devotion]. ‹ saw ‹ [God's] Eye

סָגְפָה הָאֵם וּפָרְחָה רוּחָהּ,

« did her spirit, ‹ and fly away ‹ was the mother ‹ Tormented

וְנַפְשָׁהּ הִשְׁלִימָה לַטֶּבַח אֲרוּחָה כְּאָרְחָה,

« she were preparing [for her family]. ‹ [with the same love] as if a meal ‹ to the slaughter, ‹ she submitted ‹ her soul

אֵם הַבָּנִים שְׂמֵחָה.[3]

« rejoices. ‹ of the children ‹ [And yet,] the mother

עָלְצוּ הַבָּנוֹת כְּנוּסוֹת וַאֲרוּסוֹת,

« and those betrothed, ‹ those wed « did the daughters, ‹ Exult

לְאִבְחַת חֶרֶב לְקַדֵּם דָּצוֹת וְשָׂשׂוֹת,

« and they rejoiced, ‹ they danced ‹ to rush to meet, ‹ sword ‹ to the sharpened

(1) *Isaiah* 66:8. (2) Cf. *Job* 29:11. (3) *Psalms* 113:9.

דָּמָם עַל צְחִיחַ סֶלַע לְבִלְתִּי הִכָּסוֹת.*[1]

their blood ‹ [shed] upon ‹ a rock ‹ that was smooth, « never ‹ to be covered.* «

פּוֹנֶה הָאָב בִּבְכִי וִילָלָה,

The father ‹ turns away ‹ with weeping ‹ and wailing, «

עַצְמוֹ עַל חַרְבּוֹ לִדְקוֹר וּלְהַפִּילָה,

himself ‹ on ‹ his sword ‹ to be stabbed ‹ and to be felled. «

וְהוּא מִתְגּוֹלֵל בְּדָם בְּתוֹךְ הַמְּסִלָּה.[2]

He ‹ rolls over ‹ in [his own] blood ‹ in the midst ‹ of the road. «

צִדְּקָה דִינָהּ פּוֹרִיָּה כְּהִקְרִיבָה עֲנָפֶיהָ,

Acknowledge the justice ‹ of her judgment ‹ did the fruitful [mother] ‹ as she offered ‹ her offspring. «

וּתְמוּר מִזְרָק דָּם קִבְּלָה בִּכְנָפֶיהָ,

And instead of ‹ the [consecrated] vessel ‹ for [catching the] blood [of the sacrifice], « she caught [her children's blood] ‹ in the hem of her garments, «

תִּתְיַפֵּחַ תְּפָרֵשׂ כַּפֶּיהָ.[3]

sobbing ‹ and spreading ‹ her arms [in anguish]. «

קוֹרוֹתַי מִי יָנוּד שׁוֹד וָשֶׁבֶר[4] יִשְׂתָּרֵג,

For my tragedies, « who ‹ will bewail? « wherein plunder ‹ and destruction ‹ were knitted together; «

מַחְמַד עֵינִי בְּנִמְסַר לְחֶרֶב וּלְהֶרֶג,

the delight ‹ of my eye « — when it was delivered « to sword ‹ and to slaughter. «

(1) Cf. *Ezekiel* 24:8. (2) *II Samuel* 20:12. (3) *Jeremiah* 4:31. (4) Cf. *Isaiah* 51:19.

דָּמָם עַל צְחִיחַ סֶלַע לְבִלְתִּי הִכָּסוֹת — *Their blood [shed] upon a rock that was smooth, never to be covered.* The Scriptural verse from which this fragment is borrowed reads in full: *In order to arouse fury, to incite vengeance, I have placed her blood on a smooth rock, never to be covered* (*Ezekiel* 24:8). *Rashi* explains that since the smooth rock will not absorb the blood as the soil would, the blood will remain a visible reminder that the murderer has not received his just deserts.

אִם כְּהֶרֶג הֲרוּגָיו הֹרָג.[1]

Was there ever ‹ like this slaughter ‹ of his victims ‹ another [comparable] slaughter? «

רַעְיוֹנַי נִבְהָלוּ וַאֲחָזַתְנִי פַּלָּצוּת וָשֶׁבֶר,

My thoughts ‹ are confounded ‹ for I am seized ‹ by horror ‹ and heartbreak; «

בְּאַחַת* נִמְצָא הַכָּתוּב בּוֹ תִּקְוָה וָשֶׂבֶר,

because of one [good deed],* « find ‹ did Scripture ‹ for him [Abijah] ‹ hope ‹ and positive expectation, «

כִּי זֶה לְבַדּוֹ יָבֹא לְיָרָבְעָם אֶל קָבֶר.[2]

for ‹ he ‹ alone ‹ shall come « — [of the House of] Jeroboam ‹ to ‹ [be buried in] a grave. «

שָׁלֵם נִמְצָא בְּכָל פָּעֳלוֹ,

[Yet,] one who was found to be perfect, ‹ in all ‹ of his deeds, «

נַפְשׁוֹ לָטֶבַח הִשְׁלִים מִפַּחַד חֵילוֹ,

his soul ‹ to the slaughter ‹ he surrendered ‹ out of fear ‹ of [God] Who gave him strength, «

וְגַם קְבוּרָה לֹא הָיְתָה לּוֹ.[3]

and also ‹ a [proper] burial ‹ there was not ‹ for him! «

תַּתִּי לִבִּי מְצֹא תֹּכֶן עִנְיָנָיו,

I have set ‹ my heart ‹ to finding ‹ the inner meaning ‹ of His dealings. «

יָדַעְתִּי אֲנִי צֶדֶק וְיֹשֶׁר דִּינָיו,

For I do know ‹ myself: « the righteousness ‹ and justice ‹ of His judgments, «

---

(1) *Isaiah* 27:7. (2) *I Kings* 14:13. (3) *Ecclesiates* 6:3.

בְּאַחַת — *Because of one [good deed].* In *I Kings* (Ch. 14), the prophet אֲחִיָּה, *Ahijah,* tells the wicked Jeroboam's wife that God would utterly cut off every male child from the House of Jeroboam, "*. . . and will sweep them away as one sweeps away dung . . . . The dead of Jeroboam in the city, the dogs shall eat, and the dead in the field, the birds of the heaven shall eat.*" The only exception to this curse was Jeroboam's son אֲבִיָּה, *Abijah,* who merited a proper burial because he defied his father on one point. Jeroboam had stationed armed sentries on all the roads leading to Jerusalem to prevent any member of the Ten Tribes of Israel from making the pilgrimage to Jerusalem on the three Festivals. According to the Talmud (*Moed Kattan* 28b), Prince Abijah was on sentry duty, but deserted his post and went up to

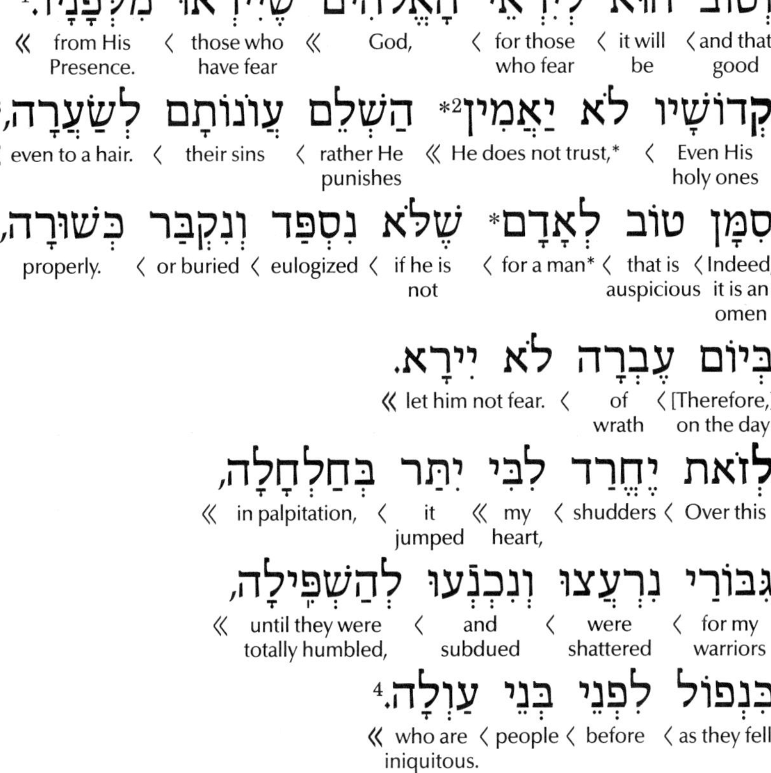

וְטוֹב הוּא לְיִרְאֵי הָאֱלֹהִים שֶׁיִּירְאוּ מִלְּפָנָיו.[1]

And that good / it will be / for those who fear / God, / those who have fear / from His Presence.

קְדוֹשָׁיו לֹא יַאֲמִין*[2] הַשְׁלֵם עֲוֹנוֹתָם לְשַׂעֲרָה,[3]

Even His holy ones / He does not trust,* / rather He punishes / their sins / even to a hair.

סִמָּן טוֹב לְאָדָם* שֶׁלֹּא נִסְפַּד וְנִקְבַּר כַּשּׁוּרָה,

Indeed, it is an omen / that is auspicious / for a man* / if he is not / eulogized / or buried / properly.

בְּיוֹם עֶבְרָה לֹא יִירָא.

[Therefore,] on the day / of wrath / let him not fear.

לְזֹאת יֶחֱרַד לִבִּי יִתַּר בְּחַלְחָלָה,

Over this / shudders / my heart, / it jumped / in palpitation,

גִּבּוֹרַי נִרְעֲצוּ וְנִכְנְעוּ לְהַשְׁפִּילָה,

for my warriors / were shattered / and subdued / until they were totally humbled,

כִּנְפוֹל לִפְנֵי בְנֵי עַוְלָה.[4]

as they fell / before / people / who are iniquitous.

(1) *Ecclesiates* 8:12. (2) Cf. *Job* 15:15. (3) Tractate *Bava Kamma* 50a. (4) *II Samuel* 3:34.

Jerusalem himself. Another opinion says that Abijah entirely abolished the sentry system his father had established.

קְדוֹשָׁיו לֹא יַאֲמִין — *Even His holy ones He does not trust.* When R' Yochanan would reach this verse (*Job* 15:15), he would weep. "If He does not trust His holy ones, whom does He trust?" One day, he came upon a man picking not-yet-completely-ripe figs while leaving the ripe figs on the tree. He explained to R' Yochanan that he was going on a long journey. The not-yet-ripe fruits could be expected to last; but the already ripe could not. Said R' Yochanan, "That must be the meaning of the verse!" Just as this man is apprehensive of how the ripe figs will fare later on, so is God apprehensive lest a young *tzaddik* spoil as he ages. Thus, He will sometimes take His holy ones from this world while they are still young, and not trust them to the vicissitudes that might break them of their righteousness (*Chagigah* 5a with *Rashi*).

סִמָּן טוֹב לְאָדָם — *Indeed, it is an omen that is auspicious for a man ....* The Talmud teaches that God will sometimes cause a righteous person anguish after his death, in order to fully purge him of any stain on his soul caused by sin. Thus, one who does not receive proper burial, or is not eulogized in accordance with his stature, or whose unburied body is attacked by a wild beast, attains atonement through this degradation. Such a person will be spared the punishments of the next world (*Sanhedrin* 47a with *Rashi* and *Tosafos* [46b]).

וְעַד מָתַי תִּהְיֶה כְּגִבּוֹר לֹא יוּכַל לְהוֹשִׁיעַ,[1]
« to save? ‹ able ‹ not ‹ like a warrior ‹ will You [continue] to be ‹ when ‹ Until

לְעֵינֵינוּ בַּגּוֹיִם נִקְמַת דַּם עֲבָדֶיךָ תּוֹדִיעַ,[2]
« — make it known; « of Your servants ‹ for the blood ‹ [Your] vengeance « among [the nations,] ‹ [Before our eyes,

אֵל נְקָמוֹת יהוה אֵל נְקָמוֹת הוֹפִיעַ.[3]
« appear! ‹ of vengeance, ‹ O God « HASHEM; ‹ of vengeance, ‹ O God

נְקוֹם נִקְמָתִי מֵאֵת מְעַנַּי,
« those who tormented me, ‹ from ‹ [with] my vengeance ‹ Avenge

עֵת נְקָמָה הִיא[4] לָדוּן דִּינַי, אֵל קַנֹּא וְנוֹקֵם יהוה.[5]
« is HASHEM. ‹ and avenging ‹ Who is jealous ‹ A God « my judgment. ‹ judge « it is, ‹ of vengeance ‹ [for] a time

יהוה כְּגִבּוֹר יֵצֵא[6] יְדֵי חוֹבָךְ פְּרַע,
« pay [to avenge the slaughtered]; ‹ of Your obligation ‹ and the full amount ‹ go forth ‹ like [mighty] warrior ‹ HASHEM,

שׁוֹבֵר כְּתוֹב שְׁטַר חוֹב תִּקְרַע,
« tear up. ‹ of [Israel's] indebtedness ‹ and the note « write, ‹ a ["paid"] receipt

שְׁבוֹר זְרוֹעַ רָשָׁע וָרָע.[7]
« and the evil one. ‹ of the wicked one ‹ the power ‹ Break

מִמָּרוֹם כְּהִסִּיק אֵשׁ[8] בְּמַעֲזִיבָה וְתִקְרָה,
« and the beam, ‹ on the plaster ‹ a fire ‹ when [God] kindled ‹ From on high

חוֹמַת אֵשׁ סָבִיב[9] שׁוֹמִירָה וּבֵית דִּירָה,
« of [Divine] Dwelling; ‹ to the House ‹ [everything from] the sentry booth ‹ all around ‹ of fire ‹ a wall

שַׁלֵּם יְשַׁלֵּם הַמַּבְעִיר אֶת הַבְּעֵרָה.[10]
« the fire. ‹ — the One Who kindled « He must surely pay ‹ pay,

---

(1) Cf. *Jeremiah* 14:9. (2) Cf. *Psalms* 79:10.(3) 94:1.(4) *Jeremiah* 51:6. (5) *Nahum* 1:2.
(6) Cf. *Isaiah* 42:13. (7) Cf. *Psalms* 10:15; some editions read גְּזַר דִּינֵנוּ הָרַע, *Break the decree of our verdict that is evil.* (8) Cf. *Eichah* 1:13. (9) *Zechariah* 2:9. (10) *Exodus* 22:5.

וּכְעַל גְּמוּלוֹת נָא שַׁלֵּם,[1]

« do repay [them]; ‹ please ‹ their [wicked] deeds, ‹ According to

(אוֹיְבַי תַּפִּיל מְהֵרָה וּתְכַלֵּם,)[2]

«and destroy them,) « speedily, ‹ humble ‹ (my enemies

כִּי אֵל גְּמוּלוֹת יהוה שַׁלֵּם יְשַׁלֵּם.[3]

« He must surely pay [them]. « is HASHEM, ‹ of retribution ‹ a God ‹ for

(שׂוֹנְאֶיךָ תַּצְמִית סַף רַעַל תַּשְׁקֵם,[4]

« give them to drink; ‹ of poison ‹ the cup « cut down, ‹ (Your enemies

הַמֵּת תַּחַת יָדוֹ נָקֹם יִנָּקֵם,[5]

« *he shall surely be avenged.* ‹ *his hand,* ‹ *under* ‹ [as Scripture states,] *If one dies*

אִם בְּכָזֶה לֹא תִתְנַקֵּם.[6])[2]

« You will not avenge? ‹ that for such as these ‹ Can it be

הַעַל כֵּן נִקְרֵאתָ אִישׁ מִלְחָמָה,[7]

« of War, ‹ the Man ‹ You are called ‹ this reason ‹ Is it for

צָרֶיךָ לְכַלּוֹת וּבָהֶם לְהִנָּקְמָה,

« You wreak vengeance? ‹ as upon them ‹ You destroy ‹ because Your enemies

נֹקֵם יהוה וּבַעַל חֵמָה.[8]

« of [His] fury. ‹ and Master ‹ is HASHEM ‹ Vengeful

קַנֵּא לְשִׁמְךָ עֲבוּרְךָ הָאֵל,

« O God! ‹ for Your sake, ‹ for Your Name, ‹ Be jealous

וּלְדַם עֲבָדֶיךָ הַשָּׁפוּךְ[9] וּלְחָרְבוֹת אֲרִיאֵל,

« of the lion-like Temple. ‹ and for the ruins « that was spilled, ‹ of Your servants ‹ And for the blood

---

(1) Cf. *Isaiah* 59:18. (2) Some editions omit the passages in parentheses.
(3) *Jeremiah* 51:56. (4) Cf. *Zechariah* 12:2. (5) Cf. *Exodus* 21:20.
(6) Cf. *Jeremiah* 5:9, 29; 9:8. (7) *Exodus* 15:3. (8) *Nahum* 1:2. (9) Cf. *Psalms* 79:10.

וּנְקוֹם נִקְמַת בְּנֵי יִשְׂרָאֵל.[1]

Avenge ‹ [with] the vengeance ‹ of the Children ‹ of Israel. «

טִפֵּי דָמָם אַחַת לְאַחַת מְנוּיוֹת,

The drops ‹ of their blood, ‹ one ‹ by one ‹ are counted, «

וְיֵז נִצְחָם[2] עַל בְּגָדֶיךָ וּבְפוּרְפְּרָךְ הֱיוֹת,

sprinkle ‹ of their lifeblood, « so that on ‹ Your garments, ‹ on Your [royal] purple ‹ it will be; «

יָדִין בַּגּוֹיִם מָלֵא גְוִיּוֹת.[3]

let Him judge ‹ the nations ‹ [on a battlefield] filled ‹ with corpses. «

נִלְאֵיתִי נְשֹׂא אֶת כָּל הַתְּלָאָה,[4]

I am weary ‹ of bearing ‹ all ‹ the hardship; «

מַהֵר גְּאֻלָּתִי וְתָחִישׁ הַמַּרְאָה,

hasten ‹ my redemption ‹ and speedily fulfill ‹ the vision: «

כִּי יוֹם נָקָם בְּלִבִּי וּשְׁנַת גְּאוּלַי בָּאָה.[5]

For ‹ the day ‹ of vengeance ‹ is in My heart, ‹ and the year ‹ of My redemption ‹ has arrived! «

---

(1) Cf. *Numbers* 31:2. (2) Cf. *Isaiah* 63:3. (3) *Psalms* 110:6; some editions do not contain this stanza, but instead read: טוֹב וּמֵטִיב קַנֵּא לִשְׁמֶךָ, *O God, One Who is good and does good for others, be zealous for Your Name,* / לְמַעַן יֵחָלְצוּן יְדִידֶיךָ, *so that may be released Your beloved ones/* הוֹשִׁיעָה יְמִינְךָ, *save us with Your right hand* (*Psalms* 60:7). (4) *Isaiah* 1:14. (5) 63:4.

KINNAH 30 / קינה ל

מְעוֹנֵי שָׁמַיִם,* שְׁחָקִים יְזַבְּלוּךְ, מְלֵאִים מֵהוֹדָךְ,
« with Your splendor, ‹ are filled « that house You, ‹ the heavens « of the skies,* ‹ The abodes

וְהֵם לֹא יְכַלְכְּלוּךְ, וְאַף כִּי הַבָּיִת.[1]
« contain You; ‹ cannot ‹ yet they « the Temple. ‹ not ‹ certainly so

מַה טּוֹב וּמַה נָּעִים,[2]
‹ pleasant ‹ and how ‹ good ‹ How

שִׁבְתְּךָ עִם רֵעִים, בְּכַנְפֵי צַעֲצוּעִים,[3]
‹ of the childlike [Cherubim] ‹ between the wings ‹ friends ‹ among ‹ was Your dwelling

יַעַן הָיָה עִם לְבָבְךָ[4] לִבְנוֹת הַבָּיִת.
« the Temple. ‹ to [have us] build ‹ of Your heart ‹ the desire ‹ it was ‹ inasmuch as

נָאוֹר, אַהֲבָתְךָ הֶרְאֵיתָ לְעַמֶּךָ, כִּי הֵם נַחֲלָתֶךָ,
« Your heritage, ‹ they are ‹ for « to Your nation, ‹ You have displayed ‹ Your love « O Awesome One,

וְלֵידַע כִּי שִׁמְךָ נִקְרָא עַל הַבָּיִת.[5]
« the Temple. ‹ upon ‹ is proclaimed ‹ Your Name ‹ that ‹ and to let it be known

נָכְרִים שָׁם בָּאוּ, וְעַמִּים הַר יִקְרָאוּ, וְאוֹתוֹתָיו רָאוּ,
« they saw, ‹ and its wondrous signs « will be summoned, ‹ to the [Temple] mountain ‹ and [foreign] peoples « came, ‹ [also] to there ‹ Gentiles

לְמַעַן יִרְאוּ כְּבוֹד יהוה עַל הַבָּיִת.[6]
« the Temple. ‹ upon ‹ of HASHEM ‹ the glory ‹ they should see ‹ in order that

(1) *I Kings* 8:27. (2) *Psalms* 133:1. (3) *II Chronicles* 3:10.
(4) Cf. 6:8. (5) Cf. *I Kings* 8:43. (6) *II Chronicles* 7:3.

מְעוֹנֵי שָׁמַיִם — *The abodes of the skies.* There was a time when God was so eager to dwell in the midst of His beloved Jewish people that He contained His unlimited Being within the limited confines of the Temple's walls. His *Shechinah,* Presence, was so manifest in the Temple that even a non-Jew who came to pray there could feel God's Presence. But later, Israel ignored God's Presence. They desecrated His earthly abode with abominable idolatry. To purify the Temple, God purged it with fiery flames that consumed it.

Today, Israel eagerly awaits God's return

חֲטָאַי כִּי עָצְמוּ, אֲכָלַתְנִי קִנְאָה,*[1]

« by God's jealous zeal,* ‹ I was consumed « they became massive, ‹ when « However, my sins,

וְעָרָה צָר הַיְסוֹד,[2] שָׂמַנִי שׁוֹאָה, וְנָתַץ אֶת הַבָּיִת.[3]

« the Temple. ‹ and demolished ‹ desolate, ‹ left me « to the [Temple's] foundation, ‹ did the tormentor ‹ and destroy

חֲמוּדֵי אוֹצְרֵיהֶם, הֵבִיאוּ בְּהֵיכְלֵיהֶם,

« into their palaces, ‹ [the enemy] brought ‹ [Israel's] most precious treasures

מִלְּאוּ כְרֵסֵיהֶם,[4] וְצִוָּה הַכֹּהֵן וּפִנּוּ אֶת הַבָּיִת.[5]

« that they empty out the Temple. ‹ did the [supreme] *Kohen* [God] ‹ For command « their bellies [from the spoils]. ‹ they filled

מַדּוּעַ נִתְּכָה, וְחֵמָה לֹא שָׁכְכָה,

« assuaged? ‹ that was not ‹ — [God's] fury « was it poured out [like molten metal] ‹ Why

עַל מָה זֶּה עָשָׂה צוּרֵנוּ כָּכָה,

‹ in such a way « — our Rock [did] — « that He acted ‹ is it ‹ what reason ‹ For

לָאָרֶץ הַזֹּאת וְלַבָּיִת.[6]

« and to the Temple? ‹ to this land

מְקוֹם כֹּהֲנַי נִגָּשׁוּ, וְשָׁם יִתְקַדָּשׁוּ, וְהֵן כָּעֵת רֻפָּסוּ,

‹ it is trampled ‹ now ‹ indeed, « they would sanctify themselves, ‹ there « would approach, ‹ where my *Kohanim* ‹ The place

(1) Cf. *Psalms* 69:10. (2) Cf. 137:7. (3) *Leviticus* 14:45.
(4) Cf. *Jeremiah* 51:34. (5) *Leviticus* 14:36. (6) *II Chronicles* 7:21.

---

when He will surround the rebuilt Temple with a wall of protective fire so that it will never again be defiled or destroyed.

The acrostic of the stanzas spells the composer's name, מְנַחֵם בַּר יַעֲקֹב חֲזַק, *Menachem son of Yaakov, may he be strong.* (R' Menachem flourished in Worms, Germany, during the last decades of the 12th century.) The fourth, final stich of each stanza is a Scriptural fragment ending with the word בַּיִת, *house* or *Temple.*

אֲכָלַתְנִי קִנְאָה — *I was consumed by God's jealous zeal.* Various interpretations are given for this line. It refers to either: God's zealous anger at "my sins" of the preceding line; or the sin of idolatry as represented by the סֵמֶל הַקִּנְאָה, *Image of Provocation,* mentioned below; or the jealousy borne by the

הֲמוֹן גּוֹיִם רָגְשׁוּ,[1] נָסַבּוּ עַל הַבָּיִת.[2]

hordes of the nations have thronged, surrounding all around the Temple.

בַּת קוֹל הִיא עוֹנָה, מַה תִּתְמְּהוּ פֶּגַע,

An echo of a voice [from heaven], it answers, *Why are you so bewildered by this affliction?*

סֶמֶל הַקִּנְאָה[3] הֲבֵאתֶם, וּכְנֶגַע נִרְאָה לִי בַּבָּיִת.[4]

The Image of Provocation you brought in[to the Sanctuary], [something] like a plague has appeared to me in the Temple.

רְבִיצַת עוֹלָם מְלֹא, שׁוֹכֵן בְּהֵיכָלוֹ,

He whose resting place is the universe in fullness, yet chose to dwell in His Temple;

הֲתַעֲשׂוּ צָרָה* לוֹ, עִוֵּר וּפִסֵּחַ לֹא יָבֹא אֶל הַבָּיִת.[5]

do you attempt to fashion a rival* to Him? *[An idol,] blind and crippled may not enter into the Temple.*

יַעַן הִשְׁחַתֶּם מְצָאוּנְכֶם רָעוֹת,

Because you grew corrupt, beset you has evil!

חֻלַּל הַמִּקְדָּשׁ וְהִנֵּה מִגְרָעוֹת נָתַן לַבָּיִת.[6]

Defiled was the Sanctuary and indeed, the lowering of its stature [God] exacted against the Temple.

קָדוֹשׁ יִתְעַשֵּׁת, אֱמֶת לָנוּ בֹּשֶׁת,[7] יְשַׁלַּח תַּחְבֹּשֶׁת,

May the Holy One change His mind, for in truth ours is the shame; May He send a bandage [for our wounds]

וְחֵטְא אַל יָשֶׁת,[8] וְחִטֵּא אֶת הַבָּיִת.[9]

and sin, do not lay [upon us]. May He purify the Temple.

בְּמָקוֹר הַנִּפְתָּח[10] וּמַעֲלֶה עַל שָׂפָה,[11] מְבַכֵּר לָחֳדָשָׁיו,

[How will He purify?] With the spring that opened up; and it will bring up on its banks [fruit trees] that ripen each month

(1) Cf. *Psalms* 2:1. (2) *Genesis* 19:4. (3) *Ezekiel* 8:3. (4) *Leviticus* 14:35. (5) *II Samuel* 5:8. (6) *I Kings* 6:6. (7) *Daniel* 9:7. (8) Cf. *Numbers* 12:11. (9) *Leviticus* 14:52. (10) *Zechariah* 13:1. (11) Cf. *Ezekiel* 47:12.

heathen nations against the *Beis HaMikdash* and which, because of my sins, they were permitted to vent by destroying the Temple.

צָרָה — *A rival.* A polygamous man's wives are called צָרוֹת, *rivals,* literally, *troubles,* to each other (see, e.g., *I Samuel* 1:6 and *Yevamos* 2a).

וְעָלֵהוּ לִתְרוּפָה, מִתַּחַת מִפְתַּן הַבָּיִת.
and whose leaves 〈 will be for healing, 《 [the spring will flow] from under 〈 the threshold 〈 of the Temple. 《

חֲמוֹל עִיר הַחֲרֵבָה, תְּמוּר מוֹקֵד שְׁבִיבָהּ,
Have mercy 〈 on the city 〈 that is ruined! 《 Instead of 〈 the pyre 〈 of her sparks [that destroyed it], 《

חוֹמַת אֵשׁ סוֹבְבָהּ, לְכָבוֹד תִּהְיֶה בָּהּ,[1]
[form] a [protecting] wall 〈 of 〈 fire 〈 to surround it, 《 and for glory will You be 〈 within it, 《

אֶל דְּבִיר הַבָּיִת.[2]
[when Your Presence returns] to 〈 the Holiest of Holies 〈 of the Temple. 《

זָרֵה וְהַעֲבֵר טֻמְאָה מִבֵּיתְךָ מַלְכִּי,
Cast out 〈 and remove 〈 all that is defiled 〈 from Your House, 《 O my King! 《

אֱלִיל כָּלִיל תַּחֲלוֹף,[3] וְתִקְרָא אָנֹכִי פִּנִּיתִי הַבָּיִת.[4]
Let the idols 〈 utterly 〈 disappear, 〈 and cry out, 《 *I [HASHEM]* 〈 *have cleared out* 〈 *[the idols from] the Temple!* 《

קַדֵּשׁ בֵּית מְעוֹנַי,* וְתָשׁוּב לִמְלוֹנַי, וְנִקְבְּצוּ לִגְיוֹנַי,
So sanctify 〈 the House 〈 of My Dwelling,* 《 and return 〈 to My Lodging; 《 let be gathered 〈 My legions 〈

וְהִנֵּה כְּבוֹד יהוה, בָּא אֶל הַבָּיִת.[5]
[and proclaim,] Behold 〈 *the glory* 〈 *of HASHEM* 〈 *has entered* 〈 *into* 〈 *the Temple!* 《

---

(1) Cf. *Zechariah* 2:9. (2) *I Kings* 8:6. (3) Cf. *Isaiah* 2:18. (4) *Genesis* 24:31. (5) *Ezekiel* 43:4.

קַדֵּשׁ בֵּית מְעוֹנַי — *Sanctify the House of My Dwelling.* The translation assumes that God is still speaking. Accordingly, God says, "I have done My part by cleansing the Sanctuary of idolatrous defilement. Now you do your part by sanctifying yourself and your environs, and by returning your thoughts to My Lodging, so that I may return to My Dwelling." Alternatively, this stanza contains Israel's plaint that God return to "the House that I built for Your dwelling."

KINNAH 31 / קינה לא

אֵשׁ תּוּקַד בְּקִרְבִּי,* בְּהַעֲלוֹתִי עַל לִבִּי,

A fire [of elation] ‹ burns ‹ within me* ‹ when I recall ‹ in ‹ my heart [what happened] ‹

בְּצֵאתִי מִמִּצְרָיִם.

when I went out ‹ from Egypt; «

קִינִים אָעִירָה, לְמַעַן אַזְכִּירָה, בְּצֵאתִי מִירוּשָׁלָיִם.

but lamentations ‹ I shall arouse, ‹ so that ‹ I will remember [what occurred] ‹ when I went out ‹ from Jerusalem. «

אָז יָשִׁיר מֹשֶׁה,[1] שִׁיר לֹא יִנָּשֶׁה, בְּצֵאתִי מִמִּצְרָיִם.

Then ‹ choose to sing, « did Moses, « a song ‹ not ‹ to be forgotten, « when I went out ‹ from Egypt; «

וַיְקוֹנֵן יִרְמְיָה,* וְנָהָה נְהִי נִהְיָה,[2]

but lament ‹ did Jeremiah;* « he lamented, ‹ *A lament* ‹ *has come to be,* «

בְּצֵאתִי מִירוּשָׁלָיִם.

when I went out ‹ from Jerusalem. «

בֵּיתִי הִתְכּוֹנָן, וְשָׁכַן הֶעָנָן,[3] בְּצֵאתִי מִמִּצְרָיִם.

My House [the Tabernacle] ‹ was established, « and rest upon it ‹ did the cloud ‹ when I went out ‹ from Egypt; «

(1) *Exodus* 15:1. (2) *Micah* 2:4. (3) See *Numbers* 9:15, 22.

⟨ אֵשׁ תּוּקַד בְּקִרְבִּי — *A fire . . . burns within me.* The Midrash cites numerous examples of the startling contrast between our triumphant Exodus from Egypt and our tragic exit from conquered Jerusalem (*Eichah Zuta* 19). When Israel left Egypt their hearts were aflame with a fire of love for God and an unquenchable desire to receive the Torah at Sinai. But as the defeated Jews trudged out of Jerusalem's ruins into captivity, their hearts were shrouded in gloom and lamentations were on their lips.

Another tragedy which occurred on Tishah B'Av was the expulsion of the Jews from Spain in 1492. At that time the Spanish rabbis allowed orchestras to play before them (even on Tishah B'Av itself), in order to strengthen the spirits of the unfortunate exiles and to thank God for giving them the courage and strength not to succumb to the pressure to convert. It was also the aim of these rabbis to teach the people that we never weep over departing from a country in exile. No matter how we prospered in that land, we weep only over our forced departure from Jerusalem (see *Sefer HaTodaah*).

The *kinnah,* of unknown authorship, follows an *aleph-beis* arrangement as the initial letters of the respective stanzas.

וַיְקוֹנֵן יִרְמְיָה — *But lament did Jeremiah.* This refers to the Book of *Eichah* that Jeremiah composed as a lament over the Destruction.

וַחֲמַת אֵל שָׁכְנָה עָלַי כַּעֲנָנָה, בְּצֵאתִי מִירוּשָׁלָיִם.

but the fury ‹ of God ‹ rested ‹ upon me ‹ like a heavy cloud ‹ when I went out ‹ from Jerusalem. «

גַּלֵּי יָם רָמוּ, וְכַחוֹמָה קָמוּ,[1] בְּצֵאתִי מִמִּצְרָיִם.

The waves ‹ of the Sea ‹ piled high ‹ and like a wall, ‹ stood up ‹ when I went out ‹ from Egypt; «

זְדוֹנִים שְׁטָפוּ, וְעַל רֹאשִׁי צָפוּ,[2]

but the treacherous enemy ‹ [like water] swept [me] away ‹ and over ‹ my head ‹ [the water] flooded ‹

בְּצֵאתִי מִירוּשָׁלָיִם.

when I went out ‹ from Jerusalem. «

דְּגַן שָׁמַיִם, וּמִצּוּר יָזוּבוּ מַיִם,[3] בְּצֵאתִי מִמִּצְרָיִם.

Grain ‹ from heaven ‹ and from a rock ‹ would flow ‹ water ‹ when I went out ‹ from Egypt; «

לַעֲנָה וּמְרוֹרִים, וּמַיִם הַמָּרִים, בְּצֵאתִי מִירוּשָׁלָיִם.

worm-wood ‹ and bitterness ‹ and the waters ‹ that are bitter when I went out ‹ from Jerusalem. «

הַשְׁכֵּם וְהַעֲרֵב, סְבִיבוֹת הַר חוֹרֵב,*

From dawn ‹ to dusk, ‹ encircling ‹ Mount ‹ Horeb,* ‹

בְּצֵאתִי מִמִּצְרָיִם.

when I went out ‹ from Egypt; «

קוֹרֵא אֶל אֵבֶל, עַל נַהֲרוֹת בָּבֶל,[4]

but a call ‹ to ‹ mourning ‹ by ‹ the rivers ‹ of Babylon, ‹

בְּצֵאתִי מִירוּשָׁלָיִם.

when I went out ‹ from Jerusalem. «

וּמַרְאֵה כְּבוֹד יהוה, כְּאֵשׁ אוֹכֶלֶת[5] לְפָנַי,

And the appearance ‹ of the glory ‹ of HASHEM ‹ was like a fire ‹ that was consuming ‹ before me ‹

(1) Cf. *Exodus* 15:8.(2) Cf. *Eichah* 3:54. (3) Cf. *Psalms* 78:24, 20. (4) 137:1. (5) *Exodus* 24:17.

הַר חוֹרֵב — *Mount Horeb.* According to the Midrash (*Tanchuma, Bamidbar* 7), Scripture records six names for Mount Sinai: (a) הַר [הָ]אֱלֹהִים, *the Mountain of Elohim* (*Exodus* 3:1; 18:5; *Psalms* 68:16); (b) הַר בָּשָׁן, *Mount Bashan* (*Psalms* 68:16); (c) הַר גַּבְנֻנִּים, *Mount Gavnunim* (ibid.); (d) הָהָר חָמַד, *the Desired Mountain* (ibid. v.

בְּצֵאתִי מִמִּצְרָיִם.

« from Egypt; ‹ when I went out

וְחֶרֶב לְטוּשָׁה, וּלְטֶבַח נְטוּשָׁה, בְּצֵאתִי מִירוּשָׁלָיִם.

« from Jerusalem. ‹ when I went out ‹ abandoned, ‹ and to the slaughter ‹ that was sharpened ‹ but to the sword

זֶבַח וּמִנְחָה, וְשֶׁמֶן הַמִּשְׁחָה, בְּצֵאתִי מִמִּצְרָיִם.

« from Egypt; ‹ when I went out ‹ of anointment, ‹ and the oil ‹ and meal-offerings, ‹ Sacrifices

סְגֻלַּת אֵל לְקוּחָה, כְּצֹאן לְטִבְחָה,

‹ to the slaughter, ‹ like sheep ‹ was taken ‹ of God ‹ but the treasure

בְּצֵאתִי מִירוּשָׁלָיִם.

« from Jerusalem. ‹ when I went out

חַגִּים וְשַׁבָּתוֹת, וּמוֹפְתִים וְאוֹתוֹת,

‹ and signs, ‹ and miracles ‹ and Sabbaths, ‹ Festivals

בְּצֵאתִי מִמִּצְרָיִם.

« from Egypt; ‹ when I went out

תַּעֲנִית וְאֵבֶל, וּרְדוֹף הַהֶבֶל, בְּצֵאתִי מִירוּשָׁלָיִם.

« from Jerusalem. ‹ when I went out ‹ of emptiness, ‹ and the pursuit ‹ and mourning ‹ but fasting

טֹבוּ אֹהָלִים, לְאַרְבָּעָה דְּגָלִים,* בְּצֵאתִי מִמִּצְרָיִם.

« from Egypt; ‹ when I went out ‹ flags,* ‹ [arranged under] four ‹ tents ‹ Goodly

וְאָהֳלֵי יִשְׁמְעֵאלִים, וּמַחֲנוֹת עֲרֵלִים,

‹ of the uncircumcised, ‹ and camps ‹ of the Ishmaelites ‹ but tents

בְּצֵאתִי מִירוּשָׁלָיִם.

« from Jerusalem. ‹ when I went out

---

17); (e) הַר חוֹרֵב, *Mount Horeb* (*Exodus* 3:1; 33:6; *I Kings* 19:8); and (f) הַר סִינַי, *Mount Sinai* (*Exodus* 19:18).

לְאַרְבָּעָה דְּגָלִים — *[Arranged under] four flags.* The Israelite camp in the Wilderness was in the shape of a square with three tribes on each side. The Torah ordained four tribes as the head of their respective sides. Thus, for example, the tribes of Judah, Issachar, and Zebulun camped on the eastern side under the דֶּגֶל מַחֲנֵה יְהוּדָה, *flag of Judah's camp.* With a similar arrangement on each side, the nation camped under four flags (see *Numbers* Ch. 2).

יוֹבֵל וּשְׁמִטָּה,[1] וְאֶרֶץ שׁוֹקֵטָה, בְּצֵאתִי מִמִּצְרָיִם.

« from Egypt; ‹ when I went out ‹ was tranquil, ‹ and the land ‹ and Sabbatical year, ‹ Jubilee year

מָכוּר לַצְּמִיתוּת,[2] וְכָרוּת וְכָתוּת,[3]

‹ and crushed, ‹ cut down ‹ for posterity; ‹ but I was sold

בְּצֵאתִי מִירוּשָׁלָיִם.

« from Jerusalem. ‹ when I went out

כַּפֹּרֶת וְאָרוֹן,[4] וְאַבְנֵי זִכָּרוֹן,[5] בְּצֵאתִי מִמִּצְרָיִם.

« from Egypt; ‹ when I went out ‹ of remembrance, ‹ and the stones ‹ and the Ark ‹ The [Ark's] Cover

וְאַבְנֵי הַקֶּלַע, וּכְלֵי הַבֶּלַע, בְּצֵאתִי מִירוּשָׁלָיִם.

« from Jerusalem. ‹ when I went out ‹ that devour, ‹ and weapons ‹ from the catapult ‹ but stones

לְוִיִּם וְאַהֲרֹנִים, וְשִׁבְעִים זְקֵנִים,[6] בְּצֵאתִי מִמִּצְרָיִם.

« from Egypt; ‹ when I went out ‹ elders, ‹ and the seventy ‹ and sons of Aaron ‹ Levites

נוֹגְשִׂים וּמוֹנִים, וּמוֹכְרִים וְקוֹנִים,

‹ and buyers, ‹ [slave-]sellers ‹ and tormentors, ‹ but tyrants

בְּצֵאתִי מִירוּשָׁלָיִם.

« from Jerusalem. ‹ when I went out

מֹשֶׁה יִרְעֵנוּ, וְאַהֲרֹן יַנְחֵנוּ, בְּצֵאתִי מִמִּצְרָיִם.

« from Egypt; ‹ when I went out ‹ would guide us, ‹ and Aaron ‹ would shepherd us, ‹ Moses

נְבוּכַדְנֶצַּר, וְאַנְדְּרִיָּנוּס* קֵיסָר, בְּצֵאתִי מִירוּשָׁלָיִם.

« from Jerusalem. ‹ when I went out ‹ the Emperor, ‹ and Hadrian* ‹ but Nebuchadnezzar

נַעֲרוֹךְ מִלְחָמָה, וַיהוה שָׁמָּה,[7] בְּצֵאתִי מִמִּצְרָיִם.

‹ from Egypt; ‹ when I went out ‹ was [with us] there, ‹ and HASHEM ‹ for battle, ‹ We arrayed

(1) See *Leviticus* 25:1-24. (2). Cf. *Leviticus* 25:23. (3). Cf. *Leviticus* 22:24 (4) See *Exodus* 25:10-22. (5) See 28:9-12.(6) See *Numbers* 11:16-17, 24-25. (7) Cf. *Exodus* 14:13.

נְבוּכַדְנֶצַּר וְאַנְדְּרִיָּנוּס — *Nebuchadnezzar and Hadrian.* The *kinnah* bewails the Destruction of both the First Temple by Nebuchadnezzar of Babylon, and the Second Temple by the Romans, here represented by Hadrian, the emperor who crushed the Bar Kochba revolution some sixty years later.

רָחֹק מִמֶּנּוּ, וְהִנֵּה אֵינֶנּוּ, בְּצֵאתִי מִירוּשָׁלָיִם.

« from Jerusalem. ‹ when I went out ‹ He [seemed] not present, ‹ and indeed, ‹ from us ‹ but He was distant

סִתְרֵי פָּרֹכֶת,[1] וְסִדְרֵי מַעֲרֶכֶת,[2] בְּצֵאתִי מִמִּצְרָיִם.

« from Egypt; ‹ when I went out ‹ array [of the Panim-bread], ‹ and the ordered ‹ by the Partition Curtain, ‹ The [Ark] concealed

חֵמָה נִתֶּכֶת, וְעָלַי סוֹכֶכֶת, בְּצֵאתִי מִירוּשָׁלָיִם.

« from Jerusalem. ‹ when I went out « hovered, ‹ and over me ‹ poured out [upon me like molten metal], ‹ but fury

עוֹלָה וּזְבָחִים, וְאִשֵּׁי נִיחוֹחִים, בְּצֵאתִי מִמִּצְרָיִם.

« from Egypt; ‹ when I went out ‹ that are pleasing, ‹ and fire offerings ‹ and sacrifices, ‹ Burnt offerings

בְּחֶרֶב מְדֻקָּרִים, בְּנֵי צִיּוֹן הַיְקָרִים,[3]

« who were precious, ‹ of Zion ‹ were the children ‹ stabbed ‹ but with the sword

בְּצֵאתִי מִירוּשָׁלָיִם.

« from Jerusalem. ‹ when I went out

פְּאֵרֵי מִגְבָּעוֹת, לְכָבוֹד נִקְבָּעוֹת,[4]

« designated, ‹ for [the priests'] honor ‹ turbans, ‹ Splendored

בְּצֵאתִי מִמִּצְרָיִם.

« from Egypt; ‹ when I went out

שְׁרִיקוֹת וּתְרוּעוֹת, וְקוֹלוֹת וּזְוָעוֹת,

‹ and trembling, ‹ loud cries ‹ and trumpet blasts, ‹ but whistle calls

בְּצֵאתִי מִירוּשָׁלָיִם.

« from Jerusalem. ‹ when I went out

צִיץ הַזָּהָב,[5] וְהַמְּשֵׁל וָרַהַב, בְּצֵאתִי מִמִּצְרָיִם.

« from Egypt; ‹ when I went out ‹ and power, ‹ sovereignty « of gold, ‹ The Head Plate

הֻשְׁלַךְ הַנֵּזֶר, וְאֶפֶס הָעֵזֶר, בְּצֵאתִי מִירוּשָׁלָיִם.

« from Jerusalem. ‹ when I went out « [Divine] help, ‹ and there was no [more] ‹ was the crown ‹ but thrown down

(1) See *Exodus* 26:31-33.(2) See *Leviticus* 24:5-9. (3) *Eichah* 4:2. (4) Cf. *Exodus* 39:28. (5) See 28:36-38.

קְדֻשָּׁה וּנְבוּאָה, וּכְבוֹד יהוה נִרְאָה,[1]
Sanctity / and prophecy, / and the glory / of HASHEM / was revealed,

בְּצֵאתִי מִמִּצְרָיִם.
when I went out / from Egypt;

נִגְאָלָה וּמוֹרְאָה,[2] וְרוּחַ הַטֻּמְאָה,
but abomination / and filth / and the spirit / of impurity,

בְּצֵאתִי מִירוּשָׁלָיִם.
when I went out / from Jerusalem.

רִנָּה וִישׁוּעָה, וַחֲצוֹצְרוֹת הַתְּרוּעָה,
Joyous song / and salvation, / and the [triumphant] trumpets / for sounding short blasts,

בְּצֵאתִי מִמִּצְרָיִם.
when I went out / from Egypt;

זַעֲקַת עוֹלָל, וְנַאֲקַת חָלָל, בְּצֵאתִי מִירוּשָׁלָיִם.
but wailing / of an infant / and groaning / of the mortally wounded, / when I went out / from Jerusalem.

שֻׁלְחָן[3] וּמְנוֹרָה,[4] וְכָלִיל וּקְטוֹרָה, בְּצֵאתִי מִמִּצְרָיִם.
[The Tabernacle's] Table / and Menorah, / burnt-offering / and incense, / when I went out / from Egypt;

אֱלִיל וְתוֹעֵבָה, וּפֶסֶל וּמַצֵּבָה, בְּצֵאתִי מִירוּשָׁלָיִם.
but idol / and abomination, / graven image / and [pagan] monument, / when I went out / from Jerusalem.

תּוֹרָה וּתְעוּדָה, וּכְלֵי הַחֶמְדָּה, בְּצֵאתִי מִמִּצְרָיִם.
Torah / and Testimony, / and the vessels / that are cherished, / when I went out / from Egypt;

שָׂשׂוֹן וְשִׂמְחָה, וְנָס יָגוֹן וַאֲנָחָה,[5]
joy / and gladness, / and the fleeing / of sadness / and sighing,

בְּשׁוּבִי לִירוּשָׁלָיִם.
when I return / to Jerusalem!

(1) Cf. *Exodus* 16:10. (2) Cf. *Zephaniah* 3:1.
(3) See *Exodus* 25:23-30.(4) See 25:31-40. (5) Cf. *Isaiah* 51:11.

KINNAH 32 / קינה לב

אֶצְבְּעוֹתַי שָׁפְלוּ,* וְאָשְׁיוֹתַי נָפְלוּ,[1] אוֹיָה.

« O woe! « fell, ‹ and my foundations ‹ were humbled* ‹ My fingers

בְּנֵי צִיּוֹן גָּלוּ, וְכָל אוֹיְבַי שָׁלוּ,[2]

« are at ease, ‹ my enemies ‹ while all ‹ were exiled ‹ of Zion ‹ The children

אוֹי מֶה הָיָה לָנוּ.

« to us! ‹ has happened ‹ What « O woe!

בַּיִת וַעֲזָרוֹת, בְּיוֹם אַף נִגָּרוֹת,[3] אוֹיָה.

« O woe! « are swept away, ‹ of anger ‹ on the day ‹ and its courtyards ‹ The Temple

פְּנֵי שָׂרִים וְשָׂרוֹת, כְּמוֹ שׁוּלֵי קְדֵרוֹת,

« of pots, ‹ the bottoms ‹ are [blackened] like ‹ and princesses ‹ of princes ‹ The faces

אוֹי מֶה הָיָה לָנוּ.

« to us! ‹ has happened ‹ What « O woe!

גֻּלַּת הַכּוֹתֶרֶת,[4] כְּנֵבֶל נִשְׁבֶּרֶת,[5] אוֹיָה.

« O woe! « are shattered, ‹ like a clay jug ‹ of the capitals ‹ The bowls

עֲטֶרֶת תִּפְאֶרֶת,[6] לָאָרֶץ נִגְרֶרֶת,

« is dragged down, ‹ to the ground « of splendor ‹ The crown

אוֹי מֶה הָיָה לָנוּ.

« to us! ‹ has happened ‹ What « O woe!

(1) Cf. *Jeremiah* 50:15. (2) *Eichah* 1:5. (3) Cf. *Job* 20:28. (4) *I Kings* 7:41. (5) Cf. *Isaiah* 30:14. (6) *Isaiah* 62:3.

אֶצְבְּעוֹתַי שָׁפְלוּ — *My fingers are humbled.* Many beautiful aspects of Jerusalem and its crowning glory, the Temple, are described and their disappearance is mourned in this *kinnah.* The greatest misfortune of all is that we once had so many opportunities to show our devotion to God and to be close to Him in the Temple, but now we are distant and alienated.

The stanzas of this *kinnah* bear an alphabetical acrostic, followed by the author's signature, בָּרוּךְ חֲזַק, *Baruch, may he be strong.* The first line of each stanza contains two stiches, and ends with the plaintive cry, אוֹיָה, *O woe!* The second line's two stiches are followed by, אוֹי מֶה

דַּרְכֵי עִיר אֲבֵלוֹת,[1] וַיֶּחְדְּלוּ הַקּוֹלוֹת[2] אוֹיָה.

The roads of the City mourn, and cease did the sounds [of her inhabitants], O woe!

אָרְחוֹת הַסְּלוּלוֹת, חֲשֵׁכוֹת וַאֲפֵלוֹת,

Her roads that are paved are darkened and gloomy

אוֹי מֶה הָיָה לָֽנוּ.

O woe! What has happened to us!

הֵיכָל וּכְתָלָיו, מֵעַי הָמוּ עָלָיו,[3] אוֹיָה.

The Sanctuary with its walls — my insides yearned for them, O woe!

וְעַל שֻׁלְחָן וְכֵלָיו, וּמְעִיל עַל שׁוּלָיו,

And for the Table and its vessels, and for the [*Kohen Gadol's*] robe [with pomegranates and bells] on its hem,

אוֹי מֶה הָיָה לָֽנוּ.

O woe! What has happened to us!

וָוֵי הָעַמּוּדִים,[4] בְּיַד בְּנֵי הָעֲבָדִים, אוֹיָה.

The hooks of the [Tabernacle's] pillars are [now] in the hand of the sons [Babylon,] of slaves O woe!

וְהֶקֵּף רוֹבְדִים, רַבִּים וְנִכְבָּדִים,[5] אוֹי מֶה הָיָה לָֽנוּ.

As are the surrounding flooring stones, many and stately O woe! What has happened to us!

זְבָחִים וּמְנָחוֹת, לְמַשּׁוּאוֹת[6] וּמַדּוּחוֹת,[7] אוֹיָה.

Sacrificial offerings and flour offerings are set for destruction and expulsion, O woe!

הֲדַר מִזְבְּחוֹת, בְּיָגוֹן וַאֲנָחוֹת, אוֹי מֶה הָיָה לָֽנוּ.

The glory of the altars is transformed into sadness and sighings, O woe! What has happened to us!

(1) Cf. *Eichah* 1:4. (2) *Exodus* 9:33. (3) *Song of Songs* 5:4.
(4) *Exodus* 27:10. (5) *Numbers* 22:15. (6) *Psalms* 73:18. (7) Cf. *Eichah* 2:14.

הָיָה לָֽנוּ, *O woe! What has happened to us!* The author, R' Baruch [probably R' Baruch ben Shmuel (died, Mainz, Germany, 1221)], was one of the Tosafists (*Ba'alei HaTosafos*) and served on the Mainz *beis din.* He wrote commentary to various tractates of the Talmud. His work *Sefer HaChochmah* is no longer extant.

חֵיל וְהַסּוֹרֵג, לְחֶרֶב וּלְהֶרֶג, אְוֹיָה.

The rampart 〈 and the [surrounding] fence 〈 were given over to sword 〈 and to slaughter, « O woe! «

בִּנְיָן הַנֶּאֱרָג, נָדַשׁ בְּמוֹרָג, אוֹי מֶה הָיָה לָנוּ.

The edifice 〈 [decorated] with weaver craft 〈 [is as if] threshed 〈 under the threshing boards, « O woe! « What 〈 has happened 〈 to us! «

טְלָאִים מְבֻקָּרִים, מֶנּוּ נֶעְדָּרִים, אְוֹיָה.

The lambs 〈 that were inspected [and found blemish free] 〈 [now] from us 〈 are missing « O woe! «

וְטַבָּעוֹת סְדוּרִים, וְנַנָּסִין הַהֲדוּרִים,

Along with the [restraining] rings 〈 in orderly rows, 〈 and the short pillars 〈 that were handsome, «

אוֹי מֶה הָיָה לָנוּ.

O woe! « What 〈 has happened 〈 to us! «

יְפִי נִבְרֶכֶת, אֵיכָה נֶהְפֶּכֶת, אְוֹיָה.

The beautiful 〈 water pool! « How 〈 has it been transformed [to ruin], « O woe! «

וְגֶפֶן וּפָרֹכֶת, וּמִנְחַת מֻרְבֶּכֶת,[1]

[Together with] the [golden] grapevine, 〈 the Partition Curtain, 〈 and the flour-offering 〈 that is scalded, «

אוֹי מֶה הָיָה לָנוּ.

O woe! « What 〈 has happened 〈 to us! «

כִּיּוֹר עִם כַּנּוֹ, הֲתָעִיף בּוֹ וְאֵינוֹ,[2] אְוֹיָה.

The Washbasin 〈 with 〈 its base, 〈 cast your eye 〈 at it 〈 and [in a blink] it is gone, « O woe! «

הַנֵּר עִם שַׁמְנוֹ, לֻקַּח מִמְּעוֹנוֹ, אוֹי מֶה הָיָה לָנוּ.

The lamp 〈 with 〈 its oil 〈 was taken 〈 from its dwelling place, « O woe! « What 〈 has happened 〈 to us! «

לֶחֶם הַפָּנִים, שְׂאוּ עָלָיו קִינִים, אְוֹיָה.

The Bread 〈 of Surfaces « — arouse 〈 for it 〈 lamentations, « O woe! «

(1) Cf. *Leviticus* 6:14. (2) Cf. *Proverbs* 23:5.

וְטוּרֵי רִמּוֹנִים, לְמִרְמָס נְתוּנִים, אוֹי מֶה הָיָה לָּנוּ.

And the rows of pomegranates [on the *Kohen Gadol's* robe] — to be trampled were given over, O woe! What has happened to us!

מְנוֹרָה הַטְּהוֹרָה, אוֹרָהּ נֶעְדָּרָה, אוֹיָה.

The Menorah that is pure — its light is missing, O woe!

וּמַגְרֵפָה יְקָרָה, נְטוּלָה וַחֲסֵרָה, אוֹי מֶה הָיָה לָּנוּ.

The coal rake that was heavy — was taken and is missing, O woe! What has happened to us!

נוֹי יָם הַנְּחֹשֶׁת,[1] לְעוֹבְדִים לַבֹּשֶׁת, אוֹיָה.

The beautiful sea of brass [was taken by] those who worship ignominious [idols], O woe!

וּמַעֲשֵׂה הָרֶשֶׁת, וְחַלּוֹת מַרְחֶשֶׁת,[2]

[Also the Altar's] work of [brass] netting and the [meal-offering] loaves, deep-pan-fried,

אוֹי מֶה הָיָה לָּנוּ.

O woe! What has happened to us!

סְלָתוֹת וּנְסָכִים, מֶנּוּ נֶחְשָׂכִים, אוֹיָה.

Fine meal-offerings and wine libations from us are witheld, O woe!

וּבוֹעַז וְגַם יָכִין,[3] לָאָרֶץ נִשְׁלָכִים,

And [the Temple pillars] Boaz as well as Yachin, to the ground they are thrown down,

אוֹי מֶה הָיָה לָּנוּ.

O woe! What has happened to us!

עַל מַחְתָּה וּמִזְרָק, אוֹיֵב שֵׁן חָרַק,[4] אוֹיָה.

Over the fire pan and the blood basin, the enemy — his teeth would gnash, O woe!

טֶנִי גַּם כּוּז זָרַק, וְאֶת חַרְבּוֹ הִבְרַק,

The basket as well as the jug [the enemy] threw down and his sword flashed,

(1) *II Kings* 25:13. (2) *Leviticus* 2:7. (3) See *I Kings* 7:21. (4) *Eichah* 2:16.

אוֹי מֶה הָיָה לָנוּ.

« to us! ‹ has happened ‹ What « O woe!

פִּשְׁפָּשִׁים וּשְׁעָרִים, אַרְצָה נִגְרָרִים, אוֹיָה.

« O woe! « are dragged, ‹ along the ground ‹ and large gates ‹ Small doors

הַתֻּמִּים וְהָאוּרִים, אֵיכָה נִסְתָּרִים,

« are they [now] hidden? ‹ where « and the Urim, ‹ The Tumim

אוֹי מֶה הָיָה לָנוּ.

« to us! ‹ has happened ‹ What « O woe!

צְפִירַת מַעֲטָפוֹת, בְּאֵיבָה נֶהְדָּפוֹת, אוֹיָה.

« O woe! « were knocked off ‹ with malice ‹ turbans ‹ The crownlike

לְשָׁכוֹת הַיָּפוֹת, וּבֵית הַחֲלָפוֹת, אוֹי מֶה הָיָה לָנוּ.

« to us! ‹ has happened ‹ What « O woe! « of the slaughtering knives ‹ and the repository ‹ that were beautiful ‹ The chambers

קִיר מָגֵן עֵרָה,[1] וְקַרְקַר הֶהָרָה,[2] אוֹיָה.

« O woe! « into the mountains, ‹ [and the Jerusalemites] ran screaming « they bared [against Jerusalem], ‹ their battle shields « [The warriors of] Kir,

וְזָרְקוּ הַמָּרָה, וְשָׂרְפוּ הַבִּירָה, אוֹי מֶה הָיָה לָנוּ.

« to us! ‹ has happened ‹ What « O woe! « the Temple, ‹ and burnt down ‹ bitterness [into the people] ‹ They injected

רָאשֵׁי מִשְׁמָרוֹת, סְבוּכִים בְּצָרוֹת, אוֹיָה.

« O woe! « in troubles, ‹ were entangled ‹ of the [Temple] watches ‹ The heads

וְשָׂרֵי הָעֲשָׂרוֹת, בְּיַד בַּעֲלֵי חֲטוֹטָרוֹת,

« staves, ‹ of those wielding ‹ [suffer] at the hand ‹ of ten ‹ And the captains

אוֹי מֶה הָיָה לָנוּ.

« to us! ‹ has happened ‹ What « O woe!

שַׁעַר בַּת רַבִּים,[3] לִזְאֵבֵי עֲרָבִים,[4] אוֹיָה.

« O woe! « of the wilderness, ‹ [is abandoned] to the wolves ‹ of the multitudes, ‹ the city ‹ The gates [of Jerusalem],

---

(1) Cf. *Isaiah* 22:6. (2) Cf. 22:5. (3) *Song of Songs* 7:5. (4) *Jeremiah* 5:6.

לֻקְּחוּ הַכְּרוּבִים, תֻּפִּים וַאֲבוּבִים,
« and flutes, ‹ [with the Levites'] drums ‹ are the Cherubim, ‹ Taken away

אוֹי מֶה הָיָה לָנוּ.
« to us! ‹ has happened ‹ What « O woe!

תָּאִים הַנָּאִים, לַבָּנִים הַשְּׂנוּאִים, אְוֹיָה.
« O woe! « who are despised, ‹ [have been given] to the sons [of Babylon] ‹ that are pleasing ‹ The rooms

בַּפָּז מְסֻלָּאִים,[1] לַחֲלָדוֹת הַסְּנָאִים,
« in the bush, ‹ are now like weasels ‹ are comparable, ‹ [While Zion's children] who to fine gold

אוֹי מֶה הָיָה לָנוּ.
« to us! ‹ has happened ‹ What « O woe!

בָּנִים הַיְּקָרִים, בַּחֲרָבוֹת נִדְקָרִים, אְוֹיָה.
« O woe! « stabbed, ‹ are by the sword ‹ who are precious ‹ [Zion's] children

לְוִיִּם הַמְּשׁוֹרְרִים, וְכֹהֲנִים מַקְטִירִים,
« who offer incense, ‹ and the *Kohanim* « the singers [in the Temple choir], « [So are] the Levites,

אוֹי מֶה הָיָה לָנוּ.
« to us! ‹ has happened ‹ What « O woe!

רוֹבִים וּפִרְחִים, לְחִצִּים וּשְׁלָחִים, אְוֹיָה.
« O woe! « and weapons of war, ‹ [were targets] for arrows ‹ and young [*Kohanim*] ‹ Youths

בְּכוֹרוֹת וְטִפּוּחִים, בְּיָגוֹן נֶאֱנָחִים, אוֹי מֶה הָיָה לָנוּ.
« to us! ‹ has happened ‹ What « O woe! « sigh, ‹ in sadness ‹ and babies they cared for ‹ Firstborn sons

וּמַפְתְּחוֹת זָרְקוּ, בְּשׁוּרָם כִּי לָקוּ, אְוֹיָה.
« O woe! « that they were beaten, ‹ when they saw ‹ [the *Kohanim* toward heaven] threw ‹ The keys [of the Temple]

(1) Cf. *Eichah* 4:2.

בְּעָוֹן נָמַקּוּ,[1] וְכַפַּיִם סָפָקוּ,[2] אוֹי מֶה הָיָה לָנוּ.

‹ Because of their iniquity, ‹ they deteriorated ‹ and [their] hands « they slapped [in anguish], « O woe! ‹ What ‹ has happened « to us!

כַּפּוֹת וּבָזִיכִים, מִנּוּ נִפְסָקִים, אוֹיָה.

‹ The incense spoons ‹ and cups [of *levonah]* ‹ from us « have been discontinued, « O woe!

וּבָנַי נֶאֱנָקִים, בְּאֶרֶץ מֶרְחַקִּים, אוֹי מֶה הָיָה לָנוּ.

‹ And my sons ‹ cry out from pain ‹ in a land « that is far off, « O woe! ‹ What ‹ has happened « to us!

חַי חוֹבוֹ גָּבָה, וְצִיץ טָהוֹר נִשְׁבָּה, אוֹיָה.

‹ The Living One ‹ His debt « He collected, ‹ and the [*Kohen Gadol's*] Head Plate ‹ of pure [gold] « was captured, « O woe!

נֵר מַעֲרָב כָּבָה, וְשִׂמְחַת בֵּית הַשּׁוֹאֵבָה, אוֹי מֶה הָיָה לָנוּ.

‹ The Lamp ‹ to the West ‹ was extinguished, ‹ as was the Rejoicing ‹ at the place « of the Water Drawing, « O woe! ‹ What ‹ has happened « to us!

זֵדִים בְּנֵי עֲדִינָה, עַל בְּנֵי מִי מָנָה,[3] אוֹיָה.

‹ The willful sinners ‹ sons [of Babylon and Edom], ‹ the pampered ones ‹ conquered ‹ the sons [of Israel] ‹ [described as] *Who* « *has counted,* « O woe!

פְּאֵר בִּגְדֵי כְהֻנָּה, בְּיָדָם נִתְּנָה, אוֹי מֶה הָיָה לָנוּ.

‹ The glorious ‹ garments ‹ of the priesthood ‹ into their hand « were given, « O woe! ‹ What ‹ has happened « to us!

קְטֹרֶת נֶעְדֶּרֶת, וְאָרוֹן וְכַפֹּרֶת, אוֹיָה.

‹ The incense offering ‹ is missing, ‹ as is the Ark « and its Cover, « O woe!

תִּכֵּן בַּזֶּרֶת,[4] תְּקַבֵּץ נִפְזֶרֶת,[5] יְשׁוּעָה תִּהְיֶה לָנוּ.

‹ [O God] Who fixed [the proportions of heaven] « with a span, ‹ gather ‹ the scattered ‹ and a salvation ‹ shall You be « unto us!

(1) Cf. *Leviticus* 26:39. (2) Cf. *Eichah* 2:15. (3) *Numbers* 23:10. (4) Cf. *Isaiah* 40:12. (5) Cf. *Jeremiah* 50:17.

KINNAH 33 / קינה לג

אֵבֶל אֲעוֹרֵר, אֲנִינוּת אֲגָרֵר, אוֹיָה לִי.

Mourning I shall arouse, grief I shall drag out — woe unto me!

בִּבְכִי אֲמָרֵר, בַּחֲמַת צוֹרֵר, דְּרָכַי סוֹרֵר,[1] אַלְלַי לִי.

Through weeping I am embittered, because of the fury of the tormentor, who my path, he has strewn with thorns — woe unto me!

גָּלוּת אָרַךְ, וְלִבִּי הֵרַךְ,[2] אוֹיָה לִי.

The exile [God] lengthened, and my heart grew fearful — woe unto me!

דָּרַךְ וּפָרַךְ, נָהֲנִי נַחְשָׁרָךְ,[3] וְצֵידוֹ חָרַךְ,[4] אַלְלַי לִי.

[The enemy] trampled and crushed in slavery, lead me [into captivity] did the hunter [Esau-Edom], and his captured prey he burned [the wings to immobilize it] — woe unto me!

הַמְעַט מַבְאִישַׁי, חִלְּלוּ מִקְדָּשַׁי, אוֹיָה לִי.

Is it insignificant that those who make me odious, also desecrated my Sanctuaries? — woe unto me!

וְהֵם בָּזוּ קֳדָשַׁי, הֵחֵלּוּ מִמְּקֻדָּשַׁי,[5] וְזִלְזְלוּ קְדוֹשַׁי, אַלְלַי לִי.

And they despoiled my holy things, beginning with my holy people [the Sages], they treated with contempt my holy ones — woe unto me!

(1) *Eichah* 3:11. (2) Cf. Job 23:16. (3) *Cf. Targum Genesis* 25:27. (4) *Cf. Proverbs* 12:27. (5) Cf. *Ezekiel* 9:6.

⊰ אֵבֶל אֲעוֹרֵר — *Mourning I shall arouse.* This *kinnah* bemoans the atrocities and calamities which befell the Jewish people during the First Crusade in the year 1096 C.E. (4856 from Creation). These events have already been described in much greater detail in *kinnah* 25. The author's signature appears in the acrostic after the *aleph-beis;* it reads אָנֹכִי מְנַחֵם הֶעָלוּב בְּרַבִּי מָכִיר, *I am Menachem, the unworthy one, the son of R' Machir.* The author's father, R' Machir, was a brother to Rabbeinu Gershom *Meor HaGolah.* His Talmudic lexicon is quoted by *Rashi.* R' Menachem, together with

זְמַן שְׁנַת תַּתְנ״ו, בְּיָ״א לְמַחֲזוֹר רְנ״ו,* אוֹיָה לִי.

《unto me! 〈 — woe 《 of 256 [years for leap years]* 〈 of the cycle 〈 in the eleventh year 〈 4856 [from Creation] 〈 was the year 〈 The time

חֲיָלוֹת זִיְּנוּ, מְקוֹמָם פִּנּוּ, כָּאַרְבֶּה נִמְנוּ, אַלְלַי לִי.

《unto me! 〈 — woe 《 were they counted 〈 like locusts 《 they emptied out, 〈 from their places 《 armed themselves, 〈 Troops of soldiers

טֶרֶף בִּקְשׁוּ,[1] וְעָלַי הִקְשׁוּ,[2] אוֹיָה לִי.

《unto me! 〈 — woe 《 they placed a severe burden 〈 upon me 《 they sought, 〈 When provisions

יִרְאָתָם קִשְׁקְשׁוּ, וְאוֹתוֹת הִקִּישׁוּ, וְאוֹתִי עִקְּשׁוּ, אַלְלַי לִי.

《they claimed was perverted 〈 and my [belief] 〈 they all were equal, 〈 with their [crucifix] symbols 《 they rallied, 〈 In the name of their deity

《unto me! 〈 — woe

כֹּפֶר מָאָסוּ, וּנְפָשׁוֹת חָמָסוּ, אוֹיָה לִי.

《unto me! 〈 — woe 《 they plundered 〈 but souls 《 they rejected, 〈 Ransom

לְוִיַּי בּוֹסָסוּ, כֹּהֲנַי בּוֹשָׁסוּ, צְנוּעַי אָנָסוּ, אַלְלַי לִי.

《unto me! 〈 — woe 《 they ravished 〈 and my modest women 《 they trampled, 〈 my priests 《 they stomped, 〈 My Levites

מְתֵי חֶרֶב מְהֻדָּמִים, בְּאֶפֶס דָּמִים, אוֹיָה לִי.

《unto me! 〈 — woe 《 blood-guilt 〈 without any 《 were cut to pieces, 〈 by the sword 〈 Those killed

(1) Some editions read טָעוּת בִּקְשׁוּ, *to misguide me they sought.*
(2) Some editions read וְעֻלִּי הִקְשׁוּ, *my yoke they made heavy.*

his brother, compiled a halachic work called *Maaseh HaMachiri*, which is extensively cited in *Sefer HaPardes* and *Sefer HaOrah*. Although primarily a halachist, R' Menachem wrote other liturgical compositions, including: אָדָם בְּקוּם, recited in the *Selichos* for Taanis Esther; and כְּהוֹשַׁעְתָּ אָדָם, recited on the Sabbath of Succos.

שְׁנַת תַּתְנ״ו בְּיָ״א לְמַחֲזוֹר רְנ״ו — *The year 4856 . . . in the eleventh year of the cycle of 256 [years for leap years].* There is a period of about eleven days by which the solar year exceeds the lunar twelve months. The calendars can be brought into alignment by intercalating a thirteenth month (of thirty days) seven times every nineteen years. 255 of these nine 19-year cycles total 4845 years. Adding eleven years to this total brings us to 4856, the eleventh year in the 256th nineteen-year cycle.

נְבֵלַת תְּמִימִים, בְּלִי מוּמִים, הָיוּ שׁוֹמֵמִים,

The corpses ‹ of the perfectly righteous, « without any ‹ blemish [from any sin], « were ‹ abandoned [without burial] «

אַלְלַי לִי.

— woe ‹ unto me! «

סָחוּב וְהֻשְׁלַךְ,[1] עֵרוֹם לְלַכְלֵךְ, אוֹיָה לִי.

They were dragged on the ground ‹ and thrown down, « [stripped] naked, ‹ to be fouled « — woe ‹ unto me! «

עוֹבְרַי בְּכָל פֶּלֶךְ,[2] חֵיל יָרֵב מֶלֶךְ,[3] וְרָדוּ בְּפֶלֶךְ,

Those who trod over me ‹ through every ‹ district, « the army ‹ that prepared to fight ‹ [God] the King, « and who controlled ‹ all of the district «

אַלְלַי לִי.

— woe ‹ unto me! «

פְּרִיעָה וּפְרִימָה, עַל תּוֹרָה תְּמִימָה,[4] אוֹיָה לִי.

Let [your hair] grow long ‹ and rend [your garments] ‹ over ‹ the [desecrated] Torah ‹ that is perfect « — woe ‹ unto me! «

צָר בְּיָד רָמָה, הַמְּסֻכָּן תְּרוּמָה,[5] נָם לְהַחֲרִימָה,

The tormentor ‹ with hand ‹ upraised, « trained [in selecting wood] ‹ to contruct an offering [to his idols], « announced [his intention] ‹ to totally consecrate [Israel to his idol] «

אַלְלַי לִי.

— woe ‹ unto me! «

קוֹל בָּתֵּי כְנֵסִיּוֹת, וּבָתֵּי תוּשִׁיּוֹת, אוֹיָה לִי.

O the outcries ‹ from the houses ‹ of prayer ‹ and the houses ‹ of study « — woe ‹ unto me! «

רַחֲמָנִיּוֹת בִּידֵיהֶן נְקִיּוֹת, זִבְחֵי רְאִיּוֹת, אַלְלַי לִי.

Compassionate [mothers] ‹ [slaughtered their children] with their own hands ‹ that were innocent, ‹ as if they were the sacrifices ‹ of the festival [when one appears before God] « — woe ‹ unto me! «

(1) *Jeremiah* 22:19. (2) Some editions read עוֹבְרַי, *those who passed;* others read עוֹבְדֵי לַמֹּלֶךְ, *those who worshiped the Molech.* (3) Cf. *Hosea* 5:13. (4) Cf. *Psalms* 19:8. (5) *Isaiah* 40:20.

שְׁלָמִים וְעוֹלוֹת, חֲתָנִים וְכַלּוֹת, אוֹיָה לִי.

[Like] peace-offerings ‹ and burnt-offerings, ‹ grooms ‹ and brides [were slaughtered] « — woe ‹ unto me! «

תּוֹדוֹת וּבְלִילוֹת, בַּחוּרִים וּבְתוּלוֹת, וְטוֹבֵי קְהִלּוֹת,

Like thanksgiving-offerings ‹ and flour-offerings that are mixed, « young men ‹ and young maidens ‹ and the elite leaders ‹ of the community [were sacrificed] «

אַלְלַי לִי.

— woe ‹ unto me! «

אַחִים גַּם יַחַד, נִשְׁפַּךְ דָּמָם כְּאֶחָד, אוֹיָה לִי.

Brothers [who lived] ‹ especially ‹ in harmony, « shed ‹ was their blood ‹ as one « — woe ‹ unto me! «

כֵּן אֲחָיוֹת בְּפַחַד, בְּיִרְאַת שֵׁם הַמְּיֻחָד,

Similarly, ‹ sisters who shared ‹ the fear [of God] ‹ in reverence ‹ for the Name ‹ of the One and Only God, «

לַטֶּבַח לְהֵאָחֵד, אַלְלַי לִי.

in their slaughter ‹ they were united « — woe ‹ unto me! «

הוֹגֵי מִלְחֲמוֹת סֵפֶר, נֶשֶׁף וָצֶפֶר, אוֹיָה לִי.

Those who were engrossed ‹ in the argumentation ‹ in the [Torah] volumes ‹ [every] evening ‹ and morning « — woe ‹ unto me! «

חֵיךְ אִמְרֵי שֶׁפֶר,[1] מָלֵא חָצָץ וָאֵפֶר,[2]

The palate [filled] ‹ with [Torah] sayings ‹ that are beautiful ‹ is full ‹ with gravel ‹ and ashes; «

וְאַיֵּה שׁוֹקֵל וְסוֹפֵר,[3] אַלְלַי לִי.

and where are ‹ [those scholars] who weighed ‹ and counted [every Torah letter]? « — woe ‹ unto me! «

הֶהָיְתָה זֹּאת מֵאָז, עָלָה עַם עָז, אוֹיָה לִי.

Has there occurred ‹ similar [tragedy] ‹ since days of yore, « that there should rise up ‹ a nation ‹ so brazen [against God]? « — Woe ‹ unto me! «

---

(1) Cf. *Genesis* 49:21. (2) Cf. *Eichah* 3:16. (3) Cf. *Isaiah* 33:18.

לְהַשְׁמִיד הוֹעֲז, וְאֶסַּף עַם נוֹעָז,[1] אֲרָם וְלוֹעֵז,[2] אַלְלַי לִי.

To destroy [the Jews] ‹ they had the audacity, « and they assembled ‹ nations ‹ fierce, « Aram ‹ and others who spoke foreign languages « — woe ‹ unto me! «

בִּקֵּשׁ עֶקֶר, רַק לַעֲקוֹר וּלְעַקֵּר, אוֹיָה לִי.

Attempt ‹ did these idolatrous nations ‹ nothing but ‹ to uproot [us] ‹ and to leave us barren « — woe ‹ unto me! «

(בְּקַר אַרְמָאִי מְשַׁקֵּר,)[3] יָזַם הַזָּר[4] לְעַקֵּר,

(In the measuring line [of justice], ‹ the Aramean ‹ acted deceitfully) « and plot ‹ did the alien ‹ to uproot [me] ‹

וְלֹא לְגָרֵם לַבֹּקֶר,[5] אַלְלַי לִי.

and not ‹ to leave a bone ‹ for the morning « — woe ‹ unto me! «

מְקַיֵּם הַבְּרִית, לוּלֵי הוֹתִיר שְׁאֵרִית,

[O God] Who upholds ‹ the covenant, « had You not ‹ left over ‹ a remnant to survive ‹

בְּגֵיא נָכְרִית, (אוֹיָה לִי.)[6]

in the valley ‹ of foreign exile; « (— woe ‹ unto me)! «

בְּשָׁר שַׁעֲרוּרִית, יְדִידַת עִבְרִית,

When He observed ‹ the wretched misery ‹ of His beloved ‹ Hebrews, «

רִחַם מֵהַכְרִית, וְיֵשׁ תִּקְוָה לְאַחֲרִית.[7]

He mercifully saved [us] ‹ from annihilation, « and there is yet ‹ hope ‹ for our future! «

---

(1) *Isaiah* 33:19. (2) Some editions read בְּנֵי נָבָל וְלוֹעֵז, *the children of the degenerate and speakers of foreign tongues,* a reading that completes the acrostic of the author's signature [see commentary].
(3) Some editions omit the words in parentheses.
(4) Some editions read אֲרַמִּי, *the Aramean,* instead of הַזָּר, *the alien.*
(5) Cf. *Zephaniah* 3:3. (6) *Cf. Isaiah* 1:9. (7) Cf. *Jeremiah* 31:16.

לוֹבֵשׁ נְקָמָה, עוּרָה וְקוּמָה,

〈 and arise 〈 awaken 《 the robes of revenge, 〈 [O You] Who dons

הָרִים שִׁפְלֵי קוֹמָה,

《 stature, 〈 those of downtrodden 〈 and elevate

יָדִין גְּוִיּוֹת רִקְמָה.

《 [that You Yourself] had knit together, 〈 for the corpses 〈 and do justice

וּשְׁכִינָה קָמָה עַל מְקוֹמָהּ.

《 its place. 〈 to 〈 rise 〈 and let the Divine Presence

KINNAH 34 / קינה לד

יוֹם אַכְפִּי הִכְבַּדְתִּי,*[1] וַיִּכְפְּלוּ עֲוֹנִי,

« was my iniquity, ‹ for doubled « I greatly increased,* ‹ my subservience ‹ On that day,

בִּשְׁלְחִי יַד בְּדַם נָבִיא בַּחֲצַר אֵל מִקְדַּשׁ יהוה,

« of HASHEM. ‹ in the Sanctuary « of God, ‹ in the Courtyard ‹ of the prophet ‹ to spill the blood ‹ my hand ‹ When I stretched out

וְלֹא כִסַּתְהוּ אֲדָמָה עַד בֹּא חֶרֶב מוֹנַי,

« of my tormentors; ‹ of the sword ‹ the arrival ‹ until ‹ would the earth ‹ cover it ‹ But not

וְלֹא שָׁקַט עֲדֵי הֻקַּם דַּם הַנָּבִיא זְכַרְיָה,

« Zechariah. ‹ of the prophet ‹ was the blood ‹ avenged ‹ until ‹ did [the blood] rest, ‹ nor

וַיֶּרֶב בְּבַת יְהוּדָה תַּאֲנִיָּה וַאֲנִיָּה.[2]

« and grief. ‹ mourning ‹ of Judah ‹ within the daughter ‹ And He multiplied

הָיָה הוֹלֵךְ וְסוֹעֵר, עַד בֹּא רַב טַבָּחִים,

« of the executioners, ‹ of the chief ‹ the arrival ‹ until ‹ to churn ‹ continue ‹ [The blood] would

וּבָא אֶל מִקְדַּשׁ יהוה, וּמָצָא דָמִים רוֹתְחִים,

« boiling. ‹ blood ‹ and found ‹ of HASHEM ‹ the Sanctuary ‹ to ‹ He came

וַיִּשְׁאַל בַּעֲבוּר זֶה, הַכֹּהֲנִים הַזּוֹבְחִים,

« who were slaughtering [offerings]. ‹ [from] the *Kohanim* ‹ this ‹ about ‹ He inquired

וַיַּעֲנוּהוּ כִּי זֶה הוּא, דַּם קָרְבַּן הַזְּבָחִים,

« that was slaughtered. ‹ of a sacrificial offering ‹ the blood ‹ is ‹ this ‹ that ‹ And they answered him

(1) Cf. *Job* 33:7. (2) *Eichah* 2:5.

⁂ **יוֹם אַכְפִּי הִכְבַּדְתִּי** — *On that day my subservience I greatly increased.* The wicked King Joash brought a pagan idol into the Holy Temple. The prophet Zechariah ben Jehoiada protested this brazen desecration, and the king ordered that he be stoned to death. By being complicit in this cold-blooded murder, the nation became guilty of a sevenfold crime: (1) The murder of an innocent person; (2) who was a *Kohen;* (3) a prophet; (4) and a judge; (5) the desecration of the Temple Courtyard; (6) on Yom Kippur, (7) which was also a Sabbath day (see *II Chronicles* 24:20-21 and *Koheles Rabbah* 3:20).

וַיְנַסֶּה בְּדַם פָּרִים וְדַם אֵילִים וְדַם מֵחִים,

« of fattened animals; ‹ and the blood ‹ of rams, ‹ the blood ‹ of cows, ‹ with the blood ‹ He tried to match [the churning blood]

וְגַם זָבַח זֶבַח רַב, לַחֲקוֹר מֶה הָיָה,

« had occurred. ‹ what ‹ to investigate ‹ many sacrifices ‹ he slaughtered ‹ in addition

וַיֶּרֶב בְּבַת יְהוּדָה תַּאֲנִיָּה וַאֲנִיָּה.

« and grief. ‹ mourning ‹ of Judah ‹ within the daughter ‹ And He multiplied

וּבְכָל זֹאת לֹא שָׁקַט, וְעוֹדוֹ כַּיָּם נִגְרָשׁ,[1]

« when it is turbulent. ‹ like the sea ‹ but continued « rest, ‹ [the blood] did not ‹ this, ‹ Despite all

וַיְבֻקַּשׁ הַדָּבָר וַיִּמָּצֵא מְפֹרָשׁ,[2]

« explicitly, ‹ and it was discovered ‹ was the matter ‹ Investigated

כִּי הוּא דַּם אִישׁ הָאֱלֹהִים עַל לֹא חָמָס[3] שֹׁרָשׁ,

« was uprooted. ‹ crime ‹ no ‹ [who] for ‹ of God ‹ of the man ‹ the blood ‹ it was ‹ that

וַיֹּאמֶר נְבוּזַרְאֲדָן, גַּם דָּמוֹ הִנֵּה נִדְרָשׁ,[4]

« *being avenged!* ‹ *is now* ‹ *his blood* ‹ *More-over,* « Nebuzaradan then declared,

אִסְפוּ לִי הַכֹּהֲנִים, וְהוֹצִיאוּם מִבֵּית יָהּ,

« *of God,* ‹ *from the House* ‹ *and take them out* ‹ *the Kohanim* ‹ *unto me* ‹ *Gather*

כִּי לֹא אֶשְׁקוֹט, עַד יִשְׁקוֹט, דַּם הַנָּבִיא זְכַרְיָה,

« *Zechariah.* ‹ *of the prophet* ‹ *is the blood* ‹ *at rest* ‹ *until* ‹ *I shall not be at rest,* ‹ *for*

וַיֶּרֶב בְּבַת יְהוּדָה תַּאֲנִיָּה וַאֲנִיָּה.

« and grief. ‹ mourning ‹ of Judah ‹ within the daughter ‹ And He multiplied

(1) Cf. *Isaiah* 57:20. (2) Cf. *Esther* 2:23. (3) *Isaiah* 53:9. (4) Cf. *Genesis* 42:22.

The blood of Zechariah lay uncovered on the stone floor of the Temple Courtyard for 250 years during which it continued to seethe and bubble as a sign of God's fury against the nation. The blood thus pointed an accusing finger, and demanded the retribution described in this *kinnah,* which is based on the following Talmudic account:

The Babylonian general Nebuzaradan was spurred on by the sight of the blood of the murdered prophet Zechariah seething on the floor of the Temple. At first, the

דָּקַר יְשִׁישִׁים לְמֵאוֹת וּבַחוּרִים לְרִבּוֹאוֹת,

He stabbed ‹ elders ‹ by the hundreds ‹ and youths ‹ by the tens of thousands, «

וַיּוֹרֶד לָטֶבַח כֹּהֲנֵי יהוה צְבָאוֹת,

and he brought down ‹ to the slaughter ‹ the *Kohanim* ‹ of HASHEM, ‹ Master of Legions. «

וְאֵין שֶׁקֶט לְדַם נָבִיא, וַיְהִי לְמוֹפֵת וָאוֹת,

Yet there was no ‹ rest ‹ for the blood ‹ of the prophet; « and this was an [amazing] wonder ‹ and a [clear] sign. «

וְהַבָּנִים נִשְׁחָטִים, וְעֵינֵי אָבוֹת רוֹאוֹת,

For the children ‹ were slaughtered ‹ while the eyes ‹ of their fathers ‹ watched, «

וְאִמּוֹתָם לַטֶּבַח, גַּם אַחֲרֵיהֶם בָּאוֹת,

and their mothers ‹ to the slaughter, ‹ too, ‹ after them ‹ came. «

וָאֹמַר לְנַפְשִׁי זֶה חַטָּאתֵךְ וְזֶה פִּרְיָהּ,

And I said ‹ to myself, « *This is your sin* ‹ *and this* ‹ *is its fruit!* «

וַיֶּרֶב בְּבַת יְהוּדָה תַּאֲנִיָּה וַאֲנִיָּה.

And He multiplied ‹ within the daughter ‹ of Judah ‹ mourning ‹ and grief. «

הוֹסִיף לַהֲרוֹג נָשִׁים עִם יוֹנְקֵי שָׁדָיִם,

He continued ‹ to kill ‹ women ‹ with ‹ those who nurse ‹ at the breast. «

וְדָם עוֹלֶה בֵּינֵיהֶם, כְּדַם יְאוֹר מִצְרָיִם,

And the blood ‹ surged up ‹ among them ‹ like the blood ‹ of the [Nile] river ‹ of Egypt [when flooding], «

עֲדֵי נָשָׂא נְבוּזַרְאֲדָן לִבּוֹ לַשָּׁמַיִם,

until ‹ lift ‹ did Nebuzaradan ‹ his heart ‹ toward heaven ‹

Jews sought to conceal the true story connected with the blood. Eventually, however, they had to confess that it was the blood of a prophet who had prophesied the Destruction of the Temple, and had been slain by the people for his candor.

"I," said Nebuzaradan, "will appease him." He ordered the scholars of the kingdom to be executed on that bloody spot, then the schoolchildren, and at last the young *Kohanim* — more than 940,000 in all.

But the blood of the prophet went on seething until Nebuzaradan exclaimed: "Zechariah, Zechariah! I have destroyed the flower of them. Do you wish me to massacre them all?"

Only then did the blood rest.

וַיֹּאמֶר, הַאֵין דַּי בִּבְנוֹת יְרוּשָׁלָיִם,

« of Jerusalem? ‹ among the daughters ‹ enough ‹ Are there not « and said,

הֲכָלָה אַתָּה עוֹשֶׂה לִשְׁאֵרִית[1] הַשְּׁבִיָּה,

« *from the captivity?* ‹ *to the remnant* ‹ *intend to do* ‹ *do you* ‹ *An annihilation*

וַיֶּרֶב בְּבַת יְהוּדָה תַּאֲנִיָּה וַאֲנִיָּה.

« and grief. ‹ mourning ‹ of Judah ‹ within the daughter ‹ And He multiplied

(לְךָ חָטָאנוּ אֱלֹהִים, הֶעֱוִינוּ וְהִרְשַׁעְנוּ,

« and we have been wicked; ‹ we have been iniquitous « O God, ‹ have we sinned, ‹ (To You

וְהָרַגְנוּ נְבִיאֶךָ וְרִשְׁעֵנוּ יָדָעְנוּ,

« we recognize. ‹ and our wickedness ‹ Your prophets ‹ we have killed

יְהִי חַסְדְּךָ לְנַחֲמֵנוּ, כִּי מִשְּׁאוֹל שִׁוַּעְנוּ,

« do we cry, ‹ from the grave ‹ for ‹ comfort us, ‹ Your kindness ‹ Let

וּמִפְּרִי מַעֲלָלֵינוּ זֶה כַּמֶּה שָׂבָעְנוּ,

« have we been sated. ‹ many years ‹ for these « of our misdeeds, ‹ and on the fruits

רַחֵם לֹא רֻחָמָה,[2] הַסֹּעֲרָה עֲנִיָּה,[3]

‹ afflicted one, ‹ the storm-tossed, « on *Not Pitied,* ‹ Have pity

עֵינֶיהָ לְךָ תִשָּׂא, וְאֶת עֶזְרָתְךָ צוֹפִיָּה.)

« anticipates.) ‹ and Your help ‹ lifts, ‹ to You ‹ who her eyes

(1) Cf. *Ezekiel* 11:13. (2) *Hosea* 2:25,1:6. (3) Cf. *Isaiah* 54:11.

Thoughts of repentance came to Nebuzaradan's mind: If the Jews, who killed one person only, have been so severely punished, what will be my fate?

He left, and ultimately converted to Judaism (*Sanhedrin* 96b).

This *kinnah* was composed by R' Yehudah HaLevi (see commentary to *Kinnah* 36), whose name יְהוּדָה forms the acrostic of the five stanzas. A sixth stanza (printed here in parentheses) appears in the Sefardic rite, and forms the acrostic לֵוִי, *Levi.*

KINNAH 35 / קינה לה

שִׁכֹּרַת וְלֹא מִיַּיִן*[1] הַשְׁלִיכִי תֻפַּיִךְ,
[O Israel] drunk, ‹ but not ‹ from wine,* « throw down your drums! «

קָרְחִי נָא וָגֹזִּי[2] וְהַשְׁחִיתִי אַפַּיִךְ,
Tear out [your hair] ‹ now ‹ and cut it off! « Mutilate ‹ your face! «

שְׂאִי עַל שְׁפָיִם קִינָה[3] וְסֹבִי אֲגַפַּיִךְ.
Call out ‹ upon ‹ the hilltops ‹ with lament, « and circle around ‹ your borders. «

וְצַעֲקִי לִפְנֵי יהוה עַל חֹרֶב סִפַּיִךְ,
And cry out ‹ before ‹ HASHEM ‹ about ‹ the destruction ‹ of your [Temple's] gateways, «

עַל חֹרֶב סִפַּיִךְ, עַל נֶפֶשׁ עוֹלָלַיִךְ,[4]
about ‹ the destruction ‹ of your [Temple's] vessels, « about ‹ the life ‹ of your young children; «

שְׂאִי אֵלָיו כַּפַּיִךְ.
lift up ‹ to Him [in prayer] ‹ your hands. «

אֵיכָה בָּא צַר וְאוֹיֵב[5] בְּצִיּוֹן עִיר מַמְלֶכֶת,
O how ‹ would there enter ‹ an adversary ‹ and an enemy ‹ into Zion, ‹ the city ‹ of royalty; «

אֵיכָה רֶגֶל זֵדִים אַדְמַת קֹדֶשׁ דּוֹרֶכֶת,
how ‹ were the feet ‹ of the willful ‹ on the ground ‹ that is holy, ‹ able to tread? «

---

(1) Cf. *Isaiah* 51:21. (2) Cf. *Micah* 1:16. (3) Cf. *Jeremiah* 7:29. (4) Cf. *Eichah* 2:19. (5) 4:12; *Esther* 7:6.

שִׁכֹּרַת וְלֹא מִיַּיִן — *Drunk, but not from wine.* The prophet Isaiah foretells of the shock which will overcome Israel after the Destruction, a trauma that will delude their intellect:

Awaken! Awaken! Stand up, O Jerusalem! You who have drunk from the hand of HASHEM the cup of His fury; you have drunk down to the very dregs the deep bowl which makes you stagger .... Therefore, now hear this, you who are afflicted, drunk, but not from wine! (*Isaiah* 51:17,21). The author here vividly describes the terrible cruelties that befell Israel and the destruction that numbed their hearts and their minds.

The author's name שְׁלֹמֹה, *Shlomo*, appears in the first four words. He is usually identified as R' Shlomo ben Yitzchak of thirteenth-century Gerona, Spain.

בְּבוֹאָם מָצְאוּ כֹּהֲנִים שׁוֹמְרֵי הַמַּעֲרֶכֶת,

When they entered ‹ they found ‹ the *Kohanim,* « the guardians ‹ of the sacrificial order; ‹

וְעַל מִשְׁמְרוֹתָם עָמְדוּ וְלֹא עָזְבוּ הַמְּלָאכֶת,

at ‹ their guard-posts ‹ they were standing, « not ‹ abandoning ‹ the service, «

עַד אֲשֶׁר שֻׁפַּךְ דָּמָם כְּמֵימֵי הַמַּהְפֶּכֶת,

until ‹ when ‹ spilled ‹ was their blood ‹ like the waters ‹ of [the Nile] that were changed [into blood]. «

וּבָא עָרֵל וְטָמֵא[1] מִבֵּית לַפָּרֹכֶת,

Then enter ‹ did the uncircumcised ‹ and defiled ‹ [the Holiest of the Holies] within ‹ the Partition Curtain, «

לַמָּקוֹם אֲשֶׁר כֹּהֵן גָּדוֹל יָרֵא שָׁם לָלֶכֶת,

the place ‹ where ‹ the *Kohen Gadol* ‹ feared ‹ there ‹ to go, «

וְהֶחֱרִיבוּ סִפַּיִךְ וְחַלּוֹנֵי שְׁקוּפַיִךְ.[2]

and they destroyed ‹ your gateways ‹ and your windows ‹ that were wide [on the outside]. «

וְצַעֲקִי לִפְנֵי יהוה עַל חֹרֶב סִפַּיִךְ,

And cry out ‹ before ‹ HASHEM ‹ about ‹ the destruction ‹ of your [Temple's] gateways, «

עַל חֹרֶב סִפַּיִךְ, עַל נֶפֶשׁ עוֹלָלַיִךְ, שְׂאִי אֵלָיו כַּפַּיִךְ.

about ‹ the destruction ‹ of your [Temple's] vessels, « about ‹ the life ‹ of your young children; « lift up ‹ to Him [in prayer] ‹ your hands. «

קוֹל יִלְלַת בַּת צִיּוֹן מֵרָחוֹק נִשְׁמַעַת,

The sound ‹ of the wailing ‹ of the daughter ‹ of Zion ‹ from afar ‹ is heard, «

תִּזְעַק זַעֲקַת חֶשְׁבּוֹן[3] תִּבְכֶּה בְּכִי מֵיפָעַת,[4]

she cries out ‹ as once cried out Cheshbon; « she weeps ‹ as once wept ‹ Mephaath. «

אֲהָהּ כִּי כּוֹס שָׁתִיתִי וּמָצִיתִי קֻבַּעַת,[5]

Ah, woe! « *For* ‹ *the cup [of retribution]* ‹ *I have drunk deeply of* ‹ *and I have sucked dry* ‹ *its bitter dregs!* «

---

(1) Some editions read וּבָא כָּל עָרֵל וְטָמֵא, *Then entered all those uncircumcised and defiled.*
(2) Cf. *I Kings* 6:4. (3) See *Jeremiah* 48:34.(4) See 48:21. (5) Cf. *Isaiah* 51:17.

אֲכָלְוּנִי אֲרָיוֹת[1] חֲדוּדֵי מַלְתָּעַת,

Consumed me ‹ have lions ‹ with sharpened ‹ molars, «

בַּת בָּבֶל הַשְּׁדוּדָה וּבַת הַמַּרְשַׁעַת,

the daughter ‹ of Babylon ‹ that was about to be violated, ‹ and the daughter [of Edom] ‹ the wicked one. «

מַה תִּתְאוֹנְנִי צִיּוֹן וְחַטֹּאתֵךְ נוֹדָעַת,

Why ‹ do you complain, ‹ O Zion, ‹ when your sins ‹ are well known! «

עַל רֹב עֲוֹנֵךְ[2] גָּלָה עַמֵּךְ מִבְּלִי דָעַת,[3]

Because of ‹ the abundance ‹ of your iniquities, « exiled ‹ was your nation, « for your lack ‹ of knowledge [of God's ways]; «

עַל עָזְבֵךְ צוֹפַיִךְ וְשָׁמְעֵךְ קוֹל תְּרָפַיִךְ.

because of ‹ your abandoning ‹ your seers, ‹ and your listening ‹ to the voice ‹ of your idolatrous oracles. «

וְצַעֲקִי לִפְנֵי יהוה עַל חֹרֶב סִפַּיִךְ,

And cry out ‹ before ‹ HASHEM ‹ about ‹ the destruction ‹ of your [Temple's] gateways, «

עַל חֹרֶב סִפַּיִךְ, עַל נֶפֶשׁ עוֹלָלַיִךְ, שְׂאִי אֵלָיו כַּפַּיִךְ.

about ‹ the destruction ‹ of your [Temple's] vessels, « about ‹ the life ‹ of your young children; « lift up ‹ to Him [in prayer] ‹ your hands. «

אַל תִּשְׂמְחִי אוֹיַבְתִּי, עַל שֶׁבֶר קַרְנִי,

Do not ‹ rejoice, ‹ O my enemy, « over the breaking ‹ of my pride, «

כִּי נָפַלְתִּי קַמְתִּי[4] וַיהוה עֲזָרָנִי,[5]

for ‹ although I have fallen, ‹ I shall arise ‹ and HASHEM ‹ shall assist me. «

הִנֵּה יַאַסְפֵנִי אֵלִי אֲשֶׁר פִּזְּרָנִי,

Indeed, ‹ gather me in ‹ shall my God ‹ Who ‹ dispersed me, «

וִיגָאֲלֵנִי מִמֵּךְ צוּרִי אֲשֶׁר מְכָרָנִי,

And redeem me ‹ from you ‹ shall my Rock ‹ Who ‹ sold me. «

---

(1) Some editions read שִׁנֵּי אֲרָיוֹת, *the teeth of the sharp-fanged lions;* some read שְׁנֵי אֲרָיוֹת, *the two ... lions,* Babylon and Edom. (2) *Jeremiah* 30:14. (3) Cf. *Isaiah* 5:13. (4) *Micah* 7:8. (5) *Psalms* 118:13.

וְגַם עָלַיִךְ תַּעֲבָר כּוֹס[1] אֲשֶׁר עֲבָרַנִי,

« passed to me, ‹ that ‹ the [bitter] cup ‹ will pass ‹ to you ‹ Also

וְאָז בְּסַלְעֵי סְעִפַּיִךְ, אֲנַפֵּץ אֶת טַפַּיִךְ.[2]

« your infants [as you did mine]. ‹ I will dash ‹ of your jagged crags ‹ upon the rocks ‹ and then

וְצַעֲקִי לִפְנֵי יהוה עַל חָרֶב סִפַּיִךְ,

« of your [Temple's] gateways, ‹ the destruction ‹ about ‹ HASHEM ‹ before ‹ And cry out

עַל חָרֶב סִפַּיִךְ, עַל נֶפֶשׁ עוֹלָלַיִךְ, שְׂאִי אֵלָיו כַּפַּיִךְ.

« your hands. ‹ to Him [in prayer] ‹ lift up « of your young children; ‹ the life ‹ about « of your [Temple's] vessels, ‹ the destruction ‹ about

(1) Cf. *Eichah* 4:21. (2) Cf. *Psalms* 137:9.

KINNAH 36 / קינה לו

צִיּוֹן הֲלֹא תִשְׁאֲלִי* לִשְׁלוֹם אֲסִירַיִךְ,

O Zion, ‹ will you not inquire* ‹ about the welfare ‹ of your imprisoned ones, «

דּוֹרְשֵׁי שְׁלוֹמֵךְ[1] וְהֵם יֶתֶר עֲדָרָיִךְ.

who seek ‹ your welfare, ‹ for they are ‹ the remnants ‹ of your flocks. «

מִיָּם וּמִזְרָח וּמִצָּפוֹן וְתֵימָן,[2]

From west ‹ and from east, « from north ‹ and from south, ‹

שְׁלוֹם רָחוֹק וְקָרוֹב,[3] שְׂאִי מִכָּל עֲבָרָיִךְ.

the welfare ‹ of the distant ‹ and the near ‹ carry [in your heart] ‹ from all ‹ of your sides. «

וּשְׁלוֹם אֲסִיר תִּקְוָה,[4] נוֹתֵן דְּמָעָיו כְּטַל חֶרְמוֹן,[5]

And the welfare ‹ of the prisoner ‹ who is yet full of hope, ‹ who gives forth ‹ his tears ‹ like the dew ‹ of [Mount] Hermon, «

וְנִכְסָף לְרִדְתָּם עַל הֲרָרָיִךְ.

and yearns ‹ to let them fall ‹ upon ‹ your hills. «

לִבְכּוֹת עֱנוּתֵךְ אֲנִי תַנִּים,[6]

When weeping ‹ over your suffering, ‹ I am ‹ like a jackal, «

וְעֵת אֶחֱלוֹם שִׁיבַת שְׁבוּתֵךְ,[7] אֲנִי כִנּוֹר לְשִׁירָיִךְ.

but when ‹ I dream ‹ of the return ‹ of your captivity, « I am ‹ a harp ‹ for your songs. «

---

(1) Cf. *Psalms* 122:6. (2) Cf. 107:3. (3) Cf. *Isaiah* 57:19. (4) Cf. *Zechariah* 9:12.
(5) *Psalms* 133:3. (6) Cf. *Micah* 1:8. (7) Cf. *Psalms* 126:1.

צִיּוֹן הֲלֹא תִשְׁאֲלִי — *O Zion, will you not inquire.* This very well-known *kinnah* was written by one of the greatest *paytanim* of all time, R' Yehudah (ben Shmuel) HaLevi. The beauty and passion of this *kinnah* reflects its author's lifelong yearning to flee from the exile and to walk on the sacred soil of the Holy Land.

R' Yehudah HaLevi was born in Toledo, Spain (circa 1080) and received an intensive Torah education at the yeshivah of R' Yitzchak Alfasi (the *Rif*) in Lucena, Spain. In addition to studying Talmud, R' Yehudah became a master of literary style in Hebrew and Arabic. *Rashba* writes of him (Responsum 418), "R' Yehudah HaLevi is foremost among all poetic singers in distinction and merit." His greatest contribution to Torah knowledge was the *Kuzari*, a philosophical work telling of the king of the Khazar tribe who sought to determine the true religion by questioning a Christian, a Moslem, and a Jewish scholar. The king was finally convinced

לִבִּי לְבֵית אֵל, וְלִפְנֵי אֵל מְאֹד יֶהֱמֶה,
« does it long, ‹ intensely ‹ God ‹ and before ‹ for the Temple of God, ‹ My heart [longs]

וּלְמַחֲנַיִם* וְכָל נִגְעֵי טְהוֹרָיִךְ.[1]
« to your purity. ‹ related ‹ and for everything ‹ and for the two encampments* [of the the *Kohanim* and Levites]

שָׁם הַשְּׁכִינָה שְׁכוּנָה לָךְ,
« for you, ‹ dwells ‹ the Divine Presence ‹ For there [in Zion]

וְיוֹצְרֵךְ פָּתַח לְמוּל שַׁעֲרֵי שַׁחַק שְׁעָרָיִךְ.[2]
« your gates [for prayer]. « of heaven, ‹ the gates ‹ opposite « has opened, ‹ and [there] your Creator

וּכְבוֹד יהוה לְבַד הָיָה מְאוֹרֵךְ,[3]
« your lamp, ‹ was ‹ alone ‹ of HASHEM ‹ And the glory

(1) Some editions read פִּגְעֵי טְהוֹרָיִךְ, *the places where your pure ones prayed, or where your pure ones met.* (2) Cf. *Genesis* 28:17. (3) Cf. *Isaiah* 60:1.

of the authenticity of Judaism, which he, together with his entire kingdom, embraced as the true religion. In the course of the disputation, the Khazar king taunts the Jewish teacher that the Jews seem to pay insincere lip service to Zion, their homeland. They pray for the restoration of Zion three times daily, yet in practice they are not willing to leave behind the prosperity and comfort of the exile to live in *Eretz Yisrael.* Humiliated, the Jewish sage of the *Kuzari* resolves to tear himself away from the lands of the gentiles and to settle in *Eretz Yisrael.*

The author of the *Kuzari* took his own words to heart and prepared to make his way to the land for which he had always yearned. Had not Rabbi Yehudah HaLevi himself written, "My heart is in the east while I am stranded in the farthest end of the west!" Despite many hardships he finally made his way to Damascus. An ancient manuscript states that R' Yehudah HaLevi composed this *kinnah* while journeying toward *Eretz Yisrael* and recited it when he reached Damascus, facing the direction of Zion. Although many historians believe that R' Yehudah HaLevi only got as far as Egypt (never even reaching Damascus), tradition has it that he finally reached Jerusalem (circa 1145). There he fell to the ground, in a state of ecstasy to fulfill the verse כִּי רָצוּ עֲבָדֶיךָ אֶת אֲבָנֶיהָ וְאֶת עֲפָרָהּ יְחֹנֵנוּ, *For Your servants had cherished her stones and been gracious to her dust (Psalms* 102:15). As he was kissing and embracing the dust near the Temple Mount he was trampled and killed by an Arab horseman.

לְבֵית אֵל וְלִפְנֵי אֵל . . . וּלְמַחֲנַיִם — *For the Temple of God, and before God . . . and for the [two] encampments.* Some editions read, לְבֵית־אֵל וְלִפְנִיאֵל, *For Beth-el and for Peniel,* treating these words as place-names. If so, מַחֲנַיִם is also a place-name, *Mahanaim.* Each of these three places was named by the Patriarch Jacob: Beth-el, after his dream of angels ascending and descending a ladder (*Genesis* 28:19); Mahanaim, after his encounter

וְאֵין סַהַר וָשֶׁמֶשׁ וְכוֹכָבִים מְאוֹרָיִךְ.[1]
« be your luminaries. ‹ and stars ‹ sun, ‹ will the moon, ‹ but no more

אֶבְחַר לְנַפְשִׁי לְהִשְׁתַּפֵּךְ,[2] בִּמְקוֹם
‹ in the place ‹ to pour itself out [in prayer], ‹ for my soul ‹ I would elect

אֲשֶׁר רוּחַ אֱלֹהִים שְׁפוּכָה עַל בְּחִירָיִךְ.
« your chosen ones. ‹ upon ‹ was poured out ‹ of God ‹ the prophetic spirit ‹ where

אַתְּ בֵּית מְלוּכָה, וְאַתְּ כִּסֵּא כְבוֹד אֵל,[3]
« of God. ‹ of the Glory ‹ the Throne ‹ and you are ‹ of royalty ‹ the palace ‹ You are

וְאֵיךְ יָשְׁבוּ עֲבָדִים עֲלֵי כִסְאוֹת גְּבִירָיִךְ.
« of your nobility? ‹ the thrones ‹ upon ‹ have slaves ‹ that sit ‹ How can it be

מִי יִתְּנֵנִי מְשׁוֹטֵט, בִּמְקוֹמוֹת
‹ in the places ‹ could wander ‹ can grant that I ‹ Who

אֲשֶׁר נִגְלוּ אֱלֹהִים לְחוֹזַיִךְ וְצִירָיִךְ.
« and your emissaries. ‹ to your seers ‹ was God ‹ revealed ‹ where

מִי יַעֲשֶׂה לִּי כְנָפַיִם[4] וְאַרְחִיק נְדוֹד,[5]
« would I wander? ‹ so that afar ‹ wings ‹ me ‹ shall make ‹ Who

אָנִיד לְבִתְרֵי לְבָבִי בֵּין בְּתָרָיִךְ.
« your shattered ruins. ‹ amidst ‹ of my heart ‹ with the broken pieces ‹ I would roam

אֶפֹּל לְאַפַּי עֲלֵי אַרְצֵךְ,
‹ your soil ‹ upon ‹ on my face ‹ I would fall

וְאֶרְצֶה אֲבָנַיִךְ לְמְאֹד וַאֲחוֹנֵן אֶת עֲפָרָיִךְ.[6]
« your dust. ‹ and I will favor ‹ intensely ‹ your stones ‹ and cherish

(1) Cf. *Isaiah* 60:19. (2) Cf. *Joel* 3:1. (3) Cf. *Jeremiah* 3:17.
(4) Cf. *Proverbs* 23:5. (5) *Psalms* 55:8. (6) Cf. 102:15.

with an encampment of angels as he returned to Canaan from Aram (ibid. 32:3); and Peniel, after he wrestled with the angel and prevailed (ibid. 32:31).

אַף כִּי בְּעָמְדִי עֲלֵי קִבְרוֹת אֲבוֹתַי,

Even 〈 as I stand 〈 by 〈 the graves 〈 of my Patriarchs, «

וְאֶשְׁתּוֹמֵם עֲלֵי חֶבְרוֹן, מִבְחַר קְבָרָיִךְ.

I am struck with wonderment 〈 over Hebron, 〈 the choicest 〈 of your burial sites. «

הַר הָעֲבָרִים[1] וְהֹר הָהָר,[2]

Mount 〈 Abarim 〈 and Mount 〈 Hor, 〈

אֲשֶׁר שָׁם שְׁנֵי אוֹרִים גְּדוֹלִים מְאוֹרַיִךְ וּמוֹרַיִךְ.

that 〈 there are [buried] 〈 the two 〈 great lights [Moses and Aaron], « your beacons 〈 and your guides. «

חַיֵּי נְשָׁמוֹת אֲוִיר אַרְצֵךְ,* וּמִמָּר דְּרוֹר

Invigorating 〈 to the souls 〈 is the air 〈 of your land;* « more [fragrant] than myrrh 〈 that is pure 〈

אַבְקַת עֲפָרֵךְ, וְנֹפֶת צוּף נְהָרָיִךְ.

is the dust 〈 of your earth, « and [sweeter] than the drippings 〈 of a honeycomb 〈 are your rivers. «

יִנְעַם לְנַפְשִׁי הָלוֹךְ עָרוֹם וְיָחֵף,[3]

It would be pleasing 〈 to my soul 〈 to walk 〈 naked 〈 and barefoot 〈

עֲלֵי חָרְבוֹת שְׁמָמָה, אֲשֶׁר הָיָה דְּבִירָיִךְ.

among 〈 the ruins 〈 and desolation, « where 〈 was located 〈 your Holiest of Holies. «

בִּמְקוֹם אֲרוֹנֵךְ אֲשֶׁר נִגְנַז וּבִמְקוֹם כְּרוּבָיִךְ,

In the place 〈 of your Ark, 〈 which 〈 was [later] hidden, 〈 and in the place 〈 of your Cherubim, «

(1) See *Deuteronomy* 32:49-50. (2) See *Numbers* 20:24-25. (3) *Isaiah* 20:2.

חַיֵּי נְשָׁמוֹת אֲוִיר אַרְצֵךְ — *Invigorating to the souls is the air of your land.* This stich can be interpreted two ways. It may refer to the souls of the living which receive an extra measure of vitality from the very air of the Holy Land. This is in accordance with the Talmudic dictum: The air of *Eretz Yisrael* makes one wise (*Bava Basra* 158b). Or it may refer to the souls of the dead who are buried in the Land of Israel. They will rise immediately at the time of the Revivification of the Dead. But those buried outside of the Land will not arise until underground passages are prepared for them to roll all the way to *Eretz Yisrael*, where they will be revived (see *Bereishis Rabbah* 96:5).

אֲשֶׁר שָׁכְנוּ חַדְרֵי חֲדָרֶיךָ.

which ‹ resided ‹ in a chamber ‹ within your chamber. «

אָגוֹז וְאַשְׁלִיךְ פְּאֵר נֶזֶר[1] וְאֶקֹּב זְמָן,

I will cut off ‹ and throw away ‹ the glorious ‹ crown [of hair] ‹ and I will curse ‹ the time ‹

חֻלַּל בְּאֶרֶץ בָּבֶל[2] אֶת נְזִירֶיךָ.

when were defiled ‹ in the land ‹ of Babylon ‹ your Nazirites. «

אֵיךְ יֶעֱרַב לִי אָכוֹל וְשָׁתוֹת בְּעֵת אֶחֱזֶה,

How can ‹ it be pleasant ‹ to me ‹ to eat ‹ and to drink, ‹ when I witness ‹

כִּי יִסְחֲבוּ הַכְּלָבִים אֶת כְּפִירֶיךָ.[3]

that ‹ drag away ‹ do the dogs ‹ [the corpse] of your young lion? «

אוֹ אֵיךְ מְאוֹר יוֹם יְהִי מָתוֹק לְעֵינַי,[4]

Or ‹ how can ‹ the light ‹ of day ‹ be ‹ sweet ‹ to my eye ‹

בְּעוֹד אֶרְאֶה בְּפִי עוֹרְבִים פִּגְרֵי בְשָׂרֶיךָ.[3]

as long as ‹ I must see ‹ in the mouth ‹ of ravens ‹ the corpses ‹ of your flesh? «

כּוֹס הַיְגוֹנִים לְאַט, הַרְפִּי מְעַט,

O cup ‹ of misery, « slow down, « slacken off ‹ a little! «

כִּי כְבָר מָלְאוּ כְסָלַי וְנַפְשִׁי[5] מִמְּרוֹרֶיךָ.

For ‹ already ‹ filled ‹ are my body ‹ and my soul ‹ of your bitterness. «

עֵת אֶזְכְּרָה אָהֳלָה[6] אֶשְׁתֶּה חֲמָרֵךְ,

When ‹ I remember ‹ Oholah [Shomron] ‹ I will drink ‹ your wine; «

וְאֶזְכּוֹר אָהֳלִיבָה, וְאֶמְצֶה אֶת שְׁמָרָיִךְ.

and when I recall ‹ Oholibah [Jerusalem] ‹ I shall suck dry ‹ the dregs. «

---

1) Cf. *Jeremiah* 7:29. (2) This seems to be the censor's emandation; some editions read בְּאֶרֶץ טְמֵאָה, *in an unclean land.* (3) Cf. *Jeremiah* 15:3. (4) Cf. *Ecclesiastes* 11:7. (5) Cf. *Psalms* 38:8. (6) See commentary to *Kinnah* 4.

צִיּוֹן כְּלִילַת יֹפִי,[1] אַהֲבָה וְחֵן עוֹרְרִי לִמְאֹד,[2]

‹ O Zion, ‹ the perfection ‹ of beauty, « with love ‹ and charm ‹ you have aroused yourself ‹ greatly, «

וּבָךְ נִקְשְׁרוּ נַפְשׁוֹת חֲבֵרָיִךְ.

‹ and with you ‹ are bound up ‹ the souls ‹ of your friends. «

הֵם הַשְּׂמֵחִים לְשַׁלְוָתֵךְ, וְהַכֹּאֲבִים

‹ It is they ‹ who rejoice ‹ over your serenity, « and who are pained ‹

עַל שׁוֹמְמוּתֵךְ, וּבוֹכִים עַל שְׁבָרָיִךְ.

‹ by ‹ your desolation, ‹ and weep ‹ over ‹ your destruction. «

מִבּוֹר שְׁבִי שׁוֹאֲפִים נֶגְדֵּךְ,

‹ From the pit ‹ of captivity, ‹ they yearn ‹ for you, «

וּמִשְׁתַּחֲוִים אִישׁ מִמְּקוֹמוֹ, עֲלֵי נוֹכַח שְׁעָרָיִךְ.

« and they prostrate themselves ‹ — everyone ‹ at his place ‹ toward ‹ facing ‹ your gates. «

עֶדְרֵי הֲמוֹנֵךְ, אֲשֶׁר גָּלוּ, וְנִתְפַּזְּרוּ

‹ The flocks ‹ of your masses ‹ who were exiled ‹ and were scattered ‹

מֵהַר לְגִבְעָה[3] וְלֹא שָׁכְחוּ גְּדֵרָיִךְ.

‹ from mountain ‹ to hilltop, « they did not forget ‹ your sheepfolds [Jerusalem]. «

הַמַּחֲזִיקִים בְּשׁוּלַיִךְ וּמִתְאַמְּצִים לַעֲלוֹת,

‹ Those who cling ‹ to your hems ‹ and exert themselves ‹ to climb ‹

וְלֶאֱחוֹז בְּסַנְסִנֵּי תְמָרָיִךְ.[4]

‹ and grasp ‹ the branches ‹ of your date palm. «

שִׁנְעָר וּפַתְרוֹס, הֲיַעַרְכוּךְ בְּגָדְלָם,

‹ Shinar [Babylon] ‹ and Pathros [Egypt] ‹ can they compare with you ‹ in their greatness, «

---

(1) *Eichah* 2:15. (2) Some editions read עוֹדְדִי, *you invigorated yourself;* some editions read תִּקְשְׁרִי, *you have bound from yore.* (3) Cf. *Jeremiah* 50:6. (4) Cf. *Song of Songs* 7:9.

וְאִם הֶבְלָם יְדַמּוּ לְתֻמֶּיךָ וְאוּרֶיךָ.*
« and Urim? ‹ to your Tumim ‹ be likened ‹ their worthless deities ‹ and can

אֶל מִי יְדַמּוּ מְשִׁיחֶיךָ, וְאֶל מִי נְבִיאֶיךָ,
« your prophets? ‹ whom ‹ and to ‹ your anointed ones ‹ can they compare ‹ whom ‹ To

וְאֶל מִי לְוִיֶּיךָ וְשִׁירֶיךָ.
« and your songs? ‹ your Levites ‹ whom ‹ And to

יְשַׁנֶּה וְיַחֲלוֹף כָּלִיל כָּל מַמְלְכוֹת הָאֱלִילִים,[1]
« that are idolatrous, ‹ kingdoms ‹ shall all ‹ totally ‹ and disappear ‹ Be changed

חָסְנֵךְ לְעוֹלָם לְדוֹר וָדוֹר נְזִירֶיךָ.[2]
« shall your crowned ones [endure]. ‹ to generation ‹ from generation « is forever; ‹ while your power, [Zion,]

אִוָּה לְמוֹשָׁב אֱלֹהָיִךְ,[3]
« did Your God, ‹ for His residence ‹ Desire [you]

וְאַשְׁרֵי אֱנוֹשׁ יִבְחַר וְיִקְרַב וְיִשְׁכּוֹן בַּחֲצֵרֶיךָ.[4]
« in your courtyards. ‹ and dwells ‹ and draws near ‹ who chooses ‹ is the man ‹ and fortunate

אַשְׁרֵי מְחַכֶּה וְיַגִּיעַ וְיִרְאֶה עֲלוֹת אוֹרֵךְ,
‹ of your light ‹ the rising ‹ and witnesses ‹ and arrives ‹ who waits ‹ Fortunate is he

וְיִבָּקְעוּ עָלָיו שְׁחָרַיִךְ.[5]
« does your dawn. ‹ over him ‹ when burst forth

(1) Cf. *Isaiah* 2:18. (2) Cf. *Proverbs* 27:24. (3) Cf. *Psalms* 132:13. (4) Cf. 65:5. (5) Cf. *Isaiah* 58:8.

לְתֻמֶּיךָ וְאוּרֶיךָ — *To your Urim and Tumim.* The חֹשֶׁן, *breastplate*, worn by the *Kohen Gadol* was made of linen; blue, purple, and red wools; and gold threads. It was folded over and the *Urim V'Tumim* (see below) was inserted in the fold. Twelve precious stones were attached to the front of the breastplate in four rows of three stones each, with each stone inscribed with the name of one of the tribes. When the *Urim V'Tumim* was consulted, the letters etched on the stones lit up and spelled out a message. Since the letters חטצק do not appear in the names of the tribes, the

לִרְאוֹת בְּטוּבַת בְּחִירֶיךָ, לַעֲלוֹת בְּשִׂמְחָתֶךָ,

« and exult in your joy « of your chosen ones, ‹ the goodness ‹ To behold

בְּשׁוּבְךָ אֱלֵי קַדְמוּת נְעוּרֶיךָ.

« of your youthfulness. ‹ the former state ‹ to ‹ when you return

---

stones were also engraved with the names of the Patriarchs אַבְרָהָם יִצְחָק יַעֲקֹב, *Abraham, Isaac, Jacob*, and the phrase שִׁבְטֵי יְשֻׁרוּן, *tribes of Yeshurun* (another name for Israel). This accounted for all twenty-two letters of the *aleph-beis*.

According to *Rashi* the *Urim V'Tumim* was a slip of parchment upon which the שֵׁם הַמְּפוֹרָשׁ, *Ineffable Four-Letter Name* of *HASHEM*, was written. This was the power that lit up the letters on the breastplate. *Ramban* (*Exodus* 28:30) adds that this Name was written by Moses in a manner entrusted by God to him alone; it was considered a heavenly handicraft. *Ritva* maintains that it was Divinely written and given to Moses.

KINNAH 37 / קינה לז

צִיּוֹן קָחִי* כָּל צֳרִי גִלְעָד[1] לְצִירָיִךְ,

« of Gilead for your pains, ‹ the balm ‹ all ‹ even if ‹ O Zion, you took*

אֵין דַּי, לְמַעַן כַּיָּם גָּדְלוּ שְׁבָרָיִךְ.[2]

« so is your devastation. ‹ is vast, ‹ as the sea ‹ because ‹ be enough, ‹ it would not

אֶרֶץ צְבִי אַתְּ[3] בְּתוֹךְ גּוֹיִם נְתוּנָה,*[4]

« have been placed,* ‹ of the nations ‹ in the center ‹ you « most desirable, ‹ O land

וּמִן עֵדֶן מְקוֹם כָּל יְקָר יָצְאוּ נְהָרָיִךְ.[5]

« your rivers. ‹ emanated « splendor, ‹ of all ‹ the source « Eden, ‹ and from

וַיְהִי לְאוֹת, נַעֲמָן* רָחַץ בְּשָׂרוֹ בְּמֵי יַרְדֵּן,

‹ of the Jordan ‹ in the waters ‹ his flesh ‹ bathed ‹ Naaman* « an indication: ‹ And this was

(1) Cf. *Jeremiah* 8:22. (3) Cf. *Eichah* 2:13. (4) Cf. *Ezekiel* 20:6. (5) Cf. 5:5. (5) See *Genesis* 2:10.

צִיּוֹן קָחִי — *O Zion, even if you took.* This beautiful composition illustrates the unique natural gifts with which the Holy Land is so abundantly blessed. Indeed, it is this country which is closest in nature to the Garden of Eden itself. The waters of the land are endowed with curative powers; the earth is filled with precious gems and metals and every type of essential resource; the fruits and grain of *Eretz Yisrael* are as delicious and nutritious as can be. In this blessed environment the Torah nation developed the most perfect society ever known to mankind. Law and order reigned throughout the land, capably governed by a noble king and taught by holy priests and prophets. Alas, all this has fallen into the rapacious hands of our enemies, but we yearn for this splendor to return!

Scholars are in dispute regarding the authorship of this *kinnah*. It is variously attributed to R' Shlomo ibn Gabirol, R' Avraham HaChozeh, R' Avraham ibn Ezra, and R' Elyah ben Menachem HaZaken.

אַתְּ בְּתוֹךְ גּוֹיִם נְתוּנָה — *You in the center of the nations have been placed. Eretz Yisrael* is positioned in the center of the world; Jerusalem is at the center of *Eretz Yisrael;* the Temple is at the center of Jerusalem; the *Heichal* hall is at the center of the Temple; and the Holy Ark is at the center of the *Heichal* (*Midrash Tanchuma, Kedoshim* 10).

נַעֲמָן — *Naaman. II Kings* Chapter 5 relates the story of Naaman, the great and victorious commander in chief of the Aramean army. Because of his excessive pride, God afflicted him with a painful leprous disease of the skin for which he could find no cure. Finally, out of sheer desperation he came to the prophet Elisha for help. At first Naaman adamantly refused to follow Elisha's instructions to bathe himself in the waters of the Jordan, exclaiming, "*Are not Amanah and Parpar, the rivers of [my homeland] Damascus, better than all the waters of Israel?*" (ibid. v. 12). Finally, Naaman relented and humbly dipped himself seven times in the Jordan

אֲזַי נֶאֱסַף אַף כִּי טְהוֹרָיִךְ.

« for your own pure people. ‹ that [the waters are curative] ‹ certainly so « he was healed; ‹ then,

אַף לֹא יְסֻלֶּה עֲפַר אַרְצֵךְ בְּזָהָב וּפָז,[1]

« or fine gold, ‹ with plain gold ‹ of your land ‹ the dust ‹ value ‹ one cannot ‹ Indeed,

יְקַר כְּמוֹ יָהֲלוֹם מַחְצַב הֲרָרָיִךְ.

« from your mountains. ‹ are even the [coarse] rocks hewn ‹ *yahalom* gems ‹ as ‹ for precious

כָּל תַּעֲנוּגִים* בְּבֹא בָסְרֵךְ, לֹא קָהֲתָה

‹ set on edge ‹ they do not ‹ your unripe fruits ‹ and even if one eats ‹ the [food] delights* [are there] ‹ All

הַשֵּׁן[2] וְאוּלָם כְּצוּף מָתְקוּ מְרוֹרָיִךְ.

« — [even] your most bitter fruits. « they were sweet « like honey, ‹ rather, « a tooth [like other unripe fruit];

פִּרְיֵךְ לְמַרְפֵּא, וְכָל עָלֶה תְּעָלָה,

« contained a cure; ‹ leaf ‹ and every ‹ had healing powers, ‹ Your fruits

הֲלֹא כְּיַעֲרַת הַדְּבַשׁ[3] הָיוּ יְעָרָיִךְ.

« your forests? ‹ were ‹ of sugar cane ‹ that like forests ‹ is it not so

עִם הַפְּתָנִים בְּרִית כָּרְתוּ מְתַיִךְ וְאֵין שָׂטָן,

« were harmed; ‹ and none ‹ by your people, ‹ was established ‹ a covenant ‹ the vipers ‹ With

(1) Cf. *Job* 28:16. (2) Cf. *Jeremiah* 31:28; *Ezekiel* 18:2. (3) *I Samuel* 14:27.

River and when he emerged, *his flesh became like the flesh of a small child* (ibid. v. 14).

כָּל תַּעֲנוּגִים — *All the [food] delights.* The finest agricultural area in the Land was adjacent to Lake Kineret and was called גִּינוֹסָר, *Ginnosar*, which is a contraction of גַּן שָׂרִים, *garden of Princes*, because its fruit and produce was desired by royalty the world over (see *Pesachim* 8b and *Rashi* to *Genesis* 49:21). The historian Josephus (*Wars of the Jews*, Book III, 10:8) reports that the soil of Ginnosar is so fruitful that every type of tree can grow on it: The temper of the air is so well mixed that it agrees well with all sorts, particularly walnuts, which require the coldest air, and flourish there in vast plenty; there are also palm trees which grow best in hot air. Fig trees and olive trees which require more temperate air grow near them. One may call this place the ambition of nature, where

אֲבָל הָשְׁלְמוּ לָהֶם כְּפִירַיִךְ.*

indeed, ‹ make peace ‹ with them ‹ did even your lions.* »

בָּךְ כָּל בְּהֵמָה וָעוֹף חָכְמוּ,

Within you ‹ every ‹ animal ‹ and bird ‹ grew wise,

עֲדֵי כַּחֲמוֹר הָיָה לְפָנִים לְבֶן יָאִיר,* חֲמוֹרַיִךְ.

to the point where ‹ [as intelligent] as the donkey ‹ that belonged ‹ of old ‹ to ben Yair* ‹ were your donkeys.* »

בָּךְ אֵל לְבַדּוֹ וְאֵין בִּלְתּוֹ, וַיֵּצֵא שְׁמֵךְ[1]

In your midst ‹ God was found, » He ruled alone ‹ with none ‹ besides Him, » and go forth ‹ did your fame

עַד כִּי אֱלֹהִים אֱמֶת נוֹדַע בְּשִׁירַיִךְ.

to the extent ‹ that ‹ God ‹ being true ‹ was revealed ‹ through your songs. »

מַה טּוֹב וְנָעִים,[2] בְּבֹא שִׁבְטֵי בְּנֵי יַעֲקֹב

How ‹ good ‹ and pleasant [it was] ‹ when enter ‹ did the tribes ‹ of the sons ‹ of Jacob

שָׁלֹשׁ פְּעָמִים[3] בְּכָל שָׁנָה בִּשְׁעָרַיִךְ.

three ‹ times ‹ every ‹ year ‹ into your gates.

בָּךְ סוֹד הַתְּעוּדָה וְסוֹד חָכְמוֹת,

Within you ‹ are the secrets ‹ of [Torah] tradition ‹ and the secrets ‹ of wisdom, »

(1) Cf. *Ezekiel* 16:14. (2) Cf. *Psalms* 133:1. (3) Cf. *Deuteronomy* 16:16.

it forces those plants which are naturally enemies to abide together; it is a happy contention of the seasons as if everyone of them laid claim to the country at once.

אֲבָל הָשְׁלְמוּ לָהֶם כְּפִירַיִךְ — *Indeed, make peace with them did even your lions.* The Torah promised the Jews: *No man shall covet your land when you go up to appear before Hashem your God three times in the year* (*Exodus* 34:24). The Talmud relates many wondrous examples of how God protected the property that the pilgrims left behind. A man once left his granary unprotected when he went to spend the festival in Jerusalem. When he returned he found everything intact because a pride of lions was patroling his premises, scaring away intruders. Another time, a person left his chickens alone, unprotected from hungry wolves. When he returned from Jerusalem, he found dead wolves that had been torn apart by his chickens. Another man came home and found deadly scorpions wrapped around the doorknobs of his home, frightening away all burglars (*Yerushalmi Peah* 3:7).

כַּחֲמוֹר ... לְבֶן יָאִיר — *As the donkey . . . of ben Yair.* The *Talmud* relates that one

וּבָאוּ בְּנֵי קֶדֶם[1] וְחַכְמֵי שְׁבָא לִכְתּוֹב סְפָרַיִךְ.

« your books. ‹ to transcribe ‹ of Sheba ‹ and the scholars ‹ of the Orient ‹ the (wise) men ‹ so there came

שׁוֹטְרִים בְּכָל הַגְּבוּל, שׁוֹפְטִים בְּכָל עִיר וָעִיר,[2]

« in each and every city; ‹ and judges ‹ your borders ‹ were [posted] within all ‹ Law enforcement officers

זִקְנֵי אֱמֶת הֵם וְאֵין מוֹרֶה כְּמוֹרַיִךְ.

« equaled your teachers. ‹ teacher ‹ and no ‹ they were ‹ men of truth ‹ these elders

מֶלֶךְ בְּקִרְבֵּךְ, וּבָךְ שָׂרֵי חֲיָלִים בְּכָל נֶשֶׁק,

« weapons. ‹ equipped with all « of the military, ‹ were officers ‹ and within you ‹ was in your midst, ‹ A king

וְעַל כָּל לְאוֹם גָּבְרוּ גְבִירַיִךְ.

«your warriors. ‹ prevailed ‹ nation ‹ every other ‹ Over

בִּימֵי בְחוּרוֹת, הֱיוֹת קֹדֶשׁ לָאֵל נִבְחָרוּ,

« you were chosen, ‹ unto God ‹ consecrated ‹ to be ‹ of your youth, [on leaving Egypt,] ‹ In the days

וּבְנֵי נְבִיאִים בְּנֵי אֵל חַי נְעָרַיִךְ.

« were your youngsters! ‹ of the Living God, ‹ children « of the prophets, ‹ and disciples

בָּךְ הַתְּקוּפָה עֲלֵי קַו הָאֱמֶת נִשְׁקָלָה,

« were balanced: ‹ that is accurate ‹ a time-line ‹ upon ‹ the seasons of the year ‹ Through you

תְּכֶן שְׁנוֹת דּוֹר וָדוֹר[3] בִּשְׁנֵי אֲדָרַיִךְ.

« months of Adar. ‹ by [intercalating] the two ‹ after generation ‹ for generation ‹ of the years ‹ the determination

(1) *I Kings* 5:10. (2) Cf. *Deuteronomy* 16:18. (3) 32:7.

night robbers stole R' Pinchas ben Yair's donkey. They hid the animal for three days during which it refused to eat a thing, because it would never eat stolen goods. In desperation, the robbers released her and she made her way home to the rabbi's house. The family gave her barley to eat but again the donkey refused to partake. R' Pinchas asked, "Are you certain that this barley was properly tithed?" The family responded, 'Father, you yourself ruled that we may follow the lenient opinion that exempts this type of produce from the tithe." To this R' Pinchas responded, "Indeed, I personally follow the lenient view, but what can I do if my donkey wishes to accept the stricter opinion?" (*Yerushalmi Shekalim* 5:1; see also *Chullin* 7a).

מוֹלַד לְבָנָה כְּפִי אָרְכֵּךְ, וְהַמַּחֲזֶה

The birth 〈 of the [new] moon 〈 [is observed] according to 〈 your longitude, 《 and its visibility 〈

שׂוּמָה לְרָחְבֵּךְ, וּבָהּ הֶרְאֵית סְתָרַיִךְ.

was designated 〈 according to your latitude, 《 and through it 〈 you displayed 〈 your secret knowledge [of the heavens]. 《

נִרְאֶה בְּתַמּוּז כְּסִיל,[1] בָּךְ יַעֲלֶה,

Visible 〈 in the month of Tammuz 〈 is the Antares 《 in you, [the Land of Israel,] 〈 it ascends 〈

כִּי שְׁאָר כָּל הֶחֳדָשִׁים לְבַד זֶה בַּחֲדָרַיִךְ.

while 〈 during the rest 〈 of all 〈 the months; 《 besides 〈 [in Tammuz] 〈 it is [concealed] in your [Southern Hemisphere] chambers. 《

אַיֵּה דְבִירֵךְ מְקוֹם אָרוֹן,

O where 〈 is your Holiest of the Holies, 〈 the resting place 〈 of the Holy Ark? 《

וְאַיֵּה הֲדַר הֵיכָל וְהַמִּזְבָּחוֹת, וְאַיֵּה חֲצֵרַיִךְ.

And where 〈 is the splendor 〈 of the Sanctuary 〈 and the Altars? 《 And where 〈 are your courtyards? 《

אַיֵּה מְשִׁיחֵךְ, בְּעַד עַמֵּךְ יְכַפֵּר,

And where 〈 is your anointed [*Kohen Gadol*] 〈 who for 〈 your people 〈 would effect atonement? 《

וּמֶה הָיָה לְיַלְדֵי קְהָת, וְאַיֵּה נְזִירַיִךְ.

And what 〈 happened 〈 to [the Levite] children 〈 of Kehath? 《 And where 〈 are your nazirites? 《

אֵיפֹה נְבִיאִים בְּנֵי עֶלְיוֹן וְכָל יוֹעֲצַיִךְ אָבָדוּ,

Where 〈 are the prophets, 〈 the sons 〈 of the Most High? 《 All 〈 of your advisers 〈 have perished; 《

וְהָלְכוּ שְׁבִי מַלְכֵּךְ וְשָׂרַיִךְ.

gone 〈 into captivity 〈 have your kings 〈 and your ministers. 《

הָיִית יְפֵה נוֹף[2] וְרֹאשׁ עַפְרוֹת תֵּבֵל,[3]

You were 〈 the fairest 〈 of sites, 《 the first 〈 of the dusts 〈 of the earth, 《

(1) *Job* 9:9; *Ibn Ezra* 38:31. (2) *Psalms* 48:3. (3) *Proverbs* 8:26.

בְּרוֹשְׁךָ לְנֵס, חֶטְאֵךְ סְחָפֵךְ, הֲלֹא קָצַר קְצִירָיִךְ.

your cypress tree [your king] ‹ is a banner; « but it is your sin ‹ that has drowned you; « has not [the enemy] ‹ harvested ‹ your harvest [your children]? «

אֶרֶץ מְאָסֵךְ וּמֵי נָכְרִים שְׁטָפוּךְ,

The land ‹ abhorred you ‹ and the waters ‹ that were alien ‹ swept you away, «

וְכָל רוּחַ הֱפִיצֵךְ, וְאֵשׁ בָּעֲרָה בְּעָרָיִךְ.

while every ‹ wind ‹ scattered you, ‹ and fires ‹ burned ‹ in your cities. «

מָרִית בְּצוּרֵךְ, אֲשֶׁר מִצָּר נְצָרֵךְ,

You rebelled ‹ against your Rock, « He who ‹ from every foe ‹ had protected you. «

וְאָז זָרִים עֲכָרוּךְ, וְאַתְּ הָיִית בְּעוֹכְרָיִךְ.[1]

Then ‹ strangers ‹ tormented you, « but you ‹ were ‹ together with those who tormented you. «

אֵל הֶאֱמִירָךְ עֲדֵי נִקְרֵאת אֲרִיאֵל,*

God ‹ has set you apart, ‹ to the point that ‹ you were given the title ‹ Ariel!* «

וְאֵיךְ עָבַר בְּנָוֵךְ אֲרִי טוֹרֵף עֲדָרָיִךְ.

How then ‹ did there pass ‹ through your dwelling ‹ the lion ‹ who would tear apart ‹ your flocks? «

שׁוּבִי לָאֵל בּוֹעֲלֵךְ, אַל תִּתְּנִי לוֹ דֳּמִי[2]

Return ‹ to God, ‹ your devoted husband; « do not ‹ give ‹ Him ‹ any rest [from entreaty], ‹

---

(1) Cf. *Judges* 11:35. (2) Cf. *Isaiah* 62:7.

אֲרִיאֵל — *Ariel* [lit., *the lion of God*]. The Temple is described thus because just as the lion is broad in chest and small behind, so is the Temple wide in front and narrow at the back.

The Midrash states: A lion came, in the month of the lion, and destroyed the lion of God.

"A lion came" refers to Nebuchadnezzar, the wicked King of Babylon, of whom it is written: *The lion has left his den* (*Jeremiah* 4:7).

"In the month of the lion" means that the Temple was destroyed in the month of Av whose symbol in the Zodiac is the lion.

"And destroyed the lion of God (Ariel)" refers to the Temple, as the prophet lamented: *"Woe Ariel, Ariel, the city where David encamped"* (*Isaiah* 29:1).

The Midrash continues: In the end of time a lion shall come in the month of the lion, and rebuild the lion of God.

"A lion shall come" refers to Almighty God Himself.

עַד שׁוּב כְּבוֹדוֹ, עַד יִבְנֶה גְּדֵרַיִךְ.

« your walls. ‹ He rebuilds ‹ until « of His glory, ‹ the return ‹ until

נַפְשִׁי מְאֹד נִכְסְפָה[1] לִרְאוֹת בְּזִיו זָהֳרֵךְ,

« of your radiance; ‹ the splendor ‹ to behold ‹ yearns ‹ intensely ‹ My soul

שָׁלוֹם יְהִי לָךְ וְרֹב שָׁלוֹם לְעוֹזְרַיִךְ.[2]

« to those who help you! ‹ peace ‹ and [may there be] abundant « yours, ‹ — may it be « peace

(1) *Psalms* 84:3. (2) *I Chronicles* 12:19.

"In the month of the lion" refers to the month of Av, which will be transformed from sorrow to rejoicing.

"And rebuild the lion of God" refers to the Temple, as it says, *The Builder of Jerusalem is* H*ASHEM*, *the outcasts of Israel He will gather in* (*Psalms* 147:2; *Pesikta* 13).

KINNAH 38 / קינה לח

צִיּוֹן עֲטֶרֶת צְבִי[1] שִׂמְחַת הֲמוֹנָיִךְ,

O Zion, crown that is most desirable, the joy of your multitudes;

שָׁלוֹם כְּנָהָר[2] קְחִי מֵאֵת אֲדוֹנָיִךְ.

blessings of peace, [endless] as the river's [flow], accept from your Lord.

אֵילֵי שְׁחָקִים אֲשֶׁר שׁוֹמְרִים לְחוֹמוֹת[3] וָחֵל,[4]

The angels of heaven who guard your walls and rampart,

לַיְלָה וָיוֹם יִדְרְשׁוּן[5] שָׁלוֹם לְמַחֲנָיִךְ.

day and night seek peace for your camp.

גַּם הַנְּפוּצִים בְּכָל אַרְבַּע קְצָוֹת,

And also those scattered [in exile] in all the four corners,

וְהֵם דּוֹרְשֵׁי שְׁלוֹמֵךְ, בְּנוֹתַיִךְ וּבָנָיִךְ.

they seek your peace, [for they are] your daughters and your sons.

שׁוֹכְנֵי קְבָרִים מְחַכִּים וּמְצַפִּים לְיוֹם יִשְׁעֵךְ,

Even those who dwell in graves await and hope for the day of your salvation,

וְאָז יִצְמְחוּ יִחְיוּ יְשֵׁנָיִךְ.

and then shall sprout forth and come [back] to life those of yours who slumber [in the earth].

וַאֲנִי בְּשָׁאֲלִי שְׁלוֹמֵךְ אֶקְרָא קוֹל בְּרֹאשׁ הָרִים,

As for me, when I seek peace for you, I shall cry out from the tops of the mountains,

וְאֶדְמֶה לְעוֹף עַל רַעֲנָנָיִךְ.

I shall be like a bird [singing aloud] atop your verdant trees.

(1) *Isaiah* 28:5. (2) Cf. 48:18. (3) Cf. 62:6. (4) Cf. *Eichah* 2:8. (5) Cf. *Isaiah* 58:2.

צִיּוֹן עֲטֶרֶת צְבִי — *O Zion, crown that is most desirable.* The Destruction of the *Beis HaMikdash* has deprived the universe of God's favorite location, His garden of delights, the Holy Temple. The composer of this *kinnah* [R' Elazar, the son of R' Moshe HaDarshan, of Wurtzburg, Germany, early 13th century] describes how he, a lover of

שָׁלוֹם לְצִיּוֹן נְוֵה צֶדֶק[1] וְשָׁלוֹם עָלַי

Peace ‹ unto Zion, « the abode ‹ of righteousness, « and peace ‹ be upon ‹

חֵילֵךְ וְחוֹמוֹת יְקַר אַבְנֵי פְנִינָיִךְ.

your ramparts ‹ and walls ‹ of more precious ‹ stones ‹ than your pearls. «

שָׁלוֹם לְאֶרֶץ צְבִי,[2] שָׁלוֹם לְכָל הַגְּבוּל

Peace ‹ unto the land ‹ that is desirable, « and peace ‹ throughout all ‹ of your borders, «

גִּלְעָד וְשׁוֹמְרוֹן, וְכָל יֶתֶר שְׁכֵנָיִךְ.

including Gilead, ‹ and Samaria, ‹ and all ‹ the rest ‹ of your dwellings. «

צִיּוֹן לְפָנִים הֲלֹא הָיִית יְפַת מַרְאֶה,

O Zion, ‹ previously, ‹ were you not ‹ of beautiful ‹ appearance? «

אֵיךְ נֶהֶפְכוּ לִשְׁחוֹר תָּאֳרֵךְ וּפָנָיִךְ.

How, then, ‹ become transfigured ‹ into blackness ‹ have your form ‹ and your face? «

כִּבְנוֹת מְלָכִים יְקָר עָטִית תְּהִלָּה,

Like the daughters ‹ of kings ‹ in precious [robes] ‹ you were enveloped, « an object of praise; «

וְאֵיךְ שַׂק תַּחְגְּרִי עַל חֲלָצַיִךְ וּמָתְנָיִךְ.

how is it ‹ that with sackcloth ‹ you must gird yourself ‹ on ‹ your loins ‹ and on your waist! «

לַחְמִי אֲנָחָה[3] בְּעֵת תַּעְדִּי אֵפֶר תַּחַת פְּאֵר,

My bread ‹ is [replaced] by sighs, « when ‹ you [Zion] adorn yourself ‹ with ashes ‹ in place ‹ of splendor; «

(אֶפְעֶה)[4] וְאֶשְׁתֶּה יְגוֹנִי עֲלֵי יְגוֹנָיִךְ.

(I shall cry out,) ‹ and drink ‹ [the cup of] my anguish ‹ for ‹ your anguish. «

(1) *Jeremiah* 50:7. (2) Cf. *Ezekiel* 20:6. (3) Cf. *Job* 3:24.
(4) Some editions omit the term in parentheses.

Zion, yearns and languishes to hear the herald of redemption and to witness the return of God to His Palace. He calls upon all the angels in heaven above to join in the lament of the Jewish people who are scattered to the four corners of the earth.

קוּמִי וְנִשָּׂא נְהִי, נִבְכֶּה דְּמָעוֹת כַּיָּם,

Arise, and let us arouse a lamentation; let us cry tears like the sea;

יִזְּלוּ נְהָרוֹת, לְמַן עֵינַי לְעֵינַיִךְ.

let there flow rivers [of tears], from my eyes to your eyes.

עַל אַלְמְנוּתֵךְ אֲשֶׁר הָלַךְ יְדִידֵךְ,

[I will cry] over your widowhood, because gone away has your Beloved,

וְהוּא הֶחֱרִיב דְּבִירוֹ וְכָל סְתָרֵי צְפוּנַיִךְ.

and He destroyed His Temple and all the secret places for you to hide.

עֵת אֶרְאֶה יָפְיֵךְ אֶקְרָא מְשׁוֹרְרִים בְּשִׁיר,

When I would behold your beauty, I would summon the singers to song;

עֵת אֶחֱזֶה עָנְיֵךְ אֶקְרָא מְקוֹנְנַיִךְ.

[but now] when I witness your affliction, I summon your lamenters.

אֶבְחַר לְקָאַת וְקִפּוֹד[1] יִשְׁכְּנוּ בָךְ,

I would prefer that the pelican and porcupine would dwell in your midst;

וְאוֹי לִי אִם אֱדוֹם וַעֲרָב קִנְּנוּ בְּקִנַּיִךְ.

but woe unto me that in Edom and Arabia nested in your nest.

עִיר הַמְּלוּכָה לְדָוִד וּשְׁלֹמֹה בְנוֹ* הָיִית בְּנוּיָה,

O City of Royalty! For David and Solomon his son* were you built,

וְהֵם קֶדֶם מְכוֹנְנַיִךְ.

and they were the first to lay down your foundations.

(1) This identification of these creatures of the wild may not be accurate.

לְדָוִד וּשְׁלֹמֹה בְנוֹ — *For David and Solomon his son.* David made all the preparations for Jerusalem and the Temple. At first the entire city was in the hands of Aravna the Jebusite. David collected fifty shekels from each of the twelve tribes of Israel, and paid a total of six hundred gold shekels for the city (*Zevachim* 116b). David also bought the place of the Altar from Aravna for fifty silver shekels. David dug the foundations of the Temple especially for the place of the Altar (*Succah* 53a),

אַתְּ הִיא לְמִקְדָּשׁ לָאֵל, אַתְּ הִיא מְנוּחָה לְצוּר,

« for the Rock; ‹ a place of rest ‹ who were ‹ it is you ‹ unto God; ‹ a Sanctuary ‹ who were ‹ It is you

אַתְּ הִיא אֲשֶׁר יוֹם בְּיוֹם יָרַד לְגַנָּיִךְ.

« to your gardens. ‹ [God] descended ‹ by day ‹ day ‹ the one that ‹ who were ‹ it is you

שָׁם שֻׁלְחָן וּמְנוֹרָה, וַאֲרוֹן הַבְּרִית,*

« of the Covenant;* ‹ and the Ark ‹ the Menorah, ‹ the Table, ‹There were [found]

אֵל בֵּין שָׁדַי* אַהֲבָה, לָן בִּמְלוֹנָיִךְ.

« in your Lodge. ‹ dwelled ‹ with love ‹the [Ark's] staves* ‹ between ‹ God

עַל מִזְבְּחֵךְ עָמְדוּ כֹּהֲנִים מְשָׁרְתִים,

‹ performing [Divine] service, ‹ the *Kohanim* ‹ stood ‹ your Altar ‹ Upon

---

and he laid down and consecrated the Temple's floor (*Zevachim* 24a). David assembled all the necessary money and materials in preparation for construction and he handed down to Solomon a comprehensive master plan describing how the Temple should be built, to the most scrupulous detail.

שֻׁלְחָן וּמְנוֹרָה וַאֲרוֹן הַבְּרִית — *The Table, the Menorah, and the Ark of the Covenant.* God performs revealed miracles as a display of His love for the beneficiary of those miracles. Thus the supernatural events that ocurred on a daily basis in the *Beis HaMikdash* were clear demonstrations of God's extraordinary love for His Jewish people. The *Panim*-Bread was baked on Friday and arranged on the Table on Saturday, where it remained until the following Saturday. In good times the bread remained fresh and steaming hot until the last day, even though it was at least eight full days since it had left the baking oven. This manifested God's intense and burning love for His people. The *Talmud (Chagigah* 26b) says that on the festivals the *Kohanim* would hold the Table aloft so that all the pilgrims could see the steaming hot bread and the *Kohanim* would say, "Behold how beloved you are to God!"

The Menorah, too, had a perpetual miracle. One of its seven lamps, called the נֵר מַעֲרָבִי, *western lamp,* would be filled with the same quantity of oil and same size wick as the other six, yet it would continue to burn throughout the following day, long after the other lights had died out in the morning. This, says the *Talmud (Shabbos* 22b), was a public demonstration to the entire world that God's Holy Spirit settled over the people of Israel and caused miracles to occur.

Finally, the *Talmud* (*Yoma* 54a) teaches that when God was pleased with the Jewish people, that close love was symbolized by the golden *Cherubim* on top of the Holy Ark, for they would then embrace each other in a display of love and affection. However, when Israel's actions were contrary to the *mitzvos* of the Torah, the *Cherubim* would face away from each another.

בֵּין שָׁדַי — *Between the Ark's staves* [lit., *between the bosoms*]. The simile of שָׁדַיִם, *bosom,* and staves of the Ark is based on *Song of Songs* (1:13) and is elaborated upon in the Talmud. Although the staves

בְּמוֹ זֶבַח וְעוֹלָה לְכַפֵּר עַל עֲוֹנֶיךָ.

« your iniquities. ‹ for ‹ to atone ‹ and burnt-offerings ‹ sacrifices ‹ with the very

רֹאשׁ הַכְּהֻנָּה אֲשֶׁר אָפוּד לְבוּשֵׁי יְקָר,

« that were precious, ‹ in garments ‹ was garbed ‹ who ‹ of the Priesthood ‹ The Leader

נִשְׁמַע בְּשׁוּלֵי מְעִיל קוֹל פַּעֲמוֹנֶיךָ.[1]

« of your bells. ‹ the sound ‹ of his robe ‹ from the edge ‹ there was heard

אַחַת בַּשָּׁנָה[2] פְּנִים הָלַךְ לְחַדְרֵי דְבִיר,

‹ of the Sanctuary ‹ into the Inner Chamber ‹ he went, ‹ inside ‹ a year [on Yom Kippur] ‹ Once

הֵבִיא קְטֹרֶת מְלֹא קֻמְצוֹ[3] וְחָפְנֶיךָ.[4]

« [so did he take] his cupped hands full. ‹ his three fingers and palm [from a meal-offering] ‹ [just as] that which fills « incense, ‹ and brought

קִדָּה וְקָנֶה, וְכָל רָאשֵׁי בְשָׂמִים,[5]

« spices, ‹ the finest ‹ and all « *kaneh* [cane], ‹ [The scent of] *kiddah* [cassia],

עֲדֵי עִיר הַתְּמָרִים, בְּבֹא רֵיחַ סַמָּנֶיךָ.[6]*

« of your spices.* ‹ the fragrance ‹ when was brought « of Palms, ‹ [Jericho] the City ‹ reached until

אַף הַלְוִיִּם אֲשֶׁר שׁוֹמְרִים שְׁעָרִים,

« of the Temple gates, ‹ the guards ‹ who were ‹ the Levites ‹ Also [heard there were]

---

(1) See *Exodus* 28:33-35. (2) 30:10. (3) Cf. *Leviticus* 2:2. (4) Cf. 16:12. See also *Yoma* 57a where the laws of חֲפִינָה, *the cupped hands full,* are derived from קְמִיצָה, *the three fingers and palm.* (5) Cf. *Exodus* 30:23. (6) Some editions read שְׁמָנַיִךְ, *your oils.*

---

were very long they were *perceivable from without but could not be actually seen* (see *I Kings* 8:8), because the twin poles pressed against the Curtain from within, and only the twin bosom-like protrusions could be discerned from without (*Yoma* 54a; *Menachos* 98a).

The word לָן, *dwelled,* infers a temporary situation, as one who "sleeps over" and then goes his way. Similarly, God "lodged" within the Sanctuary, but when Israel sinned, the *Shechinah* departed to its "heavenly abode" and took up its lodging there.

עֲדֵי עִיר הַתְּמָרִים בְּבֹא רֵיחַ סַמָּנֶיךָ — *Reached until [Jericho] the City of Palms, when was brought the fragrance of your spices.* The Talmud lists many sounds

וְגַם הַמְשׁוֹרְרִים שִׁיר בְּפֶה עִם כָּל רְנָנֶיךָ.

« the joyous instruments. ‹ of all ‹ with the accompaniment ‹ with their voices ‹ a song ‹ the [Levites] who would sing ‹ as well as

נֶגְדָּם בְּנֵי מַעֲמָד* עוֹרְכִים תְּפִלָּה,

« prayers; ‹ offering ‹ of the *maamad* delegation* ‹ were the members ‹ Facing them

וְלָךְ יַעֲלֶה הֲמוֹנֵךְ בְּכָל פַּעֲמֵי זְמַנַּיִךְ.

« of your [Pilgrimage] Festivals. ‹ occasion ‹ at every ‹ your masses ‹ ascended ‹ and to you

בָּךְ הַנְּבִיאִים, הֲלֹא הָיוּ בְּסוֹד אֵל,[1]

« of God, ‹ in the secret counsel ‹ were they not included « were the prophets, ‹ Within you

וּבָךְ חַכְמֵי תְכוּנָה, וּבָךְ שִׁבְעִים זְקֵנַיִךְ.

« your seventy elders. ‹ and within you ‹ of intercalation, ‹ were the experts ‹ and within you

(1) Cf. *Amos* 3:7.

and aromas from the Temple which were heard and smelled in Jericho, including the voice of the *Kohen Gadol* when he cried out God's Name on Yom Kippur during the Temple service. *Raavad* (comm. ibid.) explains that the smell of the incense and the sounds of the Temple were only sensed in Jericho and not in any other areas around Jerusalem. This miracle was designed to demonstrate Jericho's special status and kinship to Jerusalem. Jericho was the first city to be conquered by Joshua, so it achieved the sanctity of תְּרוּמָה, *the Kohen's due,* which is the first part of the crop that the Torah requires to be set aside. God wanted the inhabitants of Jericho to be aware of their city's status, so He gave them the ability to hear and smell things from Jerusalem, which was many miles away.

בְּנֵי מַעֲמָד — *The maamad delegation.* The Mishnah explains that all the *Kohanim* and the Levites were divided into 24 separate groups called *mishmaros* (*watches;* see commentary to *Kinnah* 10) and each one served in the Temple for two weeks of the year and on the festivals. Corresponding to these *mishmaros,* all of the Israelites were divided into 24 groups. The Mishnah teaches: These are the *maamados.* Since the Torah states: *Command the Children of Israel and say to them, "My sacrifice, My bread"* (*Numbers* 28:2,3). Now, a person's sacrifice cannot be offered if he is not present. [So we require that all of Israel be represented in the sacrificial procedure.] Therefore, the early prophets (Samuel and David) instituted 24 *mishmaros* (of *Kohanim* and Levites). Corresponding to every single *mishmar* there was a *maamad* in Jerusalem of *Kohanim,* Levites, and Israelites. When the time came for the *mishmar* to ascend, the *Kohanim* and Levites ascended to Jerusalem while the Israelites assigned to that *mishmar* would assemble in their own (specially designated) cities and read sections from the Story of Creation (in the Book of *Genesis*). Also, the men of the *maamad* would fast four days a week, from Monday through Thursday (*Taanis* 26a).

אַרְצֵךְ מְלֵאָה בְּמוֹ עֶשֶׂר קְדֻשּׁוֹת,*

Your land was permeated with the [following]: ten [levels] of sanctity;*

וְכָל מַעְשַׂר תְּרוּמָה וְגַם מִבְחַר דְּגָנַיִךְ.

and all the tithes and raised-up portions, all brought from the choicest of your grains.

עַתָּה שְׁמֵמָה בְּלִי בָנִים וּבָנוֹת,

But now you are desolate, without sons and daughters;

וְאָן מַלְכֵּךְ נְבִיאַיִךְ לְוִיַּיִךְ וְכֹהֲנַיִךְ.

and where are your kings, your prophets, your Levites, and your *Kohanim*?

מָתַי יָשׁוּבוּן וְיָבוֹאוּ בְּתוֹךְ אָהֳלֵךְ,

O when will they return [from exile] and enter the midst of your tents,

הַמִּתְאַוִּים שְׁכוֹן תַּחַת עֲנָנַיִךְ.

those who yearn to dwell under your [sheltering] clouds?

(מִי יִתְּנֵנִי לְעֵת תֵּלְדִי יְלָדִים,

(Who would grant me [to live] until the time when you will give birth to children,

כְּמוֹ שִׁפְרָה וּפוּעָה מְיַלֶּדֶת בְּאָבְנַיִךְ.[1]

[I would be] like Shifrah and Puah, the midwives at the birthstone.

זֹאת אֶתְאַוֶּה לְיוֹם יָבֹא חֲתָנֵךְ,

For this I yearn, for the day on which will arrive your bridegroom,

וְאַתְּ כַּלָּה וְהִתְפָּאֲרִי בְּעֶדִי עֲדָנַיִךְ.)[2]

and you will be the bride, and you will adorn yourself with ornaments of your jewelry.)

(1) Cf. *Exodus* 1:15-16. (2) Some editions omit the two stanzas in parentheses.

עֶשֶׂר קְדֻשּׁוֹת — *Ten [levels] of sanctity.* The Mishnah teaches that in the dimension of space there are ten levels of sanctity and enumerates them in ascending order: (1) [The Land of Israel and] its walled cities; (2) the area enclosed within the walls of Jerusalem; (3) the Temple Mount; (4) the enclosed area in front of the Temple Courtyard; (5) the Women's Courtyard; (6) the Israelites' Courtyard;

לִבִּי יְאַוֶּה לְחַבֵּק בִּזְרוֹעוֹת עֲפַר אַרְצֵךְ,

My heart ‹ yearns ‹ to embrace ‹ with my arms ‹ the dust ‹ of your Land, «

וְאֶחְשׁוֹק בְּפִי נַשֵּׁק אֲבָנָיִךְ.

and I desire « — with my mouth — « to kiss ‹ your stones! «

לוּ אֶרְאֵךְ בִּהְיוֹת נִבְנֵית בְּנֹפֶךְ וָפוּךְ,

Would ‹ that I shall see you ‹ when you will be ‹ rebuilt ‹ with gemstones ‹ and jewels, «

יֵרָאוּ לְצָפוֹן וְיָם גֹּבַהּ קְרָנָיִךְ.

when will be visible ‹ from north ‹ and west ‹ your lofty ‹ cornerstones. «

אֶכְסוֹף וְאֶחְמוֹד לְנֶחָמָה,

I yearn ‹ and I desire ‹ for consolation. «

וְתִשְׁמַעְנָה דִּבְרֵי מְבַשֵּׂר בְּקוֹל, אָזְנַי וְאָזְנָיִךְ.

O that hear « — the proclamation ‹ of the herald [of redemption] ‹ aloud — « do my ears ‹ and your ears! «

הִתְעוֹרְרִי[1] לִקְרַאת דּוֹדֵךְ וְהִתְנַעֲרִי מִן הָאֲדָמָה[2]

Wake up ‹ to greet ‹ your beloved! « Shake yourself off ‹ from ‹ [the dust] of the ground, ‹

בְּשׁוּבוֹ אֶל מְעוֹנָיִךְ.

when He returns ‹ to ‹ your palace! «

(1) *Isaiah* 51:17. (2) Cf. 52:2.

(7) the *Kohanim's* Courtyard; (8) the area between the Altar and the Sanctuary; (9) the great *Heichal* hall; and (10) the Holiest of the Holies.

KINNAH 39 / קינה לט

צִיּוֹן תְּקוֹנְנִי* עֲלֵי בֵיתֵךְ אֲשֶׁר נִשְׂרַף,

« is burnt; ‹ which ‹ your house ‹ over ‹ lament* ‹ O Zion,

צָרְחִי בְּמֶרֶר עֲלֵי שִׁמְמוֹת גְּפָנַיִךְ.*

« of your vines.* ‹ the ruination ‹ over ‹ bitterly ‹ cry out

צִיּוֹן תְּעוֹרְרִי כְּאַלְמָנָה אֲשֶׁר הָיְתָה לָמַס[1]

‹ a tribute [payer] ‹ has become ‹ who ‹ like a widow ‹ awaken [your wailing] ‹ O Zion,

לְכָל עוֹבְרִים מֵרֹב עֲוֹנַיִךְ.

« sins. ‹ because of your many ‹ who pass by ‹ to all

עַל הַגְּבָעוֹת שְׂאִי קִינָה וְתַמְרוּר,

« and bitterness; ‹ a lamentation ‹ arouse ‹ the hills ‹ On

וְגַם נְהִי בְּקוֹל רָם אֲשֶׁר הֻכּוּ הֲמוֹנַיִךְ.

« were your multitudes. ‹ smitten ‹ because « that is loud, ‹ in a voice ‹ moan ‹ also

אֵיכָה לְמוֹאָב בְּנֵי צִיּוֹן בְּאַף חֻלְּלוּ

« were killed, ‹ in anger, ‹ of Zion, ‹ the children ‹ by Moab, ‹ How is it that,

עַל רֹב גְּאוֹנֵךְ, וְקִרְאִי אֶל מְקוֹנְנַיִךְ.

« your lamentation reciters. ‹ to ‹ therefore call « stature; ‹ your great ‹ in spite of

(1) *Eichah* 1:1.

צִיּוֹן תְּקוֹנְנִי — *O Zion, lament.* In this *kinnah,* by R' Asher HaKohen, we cry out to Zion herself and implore her to weep and to wail over her own destruction, at the hand of the barbaric enemy which trampled over every one of Zion's precious treasures. The author concludes with a plea to Zion to approach the graves of the Patriarchs and Matriarchs to beg them to petition God on her behalf.

גְּפָנַיִךְ — *Your vines.* This refers to the Jewish people, who are often compared to grapevines. The prophet *Isaiah* (5:1-7) devotes a number of passages to an allegory comparing Israel to a vineyard, as does the prophet *Ezekiel* (Ch. 15).

The Sages compare Israel to a vine in three respects: (1) The vine is alive, yet it is supported by posts of dead wood; similarly, Israel is bolstered by the merit of its forefathers, who are long dead (*Shemos Rabbah* 44); (2) If the vine fails to thrive on a given plot of soil, the farmer will uproot it and replant it elsewhere; similarly, if Israel sins in one land, God will uproot them and replant them on foreign soil (ibid.); (3) The grapes of the vine produce both sweet wine and sour vinegar; simi-

הֵילֵל וְקִינָה שְׂאִי צִיּוֹן בְּמַר וּנְהִי,

Wailing and lamentation ‹ arouse, ‹ O Zion, ‹ with bitterness ‹ and moaning, «

וּבְכִי שְׁמָמוֹת עֲלֵי שִׁמְּמוֹת מְעוֹנַיִךְ.

the weeping ‹ of astonishment ‹ over ‹ the destruction ‹ of your abodes. «

קוֹנְנִי וְאַל תִּדְּמִי קוֹלֵךְ בִּבְכִי שְׂאִי,

Lament ‹ and do not ‹ be silent, « your voice ‹ in weeping ‹ raise, «

דֶּבֶר וְחֶרֶב אֲשֶׁר שֻׁלַּח לְמַחֲנַיִךְ.

[over] the plague ‹ and the sword ‹ which ‹ were unleashed ‹ against your camp. «

צָדוּ כְּצִפּוֹר[1] וְאֵין עוֹזֵר לְנֶגְדּוֹ,

The [enemy] ensnared [you] ‹ like a bird ‹ and there is no one ‹ to assist you ‹ against them, «

אֲשֶׁר פָּרְשׂוּ רְשָׁתוֹת[2] לְגַלּוֹת אֶת קְלוֹנַיִךְ.

for ‹ they have spread out ‹ nets ‹ to reveal ‹ your shame. «

וְאֵיךְ הִשְׁלִיךְ תִּפְאֶרֶת יִשְׂרָאֵל,[3]

How ‹ did [God] cast down ‹ the glory [the Temple,] ‹ of Israel, «

וְלֹא זָכַר שְׁבוּעָה אֲשֶׁר כָּרַת לְאוֹמְנַיִךְ.

and did not ‹ remember ‹ the oath-covenant ‹ which ‹ He established ‹ with [the Patriarchs] who raised you? «

קוֹלֵךְ כְּקוֹל נַהֲמַת תַּנִּים,[4]

Your voice [raise] ‹ like the sound ‹ of the howling ‹ of jackals, «

(1) Cf. *Eichah* 3:52. (2) Cf. 1:13. (3) Cf. 2:1. (4) Some editions read יְעֵנִים, *ostriches.*

larly, the fate of Israel may be sweet or it may be bitter. Under all circumstances, however, Israel blesses God for doing as He sees best (*Vayikra Rabbah* 36).

R' S. R. Hirsch (Commentary to *Psalms* 80:9) notes also that of all fruits, only the grape is so crushed and extensively altered from its natural state. But this very abuse serves to transform the grape into something far above what it had been: from an ordinary fruit into valuable and treasured wine. Ultimately, the finished product, wine, intoxicates and overpowers the one who mangled the grape.

Similarly, Israel in the crucible of exile will eventually overcome its captors and tormentors.

נְאוֹת יַעֲקֹב[1] בְּכִי וְקִינָה שְׂאִי, עַל רֹב תְּלוּנַיִךְ.

« complaints you now have [about your own actions]. ‹ the many ‹ over ‹ arouse ‹ and lamentation ‹ weeping ‹ of Jacob, ‹ O dwellings

גָּזִּי נִזְרֵךְ וְהַשְׁלִיכִי[2] לְרֹאשֵׁךְ עֲלֵי אֶרֶץ,

« the ground; ‹ upon ‹ your head ‹ and throw ‹ your beautiful hair ‹ Tear out

וְשַׂק תִּקְשְׁרִי עֲצָרִי בְּמָתְנַיִךְ.

« to your waist. ‹ and bind it ‹ tie on ‹ sackcloth

קוֹנְנִי בְּפֶשַׁע וְאַל תִּתְּנִי מְנוּחָה,

« any rest [from mourning]; ‹ give yourself ‹ and do not ‹ over [your] transgressions ‹ Lament

וְקוֹנְנֵךְ אֶל שְׁפָיִים[2] שְׂאִי מֵרֹב מְעַנַּיִךְ.

« who oppress you. ‹ because of the many ‹ raise ‹ the hilltops ‹ up to ‹ your lamentations

אֶרֶץ צְבִי צְבָאוֹת,[3] קִינָה וּנְהִי תְּעוֹרְרִי עַל שְׁפָיִים,

« the hilltops, ‹ upon ‹ arouse ‹ and moaning ‹ lamentations « by the multitude [of nations], ‹ desired ‹ O land,

הֲלֹא תַּחַת שְׂשׂוֹנַיִךְ.

« your [former] joys! ‹ [now] replace ‹ do they not

קוֹנְנוּ מְלָכִים,* וְהֵילִילוּ קְצִינִים

« O commanders! ‹ Wail, « O kings!* ‹ Lament,

וְכָל יוֹשְׁבֵי מַעֲרָב וּמִזְרָח, עַל שִׁמְלוֹנַיִךְ.

« your punishing yoke. ‹ over « and east, ‹ in west ‹ who dwell ‹ [together with] all

פִּשְׁטִי מְעִילֵךְ וְהַשְׁלִיכִי לָאָרֶץ,

« to the ground; ‹ and cast it ‹ your robe ‹ Strip off

(1) *Eichah* 2:2. (2) *Jeremiah* 7:29. (3) Cf. 3:19.

קוֹנְנוּ מְלָכִים — *Lament, O kings!* All the nations of the world and their leaders should lament the destruction of the Temple. As the Talmud states (*Succah* 55b): *R' Yochanan said, Woe to the idolaters who have lost [something precious] and do not know what they have lost! As long as the Temple stood, the Altar atoned for them, but now who will atone for them?*

וְחִגְרִי שַׂק וְגַם תְּהֶמִי תַּחַת סְדִינָיִךְ.

gird yourself ‹ with sackcloth ‹ and also ‹ start moaning « — in place of ‹ your fine linen. «

בָּחוּר וְזָקֵן וְגַם עוֹלֵל וְיוֹנֵק,[1]

Youth ‹ and elder, ‹ and also ‹ infant ‹ and nursing child, «

שְׂאוּ תַּמְרוּר נֶפֶשׁ, לְעֵינֵי כָּל זְקֵנָיִךְ.

raise a cry ‹ from the bitterness ‹ of your soul ‹ before the eyes ‹ of all ‹ of your elders. «

צִיּוֹן שׁוֹשַׁנֵּךְ[2] הֲלֹא עָבַר כְּקוֹץ עֲלֵי מַיִם,

O Zion, « your rose « — has it not gone away ‹ like a thorn ‹ upon ‹ the water, «

וְנֶהֶפְכוּ מֵרֹב זְדוֹנָיִךְ.

so have you been transformed ‹ by the enormity ‹ of your willful violations. «

חָשְׁכוּ מְאוֹרוֹת וְגַם שְׁחָקִים,*

Darkened ‹ are the celestial luminaries ‹ as well as ‹ the heavens* «

וְכָל דֶּרֶךְ מְלֹא נֶחְשַׁךְ, סָתוּם לְפָנָיִךְ.

and every ‹ path ‹ is filled ‹ with deep darkness, « [all is] sealed off ‹ before you. «

כִּי הַשְּׁחָקִים מְאֹד זָרוּ, וְאָסְפוּ לְאוֹרָם[3]

For ‹ the heavens ‹ are deeply ‹ alienated [from mankind], « and withhold ‹ their light ‹

לִפְנֵי כָּל שָׁאוֹן, עַל רֹב יְגוֹנָיִךְ.

from before ‹ the entire ‹ clamoring multitude, « because of commiseration ‹ with your tremendous ‹ grief. «

צִיּוֹן בְּשׁוֹפָר תְּקַע,[4] עַל הַר וְגֶבַע רְאִי,

O Zion, ‹ with the *shofar* ‹ sound a blast! « Upon ‹ mountain ‹ and hill ‹ gaze! «

(1) Cf. *Deuteronomy* 32:25. (2) Some editions read שְׂשׂוֹנֵךְ, *your joy.* (3) Cf. *Joel* 2:10. (4) Cf. 2:15.

חָשְׁכוּ מְאוֹרוֹת וְגַם שְׁחָקִים — *Darkened are the celestial luminaries as well as the heavens.* The *Talmud* teaches in the name of Rav Chisda: since the day that the Holy Temple

צָרְחִי בְּמַר וּבְכִי, עַל מוֹת סְרָנָיִךְ.

« of your leaders. ‹ the death ‹ over ‹ and weep ‹ bitterly ‹ Scream

שִׁלְּחוּ שְׁלָלֵךְ בָּאֵשׁ, צִיּוֹן לְמִרְמָס,

« was to be trampled, ‹ and Zion ‹ into the fire ‹ your spoils ‹ They cast

הֲלֹא טָבְעוּ שְׁעָרַיִךְ[1] בְּתוֹךְ אֶרֶץ אֲדָנָיִךְ.

« [together with] your foundations. ‹ the ground ‹ into ‹ did your gates ‹ sink ‹ indeed

הִנֵּה לְמִרְמָס נְתוּנָה בַּת יְהוּדָה,

« of Judah. ‹ the daughter ‹ has been given over ‹ to be trampled ‹ Indeed,

וְאֵין מֵשִׁיב לְנַפְשָׁהּ,[2] עֲלֵי שְׁמָמוֹת שְׁמֵנָיִךְ.

« of your fattest [finest]. ‹ the destruction ‹ after ‹ her spirits ‹ to revive ‹ There is no one

צִיּוֹן בְּמַר תִּבְכִּי מֵאֵין מְנַחֵם,[2]

« to comfort you; ‹ with no one ‹ shall you weep, ‹ bitterly ‹ O Zion,

אֲשֶׁר רָחַק מְאֹד מִקָּרוֹב נַחֵם בְּחוּנָיִךְ.

« who are Your [sorely] tested ones. ‹ to [now] comfort [the Jews] ‹ than [He was formerly] close ‹ He is much more distant ‹ since

קוֹלֵךְ כְּקוֹל יָם וְגַם תַּנִּין וְיַעֲנָה,[3]

« and the ostrich; ‹ [as loud] as the jackal ‹ and also « of the [raging] sea, ‹ should be [as loud] as the sound ‹ Your [wailing] voice

וְקוֹל נְהִי וּבְכִי אֲשֶׁר תַּחַת סִלּוֹנָיִךְ.

« your thorn[-like oppressors]. ‹ under ‹ in that you are ‹ and weeping ‹ in moaning ‹ and [raise] your voice

צִיּוֹן לַמָּרוֹם שְׂאִי עֵינַיִךְ,[4]

« your eyes ‹ raise ‹ to on high ‹ O Zion,

(1) Cf. *Eichah* 2:9. (2) Cf. 1:16. (3) Cf. *Micah* 1:8. (4) Cf. *Isaiah* 40:26.

was destroyed, the sky has never appeared in its pure (color) as it says, *I cloak the heavens with blackness, I make sackcloth their covering* (*Isaiah* 50:3; *Berachos* 59a).

וְגַם תִּרְאִי סִפְדִי וְהֵילִילִי, עֲלֵי עָזְבֵךְ תּוֹאֲנָיִךְ.

and also ‹ see [God's glory], ‹ and thus mourn ‹ and wail ‹ over ‹ your betrayal ‹ of your [God,] the First Cause. «

צִיּוֹן תְּקוֹנְנִי עֲלֵי אָבוֹת וְשַׁאֲלִי מְכוֹן בֵּיתֵךְ,

O Zion, ‹ lament ‹ to ‹ the Patriarchs ‹ and ask ‹ for the reestablishment ‹ of your House, «

וְגַם עֶזְרֵךְ, חֹסֶן קְצִינָיִךְ.

and also ‹ for the [return there of God] your Helper, « the One Who strengthens ‹ your leaders. «

אֶל הַמְּעָרָה לְכִי, צָרְחִי בְּמַר וּבְכִי,

To ‹ the Cave [of Machpelah] ‹ go, « scream ‹ bitterly ‹ and wail [to the Patriarchs], «

עִנּוּ בָנַיִךְ וּבְנוֹתַיִךְ וְנִינָיִךְ.

because [the enemy] has tormented ‹ their sons ‹ and daughters ‹ and [all] their descendants. «

שָׂרָה כְּשָׁמְעָה לְקוֹלֵךְ, גַּם מְבַכָּה עֲלֵי בָנִים,

Sarah, ‹ when she hears ‹ your voice, ‹ will also cry ‹ for ‹ [her] sons ‹

אֲשֶׁר נִשְׁבּוּ אֶל כָּל שְׁכֵנָיִךְ.

who ‹ were led captive ‹ into the midst ‹ of all ‹ your [hostile] neighbors. «

רָחֵל וְלֵאָה* בְּכוּ, בִּלְהָה וְזִלְפָּה הֲלֹא קוֹנֵנוּ,

Rachel ‹ and Leah,* ‹ cry [too]! « Bilhah ‹ and Zilpah, ‹ indeed ‹ you must lament! «

רָחֵל וְלֵאָה — *Rachel and Leah.* When the Temple was destroyed, even the merit of the Patriarchs and the Matriarchs was not enough to prevent it. However, the arguments and pleas of the Matriarch Rachel did elicit from God a solemn pledge that the exiles of Israel would someday return. The Midrash (*Pesichta* to *Eichah Rabbasi* §24) records the logical argument which Rachel put before God: You know that Your servant Jacob loved me intensely and worked for seven hard years to earn my hand in marriage. But at the end of the seven long years of waiting, my father Laban wanted me to give up my rights to my beloved Jacob in favor of my older sister Leah. My heart ached, but I didn't want my sister to be humiliated. I suppressed all of my tender feelings and emotions and revealed to Leah all the secret identification signs that Jacob and I had agreed upon as guarantees that my father Laban would not trick him. Moreover, on the wedding night I hid under the bed and

וְקִרְאוּ בְּקוֹל, מְחִי בְּפָנַיִךְ.

« on your faces. ‹ [for the enemy] has beaten ‹ with full voice ‹ Cry out

כִּי הָאֱלֹהִים הֲלֹא לָנֶצַח וְלֹא יִזְנַח,[1]

« and He will not abandon us. ‹ endures for eternity ‹ indeed, ‹ God, ‹ For

כִּי תִקְוָה הִיא וְרֹב שְׁלוֹם לְבָנַיִךְ.[2]

« for your children. ‹ will be the peace ‹ and abundant « it is, ‹ a true hope ‹ Therefore,

(1) *Eichah* 3:31. (2) Cf. *Isaiah* 54:13.

spoke instead of Leah who was together with Jacob, so that he wouldn't recognize her voice and reject her. Now, dear God, see how I acted even though I am a weak mortal of mere flesh and blood. Nevertheless, I overcame my inclination to be jealous of my rival, my sister. Certainly, You, O God, who are Infinite and Eternal and filled with compassion, can forgive my children, the Children of Israel, and not be jealous of the idols they worshiped instead of worshiping You!

KINNAH 40 / קינה מ

צִיּוֹן יְדִידוּת יָדִיד* צָעִיר לְשָׂרָיִךְ,[1]

O Zion, 〈 the beloved [Temple] 〈 of the beloved* [in the territory of Benjamin] 〈 the youngest 〈 of your [tribal] princes; 《

שָׁכַנְתְּ כְּתֵפָיו*[2] בְּרֹב עַנְוַת הֲדָרָיִךְ.

You [God] dwell 〈 between his shoulders* 《 in the great 〈 humility 〈 of Your splendor. 《

(1) Cf. *Psalms* 68:28. (2) Cf. *Deuteronomy* 33:12.

✧ **צִיּוֹן יְדִידוּת יָדִיד** — *O Zion . . . the beloved of the beloved.* Again we have a composition that sings the praises of Jerusalem and Zion, this time emphasizing the idea that the Temple was constructed on the territory of Benjamin, the youngest of Jacob's sons. The Second Temple was destroyed because of the senseless hatred which divided one Jew from another. This lack of brotherhood had its roots in the hatred displayed by Jacob's sons for their brother Joseph, many centuries earlier. The only one of the twelve brothers who had nothing to do with this bitter feud was young Benjamin, and for this reason he was especially beloved to God. And for this reason the Temple, a symbol of national unity and brotherhood, was built in Benjamin's province.

Moreover, the Second Temple was destroyed by the Romans who were descendants of Esau. When Jacob encountered Esau with his entire family, Jacob, his wives, and his sons all bowed before Esau. Only Benjamin, who was not born yet, did not bow. Therefore, the Temple was built in Benjamin's portion so that it would not bend before Esau's onslaught.

Nevertheless, Israel's sins were so great that none of these merits could protect Zion and the Temple, when God's fury was aroused and the awesome day of reckoning arrived.

The composer of this *kinnah* is the otherwise unknown R' Yaakov.

יְדִידוּת יְדִיד — *The beloved of the beloved.* The Talmud (*Menachos* 53a) teaches that when the *Beis HaMikdash* was to be built, God said, "Let the יְדִיד, *beloved,* son of the יְדִיד, come and build the יְדִיד for the יְדִיד in the portion of the יְדִיד, in order to bring atonement for the יְדִידִים." This means: Let Solomon, who is called יְדִיד (*II Samuel* 12:24) the son, [i.e., descendant] of Abraham who is called יְדִיד (*Jeremiah* 11:15), come and build the *Beis HaMikdash* which is called יְדִיד (*Psalms* 84:2), for the Holy One, Blessed is He, Who is called יְדִיד (*Isaiah* 5:1), in the portion of Benjamin who is called יְדִיד (*Deuteronomy* 33:12), to bring atonement for Israel who are called יְדִידִים (*Jeremiah* 12:7).

From the first moment when God began His creation, His prime desire was to establish a place which would allow Him to dwell in the midst of His creatures on earth: The Temple is His *beloved,* therefore, because it is, so to speak, the culmination of God's aspirations (*Alshich*).

שָׁכַנְתְּ כְּתֵפָיו — *You [God] dwell between his shoulders.* Moses gave his final blessing to the tribes of Israel. *Of Benjamin he said: May Hashem's beloved dwell securely by Him; He hovers above him all day long; and rests His Presence between his shoulders* (*Deuteronomy* 33:12). The Talmud (*Zevachim* 118b) explains that in this world God's presence was not permanently entrenched over the Temple, but in the future Third Temple of the Messianic Era, God will dwell permanently and securely between the shoulders of Benjamin.

צִיּוֹן הֲדַר כָּל חֲדַר מִטּוֹת,

« of couches [the Temple wherein God's Presence dwells], ‹ chamber ‹ of the entire ‹ [in you is] the splendor ‹ O Zion,

וְכָל מִשְׁכַּב דּוֹדִים יְדִידֵךְ בְּבֹא חַדְרֵי חֲדָרַיִךְ.

« within a chamber. ‹ your chamber ‹ when they enter ‹ [with] your beloved [Israel] « of beloveds it is, ‹ the embrace ‹ and entirely

צִיּוֹן בְּרוּכָה בְּרָכָה עֶלְיוֹנָה עֲלֵי רֹאשֵׁךְ,

« your head, ‹ which descends upon ‹ from on high ‹ with a blessing ‹ you are blessed ‹ O Zion,

לְמוּלֵךְ מְחֻטָּבִים שְׁעָרַיִךְ.

« the heavenly gates. ‹ are carved ‹ for facing you

צִיּוֹן יְרֻשַּׁת זְאֵב עֶרֶב,[1]*

« who hunts at dusk,* ‹ [who is like] the wolf ‹ you are the heir [of Benjamin] ‹ O Zion,

שְׁבִי פְּאֵרֵךְ בַּעֲדִי עֲדָיִים,[2] עֲדֵי עָלוּ כְּתָרַיִךְ.

« do your [spiritual] crowns [of Torah, priesthood and monarchy]. ‹ surpass [them] ‹ but yet ‹ and ornaments, ‹ with jewels ‹ is your coronet ‹ set

(1) Cf. *Genesis* 49:27. (2) *Ezekiel* 16:7.

Indeed, the Holy Spirit of God dwelled among the Israelites in three places and all three were in Benjamin's territory. First the Tabernacle was in Shiloh, then in Nob and Gibeon, and finally the Temple was built in Jerusalem on the land belonging not to Judah, but to the tribe of Benjamin. The Talmud (*Yoma* 12a) explains that more than any other tribe, Benjamin pined and yearned to host the Divine Presence in his territory and therefore he was granted his fervent wish. Elsewhere, the Talmud (*Sotah* 38a) says that at the Sea of Reeds the tribe of Benjamin displayed extraordinary faith and devotion to God. Even before the raging seawaters split, the Benjaminites eagerly jumped into the sea in response to God's command, and in this merit the Divine Presence dwelled in their midst. Finally, *Sifri* observes that Benjamin's advantage was that he was the only one of Jacob's sons born on the holy soil of *Eretz Yisrael* and therefore merited to host God's holy *Shechinah*.

זְאֵב עֶרֶב — *[Benjamin . . .] the wolf who hunts at dusk*. In Jacob's blessing to his son Benjamin, he said: *Benjamin is a predatory wolf; in the morning he will devour prey and in the evening he will distribute spoils* (*Genesis* 49:27). According to *Targum Onkelos* this means that Benjamin hungered for the Divine Presence as a wolf hungers for its prey. Therefore the Temple, in which the *Kohanim*

יָפִית בְּרֹב הוֹן וְהֵן רָבִית בְּדֵעוֹת,

« wisdom. ‹ and indeed you acquired vast « great wealth, ‹ through ‹ You were beautified

וְהֵן מִזִּקְנֵי צוֹעֲנִים, חָכְמוּ נְעָרַיִךְ.

« were your youths. ‹ wise « of Tzoan [Egypt], ‹ more than the elders ‹ Indeed,

הָיִית יְפֵה מִכְלָל,[1] נָאוָה בְּכָל מַהֲלָל,

« form of praise; ‹ [worthy] of every ‹ lovely, « the consummation, « of beauty, ‹ You were

עָלִית וְשָׁבִית שָׁלָל, מַלְכֵי מְגוּרָיִךְ.

« who dwelled all around you. ‹ of the kings ‹ the spoils ‹ and captured ‹ you overwhelmed

בָּךְ בִּרְוָחָה אֱנוֹשׁ לָן* מִבְּלִי חֵטְא,

« and was without sin, ‹ lodge ‹ did a person ‹ in ample space* ‹ Within you

בָּךְ כֻּפַּר בְּקָרְבַּן תָּמִיד מְכַפְּרָיִךְ.

« brought by the *Kohanim* to provide atonement. ‹ that is continual ‹ with the offering ‹ was atonement obtained ‹ for through you, [O Zion,]

יֻסַּדְתְּ בְּזִיו לְפָאֵר, חָרַבְתְּ בְּתוֹךְ אָב

‹ of the month of Av ‹ in the midst ‹ and you were destroyed « to be a splendor, ‹ in the bright [month of Iyar] ‹ You were established

בְּאַף,* אֶשְׁאַף לְזֹאת אֶשְׁאַב מֵימֵי תַמְרוּרָיִךְ.

« of your bitterness. ‹ of the waters ‹ — that I should drink deeply « for this ‹ therefore I yearn thirstily « with fury;*

(1) *Psalms* 50:2.

offered sacrifices each morning and divided the remaining sacred portions in the evening, stood in his territory.

בָּךְ בִּרְוָחָה אֱנוֹשׁ לָן — *Within you in ample space did a person lodge.* The Mishnah (*Avos* 5:7) lists ten miracles that were performed for our ancestors in the Holy Temple. One was that no man ever said to his fellow, "The space is insufficient for me to stay overnight in Jerusalem"; despite the multitudes convening in Jerusalem for the festivals, there were sufficient accommodations for them all. Moreover, because of the sanctity of the city, God provided for all residents of Jerusalem, so that no one ever had to move to another city to seek a livelihood.

אָב בְּאַף — *Of the month of Av with fury.* The author of the *piyut* is punning on the similar sound of the two words אָב and אַף as well as the words later in the line, אֶשְׁאַף and אֶשְׁאַב.

נִרְאוּ בְּעִירֵךְ פְּנֵי קוֹנֵהּ,

‹ Appear ‹ in your city ‹ to be in the presence ‹ of your Maker

בְּנֵי מַחֲנֶה, רְצוֹן לְשׁוֹכְנִי סְנֶה,[1] בִּשְׁנֵי חֲצֵרָיִךְ.

‹ did the children ‹ of your camp [the Israelites]; ‹ in order to find favor ‹ [with] He Who rested upon « the thorn bush, ‹ [they entered] into the two « courtyards [of the Temple].

עוֹשֵׂי מְלַאכְתֵּךְ בְּחוּט,

‹ Even those who did ‹ your work [in the Temple] ‹ with the [weaver's] thread

הִתְעַשְּׁרוּ בִּרְכוּשׁ, כָּל הוֹן יָקָר נִמְצָא,

‹ were enriched « with wealth; ‹ every ‹ treasure ‹ that is precious ‹ was available

לִקְהַל עֲשִׁירָיִךְ.

‹ for the community « of your rich people.

נִבְחַר מְקוֹמֵךְ לְצוּר[2] בָּחַר בְּאוּם בְּחוּרָיו,[3]

‹ Chosen ‹ was your site « for the *Rock;* ‹ He selected ‹ for His Nation « the *Chosen Ones* [Israel];

בָּחַר בְּמוֹצְאֵךְ,[4] וּבְכֹהֲנִים בְּחִירָיִךְ.[5]

‹ He chose [David] « who chose you, ‹ and for His *Kohanim* « [He chose] the finest.

בָּךְ דָּר בְּגִיל נֶהְדָּר, אַדִּירֵךְ בְּכָל דּוֹר וָדוֹר,

‹ Within you ‹ dwelt ‹ the One Who in joy « is majestic, ‹ He remained your splendor ‹ in every ‹ gener-ation « after generation;

עֶרְכֵּךְ בְּבֹא לַעֲדוֹר, עֶדְרֵי חֲבֵרָיִךְ.[6]

‹ but your true value [will be known] ‹ when return ‹ to be one flock ‹ do the [scattered] flocks « of your fellows [Israel in exile].

עָלָה גְּבוּלֵךְ[7] דְּבִיר צֶלַע יְבוּס,

‹ Ascend ‹ did the borders ‹ of your Abode ‹ from the slopes « of Yevus,

(1) Cf. *Deuteronomy* 33:16. (2) Cf. *Psalms* 132:13.
(3) Cf. *Deuteronomy* 7:6. (4) Cf. *Psalms* 78:70; 89:21; 132:5.
(5) Cf. *I Samuel* 2:28. (6) Cf. *Song of Songs* 1:7. (7) Cf. *Joshua* 15:8, 9.

לֹא לְעֵין עֵיטָם, לְבִלְתִּי שְׂאֵת כְּתֵפוֹת דְּבִירֶךְ.

but not [on the highest point] ‹ the Fountain ‹ of Eitam ‹ so that not ‹ raised too high ‹ would be the shoulders ‹ of your Abode. «

קָרָא יהוה שְׁמֵךְ עַל שֵׁם שְׁנֵי כֹּהֲנִים,*

HASHEM called ‹ your name [Jerusalem], ‹ based on ‹ the names ‹ [given by] the two ‹ priests [Shem and Abraham].* «

דָּוִד מְצָאֵךְ בְּחִיל בִּשְׂדֵי יְעָרֵיִךְ.[1]

David ‹ discovered you ‹ to be encircled [by mountains], ‹ in the fields ‹ of your forest. «

בָּנָה מְעוֹנֵךְ בְּנוֹ, וַיְחַנְּכֵךְ שֵׁם בְּשֵׁם אָבִיו*

Build ‹ your palace [the Temple] ‹ did his son [Solomon] « and he inaugurated you ‹ [giving you] a name « — the name ‹ of his father* ‹

אֲשֶׁר קִדְּמוֹ,[2] נֶחְתַּם בְּשִׁירָיִךְ.[3]

who ‹ preceded him [and built the Temple's foundation], « as is inscribed ‹ in the [introduction to] your songs. «

וּבְמַחְשְׁבוֹת בּוֹרְאֵךְ עָלִית, בְּטֶרֶם בְּרֹא תֵבֵל,

In the thoughts ‹ of your Creator ‹ you were conceived, « even before ‹ the creation ‹ of earth, ‹

וְשַׁחַק וְעוֹלָם* עַל עֲפָרָיִךְ.

heaven, ‹ and the universe* ‹ from ‹ your dust. «

(1) *Psalms* 132:6. (2) See *Succah* 53a. (3) See *Psalms* 30:1.

קָרָא ה׳ שְׁמֵךְ עַל שֵׁם שְׁנֵי כֹּהֲנִים — *Hashem called your name [Jerusalem] based on the names given by the two priests [Shem and Abraham].* The Midrash (*Bereishis Rabbah* 5:1) notes that after the *Akeidah,* we read that *Abraham named that site "Hashem Yireh [Hashem will see]"* (*Genesis* 22:14), and earlier we read that Shem the son of Noah greeted Abraham in his role as *Malchizedek, King of Shalem* (*Genesis* 14:18). Both men were in the same location and gave it different names reflecting different aspects of the unique sanctity of the holy mountain. Thus, God made a synthesis of *Yireh* and *Shalem* and called the city *Yerushalem* [יִרְאֶה שָׁלֵם = יְרוּשָׁלֵם = יְרוּשָׁלַיִם].

בְּשֵׁם אָבִיו — *The name of his father.* Midrash *Tehillim* (30) explains that when one had full intention to fulfill a mitzvah, and through circumstances beyond his control was not able to perform the mitzvah, God considers it as if he had completed it. The Midrash brings as proof that the Temple was called after David's name even though it was Solomon, his son, who actually built it.

בְּטֶרֶם בְּרֹא תֵבֵל וְשַׁחַק וְעוֹלָם — *Even before the creation of earth, heaven, and the*

וּבְמֵי מְרִיבָה בְּיוֹם זַעַם, אֲזַי טָהֳרָה אַרְצֵךְ,

And through the [flood-] waters ‹ of strife ‹ on the day ‹ of wrath, ‹ then, ‹ purified ‹ was your land, «

וְלֹא גֻשְּׁמָה*[1] בִּכְלוֹת יְצוּרָיִךְ.

and was not ‹ rained upon,* « while came to an end ‹ did the [rest of God's] creations. «

יָרַד בְּעִתּוֹ מְטַר אַרְצֵךְ, זְמַן לֵיְלָה בָּא לִבְרָכָה,

Descend ‹ in its proper time ‹ did the rain ‹ of your land, « [even] at the time ‹ of [Friday] night ‹ did it fall ‹ as a blessing, «

וְטַל לָן בִּקְצִירָיִךְ.

and [only] the dew ‹ came to rest ‹ upon your harvests. «

הָיִית לְשִׁית חוּג יְסוֹד, מִמֵּךְ תְּעוּדָה[2]

You were [the place] ‹ of the Foundation [Stone] ‹ [upon which] the universe ‹ was established; « from you went forth ‹ the Torah. «

וְסוֹד קִדּוּשׁ יַרְחֵךְ לְפִי עֵדִים מְעַבְּרָיִךְ.

The complexities ‹ of the sanctification ‹ of the New Moon ‹ according to ‹ the [testimony] of witnesses ‹ and [also] your [calculation] of intercalation. «

בָּנִים וּבָנוֹת תְּשׁוּקָה, בַּשּׁוּק שׁוֹקְקוּ,

Sons ‹ and daughters ‹ had a desire [to join the pilgrimage] ‹ and in the marketplace ‹ they merrily romped; «

שָׂחֲקוּ וְהִשְׁתַּקְשְׁקוּ[3] בַּסָּךְ עוֹבְרָיִךְ.[4]

they played ‹ and clamored ‹ amidst the throngs ‹ of the passing pilgrims. «

בְּחַג פֶּסַח נִפְלָאוּ, פּוּרִים בַּפָּז סָלָאוּ,[5]

On the Festival ‹ of Pesach ‹ they appeared wondrous; « already at Purim ‹ with the finest of gold ‹ they were adorned; «

(1) Cf. *Ezekiel* 22:24. (2) Cf. *Micah* 4:2. (3) Cf. *Nahum* 2:5. (4) Cf. *Psalms* 42:5. (5) Cf. *Eichah* 4:2.

---

universe. The Talmud lists seven things that were created before the world itself: the Torah, the concept of *teshuvah, Gan Eden, Gehinnom,* the Throne of Glory, the *Beis HaMikdash,* and the name of the Messiah (*Pesachim* 54a)

אֲזַי טָהֳרָה אַרְצֵךְ וְלֹא גֻשְּׁמָה — *Then purified was your land, and was not rained upon.* According to one view in the Talmud, the waters of Noah's Flood did not enter the area that was to become the Land of Israel (*Zevachim* 113a).

טַל אוֹר וְחֵן נִמְלָאוּ, זַכּוּ נְזִירַיִךְ.[1]

with dew, ‹ and light, ‹ and charm ‹ they were filled; « purified ‹ were your crowned people. «

אֵיךְ אֶשְׂמְחָה עוֹד בְּחַג, אֵיךְ אֶעֱלוֹז עוֹד בְּפוּר,

O how ‹ can I rejoice ‹ any more ‹ on the festivals ‹ and how ‹ can I make merry ‹ any more ‹ on Purim day, «

עַד כִּי יָבוֹאוּן יְמֵי שָׂשׂוֹן לְפוּרַיִךְ.

until ‹ when ‹ there shall come ‹ days ‹ of joy ‹ to your portion? «

אַרְצֵךְ חֲמוּדָה[2] מְאֹד, לֹא נֶחְמָדָה,[3]

Although your land ‹ was desirable ‹ to the extreme, « not coveted was it ‹

בַּעֲלוֹת בָּנִים חֲמוּדִים, לְבֵית מַחְמַד מְגוּרַיִךְ.

when ascend ‹ did [your] sons ‹ who were beloved ‹ to the House ‹ that is precious, « the place of Your residence. «

נַעֲלָה עֲנַן הַקְּטֹרֶת, מִמְּקוֹם מִקְדָּשׁ יָצָא,

There would arise ‹ the cloud ‹ of incense, « from the place ‹ of the Holy Temple ‹ it has departed, «

מְקוֹמוֹ עֲשַׁן אֵשׁ מִנְּחִירַיִךְ.

in its place ‹ is the smoke ‹ from the [furious] fire ‹ from your nostrils. «

בִּקְרוֹב מְרֵעִים בָּעִיר,[4] שִׁלְּחוּ בְּכַרְמֵךְ בְּעִיר,[5]

When there approached ‹ evildoers ‹ to the city, « they set loose [wild animals] ‹ into your vineyards ‹ in the city, «

עָרוּ וְעוֹרְרוּ,[6] בְּעִיר וְקַדִּישׁ[7] בְּעָרַיִךְ.

they destroyed, « they destroyed to the foundations ‹ the [House of] the Alert One ‹ [Whose abode is] in your City. «

בַּרְזֶל בְּלִי נִשְׁמַע קוֹלוֹ[8] בְּעֵת נִבְנֵית,*

Of iron [tools] ‹ there was not ‹ heard ‹ their sound ‹ at the time ‹ [the Temple] was being built;* «

(1) Cf. *Eichah* 4:7. (2) Cf. *Jeremiah* 3:19. (3) Cf. *Exodus* 34:24. (4) Cf. *Psalms* 27:2. (5) Cf. *Exodus* 22:4. (6) Cf. *Psalms* 137:7. (7) *Daniel* 4:10. (8) *I Kings* 6:7.

בַּרְזֶל בְּלִי נִשְׁמַע קוֹלוֹ בְּעֵת נִבְנֵית — *Of iron [tools] there was not heard their sound at the time [the Temple] was being built.* When Solomon constructed the First Temple, it is stated: *And the House, when it was being constructed, was built of stone finished at the quarry, and there was neither hammer, nor axe, nor any*

אֵיךְ חַרְבוֹת צוּרִים, בָּךְ תָּקְעוּ מְצִירָיִךְ.

how then ‹ were knives ‹ of flint ‹ into you ‹ stabbed ‹ by your tormentors? «

עַל זֹאת בַּשַּׂק עוֹבְרִים עִבְרִים,

For ‹ this, « in sackcloth ‹ wander about ‹ do the Hebrews; «

אֲבָל בּוֹטְחִים כִּי יִשְׂמְחוּ אַחֲרֵי חִתּוּךְ בְּתָרָיִךְ.[1]

yet ‹ they trust ‹ that ‹ they shall rejoice ‹ after ‹ the cutting down ‹ of the one who cut you down. «

לֵב מַדְוֶה יֶחֱלֶה, לְתַאֲוָה יִכְלֶה,

The heart ‹ that aches ‹ grows sick, « in [its] yearning ‹ it pines away, «

יִישַׁן עֲדֵי יַעֲלֶה עַמּוּד שְׁחָרָיִךְ.

[therefore] it sleeps [in exile] ‹ until ‹ the breaking ‹ of your dawn [with the coming of the Messiah]. «

יְלֵל לְקוֹלִי, אֱלִי אֵיךְ תִּתְאַפְּקִי,

Wail with me ‹ all who hear my voice; « from lamenting, « how ‹ can you restrain yourself? «

הֲלֹא קָרָא לְשַׂק וּבְכִי,[2] אַלּוּף נְעוּרָיִךְ.[3]

Has He not ‹ proclaimed [Tishah B'Av] ‹ for sackcloth ‹ and crying « — the Master ‹ of your youth [has]? «

אָקוּם חֲצוֹת לַיְלָה,[4] עַל מִשְׁמְרוֹת מַאֲפֵל,

I will arise ‹ at midnight ‹ during ‹ the nightwatch ‹ that is the gloomiest, «

לִשְׁמוֹר לְאוֹר יֶאֱתֶה בֹּקֶר[5] לְשֹׁמְרָיִךְ.

to keep vigil ‹ for the light ‹ which will arrive ‹ in the morning ‹ for those who await you. «

---

(1) Some editions read הַתּוֹר בְּתוֹרָיִךְ, *the turtledove [which was not severed] is your portion,* a reference to the Covenant Between the Parts (*Genesis* 15:9-10 with *Rashi*); some read הַתּוֹר בְּשׂוֹרָיִךְ, *the guide [the herald] will inform you [of the Messiah's arrival].*
(2) Cf. *Isaiah* 22:12. (3) Cf. *Jeremiah* 3:4. (4) Cf. *Psalms* 119:62. (5) Cf. *Isaiah* 21:12.

---

tool of iron heard in the House while it was under construction (*I Kings* 6:7). *Rashi* and *Radak* (based on *Sotah* 48b and *Gittin* 68a) explain that the stones for the Temple were hewn by a small, soft worm called שָׁמִיר, *shamir,* which has the amazing ability to cut through the hardest stones. The *shamir* was the size of a barleycorn and it was kept in a hollow lead pipe filled with rags and bran flour. This remarkable creature could split an entire mountain in half. Moses used it to cut the

אָז תִּמְצְאִי צוּף דְּבַשׁ,[1] אָז לֹא תְקוֹנְנִי בְּרֹאשׁ,

« with gall, ‹ will you lament ‹ no longer ‹ then « as honey, ‹ you will discover [a contentment] as sweet ‹ Then

כִּי תִתְכּוֹנְנִי בְּרֹאשׁ הֶהָרִים[2] הֲרָרָיִךְ.

« — your mountains. « of the mountains ‹ on the summit ‹ you will be firmly established ‹ for

יָבֹא כְּבוֹד הַלְּבָנוֹן לָךְ,[3]

« to you, ‹ of Lebanon ‹ shall the glory ‹ Return

וְתִתְלַבְּנִי כִּבְנֵי עֲדָרִים, בְּנֵי אֶדֶר גְּדֵרָיִךְ.

« your [protective] walls. ‹ of the mighty ones, [the Patriarchs], ‹ O children « of a flock. ‹ as the members ‹ and you will be whitened

עוּרִי וְהִתְנַעֲרִי[4] עֵרֶךְ יַעַר נוֹעֲרִים,

« shakes off [its dry leaves]; ‹ that a forest ‹ in the manner « and shake off [your enemies], ‹ Awaken [O Zion]

נַעַר יִתְוֶה אוֹת, לְעֵץ יַעַר[5] חֲזִירָיִךְ.[6]

« who are like a boar. ‹ left of the forest [of your enemies] ‹ [can represent] the [ten] trees ‹ even the smallest letter [*yud*] ‹ who can write ‹ then a child

(קוּמִי וְאוֹרִי לְכָל חוֹשְׁקֵי מְאוֹרֵךְ,

« your light, ‹ who seek ‹ for all ‹ and give light ‹ (Arise

וְהֵם הוֹלְכֵי בְחֹשֶׁךְ עֲדֵי אוֹרוּ מְאוֹרָיִךְ.)[7]

« your light.) ‹ will shine ‹ until « in darkness, ‹ walk ‹ for they

צִיּוֹן לְצִיּוּן וָאוֹת, עֹז עוֹד תִּהְיִ וּלְנֵס עַמִּים,[8]

« for the peoples; ‹ and a banner « will you be, ‹ yet ‹ strength « and a signpost [of majesty to the world]; ‹ will be a landmark ‹ O Zion

וְתִגְבַּהְנָה רַגְלֵי מְבַשְּׂרָיִךְ.[9]

« of your heralds. ‹ will be the footsteps ‹ and lifted on high

---

(1) *Proverbs* 16:24. (2) *Isaiah* 2:2. (3) Cf. 60:13. (4) Cf. 52:1, 2. (5) Cf. 10:19; see *Rashi*. (6) *Psalms* 80:14. (7) Some editions omit the stanza in parentheses. (8) *Isaiah* 11:10. (9) Cf. 52:7.

---

gemstones on the *Kohen Gadol's* breastplate and it was brought to Solomon from the Garden of Eden by an eagle (see also *Midrash Shocher Tov*).

נַצְּלִי עֲדִי הֶעָנִי, וּתְנִי לְבוּשֵׁךְ שָׁנִי,

Remove the cloths of the pauper, and don your garments of crimson,

תּוֹלָע[1] כְּכַלָּה עֲדִי, לִקְשׁוֹר קִשּׁוּרַיִךְ.

scarlet like a bride clothe yourself and adorn yourself with your ornaments.

אַל תֹּאמְרִי לִי, אֲשֶׁר זָקַנְתְּ הֱיוֹתֵךְ לְאִישׁ,[2]

Do not say to me that you are too old to become married to a man,

עוֹד תִּתְעַדְּנִי חֲלוֹץ הַשַּׁד לְגוּרַיִךְ.[3]

for yet you will be rejuvenated and you will draw out a breast [to nurse] your cubs.

תֵּלְדִי בְּנֵי שַׁעֲשׁוּעַיִךְ בְּעֵת עֶדְנָה,

You will bear the children of your delight at the time when you will have delicate skin,

תִּתְחַדְּשִׁי בִנְעוּרִים כִּנְשָׁרַיִךְ.[4]

and you will renew your youth as the eagles [renew their feathers].

יַטֶּה לְטוֹב יִצְרֵךְ צוּר יוֹצְרֵךְ יִצְּרֵךְ,

Incline for the good your desires, will the Rock, Who created you and will protect you;

תְּהִי נְצוּרָה, כְּעִיר חֻבְּרָה[5] לְמוֹרַיִךְ.

you will be safeguarded like a city that is united to your Teacher.

יִגְאַל בְּעֹז מִשְּׁבִי, לְהָשִׁיב לְאֶרֶץ הַצְּבִי,

He [God] will redeem [you] powerfully from captivity, to return you to the land that is desirable,

וִיהִי עֲטֶרֶת צְבִי[6] לִשְׁאָר עֲדָרַיִךְ.

and He will be a crown of delight for the remnants of your flock.

(1) Cf. *Exodus* 25:4. (2) Cf. *Ruth* 1:12. (3) Cf. *Eichah* 4:3.
(4) Cf. *Psalms* 103:5. (5) Cf. 122:3. (6) *Isaiah* 28:5.

KINNAH 41 / קינה מא

שַׁאֲלִי שְׂרוּפָה בָאֵשׁ,* לִשְׁלוֹם אֲבֵלָיִךְ,[1]

Seek* 《 [O Torah] — 〈 — consumed by fire 《 the welfare 〈 of your mourners, 《

(1) Cf. *Kinnah* 36, line 1.

שַׁאֲלִי שְׂרוּפָה בָאֵשׁ — *Seek – [O Torah] consumed by fire.* Twenty-four cartloads of the Talmud and its commentaries were publicly burned in the streets of Paris, France in the year 1242. The events leading to this tragedy give us a glimpse of the terrible persecution which hounded our ancestors in those dark times.

The French king, Louis IX (1226-1270), was a fanatical religious zealot, so much so, in fact, that he earned himself the title of Saint Louis. His piety, however, did not extend to his Jewish subjects, against whom he enacted many harsh and discriminatory laws. The king's pious zeal manifested itself most clearly in the favor he extended to apostates who abandoned Judaism. To encourage conversion, the king himself would often attend their baptisms.

Nicholas Donin of La Rochelle was an apostate who was especially vicious in his hatred for his former co-religionists, and who caused the forced baptism of the Jews of Anjou and Poitiers. Five hundred Jews from these cities surrendered before the threat of death and were baptized, while the majority of Jews, 3,000 martyrs in all, chose to meet their death while sanctifying God's Name.

Donin realized that the bulwark of firm Jewish faith was the holy Talmud, the repository of our traditions and teachings. He felt that if he could destroy the Talmud he could easily eradicate the Jews. To that end, he went to Pope Gregory IX in Rome, where he presented a formal accusation against the Talmud. He charged that it contained blasphemies against God and against Christianity, and that it alone was the cause of the Jews' steadfast refusal to accept the "true" faith.

The Pope issued orders for a seizure of all copies of the Talmud and for a thorough examination and evaluation of its contents. The churchmen of France were only too eager to obey this decree, so on March 3, 1240, while the Jews were in their synagogues, all of their sacred tomes were seized and confiscated. On June 12th of that year a public debate was held in Paris between Donin and four of the most eminent rabbinical authorities in France.

The Jewish deputation was led by R' Yechiel ben Yosef (died 1268) who headed the Yeshivah in Paris. Many of the major sages of that period studied under him. These include R' Yitzchok of Corbeil (his son-in-law) and Maharam of Rottenburg.

The other representatives were R' Moshe of Coucy, R' Yehudah ben David of Melun, and R' Shmuel ben Shlomo of Falaise.

Although R' Yechiel and his colleagues displayed great scholarship, courage, and dignity in their defense of the Talmud, the official verdict against them was a foregone conclusion. The Talmud would have been immediately consigned to the flames if not for the lone staunch ally the Jews had amongst the churchmen, the bishop of Sens (Shantz), whose arguments and pleas averted any evil decree for one year. At the year's end, while the good bishop was standing in the presence of King Louis, he suddenly convulsed and died in a most grotesque fashion. The anti-Semitic priests convinced the gullible king that this was actually an act of Divine retribution against the bishop for his heresy in defending the blasphemous Talmud. A tribunal of church elders condemned the Talmud to be burnt. Their agents eagerly searched and confiscated over 1200 manuscripts of the Talmud and commentaries. We must bear in mind that this occurred two centuries before the invention of the printing press. Each one of these volumes was a handwrit-

הַמִּתְאַוִּים שְׁכוֹן, בַּחֲצַר זְבוּלֶךָ.

« of your residence [where you studied]; ‹ in the courtyard ‹ to dwell ‹ those who yearn

ten manuscript which took months, even years to write, at tremendous effort and expense. Moreover, many of the more recent works such as novellae by the *Tosafists* of France and their correspondence and halachic decisions were transcribed only in a limited number of copies and would be lost forever.

R' Yechiel recognized that this tragedy threatened the very survival of the French Jewish community. He therefore recorded the proceedings of his disputation in a work called simply וִיכּוּחַ [*Vikuach*], *Debate*. In his introduction, paraphrasing the words of Jeremiah (*Eichah* 4:9), he states, כִּי הִנֵּה טוֹבִים חַלְלֵי חֶרֶב מֵהַיּוֹשְׁבִים שׁוֹמְמִים בְּלִי תוֹרָה, *For those put to death by the sword were better off than those who sat in desolation without Torah.*

In 1242, on Friday, 6 Tammuz, the day before the *Shabbos* when *Parashas Chukas* would be read, 24 wagonloads of holy *sefarim* were burnt.

R' Tzidkiyah ben Avrohom HaRofeh, who lived at that time, writes:

> From Torah scholars who were involved, we heard that the Rabbis inquired of heaven by means of a dream (שְׁאֵלַת חֲלוֹם), to discover whether this terrible event had been so decreed by the Almighty. The heavenly reply was given in three words: דָּא גְּזֵרַת אוֹרַיְיתָא, *This is the decree of the Torah*, the Aramaic version of the opening words of that week's Torah reading — (זֹאת חֻקַּת הַתּוֹרָה). R' Tzidkiyah further notes that, in commemoration of this tragic event, some pious people customarily fast on Erev Shabbos of *Parashas Chukas* every year (*Shibbolei HaLeket* 263).

❧ The Ashes of the Rambam's Works

R' Hillel of Verona, Italy was an eyewitness to these tragic events in Paris. He considered the burning of the Talmud as a clear sign of Divine anger and retribution for the destruction of the works of R' Moshe ben Maimon, known as the *Rambam* (Maimonides).

There were many great scholars, especially in southern France, who did not agree with many of *Rambam's* opinions in his *Moreh Nevuchim* (*Guide for the Perplexed*) and his philosophical observations in the first book of his *Yad HaChazakah* (*Sefer HaMada*). Some went so far as to place a ban on studying or even owning these works. A tremendous controversy erupted and the situation got out of control. The hysteria reached its terrible climax when members of the anti-*Rambam* camp submitted copies of his philosophical writings to the monks of the Dominican Order for the sake of determining whether these works contained heretical ideas.

The Dominicans, of course, swiftly concluded that the *Rambam's* writings were blasphemous and false. They publicly burned all copies of *Moreh Nevuchim* and *Sefer HaMada* that they could lay their hands on. This was done in Montpelier, France in 1234. In the year 1242, fanatical churchmen once again burnt the *Rambam's* works in the streets of Paris.

In a letter recording these events, R' Hillel of Verona makes the following observations:

> God looked down from heaven and avenged the honor of our holy master, *Rambam*, and his works. He poured His wrath upon the Jewish communities of France. You should not ask in wonderment, "How did God disregard twelve hundred manuscripts of Talmud and Aggadah and allow them to be burnt as retribution for the *Moreh Nevuchim* and *Sefer HaMada?*" Rather, you must bear in mind that R' Moshe ben Maimon was almost second in his generation to Moshe Rabbeinu, and the righteousness of the entire generation depended upon him . . . . If you ask; "Who can be sure that the Talmud was burned because of the burning of the *Rambam's* works?"

I will answer you. This is the sign and proof. Take note of this: Not even forty days passed between the conflagration of the works of our master and the burning of the Talmud. On the very spot where the *Rambam's* works were destroyed, the Talmud was later burnt! The ashes of the burnt Talmud mingled with the ashes of the *Rambam's* volumes, for those ashes still remained in that very place. This served as a clear lesson to one and all, Jew and gentile alike.

The destruction of the Talmud was a crushing blow to the venerable and ancient Jewish community of France. It marked the beginning of its very rapid decline and eventual disintegration.

With the conditions of the Jews in France steadily worsening, R' Yechiel immigrated to *Eretz Yisrael* in 1260 together with a large group of French Talmudists. He settled in Acre, where he established the Talmudic academy *Midrash HaGadol d' Paris.* He is believed to have died in 1267.

One of the participants in the great Talmudic debate in Paris, R' Shmuel of Falaise, summed up the enormity of the tragedy in the following elegy:

My spirit is gone, my strength is sapped, the light of my eyes has dimmed, because of the tyrant whose hand weighed very heavily upon us, when he seized the core of our soul and the delight of our eyes. Now we have no holy book in which to study and meditate. May the Almighty God avenge His people and may He say to our misery, "It is enough!" (quoted in *Teshuvos Maharam MiRottenburg* 250).

In 1306, the glorious chapter of Jewish history in medieval France came to an abrupt close, when King Philip IV (the Fair) expelled the Jews from all of France. French Jewry, which had enriched our eternal Torah legacy with the magnificent Talmudic commentaries of *Rashi* and *Tosafos*, was no longer.

◆§ The Maharam of Rottenburg

The author of this *kinnah* was R' Meir ben Baruch (1220-1293) better known as the Maharam of Rottenburg, who studied in the Yeshivah of Rabbeinu Yechiel of Paris and is said to have personally witnessed the tragic burning of the Talmud in 1242.

Born in Worms, Germany in the year 1220, Maharam first studied under the greatest *Tosafists* of that land, including R' Yitzchak (author of *Or Zarua*) in Wurtzberg and R' Yehudah ben Moshe HaKohen of Mainz.

Maharam is considered to be one of the last important *Baalei Tosafos*, but his major contribution to Rabbinic literature was his prolific responsa in all areas of halachah. Approximately one thousand of Maharam's responsa have been published and his rulings have been accepted by all subsequent generations as the opinion of a leading halachic authority.

From the seat of his rabbinate in Rottenburg, Maharam guided German Jewry throughout the second half of the thirteenth century. However, in his final years, he met with tragedy. The terrible burden of persecution was making life intolerable for the Jews of Germany. Taxation, pogroms, blood libels, harsh decrees — all of these spurred Jews to flee from this miserable exile and to make the arduous journey to *Eretz Yisrael*. Emperor Rudolph I did not wish to lose the Jews from whom he enjoyed extorting so much gold, so, in the year 1286, he declared the Jews to be his personal property — *Servi Camerae*, serfs of the Emperor's Treasury. He prohibited Jews from leaving Germany and confiscated the property of those who did.

Maharam vigorously opposed this decree and together with his family attempted to flee Germany. Unfortunately, when he reached the border with Lombardy, he was recognized by a Jewish apostate who reported him to the royal agents. The Emperor imprisoned Maharam in the Castle of Ensisheim. He demanded an exorbitant ransom from the Jewish community if they were to obtain their leader's release.

German Jewry, led by Maharam's disciple Rabbeinu Asher (the *Rosh*), began to amass the enormous sum of 23,000 talents of silver to redeem their Rav. However,

הַשּׁוֹאֲפִים בַּעֲפַר אֶרֶץ,[1]* וְהַכּוֹאֲבִים הַמִּשְׁתּוֹמְמִים,
those who yearn ‹ [to embrace] the dust ‹ of the [Holy] Land;* ‹ those pained ‹ and bewildered ‹

עֲלֵי מוֹקֵד גְּלִילַיִךְ.[2]
by ‹ the incineration ‹ of your scrolls; «

הוֹלְכִים חֲשֵׁכִים וְאֵין נֹגַהּ,[3] וְקוֹיִם לְאוֹר יוֹמָם,
those who walk ‹ in the darkness [of exile], ‹ without illumination; « those who wait hopefully ‹ for the light ‹ of day, ‹

אֲשֶׁר יִזְרַח עֲלֵיהֶם וְעָלָיִךְ.
which ‹ will shine ‹ upon them ‹ and upon you. «

וּשְׁלוֹם אֱנוֹשׁ נֶאֱנָח בּוֹכֶה בְּלֵב נִשְׁבָּר,
[Seek] the welfare ‹ of the mortal ‹ who sighs ‹ and who cries ‹ with a heart ‹ that is broken, «

תָּמִיד מְקוֹנֵן עֲלֵי צִירֵי חֲבָלָיִךְ.
who constantly ‹ laments ‹ over ‹ the labor-like pains ‹ of your suffering; «

וְיִתְאוֹנֵן כְּתַנִּים וּבְנוֹת יַעֲנָה,
who howls ‹ like a jackal ‹ and like ostriches, «

(1) Cf. *Amos* 2:7. (2) Some editions read גְּוִילַיִךְ, *your parchments.* (3) Cf. *Isaiah* 50:10.

Maharam refused to permit them to pay such an exorbitant sum, for the Mishnah (*Gittin* 45a) teaches; "For the sake of public welfare it is prohibited to redeem Jewish captives for an exorbitant sum" (lest this encourage despots to kidnap other Jews for high ransom in the future).

R' Asher disagreed with his mentor's decision. He argued that the Mishnah's ruling did not apply to the generation's greatest Torah leader, for whom no amount could be considered exorbitant. Thus, he guaranteed the Emperor that he would personally raise the full ransom. However, Maharam died in prison in the year 1293, before R' Asher was able to raise the full amount. Fearing that he would now be held hostage in Maharam's place, R' Asher fled to Spain, where he died in 1327.

Maharam died in prison in the year 1293, but his remains were not released for burial until they were ransomed fourteen years later by a wealthy Jew, Alexander Wimpfen, whose sole request was that he be buried near this great leader.

Maharam's noble act of self-sacrifice achieved its purpose. Never again in Jewish history were great Rabbinic leaders held hostage in order to extort enormous ransom payments from the Jews.

הַשּׁוֹאֲפִים בַּעֲפַר אֶרֶץ — *Those who yearn [to embrace] the dust of the [Holy] Land.* The Talmud (*Kesubos* 112a) relates that Rav Chiya bar Ganda would actually roll around in the dust of *Eretz Yisrael* to fulfill the dictate of the verse, *For Your servants had cherished her stones, and have favored her dust* (*Psalms* 102:15).

וְיִקְרָא מִסְפֵּד מַר בִּגְלָלֵךְ.

and who cries out ‹ a eulogy ‹ that is bitter ‹ on your behalf. «

אֵיכָה נְתוּנָה בְּאֵשׁ אוֹכְלָה,*[1]

How is it that ‹ you who were given ‹ [by God,] the Fire ‹ That is All-Consuming,* ‹

תְּאֻכַּל בְּאֵשׁ בָּשָׂר, וְלֹא נִכְווּ זָרִים בְּגֶחָלַיִךְ.

should be consumed ‹ by fires ‹ [made by] flesh [and blood] « — and yet, not ‹ even singed ‹ were the gentiles [who burned you] ‹ from your burning coals? «

עַד אָן עֲדִינָה[2] תְּהִי שׁוֹכְנָה בְּרֹב הַשְׁקֵט,

Until ‹ when, ‹ O pleasure-loving nations, ‹ will you ‹ dwell ‹ in excessive ‹ serenity, «

וּפְנֵי פְרָחַי הֲלֹא כִסּוּ חֲרוּלַיִךְ.[3]

while the faces ‹ of my youths « — are they not ‹ covered ‹ with thorns? «

תֵּשֵׁב בְּרֹב גַּאֲוָה, לִשְׁפּוֹט בְּנֵי אֵל בְּכָל הַמִּשְׁפָּטִים,

You sit ‹ with great ‹ arrogance ‹ to judge ‹ the children ‹ of God ‹ with every ‹ discriminatory ordinance, ‹

וְתָבִיא בִּפְלִילַיִךְ.

and you bring them ‹ [to be confirmed] by your judges. «

עוֹד תִּגְזוֹר לִשְׂרוֹף דַּת אֵשׁ* וְחֻקִּים,

In addition, ‹ you decree ‹ to burn ‹ the Law ‹ that is like fire* ‹ with its statutes; «

וְלָכֵן אַשְׁרֵי שֶׁיְּשַׁלֶּם לָךְ גְּמוּלַיִךְ.[4]

therefore ‹ praiseworthy ‹ is he who will repay ‹ you ‹ with the punishment you deserve. «

(1) *Deuteronomy* 9:3. (2) *Isaiah* 47:8. (3) Cf. *Proverbs* 24:31. (4) *Psalms* 137:8.

אֵשׁ אוֹכְלָה — *The Fire That is All-Consuming.* Scripture refers to God as אֵשׁ אֹכְלָה, *an All-Consuming Flame* (*Deuteronomy* 9:3). The Talmud (*Yoma* 21b) identifies six types of fires which have different properties. The fire of the *Shechinah*, the Divine Presence, is so powerful that it can overwhelm any other flame — even that of the fiery ministering angels.

דַּת אֵשׁ — *The Law that is like fire.* The Torah was given, מִימִינוֹ אֵשׁ דָּת לָמוֹ, *From His right hand, the fiery Law He presented to them* (*Deuteronomy* 33:2). *Rashi* explains that when the Torah was given, the top of Mount Sinai was engulfed in flames; and the Torah itself (as it appears before God in the highest celestial spheres) is black fire (in the shape of the letters) imposed upon white

צוּרִי בְּלַפִּיד וָאֵשׁ,*

« and fire!* ‹ [Who gave the Torah] with flame « O my Rock,

הַלְּבַעֲבוּר זֶה נְתָנֵךְ כִּי בְּאַחֲרִיתֵךְ,

« in the end, ‹ so that ‹ that He so gave [the Torah] to you ‹ this ‹ Was it for

תְּלַהֵט אֵשׁ בְּשׁוּלַיִךְ.

« will the edges of your [scrolls]? ‹ with fire ‹ flare

סִינַי הַעַל כֵּן בְּךְ בָּחַר אֱלֹהִים,

‹ did God choose ‹ that in you ‹ this reason ‹ was it for ‹ O Sinai,

וּמָאַס בִּגְדוֹלִים* וְזָרַח בִּגְבוּלַיִךְ.

« within your boundaries? ‹ and made His light shine ‹ taller [mountains]* ‹ while He spurned

לִהְיוֹת לְמוֹפֵת לְדָת, כִּי תִתְמַעֵט וְתֵרֵד מִכְּבוֹדָהּ,

« from its glory? ‹ and descend ‹ it would be denigrated ‹ that « for the Torah Law, ‹ an ominous sign ‹ [Was Sinai chosen] to be

וְהֵן אֶמְשׁוֹל מְשָׁלַיִךְ.

« with appropriate parables! ‹ I will illustrate [your condition] ‹ Indeed,

מָשָׁל לְמֶלֶךְ, אֲשֶׁר בָּכָה לְמִשְׁתֵּה בְנוֹ,

« of his son, ‹ at the [wedding] feast ‹ wept ‹ who ‹ to the king ‹ This may be compared

צָפָה אֲשֶׁר יִגְוַע כֵּן אַתְּ בְּמִלַּיִךְ.

« [foretold your fate] in your own words. ‹ you, [Sinai,] ‹ so too, « [his son] would die [that day], ‹ that ‹ because he foresaw

---

fire (which serves as the parchment).

בְּלַפִּיד וָאֵשׁ — *[Who gave the Torah] with flame and fire!* The Torah states: *And Mount Sinai was engulfed in smoke, because HASHEM descended upon it in fire; and its smoke ascended like the smoke from a furnace and the entire mountain shook greatly* (*Exodus* 19:18). Elsewhere it is stated: *And the appearance of the glory of HASHEM was like an All-Consuming Fire at the top of the mountain in the eyes of the Children of Israel* (ibid. 24:17).

סִינַי . . . בְּךְ בָּחַר אֱלֹהִים וּמָאַס בִּגְדוֹלִים — *Sinai . . . in you did God choose while He spurned taller [mountains].* The *Talmud* (*Sotah* 5a) teaches that God rejected lofty mountains and summits and rested His Holy Presence upon Sinai because it is the lowest of all

תַּחַת מְעִיל תִּתְכַּס, סִינַי לְבוּשְׁךָ בְּשַׂק,

« with sackcloth; ‹ you should be attired « O Sinai, « covering yourself, ‹ of with a robe ‹ Therefore, instead

תַּעֲטֶה לְבוּשׁ אַלְמְנוּת, תַּחֲלִיף שְׂמָלַיִךְ.

« your clothing! ‹ change « of a widow; ‹ in the garb ‹ cloak yourself

אוֹרִיד דְּמָעוֹת, עֲדֵי יִהְיוּ כְנַחַל,[1]

‹ like a river ‹ they flow ‹ until ‹ tears ‹ And I will shed

וְיַגִּיעוּ לְקִבְרוֹת שְׁנֵי שָׂרֵי אֲצִילַיִךְ.

« of your noble princes. ‹ of the two ‹ to the gravesites ‹ and they would reach

מֹשֶׁה וְאַהֲרֹן בְּהֹר הָהָר,

« the Mountain. ‹ [who were] on Hor, ‹ and Aaron ‹ They are Moses

וְאֶשְׁאַל הֲיֵשׁ תּוֹרָה חֲדָשָׁה, בְּכֵן נִשְׂרְפוּ גְלִילַיִךְ.

« *have your scrolls been!* ‹ *burnt* ‹ *and for that reason* « *that is new,* ‹ *a Torah* ‹ *Is there* « And I will ask:

חֹדֶשׁ שְׁלִישִׁי וְהֻקְשַׁר הָרְבִיעִי,

« in the fourth [month], ‹ but they rebelled « In the third month [they accepted the Torah],

לְהַשְׁחִית חֶמְדָּתֵךְ, וְכָל יְפִי כְּלִילַיִךְ.[2]

« that is perfect. ‹ and your beauty ‹ your delight ‹ to destroy

גָּדַע לְלֻחוֹת, וְעוֹד שָׁנָה בְּאִוַּלְתּוֹ,

« its folly, ‹ [Tammuz] repeated ‹ and additionally ‹ the Tablets ‹ [Moses] shattered

לִשְׂרוֹף בָּאֵשׁ דָּת,[3]* הֲזֶה תַּשְׁלוּם כִּפְלַיִךְ.[4]

« of your [promised] double reward? ‹ the payment ‹ Is this « the Law.* ‹ in the fire ‹ by incinerating

(1) Cf. *Eichah* 2:18. (2) Cf. 2:15. (3) Cf. *Deuteronomy* 33:2. (4) Cf. *Isaiah* 61:7.

peaks. This emphasizes that no quality is more beloved to God than genuine humility. Moreover, even after God designated Sinai for greatness, the mountain remained low and humble (see *Megillah* 29a).

לִשְׂרוֹף בָּאֵשׁ דָּת — *By incinerating in the fire the Law.* This refers to the Talmud's statement (*Taanis* 26b) that on the seventeenth of Tammuz, the gentile general Apostumus committed the terrible sacrilege of burning a *Sefer Torah.*

אֶתְמַהּ לְנַפְשִׁי אֵיךְ יֶעֱרַב לְחִכִּי אָכוֹל,

‹ to eat ‹ can it be pleasant to my palate ‹ How « to myself, ‹ I wonder

אַחֲרֵי רְאוֹתִי, אֲשֶׁר אָסְפוּ שְׁלָלַיִךְ.

all your spoils? ‹ *they gathered* ‹ *how* ‹ *I have seen* ‹ *after*

אֶל תּוֹךְ רְחוֹבָהּ כְּנִדַּחַת,* וְשָׂרְפוּ שְׁלַל עֶלְיוֹן,

« of the Most High; ‹ the spoils ‹ and burned ‹ like [the property of] an apostate city,* ‹ of the main public square [they gathered our Talmud scrolls] ‹ the midst ‹ Into

אֲשֶׁר תְּמָאֵס לָבֹא קְהָלַיִךְ.

« your congregation. ‹ from entering ‹ you would reject ‹ [perpetrated by] those whom

לֹא אֵדְעָה לִמְצוֹא דֶּרֶךְ סְלוּלָה,[1]

« that is paved [to lead me to fathom your ways]; ‹ the road ‹ how to find ‹ I do not know

הֲכִי הָיוּ אֲבֵלוֹת, נְתִיב יֹשֶׁר מְסִלָּיִךְ.

« that is the hallmark of your path? ‹ of straightness ‹ — the path « shrouded in mourning ‹ become ‹ has it

יֻמְתַּק בְּפִי מִדְּבַשׁ, לִמְסוֹךְ בְּמַשְׁקֶה דְּמָעוֹת,

« tears, ‹ into [my] drink ‹ to mix ‹ than honey ‹ to my mouth ‹ It would be sweeter

וּלְרַגְלַי הֱיוֹת כָּבוּל כְּבָלַיִךְ.

« in your shackles [to share in your sorrow]. ‹ to be chained ‹ and for my feet

יֶעֱרַב לְעֵינַי, שְׁאוֹב מֵימֵי דְמָעַי,

« of my tears, ‹ the waters ‹ to drain ‹ to my eyes ‹ It would be pleasant

(1) Cf. *Jeremiah* 18:15.

כְּנִדַּחַת — *Like [the property of] an apostate city.* If an individual Jew is guilty of idolatry, he is condemned to death by stoning. But if an entire city or a majority of its inhabitants are seduced by some of its citizens to worship idols, then this place is adjudged with the special laws of עִיר הַנִּדַּחַת, *an apostate city.* The idolaters are executed by the sword, whereas of the city the Torah says: *And you shall gather all of its contents into the middle of the main open place of the city and you shall burn with fire both the entire city and all of its contents, a total conflagration for* H*ASHEM*,

עֲדֵי כָּלוּ לְכָל מַחֲזִיק בִּכְנַף מְעִילָֽיִךְ.[1]

until [the tears] ‹ would be expended ‹ for all ‹ those who hold on ‹ to the edge ‹ of your robes. «

אַךְ יֶחֱרָֽבוּ בְּרִדְתָּם עַל לְחָיַי,

But ‹ they would dry up ‹ as they rolled down ‹ onto ‹ my cheeks, «

עֲבוּר כִּי נִכְמְרוּ רַחֲמַי לִנְדוֹד בְּעָלָֽיִךְ.

for the reason ‹ that ‹ intense ‹ is my compassion ‹ over the wanderings ‹ of your Master. «

לָקַח צְרוֹר כַּסְפּוֹ,[2]* הָלַךְ בְּדֶרֶךְ לְמֵרָחוֹק,[3]

[God] took ‹ His money-pouch ‹ [full] of silver pieces* ‹ and went ‹ on a journey ‹ to far away; «

וְעִמּוֹ הֲלֹא נָסוּ צְלָלָֽיִךְ.[4]

and with Him ‹ did they not ‹ flee « — your [sheltering] shadows. «

וַאֲנִי כְּשָׁכוּל וְגַלְמוּד,[5] נִשְׁאַרְתִּי לְבַד מֵהֶם,

And I am left ‹ like one bereft of his children, « utterly alone; « I have been left ‹ all alone ‹ without them. «

כְּתֹרֶן בְּרֹאשׁ הַר[6] מִגְדּוֹלָֽיִךְ.

[I am like a lone] flagstaff ‹ atop ‹ your mountain peak ‹ that towers above. «

לֹא אֶשְׁמַע עוֹד לְקוֹל שָׁרִים וְשָׁרוֹת,

I do not hear ‹ any longer ‹ the voice ‹ of male singers ‹ and female singers, «

עָלַי כִּי נִתְּקוּ, חֶבְלֵי תֻפֵּי חֲלִילָֽיִךְ.

because ‹ torn ‹ are the strings ‹ of your drums ‹ and flutes. «

(1) Cf. *I Samuel* 15:27. (2) Cf. *Proverbs* 7:20. (3) 7:19.
(4) Cf. *Song of Songs* 2:17. (5) Cf. *Isaiah* 49:21. (6) Cf. 30:17.

your God (*Deuteronomy* 13:17). And that is just what happened to the Talmud volumes on that fateful Friday in Paris.

לָקַח צְרוֹר כַּסְפּוֹ — *[God] took His money-pouch [full] of silver pieces.* The Talmud (*Sanhedrin* 96b) relates that Ammon and Moab are the most malicious enemies of the Jews. They heard that Nebuchadnezzar was apprehensive about destroying the Temple. He was afraid that he would meet with the same ruinous disaster as others had before him when they had attempted to harm God's Holy Sanctuary. So Ammon and Moab assured him that he had nothing to fear, for the God of the Jews had already abandoned His Temple, as we read: *For the Man is not at home, He has gone on a distant journey* (*Proverbs* 7:19). Still Nebuchadnezzar was

אֶלְבַּשׁ וְאֶתְכַּס בְּשַׂק, כִּי לִי מְאֹד יָקְרוּ,

« precious [are your martyrs], ‹ very ‹ to me ‹ because « with sackcloth, ‹ and cover myself ‹ I will clothe

עָצְמוּ כְּחוֹל יִרְבְּיוּן, נַפְשׁוֹת חֲלָלָיִךְ.

« of your corpses. ‹ are the souls ‹ is numerous ‹ as the sand ‹ and as powerful

אֶתְמַהּ מְאֹד עַל מְאוֹר הַיּוֹם,

‹ of the day ‹ the light ‹ by ‹ greatly ‹ I am astounded

אֲשֶׁר יִזְרַח אֶל כֹּל, אֲבָל יַחֲשִׁיךְ אֵלַי וְאֵלָיִךְ.

« and toward you [the Torah]. ‹ toward me ‹ it casts [only] darkness ‹ yet «every-one, ‹ toward ‹ shines ‹ which

זַעֲקִי בְּקוֹל מַר לְצוּר, עַל שִׁבְרוֹנֵךְ וְעַל חָלְיֵךְ,

« and your debilitation; ‹ your devastation ‹ over ‹ to the Rock ‹ that is bitter ‹ with voice ‹ O cry out

וְלוּ יִזְכּוֹר אַהֲבַת כְּלוּלָיִךְ.[1]

« of your wedding day. ‹ the love ‹ He would remember ‹ O if only

חִגְרִי לְבוּשׁ שַׂק[2] עֲלֵי הַהַבְעָרָה,

‹ the conflagration ‹ over ‹ of sackcloth ‹ with garments ‹ Gird yourself

אֲשֶׁר יָצְתָה לְחַלֵּק וְסָפְתָה אֶת תְּלוּלָיִךְ.

« your towering ones, [the Torah scholars]. ‹ and destroyed ‹ and divided you [into many parts], ‹ burst out ‹ which

כִּימֵי עֱנוּתֵךְ[3] יְנַחֲמֵךְ צוּר,

« — the Rock [of salvation] — « may He comfort you ‹ of your affliction, ‹ According to the days

וְיָשִׁיב שְׁבוּת שִׁבְטֵי יְשֻׁרוּן,[4] וְיָרִים אֶת שְׁפָלָיִךְ.

« your degraded ones. ‹ and may He elevate « of Jeshurun, ‹ of the Tribes ‹ the captivity ‹ and may He return

(1) Cf. *Jeremiah* 2:2. (2) Cf. 6:26. (3) Cf. *Psalms* 90:15. (4) Cf. *Jeremiah* 30:3.

reluctant. "Perhaps there are still righteous men whose prayers will save the Jews and their Temple?" Again Ammon and Moab reassured him, for it is written, *He has taken the money-pouch full of silver pieces with Him* (ibid. 7:20); in anticipation of the Destruction, God has removed the righteous who are as precious as silver coins!

עוֹד תַּעְדִּי[1] בַּעֲדִי שָׁנִי וְתֹף תִּקְחִי,

Once again ‹ you will adorn yourself ‹ with adornments ‹ of crimson, « and the drum ‹ you will take up ‹

תֵּלְכִי בְּמָחוֹל, וְצַהֲלִי בִּמְחוֹלָיִךְ.

and go out ‹ in a circle dance ‹ and rejoice ‹ in your dancing. «

יָרוּם לְבָבִי בְּעֵת צוּרֵךְ לְאוֹר לָךְ,

Uplifted ‹ will be my heart ‹ at the time ‹ when your Rock ‹ will be a light ‹ unto you, «

וְיַגִּיהַּ לְחָשְׁכֵּךְ[2] וְיָאִירוּ אֲפֵלָיִךְ.

and will illuminate ‹ your darkness ‹ and brightly lit ‹ will be your deepest gloom. «

(1) *Jeremiah* 31:3. (2) Cf. *II Samuel* 22:29.

KINNAH 42 / קינה מב

צִיּוֹן צְפִירַת פְּאֵר*¹ חֶדְוַת אֲגוּדָיִךְ,

O Zion, ‹ crown ‹ of glory,* « the delight ‹ of all who are tied to you, «

זַעֲקִי בְּרָמָה בְּקוֹלֵךְ² עַל אֲבוּדָיִךְ.

cry out ‹ to the highest [heavens] ‹ with your voice ‹ about ‹ [your people] who are lost from you. «

אֶל הַבְּנוּיָה לְבַקֵּשׁ וּלְחַנֵּן לָאֵל,

[Cry out] to ‹ the [heavenly Jerusalem that remains] built, « to request ‹ and plead ‹ with God ‹

שָׁלוֹם יִשְׁפּוֹת לָךְ³ וְגַם לִבְנֵי בְחִירָיִךְ.

that in peace ‹ He settle ‹ you, « as well as ‹ your children ‹ whom He chose. «

בַּעַל בְּחִירֵךְ אֲשֶׁר לָךְ אַהֲבָתוֹ,

[God,] the husband ‹ Who chose you, « that [once] ‹ for you exclusively ‹ was His love, «

לְזָר נֶהְפַּךְ לְנֶגְדֵּךְ וְגַם נֶגֶד גְּדוּדָיִךְ.

into a total stranger ‹ has He turned ‹ against you ‹ and also ‹ against ‹ your soldiers. «

גֻּלַּף וּפֻתַּח בְּלוּחַ לֵב, אֲזַי נִשְׁקַטְתְּ בֶּטַח

[As long as] He was inscribed ‹ and engraved ‹ upon the tablet ‹ of your heart, ‹ then ‹ you were quiet, ‹ confident, ‹

בְּשַׁלְוָה שְׁדוּכָה עַל רְדִידָיִךְ.

and tranquil, « relaxed ‹ on ‹ your mantle [the Holy Temple]. «

---

(1) Cf. *Isaiah* 28:5. (2) Cf. *Jeremiah* 31:14. (3) Cf. *Isaiah* 26:12.

צִיּוֹן צְפִירַת פְּאֵר — *O Zion, crown of glory.* The *paytan* urges terrestrial Zion to plead with its celestial counterpart that it intervene with the Heavenly Court to bring an end to Israel's exile and dispersion.

The *kinnah* is arranged according to an *aleph-beis* acrostic, each letter appearing twice: as the initial of the first word of a line, and of the last word of the preceding line. Then follows the author's signature מֵאִיר חֲזַק, *Meir, may he be strong,* in a similar manner. The composer is generally identified as R' Meir ben Elazar Lombard HaDarshan, who flourished early in the thirteenth century.

דַּבְּרִי נְכוֹחוֹת לְרֵעַיִךְ לְהָלִיץ עֲבוּרֵךְ,*
« on your behalf,* ‹ and ask them to advocate ‹ to your friends [the angels Michael and Gabriel], ‹ forthrightly ‹ So speak

אַף תְּצַפְצְפִי לְהָרִים קוֹל הֲדָרַיִךְ.
« your melodious voice [in prayer]. ‹ raising « sing [like a bird] yourself, ‹ and also

הָשֵׁב יְדִידֵךְ לְמִטָּתֵךְ וְלָלוּן בְּצִלֵּךְ,
‹ in your shade ‹ to rest « to your bed [the Temple], ‹ your Beloved ‹ [And thus] bring back

וּלְטַיֵּל בְּסֻגַּת גַּן וְרָדַיִךְ.
« formed by your roses. ‹ of the garden ‹ inside the hedges ‹ and to stroll

וְעַד בְּמֹהַר וְקִדּוּשִׁין וְגַם בִּכְתֻבָּה,
« with a marriage contract [the Torah]; ‹ and also « and betrothal [the Ten Commandments] ‹ through dowry [the Sabbath and laws at Marah] ‹ [Israel] is joined together [with God]

לָךְ וּלְעֶזְרֵךְ וְהֵם בֵּרוּר זְבָדַיִךְ.
« as Your portion. ‹ the ones chosen ‹ and they are « and as Your helpmate, ‹ [Israel] is unto You

זֶרַע וּבָנִים מְחֻטָּבִים לְאִישֵׁךְ הֲלֹא יָלַדְתְּ,
« have you not borne? ‹ for your spouse ‹ hewn to perfection ‹ and sons ‹ Offspring

וְאֵיךְ נִשְׁכַּלְתְּ מִכָּל חֲסִידַיִךְ.
« your pious ones? ‹ of all ‹ are you now bereft ‹ How, then,

חָמַק וְעָבַר[1] וְגָז מִמֵּךְ וְלֹא נִשְׁלַחַתְּ,
« were you formally released, ‹ although never ‹ from you, ‹ and severed Himself ‹ and disappeared ‹ He [God] turned His back

(1) Cf. *Song of Songs* 5:6.

דַּבְּרִי נְכוֹחוֹת לְרֵעַיִךְ לְהָלִיץ עֲבוּרֵךְ — *So speak forthrightly to your friends [the angels Michael and Gabriel] and ask them to advocate on your behalf.* This must not be misinterpreted as a prayer to the angels to pray on our behalf. *Rambam* and many others have clearly postulated that a Jew must pray to God directly without any intermediaries. Rather, *in addition* to our own fervent prayers addressed directly and exclusively to God, we

לֹא בָא בְיָדֵךְ, שְׁטַר סֵפֶר טְרוּדַיִךְ.[1]

« of your divorce. ‹ the bill « an official document, ‹ in your hand ‹ was placed ‹ for there never

טוֹעֵן בְּטַעֲנַת מְמָאֶנֶת בְּמֶרֶד,

« and rebelliousness, ‹ of defiance ‹ with the charge ‹ He [God] charges [you]

עֲלֵי כֵן נִתְקַלַּסְתְּ וְהֻשְׁפַּל עַם דּוֹדָיִךְ.

« of your Beloved. ‹ you who are the nation « and degraded, ‹ you were ridiculed ‹ that reason ‹ for

יוֹשַׁבְתְּ בְּדוּדָה דְּמוּיָה כִּי חֲשׂוּפָה קְלוֹן שׁוּלַיִךְ,

« of your hems, ‹ has been the shame ‹ for uncovered ‹ and silent, ‹ solitary ‹ Now you sit

וְנִגְלֵית וְנִדְלַל כְּבוֹדָיִךְ.

« has been your honor. ‹ and diminished « and you have been exposed,

כָּל מַחֲזִיקִים בְּנִזְרֵךְ, הֵם יְצָאוּךְ,

‹ fled from you ‹ they « your crown, ‹ who had supported ‹ All

דְּחוּפִים וּבְהוּלִים[2] וְהֵם הָיוּ לְבוֹדָיִךְ.

« attached to you. ‹ had been ‹ — even though they « and urgency ‹ in haste

לִבִּי הֲלֹא נֶחֱלַל[3] מֵאֵין הֲפוּגוֹת,[4]

« relief, ‹ without ‹ hollow within me ‹ is it not « My heart,

אֲשֶׁר הוּמַר וְנֶחְלַף לְמַר מֶתֶק מְגָדָיִךְ.

« of your fruit. ‹ is the sweetness ‹ into bitterness ‹ and turned ‹ transformed ‹ because

מְלֹא דְּמָעוֹת כַּמַּיִם נִשְׁטָפוּ,

« flowing, ‹ like [flood-] waters ‹ of tears ‹ Full

נִמְלְאוּ דְמָעוֹת לְחָיַי וְכָל עֵינֵי נְגִידָיִךְ.

« of your princes. ‹ the eyes ‹ indeed all « are my cheeks, ‹ with tears ‹ filled

---

(1) Cf. *Isaiah* 50:1. (2) Cf. *Esther* 8:14. (3) Cf. *Psalms* 109:22. (4) *Eichah* 3:49.

---

summon the defending angels to testify in our favor before the Heavenly Tribunal and to bring our good deeds and merits to God's attention in the most forceful fashion.

נַפְשִׁי עֲטוּפָה[1] בְּעֵת זָכְרִי לְאִשֵּׁךְ הֲלֹא נִכְבָּה,

« is now extinguished! ‹ that indeed ‹ your [Altar] fire ‹ I remember ‹ when ‹ grows faint ‹ My soul

וְלֹא יָכְלוּ לֶאֱפוֹת סְמִידָיִךְ.

« your fine-flour [offerings]. ‹ to bake ‹ are they able ‹ And no longer

סֶמֶךְ אֲשִׁישַׁי[2] עֵנָב מָהוּל בַּמַּיִם,*[3]

« with the water* [libation on Succos]; ‹ that mixed ‹ of grape wine [for the libations] ‹ containers ‹ [Gone are] the invigorating

וּפַס מִן הָרְפָתִים, בְּקַר זִבְחֵי עוֹבְדָיִךְ.

« of those who serve You. ‹ for the sacrifices ‹ are the cattle ‹ the pens ‹ from ‹ and absent

עֻדַּר וְנֶחֱרַשׁ יְסוּדֵךְ* לְשָׂדֶה בּוּר וְנִיר,

« yet plowed; ‹ fallow ‹ [turning it] into a field ‹ was your foundation,* [by the Roman Turnus Rufus,] ‹ and plowed under ‹ Hoed

לִחֲכָה וְאָכְלָה סְבִיבֵךְ אֵשׁ פְּלָדָיִךְ.[4]

« of your flames. ‹ did the fire ‹ all around you ‹ and consume ‹ lick at you

פֶּלֶץ וְשָׁבָץ לְבָשׁוּנִי, בְּעֵת אֶחֱזֶה מוֹנַי שְׁקֵטִים,

« in tranquility; ‹ my oppressors ‹ I observed ‹ when « clothed me, ‹ and convulsions ‹ Trembling

וְהֵם צָדוּ צְעָדָיִךְ.[5]

« those who followed in Your footsteps. ‹ who stalked ‹ they are the ones

(1) Cf. *Psalms* 107:5. (2) Cf. *Song of Songs* 2:5. (3) *Isaiah* 1:22. (4) *Nahum* 2:4. (5) Cf. *Eichah* 4:18.

עֵנָב מָהוּל בַּמַּיִם — *Grape wine . . . that mixed with the water.* This refers to the ritual of נִיסּוּךְ הַמַּיִם, *the water libation,* which took place in the Temple on the Succos festival (see *Succah* 4:9). There were two bowls atop the Altar. A *Kohen* would pour wine into one bowl and water into the other. The liquids would flow out of the bowls into two openings in the Altar's top. Eventually, they would mingle deep under the Altar. *Vilna Gaon* explains that strong wine symbolizes God's Attribute of Strict Justice whereas sweet, pure water represents God's Attribute of Mercy. When the strong wine is diluted by the water, it symbolizes God's desire to temper His Strict Justice with tender and compassionate Mercy.

עֻדַּר . . . יְסוּדֵךְ — *Hoed and plowed under was Your foundation.* Five terrible tragedies befell the Jewish people on Tishah B'Av. They culminated with the obliteration of every last vestige of the Temple by the wicked Roman governor Turnus Rufus some sixty years after the Temple

צוֹעֵק אֲנִי לִמְקוֹנְנוֹת לִבְכּוֹת,

‹ to weep ‹ to the women lamenters ‹ I scream

וּבְמַר לִזְעוֹק נְהִי נִהְיָה, הוֹי עַל קְפָדַיִךְ.

« your [people who were] cut off. ‹ for « *Ho!* « *Alas!* « *O woe!* « to cry out, ‹ and bitterly

קַלּוּ יְמֵי עָנְיִי, עֵת אֶחֱזֶה עָנְיֵךְ,

« your suffering [Jerusalem]; ‹ I see ‹ when ‹ of my suffering ‹ were the days ‹ Seemingly light

שׁוֹמְרִים מְצָאוּךְ, וְהֵם נָשְׂאוּ רְדִידַיִךְ.[1]

« of your mantle [the Temple]. ‹ stripped you ‹ and they ‹ found you ‹ the [enemy] watchmen

רָחֲפוּ עֲצָמַי[2] **עֲלֵי בָּנִים יְקָרִים**

« who were precious, ‹ the children ‹ for ‹ did my bones ‹ Tremble

אֲשֶׁר כְּשִׂיד שְׂרוּפִים בְּאוּר אוּדֵי שְׂרִידַיִךְ.

« who were your survivors [from an earlier fire]. ‹ the half-burned branches «in the fire [in exile], ‹ were burnt ‹ like limestone ash ‹ who

שָׁקְדוּ וְיָקְדוּ גְּוִילֵי דַת מְשַׂנְאַי,

« did my enemies. ‹ of the Law ‹ the parchments ‹ and set afire ‹ Hasten

אוֹי אֵיךְ נִמְשַׁלְתְּ לְפַטִּישׁ תְּעוּדַיִךְ.

« so is your Testimony? « to a hammer [that shatters even hardest rock]; ‹ for you are compared « How did this happen, ‹ Woe!

תּוֹהֶה לְבָבִי אֲשֶׁר נִרְצָה,

« You find more favorable ‹ when [I see] that ‹ is my heart ‹ Bewildered

בְּאֶרֶץ טְמֵאָה לִנְדָבָה לְנִסּוּךְ יֵין תְּמִידַיִךְ.

« of the daily [Temple] sacrifice. ‹ of the wine libations ‹ than the pouring ‹ to send beneficial rains « that are defiled — ‹ — onto the gentile lands

(1) Cf. *Song of Songs* 5:7. (2) Cf. *Jeremiah* 23:9.

was destroyed. He plowed over the Temple Mount and its surroundings in fulfillment of the prophet's threat: צִיּוֹן שָׂדֶה תֵחָרֵשׁ, *Zion will be plowed over like a field* (*Micah* 3:12; *Taanis* 29a; *Rambam, Hilchos Taanis* 5:3).

צִיּוֹן עֲדֵי אָן מְשִׂימָה אַתְּ לְפֶה אֶת יָדֵךְ,[1]
O Zion! ‹ Until ‹ when ‹ will you put ‹ to your mouth ‹ your hand [to remain silent]? «

אֵיכָה בְּיַד אוֹיְבַיִךְ נָפְּלוּ נְגִידַיִךְ.
How is it that ‹ into the hands ‹ of your enemies ‹ fell ‹ your princes? «

מִמֵּךְ אֲבוּדִים יְלָדִים חֲמוּדִים כְּפָז,
From you ‹ are lost ‹ [your] children ‹ who were as precious ‹ as the finest gold, «

עַל זֹאת בְּמֶרֶר בְּכִי יִלְלַת מְרוּדַיִךְ.
for ‹ this, ‹ with bitterness, ‹ you should weep ‹ the anguished wailing ‹ of your sorrow. «

אֵיכָה מְעֻכָּב זְמַן לְדָתֵךְ,
How is it that ‹ delayed ‹ is the time ‹ of your rebirth? «

וְעַד אָן תְּהִי אַתְּ נִקְשֶׁרֶת בְּחִיל צִירֵי אֲחוּדַיִךְ.
And until ‹ when ‹ will you be ‹ gripped ‹ by the fear ‹ of the labor pains ‹ that is your portion? «

יוֹלְדוֹת לְתִשְׁעָה יְרָחִים עֵת נְשֵׁי כֹּל,
To give birth ‹ after nine ‹ months ‹ is the [normal] time ‹ for all women, «

וְאֵיךְ רַבּוּ שְׁנוֹתַיִךְ אֲשֶׁר הָרִית יְלָדַיִךְ.
so how is it that ‹ much longer ‹ are your years ‹ that ‹ you are pregnant ‹ with your children? «

רָנִּי לְשׁוֹמֵר לְאַיָּלָה[2] חֲבָלִים,
Cry out in prayer ‹ to the One Who even watches ‹ over the deer ‹ in her labor pains, «

וְהוּא יַתִּיר לְצִירֵךְ עֲלֵי רֶבֶד רְפִידַיִךְ.
certainly He ‹ will release ‹ you from your pain ‹ over [the loss] ‹ of the ornamented ‹ couchlike Temple that was yours. «

חוֹשֵׁב זְמַן יַעֲלֵי סֶלַע[2] לְהַתִּיר,
Although He even calculates ‹ the moment ‹ the goat ‹ of the mountain ‹ delivers its offspring, «

(1) Cf. *Proverbs* 30:32, *Job* 40:4. (2) Cf. *Job* 39:1.

וְלֹא חָשַׁב זְמַנֵּךְ לְהָסִיר כָּל חֲרָדַיִךְ.

« your fear and anxiety. ‹ from all ‹ which would have spared you ‹ your time [of redemption] ‹ He did not calculate [for you]

זְמַן בְּיָדוֹ פַּתֵּחַ אַרְבַּע נְעוּלִים,*

« locked [celestial vaults];* ‹ to the four ‹ are the keys ‹ in His hands ‹ Prepared

וְגַם כֵּן יִפְתַּח גִּנְזֵי אוֹצָר זְבוּלַיִךְ.

« of your Temple Dwelling. ‹ treasures ‹ the hidden ‹ He [alone] will open ‹ in this manner ‹ and also

קוֹל יַשְׁמִיעַ לְקַבֵּץ הָאֱמוּנִים,

« the faithful, ‹ to gather in ‹ He will make heard ‹ A voice

וְאָז דְּלָתָיו פָּתוּחַ יַפְקִידֵם עַל קְלִידַיִךְ.

« the City keys. ‹ for ‹ He will make [Israel] responsible « wide open, ‹ [in order] to leave the doors [of Jerusalem] ‹ and then

צִיּוֹן מְעֻשִּׂים בְּצַעֲרֵךְ וּבְיָפְיֵךְ מְעֻשָּׁתִים,

« will be pleased, ‹ by your [future] beauty ‹ over your pains ‹ Those who are crushed by grief ‹ O Zion!

אֲשֶׁר יִזְרַח חֶרֶס חֲדוּדַיִךְ.[1]

« of your sun. ‹ the dazzling rays ‹ will shine ‹ when

צִיּוֹן בְּמִנְחָה יְכַפְּרוּן אֶת פְּנֵי זַעְמֵךְ,

« of your wrath, ‹ the face ‹ [the nations] shall attempt to appease ‹ With a gift-offering ‹ O Zion!

אָז יִשְׁתַּחֲווּ לְכַף רַגְלֵךְ חֲרָדַיִךְ.

« those who made you tremble. ‹ of your feet ‹ to the soles ‹ will bow down ‹ then

(1) Cf. *Job* 41:22.

בְּיָדוֹ פַּתֵּחַ אַרְבַּע נְעוּלִים — *In His hands are the keys to the four locked [celestial vaults].* The Talmud (*Taanis* 2a; *Sanhedrin* 113a) teaches that although God has entrusted all of the blessings of nature to angel intermediaries, three "keys" remain in His hand because these natural phenomenon require intimate Divine Providence. The three are rainfall, revivification, and childbirth. *Tur Shulchan Aruch* (*Orach Chaim* #114, based on the *Jerusalem Talmud*) adds a fourth key — that of livelihood. *Tur* notes that the word מַפְתֵּחַ, *key*, is an acronym for these four blessings: מָטָר, *rainfall;* פַּרְנָסָה, *livelihood;* תְּחִיָּה, *revivification;* and חַיָּה, *childbearing mother* (see ArtScroll, *Shemoneh Esrei*, p. 70).

צִיּוֹן עֲדִי עֶדְיֵךְ[1] רִקְמַת בִּגְדֵךְ,[2]

O Zion! ‹ Adorn yourself ‹ with your ornaments, « with your embroidered garments, «

וְגַם עֹז וּזְרוֹעַ[3] פְּאֵר בִּגְדֵי חֲמוּדָיִךְ.

and also ‹ [don] power ‹ and might ‹ and the glory ‹ of your garments ‹ that are precious. «

(1) Cf. *Jeremiah* 4:30. (2) Cf. *Ezekiel* 16:18. (3) *Isaiah* 51:9.

KINNAH 43 / קינה מג

צִיּוֹן בְּמִשְׁפָּט* לְכִי לָךְ עִם מְעוֹנְנַיִךְ,

〈 your false prophets 〈 against 〈 for yourself 〈 enter* 〈 into litigation 〈 O Zion,

הִתְעוּךְ בְּכָזָב וְלֹא גִלּוּ עֲוֹנַיִךְ.[1]

《 your iniquities, [preventing repentance]. 〈 and who did not expose 〈 with deceit 〈 who misled you

אָכֵן בְּנֵי עַוְלָה עִנּוּךְ וִירָשׁוּךְ,

《 and took possession of you, 〈 afflicted you 〈 of iniquity 〈 people 〈 Indeed,

נְוֵה צֶדֶק[2] הָיִית אֶל כָּל שְׁכֵנַיִךְ.

《 your neighbors. 〈 all 〈 for 〈 you were once 〈 of righteousness 〈 even though a haven

בָּזִית מַמְלִיכֵךְ, וְלֹא הִקְשַׁבְתְּ לְמוֹרֵךְ לְטוֹב,

《 toward goodness, 〈 to those who guided you 〈 and you did not listen 《 Who made you sovereign, 〈 You disgraced [God]

בִּשְׁכּוֹן בְּאַרְצֵךְ קְדוֹשֵׁךְ בִּמְלוֹנַיִךְ.

《 in your abode [the Temple]. 〈 did your sacred [God] 〈 in your land 〈 while dwell

גִּלִּית קְלוֹנֵךְ וְטֻמְאָתֵךְ בְּשׁוּלֵךְ,[3]

《 is on your garment-hems; 〈 and your impurity 〈 your own shame 〈 You uncovered

וְגַם טִמֵּאת דַּרְכֵּךְ, מְאֹד הִרְבֵּית זְנוּנַיִךְ.

《 your promiscuity. 〈 have you increased 〈 greatly 《 your pathway, 〈 you have defiled 〈 in addition

דֶּרֶךְ אֲחוֹתֵךְ הֲלֹא הָלַכְתְּ,

《 have you not followed, 〈 of your sister [the Northern Kingdom] 〈 In the path

(1) Cf. *Eichah* 2:14. (2) *Jeremiah* 31:22. (3) Cf. *Eichah* 1:9.

ציון במשפט — *O Zion, into litigation.* This *kinnah* was written by R' Yosef bar Chaim HaKohen who highlights the tragic fact that the Jewish people were misguided and led to sin by false prophets and corrupt leaders. Indeed, corruption and perversion of justice was one of the primary causes of our nation's decline and ultimate banishment. As the Talmud (*Shabbos* 118b) graphically describes, the leaders and judges of the Temple era were afraid to offend the rich and the power-

וְזָנִית בְּתַזְנוּתָהּ, וְהִזְנֵית בְּנוֹתַיִךְ וּבָנַיִךְ.

And have you [not] strayed 〈 after her harlotry? 《 You have even led into harlotry 〈 your daughters 〈 and your sons. 《

הֻכֵּית וְנֻגַּפְתְּ לְאֵין מַרְפֵּא,

Therefore, you were beaten 〈 and plagued 〈 beyond any 〈 cure, 《

וְהֻשְׁלַכְתְּ כְּטִיט חוּצוֹת,[1] וְהִנֵּךְ שְׂחוֹק לִבְנֵי מְעַנַּיִךְ.

and you were thrown out 〈 like mud 〈 of the streets, 《 and you have become 〈 a laughingstock 〈 for the sons 〈 of those who afflict you. 《

וַתְּהִי נְגִינָה בְּפִי זֵדִים אֲרוּרִים,

And you were 〈 the [theme of the taunting] songs 〈 in the mouths 〈 of the willful 〈 accursed ones 〈

אֲשֶׁר אָמְרוּ לְנַפְשֵׁךְ שְׁחִי[2] הֲרוֹס לְשִׁנַּיִךְ.

who 〈 said 〈 to your soul, 《 *Bend over* 〈 *so that we may smash* 〈 *your teeth!* 《

זִכְרִי עֲנִיָּה בְּלֵב נִשְׁבָּר,

Remember 〈 the impoverished one [Israel] 〈 with her heart 〈 broken, 《

וְזַעֲקִי עֲלֵי מַכֵּךְ וְנוֹגְשֵׂךְ אֲשֶׁר גָּדַע קְרָנַיִךְ.[3]

and cry out 〈 over 〈 those who beat you 〈 and your taskmasters 〈 who 〈 cut down 〈 your pride. 《

חַכִּי בֶּאֱמֶת לְאֵל צוּרֵךְ וּבוֹרְאֵךְ,

Wait in anticipation 〈 sincerely 〈 for God 〈 Who is your Rock 〈 and your Creator, 《

וְהוֹחִילִי לְמַלְכֵּךְ לְבַד כִּי הוּא אֲדוֹנַיִךְ.

and hope 〈 to your King 〈 exclusively, 《 for 〈 only He 〈 is your Lord. 《

(1) *Psalms* 18:43. (2) *Isaiah* 51:23. (3) Cf. *Eichah* 2:3.

ful, so they twisted the law in their favor.

Isaiah the prophet lamented this, saying: *How has the faithful city become a harlot? It had been filled with justice, righteousness lodged in it; but now — murderers!* (*Isaiah* 1:21). The prophet goes on to predict that in the future God will purge Jerusalem of its crooked leaders and that will lead to the redemption. *And I shall restore your judges as in earliest times and your counselors as at first. Afterwards you shall be called the City of Righteousness, the faithful City* (*Isaiah* 1:26).

This *kinnah* ends off on a note of hope that after Zion is purified it will once again be regarded as "the most precious treasure of monarchs and kingdoms."

טַהֲרִי לְבָבֵךְ וְכַפַּיִךְ,

‹ and your hands ‹ your heart ‹ Purify

וְשׁוּבִי עֲדֵי אִישֵׁךְ קְדוֹשֵׁךְ, וְלוֹ הַרְבִּי רְנָנַיִךְ.

« your prayers. ‹ increase ‹ and to Him « your Holy One; ‹ [God] your Spouse, ‹ unto ‹ and return [in penitence]

יוֹמָם וָלַיְלָה תְּנִי קוֹל בִּבְכִי מַר,

‹ that is bitter ‹ with weeping ‹ with your voice ‹ shout out ‹ and night, ‹ Day

עֲלֵי קִרְיַת מְלוּכָה[1] וְעַל תֵּל אַרְמוֹנַיִךְ.

« of your [Temple] palace. ‹ the mound [of ruins] ‹ and over ‹ of royalty ‹ the City ‹ over [Jerusalem]

כָּבוֹד וְהָדָר וְרֹב יֳפִי בְּתוֹכֵךְ,

« were in your midst, ‹ beauty ‹ and bountiful ‹ and majesty ‹ Glory

הֲלֹא נִמְצָא פְּנֵי קְדוֹשֵׁךְ וְהֵן נִתַּן לְעוֹיְנַיִךְ.

« to your enemies. ‹ have been given over ‹ but now they « your Holy One, ‹ before ‹ were displayed ‹ indeed all these

לָמָּה לְגַלִּים, מְעוֹן תַּנִּים,[2]

« of jackals, ‹ the lair ‹ a mound of rubble, ‹ Why has [Jerusalem become]

וּמוֹרַשׁ קָאַת וְקִפּוֹד,[3] וְגַם אַגְמֵי מַיִם מַעְיָנַיִךְ.

« have your springs turned. ‹ of water ‹ into marshes ‹ Even « and the hedgehog? ‹ of wild birds ‹ the domain

מֵאַנְתְּ שְׁמוֹעַ לְקוֹל מוּסַר מְיַסְּרֵךְ,

« of those who admonished you, ‹ of warning ‹ to the voice ‹ to listen ‹ You [stubbornly] refused

בְּכֵן שָׁתִית וּמָצִית,[4] שְׁמָנַיִךְ שְׁמָרַיִךְ.

« and your sediment. ‹ your fatty residue ‹ and you have sucked dry ‹ you have drunk ‹ therefore

נֹכַח פְּנֵי עֶלְיוֹן שִׁפְכִי לְבָבֵךְ[5] כְּמֵי נָהָר,

« of the river, ‹ like the waters ‹ your heart ‹ pour out « of the Most High, ‹ the Presence ‹ Before

---

(1) Cf. *Psalms* 48:3. (2) *Jeremiah* 9:10. (3) Cf. *Isaiah* 14:23, 34:11, *Zephaniah* 2:14, *Psalms* 102:7. (4) Cf. 51:17. (5) Cf. *Eichah* 2:19.

וְאַל תִּתְּנִי פוּגַת[1] לְעֵינַיִךְ.

« to your eyes. ‹ a respite ‹ give ‹ and do not

סֹבִּי וְהוֹמִי בְּעִיר,[2] קִרְאִי מְקוֹנְנוֹת[3]

‹ the women lamenters ‹ Call « all over the city. ‹ and moan ‹ Go around

וְכָל נָשִׁים מְבַכּוֹת, בְּכִי גָדוֹל מְקוֹנְנַיִךְ.

« shall your lamenters! ‹ copiously ‹ Weep « who know how to weep. ‹ the women ‹ and all

עֲלֵי צְנִיף מַלְכֵּךְ[4] עַד אָן לְמִרְמָס יְהִי,

« will it be? ‹ to be trampled ‹ when ‹ until « of your royalty, ‹ the coronet ‹ [To lament] over

עַד מָה בְּיַד צָר בְּנֵי שָׂרִים סְגָנַיִךְ.

« your ministers? ‹ of your officers, ‹ the children « of your tormentors, ‹ [will remain] in the hands ‹ when ‹ Until

פְּתַח לְבָנוֹן שְׁעָרַיִךְ,[5]* אֲשֶׁר טָבְעוּ בְּאֶרֶץ[6] נְשִׁיָּה,[7]

« of oblivion, ‹ into the land ‹ that sank ‹ The ones « your gates!* ‹ O [Levanon,] Whitened One, ‹ Open,

וְאֵין מָלוֹן לְכֹהֲנַיִךְ.

« for your priests. ‹ a lodging house ‹ for [now] there is no [longer]

צִיּוֹן עֲלֵיהֶם נְהִי נִהְיָה,[8] וְלֹא תֶחֱשִׁי,

« be silent. ‹ do not « has come to be; ‹ a lamentation ‹ over their plight « O Zion,

אִסְפִי וְקַבְּצִי זְקֵנוֹת וּזְקֵנַיִךְ.

« and old men [to lament]. ‹ your old women ‹ and assemble ‹ Gather together

---

(1) *Eichah* 2:18. (2) Cf. *Isaiah* 23:16. (3) Cf. *Jeremiah* 9:16. (4) Cf. *Isaiah* 62:3. (5) Cf. *Zechariah* 11:1. (6) *Eichah* 2:9. (7) *Psalms* 88:13. (8) *Micah* 2:4.

פְּתַח לְבָנוֹן שְׁעָרַיִךְ — *Open O [Levanon,] Whitened One, your gates!* This is based on the words of the prophet who said: פְּתַח לְבָנוֹן דְּלָתֶיךָ, *Open O [Levanon,] Whitened One, your doors!* (*Zechariah* 11:1). The Talmud (*Yoma* 39b) teaches that 40 years before the destruction of the Second Temple, the Temple itself exhibited many signs and omens of its impending doom. One of the portents was that the Temple gates would swing open all by themselves as if to invite the enemy to enter and destroy it. Rabban Yochanan ben Zakkai saw this and addressed the Temple: Sanctuary, O Sanctuary! Why do you take such pains to terrify yourself? I know full

קָרְחִי וָגֹזִּי כַּנֶּשֶׁר עַל בְּנֵי תַּעֲנוּגָיִךְ,[1]
‹ of your delight ‹ the children ‹ over « as an eagle, ‹ and tear out your hair ‹ Make yourself bald

וְעַל כָּל נְשִׂיאַיִךְ וְרוֹזְנָיִךְ.
« and your officers. ‹ your princes ‹ all ‹ and over

רָמוּ וְגָדְלוּ כְּמוֹ גַלִּים בְּלֶב יָם מְזוֹרָיִךְ,
« did your [festering] wounds, ‹ of the sea ‹ in the heart ‹ billowing waves ‹ like ‹ and distended ‹ Become swollen

בְּלֵיל שֻׁדְּדוּ[2] טוּרֵי אֲבָנָיִךְ.
« of your [precious] gems [from the *Kohen Gadol's* breastplate]. ‹ the rows ‹ when were pillaged ‹ on the night

שֻׁדַּד מְלוֹנֵךְ וְכָל מַחְמַד יְקָרֵךְ,
« among your treasures, ‹ that is precious ‹ together with all ‹ was your lodging place [the Temple] ‹ Pillaged

בְּאֵין אוּרִים וְתֻמִּים[3] אֲשֶׁר גִּלּוּ צְפוּנָיִךְ.
« all your hidden things. ‹ revealed ‹ which ‹ and the Tumim ‹ of the Urim ‹ you are bereft

תָּבוֹר וְכַרְמֶל כְּהָרֵי גִלְבּוֹעַ,*
‹ of Gilboa* ‹ have become like the mountains ‹ and Carmel ‹ Tabor

בְּלִי טַלֵּךְ וּמִטְרֵךְ,[4] וְלֹא אוֹר עֲנָנָיִךְ.[5]
« of your [protective] clouds. ‹ the light ‹ and do not have ‹ and your rain ‹ of your dew ‹ which are devoid

(1) Cf. *Micah* 1:16. (2) Cf. *Isaiah* 15:1. (3) *Exodus* 28:30. (4) Cf. *II Samuel* 1:21. (5) Cf. *Job* 37:11.

well that you are destined to be destroyed as indeed the prophet Zechariah foretold when he said, *Open O [Levanon,] Whitened One, your doors, so that the fire many consume your cedars!* [But why must you fulfill this prophecy so early and prematurely?] The *Talmud* concludes: And why is the Temple referred to as לְבָנוֹן, *Levanon* [Whitened One]? Because it is there that the Jewish nation finds atonement and the stain of their sins is whitened and cleansed!

תָּבוֹר וְכַרְמֶל כְּהָרֵי גִלְבּוֹעַ — *Tabor and Carmel have become like the mountains of Gilboa.* Tabor and Carmel were fertile mountains covered with grass and trees. Gilboa, however, was cursed and barren, for it was on Gilboa that King Saul died in his final battle with the Philistines. In his passionate eulogy for Saul, David cursed Mount Gilboa forever: *O mountains of Gilboa, let neither dew nor rain be upon you, nor fields of bounty, for there the shield of the mighty was rejected, the shield of Saul was as though not anointed with oil* [*II Samuel* 1:21].

צִיּוֹן יְגוֹנֵךְ נְשִׁי, טַהֲרִי וְהִתְקַדְּשִׁי,

« and sanctify yourself! ‹ Purify yourself « forget! ‹ Your grief « O Zion!

עֲדִי יְקָר לִבְשִׁי, תַּמְרוּק שְׁמָנַיִךְ.

« oils. ‹ and [apply] your cosmetic « don, ‹ that are precious ‹ Ornaments

צִיּוֹן וְשָׁלְמוּ יְמֵי אֶבְלֵךְ[1] בְּשָׂשׂוֹן וְגִיל,

« and jubilation, ‹ with joy ‹ of your mourning ‹ will the days ‹ Come to an end « O Zion!

כִּי תַּם עֲוֹנֵךְ וּמִשְׁנֶה שִׁבְרוֹנַיִךְ.

« Destruction [will be concluded]. ‹ and your double ‹ will your sins be ‹ entirely absolved ‹ for

צִיּוֹן סְגֻלַּת מְלָכִים וּמְדִינוֹת[2] תִּהְיִ עוֹד,

« once again, ‹ you will be [considered] ‹ and kingdoms ‹ of monarchs ‹ The most precious treasure « O Zion!

יִזְּלוּ מֵי מְנוּחוֹת[3] מַעְיָנַיִךְ.

« from your springs. ‹ that are tranquil ‹ waters ‹ and there shall flow

צִיּוֹן פְּדוּתֵךְ צַפִּי, עוֹד יִקְרָאוּךְ צְפִירַת תִּפְאָרָה,[4]

‹ of glory ‹ a coronet ‹ you will be called ‹ Once again « look forward expectantly! ‹ To your redemption « O Zion!

בְּפִי יְשָׁרִים וְנוֹגְנַיִךְ.[5]

« and by your musicians [the Levites]. ‹ of the upright ‹ by the mouth

צִיּוֹן בְּרָכָה וְחַיִּים,[6] בָּךְ אֲבִיר יַעֲקֹב,[7]

‹ of Jacob ‹ has [God] the Mighty One ‹ for you ‹ and life ‹ Blessing « O Zion!

צִוָּה לְעוֹלָם[6] וְעוֹד יֹאמְרוּ בְּאָזְנַיִךְ.

« in your ears. ‹ [mankind] will say that ‹ and what is more « forever, ‹ decreed

צִיּוֹן הֲמוֹן כֹּהֲנִים הֵמָּה יְשָׁרְתוּנֵךְ,

« shall serve you! ‹ —they « of priests ‹ A multitude « O Zion!

וְגַם יוֹסִיף יהוה קְנוֹת שֵׁנִית קְצִינַיִךְ.[8]

your leaders [from exile]. ‹ a second time ‹ to acquire ‹ HASHEM will repeat ‹ And also,

(1) *Isaiah* 60:20. (2) Cf. *Ecclesiates* 2:8. (3) *Psalms* 23:2. (4) *Isaiah* 28:5.
(5) Cf. *Psalms* 68:26. Alternatively, שָׁרִים, *singers.* (6) Cf. 133:3. (7) *Genesis* 49:24. (8) Cf. *Isaiah* 11:11.

KINNAH 44 / קינה מד

צִיּוֹן גְּבֶרֶת* לְמַמְלָכוֹת[1] מְצִירָיִךְ,

« who are now your tormentors, ‹ over the nations ‹ You who were once the queen* « O Zion!

רְבֵי שְׁלוֹמִים שְׂאִי, מֵאֵת אֲסִירָיִךְ.

« your captive [people]. ‹ from ‹ accept ‹ wishes for peace ‹ abundant

יֶחֱמַץ לְבָבִי[2] לְקוֹל נָתְנוּ רְאֵמִים,

« by the wild oxen [the kings], ‹ bellowed ‹ at the sound ‹ is my heart ‹ In ferment

בְּנֵי שֵׂעִיר וּמוֹאָב, בְּתוֹךְ הֵיכַל דְּבִירָיִךְ.

« of your Sanctuary. ‹ the hall ‹ inside ‹ and Moab, ‹ of Seir ‹ the sons

לְבְּסוּ מְשִׁיחַי בְּדַם קָדְקֹד סְגָנִים,

« of the slain [Jewish] princes. ‹ from the [smashed] skulls ‹ by the blood ‹ were my anointed ones [the *Kohen Gadol* and the king] ‹ Sullied

טְרוֹף[3] שׁוֹעַ וְקוֹעַ, רָמוֹס עַמִּי בְּחִירָיִךְ.

« your chosen ones. ‹ my nation, ‹ trampling « and the nobles, ‹ the philanthropists ‹ They tore to pieces

עָרִים בְּצוּרוֹת תָּפוּשׂ דָּיֵק וְסוֹלְלָ שָׁפוֹךְ,[4]

« pouring; ‹ and an assault ramp ‹ [building] siege towers « they seized, ‹ that were fortified ‹ The cities

אַרְזֵי לְבָנוֹן כְּרוֹת, מֵעֲצֵי יְעָרָיִךְ.

« of your forests. ‹ [as well as] from the [other] trees « they chopped down, ‹ of Lebanon ‹ the cedars

---

(1) Cf. *Isaiah* 47:5. (2) Cf. *Psalms* 73:21. (3) Cf. *Deuteronomy* 33:20. (4) Cf. *Ezekiel* 4:2.

צִיּוֹן גְּבֶרֶת — *O Zion! You who were once the queen.* In this *kinnah* we bemoan Zion's terrible fall from prominence to pitiful wretchedness. Once Zion was the center of the entire world, mistress to all the nations, but now she lies downtrodden beneath the heel of her former vassals.

Indeed it seems as if God has lost all interest in Jerusalem (Zion) and has abandoned it to heathen marauders, but in truth, God still cares deeply for Israel and Jerusalem, only He is hidden from our view. For this reason we sing *kinnos* such as this one, to arouse God to reveal His Presence once more.

The Talmud (*Menachos* 87a) states that even after the destruction of Zion, God protected this sacred site by posting guardian angels around it. As the prophet says, *Upon your walls, O Jerusalem, have I posted guardians all the day and all the night;*

חָזוּ נְבִיאִים בְּשָׁוְא דָּבָר[1]

‹ words ‹ useless ‹ did the [corrupt] prophets ‹ Envision

בְּשֵׁם עִיר קְדוֹשׁ יַעֲקֹב[2] לְשָׁלוֹם,

« [that Jerusalem] would be left in peace. « of Jacob, ‹ the Holy One « of the Divine, ‹ in the Name

וְלֹא חֻבְּשׁוּ מְזוֹרָיִךְ.

« were your festering [spiritual] wounds. ‹ bandaged [through repentance] ‹ Thus, not

יִתַּר לְבָבִי עֲלֵי אָרוֹן וּמִשְׁכָּן וְצִיץ זָהָב וְאֵפוֹד,

‹ the Ephod, ‹ of Gold, ‹ the Headplate ‹ the Tabernacle, ‹ [the loss of] the Ark, ‹ over ‹ did my heart ‹ Quiver [from terror]

וְשֵׁם קֹדֶשׁ סְתָרָיִךְ.

« that is concealed. ‹ of Holiness ‹ and Your Name

אִיִּים יְחַוּוּ לְרָז אוֹתוֹת וּמוֹפֵת,

« and the wonders [of your prophets]. ‹ through the signs [of the Urim V'Tumim] ‹ the secrets [revealed] ‹ acknowledge ‹ [Even those on remote] islands

עֲלֵי שִׁבְרֵךְ יְרַפְּאוּ, אֱלֵי מִשְׁנֶה שְׁבָרָיִךְ.[3]

« devastation! ‹ over your twofold ‹ [now instead] we lament « they could have provided healing, ‹ your wounds ‹ For

שֶׁמֶשׁ וְכָל כּוֹכְבֵי שַׁחַק בְּעֵמֶק דָּמוּ,[4]

« stood still in silence, ‹ in the Valley [of Aijalon] ‹ of heaven ‹ and all the stars ‹ The sun

קוֹלֵךְ בְּרָמָה שְׂאִי, קוֹל תַּמְרוּרָיִךְ.[5]

« of your bitter wailing. ‹ the voice « raise up, ‹ in Ramah ‹ [now] your voice

(1) Cf. *Eichah* 2:14. (2) *Isaiah* 29:23. (3) Cf. *Jeremiah* 17:18. (4) Cf. *Joshua* 10:12. (5) Cf. *Jeremiah* 31:14.

they will never be silent; all you who remind HASHEM *be not silent!* (*Isaiah* 62:6). What do these angels say as they stand guard? Either they recite the verse, *You will arise and show Zion mercy* (*Psalms* 102:14), or they recite the verse, *The builder of Jerusalem is* HASHEM (ibid. 147:2).

What did the angels say before the destruction? They recited the verse, *For* HASHEM *has chosen Zion, it He desired for His dwelling place* (ibid. 132:13). And when the Temple is rebuilt, *Rashi* comments, they will recite that verse once again.

סַהַר וְכִימָה וְעָשׁ וּכְסִיל[1] לָזֹאת יִבְכּוּ,

The moon 〈 and [the constellations of] the Pleiades, 〈 Ursa 〈 and Orion, 《 over this 〈 let them all weep, 《

נָגְהָם אֲשֶׁר אָסְפוּ,[2] כּוֹכְבֵי שְׁחָרָיִךְ.

their radiance 〈 that 〈 they have withheld 《 — the stars 〈 of your morning. 《

מַטֵּה רְשָׁעִים[3] כְּקָם, שָׂרִים בְּיָדָם תְּלוּת,

When the [powerful] staff 〈 of the wicked 〈 rose up, 《 the [Jewish] princes 〈 by their own hands 〈 they commanded to be hanged; 《

שָׁבַת מְשׂוֹשֵׂךְ[4] וְגִיל וּכְלֵי זְמָרָיִךְ.

then ceased 〈 your joy 〈 and gladness, 〈 as well as the instruments 〈 of your music. 《

אָבַל לְבָנוֹן וְגִיל כַּרְמֶל בְּלִי נִשְׁמַע חָפְרוּ סְגָנִים,

Mourn 〈 does Lebanon [the Temple], 〈 and the gladness 〈 of Carmel [the Temple] 〈 is not 〈 heard, 《 disgraced 〈 were the deputies 〈

בְּבֹא צַר בִּשְׁעָרָיִךְ.

at the entry 〈 of the enemy 〈 into your gates. 《

חָכְמַת נְבוֹנִים[5] בְּיוֹם אָבְדָה וְאֶסְּרוּ קְצִינָיִךְ,

The wisdom 〈 of the sages 〈 on that day [of the Temple's destruction] 〈 was lost 〈 and imprisoned 〈 were your leaders, 《

וְשָׁחוּ בְּנֵי צִיּוֹן יְקָרָיִךְ.[6]

and bent low 〈 were the children 〈 of Zion, 〈 your precious ones. 《

מִכְלַל מְלָכִים לְבוּשׁ בָּנוֹת רְעוּלוֹת,

The splendor 〈 of [Jewish] kings 〈 is now worn 〈 by the daughters 〈 of the uncircumcised heathens; 《

פְּאֵר רָאמוֹת וְגָבִישׁ,[7] וְאַף סַפִּיר גִּזְרָיִךְ.[8]

resplendent 〈 with precious stones, 《 even [inlaid] 〈 with sapphires 〈 skillfully cut. 《

(1) Cf. *Job* 9:9. (2) Cf. *Joel* 2:10. (3) *Isaiah* 14:5. (4) Cf. *Eichah* 5:15.
(5) Cf. *Isaiah* 29:14. (6) Cf. *Eichah* 4:2. (7) *Job* 28:18. (8) Cf. *Eichah* 4:7.

בָּזְאוּ נְהָרִים[1] בְּתוֹךְ קִרְיָה עַלִּיזָה,[2]

Utterly pillage ‹ did streams [of enemy hordes] ‹ in the midst ‹ of the City ‹ that [once] was joyous, «

לְאֵין קֵץ לַתְּכוּנָה[3] וְסוֹף, פָּרְצוּ גְּדֵרָיִךְ.[4]

without ‹ limit ‹ to the amount [of riches] ‹ or an end; « and they breached ‹ your walls. «

גִּבְעָה וְעֵץ רַעֲנָן,[5]

On every hill ‹ and [beneath] every tree ‹ that is flourishing, «

אֵלֶּה מְקוֹם פִּגּוּל מְלֵאִים מֵחֲלַל פְּגָרָיִךְ.

these are ‹ the places ‹ where [idolatrous] abominations [once] stood, « they are now filled ‹ with the corpses ‹ of your slaughtered ones. «

יֶהֱמוּ קְרָבַי כַּיָּם, יִזְּלוּ דְמָעַי כְּמֵי נִמְרִים,[6]

Churn ‹ do my innards ‹ like the sea, « flow ‹ do my tears ‹ like the waters ‹ of Nimrim, «

לְבָאִים בְּיוֹם טָרְפוּ כְּפִירָיִךְ.[7]

because of the [enemy] lions ‹ on the day ‹ they tore apart ‹ the young cubs [of Israel]. «

יִסְעַר לְבָבִי כְּמוֹ סוּפָה וָסַעַר,

In turmoil ‹ is my heart ‹ as if [struck] ‹ by a tempest ‹ and a storm, «

כְּמוֹץ גֹּרֶן יְסוֹעֵר,[8] עֲלֵי אַשְׁמוֹת כְּמָרָיִךְ.

like the chaff ‹ from the threshing floor ‹ swirling wildly, « because of ‹ the guilt ‹ of your priests [who led Israel astray]. «

הוּמַר בְּשָׂרִי לְיוֹם נֵאֵר קְדוֹשׁ יַעֲקֹב

Transformed [by suffering] ‹ has my flesh been ‹ since the day ‹ when repudiate ‹ did the Holy One ‹ of Jacob ‹

מִקְדָּשׁ וּמִזְבְּחוֹ,[9] בְּלִי בוֹא בַּחֲצֵרָיִךְ.

the Temple ‹ and its Altar, ‹ and not allowing ‹ our entry ‹ into Your courtyards. «

---

(1) *Isaiah* 18:7. (2) 22:2. (3) *Nahum* 2:10. (4) Cf. *Psalms* 80:13. (5) Cf. *Jeremiah* 2:20, *Isaiah* 17:10. (6) *Isaiah* 15:6. (7) Cf. *Nahum* 2:14. (8) Cf. *Hosea* 13:3. (9) Cf. *Eichah* 2:7.

שׂוֹרֵק וּנְטַע נַעֲמָן[1] הָיִית,

[O Israel] a choice vine, ‹ a planting ‹ that is pleasant, ‹ you were, ‹

וּבֹקֶר כְּצָץ פֶּרַח וְנִצָּה, תְּשַׂגְשֵׂגִי זְמוֹרָיִךְ.

at the dawn [of your history] ‹ after sprout ‹ did flower ‹ and blossom, « then get entangled [in the destructive thorns of sin] ‹ did your vine's tendrils. «

שׁוּבִי צְבִיָּה לְאֵל יוֹצְרֵךְ, יְכוֹנְנֵךְ לְדוֹר וָדוֹר,

Return, ‹ O deer, ‹ to God, ‹ your Creator, « and He will establish you firmly ‹ for generation ‹ after generation, «

בְּתוֹכֵךְ שְׁכוֹן בַּעַל נְעוּרָיִךְ.

when in your midst ‹ He will dwell, « the husband ‹ of your youth. «

אַרְיֵה בְּנָוֵךְ לְבַל יַעֲלֶה[2] מְסִלּוֹת,

The lion [Nebuchadnezzar] ‹ [to attack] your Temple dwelling ‹ will no longer ‹ march up ‹ the highways, «

וְצִי אַדִּיר וְשַׁיִט לְבַל יַעֲבוֹר[3] יְאוֹרָיִךְ.

and any naval fleet ‹ that is mighty ‹ or any sailing vessel ‹ will not ‹ trespass ‹ your waterways. «

נַפְשִׁי שְׁלוֹמֵךְ דְּרוֹשׁ אִוְּתָה[4] כְּחוֹם צַח עֲלֵי אוֹר,

My soul ‹ your welfare ‹ to seek ‹ does yearn, « [as people long] for warmth ‹ that is crisp ‹ after ‹ the rain, «

כְּעָב טַל בְּחוֹם[5] יוֹם, נֵד קְצִירָיִךְ.[6]

or for a mist ‹ of dew ‹ in the heat ‹ of the day, « a [breeze] rustling ‹ your harvest. «

אֶשְׂמַח וְאָשִׂישׂ בְּיוֹם אֶשְׁמַע מְבַשֵּׂר בְּקוֹל,[7]

I will be happy ‹ and rejoice ‹ on the day ‹ that I hear ‹ the herald proclaiming [the Redemption] ‹ out loud, «

שְׁלוֹם מְנוּחָה דְּרוֹשׁ, וּשְׁלוֹם אֲסִירָיִךְ.

and peace ‹ and tranquility ‹ he strives to bring ‹ and [seeks] the peace and welfare ‹ of your captives. «

(1) Cf. *Jeremiah* 2:21. (2) Cf. 4:7, 49:19. (3) Cf. *Isaiah* 33:21.
(4) Cf. *Job* 23:13. (5) *Isaiah* 18:4. (6) Cf. 17:11. (7) Cf. 52:7.

קינה לזכרון הקדושים של חורבן איירופא

IN MEMORY OF THE MARTYRS OF CHURBAN EUROPE

מאת הרב שלמה האלבערשטאם זצ"ל, האדמור מבאבאב

by Rabbi Shlomo Halberstam, זצ"ל, Bobover Rav

זִכְרוּ נָא וְקוֹנְנוּ כָּל יִשְׂרָאֵל, קוֹלְכֶם יִשָּׁמַע בָּרָמָה,

« on high. ‹ be heard ‹ let your voices « of Israel, ‹ O all ‹ and lament, ‹ please, ‹ Remember,

כִּי הִשְׁמִידָה גֶּרְמַנְיָא אֶת עַמֵּנוּ בִּימֵי זַעַם הַמִּלְחָמָה,

« of the World War; ‹ of the wrath ‹ during the days ‹ our people ‹ has Germany ‹ destroyed ‹ For

בְּמִיתוֹת מְשֻׁנּוֹת אַכְזָרִיּוֹת, בְּרָעָב וּבַצָּמָא,

« and thirst. ‹ with starvation « and cruel, ‹ horrible ‹ with killings,

אַל תִּשְׁכְּחוּ בְּכָל הַדּוֹרוֹת,

« the generations, ‹ through all ‹ forget ‹ Do not

עֲדֵי תִזְכּוּ לִרְאוֹת בַּנֶּחָמָה.

« the [ultimate] consolation. ‹ witnessing ‹ you will merit ‹ until

צַעֲקָתָם וּבִכְיוֹתֵיהֶם, צְפוּפִים וּסְגוּרִים בַּקְּרוֹנִים,

« into the train's [cattle] cars. ‹ and locked ‹ as they were tightly packed ‹ and their weeping ‹ [Remember] their screams

כַּצֹּאן לַטֶּבַח יוּבָלוּ, לִשְׂרֵפָה בַּכִּבְשׁוֹנִים,

« in the crematorium ovens. ‹ to be incinerated « they were led, ‹ to the slaughter ‹ Like sheep

קוֹל שַׁוְעָם יִזָּכֵר תָּמִיד לִפְנֵי שׁוֹכֵן מְעוֹנִים,

« in the Heavens. ‹ the One Who dwells ‹ before ‹ eternally ‹ be remembered ‹ of their pleading cries ‹ May the sound

---

זִכְרוּ נָא — *Remember, please.* The destruction of European Jewry by the Nazis during World War II was the most massive calamity to befall our people since the Destruction of the Second Temple. As explained in the prefatory notes to *Kinnah* 25, which laments the devastation of the Crusades, Torah Jews recognize that all Jewish misfortunes have their roots in the tragic events of Tishah B'Av. Therefore we designate no new days of mourning to commemorate later events, but include them in our Tishah B'Av *kinnos* service.

The Bobover Rav, Admor HaRav Shlomo Halberstam, זצ"ל, was a scion of Sanz, one of the most illustrious Rabbinic and Chassidic dynasties. The Rav lost everything in the Holocaust: family, friends, followers, disciples, and students in the thousands. The Rebbe arrived in America after the war with nothing but the clothes on his back and a burning determination

בְּקָרְאָם שְׁמַע יִשְׂרָאֵל, מָסְרוּ נַפְשָׁם לַאֲדוֹנֵי הָאֲדוֹנִים.

« of lords. ‹ to the Lord ‹ their lives ‹ they offered up ‹ *Yisrael,* ‹ *Shema* ‹ When they proclaimed,

רָאשֵׁי יְשִׁיבוֹת וְתַלְמִידֵיהֶם, וַהֲמוֹנֵי עַמְּךָ שָׁמָּה,

« were there. ‹ of Your people ‹ and the multitudes ‹ and their students, ‹ of Yeshivahs ‹ Heads

הֶעֱבִידוּם בְּעִנּוּיִים קָשִׁים, וַהֲרָגוּם בְּיָד רָמָה,

« arrogance. ‹ with high-handed ‹ and they slaughtered them « that were brutal, ‹ with tortures ‹ They enslaved them

דְּמֵי יְלָדִים רַכִּים צוֹעֲקִים אֵלֶיךָ מִן הָאֲדָמָה,

« the earth, [saying;] ‹ from ‹ to You ‹ cries out ‹ who were tender ‹ of babies ‹ The blood

נְקוֹם נִקְמַת טַף וְנָשִׁים, לֹא תְחַיֶּה כָּל נְשָׁמָה.

« *living soul!* ‹ *any* ‹ *escape alive* ‹ *let not* « *and the women;* ‹ *of the children* ‹ *the vengeance* ‹ *Avenge*

עַל שְׂרֵפַת אַלְפֵי מִדְרָשׁוֹת וּבָתֵּי כְנֵסִיּוֹת,

« and synagogues, ‹ of study halls ‹ of thousands ‹ the burning ‹ For

רִבְבוֹת סִפְרֵי תוֹרָה וְלוֹמְדֶיהָ נְקוֹנֵן בִּשְׁאִיּוֹת,

« with raised and screaming voices. ‹ we shall lament ‹ and their students ‹ of the Torah ‹ of Scrolls ‹ and for myriads

שִׁלְּחוּ בָאֵשׁ מִקְדְּשֵׁי אֵל, הִצִּיתוּ וְעֵינֵינוּ צוֹפִיּוֹת,

« witnessed. ‹ and our eyes ‹ they ignited them, « of God, ‹ the sanctuaries ‹ aflame ‹ They set

יְשַׁלֵּם הַמַּבְעִיר אֶת הַבְּעֵרָה, יָדִין בַּגּוֹיִם מָלֵא גְוִיּוֹת.

« with corpses. ‹ that are filled ‹ the nations ‹ may God judge « the raging fire; ‹ those who lit ‹ Let suffer retribution

---

to rebuild what the Nazis had destroyed. With the help of Hashem the glory of the House of Bobov has been restored and one will find dozens of Bobover institutions and thousands of Bobover Chassidim in every corner of the globe.

In 1984, the Bobover Rav composed a special *kinnah* to bemoan the tragedy of *Churban Europa,* and it is recited in many congregations. When the Rav was asked for permission to include his *kinnah* and its translation in this edition of *kinnos,* he graciously conceded. Then he explained why he had written it: "For years I had wanted to express my grief over my personal loss and *Klal Yisrael's* loss, in a special *kinnah,* but I hesitated. I felt that in order to compose a *kinnah* one must be on the exalted level of R' Elazar HaKalir, who wrote with *Ruach HaKodesh,* Divine inspiration. Moreover, he was a master of Kabbalistic secrets and knew the mystical incantations of the ministering angels. Still, many *chassidim* requested a vehicle to convey their personal sorrow on this bitter day, but I held back, because I felt

זַעֲקוּ שָׁמַיִם וַאֲדָמָה, עַל אַלְפֵי עֲיָרוֹת מִבְצְרֵי תוֹרָה,

‹ Cry out loud, ‹ O heaven ‹ and earth, ‹ for ‹ the thousands « of cities, ‹ citadels « of Torah,

אַרְצוֹת אֵירוֹפָּא וּקְהִלּוֹתֶיהָ, נוֹחֲלֵי וּמְקַיְּמֵי מְסוֹרָה,

‹ for the countries ‹ of Europe « and their [Jewish] communities, ‹ the heirs ‹ and trustees « of our traditions,

צַדִּיקִים זְקֵנִים וַחֲסִידִים, דְּבֵקֵי אֱמוּנָה טְהוֹרָה,

‹ for righteous tzaddikim, ‹ elders, « pious chassidim, ‹ all those who clung ‹ unto a faith « so pure.

מִיּוֹם גָּלִינוּ מֵאַרְצֵנוּ לֹא הָיָה כָּזֶה כִּלָּיוֹן נוֹרָא.

‹ From the day ‹ we were exiled ‹ from our homeland ‹ there was never ‹ such as this, ‹ an annihilation « so awesome.

רַחֵם עַל שְׁאֵרִיתֵנוּ, הַבֵּט נָא מִשָּׁמַיִם,

‹ Have mercy ‹ on « our remnant; ‹ look down, ‹ please, ‹ from heaven

לְמַחֲנוֹת הַקְּדוֹשִׁים, פִּי עֶשֶׂר כְּיוֹצְאֵי מִצְרַיִם,

‹ at the [death] camps « of the martyrs, ‹ ten times as many ‹ as those who left « Egypt.

קוֹמֵם בֵּית קָדְשֵׁנוּ, וְנַחֲמֵנוּ בְּכִפְלַיִם,

‹ Rebuild ‹ our holy Temple, ‹ and provide us with consolation « in a double measure,

רוֹמְמֵנוּ, וַהֲבִיאֵנוּ לְצִיּוֹן וִירוּשָׁלָיִם.

‹ Exalt us, ‹ and bring us back ‹ to Zion « and Jerusalem.

---

genuinely unworthy.

"Then, one day, I was studying the laws of Tishah B'Av in the book *Seder HaYom* [by R' Moshe ben Yehudah Makir, Rosh Yeshivah in Safed, and a colleague of the *Arizal* and *R' Yosef Karo*]. He writes as follows:

> Whoever can wail on this day should wail, and whoever can recite *kinnos* should recite *kinnos:* either those already recorded in the holy books, or the *kinnos* he himself composed with the intellect God has granted him. It is a *mitzvah* for each and every individual to compose *kinnos* for weeping and moaning and to recite them on this bitter day. One who does this is considered most righteous and is worthy of being described as one of Jerusalem's mourners and one of her holy men. But one who is *not* capable of composing his personal *kinnos* should recite the *kinnos* written by others.

"When I read these words," the Rav concluded, "I saw a clear sign from heaven that the time had come to compose a *kinnah* over the last *churban*. For doesn't the *Seder HaYom* say clearly that any person, even the smallest, should express his own feelings in his original *kinnah*?"

קינה לזכרון הקדושים של חורבן אייראפא

IN MEMORY OF THE MARTYRS OF CHURBAN EUROPE

מאת הרב שמעון שוואב זצ"ל, רב דקהל עדת ישורון

by Rabbi Shimon Schwab, זצ"ל, Rav of K'hal Adas Jeshurun

הַזּוֹכֵר* מַזְכִּירָיו, דּוֹר דּוֹר וּקְדוֹשָׁיו,

« and its holy ones ‹ after generation ‹ generation ‹ those who remember Him, ‹ He Who remembers

מֵעֵת אֲשֶׁר אָז בְּחַרְתָּנוּ,

« You chose us — ‹ then ‹ that ‹ — since the time

יִזְכּוֹר דֵּרָאוֹן, שֶׁל דּוֹר אַחֲרוֹן, אוֹיָה מֶה הָיָה לָנוּ.[1]

« to us! ‹ has happened ‹ What « Woe! « preceding this. ‹ the generation ‹ of ‹ the gruesome fate ‹ May He remember

שְׁטוּפֵי מַבּוּל דָּם, שֶׁמָּסְרוּ נַפְשׁוֹתָם,

« their lives — ‹ — who sacrificed « of blood ‹ by the flood ‹ Those who were swept away

כָּל שְׁקוּעֵי עִמְקֵי הַבָּכָא,[2]

« of tears, ‹ in valleys ‹ who were sunken ‹ All

יִפְקְדֵם אֱלֹהִים, בְּאַרְצוֹת הַחַיִּים,[3]

« of eternal life. ‹ in the lands ‹ May God think of them

וַעֲדֵי עַד זִכְרָם לִבְרָכָה.

« be for a blessing. ‹ may their memory ‹ and ever ‹ for ever

(1) *Eichah* 5:1. (2) *Cf. Psalms* 84:7. (3) 116:9.

הַזּוֹכֵר ◆ — *He Who remembers.* Rav Shimon Schwab, זצ"ל, widely recognized as an eloquent spokesman for Torah Jewry, joined the Rabbinate of Congregation K'hal Adas Jeshurun in the Washington Heights neighborhood of New York in 1958, in association with the late revered Rav Dr. Joseph Breuer, זצ"ל.

Rav Schwab was born in Frankfurt-am-Main, Germany in 1908, and studied at several well-known Eastern European yeshivos, including Telshe and Mir. In those years, Rav Schwab had the opportunity to meet with and learn from the foremost *Gedolim* of the time, including the holy Chafetz Chaim of Radin.

In the early 1930's, Rav Schwab was an eyewitness to the rise of Hitler Nazism in Germany and the systematic oppression of the Jews. In 1936, the persecution of the Nazis forced him to leave his pulpit in Germany. He came to the United States, where he assumed a position in the Baltimore Rabbinate.

Rav Schwab relates that in 1959, as Tishah B'Av approached, the late Rav

שְׂאוּ אֵלָיו כַּפַּיִם, אֲהָהּ, אֵי שָׁמַיִם,

« Heavens! ‹ O you ‹ woe « your hands, ‹ to Him ‹ Lift up

הוֹי עַל מֵיטַב שִׁבְטֵי יִשְׂרָאֵל,

« of Israel, ‹ of the tribes ‹ the best ‹ over ‹ Woe

עֵדוֹת וּקְהִלּוֹת, עָרִים וּגְלִילוֹת, חֲבוּרוֹת, מוֹסָדוֹת,

‹ organizations, ‹ fraternities, « and districts, ‹ cities « and congregations, ‹ Communities

כָּל מוֹעֲדֵי אֵל.

« for God. ‹ gatherings ‹ all

מִי יִתֵּן פַּלְגֵי מַיִם תֵּרַדְנָה עֵינַיִם[1]

‹ from eyes ‹ would pour down ‹ of water ‹ that streams ‹ can grant ‹ Who

אֶל אַשְׁדוֹת נַחֲלֵי הַדְּמָעוֹת,

« of tears, ‹ of the rivers ‹ waterfalls ‹ toward

עֲלֵי אַלְפֵי אֲלָפִים גּוּפִים נִשְׂרָפִים,

‹ consumed ‹ of bodies ‹ of thousands ‹ the thousands ‹ for

בְּמוֹ אֵשׁ[2] הַחֻרְבָּן וּזְוָעוֹת.

« and the horrors. ‹ of the destruction ‹ of fire ‹ in the midst

וְעַל שָׂרֵי הַתּוֹרָה, וּמַחֲזִיקֵי מָסוֹרָה,

« of tradition, ‹ the upholders ‹ of Torah, ‹ the princes ‹ For

וְעַל פִּרְחֵי הַכְּהוּנָּה הַצְּעִירִים,

« who are young, ‹ of the *Kehunah* ‹ the flowers ‹ for

וְעַל חוֹבְשֵׁי מִדְרָשׁוֹת, וּמוֹרִים וּמוֹרוֹת,

« and the women teachers, ‹ the men teachers « in the study hall, ‹ the [scholars] who lock themselves ‹ for

תִּינוֹקוֹת בֵּית רַבָּן יַקִּירִים.

« who are precious. ‹ of the Rabbis ‹ in the School ‹ and the children

(1) *Cf. Eichah* 3:48. (2) *Cf. Isaiah* 44:16.

Breuer made a request of him. "Please compose a special Tishah B'Av *kinnah* for our *kehillah*. Each and every one of us is either a refugee or a Holocaust survivor. We have all lost family and friends in this *churban*, and we German Jews bore the brunt of Hitler's fury. We must not forget, nor can we allow our children

עַל בָּנוֹת בּוֹטְחוֹת, וְסָבִים וְסָבוֹת,

For ‹ the daughters ‹ who are trusting, « and grandfathers ‹ and grandmothers, ‹

וְעַל זַרְעָם וְטַפָּם שֶׁיָּלְדוּ,

and for ‹ their offspring, ‹ and their infants ‹ whom they bore, «

וְגַם לְרַבּוֹת, רִבְבוֹת נֶאֱהָבִים בַּחַיִּים,

and also ‹ to include [everyone] « *— the myriads* ‹ beloved ‹ in life, «

בְּמוֹתָם לֹא נִפְרָדוּ.[1]

and in their death ‹ not ‹ parted [from God]. «

אֶת דָּמָם דְּרוֹשׁ,[2] כִּי תִשָּׂא אֶת רֹאשׁ,[3]

Their blood ‹ seek out ‹ when ‹ You take ‹ the headcount ‹

שֶׁל כָּל נִדָּף לֶעָלִים[4] הַטְּרוּפִים.

of ‹ all ‹ the scattered ones, ‹ of the leaves ‹ that are torn off, «

כָּל נַפְשׁוֹת מֵת, בִּימֵי שֶׁבֶר וָשֵׁאת,[5]

of all ‹ the souls ‹ that perished ‹ in the days ‹ of destruction ‹ and calamity «

שִׁשָּׁה אַלְפֵי פְּעָמִים אֲלָפִים.

— six ‹ thousand ‹ times ‹ a thousand. «

שְׁלִישִׁיָּה לְבָעֵר, בְּבָרָק זַעַם סוֹעֵר,

An entire third ‹ to be destroyed, « in the lightning flash ‹ of fury ‹ that stormed — [the blitzkrieg], «

מִכַּרְמֵי הַחֶמֶד[6] אָהַבְתָּ,

of the vineyards ‹ that were cherished ‹ that You loved. «

---

(1) Cf. *II Samuel* 1:23. (2) Cf. *Psalms* 9:13. (3) *Exodus* 30:12.
(4) Cf. *Leviticus* 26:36. (5) Cf. *Eichah* 3:47. (6) Cf. *Isaiah* 27:2; *Amos* 5:11.

---

to forget. Eight centuries ago German Jewry was slaughtered by the Crusaders. According to historians, how many Jews were killed? Perhaps 5,000. In World War II more than one thousand times that number were killed! In just one day at Auschwitz more than 5,000 Jews were brutally gassed and murdered. If German Jewry composed *kinnos* to commemorate the evil that befell us during the Crusades, how much more so must we compose one over the Holocaust!"

In deference to this request, Rav Schwab composed the following *kinnah* which, in K'hal Adas Jeshurun, is recited by the Rav on Tishah B'Av night at the conclu-

גּוֹאֵל הַדָּם, נָא זְכֹר צַעֲרָם אַל תִּמְחֶה מִסֵּפֶר כָּתָבְתָּ.[1]

« You have written. ‹ from the book ‹ erase ‹ do not ‹ of their misery ‹ the memory ‹ Please, « of the blood! ‹ O Avenger

זְכוֹר הַנְּאָקוֹת, וְרַעַשׁ צְעָקוֹת, אָז יוּבְלוּ לָרֶצַח,

«to slaughter — ‹ they were led ‹ from when ‹ of the screams, ‹ and the tumult ‹ the moans ‹ Remember

יְאוֹרֵי דְמֵיהֶם, וְדִמְעוֹת פְּנֵיהֶם, לֹא תִשָּׁכַחְנָה לָנֶצַח.

« ever. ‹ be forgotten ‹ not ‹ on their faces ‹ and the tears ‹ of their blood ‹ may the rivers

כָּל חִיל וּגְנִיחָה, וּנְהִי צְרִיחָה, מִשְּׁדוּדֵי לַהֲקוֹת הַכְּלָבִים,

« of dogs, ‹ by a pack ‹ of those torn asunder ‹ shriek ‹ [every] wailing ‹ and groan, ‹ tremble ‹ Every

זְכוֹר וּסְפוֹר, בְּנֹאדְךָ צְרוֹר,

«seal them, ‹ into Your flask « and count [them]; ‹ remember

עַד עֵת נְקַם עֶלְבּוֹן עֲלוּבִים.

«of the shamed ones. ‹ of the shame ‹ for the avenging ‹ the time ‹ until

בְּמַחֲנוֹת הַפְּרָאִים, כְּאֵב וּנְגָעִים, וּפַחֵי נְפָשׁוֹת עֲגוּמוֹת,

« that are despondent; ‹ souls ‹ the despairing ‹ and plagues, ‹ were pain ‹ of the barbarians ‹ In the camps

חֲרָפוֹת וּצְחוֹק, כְּלִימוֹת וָרוֹק,[2] פִּצְעֵי הַכָּאוֹת אֲיֻמּוֹת.

« that are horrific. ‹ from beatings ‹ wounds ‹ and spit, ‹ shame ‹ and mockery, ‹ insults

וּרְעָבוֹן, צִמָּאוֹן, שִׁגָּעוֹן, עִצָּבוֹן,

‹ suffering, ‹ madness, ‹ thirst, ‹ Hunger,

וְכִשְׁלוֹן נֶחֱשָׁלִים בְּלִי כֹחַ,

«strength; ‹ who have no ‹ of the weaklings ‹ the stumbling

וְכָל נַאֲקוֹת חָלָל, מִכָּל יָחִיד אֻמְלָל,

‹ who is forlorn, ‹ individual ‹ from every « of the mortally wounded, ‹ the groans ‹ all

(1) Cf. *Exodus* 32:32. (2) Cf. *Isaiah* 50:6.

sion of the *kinnos* service before the passage which begins with תְּרַחֵם צִיּוֹן, *Have mercy on Zion.* Although Rav Schwab only composed this *kinnah* to be said in his *kehillah,* many other congregations have adopted the custom of reciting it on Tishah B'Av, either at night or by day, as a memorial of our most recent *churban.*

חָלִילָה לְּךָ מִלִּשְׁכֹּחַ.

« to forget. ‹ from You ‹ far be it

וְתִימְרוֹת עָשָׁן,[1] וְקִיטוֹר מִכִּבְשָׁן,

‹ from furnace, ‹ the fumes ‹ of smoke, ‹ The pillars

תִּלֵּי תִלִּים עֲצָמוֹת וְגִידִים,

« and sinews, ‹ of bones ‹ of piles ‹ piles

וְחַדְרֵי הָרַעַל, קוֹל שְׁאָגוֹת מִקָּהָל

‹ of the congregation ‹ of the roaring ‹ the sound ‹ filled with poison, ‹ halls

הַנֶּחְנָקִים תּוֹךְ תָּאֵי הָאֵדִים.

« of gas. ‹ the chambers ‹ in ‹ of those choking

וְסִרְחוֹן גּוּפוֹת, וּגְוִיּוֹת סְגוּפוֹת,

« tortured, ‹ the corpses ‹ of the bodies, ‹ The stench

גְּלַל דֹּמֶן אַדְמַת נוֹאֲצִים,

« of the blasphemers [Nazis]. ‹ for the soil ‹ from dung ‹ fertilizer

אֵיךְ הָפְכוּ טוֹרְפֵיהֶם, לְבֹרִית חֶלְבֵּיהֶם,

« their fat, ‹ into soap « — the tormentors — « did they transform ‹ How

וְעוֹר אִישׁ לְקִשּׁוּטֵי הַנָּשִׁים.

« for women. ‹ into adornments ‹ of humans ‹ and skin

וּקְרִיצַת אֶצְבָּעוֹת, שֶׁל רָאשֵׁי הַפְּרָעוֹת,

« of the savagery. ‹ of the leaders ‹ of the fingers ‹ [Remember] the motions

לִימִין שִׁעְבּוּד פֶּרֶךְ, צַלְמָוֶת לִשְׂמֹאול.

« — to the left. « The shadow of death « that is crushing! ‹ — slavery « To the right

וְאֵיךְ יָרוּ יְרִיּוֹת עַל חוֹפְרֵי הַבּוֹרוֹת,

« [their own] graves, ‹ those digging ‹ at ‹ volleys ‹ they shot ‹ [Remember] how

בְּיִסּוּרֵי חִבּוּט קֶבֶר הוֹרִדוּם שְׁאוֹל.

« to the depths. ‹ lowering them « of the grave, ‹ of the agony ‹ in the suffering

(1) *Joel* 3:3.

אֵיךְ עִנּוּ אַחְיוֹתֵינוּ, וְסֵרְסוּ בְּנוֹתֵינוּ,

« our daughters, ‹ and mutilated ‹ our sisters ‹ they afflicted ‹ And how

כּוֹסוֹת תַּרְעֵלָה מִידֵי רוֹפְאִים אַכְזָרִים.

« who were sadistic, ‹ doctors ‹ from ‹ of poison ‹ doses

וּפְלִיטֵי הַשְּׂרִידִים בִּמְחִלּוֹת וּסְתָרִים,

« and secret hideouts, ‹ in tunnels ‹ survivors ‹ And fugitive

וְטִמְיוֹן יְלָדִים בְּבָתֵּי שְׁמַד כְּמָרִים.

« [supervised by] priests. ‹ of apostasy ‹ in houses ‹ of children ‹ and the disappearance

שֶׂה תָמִים לָעוֹלָה, דַּם בְּנֵי הַגּוֹלָה,

« of the Diaspora, ‹ of the children ‹ the blood « as a burnt-offering, ‹ unblemished, ‹ A lamb,

הוֹי אֲרִיאֵל[1] מִנִּבְלַת חֲסִידֶיךָ,

« of your devout ones. ‹ because of the corpses « Ariel [the Temple Altar], ‹ Oh

צֹאן קָדָשִׁים[2] מִי יִמְנֶה, אֲשֶׁר אִשָּׁם לֹא תִכְבֶּה,[3]

« be extinguished, ‹ will never ‹ their flame ‹ those that « could count; ‹ — who « that is sacred ‹ The flock

בְּחוּנֶיךָ הָיוּ מְקַדְּשֵׁי שְׁמֶךָ.

« of Your Name. ‹ Sanctifiers ‹ were ‹ Your tested ones

בְּקוֹל שְׁמַע יִשְׂרָאֵל מָסְרוּ נֶפֶשׁ לָאֵל שֶׁהוּא יַאַסְפֵם.

« might gather them in. ‹ so that He « for God, ‹ their lives ‹ they gave up ‹ *Yisrael,* ‹ of *Shema* ‹ With the cry

וְעַד יוֹם אַחֲרוֹן הִצְדִּיקוּ דִין, וְאַף אֲנִי מַאֲמִין עָנוּ,

« they called out, ‹ *believe ...* ‹ *I* ‹ and even « His judgment, ‹ they justified ‹ the very last day ‹ And until

וְשָׁרוּ שִׁירַת בִּטָּחוֹן.

« of trust. ‹ a song ‹ and they sang

וּבְכֵן נִשְׁאַר עָם, כְּיָתוֹם נִדְהָם, בְּלִי קְבָרִים לְהִשְׁתַּטֵּחַ,

« at which to stretch out [one's hands in prayer], ‹ graves ‹ without « is bewildered, ‹ who like an orphan « a people, ‹ there is left ‹ And now,

(1) *Isaiah* 29:1.(2) Cf. *Ezekiel* 36:37-38. (3) Cf. *Isaiah* 66:24.

וְלֹא מַצֵּבוֹת אֵיפֹה לִבְכּוֹת יְבָבוֹת לֵבָב רוֹתֵחַ.

« burning [with emotion]. ‹ of a heart ‹ the sobs ‹ to weep ‹ at which ‹ tombstones ‹ with no

רַק נִסְכֵּי הַדָּם, אַזְכָּרוֹתָם, תּוֹסְסִים בְּלִי שׁוֹכֵחַ,

« to be forgotten; ‹ not ‹ are boiling, « — their memorial portions — « of the blood ‹ the libations ‹ Only

וְהָרֵי אֶפְרֵי עֲקֵדָתָם, תְּרוּמוֹת דִּשְׁנֵי מִזְבֵּחַ.

« of the Altar. ‹ from the ashes ‹ are elevated portions ‹ from their *Akeidah,* ‹ of ashes ‹ and the mountains

מִי יְמַלֵּל צַעַר יִשְׂרָאֵל,[1] אֲשֶׁר דַּעְתּוֹ מִכְּאֵב נִטְרֶפֶת,

« is deranged? ‹ from pain ‹ their mind ‹ in that ‹ of Israel, ‹ the agony ‹ can express ‹ Who

וּשְׁאֵרִית הַפְּאֵר, כִּמְעַט מִזְּעֵיר,[2]

« of a bit, ‹ is a fraction ‹ of its splendor ‹ The remnants

וְאֵיךְ קוֹמָתָהּ הַיּוֹם נִכְפֶּפֶת.

« been bent down! ‹ today ‹ has its stature ‹ how

אֵל חַי מְרַחֵם, עֲדָתְךָ נַחֵם, אֲשֶׁר לְךָ מְאֹד נִכְסֶפֶת,

« yearns, ‹ so mightily ‹ for You ‹ — that « comfort ‹ Your congregation « Merciful One! « Who is alive! ‹ O God

אוֹר חָדָשׁ תַּזְרִיחַ, קַרְנֵי הוֹד תַּצְמִיחַ,

« grow; ‹ of glory ‹ let rays « shine through; ‹ that is new ‹ let light

וְרוּחַ אֱלֹהִים מְרַחֶפֶת.[3]

« hover [over all]. ‹ of God ‹ and may the spirit

(1) Cf. *Psalms* 106:2. (2) Cf. *Isaiah* 29:17. (3) *Genesis* 1:2.

KINNAH 45 / קינה מה

THE CONGREGATION RISES AND RECITES THE FOLLOWING *KINNAH* RESPONSIVELY WITH THE *CHAZZAN*.

אֱלִי צִיּוֹן* וְעָרֶיהָ, כְּמוֹ אִשָּׁה בְצִירֶיהָ,

« suffering from labor pains, ‹ a woman ‹ like « and her cities, ‹ O Zion* ‹ Lament,

וְכִבְתוּלָה חֲגֻרַת שַׂק עַל בַּעַל נְעוּרֶיהָ.[1]

« of her youth ... ‹ the husband ‹ [lament-ing] for « in sackcloth, ‹ wrapped around ‹ and like a maiden

עֲלֵי אַרְמוֹן אֲשֶׁר נִטַּשׁ בְּאַשְׁמַת צֹאן עֲדָרֶיהָ,

« of her flocks, ‹ of the sheep ‹ because of the sin ‹ abandoned ‹ that is ‹ the palace ‹ ... for

וְעַל בִּיאַת מְחָרְפֵי אֵל בְּתוֹךְ מִקְדַּשׁ חֲדָרֶיהָ,

« chambers. ‹ her Sanctuary's ‹ into ‹ of God ‹ of the blasphemers ‹ the entrance ‹ and for

אֱלִי צִיּוֹן וְעָרֶיהָ, כְּמוֹ אִשָּׁה בְצִירֶיהָ,

« suffering from labor pains, ‹ a woman ‹ like « and her cities, ‹ O Zion ‹ Lament,

וְכִבְתוּלָה חֲגֻרַת שַׂק עַל בַּעַל נְעוּרֶיהָ.

« of her youth ... ‹ the husband ‹ [lament-ing] for « in sackcloth, ‹ wrapped around ‹ and like a maiden

עֲלֵי גָּלוּת מְשָׁרְתֵי אֵל, מְנַעֲמֵי שִׁיר זְמָרֶיהָ,[2]

« of her praise, ‹ the song ‹ [and the Levites] who sweetly sang ‹ of God ‹ of [the *Kohanim,*] the servants ‹ the exile ‹ ... for

וְעַל דָּמָם אֲשֶׁר שֻׁפַּךְ, כְּמוֹ מֵימֵי יְאוֹרֶיהָ,

« of her canals. ‹ the waters ‹ like ‹ was spilt ‹ that ‹ their blood ‹ and for

(1) *Joel* 1:8. (2) Cf. *II Samuel* 23:1.

אֱלִי צִיּוֹן — *Lament, O Zion.* This final *kinnah* is chanted to a traditional heart-rending melody that expresses the full measure of our sorrow. Once again, in this last lament, we list all that we lost at the time of the Destruction, both materially and spiritually. However, the opening line of the *kinnah* (which is repeated either as a refrain after every second line, or once at the end of the *kinnah*) provides a ray of hope: "Lament, O Zion and her cities, like a woman suffering from labor pains." Israel's suffering is not in vain; rather the Destruction and Exile should be viewed as a period of embryonic development and gestation leading to the rebirth of our nation. No pain is more excruciating than labor pains, yet the mother accepts it because it heralds the exhilarating joy of birth. Similarly, Israel's suffering has been

אֱלִי צִיּוֹן וְעָרֶיהָ, כְּמוֹ אִשָּׁה בְצִירֶיהָ,

« suffering from labor pains, ‹ a woman ‹ like « and her cities, ‹ O Zion ‹ Lament,

וְכִבְתוּלָה חֲגֻרַת שַׂק עַל בַּעַל נְעוּרֶיהָ.

« of her youth ... ‹ the husband ‹ [lament-ing] for « in sackcloth, ‹ wrapped around ‹ and like a maiden

עֲלֵי הֶגְיוֹן מְחוֹלֶיהָ, אֲשֶׁר דָּמַם בְּעָרֶיהָ,

« in her cities, ‹ have been silenced ‹ that ‹ of her dances, ‹ the lyrics ‹ ... for

וְעַל וַעַד אֲשֶׁר שָׁמֵם וּבִטּוּל סַנְהֶדְרֶיהָ,

« of her Sanhedrin. ‹ together with the dissolution « is destroyed, ‹ that ‹ the assembly [chamber] ‹ and for

אֱלִי צִיּוֹן וְעָרֶיהָ, כְּמוֹ אִשָּׁה בְצִירֶיהָ,

« suffering from labor pains, ‹ a woman ‹ like « and her cities, ‹ O Zion ‹ Lament,

וְכִבְתוּלָה חֲגֻרַת שַׂק עַל בַּעַל נְעוּרֶיהָ.

« of her youth ... ‹ the husband ‹ [lament-ing] for « in sackcloth, ‹ wrapped around ‹ and like a maiden

עֲלֵי זִבְחֵי תְמִידֶיהָ, וּפִדְיוֹנֵי בְּכוֹרֶיהָ,*

« of her firstborn sons,* ‹ and [for] the redemption « of her daily *Tamid*, ‹ the offerings ‹ ... for

וְעַל חִלּוּל כְּלֵי הֵיכָל וּמִזְבַּח קְטוֹרֶיהָ,

« for her incense. ‹ and the Altar ‹ of the Temple ‹ of the vessels ‹ and for the desecration

אֱלִי צִיּוֹן וְעָרֶיהָ, כְּמוֹ אִשָּׁה בְצִירֶיהָ,

« suffering from labor pains, ‹ a woman ‹ like « and her cities, ‹ O Zion ‹ Lament,

וְכִבְתוּלָה חֲגֻרַת שַׂק עַל בַּעַל נְעוּרֶיהָ.

« of her youth ... ‹ the husband ‹ [lament-ing] for « in sackcloth, ‹ wrapped around ‹ and like a maiden

---

indescribable, but we must accept it as the travail which precedes the glorious rebirth of our people.

עֲלֵי זִבְחֵי תְמִידֶיהָ וּפִדְיוֹנֵי בְּכוֹרֶיהָ — *For the offerings of her daily [Tamid], and [for] the redemption of her firstborn sons.* This statement is very puzzling. True, the daily *Tamid* offerings are dependent on the existence of the Temple, but the *mitzvah* of redeeming the firstborn son is not a function of the Temple. Indeed, it is in full force today and is practiced wherever Jews may live! This question has prodded some commentaries to suggest that the text be emended from פִּדְיוֹנֵי בְּכוֹרֶיהָ to פִּרְיוֹנֵי בִּיכּוּרֶיהָ, *her bikkurim fruits*, the *mitzvah*

עֲלֵי טַפֵּי מְלָכֶיהָ, בְּנֵי דָוִד גְּבִירֶיהָ,

« her royal sovereigns, ‹ of David, ‹ the sons « of her kings, ‹ the young children ‹ ... for

וְעַל יָפְיָם אֲשֶׁר חָשַׁךְ בְּעֵת סָרוּ כְתָרֶיהָ,

« her crowns. ‹ were taken from her ‹ at the time when ‹ was darkened ‹ which ‹ their beauty ‹ and for

אֱלִי צִיּוֹן וְעָרֶיהָ, כְּמוֹ אִשָּׁה בְּצִירֶיהָ,

« suffering from labor pains, ‹ a woman ‹ like « and her cities, ‹ O Zion ‹ Lament,

וְכִבְתוּלָה חֲגֻרַת שַׂק עַל בַּעַל נְעוּרֶיהָ.

« of her youth ... ‹ the husband ‹ [lament-ing] for « in sackcloth, ‹ wrapped around ‹ and like a maiden

עֲלֵי כָּבוֹד, אֲשֶׁר גָּלָה בְּעֵת חֻרְבַּן דְּבִירֶיהָ,

« of her Temples, ‹ of the Destruction ‹ at the time ‹ was exiled ‹ which ‹ the [Divine] glory ‹ ... for

וְעַל לוֹחֵץ אֲשֶׁר לָחַץ, וְשָׂם שַׂקִּים חֲגוּרֶיהָ,

« she would wrap herself around. ‹ that with sackcloth ‹ and caused ‹ oppressed her ‹ who ‹ the oppressor ‹ and for

אֱלִי צִיּוֹן וְעָרֶיהָ, כְּמוֹ אִשָּׁה בְּצִירֶיהָ,

« suffering from labor pains, ‹ a woman ‹ like « and her cities, ‹ O Zion ‹ Lament,

וְכִבְתוּלָה חֲגֻרַת שַׂק עַל בַּעַל נְעוּרֶיהָ.

« of her youth ... ‹ the husband ‹ [lament-ing] for « in sackcloth, ‹ wrapped around ‹ and like a maiden

עֲלֵי מַחַץ וְרֹב מַכּוֹת[1] אֲשֶׁר הֻכּוּ נְזִירֶיהָ,

« her [crowned] princes, ‹ were beaten ‹ with which ‹ blows ‹ and the numerous ‹ the crushing ‹ ... for

וְעַל נִפּוּץ עֲלֵי סֶלַע עוֹלָלֶיהָ[2] וּנְעָרֶיהָ,

« and her youths. ‹ of her infants ‹ the rock ‹ upon ‹ the dashing ‹ and for

(1) Cf. *Isaiah* 30:26. (2) Cf. *Psalms* 137:9.

of bringing the first fruits to the *Kohen* in the Temple is no longer possible.

Others explain that the redemption of the firstborn here alludes to the Levites who served as the original objects by which the firstborn Israelites were redeemed in the Wilderness (see *Numbers* 3:11-13, 44-51). Thus, the first stich of this line, זִבְחֵי תְמִידֶיהָ, refers to the *Kohanim* who offered the *Tamid*, while the second stich speaks of the *Leviim*.

However, the passage may also be explained in its simplest and most literal reading. Regarding the *mitzvah* of redeem-

אֱלִי צִיּוֹן וְעָרֶיהָ, כְּמוֹ אִשָּׁה בְצִירֶיהָ,

« suffering from labor pains, ‹ a woman ‹ like « and her cities, ‹ O Zion ‹ Lament,

וְכִבְתוּלָה חֲגֻרַת שַׂק עַל בַּעַל נְעוּרֶיהָ.

« of her youth ... ‹ the husband ‹ [lament-ing] for « in sackcloth, ‹ wrapped around ‹ and like a maiden

עֲלֵי שִׂמְחַת אוֹיְבֶיהָ, שָׂחֲקוּ עַל שְׁבָרֶיהָ,

« her catastrophes, ‹ over ‹ who rejoiced ‹ of her enemies ‹ the joy ‹ ... for

וְעַל עִנּוּי בְּנֵי חוֹרִין נְדִיבֶיהָ טְהוֹרֶיהָ,

« and her pure ones. ‹ her nobles « [formerly] free; ‹ of [her] people ‹ the torturing ‹ and for

אֱלִי צִיּוֹן וְעָרֶיהָ, כְּמוֹ אִשָּׁה בְצִירֶיהָ,

« suffering from labor pains, ‹ a woman ‹ like « and her cities, ‹ O Zion ‹ Lament,

וְכִבְתוּלָה חֲגֻרַת שַׂק עַל בַּעַל נְעוּרֶיהָ.

« of her youth ... ‹ the husband ‹ [lament-ing] for « in sackcloth, ‹ wrapped around ‹ and like a maiden

עֲלֵי פֶּשַׁע אֲשֶׁר עִוְּתָה סְלוּל דֶּרֶךְ אֲשׁוּרֶיהָ,

« her footsteps, « path — ‹ —from the straight « diverted ‹ which ‹ the sin ‹ ... for

וְעַל צִבְאוֹת קְהָלֶיהָ שְׁזוּפֶיהָ שְׁחוֹרֶיהָ,

« and blackened [by the Temple's destruction]. ‹ whose [faces] are darkened ‹ of her congregations ‹ the legions ‹ and for

אֱלִי צִיּוֹן וְעָרֶיהָ, כְּמוֹ אִשָּׁה בְצִירֶיהָ,

« suffering from labor pains, ‹ a woman ‹ like « and her cities, ‹ O Zion ‹ Lament,

וְכִבְתוּלָה חֲגֻרַת שַׂק עַל בַּעַל נְעוּרֶיהָ.

« of her youth ... ‹ the husband ‹ [lament-ing] for « in sackcloth, ‹ wrapped around ‹ and like a maiden

---

ing the firstborn, the Torah states: כֹּל בְּכוֹר בָּנֶיךָ תִּפְדֶּה וְלֹא יֵרָאוּ פָנַי רֵיקָם, *Every firstborn of your sons you shall redeem, and they shall not appear before Me empty-handed* (*Exodus* 34:20). *Rabbeinu Bachya* (ibid.) comments: Why did the Torah juxtapose the *mitzvah* of redeeming the firstborn son with the *mitzvah* of appearing before God in the Temple on the festivals? To teach that the firstborn who is redeemed is assured that he will merit the privilege of seeing the construction of the Temple and he will witness God's presence therein.

Thus, the purpose of the firstborn's redemption is to prepare him for an encounter with God in the Temple so that he will "belong" to the Temple and be one of *her* firstborn sons. In this *kinnah*, we lament

עֲלֵי קוֹלוֹת מְחָרְפֶיהָ, בְּעֵת רַבּוּ פְגָרֶיהָ,

« of her corpses, ‹ there increased the number ‹ at the time when ‹ of those who vilified her ‹ the cries ‹ ... for

וְעַל רִגְשַׁת מְגַדְּפֶיהָ, בְּתוֹךְ מִשְׁכַּן חֲצֵרֶיהָ,

« Courtyards. ‹ her Tabernacle's ‹ inside ‹ of those who cursed her ‹ the thronging ‹ and for

אֱלִי צִיּוֹן וְעָרֶיהָ, כְּמוֹ אִשָּׁה בְּצִירֶיהָ,

« suffering from labor pains, ‹ a woman ‹ like « and her cities, ‹ O Zion ‹ Lament,

וְכִבְתוּלָה חֲגֻרַת שַׂק עַל בַּעַל נְעוּרֶיהָ.

« of her youth ... ‹ the husband ‹ [lament-ing] for « in sackcloth, ‹ wrapped around ‹ and like a maiden

עֲלֵי שִׁמְךָ אֲשֶׁר חֻלַּל בְּפִי קָמֵי מְצִירֶיהָ,

« to torment her, ‹ of those who arose ‹ by the mouth ‹ was profaned ‹ which ‹ Your Name ‹ ... for

וְעַל תְּחַן יְצַוְּחוּ לָךְ קְשׁוֹב וּשְׁמַע אֲמָרֶיהָ,

« to her words. ‹ and listen ‹ listen carefully « to You, ‹ which they cry out ‹ the pleading prayer ‹ and for

אֱלִי צִיּוֹן וְעָרֶיהָ, כְּמוֹ אִשָּׁה בְּצִירֶיהָ,

« suffering from labor pains, ‹ a woman ‹ like « and her cities, ‹ O Zion ‹ Lament,

וְכִבְתוּלָה חֲגֻרַת שַׂק עַל בַּעַל נְעוּרֶיהָ.

« of her youth . . . ‹ the husband ‹ [lament-ing] for « in sackcloth, ‹ wrapped around ‹ and like a maiden

---

the fact that today, in the absence of the Temple, the firstborn sons cannot achieve this encounter, the ultimate purpose of their redemption.

KINNAH 46 / קינה מו

שׁוֹמְרוֹן* קוֹל תִּתֵּן[1] מְצָאוּנִי עֲוֹנַי,[2]

« have [the punish-ments] for my sins! ‹ Befallen me ‹ raise, ‹ a voice [of lament] ‹ Shomron*

לְאֶרֶץ אַחֶרֶת יְצָאוּנִי בָּנַי,[3]

« did my children! ‹ go away from me ‹ To another land

וְאָהֳלִיבָה תִּזְעַק נִשְׂרְפוּ אַרְמוֹנַי,[4]

« were my palaces! ‹ Burnt down « screams, ‹ Then Oholivah

וַתֹּאמֶר צִיּוֹן עֲזָבַנִי יהוה.[5]

« has HASHEM! ‹ Abandoned me « And Zion says,

לֹא לָךְ אָהֳלִיבָה חָשׁוּב עָנְיֵךְ כְּעָנְיִי,

« as [equal to] my suffering! ‹ your suffering ‹ to consider « Oholivah, « [right] for you, ‹ [Oholah:] It is not

הֲתַמְשִׁילִי חָלְיֵךְ לְשִׁבְרִי וּלְחָלְיִי,

« and to my sickness? ‹ to my injury ‹ your sickness ‹ Can you compare

אֲנִי אָהֳלָה סוּרָה בָּגַדְתִּי בְּקָשְׁיִי,

« in my stub-bornness, ‹ I have rebelled « [am now] displaced, ‹ Oholah, ‹ I,

וְקָם עָלַי כַּחֲשִׁי וְעָנָה בִי מֶרְיִי,[6]

« has my defiance, ‹ against me ‹ and testified « has my deceitfulness, ‹ against me ‹ but risen

(1) Cf. *Eichah* 2:7. (2) Cf. *II Kings* 7:9; *Deuteronomy* 4:30. (3) Cf. *Jeremiah* 10:20. (4) Cf. *II Chronicles* 36:19. (5) *Isaiah* 49:14. (6) Cf. *Job* 16:8.

שׁוֹמְרוֹן — *Shomron.* This *kinnah* is based on Chapter 23 of *Ezekiel*, where God bids the prophet to expose the sins of the Jewish people. Then unfolds the shocking parable of two faithless wives who seek fulfillment of their unnatural lusts through numerous lovers. Ezekiel tells of two sisters, אָהֳלָה, *Oholah*, and אָהֳלִיבָה, *Oholivah*, who are both married to the same man. Oholah is identified as Shomron [Samaria, capital of the Northern Kingdom, also called the Kingdom of Israel, which comprised ten of the tribes] and Oholivah as Jerusalem [capital of the Southern Kingdom, also called the Kingdom of Judah, which comprised Judah and Benjamin]. Both are "wed" to one "husband," God, but both brazenly betray Him.

The names, אָהֳלָה, *Oholah*, and אָהֳלִיבָה, *Oholivah*, are both derived from אֹהֶל, a *tent* or *dwelling place*. However, אָהֳלָה is a contraction of הָאֹהֶל שֶׁלָּהּ, *her tent*, because God had no part in the tabernacles of Shomron. They were "her own tents" which she had dedicated to the golden calves Jeroboam ben

וּלְמִקְצַת הַיָּמִים[1] שִׁלַּמְתִּי נְשִׁיִי,[2]

and at the end ‹ of a short time ‹ I paid ‹ my debts [for my sins]. «

וְתִגְלַת פִּלְאֶסֶר[3] אָכַל אֶת פִּרְיִי,

[The Assyrian king] Tiglath-pileser ‹ devoured ‹ my [womb's] fruits, «

חֶמְדָּתִי פָּשַׁט וְהִצִּיל אֶת עֶדְיִי,[4]*

my precious possessions ‹ he stripped away ‹ and confiscated ‹ my jewelry,* «

וְלַחֲלַח וְחָבוֹר[5] נָשָׂא אֶת שִׁבְיִי,

then to Halah ‹ and to Habor ‹ [his successor Shalmaneser] carried away ‹ my captives. «

דֹּמִּי אָהֳלִיבָה וְאַל תִּבְכִּי כְּבִכְיִי,

[Therefore,] be silent ‹ Oholivah ‹ and do not ‹ weep ‹ as I weep! «

שְׁנוֹתַיִךְ אָרְכוּ וְלֹא אָרְכוּ שָׁנָי.*

Your years [in the Land] ‹ were prolonged, ‹ but not prolonged ‹ were my years!* «

וְאָהֳלִיבָה תִּזְעַק נִשְׂרְפוּ אַרְמוֹנַי,

Then Oholivah ‹ screams, « Burnt down ‹ were my palaces! «

וַתֹּאמֶר צִיּוֹן עֲזָבַנִי יהוה.

And Zion says, « Abandoned me ‹ has HASHEM! «

(1) *Daniel* 1:18 (2) Cf. *II Kings* 4:7. (3) 15:29. (4) Cf. *Exodus* 33:6. (5) See *II Kings* 17:3-6.

Nevat had erected (see *I Kings* 12:28). On the other hand, אָהֳלִיבָה is a contraction of הָאֹהֶל שֶׁלִּי בָהּ, *My Tent is within her* — the Tent of God, the *Beis HaMikdash*. These names place Judah, in which God's Temple stood, in sharp contrast to Shomron.

The wicked city of Shomron, with the abominations of its citizens, epitomizes all the evil of the Ten Tribes. That segment of Israel became so corrupted that to this day those tribes are lost in exile and the possibility of their ultimate return remains the subject of considerable Talmudic debate (see *Sanhedrin* 110b and *Ramban, Sefer HaGeulah, shaar* I).

In this *kinnah*, the author compares the tragedies which befell both Judah and Samaria by means of a debate raging between the two. Each capital claims — and vehemently defends its claim — that it suffered more at the hand of the marauding enemy.

The composer of the *kinnah*, R' Shlomo ibn Gabirol (11th-century Spain), used the letters of his name שְׁלֹמֹה to begin the respective stanzas.

חֶמְדָּתִי ... עֶדְיִי — *My precious possessions . . . my jewelry.* Some commentators understand these expressions as allusions to the two Temples. We have rejected that interpretation because Oholah is the speaker, but the Temples had stood in Oholivah's state.

שְׁנוֹתַיִךְ אָרְכוּ וְלֹא אָרְכוּ שָׁנָי — *Your years [in the Land] were prolonged, but not prolonged were my years!* Oholah, the North-

מְשִׁיבָה אָהֳלִיבָה אֲנִי כֵּן נֶעֱקַשְׁתִּי,

« acted crookedly, ‹ similarly ‹ I « Oholivah: ‹ Responds

וּבְאַלּוּף נְעוּרַי[1] כְּאָהֳלָה בָּגַדְתִּי,

« I rebelled! ‹ like Oholah, ‹ of my youth, ‹ and against [God,] the Mentor

דֹּמִּי אָהֳלָה כִּי יְגוֹנִי זָכַרְתִּי,

« do I remember; ‹ my agony ‹ for ‹ Oholah, ‹ Be silent,

נָדַדְתְּ אַתְּ אַחַת וְרַבּוֹת נָדַדְתִּי,

« was I exiled. ‹ while many times « but once, ‹ were you ‹ exiled

הִנֵּה בְּיַד הַכַּשְׂדִּים פַּעֲמַיִם נִלְכַּדְתִּי,

« was I taken; ‹ twice ‹ of the Chaldeans ‹ by the hands ‹ Indeed,

וּשְׁבִיָּה עֲנִיָּה לְבָבֶל יָרַדְתִּי,

« did I descend; ‹ to Babylon ‹ afflicted, ‹ as a captive,

וְנִשְׂרַף הַהֵיכָל אֲשֶׁר בּוֹ נִכְבַּדְתִּי,

« I was honored. ‹ through it ‹ that ‹ was the Temple ‹ and burnt down

וּלְשִׁבְעִים שָׁנָה בְּבָבֶל נִפְקַדְתִּי,

« I was recalled [by God]; ‹ in Babylon ‹ years ‹ After seventy

וְשַׁבְתִּי לְצִיּוֹן עוֹד וְהֵיכָל יָסַדְתִּי,

« I established. ‹ and the [Second] Temple ‹ once again ‹ to Zion ‹ I returned

גַּם זֹאת הַפַּעַם מְעַט לֹא עָמַדְתִּי,

‹ I had not lasted ‹ even a brief time ‹ time ‹ this ‹ Also

עַד לְקָחַנִי אֱדוֹם וְכִמְעַט אָבַדְתִּי,

« was I annihilated. ‹ and nearly ‹ Edom seized me ‹ before

וְעַל כָּל הָאֲרָצוֹת נָפֹצוּ הֲמוֹנַי,

« my multitudes. ‹ were dispersed ‹ the lands ‹ all ‹ Throughout

(1) Cf. *Jeremiah* 3:4.

וְאָהֳלִיבָה תִּזְעַק נִשְׂרְפוּ אַרְמוֹנַי,

« were my palaces! ‹ Burnt down « screams, ‹ Then Oholivah

וַתֹּאמֶר צִיּוֹן עֲזָבַנִי יהוה.

« has HASHEM! ‹ Abandoned me « And Zion says,

הַחוֹמֵל עַל דַּל חֲמוֹל עַל דַּלּוּתָם,*

« their poverty.* ‹ on ‹ take pity « the pauper, ‹ on ‹ O You Who takes pity

וּרְאֵה שְׁמְמוֹתָם[1] וְאֹרֶךְ גָּלוּתָם,

« of their exile. ‹ and the length ‹ their desolation ‹ See

אַל תִּקְצוֹף עַד מְאֹד[2] וּרְאֵה שִׁפְלוּתָם,

« their degradation. ‹ rather see « an extreme, ‹ to ‹ be angered ‹ Do not

וְאַל לָעַד תִּזְכּוֹר עֲוֹנָם[2] וְסִכְלוּתָם,

« and their foolishness. ‹ their sins ‹ remember ‹ forever ‹ Do not

רְפָא נָא אֶת שִׁבְרָם[3] וְנַחֵם אֲבֵלוּתָם,

« in their bereavement; ‹ and console [them] ‹ their wounds ‹ please, ‹ Heal,

כִּי אַתָּה סִבְרָם וְאַתָּה אֱיָלוּתָם,

« their Strength. ‹ and You are ‹ their Hope ‹ You are ‹ for

חַדֵּשׁ יָמֵינוּ כִּימֵי קַדְמוֹנַי,[4]

« of my youth; ‹ as the days ‹ our days ‹ Renew

כְּנֶאֱמָךְ בּוֹנֵה יְרוּשָׁלַיִם יהוה.[5]

« is HASHEM. ‹ of Jerusalem ‹ The Builder « as You have said:

(1) Cf. *Daniel* 9:18. (2) Cf. *Isaiah* 64:8. (3) Cf. *Psalms* 60:4. (4) Cf. *Eichah* 5:21. (5) *Psalms* 147:2.

ern Kingdom of Samaria, was exiled more than 130 years before Oholivah, the Southern Kingdom of Judah.

דַּלּוּתָם — *Their poverty.* Until this point, the *kinnah* has been a one-on-one debate between Oholah and Oholivah. Thus, the statements are all in first- or second-person singular. The last stanza, however, is the *paytan's* supplication for the restitution of both, and consequently is couched in third-person plural. The *paytan* prays for the reunification of the two Kingdoms with Jerusalem as the focal point as it was in "the days of [the nation's] youth."

תְּרַחֵם צִיּוֹן כַּאֲשֶׁר אָמַרְתָּ, וּתְכוֹנְנֶהָ כַּאֲשֶׁר דִּבַּרְתָּ,

« You have spoken. ‹ as ‹ and establish her « You have said, ‹ as ‹ to Zion ‹ Show mercy

תְּמַהֵר יְשׁוּעָה וְתָחִישׁ גְּאֻלָּה, וְתָשׁוּב לִירוּשָׁלַיִם

‹ to Jerusalem ‹ and return ‹ redemption ‹ and accelerate ‹ salvation ‹ Hasten

בְּרַחֲמִים רַבִּים.

« that is abundant. ‹ with mercy

כַּכָּתוּב עַל יַד נְבִיאֶךָ, לָכֵן כֹּה אָמַר יהוה, שַׁבְתִּי

‹ I shall return « HASHEM, ‹ said ‹ thus ‹ Therefore, « of Your prophet: ‹ the hand ‹ by ‹ As it is written

לִירוּשָׁלַיִם בְּרַחֲמִים, בֵּיתִי יִבָּנֶה בָּהּ, נְאֻם יהוה

‹ of HASHEM, ‹ the word « within it, ‹ shall be rebuilt ‹ My House « with mercy, ‹ to Jerusalem

צְבָאוֹת, וְקָו יִנָּטֶה עַל יְרוּשָׁלָיִם.[1] וְנֶאֱמַר, עוֹד

‹ Once again « And it is said: « Jerusalem. ‹ over ‹ shall be stretched ‹ and a [surveyor's] string « Master of Legions —

קְרָא לֵאמֹר, כֹּה אָמַר יהוה צְבָאוֹת, עוֹד תְּפוּצֶנָה

‹ *overflow* ‹ *'Once again* « *Master of Legions,* ‹ *HASHEM,* ‹ *said* ‹ *Thus* « saying, ‹ call out,

עָרַי מִטּוֹב, וְנִחַם יהוה עוֹד אֶת צִיּוֹן, וּבָחַר עוֹד

‹ *once again* ‹ *and He will choose* ‹ *Zion* ‹ *once again* ‹ *and HASHEM will comfort* « *with abundance,* ‹ *shall My cities*

בִּירוּשָׁלָיִם.[2] וְנֶאֱמַר, כִּי נִחַם יהוה צִיּוֹן, נִחַם כָּל

‹ all ‹ He will comfort ‹ Zion, ‹ HASHEM will comfort ‹ For « And it is said: « *Jerusalem.'*

חָרְבוֹתֶיהָ, וַיָּשֶׂם מִדְבָּרָהּ כְּעֵדֶן, וְעַרְבָתָהּ כְּגַן יהוה,

« of HASHEM; ‹ like a garden ‹ and her wasteland « like Eden, ‹ her wilderness ‹ He will make « her ruins,

שָׂשׂוֹן וְשִׂמְחָה יִמָּצֵא בָהּ, תּוֹדָה וְקוֹל זִמְרָה.[3]

« of music. ‹ and the sound ‹ thanksgiving « in her, ‹ will be found ‹ and gladness ‹ joy

(1) *Zechariah* 1:16. (2) 1:17. (3) *Isaiah* 51:3. See *Radak* and *Metzudos David* on the use of the past tense, as if it had already happened.

ASHREI — UVA L'TZION / אשרי – ובא לציון

אַשְׁרֵי יוֹשְׁבֵי בֵיתֶךָ, עוֹד יְהַלְלוּךָ סֶּלָה.[1] אַשְׁרֵי

Praiseworthy ‹ are those who dwell ‹ in Your house, « continually ‹ they will praise You, ‹ Selah. « Praiseworthy ‹

הָעָם שֶׁכָּכָה לּוֹ, אַשְׁרֵי הָעָם שֶׁיהוה אֱלֹהָיו.[2]

is the people ‹ that such ‹ is their lot; « praiseworthy ‹ is the people ‹ that HASHEM ‹ is their God. «

Psalm 145 / תהלים קמה

תְּהִלָּה לְדָוִד, אֲרוֹמִמְךָ אֱלוֹהַי הַמֶּלֶךְ, וַאֲבָרְכָה

A psalm of praise ‹ by David: « I will exalt You, ‹ my God ‹ the King, « and I will bless ‹

שִׁמְךָ לְעוֹלָם וָעֶד. בְּכָל יוֹם אֲבָרְכֶךָּ, וַאֲהַלְלָה

Your Name ‹ for ever ‹ and ever. « Every ‹ day ‹ I will bless You, « and I will laud ‹

שִׁמְךָ לְעוֹלָם וָעֶד. גָּדוֹל יהוה וּמְהֻלָּל מְאֹד,

Your Name ‹ for ever ‹ and ever. « Great ‹ is HASHEM ‹ and lauded ‹ exceedingly, «

וְלִגְדֻלָּתוֹ אֵין חֵקֶר. דּוֹר לְדוֹר יְשַׁבַּח מַעֲשֶׂיךָ,

and His greatness ‹ is beyond investigation. « Generation ‹ to generation ‹ will praise ‹ Your actions, «

וּגְבוּרֹתֶיךָ יַגִּידוּ. הֲדַר כְּבוֹד הוֹדֶךָ, וְדִבְרֵי

and Your mighty deeds ‹ they will recount. « The splendrous ‹ glory ‹ of Your majesty, « and Your deeds ‹

נִפְלְאוֹתֶיךָ אָשִׂיחָה. וֶעֱזוּז נוֹרְאוֹתֶיךָ יֹאמֵרוּ,

that are wondrous ‹ I shall discuss. « And of the might ‹ of Your awesome deeds ‹ they will speak, «

וּגְדוּלָּתְךָ אֲסַפְּרֶנָּה. זֵכֶר רַב טוּבְךָ יַבִּיעוּ, וְצִדְקָתְךָ

and Your greatness ‹ I shall relate. « A recollection ‹ of Your abundant goodness ‹ they will utter, « and of Your righteousness ‹

יְרַנֵּנוּ. חַנּוּן וְרַחוּם יהוה, אֶרֶךְ אַפַּיִם וּגְדָל חָסֶד.

they will sing joyfully. « Gracious ‹ and merciful ‹ is HASHEM, « slow ‹ to anger, ‹ and great ‹ in [bestowing] kindness. «

(1) *Psalms* 84:5. (2) 144:15.

טוֹב יהוה לַכֹּל, וְרַחֲמָיו עַל כָּל מַעֲשָׂיו. יוֹדְוּךָ יהוה

« HASHEM ‹ They will thank You, « His creations. ‹ all ‹ are on ‹ His mercies « to all; ‹ HASHEM is good

כָּל מַעֲשֶׂיךָ, וַחֲסִידֶיךָ יְבָרְכוּכָה. כְּבוֹד מַלְכוּתְךָ

‹ of Your kingdom ‹ Of the glory « will bless You. ‹ and Your devout ones « Your creations, ‹ — all

יֹאמֵרוּ, וּגְבוּרָתְךָ יְדַבֵּרוּ. לְהוֹדִיעַ לִבְנֵי הָאָדָם

‹ mankind ‹ To inform « they will declare. ‹ and of Your power « they will speak,

גְּבוּרֹתָיו, וּכְבוֹד הֲדַר מַלְכוּתוֹ. מַלְכוּתְךָ מַלְכוּת

‹ is a kingdom ‹ Your kingdom « of His kingdom. ‹ splendor ‹ and of the glorious « of His mighty deeds,

כָּל עֹלָמִים, וּמֶמְשַׁלְתְּךָ בְּכָל דּוֹר וָדֹר. סוֹמֵךְ יהוה

‹ HASHEM supports « after generation. ‹ generation ‹ is throughout ‹ and Your dominion « eternities, ‹ [spanning] all

לְכָל הַנֹּפְלִים, וְזוֹקֵף לְכָל הַכְּפוּפִים. עֵינֵי כֹל אֵלֶיךָ

‹ to You ‹ of all ‹ The eyes « those who are bent. ‹ all ‹ and straightens « those who are fallen, ‹ all

יְשַׂבֵּרוּ, וְאַתָּה נוֹתֵן לָהֶם אֶת אָכְלָם בְּעִתּוֹ.

« in its proper time. ‹ their food ‹ them ‹ give ‹ and You « do look with hope,

CONCENTRATE INTENTLY WHILE RECITING THE VERSE פּוֹתֵחַ, *"YOU OPEN . . . ."*

פּוֹתֵחַ אֶת יָדֶךָ, וּמַשְׂבִּיעַ לְכָל חַי רָצוֹן. צַדִּיק

‹ Righteous « [with its] desire. ‹ living thing ‹ every ‹ and satisfy « Your hand, ‹ You open

יהוה בְּכָל דְּרָכָיו, וְחָסִיד בְּכָל מַעֲשָׂיו. קָרוֹב

‹ Close « His deeds. ‹ in all ‹ and magnanimous « His ways, ‹ in all ‹ is HASHEM

יהוה לְכָל קֹרְאָיו, לְכֹל אֲשֶׁר יִקְרָאֻהוּ בֶאֱמֶת.

« sincerely. ‹ call upon Him ‹ who ‹ to all « who call upon Him, ‹ to all ‹ is HASHEM

רְצוֹן יְרֵאָיו יַעֲשֶׂה, וְאֶת שַׁוְעָתָם יִשְׁמַע וְיוֹשִׁיעֵם.

« and He will save them. ‹ He will hear, ‹ and their cry « He will do; ‹ of those who fear Him ‹ The will

שׁוֹמֵר יהוה אֶת כָּל אֹהֲבָיו, וְאֵת כָּל הָרְשָׁעִים

‹ the wicked ‹ but all « who love Him; ‹ all ‹ HASHEM protects

יַשְׁמִיד. ❖ תְּהִלַּת יהוה יְדַבֶּר פִּי, וִיבָרֵךְ כָּל בָּשָׂר

‹ flesh ‹ may all ‹ and bless « may my mouth declare, ‹ of HASHEM ‹ The praise « He will destroy.

שֵׁם קָדְשׁוֹ לְעוֹלָם וָעֶד. וַאֲנַחְנוּ נְבָרֵךְ יָהּ מֵעַתָּה

‹ from this time ‹ God ‹ will bless ‹ But we « and ever. ‹ for ever ‹ of His Holiness ‹ the Name

וְעַד עוֹלָם; הַלְלוּיָהּ.[1]

« Halleluyah! « eternity. ‹ until

PSALM 20, לַמְנַצֵּחַ, IS OMITTED.

THE PRIMARY PART OF וּבָא לְצִיּוֹן IS THE *KEDUSHAH* RECITED BY THE ANGELS. THESE VERSES ARE PRESENTED IN BOLD TYPE AND IT IS PREFERABLE THAT THE CONGREGATION RECITE THEM ALOUD AND IN UNISON. HOWEVER, THE INTERPRETIVE TRANSLATION IN ARAMAIC (WHICH FOLLOWS THE VERSES IN BOLD TYPE) SHOULD BE RECITED SOFTLY.

THE VERSE וַאֲנִי זֹאת, *"AND AS FOR ME . . .,"* IS OMITTED.

וּבָא לְצִיּוֹן גּוֹאֵל, וּלְשָׁבֵי פֶשַׁע בְּיַעֲקֹב, נְאֻם יהוה.

« of HASHEM. ‹ — the words « *among Jacob* ‹ *from willful sins* ‹ *and to those who repent* « *shall a redeemer,* ‹ *to Zion* ‹ *Come*

[...] ❖ וְאַתָּה קָדוֹשׁ יוֹשֵׁב תְּהִלּוֹת יִשְׂרָאֵל.[2] וְקָרָא זֶה

‹ And one [angel] will call « of Israel. ‹ upon the praises ‹ enthroned « the Holy One, ‹ Yet You are

אֶל זֶה וְאָמַר: **קָדוֹשׁ, קָדוֹשׁ, קָדוֹשׁ יהוה**

‹ ***is HASHEM,*** ‹ ***holy*** ‹ ***holy,*** ‹ ***Holy,*** « and say: ‹ another ‹ to

צְבָאוֹת, מְלֹא כָל הָאָרֶץ כְּבוֹדוֹ.[3] וּמְקַבְּלִין דֵּין

‹ one ‹ And they receive [permission] « ***[with] his glory.*** ‹ ***world*** ‹ ***is the whole*** ‹ ***filled*** « ***Master of Legions,***

מִן דֵּין וְאָמְרִין: קַדִּישׁ בִּשְׁמֵי מְרוֹמָא עִלָּאָה בֵּית

‹ *the abode* ‹ *on high,* ‹ *in the lofty heavens* ‹ *Holy* « and say: ‹ the other ‹ from

שְׁכִינְתֵּהּ, קַדִּישׁ עַל אַרְעָא עוֹבַד גְּבוּרְתֵּהּ, קַדִּישׁ

‹ *holy* « *of His might;* ‹ *the product* ‹ *earth,* ‹ *on* ‹ *holy* « *of His Presence;*

(1) *Psalms* 115:18. (2) 22:4. (3) *Isaiah* 6:3.

לְעָלַם וּלְעָלְמֵי עָלְמַיָּא, יהוה צְבָאוֹת מַלְיָא כָל

forever ‹ *and to all eternity* ‹ *is* HASHEM, ‹ *Master of Legions;* « *filled* ‹ *is the whole* ‹

אַרְעָא זִיו יְקָרֵהּ.[1] וַתִּשָּׂאֵנִי רוּחַ, וָאֶשְׁמַע אַחֲרַי

world ‹ *with the radiance* ‹ *of His glory.* « Lift me ‹ did a wind; « and I heard ‹ behind me ‹

קוֹל רַעַשׁ גָּדוֹל: **בָּרוּךְ כְּבוֹד יהוה מִמְּקוֹמוֹ.**[2]

the sound ‹ of a great noise: « ***Blessed*** ‹ ***is the glory*** ‹ ***of* HASHEM** ‹ ***from His place.*** «

וּנְטָלַתְנִי רוּחָא, וְשִׁמְעֵת בַּתְרַי קַל זִיעַ סַגִּיא

A wind lifted me ‹ and I heard ‹ behind me ‹ the sound ‹ of noise ‹ that was great ‹

דִּמְשַׁבְּחִין וְאָמְרִין: בְּרִיךְ יְקָרָא דַיהוה מֵאֲתַר בֵּית

of those who were praising ‹ and saying: « *Blessed* ‹ *is the glory* ‹ *of* HASHEM ‹ *from the place* ‹ *of the abode* ‹

שְׁכִינְתֵּהּ.[3] **יהוה יִמְלֹךְ לְעֹלָם וָעֶד.**[4] יהוה מַלְכוּתֵהּ

of His Presence. « **HASHEM** ‹ **shall reign** ‹ **for ever** ‹ **and ever.** « HASHEM « – His kingdom ‹

קָאֵם לְעָלַם וּלְעָלְמֵי עָלְמַיָּא.[5] יהוה אֱלֹהֵי אַבְרָהָם

stands ‹ forever ‹ and to all eternity. « HASHEM, ‹ God ‹ of Abraham, ‹

יִצְחָק וְיִשְׂרָאֵל אֲבֹתֵינוּ, שָׁמְרָה זֹּאת לְעוֹלָם,

Isaac ‹ and Israel, ‹ our forefathers, ‹ may You safeguard ‹ this ‹ forever ‹

לְיֵצֶר מַחְשְׁבוֹת לְבַב עַמֶּךָ, וְהָכֵן לְבָבָם אֵלֶיךָ.[6]

as the product ‹ of the thoughts ‹ of the heart ‹ of Your people, « and may You direct ‹ their heart ‹ to You. «

וְהוּא רַחוּם, יְכַפֵּר עָוֹן וְלֹא יַשְׁחִית, וְהִרְבָּה

And He, ‹ the Merciful One, ‹ is forgiving ‹ of iniquity ‹ and does not ‹ destroy; « frequently ‹

לְהָשִׁיב אַפּוֹ, וְלֹא יָעִיר כָּל חֲמָתוֹ.[7] כִּי אַתָּה אֲדֹנָי

He withdraws ‹ His anger, « not ‹ arousing ‹ all ‹ of His wrath. « For ‹ You, ‹ O Master, ‹

---

(1) *Targum Yonasan.* (2) *Ezekiel* 3:12. (3) *Targum Yonasan.* (4) *Exodus* 15:18.
(5) *Targum Onkelos.* (6) *II Chronicles* 29:18. (7) *Psalms* 78:38.

טוֹב וְסַלָּח, וְרַב חֶסֶד לְכָל קֹרְאֶיךָ.[1] צִדְקָתְךָ

‹ Your righteousness « who call upon You. ‹ to all ‹ kind ‹ and abundantly « and forgiving, ‹ are good

צֶדֶק לְעוֹלָם, וְתוֹרָתְךָ אֱמֶת.[2] תִּתֵּן אֱמֶת לְיַעֲקֹב,

« to Jacob, ‹ truth ‹ Grant « is truth. ‹ and Your Torah « everlasting, ‹ is a righteousness

חֶסֶד לְאַבְרָהָם, אֲשֶׁר נִשְׁבַּעְתָּ לַאֲבֹתֵינוּ מִימֵי קֶדֶם.[3]

« of old. ‹ from days ‹ to our forefathers ‹ you swore ‹ as « to Abraham, ‹ kindness

בָּרוּךְ אֲדֹנָי יוֹם יוֹם יַעֲמָס לָנוּ, הָאֵל יְשׁוּעָתֵנוּ סֶלָה.[4]

« Selah. « of our salvation, ‹ the God ‹ us [with blessings], ‹ He burdens ‹ by day ‹ day « is the Lord; ‹ Blessed

יהוה צְבָאוֹת עִמָּנוּ, מִשְׂגָּב לָנוּ אֱלֹהֵי יַעֲקֹב סֶלָה.[5]

« Selah. « of Jacob, ‹ is the God ‹ for us ‹ a Stronghold « is with us, ‹ Master of Legions, ‹ HASHEM,

יהוה צְבָאוֹת, אַשְׁרֵי אָדָם בֹּטֵחַ בָּךְ.[6] יהוה הוֹשִׁיעָה,

« save! ‹ HASHEM, « in You. ‹ who trusts ‹ is the man ‹ praiseworthy ‹ Master of Legions, ‹ HASHEM,

הַמֶּלֶךְ יַעֲנֵנוּ בְיוֹם קָרְאֵנוּ.[7] בָּרוּךְ הוּא אֱלֹהֵינוּ

‹ our God, ‹ is He, ‹ Blessed « we call. ‹ on the day ‹ answer us ‹ May the King

שֶׁבְּרָאָנוּ לִכְבוֹדוֹ, וְהִבְדִּילָנוּ מִן הַתּוֹעִים, וְנָתַן לָנוּ

‹ us ‹ and gave « those who go astray, ‹ from ‹ and separated us « for His glory, ‹ Who created us

תּוֹרַת אֱמֶת, וְחַיֵּי עוֹלָם נָטַע בְּתוֹכֵנוּ. הוּא

‹ May He « within us. ‹ implanted ‹ eternal ‹ and life « of truth, ‹ the Torah

יִפְתַּח לִבֵּנוּ בְּתוֹרָתוֹ, וְיָשֵׂם בְּלִבֵּנוּ אַהֲבָתוֹ וְיִרְאָתוֹ

‹ and awe of Him ‹ with love of Him ‹ our heart ‹ and imbue « to His Torah ‹ our heart ‹ open

וְלַעֲשׂוֹת רְצוֹנוֹ וּלְעָבְדוֹ בְּלֵבָב שָׁלֵם, לְמַעַן לֹא נִיגַע

‹ toil ‹ we do not ‹ so that « that is whole, ‹ with a heart ‹ and to serve Him ‹ His will ‹ and [the desire] to do

לָרִיק, וְלֹא נֵלֵד לַבֶּהָלָה.[8] יְהִי רָצוֹן מִלְּפָנֶיךָ, יהוה

« HASHEM, ‹ before You, ‹ the will ‹ May it be « for futility. ‹ produce ‹ nor ‹ in vain

(1) *Psalms* 86:5. (2) 119:142 (3) *Micah* 7:20. (4) *Psalms* 68:20. (5) 46:8. (6) 84:13. (7) 20:10. (8) Cf. *Isaiah* 65:23.

אֱלֹהֵינוּ וֵאלֹהֵי אֲבוֹתֵינוּ, שֶׁנִּשְׁמוֹר חֻקֶּיךָ בָּעוֹלָם הַזֶּה,

‹ in This World, ‹ Your decrees ‹ that we observe « of our forefathers, ‹ and the God ‹ our God

וְנִזְכֶּה וְנִחְיֶה וְנִרְאֶה וְנִירַשׁ טוֹבָה וּבְרָכָה לִשְׁנֵי

‹ in the years ‹ and blessing ‹ goodness ‹ and we inherit ‹ and we see ‹ that we live ‹ and that we merit

יְמוֹת הַמָּשִׁיחַ וּלְחַיֵּי הָעוֹלָם הַבָּא. לְמַעַן יְזַמֶּרְךָ

‹ sing to You ‹ So that « to Come. ‹ of the World ‹ and for the life ‹ of Messianic times

כָבוֹד וְלֹא יִדֹּם, יהוה אֱלֹהַי לְעוֹלָם אוֹדֶךָּ.[1] בָּרוּךְ

‹ Blessed « will I thank You. ‹ forever ‹ my God, ‹ HASHEM, « be silenced; ‹ and not ‹ [might] my soul,

הַגֶּבֶר אֲשֶׁר יִבְטַח בַּיהוה, וְהָיָה יהוה מִבְטַחוֹ.[2]

« his security. ‹ HASHEM be ‹ then will « in HASHEM, ‹ trusts ‹ who ‹ is the man

בִּטְחוּ בַיהוה עֲדֵי עַד, כִּי בְּיָהּ יהוה צוּר עוֹלָמִים.[3]

« of the worlds. ‹ is the strength ‹ HASHEM, ‹ in God, ‹ for « forever, ‹ in HASHEM ‹ Trust

❖ וְיִבְטְחוּ בְךָ יוֹדְעֵי שְׁמֶךָ, כִּי לֹא עָזַבְתָּ דֹּרְשֶׁיךָ,

‹ those who seek You, ‹ You have not forsaken ‹ for « Your Name, ‹ those who know « in You, ‹ And they will trust

יהוה.[4] יהוה חָפֵץ לְמַעַן צִדְקוֹ, יַגְדִּיל תּוֹרָה וְיַאְדִּיר.[5]

« and glorious. ‹ to make the Torah great ‹ of [Israel's] righteousness, ‹ for the sake ‹ desired, ‹ HASHEM « HASHEM.

THE *CHAZZAN* RECITES קַדִּישׁ שָׁלֵם בְּלֹא תִּתְקַבַּל.

יִתְגַּדַּל וְיִתְקַדַּשׁ שְׁמֵהּ רַבָּא. (Cong. — אָמֵן.) בְּעָלְמָא דִּי

‹ that ‹ in the world « (Amen.) « that is great! — ‹ may His Name ‹ and be sanctified ‹ Grow exalted

בְּרָא כִרְעוּתֵהּ. וְיַמְלִיךְ מַלְכוּתֵהּ, בְּחַיֵּיכוֹן וּבְיוֹמֵיכוֹן וּבְחַיֵּי

‹ and in the lifetimes ‹ and in your days, ‹ in your lifetimes « to His kingship, ‹ and may He give reign « according to His will, ‹ He created

דְכָל בֵּית יִשְׂרָאֵל, בַּעֲגָלָא וּבִזְמַן קָרִיב. וְאִמְרוּ: אָמֵן.

« Amen. ‹ Now respond: « that comes soon. ‹ and at a time ‹ swiftly « of Israel, ‹ Family ‹ of the entire

---

(1) *Psalms* 30:13. (2) *Jeremiah* 17:7. (3) *Isaiah* 26:4. (4) *Psalms* 9:11. (5) *Isaiah* 42:21.

CONGREGATION RESPONDS:

אָמֵן. יְהֵא שְׁמֵהּ רַבָּא מְבָרַךְ לְעָלַם וּלְעָלְמֵי עָלְמַיָּא.

« and for all eternity. ‹ forever ‹ be blessed ‹ that is great ‹ His Name ‹ May « Amen.

CHAZZAN CONTINUES:

יְהֵא שְׁמֵהּ רַבָּא מְבָרַךְ לְעָלַם וּלְעָלְמֵי עָלְמַיָּא. יִתְבָּרַךְ

‹ Blessed, « and for all eternity. ‹ forever ‹ be blessed ‹ that is great ‹ His Name ‹ May

וְיִשְׁתַּבַּח וְיִתְפָּאַר וְיִתְרוֹמַם וְיִתְנַשֵּׂא וְיִתְהַדָּר וְיִתְעַלֶּה

‹ elevated, ‹ honored, ‹ upraised, ‹ exalted, ‹ glorified, ‹ praised,

וְיִתְהַלָּל שְׁמֵהּ דְּקֻדְשָׁא בְּרִיךְ הוּא (Cong. — בְּרִיךְ הוּא) —

« is He) ‹ (Blessed « is He ‹ Blessed ‹ of the Holy One, ‹ be the Name ‹ and lauded

לְעֵלָּא מִן כָּל בִּרְכָתָא וְשִׁירָתָא תֻּשְׁבְּחָתָא וְנֶחֱמָתָא

‹ and consolation ‹ praise « and song, ‹ blessing ‹ any ‹ beyond

דַּאֲמִירָן בְּעָלְמָא. וְאִמְרוּ: אָמֵן. (Cong. — אָמֵן.)

« (Amen.) « Amen. ‹ Now respond: « in the world. ‹ that are uttered

CONGREGATION:

יְהִי שֵׁם יהוה מְבֹרָךְ, מֵעַתָּה וְעַד עוֹלָם.[1]

« eternity. ‹ until ‹ from this time « be blessed, ‹ of HASHEM ‹ the Name ‹ Let

CHAZZAN CONTINUES:

יְהֵא שְׁלָמָא רַבָּא מִן שְׁמַיָּא, וְחַיִּים עָלֵינוּ וְעַל כָּל

‹ all ‹ and upon ‹ upon us « and life, « Heaven, ‹ from ‹ that is abundant ‹ peace ‹ May there be

יִשְׂרָאֵל. וְאִמְרוּ: אָמֵן. (Cong. — אָמֵן.)

‹ (Amen.) « Amen. ‹ Now respond: « Israel.

CONGREGATION:

עֶזְרִי מֵעִם יהוה, עֹשֵׂה שָׁמַיִם וָאָרֶץ.[2]

« and earth. ‹ of heaven ‹ Maker « HASHEM, ‹ is from ‹ (My help

CHAZZAN BOWS; TAKES THREE STEPS BACK. BOWS LEFT AND SAYS ... **עֹשֶׂה שָׁלוֹם**, *"HE WHO MAKES PEACE . . ."*; BOWS RIGHT AND SAYS ... **הוּא**, *"MAY HE . . ."*; BOWS FORWARD AND SAYS ... **וְעַל כָּל יִשְׂרָאֵל**, *"AND UPON ALL ISRAEL . . ."*; REMAINS IN PLACE FOR A FEW MOMENTS, THEN TAKES THREE STEPS FORWARD.

עֹשֶׂה שָׁלוֹם בִּמְרוֹמָיו, הוּא יַעֲשֶׂה שָׁלוֹם עָלֵינוּ, וְעַל כָּל

‹ all ‹ and upon ‹ upon us, ‹ peace ‹ make ‹ may He « in His heights, ‹ peace ‹ He Who makes

יִשְׂרָאֵל. וְאִמְרוּ: אָמֵן. (Cong. — אָמֵן.)

‹ (Amen.) « Amen. ‹ Now respond: « Israel.

(1) *Psalms* 113:2. (2) 121:2.

STAND WHILE RECITING עָלֵינוּ, *"IT IS OUR DUTY . . ."*

עָלֵינוּ לְשַׁבֵּחַ לַאֲדוֹן הַכֹּל, לָתֵת גְּדֻלָּה לְיוֹצֵר

‹ to the Molder ‹ greatness ‹ to ascribe « of all, ‹ the Master ‹ to praise ‹ It is our duty

בְּרֵאשִׁית, שֶׁלֹּא עָשָׂנוּ כְּגוֹיֵי הָאֲרָצוֹת, וְלֹא

‹ and has not « of the lands, ‹ like the nations ‹ for He has not made us « of primeval creation,

שָׂמָנוּ כְּמִשְׁפְּחוֹת הָאֲדָמָה. שֶׁלֹּא שָׂם חֶלְקֵנוּ כָּהֶם,

‹ like theirs ‹ our portion ‹ assigned ‹ for He has not « of the earth; ‹ like the families ‹ established us

וְגוֹרָלֵנוּ כְּכָל הֲמוֹנָם. (שֶׁהֵם מִשְׁתַּחֲוִים לְהֶבֶל

‹ to vanity ‹ bow ‹ (For they « their multitudes. ‹ like all ‹ nor our lot

וָרִיק, וּמִתְפַּלְּלִים אֶל אֵל לֹא יוֹשִׁיעַ.[1])

« save.) ‹ who does not ‹ a god ‹ to ‹ and pray ‹ and emptiness

BOW WHILE RECITING וַאֲנַחְנוּ כּוֹרְעִים וּמִשְׁתַּחֲוִים, *"BUT WE BEND OUR KNEES, BOW"*

וַאֲנַחְנוּ כּוֹרְעִים וּמִשְׁתַּחֲוִים וּמוֹדִים, לִפְנֵי מֶלֶךְ

‹ the King ‹ before « and acknowledge our thanks ‹ bow, ‹ bend our knees, ‹ But we

מַלְכֵי הַמְּלָכִים הַקָּדוֹשׁ בָּרוּךְ הוּא. שֶׁהוּא נוֹטֶה

‹ stretches out ‹ He « He. ‹ Blessed is ‹ the Holy One, « of kings, ‹ over kings

שָׁמַיִם וְיֹסֵד אָרֶץ,[2] וּמוֹשַׁב יְקָרוֹ בַּשָּׁמַיִם מִמַּעַל,

« above, ‹ is in the heavens ‹ of His homage ‹ the seat « earth's foundation, ‹ and establishes ‹ heaven

וּשְׁכִינַת עֻזּוֹ בְּגָבְהֵי מְרוֹמִים. הוּא אֱלֹהֵינוּ, אֵין עוֹד.

« other. ‹ and there is none ‹ our God ‹ He is « heights. ‹ is in the loftiest ‹ of His power ‹ and the Presence

אֱמֶת מַלְכֵּנוּ, אֶפֶס זוּלָתוֹ, כַּכָּתוּב בְּתוֹרָתוֹ: וְיָדַעְתָּ

‹ *You are to know* « in His Torah: ‹ as it is written « beside Him, ‹ there is nothing ‹ is our King, ‹ True

הַיּוֹם וַהֲשֵׁבֹתָ אֶל לְבָבֶךָ, כִּי יהוה הוּא הָאֱלֹהִים

« *the God* ‹ *He is* ‹ *HASHEM* ‹ *that* « *your heart,* ‹ *to* ‹ *and take* ‹ *this day*

בַּשָּׁמַיִם מִמַּעַל וְעַל הָאָרֶץ מִתָּחַת, אֵין עוֹד.[3]

« *other.* ‹ *there is none* ‹ *below —* ‹ *the earth* ‹ *and on* ‹ *above* ‹ *— in heaven*

(1) *Isaiah* 45:20. (2) 51:13. (3) *Deuteronomy* 4:39.

עַל כֵּן נְקַוֶּה לְּךָ, יהוה אֱלֹהֵינוּ, לִרְאוֹת מְהֵרָה

‹ very soon ‹ that we may see « our God, ‹ HASHEM, ‹ in You, ‹ we put our hope ‹ Therefore

בְּתִפְאֶרֶת עֻזֶּךָ, לְהַעֲבִיר גִּלּוּלִים מִן הָאָרֶץ,

« the earth, ‹ from ‹ detestable idolatry ‹ to remove « of Your might, ‹ the splendor

וְהָאֱלִילִים כָּרוֹת יִכָּרֵתוּן, לְתַקֵּן עוֹלָם בְּמַלְכוּת

‹ through the sovereignty ‹ the universe ‹ to perfect « will be utterly cut off, ‹ and false gods

שַׁדַּי. וְכָל בְּנֵי בָשָׂר יִקְרְאוּ בִשְׁמֶךָ, לְהַפְנוֹת אֵלֶיךָ

‹ toward You ‹ to turn « upon Your Name, ‹ will call ‹ humanity ‹ Then all « of the Almighty.

כָּל רִשְׁעֵי אָרֶץ. יַכִּירוּ וְיֵדְעוּ כָּל יוֹשְׁבֵי תֵבֵל, כִּי

‹ That « of the world — ‹ the inhabitants ‹ — all « and know ‹ May they recognize « of the earth. ‹ the wicked ‹ all

לְךָ תִּכְרַע כָּל בֶּרֶךְ, תִּשָּׁבַע כָּל לָשׁוֹן.[1] לְפָנֶיךָ יהוה

‹ HASHEM, ‹ Before You, « tongue. ‹ every ‹ should swear « knee ‹ every ‹ should bend ‹ to You

אֱלֹהֵינוּ יִכְרְעוּ וְיִפֹּלוּ, וְלִכְבוֹד שִׁמְךָ יְקָר יִתֵּנוּ.

« they will offer, ‹ homage ‹ of Your Name ‹ and to the glory « and cast themselves down, ‹ they will bend their knees ‹ our God,

וִיקַבְּלוּ כֻלָּם אֶת עוֹל מַלְכוּתֶךָ, וְתִמְלוֹךְ עֲלֵיהֶם

‹ over them ‹ that You may reign « of Your kingship, ‹ the yoke ‹ will all ‹ and accept

מְהֵרָה לְעוֹלָם וָעֶד. כִּי הַמַּלְכוּת שֶׁלְּךָ הִיא וּלְעוֹלְמֵי

‹ and for ever « is Yours, ‹ the kingdom ‹ For « and ever. ‹ for ever ‹ very soon

עַד תִּמְלוֹךְ בְּכָבוֹד, כַּכָּתוּב בְּתוֹרָתֶךָ: יהוה יִמְלֹךְ

‹ *shall reign* ‹ *HASHEM* « in Your Torah: ‹ as it is written « in glory, ‹ You will reign ‹ and ever

לְעֹלָם וָעֶד.[2] ❖ וְנֶאֱמַר: וְהָיָה יהוה לְמֶלֶךְ עַל כָּל

‹ *all* ‹ *over* ‹ *be King* ‹ *HASHEM* ‹ *Then will* « And it is said: « *and ever.* ‹ *for ever*

הָאָרֶץ, בַּיּוֹם הַהוּא יִהְיֶה יהוה אֶחָד וּשְׁמוֹ אֶחָד.[3]

« *be One.* ‹ *and His Name* ‹ *be One* ‹ *HASHEM* ‹ *shall* ‹ *— on that day* « *the world*

(1) Cf. *Isaiah* 45:23. (2) *Exodus* 15:18. (3) *Zechariah* 14:9.

SOME CONGREGATIONS RECITE THE FOLLOWING AFTER עָלֵינוּ, *ALEINU*.

אַל תִּירָא מִפַּחַד פִּתְאֹם, וּמִשֹּׁאַת רְשָׁעִים כִּי

‹ when ‹ of the wicked ‹ nor the holocaust « [that comes] suddenly, ‹ terror ‹ Do not fear

תָבֹא.[1] עֻצוּ עֵצָה וְתֻפָר, דַּבְּרוּ דָבָר וְלֹא יָקוּם, כִּי

‹ for « stand, ‹ and it shall not ‹ your speech ‹ speak « and it will be annulled; ‹ a conspiracy ‹ Plan « it comes.

עִמָּנוּ אֵל.[2] וְעַד זִקְנָה אֲנִי הוּא, וְעַד שֵׂיבָה אֲנִי

‹ I ‹ [your] elder years, ‹ and even till « I remain unchanged; ‹ [your] old age, ‹ Even till « is God. ‹ with us

אֶסְבֹּל, אֲנִי עָשִׂיתִי וַאֲנִי אֶשָּׂא, וַאֲנִי אֶסְבֹּל וַאֲמַלֵּט.[3]

« and rescue [you]. ‹ shall carry [you] ‹ I « shall bear [you]; ‹ and I ‹ created [you] ‹ I « shall carry [you].

MOURNER'S KADDISH / קדיש יתום

IN THE PRESENCE OF A *MINYAN*, MOURNERS RECITE קַדִּישׁ יָתוֹם, THE MOURNER'S *KADDISH*.
[A TRANSLITERATION OF THIS *KADDISH* APPEARS ON P. 647.]

יִתְגַּדַּל וְיִתְקַדַּשׁ שְׁמֵהּ רַבָּא. (Cong. — אָמֵן.) בְּעָלְמָא דִּי

‹ that ‹ in the world ‹ (Amen.) « that is great! — ‹ may His Name ‹ and be sanctified ‹ Grow exalted

בְּרָא כִרְעוּתֵהּ. וְיַמְלִיךְ מַלְכוּתֵהּ, בְּחַיֵּיכוֹן וּבְיוֹמֵיכוֹן וּבְחַיֵּי

‹ and in the lifetimes ‹ and in your days, ‹ in your lifetimes « to His kingship, ‹ and may He give reign « according to His will, ‹ He created

דְכָל בֵּית יִשְׂרָאֵל, בַּעֲגָלָא וּבִזְמַן קָרִיב. וְאִמְרוּ: אָמֵן.

« Amen. ‹ Now respond: « that comes soon. ‹ and at a time ‹ swiftly « of Israel, ‹ Family ‹ of the entire

CONGREGATION RESPONDS:

אָמֵן. יְהֵא שְׁמֵהּ רַבָּא מְבָרַךְ לְעָלַם וּלְעָלְמֵי עָלְמַיָּא.

« and for all eternity. ‹ forever ‹ be blessed ‹ that is great ‹ His Name ‹ May « Amen.

MOURNER CONTINUES:

יְהֵא שְׁמֵהּ רַבָּא מְבָרַךְ לְעָלַם וּלְעָלְמֵי עָלְמַיָּא. יִתְבָּרַךְ

‹ Blessed, « and for all eternity. ‹ forever ‹ be blessed ‹ that is great ‹ His Name ‹ May

וְיִשְׁתַּבַּח וְיִתְפָּאַר וְיִתְרוֹמַם וְיִתְנַשֵּׂא וְיִתְהַדָּר וְיִתְעַלֶּה

‹ elevated, ‹ honored, ‹ upraised, ‹ exalted, ‹ glorified, ‹ praised,

---

(1) *Proverbs* 3:25. (2) *Isaiah* 8:10. (3) 46:4.

וְיִתְהַלָּל שְׁמֵהּ דְּקֻדְשָׁא בְּרִיךְ הוּא (Cong. — בְּרִיךְ הוּא)
‹ and lauded ‹ be the Name ‹ of the Holy One, ‹ Blessed « is He ‹ (Blessed « is He)

— לְעֵלָּא מִן כָּל בִּרְכָתָא וְשִׁירָתָא תֻּשְׁבְּחָתָא וְנֶחֱמָתָא
‹ beyond ‹ any ‹ blessing « and song, ‹ praise ‹ and consolation

דַּאֲמִירָן בְּעָלְמָא. וְאִמְרוּ: אָמֵן. (Cong. — אָמֵן.)
‹ that are uttered « in the world. ‹ Now respond: « Amen. « (Amen.)

יְהֵא שְׁלָמָא רַבָּא מִן שְׁמַיָּא, וְחַיִּים עָלֵינוּ וְעַל כָּל
‹ May there be ‹ peace ‹ that is abundant ‹ from « Heaven, « and life, ‹ upon us ‹ and upon ‹ all

יִשְׂרָאֵל. וְאִמְרוּ: אָמֵן. (Cong. — אָמֵן.)
« Israel. ‹ Now respond: « Amen. ‹ (Amen.)

BOW; TAKE THREE STEPS BACK. BOW LEFT AND SAY ... עֹשֶׂה שָׁלוֹם, *"HE WHO MAKES PEACE ..."*; BOW RIGHT AND SAY ... הוּא, *"MAY HE ..."*; BOW FORWARD AND SAY ... וְעַל כָּל יִשְׂרָאֵל, *"AND UPON ALL ISRAEL ..."*; REMAIN IN PLACE FOR A FEW MOMENTS, THEN TAKE THREE STEPS FORWARD.

עֹשֶׂה שָׁלוֹם בִּמְרוֹמָיו, הוּא יַעֲשֶׂה שָׁלוֹם עָלֵינוּ, וְעַל כָּל
‹ He Who makes ‹ peace « in His heights, ‹ may He ‹ make ‹ peace ‹ upon us, ‹ and upon ‹ all

יִשְׂרָאֵל. וְאִמְרוּ: אָמֵן. (Cong. — אָמֵן.)
« Israel. ‹ Now respond: « Amen. ‹ (Amen.)

THE RECITATION OF שִׁיר שֶׁל יוֹם, *"THE SONG OF THE DAY,"* IS POSTPONED UNTIL *MINCHAH*. AFTER MIDDAY, IT IT PERMISSIBLE TO SIT ON A REGULAR SEAT.

MINCHAH / מנחה

THE *PAROCHES* IS RETURNED TO THE ARK.

DONNING THE TALLIS / עטיפת טלית

BEFORE DONNING THE *TALLIS*, INSPECT THE *TZITZIS* WHILE RECITING THESE VERSES:

בָּרְכִי נַפְשִׁי אֶת יהוה, יהוה אֱלֹהַי גָּדַלְתָּ מְּאֹד,

« You are very great; ‹ my God, ‹ HASHEM, « HASHEM; ‹ O my soul, ‹ Bless,

הוֹד וְהָדָר לָבָשְׁתָּ. עֹטֶה אוֹר כַּשַּׂלְמָה, נוֹטֶה

‹ stretching out « as a garment, ‹ light ‹ donning « You have worn; ‹ and majesty ‹ glory

שָׁמַיִם כַּיְרִיעָה.[1]

« like a curtain. ‹ the heavens

MANY RECITE THE FOLLOWING DECLARATION OF INTENT BEFORE DONNING THE *TALLIS*:

לְשֵׁם יִחוּד קֻדְשָׁא בְּרִיךְ הוּא וּשְׁכִינְתֵּהּ, בִּדְחִילוּ

‹ in fear « and His Presence, « is He, ‹ Blessed « of the Holy One, ‹ of the unification ‹ For the sake

וּרְחִימוּ לְיַחֵד שֵׁם י״ה בְּו״ה בְּיִחוּדָא שְׁלִים, בְּשֵׁם

‹ in the name « that is complete, ‹ in unity ‹ with *Vav-Kei* ‹ *Yud-Kei* ‹ the Name ‹ to unify ‹ and love,

כָּל יִשְׂרָאֵל.

« Israel. ‹ of all

הֲרֵינִי מִתְעַטֵּף גּוּפִי בַּצִּיצִת, כֵּן תִּתְעַטֵּף נִשְׁמָתִי וּרְמַ״ח

‹ and my 248 « my soul, ‹ may be wrapped ‹ so « in *tzitzis;* ‹ my body ‹ wrap ‹ I am ready to

אֵבָרַי וּשְׁסָ״ה גִידַי בְּאוֹר הַצִּיצִת הָעוֹלֶה תַּרְיַ״ג. וּכְשֵׁם

‹ And just « of 613. ‹ which has the numerical value « of *tzitzis,* ‹ in the illumination « sinews ‹ and my 365 ‹ organs

שֶׁאֲנִי מִתְכַּסֶּה בְּטַלִּית בָּעוֹלָם הַזֶּה, כַּךְ אֶזְכֶּה לַחֲלוּקָא

‹ the garb ‹ may I merit ‹ so « in This World, ‹ in a *tallis* ‹ wrap myself ‹ as I

דְרַבָּנָן וּלְטַלִּית נָאָה לָעוֹלָם הַבָּא בְּגַן עֵדֶן. וְעַל יְדֵי

‹ means ‹ And by « of Eden. ‹ in the Garden ‹ to Come, ‹ in the World ‹ and a beautiful *tallis* ‹ of the rabbis

מִצְוַת צִיצִת תִּנָּצֵל נַפְשִׁי וְרוּחִי וְנִשְׁמָתִי וּתְפִלָּתִי

« and my prayer be, ‹ my soul, ‹ my spirit, « my life force, ‹ rescued may « of *tzitzis,* ‹ of the commandment

(1) *Psalms* 104:1-2.

מִן הַחִיצוֹנִים. וְהַטַּלִּית יִפְרוֹשׂ כְּנָפָיו עֲלֵיהֶם וְיַצִּילֵם כְּנֶשֶׁר

from the external forces. May the *tallis* spread its wings over them and rescue them, like an eagle

יָעִיר קִנּוֹ, עַל גּוֹזָלָיו יְרַחֵף.[1] וּתְהֵא חֲשׁוּבָה מִצְוַת צִיצִת

arousing its nest; over its eaglets hovering. May it be considered the commandment of *tzitzis* —

לִפְנֵי הַקָּדוֹשׁ בָּרוּךְ הוּא כְּאִלּוּ קִיַּמְתִּיהָ בְּכָל פְּרָטֶיהָ

before the Holy One, Blessed is He, as if I had fulfilled it in all its aspects,

וְדִקְדּוּקֶיהָ וְכַוָּנוֹתֶיהָ וְתַרְיַ״ג מִצְוֹת הַתְּלוּיִם בָּהּ. אָמֵן סֶלָה.

its details, and its intentions, as well as the 613 commandments that are dependent upon it. Amen, Selah.

UNFOLD THE *TALLIS,* HOLD IT IN READINESS TO WRAP AROUND YOURSELF, AND RECITE THE FOLLOWING BLESSING:

בָּרוּךְ אַתָּה יהוה אֱלֹהֵינוּ מֶלֶךְ הָעוֹלָם, אֲשֶׁר

Blessed are You, HASHEM, our God, King of the universe, Who

קִדְּשָׁנוּ בְּמִצְוֹתָיו, וְצִוָּנוּ לְהִתְעַטֵּף בַּצִּיצִת.

has sanctified us with His commandments, and commanded us to wrap ourselves in *tzitzis.*

WRAP THE *TALLIS* AROUND YOUR HEAD AND BODY, THEN RECITE:

מַה יָּקָר חַסְדְּךָ אֱלֹהִים, וּבְנֵי אָדָם בְּצֵל כְּנָפֶיךָ

How precious is Your kindness, O God! Mankind in the shelter of Your wings

יֶחֱסָיוּן. יִרְוְיֻן מִדֶּשֶׁן בֵּיתֶךָ, וְנַחַל עֲדָנֶיךָ תַשְׁקֵם.

takes refuge. They will be sated from the abundance of Your house, and from the stream of Your delights You give them to drink.

כִּי עִמְּךָ מְקוֹר חַיִּים, בְּאוֹרְךָ נִרְאֶה אוֹר. מְשֹׁךְ

For with You is the source of life; by Your light may we see light. Extend

חַסְדְּךָ לְיֹדְעֶיךָ, וְצִדְקָתְךָ לְיִשְׁרֵי לֵב.[2]

Your kindness to those who know You, and Your charity to the upright of heart.

(1) *Deuteronomy* 32:11. (2) *Psalms* 36:8-11.

❧ PUTTING ON TEFILLIN / סדר הנחת תפילין ❧

MANY RECITE THE FOLLOWING DECLARATION OF INTENT BEFORE PUTTING ON THE *TEFILLIN*:

לְשֵׁם יִחוּד קֻדְשָׁא בְּרִיךְ הוּא וּשְׁכִינְתֵּהּ, בִּדְחִילוּ
For the sake of the unification of the Holy One, Blessed is He, and His Presence, in fear

וּרְחִימוּ לְיַחֵד שֵׁם י״ה בְּו״ה בְּיִחוּדָא שְׁלִים, בְּשֵׁם כָּל
and love, to unify the Name *yud-kei* with *vav-kei* in unity that is complete, in the name of all

יִשְׂרָאֵל.
Israel.

הִנְנִי מְכַוֵּן בַּהֲנָחַת תְּפִלִּין לְקַיֵּם מִצְוַת בּוֹרְאִי, שֶׁצִּוָּנוּ
Behold, I intend, in putting on *tefillin,* to fulfill the commandment of my Creator, Who commanded us

לְהָנִיחַ תְּפִלִּין, כַּכָּתוּב בְּתוֹרָתוֹ: וּקְשַׁרְתָּם לְאוֹת עַל יָדֶךָ,
to put on *tefillin,* as is written in His Torah: *Bind them as a sign upon your arm,*

וְהָיוּ לְטֹטָפֹת בֵּין עֵינֶיךָ.[1] וְהֵם אַרְבַּע פַּרְשִׁיּוֹת אֵלּוּ —
and they shall be tefillin between your eyes. They [consist of] these four portions

שְׁמַע, וְהָיָה אִם שָׁמֹעַ, קַדֵּשׁ, וְהָיָה כִּי יְבִאֲךָ — שֶׁיֵּשׁ
–[1] *Shema;* [2] *And it will be, if you will hearken…;* [3] *Sanctify…;* and [4] *And it will be when He shall bring you…* –which contain

בָּהֶם יִחוּדוֹ וְאַחְדוּתוֹ יִתְבָּרַךְ שְׁמוֹ בָּעוֹלָם; וְשֶׁנִּזְכּוֹר
in them His Oneness and His Unity –blessed is His Name in the universe, and [the idea] that we should recall

נִסִּים וְנִפְלָאוֹת שֶׁעָשָׂה עִמָּנוּ בְּהוֹצִיאָנוּ מִמִּצְרַיִם; וַאֲשֶׁר
the miracles and wonders that He did for us when He took us out from Egypt, and [the idea] that

לוֹ הַכֹּחַ וְהַמֶּמְשָׁלָה בָּעֶלְיוֹנִים וּבַתַּחְתּוֹנִים לַעֲשׂוֹת בָּהֶם
He has the strength and dominion over the upper realms and the lower realms to do with them

כִּרְצוֹנוֹ. וְצִוָּנוּ לְהָנִיחַ עַל הַיָּד, לְזִכְרוֹן זְרוֹעַ הַנְּטוּיָה,
as He wishes. He commanded us to put [the *tefillin*] upon the arm as a reminder of the *outstretched arm* [of the Exodus],

וְשֶׁהִיא נֶגֶד הַלֵּב, לְשַׁעְבֵּד בָּזֶה תַּאֲוֹת וּמַחְשְׁבוֹת
and because it is opposite the heart, subjugating thereby the passions and thoughts

לִבֵּנוּ לַעֲבוֹדָתוֹ, יִתְבָּרַךְ שְׁמוֹ. וְעַל הָרֹאשׁ נֶגֶד הַמּוֹחַ,

of our heart / to His service / – Blessed / be His Name; / and upon / the head, / opposite / the brain,

שֶׁהַנְּשָׁמָה שֶׁבְּמוֹחִי, עִם שְׁאָר חוּשַׁי וְכֹחוֹתַי, כֻּלָּם יִהְיוּ

so that the soul / that is in my brain, / together with / the rest / of my senses / and faculties, / all / may be

מְשֻׁעְבָּדִים לַעֲבוֹדָתוֹ, יִתְבָּרַךְ שְׁמוֹ. וּמִשֶּׁפַע מִצְוַת תְּפִלִּין

subjugated / to His service / – Blessed / is His Name. / May some of the [spiritual] emanations / of the commandment / of *tefillin*

יִתְמַשֵּׁךְ עָלַי לִהְיוֹת לִי חַיִּים אֲרוּכִים, וְשֶׁפַע קֹדֶשׁ,

be extended / onto me, / so that I may have / a long life, / with emanations / of holiness,

וּמַחֲשָׁבוֹת קְדוֹשׁוֹת בְּלִי הִרְהוּר חֵטְא וְעָוֹן כְּלָל; וְשֶׁלֹּא

and holy thoughts, / without / thoughts / of sin / or iniquity / at all; / so that it not

יְפַתֵּנוּ וְלֹא יִתְגָּרֶה בָּנוּ יֵצֶר הָרָע, וְיַנִּיחֵנוּ לַעֲבֹד אֶת יהוה

lure us / nor / incite / against us / – the Evil Inclination – / but rather allow us / to serve / HASHEM

כַּאֲשֶׁר עִם לְבָבֵנוּ. וִיהִי רָצוֹן מִלְּפָנֶיךָ, יהוה אֱלֹהֵינוּ

as / it is in / our hearts [to do]. / May it be / the will / before You, / HASHEM, / our God

וֵאלֹהֵי אֲבוֹתֵינוּ, שֶׁתְּהֵא חֲשׁוּבָה מִצְוַת הֲנָחַת תְּפִלִּין לִפְנֵי

and the God / of our forefathers, / that it be / considered / – the commandment / of putting on / *tefillin* – / before

הַקָּדוֹשׁ בָּרוּךְ הוּא, כְּאִלּוּ קִיַּמְתִּיהָ בְּכָל פְּרָטֶיהָ וְדִקְדּוּקֶיהָ

the Holy One, / Blessed / is He, / as if / I had fulfilled it / in all / its aspects, / its details,

וְכַוָּנוֹתֶיהָ, וְתַרְיַ״ג מִצְוֹת הַתְּלוּיִם בָּהּ. אָמֵן סֶלָה.

and its intentions, / as well as the 613 / commandments / that are dependent / upon it. / Amen, / Selah.

STAND WHILE PUTTING ON *TEFILLIN*. PLACE THE ARM-*TEFILLIN* UPON THE LEFT BICEPS (OR THE RIGHT BICEPS OF ONE WHO WRITES LEFT-HANDED), HOLD IT IN PLACE READY FOR TIGHTENING, THEN RECITE THE FOLLOWING BLESSING:

בָּרוּךְ אַתָּה יהוה אֱלֹהֵינוּ מֶלֶךְ הָעוֹלָם, אֲשֶׁר

Blessed / are You, / HASHEM, / our God, / King / of the universe, / Who

קִדְּשָׁנוּ בְּמִצְוֹתָיו, וְצִוָּנוּ לְהָנִיחַ תְּפִלִּין.

has sanctified us / with His commandments / and has commanded us / to put on / *tefillin*.

TIGHTEN THE ARM-*TEFILLIN* AND WRAP THE STRAP SEVEN TIMES AROUND THE ARM. WITHOUT ANY INTERRUPTION WHATSOEVER, PUT THE HEAD-*TEFILLIN* IN PLACE, ABOVE THE HAIRLINE AND OPPOSITE THE SPACE BETWEEN THE EYES. BEFORE TIGHTENING THE HEAD-*TEFILLIN* RECITE THE FOLLOWING BLESSING:

בָּרוּךְ אַתָּה יהוה אֱלֹהֵינוּ מֶלֶךְ הָעוֹלָם, אֲשֶׁר

‹ Who « of the universe, ‹ King ‹ our God, « HASHEM, ‹ are You, ‹ Blessed

קִדְּשָׁנוּ בְּמִצְוֹתָיו, וְצִוָּנוּ עַל מִצְוַת תְּפִלִּין.

« of *tefillin.* ‹ the commandment ‹ regarding ‹ and has commanded us ‹ with His commandments ‹ has sanctified us

TIGHTEN THE HEAD-*TEFILLIN* AND RECITE:

בָּרוּךְ שֵׁם כְּבוֹד מַלְכוּתוֹ לְעוֹלָם וָעֶד.

« and ever. ‹ for ever ‹ kingdom ‹ of His glorious ‹ is the Name ‹ Blessed

AFTER THE HEAD-*TEFILLIN* IS SECURELY IN PLACE, RECITE:

וּמֵחָכְמָתְךָ אֵל עֶלְיוֹן, תַּאֲצִיל עָלַי; וּמִבִּינָתְךָ

‹ and from Your understanding « me; ‹ may You imbue « the Most High, ‹ God ‹ From Your wisdom,

תְּבִינֵנִי; וּבְחַסְדְּךָ תַּגְדִּיל עָלַי; וּבִגְבוּרָתְךָ תַּצְמִית

‹ cut down ‹ and with Your power « with me; ‹ deal greatly ‹ and with Your kindness « grant me understanding;

אֹיְבַי וְקָמַי. וְשֶׁמֶן הַטּוֹב תָּרִיק עַל שִׁבְעָה

‹ the seven ‹ upon ‹ pour out ‹ The fine oil « and those who rise against me. ‹ my foes

קְנֵי הַמְּנוֹרָה, לְהַשְׁפִּיעַ טוּבְךָ לִבְרִיּוֹתֶיךָ. פּוֹתֵחַ

‹ You open « to Your creations. ‹ Your goodness ‹ to cause to emanate « of the Menorah, ‹ branches

אֶת יָדֶךָ, וּמַשְׂבִּיעַ לְכָל חַי רָצוֹן.[1]

« [with its] desire. ‹ living thing ‹ every ‹ and satisfy ‹ Your hand

WRAP THE STRAP AROUND THE MIDDLE FINGER AND HAND ACCORDING TO YOUR CUSTOM. WHILE DOING THIS, RECITE:

וְאֵרַשְׂתִּיךְ לִי לְעוֹלָם, וְאֵרַשְׂתִּיךְ לִי בְּצֶדֶק

‹ with righteousness, ‹ to Me ‹ and I will betroth you « forever; ‹ to Me ‹ I will betroth you

(1) *Psalms* 145:16.

וּבְמִשְׁפָּט וּבְחֶסֶד וּבְרַחֲמִים. וְאֵרַשְׂתִּיךְ לִי בֶּאֱמוּנָה,
‹ with fidelity, ‹ to Me ‹ and I will betroth you « and with mercy; ‹ with kindness, ‹ with justice,

וְיָדַעַתְּ אֶת יהוה.[1]
« HASHEM. ‹ and you shall know

PORTIONS OMITTED FROM *SHACHARIS* (EXCEPT *TACHANUN* AND לַמְנַצֵּחַ) ARE RECITED HERE.

SONG OF THE DAY / שיר של יום

A DIFFERENT PSALM IS ASSIGNED AS THE *SONG OF THE DAY* FOR EACH DAY OF THE WEEK.

SUNDAY

הַיּוֹם יוֹם רִאשׁוֹן בַּשַּׁבָּת, שֶׁבּוֹ הָיוּ הַלְוִיִּם אוֹמְרִים
‹ recite ‹ the Levites would ‹ on which ‹ of the week, ‹ is the first day ‹ Today

בְּבֵית הַמִּקְדָּשׁ:
« in the Holy Temple:

Psalm 24 / תהלים כד

לְדָוִד מִזְמוֹר; לַיהוה הָאָרֶץ וּמְלוֹאָהּ, תֵּבֵל וְיִשְׁבֵי בָהּ.
« in it. ‹ and those who dwell ‹ the inhabited land « and its fullness, ‹ is the earth ‹ HASHEM's « a psalm. ‹ By David,

כִּי הוּא עַל יַמִּים יְסָדָהּ, וְעַל נְהָרוֹת יְכוֹנְנֶהָ. מִי יַעֲלֶה
‹ may ascend ‹ Who « established it. ‹ rivers ‹ and upon ‹ founded it, ‹ seas ‹ upon ‹ He ‹ For

בְהַר יהוה, וּמִי יָקוּם בִּמְקוֹם קָדְשׁוֹ. נְקִי כַפַּיִם וּבַר
‹ and pure ‹ hands ‹ One with clean « of His sanctity? ‹ in the place ‹ may stand ‹ and who ‹ of HASHEM, ‹ the mountain

לֵבָב, אֲשֶׁר לֹא נָשָׂא לַשָּׁוְא נַפְשִׁי וְלֹא נִשְׁבַּע לְמִרְמָה.
« deceitfully. ‹ sworn ‹ and has not « [by] My soul, ‹ in vain ‹ sworn ‹ has not ‹ who « heart;

יִשָּׂא בְרָכָה מֵאֵת יהוה, וּצְדָקָה מֵאֱלֹהֵי יִשְׁעוֹ. זֶה דּוֹר
‹ the generation ‹ This is « of his salvation. ‹ from the God ‹ and just kindness « HASHEM ‹ from ‹ a blessing ‹ He will receive

דֹּרְשָׁיו, מְבַקְשֵׁי פָנֶיךָ, יַעֲקֹב, סֶלָה. שְׂאוּ שְׁעָרִים
‹ O gates, ‹ Raise up, « Selah. « [the nation of] Jacob, ‹ Your Presence — ‹ those who strive for « of those who seek Him,

(1) *Hosea* 2:21-22.

רָאשֵׁיכֶם, וְהִנָּשְׂאוּ פִּתְחֵי עוֹלָם, וְיָבוֹא מֶלֶךְ הַכָּבוֹד. מִי

your heads, and be uplifted, [you] everlasting entrances, so that He may enter — the King of Glory. Who

זֶה מֶלֶךְ הַכָּבוֹד, יהוה עִזּוּז וְגִבּוֹר, יהוה גִּבּוֹר מִלְחָמָה.

is this King of Glory? HASHEM, the mighty and the strong; HASHEM, the strong in battle.

❖ שְׂאוּ שְׁעָרִים רָאשֵׁיכֶם, וּשְׂאוּ פִּתְחֵי עוֹלָם, וְיָבֹא מֶלֶךְ

Raise up, O gates, your heads, and raise up, [you] everlasting entrances, so that He may enter — the King

הַכָּבוֹד. מִי הוּא זֶה מֶלֶךְ הַכָּבוֹד, יהוה צְבָאוֹת הוּא מֶלֶךְ

of Glory. Who is He, this King of Glory? HASHEM, Master of Legions, He is the King

הַכָּבוֹד, סֶלָה.

of Glory, Selah!

THE SERVICE CONTINUES WITH קַדִּישׁ יָתוֹם, THE MOURNER'S *KADDISH* (P. 549).

TUESDAY

הַיּוֹם יוֹם שְׁלִישִׁי בַּשַּׁבָּת, שֶׁבּוֹ הָיוּ הַלְוִיִּם אוֹמְרִים

Today is the third day of the week, on which the Levites would recite

בְּבֵית הַמִּקְדָּשׁ:

in the Holy Temple:

Psalm 82 / תהלים פב

מִזְמוֹר לְאָסָף, אֱלֹהִים נִצָּב בַּעֲדַת אֵל, בְּקֶרֶב אֱלֹהִים

A psalm of Asaph: God stands in the Divine assembly, in the midst of judges

יִשְׁפֹּט. עַד מָתַי תִּשְׁפְּטוּ עָוֶל, וּפְנֵי רְשָׁעִים תִּשְׂאוּ סֶלָה.

shall He judge. Until when will you judge lawlessly and the presence of the wicked will you favor, Selah?

שִׁפְטוּ דָל וְיָתוֹם, עָנִי וָרָשׁ הַצְדִּיקוּ. פַּלְּטוּ דַל וְאֶבְיוֹן,

Dispense justice for the needy and the orphan; the poor and impoverished vindicate. Rescue the needy and destitute,

מִיַּד רְשָׁעִים הַצִּילוּ. לֹא יָדְעוּ וְלֹא יָבִינוּ, בַּחֲשֵׁכָה יִתְהַלָּכוּ,

and from the hand of the wicked deliver them. They do not know nor do they understand, in darkness they walk;

יִמּוֹטוּ כָּל מוֹסְדֵי אָרֶץ. אֲנִי אָמַרְתִּי אֱלֹהִים אַתֶּם, וּבְנֵי

collapse do all the foundations of the earth. I said, *Angelic are you, sons*

עֶלְיוֹן כֻּלְּכֶם. אָכֵן כְּאָדָם תְּמוּתוּן, וּכְאַחַד הַשָּׂרִים תִּפֹּלוּ.

of the Most High · *are you all.* · But · like men · you shall die, · and like one · of the princes · you shall fall.

❖ קוּמָה אֱלֹהִים שָׁפְטָה הָאָרֶץ, כִּי אַתָּה תִנְחַל בְּכָל הַגּוֹיִם.

Arise, · O God, · judge · the earth, · for · You · allot the portion · of all · the nations.

THE SERVICE CONTINUES WITH קַדִּישׁ יָתוֹם, THE MOURNER'S *KADDISH* (P. 549).

THURSDAY

הַיּוֹם יוֹם חֲמִישִׁי בְּשַׁבָּת, שֶׁבּוֹ הָיוּ הַלְוִיִּם אוֹמְרִים

Today · is the fifth day · of the week, · on which · the Levites would · recite

בְּבֵית הַמִּקְדָּשׁ:

in the Holy Temple:

Psalm 81 / תהלים פא

לַמְנַצֵּחַ עַל הַגִּתִּית לְאָסָף. הַרְנִינוּ לֵאלֹהִים עוּזֵּנוּ, הָרִיעוּ

For the conductor, · on · the gittis, · by Asaph. · Sing joyously · to God · our strength, · call out

לֵאלֹהֵי יַעֲקֹב. שְׂאוּ זִמְרָה וּתְנוּ תֹף, כִּנּוֹר נָעִים עִם נָבֶל.

to the God · of Jacob. · Raise up · a song · and sound · the drum, · the sweet harp · with · the lyre.

תִּקְעוּ בַחֹדֶשׁ שׁוֹפָר, בַּכֶּסֶה לְיוֹם חַגֵּנוּ. כִּי חֹק לְיִשְׂרָאֵל

Blow · at the moon's renewal · the shofar, · at the time appointed · for the day · of our festival. · Because · a decree · for Israel

הוּא, מִשְׁפָּט לֵאלֹהֵי יַעֲקֹב. עֵדוּת בִּיהוֹסֵף שָׂמוֹ, בְּצֵאתוֹ

it is, · a judgment [day] · for the God · of Jacob. · As a testimony · for Joseph · He appointed it · when He went out

עַל אֶרֶץ מִצְרָיִם, שְׂפַת לֹא יָדַעְתִּי אֶשְׁמָע. הֲסִירוֹתִי מִסֵּבֶל

over · the land · of Egypt, · a language · unknown to me · I heard. · [Says God:] *I removed* · *from the burden*

שִׁכְמוֹ, כַּפָּיו מִדּוּד תַּעֲבֹרְנָה. בַּצָּרָה קָרָאתָ, וָאֲחַלְּצֶךָּ,

his shoulder, · *his hands* · *from the kettle* · *passed.* · *In distress* · *you called out,* · *and I released you;*

אֶעֶנְךָ בְּסֵתֶר רַעַם, אֶבְחָנְךָ עַל מֵי מְרִיבָה, סֶלָה. שְׁמַע

I answered you, · *[when you called] privately,* · *with a thunderous reply.* · *I tested you* · *at* · *the Waters* · *of Strife.* · *Selah.* · *Listen,*

עַמִּי וְאָעִידָה בָּךְ, יִשְׂרָאֵל אִם תִּשְׁמַע לִי. לֹא יִהְיֶה בְךָ

My people, · *and I will attest* · *to you;* · *O Israel,* · *if you would but* · *listen* · *to Me.* · *There shall not be* · *within you*

אֵל זָר, וְלֹא תִשְׁתַּחֲוֶה לְאֵל נֵכָר. אָנֹכִי יהוה אֱלֹהֶיךָ,

[any] strange god, « *nor* ‹ *shall you bow* ‹ *before an alien god.* « *I am* ‹ *HASHEM,* ‹ *your God,* ‹

הַמַּעַלְךָ מֵאֶרֶץ מִצְרָיִם, הַרְחֶב פִּיךָ וַאֲמַלְאֵהוּ. וְלֹא שָׁמַע

Who raised you ‹ *from the land* ‹ *of Egypt.* « *Open wide* ‹ *your mouth* ‹ *and I will fill it.* « But listen not ‹

עַמִּי לְקוֹלִי, וְיִשְׂרָאֵל לֹא אָבָה לִי. וָאֲשַׁלְּחֵהוּ בִּשְׁרִירוּת

did My people ‹ to My voice; « Israel ‹ did not ‹ desire ‹ Me. « So I let them pursue ‹ the fantasies ‹

לִבָּם, יֵלְכוּ בְּמוֹעֲצוֹתֵיהֶם. לוּ עַמִּי שֹׁמֵעַ לִי, יִשְׂרָאֵל

of their heart, « that they might follow ‹ their own counsels. « If only ‹ My people ‹ would heed ‹ Me, « [if only] Israel ‹

בִּדְרָכַי יְהַלֵּכוּ. כִּמְעַט אוֹיְבֵיהֶם אַכְנִיעַ, וְעַל צָרֵיהֶם

in My ways ‹ would walk. « In an instant ‹ their foes ‹ I would subdue, « and against ‹ their tormentors ‹

אָשִׁיב יָדִי. מְשַׂנְאֵי יהוה יְכַחֲשׁוּ לוֹ, וִיהִי עִתָּם לְעוֹלָם.

I would turn ‹ My hand. « Those who hate ‹ HASHEM ‹ would lie ‹ to him; « but their time would be ‹ forever. «

❖ וַיַּאֲכִילֵהוּ מֵחֵלֶב חִטָּה, וּמִצּוּר דְּבַשׁ אַשְׂבִּיעֶךָ.

And He would feed him ‹ with the choicest ‹ wheat, « and from a rock, « with honey ‹ I would sate you. «

THE SERVICE CONTINUES WITH קַדִּישׁ יָתוֹם, THE MOURNER'S *KADDISH* (BELOW).

MOURNER'S KADDISH / קדיש יתום

IN THE PRESENCE OF A *MINYAN*, MOURNERS RECITE קַדִּישׁ יָתוֹם, THE MOURNER'S *KADDISH* (SEE *LAWS* §132-134). A TRANSLITERATION OF THIS *KADDISH* APPEARS ON PAGE 647.

יִתְגַּדַּל וְיִתְקַדַּשׁ שְׁמֵהּ רַבָּא. (Cong. — אָמֵן.) בְּעָלְמָא דִּי

Grow exalted ‹ and be sanctified ‹ may His Name ‹ that is great! — « (Amen.) ‹ — in the world ‹ that ‹

בְּרָא כִרְעוּתֵהּ. וְיַמְלִיךְ מַלְכוּתֵהּ, בְּחַיֵּיכוֹן וּבְיוֹמֵיכוֹן וּבְחַיֵּי

He created ‹ according to His will, « and may He give reign ‹ to His kingship, « in your lifetimes ‹ and in your days, ‹ and in the lifetimes ‹

דְכָל בֵּית יִשְׂרָאֵל, בַּעֲגָלָא וּבִזְמַן קָרִיב. וְאִמְרוּ: אָמֵן.

of the entire ‹ Family ‹ of Israel, « swiftly ‹ and at a time ‹ that comes soon. « Now respond: ‹ Amen. «

CONGREGATION RESPONDS:

אָמֵן. יְהֵא שְׁמֵהּ רַבָּא מְבָרַךְ לְעָלַם וּלְעָלְמֵי עָלְמַיָּא.

Amen. « May ‹ His Name ‹ that is great ‹ be blessed ‹ forever ‹ and for all eternity. «

MOURNER CONTINUES:

יְהֵא שְׁמֵהּ רַבָּא מְבָרַךְ לְעָלַם וּלְעָלְמֵי עָלְמַיָּא. יִתְבָּרַךְ

‹ Blessed, « and for all eternity. ‹ forever ‹ be blessed ‹ that is great ‹ His Name ‹ May

וְיִשְׁתַּבַּח וְיִתְפָּאַר וְיִתְרוֹמַם וְיִתְנַשֵּׂא וְיִתְהַדָּר וְיִתְעַלֶּה

‹ elevated, ‹ honored, ‹ upraised, ‹ exalted, ‹ glorified, ‹ praised,

וְיִתְהַלָּל שְׁמֵהּ דְּקֻדְשָׁא בְּרִיךְ הוּא (Cong. — בְּרִיךְ הוּא) —

« is He) ‹ (Blessed « is He ‹ Blessed ‹ of the Holy One, ‹ be the Name ‹ and lauded

לְעֵלָּא מִן כָּל בִּרְכָתָא וְשִׁירָתָא תֻּשְׁבְּחָתָא וְנֶחֱמָתָא

‹ and consolation ‹ praise « and song, ‹ blessing ‹ any ‹ beyond

דַּאֲמִירָן בְּעָלְמָא. וְאִמְרוּ: אָמֵן. (Cong. — אָמֵן.)

« (Amen.) « Amen. ‹ Now respond: « in the world. ‹ that are uttered

יְהֵא שְׁלָמָא רַבָּא מִן שְׁמַיָּא, וְחַיִּים עָלֵינוּ וְעַל כָּל

‹ all ‹ and upon ‹ upon us « and life, « Heaven, ‹ from ‹ that is abundant ‹ peace ‹ May there be

יִשְׂרָאֵל. וְאִמְרוּ: אָמֵן. (Cong. — אָמֵן.)

« (Amen.) « Amen. ‹ Now respond: « Israel.

BOW; TAKE THREE STEPS BACK. BOW LEFT AND SAY ... עֹשֶׂה שָׁלוֹם, *"HE WHO MAKES PEACE ..."*; BOW RIGHT AND SAY ... הוּא, *"MAY HE ..."*; BOW FORWARD AND SAY ... וְעַל כָּל יִשְׂרָאֵל, *"AND UPON ALL ISRAEL ..."*; REMAIN IN PLACE FOR A FEW MOMENTS, THEN TAKE THREE STEPS FORWARD.

עֹשֶׂה שָׁלוֹם בִּמְרוֹמָיו, הוּא יַעֲשֶׂה שָׁלוֹם עָלֵינוּ, וְעַל כָּל

‹ all ‹ and upon ‹ upon us, ‹ peace ‹ make ‹ may He « in His heights, ‹ peace ‹ He Who makes

יִשְׂרָאֵל. וְאִמְרוּ: אָמֵן. (Cong. — אָמֵן.)

« (Amen.) « Amen. ‹ Now respond: « Israel.

ASHREI / אשרי

אַשְׁרֵי יוֹשְׁבֵי בֵיתֶךָ, עוֹד יְהַלְלוּךָ סֶּלָה.[1] אַשְׁרֵי

‹ Praiseworthy « Selah. ‹ they will praise You, ‹ continually « in Your house, ‹ are those who dwell ‹ Praiseworthy

הָעָם שֶׁכָּכָה לּוֹ, אַשְׁרֵי הָעָם שֶׁיהוה אֱלֹהָיו.[2]

« is their God. ‹ that HASHEM ‹ is the people ‹ praiseworthy « is their lot; ‹ that such ‹ is the people

(1) *Psalms* 84:5. (2) 144:15.

Psalm 145 / תהלים קמה

תְּהִלָּה לְדָוִד, אֲרוֹמִמְךָ אֱלוֹהַי הַמֶּלֶךְ, וַאֲבָרְכָה

‹ and I will bless « the King, ‹ my God ‹ I will exalt You, « by David: ‹ A psalm of praise

שִׁמְךָ לְעוֹלָם וָעֶד. בְּכָל יוֹם אֲבָרְכֶךָּ, וַאֲהַלְלָה

‹ and I will laud « I will bless You, ‹ day ‹ Every « and ever. ‹ for ever ‹ Your Name

שִׁמְךָ לְעוֹלָם וָעֶד. גָּדוֹל יהוה וּמְהֻלָּל מְאֹד,

« exceedingly, ‹ and lauded ‹ is Hashem ‹ Great « and ever. ‹ for ever ‹ Your Name

וְלִגְדֻלָּתוֹ אֵין חֵקֶר. דּוֹר לְדוֹר יְשַׁבַּח מַעֲשֶׂיךָ,

« Your actions, ‹ will praise ‹ to generation ‹ Generation « is beyond investigation. ‹ and His greatness

וּגְבוּרֹתֶיךָ יַגִּידוּ. הֲדַר כְּבוֹד הוֹדֶךָ, וְדִבְרֵי

‹ and Your deeds « of Your majesty, ‹ glory ‹ The splendrous « they will recount. ‹ and Your mighty deeds

נִפְלְאֹתֶיךָ אָשִׂיחָה. וֶעֱזוּז נוֹרְאֹתֶיךָ יֹאמֵרוּ,

« they will speak, ‹ of Your awesome deeds ‹ And of the might « I shall discuss. ‹ that are wondrous

וּגְדוּלָּתְךָ אֲסַפְּרֶנָּה. זֵכֶר רַב טוּבְךָ יַבִּיעוּ, וְצִדְקָתְךָ

‹ and of Your righteousness « they will utter, ‹ of Your abundant goodness ‹ A recollection « I shall relate. ‹ and Your greatness

יְרַנֵּנוּ. חַנּוּן וְרַחוּם יהוה, אֶרֶךְ אַפַּיִם וּגְדָל חָסֶד.

« in [bestowing] kindness. ‹ and great ‹ to anger, ‹ slow « is Hashem, ‹ and merciful ‹ Gracious « they will sing joyfully.

טוֹב יהוה לַכֹּל, וְרַחֲמָיו עַל כָּל מַעֲשָׂיו. יוֹדוּךָ יהוה

« Hashem ‹ They will thank You, « His creations. ‹ all ‹ are on ‹ His mercies « to all; ‹ Hashem is good

כָּל מַעֲשֶׂיךָ, וַחֲסִידֶיךָ יְבָרְכוּכָה. כְּבוֹד מַלְכוּתְךָ

‹ of Your kingdom ‹ Of the glory « will bless You. ‹ and Your devout ones « Your creations, ‹ — all

יֹאמֵרוּ, וּגְבוּרָתְךָ יְדַבֵּרוּ. לְהוֹדִיעַ לִבְנֵי הָאָדָם

‹ mankind ‹ To inform « they will declare. ‹ and of Your power « they will speak,

גְּבוּרֹתָיו, וּכְבוֹד הֲדַר מַלְכוּתוֹ. מַלְכוּתְךָ מַלְכוּת

‹ is a kingdom ‹ Your kingdom « of His kingdom. ‹ splendor ‹ and of the glorious « of His mighty deeds,

כָּל עֹלָמִים, וּמֶמְשַׁלְתְּךָ בְּכָל דֹּר וָדֹר. סוֹמֵךְ יהוה

[span-ning] all ‹ eternities, ‹‹ and Your dominion ‹ throughout ‹ is ‹ gen-eration ‹ after generation. ‹‹ HASHEM supports ‹

לְכָל הַנֹּפְלִים, וְזוֹקֵף לְכָל הַכְּפוּפִים. עֵינֵי כֹל אֵלֶיךָ

all ‹ those who are fallen, ‹‹ and straightens ‹ all ‹ those who are bent. ‹‹ The eyes ‹ of all ‹ to You ‹

יְשַׂבֵּרוּ, וְאַתָּה נוֹתֵן לָהֶם אֶת אָכְלָם בְּעִתּוֹ.

do look with hope, ‹‹ and You ‹ give ‹ them ‹ their food ‹ in its proper time. ‹‹

CONCENTRATE INTENTLY WHILE RECITING THE VERSE **פּוֹתֵחַ**, *"YOU OPEN . . ."*
IT IS CUSTOMARY TO TOUCH THE ARM-*TEFILLIN* WHILE SAYING THE FIRST HALF OF THE VERSE, AND THE HEAD-*TEFILLIN* WHILE SAYING THE SECOND.

פּוֹתֵחַ אֶת יָדֶךָ, וּמַשְׂבִּיעַ לְכָל חַי רָצוֹן. **צַ**דִּיק יהוה

You open ‹ Your hand, ‹‹ and satisfy ‹ every ‹ living thing ‹ [with its] desire. ‹‹ Right-eous ‹ is HASHEM ‹

בְּכָל דְּרָכָיו, וְחָסִיד בְּכָל מַעֲשָׂיו. קָרוֹב יהוה לְכָל

in all ‹ His ways, ‹‹ and magnanimous ‹ in all ‹ His deeds. ‹‹ Close ‹ is HASHEM ‹ to all ‹

קֹרְאָיו, לְכֹל אֲשֶׁר יִקְרָאֻהוּ בֶאֱמֶת. רְצוֹן יְרֵאָיו

who call upon Him, ‹‹ to all ‹ who ‹ call upon Him ‹ sincerely. ‹‹ The will ‹ of those who fear Him ‹

יַעֲשֶׂה, וְאֶת שַׁוְעָתָם יִשְׁמַע וְיוֹשִׁיעֵם. שׁוֹמֵר יהוה

He will do; ‹‹ and their cry ‹ He will hear, ‹ and He will save them. ‹‹ HASHEM protects ‹

אֶת כָּל אֹהֲבָיו, וְאֵת כָּל הָרְשָׁעִים יַשְׁמִיד. ❖ תְּהִלַּת

all ‹ who love Him; ‹‹ but all ‹ the wicked ‹ He will destroy. ‹‹ The praise ‹

יהוה יְדַבֶּר פִּי, וִיבָרֵךְ כָּל בָּשָׂר שֵׁם קָדְשׁוֹ לְעוֹלָם

of HASHEM ‹ may my mouth declare, ‹‹ and bless ‹ may all ‹ flesh ‹ the Name ‹ of His Holiness ‹ for ever ‹

וָעֶד. וַאֲנַחְנוּ נְבָרֵךְ יָהּ מֵעַתָּה וְעַד עוֹלָם, הַלְלוּיָהּ.[1]

and ever. ‹‹ But we ‹ will bless ‹ God ‹ from this time ‹ until ‹ eternity. ‹‹ Halleluyah! ‹‹

THE *CHAZZAN* RECITES HALF-*KADDISH*:

יִתְגַּדַּל וְיִתְקַדַּשׁ שְׁמֵהּ רַבָּא. (Cong. — אָמֵן.) בְּעָלְמָא דִּי

Grow exalted ‹ and be sanctified ‹ may His Name ‹ that is great! — ‹‹ (Amen.) ‹ — in the world ‹ that ‹

(1) *Psalms* 115:18.

בְּרָא כִרְעוּתֵהּ. וְיַמְלִיךְ מַלְכוּתֵהּ, בְּחַיֵּיכוֹן וּבְיוֹמֵיכוֹן וּבְחַיֵּי

‹ and in the lifetimes ‹ and in your days, ‹ in your lifetimes « to His kingship, ‹ and may He give reign « according to His will, ‹ He created

דְכָל בֵּית יִשְׂרָאֵל, בַּעֲגָלָא וּבִזְמַן קָרִיב. וְאִמְרוּ: אָמֵן.

« Amen. ‹ Now respond: « that comes soon. ‹ and at a time ‹ swiftly « of Israel, ‹ Family ‹ of the entire

CONGREGATION RESPONDS:

אָמֵן. יְהֵא שְׁמֵהּ רַבָּא מְבָרַךְ לְעָלַם וּלְעָלְמֵי עָלְמַיָּא.

« and for all eternity. ‹ forever ‹ be blessed ‹ that is great ‹ His Name ‹ May « Amen.

CHAZZAN CONTINUES:

יְהֵא שְׁמֵהּ רַבָּא מְבָרַךְ לְעָלַם וּלְעָלְמֵי עָלְמַיָּא. יִתְבָּרַךְ

‹ Blessed, « and for all eternity. ‹ forever ‹ be blessed ‹ that is great ‹ His Name ‹ May

וְיִשְׁתַּבַּח וְיִתְפָּאַר וְיִתְרוֹמַם וְיִתְנַשֵּׂא וְיִתְהַדָּר וְיִתְעַלֶּה

‹ elevated, ‹ honored, ‹ upraised, ‹ exalted, ‹ glorified, ‹ praised,

וְיִתְהַלָּל שְׁמֵהּ דְּקֻדְשָׁא בְּרִיךְ הוּא (Cong. — בְּרִיךְ הוּא) —

« is He) ‹ (Blessed « is He ‹ Blessed ‹ of the Holy One, ‹ be the Name ‹ and lauded

לְעֵלָּא מִן כָּל בִּרְכָתָא וְשִׁירָתָא תֻּשְׁבְּחָתָא וְנֶחֱמָתָא

‹ and consolation ‹ praise « and song, ‹ blessing ‹ any ‹ beyond

דַּאֲמִירָן בְּעָלְמָא. וְאִמְרוּ: אָמֵן. (Cong. — אָמֵן.)

« (Amen.) « Amen. ‹ Now respond: « in the world. ‹ that are uttered

הוצאת ספר תורה

REMOVAL OF THE TORAH FROM THE ARK

FROM THE MOMENT THE ARK IS OPENED UNTIL THE TORAH IS RETURNED TO IT, ONE MUST CONDUCT HIMSELF WITH THE UTMOST RESPECT AND AVOID UNNECESSARY CONVERSATION. IT IS COMMENDABLE TO KISS THE TORAH AS IT IS CARRIED TO THE *BIMAH* (READING TABLE) AND BACK TO THE ARK.

ALL RISE AND REMAIN STANDING UNTIL THE TORAH IS PLACED ON THE *BIMAH*.
THE ARK IS OPENED; BEFORE THE TORAH IS REMOVED THE CONGREGATION RECITES:

וַיְהִי בִּנְסֹעַ הָאָרֹן, וַיֹּאמֶר מֹשֶׁה, קוּמָה יהוה

‹ *HASHEM,* ‹ *Arise,* « Moses would say: ‹ would the Ark ‹ that when travel ‹ It would be

וְיָפֻצוּ אֹיְבֶיךָ, וְיָנֻסוּ מְשַׂנְאֶיךָ מִפָּנֶיךָ.[1] כִּי מִצִּיּוֹן

‹ from Zion ‹ For « *from before You.* ‹ *those who hate You* ‹ *Let flee* « *be Your foes.* ‹ *and let scattered*

(1) *Numbers* 10:35.

תֵּצֵא תוֹרָה, וּדְבַר יהוה מִירוּשָׁלָיִם.[1] בָּרוּךְ שֶׁנָּתַן

‹will come forth ‹the Torah, «and the word ‹of HASHEM ‹from Jerusalem. «Blessed ‹is He Who gave

תּוֹרָה לְעַמּוֹ יִשְׂרָאֵל בִּקְדֻשָּׁתוֹ.

‹the Torah ‹to His people ‹Israel ‹in His holiness. «

Zohar, Vayakhel 206a / זוהר ויקהל רו:א

בְּרִיךְ שְׁמֵהּ דְּמָרֵא עָלְמָא, בְּרִיךְ כִּתְרָךְ וְאַתְרָךְ.

‹Blessed ‹is the Name ‹of the Master ‹of the universe; «blessed ‹is Your crown ‹and Your place. «

יְהֵא רְעוּתָךְ עִם עַמָּךְ יִשְׂרָאֵל לְעָלַם, וּפֻרְקַן

‹May Your favor be ‹with ‹Your people ‹Israel ‹forever, «and the salvation

יְמִינָךְ אַחֲזֵי לְעַמָּךְ בְּבֵית מַקְדְּשָׁךְ, וּלְאַמְטוּיֵי

‹of Your right hand ‹may You display ‹to Your people ‹in Your holy Temple, «to extend

לָנָא מִטּוּב נְהוֹרָךְ, וּלְקַבֵּל צְלוֹתָנָא בְּרַחֲמִין.

‹to us ‹of the goodness ‹of Your light, «and to accept ‹our prayers ‹with mercy. «

יְהֵא רַעֲוָא קֳדָמָךְ, דְּתוֹרִיךְ לָן חַיִּין בְּטִיבוּתָא,

‹May it be ‹the will ‹before You ‹that You extend ‹for us ‹life ‹with goodness, «

וְלֶהֱוֵי אֲנָא פְּקִידָא בְּגוֹ צַדִּיקַיָּא, לְמִרְחַם עָלַי

‹and it should be that ‹I ‹am counted ‹among ‹the righteous; «that You have mercy ‹on me «

וּלְמִנְטַר יָתִי וְיַת כָּל דִּי לִי וְדִי לְעַמָּךְ יִשְׂרָאֵל.

‹and protect ‹me, «and all ‹that ‹is mine «and [all] that ‹belongs to Your people ‹Israel. «

אַנְתְּ הוּא זָן לְכֹלָּא, וּמְפַרְנֵס לְכֹלָּא, אַנְתְּ הוּא

‹It is You ‹Who ‹nourishes ‹all ‹and sustains ‹all; «it is You ‹Who

שַׁלִּיט עַל כֹּלָּא. אַנְתְּ הוּא דְּשַׁלִּיט עַל מַלְכַיָּא,

‹rules ‹over ‹everything. «It is You ‹Who ‹rules ‹over ‹kings,

וּמַלְכוּתָא דִּילָךְ הִיא. אֲנָא עַבְדָּא דְקֻדְשָׁא בְּרִיךְ

‹and kingship ‹is Yours. «I am ‹a servant ‹of the Holy One, ‹Blessed

(1) *Isaiah* 2:3.

הוּא, דְּסָגִידְנָא קַמֵּהּ וּמִקַּמָּא דִּיקַר אוֹרַיְתֵהּ

〈 of His Torah 〈 the glory 〈 and before 〈 before Him 〈 and prostrate myself 《 is He,

בְּכָל עִדָּן וְעִדָּן. לָא עַל אֱנָשׁ רָחִיצְנָא, וְלָא עַל

〈 on 〈 nor 《 do I put trust, 〈 any man 〈 in 〈 Not 《 times. 〈 at all

בַּר אֱלָהִין סָמִיכְנָא, אֶלָּא בֶּאֱלָהָא דִשְׁמַיָּא, דְּהוּא

〈 Who is 〈 of heaven, 〈 on the God 〈 — only 《 do I rely 〈 any angel

אֱלָהָא קְשׁוֹט, וְאוֹרַיְתֵהּ קְשׁוֹט, וּנְבִיאוֹהִי קְשׁוֹט,

《 are true, 〈 Whose prophets 《 is truth, 〈 Whose Torah 《 of truth, 〈 the God

וּמַסְגֵּא לְמֶעְבַּד טַבְוָן וּקְשׁוֹט. בֵּהּ אֲנָא רָחִיץ,

《 trust, 〈 I 〈 In Him 《 and truth. 〈 with kindness 〈 acts 〈 and Who abundantly

וְלִשְׁמֵהּ קַדִּישָׁא יַקִּירָא אֲנָא אֵמַר תֻּשְׁבְּחָן. יְהֵא

〈 May it be 《 praises. 〈 declare 〈 I 〈 and glorious — 〈 — holy 〈 and to His Name,

רַעֲוָא קֳדָמָךְ, דְּתִפְתַּח לִבָּאִי בְּאוֹרַיְתָא, וְתַשְׁלִים

〈 and that You fulfill 《 to the Torah, 〈 my heart 〈 that You open 〈 before You 〈 the will

מִשְׁאֲלִין דְּלִבָּאִי, וְלִבָּא דְכָל עַמָּךְ יִשְׂרָאֵל,

〈 Israel 〈 Your people 〈 of all 〈 and the heart 〈 of my heart 〈 the wishes

לְטַב וּלְחַיִּין וְלִשְׁלָם. (אָמֵן.)

《 (Amen.) 《 and for peace. 〈 for life, 〈 for good,

THE TORAH SCROLL IS REMOVED FROM THE ARK AND PRESENTED TO THE *CHAZZAN,* WHO ACCEPTS IT IN HIS RIGHT ARM. HE THEN TURNS TO THE ARK, BOWS WHILE RAISING THE TORAH AND RECITES:

גַּדְּלוּ לַיהוה אִתִּי, וּנְרוֹמְמָה שְׁמוֹ יַחְדָּו.[1]

《 in unison. 〈 His Name 〈 and let us exalt 《 with me, 〈 of HASHEM 〈 Declare the greatness

THE *CHAZZAN* TURNS TO HIS RIGHT AND CARRIES THE TORAH TO THE *BIMAH,* AS THE CONGREGATION RESPONDS:

לְךָ יהוה הַגְּדֻלָּה וְהַגְּבוּרָה וְהַתִּפְאֶרֶת וְהַנֵּצַח

〈 the triumph, 〈 the glory, 〈 the strength, 〈 is the greatness, 〈 HASHEM, 〈 Yours,

(1) *Psalms* 34:4.

וְהַהוֹד, כִּי כֹל בַּשָּׁמַיִם וּבָאָרֶץ, לְךָ יהוה הַמַּמְלָכָה

‹ is the kingdom, ‹ HASHEM, ‹ Yours, « and on earth [is Yours]; ‹ in heaven ‹ everything ‹ for « and the majesty;

וְהַמִּתְנַשֵּׂא לְכֹל לְרֹאשׁ.[1] רוֹמְמוּ יהוה אֱלֹהֵינוּ

‹ our God, ‹ HASHEM, ‹ Exalt « leader. ‹ over every ‹ and the sovereignty

וְהִשְׁתַּחֲווּ לַהֲדֹם רַגְלָיו, קָדוֹשׁ הוּא. רוֹמְמוּ יהוה

‹ HASHEM, ‹ Exalt « is He! ‹ holy « at His footstool; ‹ and bow down

אֱלֹהֵינוּ וְהִשְׁתַּחֲווּ לְהַר קָדְשׁוֹ, כִּי קָדוֹשׁ יהוה

‹ is HASHEM, ‹ holy ‹ for « of His holiness; ‹ at the Mount ‹ and bow down ‹ our God,

אֱלֹהֵינוּ.[2]

« our God.

AS THE *CHAZZAN* CARRIES THE TORAH, THE CONGREGATION RECITES:

אַב הָרַחֲמִים, הוּא יְרַחֵם עַם עֲמוּסִים, וְיִזְכֹּר

‹ and may He remember « that is borne [by Him], ‹ on the nation ‹ have mercy ‹ May He « of compassion! ‹ Father

בְּרִית אֵיתָנִים, וְיַצִּיל נַפְשׁוֹתֵינוּ מִן הַשָּׁעוֹת

‹ the times ‹ from ‹ our souls ‹ May He rescue « of the [spiritually] mighty ones. ‹ the covenant

הָרָעוֹת, וְיִגְעַר בְּיֵצֶר הָרַע מִן הַנְּשׂוּאִים, וְיָחֹן

‹ graciously grant « [harming] those carried by Him, ‹ from ‹ the Evil Inclination ‹ and denounce « that are bad,

אוֹתָנוּ לִפְלֵיטַת עוֹלָמִים, וִימַלֵּא מִשְׁאֲלוֹתֵינוּ

‹ our requests ‹ and fulfill « eternal deliverance, ‹ us

בְּמִדָּה טוֹבָה יְשׁוּעָה וְרַחֲמִים.

« and mercy. ‹ with salvation ‹ in good measure,

THE TORAH IS PLACED ON THE *BIMAH* AND PREPARED FOR READING.
THE GABBAI USES THE FOLLOWING FORMULA TO CALL A *KOHEN* TO THE TORAH:

וְתִגָּלֶה וְתֵרָאֶה מַלְכוּתוֹ עָלֵינוּ בִּזְמַן קָרוֹב, וְיָחֹן

‹ and May He be gracious « that comes soon, ‹ at a time ‹ over us ‹ may His Kingship ‹ and become visible ‹ And be revealed

פְּלֵיטָתֵנוּ וּפְלֵיטַת עַמּוֹ בֵּית יִשְׂרָאֵל לְחֵן וּלְחֶסֶד

‹ for kindness, ‹ for graciousness, « of Israel, ‹ the Family ‹ of His people, ‹ and the remnant ‹ to our remnant

(1) *I Chronicles* 29:11. (2) *Psalms* 99:5, 9.

וּלְרַחֲמִים וּלְרָצוֹן. וְנֹאמַר אָמֵן. הַכֹּל הָבוּ גֹדֶל לֵאלֹהֵינוּ וּתְנוּ

for mercy, and for favor. And let us respond: Amen. Everyone ascribe greatness to our God and give

כָבוֹד לַתּוֹרָה. °כֹּהֵן קְרָב, יַעֲמֹד (NAME) בֶּן (FATHER'S NAME) הַכֹּהֵן.

honor to the Torah. *Kohen,* approach! Arise, (NAME) son of (FATHER'S NAME) the *Kohen!*

°IF NO *KOHEN* IS PRESENT, THE *GABBAI* SAYS:

אֵין כַּאן כֹּהֵן יַעֲמֹד (NAME) בֶּן (FATHER'S NAME) יִשְׂרָאֵל (לֵוִי)

No *Kohen* is present. Arise, (NAME) son of (FATHER'S NAME) the Israelite (the Levite),

בִּמְקוֹם כֹּהֵן.

in place of a *Kohen!*

בָּרוּךְ שֶׁנָּתַן תּוֹרָה לְעַמּוֹ יִשְׂרָאֵל בִּקְדֻשָּׁתוֹ. (תּוֹרַת יהוה

Blessed is He Who gave the Torah to His people Israel in His holiness. (The Torah of HASHEM

תְּמִימָה מְשִׁיבַת נָפֶשׁ, עֵדוּת יהוה נֶאֱמָנָה מַחְכִּימַת

is perfect, restoring the soul; the testimony of HASHEM is trustworthy, making wise

פֶּתִי. פִּקּוּדֵי יהוה יְשָׁרִים מְשַׂמְּחֵי לֵב, מִצְוַת יהוה

the simple one. The orders of HASHEM are upright, gladdening the heart; the command of HASHEM

בָּרָה מְאִירַת עֵינָיִם.[1] יהוה עֹז לְעַמּוֹ יִתֵּן, יהוה יְבָרֵךְ

is clear, enlightening the eyes. HASHEM, strength to His people will give; HASHEM will bless

אֶת עַמּוֹ בַשָּׁלוֹם.[2] הָאֵל תָּמִים דַּרְכּוֹ, אִמְרַת יהוה צְרוּפָה,

His people with peace. The God! Perfect is His way; the utterance of HASHEM is flawless;

מָגֵן הוּא לְכֹל הַחֹסִים בּוֹ.[3])

a shield He is for all who take refuge in Him).

CONGREGATION, THEN GABBAI:

וְאַתֶּם הַדְּבֵקִים בַּיהוה אֱלֹהֵיכֶם, חַיִּים כֻּלְּכֶם הַיּוֹם.[4]

And you who cling to HASHEM, your God, you are alive — all of you — today.

THE LAWS OF THE TORAH READING ARE FOUND ON PAGE 640.

---

(1) *Psalms* 19:8-9. (2) 29:11. (3) *II Samuel* 22:31; cf. *Psalms* 18:31. (4) *Deuteronomy* 4:4.

BLESSINGS FOR THE TORAH / ברכות התורה

THE READER SHOWS THE *OLEH* (PERSON CALLED TO THE TORAH) THE PLACE IN THE TORAH. THE *OLEH* TOUCHES THE TORAH WITH THE CORNER OF HIS *TALLIS*, OR THE BELT OR MANTLE OF THE TORAH, AND KISSES IT. HE THEN BEGINS THE BLESSING, BOWING AT בָּרְכוּ, AND STRAIGHTENING UP AT ה'.

בָּרְכוּ אֶת יהוה הַמְּבֹרָךְ.

Bless ‹ HASHEM, ‹ the blessed One. «

CONGREGATION, FOLLOWED BY *OLEH*, RESPONDS, BOWING AT בָּרוּךְ, AND STRAIGHTENING UP AT ה'.

בָּרוּךְ יהוה הַמְּבֹרָךְ לְעוֹלָם וָעֶד.

Blessed ‹ is HASHEM, ‹ the blessed One, ‹ for ever ‹ and ever. «

***OLEH* CONTINUES:**

בָּרוּךְ אַתָּה יהוה אֱלֹהֵינוּ מֶלֶךְ הָעוֹלָם, אֲשֶׁר בָּחַר בָּנוּ מִכָּל הָעַמִּים, וְנָתַן לָנוּ אֶת תּוֹרָתוֹ.

Blessed ‹ are You, ‹ HASHEM, « our God, ‹ King ‹ of the universe, « Who ‹ selected ‹ us ‹ from all ‹ the peoples ‹ and gave ‹ us ‹ His Torah. «

בָּרוּךְ אַתָּה יהוה, נוֹתֵן הַתּוֹרָה. (.Cong. – אָמֵן)

Blessed ‹ are You, ‹ HASHEM, « Giver ‹ of the Torah. « (Amen.) «

AFTER HIS TORAH PORTION HAS BEEN READ, THE *OLEH* RECITES:

בָּרוּךְ אַתָּה יהוה אֱלֹהֵינוּ מֶלֶךְ הָעוֹלָם, אֲשֶׁר נָתַן לָנוּ תּוֹרַת אֱמֶת, וְחַיֵּי עוֹלָם נָטַע בְּתוֹכֵנוּ.

Blessed ‹ are You, ‹ HASHEM, « our God, ‹ King ‹ of the universe, « Who ‹ gave ‹ us ‹ the Torah ‹ of truth « and the life ‹ of eternity ‹ He implanted ‹ within us. «

בָּרוּךְ אַתָּה יהוה, נוֹתֵן הַתּוֹרָה. (.Cong. – אָמֵן)

Blessed ‹ are You, ‹ HASHEM, « Giver ‹ of the Torah. « (Amen.) «

THE *MI SHEBEIRACH* PRAYER FOR A SICK PERSON APPEARS ON PAGE 198.

☙ Torah Reading

The afternoon Torah reading for Tishah B'Av is the same as that read on the other fast days. Rather than an admonition that outlines the national weaknesses that cause the sorts of tragedy commemorated by the fast day, this reading might be described as an "antidote" to the calamity.

While Moses was on Mount Sinai receiving the Torah and the Tablets of the Law, his people in the Wilderness were making the Golden Calf and giving it their allegiance. God told Moses that the purpose of his mission no longer existed; he was the representative of Israel, but his nation had betrayed God. He told Moses that He would destroy the nation, and begin anew with Moses and his offspring. But in making this chilling declaration to Moses, God asked Moses to "permit Him" to do so — this implied that Moses could prevent the destruction of Israel (see *Rashi* to *Exodus* 32:10). From this, Moses understood that his prayers could save Israel, and he immediately begged God to

TORAH READING / קריאת התורה

Exodus 32:11-14; 34:1-10 / שמות לב:יא-יד;לד:א-י

UPON REACHING THE PHRASE IN BOLD TYPE, THE READER PAUSES. THE CONGREGATION RECITES THE PHRASES, AFTER WHICH THEY ARE RECITED BY THE READER.

כהן — וַיְחַל מֹשֶׁה אֶת־פְּנֵי יְהוָה אֱלֹהָיו וַיֹּאמֶר

KOHEN Moses pleaded ‹ before the Presence ‹ of HASHEM, ‹ his God, ‹ and said, «

לָמָה יהוה יֶחֱרֶה אַפְּךָ בְּעַמֶּךָ אֲשֶׁר הוֹצֵאתָ

Why, ‹ *HASHEM,* ‹ *should flare up* ‹ *Your anger* ‹ *against Your people,* ‹ *whom* ‹ *You have taken out* ‹

מֵאֶרֶץ מִצְרַיִם בְּכֹחַ גָּדוֹל וּבְיָד חֲזָקָה: לָמָּה

of the land ‹ *of Egypt,* ‹ *with power* ‹ *that is great* ‹ *and with a hand* ‹ *that is strong?* « *Why* ‹

יֹאמְרוּ מִצְרַיִם לֵאמֹר בְּרָעָה הוֹצִיאָם לַהֲרֹג אֹתָם

should Egypt be able to say ‹ *the following:* « *With evil intent* ‹ *did He take them out,* ‹ *to kill* ‹ *them* ‹

בֶּהָרִים וּלְכַלֹּתָם מֵעַל פְּנֵי הָאֲדָמָה **שׁוּב מֵחֲרוֹן**

in the mountains ‹ *and to annihilate them* ‹ *from upon* ‹ *the face* ‹ *of the earth?* « ***Relent*** ‹ ***from the flaring*** ‹

אַפֶּךָ וְהִנָּחֵם עַל־הָרָעָה לְעַמֶּךָ: זְכֹר לְאַבְרָהָם

of Your anger ‹ ***and reconsider*** ‹ ***regarding*** ‹ ***the evil*** ‹ ***against Your people.*** « *Remember* ‹ *for [the sake of] Abraham,* ‹

לְיִצְחָק וּלְיִשְׂרָאֵל עֲבָדֶיךָ אֲשֶׁר נִשְׁבַּעְתָּ לָהֶם בָּךְ

of Isaac, ‹ *and of Israel,* ‹ *Your servants,* « *that* ‹ *You swore* ‹ *to them* ‹ *by Your very Self,* «

וַתְּדַבֵּר אֲלֵהֶם אַרְבֶּה אֶת־זַרְעֲכֶם כְּכוֹכְבֵי הַשָּׁמָיִם

and You said ‹ *to them,* « *"I shall increase* ‹ *your offspring* ‹ *like the stars* ‹ *of heaven,* «

וְכָל־הָאָרֶץ הַזֹּאת אֲשֶׁר אָמַרְתִּי אֶתֵּן לְזַרְעֲכֶם

and this entire land ‹ *of which* ‹ *I spoke,* ‹ *I shall give* ‹ *to your offspring* ‹

---

spare them.

The first portion of this reading is his prayer on the mountain; after returning to the camp, he smashed the Tablets and took charge of a mass repentance, which made Israel worthy to receive the Second Tablets. The rest of the reading skips to God's command that Moses fashion a pair of Tablets, upon which God would inscribe the Ten Commandments a second time. In the context of the fast days, the significance of the passage is that in it God

וְנָחֲלוּ לְעֹלָם: וַיִּנָּחֶם יהוה עַל־הָרָעָה אֲשֶׁר

‹ that ‹ the evil ‹ regarding ‹ HASHEM reconsidered « *forever."* ‹ *and they shall have it as a heritage*

דִּבֶּר לַעֲשׂוֹת לְעַמּוֹ:

« to His people. ‹ of doing ‹ He spoke

לוי — וַיֹּאמֶר יהוה אֶל־מֹשֶׁה פְּסָל־לְךָ שְׁנֵי־לֻחֹת

‹ *Tablets* ‹ *two* ‹ *for yourself* ‹ *Carve* « Moses, ‹ to ‹ HASHEM said ***LEVITE***

אֲבָנִים כָּרִאשֹׁנִים וְכָתַבְתִּי עַל־הַלֻּחֹת אֶת־הַדְּבָרִים

‹ *the words* ‹ *the Tablets* ‹ *on* ‹ *and I shall inscribe* « *like the first ones,* ‹ *of stone*

אֲשֶׁר הָיוּ עַל־הַלֻּחֹת הָרִאשֹׁנִים אֲשֶׁר שִׁבַּרְתָּ: וֶהְיֵה

‹ *Be* « *you shattered.* ‹ *which* ‹ *the first Tablets,* ‹ *on* ‹ *were* ‹ *that*

נָכוֹן לַבֹּקֶר וְעָלִיתָ בַבֹּקֶר אֶל־הַר סִינַי וְנִצַּבְתָּ

‹ *and you should stand waiting* ‹ *Sinai* ‹ *Mount* ‹ *to* ‹ *in the morning* ‹ *you should go up* « *for the morning;* ‹ *prepared*

לִי שָׁם עַל־רֹאשׁ הָהָר: וְאִישׁ לֹא־יַעֲלֶה עִמָּךְ

‹ *with you* ‹ *go up* ‹ *may not* ‹ *Any man* « *of the mountain.* ‹ *the top* ‹ *on* ‹ *there* ‹ *for Me*

וְגַם־אִישׁ אַל־יֵרָא בְּכָל־הָהָר גַּם־הַצֹּאן וְהַבָּקָר

‹ *and the cattle* ‹ *the flock* ‹ *Even* « *mountain.* ‹ *on the entire* ‹ *be seen* ‹ *may not* ‹ *any man* ‹ *and also*

אַל־יִרְעוּ אֶל־מוּל הָהָר הַהוּא:

« *that mountain.* ‹ *facing* ‹ *graze* ‹ *may not*

---

taught Moses the Thirteen Attributes of Mercy, which are now the central theme of the fast-day *Selichos* (except for Tishah B'Av) and of the evening and *Ne'ilah* services of Yom Kippur. According to R' Yochanan (*Rosh Hashanah* 17b), Moses thought that Israel's sin was so grievous that there was no possibility for him to intercede on their behalf. Thereupon God appeared to him in the form of a *chazzan* wrapped in a *tallis* and taught him the Thirteen Attributes. God said, "Whenever Israel sins, let them recite this in its proper order and I shall forgive them." Thus the appeal found in this Torah reading reassures us that repentance is always possible and that God always awaits our return.

Since it is axiomatic that punishment and exile are always the result of Jewish shortcomings, and as Rambam teaches, we fast to remind ourselves that no Jewish suffering is coincidental, this Torah reading teaches us the way to curtail the suffering and end the exile.

ישראל (מפטיר) — וַיִּפְסֹל שְׁנֵי־לֻחֹת אֲבָנִים כָּרִאשֹׁנִים

YISRAEL (MAFTIR) So he carved out 〈 two 〈 Tablets 〈 of stone 〈 like the first ones. 《

וַיַּשְׁכֵּם מֹשֶׁה בַבֹּקֶר וַיַּעַל אֶל־הַר סִינַי כַּאֲשֶׁר

Moses arose early 〈 in the morning 〈 and went up 〈 to 〈 Mount 〈 Sinai, 《 as 〈

צִוָּה יהוה אֹתוֹ וַיִּקַּח בְּיָדוֹ שְׁנֵי לֻחֹת אֲבָנִים׃

HASHEM had commanded 〈 him, 《 and he took 〈 in his hand 〈 two 〈 Tablets 〈 of stone. 《

וַיֵּרֶד יהוה בֶּעָנָן וַיִּתְיַצֵּב עִמּוֹ שָׁם וַיִּקְרָא בְשֵׁם

HASHEM descended 〈 in a cloud 〈 and stood 〈 with him 〈 there, 《 and He called out 〈 with the Name 〈

יהוה׃ וַיַּעֲבֹר יהוה | עַל־פָּנָיו וַיִּקְרָא **יהוה | יהוה**

HASHEM. 《 HASHEM passed 〈 before 〈 his face 〈 and He called out: 《 ***HASHEM,*** 〈 ***HASHEM,*** 〈

אֵל רַחוּם וְחַנּוּן אֶרֶךְ אַפַּיִם וְרַב־חֶסֶד וֶאֱמֶת׃

God, 〈 ***Compassionate*** 〈 ***and Gracious,*** 〈 ***Slow*** 〈 ***to Anger,*** 〈 ***and Abundant*** 〈 ***in Kindness*** 〈 ***and Truth;*** 《

נֹצֵר חֶסֶד לָאֲלָפִים נֹשֵׂא עָוֺן וָפֶשַׁע וְחַטָּאָה

Preserver 〈 ***of Kindness*** 〈 ***for thousands [of generations],*** 〈 ***Forgiver*** 〈 ***of Iniquity,*** 〈 ***Willful Sin,*** 〈 ***and inadvertent sin,*** 〈

וְנַקֵּה לֹא יְנַקֶּה פֹּקֵד | עֲוֺן אָבוֹת עַל־בָּנִים וְעַל־

and Who Absolves 《 *— but does not* 〈 *absolve [completely],* 《 *remembering* 〈 *the iniquity* 〈 *of fathers* 〈 *upon* 〈 *children* 〈 *and upon* 〈

בְּנֵי בָנִים עַל־שִׁלֵּשִׁים וְעַל־רִבֵּעִים׃ וַיְמַהֵר מֹשֶׁה

children 〈 *of children,* 〈 *and upon* 〈 *the third [generation]* 〈 *and upon* 〈 *the fourth generation.* 《 Moses hurried 〈

וַיִּקֹּד אַרְצָה וַיִּשְׁתָּחוּ׃ וַיֹּאמֶר אִם־נָא מָצָאתִי חֵן

and bowed his head 〈 toward the ground 〈 and he prostrated himself. 《 He said, 〈 *If* 〈 *now* 〈 *I have found* 〈 *favor* 〈

בְּעֵינֶיךָ אֲדֹנָי יֵלֶךְ־נָא אֲדֹנָי בְּקִרְבֵּנוּ כִּי עַם־קְשֵׁה־

in Your eyes, 〈 *O Lord,* 〈 *let the Lord go now* 〈 *in our midst* 《 *— and if* 〈 *a people* 〈 *that is stiff* 〈

עֹרֶף הוּא **וְסָלַחְתָּ לַעֲוֺנֵנוּ וּלְחַטָּאתֵנוּ וּנְחַלְתָּנוּ׃**

necked 〈 *they are,* 《 ***then You will forgive*** 〈 ***our iniquities*** 〈 ***and our sins,*** 〈 ***and make us Your heritage.*** 《

וַיֹּאמֶר הִנֵּה אָנֹכִי כֹּרֵת בְּרִית נֶגֶד כָּל־עַמְּךָ אֶעֱשֶׂה

He said, Indeed! I establish a covenant: Before your entire people I shall perform

נִפְלָאֹת אֲשֶׁר לֹא־נִבְרְאוּ בְכָל־הָאָרֶץ וּבְכָל־הַגּוֹיִם

wonders such as have never been created in the entire world and among all the nations;

וְרָאָה כָל־הָעָם אֲשֶׁר־אַתָּה בְקִרְבּוֹ אֶת־מַעֲשֵׂה

and they will see — the entire people that you are in their midst — the work

יהוה כִּי־נוֹרָא הוּא אֲשֶׁר אֲנִי עֹשֶׂה עִמָּךְ:

of HASHEM — for awesome it is — that I am about to do with you.

HAGBAHAH AND GELILAH / הגבהה וגלילה

ALL STAND. THE TORAH IS RAISED FOR ALL TO SEE. EACH PERSON LOOKS AT THE TORAH AND RECITES ALOUD:

וְזֹאת הַתּוֹרָה אֲשֶׁר שָׂם מֹשֶׁה לִפְנֵי בְּנֵי יִשְׂרָאֵל,[1] עַל פִּי יהוה בְּיַד מֹשֶׁה.[2]

This is the Torah that Moses placed before the Children of Israel, according to the word of HASHEM, through the hand of Moses.

SOME ADD:

עֵץ חַיִּים הִיא לַמַּחֲזִיקִים בָּהּ, וְתֹמְכֶיהָ מְאֻשָּׁר.[3] דְּרָכֶיהָ דַרְכֵי נֹעַם, וְכָל נְתִיבוֹתֶיהָ שָׁלוֹם.[4] אֹרֶךְ יָמִים בִּימִינָהּ, בִּשְׂמֹאלָהּ עֹשֶׁר וְכָבוֹד.[5] יהוה חָפֵץ לְמַעַן צִדְקוֹ, יַגְדִּיל תּוֹרָה וְיַאְדִּיר.[6]

A tree of life is it for those who grasp it, and its supporters are praiseworthy. Its ways are ways of pleasantness, and all its paths are peace. Length of days is at its right; at its left are wealth and honor. HASHEM desired, for the sake of [Israel's] righteousness, that He make the Torah great and [make it] glorious.

(1) *Deuteronomy* 4:44. (2) *Numbers* 9:23. (3) *Proverbs* 3:18. (4) 3:17. (5) 3:16. (6) *Isaiah* 42:21.

BLESSING BEFORE THE HAFTARAH / ברכה לפני ההפטרה

AFTER THE TORAH SCROLL HAS BEEN WOUND, TIED, AND COVERED, THE *OLEH* FOR *MAFTIR* RECITES THE *HAFTARAH* BLESSING:

בָּרוּךְ אַתָּה יהוה אֱלֹהֵינוּ מֶלֶךְ הָעוֹלָם, אֲשֶׁר

‹ Who « of the universe, ‹ King ‹ our God, « HASHEM, ‹ are You, ‹ Blessed

בָּחַר בִּנְבִיאִים טוֹבִים, וְרָצָה בְדִבְרֵיהֶם הַנֶּאֱמָרִים

‹ that were uttered ‹ with their words ‹ and was pleased ‹ good prophets ‹ has chosen

בֶּאֱמֶת, בָּרוּךְ אַתָּה יהוה, הַבּוֹחֵר בַּתּוֹרָה וּבְמֹשֶׁה

‹ and Moses, ‹ the Torah ‹ Who chooses ‹ HASHEM, ‹ are You, ‹ Blessed « with truth.

עַבְדּוֹ, וּבְיִשְׂרָאֵל עַמּוֹ, וּבִנְבִיאֵי הָאֱמֶת וָצֶדֶק.

« and righteousness. ‹ of truth ‹ and the prophets ‹ His people, ‹ and Israel, ‹ His servant,

(Cong. — אָמֵן.)

« (Amen.)

HAFTARAH / הפטרה

Isaiah 55:6-56:8 / ישעיה נה:ו-נו:ח

[ALTHOUGH THE DIVINE NAME יהוה IS PRONOUNCED AS IF IT WERE SPELLED אֲדֹנָי, WHEN IT IS VOWELIZED יֱהֹוִה, IT IS PRONOUNCED AS IF IT WERE SPELLED אֱלֹהִים.]

דִּרְשׁוּ יהוה בְּהִמָּצְאוֹ קְרָאֻהוּ בִּהְיוֹתוֹ קָרוֹב:

« near. ‹ when He is ‹ call upon Him « when He can be found; ‹ HASHEM ‹ Seek

יַעֲזֹב רָשָׁע דַּרְכּוֹ וְאִישׁ אָוֶן מַחְשְׁבֹתָיו וְיָשֹׁב

‹ and let him return « his thoughts; ‹ of iniquity ‹ and the man « his way, « Let the wicked one forsake

אֶל־יהוה וִירַחֲמֵהוּ וְאֶל־אֱלֹהֵינוּ כִּי־יַרְבֶּה לִסְלוֹחַ:

« in forgiving. ‹ He will be abundant ‹ for ‹ our God ‹ and [return] to « and He will show him mercy, ‹ HASHEM ‹ to

---

The Haftarah

As noted above, fast days represent a call to repentance and the Torah reading is the encouraging message that God is always ready — indeed, anxious — to accept our prayers. The Haftarah is an eloquent expression of that theme. It begins by urging us to seek God where He can be found and when He is near. The commentators explain that these times are before He brings punishment upon us, for then He longs for us to repent and thereby remove the root of His anger; and they are also times when we are ready to seek Him with all our hearts.

God declares that we should not project

כִּי לֹא מַחְשְׁבוֹתַי מַחְשְׁבוֹתֵיכֶם וְלֹא דַרְכֵיכֶם דְּרָכָי

« are My ways, ‹ your ways ‹ and not « are your thoughts, ‹ My thoughts ‹ not ‹ For

נְאֻם יְהוָה: כִּי־גָבְהוּ שָׁמַיִם מֵאָרֶץ כֵּן גָּבְהוּ דְרָכַי

‹ My ways ‹ are elevated ‹ so « over the earth, ‹ are the heavens ‹ elevated ‹ For as « of HASHEM. ‹ the words

מִדַּרְכֵיכֶם וּמַחְשְׁבֹתַי מִמַּחְשְׁבֹתֵיכֶם: כִּי כַּאֲשֶׁר

‹ just as ‹ For « over your thoughts. ‹ and My thoughts « over your ways,

יֵרֵד הַגֶּשֶׁם וְהַשֶּׁלֶג מִן־הַשָּׁמַיִם וְשָׁמָּה לֹא יָשׁוּב

« return, ‹ it does not ‹ and thereto « heaven ‹ from « and the snow — ‹ — the rain « they descend

כִּי אִם־הִרְוָה אֶת־הָאָרֶץ וְהוֹלִידָהּ וְהִצְמִיחָהּ וְנָתַן

‹ and it gives « and causes it to sprout, ‹ and causes it to produce ‹ the earth ‹ it fully waters ‹ rather

זֶרַע לַזֹּרֵעַ וְלֶחֶם לָאֹכֵל: כֵּן יִהְיֶה דְבָרִי אֲשֶׁר יֵצֵא

‹ emanates ‹ that ‹ My word ‹ shall be ‹ so « to the eater; ‹ and food ‹ to the sower ‹ seed

מִפִּי לֹא־יָשׁוּב אֵלַי רֵיקָם כִּי אִם־עָשָׂה אֶת־אֲשֶׁר

‹ what ‹ it will accomplish ‹ rather « unfulfilled, ‹ to Me ‹ it shall not return « from My mouth:

חָפַצְתִּי וְהִצְלִיחַ אֲשֶׁר שְׁלַחְתִּיו: כִּי־בְשִׂמְחָה תֵצֵאוּ

« shall you go out ‹ in gladness ‹ For « I sent it [to do]. ‹ in whatever ‹ and bring success « I desired

וּבְשָׁלוֹם תּוּבָלוּן הֶהָרִים וְהַגְּבָעוֹת יִפְצְחוּ לִפְנֵיכֶם

‹ before you ‹ will break out ‹ and the hills ‹ the mountains « shall you be led; ‹ and in peace

רִנָּה וְכָל־עֲצֵי הַשָּׂדֶה יִמְחֲאוּ־כָף: תַּחַת הַנַּעֲצוּץ

‹ of the thornbush ‹ In place « hands. ‹ will clap ‹ of the field ‹ the trees ‹ and all « in glad song,

יַעֲלֶה בְרוֹשׁ וְתַחַת הַסִּרְפַּד יַעֲלֶה הֲדַס וְהָיָה

‹ This will be « a myrtle. ‹ will arise ‹ of the nettle ‹ and in place « a cypress; ‹ will arise

---

our own base, human frailties onto our perceptions of Him. God is merciful. He guarantees us that everyone who is sincere and ready to serve Him wholeheartedly has a place at His table. Even those who are barren — literally or figuratively — will blossom if they join themselves to Him. The aliens who leave their origins to

לַיהוה לְשֵׁם לְאוֹת עוֹלָם לֹא יִכָּרֵת: כֹּה אָמַר

to HASHEM as a monument, as a sign for eternity, never to be cut down [or terminated]. So said

יהוה שִׁמְרוּ מִשְׁפָּט וַעֲשׂוּ צְדָקָה כִּי־קְרוֹבָה

HASHEM: Observe justice and perform righteousness, for imminent

יְשׁוּעָתִי לָבוֹא וְצִדְקָתִי לְהִגָּלוֹת: אַשְׁרֵי אֱנוֹשׁ

is My salvation to come about, and My righteousness to be revealed. Praiseworthy is the man

יַעֲשֶׂה־זֹּאת וּבֶן־אָדָם יַחֲזִיק בָּהּ שֹׁמֵר שַׁבָּת

who does this, and the son of man who holds fast to it: He who guards the Sabbath

מֵחַלְּלוֹ וְשֹׁמֵר יָדוֹ מֵעֲשׂוֹת כָּל־רָע: וְאַל־יֹאמַר

against desecrating it, and guards his hand against doing any evil. Let [him] not say

בֶּן־הַנֵּכָר הַנִּלְוָה אֶל־יהוה לֵאמֹר הַבְדֵּל יַבְדִּילַנִי

— the member of a foreign nation — who has joined himself to HASHEM, saying: *Certainly set me apart*

יהוה מֵעַל עַמּוֹ וְאַל־יֹאמַר הַסָּרִיס הֵן אֲנִי עֵץ

has HASHEM from being part of His people; and let [him] not say — the barren one: *Indeed, I am a tree*

יָבֵשׁ: כִּי־כֹה | אָמַר יהוה לַסָּרִיסִים אֲשֶׁר יִשְׁמְרוּ

that is shriveled. For so says HASHEM to the barren ones who observe

אֶת־שַׁבְּתוֹתַי וּבָחֲרוּ בַּאֲשֶׁר חָפָצְתִּי וּמַחֲזִיקִים

My Sabbaths and who choose [to keep] what I desire, and who hold fast to

בִּבְרִיתִי: וְנָתַתִּי לָהֶם בְּבֵיתִי וּבְחוֹמֹתַי יָד וָשֵׁם

My covenant. I shall give to them in My House and within My walls a memorial and a monument,

טוֹב מִבָּנִים וּמִבָּנוֹת שֵׁם עוֹלָם אֶתֶּן־לּוֹ אֲשֶׁר

better than sons and daughters; a monument for eternity shall I give him, which

---

become Jews are no longer aliens. To the contrary, they will be the forerunners of the masses who will flock to the truth when the time of redemption finally arrives.

לֹא יִכָּרֵת: וּבְנֵי הַנֵּכָר הַנִּלְוִים עַל־יהוה לְשָׁרְתוֹ

« to serve Him, ‹ HASHEM ‹ unto ‹ who have joined themselves ‹ of a foreign nation ‹ And the members « be cut down [or terminated]. ‹ will never

וּלְאַהֲבָה אֶת־שֵׁם יהוה לִהְיוֹת לוֹ לַעֲבָדִים כָּל־

‹ who- ever « as servants, ‹ to Him ‹ to become « of HASHEM, ‹ the Name ‹ and to love

שֹׁמֵר שַׁבָּת מֵחַלְּלוֹ וּמַחֲזִיקִים בִּבְרִיתִי: וַהֲבִיאוֹתִים

‹ I shall bring them « My covenant — ‹ and those who hold fast to ‹ against desecrating it ‹ the Sabbath ‹ observes

אֶל־הַר קָדְשִׁי וְשִׂמַּחְתִּים בְּבֵית תְּפִלָּתִי עוֹלֹתֵיהֶם

‹ their burnt-offerings « of prayer, ‹ in My house ‹ and I shall gladden them « of holiness, ‹ My mountain ‹ to

וְזִבְחֵיהֶם לְרָצוֹן עַל־מִזְבְּחִי כִּי בֵיתִי בֵּית־תְּפִלָּה

‹ of prayer ‹ as a house ‹ My House ‹ for « My Altar, ‹ upon ‹ will find favor ‹ and their feast-offerings

יִקָּרֵא לְכָל־הָעַמִּים: נְאֻם אֲדֹנָי יֱהֹוִה מְקַבֵּץ

‹ Who gathers in « HASHEM/ELOHIM, ‹ of the Lord, ‹ The words « the peoples. ‹ for all ‹ will be called

נִדְחֵי יִשְׂרָאֵל עוֹד אֲקַבֵּץ עָלָיו לְנִקְבָּצָיו:

« besides their own gathered ones. « to them, ‹ shall I gather ‹ Even more « of Israel: ‹ the dispersed

BLESSINGS AFTER THE HAFTARAH / ברכות לאחר ההפטרה

AFTER THE *HAFTARAH* IS READ, THE *OLEH* FOR *MAFTIR* RECITES THE FOLLOWING BLESSINGS:

בָּרוּךְ אַתָּה יהוה אֱלֹהֵינוּ מֶלֶךְ הָעוֹלָם, צוּר

‹ Rock « of the universe, ‹ King ‹ our God, « HASHEM, ‹ are You, ‹ Blessed

כָּל הָעוֹלָמִים, צַדִּיק בְּכָל הַדּוֹרוֹת, הָאֵל הַנֶּאֱמָן

« Who is trustworthy, ‹ the God « generations, ‹ in all ‹ Righteous ‹ eternities, ‹ of all

הָאוֹמֵר וְעֹשֶׂה, הַמְדַבֵּר וּמְקַיֵּם, שֶׁכָּל דְּבָרָיו אֱמֶת

‹ are true ‹ of His words ‹ Who all « and fulfills, ‹ Who speaks « and does, ‹ Who says

וָצֶדֶק. נֶאֱמָן אַתָּה הוּא יהוה אֱלֹהֵינוּ, וְנֶאֱמָנִים

‹ and trustworthy ‹ our God, ‹ HASHEM, ‹ are You, ‹ Trust- worthy « and righteous.

דְּבָרֶיךָ, וְדָבָר אֶחָד מִדְּבָרֶיךָ אָחוֹר לֹא יָשׁוּב רֵיקָם,

« unfulfilled, ‹ returns ‹ never ‹ back « of Your words ‹ [even] one word « are Your words;

כִּי אֵל מֶלֶךְ נֶאֱמָן (וְרַחֲמָן) אָתָּה. בָּרוּךְ אַתָּה

‹ are You, ‹ Blessed « are You. ‹ (and compassionate) ‹ trustworthy ‹ King, ‹ a God, ‹ for

יהוה, הָאֵל הַנֶּאֱמָן בְּכָל דְּבָרָיו. (Cong.— אָמֵן.)

« (Amen.) « His words. ‹ in all ‹ Who is trustworthy ‹ the God « HASHEM,

רַחֵם עַל צִיּוֹן כִּי הִיא בֵּית חַיֵּינוּ, וְלַעֲלוּבַת

‹ and to [Israel,] who is humiliated « [that is the focus of] our life; ‹ is the place ‹ it ‹ for ‹ Zion, ‹ on ‹ Have mercy

נֶפֶשׁ תּוֹשִׁיעַ בִּמְהֵרָה בְיָמֵינוּ. בָּרוּךְ אַתָּה יהוה,

« HASHEM, ‹ are You, ‹ Blessed « in our days. ‹ speedily, ‹ bring salvation ‹ to her very soul,

מְשַׂמֵּחַ צִיּוֹן בְּבָנֶיהָ. (Cong.— אָמֵן.)

« (Amen.) « through her children. ‹ Zion ‹ Who gladdens

שַׂמְּחֵנוּ יהוה אֱלֹהֵינוּ בְּאֵלִיָּהוּ הַנָּבִיא עַבְדֶּךָ,

« Your servant, ‹ the prophet, ‹ with Elijah ‹ our God, ‹ HASHEM, ‹ Gladden us,

וּבְמַלְכוּת בֵּית דָּוִד מְשִׁיחֶךָ, בִּמְהֵרָה יָבֹא

‹ may he come, ‹ speedily « Your anointed one; ‹ of David, ‹ of the House ‹ and with the kingdom

וְיָגֵל לִבֵּנוּ, עַל כִּסְאוֹ לֹא יֵשֶׁב זָר וְלֹא יִנְחֲלוּ

‹ and do not [allow to] inherit « any stranger, ‹ sit ‹ may there never ‹ his throne ‹ On « and then our hearts will exult.

עוֹד אֲחֵרִים אֶת כְּבוֹדוֹ, כִּי בְשֵׁם קָדְשְׁךָ נִשְׁבַּעְתָּ

‹ You swore ‹ of your Holiness ‹ by the Name ‹ for « his honor, ‹ others ‹ any longer

לּוֹ, שֶׁלֹּא יִכְבֶּה נֵרוֹ לְעוֹלָם וָעֶד. בָּרוּךְ אַתָּה

‹ are You, ‹ Blessed « and ever. ‹ forever ‹ would his lamp be ‹ extinguished ‹ that not « to him

יהוה, מָגֵן דָּוִד. (Cong.— אָמֵן.)

« (Amen.) « of David. ‹ Shield « HASHEM,

RETURNING THE TORAH / הכנסת ספר תורה

CHAZZAN TAKES THE TORAH IN HIS RIGHT ARM AND RECITES:

יְהַלְלוּ אֶת שֵׁם יהוה, כִּי נִשְׂגָּב שְׁמוֹ לְבַדּוֹ —

Let them praise ‹ the Name ‹ of HASHEM, ‹ for ‹ exalted ‹ is His Name ‹ alone; «

CONGREGATION RESPONDS:

— הוֹדוֹ עַל אֶרֶץ וְשָׁמָיִם. וַיָּרֶם קֶרֶן לְעַמּוֹ, תְּהִלָּה

His glory ‹ is above ‹ earth ‹ and heaven. « He has exalted ‹ the pride ‹ of His people, « [causing] praise ‹

לְכָל חֲסִידָיו, לִבְנֵי יִשְׂרָאֵל עַם קְרֹבוֹ, הַלְלוּיָהּ.[1]

for all ‹ His devout ones, « for the Children ‹ of Israel, ‹ the people ‹ with whom He is intimate. « Halleluyah! «

AS THE TORAH IS CARRIED TO THE ARK, THE CONGREGATION RECITES PSALM 24, לְדָוִד מִזְמוֹר.

לְדָוִד מִזְמוֹר; לַיהוה הָאָרֶץ וּמְלוֹאָהּ, תֵּבֵל

By David, ‹ a psalm. « HASHEM's ‹ is the earth ‹ and its fullness, « the inhabited land ‹

וְיֹשְׁבֵי בָהּ. כִּי הוּא עַל יַמִּים יְסָדָהּ, וְעַל נְהָרוֹת

and those who dwell ‹ in it. « For ‹ He ‹ upon ‹ seas ‹ founded it, ‹ and upon ‹ rivers ‹

יְכוֹנְנֶהָ. מִי יַעֲלֶה בְהַר יהוה, וּמִי יָקוּם בִּמְקוֹם

established it. « Who ‹ may ascend ‹ the mountain ‹ of HASHEM, ‹ and who ‹ may stand ‹ in the place ‹

קָדְשׁוֹ. נְקִי כַפַּיִם וּבַר לֵבָב, אֲשֶׁר לֹא נָשָׂא

of His sanctity? « One with clean ‹ hands ‹ and pure ‹ heart; « who ‹ has not ‹ sworn ‹

לַשָּׁוְא נַפְשִׁי וְלֹא נִשְׁבַּע לְמִרְמָה. יִשָּׂא בְרָכָה

in vain ‹ by My soul, « and has not ‹ sworn ‹ deceitfully. « He will receive ‹ a blessing ‹

מֵאֵת יהוה, וּצְדָקָה מֵאֱלֹהֵי יִשְׁעוֹ. זֶה דּוֹר

from ‹ HASHEM « and just kindness ‹ from the God ‹ of his salvation. « This is ‹ the generation ‹

דֹּרְשָׁיו, מְבַקְשֵׁי פָנֶיךָ, יַעֲקֹב, סֶלָה. שְׂאוּ שְׁעָרִים

of those who seek Him, « those who strive for ‹ Your Presence — ‹ [the nation of] Jacob, « Selah. « Raise up, ‹ O gates ‹

(1) *Psalms* 149:13-14.

רָאשֵׁיכֶם, וְהִנָּשְׂאוּ פִּתְחֵי עוֹלָם, וְיָבוֹא מֶלֶךְ

‹ — the King « so that He may enter ‹ [you] everlasting entrances, ‹ and be up-lifted, « your heads,

הַכָּבוֹד. מִי זֶה מֶלֶךְ הַכָּבוֹד, יהוה עִזּוּז וְגִבּוֹר,

« and the strong; ‹ the mighty ‹ HASHEM, « of Glory? ‹ King ‹ is this ‹ Who « of Glory.

יהוה גִּבּוֹר מִלְחָמָה. שְׂאוּ שְׁעָרִים רָאשֵׁיכֶם, וּשְׂאוּ

‹ and raise up, « your heads, ‹ O gates, ‹ Raise up, « in battle. ‹ the strong ‹ HASHEM,

פִּתְחֵי עוֹלָם, וְיָבֹא מֶלֶךְ הַכָּבוֹד. מִי הוּא זֶה מֶלֶךְ

‹ King ‹ this ‹ is He, ‹ Who « of Glory. ‹ — the King « so that He may enter ‹ [you] everlasting entrances,

הַכָּבוֹד, יהוה צְבָאוֹת הוּא מֶלֶךְ הַכָּבוֹד, סֶלָה.

« Selah! « of Glory, ‹ the King ‹ He is ‹ Master of Legions, ‹ HASHEM, « of Glory?

AS THE TORAH IS PLACED INTO THE ARK, THE CONGREGATION RECITES THE FOLLOWING VERSES:

וּבְנֻחֹה יֹאמַר, שׁוּבָה יהוה רִבְבוֹת אַלְפֵי יִשְׂרָאֵל.[1]

« *of Israel.* ‹ *thousands* ‹ *to the myriad* ‹ *HASHEM,* ‹ *Return,* « he would say: ‹ And when it rested

קוּמָה יהוה לִמְנוּחָתֶךָ, אַתָּה וַאֲרוֹן עֻזֶּךָ. כֹּהֲנֶיךָ

‹ Let Your *Kohanim* « of Your strength. ‹ and the Ark ‹ You « to Your resting place, ‹ HASHEM, ‹ Arise

יִלְבְּשׁוּ צֶדֶק, וַחֲסִידֶיךָ יְרַנֵּנוּ. בַּעֲבוּר דָּוִד עַבְדֶּךָ

« Your servant, ‹ of David, ‹ For the sake « will sing joyously. ‹ and Your devout ones « in righteousness, ‹ be clothed

אַל תָּשֵׁב פְּנֵי מְשִׁיחֶךָ.[2] כִּי לֶקַח טוֹב נָתַתִּי לָכֶם,

« you; ‹ have I given ‹ a good teaching ‹ For « of Your anointed. ‹ the face ‹ turn not away

תּוֹרָתִי אַל תַּעֲזֹבוּ.[3] ❖ עֵץ חַיִּים הִיא לַמַּחֲזִיקִים

‹ for those who grasp ‹ it is ‹ of life ‹ A tree « forsake. ‹ do not ‹ My Torah

בָּהּ, וְתֹמְכֶיהָ מְאֻשָּׁר.[4] דְּרָכֶיהָ דַרְכֵי נֹעַם, וְכָל

‹ and all « of pleasantness, ‹ are ways ‹ Its ways « are praiseworthy. ‹ and its supporters « it,

(1) *Numbers* 10:36. (2) *Psalms* 132:8-10. (3) *Proverbs* 4:2. (4) 3:18.

נְתִיבוֹתֶיהָ שָׁלוֹם.[1] הֲשִׁיבֵנוּ יהוה אֵלֶיךָ וְנָשׁוּבָה,

its paths ‹ are peace. « Bring us back, ‹ HASHEM, ‹ to You, ‹ and we shall return, «

חַדֵּשׁ יָמֵינוּ כְּקֶדֶם.[2]

renew ‹ our days ‹ as of old. «

HALF-KADDISH / חצי קדיש

THE *CHAZZAN* RECITES HALF-*KADDISH*:

יִתְגַּדַּל וְיִתְקַדַּשׁ שְׁמֵהּ רַבָּא. (Cong. — אָמֵן.) בְּעָלְמָא דִּי

Grow exalted ‹ and be sanctified ‹ may His Name ‹ that is great! — « (Amen.) ‹ in the world ‹ that ‹

בְּרָא כִרְעוּתֵהּ. וְיַמְלִיךְ מַלְכוּתֵהּ, בְּחַיֵּיכוֹן וּבְיוֹמֵיכוֹן וּבְחַיֵּי

He created ‹ according to His will, « and may He give reign ‹ to His kingship, « in your lifetimes ‹ and in your days, ‹ and in the lifetimes ‹

דְּכָל בֵּית יִשְׂרָאֵל, בַּעֲגָלָא וּבִזְמַן קָרִיב. וְאִמְרוּ: אָמֵן.

of the entire ‹ Family ‹ of Israel, « swiftly ‹ and at a time ‹ that comes soon. « Now respond: ‹ Amen. «

CONGREGATION RESPONDS:

אָמֵן. יְהֵא שְׁמֵהּ רַבָּא מְבָרַךְ לְעָלַם וּלְעָלְמֵי עָלְמַיָּא.

Amen. « May ‹ His Name ‹ that is great ‹ be blessed ‹ forever ‹ and for all eternity. «

CHAZZAN CONTINUES:

יְהֵא שְׁמֵהּ רַבָּא מְבָרַךְ לְעָלַם וּלְעָלְמֵי עָלְמַיָּא. יִתְבָּרַךְ

May ‹ His Name ‹ that is great ‹ be blessed ‹ forever ‹ and for all eternity. « Blessed, ‹

וְיִשְׁתַּבַּח וְיִתְפָּאַר וְיִתְרוֹמַם וְיִתְנַשֵּׂא וְיִתְהַדָּר וְיִתְעַלֶּה

praised, ‹ glorified, ‹ exalted, ‹ upraised, ‹ honored, ‹ elevated, ‹

וְיִתְהַלָּל שְׁמֵהּ דְּקֻדְשָׁא בְּרִיךְ הוּא (Cong. — בְּרִיךְ הוּא) —

and lauded ‹ be the Name ‹ of the Holy One, ‹ Blessed ‹ is He « (Blessed ‹ is He) «

לְעֵלָּא מִן כָּל בִּרְכָתָא וְשִׁירָתָא תֻּשְׁבְּחָתָא וְנֶחֱמָתָא

beyond ‹ any ‹ blessing ‹ and song, « praise ‹ and consolation ‹

דַּאֲמִירָן בְּעָלְמָא. וְאִמְרוּ: אָמֵן. (Cong. — אָמֵן.)

that are uttered ‹ in the world. « Now respond: ‹ Amen. « (Amen.) «

(1) *Proverbs* 3:17. (2) *Lamentations* 5:21.

SHEMONEH ESREI / שמונה עשרה — עמידה

TAKE THREE STEPS BACKWARD, THEN THREE STEPS FORWARD. REMAIN STANDING WITH FEET TOGETHER WHILE RECITING *SHEMONEH ESREI*. RECITE IT WITH QUIET DEVOTION AND WITHOUT INTERRUPTION, VERBAL OR OTHERWISE. ALTHOUGH ITS RECITATION SHOULD NOT BE AUDIBLE TO OTHERS, ONE MUST PRAY LOUDLY ENOUGH TO HEAR HIMSELF.

כִּי שֵׁם יהוה אֶקְרָא, הָבוּ גֹדֶל לֵאלֹהֵינוּ.[1]

« to our God. ‹ greatness ‹ ascribe « I call out, ‹ of HASHEM ‹ the Name ‹ When

אֲדֹנָי שְׂפָתַי תִּפְתָּח, וּפִי יַגִּיד תְּהִלָּתֶךָ.[2]

« Your praise. ‹ may declare ‹ that my mouth « open, ‹ my lips ‹ O Lord,

PATRIARCHS / אבות

BEND THE KNEES AT בָּרוּךְ; BOW AT אַתָּה; STRAIGHTEN UP AT 'ה.

בָּרוּךְ אַתָּה יהוה אֱלֹהֵינוּ וֵאלֹהֵי אֲבוֹתֵינוּ, אֱלֹהֵי

‹ God « of our forefathers, ‹ and the God ‹ our God ‹ HASHEM, ‹ are You, ‹ Blessed

אַבְרָהָם, אֱלֹהֵי יִצְחָק, וֵאלֹהֵי יַעֲקֹב, הָאֵל הַגָּדוֹל

‹ [Who is] great, ‹ God « of Jacob; ‹ and God « of Isaac, ‹ God « of Abraham,

הַגִּבּוֹר וְהַנּוֹרָא, אֵל עֶלְיוֹן, גּוֹמֵל חֲסָדִים טוֹבִים,

‹ [that are] beneficent ‹ kindnesses ‹ Who bestows « the Most High, ‹ God, ‹ and awesome; ‹ mighty,

וְקוֹנֵה הַכֹּל, וְזוֹכֵר חַסְדֵי אָבוֹת, וּמֵבִיא גוֹאֵל לִבְנֵי

‹ to the children ‹ a Redeemer ‹ and brings « of the Patriarchs, ‹ the kindnesses ‹ Who recalls « everything, ‹ and creates

בְנֵיהֶם, לְמַעַן שְׁמוֹ בְּאַהֲבָה. מֶלֶךְ עוֹזֵר וּמוֹשִׁיעַ וּמָגֵן.

« and Shield. ‹ Savior, ‹ Helper, ‹ O King, « with love. ‹ of His Name, ‹ for the sake « of their children,

BEND THE KNEES AT בָּרוּךְ; BOW AT אַתָּה; STRAIGHTEN UP AT 'ה.

בָּרוּךְ אַתָּה יהוה, מָגֵן אַבְרָהָם.

« of Abraham. ‹ Shield « HASHEM, ‹ are You, ‹ Blessed

GOD'S MIGHT / גבורות

אַתָּה גִּבּוֹר לְעוֹלָם אֲדֹנָי, מְחַיֵּה מֵתִים אַתָּה,

« are You; ‹ of the dead ‹ the Revivifier « O Lord, ‹ eternally, ‹ mighty ‹ You are

(1) *Deuteronomy* 32:3. (2) *Psalms* 51:17.

רַב לְהוֹשִׁיעַ. מְכַלְכֵּל חַיִּים בְּחֶסֶד, מְחַיֵּה מֵתִים
‹ abundantly ‹ able to save, « Who sustains ‹ the living ‹ with kindness, « Who revivifies ‹ the dead ‹

בְּרַחֲמִים רַבִּים, סוֹמֵךְ נוֹפְלִים, וְרוֹפֵא חוֹלִים,
with mercy ‹ abundant, « Who supports ‹ the fallen, « Who heals ‹ the sick, «

וּמַתִּיר אֲסוּרִים, וּמְקַיֵּם אֱמוּנָתוֹ לִישֵׁנֵי עָפָר. מִי
Who releases ‹ the confined, « and Who maintains ‹ His faith ‹ to those asleep ‹ in the dust. « Who ‹

כָמוֹךָ בַּעַל גְּבוּרוֹת, וּמִי דּוֹמֶה לָּךְ, מֶלֶךְ מֵמִית
is like You, ‹ O Master ‹ of mighty deeds, « and who ‹ is comparable ‹ to You, « O King ‹ Who causes death ‹

וּמְחַיֶּה, וּמַצְמִיחַ יְשׁוּעָה. וְנֶאֱמָן אַתָּה לְהַחֲיוֹת
and restores life ‹ and makes sprout ‹ salvation! « And faithful ‹ are You ‹ to revivify ‹

מֵתִים. בָּרוּךְ אַתָּה יהוה, מְחַיֵּה הַמֵּתִים.
the dead. « Blessed ‹ are You, ‹ HASHEM, « Who revivifies ‹ the dead. «

DURING THE *CHAZZAN'S* REPETITION, *KEDUSHAH* (BELOW) IS RECITED AT THIS POINT.

KEDUSHAH / קדושה

WHEN RECITING *KEDUSHAH*, ONE MUST STAND WITH HIS FEET TOGETHER AND AVOID ANY INTERRUPTIONS. ONE SHOULD RISE ON HIS TOES WHEN SAYING THE WORDS ,קָדוֹשׁ, קָדוֹשׁ, קָדוֹשׁ; בָּרוּךְ (OF בָּרוּךְ כְּבוֹד); AND יִמְלֹךְ.

נְקַדֵּשׁ אֶת שִׁמְךָ בָּעוֹלָם, כְּשֵׁם שֶׁמַּקְדִּישִׁים אוֹתוֹ בִּשְׁמֵי
We shall sanctify ‹ Your Name ‹ in this world « just as ‹ they sanctify ‹ it ‹ in heaven ‹

מָרוֹם, כַּכָּתוּב עַל יַד נְבִיאֶךָ, וְקָרָא זֶה אֶל זֶה וְאָמַר:
above, « *as it is written* ‹ *by* ‹ *Your prophet,* « *And one [angel] will call* ‹ *to* ‹ *another* ‹ *and say:* «

קָדוֹשׁ קָדוֹשׁ קָדוֹשׁ יהוה צְבָאוֹת, מְלֹא כָל הָאָרֶץ כְּבוֹדוֹ.[1]
Holy, ‹ *holy,* ‹ *holy* ‹ *is* HASHEM, ‹ *Master of Legions,* « *filled* ‹ *is the whole* ‹ *world* ‹ *with His glory.* «

CHAZZAN:

לְעֻמָּתָם בָּרוּךְ יֹאמֵרוּ:
Facing them, ‹ *Blessed* ‹ they proclaim: «

ALL:

בָּרוּךְ כְּבוֹד יהוה, מִמְּקוֹמוֹ.[2]
Blessed ‹ *is the glory* ‹ *of* HASHEM ‹ *from His place.* «

---

(1) *Isaiah* 6:3. (2) *Ezekiel* 3:12.

CHAZZAN:

וּבְדִבְרֵי קָדְשְׁךָ כָּתוּב לֵאמֹר:

« saying: ‹ it is written ‹ that are holy ‹ And in Your Writings

ALL:

יִמְלֹךְ יהוה לְעוֹלָם, אֱלֹהַיִךְ צִיּוֹן לְדֹר וָדֹר, הַלְלוּיָהּ.[1]

« Halleluyah! « to generation, generation ‹ from ‹ O Zion, ‹ your God, « forever; ‹ HASHEM shall reign

***CHAZZAN* ONLY CONCLUDES:**

לְדוֹר וָדוֹר נַגִּיד גָּדְלֶךָ וּלְנֵצַח נְצָחִים קְדֻשָּׁתְךָ נַקְדִּישׁ, וְשִׁבְחֲךָ אֱלֹהֵינוּ מִפִּינוּ לֹא יָמוּשׁ לְעוֹלָם וָעֶד, כִּי אֵל מֶלֶךְ גָּדוֹל וְקָדוֹשׁ אָתָּה. בָּרוּךְ אַתָּה יהוה, הָאֵל הַקָּדוֹשׁ.

« we shall sanctify. ‹ Your holiness ‹ and for all eternity « Your greatness ‹ we shall relate ‹ to generation ‹ From generation ‹ O God, ‹ for, « and ever, ‹ for ever ‹ leave ‹ shall not ‹ from our mouth « our God, ‹ Your praise, « Who is holy. ‹ the God « HASHEM, ‹ are You, ‹ Blessed « are You. ‹ and holy ‹ great ‹ a King,

***KEDUSHAH* ENDS HERE. *CHAZZAN* CONTINUES ... אַתָּה חוֹנֵן (BELOW).**

HOLINESS OF GOD'S NAME / קדושת השם

אַתָּה קָדוֹשׁ וְשִׁמְךָ קָדוֹשׁ, וּקְדוֹשִׁים בְּכָל יוֹם יְהַלְלוּךָ סֶּלָה. בָּרוּךְ אַתָּה יהוה, הָאֵל הַקָּדוֹשׁ.

‹ day ‹ every ‹ and holy ones « is holy, ‹ and Your Name ‹ are holy ‹ You « Who is Holy. ‹ the God « HASHEM, ‹ are You, ‹ Blessed « forever. ‹ praise You

INSIGHT / בינה

אַתָּה חוֹנֵן לְאָדָם דַּעַת, וּמְלַמֵּד לֶאֱנוֹשׁ בִּינָה. חָנֵּנוּ מֵאִתְּךָ דֵּעָה בִּינָה וְהַשְׂכֵּל. בָּרוּךְ אַתָּה יהוה, חוֹנֵן הַדָּעַת.

« insight. ‹ to a [frail] mortal ‹ and teach « with wisdom ‹ man ‹ graciously endow ‹ You ‹ are You, ‹ Blessed « and discernment. ‹ insight, ‹ [with] wisdom, ‹ from Yourself ‹ Endow us graciously « of wisdom. ‹ gracious Giver « HASHEM,

---

(1) *Psalms* 146:10.

REPENTANCE / **תשובה**

הֲשִׁיבֵנוּ אָבִינוּ לְתוֹרָתֶךָ, וְקָרְבֵנוּ מַלְכֵּנוּ

‹ our King, ‹ and bring us near, « to Your Torah, ‹ our Father, ‹ Bring us back,

לַעֲבוֹדָתֶךָ, וְהַחֲזִירֵנוּ בִּתְשׁוּבָה שְׁלֵמָה לְפָנֶיךָ.

« before You. ‹ in complete repentance ‹ and influence us to return « to Your service,

בָּרוּךְ אַתָּה יהוה, הָרוֹצֶה בִּתְשׁוּבָה.

« repentance. ‹ Who desires « HASHEM, ‹ are You, ‹ Blessed

FORGIVENESS / **סליחה**

STRIKE THE LEFT SIDE OF THE CHEST WITH THE RIGHT FIST WHILE RECITING THE WORDS **חָטָאנוּ**, *SINNED,* AND **פָּשָׁעְנוּ**, *WILLFULLY SINNED.*

סְלַח לָנוּ אָבִינוּ כִּי חָטָאנוּ, מְחַל לָנוּ מַלְכֵּנוּ

‹ our King, ‹ us, ‹ pardon « we have sinned; ‹ for ‹ our Father, ‹ us, ‹ Forgive

כִּי פָשָׁעְנוּ, כִּי מוֹחֵל וְסוֹלֵחַ אָתָּה. בָּרוּךְ

‹ Blessed « are You. ‹ and Forgiver ‹ a Pardoner ‹ for « we have willfully sinned; ‹ for

אַתָּה יהוה, חַנּוּן הַמַּרְבֶּה לִסְלוֹחַ.

« forgives. ‹ Who abundantly ‹ the gracious One « HASHEM, ‹ are You,

REDEMPTION / **גאולה**

רְאֵה בְעָנְיֵנוּ, וְרִיבָה רִיבֵנוּ, וּגְאָלֵנוּ[1] מְהֵרָה

‹ speedily ‹ and redeem us « our cause, ‹ champion « our affliction, ‹ Behold

לְמַעַן שְׁמֶךָ, כִּי גוֹאֵל חָזָק אָתָּה. בָּרוּךְ אַתָּה

‹ are You, ‹ Blessed « are You. ‹ Who is powerful ‹ a Redeemer ‹ for « Your Name, ‹ for the sake of

יהוה, גּוֹאֵל יִשְׂרָאֵל.

« of Israel. ‹ Redeemer « HASHEM,

DURING HIS REPETITION, THE *CHAZZAN* RECITES **עֲנֵנוּ** AT THIS POINT. SEE LAWS §61-63. [IF HE FORGOT TO RECITE IT AT THIS POINT, HE MAY INSERT IT IN **שְׁמַע קוֹלֵנוּ** (P. 580), BUT WITHOUT THE CONCLUDING BLESSING.]

עֲנֵנוּ יהוה עֲנֵנוּ, בְּיוֹם צוֹם תַּעֲנִיתֵנוּ, כִּי בְצָרָה גְדוֹלָה

‹ that is great ‹ in distress ‹ for « of our public gathering for fasting ‹ on this day « answer us, ‹ HASHEM, ‹ Answer us,

(1) Cf. *Psalms* 119:153-154.

אֲנָחְנוּ. אַל תֵּפֶן אֶל רִשְׁעֵנוּ, וְאַל תַּסְתֵּר פָּנֶיךָ מִמֶּנּוּ,

« from us, ‹ Your Face ‹ hide ‹ do not « our wickedness, ‹ to ‹ pay attention ‹ Do not « are we.

וְאַל תִּתְעַלַּם מִתְּחִנָּתֵנוּ. הֱיֵה נָא קָרוֹב לְשַׁוְעָתֵנוּ, יְהִי נָא

‹ please let « to our outcry; ‹ near ‹ Please be « our supplication. ‹ ignore ‹ and do not

חַסְדְּךָ לְנַחֲמֵנוּ, טֶרֶם נִקְרָא אֵלֶיךָ עֲנֵנוּ, כַּדָּבָר שֶׁנֶּאֱמַר:

« is said: ‹ as it « answer us, « to You ‹ we call ‹ — before « comfort us ‹ Your kindness

וְהָיָה טֶרֶם יִקְרָאוּ וַאֲנִי אֶעֱנֶה, עוֹד הֵם מְדַבְּרִים וַאֲנִי

‹ *I* ‹ *[yet] speak,* ‹ *they* ‹ *[that] while* « *will answer;* ‹ *I* ‹ *they call,* ‹ *[that] before* ‹ *And it will be*

אֶשְׁמָע.[1] כִּי אַתָּה יהוה הָעוֹנֶה בְּעֵת צָרָה, פּוֹדֶה וּמַצִּיל בְּכָל

‹ in every ‹ and rescues ‹ Who redeems « of distress, ‹ in time ‹ are the One Who responds ‹ HASHEM, ‹ You, ‹ For « *will hear.*

עֵת צָרָה וְצוּקָה. בָּרוּךְ אַתָּה יהוה, הָעוֹנֶה בְּעֵת צָרָה.

« of distress. ‹ in time ‹ Who responds « HASHEM, ‹ are You, ‹ Blessed « and woe. ‹ of distress ‹ time

HEALTH AND HEALING / רפואה

רְפָאֵנוּ יהוה וְנֵרָפֵא, הוֹשִׁיעֵנוּ וְנִוָּשֵׁעָה, כִּי תְהִלָּתֵנוּ

‹ the One we praise ‹ for « — then we will be saved, « save us « — then we will be healed; « HASHEM ‹ Heal us,

אָתָּה,[2] וְהַעֲלֵה רְפוּאָה שְׁלֵמָה לְכָל מַכּוֹתֵינוּ,°°

« our ailments, ‹ for all ‹ that is complete ‹ healing ‹ Bring « is You.

°°AT THIS POINT ONE MAY INSERT A PRAYER FOR ONE WHO IS ILL:

יְהִי רָצוֹן מִלְּפָנֶיךָ, יהוה אֱלֹהַי וֵאלֹהֵי אֲבוֹתַי, שֶׁתִּשְׁלַח מְהֵרָה

‹ quickly ‹ that You send « of my forefathers, ‹ and the God ‹ my God, ‹ HASHEM, « before You, ‹ the will ‹ May it be

רְפוּאָה שְׁלֵמָה מִן הַשָּׁמַיִם, רְפוּאַת הַנֶּפֶשׁ וּרְפוּאַת הַגּוּף

« of the body ‹ and a healing ‹ of the spirit ‹ a healing « heaven, ‹ from « which is complete, ‹ a healing

FOR A FEMALE FOR A MALE

לַחוֹלֶה / לַחוֹלָה (SICK ONE'S NAME) בֶּן / בַּת (MOTHER'S NAME) בְּתוֹךְ שְׁאָר

‹ the other ‹ among ‹ daughter of / son of ‹ to the sick one

חוֹלֵי יִשְׂרָאֵל.

« of Israel. ‹ sick ones

(1) *Isaiah* 65:24. (2) Cf. *Jeremiah* 17:14.

כִּי אֵל מֶלֶךְ רוֹפֵא נֶאֱמָן וְרַחֲמָן אָתָּה. בָּרוּךְ

‹ Blessed « are You. ‹ and compassionate ‹ Who is faithful ‹ a Healer ‹ [and] King, ‹ O God, ‹ for

אַתָּה יהוה, רוֹפֵא חוֹלֵי עַמּוֹ יִשְׂרָאֵל.

« Israel. ‹ of His people ‹ the sick ‹ Who heals « HASHEM, ‹ are You,

YEAR OF PROSPERITY / ברכת השנים

בָּרֵךְ עָלֵינוּ יהוה אֱלֹהֵינוּ אֶת הַשָּׁנָה הַזֹּאת וְאֶת

‹ and « this year « our God — ‹ — O HASHEM, ‹ on our behalf ‹ Bless

כָּל מִינֵי תְבוּאָתָהּ לְטוֹבָה, וְתֵן בְּרָכָה עַל פְּנֵי

‹ the face ‹ on ‹ a blessing ‹ and give « for goodness; ‹ of its crops ‹ of the kinds ‹ all

הָאֲדָמָה, וְשַׂבְּעֵנוּ מִטּוּבֶךָ, וּבָרֵךְ שְׁנָתֵנוּ כַּשָּׁנִים

‹ like the years ‹ our year ‹ and bless « from Your bounty, ‹ and satisfy us « of the earth,

הַטּוֹבוֹת. בָּרוּךְ אַתָּה יהוה, מְבָרֵךְ הַשָּׁנִים.

« the years. ‹ Who blesses « HASHEM, ‹ are You, ‹ Blessed « that were good.

INGATHERING OF EXILES / קיבוץ גליות

תְּקַע בְּשׁוֹפָר גָּדוֹל לְחֵרוּתֵנוּ, וְשָׂא נֵס לְקַבֵּץ

‹ to gather ‹ a banner ‹ raise « for our freedom, ‹ the great *shofar* ‹ Sound

גָּלֻיּוֹתֵינוּ, וְקַבְּצֵנוּ יַחַד מֵאַרְבַּע כַּנְפוֹת הָאָרֶץ.[1]

« of the earth. ‹ corners ‹ from the four ‹ together ‹ and gather us « our exiles,

בָּרוּךְ אַתָּה יהוה, מְקַבֵּץ נִדְחֵי עַמּוֹ יִשְׂרָאֵל.

« Israel. ‹ of His people ‹ the dispersed ‹ Who gathers in « HASHEM, ‹ are You, ‹ Blessed

RESTORATION OF JUSTICE / דין

הָשִׁיבָה שׁוֹפְטֵינוּ כְּבָרִאשׁוֹנָה, וְיוֹעֲצֵינוּ

‹ and our counselors ‹ as [they were] in earliest times, ‹ our judges ‹ Restore

כְּבַתְּחִלָּה,[2] וְהָסֵר מִמֶּנּוּ יָגוֹן וַאֲנָחָה, וּמְלוֹךְ עָלֵינוּ

‹ over us ‹ and reign « and groan; ‹ sorrow ‹ from us ‹ remove « as at the beginning;

((1) *Isaiah* 11:12. (2) Cf. 1:26.

אַתָּה יהוה לְבַדְּךָ בְּחֶסֶד וּבְרַחֲמִים, וְצַדְּקֵנוּ

‹ — You, ‹ HASHEM, ‹ alone — « with kindness ‹ and compassion, « and justify us ‹

בַּמִּשְׁפָּט. בָּרוּךְ אַתָּה יהוה, מֶלֶךְ אוֹהֵב צְדָקָה

through judgment. « Blessed ‹ are You, ‹ HASHEM, « the King ‹ Who loves ‹ righteousness ‹

וּמִשְׁפָּט.

and judgment. «

AGAINST HERETICS / ברכת המינים

וְלַמַּלְשִׁינִים אַל תְּהִי תִקְוָה, וְכָל הָרִשְׁעָה

And for slanderers ‹ let there not be ‹ hope; « and may all ‹ wickedness ‹

כְּרֶגַע תֹּאבֵד, וְכָל אוֹיְבֶיךָ מְהֵרָה יִכָּרֵתוּ, וְהַזֵּדִים

in an instant ‹ perish; « and may all ‹ Your enemies ‹ speedily ‹ be cut down. « The willful sinners «

מְהֵרָה תְעַקֵּר וּתְשַׁבֵּר וּתְמַגֵּר וְתַכְנִיעַ בִּמְהֵרָה

— may You speedily ‹ uproot, ‹ smash, ‹ cast down, ‹ and humble — « speedily ‹

בְיָמֵינוּ. בָּרוּךְ אַתָּה יהוה, שׁוֹבֵר אֹיְבִים

in our days. « Blessed ‹ are You, ‹ HASHEM, « Who breaks ‹ enemies ‹

וּמַכְנִיעַ זֵדִים.

and humbles ‹ willful sinners. «

THE RIGHTEOUS / צדיקים

עַל הַצַּדִּיקִים וְעַל הַחֲסִידִים, וְעַל זִקְנֵי עַמְּךָ בֵּית

On ‹ the righteous, ‹ on ‹ the devout, « on ‹ the elders ‹ of Your people ‹ the Family ‹

יִשְׂרָאֵל, וְעַל פְּלֵיטַת סוֹפְרֵיהֶם, וְעַל גֵּרֵי הַצֶּדֶק

of Israel, « on ‹ the remnant ‹ of their scholars, « on ‹ the converts ‹ who are righteous ‹

וְעָלֵינוּ, יֶהֱמוּ רַחֲמֶיךָ, יהוה אֱלֹהֵינוּ, וְתֵן שָׂכָר

and on ourselves « — may aroused be ‹ Your compassion, « HASHEM, ‹ our God, « and give ‹ a reward ‹

טוֹב לְכָל הַבּוֹטְחִים בְּשִׁמְךָ בֶּאֱמֶת, וְשִׂים חֶלְקֵנוּ

which is good ‹ to all ‹ who believe ‹ in Your Name ‹ in sincerity. « Put ‹ our lot ‹

עִמָּהֶם לְעוֹלָם, וְלֹא נֵבוֹשׁ כִּי בְךָ בָּטָחְנוּ. בָּרוּךְ
‹ with them ‹ forever, « and we will not ‹ feel ashamed, ‹ for ‹ in You ‹ we trust. « Blessed

אַתָּה יהוה, מִשְׁעָן וּמִבְטָח לַצַּדִּיקִים.
‹ are You, ‹ HASHEM, « Mainstay ‹ and Assurance ‹ of the righteous. «

REBUILDING JERUSALEM / בנין ירושלים

וְלִירוּשָׁלַיִם עִירְךָ בְּרַחֲמִים תָּשׁוּב, וְתִשְׁכּוֹן
‹ And to Jerusalem, ‹ Your City, ‹ in compassion ‹ may You return, « and may You rest

בְּתוֹכָהּ כַּאֲשֶׁר דִּבַּרְתָּ, וּבְנֵה אוֹתָהּ בְּקָרוֹב בְּיָמֵינוּ
‹ within it, ‹ as ‹ You have spoken. « May You rebuild ‹ it ‹ soon ‹ in our days

בִּנְיַן עוֹלָם, וְכִסֵּא דָוִד מְהֵרָה לְתוֹכָהּ תָּכִין.
‹ as a structure ‹ that is eternal, « and the throne ‹ of David, ‹ speedily, ‹ within it ‹ may You establish. «

THE FOLLOWING IS RECITED BY EVERYONE, EVEN BY ONE WHO IS NOT FASTING:

נַחֵם יהוה אֱלֹהֵינוּ אֶת אֲבֵלֵי צִיּוֹן, וְאֶת אֲבֵלֵי
‹ Console ‹ O HASHEM, ‹ our God, ‹ the mourners ‹ of Zion ‹ and the mourners ‹

יְרוּשָׁלָיִם, וְאֶת הָעִיר הָאֲבֵלָה וְהַחֲרֵבָה וְהַבְּזוּיָה
« of Jerusalem, ‹ and the city ‹ that is mournful, ‹ that is ruined, ‹ that is scorned, ‹

וְהַשּׁוֹמֵמָה. הָאֲבֵלָה מִבְּלִי בָנֶיהָ, וְהַחֲרֵבָה
« and that is desolate: ‹ mournful ‹ without « her children, ‹ ruined ‹

מִמְּעוֹנוֹתֶיהָ, וְהַבְּזוּיָה מִכְּבוֹדָהּ, וְהַשּׁוֹמֵמָה מֵאֵין
« without her abodes, ‹ scorned « without her glory, ‹ and desolate ‹ without ‹

יוֹשֵׁב. וְהִיא יוֹשֶׁבֶת וְרֹאשָׁהּ חָפוּי כְּאִשָּׁה עֲקָרָה
« inhabitant. ‹ She ‹ sits ‹ with head ‹ that is covered ‹ like a woman ‹ who is barren ‹

שֶׁלֹּא יָלָדָה. וַיְבַלְּעוּהָ לִגְיוֹנוֹת, וַיִּירָשׁוּהָ עוֹבְדֵי זָרִים,
‹ who never ‹ gave birth. « Devoured her ‹ have legions, ‹ and conquered her ‹ have idolaters; ‹

וַיָּטִילוּ אֶת עַמְּךָ יִשְׂרָאֵל לֶחָרֶב, וַיַּהַרְגוּ בְזָדוֹן
‹ they have cast ‹ Your people ‹ Israel ‹ to the sword ‹ and murdered ‹ wantonly ‹

חֲסִידֵי עֶלְיוֹן. עַל כֵּן צִיּוֹן בְּמַר תִּבְכֶּה, וִירוּשָׁלַיִם

‹ and Jerusalem ‹ weeps ‹ bitterly ‹ Zion ‹ Therefore, « of the Supreme One. ‹ the devout servants

תִּתֵּן קוֹלָהּ. לִבִּי לִבִּי עַל חַלְלֵיהֶם, מֵעַי מֵעַי

‹ my innards, ‹ My innards, « their slain! ‹ [it aches] for ‹ my heart. ‹ My heart, « her voice. ‹ raises

עַל חַלְלֵיהֶם, כִּי אַתָּה יהוה בָּאֵשׁ הִצַּתָּהּ, וּבָאֵשׁ

‹ and with fire « You consumed her, ‹ with fire ‹ HASHEM, ‹ You ‹ For « their slain! ‹ [they ache] for

אַתָּה עָתִיד לִבְנוֹתָהּ, כָּאָמוּר: וַאֲנִי אֶהְיֶה לָּהּ, נְאֻם

‹ — the words « for her ‹ will be ‹ I « as it is said: ‹ rebuild her. ‹ in the future ‹ You will

יהוה, חוֹמַת אֵשׁ סָבִיב וּלְכָבוֹד אֶהְיֶה בְתוֹכָהּ.[1]

« in her midst. ‹ will I be ‹ and glorious « surrounding ‹ of fire ‹ a wall « of HASHEM —

בָּרוּךְ אַתָּה יהוה, מְנַחֵם צִיּוֹן וּבוֹנֵה יְרוּשָׁלָיִם.

« Jerusalem. ‹ and rebuilds ‹ Zion ‹ Who consoles « HASHEM, ‹ are You, ‹ Blessed

DAVIDIC REIGN / מלכות בית דוד

אֶת צֶמַח דָּוִד עַבְדְּךָ מְהֵרָה תַצְמִיחַ, וְקַרְנוֹ

‹ and his pride « may You cause to flourish, ‹ speedily, « Your servant, ‹ of David ‹ offspring ‹ The

תָּרוּם בִּישׁוּעָתֶךָ, כִּי לִישׁוּעָתְךָ קִוִּינוּ כָּל הַיּוֹם.

« all day long. ‹ we hope ‹ for Your salvation ‹ because « through Your salvation, ‹ may You exalt

בָּרוּךְ אַתָּה יהוה, מַצְמִיחַ קֶרֶן יְשׁוּעָה.

« of salvation. ‹ the pride ‹ Who causes to flourish « HASHEM, ‹ are You, ‹ Blessed

ACCEPTANCE OF PRAYER / קבלת תפלה

שְׁמַע קוֹלֵנוּ יהוה אֱלֹהֵינוּ, חוּס וְרַחֵם עָלֵינוּ,

« on us, ‹ and have compassion ‹ pity « our God, ‹ HASHEM, ‹ our voice, ‹ Hear

וְקַבֵּל בְּרַחֲמִים וּבְרָצוֹן אֶת תְּפִלָּתֵנוּ, כִּי אֵל שׁוֹמֵעַ

‹ Who hears ‹ God ‹ for « our prayer, ‹ and with favor ‹ with compassion ‹ and accept

(1) *Zechariah* 2:9.

תְּפִלּוֹת וְתַחֲנוּנִים אָתָּה. וּמִלְּפָנֶיךָ מַלְכֵּנוּ,
‹ our King, « From before Yourself, « are You. ‹ and supplications ‹ prayers

רֵיקָם אַל תְּשִׁיבֵנוּ.
« turn us away. ‹ do not ‹ emptyhanded

DURING THE SILENT *SHEMONEH ESREI,* THE FOLLOWING IS RECITED BY ONE WHO IS FASTING. [IF FORGOTTEN, *SHEMONEH ESREI* IS NOT REPEATED. SEE *LAWS* §61-63.]

עֲנֵנוּ יהוה עֲנֵנוּ, בְּיוֹם צוֹם תַּעֲנִיתֵנוּ, כִּי בְצָרָה
‹ in distress ‹ for « of our public gathering for fasting ‹ on this day « answer us, ‹ HASHEM, ‹ Answer us,

גְדוֹלָה אֲנָחְנוּ. אַל תֵּפֶן אֶל רִשְׁעֵנוּ, וְאַל תַּסְתֵּר
‹ hide ‹ do not « our wickedness, ‹ to ‹ pay attention ‹ Do not « are we. ‹ that is great

פָּנֶיךָ מִמֶּנּוּ, וְאַל תִּתְעַלַּם מִתְּחִנָּתֵנוּ. הֱיֵה נָא קָרוֹב
‹ near ‹ Please be « our supplication. ‹ ignore ‹ and do not « from us, ‹ Your Face

לְשַׁוְעָתֵנוּ, יְהִי נָא חַסְדְּךָ לְנַחֲמֵנוּ, טֶרֶם נִקְרָא
‹ we call ‹ — before « comfort us ‹ Your kindness ‹ please let « to our outcry;

אֵלֶיךָ עֲנֵנוּ, כַּדָּבָר שֶׁנֶּאֱמַר: וְהָיָה טֶרֶם יִקְרָאוּ
‹ *they call,* ‹ *[that] before* ‹ *And it will be* « is said: ‹ as it « answer us, « to You

וַאֲנִי אֶעֱנֶה, עוֹד הֵם מְדַבְּרִים וַאֲנִי אֶשְׁמָע.[1] כִּי
‹ For « *will hear.* ‹ *I* ‹ *[yet] speak,* ‹ *they* ‹ *[that] while* « *will answer;* ‹ *I*

אַתָּה יהוה הָעוֹנֶה בְּעֵת צָרָה, פּוֹדֶה וּמַצִּיל
‹ and rescues ‹ Who redeems « of distress, ‹ in time ‹ are the One Who responds ‹ HASHEM, ‹ You,

בְּכָל עֵת צָרָה וְצוּקָה.°°
« and woe. ‹ of distress ‹ time ‹ in every

°°DURING THE SILENT *SHEMONEH ESREI* ONE MAY INSERT THE FOLLOWING PERSONAL PRAYER FOR FORGIVENESS:

אָנָּא יהוה, חָטָאתִי עָוִיתִי וּפָשַׁעְתִּי לְפָנֶיךָ, מִיּוֹם הֱיוֹתִי
‹ I have existed ‹ from the day « before You, ‹ and willfully sinned « been iniquitous, ‹ I have sinned, ‹ HASHEM, ‹ Please,

עַל הָאֲדָמָה עַד הַיּוֹם הַזֶּה (וּבִפְרַט בַּחֵטְא . . .). אָנָּא יהוה,
‹ HASHEM, ‹ Please, « with the sin of . . .). ‹ (and especially « this very day ‹ until ‹ earth ‹ on

(1) *Zechariah* 2:9.

עֲשֵׂה לְמַעַן שְׁמְךָ הַגָּדוֹל, וּתְכַפֶּר לִי עַל חֲטָאַי וַעֲוֹנַי

‹ my ‹ my inad- ‹ for ‹ to ‹ and grant « which is ‹ Your ‹ for the ‹ act
iniquities, vertent sins, me atonement great Name sake of

וּפְשָׁעַי שֶׁחָטָאתִי וְשֶׁעָוִיתִי וְשֶׁפָּשַׁעְתִּי לְפָנֶיךָ, מִנְּעוּרַי עַד

‹ until ‹ from « before ‹ and sinned ‹ been ‹ [through which] « and my
my youth You, willfully iniquitous, I have sinned, willful sins

הַיּוֹם הַזֶּה. וּתְמַלֵּא כָּל הַשֵּׁמוֹת שֶׁפָּגַמְתִּי בְּשִׁמְךָ הַגָּדוֹל.

« that is ‹ within Your ‹ that I have ‹ the [Holy] ‹ all ‹ And make « this very day.
great. Name blemished Names whole

°°DURING THE SILENT *SHEMONEH ESREI* ONE MAY INSERT THE FOLLOWING PERSONAL PRAYER FOR LIVELIHOOD:

אַתָּה הוּא יהוה הָאֱלֹהִים, הַזָּן וּמְפַרְנֵס וּמְכַלְכֵּל מִקַּרְנֵי

‹ from the « and ‹ sustains, ‹ Who ‹ the God ‹ HASHEM, ‹ Who ‹ It is You
horns supports, nourishes, are

רְאֵמִים עַד בֵּיצֵי כִנִּים. הַטְרִיפֵנִי לֶחֶם חֻקִּי,[1] וְהַמְצֵא לִי

‹ for ‹ provide « allotted ‹ the ‹ Supply me « of lice. ‹ the ‹ to ‹ of
me to me; bread with eggs *re'eimim*

וּלְכָל בְּנֵי בֵיתִי מְזוֹנוֹתַי קוֹדֶם שֶׁאֶצְטָרֵךְ לָהֶם, בְּנַחַת

‹ in con- « for it; ‹ I have need ‹ before ‹ my « of my ‹ members ‹ and
tentment food, household, for all

וְלֹא בְצַעַר, בְּהֶתֵּר וְלֹא בְאִסּוּר, בְּכָבוֹד וְלֹא בְבִזָּיוֹן,

« in ‹ but ‹ in « in a forbid- ‹ but ‹ in a permis- « in ‹ but
disgrace, not honor den manner, not sible manner pain, not

לְחַיִּים וּלְשָׁלוֹם, מִשֶּׁפַע בְּרָכָה וְהַצְלָחָה, וּמִשֶּׁפַע בְּרֵכָה

‹ of the ‹ and from « and success ‹ of ‹ from the « and for ‹ for life
spring the flow blessing flow peace;

עֶלְיוֹנָה, כְּדֵי שֶׁאוּכַל לַעֲשׂוֹת רְצוֹנֶךָ וְלַעֲסוֹק בְּתוֹרָתֶךָ

‹ in Your ‹ and « Your will ‹ to do ‹ I be ‹ so « from On
Torah engage enabled that High,

וּלְקַיֵּם מִצְוֹתֶיךָ. וְאַל תַּצְרִיכֵנִי לִידֵי מַתְּנַת בָּשָׂר וָדָם.

« and ‹ of ‹ of the gifts of ‹ make me ‹ Do « Your ‹ and
blood; flesh the hands needful not commandments. fulfill

וִיקֻיַּם בִּי מִקְרָא שֶׁכָּתוּב: פּוֹתֵחַ אֶת יָדֶךָ, וּמַשְׂבִּיעַ לְכָל

‹ *every* ‹ *and satisfy* ‹ *Your hand,* ‹ *You open* « that states, ‹ the verse ‹ in ‹ and may
me there be
fulfilled

חַי רָצוֹן.[2] וְכָתוּב: הַשְׁלֵךְ עַל יהוה יְהָבְךָ וְהוּא יְכַלְכְּלֶךָ.[3]

« *will* ‹ *and* ‹ *Your* ‹ *HASHEM* ‹ *upon* ‹ *Cast* ‹ and that « *[with its]* ‹ *living*
sustain you. *He* *burden* states, *desire,* *thing*

(1) *Proverbs* 30:8. (2) *Psalms* 145:16. (2) 55:23.

כִּי אַתָּה שׁוֹמֵעַ תְּפִלַּת עַמְּךָ יִשְׂרָאֵל בְּרַחֲמִים.

« with compassion. ‹ Israel ‹ of Your people ‹ the prayer ‹ hear ‹ You ‹ For

בָּרוּךְ אַתָּה יהוה, שׁוֹמֵעַ תְּפִלָּה.

« prayer. ‹ Who hears « HASHEM, ‹ are You, ‹ Blessed

TEMPLE SERVICE / עבודה

רְצֵה יהוה אֱלֹהֵינוּ בְּעַמְּךָ יִשְׂרָאֵל וּבִתְפִלָּתָם,

« and toward their prayer ‹ Israel ‹ toward Your people « our God, ‹ HASHEM, « Be favorable,

וְהָשֵׁב אֶת הָעֲבוֹדָה לִדְבִיר בֵּיתֶךָ. וְאִשֵּׁי יִשְׂרָאֵל

‹ of Israel ‹ The fire-offerings « of Your Temple. ‹ to the Holy of Holies ‹ the service ‹ and restore

וּתְפִלָּתָם בְּאַהֲבָה תְקַבֵּל בְּרָצוֹן, וּתְהִי לְרָצוֹן

‹ to Your favor ‹ and may it be « favorably, ‹ accept ‹ with love ‹ and their prayer

תָּמִיד עֲבוֹדַת יִשְׂרָאֵל עַמֶּךָ.

« Your people. ‹ of Israel ‹ the service ‹ always

וְתֶחֱזֶינָה עֵינֵינוּ בְּשׁוּבְךָ לְצִיּוֹן בְּרַחֲמִים. בָּרוּךְ

‹ Blessed « in compassion. ‹ to Zion ‹ Your return ‹ may our eyes ‹ Witness

אַתָּה יהוה, הַמַּחֲזִיר שְׁכִינָתוֹ לְצִיּוֹן.

« to Zion. ‹ His Presence ‹ Who restores « HASHEM, ‹ are You,

THANKSGIVING [MODIM] / הודאה

BOW AT מוֹדִים, *WE THANK YOU*; STRAIGHTEN UP AT ה׳, *HASHEM*. IN HIS REPETITION THE *CHAZZAN* RECITES THE ENTIRE מוֹדִים ALOUD, WHILE THE CONGREGATION RECITES מוֹדִים דְּרַבָּנָן (P. 583) SOFTLY.

מוֹדִים אֲנַחְנוּ לָךְ שָׁאַתָּה הוּא יהוה אֱלֹהֵינוּ

‹ our God ‹ HASHEM, ‹ Who are ‹ For it is You « You, ‹ We thank

וֵאלֹהֵי אֲבוֹתֵינוּ לְעוֹלָם וָעֶד. צוּר חַיֵּינוּ, מָגֵן

‹ Shield « of our lives, ‹ Rock « and ever; ‹ for ever ‹ of our forefathers ‹ and the God

יִשְׁעֵנוּ אַתָּה הוּא לְדוֹר וָדוֹר. נוֹדֶה לְּךָ וּנְסַפֵּר

‹ and relate ‹ You ‹ We shall thank « to generation. ‹ from generation ‹ [is what] You are « of our salvation

תְּהִלָּתֶךָ[1] עַל חַיֵּינוּ הַמְּסוּרִים בְּיָדֶךָ, וְעַל נִשְׁמוֹתֵינוּ

‹ our souls ‹ and for « into Your hands ‹ that are committed ‹ our lives ‹ for « Your praise,

הַפְּקוּדוֹת לָךְ, וְעַל נִסֶּיךָ שֶׁבְּכָל יוֹם עִמָּנוּ, וְעַל

‹ and for « are with us; ‹ day ‹ that every ‹ Your miracles ‹ and for « to You; ‹ that are entrusted

נִפְלְאוֹתֶיךָ וְטוֹבוֹתֶיךָ שֶׁבְּכָל עֵת, עֶרֶב וָבֹקֶר

‹ morning, ‹ — evening, « times ‹ that are at all ‹ and favors ‹ Your wonders

וְצָהֳרָיִם. הַטּוֹב כִּי לֹא כָלוּ רַחֲמֶיךָ, וְהַמְּרַחֵם

‹ and the Compassionate One, « are Your compassions, ‹ exhausted ‹ never ‹ for ‹ The Beneficent One, « and afternoon.

כִּי לֹא תַמּוּ חֲסָדֶיךָ,[2] מֵעוֹלָם קִוִּינוּ לָךְ.

« in You. ‹ have we put our hope ‹ — always « are Your kindnesses ‹ ended ‹ never ‹ for

MODIM OF THE RABBIS / מוֹדִים דְּרַבָּנָן

מוֹדִים אֲנַחְנוּ לָךְ, שָׁאַתָּה הוּא יהוה אֱלֹהֵינוּ וֵאלֹהֵי

‹ and the God ‹ our God ‹ HASHEM, ‹ Who are ‹ for it is You « You, ‹ We thank

אֲבוֹתֵינוּ, אֱלֹהֵי כָל בָּשָׂר, יוֹצְרֵנוּ, יוֹצֵר בְּרֵאשִׁית. בְּרָכוֹת

‹ Blessings « of the universe. ‹ the Molder ‹ our Molder, « flesh, ‹ of all ‹ the God « of our forefathers,

וְהוֹדָאוֹת לְשִׁמְךָ הַגָּדוֹל וְהַקָּדוֹשׁ, עַל שֶׁהֶחֱיִיתָנוּ וְקִיַּמְתָּנוּ.

« and You have sustained us. ‹ You have given us life ‹ for « and that is holy, ‹ that is great ‹ [are due] to Your Name ‹ and thanks

כֵּן תְּחַיֵּנוּ וּתְקַיְּמֵנוּ, וְתֶאֱסוֹף גָּלֻיּוֹתֵינוּ לְחַצְרוֹת קָדְשֶׁךָ,

« of Your Sanctuary, ‹ to the Courtyards ‹ our exiles ‹ and gather « and sustain us, ‹ may You continue to give us life ‹ So

לִשְׁמוֹר חֻקֶּיךָ וְלַעֲשׂוֹת רְצוֹנֶךָ, וּלְעָבְדְּךָ בְּלֵבָב שָׁלֵם,

« wholeheartedly. ‹ and to serve You « Your will, ‹ to do « Your decrees, ‹ to observe

עַל שֶׁאֲנַחְנוּ מוֹדִים לָךְ. בָּרוּךְ אֵל הַהוֹדָאוֹת.

« of thanksgivings. ‹ is the God ‹ Blessed « You. ‹ to thank ‹ [inspiring] us ‹ [We thank You] for

((1) Cf. *Psalms* 79:13. (2) Cf. *Lamentations* 3:22.

וְעַל כֻּלָּם יִתְבָּרַךְ וְיִתְרוֹמַם שִׁמְךָ מַלְכֵּנוּ תָּמִיד לְעוֹלָם וָעֶד.

For all these, blessed and exalted may Your Name be, our King, continually, for ever and ever.

BEND THE KNEES AT בָּרוּךְ, *BLESSED*; BOW AT אַתָּה, *YOU*; STRAIGHTEN UP AT ה׳, *HASHEM.*

וְכֹל הַחַיִּים יוֹדְוּךָ סֶּלָה, וִיהַלְלוּ אֶת שִׁמְךָ בֶּאֱמֶת, הָאֵל יְשׁוּעָתֵנוּ וְעֶזְרָתֵנוּ סֶלָה. בָּרוּךְ אַתָּה יהוה, הַטּוֹב שִׁמְךָ וּלְךָ נָאֶה לְהוֹדוֹת.

Everything alive will gratefully acknowledge You, forever! — and praise Your Name sincerely, O God of our salvation and of our help, forever! Blessed are You, HASHEM, *The Beneficent One* is Your Name, and to You it is fitting to give thanks.

THE PRIESTLY BLESSING / ברכת כהנים

THE *CHAZZAN* RECITES בִּרְכַּת כֹּהֲנִים DURING HIS REPETITION. HE FACES RIGHT AT וְיִשְׁמְרֶךָ; FACES LEFT AT אֵלֶיךָ וִיחֻנֶּךָּ; FACES THE ARK FOR THE REST OF THE BLESSINGS.

אֱלֹהֵינוּ וֵאלֹהֵי אֲבוֹתֵינוּ, בָּרְכֵנוּ בַבְּרָכָה הַמְּשֻׁלֶּשֶׁת, בַּתּוֹרָה הַכְּתוּבָה עַל יְדֵי מֹשֶׁה עַבְדֶּךָ, הָאֲמוּרָה מִפִּי אַהֲרֹן וּבָנָיו, כֹּהֲנִים עַם קְדוֹשֶׁךָ, כָּאָמוּר:

Our God and the God of our forefathers, bless us with the blessing of three verses [that is] in the Torah that was written by the hand of Moses, Your servant, that was said from the mouth of Aaron and his sons, the *Kohanim,* Your holy people, as it is said:

יְבָרֶכְךָ יהוה, וְיִשְׁמְרֶךָ. (Cong. — כֵּן יְהִי רָצוֹן.)

May HASHEM bless you and safeguard you. (May so be His will.)

יָאֵר יהוה פָּנָיו אֵלֶיךָ, וִיחֻנֶּךָּ. (Cong. — כֵּן יְהִי רָצוֹן.)

May HASHEM illuminate His countenance for you and be gracious to you. (May so be His will.)

יִשָּׂא יהוה פָּנָיו אֵלֶיךָ, וְיָשֵׂם לְךָ שָׁלוֹם.[1] (Cong. — כֵּן יְהִי רָצוֹן.)

May HASHEM turn His countenance to you and establish for you peace. (May so be His will.)

(1) *Numbers* 6:24-26

PEACE / שלום

שִׂים שָׁלוֹם, טוֹבָה, וּבְרָכָה, חֵן, וָחֶסֶד וְרַחֲמִים,

‹ Establish ‹ peace, ‹ goodness, ‹ blessing, ‹ graciousness, ‹ kindness, ‹ and compassion

עָלֵינוּ וְעַל כָּל יִשְׂרָאֵל עַמֶּךָ. בָּרְכֵנוּ אָבִינוּ,

‹ upon us ‹ and upon ‹ all ‹ of Israel ‹ Your people. « Bless us, ‹ our Father,

כֻּלָּנוּ כְּאֶחָד בְּאוֹר פָּנֶיךָ, כִּי בְאוֹר פָּנֶיךָ נָתַתָּ

« all of us « as one, ‹ with the light ‹ of Your countenance, « for ‹ with the light ‹ of Your countenance ‹ You gave

לָּנוּ, יהוה אֱלֹהֵינוּ, תּוֹרַת חַיִּים וְאַהֲבַת חֶסֶד,

‹ us, ‹ HASHEM, « our God, ‹ the Torah ‹ of life ‹ and a love ‹ of kindness,

וּצְדָקָה, וּבְרָכָה, וְרַחֲמִים, וְחַיִּים, וְשָׁלוֹם. וְטוֹב

‹ righteousness, ‹ blessing, ‹ compassion, ‹ life, ‹ and peace. « And may it be good

בְּעֵינֶיךָ לְבָרֵךְ אֶת עַמְּךָ יִשְׂרָאֵל בְּכָל עֵת וּבְכָל

‹ in Your eyes ‹ to bless ‹ Your people ‹ Israel, « at every ‹ time ‹ and at every

שָׁעָה בִּשְׁלוֹמֶךָ. בָּרוּךְ אַתָּה יהוה, הַמְּבָרֵךְ אֶת עַמּוֹ

‹ hour, ‹ with Your peace. « Blessed ‹ are You, ‹ HASHEM, « Who blesses ‹ His people

יִשְׂרָאֵל בַּשָּׁלוֹם.

‹ Israel « with peace.

ALTHOUGH THE *CHAZZAN'S* REPETITION ENDS HERE, HE SHOULD ADD THE NEXT VERSE IN AN UNDERTONE. INDIVIDUALS CONTINUE:

יִהְיוּ לְרָצוֹן אִמְרֵי פִי וְהֶגְיוֹן לִבִּי לְפָנֶיךָ,

‹ May they ‹ find favor ‹ — the expressions ‹ of my mouth ‹ and the thoughts ‹ of my heart — « before You,

יהוה צוּרִי וְגֹאֲלִי.[1]

‹ HASHEM, ‹ my Rock « and my Redeemer.

אֱלֹהַי, נְצוֹר לְשׁוֹנִי מֵרָע, וּשְׂפָתַי מִדַּבֵּר מִרְמָה,[2]

‹ My God, ‹ guard ‹ my tongue « from evil ‹ and my lips ‹ from speaking « deceitfully.

((1) *Psalms* 19:15. (2) Cf. 34:14.

וְלִמְקַלְלַי נַפְשִׁי תִדּוֹם, וְנַפְשִׁי כֶּעָפָר לַכֹּל תִּהְיֶה.

To those who curse me, ‹ let my soul ‹ be silent; « and let my soul ‹ like dust ‹ to everyone ‹ be. «

פְּתַח לִבִּי בְּתוֹרָתֶךָ, וּבְמִצְוֹתֶיךָ תִּרְדּוֹף נַפְשִׁי. וְכָל

Open ‹ my heart ‹ to Your Torah, « so that Your commandments ‹ shall my soul pursue. « As for all ‹

הַחוֹשְׁבִים עָלַי רָעָה, מְהֵרָה הָפֵר עֲצָתָם וְקַלְקֵל

who plot ‹ against me ‹ evil, « speedily ‹ nullify ‹ their counsel ‹ and disrupt ‹

מַחֲשַׁבְתָּם.[1] עֲשֵׂה לְמַעַן שְׁמֶךָ, עֲשֵׂה לְמַעַן

their scheme. « Act ‹ for the sake ‹ of Your Name; « act ‹ for the sake ‹

יְמִינֶךָ, עֲשֵׂה לְמַעַן קְדֻשָּׁתֶךָ, עֲשֵׂה לְמַעַן תּוֹרָתֶךָ.

of Your right hand; « act ‹ for the sake ‹ of Your sanctity; « act ‹ for the sake ‹ of Your Torah. «

לְמַעַן יֵחָלְצוּן יְדִידֶיךָ, הוֹשִׁיעָה יְמִינְךָ וַעֲנֵנִי.[2]

In order that ‹ released may be ‹ Your beloved ones « — save ‹ with Your right hand, ‹ and answer me. «

SOME RECITE VERSES PERTAINING TO THEIR NAMES AT THIS POINT. SEE PAGE 643.

SOME RECITE THE FOLLOWING:

רִבּוֹן כָּל הָעוֹלָמִים, גָּלוּי וְיָדוּעַ לְפָנֶיךָ, בִּזְמַן שֶׁבֵּית הַמִּקְדָּשׁ

Master ‹ of all ‹ the worlds, « it is revealed ‹ and known ‹ before You « that in the time ‹ when the Holy Temple ‹

קַיָּם אָדָם חוֹטֵא וּמֵבִיא קָרְבָּן, וְאֵין מַקְרִיבִים מִמֶּנּוּ אֶלָּא

existed, « if someone ‹ sinned, « he brought ‹ an offering. « —Although nothing ‹ was offered ‹ of it [on the Altar] ‹ except ‹

חֶלְבּוֹ וְדָמוֹ, וְאַתָּה בְּרַחֲמֶיךָ הָרַבִּים מְכַפֵּר. וְעַכְשָׁו יָשַׁבְתִּי

for its fat ‹ and its blood, « yet You ‹ in Your mercy ‹ that is abundant ‹ would grant atonement. « Now ‹ I have engaged ‹

בְתַעֲנִית, וְנִתְמַעֵט חֶלְבִּי וְדָמִי. יְהִי רָצוֹן מִלְּפָנֶיךָ, שֶׁיְּהֵא

in a fast « and diminished ‹ has my own fat ‹ and my own blood. « May it be ‹ the will ‹ before You « that [considered] should be ‹

מִעוּט חֶלְבִּי וְדָמִי שֶׁנִּתְמַעֵט הַיּוֹם, כְּאִלּוּ הִקְרַבְתִּיו לְפָנֶיךָ

the diminution ‹ of my fat ‹ and my blood ‹ that was diminished ‹ today « as if ‹ I had offered it ‹ before You ‹

עַל גַּב הַמִּזְבֵּחַ, וְתִרְצֵנִי.

on ‹ top ‹ of the Altar « and may You show me favor. «

(1) See *Berachos* 17a. (2) *Psalms* 60:7, 108:7.

יִהְיוּ לְרָצוֹן אִמְרֵי פִי וְהֶגְיוֹן לִבִּי לְפָנֶיךָ, יהוה

‹HASHEM, « before You, ‹ of my heart — ‹ and the thoughts ‹ of my mouth ‹ — the expressions ‹ find favor ‹ May they

צוּרִי וְגֹאֲלִי.[1]

« and my Redeemer. ‹ my Rock

BOW. TAKE THREE STEPS BACK. BOW LEFT AND SAY ... עֹשֶׂה, *"HE WHO MAKES . . ."*; BOW RIGHT AND SAY ... הוּא, *"MAY HE . . ."*; BOW FORWARD AND SAY ... וְעַל כָּל יִשְׂרָאֵל, *"AND UPON ALL ISRAEL . . . ."*

עֹשֶׂה שָׁלוֹם בִּמְרוֹמָיו,[2] הוּא יַעֲשֶׂה שָׁלוֹם

‹ peace ‹ make ‹ may He « in His heights, ‹ peace ‹ He Who makes

עָלֵינוּ, וְעַל כָּל יִשְׂרָאֵל.[3] וְאִמְרוּ: אָמֵן.

« Amen. ‹ Now respond: « Israel. ‹ all ‹ and upon « upon us,

יְהִי רָצוֹן מִלְּפָנֶיךָ, יהוה אֱלֹהֵינוּ וֵאלֹהֵי אֲבוֹתֵינוּ, שֶׁיִּבָּנֶה

‹ that rebuilt « of our forefathers, ‹ and the God ‹ our God ‹ HASHEM, « before You, ‹ the will, ‹ May it be

בֵּית הַמִּקְדָּשׁ בִּמְהֵרָה בְיָמֵינוּ, וְתֵן חֶלְקֵנוּ בְּתוֹרָתֶךָ.[4] וְשָׁם

‹ so that there « be in Your Torah, ‹ our portion ‹ Grant that « in our days. ‹ speedily ‹ shall the Holy Temple be,

נַעֲבָדְךָ בְּיִרְאָה, כִּימֵי עוֹלָם וּכְשָׁנִים קַדְמוֹנִיּוֹת. וְעָרְבָה

‹ And pleasing « gone by. ‹ and as in years ‹ of old ‹ as in days « with reverence, ‹ we may serve You

לַיהוה מִנְחַת יְהוּדָה וִירוּשָׁלָיִם, כִּימֵי עוֹלָם וּכְשָׁנִים

‹ and in years ‹ of old ‹ as in days « and Jerusalem, ‹ of Judah ‹ let be the offering ‹ to HASHEM

קַדְמוֹנִיּוֹת.[5]

« gone by.

THE INDIVIDUAL'S RECITATION OF *SHEMONEH ESREI* ENDS HERE.

THE INDIVIDUAL REMAINS STANDING IN PLACE UNTIL THE *CHAZZAN* RECITES KEDUSHAH — OR AT LEAST UNTIL THE *CHAZZAN* BEGINS HIS REPETITION — THEN HE TAKES THREE STEPS FORWARD. THE *CHAZZAN* HIMSELF, OR ONE WHO IS PRAYING ALONE, SHOULD REMAIN IN PLACE FOR A FEW MOMENTS BEFORE TAKING THREE STEPS FORWARD.

FULL KADDISH / קדיש שלם

THE *CHAZZAN* RECITES קַדִּישׁ שָׁלֵם, FULL *KADDISH.*

יִתְגַּדַּל וְיִתְקַדַּשׁ שְׁמֵהּ רַבָּא. (Cong. — אָמֵן.) בְּעָלְמָא דִּי

‹that ‹ in the world ‹ (Amen.) « that is great! — ‹ may His Name ‹ and be sanctified ‹ Grow exalted

(1) *Psalms* 19:15. (2) *Job* 25:2. (3) Cf. *Berachos* 16b. (4) *Ethics of the Fathers* 5:24. (5) *Malachi* 3:4.

בְּרָא כִרְעוּתֵהּ. וְיַמְלִיךְ מַלְכוּתֵהּ, בְּחַיֵּיכוֹן וּבְיוֹמֵיכוֹן וּבְחַיֵּי

He created ‹ according to His will, ‹‹ and may He give reign ‹ to His kingship, ‹‹ in your lifetimes ‹ and in your days, ‹ and in the lifetimes ‹

דְכָל בֵּית יִשְׂרָאֵל, בַּעֲגָלָא וּבִזְמַן קָרִיב. וְאִמְרוּ: אָמֵן.

of the entire ‹ Family ‹ of Israel, ‹‹ swiftly ‹ and at a time ‹ that comes soon. ‹‹ Now respond: ‹ Amen. ‹‹

CONGREGATION RESPONDS:

אָמֵן. יְהֵא שְׁמֵהּ רַבָּא מְבָרַךְ לְעָלַם וּלְעָלְמֵי עָלְמַיָּא.

Amen. ‹‹ May ‹ His Name ‹ that is great ‹ be blessed ‹ forever ‹ and for all eternity. ‹‹

CHAZZAN CONTINUES:

יְהֵא שְׁמֵהּ רַבָּא מְבָרַךְ לְעָלַם וּלְעָלְמֵי עָלְמַיָּא. יִתְבָּרַךְ

May ‹ His Name ‹ that is great ‹ be blessed ‹ forever ‹ and for all eternity. ‹‹ Blessed, ‹

וְיִשְׁתַּבַּח וְיִתְפָּאַר וְיִתְרוֹמַם וְיִתְנַשֵּׂא וְיִתְהַדָּר וְיִתְעַלֶּה

praised, ‹ glorified, ‹ exalted, ‹ upraised, ‹ honored, ‹ elevated, ‹

וְיִתְהַלָּל שְׁמֵהּ דְּקֻדְשָׁא בְּרִיךְ הוּא (Cong. — בְּרִיךְ הוּא)

and lauded ‹ be the Name ‹ of the Holy One, ‹ Blessed ‹ is He ‹‹ (Blessed ‹ is He) ‹‹

— לְעֵלָּא מִן כָּל בִּרְכָתָא וְשִׁירָתָא תֻּשְׁבְּחָתָא וְנֶחֱמָתָא

beyond ‹ any ‹ blessing ‹ and song, ‹‹ praise ‹ and consolation ‹

דַּאֲמִירָן בְּעָלְמָא. וְאִמְרוּ: אָמֵן. (Cong. — אָמֵן.)

that are uttered ‹ in the world. ‹‹ Now respond: ‹ Amen. ‹‹ (Amen.) ‹‹

CONGREGATION:

קַבֵּל בְּרַחֲמִים וּבְרָצוֹן אֶת תְּפִלָּתֵנוּ.

Accept ‹ with mercy ‹ and with favor ‹ our prayers. ‹‹

CHAZZAN CONTINUES:

תִּתְקַבֵּל צְלוֹתְהוֹן וּבָעוּתְהוֹן דְּכָל (בֵּית) יִשְׂרָאֵל קֳדָם

May accepted be ‹ the prayers ‹ and supplications ‹ of the entire ‹ (Family of) ‹ Israel ‹ before ‹

אֲבוּהוֹן דִּי בִשְׁמַיָּא. וְאִמְרוּ: אָמֵן. (Cong. — אָמֵן.)

their Father ‹ Who ‹ is in Heaven. ‹‹ Now respond: ‹ Amen. ‹‹ (Amen.) ‹

CONGREGATION:

יְהִי שֵׁם יהוה מְבֹרָךְ, מֵעַתָּה וְעַד עוֹלָם.[1]

Let ‹ the Name ‹ of HASHEM ‹ be blessed, ‹‹ from this time ‹ until ‹ eternity. ‹‹

(1) Cf. *Psalms* 113:2.

CHAZZAN CONTINUES:

יְהֵא שְׁלָמָא רַבָּא מִן שְׁמַיָּא, וְחַיִּים עָלֵינוּ וְעַל כָּל

‹ all ‹ and upon ‹ upon us « and life, « Heaven, ‹ from ‹ that is abundant ‹ peace ‹ May there be

יִשְׂרָאֵל. וְאִמְרוּ: אָמֵן. (Cong. — אָמֵן.)

‹ (Amen.) « Amen. ‹ Now respond: « Israel.

CONGREGATION:

עֶזְרִי מֵעִם יהוה, עֹשֵׂה שָׁמַיִם וָאָרֶץ.[1]

« and earth. ‹ of heaven ‹ Maker « HASHEM, ‹ is from ‹ (My help

CHAZZAN BOWS; TAKES THREE STEPS BACK. BOWS LEFT AND SAYS ... עֹשֶׂה שָׁלוֹם, *"HE WHO MAKES PEACE ..."*; BOWS RIGHT AND SAYS ... הוּא, *"MAY HE ..."*; BOWS FORWARD AND SAYS ... וְעַל כָּל יִשְׂרָאֵל, *"AND UPON ALL ISRAEL ..."*; REMAINS IN PLACE FOR A FEW MOMENTS, THEN TAKES THREE STEPS FORWARD.

עֹשֶׂה שָׁלוֹם בִּמְרוֹמָיו, הוּא יַעֲשֶׂה שָׁלוֹם עָלֵינוּ, וְעַל כָּל

‹ all ‹ and upon ‹ upon us, ‹ peace ‹ make ‹ may He « in His heights, ‹ peace ‹ He Who makes

יִשְׂרָאֵל. וְאִמְרוּ: אָמֵן. (Cong. — אָמֵן.)

‹ (Amen.) « Amen. ‹ Now respond: « Israel.

ALEINU / עלינו

STAND WHILE RECITING עָלֵינוּ, *"IT IS OUR DUTY ..."*

עָלֵינוּ לְשַׁבֵּחַ לַאֲדוֹן הַכֹּל, לָתֵת גְּדֻלָּה לְיוֹצֵר

‹ to the Molder ‹ greatness ‹ to ascribe « of all, ‹ the Master ‹ to praise ‹ It is our duty

בְּרֵאשִׁית, שֶׁלֹּא עָשָׂנוּ כְּגוֹיֵי הָאֲרָצוֹת, וְלֹא

‹ and has not « of the lands, ‹ like the nations ‹ for He has not made us « of primeval creation,

שָׂמָנוּ כְּמִשְׁפְּחוֹת הָאֲדָמָה. שֶׁלֹּא שָׂם חֶלְקֵנוּ

‹ our portion ‹ assigned ‹ for He has not « of the earth; ‹ like the families ‹ established us

כָּהֶם, וְגוֹרָלֵנוּ כְּכָל הֲמוֹנָם. (שֶׁהֵם מִשְׁתַּחֲוִים

‹ bow ‹ (For they « their multitudes. ‹ like all ‹ nor our lot ‹ like theirs

לְהֶבֶל וָרִיק, וּמִתְפַּלְּלִים אֶל אֵל לֹא יוֹשִׁיעַ.[2])

« save.) ‹ who does not ‹ a god ‹ to ‹ and pray ‹ and emptiness ‹ to vanity

(1) *Psalms* 121:2. (2) *Isaiah* 45:20.

BOW WHILE RECITING וַאֲנַחְנוּ כּוֹרְעִים וּמִשְׁתַּחֲוִים, "BUT WE BEND OUR KNEES, BOW"

וַאֲנַחְנוּ כּוֹרְעִים וּמִשְׁתַּחֲוִים וּמוֹדִים, לִפְנֵי מֶלֶךְ

〈 the King 〈 before 《 and acknowledge our thanks 〈 bow, 〈 bend our knees, 〈 But we

מַלְכֵי הַמְּלָכִים הַקָּדוֹשׁ בָּרוּךְ הוּא. שֶׁהוּא נוֹטֶה

〈 stretches out 〈 He 《 He. 〈 Blessed is 〈 the Holy One, 《 of kings, 〈 over kings

שָׁמַיִם וְיֹסֵד אָרֶץ,[1] וּמוֹשַׁב יְקָרוֹ בַּשָּׁמַיִם מִמַּעַל,

《 above, 〈 is in the heavens 〈 of His homage 〈 the seat 《 earth's foundation, 〈 and establishes 〈 heaven

וּשְׁכִינַת עֻזּוֹ בְּגָבְהֵי מְרוֹמִים. הוּא אֱלֹהֵינוּ, אֵין עוֹד.

《 other. 〈 and there is none 〈 our God 〈 He is 《 heights. 〈 is in the loftiest 〈 of His power 〈 and the Presence

אֱמֶת מַלְכֵּנוּ, אֶפֶס זוּלָתוֹ, כַּכָּתוּב בְּתוֹרָתוֹ: וְיָדַעְתָּ

〈 *You are to know* 《 in His Torah: 〈 as it is written 《 beside Him, 〈 there is nothing 〈 is our King, 〈 True

הַיּוֹם וַהֲשֵׁבֹתָ אֶל לְבָבֶךָ, כִּי יהוה הוּא הָאֱלֹהִים

《 *the God* 〈 *He is* 〈 *HASHEM* 〈 *that* 《 *your heart,* 〈 *to* 〈 *and take* 〈 *this day*

בַּשָּׁמַיִם מִמַּעַל וְעַל הָאָרֶץ מִתָּחַת, אֵין עוֹד.[2]

《 *other.* 〈 *there is none* 〈 *below —* 〈 *the earth* 〈 *and on* 〈 *above* 〈 *— in heaven*

עַל כֵּן נְקַוֶּה לְּךָ, יהוה אֱלֹהֵינוּ, לִרְאוֹת מְהֵרָה

〈 very soon 〈 that we may see 《 our God, 〈 HASHEM, 〈 in You, 〈 we put our hope 〈 Therefore

בְּתִפְאֶרֶת עֻזֶּךָ, לְהַעֲבִיר גִּלּוּלִים מִן הָאָרֶץ,

《 the earth, 〈 from 〈 detestable idolatry 〈 to remove 《 of Your might, 〈 the splendor

וְהָאֱלִילִים כָּרוֹת יִכָּרֵתוּן, לְתַקֵּן עוֹלָם בְּמַלְכוּת

〈 through the sovereignty 〈 the universe 〈 to perfect 《 will be utterly cut off, 〈 and false gods

שַׁדַּי. וְכָל בְּנֵי בָשָׂר יִקְרְאוּ בִשְׁמֶךָ, לְהַפְנוֹת אֵלֶיךָ

〈 toward You 〈 to turn 《 upon Your Name, 〈 will call 〈 humanity 〈 Then all 《 of the Almighty.

כָּל רִשְׁעֵי אָרֶץ. יַכִּירוּ וְיֵדְעוּ כָּל יוֹשְׁבֵי תֵבֵל, כִּי

〈 that 《 of the world — 〈 the inhabitants 〈 — all 《 and know 〈 May they recognize 《 of the earth. 〈 the wicked 〈 all

---

(1) *Isaiah* 51:13. (2) *Deuteronomy* 4:39.

לְךָ תִּכְרַע כָּל בֶּרֶךְ, תִּשָּׁבַע כָּל לָשׁוֹן.[1] לְפָנֶיךָ

‹ Before You, « tongue. ‹ every ‹ should swear « knee, ‹ every ‹ should bend ‹ to You

יהוה אֱלֹהֵינוּ יִכְרְעוּ וְיִפֹּלוּ, וְלִכְבוֹד שִׁמְךָ יְקָר

‹ homage ‹ of Your Name ‹ and to the glory « and cast themselves down, ‹ they will bend their knees ‹ our God, ‹ HASHEM,

יִתֵּנוּ. וִיקַבְּלוּ כֻלָּם אֶת עוֹל מַלְכוּתֶךָ, וְתִמְלֹךְ

‹ that You may reign « of Your kingship, ‹ the yoke ‹ will all ‹ and accept « they will offer,

עֲלֵיהֶם מְהֵרָה לְעוֹלָם וָעֶד. כִּי הַמַּלְכוּת שֶׁלְּךָ הִיא

« is Yours, ‹ the kingdom ‹ For « and ever. ‹ for ever ‹ very soon ‹ over them

וּלְעוֹלְמֵי עַד תִּמְלוֹךְ בְּכָבוֹד, כַּכָּתוּב בְּתוֹרָתֶךָ:

« in Your Torah: ‹ as it is written « in glory, ‹ You will reign ‹ and ever ‹ and for ever

יהוה יִמְלֹךְ לְעֹלָם וָעֶד.[2] ❖ וְנֶאֱמַר: וְהָיָה יהוה

‹ *HASHEM* ‹ *Then will* « And it is said: « *and ever.* ‹ *for ever* ‹ *shall reign* ‹ *HASHEM*

לְמֶלֶךְ עַל כָּל הָאָרֶץ, בַּיּוֹם הַהוּא יִהְיֶה יהוה

‹ *HASHEM* ‹ *shall* ‹ *— on that day* « *the world* ‹ *all* ‹ *over* ‹ *be King*

אֶחָד וּשְׁמוֹ אֶחָד.[3]

« *be One.* ‹ *and His Name* ‹ *be One*

SOME CONGREGATIONS RECITE THE FOLLOWING AFTER עָלֵינוּ, *ALEINU*.

אַל תִּירָא מִפַּחַד פִּתְאֹם, וּמִשֹּׁאַת רְשָׁעִים כִּי

‹ when ‹ of the wicked ‹ nor the holocaust « [that comes] suddenly, ‹ terror ‹ Do not fear

תָבֹא.[4] עֻצוּ עֵצָה וְתֻפָר, דַּבְּרוּ דָבָר וְלֹא יָקוּם, כִּי

‹ for « stand, ‹ and it shall not ‹ your speech ‹ speak « and it will be annulled; ‹ a conspiracy ‹ Plan « it comes.

עִמָּנוּ אֵל.[5] וְעַד זִקְנָה אֲנִי הוּא, וְעַד שֵׂיבָה אֲנִי

‹ I ‹ [your] elder years, ‹ and even till « I remain unchanged; ‹ [your] old age, ‹ Even till « is God. ‹ with us

אֶסְבֹּל, אֲנִי עָשִׂיתִי וַאֲנִי אֶשָּׂא, וַאֲנִי אֶסְבֹּל וַאֲמַלֵּט.[6]

« and rescue [you]. ‹ shall carry [you] ‹ I « shall bear [you]; ‹ and I ‹ created [you] ‹ I « shall carry [you].

(1) Cf. *Isaiah* 45:23. (2) *Exodus* 15:18. (3) *Zechariah* 14:9. (4) *Proverbs* 3:25. (5) *Isaiah* 8:10. (6) 46:4.

IN THE PRESENCE OF A *MINYAN*, MOURNERS RECITE **קַדִּישׁ יָתוֹם**, THE MOURNER'S *KADDISH* (SEE *LAWS* §132-134). [A TRANSLITERATION OF THIS *KADDISH* APPEARS ON PAGE 647.]

יִתְגַּדַּל וְיִתְקַדַּשׁ שְׁמֵהּ רַבָּא. (.Cong — אָמֵן.) בְּעָלְמָא דִּי

‹ that ‹ in the world « (Amen.) « that is great! — ‹ may His Name ‹ and be sanctified ‹ Grow exalted

בְרָא כִרְעוּתֵהּ. וְיַמְלִיךְ מַלְכוּתֵהּ, בְּחַיֵּיכוֹן וּבְיוֹמֵיכוֹן וּבְחַיֵּי

‹ and in the lifetimes ‹ and in your days, ‹ in your lifetimes « to His kingship, ‹ and may He give reign « according to His will, ‹ He created

דְכָל בֵּית יִשְׂרָאֵל, בַּעֲגָלָא וּבִזְמַן קָרִיב. וְאִמְרוּ: אָמֵן.

« Amen. ‹ Now respond: « that comes soon. ‹ and at a time ‹ swiftly « of Israel, ‹ Family ‹ of the entire

CONGREGATION RESPONDS:

אָמֵן. יְהֵא שְׁמֵהּ רַבָּא מְבָרַךְ לְעָלַם וּלְעָלְמֵי עָלְמַיָּא.

« and for all eternity. ‹ forever ‹ be blessed ‹ that is great ‹ His Name ‹ May « Amen.

MOURNER CONTINUES:

יְהֵא שְׁמֵהּ רַבָּא מְבָרַךְ לְעָלַם וּלְעָלְמֵי עָלְמַיָּא. יִתְבָּרַךְ

‹ Blessed, « and for all eternity. ‹ forever ‹ be blessed ‹ that is great ‹ His Name ‹ May

וְיִשְׁתַּבַּח וְיִתְפָּאַר וְיִתְרוֹמַם וְיִתְנַשֵּׂא וְיִתְהַדָּר וְיִתְעַלֶּה

‹ elevated, ‹ honored, ‹ upraised, ‹ exalted, ‹ glorified, ‹ praised,

וְיִתְהַלָּל שְׁמֵהּ דְּקֻדְשָׁא בְּרִיךְ הוּא (.Cong — בְּרִיךְ הוּא) —

« is He) ‹ (Blessed « is He ‹ Blessed ‹ of the Holy One, ‹ be the Name ‹ and lauded

לְעֵלָּא מִן כָּל בִּרְכָתָא וְשִׁירָתָא תֻּשְׁבְּחָתָא וְנֶחֱמָתָא

‹ and consolation ‹ praise « and song, ‹ blessing ‹ any ‹ beyond

דַּאֲמִירָן בְּעָלְמָא. וְאִמְרוּ: אָמֵן. (.Cong — אָמֵן.)

« (Amen.) « Amen. ‹ Now respond: « in the world. ‹ that are uttered

יְהֵא שְׁלָמָא רַבָּא מִן שְׁמַיָּא, וְחַיִּים עָלֵינוּ וְעַל כָּל

‹ all ‹ and upon ‹ upon us « and life, « Heaven, ‹ from ‹ that is abundant ‹ peace ‹ May there be

יִשְׂרָאֵל. וְאִמְרוּ: אָמֵן. (.Cong — אָמֵן.)

« (Amen.) « Amen. ‹ Now respond: « Israel.

BOW; TAKE THREE STEPS BACK; BOW LEFT AND SAY ... **עֹשֶׂה שָׁלוֹם**, *"HE WHO MAKES PEACE . . .";* BOW RIGHT AND SAY ... **הוּא**, *"MAY HE . . .";* BOW FORWARD AND SAY ... **וְעַל כָּל יִשְׂרָאֵל**, *"AND UPON ALL ISRAEL . . .";* REMAIN IN PLACE FOR A FEW MOMENTS, THEN TAKE THREE STEPS FORWARD.

עֹשֶׂה שָׁלוֹם בִּמְרוֹמָיו, הוּא יַעֲשֶׂה שָׁלוֹם עָלֵינוּ, וְעַל כָּל

‹ all ‹ and upon ‹ upon us, ‹ peace ‹ make ‹ may He « in His heights, ‹ peace ‹ He Who makes

יִשְׂרָאֵל. וְאִמְרוּ: אָמֵן. (.Cong — אָמֵן.)

« (Amen.) « Amen. ‹ Now respond: « Israel.

מעריב למוצאי תשעה באב

MAARIV FOR THE CONCLUSION OF TISHAH B'AV

CONGREGATION, THEN *CHAZZAN*:

וְהוּא רַחוּם יְכַפֵּר עָוֹן וְלֹא יַשְׁחִית, וְהִרְבָּה

‹ frequently « destroy; ‹ and does not ‹ of iniquity ‹ is forgiving ‹ the Merciful One, ‹ He,

לְהָשִׁיב אַפּוֹ, וְלֹא יָעִיר כָּל חֲמָתוֹ.[1] ❖ יהוה

‹ HASHEM, « His wrath. ‹ all ‹ arousing ‹ not « His anger, ‹ He withdraws

הוֹשִׁיעָה, הַמֶּלֶךְ יַעֲנֵנוּ בְיוֹם קָרְאֵנוּ.[2]

« we call. ‹ on the day ‹ answer us ‹ May the King « save!

THE *CHAZZAN* SUMMONS THE CONGREGATION TO JOIN IN THE FORTHCOMING PRAYERS, BOWING AT בָּרְכוּ, *BLESS,* AND STRAIGHTENING UP AT ה׳, *HASHEM.*

בָּרְכוּ אֶת יהוה הַמְּבֹרָךְ.

« **the blessed One.** ‹ **HASHEM,** ‹ **Bless**

THE CONGREGATION, FOLLOWED BY *CHAZZAN,* RESPONDS, BOWING AT בָּרוּךְ, *BLESS,* AND STRAIGHTENING UP AT ה׳, *HASHEM.*

בָּרוּךְ יהוה הַמְּבֹרָךְ לְעוֹלָם וָעֶד.

« **and ever.** ‹ **for ever** ‹ **the blessed One,** ‹ **HASHEM,** ‹ **Blessed is**

BLESSINGS OF THE SHEMA / ברכות קריאת שמע

בָּרוּךְ אַתָּה יהוה אֱלֹהֵינוּ מֶלֶךְ הָעוֹלָם, אֲשֶׁר

‹ Who « of the universe, ‹ King ‹ our God, ‹ HASHEM, ‹ are You, ‹ Blessed

בִּדְבָרוֹ מַעֲרִיב עֲרָבִים, בְּחָכְמָה פּוֹתֵחַ שְׁעָרִים,

« gates, ‹ opens ‹ with wisdom « evenings, ‹ brings on ‹ by His word

וּבִתְבוּנָה מְשַׁנֶּה עִתִּים, וּמַחֲלִיף אֶת הַזְּמַנִּים,

« the seasons, ‹ changes « periods, ‹ alters ‹ with understanding

וּמְסַדֵּר אֶת הַכּוֹכָבִים בְּמִשְׁמְרוֹתֵיהֶם בָּרָקִיעַ

« in the heavens ‹ in their constellations « the stars ‹ and orders

כִּרְצוֹנוֹ. בּוֹרֵא יוֹם וָלָיְלָה, גּוֹלֵל אוֹר מִפְּנֵי חֹשֶׁךְ

‹ darkness ‹ before ‹ light ‹ rolling away « and night, ‹ day ‹ He creates « as He wills.

וְחֹשֶׁךְ מִפְּנֵי אוֹר. וּמַעֲבִיר יוֹם וּמֵבִיא לָיְלָה,

« night, ‹ and brings ‹ day ‹ He removes « light. ‹ before ‹ and darkness

(1) *Psalms* 78:38. (2) 20:10.

וּמַבְדִּיל בֵּין יוֹם וּבֵין לָיְלָה, יהוה צְבָאוֹת שְׁמוֹ.

« is His Name. ‹ Master of Legions, ‹ — HASHEM, « night ‹ and between ‹ day ‹ between ‹ and separates

❖ אֵל חַי וְקַיָּם, תָּמִיד יִמְלוֹךְ עָלֵינוּ, לְעוֹלָם וָעֶד.

« and ever. ‹ for ever ‹ over us, ‹ may He reign ‹ continually « and enduring, ‹ the living ‹ God

בָּרוּךְ אַתָּה יהוה, הַמַּעֲרִיב עֲרָבִים. (Cong. – אָמֵן)

« (Amen.) « evenings. ‹ Who brings on ‹ HASHEM, ‹ are You, ‹ Blessed

אַהֲבַת עוֹלָם בֵּית יִשְׂרָאֵל עַמְּךָ אָהָבְתָּ. תּוֹרָה

‹ Torah « have You loved. ‹ Your people ‹ Israel, ‹ the Family of « that is eternal, ‹ [With] a love

וּמִצְוֹת, חֻקִּים וּמִשְׁפָּטִים, אוֹתָנוּ לִמַּדְתָּ. עַל כֵּן

‹ Therefore, « have You taught us. « and ordinances ‹ decrees ‹ and commandments,

יהוה אֱלֹהֵינוּ, בְּשָׁכְבֵנוּ וּבְקוּמֵנוּ נָשִׂיחַ בְּחֻקֶּיךָ,

« Your decrees ‹ we will discuss « and upon our arising, ‹ upon our retiring « our God, ‹ HASHEM,

וְנִשְׂמַח בְּדִבְרֵי תוֹרָתֶךָ וּבְמִצְוֹתֶיךָ לְעוֹלָם וָעֶד.

« and ever. ‹ for ever ‹ and with Your commandments « of Your Torah ‹ with the words ‹ and we will rejoice

❖ כִּי הֵם חַיֵּינוּ, וְאֹרֶךְ יָמֵינוּ, וּבָהֶם נֶהְגֶּה יוֹמָם

‹ day ‹ we will meditate ‹ and about them « of our days ‹ and the length ‹ are our life ‹ they ‹ For

וָלָיְלָה. וְאַהֲבָתְךָ, אַל תָּסִיר מִמֶּנּוּ לְעוֹלָמִים. בָּרוּךְ

‹ Blessed « forever. ‹ from us ‹ remove ‹ do not ‹ Your love « and night.

אַתָּה יהוה, אוֹהֵב עַמּוֹ יִשְׂרָאֵל. (Cong. – אָמֵן)

« (Amen.) « Israel. ‹ His people ‹ Who loves ‹ HASHEM, ‹ are You,

THE SHEMA / שמע

IMMEDIATELY BEFORE ITS RECITATION CONCENTRATE ON FULFILLING THE POSITIVE COMMANDMENT OF RECITING THE *SHEMA* TWICE DAILY. IT IS IMPORTANT TO ENUNCIATE EACH WORD CLEARLY AND NOT TO RUN WORDS TOGETHER. FOR THIS REASON, VERTICAL LINES HAVE BEEN PLACED BETWEEN TWO WORDS THAT ARE NOT SEPARATED BY A COMMA OR A DASH AND ARE APT TO BE SLURRED INTO ONE. SEE *LAWS* §95-109

WHEN PRAYING WITHOUT A *MINYAN*, BEGIN WITH THE FOLLOWING THREE-WORD FORMULA:

אֵל מֶלֶךְ נֶאֱמָן.

« Who is trustworthy. ‹ King ‹ God,

RECITE THE FIRST VERSE ALOUD, WITH THE RIGHT HAND COVERING THE EYES, AND CONCENTRATE INTENSELY UPON ACCEPTING GOD'S ABSOLUTE SOVEREIGNTY.

שְׁמַע | יִשְׂרָאֵל, יְהוָה | אֱלֹהֵינוּ, יְהוָה | אֶחָד:[1]

« the One [and Only]. ‹ HASHEM is « is our God, ‹ HASHEM « O Israel: ‹ Hear,

IN AN UNDERTONE:

בָּרוּךְ שֵׁם כְּבוֹד מַלְכוּתוֹ לְעוֹלָם וָעֶד.[2]

« and ever. ‹ for ever ‹ kingdom ‹ of His glorious ‹ is the Name ‹ Blessed

WHILE RECITING THE FIRST PARAGRAPH (*DEUTERONOMY* 6:5-9), CONCENTRATE ON ACCEPTING THE COMMANDMENT TO LOVE GOD.

וְאָהַבְתָּ אֵת | יְהוָה | אֱלֹהֶיךָ, בְּכָל־לְבָבְךָ, וּבְכָל־

‹ with all « your heart, ‹ with all « your God, ‹ HASHEM, ‹ You shall love

נַפְשְׁךָ, וּבְכָל־מְאֹדֶךָ: וְהָיוּ הַדְּבָרִים הָאֵלֶּה, אֲשֶׁר |

‹ that ‹ — these matters « They should be « your resources. ‹ and with all ‹ your soul,

אָנֹכִי מְצַוְּךָ הַיּוֹם, עַל־לְבָבֶךָ: וְשִׁנַּנְתָּם לְבָנֶיךָ,

« to your children ‹ Teach them thoroughly « your heart. ‹ upon « today— ‹ command you ‹ I

וְדִבַּרְתָּ בָּם בְּשִׁבְתְּךָ בְּבֵיתֶךָ, וּבְלֶכְתְּךָ בַדֶּרֶךְ,

« on the way, ‹ while you walk « in your home, ‹ while you sit ‹ of them ‹ and speak

וּבְשָׁכְבְּךָ וּבְקוּמֶךָ: וּקְשַׁרְתָּם לְאוֹת | עַל־יָדֶךָ,

« your arm ‹ upon ‹ as a sign ‹ Bind them « and when you arise. ‹ when you lie down,

וְהָיוּ לְטֹטָפֹת בֵּין | עֵינֶיךָ: וּכְתַבְתָּם | עַל־מְזֻזוֹת

‹ the doorposts ‹ on ‹ And write them « your eyes. ‹ between ‹ *tefillin* ‹ and they shall be

בֵּיתֶךָ וּבִשְׁעָרֶיךָ:

« and upon your gates. ‹ of your house

WHILE RECITING THE SECOND PARAGRAPH (*DEUTERONOMY* 11:13-21), CONCENTRATE ON ACCEPTING ALL THE COMMANDMENTS AND ON THE CONCEPT OF REWARD AND PUNISHMENT.

וְהָיָה, אִם־שָׁמֹעַ תִּשְׁמְעוּ אֶל־מִצְוֹתַי אֲשֶׁר |

‹ that « My commandments ‹ to ‹ you continually hearken ‹ that if ‹ And it will come to pass

---

(1) *Deuteronomy* 6:4. (2) See *Pesachim* 56a.

אָנֹכִי מְצַוֶּה | אֶתְכֶם הַיּוֹם, לְאַהֲבָה אֶת־יהוה |
‹ HASHEM, ‹ to love « today, ‹ you ‹ command ‹ I

אֱלֹהֵיכֶם וּלְעָבְדוֹ, בְּכָל־לְבַבְכֶם וּבְכָל־נַפְשְׁכֶם:
« your soul ‹ and with all ‹ your heart ‹ with all « and to serve Him, ‹ your God,

וְנָתַתִּי מְטַר־אַרְצְכֶם בְּעִתּוֹ, יוֹרֶה וּמַלְקוֹשׁ,
« and late rain, ‹ the early rain « in its proper time, ‹ for your land ‹ rain ‹ — then I will provide

וְאָסַפְתָּ דְגָנֶךָ וְתִירֹשְׁךָ וְיִצְהָרֶךָ: וְנָתַתִּי | עֵשֶׂב |
‹ grass ‹ I will provide « and your oil. ‹ your wine, ‹ your grain, ‹ that you may gather in

בְּשָׂדְךָ לִבְהֶמְתֶּךָ, וְאָכַלְתָּ וְשָׂבָעְתָּ: הִשָּׁמְרוּ לָכֶם פֶּן־
‹ lest « for yourselves ‹ Beware « and be satisfied. ‹ and you will eat « for your cattle ‹ in your field

יִפְתֶּה לְבַבְכֶם, וְסַרְתֶּם וַעֲבַדְתֶּם | אֱלֹהִים | אֲחֵרִים
‹ of others ‹ gods ‹ and serve ‹ and you turn astray « be your heart ‹ seduced

וְהִשְׁתַּחֲוִיתֶם לָהֶם: וְחָרָה | אַף־יהוה בָּכֶם, וְעָצַר |
‹ He will restrain « against you. ‹ of HASHEM ‹ the wrath ‹ Then shall blaze « to them. ‹ and bow

אֶת־הַשָּׁמַיִם וְלֹא־יִהְיֶה מָטָר, וְהָאֲדָמָה לֹא תִתֵּן
‹ yield ‹ will not ‹ and the ground « rain ‹ so there will not be ‹ the heaven

אֶת־יְבוּלָהּ, וַאֲבַדְתֶּם | מְהֵרָה מֵעַל הָאָרֶץ הַטֹּבָה |
‹ the good land ‹ from upon « swiftly ‹ And you will be banished « its produce.

אֲשֶׁר | יהוה נֹתֵן לָכֶם: וְשַׂמְתֶּם | אֶת־דְּבָרַי | אֵלֶּה
‹ these words of Mine ‹ Place « you. ‹ gives ‹ HASHEM ‹ which

עַל־לְבַבְכֶם וְעַל־נַפְשְׁכֶם, וּקְשַׁרְתֶּם | אֹתָם לְאוֹת |
‹ for a sign ‹ them ‹ bind « your soul; ‹ and upon ‹ your heart ‹ upon

עַל־יֶדְכֶם, וְהָיוּ לְטוֹטָפֹת בֵּין | עֵינֵיכֶם: וְלִמַּדְתֶּם |
‹ Teach « your eyes. ‹ between ‹ *tefillin* ‹ and they shall be « your arm ‹ upon

אֹתָם | אֶת־בְּנֵיכֶם לְדַבֵּר בָּם, בְּשִׁבְתְּךָ בְּבֵיתֶךָ,
« in your home, ‹ while you sit « them, ‹ to discuss « to your children, ‹ them

וּבְלֶכְתְּךָ בַדֶּרֶךְ, וּבְשָׁכְבְּךָ וּבְקוּמֶךָ: וּכְתַבְתָּם | עַל־

‹ on ‹ And write them « and when you arise. ‹ when you lie down « on the way, ‹ while you walk

מְזֻזוֹת בֵּיתֶךָ וּבִשְׁעָרֶיךָ: לְמַעַן | יִרְבּוּ | יְמֵיכֶם

‹ your days ‹ to prolong ‹ In order « and upon your gates. ‹ of your house ‹ the doorposts

וִימֵי בְנֵיכֶם עַל הָאֲדָמָה | אֲשֶׁר נִשְׁבַּע | יהוה

‹ HASHEM swore ‹ that ‹ the land ‹ upon « of your children ‹ and the days

לַאֲבֹתֵיכֶם לָתֵת לָהֶם, כִּימֵי הַשָּׁמַיִם | עַל־הָאָרֶץ:

« the earth. ‹ on ‹ of the heaven ‹ like the days « them, ‹ to give « to your ancestors

NUMBERS **15:37-41**

וַיֹּאמֶר | יהוה | אֶל־מֹשֶׁה לֵּאמֹר: דַּבֵּר | אֶל־בְּנֵי |

‹ the Children ‹ to ‹ Speak « saying: ‹ Moses, ‹ to ‹ HASHEM Said

יִשְׂרָאֵל וְאָמַרְתָּ אֲלֵהֶם, וְעָשׂוּ לָהֶם צִיצִת עַל־כַּנְפֵי

‹ the corners ‹ on ‹ *tzitzis* ‹ for themselves ‹ that they are to make « to them ‹ and say ‹ of Israel

בִגְדֵיהֶם לְדֹרֹתָם, וְנָתְנוּ | עַל־צִיצִת הַכָּנָף פְּתִיל

‹ a thread ‹ of the corner ‹ the *tzitzis* ‹ upon ‹ And they are to place « throughout their generations. ‹ of their garments,

תְּכֵלֶת: וְהָיָה לָכֶם לְצִיצִת, וּרְאִיתֶם | אֹתוֹ וּזְכַרְתֶּם |

‹ and remember « it ‹ that you may see « *tzitzis,* ‹ for you ‹ And it shall constitute « of *techeiles.*

אֶת־כָּל־מִצְוֹת | יהוה וַעֲשִׂיתֶם | אֹתָם, וְלֹא־תָתֻרוּ |

‹ explore ‹ and do not « them; ‹ and perform « of HASHEM ‹ the commandments ‹ all

אַחֲרֵי לְבַבְכֶם וְאַחֲרֵי | עֵינֵיכֶם אֲשֶׁר־אַתֶּם זֹנִים |

‹ stray ‹ you ‹ which ‹ your eyes ‹ and after ‹ your heart ‹ after

אַחֲרֵיהֶם: לְמַעַן תִּזְכְּרוּ וַעֲשִׂיתֶם | אֶת־כָּל־מִצְוֹתָי,

« My commandments, ‹ all ‹ and perform ‹ you may remember ‹ So that « after them.

וִהְיִיתֶם קְדֹשִׁים לֵאלֹהֵיכֶם:

« to your God. ‹ holy ‹ and be

CONCENTRATE ON THE COMMANDMENT TO REMEMBER THE EXODUS FROM EGYPT.

אֲנִי יְהֹוָה | אֱלֹהֵיכֶם אֲשֶׁר הוֹצֵאתִי | אֶתְכֶם |

‹ you ‹ has removed ‹ Who ‹ your God, ‹ HASHEM, ‹ I am

מֵאֶרֶץ מִצְרַיִם לִהְיוֹת לָכֶם לֵאלֹהִים, אֲנִי |

‹ I am « a God; ‹ to you ‹ to be ‹ of Egypt ‹ from the land

יְהֹוָה | אֱלֹהֵיכֶם: אֱמֶת —

« – It is true . . . « your God. ‹ HASHEM

ALTHOUGH THE WORD אֱמֶת, *TRUE*, BELONGS TO THE NEXT PARAGRAPH, IT IS APPENDED TO THE CONCLUSION OF THE PREVIOUS ONE.

יהוה אֱלֹהֵיכֶם אֱמֶת, — *CHAZZAN* REPEATS

« **is true,** ‹ **your God,** ‹ **HASHEM,**

וֶאֱמוּנָה כָּל זֹאת, וְקַיָּם עָלֵינוּ, כִּי הוּא יהוה

‹ is HASHEM ‹ He ‹ that « for us ‹ and it is firmly established ‹ this, ‹ is all ‹ and faithful

אֱלֹהֵינוּ וְאֵין זוּלָתוֹ, וַאֲנַחְנוּ יִשְׂרָאֵל עַמּוֹ. הַפּוֹדֵנוּ

‹ He is the One Who redeems us « His people. ‹ Israel, ‹ and we are « but Him, ‹ and there is none « our God,

מִיַּד מְלָכִים, מַלְכֵּנוּ הַגּוֹאֲלֵנוּ מִכַּף כָּל הֶעָרִיצִים.

« the cruel tyrants. ‹ of all ‹ from the hand ‹ Who delivers us ‹ our King « of kings, ‹ from the power

הָאֵל הַנִּפְרָע לָנוּ מִצָּרֵינוּ, וְהַמְשַׁלֵּם גְּמוּל לְכָל

‹ upon all ‹ just retribution ‹ and Who repays « from our foes ‹ for us ‹ Who exacts vengeance ‹ He is the God

אֹיְבֵי נַפְשֵׁנוּ. הָעֹשֶׂה גְדֹלוֹת עַד אֵין חֵקֶר, וְנִפְלָאוֹת

‹ and wonders « compre-hension, ‹ that are beyond ‹ great deeds ‹ Who performs « of our soul; ‹ the enemies

עַד אֵין מִסְפָּר.[1] הַשָּׂם נַפְשֵׁנוּ בַּחַיִּים, וְלֹא נָתַן

‹ allow ‹ and did not « in life ‹ our soul ‹ Who set « number. ‹ that are beyond

לַמּוֹט רַגְלֵנוּ.[2] הַמַּדְרִיכֵנוּ עַל בָּמוֹת אוֹיְבֵינוּ, וַיָּרֶם

‹ and raised « of our enemies ‹ the heights ‹ upon ‹ Who led us « our foot. ‹ to falter

קַרְנֵנוּ עַל כָּל שׂוֹנְאֵינוּ. הָעֹשֶׂה לָּנוּ נִסִּים וּנְקָמָה

‹ and vengeance ‹ miracles ‹ for us ‹ Who wrought « who hate us; ‹ all ‹ above ‹ our pride

(1) *Job* 9:10. (2) *Psalms* 66:9.

בְּפַרְעֹה, אוֹתוֹת וּמוֹפְתִים בְּאַדְמַת בְּנֵי חָם. הַמַּכֶּה

upon Pharaoh; « signs ‹ and wonders ‹ in the land ‹ of the offspring ‹ of Ham; « Who struck ‹

בְעֶבְרָתוֹ כָּל בְּכוֹרֵי מִצְרָיִם, וַיּוֹצֵא אֶת עַמּוֹ

in His anger ‹ all ‹ the firstborn ‹ of Egypt « and removed ‹ His people ‹

יִשְׂרָאֵל מִתּוֹכָם לְחֵרוּת עוֹלָם. הַמַּעֲבִיר בָּנָיו

Israel ‹ from their midst ‹ to freedom ‹ everlasting; « Who brought ‹ His children ‹

בֵּין גִּזְרֵי יַם סוּף, אֶת רוֹדְפֵיהֶם וְאֶת שׂוֹנְאֵיהֶם

through ‹ the split parts ‹ of the Sea ‹ of Reeds « [while] those who pursued them ‹ and those who hated them ‹

בִּתְהוֹמוֹת טִבַּע. וְרָאוּ בָנָיו גְּבוּרָתוֹ, שִׁבְּחוּ וְהוֹדוּ

into the depths ‹ He sank. « When His children perceived ‹ His power, « they praised ‹ and gave thanks ‹

לִשְׁמוֹ. ❖ וּמַלְכוּתוֹ בְּרָצוֹן קִבְּלוּ עֲלֵיהֶם. מֹשֶׁה

to His Name. « And His Kingship willingly ‹ they accepted ‹ upon themselves; « Moses ‹

וּבְנֵי יִשְׂרָאֵל לְךָ עָנוּ שִׁירָה בְּשִׂמְחָה רַבָּה, וְאָמְרוּ כֻלָּם:

and the Children ‹ of Israel ‹ to You ‹ exclaimed ‹ in song, « with great gladness ‹ and said ‹ unanimously: «

מִי כָמֹכָה בָּאֵלִם יהוה, מִי כָּמֹכָה נֶאְדָּר בַּקֹּדֶשׁ,

Who ‹ is like You ‹ among the heavenly powers, ‹ HASHEM! « Who ‹ is like You, ‹ mighty ‹ in holiness, «

נוֹרָא תְהִלֹּת, עֹשֵׂה פֶלֶא.[1] ❖ מַלְכוּתְךָ רָאוּ בָנֶיךָ

awesome ‹ [beyond] praise, ‹ doing ‹ wonders! « Your Majesty did Your children behold, «

בּוֹקֵעַ יָם לִפְנֵי מֹשֶׁה, זֶה אֵלִי[2] עָנוּ וְאָמְרוּ:

as You split ‹ the Sea ‹ before ‹ Moses, « *This ‹ is my God!* ‹ they exclaimed; « then they said: «

יהוה יִמְלֹךְ לְעֹלָם וָעֶד.[3]

HASHEM ‹ shall reign ‹ for ever ‹ and ever! «

---

(1) *Exodus* 15:11. (2) 15:2. (3) 15:18.

❖ וְנֶאֱמַר: כִּי פָדָה יהוה אֶת יַעֲקֹב, וּגְאָלוֹ מִיַּד
‹ And it is further said: ‹ For ‹ HASHEM has redeemed ‹ Jacob « and delivered him ‹ from the hand

חָזָק מִמֶּנּוּ.[1] בָּרוּךְ אַתָּה יהוה, גָּאַל יִשְׂרָאֵל.
‹ of one mightier ‹ than he. « Blessed ‹ are You, ‹ HASHEM, ‹ Who redeemed ‹ Israel. «

(אָמֵן. — Cong.)
« (Amen.)

הַשְׁכִּיבֵנוּ יהוה אֱלֹהֵינוּ לְשָׁלוֹם, וְהַעֲמִידֵנוּ
‹ Lay us down to sleep, ‹ HASHEM, ‹ our God, ‹ in peace, « and raise us up,

מַלְכֵּנוּ לְחַיִּים. וּפְרוֹשׂ עָלֵינוּ סֻכַּת שְׁלוֹמֶךָ, וְתַקְּנֵנוּ
‹ our King, ‹ to life. « Spread ‹ over us ‹ the shelter ‹ of Your peace. « Set us aright

בְּעֵצָה טוֹבָה מִלְּפָנֶיךָ, וְהוֹשִׁיעֵנוּ לְמַעַן שְׁמֶךָ. וְהָגֵן
‹ with counsel ‹ that is good ‹ from before You, « and save us ‹ for the sake ‹ of Your Name. « Shield

בַּעֲדֵנוּ, וְהָסֵר מֵעָלֵינוּ אוֹיֵב, דֶּבֶר, וְחֶרֶב, וְרָעָב,
‹ us; « remove ‹ from us ‹ foe, ‹ plague, ‹ sword, ‹ famine,

וְיָגוֹן, וְהָסֵר שָׂטָן מִלְּפָנֵינוּ וּמֵאַחֲרֵינוּ, וּבְצֵל כְּנָפֶיךָ
‹ and woe; « and remove ‹ spiritual impediment ‹ from before us ‹ and from behind us, « and in the shadow ‹ of Your wings

תַּסְתִּירֵנוּ,[2] כִּי אֵל שׁוֹמְרֵנוּ וּמַצִּילֵנוּ אָתָּה, כִּי אֵל
‹ shelter us. « For ‹ God ‹ Who protects ‹ and rescues us ‹ are You; « for ‹ God,

מֶלֶךְ חַנּוּן וְרַחוּם אָתָּה.[3] ❖ וּשְׁמוֹר צֵאתֵנוּ וּבוֹאֵנוּ,
‹ King, ‹ Gracious ‹ and Compassionate, ‹ are You. « Safeguard ‹ our going ‹ and our coming

לְחַיִּים וּלְשָׁלוֹם מֵעַתָּה וְעַד עוֹלָם.[4] בָּרוּךְ
‹ for life ‹ and for peace ‹ from now ‹ and for all ‹ eternity. « Blessed

אַתָּה יהוה, שׁוֹמֵר עַמּוֹ יִשְׂרָאֵל לָעַד. (אָמֵן. — Cong.)
‹ are You, ‹ HASHEM, « Who safeguards ‹ His people ‹ Israel ‹ forever. « (Amen.)

(1) *Jeremiah* 31:10. (2) Cf. *Psalms* 17:8. (3) Cf. *Nehemiah* 9:31. (4) Cf. *Psalms* 121:8. (5) 89: 53.

SOME CONGREGATIONS OMIT THE FOLLOWING PRAYERS AND CONTINUE WITH HALF-*KADDISH* **(P. 603).**

בָּרוּךְ יהוה לְעוֹלָם, אָמֵן וְאָמֵן.[1] בָּרוּךְ יהוה

‹ is HASHEM ‹ Blessed « and Amen. ‹ Amen « forever, ‹ is HASHEM ‹ Blessed

מִצִּיּוֹן, שֹׁכֵן יְרוּשָׁלָיִם, הַלְלוּיָהּ.[2] בָּרוּךְ יהוה

‹ is HASHEM, ‹ Blessed « Halleluyah! « in Jerusalem, ‹ He Who dwells « from Zion,

אֱלֹהִים אֱלֹהֵי יִשְׂרָאֵל, עֹשֵׂה נִפְלָאוֹת לְבַדּוֹ.

« by Himself. ‹ wondrous things ‹ Who does « of Israel, ‹ the God ‹ God,

וּבָרוּךְ שֵׁם כְּבוֹדוֹ לְעוֹלָם, וְיִמָּלֵא כְבוֹדוֹ אֶת כָּל

‹ all ‹ may His glory ‹ and fill « forever; ‹ of His glory ‹ is the Name ‹ Blessed

הָאָרֶץ, אָמֵן וְאָמֵן.[3] יְהִי כְבוֹד יהוה לְעוֹלָם,

« endure forever; ‹ of HASHEM ‹ the glory ‹ May « and Amen. ‹ Amen « the earth.

יִשְׂמַח יהוה בְּמַעֲשָׂיו.[4] יְהִי שֵׁם יהוה מְבֹרָךְ,

« be blessed, ‹ of HASHEM ‹ the Name ‹ Let « in His works. ‹ let HASHEM rejoice

מֵעַתָּה וְעַד עוֹלָם.[5] כִּי לֹא יִטֹּשׁ יהוה אֶת עַמּוֹ

« His people ‹ HASHEM will not forsake ‹ For « eternity. ‹ until ‹ from this time

בַּעֲבוּר שְׁמוֹ הַגָּדוֹל, כִּי הוֹאִיל יהוה לַעֲשׂוֹת

‹ to make ‹ HASHEM has vowed ‹ for « that is great, ‹ of His Name, ‹ for the sake

אֶתְכֶם לוֹ לְעָם.[6] וַיַּרְא כָּל הָעָם וַיִּפְּלוּ עַל פְּנֵיהֶם,

« their faces ‹ on ‹ and they fell ‹ the people ‹ did all ‹ See « a people. ‹ for Him ‹ you

וַיֹּאמְרוּ, יהוה הוּא הָאֱלֹהִים, יהוה הוּא הָאֱלֹהִים.[7]

« *is the God!* ‹ *— He* « *HASHEM* « *is the God!* ‹ *— He* « *HASHEM* « and they said,

וְהָיָה יהוה לְמֶלֶךְ עַל כָּל הָאָרֶץ, בַּיּוֹם הַהוּא

‹ — on that day « the world ‹ all ‹ over ‹ be King ‹ HASHEM ‹ Then will

יִהְיֶה יהוה אֶחָד וּשְׁמוֹ אֶחָד.[8] יְהִי חַסְדְּךָ יהוה

‹ HASHEM, ‹ Your kindness, ‹ May « be One. ‹ and His Name ‹ be One ‹ HASHEM ‹ shall

---

(1) *Psalms* 89:53. (2) 135: 21. (3) 72:18-19. (4) 104:31. (5) 113:2.
(6) *I Samuel* 12:22. (7) *I Kings* 18:39. (8) *Zechariah* 14:9.

עָלֵינוּ, כַּאֲשֶׁר יִחַלְנוּ לָךְ.[1] הוֹשִׁיעֵנוּ יהוה אֱלֹהֵינוּ,
‹ our God, ‹ HASHEM, ‹ Save us « You. ‹ we awaited ‹ just as « be upon us,

וְקַבְּצֵנוּ מִן הַגּוֹיִם, לְהוֹדוֹת לְשֵׁם קָדְשֶׁךָ לְהִשְׁתַּבֵּחַ
‹ and to glory ‹ of Your Holiness ‹ the Name ‹ to thank « among the nations, ‹ from ‹ and gather us

בִּתְהִלָּתֶךָ.[2] כָּל גּוֹיִם אֲשֶׁר עָשִׂיתָ יָבוֹאוּ וְיִשְׁתַּחֲווּ
‹ and bow down ‹ will come ‹ You have made ‹ that ‹ the nations ‹ All « in Your praise!

לְפָנֶיךָ אֲדֹנָי, וִיכַבְּדוּ לִשְׁמֶךָ. כִּי גָדוֹל אַתָּה וְעֹשֵׂה
‹ and You work ‹ are You ‹ great ‹ For « to Your Name. ‹ and they will give glory « O Lord, ‹ before You,

נִפְלָאוֹת, אַתָּה אֱלֹהִים לְבַדֶּךָ.[3] וַאֲנַחְנוּ עַמְּךָ וְצֹאן
‹ and the sheep ‹ Your people « As for us, « alone. ‹ O God ‹ You « wonders,

מַרְעִיתֶךָ, נוֹדֶה לְּךָ לְעוֹלָם, לְדוֹר וָדֹר נְסַפֵּר
‹ we shall relate ‹ after generation ‹ for generation « forever; ‹ You ‹ we shall thank « of Your pasture,

תְּהִלָּתֶךָ.[4] בָּרוּךְ יהוה בַּיּוֹם. בָּרוּךְ יהוה בַּלָּיְלָה.
« by night; ‹ is HASHEM ‹ blessed « by day; ‹ is HASHEM ‹ Blessed « Your praise.

בָּרוּךְ יהוה בְּשָׁכְבֵנוּ. בָּרוּךְ יהוה בְּקוּמֵנוּ. כִּי בְיָדְךָ
‹ in Your hand ‹ For « when we arise. ‹ is HASHEM ‹ blessed « when we retire; ‹ is HASHEM blessed

נַפְשׁוֹת הַחַיִּים וְהַמֵּתִים. אֲשֶׁר בְּיָדוֹ נֶפֶשׁ כָּל חָי,
« the living ‹ of all ‹ is the soul ‹ in His hand ‹ That « and of the dead. ‹ of the living ‹ are the souls

וְרוּחַ כָּל בְּשַׂר אִישׁ.[5] בְּיָדְךָ אַפְקִיד רוּחִי, פָּדִיתָה
‹ You redeemed « my spirit; ‹ I shall entrust ‹ In Your hand « mankind. ‹ of all ‹ and the spirit

אוֹתִי, יהוה אֵל אֱמֶת.[6] אֱלֹהֵינוּ שֶׁבַּשָּׁמַיִם, יַחֵד שִׁמְךָ,
« to Your Name; ‹ bring unity « Who is in heaven, ‹ Our God, « of truth. ‹ God ‹ O HASHEM, ‹ me,

וְקַיֵּם מַלְכוּתְךָ תָּמִיד, וּמְלוֹךְ עָלֵינוּ לְעוֹלָם וָעֶד.
« and ever. ‹ for ever ‹ over us ‹ and reign « forever ‹ Your kingdom ‹ establish

(1) *Psalms* 33:22. (2) 106:47. (3) 86:9-10. (4) 79:13. (5) *Job* 12:10. (6) *Psalms* 31:6.

יִרְאוּ עֵינֵינוּ וְיִשְׂמַח לִבֵּנוּ וְתָגֵל נַפְשֵׁנוּ בִּישׁוּעָתְךָ

‹ in Your salvation « may our soul ‹ and exult « may our heart, ‹ rejoice « may our eyes, ‹ See

בֶּאֱמֶת, בֶּאֱמֹר לְצִיּוֹן מָלַךְ אֱלֹהָיִךְ.[1] יהוה מֶלֶךְ,[2]

« reigns, ‹ HASHEM « *has Your God.* ‹ *Reigned* « to Zion, ‹ when it is told « in truth,

יהוה מָלָךְ,[3] יהוה יִמְלֹךְ לְעֹלָם וָעֶד.[4] ❖ כִּי

‹ For « and ever. ‹ for ever ‹ shall reign ‹ HASHEM « has reigned, ‹ HASHEM

הַמַּלְכוּת שֶׁלְּךָ הִיא, וּלְעוֹלְמֵי עַד תִּמְלוֹךְ בְּכָבוֹד,

« in glory, ‹ You will reign ‹ and ever ‹ and for ever « is Yours ‹ the kingdom

כִּי אֵין לָנוּ מֶלֶךְ אֶלָּא אָתָּה. בָּרוּךְ אַתָּה יהוה,

« HASHEM, ‹ are You, ‹ Blessed « You. ‹ except for ‹ King ‹ we have no ‹ for

הַמֶּלֶךְ בִּכְבוֹדוֹ תָּמִיד יִמְלוֹךְ עָלֵינוּ לְעוֹלָם וָעֶד,

‹ and ever, ‹ for ever ‹ over us ‹ will He reign ‹ always ‹ Who in His glory ‹ the King

וְעַל כָּל מַעֲשָׂיו. (.Cong. — אָמֵן)

« (Amen.) « His creation. ‹ all ‹ and over

THE *CHAZZAN* RECITES חֲצִי קַדִּישׁ, HALF-*KADDISH*:

יִתְגַּדַּל וְיִתְקַדַּשׁ שְׁמֵהּ רַבָּא. (.Cong. — אָמֵן) בְּעָלְמָא דִּי

‹ that ‹ — in the world ‹ (Amen.) « that is great! — ‹ may His Name ‹ and be sanctified ‹ Grow exalted

בְּרָא כִרְעוּתֵהּ. וְיַמְלִיךְ מַלְכוּתֵהּ, בְּחַיֵּיכוֹן וּבְיוֹמֵיכוֹן וּבְחַיֵּי

‹ and in the lifetimes ‹ and in your days, ‹ in your lifetimes « to His kingship, ‹ and may He give reign « according to His will, ‹ He created

דְכָל בֵּית יִשְׂרָאֵל, בַּעֲגָלָא וּבִזְמַן קָרִיב. וְאִמְרוּ: אָמֵן.

« Amen. ‹ Now respond: « that comes soon. ‹ and at a time ‹ swiftly « of Israel, ‹ Family ‹ of the entire

CONGREGATION RESPONDS:

אָמֵן. יְהֵא שְׁמֵהּ רַבָּא מְבָרַךְ לְעָלַם וּלְעָלְמֵי עָלְמַיָּא.

« and for all eternity. ‹ forever ‹ be blessed ‹ that is great ‹ His Name ‹ May « Amen.

CHAZZAN CONTINUES:

יְהֵא שְׁמֵהּ רַבָּא מְבָרַךְ לְעָלַם וּלְעָלְמֵי עָלְמַיָּא. יִתְבָּרַךְ

‹ Blessed, « and for all eternity. ‹ forever ‹ be blessed ‹ that is great ‹ His Name ‹ May

---

(1) *Isaiah* 52:7. (2) *Psalms* 10:16. (3) 93:1 et al. (4) *Exodus* 15:18.

וְיִשְׁתַּבַּח וְיִתְפָּאַר וְיִתְרוֹמַם וְיִתְנַשֵּׂא וְיִתְהַדָּר וְיִתְעַלֶּה

‹ praised, ‹ glorified, ‹ exalted, ‹ upraised, ‹ honored, ‹ elevated,

וְיִתְהַלָּל שְׁמֵהּ דְּקֻדְשָׁא בְּרִיךְ הוּא (Cong. — בְּרִיךְ הוּא.)

‹ and lauded ‹ be the Name ‹ of the Holy One, ‹ Blessed « is He ‹ (Blessed « is He)

— לְעֵֽלָּא מִן כָּל בִּרְכָתָא וְשִׁירָתָא תֻּשְׁבְּחָתָא וְנֶחֱמָתָא

‹ beyond ‹ any ‹ blessing « and song, ‹ praise ‹ and consolation

דַּאֲמִירָן בְּעָלְמָא. וְאִמְרוּ: אָמֵן. (Cong. — אָמֵן.)

‹ that are uttered « in the world. ‹ Now respond: « Amen. « (Amen.)

SHEMONEH ESREI / עמידה — שמונה עשרה

TAKE THREE STEPS BACKWARD, THEN THREE STEPS FORWARD. REMAIN STANDING WITH FEET TOGETHER WHILE RECITING *SHEMONEH ESREI.* RECITE IT WITH QUIET DEVOTION AND WITHOUT INTERRUPTION, VERBAL OR OTHERWISE. ALTHOUGH ITS RECITATION SHOULD NOT BE AUDIBLE TO OTHERS, ONE MUST PRAY LOUDLY ENOUGH TO HEAR HIMSELF.

אֲדֹנָי שְׂפָתַי תִּפְתָּח, וּפִי יַגִּיד תְּהִלָּתֶךָ.[1]

‹ O Lord, ‹ my lips « open, ‹ that my mouth ‹ may declare « Your praise.

PATRIARCHS / אבות

BEND THE KNEES AT בָּרוּךְ, *BLESSED*; BOW AT אַתָּה, *YOU*; STRAIGHTEN UP AT ה׳, *HASHEM.*

בָּרוּךְ אַתָּה יהוה אֱלֹהֵינוּ וֵאלֹהֵי אֲבוֹתֵינוּ, אֱלֹהֵי

‹ Blessed ‹ are You, ‹ HASHEM, ‹ our God ‹ and the God « of our forefathers, ‹ God

אַבְרָהָם, אֱלֹהֵי יִצְחָק, וֵאלֹהֵי יַעֲקֹב, הָאֵל הַגָּדוֹל

« of Abraham, ‹ God « of Isaac, ‹ and God « of Jacob; ‹ God ‹ [Who is] great,

הַגִּבּוֹר וְהַנּוֹרָא, אֵל עֶלְיוֹן, גּוֹמֵל חֲסָדִים טוֹבִים,

‹ mighty, ‹ and awesome; ‹ God « the Most High, ‹ Who bestows ‹ kindnesses ‹ [that are] beneficent

וְקוֹנֵה הַכֹּל, וְזוֹכֵר חַסְדֵי אָבוֹת, וּמֵבִיא גוֹאֵל לִבְנֵי

‹ and creates « every-thing, ‹ Who recalls ‹ the kindnesses « of the Patriarchs, ‹ and brings ‹ a Redeemer ‹ to the children

בְנֵיהֶם, לְמַעַן שְׁמוֹ בְּאַהֲבָה. מֶלֶךְ עוֹזֵר וּמוֹשִׁיעַ וּמָגֵן.

« of their children, ‹ for the sake ‹ of His Name, « with love. ‹ O King, ‹ Helper, ‹ Savior, « and Shield.

(1) *Psalms* 51:17.

BEND THE KNEES AT בָּרוּךְ, *BLESSED*; BOW AT אַתָּה, *YOU*; STRAIGHTEN UP AT 'ה, *HASHEM.*

בָּרוּךְ אַתָּה יהוה, מָגֵן אַבְרָהָם.

« of Abraham. ‹ Shield « HASHEM, ‹ are You, ‹ Blessed

GOD'S MIGHT / גבורות

אַתָּה גִּבּוֹר לְעוֹלָם אֲדֹנָי, מְחַיֵּה מֵתִים אַתָּה,

« are You; ‹ of the dead ‹ the Revivifier « O Lord, ‹ eternally, ‹ mighty ‹ You are

רַב לְהוֹשִׁיעַ. מְכַלְכֵּל חַיִּים בְּחֶסֶד, מְחַיֵּה מֵתִים

‹ the dead ‹ Who revivifies « with kindness, ‹ the living ‹ Who sustains « able to save, ‹ abundantly

בְּרַחֲמִים רַבִּים, סוֹמֵךְ נוֹפְלִים, וְרוֹפֵא חוֹלִים,

« the sick, ‹ Who heals « the fallen, ‹ Who supports « abundant, ‹ with mercy

וּמַתִּיר אֲסוּרִים, וּמְקַיֵּם אֱמוּנָתוֹ לִישֵׁנֵי עָפָר. מִי

‹ Who « in the dust. ‹ to those asleep ‹ His faith ‹ and Who maintains « the confined, ‹ Who releases

כָמוֹךָ בַּעַל גְּבוּרוֹת, וּמִי דּוֹמֶה לָּךְ, מֶלֶךְ מֵמִית

‹ Who causes death ‹ O King « to You, ‹ is comparable ‹ and who « of mighty deeds, ‹ O Master ‹ is like You,

וּמְחַיֶּה, וּמַצְמִיחַ יְשׁוּעָה. וְנֶאֱמָן אַתָּה לְהַחֲיוֹת

‹ to revivify ‹ are You ‹ And faithful « salvation! ‹ and makes sprout ‹ and restores life

מֵתִים. בָּרוּךְ אַתָּה יהוה, מְחַיֵּה הַמֵּתִים.

« the dead. ‹ Who revivifies « HASHEM, ‹ are You, ‹ Blessed « the dead.

HOLINESS OF GOD'S NAME / קדושת השם

אַתָּה קָדוֹשׁ וְשִׁמְךָ קָדוֹשׁ, וּקְדוֹשִׁים בְּכָל יוֹם

‹ day ‹ every ‹ and holy ones « is holy, ‹ and Your Name ‹ are holy ‹ You

יְהַלְּלוּךָ סֶּלָה. בָּרוּךְ אַתָּה יהוה, הָאֵל הַקָּדוֹשׁ.

« Who is Holy. ‹ the God « HASHEM, ‹ are You, ‹ Blessed « forever. ‹ praise You

INSIGHT / בינה

אַתָּה חוֹנֵן לְאָדָם דַּעַת, וּמְלַמֵּד לֶאֱנוֹשׁ בִּינָה.

« insight. ‹ to a [frail] mortal ‹ and teach « with wisdom ‹ man ‹ graciously endow ‹ You

חָנֵּנוּ מֵאִתְּךָ דֵּעָה בִּינָה וְהַשְׂכֵּל. בָּרוּךְ אַתָּה
‹ Endow us graciously ‹ from Yourself ‹ [with] wisdom, ‹ insight, ‹ and discernment. « Blessed ‹ are You,

יהוה, חוֹנֵן הַדָּעַת.
HASHEM, « gracious Giver ‹ of wisdom. «

REPENTANCE / תשובה

הֲשִׁיבֵנוּ אָבִינוּ לְתוֹרָתֶךָ, וְקָרְבֵנוּ מַלְכֵּנוּ
‹ Bring us back, ‹ our Father, ‹ to Your Torah, « and bring us near, ‹ our King, ‹

לַעֲבוֹדָתֶךָ, וְהַחֲזִירֵנוּ בִּתְשׁוּבָה שְׁלֵמָה לְפָנֶיךָ.
to Your service, « and influence us to return ‹ in complete repentance ‹ before You. «

בָּרוּךְ אַתָּה יהוה, הָרוֹצֶה בִּתְשׁוּבָה.
Blessed ‹ are You, ‹ HASHEM, « Who desires ‹ repentance. «

FORGIVENESS / סליחה

STRIKE THE LEFT SIDE OF THE CHEST WITH THE RIGHT FIST WHILE RECITING THE WORDS חָטָאנוּ, *SINNED,* AND פָּשָׁעְנוּ, *WILLFULLY SINNED.*

סְלַח לָנוּ אָבִינוּ כִּי חָטָאנוּ, מְחַל לָנוּ מַלְכֵּנוּ
‹ Forgive ‹ us, ‹ our Father, ‹ for « we have sinned; ‹ pardon ‹ us, ‹ our King,

כִּי פָשָׁעְנוּ, כִּי מוֹחֵל וְסוֹלֵחַ אָתָּה. בָּרוּךְ
‹ for ‹ we have willfully sinned; « for ‹ a Pardoner ‹ and Forgiver ‹ are You. « Blessed ‹

אַתָּה יהוה, חַנּוּן הַמַּרְבֶּה לִסְלוֹחַ.
are You, ‹ HASHEM, « the gracious One ‹ Who abundantly ‹ forgives. «

REDEMPTION / גאולה

רְאֵה בְעָנְיֵנוּ, וְרִיבָה רִיבֵנוּ, וּגְאָלֵנוּ[1] מְהֵרָה
‹ Behold ‹ our affliction, « champion ‹ our cause, « and redeem us ‹ speedily ‹

לְמַעַן שְׁמֶךָ, כִּי גוֹאֵל חָזָק אָתָּה. בָּרוּךְ אַתָּה
‹ for the sake of ‹ Your Name, « for ‹ a Redeemer ‹ Who is powerful ‹ are You. « Blessed ‹ are You, ‹

יהוה, גוֹאֵל יִשְׂרָאֵל.
HASHEM, « Redeemer ‹ of Israel. «

(1) Cf. *Psalms* 119:153-154.

HEALTH AND HEALING / רפואה

רְפָאֵנוּ יהוה וְנֵרָפֵא, הוֹשִׁיעֵנוּ וְנִוָּשֵׁעָה, כִּי

Heal us, ‹ HASHEM » — then we will be healed; » save us » — then we will be saved, » for ‹

תְהִלָּתֵנוּ אָתָּה,[1] וְהַעֲלֵה רְפוּאָה שְׁלֵמָה לְכָל

the One we praise › is You. » Bring › healing › that is complete › for all ›

מַכּוֹתֵינוּ, °°כִּי אֵל מֶלֶךְ רוֹפֵא נֶאֱמָן וְרַחֲמָן אָתָּה.

our ailments, » for › O God, › [and] King, › a Healer › Who is faithful › and compassionate › are You. »

בָּרוּךְ אַתָּה יהוה, רוֹפֵא חוֹלֵי עַמּוֹ יִשְׂרָאֵל.

Blessed › are You, › HASHEM, » Who heals › the sick › of His people › Israel. »

YEAR OF PROSPERITY / ברכת השנים

בָּרֵךְ עָלֵינוּ יהוה אֱלֹהֵינוּ אֶת הַשָּׁנָה הַזֹּאת

Bless › on our behalf › — O HASHEM, › our God — » this year »

וְאֶת כָּל מִינֵי תְבוּאָתָהּ לְטוֹבָה, וְתֵן בְּרָכָה

and › all › of the kinds › of its crops › for goodness; » and give › a blessing ›

עַל פְּנֵי הָאֲדָמָה, וְשַׂבְּעֵנוּ מִטּוּבֶךָ, וּבָרֵךְ שְׁנָתֵנוּ

on › the face › of the earth, » and satisfy us › from Your bounty, » and bless › our year ›

כַּשָּׁנִים הַטּוֹבוֹת. בָּרוּךְ אַתָּה יהוה, מְבָרֵךְ הַשָּׁנִים.

like the years › that were good. » Blessed › are You, › HASHEM, » Who blesses › the years. »

°°AT THIS POINT ONE MAY INSERT A PRAYER FOR ONE WHO IS ILL:

יְהִי רָצוֹן מִלְּפָנֶיךָ, יהוה אֱלֹהַי וֵאלֹהֵי אֲבוֹתַי, שֶׁתִּשְׁלַח מְהֵרָה

May it be › the will › before You, » HASHEM, › my God, › and the God › of my forefathers, » that You send › quickly ›

רְפוּאָה שְׁלֵמָה מִן הַשָּׁמַיִם, רְפוּאַת הַנֶּפֶשׁ וּרְפוּאַת הַגּוּף

a healing › which is complete, » from › heaven, » a healing › of the spirit › and a healing › of the body »

FOR A MALE FOR A FEMALE

לַחוֹלֶה / לַחוֹלָה (SICK ONE'S NAME) בֶּן / בַּת (MOTHER'S NAME) בְּתוֹךְ שְׁאָר

to the sick one › son of / daughter of › among › the other ›

חוֹלֵי יִשְׂרָאֵל.

sick ones › of Israel. »

CONTINUE ... כִּי אֵל (ABOVE)

---

(1) *Jeremiah* 17:14.

INGATHERING OF EXILES / קיבוץ גליות

תְּקַע בְּשׁוֹפָר גָּדוֹל לְחֵרוּתֵנוּ, וְשָׂא נֵס לְקַבֵּץ

‹to gather ‹ a banner ‹ raise «for our freedom, ‹ the great *shofar* ‹ Sound

גָּלֻיּוֹתֵינוּ, וְקַבְּצֵנוּ יַחַד מֵאַרְבַּע כַּנְפוֹת הָאָרֶץ.[1]

«of the earth. ‹ corners ‹ from the four ‹ together ‹ and gather us « our exiles,

בָּרוּךְ אַתָּה יהוה, מְקַבֵּץ נִדְחֵי עַמּוֹ יִשְׂרָאֵל.

« Israel. ‹ of His people ‹ the dispersed ‹ Who gathers in « HASHEM, ‹ are You, ‹ Blessed

RESTORATION OF JUSTICE / דין

הָשִׁיבָה שׁוֹפְטֵינוּ כְּבָרִאשׁוֹנָה, וְיוֹעֲצֵינוּ כְּבַתְּחִלָּה,[2]

« as at the beginning; ‹ and our counselors ‹ as [they were] in earliest times, ‹ our judges ‹ Restore

וְהָסֵר מִמֶּנּוּ יָגוֹן וַאֲנָחָה, וּמְלוֹךְ עָלֵינוּ אַתָּה יהוה

‹HASHEM, ‹ — You, ‹ over us ‹ and reign « and groan; ‹ sorrow ‹ from us ‹ remove

לְבַדְּךָ בְּחֶסֶד וּבְרַחֲמִים, וְצַדְּקֵנוּ בַּמִּשְׁפָּט. בָּרוּךְ

‹ Blessed « through judgment. ‹ and justify us « and compassion, ‹ with kindness « alone —

אַתָּה יהוה, מֶלֶךְ אוֹהֵב צְדָקָה וּמִשְׁפָּט.

« and judgment. ‹ righteousness ‹ Who loves ‹ the King « HASHEM, ‹ are You,

AGAINST HERETICS / ברכת המינים

וְלַמַּלְשִׁינִים אַל תְּהִי תִקְוָה, וְכָל הָרִשְׁעָה

‹ wickedness ‹ and may all « hope; ‹ let there not be ‹ And for slanderers

כְּרֶגַע תֹּאבֵד, וְכָל אוֹיְבֶיךָ מְהֵרָה יִכָּרֵתוּ, וְהַזֵּדִים

‹ The willful sinners « be cut down. ‹ speedily ‹ Your enemies ‹ and may all « perish; ‹ in an instant

מְהֵרָה תְעַקֵּר וּתְשַׁבֵּר וּתְמַגֵּר וְתַכְנִיעַ בִּמְהֵרָה

‹ speedily « and humble — ‹ cast down, ‹ smash, ‹ uproot, ‹ — may You speedily

בְיָמֵינוּ. בָּרוּךְ אַתָּה יהוה, שׁוֹבֵר אֹיְבִים וּמַכְנִיעַ

‹and humbles ‹ enemies ‹ Who breaks «HASHEM, ‹ are You, ‹ Blessed « in our days.

זֵדִים.

« willful sinners.

(1) *Isaiah* 11:12. (2) Cf. 1:26.

THE RIGHTEOUS / צדיקים

עַל הַצַּדִּיקִים וְעַל הַחֲסִידִים, וְעַל זִקְנֵי עַמְּךָ בֵּית

‹ the Family ‹ of Your people ‹ the elders ‹ on « the devout, ‹ on ‹ the righteous, ‹ On

יִשְׂרָאֵל, וְעַל פְּלֵיטַת סוֹפְרֵיהֶם, וְעַל גֵּרֵי הַצֶּדֶק

‹ who are righteous ‹ the converts ‹ on « of their scholars, ‹ the remnant ‹ on « of Israel,

וְעָלֵינוּ, יֶהֱמוּ רַחֲמֶיךָ, יהוה אֱלֹהֵינוּ, וְתֵן שָׂכָר

‹ a reward ‹ and give « our God, ‹ HASHEM, « Your compassion, ‹ — may aroused be « and on ourselves

טוֹב לְכָל הַבּוֹטְחִים בְּשִׁמְךָ בֶּאֱמֶת, וְשִׂים חֶלְקֵנוּ

‹ our lot ‹ Put « in sincerity. ‹ in Your Name ‹ who believe ‹ to all ‹ which is good

עִמָּהֶם לְעוֹלָם, וְלֹא נֵבוֹשׁ כִּי בְךָ בָּטָחְנוּ. בָּרוּךְ

‹ Blessed « we trust. ‹ in You ‹ for ‹ feel ashamed, ‹ and we will not « forever, ‹ with them

אַתָּה יהוה, מִשְׁעָן וּמִבְטָח לַצַּדִּיקִים.

« of the righteous. ‹ and Assurance ‹ Mainstay « HASHEM, ‹ are You,

REBUILDING JERUSALEM / בנין ירושלים

וְלִירוּשָׁלַיִם עִירְךָ בְּרַחֲמִים תָּשׁוּב, וְתִשְׁכּוֹן

‹ and may You rest « may You return, ‹ in compassion ‹ Your City, ‹ And to Jerusalem,

בְּתוֹכָהּ כַּאֲשֶׁר דִּבַּרְתָּ, וּבְנֵה אוֹתָהּ בְּקָרוֹב בְּיָמֵינוּ

‹ in our days ‹ soon ‹ it ‹ May You rebuild « You have spoken. ‹ as ‹ within it,

בִּנְיַן עוֹלָם, וְכִסֵּא דָוִד מְהֵרָה לְתוֹכָהּ תָּכִין.

« may You establish. ‹ within it ‹ speedily, ‹ of David, ‹ and the throne « that is eternal, ‹ as a structure

בָּרוּךְ אַתָּה יהוה, בּוֹנֵה יְרוּשָׁלָיִם.

« of Jerusalem. ‹ Builder « HASHEM, ‹ are You, ‹ Blessed

DAVIDIC REIGN / מלכות בית דוד

אֶת צֶמַח דָּוִד עַבְדְּךָ מְהֵרָה תַצְמִיחַ, וְקַרְנוֹ

‹ and his pride « may You cause to flourish, ‹ speedily, « Your servant, ‹ of David ‹ offspring ‹ The

תָּרוּם בִּישׁוּעָתֶךָ, כִּי לִישׁוּעָתְךָ קִוִּינוּ כָּל הַיּוֹם.

« all day long. ‹ we hope ‹ for Your salvation ‹ because « through Your salvation, ‹ may You exalt

בָּרוּךְ אַתָּה יהוה, מַצְמִיחַ קֶרֶן יְשׁוּעָה.

« of salvation. ‹ the pride ‹ Who causes to flourish « HASHEM, ‹ are You, ‹ Blessed

ACCEPTANCE OF PRAYER / קבלת תפלה

שְׁמַע קוֹלֵנוּ יהוה אֱלֹהֵינוּ, חוּס וְרַחֵם

‹ and have compassion ‹ have pity « our God, ‹ HASHEM, ‹ our voice, ‹ Hear

עָלֵינוּ, וְקַבֵּל בְּרַחֲמִים וּבְרָצוֹן אֶת תְּפִלָּתֵנוּ, כִּי

‹ for « our prayer, ‹ and with favor ‹ with compassion ‹ and accept « on us,

אֵל שׁוֹמֵעַ תְּפִלּוֹת וְתַחֲנוּנִים אָתָּה. וּמִלְּפָנֶיךָ

« From before Yourself, « are You. ‹ and supplications ‹ prayers ‹ Who hears ‹ God

מַלְכֵּנוּ, רֵיקָם אַל תְּשִׁיבֵנוּ.°°

« turn us away, ‹ do not ‹ empty-handed ‹ our King,

°°AT THIS POINT ONE MAY INSERT THE FOLLOWING PERSONAL PRAYER FOR FORGIVENESS:

אָנָּא יהוה, חָטָאתִי עָוִיתִי וּפָשַׁעְתִּי לְפָנֶיךָ, מִיּוֹם הֱיוֹתִי

‹ I have existed ‹ from the day « before You, ‹ and willfully « been iniquitous, ‹ I have sinned, ‹ HASHEM, ‹ Please,

עַל הָאֲדָמָה עַד הַיּוֹם הַזֶּה (וּבִפְרַט בַּחֵטְא ...). אָנָּא יהוה,

‹ HASHEM, ‹ Please, « with the sin of . . .). ‹ (and especially « this very day ‹ until ‹ earth ‹ on

עֲשֵׂה לְמַעַן שִׁמְךָ הַגָּדוֹל, וּתְכַפֶּר לִי עַל חֲטָאַי וַעֲוֹנַי

‹ my iniquities, ‹ my inadvertent sins, ‹ for ‹ to me ‹ and grant atonement « which is great ‹ Your Name ‹ for the sake of ‹ act

וּפְשָׁעַי שֶׁחָטָאתִי וְשֶׁעָוִיתִי וְשֶׁפָּשַׁעְתִּי לְפָנֶיךָ, מִנְּעוּרַי עַד

‹ until ‹ from my youth « before You, ‹ and sinned willfully ‹ been iniquitous, ‹ [through which] I have sinned, « and my willful sins

הַיּוֹם הַזֶּה. וּתְמַלֵּא כָּל הַשֵּׁמוֹת שֶׁפָּגַמְתִּי בְּשִׁמְךָ הַגָּדוֹל.

« that is great. ‹ within Your Name ‹ that I have blemished ‹ the [Holy] Names ‹ all ‹ And make whole « this very day.

CONTINUE ... כִּי אַתָּה (P. 611)

°°AT THIS POINT ONE MAY INSERT THE FOLLOWING PERSONAL PRAYER FOR LIVELIHOOD:

אַתָּה הוּא יהוה הָאֱלֹהִים, הַזָּן וּמְפַרְנֵס וּמְכַלְכֵּל מִקַּרְנֵי

‹ from the horns « and supports, ‹ sustains, ‹ Who nourishes, ‹ the God ‹ HASHEM, ‹ Who are ‹ It is You

רְאֵמִים עַד בֵּיצֵי כִנִּים. הַטְרִיפֵנִי לֶחֶם חֻקִּי,[1] וְהַמְצֵא לִי

‹ for me ‹ provide « allotted to me; ‹ the bread ‹ Supply me with « of lice. ‹ the eggs ‹ to ‹ of *re'eimim*

וּלְכָל בְּנֵי בֵיתִי מְזוֹנוֹתַי קוֹדֶם שֶׁאֶצְטָרֵךְ לָהֶם, בְּנַחַת

‹ in contentment « for it; ‹ I have need ‹ before ‹ my food, « of my household, ‹ members ‹ and for all

וְלֹא בְצַעַר, בְּהֶתֵּר וְלֹא בְאִסּוּר, בְּכָבוֹד וְלֹא בְּבִזָּיוֹן,

« in disgrace, ‹ but not ‹ in honor « in a forbidden manner, ‹ but not ‹ in a permissible manner « in pain, ‹ but not

לְחַיִּים וּלְשָׁלוֹם, מִשֶּׁפַע בְּרָכָה וְהַצְלָחָה, וּמִשֶּׁפַע בְּרֵכָה

‹ of the spring ‹ and from the flow « and success ‹ of blessing ‹ from the flow « and for peace; ‹ for life

עֶלְיוֹנָה, כְּדֵי שֶׁאוּכַל לַעֲשׂוֹת רְצוֹנֶךָ וְלַעֲסוֹק בְּתוֹרָתֶךָ

‹ in Your Torah ‹ and engage « Your will ‹ to do ‹ I be enabled ‹ so that « from On High,

וּלְקַיֵּם מִצְוֹתֶיךָ. וְאַל תַּצְרִיכֵנִי לִידֵי מַתְּנַת בָּשָׂר וָדָם.

« and blood; ‹ of flesh ‹ of the gifts of the hands ‹ make me needful ‹ Do not « Your commandments. ‹ and fulfill

וִיקֻיַּם בִּי מִקְרָא שֶׁכָּתוּב: פּוֹתֵחַ אֶת יָדֶךָ, וּמַשְׂבִּיעַ לְכָל

‹ *every* ‹ *and satisfy* ‹ *Your hand,* ‹ *You open* « that states, ‹ the verse ‹ in me ‹ and may there be fulfilled

חַי רָצוֹן.[2] וְכָתוּב: הַשְׁלֵךְ עַל יהוה יְהָבְךָ וְהוּא יְכַלְכְּלֶךָ.[3]

« *will sustain you.* ‹ *and He* ‹ *Your burden* ‹ *HASHEM* ‹ *upon* ‹ *Cast* ‹ and that states, « *[with its] desire,* ‹ *living thing*

CONTINUE ... כִּי אַתָּה (BELOW)

כִּי אַתָּה שׁוֹמֵעַ תְּפִלַּת עַמְּךָ יִשְׂרָאֵל בְּרַחֲמִים.

« with compassion. ‹ Israel ‹ of Your people ‹ the prayer ‹ hear ‹ You ‹ For

בָּרוּךְ אַתָּה יהוה, שׁוֹמֵעַ תְּפִלָּה.

« prayer. ‹ Who hears « HASHEM, ‹ are You, ‹ Blessed

(1) *Proverbs* 30:8. (2) *Psalms* 145:16. (3) 55:23.

TEMPLE SERVICE / עבודה

רְצֵה יהוה אֱלֹהֵינוּ בְּעַמְּךָ יִשְׂרָאֵל וּבִתְפִלָּתָם,
Be favorable, | HASHEM, | our God, | toward Your people | Israel | and toward their prayer

וְהָשֵׁב אֶת הָעֲבוֹדָה לִדְבִיר בֵּיתֶךָ. וְאִשֵּׁי יִשְׂרָאֵל
and restore | the service | to the Holy of Holies | of Your Temple. | The fire-offerings | of Israel

וּתְפִלָּתָם בְּאַהֲבָה תְקַבֵּל בְּרָצוֹן, וּתְהִי לְרָצוֹן
and their prayer | with love | accept | favorably, | and may it be | to Your favor

תָּמִיד עֲבוֹדַת יִשְׂרָאֵל עַמֶּךָ.
always | the service | of Israel | Your people.

וְתֶחֱזֶינָה עֵינֵינוּ בְּשׁוּבְךָ לְצִיּוֹן בְּרַחֲמִים. בָּרוּךְ
Witness | may our eyes | Your return | to Zion | in compassion. | Blessed

אַתָּה יהוה, הַמַּחֲזִיר שְׁכִינָתוֹ לְצִיּוֹן.
are You, | HASHEM, | Who restores | His Presence | to Zion.

THANKSGIVING [MODIM] / הודאה

BOW AT מוֹדִים, *WE THANK YOU*; STRAIGHTEN UP AT ה׳, *HASHEM.*

מוֹדִים אֲנַחְנוּ לָךְ שָׁאַתָּה הוּא יהוה אֱלֹהֵינוּ
We thank | You, | for it is You | Who are | HASHEM, | our God

וֵאלֹהֵי אֲבוֹתֵינוּ לְעוֹלָם וָעֶד. צוּר חַיֵּינוּ, מָגֵן
and the God | of our forefathers | for ever | and ever; | Rock | of our lives, | Shield

יִשְׁעֵנוּ אַתָּה הוּא לְדוֹר וָדוֹר. נוֹדֶה לְּךָ וּנְסַפֵּר
of our salvation | [is what] You are | from generation | to generation. | We shall thank | You | and relate

תְּהִלָּתֶךָ[1] עַל חַיֵּינוּ הַמְּסוּרִים בְּיָדֶךָ, וְעַל נִשְׁמוֹתֵינוּ
Your praise, | for | our lives | that are committed | into Your hands, | and for | our souls

הַפְּקוּדוֹת לָךְ, וְעַל נִסֶּיךָ שֶׁבְּכָל יוֹם עִמָּנוּ, וְעַל
that are entrusted | to You; | and for | Your miracles | that every | day | are with us; | and for

(1) Cf. *Psalms* 79:13.

נִפְלְאוֹתֶיךָ וְטוֹבוֹתֶיךָ שֶׁבְּכָל עֵת, עֶרֶב וָבֹקֶר

‹ morning, ‹ — evening, « times ‹ that are at all ‹ and favors ‹ Your wonders

וְצָהֳרָיִם. הַטּוֹב כִּי לֹא כָלוּ רַחֲמֶיךָ, וְהַמְּרַחֵם

‹ and the Compassionate One, « are Your compassions, ‹ exhausted ‹ never ‹ for ‹ The Beneficent One, « and afternoon.

כִּי לֹא תַמּוּ חֲסָדֶיךָ,[1] מֵעוֹלָם קִוִּינוּ לָךְ.

« in You. ‹ have we put our hope ‹ — always « are Your kindnesses ‹ ended ‹ never ‹ for

וְעַל כֻּלָּם יִתְבָּרַךְ וְיִתְרוֹמַם שִׁמְךָ מַלְכֵּנוּ

« our King, ‹ may Your Name be, ‹ and exalted ‹ blessed ‹ all these, ‹ For

תָּמִיד לְעוֹלָם וָעֶד.

« and ever. ‹ for ever ‹ continually,

BEND THE KNEES AT בָּרוּךְ, *BLESSED*; BOW AT אַתָּה, *YOU*; STRAIGHTEN UP AT ה׳, *HASHEM*.

וְכֹל הַחַיִּים יוֹדוּךָ סֶּלָה, וִיהַלְלוּ אֶת שִׁמְךָ

‹ Your Name ‹ — and praise « forever! ‹ will gratefully acknowledge You, ‹ alive ‹ Everything

בֶּאֱמֶת, הָאֵל יְשׁוּעָתֵנוּ וְעֶזְרָתֵנוּ סֶלָה. בָּרוּךְ אַתָּה

‹ are You, ‹ Blessed « forever! ‹ and of our help, ‹ of our salvation ‹ O God « sincerely,

יהוה, הַטּוֹב שִׁמְךָ וּלְךָ נָאֶה לְהוֹדוֹת.

« to give thanks. ‹ it is fitting ‹ and to You ‹ is Your Name, ‹ *The Beneficent One* « HASHEM,

PEACE / שלום

שָׁלוֹם רָב עַל יִשְׂרָאֵל עַמְּךָ תָּשִׂים לְעוֹלָם,

« forever, ‹ establish ‹ Your people ‹ Israel ‹ upon « abundant, « Peace,

כִּי אַתָּה הוּא מֶלֶךְ אָדוֹן לְכָל הַשָּׁלוֹם.

« peace. ‹ of all ‹ Master « King, ‹ Who are ‹ it is You ‹ for

וְטוֹב בְּעֵינֶיךָ לְבָרֵךְ אֶת עַמְּךָ יִשְׂרָאֵל בְּכָל

‹ at every « Israel ‹ Your people ‹ to bless ‹ in Your eyes ‹ May it be good

עֵת וּבְכָל שָׁעָה בִּשְׁלוֹמֶךָ. בָּרוּךְ אַתָּה יהוה,

« HASHEM, ‹ are You, ‹ Blessed « with Your peace. ‹ hour ‹ and at every ‹ time

(1) Cf. *Lamentations* 3:22.

הַמְּבָרֵךְ אֶת עַמּוֹ יִשְׂרָאֵל בַּשָּׁלוֹם.

« with peace. ‹ Israel ‹ His people ‹ Who blesses

יִהְיוּ לְרָצוֹן אִמְרֵי פִי וְהֶגְיוֹן לִבִּי לְפָנֶיךָ,

« before You, ‹ of my heart — ‹ and the thoughts ‹ of my mouth ‹ — the expressions ‹ find favor ‹ May they

יהוה צוּרִי וְגֹאֲלִי.[1]

« and my Redeemer. ‹ my Rock ‹ HASHEM,

אֱלֹהַי, נְצוֹר לְשׁוֹנִי מֵרָע, וּשְׂפָתַי מִדַּבֵּר מִרְמָה,[2]

« deceitfully. ‹ from speaking ‹ and my lips « from evil ‹ my tongue ‹ guard ‹ My God,

וְלִמְקַלְלַי נַפְשִׁי תִדּוֹם, וְנַפְשִׁי כֶּעָפָר לַכֹּל תִּהְיֶה.

« be. ‹ to everyone ‹ like dust ‹ and let my soul « be silent; ‹ let my soul ‹ To those who curse me,

פְּתַח לִבִּי בְּתוֹרָתֶךָ, וּבְמִצְוֹתֶיךָ תִּרְדּוֹף נַפְשִׁי.

« shall my soul pursue. ‹ so that Your commandments « to Your Torah, ‹ my heart ‹ Open

וְכָל הַחוֹשְׁבִים עָלַי רָעָה, מְהֵרָה הָפֵר עֲצָתָם

‹ their counsel ‹ nullify ‹ speedily « evil, ‹ against me ‹ who plot ‹ As for all

וְקַלְקֵל מַחֲשַׁבְתָּם.[3] עֲשֵׂה לְמַעַן שְׁמֶךָ, עֲשֵׂה לְמַעַן

‹ for the sake ‹ act « of Your Name; ‹ for the sake ‹ Act « their scheme. ‹ and disrupt

יְמִינֶךָ, עֲשֵׂה לְמַעַן קְדֻשָּׁתֶךָ, עֲשֵׂה לְמַעַן תּוֹרָתֶךָ.

« of Your Torah. ‹ for the sake ‹ act « of Your sanctity; ‹ for the sake ‹ act « of Your right hand;

לְמַעַן יֵחָלְצוּן יְדִידֶיךָ, הוֹשִׁיעָה יְמִינְךָ וַעֲנֵנִי.[4]

« and answer me. ‹ with Your right hand, ‹ — save « Your beloved ones ‹ may be released ‹ In order that

SOME RECITE THE VERSE PERTAINING TO THEIR NAMES AT THIS POINT. SEE PAGE 643.

יִהְיוּ לְרָצוֹן אִמְרֵי פִי וְהֶגְיוֹן לִבִּי לְפָנֶיךָ, יהוה

‹ HASHEM, « before You, ‹ of my heart — ‹ and the thoughts ‹ of my mouth ‹ — the expressions ‹ find favor ‹ May they

צוּרִי וְגֹאֲלִי.[1]

« and my Redeemer. ‹ my Rock

(1) *Psalms* 19:15. (2) Cf. 34:14. (3) See *Berachos* 17a. (4) *Psalms* 60:7, 108:7.

BOW. TAKE THREE STEPS BACK. BOW LEFT AND SAY ... עֹשֶׂה, *"HE WHO MAKES . . ."*; BOW RIGHT AND SAY ... הוּא, *"MAY HE . . ."*; BOW FORWARD AND SAY ... וְעַל כָּל יִשְׂרָאֵל, *"AND UPON ALL ISRAEL . . . ."*

עֹשֶׂה שָׁלוֹם בִּמְרוֹמָיו,[1] הוּא יַעֲשֶׂה שָׁלוֹם

‹ peace ‹ make ‹ may He « in His heights, ‹ peace ‹ He Who makes

עָלֵינוּ, וְעַל כָּל יִשְׂרָאֵל.[2] וְאִמְרוּ: אָמֵן.

« Amen. ‹ Now respond: « Israel. ‹ all ‹ and upon « upon us,

יְהִי רָצוֹן מִלְּפָנֶיךָ, יהוה אֱלֹהֵינוּ וֵאלֹהֵי אֲבוֹתֵינוּ, שֶׁיִּבָּנֶה

‹ that rebuilt « of our forefathers, ‹ and the God ‹ our God ‹ HASHEM, « before You, ‹ the will, ‹ May it be

בֵּית הַמִּקְדָּשׁ בִּמְהֵרָה בְיָמֵינוּ, וְתֵן חֶלְקֵנוּ בְּתוֹרָתֶךָ.[3] וְשָׁם

‹ so that there « be in Your Torah, ‹ our portion ‹ Grant that « in our days. ‹ speedily ‹ shall the Holy Temple be,

נַעֲבָדְךָ בְּיִרְאָה, כִּימֵי עוֹלָם וּכְשָׁנִים קַדְמוֹנִיּוֹת. וְעָרְבָה

‹ And pleasing « gone by. ‹ and as in years ‹ of old ‹ as in days « with reverence, ‹ we may serve You

לַיהוה מִנְחַת יְהוּדָה וִירוּשָׁלָיִם, כִּימֵי עוֹלָם וּכְשָׁנִים

‹ and in years ‹ of old ‹ as in days « and Jerusalem, ‹ of Judah ‹ let be the offering ‹ to HASHEM

קַדְמוֹנִיּוֹת.[4]

« gone by.

SHEMONEH ESREI **ENDS HERE.**

REMAIN STANDING IN PLACE FOR AT LEAST A FEW MOMENTS BEFORE TAKING THREE STEPS FORWARD.

FULL KADDISH / קדיש שלם

THE *CHAZZAN* RECITES קַדִּישׁ שָׁלֵם, FULL *KADDISH.*

יִתְגַּדַּל וְיִתְקַדַּשׁ שְׁמֵהּ רַבָּא. (Cong. — אָמֵן.) בְּעָלְמָא דִּי

‹ that ‹ in the world ‹ (Amen.) « that is great! — ‹ may His Name ‹ and be sanctified ‹ Grow exalted

בְרָא כִרְעוּתֵהּ. וְיַמְלִיךְ מַלְכוּתֵהּ, בְּחַיֵּיכוֹן וּבְיוֹמֵיכוֹן וּבְחַיֵּי

‹ and in the lifetimes ‹ and in your days, ‹ in your lifetimes « to His kingship, ‹ and may He give reign « according to His will, ‹ He created

דְכָל בֵּית יִשְׂרָאֵל, בַּעֲגָלָא וּבִזְמַן קָרִיב. וְאִמְרוּ: אָמֵן.

« Amen. ‹ Now respond: « that comes soon. ‹ and at a time ‹ swiftly « of Israel, ‹ Family ‹ of the entire

CONGREGATION RESPONDS:

אָמֵן. יְהֵא שְׁמֵהּ רַבָּא מְבָרַךְ לְעָלַם וּלְעָלְמֵי עָלְמַיָּא.

« and for all eternity. ‹ forever ‹ be blessed ‹ that is great ‹ His Name ‹ May « Amen.

---

(1) *Job* 25:2. (2) Cf. *Berachos* 16b. (3) *Ethics of the Fathers* 5:24. (4) *Malachi* 3:4.

CHAZZAN CONTINUES:

יְהֵא שְׁמֵהּ רַבָּא מְבָרַךְ לְעָלַם וּלְעָלְמֵי עָלְמַיָּא. יִתְבָּרַךְ

May ‹ His Name ‹ that is great ‹ be blessed ‹ forever ‹ and for all eternity. « Blessed, ‹

וְיִשְׁתַּבַּח וְיִתְפָּאַר וְיִתְרוֹמַם וְיִתְנַשֵּׂא וְיִתְהַדָּר וְיִתְעַלֶּה

praised, ‹ glorified, ‹ exalted, ‹ upraised, ‹ honored, ‹ elevated, ‹

וְיִתְהַלָּל שְׁמֵהּ דְּקֻדְשָׁא בְּרִיךְ הוּא (Cong. — בְּרִיךְ הוּא)

and lauded ‹ be the Name ‹ of the Holy One, ‹ Blessed ‹ is He « (Blessed ‹ is He)«

— לְעֵלָּא מִן כָּל בִּרְכָתָא וְשִׁירָתָא תֻּשְׁבְּחָתָא וְנֶחֱמָתָא

beyond ‹ any ‹ blessing ‹ and song, « praise ‹ and consolation ‹

דַּאֲמִירָן בְּעָלְמָא. וְאִמְרוּ: אָמֵן. (Cong. — אָמֵן.)

that are uttered ‹ in the world. « Now respond: ‹ Amen. « (Amen.) «

CONGREGATION:

קַבֵּל בְּרַחֲמִים וּבְרָצוֹן אֶת תְּפִלָּתֵנוּ.

Accept ‹ with mercy ‹ and with favor ‹ our prayers. «

CHAZZAN CONTINUES:

תִּתְקַבַּל צְלוֹתְהוֹן וּבָעוּתְהוֹן דְּכָל (בֵּית) יִשְׂרָאֵל קֳדָם

May accepted be ‹ the prayers ‹ and supplications ‹ of the entire ‹ (Family of) ‹ Israel ‹ before ‹

אֲבוּהוֹן דִּי בִשְׁמַיָּא. וְאִמְרוּ: אָמֵן. (Cong. — אָמֵן.)

their Father ‹ Who ‹ is in Heaven. « Now respond: ‹ Amen. « (Amen.) «

CONGREGATION:

יְהִי שֵׁם יהוה מְבֹרָךְ, מֵעַתָּה וְעַד עוֹלָם.[1]

Let ‹ the Name ‹ of HASHEM ‹ be blessed, « from this time ‹ until ‹ eternity. «

CHAZZAN CONTINUES:

יְהֵא שְׁלָמָא רַבָּא מִן שְׁמַיָּא, וְחַיִּים עָלֵינוּ וְעַל כָּל

May there be ‹ peace ‹ that is abundant ‹ from ‹ Heaven, « and life, « upon us ‹ and upon ‹ all ‹

יִשְׂרָאֵל. וְאִמְרוּ: אָמֵן. (Cong. — אָמֵן.)

Israel. « Now respond: ‹ Amen. « (Amen.) «

CONGREGATION:

עֶזְרִי מֵעִם יהוה, עֹשֵׂה שָׁמַיִם וָאָרֶץ.[2]

(My help ‹ is from ‹ HASHEM, « Maker ‹ of heaven ‹ and earth. «

(1) Cf. *Psalms* 113:2. (2) 121:2.

CHAZZAN BOWS; TAKES THREE STEPS BACK. BOWS LEFT AND SAYS ... עֹשֶׂה שָׁלוֹם, *"HE WHO MAKES PEACE ...";* BOWS RIGHT AND SAYS ... הוּא, *"MAY HE ...";* BOWS FORWARD AND SAYS ... וְעַל כָּל יִשְׂרָאֵל, *"AND UPON ALL ISRAEL ...";* REMAINS IN PLACE FOR A FEW MOMENTS, THEN TAKES THREE STEPS FORWARD.

עֹשֶׂה שָׁלוֹם בִּמְרוֹמָיו, הוּא יַעֲשֶׂה שָׁלוֹם עָלֵינוּ, וְעַל כָּל

‹ all ‹ and upon ‹ upon us, ‹ peace ‹ make ‹ may He « in His heights, ‹ peace ‹ He Who makes

יִשְׂרָאֵל. וְאִמְרוּ: אָמֵן. (Cong. — אָמֵן.)

« (Amen.) « Amen. ‹ Now respond: « Israel.

STAND WHILE RECITING עָלֵינוּ, *"IT IS OUR DUTY ..."*

עָלֵינוּ לְשַׁבֵּחַ לַאֲדוֹן הַכֹּל, לָתֵת גְּדֻלָּה לְיוֹצֵר

‹ to the Molder ‹ greatness ‹ to ascribe « of all, ‹ the Master ‹ to praise ‹ It is our duty

בְּרֵאשִׁית, שֶׁלֹּא עָשָׂנוּ כְּגוֹיֵי הָאֲרָצוֹת, וְלֹא

‹ and has not « of the lands, ‹ like the nations ‹ for He has not made us « of primeval creation,

שָׂמָנוּ כְּמִשְׁפְּחוֹת הָאֲדָמָה. שֶׁלֹּא שָׂם חֶלְקֵנוּ

‹ our portion ‹ assigned ‹ for He has not « of the earth; ‹ like the families ‹ established us

כָּהֶם, וְגוֹרָלֵנוּ כְּכָל הֲמוֹנָם. (שֶׁהֵם מִשְׁתַּחֲוִים

‹ bow ‹ (For they « their multitudes. ‹ like all ‹ nor our lot ‹ like theirs

לְהֶבֶל וָרִיק, וּמִתְפַּלְּלִים אֶל אֵל לֹא יוֹשִׁיעַ.[1])

« save.) ‹ who does not ‹ a god ‹ to ‹ and pray ‹ and emptiness ‹ to vanity

BOW WHILE RECITING וַאֲנַחְנוּ כּוֹרְעִים וּמִשְׁתַּחֲוִים, *"BUT WE BEND OUR KNEES, BOW."*

וַאֲנַחְנוּ כּוֹרְעִים וּמִשְׁתַּחֲוִים וּמוֹדִים, לִפְנֵי מֶלֶךְ

‹ the King ‹ before « and acknowledge our thanks ‹ bow, ‹ bend our knees, ‹ But we

מַלְכֵי הַמְּלָכִים הַקָּדוֹשׁ בָּרוּךְ הוּא. שֶׁהוּא נוֹטֶה

‹ stretches out ‹ He « He. ‹ Blessed is ‹ the Holy One, « of kings, ‹ over kings

שָׁמַיִם וְיֹסֵד אָרֶץ,[2] וּמוֹשַׁב יְקָרוֹ בַּשָּׁמַיִם מִמַּעַל,

« above, ‹ is in the heavens ‹ of His homage ‹ the seat « earth's foundation, ‹ and establishes ‹ heaven

וּשְׁכִינַת עֻזּוֹ בְּגָבְהֵי מְרוֹמִים. הוּא אֱלֹהֵינוּ, אֵין עוֹד.

« other. ‹ and there is none ‹ our God ‹ He is « heights. ‹ is in the loftiest ‹ of His power ‹ and the Presence

(1) *Isaiah* 45:20. (2) 51:13.

אֱמֶת מַלְכֵּנוּ, אֶפֶס זוּלָתוֹ, כַּכָּתוּב בְּתוֹרָתוֹ:

« in His Torah: ‹ as it is written « beside Him, ‹ there is nothing ‹ is our King, ‹ True

וְיָדַעְתָּ הַיּוֹם וַהֲשֵׁבֹתָ אֶל לְבָבֶךָ, כִּי יהוה הוּא

‹ He is ‹ HASHEM ‹ that « your heart, ‹ to ‹ and take ‹ this day ‹ You are to know

הָאֱלֹהִים בַּשָּׁמַיִם מִמַּעַל וְעַל הָאָרֶץ מִתָּחַת,

‹ below — ‹ the earth ‹ and on ‹ above ‹ — in heaven « the God

אֵין עוֹד.[1]

« other. ‹ there is none

עַל כֵּן נְקַוֶּה לְּךָ, יהוה אֱלֹהֵינוּ, לִרְאוֹת מְהֵרָה

‹ very soon ‹ that we may see « our God, ‹ HASHEM, ‹ in You, ‹ we put our hope ‹ Therefore

בְּתִפְאֶרֶת עֻזֶּךָ, לְהַעֲבִיר גִּלּוּלִים מִן הָאָרֶץ,

« the earth, ‹ from ‹ detestable idolatry ‹ to remove « of Your might, ‹ the splendor

וְהָאֱלִילִים כָּרוֹת יִכָּרֵתוּן, לְתַקֵּן עוֹלָם בְּמַלְכוּת

‹ through the sovereignty ‹ the universe ‹ to perfect « will be utterly cut off, ‹ and false gods

שַׁדַּי. וְכָל בְּנֵי בָשָׂר יִקְרְאוּ בִשְׁמֶךָ, לְהַפְנוֹת אֵלֶיךָ

‹ toward You ‹ to turn « upon Your Name, ‹ will call ‹ humanity ‹ Then all « of the Almighty.

כָּל רִשְׁעֵי אָרֶץ. יַכִּירוּ וְיֵדְעוּ כָּל יוֹשְׁבֵי תֵבֵל, כִּי

‹ that « of the world — ‹ the inhabitants ‹ — all « and know ‹ May they recognize « of the earth. ‹ the wicked ‹ all

לְךָ תִּכְרַע כָּל בֶּרֶךְ, תִּשָּׁבַע כָּל לָשׁוֹן.[2] לְפָנֶיךָ

‹ Before You, « tongue. ‹ every ‹ should swear « knee, ‹ every ‹ should bend ‹ to You

יהוה אֱלֹהֵינוּ יִכְרְעוּ וְיִפֹּלוּ, וְלִכְבוֹד שִׁמְךָ יְקָר

‹ homage ‹ of Your Name ‹ and to the glory « and cast themselves down, ‹ they will bend their knees ‹ our God, ‹ HASHEM,

(1) *Deuteronomy* 4:39. (2) Cf. *Isaiah* 45:23.

יִתְּנוּ. וִיקַבְּלוּ כֻלָּם אֶת עוֹל מַלְכוּתֶךָ, וְתִמְלֹךְ

they will offer, « and accept ‹ will all ‹ the yoke ‹ of Your kingship, « that You may reign ‹

עֲלֵיהֶם מְהֵרָה לְעוֹלָם וָעֶד. כִּי הַמַּלְכוּת שֶׁלְּךָ הִיא

over them ‹ very soon ‹ for ever ‹ and ever. « For ‹ the kingdom ‹ is Yours, «

וּלְעוֹלְמֵי עַד תִּמְלוֹךְ בְּכָבוֹד, כַּכָּתוּב בְּתוֹרָתֶךָ:

and for ever ‹ and ever ‹ You will reign ‹ in glory, « as it is written ‹ in Your Torah: «

יהוה יִמְלֹךְ לְעֹלָם וָעֶד.[1] ❖ וְנֶאֱמַר: וְהָיָה יהוה

HASHEM ‹ *shall reign* ‹ *for ever* ‹ *and ever.* « And it is said: « *Then will* ‹ *HASHEM* ‹

לְמֶלֶךְ עַל כָּל הָאָרֶץ, בַּיּוֹם הַהוּא יִהְיֶה יהוה

be King ‹ *over* ‹ *all* ‹ *the world* « *— on that day* ‹ *shall* ‹ *HASHEM* ‹

אֶחָד וּשְׁמוֹ אֶחָד.[2]

be One ‹ *and His Name* ‹ *be One.* «

SOME CONGREGATIONS RECITE THE FOLLOWING AFTER עָלֵינוּ, *ALEINU.*

אַל תִּירָא מִפַּחַד פִּתְאֹם, וּמִשֹּׁאַת רְשָׁעִים כִּי

Do not fear ‹ terror ‹ [that comes] suddenly, « nor the holocaust ‹ of the wicked ‹ when ‹

תָבֹא.[3] עֻצוּ עֵצָה וְתֻפָר, דַּבְּרוּ דָבָר וְלֹא יָקוּם, כִּי

it comes. « Plan ‹ a conspiracy ‹ and it will be annulled; « speak ‹ your speech ‹ and it shall not ‹ stand, « for ‹

עִמָּנוּ אֵל.[4] וְעַד זִקְנָה אֲנִי הוּא, וְעַד שֵׂיבָה אֲנִי

with us ‹ is God. « Even till ‹ [your] old age, ‹ I remain unchanged; « and even till ‹ [your] elder years, ‹ I ‹

אֶסְבֹּל, אֲנִי עָשִׂיתִי וַאֲנִי אֶשָּׂא, וַאֲנִי אֶסְבֹּל וַאֲמַלֵּט.[5]

shall carry [you]. « I ‹ created [you] ‹ and I ‹ shall bear [you]; « I ‹ shall carry [you] ‹ and rescue [you]. «

MOURNER'S KADDISH / קדיש יתום

IN THE PRESENCE OF A *MINYAN*, MOURNERS RECITE קַדִּישׁ יָתוֹם, THE MOURNER'S *KADDISH*.
[A TRANSLITERATION OF THIS *KADDISH* APPEARS ON P. 647.]

יִתְגַּדַּל וְיִתְקַדַּשׁ שְׁמֵהּ רַבָּא. (Cong. — אָמֵן.) בְּעָלְמָא דִּי

Grow exalted ‹ and be sanctified ‹ may His Name ‹ that is great! — « (Amen.) ‹ in the world ‹ that ‹

(1) *Exodus* 15:18. (2) *Zechariah* 14:9. (3) *Proverbs* 3:25. (4) *Isaiah* 8:10. (5) 46:4.

בְּרָא כִרְעוּתֵהּ. וְיַמְלִיךְ מַלְכוּתֵהּ, בְּחַיֵּיכוֹן וּבְיוֹמֵיכוֹן וּבְחַיֵּי

‹ and in the lifetimes ‹ and in your days, ‹ in your lifetimes « to His kingship, ‹ and may He give reign « according to His will, ‹ He created

דְּכָל בֵּית יִשְׂרָאֵל, בַּעֲגָלָא וּבִזְמַן קָרִיב. וְאִמְרוּ: אָמֵן.

« Amen. ‹ Now respond: « that comes soon. ‹ and at a time ‹ swiftly « of Israel, ‹ Family ‹ of the entire

CONGREGATION RESPONDS:

אָמֵן. יְהֵא שְׁמֵהּ רַבָּא מְבָרַךְ לְעָלַם וּלְעָלְמֵי עָלְמַיָּא.

« and for all eternity. ‹ forever ‹ be blessed ‹ that is great ‹ His Name ‹ May « Amen.

MOURNER CONTINUES:

יְהֵא שְׁמֵהּ רַבָּא מְבָרַךְ לְעָלַם וּלְעָלְמֵי עָלְמַיָּא. יִתְבָּרַךְ

‹ Blessed, « and for all eternity. ‹ forever ‹ be blessed ‹ that is great ‹ His Name ‹ May

וְיִשְׁתַּבַּח וְיִתְפָּאַר וְיִתְרוֹמַם וְיִתְנַשֵּׂא וְיִתְהַדָּר וְיִתְעַלֶּה

‹ elevated, ‹ honored, ‹ upraised, ‹ exalted, ‹ glorified, ‹ praised,

וְיִתְהַלָּל שְׁמֵהּ דְּקֻדְשָׁא בְּרִיךְ הוּא (Cong. — בְּרִיךְ הוּא)

« is He) ‹ (Blessed « is He ‹ Blessed ‹ of the Holy One, ‹ be the Name ‹ and lauded

— לְעֵלָּא מִן כָּל בִּרְכָתָא וְשִׁירָתָא תֻּשְׁבְּחָתָא וְנֶחֱמָתָא

‹ and consolation ‹ praise « and song, ‹ blessing ‹ any ‹ beyond

דַּאֲמִירָן בְּעָלְמָא. וְאִמְרוּ: אָמֵן. (Cong. — אָמֵן.)

« (Amen.) « Amen. ‹ Now respond: « in the world. ‹ that are uttered

יְהֵא שְׁלָמָא רַבָּא מִן שְׁמַיָּא, וְחַיִּים עָלֵינוּ וְעַל כָּל

‹ all ‹ and upon ‹ upon us « and life, « Heaven, ‹ from ‹ that is abundant ‹ peace ‹ May there be

יִשְׂרָאֵל. וְאִמְרוּ: אָמֵן. (Cong. — אָמֵן.)

« (Amen.) « Amen. ‹ Now respond: « Israel.

BOW; TAKE THREE STEPS BACK. BOW LEFT AND SAY ... עֹשֶׂה שָׁלוֹם, *"HE WHO MAKES PEACE . . ."*; BOW RIGHT AND SAY ... הוּא, *"MAY HE . . ."*; BOW FORWARD AND SAY ... וְעַל כָּל יִשְׂרָאֵל, *"AND UPON ALL ISRAEL . . ."*; REMAIN IN PLACE FOR A FEW MOMENTS, THEN TAKE THREE STEPS FORWARD.

עֹשֶׂה שָׁלוֹם בִּמְרוֹמָיו, הוּא יַעֲשֶׂה שָׁלוֹם עָלֵינוּ, וְעַל כָּל

‹ all ‹ and upon ‹ upon us, ‹ peace ‹ make ‹ may He « in His heights, ‹ peace ‹ He Who makes

יִשְׂרָאֵל. וְאִמְרוּ: אָמֵן. (Cong. — אָמֵן.)

« (Amen.) « Amen. ‹ Now respond: « Israel.

HAVDALAH / הבדלה

WHEN TISHAH B'AV FALLS ON SUNDAY, *HAVDALAH* IS RECITED. SPICES AND A FLAME ARE NOT USED.

סַבְרִי מָרָנָן וְרַבָּנָן וְרַבּוֹתַי:

By your leave, 〈 distinguished people 〈 and rabbis 〈 and gentlemen: «

בָּרוּךְ אַתָּה יהוה אֱלֹהֵינוּ מֶלֶךְ הָעוֹלָם, בּוֹרֵא

Blessed 〈 are You, 〈 HASHEM, 〈 our God, 〈 King 〈 of the universe, « Who creates 〈

פְּרִי הַגָּפֶן. (All respond – אָמֵן.)

the fruit 〈 of the vine. « (Amen.) «

בָּרוּךְ אַתָּה יהוה אֱלֹהֵינוּ מֶלֶךְ הָעוֹלָם, הַמַּבְדִּיל

Blessed 〈 are You, 〈 HASHEM, 〈 our God, 〈 King 〈 of the universe, « Who distinguishes 〈

בֵּין קֹדֶשׁ לְחוֹל, בֵּין אוֹר לְחֹשֶׁךְ, בֵּין יִשְׂרָאֵל

between 〈 the sacred 〈 and the secular, « between 〈 light 〈 and darkness, « between 〈 Israel 〈

לָעַמִּים, בֵּין יוֹם הַשְּׁבִיעִי לְשֵׁשֶׁת יְמֵי הַמַּעֲשֶׂה. בָּרוּךְ

and the nations, « between 〈 the Seventh Day 〈 and the six 〈 days 〈 of labor. « Blessed 〈

אַתָּה יהוה, הַמַּבְדִּיל בֵּין קֹדֶשׁ לְחוֹל. (All respond – אָמֵן.)

are You, 〈 HASHEM, « Who distinguishes 〈 between 〈 sacred 〈 and secular. « (Amen.) «

THE ONE WHO RECITED *HAVDALAH*, OR SOMEONE ELSE PRESENT FOR *HAVDALAH*, SHOULD DRINK MOST OF THE WINE FROM THE CUP.

Laws of *Kiddush Levanah*

It is preferable that *Kiddush Levanah* be recited: (a) under the open sky; (b) with a *minyan;* (c) at the departure of the Sabbath. When these optimal conditions are not feasible, they may be waived (e.g., a shut-in may recite it indoors if he can see the moon through a window or door; one who cannot join a *minyan;* the sky is cloudy at the departure of the Sabbath).

The earliest time for reciting *Kiddush Levanah* is 72 hours after the *molad* (new moon), although some authorities delay its recitation until seven full days after the *molad*. The latest time is mid-month, 14 days, 18 hours, and 22 minutes (some authorities extend this limit to 15 full days) after the *molad*.

During Av, *Kiddush Levanah* is generally postponed until after Tishah B'Av.

If one cannot recite *Kiddush Levanah* with a *minyan,* he should try to do so in the presence of at least three others with whom to exchange the *Shalom Aleichem* greeting. If this, too, is not possible one may recite it by himself.

✤ SANCTIFICATION OF THE MOON / קידוש לבנה ✤

Psalms 148:1-6 / תהלים קמח:א-ו

הַלְלוּיָהּ, הַלְלוּ אֶת יהוה מִן הַשָּׁמַיִם, הַלְלוּהוּ

‹ praise Him « the heavens; ‹ from ‹ HASHEM ‹ Praise « Halleluyah!

בַּמְּרוֹמִים. הַלְלוּהוּ כָל מַלְאָכָיו, הַלְלוּהוּ כָּל

‹ all ‹ praise Him, « His angels; ‹ all ‹ Praise Him, « in the heights:

צְבָאָיו. הַלְלוּהוּ שֶׁמֶשׁ וְיָרֵחַ, הַלְלוּהוּ כָּל כּוֹכְבֵי

‹ stars ‹ all ‹ praise Him, « and moon; ‹ sun ‹ Praise Him, « His legions.

אוֹר. הַלְלוּהוּ שְׁמֵי הַשָּׁמָיִם, וְהַמַּיִם אֲשֶׁר מֵעַל

‹ above ‹ that are ‹ and the waters « of the heavens ‹ the most exalted ‹ Praise Him, « that are bright.

הַשָּׁמָיִם. יְהַלְלוּ אֶת שֵׁם יהוה, כִּי הוּא צִוָּה

‹ commanded ‹ He ‹ for « of HASHEM, ‹ the Name ‹ Let them praise « the heavens.

וְנִבְרָאוּ. וַיַּעֲמִידֵם לָעַד לְעוֹלָם, חָק נָתַן וְלֹא יַעֲבוֹר.

« change. ‹ that will not ‹ He issued ‹ a decree « and ever, ‹ for ever ‹ And He established them « and they were created.

MANY RECITE THE FOLLOWING DECLARATION OF INTENT:

הֲרֵינִי מוּכָן וּמְזֻמָּן לְקַיֵּם הַמִּצְוָה לְקַדֵּשׁ הַלְּבָנָה.

« the moon. ‹ to sanctify ‹ the commandment ‹ to perform ‹ and ready ‹ prepared ‹ I am hereby

לְשֵׁם יִחוּד קֻדְשָׁא בְּרִיךְ הוּא וּשְׁכִינְתֵּיהּ עַל יְדֵי הַהוּא

‹ Him ‹ through ‹ and His Presence, ‹ is He, ‹ Blessed « of the Holy One, ‹ of the unification ‹ For the sake

טָמִיר וְנֶעְלָם, בְּשֵׁם כָּל יִשְׂרָאֵל.

« Israel. ‹ of all ‹ [I pray] in the name ‹ and Who is inscrutable ‹ Who is hidden

ONE SHOULD LOOK AT THE MOON BEFORE RECITING THIS BLESSING:

בָּרוּךְ אַתָּה יהוה אֱלֹהֵינוּ מֶלֶךְ הָעוֹלָם, אֲשֶׁר

‹ Who « of the universe, ‹ King ‹ our God, « HASHEM, ‹ are You, ‹ Blessed

בְּמַאֲמָרוֹ בָּרָא שְׁחָקִים, וּבְרוּחַ פִּיו כָּל צְבָאָם.

« their legion. ‹ all ‹ of His mouth ‹ and with the breath « the heavens, ‹ created ‹ with His utterance

חֹק וּזְמַן נָתַן לָהֶם שֶׁלֹּא יְשַׁנּוּ אֶת תַּפְקִידָם.

« their assigned task. ‹ alter ‹ that they not « them, ‹ did He give ‹ and a schedule ‹ A rule

שָׂשִׂים וּשְׂמֵחִים לַעֲשׂוֹת רְצוֹן קוֹנָם, פּוֹעֵל אֱמֶת

‹ truth, ‹ the One Who does « of their Creator, ‹ the will ‹ to perform ‹ and happy ‹ They are joyous

שֶׁפְּעֻלָּתוֹ אֱמֶת. וְלַלְּבָנָה אָמַר שֶׁתִּתְחַדֵּשׁ, עֲטֶרֶת

‹ as a crown ‹ that it should renew itself, ‹ He said ‹ To the moon « is truth. ‹ Whose deed

תִּפְאֶרֶת לַעֲמוּסֵי בָטֶן, שֶׁהֵם עֲתִידִים לְהִתְחַדֵּשׁ

‹ to renew themselves ‹ are destined ‹ those who « from the womb, ‹ for those borne [by Him] ‹ of splendor

כְּמוֹתָהּ, וּלְפָאֵר לְיוֹצְרָם עַל שֵׁם כְּבוֹד מַלְכוּתוֹ.

« kingdom. ‹ of His glorious ‹ the sake ‹ for ‹ their Molder, ‹ and to glorify « like it,

בָּרוּךְ אַתָּה יהוה, מְחַדֵּשׁ חֳדָשִׁים.

« the months. ‹ Who renews « HASHEM, ‹ are You, ‹ Blessed

RECITE THREE TIMES. RISE ON THE TOES AS IF IN DANCE:

בָּרוּךְ יוֹצְרֵךְ, בָּרוּךְ עוֹשֵׂךְ, בָּרוּךְ קוֹנֵךְ, בָּרוּךְ

‹ blessed « is your Owner; ‹ blessed « is your Maker; ‹ blessed « is your Molder; ‹ Blessed

בּוֹרְאֵךְ.

« is your Creator.

RECITE THREE TIMES. RISE ON THE TOES AS IF IN DANCE:

כְּשֵׁם שֶׁאֲנִי רוֹקֵד כְּנֶגְדֵּךְ וְאֵינִי יָכוֹל לִנְגּוֹעַ בָּךְ,

« you, ‹ to touch ‹ able ‹ but I am not ‹ opposite you, ‹ dance ‹ as I ‹ Just

כַּךְ לֹא יוּכְלוּ כָּל אוֹיְבַי לִנְגּוֹעַ בִּי לְרָעָה.

« for evil. ‹ me ‹ to touch « my enemies — ‹ — all « be able ‹ may they not ‹ so

RECITE THREE TIMES:

תִּפֹּל עֲלֵיהֶם אֵימָתָה וָפַחַד, בִּגְדֹל זְרוֹעֲךָ יִדְּמוּ

‹ let them be still ‹ of Your arm, ‹ at the greatness « and fear; ‹ terror ‹ upon them ‹ Let there fall

כָּאָבֶן.[1]

« as stone.

(1) *Exodus* 15:16.

RECITE THREE TIMES:

כָּאָבֶן יִדְּמוּ זְרוֹעֲךָ בִּגְדֹל וָפַחַד אֵימָתָה עֲלֵיהֶם תִּפֹּל.

‹ As stone ‹ let them be still, ‹ at Your arm's « greatness; ‹ fear ‹ and terror ‹ upon them « let there fall.

RECITE THREE TIMES:

דָּוִד מֶלֶךְ יִשְׂרָאֵל חַי וְקַיָּם.

‹ David, ‹ King ‹ of Israel, ‹ lives « and endures.

EXTEND GREETINGS THREE TIMES:

שָׁלוֹם עֲלֵיכֶם.

‹ Peace « upon you.

THE PERSON WHO WAS GREETED RESPONDS:

עֲלֵיכֶם שָׁלוֹם.

‹ Upon you, « peace.

RECITE THREE TIMES:

סִמָּן טוֹב וּמַזָּל טוֹב יְהֵא לָנוּ וּלְכָל יִשְׂרָאֵל. אָמֵן.

‹ A sign ‹ that is good ‹ and fortune ‹ that is good ‹ may there be ‹ for us ‹ and for all « Israel. « Amen.

קוֹל דּוֹדִי הִנֵּה זֶה בָּא מְדַלֵּג עַל הֶהָרִים מְקַפֵּץ עַל הַגְּבָעוֹת. דּוֹמֶה דוֹדִי לִצְבִי אוֹ לְעֹפֶר הָאַיָּלִים, הִנֵּה זֶה עוֹמֵד אַחַר כָּתְלֵנוּ, מַשְׁגִּיחַ מִן הַחַלֹּנוֹת, מֵצִיץ מִן הַחֲרַכִּים.[1]

‹ The voice « of my beloved ‹ — behold, ‹ it « came [suddenly], ‹ leaping ‹ over « the mountains, ‹ skipping ‹ over « the hills. ‹ Comparable ‹ is my beloved ‹ to a gazelle ‹ or ‹ a young one « of the deer. ‹ Indeed, ‹ He ‹ was standing ‹ behind « our wall, ‹ observing ‹ through « the windows, ‹ peering ‹ through « the lattices.

Psalm 121 / תהלים קכא

שִׁיר לַמַּעֲלוֹת, אֶשָּׂא עֵינַי אֶל הֶהָרִים, מֵאַיִן יָבֹא עֶזְרִי. עֶזְרִי מֵעִם יהוה, עֹשֵׂה שָׁמַיִם וָאָרֶץ. אַל יִתֵּן

‹ A song « to the ascents. ‹ I raise ‹ my eyes ‹ to « the mountains; ‹ from whence ‹ will come « my help? ‹ My help ‹ is from « HASHEM, ‹ Maker ‹ of heaven ‹ and earth. ‹ He will not allow

(1) *Song of Songs* 2:8-9.

לַמּוֹט רַגְלֶךָ, אַל יָנוּם שֹׁמְרֶךָ. הִנֵּה לֹא יָנוּם וְלֹא

‹ nor ‹ slumbers ‹ [He] neither ‹ It is so, that « will your Guardian. ‹ not slumber « of your foot; ‹ the faltering

יִישָׁן, שׁוֹמֵר יִשְׂרָאֵל. יהוה שֹׁמְרֶךָ, יהוה צִלְּךָ עַל

‹ at ‹ is your protective Shade ‹ HASHEM « is your Guardian; ‹ HASHEM « of Israel. ‹ — the Guardian « sleeps

יַד יְמִינֶךָ. יוֹמָם הַשֶּׁמֶשׁ לֹא יַכֶּכָּה וְיָרֵחַ בַּלָּיְלָה.

« by night. ‹ nor the moon « harm you, ‹ will not ‹ the sun ‹ By day « your right hand.

יהוה יִשְׁמָרְךָ מִכָּל רָע, יִשְׁמֹר אֶת נַפְשֶׁךָ. יהוה

‹ HASHEM « your soul. ‹ He will guard « evil; ‹ from every ‹ will protect you ‹ HASHEM

יִשְׁמָר צֵאתְךָ וּבוֹאֶךָ, מֵעַתָּה וְעַד עוֹלָם.

« eternity. ‹ until ‹ from this time ‹ and your arrival, ‹ your departure ‹ will guard

Psalm 150 / תהלים קנ

הַלְלוּיָהּ, הַלְלוּ אֵל בְּקָדְשׁוֹ, הַלְלְוּהוּ בִּרְקִיעַ עֻזּוֹ.

« of His power. ‹ in the firmament ‹ praise Him « in His Sanctuary; ‹ God ‹ Praise « Halleluyah!

הַלְלְוּהוּ בִגְבוּרֹתָיו, הַלְלְוּהוּ כְּרֹב גֻּדְלוֹ. הַלְלְוּהוּ

‹ Praise Him « of His greatness. ‹ as befits the abundance ‹ praise Him « for His mighty acts; ‹ Praise Him

בְּתֵקַע שׁוֹפָר, הַלְלְוּהוּ בְּנֵבֶל וְכִנּוֹר. הַלְלְוּהוּ בְּתֹף

‹ with drum ‹ Praise Him « and harp. ‹ with lyre ‹ praise Him « of the *shofar;* ‹ with the blast

וּמָחוֹל, הַלְלְוּהוּ בְּמִנִּים וְעֻגָב. הַלְלְוּהוּ בְצִלְצְלֵי

‹ with cymbals ‹ Praise Him « and flute. ‹ with organ ‹ praise Him « and dance;

שָׁמַע, הַלְלְוּהוּ בְּצִלְצְלֵי תְרוּעָה. כֹּל הַנְּשָׁמָה

‹ souls ‹ Let all « resounding. ‹ with trumpets ‹ praise Him ‹ clanging;

תְּהַלֵּל יָהּ, הַלְלוּיָהּ.

« Halleluyah! « God, ‹ praise

תָּנָא דְבֵי רַבִּי יִשְׁמָעֵאל: אִלְמָלֵי לֹא זָכוּ יִשְׂרָאֵל

‹ was Israel ‹ not privileged ‹ If it had been that « Yishmael: ‹ of Rabbi ‹ by the Academy ‹ It was taught

אֶלָּא לְהַקְבִּיל פְּנֵי אֲבִיהֶם שֶׁבַּשָּׁמַיִם פַּעַם אַחַת

except for ‹ [the mitzvah] of greeting ‹ the Countenance ‹ of their Father ‹ in Heaven ‹ once ‹

בַּחֹדֶשׁ, דַּיָּם. אָמַר אַבַּיֵי: הִלְכָּךְ צָרִיךְ לְמֵימְרָא

in a month, ‹ it would have sufficed them. « Said ‹ Abaye: « Therefore ‹ it is necessary ‹ to recite it ‹

מְעֻמָּד.[1] מִי זֹאת עֹלָה מִן הַמִּדְבָּר, מִתְרַפֶּקֶת עַל

while standing. « Who ‹ is this ‹ who rises ‹ from ‹ the desert, « clinging ‹ to ‹

דּוֹדָהּ.[2]

her Beloved? «

וִיהִי רָצוֹן מִלְּפָנֶיךָ, יהוה אֱלֹהַי וֵאלֹהֵי אֲבוֹתַי,

May it be ‹ the will ‹ before You, ‹ HASHEM, « my God ‹ and the God ‹ of my forefathers, «

לְמַלֹּאת פְּגִימַת הַלְּבָנָה, וְלֹא יִהְיֶה בָּהּ שׁוּם

to fill ‹ the flaw ‹ of the moon, « that there not ‹ be ‹ in it ‹ any ‹

מִעוּט, וִיהִי אוֹר הַלְּבָנָה כְּאוֹר הַחַמָּה, וּכְאוֹר

diminution. « And may the light ‹ of the moon « be like the light ‹ of the sun « and like the light ‹

שִׁבְעַת יְמֵי בְרֵאשִׁית[3] כְּמוֹ שֶׁהָיְתָה קוֹדֶם מִעוּטָהּ,

of the seven ‹ days ‹ of Creation, « as ‹ it was ‹ before ‹ its diminishment, «

שֶׁנֶּאֱמַר: אֶת שְׁנֵי הַמְּאֹרֹת הַגְּדֹלִים.[4] וְיִתְקַיֵּם

as it is said: « *The two* ‹ *luminaries* ‹ *that are great.* « And may there be fulfilled ‹

בָּנוּ מִקְרָא שֶׁכָּתוּב: וּבִקְשׁוּ אֶת יהוה אֱלֹהֵיהֶם,

with us ‹ the verse ‹ that is written: « *They shall seek* ‹ *HASHEM,* ‹ *their God,* ‹

וְאֵת דָּוִד מַלְכָּם.[5] אָמֵן.

and David, ‹ *their king.* « Amen. «

(1) *Sanhedrin* 42a — see *Rashi*. (2) *Song of Songs* 8:5.
(3) Cf. *Isaiah* 30:26. (4) *Genesis* 1:16. (5) *Hosea* 3:5.

Psalm 67 / תהלים סז

לַמְנַצֵּחַ בִּנְגִינֹת מִזְמוֹר שִׁיר. אֱלֹהִים יְחָנֵּנוּ

‹ favor us ‹ May God « a song. ‹ a psalm, ‹ with the neginos, ‹ For the conductor

וִיבָרְכֵנוּ, יָאֵר פָּנָיו אִתָּנוּ סֶלָה. לָדַעַת בָּאָרֶץ

‹ on earth ‹ To make known « Selah. ‹ with us, ‹ His countenance ‹ may He illuminate « and bless us,

דַּרְכֶּךָ, בְּכָל גּוֹיִם יְשׁוּעָתֶךָ. יוֹדוּךָ עַמִּים אֱלֹהִים,

« O God; ‹ will the peoples, ‹ Acknowledge You « Your salvation. ‹ nations ‹ among all « Your way,

יוֹדוּךָ עַמִּים כֻּלָּם. יִשְׂמְחוּ וִירַנְּנוּ לְאֻמִּים,

« regimes, ‹ and singing for joy will be ‹ Glad will be « — all of them. « will the peoples ‹ acknowledge You

כִּי תִשְׁפֹּט עַמִּים מִישֹׁר, וּלְאֻמִּים בָּאָרֶץ תַּנְחֵם

‹ [with fairness] you will guide, ‹ on earth ‹ and the regimes « fairly ‹ the peoples ‹ You will judge ‹ because

סֶלָה. יוֹדוּךָ עַמִּים אֱלֹהִים, יוֹדוּךָ עַמִּים כֻּלָּם.

« — all of them. ‹ will the peoples ‹ acknowledge You ‹ O God; ‹ will the peoples, ‹ Acknowledge You « Selah.

אֶרֶץ נָתְנָה יְבוּלָהּ, יְבָרְכֵנוּ אֱלֹהִים אֱלֹהֵינוּ.

« — our God. « may God bless us « its produce; ‹ will then have yielded ‹ The earth

יְבָרְכֵנוּ אֱלֹהִים, וְיִירְאוּ אוֹתוֹ כָּל אַפְסֵי אָרֶץ.

« of the earth. ‹ the ends ‹ — all « Him ‹ and may they fear ‹ May God bless us,

IN MOST CONGREGATIONS, עָלֵינוּ, *ALEINU* (PAGE 617), FOLLOWED BY THE MOURNER'S *KADDISH* (PAGE 619), IS REPEATED AT THIS POINT.

SELECTED TISHAH B'AV LAWS AND CUSTOMS

Although most of the applicable laws are cited in the main text of the prayers, in some cases they are too involved or too lengthy to be given fully where they apply. A selection of such laws is compiled here. This digest cannot cover all eventualities and should be regarded merely as a guide; in case of doubt, one should consult a competent halachic authority. When a particular *halachah* is in dispute, we generally follow the ruling of the *Mishnah Berurah.* On occasion, however (usually when *Mishnah Berurah* does not give a definitive ruling or when a significant number of congregations do not follow *Mishnah Berurah's* ruling), we cite more than one opinion. As a general rule, each congregation is bound by its tradition and the ruling of its authorities.

These laws and customs have been culled, in the main, from the most widely accepted authorities: the *Shulchan Aruch Orach Chaim* [here abbreviated *O.C.*] and *Mishnah Berurah* [*M.B.*]. We have also included many of the general laws of prayer that also apply to Tishah B'Av. They are meant only as a learning and familiarizing tool. For halachic questions, one should consult the *Shulchan Aruch* and its commentaries and/or a halachic authority.

Compiled by *Rabbi Hersh Goldwurm zt"l.*

EREV TISHAH B'AV — TISHAH B'AV EVE

The Afternoon

1. The afternoon before the Tishah B'Av fast takes on some of the mourning aspects of the fast day itself. One should not go on a pleasure trip or even on a pleasurable stroll. [Rather, one should devote his time to reflect on the theme of the upcoming day.] (*Rama O.C.* 553:2).

2. Similarly, from the hour of noon before the fast it is customary to learn only the Torah subjects that one may learn on Tishah B'Av itself (see §38); i.e., matters that pertain to the fast or to mourning. Therefore, even when Tishah B'Av falls on the Sabbath (so that the fast is observed on Sunday) or Sunday, it is customary to refrain from learning matters other than those permitted on Tishah B'Av on the Sabbath afternoon before the fast; the recitation of *Pirkei Avos* is deferred to the following week (*Rama O.C.* 553:2). However, many *poskim* point out that the custom has no Talmudic basis and argue that it is better to study whatever Torah subjects one wishes, rather than to desist from learning altogether. Therefore if one wishes to be lenient in this matter we do not deter him (*M.B.* 553:8).

Minchah

3. The *Minchah* prayer should be recited early enough to allow time to eat a small meal — the *se'udah hamafsekes* (see §5) — between the prayer and the beginning of the fast.

4. *Minchah* is recited in the usual manner; *Tachanun* is omitted. Since Tishah B'Av itself has the status of a quasi-festival on which *Tachanun* is omitted, it is also omitted at *Minchah* of the preceding afternoon (*O.C.* 552:2).

The Se'udah Hamafsekes

5. The meal that immediately precedes the fast — the *se'udah hamafsekes,* literally the *meal that interposes* — should reflect the mourning theme of the impending fast day. The *Gemara* (*Taanis* 30a) relates that on the eve of Tishah B'Av, the Tanna R' Yehudah bar Ilai's meal consisted only of stale bread with salt and a jug of water, which he would consume while seated between the oven and the stove. *Rambam* writes (*Taanis* 5:9), "The following was the practice of the devout people of ancient times: On the eve of Tishah B'Av one would be served dry bread ... and after it, drink a jug of water, in sadness, desolation, and with tears, like one who has the body of a dear one in his presence. This, or [a practice] resembling this, should be the practice of Torah scholars. In all my life I have not eaten a cooked dish on the eve of Tishah B'Av — even one of lentils — except when [Tishah B'Av or its eve] falls on the Sabbath."

6. The above practices, however, were the stringent practices of the extremely devout; they are not binding upon every Jew. The *halachah* follows the Mishnah (*Taanis* 26b), which states that at the final meal before the fast, one may not eat more than one cooked dish. Meat and wine are entirely forbidden. (The ban upon meat and wine need not concern us, since it is customary to refrain from these foods from Rosh Chodesh Av.) It should be noted that in this context fish is also categorized as meat.Thus, even fish may not be eaten at the *se'udah hamafsekes* (*O.C.* 352:2).

7. The *Gemara* (30a) applies two qualifications to the food restrictions in the meals of Tishah B'Av eve: (a) They apply only to meals eaten after the hour of noon; and (b) only to the meal that immediately precedes the fast — hence, the restrictions apply only to the *se'udah hamafsekes*, provided it is eaten in the afternoon. Hence, if one eats more than one meal in the afternoon, the restrictions apply to the final full meal of the day, and if one's last meal was eaten before noon, it is not subject to these restrictions (*O.C.* 552:9).

8. One may eat even many different types of raw fruit and vegetables (*O.C.* 552:4), but not two cooked fruit or vegetable dishes; even if they are also fit to be eaten raw (e.g., applesauce), they qualify as cooked dishes (*O.C.* 552:3). Therefore, some *poskim* prohibit hot coffee or tea at the *se'udah hamafsekes* (in addition to one cooked dish). Some permit this, arguing that the prohibition applies only to solid foods, not to drinks (*Shaarei Teshuvah* 552:1).

9. Roasted (and fried) foods are considered cooked dishes in this regard (*O.C.* 552:3), as are also pickled foods (*Shaarei Teshuvah* 552:1).

10. Even two batches of the same food could be considered two dishes in this regard: if they were cooked in two different pots and thereby differ in some way, even if the difference is only in consistency; e.g., one has a thick texture while the other is more watery. But if both batches are identical, they are considered one food (*O.C.* 552:3 with *M.B.* §8).

11. Two foods that were cooked together are considered two dishes, unless it is customary to cook these foods together year round, e.g., peas with onions (*O.C.* 552:3).

12. One should also curtail one's pleasure at this meal, by cutting down on the amount and type of drinks consumed. Beer and other intoxicating drinks should be avoided completely. One should not eat salads after the meal, as is the custom year round (*O.C.* 552:1).

13. The prevalent custom, which is also the ancient Ashkenazic custom, is to eat a regular meal in the afternoon before *Minchah*. There are no restrictions on this meal, and it is customary to eat well at this meal so that fasting will not be difficult the next day. However, if one feels that the fast will not harm him and he wishes to be stringent in this matter, he is to be commended. After *Minchah*, the *seudah hamafsekes* is eaten, subject to the restrictions noted above (*Rama O.C.* 552:9). Moreover, one should take care not to overeat at the first meal, because if one has no appetite to eat afterward, the meal may be considered as inconsequential, so that the first meal will be the actual *se'udah hamafsekes*.

◈ Customs of the Se'udah Hamafsekes

14. At the *se'udah hamafsekes* it is customary to eat [bread and] a hard-boiled egg, because eggs are a mourner's food. At the conclusion of the meal one dips a piece of bread in ashes and says, "This is the Tishah B'Av meal" (*O.C.* 552:5, 6, with *M.B.*).

15. The meal is eaten sitting on the ground or a low seat, but one need not remove one's shoes. After the meal, however, one may sit on a chair (*O.C.* 552:7).

16. Three males should not sit together during the meal, so that they will not have to recite *Birkas Hamazon* together with *zimun*. Even if they did eat together, they should nevertheless not say *zimun* (*O.C.* 552:8 with *M.B.*).

◈ After the Se'udah Hamafsekes

17. After the meal has been concluded and *Birkas Hamazon* been recited, until sundown one may still eat and do other things that are prohibited on the fast itself (*O.C.* 553:1).

18. If, however, one explicitly (i.e., orally) expressed the resolve not to eat anymore, he is considered to have taken the fast upon himself, and is obligated to observe all the strictures of the fast (eating, drinking, washing, etc.) — except for the wearing of shoes, which is permitted until sundown (*O.C.* 553:1 with *M.B.* §4). The same is true if one did not mention "eating," but said that he accepts the fast upon himself (*M.B.* §1).

19. The above-mentioned acceptance of the fast is valid only if it is done after *plag haminchah*, i.e., within approximately one and one half hours before sundown (or more precisely, 5⁄48 of the time between sunrise and sunset). Consequently, if the resolve not to eat was expressed prior to that time, one need not observe *all* the strictures of the fast, but, in accordance with his explicit vow, one is forbidden to eat (*M.B.* §4).

20. According to the *Shulchan Aruch* (*O.C.* 553:1), only an oral declaration has validity, so that if one resolved only mentally not to eat or to accept the fast, one may still eat thereafter. Some *poskim* dispute this ruling, however, and obligate one to fast even if he made merely a mental resolution to *fast;* but if he resolved mentally not to *eat,* the resolution is not binding. In view of the above, it is advisable to declare (either orally or mentally) at the conclusion of the meal that one does not wish to accept the fast prematurely (*M.B.* §2).

21. Immediately upon sundown, the fast takes effect, and all of its strictures apply. Therefore one must take care to stop eating and drinking before sundown, but there is no obligation to "add" from the daytime to the fast, as there is on the eve of the Sabbaths and festivals (*O.C.* 553:2 with *M.B.* §3).

22. Since wearing shoes is prohibited on Tishah B'Av, one must take off his shoes before sundown. Moreover if *Maariv* is recited before sundown, the shoes should be taken off before *Borchu* (i.e., the beginning of the service) is recited. Some advise that the shoes be taken off before one goes to the synagogue. However, once the sun sets one must remove them even if one has not yet gone to the synagogue (*O.C.* 553:2 with *M.B.* §5).

◆§ Tishah B'Av Eve on the Sabbath

23. When Tishah B'Av occurs on Sunday or on the Sabbath itself (so that the fast is observed on Sunday), none of the strictures regarding the *se'udah hamafsekes* apply. One may eat meat and drink wine and set the table "as King Solomon did in his time." Moreover, it is a sin to deprive oneself of these foods if one does so in observance of the mourning of Tishah B'Av (*O.C.* 552:10 with *M.B.* §23). [It goes without saying that customs such as sitting on the ground, eating a hard-boiled egg, and dipping the bread in ashes are not observed.]

24. Some say that one should not eat the third meal of Sabbath — the *se'udah shlishis* — together with a group, but others argue that if one always eats this meal together with his associates (e.g., the group meets in the synagogue for a public *se'udah shlishis*), one must also do so now, for to refrain would be a public observance of mourning on the Sabbath. All agree that at home the meal should be eaten with the family sitting together, and that *Birkas Hamazon* be recited with *zimun* (*O.C.* 552:10 with *M.B.* §23).

25. As on a weekday, the fast begins at sundown (*O.C.* 552:10 with *M.B.* §24). At this time all eating, drinking, etc. must stop, and the five restrictions are observed. However, wearing of shoes is permitted until *Borchu* is recited. The members of the congregation remove their shoes after the recitation and the *chazzan* does so before it; they should first recite the formula: בָּרוּךְ הַמַּבְדִּיל בֵּין קוֹדֶשׁ לְחוֹל, *Blessed is He Who separates between holy and secular* (*O.C.* 553:2). [Nowadays it is customary in many congregations to recite *Maariv* some time after the Sabbath has ended, so that people will have time to remove their shoes and change into their weekday clothing at home, before they go to the synagogue. They should of course recite the above-mentioned formula first.]

26. Regarding Torah study on Tishah B'Av eve when it occurs on the Sabbath, see above §2.

27. The verses of צִדְקָתְךָ, *Tzidkas'cha,* which are said at the conclusion of the *chazzan's* repetition of the Sabbath *Minchah,* are omitted (*O.C.* 552:12).

◆§ Tishah B'Av on the Sabbath

28. Even when Tishah B'Av falls on the Sabbath itself, none of the restrictions of the fast day apply, because to observe them would be a public manifestation of mourning on the Sabbath. Regarding marital relations see *O.C.* 554:19. *M.B.* §39-40.

29. Torah study is permitted until noon (*M.B.* 553:9). Thereafter, the restrictions are the same as those of a Tishah B'Av eve that falls on the Sabbath; see above §2.

30. The prayer *Av Harachamim* is recited after the Torah reading (*M.B.* 552:30).

THINGS PROHIBITED ON THE FAST DAY

◆§ The Five Restrictions

31. Fasting on Tishah B'Av is a broader concept than mere abstention from food and drink. It includes abstention from five activities: (1) eating and drinking; (2) washing one's body; (3) anointing oneself; (4) wearing leather shoes; and (5) marital relations. It is not within the scope of this summary to discuss in detail the ramifications of the restrictions that do not pertain to the prayer service. However, a few words about the restriction on washing, especially about washing the hands before a prayer service, are appropriate here.

32. It is absolutely forbidden to wash even a minute part of the body, whether in hot or cold water, or even to dip one's finger in water (*O.C.* 554:7). However, one may wash his hands three times upon arising in the morning [נְטִילַת יָדַיִם] except that one may wash only the minimum required area — the fingers, but not the palm of the hand (*O.C.* 554:10).

33. If one has performed his bodily functions and is returning to his prayers (i.e., to recite the *Shemoneh Esrei*), he may also wash his fingers (as above; *O.C.* 554:9, 613:2, *M.B.* 4). If it is his custom all year round to wash three times, he may wash his fingers three times (*Matteh Ephraim* 613:5). One may also wash his hands in preparation for *Minchah* (*M.B.* 554:21).

34. However, if one has merely urinated and will not recite the *Shemoneh Esrei,* it is questionable whether he may wash his hands. In order to avoid this problem, one should touch a covered part of the body, thus incurring an unquestionable obligation to wash his hands before reciting the blessing of אֲשֶׁר יָצַר (see *O.C.* 613:3, *M.B.* 4, 6).

35. One who merely entered a bathroom may not wash his hands, even if this is one's practice throughout the year. Rather one should wipe his hands, on a clean cloth or board, in lieu of washing (*M.E.* 613:7). However, if one is upset at praying with unwashed hands, one may wash them (*Eleph LaMatteh* 613:7). [Presumably the device of touching oneself on a covered part of the body is applicable here too.]

36. If one has touched a covered part of the body and wishes to pray or recite a blessing, one should wash all the fingers of that hand. But if one has touched dirt or mud, he may wash only the soiled area (*O.C.* 554:9, *M.B.* 613:6).

37. Although it is customary to wash one's face and rinse one's mouth every morning before praying, it is forbidden to do so on Tishah B'Av. However, if one has mucus on his eyes, he may moisten his fingers and rub them over his eyes (*O.C.* 554:11).

◆§ Other Prohibitions

38. Though we cannot detail all the laws of Tishah B'Av here, the following is a brief listing: One may not study Torah, except for things pertaining to mourning of Tishah B'Av, because the study of Torah brings joy. One may study, with commentary, the Biblical books of *Job*, the "unpleasant" passages in *Jeremiah* (omitting the verses of consolation), and *Eichah.* One may also study the Midrash to *Eichah*, the third chapter of *Moed Kattan* (which discusses the laws of mourning), the passages in the Talmud (*Gittin* 55b-58a) that discuss the destruction of the Temple, and the story of the destruction of the Temple in the book of *Yossipon* (*O.C.* 554:1-2, *M.B.* §3).

39. One does not greet his fellows on Tishah B'Av; not even to say good morning. If one is greeted by someone who is unaware of this law, one should answer quietly and with a serious mien. It is better to tell him that on Tishah B'Av one does not extend greetings. One should also not give a present on Tishah B'Av (*O.C.* 554:20; *M.B.* 41-2).

40. Work should be avoided until noon. See *O.C.* 554:22-4. If possible, one should refrain from smoking on Tishah B'Av. If this is very difficult, one may smoke in private after the hour of noon (*M.B.* 555:8).

41. On the night of Tishah B'Av and on the morning, until noon, one sits on the ground or on a low stool (*O.C.* 559:3; *M.B.* §3).

MAARIV

42. *Maariv* begins in the usual manner. After בָּרְכוּ the congregation sits on the floor or on low stools and the lights are dimmed. The *paroches* is removed from the front of the Holy Ark. On Tishah B'Av the prayers are said slowly and tearfully, in the manner of mourners (*O.C.* 559:1).

43. The regular *Maariv* service is recited [on Saturday night with the addition of אַתָּה חוֹנַנְתָּנוּ]. After *Shemoneh Esrei* the Full *Kaddish* is recited [including the verse תִּתְקַבֵּל] (*M.B.* 559:4).

44. On Saturday night, although *Havdalah* is not recited [see below], a multi-wicked candle is lit and the blessing בּוֹרֵא מְאוֹרֵי הָאֵשׁ is recited (*O.C.* 556:1).

45. *Eichah* (the Book of *Lamentations*) is chanted aloud by the reader. The prevalent custom is that the entire congregation reads along in an undertone (see *M.B.* 559:15. See also *Taz, Magen Avraham,* and *Pri Megadim* to 559:4). After *Eichah* has been concluded, the evening *Kinnos* are recited.

46. After the *Kinnos,* the congregation recites וְאַתָּה קָדוֹשׁ; the reader recites the Full *Kaddish,* but omits the verse תִּתְקַבֵּל; and the congregation recites עָלֵינוּ, followed by the Mourner's *Kaddish.* [At the end of the Sabbath, וִיהִי נֹעַם and וְיִתֶּן לְךָ are omitted, and *Havdalah* is postponed until Sunday night.]

SHACHARIS

47. Candles are not lit at the *chazzan's* lectern for *Shacharis,* but they are lit for *Minchah* (*M.B.* 559:15).

48. Donning of the *tallis* and *tefillin* is postponed until *Minchah.* The *tallis kattan (tzitzis)* is worn, however, but the accompanying blessing is omitted(*O.C.* 555:1).

49. The morning blessings (p. 72) are recited as usual. Although the blessing שֶׁעָשָׂה לִי כָּל צָרְכִּי was instituted to thank God for providing us with shoes, it is the general custom among Ashkenazim to recite it even though shoes are not worn on Tishah B'Av (*M.B.* 554:31, see *Shaarei Teshuvah* and *Pri Megadim* to *O.C.* 46:8). However, Sephardim omit the blessing (see *Kaf HaChaim* 46:17), and the Vilna Gaon (*Maaseh Rav*) is reported to have recited the blessing only at night, after the fast.

50. The entire prayer service which precedes פְּסוּקֵי דְזִמְרָה (the *Verses of Praise*), including אֵיזֶהוּ מְקוֹמָן, may be said. [Although *Eizehu Mekoman* is a chapter of Mishnah — which may not be studied on Tishah B'Av — it is part of the regular prayer order, and is therefore not omitted.] (*O.C.* 554:4, *M.B.* 7). However, *Rama* states (*O.C.* 559:4) that פְּטוּם הַקְּטֹרֶת is omitted (because, *M.B.* explains, its recitation is not considered to be sufficiently widespread for it to be considered part of the "order of the day").

Mishnah Berurah (554:7) maintains that according to *Rama's* view, the passage of

Tamid is the only Scriptural passage referring to offerings that may be recited. Nevertheless, in many communities the entire service is recited, without omission, as already indicated.

51. Individuals recite *Shemoneh Esrei* at *Shacharis* as usual, without any additions. The *chazzan,* however, inserts the blessing עֲנֵנוּ in his repetition. See §61 for laws pertaining to this blessing. *Birkas Kohanim* is omitted (see *Dagul Merevavah* to *O.C.* 559) as is *Tachanun.*

52. The prayer service continues with reading from the Torah, followed by the Half *Kaddish* and *Haftarah.* The Torah is returned to the Ark and *Kinnos* are recited. It is preferable that their recitation extend until close to noon (*O.C.* 559:2).

53. After the recitation of *Kinnos,* the prayer service continues with אַשְׁרֵי and וּבָא לְצִיּוֹן (with the omission of the verse וַאֲנִי זֹאת ...), the Full *Kaddish,* with the omission of תִּתְקַבֵּל; followed by עָלֵינוּ and the Mourner's *Kaddish.* The Song of the Day is deferred until *Minchah.*

54. During the recitation of *Kinnos,* one should not talk about extraneous matters nor leave the synagogue, in order to fully concentrate on mourning for the destruction of the Temple (*O.C.* 559:5).

55. It is commendable that every individual read *Eichah* again during the daytime (*Shelah* cited by *Magen Avraham,* beginning of 559).

MINCHAH

56. Candles are lit at the *chazzan's* lectern for *Minchah* (*Pri Megadim* in *Eishel Avraham* 559:3). The *paroches* [*Ark* curtain] is put back in place (*Kaf HaChaim* 559:19).

57. The *talis* and *tefillin* are donned (*O.C.* 555:1), and the remainder of the *Shacharis* prayer is said.

58. *Minchah* on Tishah B'Av is the same as that of a regular fast day (except that נַחֵם, *Nacheim,* is inserted in the *Shemoneh Esrei* (see §64). The Torah reading and the *Haftarah* are identical to that of a regular fast day, with the exception of *Avinu Malkeinu* and *Tachanun,* which are omitted.

59. In *Shemoneh Esrei,* עֲנֵנוּ, *Aneinu,* [*Answer us*] is inserted, as on other fast days. In addition, נַחֵם, *Nacheim,* [*Comfort,*] is inserted. See below §64.

60. The *chazzan* repeats the *Shemoneh Esrei* as usual and inserts the above two prayers (see below). He also recites the Priestly Blessing, as on other fast days (*Kitzur Shulchan Aruch* 124:19). The *Shemoneh Esrei* is followed by the Full *Kaddish* (with תִּתְקַבֵּל), then עָלֵינוּ, and the Mourner's *Kaddish.*

◆§ עֲנֵנוּ / Aneinu

61. A special fast-day prayer — עֲנֵנוּ — is inserted both in the silent *Shemoneh Esrei* and in the *chazzan's* repetition. This prayer may be recited only by one who is fasting; for someone not fasting to recite this prayer which refers specifically to "our public fast" would be fraudulent (see *O.C.* 565:3 in *Rama*). This insertion is made by the *chazzan* in his repetition of both *Shacharis* and *Minchah,* but in the silent *Shemoneh Esrei* it is recited only during *Minchah* (*O.C.* 565:3). In the *chazzan's* prayer, *Aneinu* takes the form of a complete benediction, concluding with הָעוֹנֶה בְּעֵת צָרָה, *Blessed ... Who responds in time of distress* (*O.C.* 566:1), בָּרוּךְ ... גּוֹאֵל יִשְׂרָאֵל, and רְפָאֵנוּ. The individual's recitation is included in the benediction שְׁמַע קוֹלֵנוּ (*O.C.* 565:1). In order for the *chazzan* to recite the blessing in his repetition of the *Shemoneh Esrei,* there must be ten congregants who are fasting. Some authorities rule that it is sufficient that there be seven fasting individuals (*O.C.* 566:3, *M.B.* §14). Individuals recite *Aneinu* in their own *Shemoneh Esrei* even if no one else is fasting.

62. If an individual forgot to insert עֲנֵנוּ in its proper place and has already said the word *HASHEM* in the concluding blessing of שְׁמַע קוֹלֵנוּ, he must conclude with שׁוֹמֵעַ תְּפִלָּה and continue with רְצֵה. He may insert עֲנֵנוּ at the end of the *Shemoneh Esrei* before אֱלֹהַי נְצוֹר. If he finished *Shemoneh Esrei* before realizing his error, he should not repeat the *Shemoneh Esrei* (*M.B.* 119:16,19).

63. If the *chazzan* forgot to insert עֲנֵנוּ in its proper place, but has not yet said the word *HASHEM* of the concluding blessing of רְפָאֵנוּ, he should interrupt his recitation, and recite עֲנֵנוּ. Thereafter he should begin רְפָאֵנוּ again and continue. If he has already uttered the word *HASHEM*, he must conclude the blessing רוֹפֵא חוֹלֵי and continue his prayer as usual. In this case, the *chazzan* inserts עֲנֵנוּ in the benediction שְׁמַע קוֹלֵנוּ, as do individuals in the silent prayer, but omits the concluding formula בָּרוּךְ הָעוֹנֶה בְּעֵת צָרָה. If he realized his error after he uttered the word *HASHEM* in the concluding formula of שְׁמַע קוֹלֵנוּ, he must continue with שׁוֹמֵעַ תְּפִלָּה. In that case, he may recite עֲנֵנוּ (omitting the concluding blessing) after הַמְבָרֵךְ אֶת עַמּוֹ יִשְׂרָאֵל בַּשָּׁלוֹם (*O.C.* 119:4 *M.B.* §16,19).

נַחֵם / Nacheim

64. In addition to עֲנֵנוּ, a special prayer (נַחֵם, *Comfort*), mourning the destruction of the Holy Temple and supplicating that it be rebuilt, is inserted in the benediction וְלִירוּשָׁלַיִם, *and to Jerusalem* (both in the silent and *chazzan's Shemoneh Esrei*) of *Minchah*. The concluding blessing of וְלִירוּשָׁלַיִם is changed (both for individuals and for the *chazzan*) to בָּרוּךְ ... מְנַחֵם צִיּוֹן וּבוֹנֵה יְרוּשָׁלָיִם, *Blessed ... Who consoles Zion and rebuilds Jerusalem*. If one forgot to recite this prayer in its appropriate place, he inserts it in the benediction רְצֵה, before the word וְתֶחֱזֶינָה, but in that case one omits the concluding formula ... מְנַחֵם צִיּוֹן (*O.C.* 557:1, *M.B.* §2). However, if one recited נַחֵם erroneously in the benediction שְׁמַע קוֹלֵנוּ, it need not be repeated in רְצֵה (*Be'ur Halachah*). If one has already concluded the רְצֵה benediction with הַמַּחֲזִיר שְׁכִינָתוֹ לְצִיּוֹן (or even said the word *HASHEM*), he continues his prayer, and need not repeat *Shemoneh Esrei* (*O.C.* 557).

AFTERNOON

65. Although some restrictions are relaxed in the afternoon, e.g., one may sit on a chair, etc., this applies only to practices that are based on custom. However, all halachic strictures that apply to the fast, i.e., eating, drinking, wearing shoes, studying Torah, et al. are in force until nightfall, when stars become visible (*M.B.* 553:3).

MAARIV

66. The regular *Maariv* is recited. On Sunday night, *Havdalah* is recited, with the following exceptions: a) *Havdalah* commences with the blessing over wine; the preliminary verses that are recited at the end of the Sabbath are omitted; b) the blessings over spices and the candles are omitted. Even those who do not drink the *Havdalah* wine during the Nine Days may do so now; they need not give the wine to a child to drink. [One should not eat before reciting *Havdalah*.] (*O.C.* 556:1, *M.B.* §3).

Kiddush Levanah

67. According to *Rama* (*O.C.* 426:2), *Kiddush Levanah* should not be recited on the night following Tishah B'Av, because it should be recited joyously, but we are still in mourning. However, many *poskim* dispute this ruling and permit the recitation of *Kiddush Levanah*. Nevertheless, one should first eat something and don his shoes (*M.B.* §11). However, if this is the only time he will be able to recite *Kiddush Levanah* with a *minyan*, some permit its recitation even if one has not yet broken his fast (*Shaar HaTziyun* §9).

The Night After the Fast

68. The strictures that were observed during the Nine Days apply also to the night following Tishah B'Av and the next day until noon. Thus, one does not eat meat, take a haircut, launder clothing, etc. until noon of the next day (*O.C.* 558:1, *M.B.* §3).

However if Tishah B'Av was on Thursday, one may wash clothing and take a haircut or shave on Friday morning in preparation for the Sabbath (*M.B.* 558:3, *Shaarei Teshuvah* §2).

69. If Tishah B'Av fell on the Sabbath so that the fast was observed on the tenth of Av, one need not observe the strictures of the Nine Days [e.g., bathing, haircut, laundering] on the night after the fast. However, one should abstain from meat and wine [except for the *Havdalah* wine] on the night itself (*O.C.* 558:1, *M.B.* §4).

GENERAL LAWS OF PRAYER

☙ The Obligation

70. Prayer is a major ingredient of every Jew's daily religious life. The Sages teach us that in the post-Temple era, prayer was substituted for the Temple service, and according to some authorities it is a Scriptural obligation to pray every single day (see *Rambam, Hil. Tefillah* 1:1).

71. Before praying, one should set aside a few minutes to collect his thoughts and to prepare himself mentally to stand before his Maker. Also, one should not rush away immediately after ending his prayer so as not to give the impression that he regards prayer as a burdensome task (*O.C.* 93:1).

72. Before beginning to pray, one should meditate upon God's infinite greatness and man's insignificance, and thereby remove from his heart any thoughts of physical pleasure (*O.C.* 98:1). By pondering God's works, man recognizes His infinite wisdom and comes to love and laud Him. This makes man cognizant of his own puny intelligence and flawed nature and puts him in a proper frame of mind to plead for God's mercy (*Rambam, Yesodei HaTorah* 2:2).

73. The prayers should be said with a feeling of awe and humility, and surely not in an atmosphere of levity, frivolity, or mundane concerns, nor should one pray while angry. Rather, one should pray with the feeling of happiness brought on by the knowledge of God's historic kindness to Israel and His mercy to all creatures (*O.C.* 93:2).

☙ Concentration on the Prayers

74. During *Shemoneh Esrei* one should imagine that he is in the Holy Temple and concentrate his feelings and thoughts toward Heaven, clearing his mind of all extraneous matters (*O.C.* 95:2). His eyes should be directed downward, either closed or reading from the *siddur* (*O.C.* 95:2, *M.B.* 5). One should not look up during *Shemoneh Esrei*, but when he feels his concentration failing, he should raise his eyes heavenward to renew his inspiration (*M.B.* 90:8).

75. One should know the meaning of his prayers. If one had an audience with a human ruler he would take the utmost care in his choice of words and be aware of their meaning. Surely, therefore, when one stands before the King of kings Who knows his innermost thoughts, he must be careful how he speaks (*O.C.* 98:1). Especially in regard to the benedictions of *Shemoneh Esrei*, one should at least meditate on the meaning of the concluding sentence of each benediction, which summarizes its theme (e.g., בָּרוּךְ ... הָאֵל הַקָּדוֹשׁ , *Blessed ... the holy God*; *M.B.* 101:1). The first benediction of the *Shemoneh Esrei* is treated with special stringency in this regard. According to the *halachah* as stated in the Talmud, this benediction must be repeated if it was said without concentration on its meaning (*O.C.* 101:1). However, *Rama* (loc. cit.) rules that it is best *not* to repeat the benediction because it is likely that one will not concentrate properly even during the repetition. *Chayei Adam* (cited in *M.B.* 101:4) advises that if one realized his inattentiveness before saying the word HASHEM in the concluding formula of the first blessing (בָּרוּךְ ... מָגֵן אַבְרָהָם), he should start over from אֱלֹהֵי אַבְרָהָם. Thus, it is of utmost importance that one learn the meaning of the prayers in order to develop his power of concentration (*M.B.* 101:2).

76. On Tishah B'Av a lengthy selection of lamentation liturgy — *Kinnos* — is a central part of the *Shacharis* service. It is important that one familiarize himself with these prayers prior to the fast day, some of which use unfamiliar language and contain numerous allusions to Midrashic sources.

☙ Women's Obligation to Pray

77. Women are obligated to pray, and according to *Rambam* and *Shulchan Aruch* (*O.C.* 106:1) this obligation has Scriptural status. However, there are various opinions regarding the extent of their obligation.

According to the views preferred by *M.B.* (106:4), women are required to recite the *Shemoneh Esrei* of *Shacharis* and *Minchah*; they must recall the Exodus by reciting אֱמֶת וְיַצִּיב, *true and certain* (the prayer after the *Shacharis* recitation of *Shema*), and אֱמֶת וֶאֱמוּנָה, *true and faithful* (the parallel prayer after the *Maariv* recitation of *Shema*), because it recalls the Exodus (*M.B.* 70:2); and it is urged that they recite at least the first verse of *Shema* because it constitutes קַבָּלַת עוֹל מַלְכוּת שָׁמַיִם, *acceptance of God's sovereignty* (*O.C.* 70:1).

Some authorities rule that women should also recite all the morning benedictions. According to one view, *Pesukei D'Zimrah* is introductory to *Shemoneh Esrei* and, consequently, is obligatory upon women too (*M.B.* 70:2).

Women should recite בִּרְכַּת הַתּוֹרָה, *blessings of the Torah* (*O.C.* 47:14, see *Be'ur Halachah*).

According to *Magen Avraham* (*O.C.* 106:2), women are required by the Torah to pray once a day and they may formulate the prayer as they wish. In many countries, this ruling became the basis for the custom that women recite a brief prayer early in the morning and do not recite any of the formal prayers from the *Siddur.*

☙ Miscellaneous Laws

78. One may not pray in the presence of immodestly clad women, or facing a window through which they can be observed (see *O.C.* 75 for details).

79. It is forbidden to pray while one feels the need to discharge his bodily functions (*O.C.* 92:1-3).

80. One must wash his hands before praying, but no benediction is required (*O.C.* 92:4).

On Tishah B'Av, certain strictures must be observed when washing one's hands before prayer; see §32-36.

PRAYER WITH THE CONGREGATION

☙ Prayer with a Minyan of Ten

81. One should do his utmost to pray in the synagogue together with the congregation (*O.C.* 90:9), for the Almighty does not reject the prayer of the many. Contrary to the popular misconception that it is sufficient to respond to בָּרְכוּ and קְדוּשָּׁה, the main objective of prayer with a *minyan* is to recite *Shemoneh Esrei* with the *minyan*. Therefore one must arrive at the synagogue early enough to keep up with the congregation (*M.B.* §28).

☙ Instructions for Latecomers

82. If one arrived at the synagogue too late to recite the entire order of the prayer and still recite the *Shemoneh Esrei* together with the congregation, he may omit certain parts of the service and recite them after the end of *Shacharis*. If time is extremely short, it suffices to recite the benedictions עַל נְטִילַת יָדָיִם; אֲשֶׁר יָצַר; אֱלֹהַי נְשָׁמָה; the benedictions over the Torah; בָּרוּךְ שֶׁאָמַר; אַשְׁרֵי; and from יִשְׁתַּבַּח through *Shemoneh Esrei*. If time permits, the following sections (listed in descending order of importance) should be recited:

(1) הַלְלוּיָהּ הַלְלוּ אֵל בְּקָדְשׁוֹ;
(2) הַלְלוּיָהּ הַלְלוּ אֶת ה' מִן הַשָּׁמַיִם;
(3) the other three הַלְלוּיָהּ psalms;
(4) from וַיְבָרֶךְ דָּוִיד until לְשֵׁם תִּפְאַרְתֶּךָ;
(5) הוֹדוּ until וְהוּא רַחוּם;
(6) the rest of *Pesukei D'Zimrah* (*O.C.* 52:1, *M.B.* §4, *Ba'er Heitev* §3).

83. The above is only an emergency solution. One should not rely on this to arrive late for the *Pesukei D'Zimrah*, because the proper order of the prayers is of utmost importance. Indeed, some authorities contend that recitation of the prayers in their proper order takes priority over the obligation to recite *Shemoneh Esrei* together with the congregation (*M.B.* 52:1).

RESPONSES DURING THE PRAYER

☙ During Pesukei D'Zimrah

84. Other than the exceptions noted below, it is prohibited to interrupt from the beginning of בָּרוּךְ שֶׁאָמַר until the conclusion of the *Shemoneh Esrei* (*O.C.* 51:4). Wherever one may not talk, it is forbidden to do so even in Hebrew (*M.B.* 51:7).

85. With the exception of *Shemoneh Esrei*, parts of *Shacharis* may be interrupted for certain responses to the *chazzan* or for certain blessings, but the rules vary widely, depending on the section of *Shacharis* and the response. In this regard, the most lenient part of *Shacharis* is *Pesukei D'Zimrah*, i.e., the unit that includes the verses between בָּרוּךְ שֶׁאָמַר and יִשְׁתַּבַּח. There, one may respond with *Amen* to any benediction, but may not say בָּרוּךְ הוּא וּבָרוּךְ שְׁמוֹ. It is permitted to respond to *Kedushah* and מוֹדִים (in the repetition of *Shemoneh Esrei*), בָּרְכוּ, and *Kaddish*. If the congregation is reciting the *Shema*, one should recite the first verse (*Shema Yisrael ...*) together with them. If one discharged his bodily functions, he may recite the benediction אֲשֶׁר יָצַר (*M.B.* 51:8).

86. If one did not yet recite the *Shema* and calculates that the congregation will reach it after the deadline (see §109 below) or if he had forgotten to say the daily *berachos* on the Torah, he should say them in the *Pesukei D'Zimrah* (*M.B.* 51:10).

❧ During the Pesukei D'Zimrah Blessings

87. The second level of stringency regarding interruptions includes the two benedictions of *Pesukei D'Zimrah*: בָּרוּךְ שֶׁאָמַר and יִשְׁתַּבַּח.

❑ בָּרוּךְ שֶׁאָמַר is composed of three parts:

(a) From בָּרוּךְ שֶׁאָמַר until the first בָּרוּךְ אַתָּה ה' is but a preamble; all responses are permitted.

(b) From the first בָּרוּךְ אַתָּה ה' until the final one, all the interruptions permitted in §85 for the rest of *Pesukei D'Zimrah* are also permitted here. However, the following interruptions are *not* permitted at this point: אֲשֶׁר יָצַר and the *Amen* after the benedictions בָּרוּךְ שֶׁאָמַר and יִשְׁתַּבַּח.

(c) The last, brief blessing, בָּרוּךְ ... בַּתִּשְׁבָּחוֹת, during which no interruption at all is permitted (*M.B.* 51:2).

❑ יִשְׁתַּבַּח is composed of two parts:

(a) From the beginning of יִשְׁתַּבַּח to בָּרוּךְ אַתָּה ה', which has the same rules as (b) above.

(b) From בָּרוּךְ אַתָּה ה' to the end, which has the same rules as (c) above (*M.B.* 51:2, 65:11, 54:11).

❧ Between the Shema Blessings of Shacharis and Maariv

88. The third level of stringency concerns the "intervals" between the various sections of the *Shema* and the benedictions bracketing it. The intervals are as follows: After בָּרוּךְ ... יוֹצֵר הַמְּאוֹרוֹת; after בָּרוּךְ ... בְּאַהֲבָה; and after the first and second sections of the *Shema*. [The end of the *Shema* is immediately followed by the first word of the following paragraph (אֱמֶת) so that there is no "interval" there. Similarly, it is forbidden to interrupt between the benediction גָּאַל יִשְׂרָאֵל and *Shemoneh Esrei* (*O.C.* 66:5, 9).]

Corresponding "intervals" exist in *Maariv* following each blessing and after the first and second sections of the *Shema* (*M.B.* 66:27; *Be'ur Halachah* there).

89. During the "intervals" one may respond with *Amen* to all benedictions (*M.B.* 66:23). Regarding קַדִּישׁ, קְדוּשָׁה, בָּרְכוּ, and other interruptions, the "intervals" are treated in the same way as are interruptions in the fourth level (see below §90). During the interval between בְּאַהֲבָה and שְׁמַע, however, only the *Amen* after בְּאַהֲבָה as permitted (*Derech HaChaim*; see *M.B.* 59:25).

❧ During the Shema and Its Blessings in Shacharis and Maariv

90. The fourth level concerns the *Shema* itself and the benedictions bracketing it. The benedictions may be separated into two parts for this purpose: (1) During the concluding, brief blessing, and during the verses of שְׁמַע ... אֶחָד and בָּרוּךְ שֵׁם, no interruption whatever is permitted (*O.C.* 66:1; *M.B.* §11, 12). (2) During the rest of the fourth level, one may respond with *Amen* only to the two blessings הָאֵל הַקָּדוֹשׁ and שׁוֹמֵעַ תְּפִלָּה in *Shemoneh Esrei*. It is permitted to respond to בָּרְכוּ of both the *chazzan* and one who is called up to the Torah. In *Kaddish* one may respond with אָמֵן יְהֵא שְׁמֵהּ רַבָּא... and with the *Amen* to דַּאֲמִירָן בְּעָלְמָא. In *Kedushah* one may say only the verses beginning קָדוֹשׁ and בָּרוּךְ. To *Modim*, one may respond only with the three words מוֹדִים אֲנַחְנוּ לָךְ (*O.C* 66:3; *M.B.* §17, 18).

A person who is reciting the *Shema* or its benedictions should not be called up to the Torah, even if he is the only *Kohen* or Levite present; in such a case it is preferable that he leave the room. However, if he *was* called up to the Torah, he may recite the benedictions, but should not read along with the reader. If possible he should attempt to get to an "interval" in his prayers before doing so (*M.B.* 66:26).

If one had to discharge his bodily functions he should merely wash his hands and defer the recitation of אֲשֶׁר יָצַר until after *Shemoneh Esrei* (*M.B.* 66:23).

91. If one has not yet responded to בָּרְכוּ, קְדוּשָׁה, or מוֹדִים and is nearly up to *Shemoneh Esrei,* he should stop before שִׁירָה חֲדָשָׁה in order to make the responses. If he has already said שִׁירָה חֲדָשָׁה, but has not yet concluded the benediction, he may respond, but after the response he should start again from שִׁירָה חֲדָשָׁה (*M.B.* 66:52).

92. Regarding גָּאַל יִשְׂרָאֵל of *Shacharis, Rama,* followed by most Ashkenazic congregations, rules that it is permitted to answer *Amen,* while others, particularly Chassidic congregations, follow R' Yosef Caro's ruling against *Amen* at this point. To avoid the controversy, many individuals recite the blessing in unison with the *chazzan* (*O.C.* 66:7, *M.B.* §35).

93. The fifth level concerns the *Shemoneh Esrei* prayer. Here, any interruption is forbidden. Even motioning to someone is prohibited (*O.C.* 104:1; *M.B.* §1). If the *chazzan* is up to קַדִּישׁ, קְדוּשָׁה, or בָּרְכוּ, one should stop and listen silently to the *chazzan's* recitation; his own silent concentration is considered as if he had responded (*O.C.* 104:7; *M.B.* §26-28).

94. From the time one has concluded the last benediction of *Shemoneh Esrei* with בַּשָּׁלוֹם until the end of the standard prayers (i.e., יִהְיוּ לְרָצוֹן at the end of אֱלֹהַי נְצוֹר), one is restricted to the responses listed in level four. However, whenever possible, one should hurry to say the verse יִהְיוּ לְרָצוֹן ... וְגוֹאֲלִי before making any kind of response. It is preferable to take the usual three steps backward before making the responses (*O.C.* 122:1; *M.B.* §2-4). [Once one has concluded the *Shemoneh Esrei* by taking three steps backward, he may make any response, even if he has not yet recited אֱלֹהַי נְצוֹר.]

LAWS OF RECITING THE SHEMA

95. It is a Scriptural precept to recite the *Shema* twice daily, once in the morning and again in the evening. When one recites the *Shema* he must have in mind that he is fulfilling a Scriptural precept; otherwise it must be repeated (*O.C.* 60:4). However, if the circumstances make it obvious that the intention was present — e.g., he recited it during the prayer with the benedictions preceding and following it — he need not repeat the *Shema* even if he did not make a mental declaration of purpose (*M.B.* 60:10).

96. The third section of *Shema,* whose recitation is Rabbinical in origin according to almost all authorities, contains a verse whose recitation fulfills the Scriptural obligation to commemorate the Exodus from Egypt twice daily (see *Berachos* 12b; *Rambam, Hil. Kerias Shema* 1:3). The above rule concerning a mental declaration of intent applies here, too.

97. One should concentrate on the meaning of all the words, and read them with awe and trepidation (*O.C.* 61:1). He should read the *Shema* as if it were a new proclamation containing teachings never yet revealed (*O.C.* 61:2). The first verse of *Shema* is the essential profession of our faith. Therefore, the utmost concentration on its meaning is necessary. If one said it without such concentration, he has not fulfilled his obligation and must repeat it (*O.C.* 60:5, 63:4), but he should repeat the verse quietly, for one may not (publicly) say the first verse of *Shema* repeatedly (ibid.).

98. While reciting the first verse, it is customary to cover the eyes with the right hand to avoid distraction and to enhance concentration (*O.C.* 61:5).

99. Although *Shema* may be recited quietly, one should recite it loudly enough to hear himself. However, one has discharged his obligation even if he does not hear himself, as long as he has enunciated the words (*O.C.* 62:3).

100. The last word of the first verse, אֶחָד, must be pronounced with special emphasis, while one meditates on God's exclusive sovereignty over the seven heavens and earth, and the four directions: east, south, west, and north (*O.C.* 61:6).

101. Some consider it preferable to recite the entire *Shema* aloud (except for the passage בָּרוּךְ שֵׁם) while others say it quietly; our custom follows the latter usage. However, the first verse should be said aloud in order to arouse one's full concentration (*O.C.* 61:4, 26). It is customary for the *chazzan* to lead the congregation in the recitation of the first verse so that they all proclaim the Kingdom of Heaven together (*Kol Bo* cited in *Darkei Moshe* to *O.C.* 61; *Levush*).

102. Every word must be enunciated clearly and uttered with the correct grammatical pronunciation (*O.C.* 62:1, 61:23, 16-19). It is especially important to enunciate each word clearly and to avoid run-on words by pausing briefly between words ending and beginning with the same consonant, such as וַאֲבַדְתֶּם מְהֵרָה, בְּכָל לְבַבְכֶם, and to pause between a word that ends with a consonant and the next one that begins with a silent letter [i.e., א or ע], such as אֲשֶׁר אָנֹכִי, הַיּוֹם עַל, וּרְאִיתֶם אֹתוֹ (*O.C.* 61:20, 21).

103. Although it is not the universal custom to chant the *Shema* with the cantillation melody used during the synagogue Torah reading, it is laudable to do so, unless one finds that such chanting interferes with his concentration. In any event, the proper punctuation must be followed so that words are grouped into the proper phrases in accordance with the syntax of each word-group and verse (*O.C.* 61:24, *M.B.* §37, 38).

104. While reciting the first two portions of the *Shema*, one may not communicate with someone else by winking or motioning with his lips or fingers (*O.C.* 63:6, *M.B.* §18).

105. It is incumbent that each paragraph of the *Shema* be read word for word as it appears in the Torah. If one erred and skipped a word, he must return to the place of his error and continue the section from there (*O.C.* 64:1-2).

106. The *Shema* should be said in one uninterrupted recitation, but, if one interrupted, whether by talking or waiting silently, he does not have to repeat the *Shema*. However, if the interruption was involuntary in nature [e.g., one had to relieve himself], and the interruption was long enough for him to have recited all three paragraphs of the *Shema* at his own normal speed, he must repeat the entire *Shema* (*Rama O.C.* 65:1). Multiple interruptions interspersed in the recitation of *Shema* are not added together to constitute one long, invalidating interruption (*M.B.* 65:4).

107. If one is present in the synagogue when the congregation recites the *Shema*, he must recite at least the first verse and the verse בָּרוּךְ שֵׁם together with them. If he is in the midst of a prayer that he may not interrupt (see above §87-92), he should at least give the appearance of saying *Shema* by praying loudly in the tune the congregation uses for the *Shema* (*O.C.* 65:2, 3; *M.B.* §10).

108. During morning services, one ordinarily gathers together the four *tzitzis* when he says the words וַהֲבִיאֵנוּ לְשָׁלוֹם מֵאַרְבַּע כַּנְפוֹת הָאָרֶץ, *Bring us in peacefulness from the four corners of the earth*, in the paragraph preceding the *Shema*. [The *tzitzis* are then held in the hand and kissed at specific points of the *Shema* recitation and the blessing which follows it. On Tishah B'Av, however, this is not done.]

109. It is absolutely required that the *Shema* be recited within the requisite time: the first quarter of the day. There are various opinions among the *poskim* as to how to calculate the first quarter of a day, and these are noted in many Jewish calendars. If the congregation begins *Shacharis* late, one should be careful to check the deadline for *K'rias Shema* and, if necessary, recite all three passages of the *Shema* before the communal prayers.

☙ The Chazzan's Repetition of the Shemoneh Esrei

110. The *chazzan's* repetition of *Shemoneh Esrei* is a congregational, rather than an individual, worship. By definition, a "congregation" consists of a *minyan* (quorum of at least ten males over *bar mitzvah*, including the *chazzan*), present and listening to the recitation. If the congregants do not pay attention, it is almost as if the *chazzan* were taking God's Name in vain. Every person should imagine that there are only ten congregants present and that he is one of the nine whose attentive listening is vital to the recitation (*O.C.* 124:4).

If one of the ten is in the middle of the silent *Amidah*, he may still be counted as part of the *minyan*. However, it is preferable that not more than one such person be included (*M.B.* 55:32-34).

111. One should respond with *Amen* to every benediction he hears, and should teach his young children to do so (*O.C.* 124:6, 7).

112. When one says *Amen*, it is important to enunciate all of the vowels and consonants distinctly. One should not respond until the *chazzan* has concluded the benediction, and then the response should be immediate (*O.C.* 124:8). *Mishnah Berurah* (§17) cautions even against Torah study or recitation of psalms and other prayers during the *chazzan's* recitation of the *Shemoneh Esrei*.

113. It is absolutely forbidden to talk during the repetition of *Shemoneh Esrei* even if one makes sure to respond with *Amen* at the conclusion of each benediction (*O.C.* 124:7).

THE READING OF THE TORAH

114. On Tishah B'Av, as on every fast day, three people are called to the Torah at the *Shacharis* prayer, and three at the *Minchah* prayer. One may not add to the prescribed number of *aliyos* (*O.C.* 282:1, *M.B.* §6).

115. The first *aliyah* belongs to a *Kohen* and the second to a *Levi* (if any are present). If no *Kohen* is present, there is no obligation to call a *Levi* in his place, but if no *Levi* is present the same *Kohen* who has been called for his own *aliyah* is called again to replace the *Levi*. He recites both blessings again (*O.C.* 135:10; *M.B.* §35).

◆§ Procedure of the Aliyah

116. Before the person called to the Torah for an *aliyah* recites the benediction, he must open the Torah and find the passage that will be read for him (*O.C.* 139:4). In order to dispel any notion that he is reading the benedictions from the Torah, one should avert his face while reciting them; it is preferable to turn to the left side (*Rama* there). Some authorities maintain that it is better to face the Torah while saying the benedictions but to close his eyes (*M.B.* §19). Others say that it is better to close the Torah during the recitation of the benedictions (*Be'ur Halachah* there). All three modes are practiced today in various congregations.

117. In many congregations it is customary to touch the Torah with a *tallis* (or the Torah's mantle or girdle) at the beginning of the passage to be read, and to kiss the edge which touched the Torah (*Sha'arei Ephraim* 4:3). One should be careful not to rub on the Torah script forcefully for this can cause words to become erased and thus invalidate the Torah Scroll.

118. It is extremely important that the benedictions be said loudly enough for the congregation to hear (*O.C.* 139:6). If the congregation did not hear the recitation of בָּרְכוּ, they may not respond with בָּרוּךְ ... וָעֶד (*Be'ur Halachah* to *O.C.* 57:1). However, if the congregation (or at least a *minyan*) heard בָּרְכוּ, then even someone who has not heard בָּרְכוּ may respond along with the congregation (*M.B.* 57:2).

119. While reciting the benedictions, one should hold the poles (*atzei chaim*) upon which the Torah is rolled. During the reading, the reader holds one pole and the person called to the Torah holds the other one (*O.C.* 139:11; *M.B.* §35). *Arizal* says one should hold the *atzei chaim* with both hands during the benedictions and with the right hand only during the reading (cited in *Magen Avraham* 139:13).

120. Upon completion of the reading, it is customary for the person who has been called up to touch the Torah with a *tallis* (or the Torah's mantle or girdle) and to kiss the edge that has touched the Torah (see *M.B.* 139:35).

121. After the Torah passage has been read, he closes the Torah Scroll and then recites the benediction (*Rama O.C.* 139:5). If the Torah reading will not be resumed immediately (e.g., a מִי שֶׁבֵּרַךְ is said), then a covering should be spread out over the Torah (*M.B.* 139:21).

122. In Talmudic times the person called for an *aliyah* would also read aloud from the Torah. This practice was still followed in Greek and Turkish communities up to the sixteenth century (see *Beis Yosef* to *Tur O.C.* 141), and the tradition persists to this day in Yemenite communities. However, since ancient times the Ashkenazic custom has been for a designated reader (*baal korei*) to read the Torah aloud to the congregation (see *Rosh* cited in *Tur* loc. cit). Nevertheless, the person who recites the benedictions should read quietly along with the reader (*O.C.* 141:2).

123. The reader and the one called up to the Torah must stand while reading the Torah in public. It is forbidden even to lean upon something (*O.C.* 141:1).

124. When going up to the *bimah* to recite the benedictions, one should pick the shortest route possible, and when returning to his seat, he should take a longer route. If two routes are equidistant, one should go to the *bimah* via the route which is to his right and descend via the opposite route (*O.C.* 141:7).

125. After one has finished reciting the concluding benediction, he should not return to his place at least until the next person called up to the Torah has come to the *bimah* (*O.C.* 141:7). However, it is customary to wait until the next person has finished his passage of the Torah (*M.B.* §26).

126. It is forbidden to talk or even to discuss Torah topics while the Torah is being read (*O.C.* 146:2).

127. It is forbidden to leave the synagogue while the Torah is being read (*O.C.* 146:1), even if one has already heard the reading of the passage elsewhere (*M.B.* §1). However, if necessary, one may leave during the pause between one portion and the next (*O.C.* 146:1), provided that a *minyan* remains in the synagogue (*M.B.* §2).

KADDISH

128. The conclusion of a section of prayer is usually signified by the recitation of the *Kaddish*. Many of these *Kaddish* recitations are the privilege of mourners (within the eleven months following the death or burial of a parent, or in some instances, of other close relatives), or of those observing *yahrzeit*, i.e., the anniversary of the death of a parent (and in some congregations, of a grandparent who has no living sons; see *Matteh Ephraim, Dinei Kaddish* 3:14). However, many recitations of *Kaddish* are exclusively the prerogative of the *chazzan*.

129. Basically there are four types of *Kaddish*:

(a) חֲצִי קַדִּישׁ, Half-*Kaddish*, which ends with דַּאֲמִירָן בְּעָלְמָא וְאִמְרוּ אָמֵן;

(b) קַדִּישׁ יָתוֹם, the Mourner's *Kaddish*, which consists of the Half-*Kaddish*, with the addition of יְהֵא שְׁלָמָא and עוֹשֶׂה שָׁלוֹם;

(c) קַדִּישׁ שָׁלֵם, the Full *Kaddish*, the same as the Mourner's *Kaddish* with the addition of תִּתְקַבֵּל before יְהֵא שְׁלָמָא; and

(d) קַדִּישׁ דְּרַבָּנָן, the Rabbis' *Kaddish*, the same as the Mourner's *Kaddish* with the addition of עַל יִשְׂרָאֵל.

130. The function of the Half-*Kaddish* is to link different segments of the prayer, e.g., it is recited between *Pesukei D'Zimrah* and the *Shema* benedictions, between *Shemoneh Esrei* (or *Tachanun*) and the prayers that conclude the service (*Pri Megadim* in *Mishbetzos Zahav, Orach Chaim* 55:1). Thus, it is recited by the *chazzan*.

Nevertheless, in some congregations it is customary for a mourner to recite the *Kaddish* following the reading of the Torah if he has been called to the Torah for the concluding segment (*Sha'arei Ephraim* 10:9). The rationale for this custom is that the person called to the Torah is also a *chazzan* of sorts, since he too must read from the Torah, albeit quietly. In some congregations, a mourner recites this *Kaddish* even if he was not called to the Torah.

131. The Full *Kaddish* is recited only after the communal recitation of *Shemoneh Esrei* (or *Selichos*). It includes the *chazzan's* prayer that the just-concluded service be accepted by God. Consequently it must be recited by the *chazzan*.

132. The Mourner's *Kaddish* is recited after the recital of Scriptural verses that supplement the main body of prayer. The recital of *Kaddish* after this portion of the service is not obligatory, and is not recited if no mourners are present. Since *Kaddish* in these parts of the service is recited exclusively by mourners, it has become customary that one whose parents are living should not recite it, since this would be a mark of disrespect to his parents (see *Rama O.C.* 132:2; *Pis'chei Teshuvah, Yoreh Deah* 376:4).

If no mourners are present, the Mourner's *Kaddish* is not recited, with one exception. After *Aleinu*, which also contains Scriptural verses, *Kaddish* should be recited even if no mourner is present. In such a case, it should be recited by the *chazzan* or one of the congregants, preferably one whose parents are no longer alive, or one whose parents have not explicitly expressed their opposition to his recitation of *Kaddish* (*O.C.* 132:2 with *M.B.* §11).

133. Ideally, each Mourner's *Kaddish* should be recited by only one person. Where more than one mourner is present, the *poskim* developed a system of rules establishing an order of priorities for those who must recite *Kaddish* (see *M.B.* in *Be'ur Halachah* to *O.C.* 132, et al.). However, since adherence to these rules can often cause discord in the congregation, it has become widely accepted for all the mourners to recite the *Kaddish* simultaneously (see *Aruch HaShulchan O.C.* 132:8; *Siddur R' Yaakov Emden*; *Teshuvos Chasam Sofer, O. C.* 159).

134. In many congregations it is customary that someone observing a *yahrzeit* is given the exclusive privilege of reciting a *Kaddish*, usually the one after *Aleinu*. In that case, an additional psalm (usually Psalm 24) is recited at the conclusion of the services so that all the mourners can recite *Kaddish* after it.

135. The Rabbis' *Kaddish* (*Kaddish D'Rabbanan*) is recited after segments of the Oral Torah (e.g., Talmud) have been studied or recited by a quorum of ten adult males (*Rambam, Seder Tefillos Kol HaShanah*). The Talmud (*Sotah* 49a) refers to the great significance of יְהֵא שְׁמֵיהּ רַבָּא (a reference to *Kaddish*) that is said after *Aggadah*, indicating that this *Kaddish* has a special relevance to the Midrashic portion of the Torah. Therefore, it is customary to append a brief Aggadic selection to Torah study and then to recite the Rabbis' *Kaddish* (*M.B.* 54:9).

136. Although *Kaddish D'Rabbanan* is not reserved for mourners and may be recited even by one whose parents are alive (*Pischei Teshuvah, Yoreh Deah* 376:4), it is generally recited by mourners. However, when one celebrates the completion of a tractate of the Talmud, or when the rabbi delivers a *derashah* (homiletical discourse), it is customary for the celebrant or the rabbi to recite the *Kaddish* himself.

VERSES FOR PEOPLE'S NAMES / פסוקים לשמות אנשים

Kitzur Shelah teaches that it is a source of merit to recite a Scriptural verse representing one's name before יִהְיוּ לְרָצוֹן at the end of *Shemoneh Esrei*. The verse should either contain the person's name, or else begin and end with the first and last letters of the name.

Following is a selection of first and last letters of names, with appropriate verses:

א...א אָנָּא יהוה הוֹשִׁיעָה נָּא, אָנָּא יהוה הַצְלִיחָה נָּא.[1]

א...ה אַשְׁרֵי מַשְׂכִּיל אֶל דָּל, בְּיוֹם רָעָה יְמַלְּטֵהוּ יהוה.[2]

א...ו אַשְׁרֵי שֶׁאֵל יַעֲקֹב בְּעֶזְרוֹ, שִׂבְרוֹ עַל יהוה אֱלֹהָיו.[3]

א...י אֲמָרַי הַאֲזִינָה יהוה, בִּינָה הֲגִיגִי.[4]

א...ך אָמַרְתְּ לַיהוה, אֲדֹנָי אָתָּה, טוֹבָתִי בַּל עָלֶיךָ.[5]

א...ל אֶרֶץ רָעָשָׁה, אַף שָׁמַיִם נָטְפוּ מִפְּנֵי אֱלֹהִים; זֶה סִינַי, מִפְּנֵי אֱלֹהִים אֱלֹהֵי יִשְׂרָאֵל.[6]

א...ם אַתָּה הוּא יהוה הָאֱלֹהִים, אֲשֶׁר בָּחַרְתָּ בְּאַבְרָם, וְהוֹצֵאתוֹ מֵאוּר כַּשְׂדִּים, וְשַׂמְתָּ שְּׁמוֹ אַבְרָהָם.[7]

א...ן אֵלֶיךָ יהוה אֶקְרָא, וְאֶל אֲדֹנָי אֶתְחַנָּן.[8]

א...ע אָמַר בְּלִבּוֹ בַּל אֶמּוֹט, לְדֹר וָדֹר אֲשֶׁר לֹא בְרָע.[9]

א...ר אֵלֶּה בָרֶכֶב וְאֵלֶּה בַסּוּסִים, וַאֲנַחְנוּ בְּשֵׁם יהוה אֱלֹהֵינוּ נַזְכִּיר.[10]

ב...א בְּרִיתִי הָיְתָה אִתּוֹ הַחַיִּים וְהַשָּׁלוֹם, וָאֶתְּנֵם לוֹ מוֹרָא וַיִּירָאֵנִי, וּמִפְּנֵי שְׁמִי נִחַת הוּא.[11]

ב...ה בַּעֲבוּר יִשְׁמְרוּ חֻקָּיו, וְתוֹרֹתָיו יִנְצֹרוּ, הַלְלוּיָהּ.[12]

ב...ז בְּיוֹם קָרָאתִי וַתַּעֲנֵנִי, תַּרְהִבֵנִי בְנַפְשִׁי עֹז.[13]

ב...ך בָּרוּךְ אַתָּה יהוה, לַמְּדֵנִי חֻקֶּיךָ.[14]

ב...ל בְּמַקְהֵלוֹת בָּרְכוּ אֱלֹהִים, אֲדֹנָי מִמְּקוֹר יִשְׂרָאֵל.[15]

ב...ם בְּךָ יהוה חָסִיתִי, אַל אֵבוֹשָׁה לְעוֹלָם.[16]

ב...ן בָּרוּךְ יהוה אֱלֹהֵי יִשְׂרָאֵל מֵהָעוֹלָם וְעַד הָעוֹלָם, אָמֵן וְאָמֵן.[17]

ב...ע בְּחֶסֶד וֶאֱמֶת יְכֻפַּר עָוֹן, וּבְיִרְאַת יהוה סוּר מֵרָע.[18]

ג...ה גּוֹל עַל יהוה דַּרְכֶּךָ, וּבְטַח עָלָיו וְהוּא יַעֲשֶׂה.[19]

ג...ל גַּם אֲנִי אוֹדְךָ בִכְלִי נֶבֶל אֲמִתְּךָ אֱלֹהָי, אֲזַמְּרָה לְךָ בְכִנּוֹר, קְדוֹשׁ יִשְׂרָאֵל.[20]

ג...ן גַּם בְּנֵי אָדָם גַּם בְּנֵי אִישׁ, יַחַד עָשִׁיר וְאֶבְיוֹן.[21]

ד...ב דִּרְשׁוּ יהוה בְּהִמָּצְאוֹ, קְרָאֻהוּ בִּהְיוֹתוֹ קָרוֹב.[22]

ד...ד דִּרְשׁוּ יהוה וְעֻזּוֹ, בַּקְּשׁוּ פָנָיו תָּמִיד.[23]

ד...ה דְּאָגָה בְלֶב אִישׁ יַשְׁחֶנָּה, וְדָבָר טוֹב יְשַׂמְּחֶנָּה.[24]

ד...ל דָּן יָדִין עַמּוֹ, כְּאַחַד שִׁבְטֵי יִשְׂרָאֵל.[25]

ה...א הַצּוּר תָּמִים פָּעֳלוֹ, כִּי כָל דְּרָכָיו מִשְׁפָּט, אֵל אֱמוּנָה וְאֵין עָוֶל, צַדִּיק וְיָשָׁר הוּא.[26]

ה...ה הַסְתֵּר פָּנֶיךָ מֵחֲטָאָי, וְכָל עֲוֹנֹתַי מְחֵה.[27]

ה...ל הַקְשִׁיבָה לְקוֹל שַׁוְעִי מַלְכִּי וֵאלֹהָי, כִּי אֵלֶיךָ אֶתְפַּלָּל.[28]

ז...ב זֵכֶר צַדִּיק לִבְרָכָה, וְשֵׁם רְשָׁעִים יִרְקָב.[29]

ז...ה זֹאת מְנוּחָתִי עֲדֵי עַד, פֹּה אֵשֵׁב כִּי אִוִּתִיהָ.[30]

ז...ח זָכַרְתִּי יָמִים מִקֶּדֶם, הָגִיתִי בְכָל פָּעֳלֶךָ, בְּמַעֲשֵׂה יָדֶיךָ אֲשׂוֹחֵחַ.[31]

ז...ן זְבוּלֻן לְחוֹף יַמִּים יִשְׁכֹּן, וְהוּא לְחוֹף אֳנִיֹּת, וְיַרְכָתוֹ עַל צִידֹן.[32]

ח...ה חָגְרָה בְעוֹז מָתְנֶיהָ, וַתְּאַמֵּץ זְרוֹעֹתֶיהָ.[33]

ח...ך חֲצוֹת לַיְלָה אָקוּם לְהוֹדוֹת לָךְ, עַל מִשְׁפְּטֵי צִדְקֶךָ.[34]

(1) *Psalms* 118:25. (2) 41:2. (3) 146:5. (4) 5:2. (5) 16:2. (6) 68:9. (7) *Nehemiah* 9:7. (8) *Psalms* 30:9. (9) 10:6. (10) 20:8. (11) *Malachi* 2:5. (12) *Psalms* 105:45. (13) 138:3. (14) 119:12. (15) 68:27. (16) 71:1. (17) 41:14. (18) *Proverbs* 16:6. (19) *Psalms* 37:5. (20) 71:22. (21) 49:3. (22) *Isaiah* 55:6. (23) *Psalms* 105:4. (24) *Proverbs* 12:25. (25) *Genesis* 49:16. (26) *Deuteronomy* 32:4. (27) *Psalms* 51:11. (28) 5:3. (29) *Proverbs* 10:7. (30) *Psalms* 132:14. (31) 143:5. (32) *Genesis* 49:13. (33) *Proverbs* 31:17. (34) *Psalms* 119:62.

ח...ל חָדְלוּ פְרָזוֹן בְּיִשְׂרָאֵל חָדֵלּוּ, עַד שַׁקַּמְתִּי דְּבוֹרָה, שַׁקַּמְתִּי אֵם בְּיִשְׂרָאֵל.[1]
ח...ם חֹנֶה מַלְאַךְ יהוה סָבִיב לִירֵאָיו, וַיְחַלְּצֵם.[2]
ט...א טוֹב יַנְחִיל בְּנֵי בָנִים, וְצָפוּן לַצַּדִּיק חֵיל חוֹטֵא.[3]
ט...ה טָמְנוּ גֵאִים פַּח לִי וַחֲבָלִים, פָּרְשׂוּ רֶשֶׁת לְיַד מַעְגָּל, מֹקְשִׁים שָׁתוּ לִי סֶלָה.[4]
י...א יִשְׂרָאֵל בְּטַח בַּיהוה, עֶזְרָם וּמָגִנָּם הוּא.[5]
י...ב יַעַנְךָ יהוה בְּיוֹם צָרָה, יְשַׂגֶּבְךָ שֵׁם אֱלֹהֵי יַעֲקֹב.[6]
י...ד יָסַד אֶרֶץ עַל מְכוֹנֶיהָ, בַּל תִּמּוֹט עוֹלָם וָעֶד.[7]
י...ה יהוה הַצִּילָה נַפְשִׁי מִשְּׂפַת שֶׁקֶר, מִלָּשׁוֹן רְמִיָּה.[8]
י...י יהוה לִי בְּעֹזְרָי, וַאֲנִי אֶרְאֶה בְשֹׂנְאָי.[9]
י...ל יְמִין יהוה רוֹמֵמָה, יְמִין יהוה עֹשָׂה חָיִל.[10]
י...ם יַעְלְזוּ חֲסִידִים בְּכָבוֹד, יְרַנְּנוּ עַל מִשְׁכְּבוֹתָם.[11]
י...ן יָשֵׂם נְהָרוֹת לְמִדְבָּר, וּמֹצָאֵי מַיִם לְצִמָּאוֹן.[12]
י...ע יָחֹס עַל דַּל וְאֶבְיוֹן, וְנַפְשׁוֹת אֶבְיוֹנִים יוֹשִׁיעַ.[13]
י...ף יהוה יִגְמֹר בַּעֲדִי, יהוה חַסְדְּךָ לְעוֹלָם, מַעֲשֵׂי יָדֶיךָ אַל תֶּרֶף.[14]
י...ץ יְבָרְכֵנוּ אֱלֹהִים, וְיִירְאוּ אוֹתוֹ כָּל אַפְסֵי אָרֶץ.[15]
י...ק יוֹצִיאֵם מֵחֹשֶׁךְ וְצַלְמָוֶת, וּמוֹסְרוֹתֵיהֶם יְנַתֵּק.[16]
י...ר יהוה שִׁמְךָ לְעוֹלָם, יהוה זִכְרְךָ לְדֹר וָדֹר.[17]
י...ת יהוה שֹׁמֵר אֶת גֵּרִים, יָתוֹם וְאַלְמָנָה יְעוֹדֵד, וְדֶרֶךְ רְשָׁעִים יְעַוֵּת.[18]
כ...ב כִּי לֹא יִטֹּשׁ יהוה עַמּוֹ, וְנַחֲלָתוֹ לֹא יַעֲזֹב.[19]
כ...ל כִּי מֶלֶךְ כָּל הָאָרֶץ אֱלֹהִים זַמְּרוּ מַשְׂכִּיל.[20]
ל...א לֹא תִהְיֶה מְשַׁכֵּלָה וַעֲקָרָה בְּאַרְצֶךָ, אֶת מִסְפַּר יָמֶיךָ אֲמַלֵּא.[21]
ל...ה לְדָוִד, בָּרוּךְ יהוה צוּרִי, הַמְלַמֵּד יָדַי לַקְרָב, אֶצְבְּעוֹתַי לַמִּלְחָמָה.[22]
ל...י לוּלֵי תוֹרָתְךָ שַׁעֲשֻׁעָי, אָז אָבַדְתִּי בְעָנְיִי.[23]
ל...ת לַמְנַצֵּחַ עַל שֹׁשַׁנִּים לִבְנֵי קֹרַח, מַשְׂכִּיל שִׁיר יְדִידֹת.[24]
מ...א מִי כָמֹכָה בָּאֵלִם יהוה, מִי כָּמֹכָה נֶאְדָּר בַּקֹּדֶשׁ, נוֹרָא תְהִלֹּת עֹשֵׂה פֶלֶא.[25]
מ...ה מַחֲשָׁבוֹת בְּעֵצָה תִכּוֹן, וּבְתַחְבֻּלוֹת עֲשֵׂה מִלְחָמָה.[26]
מ...ו מַה דּוֹדֵךְ מִדּוֹד הַיָּפָה בַּנָּשִׁים, מַה דּוֹדֵךְ מִדּוֹד שֶׁכָּכָה הִשְׁבַּעְתָּנוּ.[27]
מ...י מָה אָהַבְתִּי תוֹרָתֶךָ, כָּל הַיּוֹם הִיא שִׂיחָתִי.[28]
מ...ל מַה טֹּבוּ אֹהָלֶיךָ יַעֲקֹב, מִשְׁכְּנֹתֶיךָ יִשְׂרָאֵל.[29]
מ...ם מְאוֹר עֵינַיִם יְשַׂמַּח לֵב, שְׁמוּעָה טוֹבָה תְּדַשֶּׁן עָצֶם.[30]
מ...ר מִי זֶה הָאִישׁ יְרֵא יהוה, יוֹרֶנּוּ בְּדֶרֶךְ יִבְחָר.[31]
נ...א נַפְשֵׁנוּ חִכְּתָה לַיהוה, עֶזְרֵנוּ וּמָגִנֵּנוּ הוּא.[32]
נ...ה נָחַלְתִּי עֵדְוֹתֶיךָ לְעוֹלָם, כִּי שְׂשׂוֹן לִבִּי הֵמָּה.[33]
נ...ח נָסוּ וְאֵין רֹדֵף רָשָׁע, וְצַדִּיקִים כִּכְפִיר יִבְטָח.[34]
נ...י נִדְבוֹת פִּי רְצֵה נָא יהוה, וּמִשְׁפָּטֶיךָ לַמְּדֵנִי.[35]
נ...ל נֶחְשַׁבְתִּי עִם יוֹרְדֵי בוֹר, הָיִיתִי כְּגֶבֶר אֵין אֱיָל.[36]
נ...ם נַחֲמוּ נַחֲמוּ עַמִּי, יֹאמַר אֱלֹהֵיכֶם.[37]
נ...ן נֵר יהוה נִשְׁמַת אָדָם, חֹפֵשׂ כָּל חַדְרֵי בָטֶן.[38]

(1) *Judges* 5:7. (2) *Psalms* 34:8. (3) *Proverbs* 13:22. (4) *Psalms* 140:6. (5) 115:9. (6) 20:2. (7) 104:5. (8) 120:2. (9) 118:7. (10) 118:16. (11) 149:5. (12) 107:33. (13) 72:13. (14) 138:8. (15) 67:8. (16) 107:14. (17) 135:13. (18) 146:9. (19) 94:14. (20) 47:8. (21) *Exodus* 23:26. (22) *Psalms* 144:1. (23) 119:92. (24) 45:1. (25) *Exodus* 15:11. (26) *Proverbs* 20:18. (27) *Song of Songs* 5:9. (28) *Psalms* 119:97. (29) *Numbers* 24:5. (30) *Proverbs* 15:30. (31) *Psalms* 25:12. (32) 33:20. (33) 119:111. (34) *Proverbs* 28:1. (35) *Psalms* 119:108. (36) 88:5. (37) *Isaiah* 40:1. (38) *Proverbs* 20:27.

ס...ה סֹבּוּ צִיּוֹן וְהַקִּיפוּהָ, סִפְרוּ מִגְדָּלֶיהָ.[1]

ס...י סֵעֲפִים שָׂנֵאתִי, וְתוֹרָתְךָ אָהָבְתִּי.[2]

ע...א עַתָּה אָקוּם, יֹאמַר יהוה, עַתָּה אֵרוֹמָם, עַתָּה אֶנָּשֵׂא.[3]

ע...ב עַד אֶמְצָא מָקוֹם לַיהוה, מִשְׁכָּנוֹת לַאֲבִיר יַעֲקֹב.[4]

ע...ה עָזִּי וְזִמְרָת יָהּ, וַיְהִי לִי לִישׁוּעָה.[5]

ע...ל עַל דַּעְתְּךָ כִּי לֹא אֶרְשָׁע, וְאֵין מִיָּדְךָ מַצִּיל.[6]

ע...ם עֲרֹב עַבְדְּךָ לְטוֹב, אַל יַעַשְׁקֻנִי זֵדִים.[7]

ע...ר עֹשֶׂה גְדֹלוֹת וְאֵין חֵקֶר, נִפְלָאוֹת עַד אֵין מִסְפָּר.[8]

פ...א פָּתוֹת אֹתָהּ פִּתִּים וְיָצַקְתָּ עָלֶיהָ שָׁמֶן, מִנְחָה הִיא.[9]

פ...ה פִּתְחוּ לִי שַׁעֲרֵי צֶדֶק, אָבֹא בָם אוֹדֶה יָהּ.[10]

פ...ל פֶּן יִטְרֹף כְּאַרְיֵה נַפְשִׁי, פֹּרֵק וְאֵין מַצִּיל.[11]

פ...ס פֶּלֶס וּמֹאזְנֵי מִשְׁפָּט לַיהוה, מַעֲשֵׂהוּ כָּל אַבְנֵי כִיס.[12]

פ...ץ פִּנִּיתָ לְפָנֶיהָ, וַתַּשְׁרֵשׁ שָׁרָשֶׁיהָ, וַתְּמַלֵּא אָרֶץ.[13]

צ...ה צִיּוֹן בְּמִשְׁפָּט תִּפָּדֶה, וְשָׁבֶיהָ בִּצְדָקָה.[14]

צ...ח צִיּוֹן יִשְׁאָלוּ דֶּרֶךְ הֵנָּה פְנֵיהֶם, בֹּאוּ וְנִלְווּ אֶל יהוה, בְּרִית עוֹלָם לֹא תִשָּׁכֵחַ.[15]

צ...י צַר וּמָצוֹק מְצָאוּנִי, מִצְוֹתֶיךָ שַׁעֲשֻׁעָי.[16]

צ...ל צַהֲלִי וָרֹנִּי יוֹשֶׁבֶת צִיּוֹן, כִּי גָדוֹל בְּקִרְבֵּךְ קְדוֹשׁ יִשְׂרָאֵל.[17]

ק...א קָרַבְתָּ בְּיוֹם אֶקְרָאֶךָּ, אָמַרְתָּ אַל תִּירָא.[18]

ק...ל קַמְתִּי אֲנִי לִפְתֹּחַ לְדוֹדִי, וְיָדַי נָטְפוּ מוֹר וְאֶצְבְּעֹתַי מוֹר עֹבֵר עַל כַּפּוֹת הַמַּנְעוּל.[19]

ק...ן קוֹלִי אֶל יהוה אֶזְעָק, קוֹלִי אֶל יהוה אֶתְחַנָּן.[20]

ק...ת קָרוֹב אַתָּה יהוה, וְכָל מִצְוֹתֶיךָ אֱמֶת.[21]

ר...ה רִגְזוּ וְאַל תֶּחֱטָאוּ, אִמְרוּ בִלְבַבְכֶם עַל מִשְׁכַּבְכֶם, וְדֹמּוּ סֶלָה.[22]

ר...ל רְאוּ עַתָּה כִּי אֲנִי אֲנִי הוּא, וְאֵין אֱלֹהִים עִמָּדִי, אֲנִי אָמִית וַאֲחַיֶּה, מָחַצְתִּי וַאֲנִי אֶרְפָּא,
וְאֵין מִיָּדִי מַצִּיל.[23]

ר...ן רְאֵה זֶה מָצָאתִי, אָמְרָה קֹהֶלֶת, אַחַת לְאַחַת לִמְצֹא חֶשְׁבּוֹן.[24]

ר...ת רָאוּךָ מַּיִם אֱלֹהִים, רָאוּךָ מַּיִם יָחִילוּ, אַף יִרְגְּזוּ תְהֹמוֹת.[25]

ש...א שַׂמֵּחַ נֶפֶשׁ עַבְדֶּךָ, כִּי אֵלֶיךָ אֲדֹנָי נַפְשִׁי אֶשָּׂא.[26]

ש...ה שְׂאוּ יְדֵכֶם קֹדֶשׁ, וּבָרְכוּ אֶת יהוה.[27]

ש...ח שָׁמַע יהוה תְּחִנָּתִי, יהוה תְּפִלָּתִי יִקָּח.[28]

ש...י שָׂנֵאתִי הַשֹּׁמְרִים הַבְלֵי שָׁוְא, וַאֲנִי אֶל יהוה בָּטָחְתִּי.[29]

ש...ל שָׁלוֹם רָב לְאֹהֲבֵי תוֹרָתֶךָ, וְאֵין לָמוֹ מִכְשׁוֹל.[30]

ש...ם שְׁמָר תָּם וּרְאֵה יָשָׁר, כִּי אַחֲרִית לְאִישׁ שָׁלוֹם.[31]

ש...ן שִׁיתוּ לִבְּכֶם לְחֵילָה, פַּסְּגוּ אַרְמְנוֹתֶיהָ, לְמַעַן תְּסַפְּרוּ לְדוֹר אַחֲרוֹן.[32]

ש...ר שְׂפַת אֱמֶת תִּכּוֹן לָעַד, וְעַד אַרְגִּיעָה לְשׁוֹן שָׁקֶר.[33]

ש...ת שִׁיר הַמַּעֲלוֹת, הִנֵּה בָּרְכוּ אֶת יהוה כָּל עַבְדֵי יהוה, הָעֹמְדִים בְּבֵית יהוה בַּלֵּילוֹת.[34]

ת...ה תַּעֲרֹךְ לְפָנַי שֻׁלְחָן נֶגֶד צֹרְרָי, דִּשַּׁנְתָּ בַשֶּׁמֶן רֹאשִׁי, כּוֹסִי רְוָיָה.[35]

ת...י תּוֹצִיאֵנִי מֵרֶשֶׁת זוּ, טָמְנוּ לִי, כִּי אַתָּה מָעוּזִּי.[36]

ת...ם תְּנוּ עֹז לֵאלֹהִים, עַל יִשְׂרָאֵל גַּאֲוָתוֹ, וְעֻזּוֹ בַּשְּׁחָקִים.[37]

---

(1) *Psalms* 48:13. (2) 119:113. (3) *Isaiah* 33:10. (4) *Psalms* 132:5. (5) 118:14. (6) *Job* 10:7. (7) *Psalms* 119:122. (8) *Job* 5:9. (9) *Leviticus* 2:6. (10) *Psalms* 118:19. (11) 7:3. (12) *Proverbs* 16:11. (13) *Psalms* 80:10. (14) *Isaiah* 1:27. (15) *Jeremiah* 50:5. (16) *Psalms* 119:143. (17) *Isaiah* 12:6. (18) *Lamentations* 3:57. (19) *Song of Songs* 5:5. (20) *Psalms* 142:2. (21) 119:151. (22) 4:5. (23) *Deuteronomy* 32:39. (24) *Ecclesiastes* 7:27. (25) *Psalms* 77:7. (26) 86:4. (27) 134:2. (28) 6:10. (29) 31:7. (30) 119:165. (31) 37:37. (32) 48:14. (33) *Proverbs* 12:19. (34) *Psalms* 134:1. (35) 23:5. (36) 31:5. (37) 68:35.

THE RABBIS' KADDISH / KADDISH D'RABBANAN

TRANSLITERATED WITH ASHKENAZIC PRONUNCIATION

Yisgadal v'yiskadash sh'mei rabbaw (Cong.— *Amein*).
b'allmaw dee v'raw chir'usei v'yamlich malchusei,
b'chayeichon, uv'yomeichon, uv'chayei d'chol beis yisrawel,
ba'agawlaw u'vizman kawriv. V'imru: Amein.
(Cong. – *Amein. Y'hei sh'mei rabbaw m'vawrach l'allam ul'allmei allmayaw.*)
Y'hei sh'mei rabbaw m'vawrach, l'allam ul'allmei allmayaw.

Yisbawrach, v'yishtabach, v'yispaw'ar, v'yisromam, v'yisnasei,
v'yis'hadar, v'yis'aleh, v'yis'halawl
sh'mei d'kudshaw b'rich hu (Cong.— *b'rich hu*)
l'aylaw °min kawl
bir'chawsaw v'shirawsaw,
tushb'chawsaw v'nechemawsaw
da'amirawn b'allmaw, v'imru: Amein (Cong.— *Amein*).

Al yisrawel v'al rabawnawn v'al talmideihon,
v'al kol talmidei salmideihon, v'al kol mawn d'awskin b'oraysaw,
dee v'asraw hawdain, v'dee b'chol asar va'asar.
Y'hei l'hon ulchon sh'lawmaw rabbaw,
cheenaw v'chisdaw v'rachamin, v'chayin arichin, umzonei r'vichei,
u'furkawnaw min kawdawm avuhone dee vishmayaw.
V'imru: Amein (Cong.— *Amein*).

Y'hei sh'lawmaw rabbaw min sh'mayaw, v'chayim awleinu
v'al kawl yisrawel. V'imru: Amein (Cong.— *Amein*).

Take three steps back, bow left and say, *"Oseh . . ."*; bow right and say, *"hu b'rachamawv ya'aseh . . ."*; bow forward and say, *"v'al kawl yisrawel v'imru: Amein."*

Oseh shawlom bimromawv,
hu ya'aseh shawlom awleinu,
v'al kawl yisrawel. V'imru: Amein (Cong.— *Amein*).

Remain standing in place for a few moments, then take three steps forward.

THE MOURNER'S KADDISH

TRANSLITERATED WITH ASHKENAZIC PRONUNCIATION

Yisgadal v'yiskadash sh'mei rabbaw (Cong.— *Amein*).
b'allmaw dee v'raw chir'usei v'yamlich malchusei,
b'chayeichon, uv'yomeichon, uv'chayei d'chol beis yisrawel,
ba'agawlaw u'vizman kawriv. V'imru: Amein.
(Cong.— *Amein. Y'hei sh'mei rabbaw m'vawrach l'allam ul'allmei allmayaw.*)
Y'hei sh'mei rabbaw m'vawrach, l'allam ul'allmei allmayaw.

Yisbawrach, v'yishtabach, v'yispaw'ar,
v'yisromam, v'yisnasei,
v'yis'hadar, v'yis'aleh, v'yis'halawl
sh'mei d'kudshaw b'rich hu (Cong.— *b'rich hu*)
l'aylaw °*min kawl*
(°from Rosh Hashanah to Yom Kippur substitute: *u'l'aylaw mikawl*)
bir'chawsaw v'shirawsaw,
tushb'chawsaw v'nechemawsaw
da'amirawn b'allmaw, v'imru: Amein (Cong.— *Amein*).

Y'hei sh'lawmaw rabbaw min sh'mayaw,
v'chayim awleinu v'al kawl yisrawel. V'imru: Amein (Cong.— *Amein*).

Take three steps back, bow left and say, *"Oseh . . ."*; bow right and say, *"hu ya'aseh . . ."*; *bow forward and say, "v'al kawl yisrawel v'imru: Amein."*

Oseh shawlom bimromawv,
hu ya'aseh shawlom awleinu,
v'al kawl yisrawel. V'imru: Amein (Cong.— *Amein*).

Remain standing in place for a few moments, then take three steps forward.

K'INNOS
WITH AN INTERLINEAR TRANSLATION